W9-BIL-921

USED

33 75

# Financial Accounting

*Fifth Edition*

# Financial Accounting

## An Introduction to Concepts, Methods, and Uses

*Fifth Edition*

**Sidney Davidson, Ph.D., CPA**
University of Chicago

**Clyde P. Stickney, D.B.A., CPA**
Dartmouth College

**Roman L. Weil, Ph.D., CPA, CMA**
University of Chicago

**The Dryden Press**
Chicago New York San Francisco Philadelphia
Montreal Toronto London Sydney Tokyo

Acquisitions Editor: Mike Reynolds
Project Editor: Paula Ransdell
Design Director: Alan Wendt
Production Manager: Barb Bahnsen
Permissions Editor: Doris Milligan
Director of Editing, Design, and Production: Jane Perkins

Text and Cover Designer: C. J. Petlick
Copy Editor: Judith Lary
Indexer: Cherie Weil
Compositor: York Graphic Services, Inc.
Text Type: 10/12 Times Roman

Library of Congress Cataloging-in-Publication Data

Davidson, Sidney, 1919–
  Financial accounting.

  Includes bibliographical references and index.
  1. Accounting.  I. Stickney, Clyde P., 1944–
II. Weil, Roman L.   III. Title.
HF5635.D228   1988      657      87-9135
ISBN 0-03-011522-1

Printed in the United States of America
789-039-9876543
Copyright © 1988, 1985, 1982, 1979, 1976 by The Dryden Press,
a division of Holt, Rinehart and Winston, Inc.

All rights reserved. No part of this publication may be
reproduced or transmitted in any form or by any means, electronic
or mechanical, including photocopy, recording, or any information
storage and retrieval system, without permission in writing from
the publisher.

Requests for permission to make copies of any part of the work
should be mailed to: Permissions, Holt, Rinehart and Winston,
Inc., Orlando, Florida 32887.

Address orders:
The Dryden Press
Orlando, Florida 32887

Address editorial correspondence:
The Dryden Press
908 N. Elm St.
Hinsdale, IL 60521

The Dryden Press
Holt, Rinehart and Winston
Saunders College Publishing

*For our students, with thanks.*

Whatever be the detail with which you cram
your students, the chance of their meeting in
after-life exactly that detail is almost
infinitesimal; and if they do meet it, they will
probably have forgotten what you taught them
about it. The really useful training yields a
comprehension of a few general principles with
a thorough grounding in the way they apply to
a variety of concrete details. In subsequent
practice the students will have forgotten your
particular details; but they will remember by an
unconscious common sense how to apply
principles to immediate circumstances.

**Alfred North Whitehead**
*The Aims of Education and Other Essays*

# The Dryden Press Series in Accounting

# Preface

The fifth edition of this book has the same principal objectives as the previous editions. The introductory course in financial accounting has two main purposes:

- To help the student develop a sufficient understanding of the basic concepts underlying financial statements so that the concepts can be applied to new and different situations.

- To train the student in accounting terminology and methods so that financial statements currently published in corporate annual reports can be interpreted, analyzed, and evaluated.

Most introductory financial accounting textbooks share these, or similar, objectives. The critical differences among textbooks relate to the relative emphases on concepts, methods, and uses.

**1. Concepts** This book emphasizes the rationale for, and implications of, important accounting concepts. The ability to conceptualize material covered is an important part of the learning process. Without such conceptualization, students will have difficulty focusing on relevant issues in new and different situations. Accordingly, important accounting concepts are identified early in each chapter. Following these are several numerical examples illustrating their application. Numerous short exercises are included at the end of each chapter to check the students' ability to apply the concepts to still different problem situations.

**2. Methods** Sufficient emphasis is placed on accounting procedures so that students can interpret, analyze, and evaluate published financial statements. However, procedures are not emphasized to such an extent that students bog down in detail. The determination of just how much accounting procedure is enough is a problem faced by all writers of accounting textbooks. Many believe, as we do, that the most effective way to learn accounting concepts is to work numerous problems and exercises. When too much emphasis is placed on accounting procedures, however, there is a tendency for students to be lulled into the security of thinking they understand accounting concepts when they actually do not. The mixture of concepts and procedures in this book is one with which we have experimented extensively, and we have found it to be effective in classroom use.

Understanding the accounting implications of an event requires that students be able to construct the journal entry for that event. Throughout this book, journal entries are used in describing the nature of accounting events. Moreover, most chapters contain exercises and problems that require the analysis of transactions with debits and credits. Do not conclude by a glance at this text, however, that it is primarily procedural. The principal objective is that students learn concepts; the procedures are required for learning the concepts.

**3. Uses** An attempt is made to bridge the gap between the preparation of financial statements and the uses to which the statements may be put. Extensive consideration is given to the effects of alternative accounting principles on the measurement of earnings and financial position and to the types of interpretations that should and should not be made. Numerous user-oriented cases appear at the end of most chapters.

## Changes in This Edition _____

The major changes in the fifth edition are as follows:

1. Chapter 5 introduces the statement of cash flows, previously called the statement of changes in financial position, describing and illustrating the new concepts, definitions, and reporting formats of the recent FASB statement.

2. Chapter 14 in the fourth edition on changing prices has been eliminated. Discussions of the impact of changing prices have been included in Chapters 2, 8, and 9.

3. The new Chapter 14, "Statement of Cash Flows: Another Look," expands the elementary discussion of this topic in Chapter 5 by illustrating the effect of materials discussed in Chapters 7 through 13 on this financial statement.

4. The treatment of the material covered in Chapters 7 through 13 on the statement of cash flows has been placed in an appendix to each chapter rather than in the body of the chapter.

5. Relevant aspects of the Tax Reform Act of 1986 have been incorporated throughout the book, particularly in Chapters 9 and 11.

6. Based on a review of course assignments made by a sample of instructors using the previous edition, new exercises and problems that are similar to the ones most frequently assigned have been added.

## Organization _____

This book comprises four major parts. Part One, "Overview of Financial Statements," includes Chapter 1; Part Two, "Accounting Concepts and Methods," Chapters 2 through 6; Part Three, "Measuring and Reporting Assets and Equities," Chapters 7 through 14; and Part Four, "Synthesis," Chapter 15. The four parts may be viewed as four tiers, or steps, for covering the material. Part One presents a general overview of the principal financial statements. Part Two discusses the basic accounting model used to generate the principal financial statements. Part Three considers the specific accounting principles or methods used in preparing the financial statements. Finally, Part Four serves as a synthesis for the entire book. This organization reflects the view that learning can take place most effectively when the student starts with a broad picture, then breaks up that broad picture into smaller pieces until the desired depth is achieved, and finally synthesizes so that the relation between the parts and the whole is kept in perspective.

Chapter 1 presents a brief description of the principal activities of a business firm (investing, financing, and operating) and shows how the results of these activities are reported in the three principal financial statements: the balance sheet, the income statement, and the statement of cash flows.

Many students feel deluged with the multitude of new terms and concepts after reading Chapter 1. Most of these same students admit later, however, that the broad overview was useful in piecing material together as they later explored individual topics at greater length.

Chapters 2 through 5 present the basic accounting model that generates the three principal financial statements. In each case, the discussion begins with a description of the important concepts underlying each statement. The accounting procedures employed to generate the statements are then described and illustrated. One of the unique features of the book is the integration in Chapter 3 of the accounting entries for transactions during a period with the related adjusting entries at the end of the period. When these two types of entries are discussed in separate chapters, students lose sight of the fact that both kinds of entries are required to measure net income and financial position.

Another unique aspect of the text is the early coverage, in Chapter 5, of the statement of cash flows. Two purposes are served by placing it here. First, this placement elevates the statement to its rightful place among the three principal financial statements. Students can thereby integrate the concepts of profitability and cash flow more effectively and begin to understand that one does not necessarily accompany the other. When this statement is covered at the end of the course (in many cases, when time is running out), there is a tendency for the student to think it is less important. A second purpose for placing this chapter early in the book is that it serves to cement understanding of the basic accounting model in Chapters 2 through 4. Preparing the statement of cash flows requires the student to work "backward" from the balance sheet and income statement to reconstruct the transactions that took place.

Chapter 6 introduces the topic of financial statement analysis. This topic is placed here to serve as a partial synthesis of the first five chapters. Students at this point ask how information in the statements may be used. This chapter presents an opportunity to answer some of these questions, even if at only an elementary level. Effective financial statement analysis requires an understanding of the specific accounting methods discussed in Part Three. Chapter 6 therefore serves as a springboard for what is to come.

Chapters 7 through 13 discuss the various generally accepted accounting principles employed in generating financial statements. Each chapter not only describes and illustrates the application of the various accounting methods but also considers their effects on the financial statements. This approach reflects the view that students should be able to interpret and analyze published financial statements and to understand the effect of alternative accounting methods on such assessments. Some of the more complicated topics have been placed in end-of-chapter appendixes to provide flexibility in coverage. Some instructors may not wish to use this more advanced material.

Chapter 14 explores the statement of cash flows in greater depth than in Chapter 5. A comprehensive illustration using transactions covered in Chapters 7 through 13 is presented, with each item in the statement discussed fully. Instructors are offered considerable flexibility in the manner in which the statement of cash flows can be covered.

The students who have used the previous editions of this book have found Chapter 15, which synthesizes much of the material in the first fourteen chapters, in many ways the most useful in the book. Explicit consideration is given to the combined effects of alternative accounting methods on financial statement analysis. The self-study problem and problems 21 and 22 at the end of Chapter 15 are major review problems for the entire book.

A comprehensive glossary of accounting terms is included at the end of the book. It serves as a useful reference tool for accounting and other business terms and provides additional descriptions of a few topics considered only briefly in the text, such as accounting changes.

## Related Materials Accompanying the Text _____

The following materials have been prepared for use with the text:

**Instructor's Manual and Test Bank** The instructor's manual, in addition to including responses to all questions, exercises, problems, and cases, presents suggested outlines for courses of varying lengths, a list of chapter objectives, helpful teaching hints, detailed lecture and discussion outlines including the numbers of particularly germane problems, and sample examination questions and problems. The instructor's manual also includes a list of check figures for various problems in the text. These check figures can be photocopied and distributed to students if the instructor so desires.

**Study Guide** A study guide has been prepared by LeBrone C. Harris and James E. Moon. This study guide includes a listing of highlights from each chapter and is then followed by numerous short true/false, matching, multiple-choice questions, and exercises, with answers.

**Transparencies** A set of transparencies is available for many of the exhibits in the text and the end-of-chapter problems.

# Acknowledgments ————————————————

We gratefully acknowledge the helpful criticisms and suggestions of the following people who reviewed the manuscript at various stages: Mike Bohman (University of Santa Clara), Richard Church (Plymouth State College), Dennis Daly (University of Minnesota), Carlos del Portal (Florida Atlantic University), Susan Gill (Central Michigan University), V. Govindarajan (Dartmouth College), Patricia King (University of Arizona), John Martinelli (California State University at Long Beach), Katherine Schipper (University of Chicago), Tom Selling (Dartmouth College), John Shank (Dartmouth College), Peter Wilson (New York University), G. Peter Wilson (Stanford University), and Steve Zeff (Rice University).

Thomas Horton and Daughters, Inc., has graciously given us permission to reproduce material from *Accounting: The Language of Business*. Problems 47 through 49 in Chapter 3 were adapted from ones prepared by George H. Sorter. These problems involve working backwards from one financial statement to another, and we have found them useful in cementing understanding. Stan Baiman provided us with a series of excellent problems on the statements of cash flows for use in Chapters 7 through 13.

We thank the following people for their hard work in helping us to prepare the manuscript for this book: Peg McGann, Karen Rainey, and K. Xenophon-Rybowiak. Cherie Weil prepared the index.

Finally, we thank Penny Gaffney, Diana Gunderson, Judith Lary, Mike Reynolds, Alan Wendt, and particularly Paula Ransdell of The Dryden Press for their assistance and patience in the preparation of this book.

**S. D.**
**C. P. S.**
**R. L. W.**

# Contents _____

**Chapter 8**  **Inventories: The Source of Operating Profits** ———————————— 314

**Chapter 9**  **Plant, Equipment, and Intangible Assets: The Source of Operating
Capacity** ——————————————————————————————— 364

# Part One

# Overview of Financial Statements ─────

# Chapter 1 Introduction to Business Activities and Overview of Principal Financial Statements _____

Accounting is a system for measuring the results of business activities and communicating those measurements to interested users. You are about to begin a study of (1) the concepts and procedures used by accountants to make these measurements and (2) the principal financial statements through which the measurements are communicated. You probably will not become an accountant yourself. Rather, you will use accounting as a tool in making production, marketing, investment, financing or other business decisions. The goal of your study (and this book) is to help you gain sufficient understanding of accounting concepts and procedures so that you can use accounting data effectively.

## Distinction between Managerial and Financial Accounting _____

The field of accounting divides into two parts: managerial accounting and financial accounting.

*Managerial accounting* is concerned with the preparation of reports for use by persons within a firm. For example, a corporate treasurer might use a statement of projected cash receipts and disbursements in deciding if short-term borrowing is necessary. A production manager might use a report on the productivity of various employees in deciding how a special order is to be routed through a factory. A sales manager might use a report on the cost of producing and selling different product lines in recommending the prices to be charged and the products to be emphasized by the sales staff. Users of information within a firm can specify the types of information they need for their decisions; managerial accounting reports are designed to satisfy these needs.

In contrast, *financial accounting* is concerned with the preparation of reports for use by persons outside a firm. For example, a bank may desire information on the cash-generating ability of a firm when deciding whether to grant a bank loan. A potential investor may desire information on a firm's profitability before deciding whether to invest in the firm.

The format and content of financial accounting reports are more standardized than those used in managerial accounting. The large number of uses and users of financial accounting reports creates the need for some degree of uniformity in reporting among firms.

The most common reports for external use are the financial statements included in the annual report to shareholders (owners) and potential investors. These financial statements are prepared to conform with *generally accepted accounting principles*. Such principles have evolved over time or have been made acceptable by decree from an official rule-making body. The *Financial Accounting Standards Board (FASB),* an independent body in the private sector, and the *Securities and Exchange Commission (SEC),* an agency of the federal government, are the principal rule-making bodies in the United States.

This text discusses the principles that underlie the financial statements prepared by firms for external users. We begin by studying how a typical firm carries out its business activities. We then see how the results of these business activities are measured and reported in the principal financial statements. This chapter introduces material to be covered in greater depth in later chapters. The objective is to develop the big picture so that a perspective is provided for the concepts and procedures discussed later.

# Overview of Business Activities ————————————

Financial statements for external users attempt to present in a meaningful way the results of a firm's business activities. Understanding these financial statements requires an understanding of the business activities that they attempt to portray.

**Example 1**  Janet Marsh and Bill Nelson, while working toward degrees in engineering, developed a computerized mechanism for monitoring automobile engine performance. They received a patent on the device and, having recently graduated, want to set up their own firm to manufacture and sell it. The firm will be called Marnel Corporation.

Some of the more important processes through which Marnel Corporation must go are described in the following sections.

## Establishing Corporate Goals and Strategies

The *goals* of any firm are the targets, or end results, toward which the energies of the firm are directed. The *strategies* of the firm are the means for achieving these goals.

The detail in which goals and strategies are stated varies among firms. Some firms prefer to state goals and strategies only in general terms. For example, a firm might express its goal as "to be more profitable than our leading competitors." Its strategy might be to mechanize production so that it can manufacture quality products at a cost lower than its competitors.

Often firms might be more explicit. The goal might be to achieve a certain rate of profitability. The goals might also be broader than profitability alone and include concerns for employee welfare, environmental protection, and community involvement. Strategies might likewise be spelled out in detail, including step-by-step actions to accomplish the goals.

Marnel Corporation's goal is to develop a continuing stream of quality electronic products that can be manufactured and marketed profitably, thereby increasing the value of the firm and the wealth of its owners. Its strategies include the following:

1. All electronic devices will be manufactured by Marnel Corporation so as to ensure quality and provide some protection against other firms' attempts to imitate the devices.

2. The sale and servicing of the devices will be carried out by the firm's sales staff to provide close working relations with customers.

3. Investments will be made in research and development to ensure the ongoing creation of new products.

## Obtaining Financing

Before Marnel Corporation can embark on its business activities, it must obtain the necessary financing. Such *financing activities* involve obtaining funds from two principal sources: owners and creditors.

**Owners**   Owners provide funds to a firm and in return receive some evidence of their ownership. When a firm is organized as a corporation, ownership is evidenced by shares of common stock, and the owners are called *shareholders* or *stockholders*. The firm need not repay the owners at a particular future date. Instead, the owners receive dividends if and when the firm decides to pay them. The owners also have a claim on all increases in the value of the firm resulting from future profitable operations.

**Creditors**   Unlike owners, creditors provide funds but require that the funds be repaid, often with interest, at a specific date. The length of time that elapses until repayment varies. Long-term creditors may provide funds and not require repayment for 20 years or more. Such borrowings are usually evidenced by a *bond*. A bond is simply an agreement in which the borrowing company promises to pay the creditors interest on the amounts borrowed at specific dates in the future and then to repay the amount borrowed at the end of some stated period of years. Banks usually lend for periods between several months and several years. Bank borrowings are usually evidenced by a *note* in which the borrowing company promises to repay the amount borrowed plus interest at some future date. Suppliers of raw materials may not view themselves as sources of funds for a firm. Yet, when they supply raw materials but do not require payment for 30 days, they implicitly provide funds. Likewise, employees who are paid weekly or monthly and governmental units that require only monthly or quarterly payment of taxes provide funds.

All firms must choose the proportion of funds to be obtained from owners, long-term creditors, and short-term creditors. Finance courses cover such financing decisions.

## Making Investments

Once a firm has obtained funds, it usually invests them in various items needed to carry out its business activities. Such *investing activities* involve acquisitions of the following:

1. Land, buildings, and equipment — Such investments provide a firm with a capacity to manufacture and sell its products and usually take many years to provide all of the potential services for which they were acquired.

2. Patents, licenses, and other contractual rights — Such investments provide a firm with the legal right to use certain property or processes in pursuing its business activities.

3. Common stock or bonds of other firms — A firm might invest in other firms (thereby becoming one of its owners or creditors). Such investments might be made for a few months with temporarily excess cash or for more long-term purposes.

4. Inventories — The principal goal of most business firms is to sell its products to customers. To satisfy the needs of customers as they arise, an inventory of products must be on hand. Funds are usually not invested in specific inventory items for very long, because the items will soon be sold to customers. However, since a certain amount of inventory must always be on hand, firms must continually invest some amount of their funds in inventory items.

5. Accounts receivable from customers — When a firm sells its products to customers who are not required to pay immediately, the firm is providing financing to its customers. Carrying a certain amount of accounts receivable may be in the best interest of the firm if by doing so the firm increases its sales and profits. In extending credit to customers, the firm forgoes collecting its cash right away. Funds to acquire other assets must be obtained elsewhere. Carrying accounts receivable, therefore, requires an investment of funds.

6. Cash — Most firms will leave a portion of their funds in the form of cash in checking or savings accounts so that they can pay their current bills.

Managerial accounting courses cover the techniques for making proper investment decisions.

## Carrying Out Operations

A firm obtains financing and invests the funds in various resources to generate profit. The following comprises the *operating activities* of a firm:

1. Purchasing — The purchasing department of a merchandising firm acquires the amounts and types of products needed by its retail stores. The purchasing department of a manufacturing firm acquires the amounts and types of raw materials needed in production.

2. Production — The production department in a manufacturing firm combines raw materials, labor services, and other manufacturing inputs to produce the products, or outputs, of a firm.

3. Marketing — The marketing department oversees selling the product to customers.

4. Administration — The administrative activity of a firm supports purchasing, production, marketing, and other operating departments. Administration might include data processing, legal services, research and development, and other activities.

Managerial accounting, marketing, and production courses cover the appropriate basis for making operating decisions.

## Summary of Business Activities

Figure 1.1 summarizes the four principal business activities discussed in this section. Figure 1.1 distinguishes between the short term and the long term. Although the time line dividing short- from long-term activities varies somewhat among firms, 1 year is generally the dividing line used.

# Principal Financial Statements _____

The annual report to shareholders typically includes a letter from the firm's president summarizing activities of the past year and assessing the firm's prospects for the coming year. Also frequently included are promotional materials, such as pictures of the firm's products and employees. The section of the annual report containing the financial statements comprises the following:

1. Balance sheet.
2. Income statement.
3. Statement of cash flows.
4. Notes to the financial statements, including various supporting schedules.
5. Opinion of the independent certified public accountant.

The following sections of this chapter discuss briefly each of these five items.

**Figure 1.1** _____

**Summary of Business Activities**

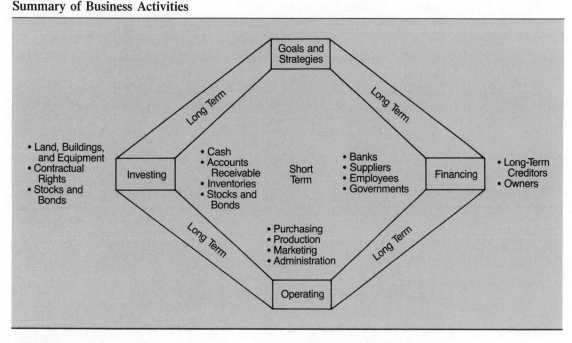

## Balance Sheet

The *balance sheet* presents a snapshot of the investing and financing activities of a firm as of a moment in time. Exhibit 1.1 presents a comparative balance sheet for Marnel Corporation as of January 1, Year 1, and December 31, Year 1.

The balance sheet on January 1, Year 1, depicts Marnel Corporation on the day it was organized. Owners provided $500,000 in funds, long-term creditors provided $400,000, and suppliers provided $100,000. These funds were invested in inventories, land, building, equipment, and a patent; $70,000 was left in the firm's checking account.

The balance sheet on December 31, Year 1, presents the financial position of Marnel Corporation at the end of the first year. The amounts for most items in the balance sheet changed between the beginning and end of the year.

Note several aspects of the balance sheet:

**Concepts of Assets, Liabilities, and Shareholders' Equity**  The balance sheet presents a listing of a firm's assets, liabilities, and shareholders' equity.

*Assets* are economic resources. An asset is an item that has the ability or potential to provide future benefits to a firm. For example, cash can be used to purchase inventory or equipment. Inventory can be sold to customers for an amount the firm hopes will provide a profit. Equipment can be used in transporting inventory to customers.

*Liabilities* are creditors' claims on the assets of a firm. Marnel Corporation has purchased inventories from its suppliers but has not paid for a portion of the pur-

Exhibit 1.1 _____

**MARNEL CORPORATION**
**Comparative Balance Sheet**

| | January 1, Year 1 | December 31, Year 1 |
|---|---|---|
| **Assets** | | |
| **Current Assets:** | | |
| Cash ............................................. | $ 70,000 | $ 200,000 |
| Accounts Receivable from Customers ................ | — | 180,000 |
| Inventories (at manufacturing cost) ................... | 100,000 | 270,000 |
| Total Current Assets ............................. | $ 170,000 | $ 650,000 |
| **Noncurrent Assets (at acquisition cost):** | | |
| Land ............................................ | $ 30,000 | $ 30,000 |
| Buildings (net of accumulated depreciation) ........... | 400,000 | 380,000 |
| Equipment (net of accumulated depreciation) .......... | 250,000 | 230,000 |
| Patent (net of accumulated amortization) .............. | 150,000 | 120,000 |
| Total Noncurrent Assets ......................... | $ 830,000 | $ 760,000 |
| Total Assets .................................... | $1,000,000 | $1,410,000 |
| **Liabilities and Shareholders' Equity** | | |
| **Current Liabilities:** | | |
| Accounts Payable to Suppliers ....................... | $ 100,000 | $ 130,000 |
| Salaries Payable to Employees ...................... | — | 30,000 |
| Income Taxes Payable to Federal Government ........ | — | 40,000 |
| Total Current Liabilities ........................... | $ 100,000 | $ 200,000 |
| **Noncurrent Liabilities:** | | |
| Bonds Payable to Lenders (due Year 20) ............. | 400,000 | 450,000 |
| Total Liabilities .................................. | $ 500,000 | $ 650,000 |
| **Shareholders' Equity:** | | |
| Common Stock..................................... | $ 500,000 | $ 600,000 |
| Retained Earnings ................................. | — | 160,000 |
| Total Shareholders' Equity ........................ | $ 500,000 | $ 760,000 |
| Total Liabilities and Shareholders' Equity ............ | $1,000,000 | $1,410,000 |

chases. As a result, these creditors have provided funds to the firm and have a claim on its assets. Labor services have been provided by employees for which payment has not been made as of December 31, Year 1. These employees likewise have provided funds to the firm and have a claim on its assets. Creditors' claims, or liabilities, result from a firm having previously received benefits (cash, inventories, labor services), and typically they have a specified amount and date at which they must be paid.

*Shareholders' equity* is the owners' claim on the assets of a firm. Unlike creditors, the owners have only a residual interest; that is, owners have a claim on all assets in excess of those required to meet creditors' claims. The shareholders' equity generally comprises two parts: contributed capital and retained earnings. *Con-*

*tributed capital* reflects the funds invested by shareholders for an ownership inter-est. The owners initially contributed $500,000 for shares of Marnel Corporation's common stock. They invested an additional $100,000 during Year 1 for more shares of stock. *Retained earnings* represent the earnings realized by a firm since its forma-tion in excess of dividends distributed to shareholders. In other words, retained earnings are earnings reinvested by management for the benefit of shareholders. Management directs the use of a firm's assets so that over time more assets are received than are consumed in operations. This increase in assets, after any claims of creditors, belongs to the firm's owners. Most firms reinvest a large percentage of the assets generated by earnings for replacement of assets and growth rather than for payment of dividends.

**Equality of Assets and Liabilities Plus Shareholders' Equity**  As the balance sheet for Marnel Corporation shows, there is an equality between (1) assets and (2) liabilities plus shareholders' equity. That is,

$$\text{Assets} = \text{Liabilities} + \text{Shareholders' Equity.}$$

The component structure of assets reflects a firm's investment decisions, and the components of liabilities plus shareholders' equity reflect a firm's financing deci-sions. Every dollar of funds obtained must be invested in something. Thus we are viewing the same resources from two angles: a listing of the forms in which they are held (assets) and a listing of the parties (creditors and owners) who have provided financing and who, therefore, have a claim on those assets. Thus

$$\text{Assets} = \text{Liabilities} + \text{Shareholders' Equity,}$$

or

$$\text{Investing} = \text{Financing.}$$

**Balance Sheet Classification**  The balance sheet classifies assets and liabilities as being either current or noncurrent.

*Current assets* include cash and assets that are expected to be turned into cash, sold, or consumed within approximately 1 year from the date of the balance sheet. Cash, temporary investments in securities, accounts receivable from customers, and inventories are the most common current assets. *Current liabilities* include liabili-ties that are expected to be paid within 1 year. Notes payable to banks, accounts payable to suppliers, salaries payable to employees, and taxes payable to govern-ments are examples.

*Noncurrent assets,* typically held and used for several years, include land, buildings, equipment, patents, and long-term investments in securities. *Noncurrent liabilities* and *shareholders' equity* are a firm's longer-term sources of funds.

**Valuation**  The dollar amount at which each asset and liability appears on the balance sheet is based on one of two valuation bases: (1) *cash,* or *cash equivalent, valuation,* or (2) *acquisition,* or *historical, cost valuation.*

Cash is stated at the amount of cash on hand or in the bank. Accounts receiva-ble are shown at the present value of the amount of cash expected to be collected from customers. Liabilities are generally shown at the present value of the cash required to pay the liabilities. These assets and liabilities are sometimes referred to as *monetary items* because they are valued on a cash, or cash equivalent, basis.

The remaining assets are shown either at acquisition cost or at acquisition cost net of accumulated depreciation or amortization. For example, inventories and land are stated at the amount of cash or other resources that the firm originally sacrificed to acquire those assets. Buildings, equipment, and patents are likewise stated at acquisition cost, but this amount is adjusted downward to reflect the portion of the assets' services that has been used up since acquisition.

Common stock is reported at the amount invested by owners when the firm's common stock was first issued. Retained earnings is the sum of all prior years' earnings in excess of dividends.

## Income Statement

The second principal financial statement is the *income statement,* which presents the results of the operating activities of a firm for a period of time. Exhibit 1.2 shows the income statement for Marnel Corporation for Year 1. This statement indicates the *net income, earnings,* or *profits* of a firm for a period of time. Net income is the difference between revenues and expenses. Note several aspects of the income statement.

**Concepts of Net Income, Revenue, and Expense**  The terms *net income, earnings,* and *profits* are synonyms used interchangeably in corporate annual reports and throughout this text. Generating a profit from operating activities is the primary goal of most business firms. The income statement provides a measure of how successful a firm was in achieving this goal for a given time span. The income statement also

**Exhibit 1.2** ——————————————————————————————

**MARNEL CORPORATION**
**Income Statement for Year 1**

| | |
|---|---:|
| **Revenues:** | |
| Sale of Electronic Devices | $2,250,000 |
| Sale of Engineering Services | 140,000 |
| Interest on Accounts Receivable from Customers | 10,000 |
| Total Revenues | $2,400,000 |
| | |
| **Expenses:** | |
| Cost of Goods Sold | $1,465,000 |
| Selling Expenses | 400,000 |
| Administrative Expenses | 200,000 |
| Interest Expense | 50,000 |
| Income Tax Expense | 85,000 |
| Total Expenses | $2,200,000 |
| | |
| **Net Income** | $  200,000 |

reports the sources and amounts of a firm's revenues and the nature and amount of a firm's expenses that net to earnings for the period.

*Revenues* measure the inflows of assets (or reductions in liabilities) from selling goods and providing services to customers. During Year 1, Marnel Corporation sold electronic devices and provided engineering and financing services. From its customers Marnel Corporation received either cash or promises to pay cash in the future, called Accounts Receivable from Customers. Both are assets. Thus revenues were generated and assets increased.

*Expenses* measure the outflow of assets (or increases in liabilities) used up in generating revenues. Cost of Goods Sold (an expense) is a measure of the cost of inventories sold to customers. Selling expenses measure the cash payments made or the liabilities incurred to make future cash payments for marketing services received during the period. For each expense, either an asset decreases or a liability increases.

A firm strives to generate an excess of net asset inflows from revenues over net asset outflows from expenses required in generating the revenues. Net income indicates a firm's accomplishments (revenues) relative to the efforts required (expenses) in pursuing its operating activities. When expenses for a period exceed revenues, a firm incurs a *net loss*.

**Classification of Revenues and Expenses**  The income statement for Marnel Corporation classifies revenues by the nature of the good or service sold (electronic devices, engineering services, financing services) and classifies expenses by the department within the firm that carried out the firm's operating activities (production, marketing, administration). Depreciation and amortization on buildings, equipment, and patents are included in cost of goods sold, selling expenses, and administrative expenses. Interest expense on long-term bonds and income tax expense appear separately. Firms classify revenues and expenses in their income statements in many different ways.

**Relationship to Balance Sheet**  The income statement links the balance sheet at the beginning with that at the end of the period. Recall that retained earnings represent the sum of prior earnings of a firm in excess of *dividends*. The amount of net income helps explain the change in retained earnings between the beginning and end of the period. During Year 1, Marnel Corporation had net income of $200,000. Dividends declared and paid were $40,000. The change in retained earnings during Year 1 can, therefore, be explained as follows:

| | |
|---|---:|
| Retained Earnings, January 1, Year 1 ................................... | $      0 |
| Add Net Income for Year 1 ............................................ | 200,000 |
| Subtract Dividends Declared and Paid during Year 1 ...................... | ( 40,000) |
| Retained Earnings, December 31, Year 1 ............................... | $160,000 |

## Summary of Balance Sheet and Income Statement

Recall that Figure 1.1 summarizes the principal business activities of a firm: financing, investing, and operating. Figure 1.2 now summarizes the relation between these business activities and the balance sheet and income statement.

## Statement of Cash Flows

The third principal financial statement is the statement of cash flows. This statement reports the net cash flows relating to operating, investing, and financing activities for a period of time. Exhibit 1.3 presents a statement of cash flows for Marnel Corporation for Year 1. Operations lead to an increase in cash of $50,000. (Recall that not all revenues result in an immediate increase in cash and that not all expenses result in an immediate decrease in cash.) Cash of $30,000 was used in acquiring noncurrent assets. Financing activities led to a $110,000 net increase in cash. Of what significance is a statement explaining or analyzing the change in cash during a period of time? This might be best understood with an example.

**Example 2** Diversified Technologies Corporation began business 4 years ago. In its first 4 years of operations, net income was $100,000; $300,000; $800,000; and $1,500,000; respectively. The company retained all of its earnings for growth.

**Figure 1.2**

**Relation between Business Activities and Balance Sheet and Income Statement**

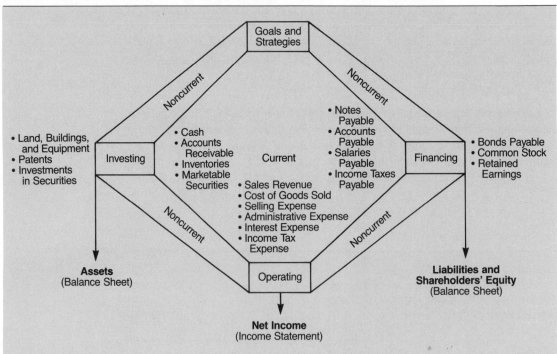

## Exhibit 1.3 ———————————————————————————————————————
### MARNEL CORPORATION
### Statement of Cash Flows for Year 1

| | | |
|---|---:|---:|
| Cash Flow from Operations................................ | | $ 50,000[a] |
| Investing: | | |
| Sale of Noncurrent Assets................................ | — | |
| Acquisition of Noncurrent Assets ......................... | ( 30,000) | |
| Cash Flow from Investing ................................ | | ( 30,000) |
| Financing: | | |
| Issue of Bonds......................................... | $ 50,000 | |
| Issue of Common Stock.................................. | 100,000 | |
| Dividends.............................................. | ( 40,000) | |
| Reduction in Financing.................................. | — | |
| Cash Flow from Financing................................ | | $110,000 |
| Net Change in Cash for Year 1 .......................... | | $130,000 |

[a]The computation of cash generated from operations and its relation to net income are discussed in Chapter 5.

Early in the fifth year, the company learned that despite the retention of all of its earnings, it was running out of cash. A careful study of the problem revealed that the company was expanding accounts receivable, inventories, buildings, and equipment so fast that funds were not being generated quickly enough by operations and external financing to keep pace with its growth.

This example illustrates a common phenomenon for business firms. Cash may not be generated in sufficient amounts or at the proper times to finance all ongoing or growing operations. If the firm is to continue operating successfully, it must generate more funds than it spends. In some cases the firm can borrow from creditors to replenish its cash, but future operations must generate funds to repay these loans.

**Classification of Items in the Statement of Cash Flows**   Exhibit 1.3 classifies the inflows and outflows of cash in parallel with the three principal business activities described earlier in the chapter. Figure 1.3 depicts these various sources and uses graphically.

1. Operations: The excess of cash received from customers over the amount of cash paid to suppliers, employees, and others in carrying out a firm's operating activities is a primary source of funds for most firms.

2. Investing: Firms that expect either to maintain current operating levels or to grow must continually acquire buildings, equipment, and other noncurrent assets. Some of the cash needed can be obtained from selling existing land, buildings, and equipment. The cash proceeds, however, are seldom sufficient to replace the assets sold.

3. Financing: Firms obtain additional financing to support operating and investing activities by issuing bonds or common stock. Cash is used for dividends and retiring old financing.

**Figure 1.3** _____
Inflows and Outflows of Cash

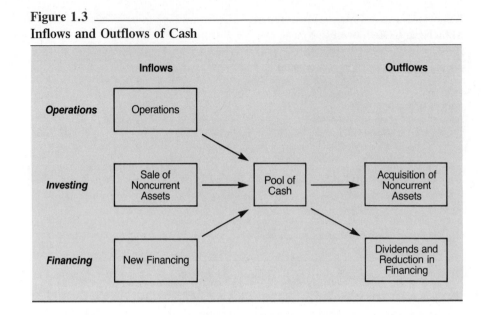

**Relation to Balance Sheet and Income Statement**  The statement of cash flows explains the change in cash between the beginning and end of the period. The statement also sets forth the major investing and financing activities of the period. Thus, the statement of cash flows helps explain changes in various items on the comparative balance sheet.

The statement of cash flows also relates to the income statement in that it shows how operations affected cash for the period.

# Other Items in Annual Reports _____

## Supporting Schedules and Notes

The balance sheet, income statement, and statement of cash flows in the annual report are condensed for easy comprehension by the average reader. Some readers are interested in details omitted from these condensed versions. The annual report, therefore, typically includes schedules that provide more detail for some of the items reported in the three main statements. For example, separate schedules must be provided to explain the change in contributed capital and retained earnings, and may be provided to explain changes in other items in the balance sheet.

Every set of published financial statements also contains explanatory notes that are an integral part of the statements. As later chapters make clear, a firm must select the accounting methods followed in preparing its financial statements from a set of generally accepted methods. The notes indicate the actual accounting methods used by the firm and also disclose additional information that elaborates on items presented in the three principal statements. To understand fully a firm's balance sheet, income statement, and statement of cash flows requires a careful reading of the notes. No such notes are presented for the financial statements of Marnel Corporation because they would not mean much at this stage. Do not conclude, however, that the notes are unimportant merely because they have been omitted from the statements presented in this chapter.

## Auditor's Opinion

The annual report to the shareholders contains the opinion of the independent auditor, or certified public accountant, on the financial statements, supporting schedules, and notes.

The auditor's opinion generally follows a standard format, with some variations to meet specific circumstances. An auditor's opinion on the financial statements of Marnel Corporation might be as follows:

> We have examined the comparative balance sheet of Marnel Corporation as of January 1 and December 31, Year 1, and the related statements of net income and cash flows for Year 1. Our examination was made in accordance with generally accepted auditing standards, and accordingly included such tests of the accounting records and such other auditing procedures as we considered necessary in the circumstances.
>
> In our opinion, the aforementioned financial statements present fairly the financial position of Marnel Corporation at January 1 and December 31, Year 1, and the results of its operations and cash flows for Year 1 in conformity with generally accepted accounting principles applied on a consistent basis.

The opinion usually contains two paragraphs — a scope paragraph and an opinion paragraph. The scope paragraph indicates the financial presentations covered by the opinion and affirms that auditing standards and practices generally accepted by the accounting profession have been followed unless otherwise noted and described. Exceptions to the statement that the auditor's "examination was made in accordance with generally accepted auditing standards" are seldom seen in published annual reports. There are occasional references to the auditor's having relied on financial statements examined by other auditors, particularly for subsidiaries or for data from prior periods.

The opinion expressed by the auditor in the second paragraph is the heart of the report. It may be an *unqualified* or *qualified opinion*. The great majority of opinions are unqualified; that is, there are no exceptions or qualifications to the auditor's opinion that the statements "present fairly the financial position . . . and the results of operations and the changes in cash flows . . . in conformity with generally accepted accounting principles applied on a consistent basis."

Qualifications to the opinion result primarily from material uncertainties regarding realization or valuation of assets, outstanding litigation or tax liabilities, or accounting inconsistencies between periods caused by changes in the application of accounting principles. An opinion qualified as to fair presentation is usually noted by the phrase *subject to;* an opinion qualified as to consistency in application of accounting principles is usually noted by *except for,* with an indication of the auditor's approval of the change in principles.

Figure 1.4
**Summary of Reporting Process and Principal Financial Statements**

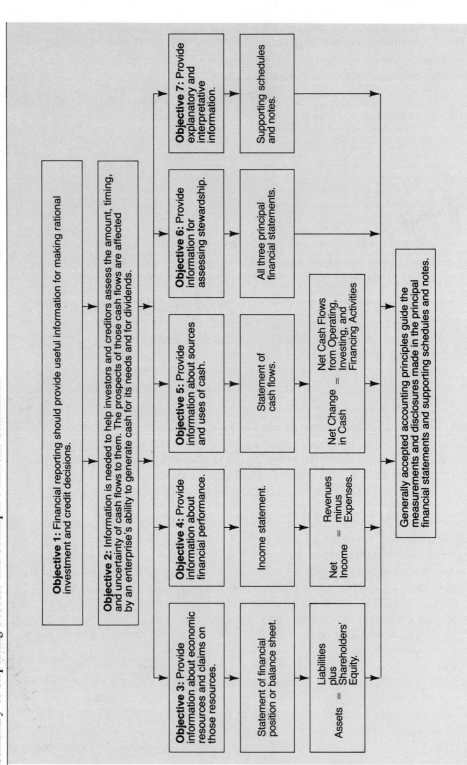

A qualification so material that the auditor feels an opinion cannot be expressed as to the fairness of the financial statements as a whole must result in either a *disclaimer of opinion* or an *adverse opinion*. Adverse opinions and disclaimers of opinion are extremely rare in published reports.

## Objectives of Financial Reporting ————————————————

Financial statements such as those discussed in this chapter provide information to investors, creditors, and others who commit funds to a firm. The Financial Accounting Standards Board, the official rule-making body in the private sector, has established a broad set of *financial reporting objectives* to guide the financial reporting process. Figure 1.4 summarizes these objectives (described briefly below) and their relation to the principal financial statements.

1.  Financial reporting should provide information useful for making rational investment and credit decisions. This general-purpose objective states simply that financial reporting should be aimed primarily at investors and creditors and should strive to be useful to these individuals in their decision making.

2.  Financial reporting should provide information to help investors and creditors assess the amount, timing, and uncertainty of cash flows. This objective flows from the first by defining "useful" information more fully. It states that investors and creditors are interested primarily in the cash they will receive from investing in a firm. That cash is affected by the ability of the firm to generate cash flows.

3.  Financial reporting should provide information about the economic resources of a firm and the claims on those resources. The balance sheet satisfies this objective.

4.  Financial reporting should provide information about a firm's operating performance during a period. The income statement accomplishes this objective.

5.  Financial reporting should provide information about how an enterprise obtains and uses cash. The statement of cash flows accomplishes this objective.

6.  Financial reporting should provide information about how management has discharged its stewardship responsibility to owners. Stewardship refers to the prudent use of resources entrusted to a firm. No single statement helps in assessing stewardship. Rather, owners assess stewardship using information from all three financial statements and the notes.

7.  Financial reporting should include explanations and interpretations to help users understand the financial information provided. Supporting schedules and notes to the financial statements satisfy this objective.

## Summary ————————————————————————

This chapter provided an overview of business activities and related them to the principal financial statements included in annual reports to shareholders. Perhaps more questions have been raised than-answered. It is helpful, however, to have a broad overview of the various financial statements before examining the concepts and procedures that underlie each statement.

Chapters 2 through 5 discuss and illustrate the concepts and procedures underlying the balance sheet, income statement, and statement of cash flows. Chapter 6 considers techniques for analyzing and interpreting these financial statements. Chapters 7 through 14 explore more fully the principles of accounting for individual assets, liabilities, and shareholders' equities. Chapter 15 provides a synthesis for the book.

Now we turn to the study of financial accounting. One of the most effective means of comprehending the concepts and procedures in the book is the careful study of the numerical examples presented in each chapter and the diligent working of several problems, including the self-study problem(s), at the end of each chapter. Frequent reference should also be made to the glossary of terms at the back of the book.

## Problem for Self-Study _____

The accounting records of Digital Electronics Corporation reveal the following:

|  | December 31 | |
| --- | --- | --- |
|  | Year 1 | Year 2 |
| **Balance Sheet Items:** | | |
| Accounts Payable to Suppliers ........................... | $250,000 | $295,000 |
| Accounts Receivable from Customers ................... | 240,000 | 320,000 |
| Bonds Payable ......................................... | 100,000 | 120,000 |
| Buildings (net of accumulated depreciation) ............... | 150,000 | 140,000 |
| Cash ................................................. | 30,000 | 50,000 |
| Common Stock ........................................ | 100,000 | 100,000 |
| Equipment (net of accumulated depreciation) .............. | 140,000 | 220,000 |
| Income Taxes Payable ................................. | 40,000 | 70,000 |
| Land ................................................. | 60,000 | 70,000 |
| Merchandise Inventory ................................ | 380,000 | 400,000 |
| Retained Earnings .................................... | 500,000 | 600,000 |
| Salaries Payable ..................................... | 10,000 | 15,000 |
| **Income Statement Items for Year 2:** | | |
| Cost of Merchandise Sold ............................. |  | $   620,000 |
| Depreciation Expense ................................. |  | 40,000 |
| Income Tax Expense ................................. |  | 100,000 |
| Insurance Expense ................................... |  | 3,000 |
| Interest Expense ..................................... |  | 10,000 |
| Property Tax Expense ................................ |  | 2,000 |
| Rental Revenue (rental of part of building) ............... |  | 30,000 |
| Salary Expense ...................................... |  | 135,000 |
| Sales Revenue ....................................... |  | 1,000,000 |
| **Dividend Information for Year 2:** | | |
| Dividends Declared and Paid ........................... |  | $    20,000 |

a.  Prepare a comparative balance sheet for Digital Electronics Corporation as of December 31, Year 1 and Year 2. Classify the balance sheet items into the following categories: current assets, noncurrent assets, current liabilities, noncurrent liabilities, and shareholders' equity.

b.  Prepare an income statement for Digital Electronics Corporation for Year 2. Separate income statement items into revenues and expenses.

c.  Prepare a schedule explaining the changes in retained earnings during Year 2.

## Suggested Solution

Exhibit 1.4 presents a comparative balance sheet, Exhibit 1.5 presents an income statement, and Exhibit 1.6 analyzes the change in retained earnings for Digital Electronics Corporation for Year 2.

**Exhibit 1.4** —————————————————————————————————
DIGITAL ELECTRONICS CORPORATION
Comparative Balance Sheet
December 31, Year 1 and Year 2

|  | December 31 | |
|---|---|---|
|  | Year 1 | Year 2 |
| **Assets** | | |
| **Current Assets:** | | |
| Cash | $ 30,000 | $ 50,000 |
| Accounts Receivable from Customers | 240,000 | 320,000 |
| Merchandise Inventory | 380,000 | 400,000 |
| Total Current Assets | $ 650,000 | $ 770,000 |
| **Noncurrent Assets:** | | |
| Land | $ 60,000 | $ 70,000 |
| Equipment (net of accumulated depreciation) | 140,000 | 220,000 |
| Buildings (net of accumulated depreciation) | 150,000 | 140,000 |
| Total Noncurrent Assets | $ 350,000 | $ 430,000 |
| Total Assets | $1,000,000 | $1,200,000 |
| **Liabilities and Shareholders' Equity** | | |
| **Current Liabilities:** | | |
| Accounts Payable to Suppliers | $ 250,000 | $ 295,000 |
| Salaries Payable | 10,000 | 15,000 |
| Income Taxes Payable | 40,000 | 70,000 |
| Total Current Liabilities | $ 300,000 | $ 380,000 |
| **Noncurrent Liabilities:** | | |
| Bonds Payable | 100,000 | 120,000 |
| Total Liabilities | $ 400,000 | $ 500,000 |
| **Shareholders' Equity:** | | |
| Common Stock | $ 100,000 | $ 100,000 |
| Retained Earnings | 500,000 | 600,000 |
| Total Shareholders' Equity | $ 600,000 | $ 700,000 |
| Total Liabilities and Shareholders' Equity | $1,000,000 | $1,200,000 |

Exhibit 1.5 _____

**DIGITAL ELECTRONICS CORPORATION**
**Income Statement for Year 2**

**Revenues:**

| | | |
|---|---:|---:|
| Sales Revenue . . . . . . . . . . . . . . . . . . . . . . . . . . . . . . . . . . . . . . . . | $1,000,000 | |
| Rental Revenue . . . . . . . . . . . . . . . . . . . . . . . . . . . . . . . . . . . . . | 30,000 | |
| Total Revenues . . . . . . . . . . . . . . . . . . . . . . . . . . . . . . . . . . | | $1,030,000 |

**Expenses:**

| | | |
|---|---:|---:|
| Cost of Merchandise Sold . . . . . . . . . . . . . . . . . . . . . . . . . . . . . | $ 620,000 | |
| Salary Expense . . . . . . . . . . . . . . . . . . . . . . . . . . . . . . . . . . . . . | 135,000 | |
| Property Tax Expense . . . . . . . . . . . . . . . . . . . . . . . . . . . . . . . | 2,000 | |
| Insurance Expense . . . . . . . . . . . . . . . . . . . . . . . . . . . . . . . . . . | 3,000 | |
| Depreciation Expense . . . . . . . . . . . . . . . . . . . . . . . . . . . . . . . | 40,000 | |
| Interest Expense . . . . . . . . . . . . . . . . . . . . . . . . . . . . . . . . . . . | 10,000 | |
| Income Tax Expense . . . . . . . . . . . . . . . . . . . . . . . . . . . . . . . . | 100,000 | |
| Total Expenses. . . . . . . . . . . . . . . . . . . . . . . . . . . . . . . . . . . . | | $ 910,000 |
| **Net Income**. . . . . . . . . . . . . . . . . . . . . . . . . . . . . . . . . . . . . . . . . | | $ 120,000 |

Exhibit 1.6 _____

**DIGITAL ELECTRONICS CORPORATION**
**Analysis of Change in Retained Earnings for Year 2**

| | |
|---|---:|
| Retained Earnings, December 31, Year 1 . . . . . . . . . . . . . . . . . . . . . . . . . . . . . . | $500,000 |
| Plus Net Income . . . . . . . . . . . . . . . . . . . . . . . . . . . . . . . . . . . . . . . . . . | 120,000 |
| Less Dividends Declared and Paid . . . . . . . . . . . . . . . . . . . . . . . . . . . . . . . . . | (20,000) |
| Retained Earnings, December 31, Year 2 . . . . . . . . . . . . . . . . . . . . . . . . . . . . . | $600,000 |

# Questions, Exercises, Problems, and Cases _____

## Questions

1. Review the meaning of the following concepts or terms discussed in this chapter.

   **a.** Managerial accounting.

   **b.** Financial accounting.

   **c.** Generally accepted accounting principles.

   **d.** Financial Accounting Standards Board.

   **e.** Securities and Exchange Commission.

   **f.** Goals and strategies.

   **g.** Financing activities.

   **h.** Investing activities.

   **i.** Operating activities.

   **j.** Balance sheet.

   **k.** Assets.

   **l.** Liabilities.

   **m.** Shareholders' equity.

   **n.** Contributed capital.

   **o.** Retained earnings.

   **p.** Cash equivalent valuation.

   **q.** Acquisition (or historical) cost.

   **r.** Income statement.

   **s.** Net income, earnings, profits.

| | | | |
|---|---|---|---|
| **t.** | Revenue. | **x.** | Statement of cash flows. |
| **u.** | Expense. | **y.** | Unqualified, qualified, and ad- |
| **v.** | Net loss. | | verse opinions. |
| **w.** | Dividends. | **z.** | Financial reporting objectives. |

2. Distinguish between financial accounting and managerial accounting. Suggest several ways in which the managers of a firm might use information presented in the three principal externally directed financial statements discussed in this chapter.

3. Suggest reasons why the format and content of financial accounting reports tend to be more standardized than is the case for managerial accounting reports.

4. What purpose is served by having a broad set of financial reporting objectives, such as those issued by the Financial Accounting Standards Board?

5. "Asset valuation and income measurement are closely related." Explain.

6. Does the unqualified or "clean" opinion of a certified public accountant indicate that the financial statements are free of errors and misrepresentations? Explain.

## Exercises

7. *Preparation of personal balance sheet.* Prepare a balance sheet of your personal assets, liabilities, and owner's equity. How does the presentation of owner's equity on your balance sheet differ from that in Exhibit 1.1?

8. *Account classification.* Various items are classified on the balance sheet or income statement in one of the following ways:

CA — Current assets.

NA — Noncurrent assets.

CL — Current liabilities.

NL — Noncurrent liabilities.

CC — Contributed capital.

RE — Retained earnings.

NI — Income statement item (revenue or expense).

X — Item would generally not appear on a balance sheet or income statement.

Using the letters above, indicate the classification of each of the following items:

a. Factory.
b. Interest revenue.
c. Common stock issued by a corporation.
d. Goodwill developed by a firm (see glossary).
e. Automobiles used by sales staff.
f. Cash on hand.
g. Unsettled damage suit against a firm.

 **h.** Commissions earned by sales staff.
 **i.** Supplies inventory.
 **j.** Note payable, due in 3 months.
 **k.** Increase in market value of land held.
 **l.** Dividends.
 **m.** Employee payroll taxes payable.
 **n.** Note payable, due in 6 years.

**9.** *Balance sheet relations*. Compute the missing balance sheet amounts in each of the four independent cases that follow.

|  | a | b | c | d |
|---|---|---|---|---|
| Noncurrent Assets . . . . . . . . . . . . | $400,000 | $500,000 | $340,000 | ? |
| Shareholders' Equity . . . . . . . . . . | ? | 250,000 | 290,000 | $140,000 |
| Total Assets . . . . . . . . . . . . . . . . | ? | ? | 500,000 | ? |
| Current Liabilities . . . . . . . . . . . . | 500,000 | 150,000 | ?* | ?** |
| Current Assets . . . . . . . . . . . . . . | 600,000 | ? | ?* | ?** |
| Noncurrent Liabilities . . . . . . . . . . | 100,000 | ? | ? | 160,000 |
| Total Liabilities and Shareholders' Equity . . . . . | ? | 700,000 | ? | 550,000 |

*Current Assets − Current Liabilities = $70,000.
**Current Assets − Current Liabilities = $80,000.

**10.** *Balance sheet relations*. Compute the missing balance sheet amounts in each of the four independent cases that follow.

|  | a | b | c | d |
|---|---|---|---|---|
| Noncurrent Assets . . . . . . . . . . | $700,000 | $2,000,000 | $340,000 | ? |
| Shareholders' Equity . . . . . . . . | ? | 1,550,000 | 380,000 | $370,000 |
| Total Assets . . . . . . . . . . . . . . | ? | ? | 500,000 | ? |
| Current Liabilities . . . . . . . . . . . | 250,000 | 400,000 | ?* | ?** |
| Current Assets . . . . . . . . . . . . | 300,000 | ? | ?* | ?** |
| Noncurrent Liabilities . . . . . . . . | 300,000 | ? | ? | 400,000 |
| Total Liabilities and Shareholders' Equity . . . . . . . | ? | 2,650,000 | ? | 950,000 |

*Current Assets − Current Liabilities = $40,000.
**Current Assets − Current Liabilities = $70,000.

**11.** *Balance sheet relations*. Compute the missing balance sheet amounts in each of the four independent cases that follow.

|  | a | b | c | d |
|---|---|---|---|---|
| Total Assets . . . . . . . . . . . . . . | $1,000,000 | ? | ? | $270,000 |
| Noncurrent Liabilities . . . . . . . . | 350,000 | $ 25,000 | ? | 230,000 |
| Noncurrent Assets . . . . . . . . . . | ? | 50,000 | $600,000 | ? |
| Total Liabilities and Shareholders' Equity . . . . . . . | ? | 300,000 | ? | ? |
| Current Liabilities . . . . . . . . . . . | 250,000 | ? | 40,000 | 60,000 |
| Shareholders' Equity . . . . . . . . | ? | 75,000 | 110,000 | ? |
| Current Assets . . . . . . . . . . . . | 350,000 | ? | 50,000 | 30,000 |

**12.** *Retained earnings relations.* Compute the missing amount affecting retained earnings for Year 2 in each of the independent cases that follow.

|  | a | b | c | d | e |
|---|---|---|---|---|---|
| Retained Earnings, Dec. 31, Year 1 ......... | $80,000 | ? | $458,000 | $120,000 | $240,000 |
| Net Income ............... | 30,000 | $260,000 | 260,000 | ? | (60,000)* |
| Dividends Declared and Paid ............... | 10,000 | 145,000 | ? | 35,000 | ? |
| Retained Earnings, Dec. 31, Year 2 ......... | ? | 766,000 | 598,000 | 110,000 | 180,000 |

*Net loss.

**13.** *Retained earnings relations.* Compute the missing amount affecting retained earnings for Year 2 in each of the independent cases that follow.

|  | a | b | c | d | e |
|---|---|---|---|---|---|
| Retained Earnings, Dec. 31, Year 1 ......... | $150,000 | ? | $320,000 | $75,000 | $ 40,000 |
| Net Income ............... | 50,000 | $125,000 | 180,000 | ? | (30,000)* |
| Dividends Declared and Paid ............... | 20,000 | 75,000 | ? | 30,000 | ? |
| Retained Earnings, Dec. 31, Year 2 ......... | ? | 500,000 | 470,000 | 90,000 | 10,000 |

*Net loss.

**14.** *Relation of net income to balance sheet changes.* The comparative balance sheets of the Sweet Corporation as of December 31, Year 1, and December 31, Year 2, are presented as follows.

**SWEET CORPORATION**
**Comparative Balance Sheets**
**December 31, Year 1 and Year 2**

|  | December 31 | |
|---|---|---|
|  | Year 1 | Year 2 |
| Total Assets ......................................... | $500,000 | $800,000 |
| Liabilities ............................................ | $100,000 | $160,000 |
| Common Stock....................................... | 250,000 | 290,000 |
| Retained Earnings .................................... | 150,000 | 350,000 |
| Total Liabilities and Shareholders' Equity................. | $500,000 | $800,000 |

Dividends declared and paid during Year 2 were $60,000.

**a.** Compute net income for the year ending December 31, Year 2, by analyzing the change in retained earnings.

**b.** Demonstrate that the following relation holds:

Net Income = Increase in Assets − Increase in Liabilities
  −Increase in Contributed Capital + Dividends.

**15.** *Income statement relations*. Compute the missing amounts affecting the net income for Year 1 in each of the independent cases that follow.

|  | a | b | c | d |
|---|---|---|---|---|
| Sales Revenue................................ | $500 | ? | $390 | $260 |
| Cost of Goods Sold........................... | 250 | $60 | ? | 190 |
| Selling and Administrative Expenses............ | 120 | 30 | 70 | ? |
| Income Tax Expense ......................... | 60 | 20 | 35 | 0 |
| Net Income ................................... | ? | 15 | 35 | (15)* |

*Net loss.

**16.** *Statement of cash flows*. Compute the missing amounts affecting the change in cash for Year 1 in each of the independent cases that follow.

|  | a | b | c | d |
|---|---|---|---|---|
| **Inflows of Cash:** | | | | |
| Operations................................... | $500 | $250 | $600 | $(200)* |
| New Financing ............................... | 200 | 100 | ? | 300 |
| Sale of Noncurrent Assets.................. | 50 | 20 | 0 | 100 |
| **Outflows of Cash:** | | | | |
| Dividends.................................... | 100 | 75 | 200 | 0 |
| Reduction in Financing...................... | 80 | 0 | 50 | 50 |
| Acquisition of Noncurrent Assets ........... | 550 | ? | 800 | 120 |
| Change in Cash............................. | ? | 20 | (50)** | ? |

*Net use of cash for operations.
**Decrease in cash.

**17.** *Relations between financial statements*. Compute the missing information in each of the four independent cases below. The letters in parentheses refer to the following:

   BS — Balance sheet.

    IS — Income statement.

   SCF — Statement of cash flows.

| | |
|---|---|
| **a.** Accounts Receivable, Jan. 1, Year 2 (BS) .......................... | $ 450 |
|    Sales on Account for Year 2 (IS) .................................... | 1,700 |
|    Collections from Customers on Account during Year 2 (SCF) .......... | 1,350 |
|    Accounts Receivable, Dec. 31, Year 2 (BS)......................... | ? |
| **b.** Salaries Payable, Jan. 1, Year 2 (BS)............................... | $ 120 |
|    Salary Expense for Year 2 (IS) ...................................... | ? |
|    Payments to Salaried Employees during Year 2 (SCF)................ | 660 |
|    Salaries Payable, Dec. 31, Year 2 (BS) ............................. | 90 |

*continued*

c. Equipment (net of depreciation), Jan. 1, Year 2 (BS) ................. $ 800
   Depreciation Expense for Year 2 (IS) .............................. ?
   Sales of Equipment during Year 2 (SCF) ........................... 0
   Acquisition of Equipment during Year 2 (SCF) ...................... 250
   Equipment (net of depreciation), Dec. 31, Year 2 (BS) .............. 900

d. Retained Earnings, Jan. 1, Year 2 (BS) .......................... $1,250
   Net Income for Year 2 (IS)........................................ 300
   Dividends Declared and Paid during Year 2 (SCF) .................. ?
   Retained Earnings, Dec. 31, Year 2 (BS).......................... 1,430

## Problems and Cases

**18.** *Preparation of balance sheet and income statement.* B. Stephens, L. Harris, and G. Winkle, recent graduates, set up a management consulting practice on December 31, Year 1, by issuing common stock for $750,000. The accounting records of the S, H & W Corporation as of December 31, Year 2, reveal the following.

**Balance Sheet Items:**

| | |
|---|---:|
| Cash ....................................................... | $ 50,000 |
| Accounts Receivable from Clients .................................... | 165,000 |
| Supplies Inventory ................................................ | 5,000 |
| Office Equipment (net of depreciation) ............................... | 85,000 |
| Office Building (net of depreciation)................................. | 500,000 |
| Accounts Payable to Suppliers .................................... | 10,000 |
| Payroll Taxes Payable ........................................... | 12,000 |
| Income Taxes Payable ............................................ | 13,000 |
| Common Stock............................,..................... | 750,000 |

**Income Statement Items:**

| | |
|---|---:|
| Revenue from Consulting Services .................................... | $300,000 |
| Rental Revenue (from renting part of building) ......................... | 30,000 |
| Salaries Expense................................................ | 222,000 |
| Property Taxes and Insurance Expense .............................. | 30,000 |
| Supplies Expense ................................................ | 10,000 |
| Depreciation Expense............................................ | 25,000 |
| Income Tax Expense ............................................. | 13,000 |

**Dividend Information:**

| | |
|---|---:|
| Dividends Declared and Paid ...................................... | $ 10,000 |

a. Prepare an income statement for S, H & W Corporation for the year ending December 31, Year 2. Refer to Exhibit 1.2 for help in designing the format of the statement.

b. Prepare a comparative balance sheet for S, H & W Corporation on December 31, Year 1, and December 31, Year 2. Refer to Exhibit 1.1 for help in designing the format of the statement.

c. Prepare an analysis of the change in retained earnings during Year 2.

**19.** *Preparation of balance sheet and income statement.* Keyes Manufacturing Corporation was organized on January 1, Year 1. The company issued common stock for $600,000 and long-term bonds for $400,000. The accounting records of Keyes Manufacturing Corporation as of December 31, Year 1, reveal the following.

**Balance Sheet Items:**

| | |
|---|---:|
| Cash . . . . . . . . . . . . . . . . . . . . . . . . . . . . . . . . . . . . . . . . . . . . . . . . . . | $    50,000 |
| Accounts Receivable from Customers . . . . . . . . . . . . . . . . . . . . . . . . . . . | 350,000 |
| Inventories . . . . . . . . . . . . . . . . . . . . . . . . . . . . . . . . . . . . . . . . . . . . . . | 300,000 |
| Land . . . . . . . . . . . . . . . . . . . . . . . . . . . . . . . . . . . . . . . . . . . . . . . . . . . | 50,000 |
| Buildings (net of depreciation) . . . . . . . . . . . . . . . . . . . . . . . . . . . . . . . | 400,000 |
| Equipment (net of depreciation) . . . . . . . . . . . . . . . . . . . . . . . . . . . . . . . | 350,000 |
| Accounts Payable to Suppliers . . . . . . . . . . . . . . . . . . . . . . . . . . . . . . . . | 120,000 |
| Salaries Payable to Workers . . . . . . . . . . . . . . . . . . . . . . . . . . . . . . . . . . | 75,000 |
| Bonds Payable . . . . . . . . . . . . . . . . . . . . . . . . . . . . . . . . . . . . . . . . . . . . | 400,000 |
| Common Stock . . . . . . . . . . . . . . . . . . . . . . . . . . . . . . . . . . . . . . . . . . . . | 700,000 |

**Income Statement Items:**

| | |
|---|---:|
| Sales Revenue . . . . . . . . . . . . . . . . . . . . . . . . . . . . . . . . . . . . . . . . . . . . | $2,000,000 |
| Cost of Goods Sold . . . . . . . . . . . . . . . . . . . . . . . . . . . . . . . . . . . . . . . . . | 1,200,000 |
| Selling Expenses . . . . . . . . . . . . . . . . . . . . . . . . . . . . . . . . . . . . . . . . . . | 200,000 |
| Administrative Expenses . . . . . . . . . . . . . . . . . . . . . . . . . . . . . . . . . . . . | 210,000 |
| Interest Expense . . . . . . . . . . . . . . . . . . . . . . . . . . . . . . . . . . . . . . . . . . | 40,000 |
| Income Tax Expense . . . . . . . . . . . . . . . . . . . . . . . . . . . . . . . . . . . . . . . | 100,000 |

**Dividend Information:**

| | |
|---|---:|
| Dividends Declared and Paid . . . . . . . . . . . . . . . . . . . . . . . . . . . . . . . . . | $    45,000 |

a.  Prepare an income statement for Keyes Manufacturing Corporation for the year ending December 31, Year 1. Refer to Exhibit 1.2 for help in designing the format of the statement.

b.  Prepare a comparative balance sheet for Keyes Manufacturing Corporation on January 1, Year 1, and December 31, Year 1. Refer to Exhibit 1.1 for help in designing the format of the statement.

c.  Prepare an analysis of the change in retained earnings during Year 1.

20.  *Preparation of balance sheet and income statement.* The accounting records of Laser Sales Corporation reveal the following:

| | December 31 | |
|---|---:|---:|
| | **Year 1** | **Year 2** |
| **Balance Sheet Items:** | | |
| Accounts Payable . . . . . . . . . . . . . . . . . . . . . . . . . . . . . . . | $1,247,000 | $1,513,000 |
| Accounts Receivable . . . . . . . . . . . . . . . . . . . . . . . . . . . . . | 740,000 | 820,000 |
| Bank Loan Payable (due April 10, Year 3) . . . . . . . . . . . | — | 15,000 |
| Bonds Payable (due Year 16) . . . . . . . . . . . . . . . . . . . . . . | 80,000 | 100,000 |
| Building (net of accumulated depreciation) . . . . . . . . . . . | 460,000 | 440,000 |
| Cash . . . . . . . . . . . . . . . . . . . . . . . . . . . . . . . . . . . . . . . . . | 270,000 | 315,000 |
| Common Stock . . . . . . . . . . . . . . . . . . . . . . . . . . . . . . . . . | 1,190,000 | 1,240,000 |
| Equipment (net of accumulated depreciation) . . . . . . . . . | 825,000 | 1,023,000 |
| Income Taxes Payable . . . . . . . . . . . . . . . . . . . . . . . . . . . | 25,000 | 30,000 |

*continued*

| | | |
|---|---:|---:|
| Land .......................................... | 40,000 | 50,000 |
| Merchandise Inventory ........................... | 550,000 | 610,000 |
| Note Receivable (due June 15, Year 3) .............. | — | 20,000 |
| Note Receivable (due December 31, Year 10) ........ | 100,000 | 100,000 |
| Retained Earnings ................................ | 430,000 | 470,000 |
| Salaries Payable ................................. | 28,000 | 32,000 |
| Supplies Inventory ................................ | 15,000 | 22,000 |

**Income Statement Items for Year 2:**

| | |
|---|---:|
| Cost of Merchandise Sold ......................... | $2,611,000 |
| Depreciation Expense ............................. | 45,000 |
| Income Tax Expense ............................. | 25,000 |
| Insurance Expense ............................... | 8,000 |
| Interest Expense ................................. | 16,000 |
| Interest Revenue ................................. | 15,000 |
| Payroll Tax Expense .............................. | 80,000 |
| Salary Expense .................................. | 670,000 |
| Sales Revenue ................................... | 3,500,000 |

**Dividend Information:**

| | |
|---|---:|
| Dividends Declared and Paid during Year 2 ........... | $   20,000 |

a. Prepare a comparative balance sheet for Laser Sales Corporation as of December 31, Year 1 and Year 2. Classify the balance sheet items into one of the following categories: current assets, noncurrent assets, current liabilities, noncurrent liabilities, or shareholders' equity.

b. Prepare an income statement for Laser Sales Corporation for Year 2. Separate income items into revenues and expenses.

c. Prepare a schedule explaining, or accounting for, the change in retained earnings between the beginning and end of Year 2.

21. *Relations among principal financial statements.* This problem illustrates the relations among the three principal financial statements. Exhibit 1.7 presents a comparative balance sheet for Articulation Corporation as of December 31, Year 1 and Year 2. Exhibit 1.8 presents an income statement and Exhibit 1.9 presents a statement of cash flows for Articulation Corporation for Year 2.

Using amounts from these three financial statements, demonstrate that the following relations are correct:

a. Retained earnings at the end of Year 1 plus net income for Year 2 minus dividends declared and paid for Year 2 equals retained earnings at the end of Year 2.

b. Change in total assets equals change in total liabilities plus change in common stock plus net income minus dividends.

c. Accounts receivable at the end of Year 1 plus sales to customers (all on account) less cash collections from customers (see statement of cash flows) equals accounts receivable at the end of Year 2.

d. Buildings and equipment at the end of Year 1 plus acquisitions of buildings and equipment minus dispositions of buildings and equipment minus depreciation for Year 2 equals buildings and equipment at the end of Year 2.

Exhibit 1.7 _____

**ARTICULATION CORPORATION**
Comparative Balance Sheets
December 31, Year 1 and Year 2

|  | December 31 | |
|---|---|---|
|  | Year 1 | Year 2 |

# Assets

| | | |
|---|---|---|
| **Current Assets:** | | |
| Cash . . . . . . . . . . . . . . . . . . . . . . . . . . . . . . . . . . . . . . . . . . . . . . . . . | $ 80 | $180 |
| Accounts Receivable from Customers . . . . . . . . . . . . . . . . . . . . . . . | 300 | 340 |
| Merchandise Inventory . . . . . . . . . . . . . . . . . . . . . . . . . . . . . . . . . . . | 150 | 160 |
| Total Current Assets . . . . . . . . . . . . . . . . . . . . . . . . . . . . . . . . . . . | $530 | $680 |
| **Noncurrent Assets:** | | |
| Land . . . . . . . . . . . . . . . . . . . . . . . . . . . . . . . . . . . . . . . . . . . . . . . . . . | $ 40 | $ 55 |
| Buildings and Equipment (net of accumulated depreciation) . . . . . | 130 | 165 |
| Total Noncurrent Assets . . . . . . . . . . . . . . . . . . . . . . . . . . . . . . . . | $170 | $220 |
| Total Assets . . . . . . . . . . . . . . . . . . . . . . . . . . . . . . . . . . . . . . . . . | $700 | $900 |

# Liabilities and Shareholders' Equity

| | | |
|---|---|---|
| **Current Liabilities:** | | |
| Accounts Payable . . . . . . . . . . . . . . . . . . . . . . . . . . . . . . . . . . . . . . . | $310 | $350 |
| Income Taxes Payable . . . . . . . . . . . . . . . . . . . . . . . . . . . . . . . . . . . | 40 | 60 |
| Total Current Liabilities . . . . . . . . . . . . . . . . . . . . . . . . . . . . . . . . | $350 | $410 |
| **Noncurrent Liabilities:** | | |
| Bonds Payable . . . . . . . . . . . . . . . . . . . . . . . . . . . . . . . . . . . . . . . . . | 20 | 25 |
| Total Liabilities . . . . . . . . . . . . . . . . . . . . . . . . . . . . . . . . . . . . . . | $370 | $435 |
| **Shareholders' Equity:** | | |
| Common Stock . . . . . . . . . . . . . . . . . . . . . . . . . . . . . . . . . . . . . . . . . | $200 | $245 |
| Retained Earnings . . . . . . . . . . . . . . . . . . . . . . . . . . . . . . . . . . . . . . | 130 | 220 |
| Total Shareholders' Equity . . . . . . . . . . . . . . . . . . . . . . . . . . . . . . | $330 | $465 |
| Total Liabilities and Shareholders' Equity . . . . . . . . . . . . . . . . . . | $700 | $900 |

Exhibit 1.8 _____

**ARTICULATION CORPORATION**
Income Statement for Year 2

| | | |
|---|---|---|
| **Sales Revenue** . . . . . . . . . . . . . . . . . . . . . . . . . . . . . . . . . . . . . . . . . |  | $1,000 |
| **Expenses:** | | |
| Cost of Merchandise Sold . . . . . . . . . . . . . . . . . . . . . . . . . . . . . . . . | $600 | |
| Salary Expense . . . . . . . . . . . . . . . . . . . . . . . . . . . . . . . . . . . . . . . . | 100 | |
| Depreciation Expense . . . . . . . . . . . . . . . . . . . . . . . . . . . . . . . . . . . | 50 | |
| Interest Expense . . . . . . . . . . . . . . . . . . . . . . . . . . . . . . . . . . . . . . . | 20 | |
| Income Tax Expense . . . . . . . . . . . . . . . . . . . . . . . . . . . . . . . . . . . . | 120 | |
| Total Expenses . . . . . . . . . . . . . . . . . . . . . . . . . . . . . . . . . . . . . . . |  | $ 890 |
| **Net Income** . . . . . . . . . . . . . . . . . . . . . . . . . . . . . . . . . . . . . . . . . . . |  | $ 110 |

Exhibit 1.9 _____

**ARTICULATION CORPORATION**
**Statement of Cash Flows for Year 2**

---

**Operations:**

| | | |
|---|---|---|
| Revenues Increasing Cash ................................... | $960 | |
| Expenses Decreasing Cash ................................. | 790 | |
|     Cash Flow from Operations.............................. | | $170 |

**Investing:**

| | | |
|---|---|---|
| Land Acquired .......................................... | $( 15) | |
| Buildings and Equipment Acquired ......................... | ( 85) | |
|     Cash Flow from Investing .............................. | | (100) |

**Financing:**

| | | |
|---|---|---|
| Issue of Bonds ......................................... | $  5 | |
| Issue of Common Stock................................... | 45 | |
| Dividends Declared and Paid .............................. | ( 20) | |
|     Cash Flow from Financing.............................. | | 30 |
| **Net Change in Cash** ...................................... | | $100 |

---

   **e.**   Bonds payable at the end of Year 1 plus new bonds issued during Year 2 minus outstanding bonds redeemed during Year 2 equals bonds payable at the end of Year 2.

   **f.**   Common stock at the end of Year 1 plus common stock issued during Year 2 minus outstanding common stock redeemed during Year 2 equals common stock at the end of Year 2.

**22.** *Relations between net income and cash flows.* The ABC Company started the year in fine shape. The firm made widgets — just what the customer wanted. It made them for $0.75 each and sold them for $1.00. The ABC Company kept an inventory equal to shipments of the past 30 days, paid its bills promptly, and collected cash from customers within 30 days after the sale. The sales manager predicted a steady increase of 500 widgets each month beginning in February. It looked like a great year, and it began that way.

January 1      Cash, $875; receivables, $1,000; inventory, $750.

January        In January, 1,000 widgets costing $750 were sold on account for $1,000. Receivables outstanding at the beginning of the month were collected. Production equaled 1,000 units at a total cost of $750. Net income for the month was $250. The books at the end of January showed:

February 1    Cash, $1,125; receivables, $1,000; inventory $750.

February      This month's sales jumped, as predicted, to 1,500 units. With a corresponding step-up in production to maintain the 30-day inventory, ABC Company made 2,000 units at a cost of $1,500. All receivables from January sales were collected. Net income so far, $625. Now the books looked like this:

March 1      Cash, $625; receivables, $1,500; inventory, $1,125.

March        March sales were even better—2,000 units. Collections, on time; Production, to adhere to the inventory policy, 2,500 units; Operating results for the month, net income of $500; Net income to date, $1,125. The books:

April 1      Cash, $250; receivables, $2,000; inventory, $1,500.

April        In April, sales jumped another 500 units to 2,500, and the manager of ABC Company patted the sales manager on the back. Customers were paying right on time. Production was pushed to 3,000 units, and the month's business netted $625 for a net income to date of $1,750. The manager of ABC Company took off for Miami before the accountant's report was issued. Suddenly a phone call came from the treasurer: "Come home! We need money!"

May 1        Cash, $0; receivables, $2,500; inventory, $1,875.

a.   Prepare an analysis that explains what happened to ABC Company. (Hint: Compute the amount of cash receipts and cash disbursements for each month during the period January 1 to May 1.)

b.   How can a firm show increasing net income but a decreasing amount of cash?

c.   What insights are provided by the problem about the need for all three financial statements—balance sheet, income statement, and statement cash flows?

# Part Two
## Accounting Concepts and Methods

# Chapter 2 Balance Sheet: Presenting the Investments and Financing of a Firm _____

Chapter 1 introduced the balance sheet, one of the three principal financial statements. Recall that the balance sheet presents a snapshot of the investments of a firm (assets) and the financing of those investments (liabilities and shareholders' equity) as of a specific time. The balance sheet shows the following balance, or equality:

$$\text{Assets} = \text{Liabilities} + \text{Shareholders' Equity}.$$

This means that a firm's assets are in balance with, or equal to, the financing of those assets by creditors and owners. In the balance sheet, we view resources from two angles: a listing of the specific forms in which they are held (for example, cash, inventory, equipment); and a listing of the persons or interests that provided the financing and therefore have a claim on them (for example, suppliers, employees, governments, shareholders). The introduction to the balance sheet in Chapter 1 left several questions unanswered.

1. Which resources of a firm are recognized as assets?

2. What valuations are placed on these assets?

3. How are assets classified, or grouped, within the balance sheet?

4. Which claims against a firm's assets are recognized as liabilities?

5. What valuations are placed on these liabilities?

6. How are liabilities classified within the balance sheet?

7. What valuation is placed on the owners' equity in a firm, and how is the owners' equity disclosed?

In answering these questions, several accounting concepts underlying the balance sheet must be considered. This discussion not only provides a background for understanding the statement as it is currently prepared, but also permits an assessment of alternative methods of measuring financial position. After this introduction to important accounting concepts, the accounting procedures used in recording transactions and events for presentation in a balance sheet are described and illustrated.

# Underlying Concepts

## Asset Recognition

Assets are resources that have the potential for providing a firm with a future economic benefit. That benefit is the ability to generate future cash inflows or to reduce future cash outflows. The resources that are recognized as assets are those (1) for which the firm has acquired rights to their use in the future as a result of a past transaction or exchange and (2) for which the value of the future benefits can be measured, or quantified, with a reasonable degree of precision.[1]

**Example 1**  Miller Corporation sold merchandise and received a note from the customer, who agreed to pay $2,000 within 4 months. This note receivable is an asset of Miller Corporation because a right has been established to receive a definite amount of cash in the future as a result of the previous sale of merchandise.

**Example 2**  Miller Corporation acquired manufacturing equipment costing $40,000 and agreed to pay the seller over 3 years. After the final payment, legal title to the equipment will be transferred to Miller Corporation. Even though Miller Corporation does not possess legal title, the equipment is Miller's asset because it has obtained the rights and responsibilities of ownership and can maintain those rights as long as the payments are made on schedule.

**Example 3**  Miller Corporation has developed a good reputation with its employees, customers, and citizens of the community. This good reputation is expected to provide benefits to the firm in its future business activities. A good reputation, however, is generally *not* recognized as an asset. Although Miller Corporation has made various expenditures in the past to develop the reputation, the future benefits are considered to be too difficult to quantify with a sufficient degree of precision to warrant recognition as an asset.

**Example 4**  Miller Corporation plans to acquire a fleet of new trucks next year to replace those wearing out. These new trucks are not assets now because no exchange has taken place between Miller Corporation and a supplier, and, therefore, no right to the future use of the trucks has been established.

Most of the difficulties in deciding which items to recognize as assets are related to unexecuted or partially executed contracts. In Example 4, suppose that Miller Corporation entered into a contract with a local truck dealer to acquire the trucks next year at a cash price of $60,000. Miller Corporation has acquired rights to future benefits, but the contract has not been executed. Unexecuted contracts of this nature, sometimes called *executory contracts,* are generally not recognized as assets in

---

[1]Financial Accounting Standards Board, *Statement of Financial Accounting Concepts No. 6,* ''Elements of Financial Statements,'' 1985, par. 25. See glossary for the Board's specific definition of an asset.

accounting. Miller Corporation will recognize an asset for the trucks when they are received next year.

To take the illustration one step further, assume that Miller Corporation advances the truck dealer $15,000 of the purchase price upon signing the contract. Miller Corporation has acquired rights to future benefits and has exchanged cash. Current accounting practice treats the $15,000 as an advance on the purchase of equipment and reports it as an asset under a title such as Advances to Suppliers. The trucks would not be shown as assets at this time, however, because Miller Corporation is not yet deemed to have received sufficient future rights to justify their inclusion in the balance sheet. Similar asset recognition questions arise when a firm leases buildings and equipment for its own use under long-term leases or manufactures custom-design products for particular customers. Later chapters discuss these issues more fully.

## Asset Valuation Bases

An amount must be assigned to each asset in the balance sheet. Several methods of computing this amount might be used.

**Acquisition or Historical Cost**  The amount of cash payment (or cash equivalent value of other forms of payment) made in acquiring an asset is the *acquisition,* or *historical, cost* of an asset. This amount can generally be found by referring to contracts, invoices, and canceled checks. Because a firm is not compelled to acquire a given asset, it must expect the future benefits from that asset to be at least as large as its acquisition cost. Historical cost, then, is a lower limit on the amount that a firm considered the future benefits of the asset to be worth at the time of acquisition.

**Current Replacement Cost**  Each asset might be shown on the balance sheet at the current cost of replacing it. *Current replacement cost* is often referred to as an *entry value,* because it represents the amount currently required to acquire, or enter into, the rights to receive future benefits from the asset.

For assets purchased frequently, such as merchandise inventory, current replacement cost can often be calculated by consulting suppliers' catalogs or price lists. The replacement cost of assets purchased less frequently, such as land, buildings, and equipment, is more difficult to ascertain. A major obstacle to implementing current replacement cost is the absence of well-organized secondhand markets for many used assets. Ascertaining current replacement cost in these cases requires finding the cost of a similar new asset and then adjusting that amount downward somehow for the services of the asset already used. There may be difficulties, however, in finding a similar asset. With technological improvements and other quality changes, equipment purchased currently will likely differ from equipment still being used but acquired 10 years previously. Thus there may be no similar equipment on the market for which replacement cost can be found. Alternatively, the current replacement cost of an asset capable of rendering equivalent services might be substituted when the replacement cost of the specific asset is not readily available. This approach, however, requires subjectivity in identifying assets with equivalent service potential.

**Current Net Realizable Value** The net amount of cash (selling price less selling costs) that the firm would receive currently if it sold each asset separately is the *current net realizable value*. This amount is often referred to as an *exit value*, because it reflects the amount obtainable if the firm currently disposed of the asset, or exited ownership. In measuring net realizable value, one generally assumes that the asset is sold in an orderly fashion rather than through a forced sale at some distress price.

Measuring net realizable value entails difficulties similar to those in measuring current replacement cost. There may be no well-organized secondhand market for used equipment, particularly when the equipment is specially designed for a single firm's needs. In this case, the current selling price of the asset (value in exchange) may be substantially less than the value of the future benefits to the firm from using the asset (value in use).

**Present Value of Future Net Cash Flows** Another possible valuation basis is the *present value of future net cash flows*. An asset is a resource that provides a future benefit. This future benefit is the ability of an asset either to generate future net cash receipts or to reduce future cash expenditures. For example, accounts receivable from customers will lead directly to future cash receipts. Merchandise inventory can be sold for cash or promises to pay cash. Equipment can be used to manufacture products that can then be sold for cash. A building that is owned reduces future cash outflows for rental payments. Because these cash flows represent the future services, or benefits, of assets, they might be used in the valuation of assets.

Because cash can be invested to earn interest over time, today's value of a stream of future cash flows, called the *present value,* is worth less than the sum of the cash amounts to be received or saved over time. The balance sheet is to be prepared as of a current date. If future cash flows are to be used to measure an asset's value, then the future net cash flows must be discounted to find their present value as of the date of the balance sheet. Chapters 10 and 11 and Appendix A discuss the discounting methodology. The following example presents the general approach.

**Example 5** Miller Corporation sold merchandise to a reliable customer, General Models Company, who promised to pay $10,000 one year from the date of sale. General Models Company signed a promissory note to that effect and gave the note to Miller Corporation. Miller Corporation judges that the current borrowing rate of General Models Company is 10 percent per year; that is, a loan to General Models Company should yield a return to Miller Corporation of 10 percent. Miller Corporation is to receive $10,000 one year from today. The $10,000 includes both the amount lent initially plus interest on that amount for 1 year. Today's value of the $10,000 to be received 1 year hence is not $10,000 but about $9,090; that is, $9,090 plus 10 percent interest on $9,090 equals $10,000. Hence, the present value of $10,000 to be received 1 year from today is $9,090. (Miller Corporation is indifferent between receiving approximately $9,090 today and $10,000 one year from today.) The asset represented by General Models Company's promissory note has a present value of $9,090. If the note were stated on the balance sheet at the present value of the future cash flows, it would be shown at approximately $9,090 on the date of sale.

Using discounted cash flows in the valuation of individual assets requires solving several problems. One is the difficulty caused by the uncertainty of the amounts of future cash flows. The amounts to be received can depend on whether competitors introduce new products, the rate of inflation, and many other factors. A second problem is allocating the cash receipts from the sale of a single item of merchandise inventory to all of the assets involved in its production and distribution (for example, equipment, buildings, sales staff's automobiles). A third problem is selecting the appropriate rate to use in discounting the future cash flows to the present. Is the interest rate at which the firm could borrow the appropriate one? Or is the rate at which the firm could invest excess cash the one that should be used? Or is the appropriate rate the firm's cost of capital (a concept introduced in managerial accounting and finance courses)? In the example above, the appropriate rate is General Models' borrowing rate.

## Selecting the Appropriate Valuation Basis

The valuation basis selected depends on the financial report being prepared.

**Example 6**  Miller Corporation is preparing its income tax return for the current year. The Internal Revenue Code and Regulations specify that acquisition or adjusted acquisition cost valuation must be used in most instances.

**Example 7**  A fire recently destroyed the manufacturing plant, equipment, and inventory of Miller Corporation. The firm's fire insurance policy provides coverage in an amount equal to the cost of replacing the assets that were destroyed. Current replacement cost at the time of the fire is appropriate for supporting the insurance claim.

**Example 8**  Miller Corporation plans to dispose of one of its manufacturing divisions because it has been operating unprofitably. In deciding on the lowest price to accept for the division, the firm considers the net realizable value of each asset.

**Example 9**  Brown Corporation is considering the purchase of Miller Corporation. In deciding on the highest price to be paid, Brown Corporation would be interested in the present value of the future net cash flows to be realized from owning Miller Corporation.

## Generally Accepted Accounting Asset Valuation Bases

The asset valuation basis appropriate for financial statements issued to shareholders and other investors is perhaps less obvious. The financial statements currently prepared by publicly held firms are based on one of two valuation bases — one for monetary assets and one for nonmonetary assets.

*Monetary assets,* such as cash and accounts receivable, are generally shown on the balance sheet at their net present value — their current cash, or cash equivalent, value. Cash is stated at the amount of cash on hand or in the bank. Accounts receivable from customers are stated at the amount of cash expected to be collected in the future. If the period of time until a receivable is to be collected spans more than 1 year, the expected future cash receipt is discounted to a present value. Most accounts receivable, however, are collected within 1 to 3 months. The amount of future cash flows is approximately equal to the present value of these flows, and the discounting process is ignored.

*Nonmonetary assets,* such as merchandise inventory, land, buildings, and equipment, are stated at acquisition cost, in some cases adjusted downward for depreciation to reflect the services of the assets that have been consumed.

The acquisition cost of an asset includes more than its invoice price. Cost includes all expenditures made or obligations incurred in order to put the asset into usable condition. Transportation cost, costs of installation, handling charges, and any other necessary and reasonable costs incurred in connection with the asset up to the time it is put into service should be considered as part of the total cost assigned to the asset. For example, the cost of an item of equipment might be calculated as follows:

| | |
|---|---:|
| Invoice Price of Equipment ............................................... | $12,000 |
| Less: 2 Percent Discount for Prompt Cash Payment ....................... | (240) |
| Net Invoice Price ....................................................... | $11,760 |
| Transportation Cost ..................................................... | 326 |
| Installation Costs ...................................................... | 735 |
| Total Cost of Equipment ................................................. | $12,821 |

The acquisition cost of this equipment to be recorded in the accounting records is $12,821.

Instead of disbursing cash or incurring a liability, other forms of consideration (for example, common stock, merchandise inventory, land) may be given in acquiring an asset. In these cases, acquisition cost is measured by the market value of the consideration given or the market value of the asset received, depending on which market value is more reliably measured.

**Foundations for Acquisition Cost** Accounting's use of acquisition cost valuations for nonmonetary assets rests on three important concepts or conventions. First, a firm is assumed to be a *going concern.* In other words, the firm is assumed to remain in operation long enough for all of its current plans to be carried out. Any increases in the market value of assets held will be realized in the normal course of business when the firm receives higher prices for its products. Current values of the individual assets are therefore assumed to be largely unimportant. Second, acquisition cost valuations are more objective than those obtained from using the other valuation methods. *Objectivity* in accounting refers to the ability of several independent measurers to come to the same conclusion about the valuation of an asset. Obtaining consensus on what constitutes the acquisition cost of an asset is relatively easy. Differences among measurers can arise in ascertaining an asset's current replacement cost, current net realizable value, or present value of future cash flows. Objectivity is necessary if financial statements are to be subject to audits by independent accountants. Third, acquisition cost generally provides more conservative valuations of assets (and measures of earnings) relative to the other valuation methods. Many accountants believe that the possibility of misleading financial statement users will be minimized when assets are stated at lower rather than higher amounts. Thus, *conservatism* has evolved as a convention to justify acquisition cost valuations.

The general acceptance of these valuation bases does not justify them. The valuation basis most relevant to users — acquisition cost, current replacement cost, current net realizable value, or present value of future cash flows — is an empirical issue for which convincing evidence has not yet been provided. As Chapters 8 and 9 discuss, some large, publicly held firms provide supplementary information on the current cost of their inventories, property, plant, and equipment. The disclosure of such information is, to some extent, a response to the recognized deficiencies of historical cost valuations during periods of changing prices.

## Asset Classification

The classification of assets within the balance sheet varies widely in published annual reports. The following discussion gives the principal asset categories.

**Current Assets**  Cash and other assets that are expected to be realized in cash or sold or consumed during the normal operating cycle of the business, usually 1 year, are *current assets*. The operating cycle refers to the period of time that elapses for a given firm during which cash is converted into salable goods and services, goods and services are sold to customers, and customers pay for their purchases with cash. Included in current assets are cash, marketable securities held for the short term, accounts and notes receivable, inventories of merchandise, raw materials, supplies, work in process, and finished goods and prepaid operating costs (for example, prepaid insurance and prepaid rent). Prepaid costs, or prepayments, are current assets because if they were not paid in advance, current assets would be required within the next operating cycle to acquire those services.

**Investments**  A second section of the balance sheet, labeled "Investments," includes long-term investments in securities of other firms. For example, a firm might purchase shares of common stock of a supplier to help assure continued availability of raw materials. Or shares of common stock of a firm in another area of business activity might be acquired to permit the acquiring firm to diversify its operations. When one corporation (the parent) owns more than 50 percent of the voting stock in another corporation (the subsidiary), a single set of consolidated financial statements is usually prepared; that is, the specific assets, liabilities, revenues, and expenses of the subsidiary are merged, or consolidated, with those of the parent corporation. The securities shown in the Investments section of the balance sheet are therefore investments in firms whose assets and liabilities have *not* been consolidated with the parent or investor firm. Chapter 13 discusses consolidated financial statements.

The holders of a firm's long-term bonds may require that cash be set aside periodically so that sufficient funds will be available to retire the bonds at maturity. The funds are typically given to a trustee, such as a bank or insurance company, which invests the funds received. Funds set aside for this purpose are shown in a Sinking Fund account and classified under Investments on the balance sheet.

**Property, Plant, and Equipment** Property, plant, and equipment (sometimes called *plant assets* or *fixed assets*) designates the tangible, long-lived assets used in a firm's operations over a period of years and generally not acquired for resale. This category includes land, buildings, machinery, automobiles, furniture, fixtures, computers, and other equipment. The amount shown on the balance sheet for each of these items (except land) is acquisition cost less accumulated depreciation since the asset was acquired. Frequently, only the net balance, or book value, appears on the balance sheet. Land is shown at acquisition cost.

**Intangible Assets** Such items as patents, trademarks, franchises, and goodwill are *intangible assets*. The expenditures made by a firm in developing intangible assets are usually not recognized as assets because of the difficulty of ascertaining the existence of future benefits. Only specifically identifiable intangible assets acquired in market exchanges from other entities, such as a patent acquired from its holder, are recognized as assets.

## Liability Recognition

A liability arises when a firm receives benefits or services and in exchange promises to pay the provider of those goods and services a reasonably definite amount at a reasonably definite future time. The payment is usually in cash but may be made in goods or services.[2]

**Example 10** Miller Corporation purchased merchandise inventory and agreed to pay the supplier $8,000 within 30 days. This obligation is a liability because Miller Corporation has received the goods and must pay a definite amount at a reasonably definite future time.

**Example 11** Miller Corporation borrowed $4 million by issuing long-term bonds. Annual interest payments of 10 percent must be made on December 31 of each year, and the $4 million principal must be repaid in 20 years. This obligation is a liability because Miller Corporation has received the cash and must repay the debt in a definite amount at a definite future time.

**Example 12** Miller Corporation provides a 3-year warranty on its products. The obligation to maintain the products under warranty plans creates a liability. The selling price for its products implicitly includes a charge for future warranty ser-

---

[2]Financial Accounting Standards Board, *Statement of Financial Accounting Concepts No. 6*, "Elements of Financial Statements," 1985, par. 35. See glossary for the Board's specific definition of a liability.

vices. As customers pay the selling price, Miller Corporation receives a benefit (that is, the cash received). Past experience provides a basis for estimating the amount of the liability. Miller Corporation can estimate the proportion of customers who will seek services under the warranty agreement and the expected cost of providing warranty services. Thus, Miller Corporation can measure the amount of the obligation with a reasonable degree of accuracy and will show it as a liability.

**Example 13**  Miller Corporation has signed an agreement with its employees' labor union, promising to increase wages by 6 percent and to provide for medical and life insurance. Although this agreement creates an obligation, it does *not* immediately create a liability. Services have not yet been received from employees that would require any payments for wages and insurance. As labor services are received, a liability will arise.

The most troublesome questions of liability recognition relate to obligations under unexecuted contracts. The labor union agreement in Example 13 is an unexecuted contract. Other examples include some leases, purchase order commitments, and employment contracts. Accounting does not currently recognize the obligations created by unexecuted contracts to be liabilities, although the issue continues to be controversial.

## Liability Valuation

Most liabilities are monetary, requiring payments of specific amounts of cash. Those due within 1 year or less are stated at the amount of cash expected to be paid to discharge the obligation. If the payment dates extend more than 1 year into the future (for example, as in the case of the bonds in Example 11), the liability is stated at the present value of the future cash outflows.

A liability that requires delivering goods or rendering services rather than paying cash is nonmonetary. For example, magazine publishers typically collect cash for subscriptions, promising delivery of magazines over many months. Cash is received currently, whereas the obligation under the subscription is discharged by delivering magazines in the future. Theaters and football teams receive cash for season tickets and promise to admit the ticket holder to future performances. Landlords receive cash in advance and promise to let the tenant use the property. Such nonmonetary obligations appear among liabilities. They are stated, however, at the amount of cash received rather than at the expected cost of publishing the magazines or of providing the theatrical or sporting entertainment. The title frequently used for liabilities of this type is Advances from Customers.

## Liability Classification

Liabilities in the balance sheet are typically classified in one of the following categories.

**Current Liabilities**  Obligations expected to be paid or discharged during the normal operating cycle of the firm, usually 1 year, are *current liabilities*. In general, current liabilities are paid using current assets. Included in this category are liabilities to merchandise suppliers, employees, and governmental units. Notes and bonds payable are also included to the extent that they will require the use of current assets within the next year.

**Long-Term Debt**  Obligations having due dates, or maturities, more than 1 year after the balance sheet date are classified as *long-term debt*. Included are bonds, mortgages, and similar debts, as well as some obligations under long-term leases.

**Other Long-Term Liabilities**  Obligations not properly considered as current liabilities or long-term debt are classified as *other long-term liabilities*. Included are such items as deferred income taxes and some pension obligations.

## Owners' Equity Valuation and Disclosure

The owners' equity in a firm is a residual interest[3]—that is, the owners have a claim on all assets not required to meet the claims of creditors.[4] The valuation of the assets and liabilities included in the balance sheet therefore determines the valuation of total owners' equity.

The remaining question concerns the manner of disclosing this total owners' equity. Accounting draws a distinction between contributed capital and earnings retained by a firm. The balance sheet for a corporation generally separates the amounts contributed directly by shareholders for an interest in the firm (that is, common stock) from earnings subsequently realized by the firm in excess of dividends declared (that is, retained earnings).

In addition, the amount received from shareholders is usually further disaggregated into the *par* or *stated value* of the shares and *amounts contributed in excess of par value or stated value*. The par or stated value of a share of stock is a somewhat arbitrary amount assigned to comply with corporation laws of each state and will rarely equal the market price of the shares at the time they are issued. As a result, the distinction between par or stated value and amounts contributed in excess of par or stated value contains little information, but this distinction is typically shown nonetheless. (Chapter 12 discusses these fine points of accounting for owners' equity.)

**Example 14**  Stephens Corporation was formed on January 1, Year 1. It issued 15,000 shares of $10 par value common stock for $10 cash per share. During Year 1, Stephens Corporation had net income of $30,000 and paid dividends of $10,000 to shareholders. The shareholders' equity section of the balance sheet of Stephens Corporation on December 31, Year 1, is as follows:

---

[3]Although owners' equity is equal to assets minus liabilities, accounting provides an independent method for computing the amount. This method is presented in this and the next two chapters.

[4]Financial Accounting Standards Board, *Statement of Financial Accounting Concepts No. 6,* "Elements of Financial Statements," 1985, par. 49. See glossary for the Board's specific definition of owners' equity.

| Common Stock (par value of $10 per share, 15,000 shares issued and outstanding) | $150,000 |
|---|---|
| Retained Earnings | 20,000 |
| Total Shareholders' Equity | $170,000 |

**Example 15**  Instead of issuing $10 par value common stock as in Example 14, assume that Stephens Corporation issued 15,000 shares of $1 par value common stock for $10 cash per share. (The market price of a share of common stock depends on the economic value of the firm and not on the par value of the shares.) The shareholders' equity section of the balance sheet of Stephens Corporation on December 31, Year 1, is as follows:

| Common Stock (par value of $1 per share, 15,000 shares issued and outstanding) | $ 15,000 |
|---|---|
| Capital Contributed in Excess of Par Value | 135,000 |
| Retained Earnings | 20,000 |
| Total Shareholders' Equity | $170,000 |

## Accounting Procedures for Preparing the Balance Sheet

Now that the concepts underlying the balance sheet have been discussed, the manner in which these concepts are applied in preparing the statement can be considered. The objective is to develop a sufficient understanding of the accounting process that generates the balance sheet so that the resulting statement can be interpreted and analyzed.

### Dual Effects of Transactions on the Balance Sheet Equation

The equality between total assets and total liabilities plus shareholders' equity in the balance sheet equation is maintained by reporting the effects of *each* transaction in a way that maintains the equation. Any single transaction will have one of the following four effects or some combination of these effects:

1.  It increases both an asset and a liability or shareholders' equity.

2.  It decreases both an asset and a liability or shareholders' equity.

3.  It increases one asset and decreases another asset.

4.  It increases one liability or shareholders' equity and decreases another liability or shareholders' equity.

To illustrate the dual effects of various transactions on the balance sheet equation, consider the following selected transactions for Miller Corporation during January.

1.  On January 1, 10,000 shares of $10 par value common stock are issued for $100,000 cash.

2.  Equipment costing $60,000 is purchased for cash on January 5.

3.  Merchandise inventory costing $15,000 is purchased from a supplier on account on January 15.

4.  The supplier in **(3)** is paid $8,000 of the amount due on January 21.

5.  The supplier in **(3)** accepts 700 shares of common stock at par value in settlement of the $7,000 amount owed.

6.  A 1-year insurance premium of $600 for coverage beginning February 1 is paid in cash on January 31.

7.  Cash of $3,000 is received from a customer on January 31 for merchandise to be delivered during February.

Exhibit 2.1 illustrates the dual effects of these transactions on the balance sheet equation. Note that after each transaction, assets equal liabilities plus shareholders' equity.

The dual effects reported for each transaction may be viewed as an outflow and an inflow. For example, common stock is issued to shareholders and cash is received. A cash expenditure is made and equipment is received. A promise to make a future cash payment is given to a supplier and merchandise inventory is received. Most transactions and events recorded in the accounting system result from exchanges. The accounting records reflect the inflows and outflows arising from these exchanges.

## Purpose and Use of Accounts

A balance sheet could be prepared for Miller Corporation as of January 31 using information from the preceding analysis. Total assets are $110,000. To prepare a balance sheet, however, it would be necessary to retrace the effects of each transaction on total assets to ascertain what portion of the $110,000 represents cash, merchandise inventory, and equipment. Likewise, the effects of each transaction on total liabilities and shareholders' equity would have to be retraced to ascertain which liability and shareholders' equity amounts comprise the $110,000 total. Even with just a few transactions during the accounting period, this approach to preparing a balance sheet would be cumbersome. Considering the thousands of transactions during the accounting period for most firms, some more practical approach to accumulating amounts for the balance sheet is necessary. To accumulate the changes that take place in each balance sheet item, the accounting system uses a device known as an *account*.

**Requirement for an Account**  Because a changing balance sheet item can only increase or decrease, all an account needs to do is to provide for accumulating the increases and decreases that have taken place during the period for a single balance

## Exhibit 2.1 ——————————————————————

## Illustration of Dual Effects of Transactions on Balance Sheet Equation

| Transaction | Assets = | Liabilities + | Shareholders' Equity |
|---|---|---|---|
| (1) On January 1, 10,000 shares of $10 par value common stock are issued for $100,000 cash (increase in both an asset and shareholders' equity). | + $100,000 | $    0 + | $100,000 |
| Subtotal . . . . . . . . . . . . . . . . . . . . . . . . . . . | $100,000 = | $    0 + | $100,000 |
| (2) Equipment costing $60,000 is purchased for cash on January 5 (increase in one asset and decrease in another asset). | –    60,000 +    60,000 | | |
| Subtotal . . . . . . . . . . . . . . . . . . . . . . . . . . . | $100,000 = | $    0 + | $100,000 |
| (3) Merchandise inventory costing $15,000 is purchased from a supplier on account on January 15 (increase in both an asset and a liability). | +    15,000 | +.  15,000 | |
| Subtotal . . . . . . . . . . . . . . . . . . . . . . . . . . . | $115,000 = | $15,000 + | $100,000 |
| (4) The supplier in (3) is paid $8,000 of the amount due on January 21 (decrease in both an asset and a liability). | –    8,000 | –    8,000 | |
| Subtotal . . . . . . . . . . . . . . . . . . . . . . . . . . . | $107,000 = | $ 7,000 + | $100,000 |
| (5) The supplier in (3) accepts 700 shares of common stock at par value in settlement of the $7,000 amount owed (increase in shareholders' equity and decrease in a liability). | | –    7,000 + | 7,000 |
| Subtotal . . . . . . . . . . . . . . . . . . . . . . . . . . . | $107,000 = | $    0 + | $107,000 |
| (6) A one-year fire insurance premium of $600 for coverage beginning February 1 is paid in cash on January 31 (increase in one asset and decrease in another asset). | +    600 –    600 | | |
| Subtotal . . . . . . . . . . . . . . . . . . . . . . . . . . . | $107,000 = | $    0 + | $107,000 |
| (7) Cash of $3,000 is received from a customer on January 31 for merchandise to be delivered during February (increase in both an asset and a liability). | +    3,000 | +    3,000 | |
| Total—January 31 . . . . . . . . . . . . . . . . . . . | $110,000 = | $ 3,000 + | $107,000 |

sheet item. The balance carried forward from the previous statement is added to the total increases; the total decreases are deducted, and the result is the amount of the new balance for the current balance sheet.

**Form of an Account**  The account may take many possible forms, and several are commonly used in accounting practice.

Perhaps the most useful form of the account for textbooks, problems, and examinations is the *T-account*. This form of the account is not used in actual practice, except perhaps for memorandums or preliminary analyses. However, it satisfies the requirement of an account and it is easy to use. As the name indicates, the T-account is shaped like the letter T and consists of a horizontal line bisected by a vertical line. The name or title of the account is written on the horizontal line. One side of the space formed by the vertical line is used to record increases in the item and the other side to record the decreases. Dates and other information can appear as well.

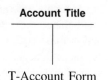

**Account Title**

T-Account Form

The form that the account takes in actual records depends on the type of accounting system being used. In manual systems the account may take the form of a single ledger sheet with columns for recording increases and decreases; in computer systems it may be a group of similarly coded items in a file. Whatever its form, an account contains the opening balance as well as the increases and decreases in the balance that result from the transactions of the period.

**Placement of Increases and Decreases in the Account**  Given the two-sided account, we must choose which side will be used to record increases and which decreases. By long-standing custom, the following rules are used:

1.  Increases in assets are entered on the left side and decreases in assets on the right side.
2.  Increases in liabilities are entered on the right side and decreases in liabilities on the left side.
3.  Increases in shareholders' equity are entered on the right side and decreases in shareholders' equity on the left side.

This custom reflects the fact that a common format for a balance sheet shows assets on the left and liabilities and shareholders' equity on the right. Following this format, asset balances should appear on the left side of accounts; liability and shareholders' equity balances should appear on the right. Asset balances will appear on the left only if asset increases are recorded on the left side of the account. Similarly, right-hand liability and shareholders' equity balances can be produced only by recording liability and shareholders' equity increases on the right. When each transaction is properly analyzed into its dual effects on the accounting equation, and when the three rules for recording the transaction are followed, every transaction results in equal amounts in entries on the left- and right-hand sides of various accounts.

**Debit and Credit**  Two terms may now be introduced — debit (Dr.) and credit (Cr.). These terms are convenient abbreviations. *Debit* is an abbreviation for ''record an entry on the left side of an account'' when used as a verb and is an abbreviation for "an entry on the left side of an account" when used as a noun or adjective. *Credit* is an abbreviation for "record an entry on the right side of an account" when used as a verb and is an abbreviation for "an entry on the right side of an account" when used as a noun or adjective. Often, however, the word *charge* is used instead of *debit,* both as a noun and as a verb. In terms of balance sheet categories, a debit or charge indicates (1) an increase in an asset, (2) a decrease in a liability, or (3) a decrease in a shareholders' equity item. A credit indicates (1) a decrease in an asset, (2) an increase in a liability, or (3) an increase in a shareholders' equity item.

To maintain the equality of the balance sheet equation, the amounts debited to various accounts for each transaction must equal the amounts credited to various accounts. Likewise, the sum of balances in accounts with debit balances at the end of each period must equal the sum of balances in accounts with credit balances.

**Summary of Account Terminology and Procedure**   The conventional use of the account form and the terms debit and credit can be summarized graphically with the use of the T-account form, as follows:

| Any Asset Account | | Any Liability Account | |
|---|---|---|---|
| ✔ Beginning Balance Increases + Dr. | Decreases − Cr. | Decreases − Dr. | Beginning Balance Increases + Cr. ✔ |
| ✔ Ending Balance | | | Ending Balance ✔ |

| Any Shareholders' Equity Account | |
|---|---|
| Decreases − Dr. | Beginning Balance Increases + Cr. ✔ |
| | Ending Balance ✔ |

Customarily, a checkmark in an account indicates a balance.

## Reflecting the Dual Effects of Transactions in the Accounts

The manner in which the dual effects of transactions change the accounts can now be illustrated. Three separate T-accounts are created: one for assets, one for liabilities, and one for shareholders' equity. The dual effects of the transactions of Miller Corporation for January, described earlier in the chapter, are entered in the T-accounts shown in Exhibit 2.2.

The amount entered on the left side of (or debited to) the accounts for each transaction is equal to the amount entered on the right side of (or credited to) the

**Exhibit 2.2** ————————————————————————————————————————

## MILLER CORPORATION
## Summary T-Accounts Showing Transactions

| | Assets | | = | Liabilities | | + | Shareholders' Equity | |
|---|---|---|---|---|---|---|---|---|
| | Increases (Dr.) | Decreases (Cr.) | | Decreases (Dr.) | Increases (Cr.) | | Decreases (Dr.) | Increases (Cr.) |
| (1) Issue of Common Stock for Cash ............... | 100,000 | | | | | | | 100,000 |
| (2) Purchase of Equipment for Cash ............... | 60,000 | 60,000 | | | | | | |
| (3) Purchase of Merchandise on Account .............. | 15,000 | | | | 15,000 | | | |
| (4) Payment of Cash to Supplier in (3) ........... | | 8,000 | | 8,000 | | | | |
| (5) Issuance of Common Stock to Supplier in (3) .... | | | | 7,000 | | | | 7,000 |
| (6) Payment of Insurance Premium in Advance ...... | 600 | 600 | | | | | | |
| (7) Cash Received from Customer in Advance ...... | 3,000 | | | | 3,000 | | | |
| Balance ................... | 110,000 | | | | 3,000 | | | 107,000 |

accounts. Recording equal amounts of debits and credits for each transaction ensures that the balance sheet equation will always be in balance. At the end of January, the assets account has a debit balance of $110,000. The sum of the balances in the liabilities and shareholders' equity accounts is a credit balance of $110,000.

A balance sheet could be prepared for Miller Corporation from the information in the T-accounts. However, as was the case in the earlier illustration, it would be necessary to retrace the entries in the accounts during the period to ascertain which individual assets, liabilities, and shareholders' equity items made up the total assets of $110,000 and the total equities of $110,000.

So that the amount of each asset, liability, and shareholders' equity item can be computed directly, a separate account is used for each balance sheet item rather than for the three broad categories alone. The recording procedure is the same, except that specific asset or equity accounts are debited and credited.

The transactions of Miller Corporation for January are recorded in Exhibit 2.3 using separate T-accounts for each balance sheet item. The number in parentheses refers to the seven transactions we have been considering for Miller Corporation.

The total assets of Miller Corporation of $110,000 as of January 31 comprise $34,400 in cash, $15,000 in merchandise inventory, $600 of prepaid insurance, and $60,000 in equipment. Total liabilities plus shareholders' equity of $110,000 comprise $3,000 of advances from customers and $107,000 of common stock.

The balance sheet can be prepared using the amounts shown as balances in the T-accounts. The balance sheet of Miller Corporation after the seven transactions of January appears in Exhibit 2.4.

**Exhibit 2.3**

**MILLER CORPORATION**
**Individual T-Accounts Showing Transactions**

| Cash (Asset) | | | Accounts Payable (Liability) | | |
|---|---|---|---|---|---|
| Increases (Dr.) | Decreases (Cr.) | | Decreases (Dr.) | Increases (Cr.) | |
| (1) 100,000 | 60,000 (2) | | (4) 8,000 | 15,000 (3) | |
| (7) 3,000 | 8,000 (4) | | (5) 7,000 | | |
| | 600 (6) | | | | |
| Balance 34,400 | | | | 0 Balance | |

| Merchandise Inventory (Asset) | | | Advance from Customer (Liability) | | |
|---|---|---|---|---|---|
| Increases (Dr.) | Decreases (Cr.) | | Decreases (Dr.) | Increases (Cr.) | |
| (3) 15,000 | | | | 3,000 (7) | |
| Balance 15,000 | | | | 3,000 Balance | |

| Prepaid Insurance (Asset) | | | Common Stock (Shareholders' Equity) | | |
|---|---|---|---|---|---|
| Increases (Dr.) | Decreases (Cr.) | | Decreases (Dr.) | Increases (Cr.) | |
| (6) 600 | | | | 100,000 (1) | |
| | | | | 7,000 (5) | |
| Balance 600 | | | | 107,000 Balance | |

| Equipment (Asset) | | |
|---|---|---|
| Increases (Dr.) | Decreases (Cr.) | |
| (2) 60,000 | | |
| Balance 60,000 | | |

# An Overview of the Accounting Process

The double-entry recording framework is used in processing the results of various transactions and events through the accounts so that financial statements can be prepared periodically. The accounting system designed around this recording framework generally involves the following operations:

1. Entering the results of each transaction in the general journal in the form of a journal entry, a process called *journalizing*.

2. Posting the journal entries from the general journal to the accounts in the general ledger.

3. Preparing a trial balance of the accounts in the general ledger.

4. Making adjusting and correcting journal entries to accounts listed in the trial balance and posting them to the appropriate general ledger accounts.

Exhibit 2.4 —————————————————————————

MILLER CORPORATION
Balance Sheet, January 31

# Assets

**Current Assets:**

| | |
|---|---:|
| Cash ............................................. | $ 34,400 |
| Merchandise Inventory ............................. | 15,000 |
| Prepaid Insurance .................................. | 600 |
| Total Current Assets .............................. | $ 50,000 |

**Property, Plant, and Equipment:**

| | |
|---|---:|
| Equipment ......................................... | 60,000 |
| Total Assets ...................................... | $110,000 |

# Liabilities and Shareholders' Equity

**Current Liabilities:**

| | |
|---|---:|
| Advance from Customer............................... | $ 3,000 |

**Shareholders' Equity:**

| | |
|---|---:|
| Common Stock...................................... | 107,000 |
| Total Liabilities and Shareholders' Equity............... | $110,000 |

**5.** Preparing financial statements from a trial balance after adjusting and correcting entries.

Figure 2.1 shows these operations. Each operation is described further and illustrated using the transactions of Miller Corporation during January.

## Journalizing

Each transaction is initially recorded in the general journal in the form of a *journal entry*. The standard journal entry format is as follows:

| | | |
|---|---|---|
| Date | Account Debited ...................... | Amount Debited |
| | Account Credited.................... | Amount Credited |
| | Explanation of transaction or event being journalized | |

Figure 2.1 ———————————————————————————————————————

**Summary of the Accounting Process**

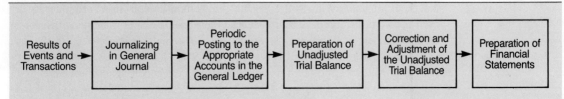

The *general journal* is merely a book or other record containing a listing of journal entries. The general journal is often referred to as the *book of original entry,* because transactions initially enter the accounting system through it.

The journal entries for the seven transactions of Miller Corporation during January are presented as follows:

| | | | | |
|---|---|---|---|---|
| (1) Jan. 1 | Cash ........................................ | 100,000 | |
| | Common Stock .............................. | | 100,000 |
| | 10,000 shares of $10 par value common stock are issued for cash. | | |
| (2) Jan. 5 | Equipment ................................... | 60,000 | |
| | Cash ....................................... | | 60,000 |
| | Equipment costing $60,000 is purchased for cash. | | |
| (3) Jan. 15 | Merchandise Inventory ......................... | 15,000 | |
| | Accounts Payable............................ | | 15,000 |
| | Merchandise inventory costing $15,000 is purchased on account. | | |
| (4) Jan. 21 | Accounts Payable............................. | 8,000 | |
| | Cash ....................................... | | 8,000 |
| | Liabilities of $8,000 are paid with cash. | | |
| (5) Jan. 21 | Accounts Payable............................. | 7,000 | |
| | Common Stock .............................. | | 7,000 |
| | 700 shares of $10 par value common stock are issued in settlement of an account payable of $7,000. | | |
| (6) Jan. 31 | Prepaid Insurance ............................ | 600 | |
| | Cash ....................................... | | 600 |
| | One-year fire insurance premium of $600 is paid in advance. | | |
| (7) Jan. 31 | Cash ........................................ | 3,000 | |
| | Advance from Customer....................... | | 3,000 |
| | Advance of $3,000 is received from customer for merchandise to be delivered in February. | | |

Journal entries are useful for indicating the effects of various transactions on a firm's financial statements and for preparing solutions to the problems at the end of each chapter. You cannot be sure that you understand a business transaction until you can analyze it into its required debits and credits and prepare the proper journal entry. Consequently, this text uses journal entries as tools of analysis throughout.

## Posting

At periodic intervals (for example, weekly or monthly), the transactions recorded in the general journal are entered, or posted, to the individual accounts in the general ledger. In manual systems, the *general ledger* is a book with a separate page for each account. In computerized systems, the general ledger takes the form of an access number in a computer's file. The T-account described earlier serves as a useful surrogate for a general ledger account. The journal entries from the general journal of Miller Corporation would be posted to the general ledger accounts in the manner shown previously in Exhibit 2.3.

As with journal entries, T-accounts are useful tools in preparing solutions to accounting problems and appear throughout this text.

## Trial Balance Preparation

A *trial balance* is a listing of each of the accounts in the general ledger with its balance as of a particular date. The trial balance of Miller Corporation on January 31 appears in Exhibit 2.5.

An equality between the sum of debit account balances and the sum of credit account balances helps check the arithmetic accuracy of the dual-entry recording procedure carried out during the period. If the trial balance fails to balance, one must retrace the steps followed in processing the accounting data to locate the source of the error.

## Trial Balance after Adjustment and Correction

Any errors detected in the processing of accounting data must be corrected. Often a more frequent type of adjustment is necessary to account for unrecorded events that help to measure net income for the period and financial position at the end of the period. For example, at the end of February, the Prepaid Insurance account will be adjusted downward to reflect the coverage that expired during February. Chapters 3 and 4 discuss this type of adjustment more fully. Most corrections and adjustments are made by preparing a journal entry, entering it in the general journal, and then posting it to the general ledger accounts.

## Financial Statement Preparation

The balance sheet and income statement can be prepared from the trial balance after adjustments and corrections. Because correcting or adjusting entries are not required for Miller Corporation, the balance sheet presented in Exhibit 2.4 is correct as presented. In subsequent chapters, the accounting procedures for preparing the income statement and the statement of cash flows will be considered.

The results of various transactions and events are processed through the accounting system in a flow beginning with the journalizing operation and ending with the financial statements. The audit of the financial statements by the independent auditor typically flows in the opposite direction. The auditor begins with the finan-

Exhibit 2.5 ————————————————

**MILLER CORPORATION**
**Unadjusted Trial Balance, January 31**

| Account | Amounts in Accounts with Debit Balances | Amounts in Accounts with Credit Balances |
|---|---|---|
| Cash | $ 34,400 | |
| Merchandise Inventory | 15,000 | |
| Prepaid Insurance | 600 | |
| Equipment | 60,000 | |
| Advance from Customer | | $ 3,000 |
| Common Stock | | 107,000 |
| Totals | $110,000 | $110,000 |

cial statements prepared by management and then traces various items back through the accounts to the source documents (for example, sales invoices, canceled checks) that support the entries made in the general journal. Thus it is possible to move back and forth among source documents, journal entries, general ledger postings, and the financial statements.

## Balance Sheet Account Titles

The following list shows balance sheet account titles commonly used. The descriptions should help in understanding the nature of various assets, liabilities, and shareholders' equities as well as in selecting appropriate account names to use when solving problems. Alternative account titles can be devised easily. The list does not show all the account titles that are used in this book or that appear in the financial statements of publicly held firms.

### Assets

**Cash**   Coins and currency and items such as bank checks and money orders. (The latter items are merely claims against individuals or institutions but by custom are called cash.) Bank deposits against which checks can be drawn, and time deposits, usually savings accounts and certificates of deposit.

**Marketable Securities**   Government bonds, or stocks and bonds of corporations, which the firm plans to hold for a relatively short time. The word *marketable* implies that they can be bought and sold readily through a security exchange such as the New York Stock Exchange.

**Accounts Receivable**   Amounts due from customers of a business from the sale of goods or services. The collection of cash occurs some time after the sale. These accounts are also known as *charge accounts* or *open accounts*. The general term Accounts Receivable is used in financial statements to describe the figure representing the total amount receivable from all customers, but, of course, the firm keeps a separate record for each customer.

**Notes Receivable**   Amounts due from customers or from others to whom loans have been made or credit extended, when the claim has been put into writing in the form of a formal note (which distinguishes it from an open account receivable).

**Interest Receivable**   Interest on assets such as promissory notes or bonds that has accrued (or come into existence) through the passing of time but that has not been collected as of the date of the balance sheet.

**Merchandise Inventory**   Goods on hand that have been purchased for resale, such as canned goods on the shelves of a grocery store or suits on the racks of a clothing store.

**Raw Materials Inventory**   Unused materials from which manufactured products are to be made.

**Finished Goods Inventory**   Completed but unsold manufactured products.

**Work-in-Process Inventory**   Partially completed manufactured products.

**Supplies Inventory**   Lubricants, abrasives, and other incidental materials used in manufacturing operations. Stationery, computer disks, pens, and other office supplies. Bags, twine, boxes, and other store supplies. Gasoline, oil, spare parts, and other delivery supplies.

**Prepaid Insurance**   Insurance premiums paid for future coverage. May be called Advances to Insurance Company.

**Prepaid Rent**   Rent paid in advance for future use of land, buildings, or equipment. May be called Advances to Landlord.

**Advances to Suppliers**   The general name used to indicate payments made in advance for goods to be received at a later date. If no cash is paid by a firm when it places an order, no asset is recognized.

**Investment in Securities**   The cost of shares of bonds or stock in other companies where the firm plans to hold the securities for a relatively long time.

**Land**   Land occupied by buildings or used in operations.

**Buildings**   Factory buildings, store buildings, garages, warehouses, and so forth.

**Equipment**   Lathes, ovens, tools, boilers, computers, motors, bins, cranes, conveyors, automobiles, and so forth.

**Furniture and Fixtures**   Desks, tables, chairs, counters, showcases, scales, and other store and office equipment.

**Accumulated Depreciation**   The cumulative amount of the cost of long-term assets (such as buildings and equipment) that has been allocated to the costs of production or to current and prior periods in measuring net income. The amount in this account is subtracted from the acquisition cost of the long-term asset to which it relates when ascertaining the *net book value* of the asset to be shown in the balance sheet.

**Leasehold**   The right to use property owned by someone else.

**Organization Costs**   Amounts paid for legal and incorporation fees, for printing the certificates for shares of stock, and for accounting and other costs incurred in organizing the business so that it can begin to function.

**Patents** Rights granted for up to 17 years by the federal government to exclude others from manufacturing, using, or selling certain processes or devices. Under current generally accepted accounting principles, research and development costs must be treated as expenses in the year incurred rather than being recognized as assets with future benefits.[5] As a result, a firm that develops a patent will not normally show it as an asset. On the other hand, a firm that purchases a patent from another firm or from an individual will recognize the patent as an asset. Chapter 9 discusses this inconsistent treatment of internally developed and externally purchased patents.

**Goodwill** An amount paid by one firm in acquiring another business enterprise that is greater than the sum of the then-current values assignable to individual identifiable assets. A good reputation and other desirable attributes are generally not recognized as assets by the firm that creates or develops them. However, when one firm acquires another firm, these desirable attributes become recognized as assets insofar as they cause the value of the acquired firm to exceed the values assigned to the individual identifiable assets.

## Liabilities

**Accounts Payable** Amounts owed for goods or services acquired under an informal credit agreement. These accounts are usually payable within 1 or 2 months. The same items appear as Accounts Receivable on the creditor's books.

**Notes Payable** The face amount of promissory notes given in connection with loans from a bank or the purchase of goods or services. The same items appear as Notes Receivable on the creditor's books.

**Interest Payable** Interest on obligations that has accrued or accumulated with the passage of time but that has not been paid as of the date of the balance sheet. The liability for interest is customarily shown separately from the face amount of the obligation.

**Income Taxes Payable** The estimated liability for income taxes, accumulated and unpaid, based on the taxable income of the business from the beginning of the taxable year to the date of the balance sheet.

**Advances from Customers** The general name used to indicate payments received in advance for goods or services to be furnished to customers in the future; a nonmonetary liability. If no cash is received when a customer places an order, no liability is recorded.

**Advances from Tenants or Rent Received in Advance** Another example of a nonmonetary liability. For example, the business owns a building that it rents to a tenant. The tenant has prepaid the rental charge for several months in advance. The

---

[5]Financial Accounting Standards Board, *Statement of Financial Accounting Standards No. 2,* "Accounting for Research and Development Costs," 1974.

amount applicable to future months cannot be considered a component of income until the rent is earned as service is rendered with the passage of time. Meanwhile the advance payment results in a liability payable in services (that is, in the use of the building). On the records of the tenant, the same amount would appear as an asset, Prepaid Rent.

**Mortgage Payable**   Long-term promissory notes that have been given greater protection by the pledge of specific pieces of property as security for their payment. If the loan or interest is not paid according to the agreement, the property can be sold for the benefit of the creditor.

**Bonds Payable**   Amounts borrowed by the business for a relatively long period of time under a formal written contract or indenture. The loan is usually obtained from a number of lenders, all of whom receive one or more bond certificates as written evidence of their share of the loan.

**Convertible Bonds Payable**   Bonds that the holder can convert into or trade in for shares of common stock. The bond indenture specifies the number of shares to be received when the bond is converted into stock, the dates when conversion can occur, and other details.

**Capitalized Lease Obligations**   The present value of future commitments for cash payments to be made in return for the right to use property owned by someone else.

**Deferred Income Taxes**   Certain income tax obligations that are delayed beyond the current accounting period. Chapter 11 discusses this item, which appears on the balance sheet of most U.S. corporations.

## Shareholders' Equity

**Common Stock**   Amounts received for the par or stated value of a firm's principal class of voting stock.

**Preferred Stock**   Amounts received for the par value of a class of a firm's stock that has some preference relative to the common stock. This preference is usually with respect to dividends and to assets in the event the corporation is liquidated. Sometimes preferred stock is convertible into common stock.

**Capital Contributed in Excess of Par or Stated Value**   Amounts received from the issuance of common or preferred stock in excess of such shares' par value or stated value. This account is also referred to as *Additional Paid-in Capital* or sometimes as *Premium on Preferred* (or *Common*) *Stock*.

**Retained Earnings**   The increase in net assets since a business was organized as a result of its generating earnings in excess of dividend declarations. When dividends are declared, net assets decrease, and retained earnings decrease by an equal amount. As Chapters 5 and 12 discuss, the net assets generated are generally *not* held as cash.

**Treasury Shares**   The cost of shares of stock originally issued but subsequently reacquired by a corporation. Treasury shares are not entitled to dividends and are not considered to be outstanding shares. The cost of treasury shares is almost always shown on the balance sheet as a deduction from the total of the other shareholders' equity accounts. Chapter 12 discusses the accounting for treasury shares.

## Analysis of Balance Sheet ————————————————————

The balance sheet reflects the effects of a firm's investment and financing decisions. In general, firms attempt to balance the term structure of their financing with the term structure of their investments. For example, firms such as retail stores, with large investments in current assets (receivables and inventories), tend to use significant amounts of short-term financing. Highly capital-intensive firms, such as electric utilities and steel manufacturers, tend to rely heavily on long-term debt and common stock.

Short-term financing must be paid within approximately 1 year. A firm will want to be sure that it has sufficient cash available within that time period to pay the obligations. Assets classified as current will be the assets most likely to generate the cash needed. Likewise, long-term financing is repaid, if at all, over a longer period. Because noncurrent assets tend to generate cash over a longer period of years, long-term financing for these assets is appropriate.

A potential cause for concern occurs when the percentage of short-term financing begins to exceed the percentage of current assets. In this case, the firm is using short-term financing for noncurrent assets, and it may face difficulties in obtaining sufficient cash from these assets to meet required payments on short-term debt.

## Summary ————————————————————————————

The balance sheet comprises three major classes of items — assets, liabilities, and shareholders' equity.

Resources are recognized as assets when a firm has acquired rights to their future use as a result of a past transaction or exchange and when the value of the future benefits can be measured with a reasonable degree of precision. Monetary assets are, in general, stated at their current cash, or cash equivalent, values. Nonmonetary assets are stated at acquisition cost, in some cases adjusted downward for the cost of services that have been consumed. Liabilities represent obligations of a firm to make payments of a reasonably definite amount at a reasonably definite future time for benefits already received. Shareholders' equity, the difference between total assets and total liabilities, is typically segregated for corporations into contributed capital and retained earnings.

The equality of total assets and total liabilities plus shareholders' equity is maintained by recording the effects of each transaction in a dual manner in the accounts. The double-entry recording framework is summarized as follows:

| Asset Accounts | | = | Liability Accounts | | + | Shareholders' Equity Accounts | |
|---|---|---|---|---|---|---|---|
| Increases (Debits) | Decreases (Credits) | | Decreases (Debits) | Increases (Credits) | | Decreases (Debits) | Increases (Credits) |

The dual effects of each transaction are initially recorded in journal entry form in the general journal. These journal entries are then posted to the appropriate asset, liability, and shareholders' equity accounts in the general ledger. A trial balance of the ending balances in the general ledger accounts is prepared periodically as a check on the arithmetic accuracy of the double-entry recording procedure. Any necessary adjustments or corrections of the account balances in the trial balance are then made in the general journal and posted to the accounts in the general ledger. The financial statements are prepared from the adjusted and corrected trial balance. Chapters 3 and 4 discuss the procedures for preparing the income statement. Chapter 5 discusses the statement of cash flows.

When analyzing a balance sheet, one looks for a reasonable balance between the term structure of assets and the term structure of liabilities plus shareholders' equity. The proportion of short- versus long-term financing should bear some relation to the proportion of current versus noncurrent assets.

# Problem for Self-Study _____

The Electronics Appliance Corporation was organized on September 1. The following transactions occur during the month of September.

1. The firm issues 4,000 shares of $10 par value common stock for $12 cash per share on September 1.

2. The firm's attorney is given 600 shares of $10 par value common stock on September 2 in payment for legal services rendered in the organization of the corporation. The bill for the services is $7,200.

3. A factory building is leased for the 3 years beginning October 1. Monthly rental payments are $5,000. The firm pays 2 months' rent in advance on September 5.

4. Raw materials are purchased on account for $6,100 on September 12.

5. A check for $900 is received from a customer on September 15 as a deposit on a special order for equipment that Electronics plans to manufacture. The contract price is $4,800.

6. Office equipment with a list price of $950 is acquired on September 20. After deducting a discount of $25 for prompt payment, a check is issued in full payment.

7. The company hires three employees to begin work October 1. A cash advance of $200 is given to one of the employees on September 28.

8. Factory equipment costing $27,500 is purchased on September 30. A check for $5,000 is issued, and a long-term mortgage liability is assumed for the balance.

9. The labor costs of installing the new equipment in (8) are $450 and are paid in cash on September 30.
   a. Prepare journal entries for each of the nine transactions.

**b.** Set up T-accounts and enter each of the nine transactions.

**c.** Prepare a balance sheet for Electronics Appliance Corporation as of September 30.

## Suggested Solution

The journal entries for the nine transactions are as follows:

| | | | | |
|---|---|---|---:|---:|
| (1) Sept. 1 | Cash...................................... | | 48,000 | |
| | Common Stock............................... | | | 40,000 |
| | Additional Paid-in Capital...................... | | | 8,000 |
| | Four thousand shares of $10 par value common stock are issued for $12 cash per share. | | | |
| (2) Sept. 2 | Organization Costs............................ | | 7,200 | |
| | Common Stock............................... | | | 6,000 |
| | Additional Paid-in Capital...................... | | | 1,200 |
| | Six hundred common shares of $10 par value common stock are issued in settlement of $7,200 attorney's bill connected with organization of the corporation. | | | |
| (3) Sept. 5 | Prepaid Rent................................. | | 10,000 | |
| | Cash...................................... | | | 10,000 |
| | Rent for October and November on factory building is prepaid. | | | |
| (4) Sept. 12 | Raw Material Inventory......................... | | 6,100 | |
| | Accounts Payable............................ | | | 6,100 |
| | Raw materials costing $6,100 are purchased on account. | | | |
| (5) Sept. 15 | Cash...................................... | | 900 | |
| | Advances from Customers..................... | | | 900 |
| | An advance of $900 is received from a customer as a deposit on equipment to be manufactured in the future. | | | |
| (6) Sept. 20 | Equipment.................................. | | 925 | |
| | Cash...................................... | | | 925 |
| | Equipment with a list price of $950 is acquired, after a discount, for $925. | | | |
| (7) Sept. 28 | Advance to Employee.......................... | | 200 | |
| | Cash...................................... | | | 200 |
| | A cash advance of $200 is given to an employee beginning work on October 1. | | | |
| (8) Sept. 30 | Equipment.................................. | | 27,500 | |
| | Cash...................................... | | | 5,000 |
| | Mortgage Payable............................ | | | 22,500 |
| | Equipment is acquired for $5,000 cash and a $22,500 mortgage for the balance of the purchase price is assumed. | | | |
| (9) Sept. 30 | Equipment.................................. | | 450 | |
| | Cash...................................... | | | 450 |
| | Installation cost on equipment acquired in (8) of $450 is paid in cash. | | | |

Exhibit 2.6 presents T-accounts for Electronics Appliance Corporation and shows the recording of the nine entries in the accounts. The letters A, L, and SE are added after the account titles to indicate the balance sheet category of the accounts. Exhibit 2.7 presents a balance sheet as of September 30.

Exhibit 2.6 _____

**ELECTRONICS APPLIANCE CORPORATION**
**T-Accounts and Transactions during September**

| Cash (A) | | Advances to Employees (A) | | Raw Materials Inventory (A) | | Prepaid Rent (A) | |
|---|---|---|---|---|---|---|---|
| (1) 48,000 | 10,000 (3) | (7) 200 | | (4) 6,100 | | (3) 10,000 | |
| (5) 900 | 925 (6) | | | | | | |
| | 200 (7) | | | | | | |
| | 5,000 (8) | | | | | | |
| | 450 (9) | | | | | | |
| 32,325 | | 200 | | 6,100 | | 10,000 | |

| Equipment (A) | | Organization Costs (A) | | Accounts Payable (L) | | Advances from Customers (L) | |
|---|---|---|---|---|---|---|---|
| (6) 925 | | (2) 7,200 | | | 6,100 (4) | | 900 (5) |
| (8) 27,500 | | | | | | | |
| (9) 450 | | | | | | | |
| 28,875 | | 7,200 | | | 6,100 | | 900 |

| Mortgage Payable (L) | | Common Stock (SE) | | Additional Paid-in Capital (SE) | |
|---|---|---|---|---|---|
| | 22,500 (8) | | 40,000 (1) | | 8,000 (1) |
| | | | 6,000 (2) | | 1,200 (2) |
| | 22,500 | | 46,000 | | 9,200 |

Exhibit 2.7 _____

**ELECTRONICS APPLIANCE CORPORATION**
**Balance Sheet, September 30**

## Assets

**Current Assets:**

| | |
|---|---|
| Cash .......................... | $32,325 |
| Advances to Employees .......... | 200 |
| Raw Materials Inventory .......... | 6,100 |
| Prepaid Rent .................... | 10,000 |
| Total Current Assets ........... | $48,625 |

**Property, Plant, and Equipment:**

| | |
|---|---|
| Equipment ...................... | 28,875 |

**Intangibles:**

| | |
|---|---|
| Organization Costs ............. | 7,200 |
| Total Assets ................. | $84,700 |

## Liabilities and Shareholders' Equity

**Current Liabilities:**

| | | |
|---|---|---|
| Accounts Payable ............... | $ 6,100 | |
| Advances from Customers ....... | 900 | |
| Total Current Liabilities ........ | | $ 7,000 |

**Long-Term Debt:**

| | | |
|---|---|---|
| Mortgage Payable .............. | | 22,500 |
| Total Liabilities ............... | | $29,500 |

**Shareholders' Equity:**

| | | |
|---|---|---|
| Common Stock, $10 Par Value ... | $46,000 | |
| Additional Paid-in Capital ........ | 9,200 | |
| Total Shareholders' Equity ..... | | 55,200 |
| Total Liabilities and Shareholders' Equity ........ | | $84,700 |

# Questions, Exercises, Problems, and Cases ——————————

## Questions

1. Review the meaning of the following concepts or terms discussed in this chapter.

   | | | | |
   |---|---|---|---|
   | **a.** | Executory contract. | **j.** | Plant, or fixed, assets. |
   | **b.** | Acquisition (historical) cost. | **k.** | Intangible assets. |
   | **c.** | Current replacement cost (entry value). | **l.** | Par or stated value. |
   | | | **m.** | T-account. |
   | **d.** | Current net realizable value (exit value). | **n.** | Debit. |
   | | | **o.** | Credit. |
   | **e.** | Monetary assets. | **p.** | Charge. |
   | **f.** | Nonmonetary assets. | **q.** | Journal entry. |
   | **g.** | Going concern. | **r.** | General journal. |
   | **h.** | Objectivity. | **s.** | General ledger. |
   | **i.** | Conservatism. | **t.** | Trial balance. |

2. Conservatism is generally regarded as a convention in accounting. Indicate who might be hurt by conservatively stated accounting reports.

3. One of the criteria for the recognition of an asset or a liability is that there be an exchange. What justification can you see for this requirement?

4. Accounting typically does not recognize either assets or liabilities for mutually unexecuted contracts. What justification can you see for this treatment?

5. Cash discounts taken on the purchase of merchandise or equipment are treated as a reduction in the amount recorded for the assets acquired. What justification can you see for this treatment?

6. A group of investors owns an office building, which is rented unfurnished to tenants. The building was purchased 5 years previously from a construction company and at that time was expected to have a useful life of 40 years. Indicate the procedures that might be followed in ascertaining the amount at which the building would be stated under each of the following valuation methods.

   **a.** Acquisition cost.
   **b.** Adjusted acquisition cost.
   **c.** Current replacement cost.
   **d.** Current net realizable value.
   **e.** Present value of future cash flows.

7. Some of the assets of one firm correspond to the liabilities of another firm. For example, an account receivable on the seller's balance sheet would be an account payable on the buyer's balance sheet. For each of the following items, indicate whether it is an asset or a liability and give the corresponding account title on the balance sheet of the other party to the transaction.

   **a.** Advances by Customers.
   **b.** Bonds Payable.

c. Interest Receivable.
d. Prepaid Insurance.
e. Rental Fees Received in Advance.

# Exercises

8. *Asset recognition*. Indicate whether or not each of the following items would be recognized as an asset by a firm according to generally accepted accounting principles.
   a. A patent on a new invention purchased from its creator.
   b. A firm's chief scientist, who has twice won the Nobel prize.
   c. The right to use a building during the coming year. The rent for the period has already been paid.
   d. An automobile acquired with the issue of a note payable. Because the note has not been paid, the title document for the automobile is retained in the vault of the dealer.
   e. A degree in engineering from a reputable university, earned by the firm's chief executive.
   f. A contract, signed by a customer, to purchase $1,000 worth of goods next year.
   g. A favorable reputation.

9. *Asset recognition and valuation*. Indicate whether or not each of the following immediately gives rise to an asset under generally accepted accounting principles. If an asset is recognized, state the account title and amount.
   a. A check for $300 has been sent to an insurance company for property insurance. The period of coverage begins next month (consider from the standpoint of the firm making the cash expenditure).
   b. A check for $3,000 is issued as a deposit on specially designed equipment. The equipment is to have a total purchase price of $20,000 and will be completed and delivered next year (consider from the standpoint of the firm making the cash expenditure).
   c. Shares of common stock of General Electric Company are acquired for $12,000 with temporarily excess cash.
   d. Merchandise inventory with a list price of $800 is acquired, with payment made in time to secure a 3 percent discount for prompt payment. Cash discounts are treated as a reduction in the acquisition cost of the inventory.
   e. A well-known scientist has been hired to manage the firm's research and development activities. Employment begins next month. One-twelfth of the annual salary of $90,000 is payable at the end of each month worked.
   f. Bonds with a face value of $200,000 are purchased for $206,000. The bonds mature in 20 years. Interest is payable by the issuer at the rate of 10 percent annually.
   g. An order for $700 worth of merchandise is received from a customer.
   h. Notice has been received from a manufacturer that raw materials billed at $2,000, with payment due in 30 days, have been shipped by freight. The buyer obtains title to the goods as soon as they are shipped by the seller.

10. *Asset recognition and valuation.* Indicate whether or not each of the following events immediately gives rise to the recognition of an asset under generally accepted accounting principles. If an asset is recognized, state the account title and amount.

    a. Raw materials with an invoice price of $4,800 are purchased on account from Greer Wholesalers.

    b. Defective raw material purchased in part **a** for $400 is returned to Greer Wholesalers, and full credit is received.

    c. The bill of Greer Wholesalers (see parts **a** and **b**) is paid promptly. A discount of 2 percent offered by the seller for prompt payment is taken. Cash discounts are treated as a reduction in the acquisition cost of the raw materials.

    d. A machine is purchased for $25,000 cash.

    e. The cost of transporting the new machine in part **d** to the plant site is $450 and is paid in cash.

    f. Material and labor costs incurred in installing the machine in part **d** total $300 and are paid in cash.

11. *Asset recognition and valuation.* Indicate whether or not each of the following events immediately gives rise to an asset under generally accepted accounting principles. If an asset is recognized, state the account title and amount.

    a. An investment of $8,000 is made in a government bond. The bond will have a maturity value of $10,000 in 3 years. The firm intends to hold the bond to maturity.

    b. A check for $900 is sent to a landlord for 2 months' rent in advance (consider from the standpoint of the firm issuing the check).

    c. A check for $1,000 is written to obtain an option to purchase a tract of land. The price of the land is $32,500 (consider from the standpoint of the firm issuing the check).

    d. A firm signs a 4-year employment agreement with its president for $500,000 per year. The contract period begins next month (consider from the standpoint of the firm).

    e. A patent has been purchased from its creator for $40,000.

    f. A patent has been received on a new invention developed by a firm. Expenditures of $40,000 have been made to develop the patented invention.

    g. Notice has been received from a supplier that materials billed at $4,000, with payment due in 30 days, have been shipped by freight. The seller retains title to the materials until received by the buyer.

12. *Asset recognition and valuation.* In each of the following transactions, give the title(s) and amount(s) of the asset(s) that would appear on the balance sheet.

    a. A firm purchases an automobile with a list price of $8,000. The dealer allows a discount of $850 from the list price for payment in cash. Dealer preparation charges on the automobile amount to an extra $200. The dealer collects a 4 percent sales tax on the price paid for the automobile and preparation charges. In addition, the dealer collects a $75 fee to be remitted to the state for this year's license plates and $300 for a 1-year insurance policy provided by the dealer's insurance agency. The firm pays a body shop $75 for painting the firm's name on the automobile.

    **b.** A firm acquires land that has been appraised at $2 million by a certified real estate appraiser. The firm pays for the land by giving up shares in the Xerox Corporation at a time when equivalent shares traded on the New York Stock Exchange have a market value of $2,100,000.

    **c.** A firm acquires land that has been appraised at $2 million by a certified real estate appraiser. The firm pays for the land by giving up shares in Small Timers, Inc., whose shares are traded only on the Pacific Stock Exchange. The last transaction in shares of Small Timers, Inc. occurred 4 days prior to this asset swap. Using the prices of the most recent trades, the shares of stock of Small Timers, Inc. given in exchange for the land have a market value of $2,100,000.

13. *Liability recognition.* Indicate whether or not each of the following items is recognized as a liability according to generally accepted accounting principles.

    **a.** An obligation to provide magazines next year to subscribers who have paid 1 year's subscription fees in advance (consider from the standpoint of the magazine publisher).

    **b.** The reputation for poor quality control on products manufactured.

    **c.** An obligation to provide warranty services for 3 years after customers purchase the firm's products.

    **d.** The outstanding common stock of a corporation.

    **e.** Unpaid property taxes for the preceding year.

    **f.** The amount payable by a firm for a television advertisement that has appeared but for which payment is not due for 30 days.

    **g.** A tenant's obligation to maintain a rented warehouse in good repair.

    **h.** The firm president's incompetent son, who is employed in the business.

14. *Liability recognition and valuation.* Indicate whether or not each of the following events immediately gives rise to the recognition of a liability under generally accepted accounting principles. If a liability is recognized, state the account title and amount.

    **a.** A company hires its president under a 5-year contract beginning next month. The contract calls for $300,000 compensation per year.

    **b.** An insurance company receives $2,000 for 6 months' insurance coverage in advance (consider from the standpoint of the insurance company).

    **c.** A manufacturer agrees to produce a specially designed piece of equipment for $3 million. A down payment of $300,000 is received upon signing the contract, and the remainder is due when the equipment is completed (consider from the standpoint of the manufacturer).

    **d.** Additional common stock with a par value of $75,000 is issued for $80,000.

    **e.** Employees earned wages totaling $6,000 during the last pay period for which they have not been paid. The employer is also liable for payroll taxes of 8 percent of the wages earned.

    **f.** A firm signs a contract agreeing to sell $6,000 of merchandise to a particular customer.

15. *Liability recognition and valuation.* Indicate whether or not each of the following events immediately gives rise to the recognition of a liability under gener-

ally accepted accounting principles. If a liability is recognized, indicate the account title and amount.

**a.** A $600 check is received from a tenant for 3 months' rent in advance (consider from the standpoint of the lessor, or owner, of the building).

**b.** Utility services of $240, received during the past month, have not been paid (consider from the standpoint of the firm using the utility services).

**c.** A $10,000 loan has been received from the bank, with the firm signing a note agreeing to repay the loan in 6 months with interest at 8 percent.

**d.** A firm has signed an agreement with its employees' labor union agreeing to increase the firm's contribution to the union pension fund by $20,000 per month, beginning next month (consider from the standpoint of the firm).

**e.** Income taxes on last year's earnings totaling $15,000 have not been paid.

**f.** A firm has signed an employment contract with its controller for a 3-year period, beginning next month, at a contract price of $200,000 per year (consider from the standpoint of the firm).

16. *Liability recognition and valuation.* Indicate whether or not each of the following events immediately gives rise to a liability under generally accepted accounting principles. If a liability is recognized, state the account title and amount.

**a.** A landscaper agrees to improve land owned by a firm. The agreed price for the work is $2,500 (consider from the standpoint of the firm owning the land).

**b.** A check for $36 is received for a 2-year, future subscription to a magazine (consider from the standpoint of the magazine publisher).

**c.** A construction company agrees to build a bridge for $2 million. A down payment of $200,000 is received upon signing the contract, and the remainder is due when the bridge is completed.

**d.** Additional common stock with a par value of $60,000 is issued for $80,000.

**e.** A firm receives a 60-day, 10 percent loan of $10,000 from a local bank.

**f.** A firm signs a contract to purchase at least $6,000 worth of merchandise during the next year.

**g.** Refer to part **f.** An order for $1,500 of merchandise is placed with the supplier.

17. *Balance sheet classification.* Information may be classified with respect to a balance sheet in one of the following ways:

**(1)** Asset.

**(2)** Liability.

**(3)** Shareholders' equity.

**(4)** Item would not appear on the balance sheet as conventionally prepared.

Using these numbers, indicate the appropriate classification of each of the following items:

**a.** Salaries payable.

**b.** Retained earnings.

**c.** Notes receivable.

    **d.**  Unfilled customers' orders.
    **e.**  Land.
    **f.**  Interest payable.
    **g.**  Work-in-process inventory.
    **h.**  Mortgage payable.
    **i.**  Organization costs.
    **j.**  Advances by customers.
    **k.**  Advances to employees.
    **l.**  Patents.
    **m.**  Good credit standing.
    **n.**  Common stock.

18. *Balance sheet classification.* Information may be classified with respect to a balance sheet in one of the following ways:
    **(1)** Asset.
    **(2)** Liability.
    **(3)** Shareholders' equity.
    **(4)** Item would not appear on the balance sheet as conventionally prepared.
Using these numbers, indicate the appropriate classification of each of the following items:
    **a.**  Preferred stock.
    **b.**  Furniture and fixtures.
    **c.**  Potential liability under lawsuit (case has not yet gone to trial).
    **d.**  Prepaid rent.
    **e.**  Capital contributed in excess of par value.
    **f.**  Cash on hand.
    **g.**  Goodwill.
    **h.**  Estimated liability under warranty contract.
    **i.**  Raw materials inventory.
    **j.**  Rental fees received in advance.
    **k.**  Bonds payable.
    **l.**  Prepaid insurance.

## Problems and Cases

19. *Journal entries for various transactions.* Present journal entries for each of the following transactions of Mailor Corporation during April, its first month of operations.
    **(1)** April 2: The firm issues 250,000 shares of $5 par value common stock for $8 cash per share.
    **(2)** April 3: A building costing $800,000 is acquired. A down payment of $200,000 is made in cash, and a 10 percent note maturing in 3 years is signed for the balance.
    **(3)** April 8: A machine costing $15,000 is acquired for cash.
    **(4)** April 15: Merchandise inventory costing $120,000 is acquired on account from various suppliers.

(5) April 18: A check for $400 is issued for insurance coverage for the period beginning May 1.

(6) April 20: A check for $800 is received from a customer for merchandise to be delivered on May 5.

(7) April 26: Invoices totaling $80,000 from the purchases on April 15 are paid after deducting a 2 percent discount for prompt payment. Cash discounts are treated as a reduction in the acquisition cost of inventory.

(8) April 30: The remaining invoices from the purchases on April 15 are paid after the discount period has lapsed.

20. *Journal entries for various transactions.* Present journal entries for each of the following transactions of Area Corporation. You may omit dates and explanations for the journal entries.

(1) The firm issues 20,000 shares of $10 par value common stock at par value for cash.

(2) Land and building costing $90,000 are acquired with the payment of $25,000 cash and the assumption of a 20-year, 8 percent mortgage for the balance. The land is to be stated at $30,000 and the building at $60,000.

(3) A used lathe is purchased for $4,620 cash.

(4) Raw materials costing $3,600 are acquired on account.

(5) Defective raw materials purchased in (4) and costing $650 are returned to the supplier. The account has not yet been paid.

(6) The supplier in (4) is paid the amount due, less a 2 percent discount for prompt payment. Cash discounts are treated as a reduction in the acquisition cost of raw materials.

(7) A fire insurance policy providing $100,000 coverage beginning next month is obtained. The 1-year premium of $625 is paid in cash.

(8) A check for $2,000 is issued to Roger White to reimburse him for costs incurred in organizing and promoting the corporation.

(9) A check for $600 is issued for 3 months' rent in advance for office space.

(10) A patent on a machine process is purchased for $35,000 cash.

(11) Office equipment is purchased for $950. A down payment of $250 is made, with the balance payable in 30 days.

(12) $275 is paid to Express Transfer Company for delivering the equipment purchased in (3).

21. *Journal entries for various transactions.* Express the following transactions of the Winkle Grocery Store, Inc. in journal entry form. You may omit explanations for the journal entries.

(1) John Winkle contributes $50,000 cash for 1,000 shares of $50 par value common stock.

(2) A 60-day, 8 percent note is signed in return for a $10,000 loan from the bank.

(3) A building is rented, with the annual rental of $6,000 paid in advance.

(4) Display equipment costing $16,000 is acquired. A check is issued.

(5) Merchandise inventory costing $35,000 is acquired. A check for $8,000 is issued, with the remainder payable in 30 days.

(6) A contract is signed with a nearby restaurant under which the restaurant

agrees to purchase $6,000 of groceries each week. A check is received for the first 2 weeks' orders in advance.

22. *Journal entries for various transactions.* Express the following independent transactions in journal entry form. If an entry is not required, indicate the reason. You may omit explanations for the journal entries.

(1) Bonds of the Sommers Company with a face value of $60,000 and annual interest at the rate of 8 percent are purchased for $58,500 cash.

(2) A check for $2,600 is received by a fire insurance company for premiums on policy coverage over the next 2 years.

(3) A corporation issues 20,000 shares of $12 par value common stock in exchange for land, building, and equipment. The land is to be stated at $30,000, the building at $180,000, and the equipment at $75,000.

(4) A contract is signed by a manufacturing firm agreeing to purchase 100 dozen machine tool parts over the next 2 years at a price of $60 per dozen.

(5) A firm issues 5,000 shares of $1 par value preferred stock to an attorney for legal services rendered in the organization of the corporation. The bill for the services is $9,500.

(6) A coupon book, redeemable in future movie viewings, is issued for $60 cash by a movie theatre.

(7) A firm has been notified that it is being sued for $30,000 damages by a customer who incurred losses as a result of purchasing defective merchandise.

(8) Merchandise inventory costing $2,000, purchased on account, is found to be defective and returned to the supplier for full credit.

23. *Effect of transactions on balance sheet equation.* Indicate the effects of the following transactions on the balance sheet equation using this format:

| Transaction Number | Assets | = | Liabilities | + | Shareholders' Equity |
|---|---|---|---|---|---|
| (1) | +$50,000 | | $0 | | +$50,000 |
| Subtotal | $50,000 | = | $0 | + | $50,000 |

(1) A firm issues 5,000 shares of $10 par value common stock at par for cash.

(2) Equipment costing $12,000 is acquired. A down payment of $4,000 is made, with the remainder payable in 6 months with interest at 9 percent.

(3) Raw materials costing $6,000 are acquired on account.

(4) Installation cost of $800 on the equipment in (2) is paid in cash.

(5) The property insurance premium of $420 for the year, beginning on the first day of next month, is paid.

(6) Raw materials acquired in (3) for $700 are found to be defective and returned to the supplier for full credit. The account has not yet been paid.

(7) Invoices from the purchases in (3) totaling $4,000 are paid after deducting a 1 percent discount for prompt payment. Cash discounts are treated as a reduction in the acquisition cost of raw materials.

(8) One hundred shares of $10 par value common stock are issued to the firm's attorney for services rendered in organizing the corporation. The attorney's bill is $1,000.

**(9)** Customers advance the firm $250 for merchandise to be delivered next month.

**24.** *Effect of transactions on balance sheet equation.* Indicate the effects of the following transactions on the balance sheet equation using this format:

| Transaction Number | Assets | = | Liabilities | + | Shareholders' Equity |
|---|---|---|---|---|---|
| (1) | +$30,000 | | $0 | | +$30,000 |
| Subtotal | $30,000 = | | $0 | + | $30,000 |

**(1)** A firm issues 3,000 shares of $10 par value common stock at par for cash.
**(2)** Merchandise costing $24,300 is purchased on account.
**(3)** Store equipment costing $4,800 is acquired. A check for $1,000 is issued, and the balance is payable over 3 years under an installment contract.
**(4)** A check is issued for $900 covering 2 months' rent in advance.
**(5)** Refer to transaction **(3)**. Common stock with a market value of $3,800 is issued in full settlement of the installment contract.
**(6)** The merchandise supplier in transaction **(2)** is paid the amount due.

**25.** *T-account entries for various transactions.* Set up T-accounts for the following accounts. Indicate whether each account is an asset, liability, or shareholders' equity item, and enter the transactions described below.

- Cash
- Merchandise Inventory
- Prepaid Insurance
- Building
- Equipment

- Accounts Payable
- Note Payable
- Mortgage Payable
- Common Stock — Par Value
- Additional Paid-in Capital

**(1)** A firm issues 30,000 shares of $5 par value stock for $8 cash per share.
**(2)** A building costing $300,000 is acquired. A cash payment of $60,000 is made, and a long-term mortgage is assumed for the balance of the purchase price.
**(3)** Equipment costing $5,000 and merchandise inventory costing $7,000 are acquired on account.
**(4)** A 3-year fire insurance policy is taken out, and the $900 premium is paid in advance.
**(5)** A 90-day, 6 percent note is issued to the bank for a $10,000 loan.
**(6)** Payments of $8,000 are made to the suppliers in **(3)**.

**26.** *T-account entries and balance sheet preparation.* The Patterson Manufacturing Corporation is organized on January 1. During January, the following transactions occur:

**(1)** The corporation issues 15,000 shares of $10 par value common stock for $210,000 in cash.
**(2)** The corporation issues 28,000 shares of common stock in exchange for land, building, and equipment. The land is to be stated at $80,000, the building at $220,000, and the equipment at $92,000.
**(3)** The corporation issues 2,000 shares of common stock to an attorney in payment for legal services rendered in obtaining the corporate charter.

**(4)** Raw materials costing $75,000 are acquired on account from various suppliers.

**(5)** Manufacturing equipment with a list price of $6,000 is acquired. After deducting a $600 discount, the net amount is paid in cash. Cash discounts are treated as a reduction in the acquisition cost of equipment.

**(6)** Freight charges of $350 for delivery of the equipment in (5) are paid in cash.

**(7)** Raw materials costing $800 are found to be defective and returned to the supplier for full credit. The raw materials had been purchased on account [see **(4)**], and no payment had been made as of the time that the goods were returned.

**(8)** A contract is signed for the rental of a fleet of automobiles beginning February 1. The rental for February of $1,400 is paid in advance.

**(9)** Invoices for $60,000 of raw materials purchased in **(4)** are paid after deducting a discount of 3 percent for prompt payment. Cash discounts are treated as a reduction in the acquisition cost of raw materials.

**(10)** Fire and liability insurance coverage is obtained from Southwest Insurance Company. The 2-year policy, beginning February 1, carries a $400 premium that has not yet been paid.

**(11)** A contract is signed with a customer for $20,000 of merchandise that Patterson plans to manufacture. The customer advances $4,500 toward the contract price.

**(12)** A warehouse costing $60,000 is acquired. A down payment of $7,000 is made, and a long-term mortgage is assumed for the balance.

**(13)** Raw materials inventory with an original list price of $1,500 is found to be defective and returned to the supplier. This inventory has already been paid for in **(9)**. The returned raw materials are the only items purchased from this particular supplier during January. A cash refund has not yet been received from the supplier.

**(14)** The firm purchases 6,000 shares of $10 par value common stock of the General Cereal Corporation for $95,000. This investment is made as a short-term investment of excess cash. The shares of General Cereal Corporation are traded on the New York Stock Exchange.

The following assumptions will help you resolve certain accounting uncertainties: (i) Transactions **(2)** and **(3)** occurred on the same day as transaction **(1)**. (ii) The invoices paid in **(9)** are the only purchases for which discounts were made available to the purchaser.

**a.** Enter these transactions in T-accounts. Indicate whether each account is an asset, liability, or shareholders' equity item. Cross-reference each entry to the appropriate transaction number.

**b.** Prepare a balance sheet as of January 31.

27. *T-account entries and balance sheet preparation*. The Scott Products Corporation is organized on October 1. During October, the following transactions occur:

**(1)** The corporation issues 20,000 shares of $5 par value common stock for $7 per share in cash.

**(2)** The corporation issues 200 shares of $100 par value preferred stock at par value for cash.

(3) The corporation gives $40,000 in cash and 5,000 shares of common stock in exchange for land and building. The land is to be stated at $5,000 and the building at $70,000.

(4) Equipment costing $26,000 is acquired. A cash payment of $3,000 is made, and an 8 percent note, due in 1 year, is given for the balance.

(5) Transportation costs of $800 on the equipment in (4) are paid in cash.

(6) Installation costs of $1,100 on the equipment in (4) are paid in cash.

(7) Merchandise inventory costing $45,000 is acquired on account.

(8) License fees of $800 for the year beginning November 1 are paid in advance.

(9) Merchandise costing $1,300 from the acquisition in (7) are found to be defective and returned to the supplier for full credit. The account had not been paid.

(10) A patent is purchased from its creator for $15,000.

(11) The corporation signed an agreement to manufacture a specially designed machine for a customer for $60,000, to be delivered in January of next year. At the time of signing, the customer advances $6,000 of the contract price.

(12) Invoices totaling $30,000 from the purchases in (7) are paid after deducting a 2 percent discount for prompt payment. Cash discounts are treated as a reduction in the acquisition cost of inventory.

a.  Enter the transactions in T-accounts. Indicate whether each account is an asset, liability, or shareholders' equity item. Cross-reference each entry to the appropriate transaction number.

b.  Prepare a balance sheet for Scott Products Corporation as of October 31.

28. *T-account entries and balance sheet preparation.* The Sarwark Corporation is organized on January 1. During January, the following transactions occur:

(1) The corporation issues 10,000 shares of $10 par value common stock for $150,000.

(2) Bonds with a face and maturity value of $100,000 are issued at face value for cash.

(3) Land and a building costing $200,000 are acquired. A check for $80,000 is issued, with the remainder payable over 20 years. The land is assigned $20,000 and the building is assigned $180,000 of the acquisition cost.

(4) Equipment costing $40,000 is acquired. After deducting a discount of 2 percent for immediate cash payment, the net amount due is paid.

(5) Merchandise costing $25,000 is acquired on account.

(6) Merchandise costing $2,000 is found to be defective and returned to the supplier. No cash payments have yet been made to this supplier.

(7) An insurance policy for a 1-year period beginning February 1 is obtained. The premium for the 1-year period of $1,200 is paid.

(8) A customer places an order for $1,500 of merchandise to be delivered in February. The customer sends a check of $300 with the order.

(9) Merchandise suppliers in (5) are paid $18,000 of the amounts due. The remaining suppliers will be paid in February.

**a.** Enter these transactions in T-accounts. Indicate whether each account is an asset, liability, or shareholders' equity item. Cross-reference each entry to the appropriate transaction number.

**b.** Prepare a balance sheet as of January 31.

29. *T-account entries and balance sheet preparation.* The following transactions occur during March for Dryden's Book Store, Inc. in preparation for its opening for business on April 1.

(1) H. R. Dryden contributes $6,000 in cash, 100 shares of Western Corporation common stock, and an inventory of books to be sold. The stock of Western Corporation is quoted on the New York Stock Exchange at $15 per share on the day it is contributed, and will be sold when additional cash is needed. The books are to be stated at $2,750. H. R. Dryden receives 8,000 shares of $1 par value common stock of Dryden's Book Store, Inc.

(2) Two months' rent on a store building is paid in advance in cash. The bookstore will occupy the building on April 1. The monthly rental is $400.

(3) Store fixtures are purchased for $4,000, of which $800 is paid in cash. A note, to be paid in 10 equal monthly installments beginning May 1, is signed for the balance.

(4) Books with an invoice price of $2,600 are purchased on account.

(5) A 1-year insurance policy on the store's contents, beginning April 1, is purchased. The premium of $160 is paid by check.

(6) A check for $320 is issued to the Darwin Equipment Co. for a cash register and other operating equipment.

(7) Merchandise costing $1,800 is ordered from a publisher. Delivery is scheduled for April 15.

(8) The merchandise purchased in (4) is paid for by check. Payment is made in time to obtain a 2 percent cash discount for prompt payment. This is the only purchase for which a discount is available. Cash discounts are treated as a reduction in the acquisition cost of merchandise.

(9) An operating license for the year, beginning April 1, is obtained. A fee of $250 is paid by check.

**a.** Enter these transactions in T-accounts. Indicate whether each account is an asset, liability, or shareholders' equity item. Cross-reference each entry to the appropriate transaction number.

**b.** Prepare a balance sheet for this firm as of March 31.

30. *T-account entries and balance sheet preparation.* Priscilla Mullins and Miles Standish form a corporation to operate a laundry and cleaning business to be known as Pilgrim's One Day Laundry and Cleaners, Inc. The following transactions occur in late June, prior to the grand opening on July 1.

(1) Standish contributes $400 cash and cleaning equipment that is to be stated at $5,600, in exchange for 6,000 shares of $1 par value common stock.

(2) Mullins contributes $3,000 cash and a delivery truck to be stated at $2,500, in exchange for 5,500 shares of $1 par value common stock.

(3) The July rent of $400 for the business premises is paid in advance.

(4) Cleaning supplies are purchased on account from the Wonder Chemical Company for $2,500.

**(5)** Insurance coverage on the equipment and truck for a 1-year period beginning July 1 is purchased for $425 cash.

**(6)** The firm borrows $2,000 from the First National Bank. A 90-day, 8 percent note is signed, with principal and interest payable at maturity.

**(7)** The Wonder Chemical Company account is paid in full after deducting a 2 percent discount for prompt payment. Cash discounts are treated as a reduction in the acquisition cost of supplies.

**(8)** A cash register is purchased for $700. A down payment of $100 is made, and a note is signed for the remainder, payable in 10 equal installments beginning August 1.

**a.** Enter these transactions in T-accounts. Indicate whether each account is an asset, liability, or shareholders' equity item. Cross-reference each entry to the appropriate transaction number.

**b.** Prepare a balance sheet for the partnership as of June 30.

**31.** *Effect of recording errors on balance sheet equation.* Using the notation O/S (overstated), U/S (understated), or No (no effect), indicate the effects on assets, liabilities, and shareholders' equity of failing to record each of the following independent transactions or events. For example, a failure to record the issuance of common stock for $10,000 cash would be

- Assets — U/S $10,000

- Liabilities — No

- Shareholders' equity — U/S $10,000

**(1)** Merchandise costing $6,000 is purchased on account.

**(2)** A machine costing $10,000 is acquired. A 25 percent down payment is made, with the remainder payable over 5 years.

**(3)** An order for $3,500 of merchandise is placed with a supplier.

**(4)** A check for $300 is received from a customer for merchandise to be delivered next month.

**(5)** A check for $800 was issued to cover rental of a warehouse for the next 2 months.

**(6)** Common stock with a market value of $1,500 is issued to attorneys for services rendered in setting up the firm.

**(7)** A note payable for $2,000, which had previously been correctly recorded on the books, is now paid in the amount of $2,000.

**(8)** A check for $1,000 is issued for an option to purchase a tract of land. The price of the land is $30,000. The option can be exercised within 90 days.

# Chapter 3    Income Statement: Reporting the
Results of Operating Activities _____

The second principal financial statement is the income statement, which provides a measure of the operating performance of a firm for some particular period of time. *Net income,* or *earnings,* is equal to revenues minus expenses.

*Revenues* measure the net assets (assets less liabilities) that flow into a firm when goods are sold or services are rendered. *Expenses* measure the net assets used up in the process of generating revenues. As a measure of operating performance, revenues reflect the services rendered by the firm, and expenses indicate the efforts required.

This chapter considers the measurement principles and accounting procedures that underlie the income statement. We begin by considering the concept of an accounting period, the span of time over which operating performance is measured. Next, two common approaches to measuring operating performance, the cash basis and the accrual basis, are described and illustrated. Finally, the accounting procedures used in applying the accrual basis of accounting are illustrated for a merchandising firm. Chapter 4 explores more fully the application of the accrual basis of accounting for manufacturing, construction, and other types of businesses.


## The Accounting Period Convention _____

The income statement reports operating performance for a specific period of time. Years ago, the length of this period varied substantially among firms. Income statements were prepared at the completion of some activity, such as after the round-trip voyage of a ship between England and the Colonies, or at the completion of a construction project.

The operating activities of most modern firms do not divide so easily into distinguishable projects. Instead, the income-generating activity occurs continually. For example, a plant is acquired and used in manufacturing products for a period of 40 years or more. Delivery equipment is purchased and used in transporting merchandise to customers for 4, 5, or more years. If the preparation of the income statement were postponed until all operating activities were completed, the report might be prepared only when the firm ceased to exist and, in any case, would be too late to help a reader appraise operating performance. An *accounting period* of uniform length facilitates timely comparisons and analyses among firms.

An accounting period of 1 year underlies the principal financial statements distributed to shareholders and potential investors. Most firms prepare their annual reports using the calendar year as the accounting period. A growing number of firms, however, use a *natural business year* in an attempt to measure performance at a time when most operating activities have been substantially concluded. The ending date of a natural business year varies from one firm to another. For example, J. C. Penney uses a natural business year ending near the end of January, which comes after completion of the Christmas shopping season and before the start of the Easter season. Winnebago Industries uses a year ending August 31, the end of its model year. A. C. Nielsen (producers of television ratings and other surveys) uses a year ending August 31, just before the beginning of the new television season.

Reports of performance for periods shorter than a year are frequently prepared as indicators of progress during the year. These are known as *interim reports* or *reports for interim periods*. Preparing interim reports does not remove the need to prepare an annual report.

# Accounting Methods for Measuring Performance ————

Some operating activities both start and finish within a given accounting period. For example, merchandise may be purchased from a supplier and sold to a customer on account, and the account may be collected in cash, all within a particular accounting period. Few difficulties are encountered in measuring performance in these cases. The difference between the cash received from customers and the cash disbursed to acquire, sell, and deliver the merchandise represents earnings from this series of transactions.

Many operating activities, however, start in one accounting period and finish in another. Buildings and equipment are acquired in one period but used over several years. Merchandise is sometimes purchased in one accounting period and sold during the next period, with cash being collected from customers during a third period. A significant problem in measuring performance for a specific accounting period is measuring the amount of revenues and expenses from operating activities that are in process at the beginning of the period or are incomplete at the end of the period. Two approaches to measuring operating performance are (1) the cash basis of accounting and (2) the accrual basis of accounting.

## Cash Basis of Accounting

Under the *cash basis of accounting*, revenues from selling goods and providing services are recognized in the period when cash is received from customers. Expenses are reported in the period in which expenditures are made for merchandise, salaries, insurance, taxes, and similar items. To illustrate the measurement of performance under the cash basis of accounting, consider the following example.

**Exhibit 3.1** _____

## ALLENS' HARDWARE STORE
### Performance Measurement on a Cash Basis
### for the Month of January, Year 1

| | | |
|---|---:|---:|
| Cash Receipts from Sales of Merchandise .................... | | $34,000 |
| Less Cash Expenditures for Merchandise and Services: | | |
|    Merchandise ............................................. | $26,000 | |
|    Salaries ................................................ | 5,000 | |
|    Rent .................................................... | 4,000 | |
|    Insurance ............................................... | 2,400 | |
|      Total Cash Expenditures .............................. | | 37,400 |
| Excess of Cash Expenditures over Cash Receipts ............. | | ($ 3,400) |

Donald and Joanne Allens open a hardware store on January 1, Year 1. They contribute $20,000 in cash and borrow $12,000 from a local bank. The loan is repayable on June 30, Year 1, with interest charged at the rate of 12 percent per year. A store building is rented on January 1, and 2 months' rent of $4,000 is paid in advance. The premium of $2,400 for property and liability insurance coverage for the year ending December 31, Year 1, is paid on January 1. During January, merchandise costing $40,000 is acquired, of which $26,000 is purchased for cash and $14,000 is purchased on account. Sales to customers during January total $50,000, of which $34,000 is sold for cash and $16,000 is sold on account. The acquisition cost of the merchandise sold during January is $32,000, and various employees are paid $5,000 in salaries.

Exhibit 3.1 presents a performance report for Allens' Hardware Store for the month of January Year 1, using the cash basis. Cash receipts from sales of merchandise of $34,000 represent the portion of the total sales of $50,000 made during January that was collected in cash. Whereas merchandise costing $40,000 was acquired during January, only $26,000 cash was disbursed to suppliers, and only this amount is subtracted in measuring performance under the cash basis. Cash expenditures during January for salaries, rent, and insurance are also subtracted in measuring performance, without regard to whether the services acquired were fully consumed by the end of the month. Cash expenditures made for merchandise and services exceeded cash receipts from customers during January by $3,400.[1]

As a basis for measuring performance for a particular accounting period (for example, January, Year 1, for Allens' Hardware Store), the cash basis of accounting has two weaknesses. First, the cost of the efforts required in generating revenues is not adequately matched with those revenues. The performance of one period gets mingled with the performance of preceding and succeeding periods. The store rental payment of $4,000 provides rental services for both January and February, but under the cash basis the full amount is subtracted in measuring performance during January. Likewise, the annual insurance premium provides coverage for the full

_____

[1]Note that, under the cash basis, cash received from owners and through borrowing (financing transactions) is not included in the performance report.

Exhibit 3.2 ————————————————————————————————

## ALLENS' HARDWARE STORE
### Income Statement for the Month of January, Year 1
### (Accrual Basis of Accounting)

| | | |
|---|---:|---:|
| Sales Revenue . . . . . . . . . . . . . . . . . . . . . . . . . . . . . . . . . . . . . . . . . . . . . . . . | | $50,000 |
| Less Expenses: | | |
| Cost of Goods Sold . . . . . . . . . . . . . . . . . . . . . . . . . . . . . . . . . . . . . . . | $32,000 | |
| Salaries Expense . . . . . . . . . . . . . . . . . . . . . . . . . . . . . . . . . . . . . . . . . | 5,000 | |
| Rent Expense . . . . . . . . . . . . . . . . . . . . . . . . . . . . . . . . . . . . . . . . . . . . . | 2,000 | |
| Insurance Expense . . . . . . . . . . . . . . . . . . . . . . . . . . . . . . . . . . . . . . . | 200 | |
| Interest Expense . . . . . . . . . . . . . . . . . . . . . . . . . . . . . . . . . . . . . . . . . | 120 | |
| Total Expenses . . . . . . . . . . . . . . . . . . . . . . . . . . . . . . . . . . . . . . . . . | | 39,320 |
| Net Income . . . . . . . . . . . . . . . . . . . . . . . . . . . . . . . . . . . . . . . . . . . . . . . . | | $10,680 |

year, whereas under the cash basis of accounting, none of this insurance cost will be subtracted in measuring performance during February through December.

The longer the period over which future benefits are received, the more serious is this criticism of the cash basis of accounting. Consider, for example, the investments of a capital-intensive firm in buildings and equipment that might be used for 10, 20, or more years. The length of time between the purchase of these assets and the collection of cash for goods produced and sold can span many years.

Second, the cash basis of accounting postpones unnecessarily the time when revenue is recognized. In most cases, the sale (delivery) of goods or rendering of services is the important event in generating revenue. Collecting cash is relatively routine or at least highly predictable. In these cases, recognizing revenue at the time of cash collection may result in reporting the effects of operating activities one or more periods after the critical revenue-generating activity has occurred. For example, sales to customers during January by Allens' Hardware Store totaled $50,000. Under the cash basis of accounting, $16,000 of this amount will not be recognized until the cash is collected, during February or even later. If the creditworthiness of customers has been checked prior to making sales on account, the cash will probably be collected, and there is little reason to postpone recognition of the revenue.

The cash basis of accounting is used principally by lawyers, accountants, and other professional people. These professionals have relatively small investments in multiperiod assets such as buildings and equipment, and they usually collect cash from their clients soon after services are rendered. Most of these firms actually use a *modified* cash basis of accounting, under which the costs of buildings, equipment, and similar items are treated as assets when purchased. A portion of the acquisition cost is then recognized as an expense when services of these assets are consumed. Except for the treatment of these long-lived assets, revenues are recognized at the time cash is received and expenses are reported when cash is disbursed.

Most individuals use the cash basis of accounting for the purpose of computing personal income and personal income taxes. Where inventories are an important factor in generating revenues, such as for a merchandising or manufacturing firm, the Internal Revenue Code prohibits a firm from using the cash basis of accounting in its income tax returns.

## Accrual Basis of Accounting

The *accrual basis of accounting* typically recognizes revenue when goods are sold or services are rendered. Costs incurred are reported as expenses in the period when the revenues that the costs helped produce are recognized. Thus accrual accounting attempts to match expenses with associated revenues. Costs incurred that cannot be closely identified with specific revenue streams are treated as expenses of the period in which services of an asset are consumed and the future benefits of an asset disappear.

Exhibit 3.2 presents an income statement for Allens' Hardware Store for January of Year 1 using the accrual basis of accounting. The entire $50,000 of sales during January is recognized as revenue, even though cash in that amount has not yet been received. Because the outstanding accounts receivable will probably be collected, the sale of the goods, rather than the collection of cash from customers, triggers the recognition of revenue. The merchandise sold during January costs $32,000. Recognizing this amount as an expense (cost of goods sold) matches the cost of the merchandise sold with revenue from sales. Of the advance rental payment of $4,000, only $2,000 applies to the cost of services consumed during January. The remaining rental of $2,000 applies to the month of February. Likewise, only $200 of the $2,400 insurance premium represents coverage used up during January. The remaining $2,200 of the insurance premium provides coverage for February through December and will be recognized as an expense during those months. The interest expense of $120 represents 1 month's interest on the $12,000 bank loan at an annual rate of 12 percent ($= \$12,000 \times .12 \times 1/12$). Although the interest will not be paid until the loan becomes due on June 30, Year 1, the firm benefited from having the funds available for its use during January; an appropriate portion of the total interest cost on the loan should therefore be recognized as an expense of January. The salaries, rental, insurance, and interest expenses, unlike the cost of merchandise sold, cannot be associated directly with revenues recognized during the period. These costs are therefore reported as expenses of January to the extent that services were consumed during the month.

The accrual basis of accounting provides a better measure of operating performance for Allens' Hardware Store for the month of January than does the cash basis for two reasons:

1. Revenues more accurately reflect the results of sales activity during January.

2. Expenses are associated more closely with reported revenues.

Likewise, the accrual basis will provide a superior measure of performance for future periods, because activities of those periods will be charged with their share of the costs of rental, insurance, and other services to be consumed. Thus the accrual basis focuses on *inflows of net assets* from operations (revenues) and the *use of net assets* in operations (expenses), regardless of whether those inflows and outflows currently produce or use cash.

Most business firms, particularly those involved in merchandising and manufacturing activities, use the accrual basis of accounting. The next section examines the measurement principles of accrual accounting.

# Measurement Principles of Accrual Accounting ———

Under the accrual basis of accounting, one must consider *when* revenues and expenses are recognized (timing questions) and *how much* is recognized (measurement questions).

## Timing of Revenue Recognition

The operating process for the acquisition and sale of merchandise might be depicted as shown in Figure 3.1. Revenue, a measure of the increase in net assets from selling goods or providing services, could be recognized at the time of purchase, sale, or cash collection, at some point(s) between these events, or even continually. Answering the timing question requires a set of criteria for revenue recognition.

**Criteria for Revenue Recognition**   Revenue is recognized under the accrual basis of accounting when:

1.  All, or a substantial portion, of the services to be provided have been performed.
2.  Either cash, or a receivable, or some other asset susceptible to reasonably precise measurement has been received.

For the majority of firms involved in selling goods and services, revenue is recognized at the time of sale (delivery). The goods have been transferred to a buyer or the services have been performed. Future services, such as for warranties, are either insignificant or, if significant, can be estimated with reasonable precision. An exchange between an independent buyer and seller provides an objective measure of the amount of revenue. If the sale is made on account, past experience and an assessment of credit standings of customers provide a basis for predicting the amount of cash that will be collected. Thus the criteria for revenue recognition are usually met at the time of sale.

## Measurement of Revenue

The amount of revenue recognized is measured by the cash or cash-equivalent value of other assets received from customers. As a starting point, this amount is the agreed-upon price between buyer and seller at the time of sale. Some adjustments to this amount may be necessary, however, if revenue is recognized in a period before the collection of cash.

**Figure 3.1** ————————————————————————

**Operating Process for the Acquisition and Sale of Merchandise**

| Purchase of Merchandise | Sale of Merchandise | Collection of Cash |
|---|---|---|

**Uncollectible Accounts**  If some portion of the sales for a period is expected not to be collected, the amount of revenue recognized for that period must be adjusted for estimated uncollectible accounts arising from those sales. This adjustment of revenue occurs in the period when revenue is recognized and not in a later period when specific customers' accounts are found to be uncollectible. If the adjustment were postponed, reported income of subsequent periods would be affected by earlier decisions to extend credit to customers. Thus the performance of the firm for both the period of sale and the period when the account is judged uncollectible would be measured inaccurately. Chapter 7 considers these problems further.

**Sales Discounts and Allowances**  Customers may take advantage of discounts for prompt payment, and the seller may grant allowances for unsatisfactory merchandise. In these cases, the amount of cash eventually to be received can be expected to be less than the stated selling price. Appropriate reductions should therefore be made at the time of sale in measuring the amount of revenue to be recognized.

**Delayed Payments**  When the period between the sale of the goods or services and the time of cash collection extends beyond a year, and there is no provision for explicit interest payments, the selling price probably includes an implicit interest charge for the right to delay payment. Under the accrual basis of accounting, this interest element is recognized as interest revenue during the periods between sale and collection. To recognize all revenue entirely in the period of sale would be to recognize too soon the return for services rendered over time in lending money. Thus, when cash collection is to be delayed beyond 1 year, the measure of revenue for the current period is the selling price reduced to account for interest between sale and cash collection. Only the present value at the time of sale of the amount to be received should be recognized as revenue during the period of sale.

For most accounts receivable, the period between sale and collection spans only 2 to 3 months. The interest element is likely to be relatively insignificant in these cases. As a result, in accounting practice no reduction for interest on delayed payments is made for receivables to be collected within 1 year or less. This procedure is a practical expedient rather than a strict adherence to the underlying accounting theory.

## Timing of Expense Recognition

Assets provide future benefits to the firm. Expenses measure the assets consumed in generating revenue. Assets are *unexpired costs,* and expenses are *expired costs* or "gone assets." Our attention focuses on *when* the asset expiration takes place. The critical question is "When do asset benefits expire—leaving the balance sheet—and become expenses—entering the income statement as reductions in owners' equity?" Thus:

| Balance Sheet | | Income Statement |
|---|---|---|
| Assets or Unexpired Costs | → | Expenses or Expired Costs (which reduce owners' equity on the balance sheet). |

**Expense Recognition**   Expenses are recognized as follows:

1.  Asset expirations associated directly with particular types of revenues are expenses in the period in which the revenues are recognized. This treatment is called the *matching convention*, because cost expirations are matched with revenues.

2.  Asset expirations not associated with revenues are expenses of the period in which services are consumed in operations.

**Product Costs**   The cost of goods or merchandise sold is perhaps the easiest expense to associate with revenue. At the time of sale, the asset physically changes hands. Revenue is recognized, and the cost of the merchandise transferred is an expense.

A merchandising firm purchases inventory and later sells it without changing its physical form. The inventory appears as an asset stated at acquisition cost on the balance sheet. Later, when the inventory is sold, the same amount of acquisition cost appears as an expense (cost of goods sold) on the income statement.

A manufacturing firm, on the other hand, incurs various costs in changing the physical form of the goods it produces. Three types of costs are (1) direct material, (2) direct labor, and (3) manufacturing overhead (sometimes called indirect manufacturing costs). Direct material and direct labor costs are associated with particular products manufactured. Manufacturing overhead includes a mixture of costs that provide a firm with a capacity to produce. Examples of manufacturing overhead costs are expenditures for supervisors' salaries, utilities, property taxes, and insurance on the factory, as well as depreciation on manufacturing plant and equipment. The services of each of these items are used up during the period while the firm is creating new assets—the inventory of goods being worked on or held for sale. Benefits from direct material, direct labor, and manufacturing overhead are transferred to, or become embodied in, the asset represented by units of inventory. Because the inventory items are assets until sales are made to customers, the various direct material, direct labor, and manufacturing overhead costs incurred in producing the goods are included in the manufacturing inventory under the titles Work-in-Process Inventory and Finished Goods Inventory. Such costs, which are assets transformed from one form to another, are called *product costs*. Product costs are assets; they become expenses only when the goods in which they are embodied are sold. Chapter 4 discusses more fully the accounting for manufacturing costs.

**Selling Costs**   In most cases, the costs incurred in selling or marketing a firm's products relate to the units sold during the period. For example, salaries and commissions of the sales staff, sales literature used, and most advertising costs are incurred in generating revenue currently. Because these selling costs are associated with the revenues of the period, they are reported as expenses in the period when their services are used. Some argue that part of some selling costs, such as advertising and other sales promotion, provide future-period benefits for a firm and should continue to be treated as assets. However, distinguishing the portion of the cost relating to the current period (to be recognized as an expense) from the portion relating to future periods (to be treated as an asset) can be extremely difficult. Accountants, therefore, treat selling and other marketing activity costs as expenses of the period when the services are used. Even though they may enhance the future marketability of a firm's products, these selling costs are treated as *period expenses* rather than as assets.

**Administrative Costs**  The costs incurred in administering the activities of the firm cannot be closely associated with units produced or sold and, like selling costs, are treated as period expenses. Examples include the president's salary, accounting and data processing costs, and the costs of conducting various supportive activities, such as legal services and corporate planning.

## Measurement of Expenses

Expenses represent assets consumed during the period. The amount of an expense is therefore the cost of the expired asset. Thus the basis for expense measurement is the same as that for asset valuation. Because assets are stated primarily at acquisition cost on the balance sheet, expenses are measured by the acquisition cost of the assets that were either sold or used during the period.

## Summary

Over sufficiently long time periods, income equals cash in less cash out; that is, the amount of income from operating activities is equal to the difference between the cash received from customers and the amount of cash paid to suppliers, employees, and other providers of goods and services. Cash receipts from customers do not, however, always occur in the same accounting period as the related cash expenditures to the providers of goods and services. The accrual basis of accounting provides a measure of operating performance in which outflows are more closely matched to inflows than under the cash basis.

The accrual basis determines the *timing* of income recognition. Revenue is typically recognized at the time of sale under the accrual basis. Costs that can be associated directly with particular revenues become expenses in the period when the revenues are recognized. The cost of acquiring or manufacturing inventory items is treated in this manner. Costs that cannot be closely associated with particular revenue streams become expenses of the period when the goods or services are consumed in operations. Most selling and administrative costs are treated in this manner.

The accounting procedures for preparing the income statement are considered next.

# Overview of Accounting Procedures ————————————————

## Relation between Balance Sheet and Income Statement

Net income (or earnings) for a period measures the excess of revenues (net asset inflows) over expenses (net asset outflows) from selling goods and providing services. Dividends measure the net assets distributed to shareholders. The Retained Earnings account on the balance sheet measures the cumulative excess of earnings over dividends since the firm began operations. The following disaggregation of the balance sheet equation shows the relation of revenues, expenses, and dividends to the components of the balance sheet.

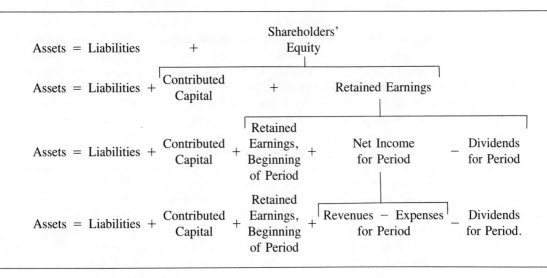

## Purpose and Use of Individual Revenue and Expense Accounts

Revenue and expense amounts could be recorded directly in the Retained Earnings account. For example, the sale of merchandise on account results in an increase in assets (accounts receivable) and retained earnings (sales revenue) and a decrease in assets (merchandise inventory) and retained earnings (cost of goods sold). Measuring the amount of net income would be relatively simple if revenues and expenses were recorded directly in the Retained Earnings account. Net income would be computed from the following equation:

$$\text{Net Income} = \frac{\text{Retained Earnings,}}{\text{End of Period}} - \frac{\text{Retained Earnings,}}{\text{Beginning of Period}} + \text{Dividends.}$$

The income statement is not designed primarily to report net income; as the equation indicates, the amount of net income can be deduced from the change in the Retained Earnings account. Rather, the income statement is designed to report the sources and amounts of a firm's revenues and the nature and amounts of a firm's expenses that total income for the period. Knowledge of the components of a firm's net income is helpful both in appraising past performance and in forecasting future performance.

To help prepare the income statement, individual revenue and expense accounts are maintained during the accounting period. These accounts begin the accounting period with a zero balance. During the period, revenues and expenses are recorded in the accounts as they arise. At the end of the period, the balance in each revenue and expense account represents the cumulative revenues and expenses *for the period*. These amounts are reported in the income statement, which shows the period's revenues, expenses, and net income.

Because revenues and expenses are basically components of retained earnings, the balance in each revenue and expense account is transferred at the end of the period to the Retained Earnings account. Each revenue and expense account will then have a zero balance after the transfer. Retained earnings will be increased by the amount of net income (or decreased by the net loss) for the period.

The end result of maintaining separate revenue and expense accounts during the period and transferring their balances to the Retained Earnings account at the end of the period is the same as it would be if revenues and expenses were initially recorded directly in the Retained Earnings account. Using separate revenue and expense accounts facilitates preparation of the income statement, which shows specific types of revenues and expenses. Once this purpose has been served, the need for separate accounts for a given accounting period has ended. These accounts begin the following accounting period with a zero balance and are therefore ready for the entry of the revenue and expense amounts of the new period.

The process of transferring the balances in revenue and expense accounts to retained earnings is referred to as the *closing process,* because each account is closed, or reduced to a zero balance. Revenue and expense accounts accumulate amounts for only a single accounting period and are therefore *temporary accounts.* On the other hand, the accounts on the balance sheet reflect the cumulative changes in each account from the time the firm was first organized, and they are not closed each period. The balances in these accounts at the end of one period carry over as the beginning balances of the following period. Balance sheet accounts are *permanent accounts.*

## Debit and Credit Procedures for Revenues, Expenses, and Dividends

Because revenues, expenses, and dividends are components of retained earnings, the recording procedures for these items are the same as for any other transaction affecting shareholders' equity accounts.

| Shareholders' Equity | |
|---|---|
| Decreases (Debit) | Increases (Credit) Issues of Capital Stock |
| Expenses Dividends | Revenues |

The transaction giving rise to revenue results in an increase in net assets (increase in assets or decrease in liabilities) and an increase in shareholders' equity. The usual journal entry to record a revenue transaction is therefore

Asset (A) Increase or Liability (L) Decrease ..................... Amount
  Revenue (SE)............................................  Amount
Typical entry to recognize revenue.

The transaction giving rise to an expense results in a decrease in net assets (decrease in assets or increase in liabilities) and a decrease in shareholders' equity. The usual journal entry to record an expense is therefore

---

Expense (SE) .............................................    Amount
   Asset (A) Decrease or Liability (L) Increase ..................    Amount
Typical entry to record expense.

---

Dividends result in a decrease in net assets and a decrease in shareholders' equity. As Chapter 12 discusses, dividends may be paid either in cash or in other assets. Although the accounting procedures for dividends are similar regardless of the form of the distribution, we assume that cash is used unless information is provided to the contrary. The usual entry to record the declaration of a dividend by the board of directors of a corporation is

---

Retained Earnings (SE) ....................................    Amount
   Dividends Payable (L).....................................    Amount
Typical entry to record dividend declaration.

---

When the dividend is paid, the journal entry is

---

Dividends Payable (L).......................................    Amount
   Cash (A) .................................................    Amount
Typical entry to record dividend payment.

---

A conceptual error sometimes made is that of treating dividends as expenses on the income statement. *Dividends are not expenses.* They are not costs incurred in *generating* revenues. Rather, they represent *distributions* of assets arising from current and previous years' operations to the owners of the firm.[2]

Before illustrating the recording procedures for revenues and expenses, it may be helpful to review briefly the steps in the accounting process.

---

[2]An alternative method for recording dividends is to debit an account, Dividends Declared. At the end of the accounting period, the balance in the Dividends Declared account is closed to the Retained Earnings account, thereby reducing the balance of Retained Earnings. The end result is a debit to Retained Earnings and a credit to Dividends Payable for the amount of dividends declared during the period. Because the account Dividends Declared is closed in a manner similar to an expense account at the end of the accounting period, this method of recording the dividend sometimes leads to the erroneous treatment of dividends as expenses. In this book, declarations of dividends are debited directly to Retained Earnings.

### Review of the Accounting Process

The steps in the accounting process, discussed in Chapter 2, are as follows:

**Journalizing**  Each transaction or series of transactions during the period is recorded in journal entry form in the general journal (or in a special journal that supplements the general journal).

**Posting**  Periodically, the *general journal entries* are posted to the accounts in the general ledger.

**Trial Balance**  At the end of the accounting period, the balance in each general ledger account is calculated and a trial balance is prepared. A trial balance is a listing of all accounts in the general ledger and their balances. If the recording process has been carried out properly, the total of amounts in accounts having debit balances must equal the total of amounts in accounts having credit balances.

**Adjusting Entries**  During the period, some accounting events may be only partially recorded, not recorded at all, or recorded incorrectly. Before the financial statements can be prepared at the end of the period, the omissions must be accounted for and the errors corrected. The entries to do this are known as *adjusting entries*. They are made so that revenues and expenses are reported in appropriate accounts with correct amounts and so that balance sheet accounts show correct amounts of assets and equities at the end of the period. The income statement can be prepared after adjusting entries have been made.

**Closing Entries**  The revenue and expense accounts are closed at the end of the accounting period by transferring the balance in each account to Retained Earnings.

**Statement Preparation**  The balance sheet, statement of cash flows, and any desired supporting schedules (for example, an analysis of changes in the Cash, Buildings and Equipment, or Retained Earnings, accounts) are then prepared.

### Illustration of the Accounting Process for a Merchandising Firm

Stephen's Shoe Store, Inc., has been in business since Year 1. A trial balance taken from its general ledger accounts on January 1, Year 4, the first day of an accounting period, appears in Exhibit 3.3. The asset accounts are designated (A), the liability accounts (L), and the shareholders' equity (including revenue and expense) accounts (SE). Trial balances do not usually contain such designations.

   Note that the revenue and expense accounts do not appear in this trial balance; they have zero balances at the beginning of an accounting period. One of the accounts in the trial balance, Accumulated Depreciation, has not previously been considered. This account is presented on the balance sheet as a deduction from

**Exhibit 3.3** ————————————————————————————————————
**STEPHEN'S SHOE STORE, INC.**
**Trial Balance**
**January 1, Year 4**

|  | Accounts with Debit Balances | Accounts with Credit Balances |
|---|---|---|
| Cash (A) ..................................... | $ 30,000 | |
| Accounts Receivable (A) ...................... | 63,000 | |
| Merchandise Inventory (A)..................... | 175,000 | |
| Land (A)...................................... | 100,000 | |
| Building and Equipment (A).................... | 525,000 | |
| Accumulated Depreciation (XA) ................ | | $ 85,000 |
| Accounts Payable (L) ......................... | | 135,000 |
| Bonds Payable (L)............................. | | 100,000 |
| Common Stock (SE) ........................... | | 250,000 |
| Additional Paid-in Capital (SE) ................ | | 200,000 |
| Retained Earnings (SE) ....................... | | 123,000 |
| Total ..................................... | $893,000 | $893,000 |

Building and Equipment. (See Exhibit 3.8 for balance sheet presentation of this account.) Because of its manner of disclosure, this account is referred to as a *contra account*. A contra account accumulates amounts that are subtracted from the amount in another account. The nature and use of these contra accounts are discussed later in this illustration. An asset contra account is designated XA in the trial balance.

## Journalizing

The transactions of Stephen's Shoe Store during Year 4 and the appropriate journal entries at the time of the transactions follow.

**1.** The firm purchases merchandise on account costing $355,000.

| | | |
|---|---|---|
| (1) Merchandise Inventory (A) .......................... | 355,000 | |
| Accounts Payable (L).............................. | | 355,000 |

**2.** Sales during the year are $625,000, of which $225,000 is for cash collected at the time of sale and the remainder is on account.

| | | |
|---|---|---|
| (2) Cash (A) ......................................... | 225,000 | |
| Accounts Receivable (A) ........................... | 400,000 | |
| Sales Revenue (SE).............................. | | 625,000 |

**3.** The cost of merchandise sold during Year 4 is $390,000.

| | | |
|---|---|---|
| (3) Cost of Goods Sold (SE) .......................... | 390,000 | |
| Merchandise Inventory (A) ...................... | | 390,000 |

**4.** The firm pays salaries in cash of $110,000 for work performed during the year.

| | | |
|---|---|---|
| (4) Salaries Expense (SE)............................. | 110,000 | |
| Cash (A) ...................................... | | 110,000 |

**5.** The firm collects cash of $325,000 from customers who had made purchases on account.

| | | |
|---|---|---|
| (5) Cash (A) ........................................ | 325,000 | |
| Accounts Receivable (A) ......................... | | 325,000 |

**6.** The firm makes payments of $270,000 to merchandise suppliers for purchases on account.

| | | |
|---|---|---|
| (6) Accounts Payable (L).............................. | 270,000 | |
| Cash (A) ...................................... | | 270,000 |

**7.** The firm makes a premium payment of $1,500 on January 1, Year 4, for a 3-year property and liability insurance policy.

| | | |
|---|---|---|
| (7) Prepaid Insurance (A) ............................ | 1,500 | |
| Cash (A) ...................................... | | 1,500 |

The debit in this entry, made on January 1, Year 4, is to an asset account, because the insurance provides 3 years of coverage beginning on that date. The entry to reduce the Prepaid Insurance account and to record the insurance expense for Year 4 is one of the adjusting entries made at the end of the accounting period and is illustrated later.

**8.** Warehouse space not needed in the company's operations is rented out for 1 year beginning December 1, Year 4. The firm receives the annual rental of $600 at that time.

| | | |
|---|---|---|
| (8) Cash (A) .......................................... | 600 | |
|     Advances from Tenants (L)........................ | | 600 |

**9.** On December 31, Year 4, the firm pays annual interest at 8 percent on the long-term bonds outstanding; $.08 \times \$100{,}000 = \$8{,}000$.

| | | |
|---|---|---|
| (9) Interest Expense (SE) ............................. | 8,000 | |
|     Cash (A) ......................................... | | 8,000 |

**10.** A customer who had purchased merchandise on account for $10,000 has experienced financial difficulty and has been unable to pay for the goods on time. The customer now promises to pay $10,000 in 90 days with interest at 9 percent per year. As evidence of that promise, the customer gives a promissory note. On November 1, Year 4, Stephen's Shoe Store accepts the 90-day note for $10,000 bearing interest at 9 percent in settlement of the open account receivable.

| | | |
|---|---|---|
| (10) Notes Receivable (A)............................. | 10,000 | |
|     Accounts Receivable (A)......................... | | 10,000 |

**11.** The board of directors declares a cash dividend of $15,000 on December 28, Year 4. The dividend is to be paid on January 20, Year 5.

| | | |
|---|---|---|
| (11) Retained Earnings (SE)........................... | 15,000 | |
|     Dividends Payable (L) ........................... | | 15,000 |

## Posting

The entries in the general journal are posted to the appropriate general ledger accounts. In this illustration, the posting operation takes place on December 31, Year 4. The T-accounts in Exhibit 3.4 show the opening balances from the trial balance in Exhibit 3.3 and the effects of transactions **(1)** through **(11)**.

Exhibit 3.4

# STEPHEN'S SHOE STORE, INC.
T-Accounts Showing Beginning Balances, Transactions during Year 4, and Ending Balance before Adjusting Entries
Balance Sheet Accounts (Permanent)

## Cash (A)

| Bal. 1/1 | 30,000 | | |
|---|---|---|---|
| (2) | 225,000 | 110,000 | (4) |
| (5) | 325,000 | 270,000 | (6) |
| (8) | 600 | 1,500 | (7) |
| | | 8,000 | (9) |
| Bal. 12/31 | 191,100 | | |

## Accounts Receivable (A)

| Bal. 1/1 | 63,000 | | |
|---|---|---|---|
| (2) | 400,000 | 325,000 | (5) |
| | | 10,000 | (10) |
| Bal. 12/31 | 128,000 | | |

## Notes Receivable (A)

| Bal. 1/1 | 0 | | |
|---|---|---|---|
| (10) | 10,000 | | |
| Bal. 12/31 | 10,000 | | |

## Merchandise Inventory (A)

| Bal. 1/1 | 175,000 | | |
|---|---|---|---|
| (1) | 355,000 | 390,000 | (3) |
| Bal. 12/31 | 140,000 | | |

## Prepaid Insurance (A)

| Bal. 1/1 | 0 | | |
|---|---|---|---|
| (7) | 1,500 | | |
| Bal. 12/31 | 1,500 | | |

## Land (A)

| Bal. 1/1 | 100,000 | | |
|---|---|---|---|
| Bal. 12/31 | 100,000 | | |

## Building and Equipment (A)

| Bal. 1/1 | 525,000 | | |
|---|---|---|---|
| Bal. 12/31 | 525,000 | | |

## Accumulated Depreciation (XA)

| | | 85,000 | Bal. 1/1 |
|---|---|---|---|
| | | 85,000 | Bal. 12/31 |

## Accounts Payable (L)

| | | 135,000 | Bal. 1/1 |
|---|---|---|---|
| (6) | 270,000 | 355,000 | (1) |
| | | 220,000 | Bal. 12/31 |

## Advances from Tenants (L)

| | | 0 | Bal. 1/1 |
|---|---|---|---|
| | | 600 | (8) |
| | | 600 | Bal. 12/31 |

## Bonds Payable (L)

| | | 100,000 | Bal. 1/1 |
|---|---|---|---|
| | | 100,000 | Bal. 12/31 |

## Dividends Payable (L)

| | | 0 | Bal. 1/1 |
|---|---|---|---|
| | | 15,000 | (11) |
| | | 15,000 | Bal. 12/31 |

**Common Stock (SE)**

| | |
|---|---|
| | 250,000 Bal. 1/1 |
| | 250,000 Bal. 12/31 |

**Additional Paid-In Capital (SE)**

| | |
|---|---|
| | 200,000 Bal. 1/1 |
| | 200,000 Bal. 12/31 |

**Retained Earnings (SE)**

| | |
|---|---|
| (11) 15,000 | 123,000 Bal. 1/1 |
| | 108,000 Bal. 12/31 |

**Sales Revenue (SE)**

| | |
|---|---|
| | 0 Bal. 1/1 |
| | 625,000 (2) |
| | 625,000 Bal. 12/31 |

**Cost of Goods Sold (SE)**

| | |
|---|---|
| Bal. 1/1 0 | |
| (3) 390,000 | |
| Bal. 12/31 390,000 | |

**Salaries Expense (SE)**

| | |
|---|---|
| Bal. 1/1 0 | |
| (4) 110,000 | |
| Bal. 12/31 110,000 | |

**Interest Expense (SE)**

| | |
|---|---|
| Bal. 1/1 0 | |
| (9) 8,000 | |
| Bal. 12/31 8,000 | |

## Trial Balance Preparation

The trial balance prepared at the end of the accounting period before adjusting and closing entries is called an *unadjusted trial balance*. Exhibit 3.5 presents the unadjusted trial balance of Stephen's Shoe Store as of December 31, Year 4. The amounts in the unadjusted trial balance are taken directly from the ending balances in the T-accounts in Exhibit 3.4.

## Adjusting Entries

The entries in the general journal made during the year result from transactions between the firm and outsiders (for example, suppliers, employees, customers, and governmental units). Other events continually occur, however, for which no specific transaction signals the requirement for a journal entry but that must be considered in measuring net income for the period and financial position at the end of the period. For example, building and equipment are continually used in the process of generating revenue. Because the services of these assets are consumed during the period, a portion of their acquisition cost must be recorded as an expense. Similarly, insurance coverage expires continually throughout the year. Because the services of the asset are gradually consumed, a portion of the asset, Prepaid Insurance, must be recorded as an expense.

Exhibit 3.5 ————————————————————————————————————

**STEPHEN'S SHOE STORE, INC.**
**Unadjusted Trial Balance**
**December 31, Year 4**

| | Accounts with Debit Balances | Accounts with Credit Balances |
|---|---|---|
| Cash (A) ..................................... | $ 191,100 | |
| Accounts Receivable (A) ....................... | 128,000 | |
| Notes Receivable (A) .......................... | 10,000 | |
| Merchandise Inventory (A) ...................... | 140,000 | |
| Prepaid Insurance (A) .......................... | 1,500 | |
| Land (A)...................................... | 100,000 | |
| Building and Equipment (A)..................... | 525,000 | |
| Accumulated Depreciation (XA) ................. | | $   85,000 |
| Accounts Payable (L) .......................... | | 220,000 |
| Dividends Payable (L)........................... | | 15,000 |
| Advances from Tenants (L) ..................... | | 600 |
| Bonds Payable (L).............................. | | 100,000 |
| Common Stock (SE) ............................ | | 250,000 |
| Additional Paid-in Capital (SE) .................. | | 200,000 |
| Retained Earnings (SE) ......................... | | 108,000 |
| Sales Revenue (SE) ............................ | | 625,000 |
| Cost of Goods Sold (SE) ....................... | 390,000 | |
| Salaries Expense (SE) .......................... | 110,000 | |
| Interest Expense (SE).......................... | 8,000 | |
| Totals ..................................... | $1,603,600 | $1,603,600 |

Other kinds of events occur that affect the revenues and expenses of the period but for which a cash transaction with an outsider will not occur until a subsequent period. For example, salaries and wages are earned by administrative employees during the last several days of the current accounting period, but they will not be paid until the following accounting period. Such salaries and wages, although paid in the next period, are expenses of the current period when the labor services are consumed. Similarly, interest accrues on a firm's notes receivable or payable. Interest will be collected or paid in a subsequent period, but a portion of the interest should be recognized as revenue or expense in the current period.

Adjusting entries prepared at the end of the accounting period change the balances in the general ledger accounts to recognize all revenues and expenses for the proper reporting of net income and financial position. The following sections illustrate several examples of adjusting entries for Stephen's Shoe Store.

**Recognition of Accrued Revenues and Receivables** Revenue is earned as services are rendered. For example, rent is earned as a tenant uses the rental property. Interest, a rent for the use of money, is earned from a loan as time passes. Recording these amounts as they accrue day by day is usually not convenient, however. At the end of the accounting period, there may be some situations in which revenue has been earned but for which no entry has been made, either because cash has not been received or the time has not arrived for a formal invoice to be sent to the customer. A claim has come into existence that, although it may not be due immediately, should appear on the balance sheet as an asset and be reflected in the revenues of the period. The purpose of the adjusting entry for interest eventually receivable by the lender is to recognize on the balance sheet the right to receive cash in an amount equal to the interest already earned and to recognize the same amount as revenue on the income statement for the period.

Stephen's Shoe Store received a 90-day note from a customer on November 1, Year 4. At year-end, the note already appears on the trial balance. Interest earned during November and December, however, does not appear in the unadjusted trial balance. The note earns interest at the rate of 9 percent per year. By convention in business practice, interest rates on loans are almost always stated as annual interest rates. Also by convention, a year equal to 12 months of 30 days each, or 360 days, is usually assumed to simplify the calculation of interest earned. Interest of $150 is earned by Stephen's Shoe Store, Inc., during November and December. This amount is equal to the $10,000 principal times the 9 percent annual interest rate times the elapsed 60 days divided by 360 days ($150 = $10,000 × .09 × 60/360). The adjusting entry to recognize the asset, Interest Receivable, and the interest earned, is

---

(12) Interest Receivable (A) .................................... 150
　　　Interest Revenue (SE) .................................. 　　　150

---

**Recognition of Accrued Expenses and Payables** As various services are received, their cost should be reflected in the financial statements, whether or not payment has been made or an invoice received. Here also, recording these amounts day by day is frequently not convenient. Some adjustment of expenses and liabilities will probably be necessary at the end of the accounting period.

Salaries and wages that are earned during the last several days of the accounting period but that will not be paid until the following accounting period illustrate this type of adjustment. According to payroll records, employees of Stephen's Shoe Store earned salaries of $6,000 during the last several days of Year 4 that were not recorded at year-end. The adjusting entry is

---

| | | |
|---|---|---|
| (13) Salaries Expense (SE) ................................... | 6,000 | |
| Salaries Payable (L).................................... | | 6,000 |

---

Other examples of this type of adjusting entry include costs incurred for utilities, taxes, and interest.

**Allocation of Prepaid Operating Costs**  Another type of adjustment arises because assets are acquired for use in the operations of the firm but are not completely used during the accounting period in which they are acquired. For example, Stephen's Shoe Store paid $1,500 on January 1, Year 4, for a 3-year insurance policy. During Year 4, one-third of the coverage expired, so $500 of the premium should be removed from the asset account and reflected as insurance expense. The balance sheet on December 31, Year 4, should show only $1,000 of prepaid insurance as an asset, because this portion of the premium is a future benefit — the asset of insurance coverage to be received over the next 2 years.

The nature of the adjusting entry to record an asset expiration as an expense depends on the recording of the original payment. If the payment resulted in a debit to an asset account, the adjusting entry must reduce the asset and increase the expense for the services used up during the accounting period. Stephen's Shoe Store had recorded in entry (7) (as discussed on page 88) the payment of the insurance premium on January 1, Year 4, as follows:

---

| | | |
|---|---|---|
| (7) Prepaid Insurance (A) ..................................... | 1,500 | |
| Cash (A) ............................................... | | 1,500 |

---

The adjusting entry is, therefore,

---

| | | |
|---|---|---|
| (14) Insurance Expense (SE) ................................... | 500 | |
| Prepaid Insurance (A) ................................. | | 500 |

---

Insurance expense for Year 4 is $500, and prepaid insurance of $1,000 appears as an asset on the balance sheet on December 31, Year 4.

***Alternative Procedure***   Instead of debiting an asset account at the time the premium is paid, some firms debit an expense account. For example, Stephen's Shoe Store may have recorded the original premium payment as follows:

| | | |
|---|---|---|
| (7a) Insurance Expense (SE) ................................. | 1,500 | |
|     Cash (A) ............................................. | | 1,500 |

Because many operating costs become expenses in the period in which the expenditure is made (for example, monthly rent), this second procedure for recording expenditures during the year sometimes reduces the number of adjusting entries that must be made at year-end. In the situation with the insurance policy, however, not all of the $1,500 premium paid is an expense of Year 4. If the original journal entry had been (7a), the adjusting entry would then have been

| | | |
|---|---|---|
| (14a) Prepaid Insurance (A) ................................. | 1,000 | |
|      Insurance Expense (SE) .............................. | | 1,000 |

After the original entry in (7a) and the adjusting entry in (14a), insurance expense for Year 4 is reflected in the accounts at $500 and prepaid insurance at $1,000. The end result of these two approaches to recording the original payment of the premium is the same. The adjusting entries, however, are quite different. (See Problem 3 for Self-Study at the end of the chapter.)

**Recognition of Depreciation**   When assets such as buildings, machinery, furniture, and trucks are purchased, their acquisition cost is debited to appropriate asset accounts. Although these assets may provide services for a number of years, their future benefits expire as time passes. The portion of an asset's cost that will expire is spread systematically over its estimated useful life. The charge made to the current operations for the portion of the cost of such assets consumed during the current period is called *depreciation*. Depreciation involves nothing new in principle; it is identical with the procedure for prepaid operating costs presented previously. For example, the cost of a building is a prepayment for a series of future services, and depreciation allocates the cost of the services to the periods in which services are received and used.

   Various accounting methods are used in allocating the acquisition cost of long-lived assets to the periods of benefit. The most widely used method is the *straight-line method*. Under this procedure, an equal portion of the acquisition cost, less estimated salvage value, is allocated to each period of the asset's estimated useful life. The depreciation charge for each period is computed as follows:

$$\frac{\text{Acquisition Cost} - \text{Estimated Salvage Value}}{\text{Number of Periods in Estimated Useful Life}} = \frac{\text{Depreciation Charge for}}{\text{Each Period.}}$$

Internal records indicate that the Building and Equipment account of Stephen's Shoe Store comprises a store building with an acquisition cost of $400,000 and a group of items of equipment with an acquisition cost of $125,000. At the time the building was acquired, it had an estimated 40-year useful life and a zero salvage value. Depreciation expense for each year of the building's life is calculated to be

$$\frac{\$400,000 - \$0}{40 \text{ years}} = \$10,000 \text{ per year.}$$

At the time the equipment was acquired, it had an estimated useful life of 6 years and an estimated salvage value of $5,000. Annual depreciation is, therefore,

$$\frac{\$125,000 - \$5,000}{6 \text{ years}} = \$20,000 \text{ per year.}$$

The adjusting entry to record depreciation of $30,000 (= $10,000 + $20,000) for Year 4 is

---

| | | |
|---|---|---|
| (15) Depreciation Expense (SE) .............................. | 30,000 | |
| Accumulated Depreciation (XA)......................... | | 30,000 |

---

The credit in entry (15) could have been made directly to the Building and Equipment account, because the credit records the portion of the asset's cost that has expired, or become an expense, during Year 4. The same end result is achieved by crediting the Accumulated Depreciation account, a contra-asset account, and then deducting the balance in this account from the acquisition cost of the assets in the Building and Equipment account on the balance sheet. Using the contra account enables the financial statements to show both the acquisition cost of the assets in use and the portion of that amount that has previously been recognized as an expense. Showing both acquisition cost and accumulated depreciation amounts separately provides a rough indication of the relative age of the firm's long-lived assets. (See Exercise 29 at the end of the chapter.)

Note that the Depreciation Expense account includes depreciation for the current accounting period only, whereas the Accumulated Depreciation account includes the cumulative depreciation charges since acquisition. The Accumulated Depreciation account is sometimes referred to as Allowance for Depreciation.

**Valuation of Liabilities**  When a firm receives cash from customers before it sells merchandise or renders services, it incurs a liability. For example, Stephen's Shoe Store received $600 on December 1, Year 4, as 1 year's rent on warehouse space. When the cash was received, the liability account, Advances from Tenants, was credited. One month's rent has been earned as of December 31, Year 4. The adjusting entry is

---

| | | |
|---|---|---|
| (16) Advances from Tenants (L) .............................. | 50 | |
| Rent Revenue (SE) ..................................... | | 50 |
| Recognizes 1 month's rent revenue and reduces liability from $600 to $550. | | |

---

The remaining $550 of the collections for rent is yet to be earned and appears on the December 31, Year 4, balance sheet as a liability.

**Correction of Errors**   Various errors and omissions may be discovered at the end of the accounting period as the process of checking, reviewing, and auditing is carried out. For example, 1 month's sales during the year might have been recorded as $38,700 instead of $37,800. Or the sale to a specific customer might not have been recorded. Entries must be made at the end of the accounting period to correct for these errors. There were no such errors in the accounts of Stephen's Shoe Store.

**Trial Balance after Adjusting Entries**   The adjusting entries are posted in the general ledger in the same manner as entries made during the year. A trial balance of the general ledger accounts after adjusting entries are made is called an *adjusted trial balance* and helps in preparing the financial statements. Exhibit 3.6 presents the trial balance data before and after adjusting entries for Stephen's Shoe Store. The exhibit indicates the effect of the adjustment process on the various accounts. The parenthetical number identifies the debit and credit components of each adjusting entry.

**Preparing Income Statement**   The adjusted trial balance shows all revenue and expense accounts with their correct amounts for the period. The income statement can be prepared by listing all the revenue accounts, listing all the expense accounts, and showing the difference between the sum of the revenues and the sum of the expenses as net income. Revenue and expense accounts are temporary labels for portions of retained earnings. Once the adjusted trial balance has been prepared, the revenue and expense accounts have served their purpose for the current period and are closed.

## Closing of Temporary Accounts

The closing process transfers the balances in the temporary revenue and expense accounts to Retained Earnings. A temporary account with a debit balance is closed by crediting it with the amount equal to its balance at the end of the period and debiting Retained Earnings. The usual closing entry for a temporary account with a debit balance is

---

| | | |
|---|---|---|
| Retained Earnings (SE) . . . . . . . . . . . . . . . . . . . . . . . . . . . . . . . . . . . . . | X | |
|     Account with Debit Balance (SE) (use specific account title) . . . . . | | X |

---

A temporary account with a credit balance is closed by debiting the temporary account and crediting Retained Earnings. The usual closing entry for a temporary account with a credit balance is the entry at the top of page 99.

## Exhibit 3.6

**STEPHEN'S SHOE STORE, INC.**
Trial Balance before and after Adjusting Entries[a]
December 31, Year 4

| Accounts | Unadjusted Trial Balance Debit | Unadjusted Trial Balance Credit | Adjusting Entries Debit | Adjusting Entries Credit | Adjusted Trial Balance Debit | Adjusted Trial Balance Credit |
|---|---|---|---|---|---|---|
| Cash (A) | $ 191,100 | | | | $ 191,100 | |
| Accounts Receivable (A) | 128,000 | | | | 128,000 | |
| Notes Receivable (A) | 10,000 | | | | 10,000 | |
| Interest Receivable (A) | | | $ 150 (12) | | 150 | |
| Merchandise Inventory (A) | 140,000 | | | | 140,000 | |
| Prepaid Insurance (A) | 1,500 | | | $ 500 (14) | 1,000 | |
| Land (A) | 100,000 | | | | 100,000 | |
| Building and Equipment (A) | 525,000 | | | | 525,000 | |
| Accumulated Depreciation (XA) | | $ 85,000 | | 30,000 (15) | | $ 115,000 |
| Accounts Payable (L) | | 220,000 | | | | 220,000 |
| Salaries Payable (L) | | | | 6,000 (13) | | 6,000 |
| Dividends Payable (L) | | 15,000 | | | | 15,000 |
| Advances from Tenants (L) | | 600 | 50 (16) | | | 550 |
| Bonds Payable (L) | | 100,000 | | | | 100,000 |
| Common Stock (SE) | | 250,000 | | | | 250,000 |
| Additional Paid-in Capital (SE) | | 200,000 | | | | 200,000 |
| Retained Earnings (SE) | | 108,000 | | | | 108,000 |
| Sales Revenue (SE) | | 625,000 | | | | 625,000 |
| Interest Revenue (SE) | | | | 150 (12) | | 150 |
| Rent Revenue (SE) | | | | 50 (16) | | 50 |
| Cost of Goods Sold (SE) | 390,000 | | | | 390,000 | |
| Salaries Expense (SE) | 110,000 | | 6,000 (13) | | 116,000 | |
| Interest Expense (SE) | 8,000 | | | | 8,000 | |
| Insurance Expense (SE) | | | 500 (14) | | 500 | |
| Depreciation Expense (SE) | | | 30,000 (15) | | 30,000 | |
| Totals | $1,603,600 | $1,603,600 | $36,700 | $36,700 | $1,639,750 | $1,639,750 |

[a]This convenient tabular form is often called a work sheet.

| | | |
|---|---|---|
| Account with Credit Balance (SE) (use specific account title) ...... | **X** | |
| Retained Earnings (SE) ..................................... | | **X** |

After closing entries, the balances in all temporary accounts are zero. The former debit (credit) balances in temporary accounts become debits (credits) in the Retained Earnings account.

Each temporary revenue and expense account could be closed by a separate entry. Some recording time is saved, however, by closing all revenue and expense accounts in a single entry as follows:

| | | |
|---|---|---|
| (17) Sales Revenue (SE) ..................................... | 625,000 | |
| Interest Revenue (SE) .................................... | 150 | |
| Rent Revenue (SE) ....................................... | 50 | |
| Cost of Goods Sold (SE) .............................. | | 390,000 |
| Salaries Expense (SE) ................................ | | 116,000 |
| Interest Expense (SE) ................................. | | 8,000 |
| Insurance Expense (SE) ............................... | | 500 |
| Depreciation Expense (SE) ............................ | | 30,000 |
| Retained Earnings (SE)................................. | | 80,700 |

The amount credited to Retained Earnings is the difference between the amounts debited to revenue accounts and the amounts credited to expense accounts. This amount is the net income for the period.[3]

*Alternative Closing Procedure* An alternative closing procedure uses a temporary Income Summary account. Individual revenue and expense accounts are first closed to the Income Summary account. The income statement is prepared using information on the individual revenues and expenses in the Income Summary account. The balance in the Income Summary account, representing net income for the period, is then closed to Retained Earnings.

For example, the entry to close the Sales Revenue account under this alternative procedure is

| | | |
|---|---|---|
| (17a) Sales Revenue (SE) ..................................... | 625,000 | |
| Income Summary (SE) ............................... | | 625,000 |

---

[3]The amount credited to Retained Earnings in the closing entry is called a *plug*. Often when making some journal entries in accounting all debits are known, as are all but one of the credits (or vice versa). Because double-entry recording procedure requires equal debits and credits, the unknown quantity can be found by subtracting the sum of the known credits from the sum of all debits (or vice versa). This process is known as *plugging*.

The entry to close the Cost of Goods Sold account is

| | | |
|---|---|---|
| (17b) Income Summary (SE) ................................. | 390,000 | |
| Cost of Goods Sold (SE) ............................ | | 390,000 |

Similar closing entries are made for the other revenue and expense accounts. The Income Summary account will have a credit balance of $80,700 after all revenue and expense accounts have been closed. Its balance is then transferred to Retained Earnings:

| | | |
|---|---|---|
| (17c) Income Summary (SE) ................................. | 80,700 | |
| Retained Earnings (SE)............................... | | 80,700 |

The end result of both closing procedures is the same. Revenue and expense accounts, as well as the Income Summary account (if one is used), have zero balances after closing entries, and the Retained Earnings account is increased by the net income for the period of $80,700. Exhibit 3.7 shows the Income Summary account for Stephen's Shoe Store after all revenue and expense accounts have been closed at the end of the period.

## Financial Statement Preparation

The income statement, balance sheet, and any desired supporting schedules can be prepared from information in the adjusted trial balance. Exhibit 3.8 gives the comparative balance sheets for December 31, Year 3 and Year 4. Exhibit 3.9 shows the income statement of Stephen's Shoe Store for Year 4. Exhibit 3.10 presents an analysis of changes in retained earnings.

Exhibit 3.7 ————————————————————————————————————————————

**STEPHEN'S SHOE STORE, INC.**
**Illustration of Income Summary Account**

| Income Summary Account (SE) | | | | Retained Earnings (SE) | | |
|---|---|---|---|---|---|---|
| Cost of Goods Sold | 390,000 | 625,000 Sales Revenue | | | 123,000 Beginning Balance | |
| Salaries Expense | 116,000 | 150 Interest Revenue | | | | |
| Interest Expense | 8,000 | 50 Rent Revenue | Dividends | 15,000 | 80,700 Net Income | |
| Insurance Expense | 500 | 625,200 | | | | |
| Depreciation Expense | 30,000 | | | | 188,700 Ending Balance | |
| To Close Income Summary Account | 80,700 | | | | | |
| | 625,200 | | | | | |

Exhibit 3.8 ————————————————————————————

STEPHEN'S SHOE STORE, INC.
Comparative Balance Sheet
December 31, Year 3 and Year 4

| | December 31, Year 3 | | December 31, Year 4 | |
|---|---|---|---|---|

## Assets

**Current Assets:**

| | | | | |
|---|---|---|---|---|
| Cash | | $ 30,000 | | $191,100 |
| Accounts Receivable | | 63,000 | | 128,000 |
| Notes Receivable | | — | | 10,000 |
| Interest Receivable | | — | | 150 |
| Merchandise Inventory | | 175,000 | | 140,000 |
| Prepaid Insurance | | — | | 1,000 |
| Total Current Assets | | $268,000 | | $470,250 |
| | | | | |
| **Property, Plant, and Equipment:** | | | | |
| Land | | $100,000 | | $100,000 |
| Building and Equipment (at acquisition cost) | $525,000 | | $525,000 | |
| Less Accumulated Depreciation | 85,000 | | 115,000 | |
| Building and Equipment (net) | | 440,000 | | 410,000 |
| Total Property, Plant, and Equipment | | $540,000 | | $510,000 |
| Total Assets | | $808,000 | | $980,250 |

## Liabilities and Shareholders' Equity

**Current Liabilities:**

| | | | | |
|---|---|---|---|---|
| Accounts Payable | | $135,000 | | $220,000 |
| Salaries Payable | | — | | 6,000 |
| Dividends Payable | | — | | 15,000 |
| Advances from Tenants | | — | | 550 |
| Total Current Liabilities | | $135,000 | | $241,550 |
| | | | | |
| **Long-Term Debt:** | | | | |
| Bonds Payable | | 100,000 | | 100,000 |
| Total Liabilities | | $235,000 | | $341,550 |
| | | | | |
| **Shareholders' Equity:** | | | | |
| Common Stock (at par value) | | $250,000 | | $250,000 |
| Additional Paid-in Capital | | 200,000 | | 200,000 |
| Retained Earnings | | 123,000 | | 188,700 |
| Total Shareholders' Equity | | $573,000 | | $638,700 |
| Total Liabilities and Shareholders Equity | | $808,000 | | $980,250 |

Exhibit 3.9 ———————————————————————

**STEPHEN'S SHOE STORE, INC.**
**Income Statement for the Year Ending December 31, Year 4**

| | | |
|---|---:|---:|
| **Revenues:** | | |
| Sales Revenue........................................ | $625,000 | |
| Interest Revenue..................................... | 150 | |
| Rent Revenue........................................ | 50 | |
|   Total Revenues................................. | | $625,200 |
| **Less Expenses:** | | |
| Cost of Goods Sold................................... | $390,000 | |
| Salaries Expense..................................... | 116,000 | |
| Interest Expense .................................... | 8,000 | |
| Insurance Expense ................................... | 500 | |
| Depreciation Expense ................................ | 30,000 | |
|   Total Expenses................................. | | 544,500 |
| **Net Income**........................................ | | $ 80,700 |

Exhibit 3.10 ———————————————————————

**STEPHEN'S SHOE STORE, INC.**
**Analysis of Changes in Retained Earnings for the**
**Year Ending December 31, Year 4**

| | | |
|---|---:|---:|
| Retained Earnings, December 31, Year 3 ..................... | | $123,000 |
| Net Income ............................................... | $80,700 | |
| Less Dividends............................................ | 15,000 | |
| Increase in Retained Earnings ............................... | | 65,700 |
| Retained Earnings, December 31, Year 4 ..................... | | $188,700 |

# Summary ———————————————————————————

Measurements of net income *for the period* and of financial position *at the end of the period* are interrelated. Revenues result from selling goods or rendering services to customers and lead to increases in assets or decreases in liabilities. Expenses indicate that services have been used in generating revenue and result in decreases in assets or increases in liabilities. Because revenues represent increases in shareholders' equity, revenue transactions are recorded by crediting (increasing) a shareholders' equity account for the specific type of revenue and debiting either an asset or liability account. Expenses represent decreases in shareholders' equity and are recorded by debiting (decreasing) a shareholders' equity account for the specific type of expense and crediting either an asset or a liability account. The revenue and expense accounts accumulate the revenues earned and expenses recognized during the period. After an adjusted trial balance has been prepared, the balances in these temporary accounts are transferred, or closed, to the Retained Earnings account.

**Exhibit 3.11** _____

**Relation of Cash Flows (Receipts and Expenditures)
to Recognition of Revenues and Expenses**

| Transaction | Year 1 | Year 2 | Year 3 |
|---|---|---|---|
| | | Journal Entry Each Year | |
| 1. Cash received from customer in Year 1 for services to be performed in Year 2 . . . . . . . . . . | (T)[a] Cash . . . . . . . X  Liability . . . X | (A)[b] Liability . . . . . . . . X  Revenue . . . . . X | |
| 2. Cash received from customer in Year 2 for services performed in Year 2 . . . . . . . . . . | | (T) Cash . . . . . . . . . X  Revenue . . . . . X | |
| 3. Services performed in Year 2 for which cash will not be received until Year 3 . . . . . . . . . | | (A) Accounts Receivable . . . . . X  Revenue . . . . . X | (T) Cash . . . . . . . . . . . . X  Accounts Receivable . . . . X |
| 4. Cash expended in Year 1 for services consumed in Year 2 . . . . . . . . . . . . . . . . . . . . . . | (T) Asset . . . . . . X  Cash . . . . . X | (A) Expense . . . . . . . X  Asset . . . . . . . . X | |
| 5. Cash expended in Year 2 for services consumed in Year 2 . . . . . . . . . . . . . . . . . . . . . . | | (T) Expense . . . . . . . X  Cash . . . . . . . . X | |
| 6. Services consumed in Year 2 for which cash will not be expended until Year 3 . . . . . . . . | | (A) Expense . . . . . . X  Liability . . . . . . X | (T) Liability . . . . . . . . . . X  Cash . . . . . . . . . . X |

[a](T) is a transaction entry made during the period.

[b](A) is an adjusting entry made at the end of a period.

Some events will not be entered as part of the regular day-to-day recording process during the period because no explicit transaction between the firm and some external party (such as a customer, creditor, or governmental unit) has taken place to require a journal entry. Such events require adjusting entries at the end of the period so that the firm's periodic income and financial position can be properly reported on an accrual basis. Exhibit 3.11 summarizes the relation between cash inflows and outflows and the recognition of revenues and expenses.

# Problem 1 for Self-Study _____

Harris Equipment Corporation was organized on January 2, Year 2, with the issuance of 10,000 shares of $10-par value common stock for $15 cash per share. The following transactions occurred during Year 2:

**(1)** January 2, Year 2: The firm acquired a building costing $80,000 and equipment costing $40,000. It paid cash in the amount of $60,000 and assumed a 10 percent mortgage for the balance of the purchase price. Interest is payable on January 2 of each year, beginning 1 year after the purchase.

**(2)** January 2, Year 2: The firm bought a 2-year fire insurance policy on the building and equipment. It paid the insurance premium of $1,200 for the 2-year period in advance (debit an asset account).

(3) During Year 2: Merchandise acquired on account totaled $320,000. Payments to these suppliers during Year 2 totaled $270,000.

(4) During Year 2: Sales of merchandise totaled $510,000, of which $80,000 was for cash and $430,000 was on account. Collections from credit customers during Year 2 totaled $360,000.

(5) During Year 2: Salaries paid to employees totaled $80,000.

(6) During Year 2: Utility bills totaling $1,300 were paid.

(7) November 1, Year 2: A customer advanced $600 toward the purchase price of merchandise to be delivered during January, Year 3.

(8) November 1, Year 2: A customer gave a $1,000, 9 percent, 90-day note to settle an open account receivable.

(9) December 1, Year 2: The firm rented out a portion of the building for a 3-month period. It received the rent for the period of $900 in advance (credit a revenue account).

Give the journal entries to record these nine transactions *during Year 2*. (Adjusting entries at the end of Year 2 are analyzed in the next self-study problem.) Omit explanations for the journal entries.

## Suggested Solution

| | | Debit | Credit |
|---|---|---|---|
| (1) Jan. 2, Year 2 | Building | 80,000 | |
| | Equipment | 40,000 | |
| | Cash | | 60,000 |
| | Mortgage Payable | | 60,000 |
| (2) Jan. 2, Year 2 | Prepaid Insurance | 1,200 | |
| | Cash | | 1,200 |
| (3) During Year 2 | Merchandise Inventory | 320,000 | |
| | Accounts Payable | | 320,000 |
| During Year 2 | Accounts Payable | 270,000 | |
| | Cash | | 270,000 |
| (4) During Year 2 | Cash | 80,000 | |
| | Accounts Receivable | 430,000 | |
| | Sales Revenue | | 510,000 |
| During Year 2 | Cash | 360,000 | |
| | Accounts Receivable | | 360,000 |
| (5) During Year 2 | Salaries Expense | 80,000 | |
| | Cash | | 80,000 |
| (6) During Year 2 | Utilities Expense | 1,300 | |
| | Cash | | 1,300 |
| (7) Nov. 1, Year 2 | Cash | 600 | |
| | Advances from Customers | | 600 |
| (8) Nov. 1, Year 2 | Note Receivable | 1,000 | |
| | Accounts Receivable | | 1,000 |
| (9) Dec. 1, Year 2 | Cash | 900 | |
| | Rent Revenue | | 900 |

# Problem 2 for Self-Study _____

Refer to the data for Harris Equipment Corporation in the preceding self-study problem. Give the adjusting entries on December 31, Year 2, to reflect the following items. You may omit explanations to the journal entries.

**(10)** The building acquired on January 2, Year 2, has a 20-year estimated life and zero salvage value. The equipment has a 7-year estimated life and $5,000 salvage value. The straight-line depreciation method is used.

**(11)** After a physical inventory is taken at the end of the year, the cost of merchandise sold during Year 2 is found to be $180,000.

**(12)** Interest expense on the mortgage liability for Year 2 is recognized.

**(13)** Salaries earned by employees during the last 3 days of December total $800 and will be paid on January 4, Year 3.

**(14)** Interest revenue is recognized on the note receivable [see transaction **(8)** in the preceding self-study problem].

**(15)** An adjusting entry is made to record the proper amount of rent revenue for Year 2 [see transaction **(9)** in the preceding self-study problem].

**(16)** Dividends of $25,000 are declared. The dividend will be paid on January 15, Year 3 (debit Retained Earnings).

## Suggested Solution

| | | |
|---|---:|---:|
| (10) Depreciation Expense | 9,000 | |
| Accumulated Depreciation | | 9,000 |
| ($80,000 − $0)/20 = $4,000; ($40,000 − $5,000)/7 = $5,000. | | |
| (11) Cost of Goods Sold | 180,000 | |
| Merchandise Inventory | | 180,000 |
| (12) Interest Expense | 6,000 | |
| Interest Payable | | 6,000 |
| $60,000 × 0.10 = $6,000. | | |
| (13) Salaries Expense | 800 | |
| Salaries Payable | | 800 |
| (14) Interest Receivable | 15 | |
| Interest Revenue | | 15 |
| $1,000 × 0.09 × 60/360. | | |
| (15) Rent Revenue | 600 | |
| Advances from Tenants | | 600 |
| (16) Retained Earnings | 25,000 | |
| Dividends Payable | | 25,000 |

# Problem 3 for Self-Study _____

To achieve efficient recording of day-to-day cash receipts and disbursements relating to operations, a firm may credit all cash receipts to revenue accounts and debit all cash disbursements to expense accounts. The efficiency stems from treating all receipts in the same way and all disbursements in the same way. As a result, lower-paid clerks can be employed to make the routine and repetitive entries for receipts and disbursements. In the day-to-day recording of transactions, the clerk does not need to be concerned with whether a specific cash transaction reflects settlement of a past accrual, a revenue or expense correctly assigned to the current period, or a prepayment relating to a future period. Higher-paid accountants would need to be employed only at the end of the period to analyze the existing account balances and to construct the adjusting entries required to correct them. This process results in temporarily incorrect balances in some balance sheet and income statement accounts during the accounting period.

Construct the adjusting entry required for each of the following scenarios.

**a.** On September 1, Year 2, a tenant paid $24,000 rent for the 1-year period starting at that time. The tenant debited the entire amount to Rent Expense and credited Cash. The tenant made no adjusting entries for rent between September 1 and December 31. Construct the adjusting entry to be made on December 31, Year 2, to recognize the proper balances in the Prepaid Rent and Rent Expense accounts. What is the amount of Rent Expense for Year 2?

**b.** The tenant's books for December 31, Year 2, after adjusting entries, show a balance in the Prepaid Rent account of $16,000. This amount represents rent for the period January 1 through August 31, Year 3. On September 1, Year 3, the tenant paid $30,000 for rent for the 1-year period starting September 1, Year 3. The tenant debited this amount to Rent Expense and credited Cash, but made no adjusting entries for rent during Year 3. Construct the adjusting entry required on December 31, Year 3. What is Rent Expense for Year 3?

**c.** The tenant's books for December 31, Year 3, after adjusting entries, show a balance in the Prepaid Rent account of $20,000. This amount represents rent for the period January 1 through August 31, Year 4. On September 1, Year 4, the tenant paid $18,000 for rent for the *6-month period* starting September 1, Year 4. The tenant debited this amount to Rent Expense and credited Cash, but made no adjusting entries during Year 4. Construct the adjusting entry required on December 31, Year 4. What is Rent Expense for Year 4?

**d.** Whenever the firm makes payments for wages, it debits Wage Expense. At the start of April, the Wages Payable account had a balance of $5,000, representing wages earned but not paid during the last few days of March. During April, the firm paid $30,000 in wages, debiting the entire amount to Wage Expense. At the end of April, analysis of amounts earned since the last payday indicates that wages of $4,000 have been earned but not yet paid. These are the only unpaid wages at the end of April. Construct the required adjusting entry. What is Wage Expense for April?

**e.** A firm purchased an insurance policy providing 1 year's coverage from May 1, Year 1, and debited the entire amount to Insurance Expense. After the firm made adjusting entries, the balance sheet for December 31, Year 1, correctly showed Prepaid Insurance of $3,000. Construct the adjusting entry that must be made on January 31, Year 2, if the books are closed monthly and a balance sheet is to be prepared for January 31, Year 2.

**f.** The record-keeping system for an apartment building instructs the bookkeeper always to credit rent revenue when a payment is received from tenants. At the beginning of Year 3, the liability account Advances from Tenants had a credit balance of $25,000, representing collections from tenants for rental services to be received during Year 3. During Year 3, collections from tenants of $250,000 were all debited to Cash and credited to Rent Revenue. No adjusting entries were made during Year 3. At the end of Year 3, analysis of the individual accounts indicates that of the amounts already collected, $30,000 represents collections for rental services to be provided to tenants during Year 4. Present the required adjusting entry. What is Rent Revenue for Year 3?

**g.** When the firm acquired new equipment costing $10,000 on January 1, Year 1, the bookkeeper debited Depreciation Expense and credited Cash for $10,000, but made no further entries for this equipment during Year 1. The equipment has an expected service life of 5 years and an estimated salvage value of zero. Construct the adjusting entry required before a balance sheet for December 31, Year 1, can be prepared.

## Suggested Solution

**a.** The Prepaid Rent account on the year-end balance sheet should represent 8 months of prepayments. The rent per month is $2,000 (= $24,000/12), so the balance required in the Prepaid Rent account is $16,000 (= 8 × $2,000). Rent Expense for Year 2 is $8,000 (= 4 × $2,000 = $24,000 − $16,000).

| | | |
|---|---|---|
| Prepaid Rent.......................................... | 16,000 | |
|    Rent Expense......................................... | | 16,000 |
| To increase the balance in the Prepaid Rent account, reducing the amount in the Rent Expense account. | | |

**b.** The Prepaid Rent account on the balance sheet for the end of Year 3 should represent 8 months of prepayments. The rent per month is $2,500 (= $30,000/12), so the required balance in the Prepaid Rent account is $20,000 (= 8 × $2,500). The balance in that account is already $16,000, so the adjusting entry must increase it by $4,000 (= $20,000 − $16,000).

| | | |
|---|---|---|
| Prepaid Rent.......................................... | 4,000 | |
|    Rent Expense......................................... | | 4,000 |
| To increase the balance in the Prepaid Rent account, reducing the amount in the Rent Expense account. | | |

The Rent Expense account will have a balance at the end of Year 3 before closing entries of $26,000 (= $30,000 − $4,000). This amount comprises $16,000 (= $2,000 × 8) for rent from January through August and $10,000 (= $2,500 × 4) for rent from September through December.

**c.** The Prepaid Rent account on the balance sheet at the end of Year 4 should represent 2 months of prepayments. The rent per month is \$3,000 (= \$18,000/6), so the required balance in the Prepaid Rent account is \$6,000 (= 2 × \$3,000). The balance in that account is \$20,000, so the adjusting entry must reduce it by \$14,000 (= \$20,000 − \$6,000).

| | | |
|---|---|---|
| Rent Expense ........................................... | 14,000 | |
|    Prepaid Rent ......................................... | | 14,000 |
| To reduce the balance in the Prepaid Rent account, increasing the amount in the Rent Expense account. | | |

The Rent Expense account will have a balance at the end of Year 4 before closing entries of \$32,000 (= \$18,000 + \$14,000). This amount comprises \$20,000 (= \$2,500 × 8) for rent from January through August and \$12,000 (= \$3,000 × 4) for rent from September through December.

**d.** The Wages Payable account should have a credit balance of \$4,000 at the end of April, but it has a balance of \$5,000 carried over from the end of March. The adjusting entry must reduce the balance by \$1,000, which requires a debit to the Wages Payable account.

| | | |
|---|---|---|
| Wages Payable ......................................... | 1,000 | |
|    Wage Expense ........................................ | | 1,000 |
| To reduce the balance in the Wages Payable account, reducing the amount in the Wage Expense account. | | |

Wage Expense is \$29,000 (= \$30,000 − \$1,000).

**e.** The Prepaid Insurance account balance of \$3,000 represents 4 months of coverage. Thus the cost of insurance is \$750 (= \$3,000/4) per month. The adjusting entry for a single month is

| | | |
|---|---|---|
| Insurance Expense ..................................... | 750 | |
|    Prepaid Insurance .................................... | | 750 |

**f.** The Advances from Tenants account has a balance of \$25,000 carried over from the start of the year. At the end of Year 3, it should have a balance of \$30,000. Thus the adjusting entry must increase the balance by \$5,000, which requires a credit to the liability account.

| | | |
|---|---|---|
| Rent Revenue .......................................... | 5,000 | |
|    Advances from Tenants ............................... | | 5,000 |
| To increase the balance in the Advances from Tenants account, reducing the amount in the Rent Revenue account. | | |

Rent Revenue for Year 3 is \$245,000 (= \$250,000 − \$5,000).

**g.** The Depreciation Expense for the year should be $2,000 (= $10,000/5). The balance in the Accumulated Depreciation account should also be $2,000 and, thus, the Depreciation Expense account must be reduced (credited) by $8,000 (= $10,000 − $2,000). The adjusting entry not only reduces recorded Depreciation Expense, but it sets up the asset account and its accumulated depreciation contra account.

| | | |
|---|---|---|
| Equipment . . . . . . . . . . . . . . . . . . . . . . . . . . . . . . . . . . . . . . . . . . . . . . . | 10,000 | |
| Accumulated Depreciation . . . . . . . . . . . . . . . . . . . . . . . . . . . . . | | 2,000 |
| Depreciation Expense . . . . . . . . . . . . . . . . . . . . . . . . . . . . . . . . . | | 8,000 |
| To reduce Depreciation Expense, setting up the asset and its contra account. | | |

# Questions, Exercises, Problems, and Cases _____

## Questions

**1.** Review the meaning of the following concepts or terms discussed in this chapter.

   **a.** Net income or net loss.

   **b.** Revenue.

   **c.** Expense.

   **d.** Accounting period.

   **e.** Natural business year or fiscal period.

   **f.** Cash basis of accounting.

   **g.** Accrual basis of accounting.

   **h.** Unexpired costs.

   **i.** Expired costs.

   **j.** Matching convention.

   **k.** Product cost.

   **l.** Period expense.

   **m.** Closing process.

   **n.** Temporary and permanent accounts.

   **o.** Expense versus dividend.

   **p.** General journal entries.

   **q.** Adjusting entries.

   **r.** Contra account.

   **s.** Unadjusted trial balance.

   **t.** Adjusted trial balance.

**2.** What factors would a firm be likely to consider in its decision to use the calendar year versus a fiscal (natural business) year as its accounting period?

**3.** Which of the following types of businesses are likely to have a natural business year different from the calendar year?

   **a.** A ski resort in Vermont.

   **b.** A professional basketball team.

   **c.** A grocery store.

**4.** Distinguish between a revenue and a cash receipt. Under what conditions will they be the same?

**5.** Distinguish between an expense and a cash expenditure. Under what conditions will they be the same?

**6.** ''Cash flows determine the *amount* of revenue and expense but not the *timing* of their recognition.'' Explain.

7. "Accrual accounting focuses on the use, rather than the financing, of assets." Explain.

8. "Depreciation on equipment may be a product cost or a period expense, depending on the type of equipment." Explain.

9. "Revenue and expense accounts are useful accounting devices, but they could be dispensed with." What is an alternative to using them?

10. Why are revenue and expense accounts closed at the end of each accounting period?

11. Before the books have been closed for an accounting period, what types of accounts will have nonzero balances? After the books have been closed, what types of accounts will have nonzero balances?

12. If each transaction occurring during an accounting period has been recorded properly, why is there a need for adjusting entries at the end of the period?

13. What is the purpose of using contra accounts? What is the alternative to using them?

## Exercises

14. *Revenue recognition.* Assume that the accrual basis of accounting is used and that revenue is recognized at the time the goods are sold or services are rendered. How much revenue is recognized during the month of May in each of the following transactions?
   a. Collection of cash from customers during May for merchandise sold and delivered in April, $8,200.
   b. Sales of merchandise during May for cash, $9,600.
   c. Sales of merchandise to customers during May to be collected in June, $2,400.
   d. Collection of cash from customers during May for merchandise to be sold and delivered in June.
   e. A store building is rented to a toy shop for $800 a month, effective May 1 (a check for $1,600 for 2 months' rent is received on May 1).
   f. Data in part **e**, except that collection is received from the tenant in June.

15. *Revenue recognition.* Assume that the accrual basis of accounting is used and that revenue is recognized at the time goods are sold or services are rendered. Indicate the amount of revenue recognized in each of the months of April, May, and June relating to the following cash receipts during May.
   a. $4,600 collected from customers for merchandise sold and delivered in April.
   b. $8,900 collected from customers for merchandise sold and delivered in May.
   c. $1,800 collected from customers for merchandise to be delivered in June.
   d. $3,600 collected from subscribers for subscription fees to monthly magazines for the 1-year period beginning April 1.
   e. Same as Part **d**, except that the subscription period begins May 1.
   f. Same as Part **d**, except that the subscription period begins June 1.

**16.** *Revenue recognition.* Indicate the amount of revenue recognized (if any) from each of the following related events, assuming that the accrual basis of accounting is used.

**a.** A firm receives purchase orders from regular customers for $8,400 of merchandise. A 2 percent discount is allowed, and generally is taken, for prompt payment.

**b.** The customers' orders are filled and shipped by way of the company's trucking division.

**c.** The firm sends invoices totaling $8,400 to the customers.

**d.** The merchandise is received by customers in the correct quantities and according to specifications.

**e.** The firm receives checks in the amount of $8,232 (= .98 × $8,400) from customers in payment for the merchandise.

**f.** Upon reinspection several days later, merchandise with a gross invoice price of $600 is found to be defective by customers and is returned for appropriate credit.

**17.** *Revenue recognition.* Indicate which of the following transactions or events immediately gives rise to the recognition of revenue under the accrual basis of accounting.

**a.** The receipt of an order from a customer for merchandise.

**b.** The shipment of goods that have been paid for in advance.

**c.** The issue of additional shares of common stock.

**d.** The completion of a batch of men's suits by a clothing factory.

**e.** The sale of tickets by a major league baseball team for a game in 2 weeks.

**f.** Same as part **e**, except that sale was made by Ticketron, a ticket agent.

**g.** The earning of interest on a savings account between interest dates.

**h.** The collection of cash from accounts receivable debtors.

**i.** The rendering of accounting services to a customer on account.

**18.** *Expense recognition.* Give the amount of expense recognized (if any) from each of the following related events, assuming that the accrual basis of accounting is used.

**a.** The purchasing department notifies the stockroom that the supply of $\frac{1}{2}$-inch plywood has reached the minimum point and should be reordered.

**b.** The firm sends a purchase order to Central Lumber Company for $10,000 of the material.

**c.** The firm receives an acknowledgment of the order. It indicates that delivery will be made in 15 days but that the price has been raised to $10,200.

**d.** The shipment of plywood arrives and is checked by the receiving department. The correct quantity has been delivered.

**e.** The purchase invoice arrives. The amount of $10,200 is subject to a 2 percent discount if paid within 10 days. Cash discounts are treated as a reduction in the acquisition cost of inventory.

**f.** Upon reinspection, the firm finds plywood with a gross invoice price of $200 to be defective and returns it to the supplier.

**g.** The balance of the amount due the Central Lumber Company is paid in time to obtain the discount.

**h.** The firm sells the plywood to customers for $12,000.

**19.** *Expense recognition.* Assume that the accrual basis of accounting is used and that revenue is recognized at the time goods are sold or services are rendered. Indicate the amount of expense recognized during March (if any) from each of the following transactions or events.

  **a.** An insurance premium of $1,800 was paid on March 1 for 1 year's coverage beginning on that date.

  **b.** On April 3, a utilities bill totaling $460 for services during March was received.

  **c.** Supplies were purchased for $700 on account during March. Payment was made for $500 of these purchases on account in March, and the remainder was paid in April. On March 1, supplies were on hand that cost $300. On March 31, supplies that cost $350 were still on hand.

  **d.** Data in **c**, except that $200 of supplies was on hand March 1.

  **e.** Property taxes of $4,800 on an office building for the year were paid in January.

  **f.** An advance of $250 on the April salary was paid to an employee on March 29.

**20.** *Expense recognition.* Assume that the accrual basis of accounting is used and that revenue is recognized at the time goods are sold or services are rendered. Indicate the amount of expense recognized in each of the months of April, May, and June relating to the following cash expenditures during May.

  **a.** $1,900 for advertising that appeared on television programs during April.

  **b.** $3,200 for sales commissions on sales made during May.

  **c.** $500 for rent on delivery equipment for the month of June.

  **d.** $600 for an insurance premium for coverage from May 1 until October 30.

  **e.** $800 as a deposit on equipment to be delivered on June 30.

  **f.** $1,200 for property taxes on an office building for the current calendar year.

**21.** *Allocation of Cost.* How should the cost of the following assets be allocated over their useful lives?

  **a.** A building with an estimated useful life of 30 years.

  **b.** A road leading to a timber tract. The road would normally last for 14 years before extensive reconstruction would be necessary, but it is expected that the timber will all be cut in 5 years.

  **c.** Rent prepaid for 2 years on a warehouse in Minneapolis.

  **d.** A truck with an estimated service life of 90,000 miles.

  **e.** Rent prepaid for a year on a shop used for boat repairs at a summer resort. The shop is open only from June 1 to September 1.

  **f.** An ore deposit owned by a mining company.

**22.** *Income recognition.* Feltham Company acquired used machine tools costing $75,000 from various sources. These machine tools were then sold to Mock Corporation. Delivery costs paid by Feltham Company totaled $4,500. Mock Corporation had agreed to pay $100,000 cash for these tools. Finding itself short of cash, however, Mock Corporation offered some of its bonds to Feltham Company. The bonds have a face value of $110,000, mature in 5 years, and promise 8 percent interest per year. At the time the offer was made, the bonds could have been sold in public bond markets for $98,000.

Feltham Company accepted the offer and held the bonds for 3 years. During the 3 years, it received interest payments of $8,800 per year, or $26,400 total. At the end of the third year, Feltham Company sold the bonds for $95,000.

a.  What profit or loss did Feltham Company recognize at the time of sale of machine tools to Mock Corporation?

b.  What profit or loss would Feltham Company have recognized at the time of the sale of machine tools if it had sold the bonds for $98,000 immediately upon receiving them?

c.  What profit or loss would Feltham Company have recognized at the time of the sale of machine tools if it had held the bonds to maturity, receiving $8,800 each year for another 5 years and $110,000 at the time the bonds matured?

23. *Identifying missing half of journal entries.* In the business world, many transactions are routine and repetitive. Because accounting records business transactions, many accounting entries are also routine and repetitive. Knowing one-half of an entry in the double-entry recording system often permits a reasoned guess about the other half. The items below give the account name for one-half of an entry. Indicate your best guess as to the nature of the transaction being recorded and the name of the account of the *routine* other half of the entry. Also indicate whether the other account is increased or decreased by the transaction.

a.  Debit: Cost of Goods Sold.

b.  Debit: Accounts Receivable.

c.  Credit: Accounts Receivable.

d.  Debit: Accounts Payable.

e.  Credit: Accounts Payable.

f.  Credit: Accumulated Depreciation.

g.  Debit: Retained Earnings.

h.  Credit: Prepaid Insurance.

i.  Debit: Property Taxes Payable.

j.  Debit: Merchandise Inventory.

24. *Asset versus expense recognition.* Give the journal entry that should be made upon the receipt of each of the following invoices by the South Appliance Company, assuming that no previous entry has been made.

(1)  From Western Electric Supply Company, $385, for repair parts purchased.

(2)  From Touch & Rose, certified public accountants, $800, for services in filing income tax returns.

(3)  From the General Electric Company, $12,365, for refrigerators purchased.

(4)  From the White Stationery Company, $250, for office supplies purchased.

(5)  From the Showy Sign Company, $540, for a neon sign acquired.

(6)  From Schutheis and Schutheis, attorneys, $1,000, for legal services in changing from the corporate to the partnership form of organization.

(7)  From the Bell Telephone Company, $65, for telephone service for next month.

**(8)** From the Madison Avenue Garage, $43, for gasoline and oil used by the delivery truck.

**(9)** From the Municipal Electric Department, $105, for electricity used for lighting last month.

25. *Journal entries for notes receivable and notes payable.* The General Supply Company received a $10,000, 3-month, 9 percent promissory note, dated December 1, Year 6, from Widen Stores to apply on its open accounts receivable.

   **a.** Present journal entries for the General Supply Company from December 1, Year 6, through collection at maturity. The books are closed quarterly. Include the closing entry.

   **b.** Present journal entries for Widen Stores from December 1, Year 6, through payment at maturity. The books are closed quarterly. Include the closing entry.

26. *Journal entries for notes payable.* Selected transactions of the Burlson Company are described below. Present dated journal entries for these transactions and adjusting entries at the end of each month from January 15, Year 2, through July 1, Year 2. Assume that only the notes indicated were outstanding during this period. The accounting period is 1 month.

   **(1)** The company issued a $6,000, 2-month, 10 percent promissory note on January 15, Year 2, in lieu of payment on an account due that date to the Grey Wholesale Company.

   **(2)** The note in **(1)** and interest were paid at maturity.

   **(3)** The company issued a $2,000, 3-month, 9 percent promissory note to the Grey Wholesale Company on the date of purchase of merchandise, April 1, Year 2.

   **(4)** The note in **(3)** and interest were paid at maturity.

27. *Journal entries for office supply inventories.* On January 1, Year 4, the Office Supplies Inventory account of the Harris Company had a balance of $4,200. During the ensuing quarter, supplies were acquired on account in the amount of $9,000. On March 31, Year 4, the inventory was taken and calculated to amount to $2,500.

   Present journal entries to record these acquisitions and adjustments at the end of March in accordance with each of the following sets of instructions, which might be established in an accounting systems manual.

   **a.** An expense account is to be debited at the time supplies are acquired.

   **b.** An asset account is to be debited at the time supplies are acquired.

28. *Journal entries for rental receipts and payments.* The Florida Realty Company rents office space to Maddox Consultants at the rate of $600 per month. Collections have been made for rental through April 30, Year 3. The following transactions occurred on the dates indicated:

   **(1)** May 1, Year 3: Collection, $600.

   **(2)** June 1, Year 3: Collection, $1,200.

   **(3)** August 1, Year 3: Collection, $1,800.

   Present journal entries for these transactions and for adjusting and closing entries from May 1 to August 31 (inclusive) as they relate to both companies, assuming that each company closes its books monthly.

29. *Using accumulated depreciation to estimate asset age.*
   a. Machine A costs $10,000, has accumulated depreciation of $4,000 as of year-end, and is being depreciated on a straight-line basis over 10 years with an estimated salvage value of zero. How long ago was machine A acquired?
   b. Machine B has accumulated depreciation (straight-line basis) of $6,000 at year-end. The depreciation charge for the year is $2,000. The estimated salvage value of the machine at the end of its useful life is $1,000. How long ago was machine B acquired?

30. *Effect of recording errors on financial statements.* In recording transactions of Rogow Corporation during Year 7, the following errors were made:
   (1) An expenditure of $2,000 to acquire a tract of land was debited to Administrative Expenses.
   (2) Cash collections during Year 7 of $1,500 relating to sales made during Year 6 were credited to Sales Revenue of Year 7.
   (3) An expenditure of $1,200 for insurance coverage from October 1, Year 7, to September 30, Year 8, was debited to Administrative Expenses on October 1, Year 7.
   (4) Cash collections during Year 7 of $1,000 for goods to be delivered during Year 8 were credited to Sales Revenue of Year 7.
   Indicate the effect (exclusive of income tax implications) of these errors on the following items in the financial statements prepared on December 31, Year 7:
   a. Current assets.
   b. Property, plant, and equipment.
   c. Current liabilities.
   d. Sales Revenue.
   e. Administrative expenses.
   f. Net income.
   g. Retained earnings.

31. *Effect of recording errors on financial statements.* In recording the adjusting entries of the Hammond Sales Company, Inc., at the end of Year 7, the following adjustments were omitted:
   (1) Depreciation on the delivery truck of $3,000.
   (2) Insurance expired on the delivery truck of $600.
   (3) Interest accrued on notes payable of $150.
   (4) Interest accrued on notes receivable of $330.
   Indicate the collective effect (exclusive of income tax implications) of these omissions on the following items in the financial statements prepared on December 31, Year 7:
   a. Current assets.
   b. Property, plant, and equipment.
   c. Current liabilities.
   d. Selling and administrative expenses.
   e. Net income.
   f. Retained earnings.

**32.** *Effect of recording errors on financial statements.* Using the notation O/S (overstated), U/S (understated), and NO (no effect), indicate the effects on assets, liabilities, and shareholders' equity as of December 31, Year 3, of the following independent errors or omissions. Ignore income tax implications.

**a.** An expenditure of $600 made on December 1, Year 3, for 6 months' rent on an automobile was debited to Prepaid Rent. No adjusting entry was made on December 31, Year 3.

**b.** A microcomputer acquired on July 1, Year 3, for $6,000 was debited to Administrative Expenses. The microcomputer has an expected useful life of 3 years and zero estimated salvage value.

**c.** The company rented out excess office space for the 6-month period beginning January 1, Year 3. A rental check for this period of $600 was received on December 26, Year 2, and correctly credited to Rental Fees Received in Advance. No further journal entries were made relating to this rental during Year 3.

**d.** Interest accrued on Notes Receivable of $500 as of December 31, Year 3, was not recorded.

**e.** A check for $250 was received from a customer on December 31, Year 3, in settlement of an account receivable. No journal entries were made to record this check.

**f.** An expenditure of $740 for travel during December 31, Year 3, was recorded as $470.

**33.** *Reconstructing accounting records.* Most of the financial records of the Rowland Novelty Company were removed by an employee who apparently took all the cash on hand from the store on October 31. From supplementary records, the following information is obtained:

**(1)** According to the bank, cash in bank was $5,730.

**(2)** Amounts payable to creditors were $4,720.

**(3)** Rowland's initial contribution to the business was $15,000, and the total shareholders' equity at the time of the theft was $17,500.

**(4)** Cost of merchandise on hand was $11,380.

**(5)** A 1-year fire insurance policy was purchased on September 1 for $900.

**(6)** Furniture and fixtures are rented from the Anderson Office Supply Company for $200 per month. The rental for October has not been paid.

**(7)** A note for $1,200 was given by a customer. Interest due at October 31 was $45.

**(8)** Payments due from other customers amounted to $1,915.

**(9)** Rowland purchased a license from the city for $300 on July 1. The license allows retail operations for 1 year.

**a.** Determine the probable cash shortage.

**b.** Prepare a well-organized balance sheet presenting the financial position immediately preceding the theft.

## Problems and Cases

**34.** *Cash versus accrual basis of accounting.* J. Thompson opened a hardware store on January 1, Year 5. Thompson invested $10,000 and borrowed $8,000 from a local bank. The loan is repayable on June 30, Year 5, with interest at the rate of 9 percent per year.

Thompson rented a building on January 1 and paid 2 months' rent in advance in the amount of $2,000. Property and liability insurance coverage for the year ending December 31, Year 5, was paid on January 1 in the amount of $1,200.

Thompson purchased $28,000 of merchandise inventory on account on January 2 and paid $10,000 of this amount on January 25. The cost of merchandise on hand on January 31 was $15,000.

During January, cash sales to customers totaled $20,000 and sales on account totaled $9,000. Of the sales on account, $2,000 had been collected as of January 31.

Other costs incurred and paid in cash during January were as follows: utilities, $400; salaries, $650; and taxes, $350.

**a.** Prepare an income statement for January, assuming that Thompson uses the accrual basis of accounting, with revenue recognized at the time goods are sold (delivered).

**b.** Prepare an income statement for January, assuming that Thompson uses the cash basis of accounting.

**c.** Which basis of accounting do you believe provides a better indication of the operating performance of the hardware store during January? Why?

**35.** *Cash versus accrual basis of accounting.* Management Consultants, Inc., opened a consulting business on July 1, Year 2. Roy Bean and Sarah Bower each contributed $7,000 cash for shares of the firm's common stock. The corporation borrowed $8,000 from a local bank on August 1, Year 2. The loan is repayable on July 31, Year 3, with interest at the rate of 9 percent per year.

Office space was rented on August 1, with 2 months' rent paid in advance. The remaining monthly rental fees of $900 per month were made on the first of each month, beginning October 1. Office equipment with a 4-year life was purchased for cash on August 1 for $4,800.

Consulting services rendered for clients between August 1 and December 31, Year 2, were billed at $15,000. Of this amount, $9,000 was collected by year-end.

Other costs incurred and paid in cash by the end of the year were as follows: utilities, $450; salary of secretary, $7,500; supplies, $450. Unpaid bills at year-end were as follows: utilities, $80; salary of secretary, $900; supplies, $70. All supplies acquired were used.

**a.** Prepare an income statement for the 5 months ended December 31, Year 2, assuming that the corporation uses the accrual basis of accounting, with revenue recognized at the time services are rendered.

**b.** Prepare an income statement for the 5 months ended December 31, Year 2, assuming that the corporation uses the cash basis of accounting.

**c.** Which basis of accounting do you believe provides a better indication of operating performance of the consulting firm for the period? Why?

**36.** *Cash versus accrual basis of accounting.* J. Hennessey opened a retail store on January 1, Year 8. Hennessey invested $20,000 and borrowed $10,000 from a local bank. The loan is repayable on December 31, Year 9, with interest at the rate of 12 percent per year.

Hennessey purchased $84,000 of merchandise on account during Year 8 and paid $76,000 of the amount by the end of Year 8. The cost of merchandise on hand on December 31, Year 8 was $12,000.

During year 8, cash sales to customers were $30,000 and sales on account totaled $70,000. Of the sales on account, $62,000 was collected by December 31, Year 8.

Other costs incurred and paid in cash were salaries, $20,000, and utilities, $1,500. Unpaid bills at year-end included salaries, $1,200, and utilities, $120.

**a.** Prepare an income statement for Year 8 assuming that the company uses the accrual basis of accounting, with revenue recognized at the time of sale.

**b.** Prepare an income statement for Year 8 assuming that the company uses the cash basis of accounting.

**c.** Which basis of accounting do you believe provides a better indication of operating performance for the retail store during Year 8? Why?

**37.** *Miscellaneous transactions and adjusting entries.* Present journal entries for each of the following separate sets of data.

**a.** On January 15, Year 2, a $6,000, 2-month, 12 percent note was received by the company. Present adjusting entries at the end of each month and the entry for collection at maturity.

**b.** The company uses one Merchandise Inventory account to record the beginning inventory and purchases during the period. The balance in this account on December 31, Year 2, was $580,000. The inventory of merchandise on hand at that time was $60,000. Present the adjusting entry.

**c.** The company rents out part of its building for office space at the rate of $900 a month, payable in advance for each calendar quarter of the year. The quarterly rental for the first quarter was received 1 month late on February 1, Year 2. Present collection and adjusting entries for the quarter. Assume that the books are closed monthly.

**d.** The company leases branch office space at $3,000 a month. Payment is made by the company on the first day of each 6-month period. Payment of $18,000 was made on July 1, Year 2. Present payment and adjusting entries through August 31, Year 2. Assume that the books are closed monthly.

**e.** The balance of the Prepaid Insurance account on October 1, Year 2, was $400. On December 1, Year 2, the company renewed its only insurance policy for another 2 years, beginning on that date, by payment of $3,000. Present journal entries for renewal and adjusting entries through December 31, Year 2. Assume that the books are closed quarterly.

**f.** The Office Supplies on Hand account had a balance of $400 on December 31, Year 2. Purchases of supplies in the amount of $580 were recorded in the Office Supplies Expense account during the month. The physical inventory of office supplies on December 31, Year 2, was $340. Present any necessary adjusting entry at December 31, Year 2.

**g.** An office building was constructed at a cost of $560,000. It was estimated that it would have a useful life of 50 years from the date of occupancy, October 31, Year 2, and a residual value of $80,000. Present the adjusting entry for the depreciation of the building in Year 2. Assume that the books are closed annually on December 31.

38. *Miscellaneous transactions and adjusting entries.* Give the journal entry to record each of the transactions that follow as well as any necessary adjusting entries on December 31, Year 6, assuming that the accounting period is the calendar year and the books are closed on December 31.

   **a.** Harrison's Supply Company received a 90-day note from a customer on December 1, Year 6. The note in the face amount of $3,000 replaced an open account receivable of the same amount. The note is due on March 1, Year 7, with interest at 9 percent per year.

   **b.** Thompson's Wholesale Company purchased a 2-year insurance policy on September 1, Year 6, paying the 2-year premium of $9,600 in advance.

   **c.** William's Products Company acquired a machine on July 1, Year 6, for $20,000 cash. The machine is expected to have a $4,000 salvage value and a 4-year life.

   **d.** Greer Electronics Company acquired an automobile on September 1, Year 5, for $5,000 cash. The automobile is expected to have $1,400 salvage value and a 4-year life.

   **e.** Devine Company rented out excess office space for the 3-month period beginning December 15, Year 6. The first month's rent of $6,400 was received on this date.

   **f.** Prentice Products Corporation began business on November 1, Year 6. It acquired office supplies costing $5,000 on account. Of this amount, $4,000 was paid by year-end. A physical inventory indicates that office supplies costing $2,400 were on hand on December 31, Year 6.

39. *Miscellaneous transactions and adjusting entries.* Prepare journal entries for each of the following sets of data.

   **a.** The company rents out excess office space at a rate of $3,000 per month, payable in advance at the beginning of each calendar quarter of the year. The rental payment for the first quarter was received 2 months late on March 1. Assume that the books are closed monthly. Present the collection entry on March 1 and the adjusting entry made at the end of each month.

   **b.** On March 16, a $20,000, 2-month, 9-percent note was received by the company in full payment of an open account receivable. Assume that the books are closed monthly. Give all journal entries relating to the note, from March 16 until payment at maturity on May 15.

   **c.** The balance in the Prepaid Insurance account on January 1, Year 4, was $600. On March 1, Year 4, the company renewed its only insurance policy for another 3 years, beginning on that date, by payment of $14,400. Assume that the books are closed quarterly. Present journal entries for the renewal and adjusting entries for Year 4.

   **d.** The Repair Parts Inventory account showed a balance of $3,000 on January 1. During January, parts costing $8,000 were purchased and charged to

Repair Expense. An inventory of repair parts at the end of January revealed that parts costing $3,800 were on hand. Present the adjusting entry required at the end of January.

**e.** An office machine was acquired on July 1, Year 6, at a cost of $100,000. It was estimated to have a 10-year life and a $20,000 residual value. Assume that the books are closed annually. Present the adjusting entries on December 31, Year 6, and December 31, Year 7.

**f.** Property taxes for the calendar year are assessed on January 1 but are paid on April 1. The company's property taxes for Year 8 of $24,000 were paid as required. Assume that the books are closed quarterly. Give the journal entries relating to property taxes for Year 8.

**40.** *Preparation of T-account entries and adjusted trial balance.* A corporation known as the Kirby Collection Agency is organized by Betty Kirby and Charles Stevens on January 1, Year 3. The business of the firm is to collect overdue accounts receivable of various clients on a commission basis. The following transactions occurred during January:

**(1)** Kirby contributes office supplies at $3,000 and cash of $12,000. She is issued stock certificates for 500 shares with a par value of $30 a share.

**(2)** Stevens contributes $3,000 in cash and office equipment valued at $9,000. He is issued stock certificates for 400 shares.

**(3)** The Kirby agency collects $400 on an account that was turned over to it by the Jiggly Market. The commission earned is 50 percent of the amount collected.

**(4)** The stenographer's salary during the month, $600, is paid.

**(5)** A bill is received from Lyband and Linn, certified public accountants, for $400 to cover the cost of installing a computer system.

**(6)** The amount due the Jiggly Market is paid [see **(3)**].

**(7)** An office is leased for the year beginning February 1, Year 3, and the rent for 2 months is paid in advance. A check is drawn for $900.

**(8)** An automobile is purchased on January 30 for $4,500; $2,500 is paid by check, and an installment contract, payable to the Scotch Automobile Sales Company, is signed for the balance.

**a.** Open T-accounts and record the transactions during January.

**b.** Prepare an adjusted, preclosing trial balance as of January 31, Year 3. Indicate, by R or E, accounts that are revenue or expense accounts.

**41.** *Preparation of T-account entries, adjusted trial balance, income statement, and balance sheet.* The trial balance of Safety Cleaners and Dyers, Inc., at February 28, Year 6, follows. The books have not been closed nor have adjusting entries been made since December 31, Year 5.

| | | |
|---|---:|---:|
| Cash | $ 3,400 | |
| Accounts Receivable | 15,200 | |
| Supplies on Hand | 4,800 | |
| Prepaid Insurance | 1,200 | |
| Equipment | 65,000 | |
| Accumulated Depreciation | | $ 9,680 |
| Accounts Payable | | 7,900 |
| Common Stock | | 20,000 |

| | | |
|---|---:|---:|
| Retained Earnings . . . . . . . . . . . . . . . . . . . . . . . . . . . . . . . . . . . . . . . | | 40,000 |
| Sales Revenue . . . . . . . . . . . . . . . . . . . . . . . . . . . . . . . . . . . . . . . . . | | 46,060 |
| Salaries and Wages Expense . . . . . . . . . . . . . . . . . . . . . . . . . . . | 26,600 | |
| Cost of Outside Work . . . . . . . . . . . . . . . . . . . . . . . . . . . . . . . . . . | 2,040 | |
| Advertising Expense . . . . . . . . . . . . . . . . . . . . . . . . . . . . . . . . . . . | 400 | |
| Repairs Expense . . . . . . . . . . . . . . . . . . . . . . . . . . . . . . . . . . . . . . | 500 | |
| Rent Expense . . . . . . . . . . . . . . . . . . . . . . . . . . . . . . . . . . . . . . . . . | 1,200 | |
| Power, Gas, and Water Expense . . . . . . . . . . . . . . . . . . . . . . . | 880 | |
| Supplies Used . . . . . . . . . . . . . . . . . . . . . . . . . . . . . . . . . . . . . . . . | — | |
| Depreciation Expense . . . . . . . . . . . . . . . . . . . . . . . . . . . . . . . . . . | — | |
| Miscellaneous Expense . . . . . . . . . . . . . . . . . . . . . . . . . . . . . . . . | 2,420 | |
| | $123,640 | $123,640 |

A summary of the transactions for the month of March Year 6 is as follows:

**(1)** Sales: For cash, $14,000; on account, $5,800.

**(2)** Collections on account, $10,000.

**(3)** Purchases of outside work (cleaning done by wholesale cleaners), $800, on account.

**(4)** Purchases of supplies, on account, $2,800.

**(5)** Payments on account, $4,000.

**(6)** March rent paid, $600.

**(7)** Supplies used (for the quarter), $5,340.

**(8)** Depreciation (for the quarter), $2,420.

**(9)** March salaries and wages paid, $11,120.

**(10)** Bills received but not recorded or paid by the end of the month: advertising, $200; maintenance on equipment, $60; power, gas, and water, $380.

**(11)** Insurance expired (for the quarter), $400.

**a.** Open T-accounts and enter the trial balance amounts.

**b.** Record the transactions for the month of March in the T-accounts, opening additional T-accounts as needed. Cross-number the entries.

**c.** Prepare an adjusted, preclosing trial balance at March 31, Year 6, an income statement for the 3 months ending March 31, Year 6, and a balance sheet as of March 31, Year 6.

**d.** Enter closing entries in the T-accounts using an Income Summary account.

**42.** *Preparation of T-account entries, adjusted trial balance, income statement, and balance sheet.* The balance sheet accounts of Hanover Camera Repair Shop, Inc., at June 30, Year 8, are as follows:

| | | |
|---|---:|---:|
| Cash . . . . . . . . . . . . . . . . . . . . . . . . . . . . . . . . . . . . . . . . . . . . . . . . . | $1,920 | |
| Repair Parts Inventory . . . . . . . . . . . . . . . . . . . . . . . . . . . . . . . . . | 600 | |
| Office Supplies Inventory . . . . . . . . . . . . . . . . . . . . . . . . . . . . . . . | 80 | |
| Equipment . . . . . . . . . . . . . . . . . . . . . . . . . . . . . . . . . . . . . . . . . . . . | 2,200 | |
| Accumulated Depreciation . . . . . . . . . . . . . . . . . . . . . . . . . . . . . . | | $  300 |
| Accounts Payable . . . . . . . . . . . . . . . . . . . . . . . . . . . . . . . . . . . . . . | | 2,500 |
| Common Stock . . . . . . . . . . . . . . . . . . . . . . . . . . . . . . . . . . . . . . . . | | 500 |
| Retained Earnings . . . . . . . . . . . . . . . . . . . . . . . . . . . . . . . . . . . . . | | 1,500 |
| | $4,800 | $4,800 |

A summary of the transactions during July is as follows:

**(1)** Performed repair services, for which $900 in cash was received immediately.

**(2)** Performed additional repair work, $200, and sent bills to customers for this amount.

**(3)** Paid creditors $400.

**(4)** Took out insurance on equipment on July 1, and issued a check to cover 1 year's premium of $96.

**(5)** Paid $60 for a series of advertisements that appeared in the local newspaper during July.

**(6)** Issued a check for $130 for rent of shop space for July.

**(7)** Paid telephone bill of $35 for the month.

**(8)** Collected $100 of the amount charged to customers in item **(2)**.

Adjusting entries required at the end of July relate to the following:

**(9)** The insurance expired during July is calculated at $8.

**(10)** Cost of repair parts used during the month is $180.

**(11)** Cost of office supplies used during July is $40.

**(12)** Depreciation of equipment for the month is $30.

**a.** Open T-accounts and insert the July 1 balances. Record the transactions for the month in the T-accounts, opening additional T-accounts for individual revenue and expense accounts as needed.

**b.** Prepare an adjusted, preclosing trial balance at July 31, Year 8.

**c.** Enter closing entries in the T-accounts using an Income Summary account.

**d.** Prepare an income statement for the month of July and a balance sheet as of July 31, Year 8.

**43.** *Preparation of T-account entries, adjusted trial balance, income statement, and balance sheet.* The trial balance of Jones Shoe Repair Shop, Inc., at February 28, Year 2, follows. The books have not been closed since December 31, Year 1.

| | | |
|---|---:|---:|
| Cash | $ 6,060 | |
| Accounts Receivable | 15,200 | |
| Supplies Inventory | 4,800 | |
| Prepaid Insurance | 900 | |
| Equipment | 65,000 | |
| Accumulated Depreciation | | $ 11,460 |
| Accounts Payable | | 6,120 |
| Common Stock | | 15,000 |
| Retained Earnings | | 47,360 |
| Sales Revenue | | 46,060 |
| Salaries and Wages Expense | 26,600 | |
| Cost of Outside Work | 2,040 | |
| Advertising Expense | 900 | |
| Rent Expense | 1,200 | |
| Power, Gas, and Water Expense | 880 | |
| Supplies Used | — | |
| Depreciation Expense | — | |
| Miscellaneous Expense | 2,420 | |
| | $126,000 | $126,000 |

A summary of the transactions during the month of March, Year 2 is as follows:

(1)  Sales: for cash, $26,000; on account, $17,600.

(2)  Collections on account, $22,000.

(3)  Purchases of outside work (repair work done by another shoe repair shop for Jones), $1,600, on account.

(4)  Purchases of supplies, on account, $2,800.

(5)  Payments on account, $6,000.

(6)  March rent paid, $1,200.

(7)  March salaries and wages paid, $13,290.

Adjusting entries required at the end of March relate to the following:

(8)  Supplies used (for the quarter), $4,960.

(9)  Depreciation (for the quarter), $3,820.

(10)  Bills received but not yet recorded or paid by the end of the month: advertising, $300; power, gas, and water, $620.

(11)  Insurance expired (for the quarter), $300.

a.   Open T-accounts and enter the trial balance amounts.

b.   Record the transactions for the month of March in the T-accounts, opening additional T-accounts as needed. Cross-number the entries.

c.   Enter closing entries in the T-accounts using an Income Summary account.

d.   Prepare an adjusted, preclosing trial balance at March 31, Year 2, an income statement for the 3 months ending March 31, Year 2, and a balance sheet as of March 31, Year 2.

**44.** *Preparation of journal entries, T-accounts, adjusted trial balance, income statement, and balance sheet.* The post-closing trial balance of Cunningham's Hardware Store on September 30, Year 4, is as follows:

| | | |
|---|---:|---:|
| Cash | $ 88,400 | |
| Accounts Receivable | 54,500 | |
| Merchandise Inventory | 136,300 | |
| Prepaid Insurance | 800 | |
| Equipment | 420,000 | |
| Accumulated Depreciation | | $168,000 |
| Accounts Payable | | 66,200 |
| Note Payable | | 10,000 |
| Salaries Payable | | 2,500 |
| Common Stock | | 300,000 |
| Retained Earnings | | 153,300 |
| Total | $700,000 | $700,000 |

Transactions during October and additional information are as follows:

(1)  Sales, all on account, total $170,000.

(2)  Merchandise inventory purchased on account from various suppliers is $92,600.

(3)  Rent for the month of October of $23,500 is paid.

(4)  Salaries paid to employees during October are $41,200.

**(5)** Accounts receivable of $68,300 are collected.

**(6)** Accounts payable of $77,900 are paid.

**(7)** Miscellaneous expenses of $6,400 are paid in cash.

Adjusting entries required at the end of October relate to the following:

**(8)** The premium on a 1-year insurance policy was paid on June 1, Year 4. This is the only insurance policy in force on September 30, Year 4.

**(9)** Equipment is depreciated over a 10-year life. Estimated salvage value of the equipment is considered to be negligible.

**(10)** Employee salaries earned during the last 2 days of October but not paid are $3,200. These are the only unpaid salaries at the end of October.

**(11)** The note payable is a 90-day, 12 percent note issued on September 30, Year 4.

**(12)** Merchandise inventory on hand on October 31, Year 4, totals $155,900.

**a.** Prepare general journal entries to reflect the transactions and other events during October. Indicate whether each entry records a transaction (T) during the month or is an adjusting entry (A) at the end of the month.

**b.** Set up T-accounts and enter the opening balances in the accounts on September 30, Year 4. Record the entries from part **a** in the T-accounts, creating additional accounts as required.

**c.** Prepare an adjusted, preclosing trial balance at October 31, Year 4.

**d.** Prepare an income statement for the month of October.

**e.** Enter the appropriate closing entries at the end of October in the T-accounts, assuming that the books are closed each month. Use an Income Summary account. Prepare a balance sheet as of October 31, Year 4.

**45.** *Preparation of adjusting entries.* The following unadjusted trial balance is taken from the books of the Kathleen Clothing Company at July 31, Year 3. The company closes its books monthly.

| | | |
|---|---:|---:|
| Accounts Payable | | $ 12,952 |
| Accounts Receivable | $ 18,257 | |
| Accumulated Depreciation | | 8,214 |
| Advances by Customers | | 540 |
| Common Stock | | 40,000 |
| Cash | 9,000 | |
| Equipment | 2,640 | |
| Depreciation Expense | — | — |
| Dividends Payable | — | — |
| Furniture and Fixtures | 12,000 | |
| Income Tax Expense | — | |
| Income Tax Payable | | 3,500 |
| Insurance Expense | — | — |
| Leasehold | 10,800 | |
| Merchandise Cost of Goods Sold | — | — |
| Merchandise Inventory | 49,500 | |
| Miscellaneous Expense | 188 | |
| Prepaid Insurance | 450 | |
| Rent Expense | — | — |
| Retained Earnings | | 14,294 |
| Salaries and Commissions Expense | 2,020 | |

| | | |
|---|---:|---:|
| Salaries and Commissions Payable...................... | | 500 |
| Sales............................................... | | 25,000 |
| Supplies Inventory ..................................... | 145 | |
| | $105,000 | $105,000 |

Additional data include the following:

**(1)** Depreciation on equipment is to be calculated at 10 percent of cost per year (assume zero salvage value).

**(2)** Depreciation on furniture and fixtures is to be calculated at 20 percent of cost per year (assume zero salvage value).

**(3)** The leasehold represents long-term rent paid in advance by Kathleen. The monthly rental charge is $600.

**(4)** One invoice of $420 for the purchase of merchandise on account from the Peoria Company was recorded during the month as $240. The account has not yet been paid.

**(5)** Commissions unpaid at July 31, Year 3, were $340. All salaries have been paid. The balance in the Salaries and Commissions Payable account represents the amount of commissions unpaid at July 1.

**(6)** Merchandise with a sales price of $350 was recently delivered to a customer and charged to Accounts Receivable, although the customer had paid $350 in advance.

**(7)** The balance in the Prepaid Insurance account relates to a 3-year policy that went into effect on January 1, Year 3.

**(8)** A dividend of $3,000 was declared on July 31, Year 3.

**(9)** The inventory of merchandise on July 31, Year 3, was $33,600.

Present adjusting journal entries at July 31, Year 3. Use only the accounts listed in the trial balance.

**46.** *Preparation of closing entries.* The adjusted trial balance of Life Photographers, Inc., at June 30, Year 2, is presented in Exhibit 3.12.

   **a.** Present the journal entries to close the revenue and expense accounts directly to Retained Earnings as of June 30, Year 2.

   **b.** Set up in T-account form the revenue, expense, and retained earnings accounts. Insert the trial balance amounts and record the closing entries from part **a**.

**47.** *Working backwards to balance sheet at beginning of period.* (Problems 47 through 49 are adapted from problems by George H. Sorter.) The following data relate to the Prima Company.

   **(1)** Post-closing trial balance at December 31, Year 2:

**Debits:**

| | |
|---|---:|
| Cash .......................................................... | $ 10,000 |
| Marketable Securities ................................................ | 20,000 |
| Accounts Receivable................................................. | 25,000 |
| Merchandise Inventory ............................................ | 30,000 |
| Prepayments for Miscellaneous Services ............................ | 3,000 |
| Land, Buildings, and Equipment...................................... | 40,000 |
|    Total Debits ...................................................... | $128,000 |

*continued*

Exhibit 3.12 ───────────────────────────

**LIFE PHOTOGRAPHERS, INC.**
**Adjusted Trial Balance**
**June 30, Year 2**
**(Problem 46)**

| | | |
|---|---:|---:|
| Accounts Payable ........................................ | | $ 3,641 |
| Accounts Receivable..................................... | $ 3,900 | |
| Accumulated Depreciation ............................... | | 1,995 |
| Advertising Expense .................................... | 1,500 | |
| Cameras and Equipment ................................ | 15,500 | |
| Cash.................................................... | 2,994 | |
| Common Stock.......................................... | | 10,000 |
| Depreciation Expense—Cameras and Equipment........... | 180 | |
| Depreciation Expense—Furniture and Fixtures ............. | 105 | |
| Electricity Expense ..................................... | 300 | |
| Equipment Repairs Expense ............................. | 180 | |
| Furniture and Fixtures................................... | 9,600 | |
| Insurance Expense ..................................... | 330 | |
| Photographic Supplies Expense .......................... | 1,950 | |
| Photographic Supplies on Hand .......................... | 3,390 | |
| Prepaid Insurance ...................................... | 270 | |
| Rent Expense........................................... | 1,425 | |
| Retained Earnings ...................................... | | 14,138 |
| Revenue—Commercial Photography ...................... | | 18,090 |
| Revenue—Printing Service............................... | | 4,680 |
| Salaries Expense........................................ | 10,800 | |
| Telephone Expense...................................... | 120 | |
| | $52,544 | $52,544 |

**(1)** *(continued)*

**Credits:**

| | |
|---|---:|
| Accounts Payable (for merchandise) ................................ | $ 25,000 |
| Interest Payable ................................................. | 300 |
| Taxes Payable ................................................... | 4,000 |
| Notes Payable (6 percent, long-term) ................................ | 20,000 |
| Accumulated Depreciation ......................................... | 16,000 |
| Capital Stock.................................................... | 50,000 |
| Retained Earnings ............................................... | 12,700 |
| Total Credits ............................................... | $128,000 |

**(2)** Income and retained earnings data for Year 2:

| | | |
|---|---:|---:|
| Sales.................................................... | | $200,000 |
| Less Expenses: | | |
| Cost of Goods Sold.................................. | $130,000 | |
| Depreciation Expense ............................... | 4,000 | |
| Taxes Expense...................................... | 8,000 | |

| | | |
|---|---:|---:|
| Other Operating Expenses .......................... | 47,700 | |
| Interest Expense ..................................... | 1,200 | |
| Total Expenses....................................... | | 190,900 |
| Net Income ........................................... | | $ 9,100 |
| Less Dividends....................................... | | 5,000 |
| Increase in Retained Earnings ......................... | | $ 4,100 |

**(3)** Summary of cash receipts and disbursements in Year 2:

**Cash Receipts:**

| | | |
|---|---:|---:|
| Cash Sales ......................................... | $ 47,000 | |
| Collection from Credit Customers...................... | 150,000 | |
| Total Receipts...................................... | | $197,000 |

**Cash Disbursements:**

| | | |
|---|---:|---:|
| Payment to Suppliers of Merchandise.................... | $128,000 | |
| Payment to Suppliers of Miscellaneous Services .......... | 49,000 | |
| Payment of Taxes ..................................... | 7,500 | |
| Payment of Interest.................................... | 1,200 | |
| Payment of Dividends................................... | 5,000 | |
| Purchase of Marketable Securities....................... | 8,000 | |
| Total Disbursements ................................. | | 198,700 |
| **Excess of Disbursements over Receipts** .............. | | $ 1,700 |

**(4)** Purchases of merchandise during the period, all on account, were $127,000. All "Other Operating Expenses" were credited to Prepayments.

Prepare a balance sheet for January 1, Year 2. (*Hint:* Set up T-accounts for each of the accounts in the trial balance and enter the *ending* balances in the T-accounts. Starting with information from the income statement and statement of cash receipts and disbursements, reconstruct the transactions that took place during the year and enter the amounts in the appropriate T-accounts.)

**48.** *Working backwards to cash receipts and disbursements.* The Secunda Company's trial balance at the beginning of Year 2 and the adjusted, preclosing trial balance at the end of Year 2 are presented as follows:

| | 1/1/Year 2 | 12/31/Year 2 |
|---|---:|---:|
| **Debits:** | | |
| Cash............................................. | $ 20,000 | $ 9,000 |
| Accounts Receivable............................... | 36,000 | 51,000 |
| Merchandise Inventory ............................ | 45,000 | 60,000 |
| Prepayments...................................... | 2,000 | 1,000 |
| Land, Buildings, and Equipment.................... | 40,000 | 40,000 |

*continued*

| | | |
|---|---|---|
| Cost of Goods Sold......................... | — | 50,000 |
| Interest Expense ......................... | — | 3,000 |
| Other Operating Expenses ................ | — | 29,000 |
| Total Debits......................... | $143,000 | $243,000 |

**Credits:**

| | | |
|---|---|---|
| Accumulated Depreciation ................ | $ 16,000 | $ 18,000 |
| Interest Payable ......................... | 1,000 | 2,000 |
| Accounts Payable ....................... | 30,000 | 40,000 |
| Mortgage Payable ....................... | 20,000 | 17,000 |
| Capital Stock............................ | 50,000 | 50,000 |
| Retained Earnings ...................... | 26,000 | 16,000 |
| Sales.................................. | — | 100,000 |
| Total Credits ......................... | $143,000 | $243,000 |

All goods and services acquired during the year were purchased on account. The Other Operating Expenses account includes depreciation charges and expirations of prepayments. Dividends declared during the year were debited to Retained Earnings.

Prepare a schedule showing all cash transactions for Year 2. (*Hint:* Set up T-accounts for each of the accounts listed in the trial balance and enter the amounts shown as of January 1, Year 2, and December 31, Year 2. Starting with the entries in revenue and expense accounts, reconstruct the transactions that took place during the year, and enter the amounts in the appropriate T-accounts. The effect of earnings activities is not yet reflected in the Retained Earnings account because the trial balance is before closing entries.)

49. *Working backwards to income statement.* Tertia Company presents the following incomplete post-closing trial balances, as well as a statement of cash receipts and disbursements:

| | 1/1/Year 2 | 12/31/Year 2 |
|---|---|---|
| **Debits:** | | |
| Cash ....................................... | $   ? | $   ? |
| Accounts and Notes Receivable.................... | 36,000 | 41,000 |
| Merchandise Inventory ........................... | 55,000 | 49,500 |
| Interest Receivable ............................ | 1,000 | 700 |
| Prepaid Miscellaneous Services .................... | 4,000 | 5,200 |
| Building, Machinery, and Equipment ................ | 47,000 | 47,000 |
| Total Debits ..................................... | $   ? | $   ? |
| **Credits:** | | |
| Accounts Payable (miscellaneous services)........... | $  2,000 | $  2,500 |
| Accounts Payable (merchandise) ................... | 34,000 | 41,000 |
| Property Taxes Payable ........................... | 1,000 | 1,500 |
| Accumulated Depreciation ........................ | 10,000 | 12,000 |
| Mortgage Payable ................................ | 35,000 | 30,000 |
| Capital Stock..................................... | 25,000 | 25,000 |
| Retained Earnings ............................... | 76,000 | ? |
| Total Credits ..................................... | $183,000 | $211,200 |

|                                                          | Year 2    |
| -------------------------------------------------------- | --------- |
| **Cash Receipts:**                                       |           |
| 1. Collection from Credit Customers ................     | $144,000  |
| 2. Cash Sales ...................................        | 63,000    |
| 3. Collection of Interest .........................      | 1,000     |
|                                                          | $208,000  |
|                                                          |           |
| **Less Cash Disbursements:**                             |           |
| 4. Payment to Suppliers of Merchandise ............      | $114,000  |
| 5. Repayment on Mortgage .......................         | 5,000     |
| 6. Payment of Interest ...........................       | 500       |
| 7. Prepayment to Suppliers of Miscellaneous              |           |
|    Services .....................................        | 57,500    |
| 8. Payment of Property Taxes .....................       | 1,200     |
| 9. Payment of Dividends ..........................       | 2,000     |
|                                                          | $180,200  |
| Increase in Cash Balance for Year .................      | $ 27,800  |

Prepare a combined statement of income and retained earnings for Year 2. (*Hint:* Set up T-accounts for each of the balance sheet accounts listed in the trial balance and enter the amounts shown as of January 1, Year 2, and December 31, Year 2. Starting with the cash receipts and disbursements for the year, reconstruct the transactions that took place during the year and enter them in the appropriate T-accounts. The effect of earnings activities for the year is already reflected in the Retained Earnings account, because the trial balance shown is after closing entries.)

# Chapter 4  Income Statement: Extensions of the Accrual Concept ⎯⎯⎯⎯

Chapter 3 points out that over sufficiently long time periods, accounting income is equal *in amount* to cash in less cash out. Most business firms, however, do not recognize revenue when cash is received or recognize expenses when cash is disbursed. Instead, they use the accrual basis of accounting. The two distinguishing features of the accrual basis are the following:

1. Revenue is recognized when all (or a substantial portion) of the services to be provided have been performed and when cash, a receivable, or some other asset whose cash equivalent value can be measured objectively has been received.

2. Expenses are recognized in the period when related revenues are recognized, or, if not associated with a particular revenue stream, expenses are recognized in the period when goods or services are consumed in operations.

For most merchandising firms, revenue is recognized in the period when goods are sold. Expenses are then matched either directly with the revenue or with the period when goods or services are consumed. This chapter explores the application of the accrual concept to other types of businesses: firms involved in manufacturing, firms involved in long-term contract activities, and firms selling goods on an installment basis.

## Accrual Basis for Manufacturers ⎯⎯⎯⎯⎯⎯⎯⎯⎯⎯⎯⎯⎯⎯⎯⎯⎯⎯⎯

A manufacturing firm incurs various costs in changing the physical form of the goods it produces. Figure 4.1 depicts the operating process for a typical manufacturing firm. A firm acquires productive facilities (plant and equipment) to provide capacity to manufacture goods. Raw materials for use in production are also acquired. Converting raw materials into a salable product requires labor and other manufacturing services (for example, utilities, insurance, taxes, and depreciation on production facilities) during the period of production. The finished product is held

**Figure 4.1** _____

**Operating Process for Manufacturing Firm**

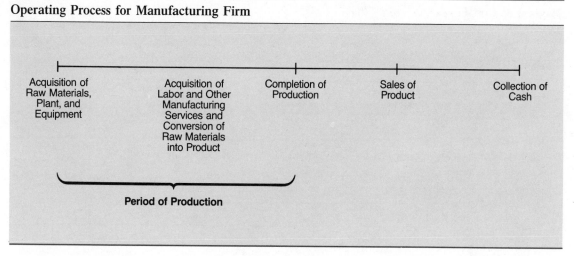

in inventory until sold. When the good is sold, either cash is collected or a receivable from the customer arises.

Most manufacturing firms recognize revenue at the time goods are sold. At this time, the production activity has been completed, a customer has been identified and a selling price agreed upon, and an assessment of the customer's credit standing provides a reasonable basis for estimating the present value of the amount of cash that will be collected.

## Accounting for Manufacturing Costs

As was noted in Chapter 3, a merchandising firm acquires inventory items in finished form ready for sale. The acquisition cost of these items remains in the asset account, Merchandise Inventory, until the units are sold. At the time of sale, the cost of the items sold is transferred from the asset account Merchandise Inventory to the expense account Cost of Goods Sold.

A manufacturing firm, in contrast, incurs various costs in converting raw materials into finished products. These manufacturing costs are generally classified into *direct material* (or raw material), *direct labor,* and *manufacturing overhead*. Manufacturing overhead includes a variety of indirect costs (depreciation, insurance, and taxes on manufacturing facilities, supervisory labor, and supplies for factory equipment) that provide a firm with productive capacity. Until the units are sold and revenue is recognized, manufacturing costs are treated as *product costs* — assets — and accumulated in various inventory accounts.

A manufacturing firm, like a merchandising firm, also incurs various selling costs (commissions for the sales staff, depreciation, insurance and taxes on the sales staff's automobiles) and administrative costs (salary of president, depreciation on computer facilities). Selling and administrative costs are treated as *period expenses*

**Figure 4.2** _____

**Diagram of Cost Flows**

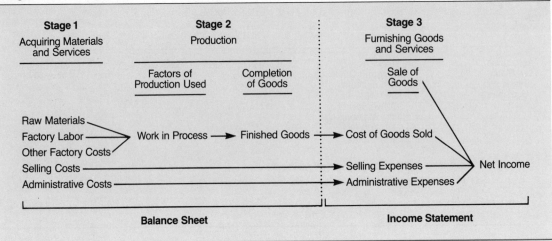

by both merchandising and manufacturing firms. Figure 4.2 summarizes the nature and *flow of costs* for a manufacturing firm.

Separate inventory accounts are maintained by a manufacturing firm for product costs incurred at various stages of completion. The *Raw Materials Inventory* account includes the cost of raw materials purchased but not yet transferred to production. The balance in the Raw Materials Inventory account indicates the cost of raw materials on hand in the raw materials storeroom or warehouse. When raw materials are issued to producing departments, the cost of the materials is transferred from the Raw Materials Inventory account to the *Work-in-Process Inventory* account, which accumulates the costs incurred in producing units during the period. The Work-in-Process Inventory account is debited for the cost of raw materials transferred from the raw materials storeroom, the cost of direct labor services used, and the manufacturing overhead costs incurred; the account is credited for the total manufacturing cost of units completed in the factory and transferred to the finished goods storeroom. The *Finished Goods Inventory* account includes the total manufacturing cost of units completed but not yet sold. The cost of units sold during the period is transferred from the Finished Goods Inventory account to the Cost-of-Goods-Sold expense account. Figure 4.3 on page 134 shows the flow of manufacturing costs through the various inventory and other accounts.

## Illustration of the Accounting Process for a Manufacturing Firm

The accounting process for a manufacturing firm is illustrated with information about the operations of the Moon Manufacturing Company. The company was formed on January 1 with the issuance of 10,000 shares of $10-par value common stock for $30 per share. Transactions during January are described, and the appropriate journal entries are provided, as follows:

**1.** A building costing $200,000 and equipment costing $50,000 are acquired for cash.

| | | |
|---|---|---|
| (1) Building (A)........................................ | 200,000 | |
|     Equipment (A) ...................................... | 50,000 | |
|         Cash (A) ....................................... | | 250,000 |

**2.** Raw materials costing $25,000 are purchased on account.

| | | |
|---|---|---|
| (2) Raw Materials Inventory (A) ........................... | 25,000 | |
|     Accounts Payable (L)................................ | | 25,000 |

**3.** Raw materials costing $20,000 are issued to producing departments.

| | | |
|---|---|---|
| (3) Work-in-Process Inventory (A) ......................... | 20,000 | |
|     Raw Materials Inventory (A) .......................... | | 20,000 |

**4.** The total payroll for January is $60,000. Of this amount, $40,000 is paid to factory workers and $20,000 is paid to selling and administrative personnel.

| | | |
|---|---|---|
| (4) Work-in-Process Inventory (A) ......................... | 40,000 | |
|     Salaries Expense (SE)................................ | 20,000 | |
|         Cash (A) ....................................... | | 60,000 |

Recall that nonmanufacturing costs are recorded as expenses of the period in which the services are consumed, because these costs rarely create assets with future benefits. Journal entry (4) [as well as entries (5) and (6) that follow] illustrates the difference between the recording of a product cost and a period expense.

**5.** The expenditures for utilities during January are $1,200. Of this amount, $1,000 is attributable to manufacturing and $200 to selling and administrative activities.

| | | |
|---|---|---|
| (5) Work-in-Process Inventory (A) ......................... | 1,000 | |
|     Utilities Expense (SE) ............................... | 200 | |
|         Cash (A) ....................................... | | 1,200 |

**Figure 4.3**
**Flow of Manufacturing Costs through the Accounts**

| Raw Materials Inventory (A) | | Work-In-Process Inventory (A) | | Finished Goods Inventory (A) | | Cost of Goods Sold (SE) |
|---|---|---|---|---|---|---|
| Cost of Raw Materials Purchased | Raw Materials Costs Incurred in Manufacturing → | Raw Materials Costs Incurred in Manufacturing | Manufacturing Cost of Units Completed and Transferred to Storeroom → | Manufacturing Cost of Units Transferred from Factory → | Manufacturing Cost of Units Sold → | Manufacturing Cost of Units Sold |

**Cash (A) or Wages Payable (L)**

Direct Labor Costs Incurred in Manufacturing → | Direct Labor Costs Incurred in Manufacturing

**Cash (A), Accumulated Depreciation (XA), Other Accounts**

Overhead Costs Incurred in Manufacturing → | Overhead Costs Incurred in Manufacturing

6. Depreciation on building and equipment during January is as follows: factory, $8,000; selling and administrative, $2,000.

| (6) Work-in-Process Inventory (A) ......................... | 8,000 | |
|---|---|---|
| Depreciation Expense (SE)............................. | 2,000 | |
| Accumulated Depreciation (XA) ....................... | | 10,000 |

7. The manufacturing cost of units completed during January and transferred to the finished goods storeroom is $48,500.

| (7) Finished Goods Inventory (A)......................... | 48,500 | |
|---|---|---|
| Work-in-Process Inventory (A) ...................... | | 48,500 |

8. Sales during January total $75,000, of which $25,000 is on account.

| (8) Cash (A) .............................................. | 50,000 | |
|---|---|---|
| Accounts Receivable (A) .............................. | 25,000 | |
| Sales Revenue (SE)................................... | | 75,000 |

9. The cost of the goods sold during January is $42,600.

| (9) Cost of Goods Sold (SE) ............................. | 42,600 | |
|---|---|---|
| Finished Goods Inventory (A)......................... | | 42,600 |

Exhibit 4.1 shows how the various manufacturing and other costs incurred flow through the accounts. Exhibit 4.2 presents an income statement for Moon Manufacturing Company for January.

## Summary of the Accounting for Manufacturing Operations

The accounting procedures for the selling and administrative costs of manufacturing firms resemble those for merchandising firms. These costs are expenses of the period in which services are consumed. The accounting procedures for a manufacturing firm differ from those of a merchandising firm primarily in the treatment of inventories. A manufacturing firm incurs various costs in transforming raw materials into finished products. Until the units produced are sold, manufacturing costs are accumulated in inventory accounts — the Work-in-Process Inventory account or the Finished Goods Inventory account — depending on the stage of completion of each unit being produced. Product costs are therefore debited to inventory (asset) accounts until the time of sale.

Exhibit 4.1 _____

## MOON MANUFACTURING COMPANY
T-Accounts Showing Transactions during January

| Raw Materials Inventory (A) | |
|---|---|
| (2) 25,000 | 20,000 (3) ▶──────── |
| | |
| Bal. 1/31   5,000 | |

| Work-in-Process Inventory (A) | |
|---|---|
| ▶(3) 20,000 | 48,500 (7) ▶──── |
| (4) 40,000 | |
| (5)  1,000 | |
| (6)  8,000 | |
| Bal. 1/31   20,500 | |

| Finished Goods Inventory (A) | |
|---|---|
| ▶(7) 48,500 | 42,600 (9) ▶──────── |
| Bal. 1/31   5,900 | |

| Cost of Goods Sold (SE) | |
|---|---|
| ▶(9) 42,600 | |
| Bal. 1/31   42,600 | |

| Cash (A) | |
|---|---|
| Bal. 1/1   300,000 | 250,000 (1) |
| (8)  50,000 | 60,000 (4) |
| | 1,200 (5) |
| Bal. 1/31   38,800 | |

| Accounts Receivable (A) | |
|---|---|
| (8) 25,000 | |
| Bal. 1/31   25,000 | |

| Building (A) | |
|---|---|
| (1) 200,000 | |
| Bal. 1/31   200,000 | |

| Equipment (A) | |
|---|---|
| (1) 50,000 | |
| Bal. 1/31   50,000 | |

| Accumulated Depreciation (XA) | |
|---|---|
| | 10,000 (6) |
| | 10,000   Bal. 1/31 |

| Salaries Expense (SE) | |
|---|---|
| (4) 20,000 | |
| Bal. 1/31   20,000 | |

| Sales Revenue (SE) | |
|---|---|
| | 75,000 (8) |
| | 75,000   Bal. 1/31 |

| Accounts Payable (L) | |
|---|---|
| | 25,000 (2) |
| | 25,000   Bal. 1/31 |

| Utilities Expense (SE) | |
|---|---|
| (5)   200 | |
| Bal. 1/31   200 | |

| Depreciation Expense (SE) | |
|---|---|
| (6)  2,000 | |
| Bal. 1/31   2,000 | |

Exhibit 4.2 ⎯⎯⎯⎯⎯⎯⎯⎯⎯⎯⎯⎯⎯⎯⎯⎯⎯⎯⎯⎯⎯⎯⎯⎯⎯
**MOON MANUFACTURING COMPANY**
**Income Statement for the Month of January**

| | | |
|---|---:|---:|
| Sales Revenue . . . . . . . . . . . . . . . . . . . . . . . . . . . . . . . . . . . . . . . . . . . . . . . . | | $75,000 |
| Less Expenses: | | |
|    Cost of Goods Sold . . . . . . . . . . . . . . . . . . . . . . . . . . . . . . . . . . . . . . | $42,600 | |
|    Salaries Expense . . . . . . . . . . . . . . . . . . . . . . . . . . . . . . . . . . . . . . . . | 20,000 | |
|    Utilities Expense . . . . . . . . . . . . . . . . . . . . . . . . . . . . . . . . . . . . . . . . . | 200 | |
|    Depreciation Expense . . . . . . . . . . . . . . . . . . . . . . . . . . . . . . . . . . . . . | 2,000 | |
|      Total Expenses . . . . . . . . . . . . . . . . . . . . . . . . . . . . . . . . . . . . . . . | | 64,800 |
| Net Income . . . . . . . . . . . . . . . . . . . . . . . . . . . . . . . . . . . . . . . . . . . . . . . . | | $10,200 |

# Accrual Basis for Long-Term Contractors ⎯⎯⎯⎯⎯⎯

The operating process for a long-term contractor (for example, building construction, shipbuilding) differs from that of a manufacturing firm (depicted in Figure 4.1) in three important respects:

1. The period of construction (production) may span several accounting periods.

2. A customer is identified and a contract price agreed upon in advance (or at least in the early stages of construction).

3. Periodic payments of the contract price are often made by the buyer as work progresses.

The criteria for the recognition of revenue from long-term contracts are often satisfied during the period of construction. The existence of a contract indicates that a buyer has been identified and a price agreed upon. Either cash is collected in advance or an assessment of the customer's credit standing leads to a reasonable expectation that the contract price will be received in cash after construction is completed. Although future services required on these long-term construction contracts can be substantial at any given time, the costs to be incurred in providing these services can often be estimated with reasonable precision. In agreeing to a contract price, the firm must have some confidence in its estimates of the total costs to be incurred on the contract.

When the criteria for revenue recognition are met as construction progresses, revenue is usually recognized during the period of construction using the *percentage-of-completion method*. Under the percentage-of-completion method, a portion of the total contract price, based on the degree of completion of the work during the period, is recognized as revenue for the period. This proportion is based either on engineers' or architects' estimates of the degree of completion or on the ratio of costs incurred to date to the total expected costs for the contract. The actual schedule of cash collections is *not* significant for the revenue recognition process when the percentage-of-completion method is used. Even if all of the contract price is to be collected at completion of construction, the percentage-of-completion method may still be used as long as reasonable estimates of the amount of cash to be collected and of the costs remaining to be incurred can be made as construction progresses.

As portions of the contract price are recognized as revenues, corresponding proportions of the total estimated costs of the contract are recognized as expenses. Thus the percentage-of-completion method follows the accrual basis of accounting, because expenses are matched with related revenues.

To illustrate the percentage-of-completion method, assume that a firm agrees to construct a bridge for $5,000,000. Estimated costs are as follows: Year 1, $1,500,000; Year 2, $2,000,000; and Year 3, $500,000. Thus the expected profit from the contract is $1,000,000 (= $5,000,000 − $1,500,000 − $2,000,000 − $500,000).

Assuming that the degree of completion is based on the percentage of total costs incurred and that actual costs are incurred as anticipated, revenue and expense from the contract are as follows:

| Year | Degree of Completion | Revenue | Expense | Profit |
|------|---------------------|---------|---------|--------|
| 1 ....... | $1,500,000/$4,000,000 = 37.5% | $1,875,000 | $1,500,000 | $  375,000 |
| 2 ....... | $2,000,000/$4,000,000 = 50.0% | 2,500,000 | 2,000,000 | 500,000 |
| 3 ....... | $500,000/$4,000,000 = 12.5% | 625,000 | 500,000 | 125,000 |
|  |  | $5,000,000 | $4,000,000 | $1,000,000 |

Some firms involved with construction contracts postpone the recognition of revenue until the construction project and the sale are completed. This method is the same as the *completed sale* basis but is often referred to as the *completed contract method* of recognizing revenue. If the completed contract method were used in the previous example, no revenue or expense from the contract would be recognized during Year 1 or Year 2. In Year 3, contract revenue of $5,000,000 and contract expenses of $4,000,000 would be recognized in measuring net income. Note that total income, or profit, is $1,000,000 under both the percentage-of-completion and completed contract methods, equal to cash in of $5,000,000 less cash out of $4,000,000.

In some cases the completed contract method is used because the contracts are of such short duration (such as a few months) that earnings reported with the percentage-of-completion method and the completed contract method are not significantly different. In these cases the completed contract method is used because it is generally easier to implement. Firms use the completed contract method in situations when a specific buyer has not been obtained while construction is progressing, as is sometimes the case in the construction of residential housing. In these cases future selling efforts are required, and substantial uncertainty may exist regarding the contract price that will ultimately be established and the amount of cash that will be received.

The primary reason that a contractor would not use the percentage-of-completion method when a contract exists is that there is substantial uncertainty regarding the total costs to be incurred in carrying out the project. If total costs cannot be reasonably estimated, the percentage of total costs incurred by a given date also cannot be estimated, and the percentage of services already rendered (revenue) cannot be measured.

# Accrual Basis When Cash Collectibility Is Uncertain

Occasionally, estimating the amount of cash or cash equivalent value of other assets that will be received from customers is difficult. This may be because the future financial condition of the buyer is highly uncertain or because the buyer may have the right to return the items purchased, thereby avoiding making payments. Therefore, an objective measure of the present value of the cash to be received cannot be made at the time of the sale. Under such circumstances, revenue is recognized at the time of cash collection using either the installment method or the cost-recovery-first method. Unlike the cash method of accounting, however, there is an attempt to match expenses with revenues.

## Installment Method

Under the *installment method,* revenue is recognized as parts of the selling price are collected in cash. At the same time, corresponding parts of the cost of the good or service sold are recognized as expenses. For example, assume that merchandise costing $60 is sold for $100. The buyer agrees to pay (ignoring interest) $20 per month for 5 months. Under the installment method, revenue of $20 is recognized each month as cash is received. Likewise, cost of goods sold is $12 (= $20/ $100 × $60) each month. By the end of 5 months, total income of $40 [= 5 × ($20 − $12)] would be recognized.

The installment method is sometimes used by land development companies, which typically sell undeveloped land and promise to develop it over several future years. The buyer makes a nominal down payment and agrees to pay the remainder of the purchase price in installments over 10, 20, or more years. In these cases, future development of the land is a significant aspect of the earnings process. Also, substantial uncertainty often exists as to the ultimate collectibility of the installment notes, particularly those not due until several years in the future. The customer can always elect to stop making payments, losing the right to own the land.

## Cost-Recovery-First Method

Under circumstances where there is substantial uncertainty about cash collection, the *cost-recovery-first method* of income recognition can also be used. When this method is used, costs of generating revenues are matched dollar for dollar with cash receipts until all such costs are recovered. Revenues and expenses are equal in each period until all costs are recovered. Only when cumulative cash receipts exceed total costs will profit (that is, revenue without any matching expenses) be shown in the income statement.

To illustrate the cost-recovery-first method, refer to the previous example relating to the sale of merchandise for $100. During the first 3 months, revenue of $20 and expenses of $20 would be recognized. By the end of the third month, cumulative cash receipts of $60 would be exactly equal to the cost of the merchandise sold. During the fourth and fifth months, revenue of $20 per month would be recognized but without an offsetting expense. For the 5 months as a whole, total income of $40 would again be recognized (equal to cash in of $100 less cash out of $60) but in a different pattern than under the installment method.

## Use of Installment and Cost-Recovery-First Methods

Generally accepted accounting principles permit the installment method and the cost-recovery-first method to be used only when substantial uncertainty exists about cash collection. For most sales of goods and services, past experience and an assessment of customers' credit standings provide a sufficient basis for estimating the amount of cash to be received. If a reasonable estimate of the amount of cash to be received can be made, the installment method and the cost-recovery-first method are not allowed for financial reporting, and revenue must be recognized no later than the time of sale.[1]

The installment method is allowed for income tax reporting under some circumstances, even when cash collections are assured. Manufacturing firms selling on extended payment plans often use the installment method for income tax reporting (while recognizing revenue at the time of sale for financial reporting). The cost-recovery-first method is sometimes used in tax reporting but only in special circumstances, such as for pension benefits received.

# Recognition of Revenue between Purchase and Sale ——

The period between the acquisition or production of inventory items and the sale of the items to customers is referred to as a *holding period*. The current market prices of these assets could change during this holding period while the items are held in inventory. Such changes are described as *unrealized holding gains and losses,* because transactions or exchanges have not taken place.

Unrealized holding gains could be recognized as they occur. Accountants typically wait, however, until the asset is sold or exchanged in an arm's-length transaction before recognizing any gain. At that time, an inflow of net assets subject to objective measurement takes place. Because the accountant assumes that the firm is a going concern, the unrealized gain will eventually be recognized as revenue in the ordinary course of business in a future period. The recognition of revenue and the valuation of assets are therefore closely associated. Nonmonetary assets are typically stated at acquisition cost until sold. At the time of sale, an inflow of net assets occurs (for example, cash, accounts receivable), and revenue reflecting the previously unreported unrealized gain is recognized. This treatment of unrealized holding gains has the effect of shifting income from periods when the asset is held and the market value increases to the later period of sale. The longer the holding period

---

[1]Accounting Principles Board, *Opinion No. 10,* ''Omnibus Opinion—1966,'' par. 12, footnote 8. When cash collection is sufficiently uncertain that either of these methods is allowed by generally accepted accounting principles, the cost-recovery-first method seems to reflect more accurately the substance of the uncertainty. The installment method assumes that all cash will eventually be received or, if not, that when payments cease, the goods can be repossessed while still having substantial value.

(as, for example, land held for several decades), the more likely reported income is to be shifted to later periods.

Current accounting practices do not treat all unrealized holding losses in the same way as unrealized holding gains. If the current market prices of inventory items or marketable securities decrease below acquisition cost during the holding period, the asset is usually written down with a credit to the asset account. The matching debit recognizes the unrealized loss in measuring net income in the period of price decline. This treatment of losses rests on the convention of using *conservatism* in reporting earnings. Considering the estimates and predictions required in measuring revenues and expenses, some accountants prefer to provide a conservative measure of earnings so that statement users will not be misled into thinking the firm is doing better than it really is.

The inconsistent treatment of unrealized gains and unrealized losses does not seem warranted. The arguments used against recognizing unrealized gains apply equally well to unrealized losses. If gains cannot be measured objectively before a sale, how can losses be measured before the sale? If losses can be measured objectively before the sale, why cannot gains? The accounting treatment of unrealized holding gains and losses is considered further in Chapters 7, 8, and 13.

# Summary Illustration of Income Recognition Methods

Exhibit 4.3 illustrates various methods of income recognition discussed in Chapters 3 and 4. The illustration relates to a contract for the construction of a bridge for $12 million. The expected and actual pattern of cash receipts and disbursements under the contract is as follows:

| Period | Expected and Actual Cash Receipts | Expected and Actual Cash Expenditures |
|---|---|---|
| 1 | $ 1,000,000 | $1,600,000 |
| 2 | 1,000,000 | 4,000,000 |
| 3 | 2,000,000 | 4,000,000 |
| 4 | 4,000,000 | — |
| 5 | 4,000,000 | — |
| Total | $12,000,000 | $9,600,000 |

The bridge was completed in Period 3. Exhibit 4.3 indicates the revenues, expenses, and income recognized during each period under the contract using the cash basis of accounting, the percentage-of-completion method, the completed contract (completed sale) method, the installment method, and the cost-recovery-first method. Not all of the five methods of income recognition could be justified for financial reporting; they are presented merely for illustrative purposes. Note that the total revenues, expenses, and income recognized for the 5 years are the same for all

## Exhibit 4.3 ————————————————————————————

## Comprehensive Illustration of Revenue and Expense Recognition
(all dollar amounts in thousands)

| Period | Cash Basis of Accounting[a] | | |
|---|---|---|---|
| | Revenue | Expense | Income |
| 1 ............................................. | $ 1,000 | $1,600 | $ (600) |
| 2 ............................................. | 1,000 | 4,000 | (3,000) |
| 3 ............................................. | 2,000 | 4,000 | (2,000) |
| 4 ............................................. | 4,000 | — | 4,000 |
| 5 ............................................. | 4,000 | — | 4,000 |
| Total ........................................ | $12,000 | $9,600 | $2,400 |

| Period | Percentage-of-Completion Method | | | Completed Contract Method | | |
|---|---|---|---|---|---|---|
| | Revenue | Expense | Income | Revenue | Expense | Income |
| 1 ........ | $ 2,000[d] | $1,600 | $ 400 | $ — | $ — | $ — |
| 2 ........ | 5,000[e] | 4,000 | 1,000 | — | — | — |
| 3 ........ | 5,000[e] | 4,000 | 1,000 | 12,000 | 9,600 | 2,400 |
| 4 ........ | — | — | — | — | — | — |
| 5 ........ | — | — | — | — | — | — |
| Total ... | $12,000 | $9,600 | $2,400 | $12,000 | $9,600 | $2,400 |

| Period | Installment Method[b] | | | Cost-Recovery-First Method[c] | | |
|---|---|---|---|---|---|---|
| | Revenue | Expense | Income | Revenue | Expense | Income |
| 1 ........ | $ 1,000 | $ 800[f] | $ 200 | $ 1,000 | $1,000 | $ 0 |
| 2 ........ | 1,000 | 800[f] | 200 | 1,000 | 1,000 | 0 |
| 3 ........ | 2,000 | 1,600[g] | 400 | 2,000 | 2,000 | 0 |
| 4 ........ | 4,000 | 3,200[h] | 800 | 4,000 | 4,000 | 0 |
| 5 ........ | 4,000 | 3,200[h] | 800 | 4,000 | 1,600 | 2,400 |
| Total ... | $12,000 | $9,600 | $2,400 | $12,000 | $9,600 | $2,400 |

[a]The cash basis is not allowed for tax or financial reporting if inventories are a material factor in generating income.

[b]The installment method is allowed for financial reporting only if extreme uncertainty exists as to the amount of cash to be collected from customers. Its use for tax purposes is independent of the collectibility of cash.

[c]The cost-recovery-first method is allowed for financial reporting only if extreme uncertainty exists as to the amount of cash to be collected from customers. It is sometimes used for tax purposes.

[d]$1,600/$9,600 × $12,000.

[e]$4,000/$9,600 × $12,000.

[f]$1,000/$12,000 × $9,600.

[g]$2,000/$12,000 × $9,600.

[h]$4,000/$12,000 × $9,600.

methods. In historical cost accounting over sufficiently long time periods, income is equal to cash inflows less cash outflows. The time patterns of annual income differ, however, depending on the accounting method.

## Format and Classification within the Income Statement _____

The income statement might contain some or all of the following sections or categories, depending on the nature of the firm's income for the period:

**1.** Income from continuing operations.

**2.** Income, gains, and losses from discontinued operations.

**3.** Adjustments for changes in accounting principles.

**4.** Extraordinary gains and losses.

**5.** Earnings per share.

The majority of income statements include only the first and fifth sections. The other sections are added if necessary.

**Income from Continuing Operations**  Revenues, gains, expenses, and losses from the continuing areas of business activity of a firm appear in the first section of the income statement, which is titled *Income from Continuing Operations*.

**Income, Gains, and Losses from Discontinued Operations**  If a firm sells a major division or segment of its business during the year or contemplates its sale within a short time after the end of the accounting period, any income, gains, and losses related to that segment must be disclosed separately from ordinary continuing operations in a section of the income statement titled *Income, Gains, and Losses from Discontinued Operations.*[2] This section follows the section presenting Income from Continuing Operations.

**Adjustments for Changes in Accounting Principles**  A firm that changes its principles (or methods) of accounting during the period is required in some cases to disclose the effects of the change on current and previous years' net income.[3] This information is presented in a separate section, titled *Adjustments for Changes in Accounting Principles,* after Income, Gains, and Losses from Discontinued Operations.

---

[2]Accounting Principles Board, *Opinion No. 30,* "Reporting the Results of Operations," 1973.
[3]Accounting Principles Board, *Opinion No. 20,* "Accounting Changes," 1971.

**Extraordinary Gains and Losses**  A separate section of the income statement presents extraordinary gains and losses. For an item to be extraordinary, it must generally meet both of the following criteria:

**1.** It is unusual in nature.

**2.** It is infrequent in occurrence.[4]

An example of an item likely to be extraordinary for most firms would be a loss from expropriation or confiscation of assets by a foreign government. Such items are likely to be rare. Since 1973, when Accounting Principles Board *Opinion No. 30* was issued, extraordinary items have seldom been seen in published annual reports (except for gains or losses on bond retirements,[5] which are discussed in Chapter 10).

**Earnings per Share**  Earnings-per-share data must be shown by publicly held firms in the body of the income statement to receive an unqualified accountant's opinion.[6] Earnings per common share is conventionally calculated by dividing net income minus preferred stock dividends by the average number of outstanding common shares during the accounting period. For example, assume that a firm had net income of $500,000 during the year. Dividends declared and paid on outstanding preferred stock were $100,000. The average number of shares of outstanding common stock during the year was 1 million shares. Earnings per common share would be $.40 [= ($500,000 − $100,000)/1,000,000].

If a firm has securities outstanding that can be converted into common stock (for example, convertible bonds) or exchanged for common stock (for example, stock options), it may be required to present two sets of earnings-per-share amounts — *primary earnings per share* and *fully diluted earnings per share*.[7] Chapter 6 discusses the calculation of primary and fully diluted earnings per share.

# Problem 1 for Self-Study _____

The following data relate to the manufacturing activities of the Haskell Corporation during March.

|  | March 1 | March 31 |
|---|---|---|
| Raw Materials Inventory | $42,400 | $ 46,900 |
| Work-in-Process Inventory | 75,800 | 63,200 |
| Finished Goods Inventory | 44,200 | 46,300 |
| **Factory Costs Incurred during the Month:** | | |
| Raw Materials Purchased | | $ 60,700 |
| Labor Services Received | | 137,900 |

---

[4]Accounting Principles Board, *Opinion No. 30.*

[5]Financial Accounting Standards Board, *Statement of Financial Accounting Standards No. 4,* "Reporting Gains and Losses from Extinguishment of Debt," 1975.

[6]Accounting Principles Board, *Opinion No. 15,* "Earnings per Share," 1969.

[7]Accounting Principles Board, *Opinion No. 15.*

| | | |
|---|---|---:|
| Heat, Light, and Power...................................... | | 1,260 |
| Rent .................................................... | | 4,100 |
| **Expirations of Previous Factory Acquisitions and Prepayments:** | | |
| Depreciation of Factory Equipment ......................... | $ | 1,800 |
| Prepaid Insurance Expired................................. | | 1,440 |
| **Other Data Relating to the Month:** | | |
| Sales.................................................... | | $400,000 |
| Selling and Administrative Expenses......................... | | 125,000 |

**a.**  Calculate the cost of raw materials used during March.

**b.**  Calculate the cost of units completed during March and transferred to the finished goods storeroom.

**c.**  Calculate the cost of goods sold during March.

**d.**  Calculate income before taxes for March.

## Suggested Solution

The transactions and events relating to manufacturing activities are shown in the appropriate T-accounts in Exhibit 4.4.

**Exhibit 4.4** _____

## HASKELL CORPORATION
## T-Accounts and Transactions

| Raw Materials Inventory | | | |
|---|---|---|---|
| Bal. | 42,400 | | |
| (1) | 60,700 | 56,200 | (2)ᵃ |
| Bal. | 46,900 | | |

| Finished Goods Inventory | | | |
|---|---|---|---|
| Bal. | 44,200 | | |
| (8) | 215,300 | 213,200 | (9)ᵃ |
| Bal. | 46,300 | | |

| Cash or Various Liabilities | | |
|---|---|---|
| | 60,700 | (1) |
| | 137,900 | (3) |
| | 1,260 | (4) |
| | 4,100 | (5) |

| Work-in-Process Inventory | | | |
|---|---|---|---|
| Bal. | 75,800 | | |
| (2) | 56,200 | 215,300 | (8)ᵃ |
| (3) | 137,900 | | |
| (4) | 1,260 | | |
| (5) | 4,100 | | |
| (6) | 1,800 | | |
| (7) | 1,440 | | |
| Bal. | 63,200 | | |

| Cost of Goods Sold | |
|---|---|
| (9) | 213,200 |

| Prepaid Insurance | | |
|---|---|---|
| | 1,440 | (7) |

| Accumulated Depreciation | | |
|---|---|---|
| | 1,800 | (6) |

ᵃAmounts calculated by plugging.

a. The cost of raw materials used is $56,200.

b. The cost of units completed during March is $215,300.

c. The cost of units sold during March is $213,200.

d. Income before taxes is $61,800 (= $400,000 − $213,200 − $125,000).

## Problem 2 for Self-Study ——————————————————

The Brennan Construction Company contracted on May 15, Year 2, to build a bridge for the city for $4,500,000. Brennan estimated that the cost of constructing the bridge would be $3,600,000. Brennan incurred $1,200,000 in construction costs during Year 2, $2,000,000 during Year 3, and $400,000 during Year 4 in completing the bridge. The city paid $1,000,000 during Year 2, $1,500,000 during Year 3, and the remaining $2,000,000 of the contract price at the time the bridge was completed and approved in Year 4.

a. Calculate Brennan's net income (revenue less expenses) on the contract during Year 2, Year 3, and Year 4, assuming that the percentage-of-completion method is used.

b. Repeat part a, assuming that the completed contract method is used.

c. Repeat part a, assuming that the installment method is used.

d. Repeat part a, assuming that the cost-recovery-first method is used.

### Suggested Solution

a. Percentage-of-completion method:

| Year | Incremental Percentage Complete | Revenue Recognized | Expenses Recognized | Net Income |
|------|---------------------------------|--------------------|--------------------|------------|
| 2 ............... | 12/36 ( .333) | $1,500,000 | $1,200,000 | $300,000 |
| 3 ............... | 20/36 ( .556) | 2,500,000 | 2,000,000 | 500,000 |
| 4 ............... | 4/36 ( .111) | 500,000 | 400,000 | 100,000 |
| Total .......... | 36/36 (1.000) | $4,500,000 | $3,600,000 | $900,000 |

b. Completed contract method:

| Year | Revenue Recognized | Expenses Recognized | Net Income |
|------|--------------------|--------------------|------------|
| 2 .......... | $ 0 | $ 0 | $ 0 |
| 3 .......... | 0 | 0 | 0 |
| 4 .......... | 4,500,000 | 3,600,000 | 900,000 |
| Total ....... | $4,500,000 | $3,600,000 | $900,000 |

**c.** Installment method:

| Year | Cash Collected (= revenue) | Fraction of Cash Collected | Expenses (= fraction × total cost) | Net Income |
|------|------|------|------|------|
| 2 ................. | $1,000,000 | 2/9 | $  800,000 | $200,000 |
| 3 ................. | 1,500,000 | 3/9 | 1,200,000 | 300,000 |
| 4 ................. | 2,000,000 | 4/9 | 1,600,000 | 400,000 |
| Total ............ | $4,500,000 | 1.0 | $3,600,000 | $900,000 |

**d.** Cost-recovery-first method:

| Year | Cash Collected (= revenue) | Expenses Recognized | Net Income |
|------|------|------|------|
| 2 .......................... | $1,000,000 | $1,000,000 | $      0 |
| 3 .......................... | 1,500,000 | 1,500,000 | 0 |
| 4 .......................... | 2,000,000 | 1,100,000 | 900,000 |
| Total ..................... | $4,500,000 | $3,600,000 | $900,000 |

# Questions, Exercises, Problems, and Cases _____

## Questions

**1.** Review the meaning of the following concepts or terms discussed in this chapter.

- **a.** Direct material.
- **b.** Direct labor.
- **c.** Manufacturing overhead.
- **d.** Product cost.
- **e.** Period expense.
- **f.** Flow of costs.
- **g.** Raw materials inventory.
- **h.** Work-in-process inventory.
- **i.** Finished goods inventory.
- **j.** Percentage-of-completion method.
- **k.** Completed sales, or completed contract, method.
- **l.** Installment method.
- **m.** Cost-recovery-first method.
- **n.** Unrealized holding gain or loss.
- **o.** Conservatism.
- **p.** Income from continuing operations.
- **q.** Income, gains, and losses from discontinued operations.
- **r.** Adjustments for changes in accounting principles.
- **s.** Extraordinary gains and losses.
- **t.** Primary earnings per share.
- **u.** Fully diluted earnings per share.

**2.** "Depreciation on equipment may be a product cost or a period expense, depending on the type of equipment." Explain.

**3.** Compare and contrast the Merchandise Inventory account of a merchandising firm and the Finished Goods Inventory account of a manufacturing firm.

**4.** The percentage-of-completion method is often used by construction companies. Why isn't this method of income recognition used by a typical manufacturing firm?

5. Under both the installment method and the cost-recovery-first method, revenue is recognized when cash is received. Why, then, is the pattern of income (that is, revenues minus expenses) over time different under these two methods?

6. Compare and contrast the installment method and the cash basis of accounting.

7. "When the *total* amount of cash to be collected from a customer is highly uncertain, the cost-recovery-first method seems more appropriate than the installment method." Explain.

8. Economists typically define income as an increase in value, or wealth, while assets are held. Accountants typically recognize income when the criteria for revenue recognition are satisfied. Why does the accountants' approach to income recognition differ from that of the economists?

9. Why do income statements separate income relating to continuing operations from income relating to discontinued operations?

## Exercises

10. *Identifying product costs and period expenses*. Indicate whether each of the following types of wages and salaries is (1) a product cost or (2) a period expense:

    a. Cutting-machine operators.
    b. Delivery labor.
    c. Factory janitors.
    d. Factory payroll clerks.
    e. Factory superintendent.
    f. General office secretaries.
    g. Guards at factory gate.
    h. Inspectors in factory.
    i. Maintenance workers who service factory machinery.
    j. Night watch force at the factory.
    k. General office clerks.
    l. Operator of a lift truck in the shipping room.
    m. President of the firm.
    n. Sales manager.
    o. Shipping room workers.
    p. Sweepers who clean retail store.
    q. Traveling salespersons.

11. *Identifying product costs and period expenses*. Indicate whether each of the following types of materials and supplies is (1) a product cost or (2) a period expense:

    a. Cleaning lubricants for factory machines.
    b. Paper for central office computer.
    c. Glue used in assembling products.
    d. Supplies used by factory janitor.
    e. Gasoline used by salespersons.
    f. Sales promotion pamphlets distributed.
    g. Materials used in training production workers.

12. *Identifying product costs, period expenses, and assets*. Indicate whether each of the following costs is (1) a period expense, (2) a product cost, or (3) some other balance sheet account other than those for product costs.

    a. Office supplies used.
    b. Salary of the factory supervisor.
    c. Purchase of a fire insurance policy on the store building for the 3-year period beginning next month.

    **d.**  Expiration of 1 month's protection of the insurance in part **c.**

    **e.**  Property taxes for the current year on the factory building.

    **f.**  Wages of truck drivers who deliver finished goods to customers.

    **g.**  Wages of factory workers who install a new machine.

    **h.**  Wages of mechanics who repair and service factory machines.

    **i.**  Salary of the president of the company.

    **j.**  Depreciation of office equipment.

    **k.**  Factory supplies used.

**13.** *Raw materials inventory transactions.* Compute the missing item in each of the independent cases that follow.

|  | a | b | c | d |
|---|---|---|---|---|
| Raw Materials Inventory, Jan. 1 .......... | $ 15,000 | $ 76,900 | $ 28,700 | ? |
| Purchases of Raw Materials ............. | 297,000 | 696,000 | ? | $76,700 |
| Raw Materials Used ................... | 290,000 | ? | 467,300 | 71,700 |
| Raw Materials Inventory, Dec. 31 ........ | ? | 72,100 | 37,900 | 12,300 |

**14.** *Work-in-process inventory transactions.* Compute the missing item in each of the independent cases that follow.

|  | a | b | c | d |
|---|---|---|---|---|
| Work-in-Process Inventory, Jan. 1 ..... | $ 26,000 | $ 55,600 | $ 39,400 | ? |
| Raw Materials Used ................ | 290,000 | 700,800 | 467,300 | $ 71,700 |
| Direct Labor Costs................. | 260,000 | 675,800 | ? | 87,300 |
| Manufacturing Overhead Costs ....... | 180,000 | 267,900 | 136,900 | 42,900 |
| Cost of Units Completed ............ | 724,000 | ? | 1,206,600 | 193,400 |
| Work-in-Process Inventory, Dec. 31.... | ? | 72,300 | 35,900 | 41,700 |

**15.** *Finished goods inventory transactions.* Compute the missing item in each of the independent cases that follow.

|  | a | b | c | d |
|---|---|---|---|---|
| Finished Goods Inventory, Jan. 1 ... | $ 71,000 | $ 189,300 | $ 110,300 | ? |
| Cost of Units Completed .......... | 724,000 | 1,627,800 | ? | $193,400 |
| Cost of Units Sold ............... | 701,000 | ? | 1,197,900 | 187,200 |
| Finished Goods Inventory, Dec. 31 .. | ? | 179,600 | 119,000 | 22,100 |

**16.** *Income computation for a manufacturing firm.* The following data relate to a manufacturing firm for a period.

| | |
|---|---|
| Sales....................................................... | $250,000 |
| Cost of Units Completed ........................................ | 240,000 |
| Cost of Units Sold ............................................. | 210,000 |
| Selling and Administrative Expenses.................................. | 30,000 |

Compute net income for the period.

**17.** *Income computation for a manufacturing firm.* The following data relate to the United Manufacturing Corporation for the month of April.

|  | April 1 | April 30 |
|---|---|---|
| Raw Materials Inventory................................ | $0 | $10,000 |
| Work-in-Process Inventory .............................. | 0 | 25,000 |
| Finished Goods Inventory ............................... | 0 | 22,000 |

Manufacturing costs (direct material used, direct labor, and manufacturing overhead) incurred during April totaled $65,000. Sales revenue for April was $25,000, and selling and administrative expenses were $2,000.

Compute net income for April.

**18.** *Percentage-of-completion and completed contract methods of income recognition.* A construction company agreed to build a warehouse for $2,500,000. Expected and actual costs to construct the warehouse were as follows: Year 1, $600,000; Year 2, $1,000,000; and Year 3, $400,000. The warehouse was completed in Year 3.

Compute revenue, expense, and net income for Year 1, Year 2, and Year 3 using the percentage-of-completion method and the completed contract method.

**19.** *Installment and cost-recovery-first methods of income recognition.* A real estate firm sold a tract of land costing $80,000 to a manufacturing firm for $100,000. The manufacturing firm agreed to pay $25,000 per year for 4 years (plus interest).

Compute revenue, expense, and net income for each of the 4 years using the installment method and the cost-recovery-first method. Ignore interest.

## Problems and Cases

**20.** *Preparation of journal entries and income statement for a manufacturing firm.* Westside Products showed the following amounts in its inventory accounts on January 1.

| | |
|---|---|
| Raw Materials Inventory............................................. | $15,000 |
| Work-in-Process Inventory .......................................... | 65,000 |
| Finished Goods Inventory............................................ | 32,000 |

The following transactions occurred during January.
**(1)** Raw materials costing $28,500 were acquired on account.
**(2)** Raw materials costing $31,600 were issued to producing departments.
**(3)** Salaries and wages paid during January for services received during the month were as follows:

| | |
|---|---|
| Factory Workers............................................. | $46,900 |
| Sales Personnel............................................. | 14,300 |
| Administrative Officers ....................................... | 20,900 |

**(4)** Depreciation on buildings and equipment during January was as follows:

| | |
|---|---|
| Manufacturing Facilities ....................................... | $12,900 |
| Selling Facilities............................................. | 2,300 |
| Administrative Facilities ....................................... | 1,800 |

**(5)** Other operating costs incurred and paid in cash were as follows:

| | |
|---|---|
| Manufacturing............................................... | $15,600 |
| Selling .................................................... | 4,900 |
| Administrative............................................... | 3,700 |

**(6)** The cost of goods manufactured and transferred to the finished goods storeroom totaled $85,100.

**(7)** Sales on account during January totaled $150,000.

**(8)** A physical inventory taken on January 31 revealed a finished goods inventory of $35,200.

**a.** Present journal entries to record the transactions and events during January.

**b.** Prepare an income statement for Westside Products for January.

**21.** *Preparation of journal entries and an income statement for a manufacturing firm.* Southside Products showed the following amounts in its inventory accounts on January 1.

| | |
|---|---|
| Raw Materials Inventory ....................................... | $40,000 |
| Work-in-Process Inventory ..................................... | 96,000 |
| Finished Goods Inventory...................................... | 73,000 |

The following transactions occurred during January.

**(1)** Raw materials costing $122,700 were acquired on account.

**(2)** Raw materials costing $119,200 were issued to production.

**(3)** Salaries and wages paid during January for services received during the month were as follows:

| | |
|---|---|
| Factory Workers............................................... | $87,600 |
| Sales Personnel................................................ | 18,900 |
| Administrative Personnel....................................... | 27,400 |

**(4)** Depreciation on buildings and equipment during January was as follows:

| | |
|---|---|
| Manufacturing Facilities ....................................... | $14,700 |
| Selling Facilities.............................................. | 2,400 |
| Administrative Facilities ...................................... | 2,900 |

**(5)** Other operating costs incurred and paid in cash were as follows:

| | |
|---|---|
| Manufacturing................................................. | $18,200 |
| Selling ...................................................... | 7,300 |
| Administrative................................................ | 4,400 |

**(6)** The cost of goods completed and transferred to the finished goods store-room totaled $234,000.

**(7)** Sales on account during January totaled $325,000.

**(8)** A physical inventory taken on January 31 revealed a finished goods inventory of $68,000.

**a.** Present journal entries to record the transactions and events during January.

**b.** Prepare an income statement for Southside Products for January.

**22.** *Flow of manufacturing costs through the accounts.* The following data relate to the manufacturing activities of the Cornell Company during June.

| | June 1 | June 30 |
|---|---|---|
| Raw Materials Inventory............................... | $ 46,900 | $ 43,600 |
| Factory Supplies Inventory ........................... | 7,600 | 7,700 |
| Work-in-Process Inventory ............................ | 110,900 | 115,200 |
| Finished Goods Inventory ............................. | 76,700 | 71,400 |

Factory costs incurred during the month were as follows:

| | |
|---|---|
| Raw Materials Purchased.......................................... | $429,000 |
| Supplies Purchased............................................... | 22,300 |
| Labor Services Received .......................................... | 362,100 |
| Heat, Light, and Power............................................ | 10,300 |
| Insurance........................................................ | 4,200 |

Expirations of previous factory acquisitions and prepayments were as follows:

| | |
|---|---:|
| Depreciation on Factory Equipment..................................... | $36,900 |
| Prepaid Rent Expired ................................................ | 3,600 |

**a.** Calculate the cost of raw materials and factory supplies used during June.
**b.** Calculate the cost of units completed during June and transferred to the finished goods storeroom.
**c.** Calculate the cost of goods sold during June.

**23.** *Flow of manufacturing costs through the accounts.* The following data relate to the activities of Myers Corporation during April.

| | April 1 | April 30 |
|---|---:|---:|
| Raw Materials Inventory..................................... | $18,700 | $16,400 |
| Work-in-Process Inventory ................................. | 66,800 | 72,400 |
| Finished Goods Inventory ................................. | 32,900 | 29,800 |

Factory costs incurred during the month comprised the following:

| | |
|---|---:|
| Raw Materials Purchased......................................... | $87,300 |
| Labor Services Received ......................................... | 66,100 |
| Heat, Light and Power ........................................... | 2,700 |
| Depreciation...................................................... | 15,600 |

Other data relating to the month included the following:

| | |
|---|---:|
| Sales............................................................. | $250,000 |
| Selling and Administrative Expenses............................. | 38,100 |

**a.** Calculate the cost of raw materials used during April.
**b.** Calculate the cost of units completed during April and transferred to the finished goods storeroom.
**c.** Calculate net income for April.

**24.** *Flow of manufacturing costs through the accounts.* The following data relate to the manufacturing activities of Quilt Manufacturing Company during July.

| | July 1 | July 31 |
|---|---:|---:|
| Raw Materials Inventory..................................... | $ 56,300 | $ 62,900 |
| Factory Supplies Inventory ................................ | 15,900 | 13,700 |
| Work-in-Process Inventory ................................. | 297,200 | 257,200 |
| Finished Goods Inventory ................................. | 83,700 | 86,200 |

Factory costs incurred during the month were as follows:

| | |
|---|---:|
| Raw Materials Purchased. . . . . . . . . . . . . . . . . . . . . . . . . . . . . . . . . . . . . . . . | $ 42,700 |
| Supplies Purchased. . . . . . . . . . . . . . . . . . . . . . . . . . . . . . . . . . . . . . . . . . . . | 9,200 |
| Labor Services Received . . . . . . . . . . . . . . . . . . . . . . . . . . . . . . . . . . . . . . . . | 187,600 |
| Heat, Light, and Power. . . . . . . . . . . . . . . . . . . . . . . . . . . . . . . . . . . . . . . . . | 12,100 |
| Insurance . . . . . . . . . . . . . . . . . . . . . . . . . . . . . . . . . . . . . . . . . . . . . . . . . . . . | 6,000 |

Expirations of previous factory acquisitions and prepayments were as follows:

| | |
|---|---:|
| Depreciation on Factory Equipment . . . . . . . . . . . . . . . . . . . . . . . . . . . . . . . . | $15,000 |
| Prepaid Rent Expired . . . . . . . . . . . . . . . . . . . . . . . . . . . . . . . . . . . . . . . . . . . | 2,000 |

   **a.**  Calculate the cost of raw materials and factory supplies used during July.

   **b.**  Calculate the cost of units completed during July and transferred to the finished goods storeroom.

   **c.**  Calculate the cost of goods sold during July.

**25.** *Preparing T-account entries, adjusted trial balance, income statement, and balance sheet for a manufacturing firm.* On July 1, the accounts of the Tampa Manufacturing Company contained the following balances:

| Debit Balances | | Credit Balances | |
|---|---:|---|---:|
| Cash . . . . . . . . . . . . . . . . . . | $ 110,000 | Accumulated Depreciation | $ 30,000 |
| Accounts Receivable . . . . . | 220,000 | Accounts Payable . . . . . . . | 56,000 |
| Raw Materials Inventory . . | 80,000 | Wages Payable . . . . . . . . . | 24,000 |
| Work-in-Process Inventory | 230,000 | Capital Stock . . . . . . . . . . . | 1,000,000 |
| Finished Goods Inventory | 170,000 | Retained Earnings . . . . . . . | 200,000 |
| Factory Supplies Inventory | 20,000 | | |
| Manufacturing Equipment . | 480,000 | | |
| Total . . . . . . . . . . . . . . . . | $1,310,000 | Total . . . . . . . . . . . . . . . | $1,310,000 |

Transactions for the month of July are listed below in summary form.

   **(1)**  Sales, all on account, totaled $310,000.

   **(2)**  Labor services furnished by employees during the period (but as yet unpaid) amounted to $80,000. All labor is employed in the factory.

   **(3)**  Factory supplies were purchased for $8,500; payment was made by check.

   **(4)**  Raw materials purchased on account came to $100,000.

   **(5)**  Collections from customers were $335,000.

   **(6)**  Payment of $108,000 was made to raw materials suppliers.

   **(7)**  Payments to employees totaled $78,500.

   **(8)**  Rent of the factory building for the month, $8,000, was paid.

   **(9)**  Depreciation of manufacturing equipment for the month was $12,000.

**(10)** Other manufacturing costs incurred and paid totaled $40,000.

**(11)** All selling and administrative services are furnished by Clark and Company for $10,000 per month. Their bill was paid by check.

**(12)** Raw materials used during the month amounted to $115,000.

**(13)** Factory supplies used during the month totaled $8,000.

**(14)** Cost of goods completed during the month totaled $258,000.

**(15)** Goods costing $261,500 were shipped to customers during the month.

**a.** Open T-accounts and record the July 1 amounts. Record transactions **(1)** through **(15)** in the T-accounts, opening additional accounts as needed.

**b.** Prepare an adjusted, preclosing trial balance as of July 31.

**c.** Prepare a combined statement of income and retained earnings for July.

**d.** Enter closing entries in the T-accounts using an Income Summary account.

**e.** Prepare a balance sheet as of July 31.

**26.** *Preparing T-account entries, income statement, and balance sheet for a manufacturing firm.* Melton Plastics Company was incorporated on September 16. By September 30, the firm was ready to begin operations. The trial balance at that date was as follows:

| | | |
|---|---|---|
| Cash | $387,200 | |
| Raw Materials Inventory | 19,200 | |
| Factory Equipment | 136,000 | |
| Accounts Payable | | $ 22,400 |
| Capital Stock | | 520,000 |
| | $542,400 | $542,400 |

The following data relate only to the manufacturing operations of the firm during October:

**(1)** Materials were purchased on account for $161,600.

**(2)** Wages and salaries earned during the month amounted to $148,000.

**(3)** Raw materials requisitioned and put into process during the month cost $168,800.

**(4)** Equipment was acquired during the month at a cost of $112,000. A check for $40,000 was issued, and an equipment contract payable in eight equal monthly installments was signed for the remainder.

**(5)** Additional payments by check were as follows:

| | |
|---|---|
| Raw Materials Suppliers | $140,000 |
| Payrolls | 112,420 |
| Building Rent | 6,000 |
| Utilities | 2,920 |
| Insurance Premiums (for 1 year from October 1) | 9,600 |
| Miscellaneous Factory Costs | 26,400 |
| | $297,340 |

**(6)** Invoices received but unpaid at October 31 included the following:

| | |
|---|---:|
| City Water Department.......................................... | $ 120 |
| Hoster Machine Supply Company, for additional equipment......... | 2,400 |

**(7)** Depreciation on equipment for the month was $1,200.

**(8)** One month's insurance expiration was recorded.

**(9)** The cost of parts finished during October was $281,750.

In addition to these manufacturing activities, the following transactions relating to selling and administrative activities occurred during October.

**(10)** Sales, on account, totaled $340,600.

**(11)** Collections from customers were $330,000.

**(12)** Salaries earned during the month were broken down into: sales, $30,800; and office, $31,200.

**(13)** Payments by check were made as follows:

| | |
|---|---:|
| Sales Salaries ............................................... | $27,630 |
| Office Salaries............................................... | 27,550 |
| Advertising during October ..................................... | 7,200 |
| Rent of Office and Office Equipment for October ................... | 2,200 |
| Office Supplies .............................................. | 1,600 |
| Miscellaneous Office Costs..................................... | 1,400 |
| Miscellaneous Selling Costs.................................... | 2,800 |
| Total...................................................... | $70,380 |

**(14)** The inventory of office supplies on October 31 was $800.

**(15)** The inventory of finished goods on October 31 was $59,000.

**a.** Open T-accounts and enter the amounts from the opening trial balance.

**b.** Record the transactions during the month in the T-accounts, opening additional accounts as needed.

**c.** Enter closing entries in the T-accounts, using an Income Summary account.

**d.** Prepare a combined statement of income and retained earnings for the month.

**e.** Prepare a balance sheet as of October 31.

**27.** *Income recognition for shipbuilder.* Maine Shipbuilding Company agreed on June 15, Year 2, to construct an oil tanker for Global Petroleum Company. The contract price of $80 million is to be paid as follows: at the time of signing, $8 million; on December 31, Year 3, $32 million; and at completion on June 30, Year 4, $40 million. Maine Shipbuilding Company incurred the following costs in constructing the tanker: Year 2, $21.6 million; Year 3, $36 million; and Year 4, $14.4 million. These amounts conformed to original expectations.

a.  Calculate the amount of revenue, expense, and net income for Year 2, Year 3, and Year 4 under each of the following revenue recognition methods:
1.  Percentage-of-completion method.
2.  Completed contract method.
3.  Installment method.
4.  Cost-recovery-first method.
b.  Which method do you believe provides the best measure of Maine Shipbuilding Company's performance under the contract? Why?

28. *Income recognition for contractor.* The Humbolt Electric Company received a contract late in Year 1 to build a small electricity-generating unit. The contract price was $700,000, and it was estimated that total costs would be $600,000. Estimated and actual construction time was 15 months, and it was agreed that payments would be made by the purchaser as follows:

| | |
|---|---|
| March 31, Year 2 | $ 70,000 |
| June 30, Year 2 | 105,000 |
| September 30, Year 2 | 203,000 |
| December 31, Year 2 | 161,000 |
| March 31, Year 3 | 161,000 |
| | $700,000 |

Estimated and actual costs of construction incurred by the Humbolt Electric Company were as follows:

| | |
|---|---|
| January 1–March 31, Year 2 | $120,000 |
| April 1–June 30, Year 2 | 120,000 |
| July 1–September 30, Year 2 | 180,000 |
| October 1–December 31, Year 2 | 120,000 |
| January 1–March 31, Year 3 | 60,000 |
| | $600,000 |

The Humbolt Electric Company prepares financial statements quarterly at March 31, June 30, and so forth.
a.  Calculate the amount of revenue, expense, and net income for each quarter under each of the following methods of revenue recognition:
1.  Percentage-of-completion method.
2.  Completed contract method.
3.  Installment method.
4.  Cost-recovery-first method.
b.  Which method do you believe provides the best measure of Humbolt's performance under this contract? Why?
c.  Under what circumstances would the methods not selected in part **b** provide a better measure of performance?

29. *Income recognition for contractor.* On March 15, Year 1, Fuller Construction Company contracted to build a shopping center at a contract price of $10 million. The schedule of expected and actual cash collections and contract costs is as follows:

| Year | Cash Collections from Customers | Estimated and Actual Cost Incurred |
|------|---------------------------------|-------------------------------------|
| 1 ............................ | $ 2,000,000 | $1,200,000 |
| 2 ............................ | 3,000,000 | 3,200,000 |
| 3 ............................ | 4,000,000 | 1,600,000 |
| 4 ............................ | 1,000,000 | 2,000,000 |
|  | $10,000,000 | $8,000,000 |

a. Calculate the amount of revenue, expense, and net income for each of the 4 years under the following revenue recognition methods:
   1. Percentage-of-completion method.
   2. Completed-contract method.
   3. Installment method.
   4. Cost-recovery-first method.
b. Which method do you believe provides the best measure of Fuller Construction Company's performance under the contract? Why?

30. *Point-of-sale versus installment method of income recognition.* The Freda Company begins business on January 1, Year 8. Activities of the company for the first 2 years are summarized as follows:

|  | Year 8 | Year 9 |
|--|--------|--------|
| Sales, All on Account .................................. | $100,000 | $150,000 |
| Collections from Customers |  |  |
|   On Year 8 Sales ..................................... | 45,000 | 55,000 |
|   On Year 9 Sales ..................................... |  | 60,000 |
| Purchases of Merchandise ........................... | 90,000 | 120,000 |
| Inventory of Merchandise at 12/31...................... | 30,000 | 57,000 |
| All Expenses Other than Merchandise, Paid in Cash ...... | 16,000 | 22,000 |

a. Prepare income statements for Year 8 and Year 9, assuming that the company uses the accrual basis of accounting and that revenue is recognized at the time of sale.
b. Prepare income statements for Year 8 and Year 9, assuming that the company uses the installment method of accounting.

31. *Classifying items in income statement.* The results of various transactions and events are usually classified within the income statement in one of the following three sections: (1) income from continuing operations; (2) income, gains, and losses from discontinued operations; and (3) extraordinary items. Using the appropriate number, identify the classification of each of the transactions or events that follow. State any assumptions you believe are necessary.

    **a.** Depreciation expense for the year on a company's automobile used by its president.

    **b.** Uninsured loss of a factory complex in Louisiana as a result of a hurricane.

    **c.** Gain from the sale of marketable securities.

    **d.** Loss from the sale of a delivery truck.

    **e.** Loss from the sale of a division that conducted all of the firm's research activities.

    **f.** Earnings during the year up to the time of the sale of the division in part **e.**

    **g.** Loss in excess of insurance proceeds on an automobile destroyed during an accident.

    **h.** Loss of plant, equipment, and inventory held in a South American country when they were confiscated by the government of that country.

**32.** *Classifying items in income statement.* Comment on any unusual features of the income statement of Nordic Enterprises, Inc., shown in Exhibit 4.5.

**33.** *Revenue recognition for various types of businesses.* Discuss when revenue is likely to be recognized by firms in each of the following types of businesses:

    **a.** A shoe store.

    **b.** A shipbuilding firm constructing an aircraft carrier under a government contract.

    **c.** A real estate developer selling lots on long-term contracts with small down payments.

    **d.** A barber shop.

    **e.** A citrus-growing firm.

    **f.** A producer of television movies working under the condition that the rights

Exhibit 4.5 _____

**NORDIC ENTERPRISES, INC.**
**Income Statement**
**December 31, Year 5**

| | | |
|---|---:|---:|
| **Revenues and Gains:** | | |
| Sales Revenue . . . . . . . . . . . . . . . . . . . . . . . . . . . . . . . . . . . . | $1,964,800 | |
| Rental Revenue . . . . . . . . . . . . . . . . . . . . . . . . . . . . . . . . . . | 366,900 | |
| Interest Revenue . . . . . . . . . . . . . . . . . . . . . . . . . . . . . . . . . | 4,600 | |
| Gain on Sale of Equipment . . . . . . . . . . . . . . . . . . . . . . . . | 2,500 | |
| Gain on Sale of Subsidiary . . . . . . . . . . . . . . . . . . . . . . . . | 643,200 | $2,982,000 |
| | | |
| **Expenses and Losses:** | | |
| Cost of Goods Sold . . . . . . . . . . . . . . . . . . . . . . . . . . . . . . . | $1,432,900 | |
| Depreciation Expense . . . . . . . . . . . . . . . . . . . . . . . . . . . . . | 226,800 | |
| Salaries Expense . . . . . . . . . . . . . . . . . . . . . . . . . . . . . . . . . | 296,900 | |
| Interest Expense . . . . . . . . . . . . . . . . . . . . . . . . . . . . . . . . . | 6,600 | |
| Loss of Plant Due to Fire . . . . . . . . . . . . . . . . . . . . . . . . . . | 368,800 | |
| Income Tax Expense . . . . . . . . . . . . . . . . . . . . . . . . . . . . | 200,000 | |
| Dividends Expense . . . . . . . . . . . . . . . . . . . . . . . . . . . . . . | 100,000 | 2,632,000 |
| | | |
| **Net Income** . . . . . . . . . . . . . . . . . . . . . . . . . . . . . . . . . . . . | | $   350,000 |

to the movies are sold to a television network for the first 3 years and all rights thereafter revert to the producer.

g. A residential real estate developer who constructs only ''speculative'' houses and later sells the houses to buyers.

h. A producer of fine whiskey that is aged from 6 to 12 years before sale.

i. A savings and loan association lending money for home mortgages.

j. A travel agency.

k. A printer who prints only custom-order stationery.

l. A seller to food stores of trading stamps redeemable by food store customers for various household products.

m. A wholesale food distributor.

n. A livestock rancher.

o. A shipping company that loads cargo in one accounting period, carries cargo across the ocean in a second accounting period, and unloads the cargo in a third period. The shipping is all done under contract, and cash collection of shipping charges is relatively certain.

34. *Revenue recognition for franchise.* Pickin Chicken, Incorporated, and Country Delight, Incorporated, both sell franchises for their chicken restaurants. The franchisee receives the right to use the franchisor's products and to benefit from national training and advertising programs. The franchisee agrees to pay $50,000 for exclusive franchise rights in a particular city. Of this amount, $20,000 is paid upon signing the franchise agreement and the remainder is payable in five equal annual installments of $6,000 each.

Pickin Chicken, Incorporated, recognizes franchise revenue as franchise agreements are signed, whereas Country Delight, Incorporated, recognizes franchise revenue on an installment basis. In Year 2, both companies sold eight franchises. In Year 3, they both sold five franchises. In Year 4, neither company sold a franchise.

a. Calculate the amount of revenue recognized by each company during Year 2, Year 3, Year 4, Year 5, Year 6, Year 7, and Year 8.

b. When do you think franchise revenue should be recognized? Why?

# Chapter 5    Statement of Cash Flows: Reporting the Effects of Operating, Investing, and Financing Activities on Cash Flows ____

Chapter 1 pointed out that three major financial statements are useful to those interested in understanding the financial activities of a business. Chapter 2 discussed the balance sheet, a snapshot of the investments and financing of a firm at a moment in time. Chapters 3 and 4 considered the income statement, a report on the revenues and expenses related to operations for a period of time. This chapter discusses a third major statement, the statement of cash flows, which reports the impact of a firm's operating, investing, and financing activities on cash flows during a period of time.[1]

## Rationale for the Statement of Cash Flows ____

Chapter 1 introduced the relation between the principal activities of a business — investing, financing, and operating — and the two financial statements already discussed — the balance sheet and the income statement. The principal business activities might be thought of as three interconnected cogwheels, each turning on its own yet connected in important ways with the other activities.

Cash flows tie these three activities together and keep them running smoothly. If cash cannot be generated in sufficient amounts and at the right times, a firm faces financial difficulty and even bankruptcy.

**Example**    Solinger Electric Corporation was formed during January, Year 1, to operate a retail electrical supply business. It obtained financing from creditors and owners and invested the funds in buildings and equipment. The firm has operated

---

[1]The FASB requires that the statement of cash flows should explain changes in cash and cash equivalents. Cash equivalents represent short-term, highly liquid investments in which a firm has temporarily placed excess cash. Throughout this text, we use the term *cash flows* to refer to cash and cash equivalents. See Financial Accounting Standards Board, *Statement of Financial Accounting Standards No. 95*, "Statement of Cash Flows," 1987.

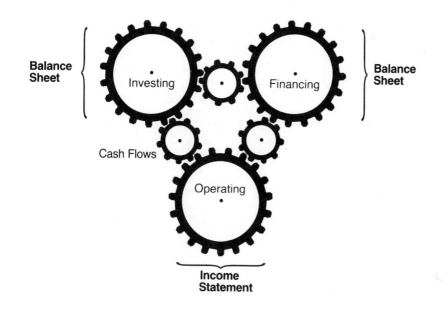

profitably since opening, with net income increasing from $3,000 in Year 1 to $20,000 in Year 4. However, the firm has had increasing difficulty paying its monthly bills as they become due. Management is puzzled as to how net income can be increasing while, at the same time, the firm continually finds itself strapped for cash.

## Relation between Income Flows and Cash Flows

Revenues and expenses reported in the income statement for a period differ in amount from the cash receipts and disbursements for the period. The differences arise for two principal reasons.

1. The accrual basis of accounting is used in measuring net income. Thus the recognition of revenues does not necessarily coincide with receipts of cash from customers. Likewise, the recognition of expenses does not necessarily coincide with disbursements of cash to suppliers, employees, and other creditors. As Chapter 3 pointed out, the accrual basis of accounting focuses on the use of assets in generating earnings, not on their associated cash receipts and disbursements.

2. The firm receives cash from sources that are not related directly to operations, such as issuing capital stock or bonds. Similarly, the firm makes cash disbursements for such things as dividends and the acquisition of equipment that are not related directly to operations during the current period. These investing and financing activities also generate or use cash.

To illustrate the relation between income flows and cash flows, refer to the data for Solinger Electric Corporation for Year 4 in Exhibit 5.1. Sales revenue reported in the income statement totaled $125,000. However, only $90,000 in cash was

Exhibit 5.1 _____

## SOLINGER ELECTRIC CORPORATION
Income Statement and Statement of Cash Receipts and Disbursements for
Year 4

| | Income Statement | Statement of Cash Receipts and Disbursements | |
|---|---|---|---|
| Sales Revenue . . . . . . . . . . | $125,000 | $ 90,000 | . . . . . Collections from Customers |
| *Less Expenses:* | | | *Less Disbursements:* |
| Cost of Goods Sold . . . . | $ 60,000 | $ 50,000 | . . . . . To Merchandise Suppliers |
| Salaries . . . . . . . . . . . . . | 20,000 | 19,000 | . . . . . To Employees |
| Depreciation . . . . . . . . . | 10,000 | 0 | . . . . .    — |
| Other. . . . . . . . . . . . . . . | 15,000 | 13,000 | . . . . . To Other Suppliers |
| Total Expenses . . . . . . | $105,000 | $ 82,000 | . . . . . Total Disbursements to Suppliers and Employees |
| Net Income . . . . . . . . . . . . | $ 20,000 | $  8,000 | . . . . . Cash Flow from Operations |
| | | $(125,000) | . . . . . Cash Flow from Investments in Plant and Equipment |
| | | $  (8,000) | . . . . . Disbursement for Dividends |
| | | 100,000 | . . . . . Receipts from Issuing Long-Term Bonds |
| | | $ 92,000 | . . . . . Cash Flow from Financing |
| | | $ (25,000) | . . . . . Net Change in Cash |

collected from customers. The remaining amount of sales was not collected by the
end of the year and is reflected in the increase in the Accounts Receivable account
on the balance sheet.[2] Likewise, the cost of goods sold shown on the income
statement totaled $60,000, but only $50,000 cash was disbursed to suppliers during
the year. Similar differences between income flows and cash flows can be seen for
salaries and for other expenses.

Note that there is no specific cash flow associated with depreciation expense
during Year 4. Cash was used in some earlier period for the acquisition of buildings
and equipment, but the amount of cash spent earlier was not reported at that time as
an expense in accrual accounting. Rather, it was reflected in the balance sheet as an
increase in the asset account for buildings and equipment and shown in the statement of cash flows as a use of cash for investing activities. Now, as the buildings
and equipment are being used, the cost of the assets' services used is reported as an
expense of the period even though there is now no outflow of cash. Although the
operating activities generated $20,000 in net income, these activities led to an
increase in cash of only $8,000 during Year 4.

_____

[2]This example has been simplified for the purpose of illustration. In a realistic situation, some of the
receipts would have been from collection of receivables existing at the start of the year. Similarly, some
of the payments would have been for liabilities existing at the start of the year.

Solinger Electric Corporation engaged in investing and financing activities that affected cash during Year 4, as is reported in the lower portion of Exhibit 5.1. Cash in the amount of $125,000 was disbursed for the acquisition of new equipment, $8,000 was disbursed for dividends, and $100,000 was received from the issue of bonds. The result of all of the firm's activities was a decrease in cash of $25,000.

The experience of Solinger Electric Corporation is not unusual. Many firms, particularly those growing rapidly, discover that their cash position is deteriorating despite an excellent earnings record. The statement of cash flows explains the major reasons for the change in cash for a period.

## Objective of the Statement of Cash Flows

The statement of cash flows reports the amount of cash flow from a firm's operating, investing, and financing activities. It also shows the principal inflows and outflows of cash from each of these three activities. Figure 5.1 presents the major types of cash flows, which the following sections describe.

**Operations**  Selling goods and providing services are among the most important ways of generating cash for a financially healthy company. When assessed over several years, *cash flow from operations* indicates the extent to which operating activities have generated more cash than has been used. The excess from operations

**Figure 5.1** _____

**Components of Statement of Cash Flows**

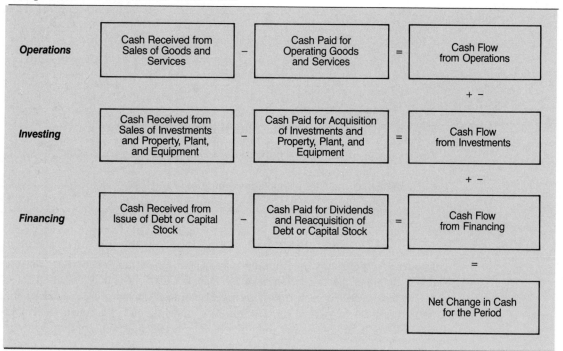

can then be used for dividends, acquisition of buildings and equipment, repayment of long-term debt, and other investing and financing activities.

**Investing**  The acquisition of noncurrent assets, particularly property, plant, and equipment, usually represents a major ongoing use of cash. Such assets must be replaced as they wear out, and additional noncurrent assets must be acquired if a firm is to grow. A portion of the cash needed to acquire noncurrent assets is obtained from sales of existing noncurrent assets. However, such cash inflows are seldom sufficient to cover the cost of new acquisitions.

**Financing**  A firm obtains cash from short- and long-term borrowing and from issues of capital stock. Cash is used to pay dividends to shareholders, to repay short- or long-term borrowing, and to reacquire shares of outstanding capital stock. The amount of cash flow from these financing activities is the third major component reported in the statement of cash flows.

Firms sometimes engage in investing and financing transactions that do not directly involve cash. For example, a building may be acquired by assuming a mortgage obligation. A tract of land might be exchanged for equipment. Long-term debt might be converted into shares of common stock. These transactions are disclosed either in the statement of cash flows or in a supplementary schedule, in a way that clearly indicates that they are investing and financing transactions that do not affect cash. For example, the acquisition of a building by assuming a mortgage might be disclosed in the statement of cash flows as follows:

| | |
|---|---|
| *Investing:* | |
| Acquisition of a Building by Assuming Mortgage......................... | $100,000 |
| *Financing:* | |
| Mortgage Assumed in Acquisition of a Building........................... | $100,000 |

## Uses of Information in the Statement of Cash Flows

The statement of cash flows provides information that may be used in

1. assessing the impact of operations on liquidity.

2. assessing the relations among cash flows from operating, investing, and financing activities.

**Impact of Operations on Liquidity**  Perhaps the most important factor not reported on either the balance sheet or the income statement is how operations of a period have affected cash flows. Increased earnings do not always generate increased cash flow. A growing, successful firm may find that its accounts receivable and inventories are increasing, resulting in a lag between earnings and cash flows.

On the other hand, increased cash flow can accompany reduced earnings. Consider, for example, a firm that is experiencing operating problems and reducing the scope of its activities. Such a firm is likely to report reduced net income or even losses. However, it might experience positive cash flow from operations because accounts receivable from prior periods are being collected and inventories are not being replaced, saving cash.

**Relations among Cash Flows from Operations, Investing, and Financing Activities**   The relations among the cash flows from each of the three principal business activities are likely to differ depending on the characteristics of the firm's products and the maturity of its industry. Consider each of the four following patterns of cash flows.

| Cash Flows from: | A | B | C | D |
|---|---|---|---|---|
| Operations..................................... | $ (3) | $ 7 | $ 15 | $ 8 |
| Investing...................................... | (15) | (12) | (8) | (2) |
| Financing..................................... | 18 | 5 | (7) | (3) |
| Net Cash Flow ............................ | $ 0 | $ 0 | $ 0 | $ 3 |

Case A is typical of a new, rapidly growing firm. It is not yet operating profitably and is experiencing buildups of its accounts receivable and inventories. Thus its cash flow from operations is negative. To sustain its rapid growth, the firm must invest heavily in plant and equipment. During this stage, the firm must rely on external sources of cash to finance both its operating and investing activities.

Case B illustrates a firm that is somewhat more seasoned than in Case A, but that is still in a growth stage. It is operating profitably, and because its rapid growth is beginning to slow, it finds that it generates positive cash flow from operations. However, this cash flow from operations is not sufficient to finance acquisitions of plant and equipment. External financing is therefore required.

Case C illustrates the cash flow pattern of a mature, stable-growth firm. It generates a healthy cash flow from operations, which is more than sufficient to cover acquisitions of plant and equipment. The excess cash flow is used to repay financing from earlier periods.

Case D illustrates a firm in the early stages of decline. Its cash from operations begins to decrease but is still positive because of decreases in accounts receivable and inventories. It has cut back significantly on capital expenditures because it is in a declining industry. It uses some of its excess cash flow to repay any outstanding financing, and the remainder is available for investment in new products or industries.

These four cases do not, of course, cover all of the patterns of cash flows likely to be found in corporate annual reports. They do illustrate, however, how the characteristics of a firm's products and industry can affect the interpretation of information in the statement of cash flows.

# Analysis of the Effects of Transactions on Cash ————

## Algebraic Formulation

The effects of various transactions on cash might be seen by reexamining the accounting equation. In doing so, the following notation is used:

C — cash

NCA — noncash assets

L — liabilities

SE — shareholders' equity

Δ — the change in an item, whether positive (an increase) or negative (a decrease) from the beginning of a period to the end of the period

The accounting equation states that

$$\text{Assets} = \text{Liabilities} + \text{Shareholders' Equity}$$
$$C + NCA = L + SE$$

Furthermore, this equation must be true for balance sheets constructed at both the start of the period and the end of the period. If the start-of-the-period and end-of-the-period balance sheets maintain the accounting equation, the following equation must also be valid:

$$\Delta C + \Delta NCA = \Delta L + \Delta SE.$$

Rearranging terms in this equation, we obtain the equation for changes in cash.

$$\Delta C = \Delta L + \Delta SE - \Delta NCA.$$

The left-hand side of this equation represents the change in cash. The right-hand side of the equation, reflecting changes in all noncash accounts, must also be equal in amount to the net change in cash. The equation states that increases in cash (left-hand side) are equal to, or caused by, the increases in liabilities plus the increases in shareholders' equity less the increases in noncash assets (right-hand side). Next we illustrate how the changes in the accounts on the right-hand side bring about the change in cash on the left-hand side.

## Illustration of Transactions Analysis

We can analyze some typical transactions to demonstrate how the equation is maintained and how cash is affected.

Assume that the following events occur during Year 4 for the Solinger Electric Corporation, considered earlier in Exhibit 5.1.

**1.** Merchandise costing $70,000 is acquired on account.

**2.** Merchandise costing $60,000 is sold to customers on account for $125,000.

**3.** Salaries of $19,000 are paid in cash.

**4.** Other expenses of $13,000 are paid in cash.

5. Cash collections of customers' accounts total $90,000.

6. Cash payments to suppliers of merchandise total $50,000.

7. Salaries earned but not paid as of December 31, Year 4, are accrued, $1,000.

8. Other expenses not paid as of December 31, Year 4, are accrued, $2,000.

9. Depreciation for Year 4 is recorded, $10,000.

10. Long-term debt is issued for cash, $100,000.

11. Dividends of $8,000 are declared and paid.

12. Equipment costing $125,000 is acquired for cash.

Exhibit 5.2 analyzes the effects of these transactions on cash, which decreased by $25,000 during Year 4. Both sides of the equation show this net change. The net change in cash during a period (left-hand side of the equation) can therefore be explained by focusing on the changes in noncash accounts (right-hand side of the equation). For Solinger Electric Corporation, the net decrease in cash of $25,000 is explained as follows:

| | |
|---|---:|
| From Operations.................................................... | $    8,000 |
| From Investing Activities............................................. | (125,000) |
| From Financing Activities............................................ | 92,000 |
| Net Decrease in Cash............................................... | $  (25,000) |

# Preparation of the Statement of Cash Flows _____

The statement of cash flows could be prepared by examining every transaction affecting the Cash account, as is done in Exhibit 5.2, and classifying each one as an operating, investing, or financing activity. If a firm's record keeping system incorporates the appropriate classification codes into the initial recording of transactions in the Cash account, preparation of the statement of cash flows becomes straightforward.

Given the large number of transactions affecting the Cash account during a period, however, most firms find it easier to prepare the statement of cash flows after the balance sheet and income statement have been prepared. This section presents a step-by-step procedure for preparing the statement of cash flows using the transactions of Solinger Electric Corporation for Year 4.

## The Procedure and an Illustration

**Step 1**  Obtain balance sheets for the beginning and end of the period covered by the statement of cash flows. Exhibit 5.3 presents the comparative balance sheets of Solinger Electric Corporation for December 31, Year 3 and Year 4.

**Step 2**  Prepare a *T-account work sheet*. An example of such a T-account work sheet appears in Exhibit 5.4. At the top of the work sheet is a master T-account

## Exhibit 5.2 ————————————————————————————————————————————

## SOLINGER ELECTRIC CORPORATION
### Analysis of the Effects of Transactions during Year 4 on Cash and Noncash Accounts

| Transactions | Changes in Cash $\Delta C$ | = | $\Delta L$ | + | Changes in Noncash Accounts $\Delta SE$ | − | $\Delta NCA$ |
|---|---|---|---|---|---|---|---|
| | | | | | **Effect on Cash** | | |
| (1) Merchandise costing $70,000 is acquired on account, increasing a noncash asset and a noncash liability .......................... | $ 0 | = | $ 70,000 | + | 0 | − | (+$ 70,000) |
| (2) Merchandise costing $60,000 is sold to customers on account for $125,000, increasing a noncash asset, accounts receivable, by $125,000, decreasing the noncash asset, inventory, by $60,000, and increasing shareholders' equity by $65,000 ...................... | 0 | = | 0 | + | $65,000 | − | (+$125,000) (−$ 60,000) |
| (3) Salaries of $19,000 are paid in cash, decreasing cash and shareholders' equity .............. | (−$ 19,000) | = | 0 | + | (−$19,000) | − | 0 |
| (4) Other expenses of $13,000 are paid in cash, decreasing cash and shareholders' equity .............. | (−$ 13,000) | = | 0 | + | (−$13,000) | − | 0 |
| (5) Cash collections of customers' accounts total $90,000, increasing cash and decreasing the noncash asset, accounts receivable ......... | $ 90,000 | = | 0 | + | 0 | − | (−$ 90,000) |
| (6) Payments to suppliers of merchandise total $50,000, decreasing cash and a liability...... | (−$ 50,000) | = | (−$ 50,000) | + | 0 | − | 0 |
| (7) Salaries of $1,000 earned but not paid as of December 31, Year 4, are accrued, increasing a liability and decreasing shareholders' equity .......................... | 0 | = | $ 1,000 | + | (−$ 1,000) | − | 0 |
| (8) Other expenses of $2,000 not paid as of December 31, Year 4, are accrued, increasing a liability and decreasing shareholders' equity .............. | 0 | = | $ 2,000 | + | (−$ 2,000) | − | 0 |
| (9) Depreciation for Year 4 of $10,000 is recorded, decreasing shareholders' equity and noncash assets .......................... | 0 | = | 0 | + | (−$10,000) | − | (−$ 10,000) |
| Total from operations ........... | $ 8,000 | = | $ 23,000 | + | $20,000 | − | $ 35,000 |
| (10) Long-term debt is issued for $100,000, increasing cash and a liability ....................... | $100,000 | = | $100,000 | + | 0 | − | 0 |
| (11) Dividends of $8,000 are declared and paid, decreasing cash and shareholders' equity .............. | (−$ 8,000) | = | 0 | + | (−$ 8,000) | − | 0 |
| (12) Equipment costing $125,000 is acquired for cash, decreasing cash and increasing noncash assets .......................... | (−$125,000) | = | 0 | + | 0 | − | (+$125,000) |
| Net change in cash and noncash accounts............. | −$ 25,000 | = | $123,000 | + | $12,000 | − | $160,000 |

**Exhibit 5.3** _____

## SOLINGER ELECTRIC CORPORATION
Comparative Balance Sheets for December 31, Year 3 and Year 4

| | December 31, Year 3 | December 31, Year 4 |
|---|---|---|
| **Assets** | | |
| **Current Assets:** | | |
| Cash................................................... | $ 30,000 | $ 5,000 |
| Accounts Receivable..................................... | 20,000 | 55,000 |
| Merchandise Inventory ................................. | 40,000 | 50,000 |
| Total Current Assets ................................ | $ 90,000 | $110,000 |
| **Noncurrent Assets:** | | |
| Buildings and Equipment (cost) .......................... | $100,000 | $225,000 |
| Accumulated Depreciation ............................... | (30,000) | (40,000) |
| Total Noncurrent Assets.............................. | $ 70,000 | $185,000 |
| Total Assets ........................................ | $160,000 | $295,000 |
| **Equities** | | |
| **Current Liabilities:** | | |
| Accounts Payable—Merchandise Suppliers ................. | $ 30,000 | $ 50,000 |
| Accounts Payable—Other Suppliers....................... | 10,000 | 12,000 |
| Salaries Payable ...................................... | 5,000 | 6,000 |
| Total Current Liabilities ................................ | $ 45,000 | $ 68,000 |
| **Noncurrent Liabilities:** | | |
| Bonds Payable ........................................ | $ 0 | $100,000 |
| **Shareholders' Equity:** | | |
| Common Stock......................................... | $100,000 | $100,000 |
| Retained Earnings ..................................... | 15,000 | 27,000 |
| Total Shareholders' Equity............................. | $115,000 | $127,000 |
| Total Equities ....................................... | $160,000 | $295,000 |

titled Cash. Note that this T-account has sections labeled Operations, Investing, and Financing. Transactions affecting cash during the period are classified under one of these headings to aid in the preparation of the statement of cash flows. This procedure is explained later in this section. The beginning and ending amounts of cash are then entered in the master T-account. (The beginning and ending amounts of cash for Solinger Electric Corporation are $30,000 and $5,000, respectively.) The number at the top of the T-account is the opening balance; the one at the bottom is the closing balance. The check marks indicate that the figures are balances. Note that the master T-account, Cash, is another means of expressing the left-hand side of the equation for changes in cash in Exhibit 5.2.

After the master T-account for Cash has been prepared (as at the top of Exhibit 5.4), the work sheet is completed by preparing T-accounts for *each* noncash asset,

## Exhibit 5.4 _____

### SOLINGER ELECTRIC CORPORATION
T-Account Work Sheet

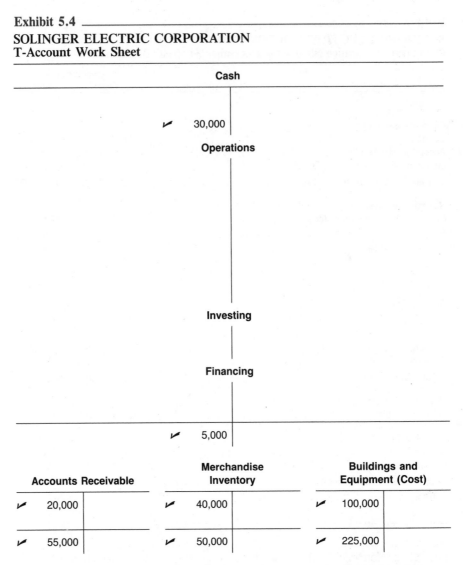

| | Cash | |
|---|---|---|
| ✔ 30,000 | | |
| | **Operations** | |
| | | |
| | **Investing** | |
| | **Financing** | |
| ✔ 5,000 | | |

| Accounts Receivable | | Merchandise Inventory | | Buildings and Equipment (Cost) | |
|---|---|---|---|---|---|
| ✔ 20,000 | | ✔ 40,000 | | ✔ 100,000 | |
| ✔ 55,000 | | ✔ 50,000 | | ✔ 225,000 | |

| Accumulated Depreciation | | Accounts Payable— Merchandise Suppliers | | Accounts Payable— Other Suppliers | |
|---|---|---|---|---|---|
| | 30,000 ✔ | | 30,000 ✔ | | 10,000 ✔ |
| | 40,000 ✔ | | 50,000 ✔ | | 12,000 ✔ |

| Salaries Payable | | Bonds Payable | | Retained Earnings | |
|---|---|---|---|---|---|
| | 5,000 ✔ | | 0 ✔ | | 15,000 ✔ |
| | 6,000 ✔ | | 100,000 ✔ | | 27,000 ✔ |

liability, and shareholders' equity account. Enter the beginning and ending balances in each account for the period as given in Exhibit 5.3. The lower portion of Exhibit 5.4 shows the T-accounts for each noncash account. Note that the sum of the changes in these individual T-accounts is another means of expressing the right-hand side of the equation for changes in cash in Exhibit 5.2.

**Step 3**  Explain the change in the master cash account between the beginning and end of the period by accounting for the change in the balance of each noncash account during the period. This step is accomplished by *reconstructing the entries originally recorded in the accounts during the period*. The reconstructed entries are written in the appropriate T-accounts on the work sheet. Once the net change in each of the noncash accounts has been accounted for, sufficient information will have been generated to account for the net change in cash. In other words, if the changes in the right-hand side of the cash equation have been explained, the causes of the changes in cash itself on the left-hand side will also have been explained.

The process of reconstructing the transactions during the year is usually easiest if information supplementary to the balance sheet is accounted for first. Assume the following information concerning the Solinger Electric Corporation for Year 4:

1.  Net income is $20,000.
2.  Depreciation expense is $10,000.
3.  Dividends declared and paid total $8,000.

The analytic entry to record the information concerning net income is

---

| | | |
|---|---|---|
| (1) Cash (Operations—Net Income) .......................... | 20,000 | |
| Retained Earnings ...................................... | | 20,000 |
| Entry recorded in T-account work sheet. | | |

---

To understand this entry, review the process of recording revenues and expenses and the closing entries for those temporary accounts from Chapter 3. All of the journal entries that together record the process of earning $20,000 net income are equivalent to the following single journal entry:

---

| | | |
|---|---|---|
| Net Assets (= All Assets Minus All Liabilities) ................... | 20,000 | |
| Retained Earnings ....................................... | | 20,000 |
| Summary entry equivalent to recording earnings of $20,000. | | |

---

The summary journal entry debits Net Assets. At this stage of preparing the statement of cash flows, the assumption is that all of the net assets generated by the earnings process were cash. Thus, in analytic entry (1), the debit results in showing a provisional increase in cash from operations in an amount equal to net income for the period.

However, not all of the items recognized as expenses and deducted in calculating net income decrease cash (refer to Exhibit 5.1). The portion of the expenses that does not affect cash should be added to the provisional increase in cash to calculate the net amount of cash from operations. For example, one expense not using cash is depreciation, illustrated in entry (2).

---

(2) Cash (Operations—Depreciation Expense Addback)..........    10,000
     Accumulated Depreciation................................        10,000
    Entry recorded in T-account work sheet.

---

Because depreciation expense was deducted in calculating net income but did not reduce cash, the amount of depreciation expense must be added back to net income in calculating the amount of cash provided by operations.

The supplementary information concerning dividends of $8,000 declared and paid is recorded as follows:

---

(3) Retained Earnings .......................................    8,000
    Cash (Financing—Dividends) ...........................        8,000
    Entry recorded in T-account work sheet. Dividends reduce retained earnings and cash.

---

Because paying dividends generally increases the need for other forms of financing, this transaction is classified on the statement of cash flows as a financing activity.

Once the supplementary information has been reflected in the T-account work sheet, it is necessary to make inferences about the reasons for the remaining changes in the noncash accounts on the balance sheet. (If the statement of cash flows is being prepared for an actual firm, such inferences may not be necessary, because sufficient information regarding the change in each account is likely to be available from the firm's accounting records.) The changes in noncash accounts are explained in the order of their appearance.

The Accounts Receivable account shows an increase of $35,000. The analytic entry to record this information in the work sheet is as follows:

---

(4) Accounts Receivable ......................................    35,000
    Cash (Operations—Subtractions) .......................        35,000
    Entry recorded in T-account work sheet.

---

The operations of the period generated sales, but not all of these sales resulted in an increase in cash. Some of the sales increased Accounts Receivable. Because we start the statement of cash flows with net income, in deriving the amount of cash from operations we must subtract that portion of revenues not producing cash (that is, the excess of sales on account over cash collections from customers).

The next noncash account showing a change is Merchandise Inventory, which shows an increase during the year of $10,000. As the operations of the firm have expanded, so has the amount carried in inventory. The analytic entry in the work sheet to explain the change in Merchandise Inventory is as follows:

---

(5) Merchandise Inventory.................................... 10,000
      Cash (Operations — Subtractions)........................     10,000
      Entry recorded in T-account work sheet.

---

Solinger Electric Corporation found it necessary to increase the amount of inventory carried to make possible increased future sales. An increase in inventory is ordinarily an operating use of cash. Because we start the statement of cash flows with net income, in deriving cash from operations we must subtract from net income the increase in inventories during the year (that is, the excess of purchases over the cost of goods sold).

The next noncash account, Buildings and Equipment (Cost), shows a net increase of $125,000 (= $225,000 − $100,000). Because we have no other information, we must assume that buildings and equipment costing $125,000 were acquired during the year. The analytic entry is as follows:

---

(6) Buildings and Equipment (Cost) ........................... 125,000
      Cash (Investing — Acquisitions of Buildings and Equipment) .     125,000

---

Another noncash account showing a change is Accounts Payable — Merchandise Suppliers. As the amounts carried in inventory have increased, so have the amounts owed to suppliers of inventory. The analytic entry to explain the increase in the amount of Accounts Payable — Merchandise Suppliers is as follows:

---

(7) Cash (Operations — Additions)............................. 20,000
      Accounts Payable — Merchandise Suppliers................     20,000
      Entry recorded in T-account work sheet.

---

Ordinarily, acquiring inventory requires cash. Suppliers who allow a firm to pay later for goods and services received now are in effect supplying the firm with cash. Thus an increase in the amount of accounts payable for inventory results from a transaction where inventory increases but cash does not decrease. This is equivalent to saying that an increase in payables provides cash, even if it is only temporary. The increase in cash resulting from increased payables for inventory is an operating source of funds.

The next noncash account showing a change is Accounts Payable — Other Suppliers. As the scope of operations has increased, so has the amount owed to others.

The analytic entry to explain the increase in the amount of Accounts Payable—Other Suppliers is as follows:

---

| | | |
|---|---|---|
| (8) Cash (Operations—Additions)............................. | 2,000 | |
|        Accounts Payable—Other Suppliers ..................... | | 2,000 |
|        Entry recorded in T-account work sheet. | | |

---

The reasoning behind this entry is the same as for entry (7). Creditors who permit a firm to increase amounts owed are in effect providing cash. The same reasoning applies to an increased amount of Salaries Payable, the next noncash account showing a change. The analytic entry to record the increase in Salaries Payable is as follows:

---

| | | |
|---|---|---|
| (9) Cash (Operations—Additions)............................. | 1,000 | |
|        Salaries Payable ....................................... | | 1,000 |
|        Entry recorded in T-account work sheet. | | |

---

Employees who do not demand immediate payment for salaries earned have provided their employer with cash, at least temporarily.

Bonds Payable, the final noncash account showing a change not yet explained, shows a net increase of $100,000 for the year. Because no other information is given, one can deduce that long-term bonds were issued during the year. The analytic entry is as follows:

---

| | | |
|---|---|---|
| (10) Cash (Financing—Long-Term Bond Issue) ................ | 100,000 | |
|        Bonds Payable ........................................ | | 100,000 |

---

Exhibit 5.5 presents the completed T-account work sheet for Solinger Electric Corporation for Year 4. All changes in the noncash T-accounts have been explained with the ten entries. If the work is correct, the causes of the change in the Cash account will have been presented in the entries in the master Cash account.

**Step 4**  The final step is the preparation of a formal statement of cash flows. Exhibit 5.6 presents the statement for Solinger Electric Corporation, which has been prepared directly from the information provided in the master T-account for Cash in the completed work sheet.

The first item disclosed in the statement is the amount of cash generated by operations. In deriving cash from operations, all revenues providing cash could be listed, followed by all expenses using cash. This is referred to as the *direct method* of computing cash flow from operations. This is the format shown in the right-hand column of Exhibit 5.1.

## Exhibit 5.5 ——————————————————————

## SOLINGER ELECTRIC CORPORATION
## T-Account Work Sheet

### Cash

| | | | | |
|---|---|---|---|---|
| ✔ | 30,000 | | | |

#### Operations

| | | | | |
|---|---|---|---|---|
| Net Income | (1) | 20,000 | 35,000 (4) | Increased Accounts Receivable |
| Depreciation Expense Addback | (2) | 10,000 | 10,000 (5) | Increased Merchandise Inventory |
| Increased Accounts Payable to Merchandise Suppliers | (7) | 20,000 | | |
| Increased Accounts Payable to Other Suppliers | (8) | 2,000 | | |
| Increased Salaries Payable | (9) | 1,000 | | |

#### Investing

| | | | | |
|---|---|---|---|---|
| | | | 125,000 (6) | Acquisition of Buildings and Equipment |

#### Financing

| | | | | |
|---|---|---|---|---|
| Long-Term Bond Issue | (10) | 100,000 | 8,000 (3) | Dividends |
| ✔ | | 5,000 | | |

| Accounts Receivable | | | Merchandise Inventory | | | Buildings and Equipment (Cost) | |
|---|---|---|---|---|---|---|---|
| ✔ | 20,000 | | ✔ | 40,000 | | ✔ | 100,000 |
| (4) | 35,000 | | (5) | 10,000 | | (6) | 125,000 |
| ✔ | 55,000 | | ✔ | 50,000 | | ✔ | 225,000 |

| Accumulated Depreciation | | | Accounts Payable— Merchandise Suppliers | | | Accounts Payable— Other Suppliers | |
|---|---|---|---|---|---|---|---|
| | 30,000 ✔ | | | 30,000 ✔ | | | 10,000 ✔ |
| | 10,000 (2) | | | 20,000 (7) | | | 2,000 (8) |
| | 40,000 ✔ | | | 50,000 ✔ | | | 12,000 ✔ |

| Salaries Payable | | | Bonds Payable | | | Retained Earnings | |
|---|---|---|---|---|---|---|---|
| | 5,000 ✔ | | | 0 ✔ | | | 15,000 ✔ |
| | 1,000 (9) | | | 100,000 (10) | (3)   8,000 | 20,000 (1) |
| | 6,000 ✔ | | | 100,000 ✔ | | | 27,000 ✔ |

Exhibit 5.6 ———————————————————————————————

## SOLINGER ELECTRIC CORPORATION
### Statement of Cash Flows for Year 4

| | | |
|---|---:|---:|
| *Operations:* | | |
| Net Income . . . . . . . . . . . . . . . . . . . . . . . . . . . . . . . . . . . . . . . . . . . . . . . | $20,000 | |
| Additions: | | |
| Depreciation Expense Not Using Cash . . . . . . . . . . . . . . . . . . . . | 10,000 | |
| Increased Accounts Payable: | | |
| To Suppliers of Merchandise . . . . . . . . . . . . . . . . . . . . . . . . . . | 20,000 | |
| To Other Suppliers . . . . . . . . . . . . . . . . . . . . . . . . . . . . . . . . . | 2,000 | |
| Increased Salaries Payable . . . . . . . . . . . . . . . . . . . . . . . . . . . . | 1,000 | |
| Subtractions: | | |
| Increased Accounts Receivable . . . . . . . . . . . . . . . . . . . . . . . . | (35,000) | |
| Increased Merchandise Inventory . . . . . . . . . . . . . . . . . . . . . . . | (10,000) | |
| Cash Flow from Operations . . . . . . . . . . . . . . . . . . . . . . . . . . . . . | | $   8,000 |
| *Investing:* | | |
| Acquisition of Buildings and Equipment . . . . . . . . . . . . . . . . . . | | $(125,000) |
| *Financing:* | | |
| Dividends Paid . . . . . . . . . . . . . . . . . . . . . . . . . . . . . . . . . . . . . | | $  (8,000) |
| Proceeds from Long-Term Bonds Issued . . . . . . . . . . . . . . . . . | | 100,000 |
| Cash Flow from Financing . . . . . . . . . . . . . . . . . . . . . . . . . . . . . | | $  92,000 |
| Net Change in Cash for Year . . . . . . . . . . . . . . . . . . . . . . . . . . . . | | ($  25,000) |

An alternative acceptable format is to begin with net income, subtract revenues not providing cash, and add expenses not using cash. This is referred to as the *indirect method* of computing cash flow from operations and is illustrated in Exhibit 5.6.

Because depreciation expense is added to net income to calculate cash provided by operations under the indirect method, readers of financial statements might incorrectly conclude that depreciation expense is a source of cash. However, as Exhibit 5.2 illustrates, the recording of depreciation expense does not affect cash. A noncash asset is decreased and a shareholders' equity account is decreased. Cash from operations results from selling goods and services to customers. If no sales are made, there will be no cash provided by operations regardless of how large the depreciation charge may be.

**Depreciation Is Not a Source of Cash**   To demonstrate that depreciation is not a source of cash, refer to the income statement of Solinger Electric Corporation (Exhibit 5.1) and the operations section of the statement of cash flows (Exhibit 5.6). Exhibit 5.7 reproduces them in condensed form. Ignore income taxes for a moment. Suppose that depreciation for Year 4 had been $25,000 rather than $10,000. The condensed income statement and cash flow from operations would then appear as in Exhibit 5.8. Note that the total cash flow from operations, which is the difference between receipts from revenues and all expenses that did use cash, remains $8,000. The only effects on cash of transactions involving long-term assets are that (1) cash

## Exhibit 5.7 _____

**SOLINGER ELECTRIC CORPORATION**
Year 4
Depreciation, $10,000

| Income Statement | | Cash Flow from Operations | |
|---|---:|---|---:|
| Revenues.................... | $125,000 | Net Income ................. | $20,000 |
| Expenses Except Depreciation .. | (95,000) | Additions: | |
| | $ 30,000 |   Depreciation ............... | 10,000 |
| Depreciation Expense ......... | (10,000) |   Other .................... | 23,000 |
| | | Subtractions:................ | (45,000) |
| | | Cash Flow Provided by | |
| Net Income .................. | $ 20,000 |   Operations................ | $ 8,000 |

## Exhibit 5.8 _____

**SOLINGER ELECTRIC CORPORATION**
Year 4
Depreciation, $25,000

| Income Statement | | Cash Flow from Operations | |
|---|---:|---|---:|
| Revenues.................... | $125,000 | Net Income ................. | $ 5,000 |
| Expenses Except Depreciation .. | (95,000) | Additions: | |
| | $ 30,000 |   Depreciation ............... | 25,000 |
| Depreciation Expense ......... | (25,000) |   Other .................... | 23,000 |
| | | Subtractions:................ | (45,000) |
| | | Cash Flow Provided by | |
| Net Income .................. | $ 5,000 |   Operations................ | $ 8,000 |

is typically used when a long-term asset is acquired and (2) cash is provided when the asset is sold.

At a more sophisticated level, when income taxes are a factor, depreciation does affect cash flow. Depreciation is a factor in the calculation of net income reported in the financial statements, and it is also a deduction from otherwise taxable income on tax returns. The larger the amount of depreciation on tax returns, the smaller the taxable income and the smaller the current payment for income taxes. Chapters 9 and 11 discuss the effect of depreciation on income taxes.

To overcome some of these interpretative problems of the indirect method, the FASB permits the direct method to be used in reporting cash flow from operations in the statement of cash flows, but a note to the financial statements must reconcile net income with cash flow from operations (that is, the indirect method). To simplify the illustrations in this book, we use the indirect method in preparing the statement of cash flows. Intermediate accounting texts illustrate the procedures for preparing the statement of cash flows under the direct method.

## Extension of the Illustration

The illustration for Solinger Electric Corporation considered so far in this chapter is simpler than the typical published statement of cash flows in at least four respects.

1. There are only a few balance sheet accounts whose changes are to be explained.
2. Several types of more complex transactions that affect the sources of cash from operations are not involved.
3. Each transaction recorded in step 3 involves only one debit and one credit.
4. Each explanation of a noncash account change involves only one analytic entry on the work sheet, except for the Retained Earnings account.

Most of the complications that arise in interpreting published statements of cash flows relate to accounting events discussed in later chapters. As these transactions are discussed, their effects on the statement of cash flows will be illustrated. One complication caused by supplementary disclosure can be illustrated at this time, however. Suppose that the firm sold some of its buildings and equipment during the year. For now, and until the issue is addressed again in Chapter 9, assume that the firm disposes of existing buildings and equipment at their book value; the cash proceeds from disposition are equal to acquisition cost less accumulated depreciation of the assets. With this assumption, there will be no gain or loss on disposition.

Reconsider the Solinger Electric Corporation example with the following new information. Solinger Electric Corporation sold some equipment during Year 4. This equipment cost $10,000 and was sold for $3,000 at a time when accumulated depreciation on the equipment sold was $7,000. The actual entry made during the year to record the sale of the equipment was as follows:

| | | |
|---|---:|---:|
| Cash . . . . . . . . . . . . . . . . . . . . . . . . . . . . . . . . . . . . . . . . . . . . . . . . . . . . . | 3,000 | |
| Accumulated Depreciation . . . . . . . . . . . . . . . . . . . . . . . . . . . . . . . . . . . . | 7,000 | |
|    Buildings and Equipment (Cost) . . . . . . . . . . . . . . . . . . . . . . . . . . . . | | 10,000 |
| Journal entry for sale of equipment. | | |

Assume that the comparative balance sheets as shown in Exhibit 5.3 are correct and thus that the net decrease in cash for Year 4 is still $25,000. The entries in the T-accounts must be altered to reflect this new information. The following entry in the T-account work sheet is required to recognize the effect of the sale of equipment:

| | | |
|---|---:|---:|
| (1a) Cash (Investing: Sale of Equipment) . . . . . . . . . . . . . . . . . . . . . . | 3,000 | |
|      Accumulated Depreciation . . . . . . . . . . . . . . . . . . . . . . . . . . . . . . | 7,000 | |
|        Buildings and Equipment (Cost) . . . . . . . . . . . . . . . . . . . . . . . . | | 10,000 |
|      Entry recorded in T-account work sheet. | | |

The debit to Cash (Investing: Sale of Equipment) shows the proceeds of the sale.

As a result of entry (1a), the T-accounts for Buildings and Equipment (Cost) and Accumulated Depreciation would appear as follows:

| Buildings and Equipment (Cost) | | | | Accumulated Depreciation | | |
|---|---|---|---|---|---|---|
| ✔ | 100,000 | | | | 30,000 | ✔ |
| | | 10,000 (1a) | (1a) | 7,000 | | |
| ✔ | 225,000 | | | | 40,000 | ✔ |

When the time comes to explain the change in Buildings and Equipment (Cost) account, the T-account indicates that there is an increase of $125,000 and a credit entry (1a) of $10,000 to recognize the sale of equipment. The net increase in the Buildings and Equipment (Cost) account can be accounted for, given the decrease already entered, only by assuming that new buildings and equipment have been acquired for $135,000 during the period.

The reconstructed entry to complete the explanation of the change in this account would be as follows:

---

(6a) Buildings and Equipment (Cost) ........................... 135,000
      Cash (Investing: Acquisition of Buildings and Equipment)...       135,000
      Entry recorded in T-account work sheet.

---

Likewise, when the change in the T-account for Accumulated Depreciation is explained, there is a net credit change of $10,000 and a debit entry (1a) of $7,000 to recognize the sale. Thus the depreciation charge for Year 4 must have been $17,000. The reconstructed entry to complete the explanation of the change in the Accumulated Depreciation account would be as follows:

---

(2a) Cash (Operations—Depreciation Expense Addback) ........ 17,000
      Accumulated Depreciation .............................       17,000
      Entry recorded in T-account work sheet.

---

Exhibit 5.9 presents a revised T-account work sheet for Solinger Electric Corporation incorporating the new information on the sale of equipment.

## Summary _____

The statement of cash flows reports the effects of a firm's operating, investing, and financing activities on cash flows. Information in the statement helps in understanding (1) how operations affect the liquidity of a firm, (2) the level of capital expenditures needed to support ongoing and growing levels of activity, and (3) the major changes in the financing of a firm.

## Exhibit 5.9

### SOLINGER ELECTRIC CORPORATION
### Revised T-Account Work Sheet

**Cash**

| | | |
|---|---|---|
| ✔ | 30,000 | |

**Operations**

| | | | | | |
|---|---|---|---|---|---|
| Net Income | (1) | 20,000 | 35,000 | (4) | Increased Accounts Receivable |
| Depreciation Expense Addback | (2a) | 17,000 | 10,000 | (5) | Increased Merchandise Inventory |
| Increased Accounts Payable to Merchandise Suppliers | (7) | 20,000 | | | |
| Increased Accounts Payable to Other Suppliers | (8) | 2,000 | | | |
| Increased Salaries Payable | (9) | 1,000 | | | |

**Investing**

| | | | | | |
|---|---|---|---|---|---|
| Sale of Equipment | (1a) | 3,000 | 135,000 | (6a) | Acquisition of Buildings and Equipment |

**Financing**

| | | | | | |
|---|---|---|---|---|---|
| Long-Term Bond Issue | (10) | 100,000 | 8,000 | (3) | Dividends |

| | | |
|---|---|---|
| ✔ | 5,000 | |

**Accounts Receivable**

| | | |
|---|---|---|
| ✔ | 20,000 | |
| (4) | 35,000 | |
| ✔ | 55,000 | |

**Merchandise Inventory**

| | | |
|---|---|---|
| ✔ | 40,000 | |
| (5) | 10,000 | |
| ✔ | 50,000 | |

**Buildings and Equipment (Cost)**

| | | | | |
|---|---|---|---|---|
| ✔ | 100,000 | | | |
| (6a) | 135,000 | 10,000 | (1a) | |
| ✔ | 225,000 | | | |

**Accumulated Depreciation**

| | | | | |
|---|---|---|---|---|
| | | 30,000 | ✔ | |
| (1a) | 7,000 | 17,000 | (2a) | |
| | | 40,000 | ✔ | |

**Accounts Payable— Merchandise Suppliers**

| | | |
|---|---|---|
| 30,000 | ✔ | |
| 20,000 | (7) | |
| 50,000 | ✔ | |

**Accounts Payable— Other Suppliers**

| | | |
|---|---|---|
| 10,000 | ✔ | |
| 2,000 | (8) | |
| 12,000 | ✔ | |

**Salaries Payable**

| | | |
|---|---|---|
| 5,000 | ✔ | |
| 1,000 | (9) | |
| 6,000 | ✔ | |

**Bonds Payable**

| | | | |
|---|---|---|---|
| | 0 | ✔ | |
| | 100,000 | (10) | |
| | 100,000 | ✔ | |

**Retained Earnings**

| | | | | |
|---|---|---|---|---|
| | | 15,000 | ✔ | |
| (3) | 8,000 | 20,000 | (1) | |
| | | 27,000 | ✔ | |

The statement of cash flows is usually prepared by analyzing changes in balance sheet accounts during the accounting period. If the double-entry recording process has been applied properly, the net change in cash will equal the net change in all noncash accounts. Reconstructing the entries made in the noncash accounts and explaining their net change during the period will also explain the net change in cash.

The statement of cash flows usually begins with net income for the period. Adjustments are then made for revenues not providing cash, for expenses not using cash, and for changes in operating working capital accounts. The result is cash flow from operations. Some firms follow a more direct approach to calculating cash flow from operations by listing all revenues that provide cash and subtracting all expenses that use cash. The cash flows from investing activities and financing activities appear after cash flow from operations.

## Problem 1 for Self-Study _____

Exhibit 5.10 presents a comparative balance sheet for Robbie Corporation as of December 31, Year 1 and Year 2. During Year 2, no plant and equipment was sold and no dividends were declared or paid.

Prepare a T-account work sheet for the preparation of a statement of cash flows.

**Exhibit 5.10** _____
**ROBBIE CORPORATION**
**Comparative Balance Sheet**
**December 31, Year 1 and Year 2**
**(all dollar amounts in thousands)**
**(Problem 1 for Self-Study)**

| | December 31, Year 1 | December 31, Year 2 | | December 31, Year 1 | December 31, Year 2 |
|---|---|---|---|---|---|
| **Assets** | | | **Liabilities and Shareholders' Equity** | | |
| **Current Assets:** | | | **Current Liabilities:** | | |
| Cash ........................ | $10 | $ 25 | Accounts Payable ............. | $30 | $ 40 |
| Accounts Receivable............ | 15 | 20 | Total Current Liabilities ....... | $30 | $ 40 |
| Merchandise Inventories......... | 20 | 25 | | | |
| Total Current Assets .......... | $45 | $ 70 | **Long-Term Debt:** | | |
| | | | Bonds Payable ............... | $10 | $ 15 |
| **Property, Plant, and Equipment:** | $50 | $ 60 | Total Liabilities .............. | $40 | $ 55 |
| **Less Accumulated Depreciation:** | (25) | (30) | | | |
| Total Property, Plant, and Equipment ................. | $25 | $ 30 | **Shareholders' Equity:** | | |
| Total Assets ................ | $70 | $100 | Common Stock................ | $10 | $ 20 |
| | | | Retained Earnings ............. | 20 | 25 |
| | | | Total Shareholders' Equity .... | $30 | $ 45 |
| | | | Total Liabilities and Shareholders' Equity .................. | $70 | $100 |

## Suggested Solution

Exhibit 5.11 presents a completed T-account work sheet for Robbie Corporation.

**Exhibit 5.11** _____

**ROBBIE CORPORATION**
**T-Account Work Sheet**
**(all dollar amounts in thousands)**

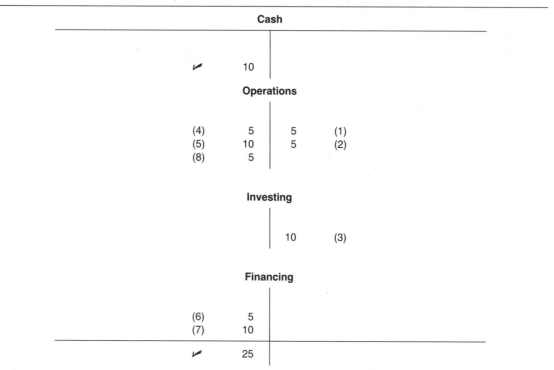

# Problem 2 for Self-Study _____

Exhibit 5.12 presents a comparative balance sheet for Gordon Corporation as of December 31, Year 1 and Year 2. The following information pertains to Gordon Corporation for Year 2.

**1.** Net income was $200,000.

**2.** Dividends declared and paid were $120,000.

**Exhibit 5.12** _____

GORDON CORPORATION
Comparative Balance Sheet
December 31, Year 1 and Year 2
(all dollar amounts in thousands)
(Problem 2 for Self-Study)

|  | December 31, Year 1 | December 31, Year 2 |
|---|---|---|
| **Assets** | | |
| **Current Assets:** | | |
| Cash | $ 70 | $ 40 |
| Accounts Receivable | 320 | 420 |
| Merchandise Inventories | 360 | 470 |
| Prepayments | 50 | 70 |
| Total Current Assets | $ 800 | $1,000 |
| **Property, Plant, and Equipment:** | | |
| Land | $ 200 | $ 250 |
| Buildings and Equipment (net of accumulated depreciation of $800 and $840) | 1,000 | 1,150 |
| Total Property, Plant, and Equipment | $1,200 | $1,400 |
| Total Assets | $2,000 | $2,400 |
| **Liabilities and Shareholders' Equity** | | |
| **Current Liabilities:** | | |
| Accounts Payable | $ 320 | $ 440 |
| Income Taxes Payable | 60 | 80 |
| Other Current Liabilities | 170 | 360 |
| Total Current Liabilities | $ 550 | $ 880 |
| **Noncurrent Liabilities:** | | |
| Bonds Payable | $ 250 | $ 200 |
| Total Liabilities | $ 800 | $1,080 |
| **Shareholders' Equity:** | | |
| Common Stock | $ 500 | $ 540 |
| Retained Earnings | 700 | 780 |
| Total Shareholders' Equity | $1,200 | $1,320 |
| Total Liabilities and Shareholders' Equity | $2,000 | $2,400 |

3. Depreciation expense totaled $80,000.

4. Buildings and equipment originally costing $50,000 and with accumulated depreciation of $40,000 were sold for $10,000.

a. Prepare a T-account work sheet for the preparation of a statement of cash flows.

b. Prepare a formal statement of cash flows.

## Suggested Solution

Exhibit 5.13 presents a completed T-account work sheet for Gordon Corporation. Exhibit 5.14 presents a formal statement of cash flows.

Exhibit 5.13 ─────────────────────────────────────────────────────────

GORDON CORPORATION
T-Account Work Sheet
Funds Defined as Cash
(all dollar amounts in thousands)

### Cash

|  |  |
|---|---|
| ✔ 70 |  |

### Operations

| | | | | |
|---|---|---|---|---|
| (1) | 200 | 100 | (5) |
| (3) | 80 | 110 | (6) |
| (10) | 120 | 20 | (7) |
| (11) | 20 | | |
| (12) | 190 | | |

### Investing

| | | | | |
|---|---|---|---|---|
| (4) | 10 | 50 | (8) |
| | | 240 | (9) |

### Financing

| | | | | |
|---|---|---|---|---|
| (14) | 40 | 120 | (2) |
| | | 50 | (13) |
| ✔ | 40 | | |

| Accounts Receivable | | Merchandise Inventory | | Prepayments | |
|---|---|---|---|---|---|
| ✔ 320 | | ✔ 360 | | ✔ 50 | |
| (5) 100 | | (6) 110 | | (7) 20 | |
| ✔ 420 | | ✔ 470 | | ✔ 70 | |

*continued*

**Exhibit 5.13** (*continued*) ————————————————————————————————————

| Land | | | Buildings and Equipment—Net | | | Accounts Payable | | |
|---|---|---|---|---|---|---|---|---|
| ✔ | 200 | | ✔ | 1,000 | | | | 320 ✔ |
| (8) | 50 | | (4) | 40 | 80 (3) | | | 120 (10) |
| | | | (9) | 240 | 50 (4) | | | |
| ✔ | 250 | | ✔ | 1,150 | | | | 440 ✔ |

| Income Taxes Payable | | | Other Current Liabilities | | | Bonds Payable | | |
|---|---|---|---|---|---|---|---|---|
| | | 60 ✔ | | | 170 ✔ | | | 250 ✔ |
| | | 20 (11) | | | 190 (12) | (13) | 50 | |
| | | 80 ✔ | | | 360 ✔ | | | 200 ✔ |

| Common Stock | | | Retained Earnings | | |
|---|---|---|---|---|---|
| | | 500 ✔ | | | 700 ✔ |
| | | 40 (14) | (2) | 120 | 200 (1) |
| | | 540 ✔ | | | 780 ✔ |

**Exhibit 5.14** ————————————————————————————————————

## GORDON CORPORATION
## Statement of Cash Flows for Year 2
## (all dollar amounts in thousands)

**Sources of Cash**
*Operations:*

| | | |
|---|---|---|
| Net Income . . . . . . . . . . . . . . . . . . . . . . . . . . . . . . . . . . . . . . . . . . . . . . . . . . | $200 | |
| Additions: | | |
|   Depreciation Expense . . . . . . . . . . . . . . . . . . . . . . . . . . . . . . . . . . . . . . . | 80 | |
|   Increase in Accounts Payable . . . . . . . . . . . . . . . . . . . . . . . . . . . . . . . . | 120 | |
|   Increase in Income Taxes Payable . . . . . . . . . . . . . . . . . . . . . . . . . . . | 20 | |
|   Increase in Other Current Liabilities . . . . . . . . . . . . . . . . . . . . . . . . . | 190 | |
| Subtractions: | | |
|   Increase in Accounts Receivable . . . . . . . . . . . . . . . . . . . . . . . . . . . . . | (100) | |
|   Increase in Merchandise Inventories . . . . . . . . . . . . . . . . . . . . . . . . . . | (110) | |
|   Increase in Prepayments . . . . . . . . . . . . . . . . . . . . . . . . . . . . . . . . . . . . | (20) | |
| Cash Provided by Operations . . . . . . . . . . . . . . . . . . . . . . . . . . . . . . . . . . . . | | $380 |
| *Investing:* | | |
|   Buildings and Equipment Sold . . . . . . . . . . . . . . . . . . . . . . . . . . . . . . . . | $ 10 | |
|   Acquisition of Land . . . . . . . . . . . . . . . . . . . . . . . . . . . . . . . . . . . . . . . . . | (50) | |
|   Acquisition of Buildings and Equipment . . . . . . . . . . . . . . . . . . . . . . . | (240) | |
| Cash Used for Investing . . . . . . . . . . . . . . . . . . . . . . . . . . . . . . . . . . . . . . . . | | (280) |

*continued*

**Exhibit 5.14** *(continued)* ————————————————————————————

*Financing:*

| | | |
|---|---|---|
| Common Stock Issued | $ 40 | |
| Dividends Paid | (120) | |
| Repayment of Bonds | (50) | |
| Cash Used for Financing | | (130) |
| Net Decrease in Cash | | $ (30) |

## Problem 3 for Self-Study ————————————————————————

Exhibit 5.15 shows a simplified statement of cash flows for a period. Eleven of the lines in the statement are numbered. Other lines are various subtotals and grand totals; these are to be ignored in the remainder of the problem. Assume that the accounting cycle is complete for the period and that all of the financial statements have been prepared. It is then discovered that a transaction has been overlooked. That transaction is recorded in the accounts, and all of the financial statements are corrected. For each of the following transactions, indicate which of the numbered lines of the statement of cash flows are affected. Define funds as cash. If net income, line (1), is affected, be sure to indicate whether it decreases or increases. Ignore income tax effects.

**Exhibit 5.15** ————————————————————————————————

**Simplified Statement of Cash Flows**

*Operating:*

| | |
|---|---|
| Net Income | (1) |
| Addback for Expenses and Losses Not Using Working Capital | +(2) |
| Subtractions for Revenues and Gains Not Producing Working Capital | −(3) |
| Additions for Decreases in Current Asset Accounts Other than Cash and for Increases in Current Liability Accounts | +(4) |
| Subtractions for Increases in Current Asset Accounts Other than Cash and for Decreases in Current Liability Accounts | −(5) |
| Cash Flow from Operations [ = (1) + (2) − (3) + (4) − (5)] | S1 |

*Investing:*

| | |
|---|---|
| Proceeds from Dispositions of Noncurrent Assets | +(6) |
| Acquisition of Noncurrent Assets | −(7) |
| Cash Flow from Investing [ = (6) − (7)] | S2 |

*Financing:*

| | |
|---|---|
| Increases in Debt or Capital Stock | +(8) |
| Dividends | −(9) |
| Reduction in Debt or Capital Stock | −(10) |
| Cash Flow from Financing [ = (8) − (9) − (10)] | S3 |
| Net Change in Cash for the Period ( = S1 + S2 + S3) | (11) |

a.   Depreciation expense on an office computer.

b.   Purchase of machinery for cash.

c.   Declaration of a cash dividend on common stock. The dividend was paid by the end of the fiscal year.

d.   Issue of common stock for cash.

e.   Proceeds of the sale of a common stock investment, a noncurrent asset, for cash. The investment was sold for book value.

## Suggested Solution

a.   (1) decreases; reduction in net income for depreciation expense.
     (2) increases; amount of expense is added back to net income in deriving cash flow from operations.

b.   (7) increases; decrease in cash to acquire noncurrent asset.
     (11) decreases.

c.   (9) increases; decrease in cash for dividend.
     (11) decreases.

d.   (8) increases; increase in cash from security issue.
     (11) increases.

e.   (6) increases; increase in cash from disposition of noncurrent asset.
     (11) increases.

# Questions, Exercises, Problems, and Cases _____
## Questions

1.  Review the meaning of the following concepts or terms discussed in this chapter.
    a.   Relation between income flows and cash flows.
    b.   Cash flow from operations.
    c.   T-account work sheet.
    d.   Depreciation is not a source of cash.

2.  "The reporting objective of the income statement under the accrual basis of accounting and the reporting objective of the statement of cash flows could be more easily accomplished by issuing a single income statement using the cash basis of accounting." Evaluate this proposal.

3.  "The statement of cash flows provides information about changes in the structure of a firm's assets and equities." Explain.

4.  The acquisition of equipment by assuming a mortgage is a transaction that must be disclosed either in the statement of cash flows or in a supplemental schedule. Of what value is information about the disclosure of this type of transaction?

**5.** One writer stated:

> Depreciation expense is the chief source of cash for growth in industries.

A reader criticized this statement by replying:

> The fact remains that if the companies listed had elected, in any year, to charge off $10 million more depreciation than they did charge off, they would not thereby have added one dime to the total of their cash available for plant expansion or for increasing inventories or receivables. Therefore, to speak of depreciation expense as a source of cash has no significance in a discussion of fundamentals.

Comment on these statements, including income tax effects.

**6.** A firm generated net income for the current year, but cash flow from operations was negative. How can this happen?

**7.** A firm operated at a net loss for the current year, but cash flow from operations was positive. How can this happen?

## Exercises

**8.** *Effect of various transactions on cash.* Prepare a work sheet with the following headings:

### Effect of Transaction or Event on

| Transaction or Event | Cash | Other Current Assets | Noncurrent Assets | Current Liabilities | Noncurrent Liabilities | Shareholders' Equity |
|---|---|---|---|---|---|---|

**a.** For each of the transactions or events that follow, indicate the effect on the balance sheet categories shown in the work sheet.

**(1)** Merchandise is purchased on account for $5,000.

**(2)** Of amount due for purchases in **(1)**, $4,000 is paid.

**(3)** Merchandise is sold to customers on credit. Selling price is $7,000; cost of goods sold is $3,500.

**(4)** Of amount due from customers from sales in **(3)**, $5,500 is collected.

**(5)** Depreciation expense for the period is $600.

**(6)** Employees earn salaries of $1,200 [also see transaction **(7)**].

**(7)** Employees are paid $1,100 of amount due in **(6)**.

**(8)** Insurance premium of $200 is paid for coverage to begin next accounting period.

**(9)** Income taxes for the period are accrued, $900 [also see transaction **(10)**].

**(10)** Income taxes of $600 are paid.

**(11)** Bonds payable of $200 are issued.

**(12)** Equipment costing $1,500, and on which $1,000 of depreciation had been taken, is sold for $500.

**(13)** Equipment costing $300 is acquired for cash.

(**14**) Equipment costing $200 is acquired and a noncurrent liability of $200 is assumed for the purchase price.

(**15**) Dividends of $700 are declared and paid.

**b.** Indicate whether each of the transactions or events affecting cash relates to an operating, investing, or financing activity.

**9.** *Calculating cash flow from operations.* The following items were found in the financial statements of Maher Company for Year 2.

| | |
|---|---:|
| Sales. . . . . . . . . . . . . . . . . . . . . . . . . . . . . . . . . . . . . . . . . . . . . . . . . . . . . . . . . | $90,000 |
| Depreciation Expense . . . . . . . . . . . . . . . . . . . . . . . . . . . . . . . . . . . . . . . . . . . | 45,000 |
| Income Taxes . . . . . . . . . . . . . . . . . . . . . . . . . . . . . . . . . . . . . . . . . . . . . . . . . . | 10,000 |
| Other Expenses . . . . . . . . . . . . . . . . . . . . . . . . . . . . . . . . . . . . . . . . . . . . . . . . | 20,000 |
| Common Stock Issued during Year . . . . . . . . . . . . . . . . . . . . . . . . . . . . . . . . | 17,500 |

The changes in current asset and current liability accounts were as follows:

| | |
|---|---:|
| Accounts Receivable . . . . . . . . . . . . . . . . . . . . . . . . . . . . . . . . . . . . . . . . . . . | $45,000 Increase |
| Merchandise Inventories . . . . . . . . . . . . . . . . . . . . . . . . . . . . . . . . . . . . . . . . | 30,000 Increase |
| Prepayments . . . . . . . . . . . . . . . . . . . . . . . . . . . . . . . . . . . . . . . . . . . . . . . . . . | 5,000 Decrease |
| Accounts Payable . . . . . . . . . . . . . . . . . . . . . . . . . . . . . . . . . . . . . . . . . . . . . | 15,000 Increase |
| Income Taxes Payable . . . . . . . . . . . . . . . . . . . . . . . . . . . . . . . . . . . . . . . . . | 7,500 Decrease |

Compute the amount of cash flow from operations.

**10.** *Calculating cash flow from operations.* Compute the amount of cash flow from operations in each of the independent cases that follow.

| | a | b | c | d |
|---|---:|---:|---:|---:|
| Net Income (Loss) . . . . . . . . . . . . . . . . . . . . . . . . . . | $100 | $50 | $70 | $(40) |
| Depreciation Expense . . . . . . . . . . . . . . . . . . . . . . . | 15 | 10 | 12 | 18 |
| Increase (Decrease) In: | | | | |
|    Accounts Receivable . . . . . . . . . . . . . . . . . . . . . . . | 20 | 15 | (10) | 12 |
|    Merchandise Inventories . . . . . . . . . . . . . . . . . . . . | 25 | (10) | 15 | 15 |
|    Prepayments . . . . . . . . . . . . . . . . . . . . . . . . . . . . . . | 10 | (3) | 4 | (6) |
|    Accounts Payable . . . . . . . . . . . . . . . . . . . . . . . . . | 15 | 10 | (20) | 14 |
|    Income Taxes Payable . . . . . . . . . . . . . . . . . . . . . | 18 | (8) | 14 | (16) |
|    Other Current Liabilities . . . . . . . . . . . . . . . . . . . . | 12 | (9) | (7) | 11 |

**11.** *Working backwards from changes in Buildings and Equipment account.* The comparative balance sheet of the Kanodia Company showed a balance in the Buildings and Equipment account at December 31, Year 5, of $24,600,000; at December 31, Year 4, the balance was $24,000,000. The Accumulated Depreciation account showed a balance of $8,600,000 at December 31, Year 5, and of $7,600,000 at December 31, Year 4. The statement of cash flows reports that expenditures for buildings and equipment for the year totaled $1,300,000. The income statement indicates a depreciation charge of $1,200,000 for the year. Buildings and equipment were sold during the year at their book value.

Calculate the acquisition cost and accumulated depreciation of the buildings and equipment retired during the year and the proceeds from their disposition.

**12.** *Preparing statement of cash flows; working backwards from changes in plant asset accounts.* The balance in the Property, Plant, and Equipment (Cost) account was $200 on January 1 and $260 on December 31. The balance in the Accumulated Depreciation account was $120 on January 1 and $140 on December 31. During the year, equipment costing $25 and with accumulated depreciation of $15 was sold for $10. No dividends were paid during the year, nor were there any changes in the Bonds Payable or the Common Stock accounts. Cash flow from operations totaled $80, and the net change in cash for the year was an increase of $5.

Prepare a statement of cash flows for the year.

**13.** *Preparing statement of cash flows using changes in balance sheet accounts.* The accounting records of Kropp Corporation reveal the following for the current year.

| Account | Change Amount | Direction |
|---|---|---|
| Cash ..................................................... | $120 | Increase |
| Accounts Receivable.................................... | 15 | Increase |
| Merchandise Inventories................................ | 20 | Decrease |
| Property, Plant, and Equipment ......................... | 50[a] | Increase |
| Accumulated Depreciation .............................. | 10 | Increase |
| Accounts Payable ...................................... | 25 | Increase |
| Bonds Payable ......................................... | 20 | Increase |
| Common Stock.......................................... | 30 | Increase |
| Retained Earnings ..................................... | 80[b] | Increase |

[a]There were no dispositions of property, plant, and equipment during the year.
[b]Net income was $130; dividends were $50.

Prepare a statement of cash flows.

**14.** *Preparing statement of cash flows using changes in balance sheet accounts.* The accounting records of Baker Corporation reveal the following for the current year.

| Account | Change Amount | Direction |
|---|---|---|
| Cash ..................................................... | $75 | Decrease |
| Accounts Receivable.................................... | 40 | Increase |
| Merchandise Inventories................................ | 30 | Increase |
| Property, Plant, and Equipment ......................... | 60[a] | Increase |
| Accumulated Depreciation .............................. | 20[a] | Increase |
| Accounts Payable ...................................... | 25 | Decrease |

| Bonds Payable ....................................... | 35[b] | Decrease |
| Common Stock........................................ | 45 | Increase |
| Retained Earnings ................................... | 50[c] | Increase |

[a]Equipment costing $15 and with accumulated depreciation of $12 was sold for $3 during the year.

[b]Bonds with a face value and book value of $50 were retired during the year at no gain or loss.

[c]Dividends declared and paid totaled $20 during the year.

Prepare a statement of cash flows.

15. *Reformatting statement of cash flows.* Guerrero Corporation has prepared the statement of cash flows appearing in Exhibit 5.16. Recast this statement into a properly formatted statement of cash flows.

Exhibit 5.16 _____

**GUERRERO CORPORATION**
**Statement of Cash Flows for the Current Year**
**(Exercise 15)**

| | |
|---|---:|
| **Sources of Cash:** | |
| Proceeds from Issue of Bonds ....................................... | $ 20,000 |
| Proceeds from Issue of Common Stock ............................. | 30,000 |
| Proceeds from Sale of Equipment ................................... | 4,000 |
| Net Income ............................................................. | 40,000 |
| Depreciation Expense ................................................ | 10,000 |
| Increase in Accounts Payable....................................... | 15,000 |
| Total Sources ...................................................... | $119,000 |
| | |
| **Uses of Cash:** | |
| Acquisition of Equipment[a] ......................................... | $ 60,000 |
| Payment of Dividends................................................. | 12,000 |
| Repayment of Bonds Payable....................................... | 8,000 |
| Increase in Accounts Receivable ................................... | 16,000 |
| Increase in Merchandise Inventory ................................ | 11,000 |
| Total Uses ......................................................... | $107,000 |
| **Net Change in Cash** ............................................. | $ 12,000 |

[a]In addition, equipment costing $25,000 was acquired and a noncurrent liability was assumed for the purchase price.

16. *Effect of various transactions on statement of cash flows.* Exhibit 5.15 shows a simplified statement of cash flows for a period. Eleven of the lines in the statement are numbered. Other lines are various subtotals and grand totals; these are to be ignored in the rest of the problem. Assume that the accounting cycle is complete for the period and that all of the financial statements have been prepared. It is then discovered that a transaction has been overlooked. That transaction is recorded in the accounts, and all of the financial statements are corrected. For each of the following transactions, indicate which of the numbered lines of the statement of cash flows are affected. If net income, line (1), is affected, be sure to indicate whether it decreases or increases. Ignore income tax effects.

a. Amortization of a patent, treated as an expense.
b. Amortization of a patent, charged to production activities. The items being produced have not yet been completed.
c. Acquisition of a factory site by the issue of capital stock.
d. Purchase of inventory on account.
e. Uninsured fire loss of merchandise inventory.
f. Collection of an account receivable.
g. Issue of bonds for cash.
h. Proceeds from sale of equipment. The equipment was sold for its book value.

## Problems and Cases

17. *Preparing statement of cash flows*. Exhibit 5.17 presents a comparative balance sheet for Bragg Corporation as of the beginning and end of the current year. During the year there were no dispositions of property, plant, and equipment, and no dividends were declared or paid.

   Prepare a statement of cash flows for Bragg Corporation for the current year, supporting the statement with a T-account work sheet.

Exhibit 5.17 _____
**BRAGG CORPORATION**
**Comparative Balance Sheet**
**(Problem 17)**

|  | January 1 | December 31 |
|---|---|---|
| **Assets** | | |
| **Current Assets:** | | |
| Cash ............................................. | $ 6,000 | $ 10,000 |
| Accounts Receivable............................. | 72,000 | 82,000 |
| Merchandise Inventories......................... | 95,000 | 110,000 |
| Total Current Assets ............................ | $173,000 | $202,000 |
| Property, Plant, and Equipment .................... | $350,000 | $425,000 |
| Less Accumulated Depreciation .................... | (123,000) | (135,000) |
| Total Property, Plant and Equipment.............. | $227,000 | $290,000 |
| Total Assets .................................. | $400,000 | $492,000 |
| **Liabilities and Shareholders' Equity** | | |
| **Current Liabilities:** | | |
| Accounts Payable ................................ | $ 95,000 | $121,000 |
| Income Taxes Payable ........................... | 10,000 | 15,000 |
| Total Current Liabilities ........................ | $105,000 | $136,000 |

*continued*

**Exhibit 5.17** *(continued)* _____

|  | January 1 | December 31 |
|---|---|---|
| **Long-Term Debt:** | | |
| Bonds Payable . . . . . . . . . . . . . . . . . . . . . . . . . . . . . . . . . . . | 50,000 | 75,000 |
| Total Liabilities . . . . . . . . . . . . . . . . . . . . . . . . . . . . . . . . . | $155,000 | $211,000 |
| **Shareholders' Equity:** | | |
| Common Stock. . . . . . . . . . . . . . . . . . . . . . . . . . . . . . . . . . . | $105,000 | $106,000 |
| Retained Earnings . . . . . . . . . . . . . . . . . . . . . . . . . . . . . . . . | 140,000 | 175,000 |
| Total Shareholders' Equity . . . . . . . . . . . . . . . . . . . . . . . | $245,000 | $281,000 |
| Total Liabilities and Shareholders' Equity . . . . . . . . . . | $400,000 | $492,000 |

18. *Preparing statement of cash flows.* Condensed financial statement data for the Harris Company for the current year appear in Exhibits 5.18 and 5.19. During the current year, equipment costing $10,000 and with $8,000 of accumulated depreciation was sold for $2,000.

Prepare a statement of cash flows for the year, supporting the statement with a T-account work sheet. Define funds as cash.

**Exhibit 5.18** _____

**HARRIS COMPANY**
**Comparative Balance Sheets**
**(Problem 18)**

|  | January 1 | December 31 |
|---|---|---|
| # Assets | | |
| Cash . . . . . . . . . . . . . . . . . . . . . . . . . . . . . . . . . . . . . . . . . . | $ 20,000 | $ 24,000 |
| Accounts Receivable. . . . . . . . . . . . . . . . . . . . . . . . . . . . . | 52,000 | 58,000 |
| Inventory . . . . . . . . . . . . . . . . . . . . . . . . . . . . . . . . . . . . . . | 79,000 | 81,000 |
| Land . . . . . . . . . . . . . . . . . . . . . . . . . . . . . . . . . . . . . . . . . . | 15,000 | 15,000 |
| Buildings and Equipment (Cost) . . . . . . . . . . . . . . . . . . . | 400,000 | 415,000 |
| Less Accumulated Depreciation . . . . . . . . . . . . . . . . . . . | (240,000) | (252,000) |
| Total Assets . . . . . . . . . . . . . . . . . . . . . . . . . . . . . . . . | $326,000 | $341,000 |
| # Liabilities and Shareholders' Equity | | |
| Accounts Payable for Inventory . . . . . . . . . . . . . . . . . . . . | $ 62,000 | $ 65,000 |
| Interest Payable . . . . . . . . . . . . . . . . . . . . . . . . . . . . . . . . | 6,000 | 4,000 |
| Mortgage Payable . . . . . . . . . . . . . . . . . . . . . . . . . . . . . . | 60,000 | 55,000 |
| Common Stock. . . . . . . . . . . . . . . . . . . . . . . . . . . . . . . . . . | 120,000 | 130,000 |
| Retained Earnings . . . . . . . . . . . . . . . . . . . . . . . . . . . . . . | 78,000 | 87,000 |
| Total Liabilities and Shareholders' Equity . . . . . . . . . | $326,000 | $341,000 |

Exhibit 5.19 _____

**HARRIS COMPANY**
**Statement of Income and Retained Earnings for the Current Year**
**(Problem 18)**

| | | |
|---|---:|---:|
| Revenues........................................ | | $200,000 |
| Expenses: | | |
| Cost of Goods Sold........................ | $80,000 | |
| Wages and Salaries ...................... | 26,000 | |
| Depreciation ............................ | 20,000 | |
| Interest................................ | 8,000 | |
| Income Taxes........................... | 27,000 | |
| Total .................................. | | 161,000 |
| Net Income .............................. | | $ 39,000 |
| Dividends on Common Stock ............... | | 30,000 |
| Addition to Retained Earnings for Year..... | | $ 9,000 |
| Retained Earnings, January 1............. | | 78,000 |
| Retained Earnings, December 31 .......... | | $ 87,000 |

19. *Preparing statement of cash flows.* Financial statement data for the Perkerson Supply Company for the current year appear in Exhibit 5.20.

Exhibit 5.20 _____

**PERKERSON SUPPLY COMPANY**
**Comparative Balance Sheets**
**(Problem 19)**

| | January 1 | December 31 |
|---|---:|---:|
| **Assets** | | |
| **Current Assets:** | | |
| Cash .......................................... | $ 179,000 | $ 162,000 |
| Accounts Receivable............................ | 473,000 | 526,000 |
| Inventory ...................................... | 502,000 | 604,000 |
| Total Current Assets ......................... | $1,154,000 | $1,292,000 |
| **Noncurrent Assets:** | | |
| Land .......................................... | $ 297,000 | $ 315,000 |
| Buildings and Machinery ........................ | 4,339,000 | 4,773,000 |
| Less Accumulated Depreciation .................. | (1,987,000) | (2,182,000) |
| Total Noncurrent Assets ...................... | $2,649,000 | $2,906,000 |
| Total Assets ................................. | $3,803,000 | $4,198,000 |
| **Liabilities and Shareholders' Equity** | | |
| **Current Liabilities:** | | |
| Accounts Payable .............................. | $ 206,000 | $ 279,000 |
| Taxes Payable ................................. | 137,000 | 145,000 |
| Other Short-Term Payables ..................... | 294,000 | 363,000 |
| Total Current Liabilities ...................... | $ 637,000 | $ 787,000 |

*continued*

**Exhibit 5.20** *(continued)* _____

| | January 1 | December 31 |
|---|---|---|
| **Noncurrent Liabilities:** | | |
| Bonds Payable .................................. | 992,000 | 967,000 |
| Total Liabilities ............................. | $1,629,000 | $1,754,000 |
| | | |
| **Shareholders' Equity:** | | |
| Common Stock................................. | $  836,000 | $  852,000 |
| Retained Earnings ............................. | 1,338,000 | 1,592,000 |
| Total Shareholders' Equity ..................... | $2,174,000 | $2,444,000 |
| Total Liabilities and Shareholders' Equity ......... | $3,803,000 | $4,198,000 |

Additional information includes the following:

**(1)** Net income for the year was $324,000; dividends declared and paid were $70,000.

**(2)** Depreciation expense for the year was $305,000 on buildings and machinery.

**(3)** Machinery originally costing $125,000 and with accumulated depreciation of $110,000 was sold for $15,000.

Prepare a statement of cash flows for the Perkerson Supply Company for the year. Support the statement with a T-account work sheet.

**20.** *Preparing income statement and statement of cash flows.* The year's condensed financial statement data for the Victoria Company appear in Exhibit 5.21.

Expenditures on new plant and equipment for the year amounted to $121,000. Old plant and equipment that had cost $94,000 were sold for cash during the year at book value.

**Exhibit 5.21** _____

**VICTORIA COMPANY**
**Post-Closing Trial Balance**
**Comparative Data**
**(Problem 20)**

| | January 1 | December 31 |
|---|---|---|
| **Debits:** | | |
| Cash .......................................... | $   62,000 | $   55,000 |
| Accounts Receivable ........................... | 135,000 | 163,000 |
| Merchandise Inventory ......................... | 247,000 | 262,000 |
| Plant and Equipment (cost) ..................... | 1,362,000 | 1,389,000 |
| Total Debits .................................. | $1,806,000 | $1,869,000 |

*continued*

**Exhibit 5.21** (continued) _____

| | January 1 | December 31 |
|---|---|---|
| **Credits:** | | |
| Accounts Payable ............................... | $  72,000 | $   75,000 |
| Accumulated Depreciation ........................ | 508,000 | 573,000 |
| Long-Term Debt .................................. | 200,000 | 215,000 |
| Capital Stock.................................... | 509,000 | 509,000 |
| Retained Earnings ............................... | 517,000 | 497,000 |
| Total Credits ................................ | $1,806,000 | $1,869,000 |
| | | |
| **Income Statement Data:** | | |
| Sales............................................ | | $1,338,000 |
| Cost of Goods Sold (excluding depreciation) ....... | | 932,000 |
| Selling and Administrative Expenses............... | | 298,000 |
| Depreciation Expense............................. | | 93,000 |
| Interest Expense ................................ | | 20,000 |
| Other Expenses ................................. | | 15,000 |

a. Prepare an income statement (including a reconciliation of retained earnings) for the year.

b. Prepare a statement of cash flows for the Victoria Company for the year. Support the statement of cash flows with a T-account work sheet.

21. *Preparing statement of cash flows.* Exhibit 5.22 presents a comparative balance sheet for Psilos Corporation as of the beginning and end of the current year. Additional information related to the year is as follows:

| | |
|---|---|
| Net Income ...................................................... | $40,000 |
| Dividends Declared and Paid ....................................... | 50,000 |
| Property, Plant and Equipment Acquired: | |
| For Cash ....................................................... | 40,000 |
| By Assuming Long-Term Debt ..................................... | 15,000 |
| Proceeds from Sale of Property, Plant, and Equipment at Book Value..... | 5,000 |

Prepare a statement of cash flows for Psilos Corporation for the current year, supporting the statement with a T-account work sheet.

Exhibit 5.22 _____

PSILOS CORPORATION
Comparative Balance Sheet
(Problem 21)

| | January 1 | December 31 |
|---|---|---|
| **Assets** | | |
| **Current Assets:** | | |
| Cash............................................. | $ 28,000 | $ 16,000 |
| Accounts Receivable............................ | 125,000 | 109,000 |
| Merchandise Inventories........................ | 147,000 | 163,000 |
|    Total Current Assets ........................... | $300,000 | $288,000 |
| Property, Plant, and Equipment ................... | $210,000 | $240,000 |
| Less Accumulated Depreciation ................... | (87,000) | (85,000) |
|    Total Property, Plant, and Equipment ............ | $123,000 | $155,000 |
|    Total Assets ................................. | $423,000 | $443,000 |
| **Liabilities and Shareholders' Equity** | | |
| **Current Liabilities:** | | |
| Accounts Payable .............................. | $177,000 | $175,000 |
| Income Taxes Payable .......................... | 23,000 | 30,000 |
|    Total Current Liabilities ........................ | $200,000 | $205,000 |
| **Long-Term Debt:** | | |
| Bonds Payable ................................. | 50,000 | 75,000 |
|    Total Liabilities ............................... | $250,000 | $280,000 |
| **Shareholders' Equity:** | | |
| Common Stock.................................. | $ 10,000 | $ 10,000 |
| Retained Earnings .............................. | 163,000 | 153,000 |
|    Total Shareholders' Equity ...................... | $173,000 | $163,000 |
|    Total Liabilities and Shareholders' Equity .......... | $423,000 | $443,000 |

**22.** *Preparing statement of cash flows over 2-year period.* Condensed financial statement data of the Alberta Company for December 31, Year 1, Year 2, and Year 3, are presented in Exhibits 5.23 and 5.24.

   **a.** Prepare a statement of cash flows for Year 2. Support the statement with a T-account work sheet. The original cost of the property, plant, and equipment sold during Year 2 was $108,000. These assets were sold for cash at their net book value.

   **b.** Prepare a T-account work sheet and a statement of cash flows for Year 3. Property, plant, and equipment were sold during the year at book value. Expenditures on new property, plant, and equipment amounted to $318,000 during Year 3.

Exhibit 5.23 _____

**ALBERTA COMPANY**
**Post-Closing Trial Balance**
**Comparative Data**
**(Problem 22)**

|  | 12/31/Year 1 | 12/31/Year 2 | 12/31/Year 3 |
|---|---|---|---|
| **Debits:** | | | |
| Cash ......................... | $  55,000 | $  87,000 | $  97,000 |
| Accounts Receivable ............ | 110,000 | 120,000 | 105,000 |
| Merchandise Inventories ......... | 125,000 | 115,000 | 140,000 |
| Total Current Assets .......... | $ 290,000 | $ 322,000 | $ 342,000 |
| Property, Plant, and Equipment ... | 1,616,000 | 1,679,000 | 1,875,000 |
| Total Debits ................. | $1,906,000 | $2,001,000 | $2,217,000 |
| **Credits:** | | | |
| Accounts Payable ............... | $  81,000 | $  80,000 | $  83,000 |
| Accumulated Depreciation ........ | 697,000 | 720,000 | 745,000 |
| Bonds Payable .................. | 106,000 | 90,000 | 135,000 |
| Common Stock ................... | 377,000 | 423,000 | 514,000 |
| Retained Earnings .............. | 645,000 | 688,000 | 740,000 |
| Total Credits ................. | $1,906,000 | $2,001,000 | $2,217,000 |

Exhibit 5.24 _____

**ALBERTA COMPANY**
**Income and Retained Earnings**
**Statement Data**
**(Problem 22)**

|  | Year 2 | Year 3 |
|---|---|---|
| Sales .............................................. | $910,000 | $970,000 |
| Interest and Other Revenue .......................... | 5,000 | 7,000 |
| Cost of Goods Sold (excluding depreciation) ............ | 370,000 | 413,000 |
| Selling and Administrative Expenses .................... | 320,000 | 301,000 |
| Depreciation ....................................... | 87,000 | 98,000 |
| Federal Income Taxes ............................... | 55,000 | 66,000 |
| Dividends Declared ................................. | 40,000 | 47,000 |

23. *Working backwards through statement of cash flows.* The Quinta Company presents the post-closing trial balance shown in Exhibit 5.25 and the statement of cash flows shown in Exhibit 5.26 for Year 5.

Investments, equipment, and land were sold for cash at their net book value. The accumulated depreciation of the equipment sold was $20,000.

Prepare a balance sheet for the beginning of the year, January 1, Year 5.

**Exhibit 5.25** _____

## QUINTA COMPANY
Post-Closing Trial Balance
December 31, Year 5
(Problem 23)

**Debit Balances:**

| | |
|---|---:|
| Cash | $ 25,000 |
| Accounts Receivable | 220,000 |
| Merchandise Inventories | 320,000 |
| Land | 40,000 |
| Buildings and Equipment | 500,000 |
| Investments (noncurrent) | 100,000 |
| Total Debits | $1,205,000 |

**Credit Balances:**

| | |
|---|---:|
| Accumulated Depreciation | $ 200,000 |
| Accounts Payable | 280,000 |
| Other Current Liabilities | 85,000 |
| Bonds Payable | 100,000 |
| Common Stock | 200,000 |
| Retained Earnings | 340,000 |
| Total Credits | $1,205,000 |

**Exhibit 5.26** _____

## QUINTA COMPANY
Statement of Cash Flows for Year 5
(Problem 23)

| | | |
|---|---:|---:|
| *Operations:* | | |
| Net Income | $200,000 | |
| Additions: | | |
| Depreciation Expense | 60,000 | |
| Increase in Accounts Payable | 25,000 | |
| Subtractions: | | |
| Increase in Accounts Receivable | (30,000) | |
| Increase in Merchandise Inventories | (40,000) | |
| Decrease in Other Current Liabilities | (45,000) | |
| Cash Flow from Operations | | $170,000 |
| *Investing:* | | |
| Sale of Investments | $ 40,000 | |
| Sale of Buildings and Equipment | 15,000 | |
| Sale of Land | 10,000 | |
| Acquisition of Buildings and Equipment | (130,000) | |
| Cash Flow from Investing | | (65,000) |
| *Financing:* | | |
| Common Stock Issued | $ 60,000 | |
| Bonds Issued | 40,000 | |
| Dividends Paid | (200,000) | |
| Cash Flow from Financing | | (100,000) |
| Net Change in Cash | | $ 5,000 |

**24.** *Interpretative case using statement of cash flows (adapted from a problem by L. Morrissey).* RV Suppliers, Incorporated, founded in January, Year 1, manufactures "Kaps." A "Kap" is a relatively low-cost camping unit attached to a pickup truck. Most units consist of an extruded aluminum frame and a fiberglass skin.

   After a loss in its initial year, the company was barely profitable in Year 2 and Year 3. More substantial profits were realized in Years 4 and 5, as indicated in the financial statements shown in Exhibits 5.27 and 5.28.

Exhibit 5.27 ─────────────────────────────────────────────

**RV SUPPLIERS, INCORPORATED**
**Balance Sheets**
**(all dollar amounts in thousands)**
**(Problem 24)**

| | Dec. 31 Year 4 | Dec. 31 Year 5 | Dec. 31 Year 6 |
|---|---|---|---|
| **Assets** | | | |
| **Current Assets:** | | | |
| Cash . . . . . . . . . . . . . . . . . . . . . . . . . . . . . . . . . . . . . . . . | $ 14.0 | $ 12.0 | $  5.2 |
| Accounts Receivable . . . . . . . . . . . . . . . . . . . . . . . . . | 28.8 | 55.6 | 24.2 |
| Inventories . . . . . . . . . . . . . . . . . . . . . . . . . . . . . . . . . . | 54.0 | 85.6 | 81.0 |
| Tax Refund Receivable . . . . . . . . . . . . . . . . . . . . . . | 0 | 0 | 5.0 |
| Prepayments . . . . . . . . . . . . . . . . . . . . . . . . . . . . . . . . | 4.8 | 7.4 | 5.6 |
| Total Current Assets . . . . . . . . . . . . . . . . . . . . . . | $101.6 | $160.6 | $121.0 |
| Property, Plant, Equipment — Net (Note 1) . . . . . . | 30.2 | 73.4 | 72.2 |
| Total Assets . . . . . . . . . . . . . . . . . . . . . . . . . . . . . | $131.8 | $234.0 | $193.2 |
| **Liabilities and Shareholders' Equity** | | | |
| **Current Liabilities:** | | | |
| Bank Notes Payable . . . . . . . . . . . . . . . . . . . . . . . . | $ 10.0 | $ 52.0 | $ 70.0 |
| Accounts Payable . . . . . . . . . . . . . . . . . . . . . . . . . . | 31.6 | 53.4 | 17.4 |
| Income Taxes Payable . . . . . . . . . . . . . . . . . . . . . . . | 5.8 | 7.0 | 0 |
| Other Current Liabilities . . . . . . . . . . . . . . . . . . . . . | 4.2 | 6.8 | 4.4 |
| Total Current Liabilities . . . . . . . . . . . . . . . . . . . . | $ 51.6 | $119.2 | $ 91.8 |
| **Shareholders' Equity:** | | | |
| Capital Stock . . . . . . . . . . . . . . . . . . . . . . . . . . . . . . . | $ 44.6 | $ 44.6 | $ 44.6 |
| Retained Earnings . . . . . . . . . . . . . . . . . . . . . . . . . . | 35.6 | 70.2 | 56.8 |
| Total Shareholders' Equity . . . . . . . . . . . . . . . . . . | $ 80.2 | $114.8 | $101.4 |
| Total Liabilities and Shareholders' Equity . . . . . . | $131.8 | $234.0 | $193.2 |

| Note 1 | Year 4 | Year 5 | Year 6 |
|---|---|---|---|
| Acquisitions . . . . . . . . . . . . . . . . . . . . . . . . . . . . . . . . . | $ 13.4 | $ 48.4 | $ 11.8 |
| Depreciation Expense . . . . . . . . . . . . . . . . . . . . . . . . | (1.7) | (4.8) | (7.6) |
| Book Value and Sales Proceeds from Retirements | (.4) | (.4) | (5.4) |
| Net Change in Property, Plant, and Equipment . . | $ 11.3 | $ 43.2 | $  1.2 |

**Exhibit 5.28**

**RV SUPPLIERS, INCORPORATED**
**Income Statements**
**(all dollar amounts in thousands)**
**(Problem 24)**

|  | Year 4 | Year 5 | Year 6 |
|---|---|---|---|
| Net Sales..................................... | $266.4 | $424.0 | $247.4 |
| Cost of Goods Sold............................ | 191.4 | 314.6 | 210.6 |
| Gross Margin ................................. | $ 75.0 | $109.4 | $ 36.8 |
| Operating Expenses[a] .......................... | 35.5 | 58.4 | 55.2 |
| Income (loss) before Income Taxes................ | $ 39.5 | $ 51.0 | $ (18.4) |
| Income Taxes.................................. | 12.3 | 16.4 | 5.0 |
| Net Income (loss) ............................. | $ 27.2 | $ 34.6 | $ (13.4) |

[a]Includes depreciation expense of $1.7 in Year 4, $4.8 in Year 5, and $7.6 in Year 6.

However, in Year 6, ended just last month, the company suffered a loss of $13,400. Sales dropped from $424,000 in Year 5 to $247,400 in Year 6. The outlook for Year 7 is not encouraging. Potential buyers continue to shun pickup trucks in preference to more energy-efficient small foreign and domestic automobiles.

How did the company finance its rapid growth during the year ended December 31, Year 5? What were the sources and uses of cash during the year? Similarly, how did the company manage its financial affairs during the abrupt contraction in business during the year just ended last month?

# Chapter 6 Introduction to Financial Statement Analysis

Chapters 1 through 5 discussed the three principal financial statements provided to report the financial activities of a business: the balance sheet, the income statement, and the statement of cash flows. These chapters considered the purpose, underlying concepts, and procedures for preparing each statement, and discussed some of the uses for information contained in the statements.

Chapters 7 through 13 explore the generally accepted accounting principles used in preparing these financial statements. Before embarking on a study of these principles, it will be useful to introduce some of the techniques that can be used in analyzing financial statements. Such analysis can be done at only an elementary level at this point; effective financial statement interpretation and analysis require a fuller understanding of the impact of accounting principles on the reported amounts. Introducing the tools and techniques of financial statement analysis at this time, however, provides an opportunity to synthesize the material in the five preceding chapters.

## Objectives of Financial Statement Analysis

The first question likely to be raised in analyzing a set of financial statements is "What do I look for?" The response to this question requires an understanding of investment decisions.

To illustrate, assume that you recently have inherited $25,000 and must decide what to do with the bequest. You have narrowed the investment decision to purchasing either a certificate of deposit at a local bank or shares of common stock of Horrigan Corporation, currently selling for $40 per share. Your decision will be based on the *return* anticipated from each investment and the *risk* associated with that return.

The bank is currently paying interest at the rate of 8 percent annually on certificates of deposit. Because it is unlikely that the bank will go out of business, you are virtually certain of earning 8 percent each year.

The return from investing in the shares of Horrigan Corporation's common stock has two components. First, the firm paid a cash dividend in its most recent year of $.625 per share, and you anticipate that this dividend will continue in the future. Also, the market price of the stock is likely to change between the date the shares are purchased and the date in the future when they are sold. The difference between the eventual selling price and the purchase price, often called a *holding gain* (or *loss*), is a second component of the return from buying the stock.

The return from the common stock investment is riskier than the interest on the certificate of deposit. Future dividends and market price changes are likely to be associated, at least partially, with the profitability of the firm. Future income might be less than is currently anticipated if competitors introduce new products that erode Horrigan Corporation's share of its sales market. Future income might be greater than currently anticipated if Horrigan Corporation makes important discoveries or introduces successful new products.

The market price of Horrigan Corporation's shares will probably also be affected by economy-wide factors such as inflation and changes in international tensions. Also, specific industry factors, such as raw materials shortages or government regulation actions, may influence the market price of the shares. Because most individuals prefer less risk to more risk, you will probably demand a higher expected return if you purchase the Horrigan Corporation's shares than if you invest in a certificate of deposit.

Theoretical and empirical research has shown that the expected return from investing in a firm is, in part, related to the expected profitability of the firm.[1] A firm's past operating, or earnings, performance is analyzed as a basis for forecasting its future profitability.

Investment decisions also require that the risk associated with the expected return be assessed.[2] A firm may find itself with a shortage of cash and be unable to repay a short-term loan coming due. Or the amount of long-term debt in the capital structure may be so large that the firm has difficulty meeting the required interest and principal payments. The financial statements provide information for assessing how these and other elements of risk affect expected return.

Most financial statement analysis, therefore, explores some aspect of a firm's profitability or its risk, or both.

## Usefulness of Ratios _____

The various items in financial statements may be difficult to interpret in the form in which they are presented. For example, the profitability of a firm may be difficult to assess by looking at the amount of net income alone. It is helpful to compare earnings with the assets or capital required to generate those earnings. This relation, and other important ones between various items in the financial statements, can be expressed in the form of ratios. Some ratios compare items within the income

[1]Ray Ball and Phillip Brown, "An Empirical Evaluation of Accounting Income Numbers," *Journal of Accounting Research* (Autumn 1968): 159–178.

[2]Modern finance makes a distinction between systematic (market) risk and nonsystematic (firm-specific) risk. The discussion in this chapter does not differentiate between these two dimensions of risk.

statement; some use only balance sheet data; others relate items from more than one of the three principal financial statements. Ratios are useful tools of financial statement analysis because they conveniently summarize data in a form that is easily understood, interpreted, and compared.

Ratios are, by themselves, difficult to interpret. For example, does a rate of return on common shareholders' equity of 8.6 percent reflect a good performance? Once calculated, the ratios must be compared with some standard. Several of the following possible standards may be used:

1. The planned ratio for the period being analyzed.
2. The corresponding ratio during the preceding period for the same firm.
3. The corresponding ratio for a similar firm in the same industry.
4. The average ratio for other firms in the same industry.

Difficulties encountered in using each of these bases for comparison are discussed later.

The sections that follow describe several ratios useful for assessing profitability and various dimensions of risk. To demonstrate the calculation of various ratios, we use data for Horrigan Corporation for Years 2 through 4 appearing in Exhibit 6.1 (comparative balance sheets), Exhibit 6.2 (comparative income statements), and Exhibit 6.3 (comparative statements of cash flows). Our analysis for Horrigan Corporation studies changes in its various ratios over the 3-year period. Such an analysis is referred to as a *time-series analysis*. Comparison of a given firm's ratios with those of other firms for a particular period is referred to as a *cross-section analysis*. Cross-section analysis requires an understanding of the accounting principles used by different firms and is considered in Chapter 15.

## Analysis of Profitability _____

A firm engages in operations to generate net income. Three measures of *profitability* discussed in this section are

1. Rate of return on assets.
2. Rate of return on common shareholders' equity.
3. Earnings per common share.

### Rate of Return on Assets

The *rate of return on assets* is a measure of a firm's performance in using assets to generate earnings independent of the financing of those assets. In terms of the three principal business activities (investing, financing, and operating) discussed in previous chapters, the rate of return on assets relates the results of *operating* performance to the *investments* that a firm has made without regard to how the acquisition of those investments was *financed*.

The rate of return on assets is calculated as follows:

$$\frac{\text{Net Income plus Interest Expense Net of Income Tax Savings}}{\text{Average Total Assets}}.$$

Exhibit 6.1 ————————————————————————

**HORRIGAN CORPORATION**
**Comparative Balance Sheets**
**(all dollar amounts in millions)**

| | December 31 | | | |
| --- | --- | --- | --- | --- |
| | Year 1 | Year 2 | Year 3 | Year 4 |
| **Assets** | | | | |
| Cash . . . . . . . . . . . . . . . . . . . . . . . . . . . . . . . . . . . . . . . | $ 10 | $ 14 | $ 8 | $ 12 |
| Accounts Receivable (net) . . . . . . . . . . . . . . . . . . . . . . | 26 | 36 | 46 | 76 |
| Inventories . . . . . . . . . . . . . . . . . . . . . . . . . . . . . . . . . . | 14 | 30 | 46 | 83 |
| Total Current Assets . . . . . . . . . . . . . . . . . . . . . . . . | $ 50 | $ 80 | $100 | $171 |
| Land . . . . . . . . . . . . . . . . . . . . . . . . . . . . . . . . . . . . . . . | $ 20 | $ 30 | $ 60 | $ 60 |
| Building . . . . . . . . . . . . . . . . . . . . . . . . . . . . . . . . . . . . | 150 | 150 | 150 | 190 |
| Equipment . . . . . . . . . . . . . . . . . . . . . . . . . . . . . . . . . . | 70 | 192 | 276 | 313 |
| Less Accumulated Depreciation . . . . . . . . . . . . . . . . . | (40) | (52) | (66) | (84) |
| Total Noncurrent Assets . . . . . . . . . . . . . . . . . . . . . | $200 | $320 | $420 | $479 |
| Total Assets . . . . . . . . . . . . . . . . . . . . . . . . . . . . . . | $250 | $400 | $520 | $650 |
| **Liabilities and Shareholders' Equity** | | | | |
| Accounts Payable . . . . . . . . . . . . . . . . . . . . . . . . . . . . | $ 25 | $ 30 | $ 35 | $ 50 |
| Salaries Payable . . . . . . . . . . . . . . . . . . . . . . . . . . . . . | 10 | 13 | 15 | 20 |
| Income Taxes Payable . . . . . . . . . . . . . . . . . . . . . . . . | 5 | 7 | 10 | 20 |
| Total Current Liabilities . . . . . . . . . . . . . . . . . . . . . . | $ 40 | $ 50 | $ 60 | $ 90 |
| Bonds Payable . . . . . . . . . . . . . . . . . . . . . . . . . . . . . . | 50 | 50 | 100 | 150 |
| Total Liabilities . . . . . . . . . . . . . . . . . . . . . . . . . . . . | $ 90 | $100 | $160 | $240 |
| Common Stock ($10 par value) . . . . . . . . . . . . . . . . . | $100 | $150 | $160 | $160 |
| Additional Paid-in Capital . . . . . . . . . . . . . . . . . . . . . . | 20 | 100 | 120 | 120 |
| Retained Earnings . . . . . . . . . . . . . . . . . . . . . . . . . . . . | 40 | 50 | 80 | 130 |
| Total Shareholders' Equity . . . . . . . . . . . . . . . . . . . . | $160 | $300 | $360 | $410 |
| Total Liabilities and Shareholders' Equity . . . . . . . . | $250 | $400 | $520 | $650 |

The earnings figure used in calculating the rate of return on assets is income before
deducting any payments or distributions to the providers of capital. Because interest
is a payment to a furnisher of capital, interest expense should not be deducted in
measuring the return on total assets. To derive income before interest charges, it is
usually easier to start with net income and add to that figure. However, the amount
added to net income is not the interest expense shown on the income statement.
Because interest expense is deductible in calculating taxable income, it does not
reduce *aftertax* net income by the full amount of interest expense. The amount
added back to net income is interest expense reduced by income tax savings.

For example, interest expense for Horrigan Corporation for year 4, as shown in
Exhibit 6.2, is $16 million. The income tax rate is assumed to be 30 percent of
pretax income. The income taxes saved, because interest is deductible in computing
taxable income, equal $4.8 million (= .30 × $16 million). The amount of interest
expense net of income tax savings that is added back to net income is therefore
$11.2 million (= $16 million − $4.8 million). There is no need to add back divi-

Exhibit 6.2 ————————————————————————————————————

## HORRIGAN CORPORATION
## Comparative Income Statements
## (all dollar amounts in millions)

|  | Years Ended December 31 | | |
|  | Year 2 | Year 3 | Year 4 |
|---|---|---|---|
| Sales Revenue | $210 | $310 | $475 |
| Less Expenses: | | | |
| Cost of Goods Sold | $119 | $179 | $280 |
| Selling | 36 | 42 | 53 |
| Administrative | 15 | 17 | 22 |
| Depreciation | 12 | 14 | 18 |
| Interest | 5 | 10 | 16 |
| Total | $187 | $262 | $389 |
| Net Income before Taxes | $ 23 | $ 48 | $ 86 |
| Income Tax Expense | 7 | 14 | 26 |
| Net Income | $ 16 | $ 34 | $ 60 |

Exhibit 6.3 ————————————————————————————————————

## HORRIGAN CORPORATION
## Comparative Statements of Cash Flows
## (all dollar amounts in millions)

|  | For the Year Ended December 31 | | |
|  | Year 2 | Year 3 | Year 4 |
|---|---|---|---|
| *Operations:* | | | |
| Net Income | $ 16 | $ 34 | $ 60 |
| Additions: | | | |
| Depreciation Expense | 12 | 14 | 18 |
| Increase in Accounts Payable | 5 | 5 | 15 |
| Increase in Salaries Payable | 3 | 2 | 5 |
| Increase in Income Taxes Payable | 2 | 3 | 10 |
| Subtractions: | | | |
| Increase in Accounts Receivable | (10) | (10) | (30) |
| Increase in Inventories | (16) | (16) | (37) |
| Cash Flow from Operations | $ 12 | $ 32 | $ 41 |
| *Investing:* | | | |
| Purchase of Land | $ (10) | $ (30) | — |
| Purchase of Building | — | — | $(40) |
| Purchase of Equipment | (122) | (84) | (37) |
| Cash Flow from Investing | $(132) | $(114) | $(77) |
| *Financing:* | | | |
| Issuance of Bonds | — | $ 50 | $ 50 |
| Issuance of Common Stock | $ 130 | 30 | — |
| Dividends | (6) | (4) | (10) |
| Cash Flow from Financing | $ 124 | $ 76 | $ 40 |
| Net Change in Cash | $ 4 | $ (6) | $ 4 |

dends paid to shareholders, because they are not deducted as an expense in calculating net income.

Because the earnings rate *during the year* is being computed, the measure of investment should reflect the average amount of assets in use during the year. A crude but usually satisfactory figure for average total assets is one-half the sum of total assets at the beginning and at the end of the year.

The calculation of rate of return on assets for Horrigan Corporation for year 4 is as follows:[3]

$$\frac{\text{Net Income plus Interest Expense Net of Income Tax Savings}}{\text{Average Total Assets}} = \frac{\$60 + (\$16 - \$4.8)}{\frac{1}{2}(\$520 + \$650)} = 12.2 \text{ percent.}$$

Thus, for each dollar of assets used, the management of Horrigan Corporation was able to earn $.122 during Year 4 before payments to the suppliers of capital. The rate of return on assets was 8.9 percent in Year 3 and 6.0 percent in Year 2. Thus the rate of return has increased steadily during this 3-year period.

One might question the rationale for a measure of return that is independent of the means of financing. After all, the assets must be financed and the cost of that financing must be covered if the firm is to be profitable.

The rate of return on assets is of particular concern to lenders, or creditors, of a firm. These creditors have a senior claim on earnings and assets relative to common shareholders. Creditors receive their return in the form of interest. This return typically comes from earnings generated from assets before any other suppliers of capital receive a return (for example, dividends). When extending credit or providing debt capital to a firm, creditors want to be sure that the return generated by the firm on that capital (assets) exceeds its cost.

The rate of return on assets is also useful to common shareholders in assessing financial leverage, a topic discussed later in this chapter.

## Disaggregating the Rate of Return on Assets

One means of studying changes in the rate of return on assets is to disaggregate the ratio into two other ratios, as follows:

$$\frac{\text{Rate of}}{\text{Return on Assets}} = \frac{\text{Profit Margin Ratio}}{\text{(before interest expense and related income tax effects)}} \times \frac{\text{Total Assets}}{\text{Turnover Ratio,}}$$

or

$$\frac{\text{Net Income plus Interest Expense Net of Income Tax Savings}}{\text{Average Total Assets}} = \frac{\text{Net Income plus Interest Expense Net of Income Tax Savings}}{\text{Revenues}} \times \frac{\text{Revenues}}{\text{Average Total Assets}}.$$

---

[3]Throughout the remainder of this chapter, we omit reference to the fact that the amounts for Horrigan Corporation are in millions of dollars.

Exhibit 6.4 ———————————————————————————————————————

## HORRIGAN CORPORATION
## Disaggregation of Rate of Return on Assets for Year 2, Year 3, and Year 4

| | Net Income plus Interest Expense Net of Income Tax Savings / Average Total Assets | = | Net Income plus Interest Expense Net of Income Tax Savings / Revenues | × | Revenues / Average Total Assets |
|---|---|---|---|---|---|
| Year 2: | $\dfrac{\$16 + (\$5 - \$1.5)}{\frac{1}{2}(\$250 + \$400)}$ | = | $\dfrac{\$16 + (\$5 - \$1.5)}{\$210}$ | × | $\dfrac{\$210}{\frac{1}{2}(\$250 + \$400)}$ |
| | 6.0% | = | 9.3% | × | .65 |
| Year 3: | $\dfrac{\$34 + (\$10 - \$3)}{\frac{1}{2}(\$400 + \$520)}$ | = | $\dfrac{\$34 + (\$10 - \$3)}{\$310}$ | × | $\dfrac{\$310}{\frac{1}{2}(\$400 + \$520)}$ |
| | 8.9% | = | 13.2% | × | .67 |
| Year 4: | $\dfrac{\$60 + (\$16 - \$4.8)}{\frac{1}{2}(\$520 + \$650)}$ | = | $\dfrac{\$60 + (\$16 - \$4.8)}{\$475}$ | × | $\dfrac{\$475}{\frac{1}{2}(\$520 + \$650)}$ |
| | 12.2% | = | 15.0% | × | .81 |

The *profit margin ratio* is a measure of a firm's ability to control the level of expenses relative to revenues generated. By holding down costs, a firm will be able to increase the profits from a given amount of revenue and thereby improve its profit margin ratio. The *total assets turnover ratio* is a measure of a firm's ability to generate revenues from a particular level of investment in assets, or, to put it another way, the total assets turnover measures a firm's ability to control the level of investment in assets for a particular level of revenues.

Exhibit 6.4 shows the disaggregation of the rate of return on assets for Horrigan Corporation into profit margin and total assets turnover ratios for Year 2, Year 3, and Year 4. Much of the improvement in the rate of return on assets between Year 2 and Year 3 resulted from an increase in the profit margin ratio from 9.3 percent to 13.2 percent. The total assets turnover ratio remained relatively stable between these two years. On the other hand, most of the improvement in the rate of return on assets between Year 3 and Year 4 could be attributed to the increased total assets turnover. The firm was able to generate $.81 of sales from each dollar invested in assets during Year 4 as compared to $.67 of sales per dollar of assets in Year 3. The increased total assets turnover, coupled with an improvement in the profit margin ratio, permitted Horrigan Corporation to increase its rate of return on assets during Year 4. We must analyze the changes in the profit margin ratio and total assets turnover ratio in greater depth to pinpoint the causes of the changes in Horrigan Corporation's profitability over this 3-year period. We will return to this analysis shortly.

Improving the rate of return on assets can be accomplished by increasing the profit margin ratio, the rate of asset turnover, or both. Some firms, however, may have little flexibility in altering one of these components. For example, a firm committed under a 3-year labor union contract may have little control over wage rates paid. Or a firm operating under market- or government-imposed price controls may not be able to increase the prices of its products. In these cases, the opportunities for improving the profit margin ratio may be limited. To increase the rate of return on assets, the level of investment in assets such as inventory, plant, and equipment must be reduced, or, to put it another way, revenues per dollar of assets must be increased.

## Analyzing Changes in the Profit Margin Ratio

Profit, or net income, is measured by subtracting various expenses from revenues. To identify the reasons for a change in the profit margin ratio, changes in a firm's expenses relative to revenues must be examined. One approach is to express individual expenses and net income as a percentage of revenues. Such an analysis is presented in Exhibit 6.5 for Horrigan Corporation. Note that we have altered somewhat the conventional income statement format in this analysis by subtracting interest expense (net of its related income tax effects) as the last expense item. The percentages on the line titled Income before Interest and Related Income Tax Effect correspond to the profit margin ratios (before interest and related tax effects) in Exhibit 6.4.

The analysis in Exhibit 6.5 indicates that the improvement in Horrigan Corporation's profit margin ratio over the 3 years can be attributed primarily to decreases in selling, administrative, and depreciation expenses as a percentage of sales. The reasons for these decreasing percentages should be explored further with management. Does the decrease in selling expenses as a percentage of sales reflect a reduction in advertising expenditures that could hurt future sales? Does the decrease in depreciation expense as a percentage of sales reflect a failure to expand plant and

**Exhibit 6.5** ————————————————————————————————————

**HORRIGAN CORPORATION**
**Net Income and Expenses as a Percentage of Revenues for Year 2, Year 3, and Year 4**

| | Years Ended December 31 | | |
| --- | --- | --- | --- |
| | Year 2 | Year 3 | Year 4 |
| Sales Revenue . . . . . . . . . . . . . . . . . . . . . . . . . . . . . . . . . . . . . . | 100.0% | 100.0% | 100.0% |
| Less Operating Expenses: | | | |
|   Cost of Goods Sold . . . . . . . . . . . . . . . . . . . . . . . . . . . . . . | 56.7% | 57.7% | 58.9% |
|   Selling . . . . . . . . . . . . . . . . . . . . . . . . . . . . . . . . . . . . . . . . . . | 17.1 | 13.6 | 11.2 |
|   Administrative . . . . . . . . . . . . . . . . . . . . . . . . . . . . . . . . . . | 7.1 | 5.5 | 4.6 |
|   Depreciation . . . . . . . . . . . . . . . . . . . . . . . . . . . . . . . . . . . | 5.7 | 4.5 | 3.8 |
|     Total . . . . . . . . . . . . . . . . . . . . . . . . . . . . . . . . . . . . . . . . | 86.6% | 81.3% | 78.5% |
| Income before Income Taxes and Interest . . . . . . . . . . . . . | 13.4% | 18.7% | 21.5% |
| Income Taxes at 30 Percent . . . . . . . . . . . . . . . . . . . . . . . . . | 4.1 | 5.5 | 6.5 |
| Income before Interest and Related Income Tax Effect | 9.3% | 13.2% | 15.0% |
| Interest Expense Net of Income Tax Effect . . . . . . . . . . . . | 1.7 | 2.2 | 2.4 |
| Net Income . . . . . . . . . . . . . . . . . . . . . . . . . . . . . . . . . . . . . . | 7.6% | 11.0% | 12.6% |

equipment as sales have increased? On the other hand, do these decreasing percentages merely reflect the realization of economies of scale as fixed selling, administrative, and depreciation expenses are being spread over a larger number of units?[4] The amount or trend in a particular ratio cannot, by itself, be the basis for investing or not investing in a firm. Ratios merely indicate areas where additional analysis is required. For example, the increasing percentage of cost of goods sold to sales should be explored further. It may reflect a successful, planned pricing policy of reducing gross margin (selling price less cost of goods sold) to increase the volume of sales. On the other hand, the replacement cost of inventory items may be increasing without corresponding increases being made in selling prices. Or the firm may be accumulating excess inventories that are physically deteriorating or becoming obsolete.

## Analyzing Changes in the Total Assets Turnover Ratio

The total assets turnover ratio depends on the turnover ratios for its individual asset components. Three turnover ratios are commonly calculated: accounts receivable turnover, inventory turnover, and fixed asset turnover.

**Accounts Receivable Turnover** The rate at which accounts receivable turn over gives an indication of their nearness to being converted into cash. The *accounts receivable turnover ratio* is calculated by dividing net sales on account by average accounts receivable. For Horrigan Corporation, the accounts receivable turnover for Year 4, assuming that all sales are on account (that is, none are for immediate cash), is calculated as follows:

$$\frac{\text{Net Sales on Account}}{\text{Average Accounts Receivable}} = \frac{\$475}{\frac{1}{2}(\$46 + \$76)} = 7.8 \text{ times per year.}$$

The concept of accounts receivable turnover is often expressed in terms of the average number of days that receivables are outstanding before cash is collected. For the calculation, 365 days is divided by the accounts receivable turnover ratio. The average number of days that accounts receivable are outstanding for Horrigan Corporation for Year 4 is 46.8 days (= 365 days/7.8 times per year). Thus, on average, accounts receivable are collected approximately $1\frac{1}{2}$ months after the date of sale. The interpretation of this average collection period depends on the terms of sale. If the terms of sale are "net 30 days," the accounts receivable turnover indicates that collections are not being made in accordance with the stated terms. Such a ratio would warrant a review of the credit and collection activity for an explanation and for possible corrective action. If the firm offers terms of "net 45 days," the results indicate that accounts receivable are being handled better.

**Inventory Turnover** The *inventory turnover ratio* is considered to be a significant indicator of the efficiency of operations for many businesses. It is calculated by

───────────────

[4]This phenomenon is called operating leverage and is discussed more fully in managerial accounting and managerial economics textbooks.

dividing cost of goods sold by the average inventory during the period. The inventory turnover for Horrigan Corporation for Year 4 is calculated as follows:

$$\frac{\text{Cost of Goods Sold}}{\text{Average Inventory}} = \frac{\$280}{\frac{1}{2}(\$46 + \$83)} = 4.3 \text{ times per year.}$$

Thus inventory is typically on hand an average of 84.9 days (= 365 days/4.3 times per year) before it is sold.

The interpretation of the inventory turnover figure involves two opposing considerations. Management would like to sell as many goods as possible with a minimum of capital tied up in inventories. An increase in the rate of inventory turnover between periods may seem to indicate more profitable use of the investment in inventory. On the other hand, management does not want to have so little inventory on hand that shortages result. An increase in the rate of inventory turnover in this case may mean a loss of customers, thereby offsetting any advantage gained by decreased investment in inventory. Some trade-offs are therefore required in deciding the optimum level of inventory for each firm and thus the desirable rate of inventory turnover.

The inventory turnover ratio is sometimes calculated by dividing sales, rather than cost of goods sold, by the average inventory. As long as there is a relatively constant relationship between selling prices and cost of goods sold, changes in the trend of the inventory can usually be identified with either measure. It is inappropriate to use sales in the numerator if the inventory turnover ratio is to be used to calculate the average number of days inventory is on hand until sale.

**Plant Asset Turnover** The *plant asset turnover ratio* is a measure of the relation between sales and the investment in plant assets such as property, plant, and equipment. It is calculated by dividing revenues by average plant assets during the year. The plant assets turnover ratio for Horrigan Corporation for Year 4 is

$$\frac{\text{Revenues}}{\text{Average Plant Assets}} = \frac{\$475}{\frac{1}{2}(\$420 + \$479)} = 1.1 \text{ times per year.}$$

Thus for each dollar invested in plant assets during Year 4, $1.10 was generated in revenues.

Changes in the plant asset turnover ratio must be interpreted carefully. Investments in plant assets (for example, production facilities) are often made several periods before sales are generated from products manufactured in the plant. Thus a low or decreasing rate of plant asset turnover may indicate an expanding firm preparing for future growth. On the other hand, a firm may cut back its capital expenditures if the near-term outlook for its products is poor. Such an action could lead to an increase in the plant asset turnover ratio.

We noted earlier that the total assets turnover for Horrigan Corporation was relatively steady between Year 2 and Year 3 but increased dramatically in Year 4. Exhibit 6.6 presents the four turnover ratios we have discussed for Horrigan Corporation over this 3-year period. The accounts receivable turnover ratio increased steadily over the 3 years, indicating either more careful screening of credit applications or more effective collection efforts. The inventory turnover ratio decreased

Exhibit 6.6 _____

**HORRIGAN CORPORATION**
Asset Turnover Ratios for
Year 2, Year 3, and Year 4

|                              | Year 2 | Year 3 | Year 4 |
| ---------------------------- | ------ | ------ | ------ |
| Total Assets Turnover ...................................... | .65    | .67    | .81    |
| Accounts Receivable Turnover .......................... | 6.8    | 7.6    | 7.8    |
| Inventory Turnover ..................................... | 5.4    | 4.7    | 4.3    |
| Plant Asset Turnover .................................. | .8     | .8     | 1.1    |

during the 3 years. Coupling this result with the increasing percentage of cost of goods sold to sales shown in Exhibit 6.5 indicates that there may be excessive investments in inventories that are physically deteriorating or becoming obsolete.

Most of the increase in the total assets turnover between Year 3 and Year 4 can be attributed to an increase in the plant assets turnover. We note in the statement of cash flows for Horrigan Corporation in Exhibit 6.3 that total capital expenditures on land, buildings, and equipment have decreased over the 3-year period, possibly accounting for the increase in the plant assets turnover. The reasons for this decrease should be investigated.

## Summary of the Analysis of the Rate of Return on Assets

This section began by stating that the rate of return on assets is a useful measure for assessing a firm's performance in using assets to generate earnings. The rate of return on assets was then disaggregated into profit margin and total assets turnover components. The profit margin ratio was, in turn, disaggregated by relating various expenses and net income to sales. The total assets turnover was further analyzed by calculating turnover ratios for accounts receivable, inventory, and plant assets.

The analysis for Horrigan Corporation revealed the following:

1.  The rate of return on assets increased steadily over the 3-year period from Year 2 to Year 4.

2.  The improved rate of return on assets can be attributed to an increasing profit margin over all 3 years and an improved total asset turnover during Year 4.

3.  The improved profit margin is in large measure attributable to decreases in the percentages of selling and administrative expenses to sales. The reasons for these decreases should be explored further to ascertain whether there are selling and administrative efforts currently being curtailed that might adversely affect future sales and operations.

4.  The changes in the total assets turnover reflect the effects of increasing accounts receivable and plant asset turnover ratios and a decreasing inventory turnover. The increasing plant asset turnover might be attributable to a reduced level of investment in new property, plant, and equipment that could hurt future productive capacity. The decreasing rate of inventory turnover coupled with the

increasing percentage of cost of goods sold to sales may indicate inventory control problems (build-up of obsolete inventory). All of these changes should be explored further.

## Rate of Return on Common Shareholders' Equity

The *rate of return on common shareholders' equity* measures a firm's performance in using assets to generate earnings, but, unlike the rate of return on assets, it explicitly considers the financing of those assets. Thus this measure of profitability incorporates the results of operating, investing, and financing decisions. It is of primary interest to investors in a firm's common stock. The rate of return on common shareholders' equity is calculated as follows:

$$\frac{\text{Net Income} - \text{Dividends on Preferred Stock}}{\text{Average Common Shareholders' Equity}}.$$

To calculate the amount of earnings assignable to common shareholders' equity, the earnings allocable to any preferred stock equity — usually the dividends on preferred stock declared during the period — must be deducted from net income. The capital provided by common shareholders during the period can be computed by averaging the aggregate par value of common stock, capital contributed in excess of par value on common stock, and retained earnings (or by deducting preferred shareholders' equity from total shareholders' equity) at the beginning and end of the period.

The rate of return on common shareholders' equity of Horrigan Corporation for Year 4 is calculated as

$$\frac{\text{Net Income} - \text{Dividends on Preferred Stock}}{\text{Average Common Shareholders' Equity}} = \frac{\$60 - \$0}{\frac{1}{2}(\$360 + \$410)} = 15.6 \text{ percent.}$$

The rate of return on common shareholders' equity was 7.0 percent in Year 2 and 10.3 percent in Year 3. Thus, like the rate of return on assets, the rate of return on common shareholders' equity increased dramatically over the 3 years.

## Relation between Return on Assets and Return on Common Shareholders' Equity

Figure 6.1 graphs the two measures of rate of return discussed thus far for Horrigan Corporation for Year 2, Year 3, and Year 4. In each year, the rate of return on common shareholders' equity exceeded the rate of return on assets. What accounts for this relation?

Recall that the rate of return on assets measures the profitability of a firm before any payments to the suppliers of capital. This return on assets must then be allocated among the various providers of capital. Creditors are allocated an amount equal to any contractual interest to which they have a claim. Preferred shareholders, if any, are allocated an amount equal to the stated dividend rate on the preferred stock. Any remaining return belongs to the common shareholders; that is, common sharehold-

**Figure 6.1** _____

**Rates of Return for Horrigan Corporation**

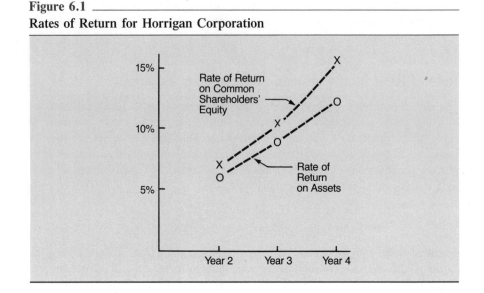

ers have a residual claim on all earnings after creditors and preferred shareholders have received amounts contractually owed them. Thus

$$\begin{array}{c}\text{Rate of Return} \\ \text{on Assets}\end{array} \rightarrow \begin{array}{c}\text{Return to} \\ \text{Creditors} \\ \text{(interest)}\end{array} + \begin{array}{c}\text{Return to} \\ \text{Preferred} \\ \text{Shareholders} \\ \text{(dividends)}\end{array} + \begin{array}{c}\text{Return to} \\ \text{Common} \\ \text{Shareholders} \\ \text{(residual).}\end{array}$$

We can now see how the rate of return on common shareholders' equity can be larger than the rate of return on assets. The rate of return on assets must exceed the aftertax cost of debt (Horrigan Corporation has no preferred stock outstanding). For Year 4, the rate of return on assets was 12.2 percent and the aftertax cost of debt was 5.6 percent [= (1 − .3)($16)/.5($160 + $240); see Exhibits 6.1 and 6.2]. This excess return belongs to the common shareholders.

The common shareholders earned a higher return only because they undertook more risk in their investment. They were placed in a riskier position because the firm incurred debt obligations with fixed payment dates. The phenomenon of common shareholders trading extra risk for a potentially higher return is called *financial leverage*.

## Financial Leverage: Trading on the Equity

Financing with debt and preferred stock to increase the potential return to the residual common shareholders' equity is referred to as *financial leverage* or *trading on the equity*. As long as a higher rate of return can be earned on assets than is paid for the capital used to acquire those assets, the rate of return to common shareholders can be increased. Exhibit 6.7 explores this phenomenon. Leveraged Company and No-Debt Company both have $100,000 in assets. Leveraged Company borrows

## Exhibit 6.7 ————————————————————————————————————————————

## Effects of Financial Leverage on Rate of Return of Shareholders' Equity
## (income tax rate is 30 percent of pretax income)

| | Long-Term Equities | | Income after Taxes but before Interest Charges[a] | Aftertax Interest Charges[b] | Net Income | Rate of Return on Total Assets[c] (percent) | Rate of Return on Common Shareholders' Equity (percent) |
|---|---|---|---|---|---|---|---|
| | Long-Term Borrowing at 10 Percent per Year | Shareholders' Equity | | | | | |
| **Good Earnings Year** | | | | | | | |
| Leveraged Company.. | $40,000 | $ 60,000 | $10,000 | $2,800 | $ 7,200 | 10.0% | 12.0% |
| No-Debt Company.... | — | 100,000 | 10,000 | — | 10,000 | 10.0 | 10.0 |
| **Neutral Earnings Year** | | | | | | | |
| Leveraged Company.. | 40,000 | 60,000 | 7,000 | 2,800 | 4,200 | 7.0 | 7.0 |
| No-Debt Company.... | — | 100,000 | 7,000 | — | 7,000 | 7.0 | 7.0 |
| **Bad Earnings Year** | | | | | | | |
| Leveraged Company.. | 40,000 | 60,000 | 4,000 | 2,800 | 1,200 | 4.0 | 2.0 |
| No-Debt Company.... | — | 100,000 | 4,000 | — | 4,000 | 4.0 | 4.0 |

[a]Not including any income tax savings caused by interest charges. Income before taxes and interest for *good* year is $14,286; for *neutral* year is $10,000; for *bad* year is $5,714.

[b]$40,000 (borrowed) × .10 (interest rate) × [1 − .30 (income tax rate)]. The numbers shown in the preceding column for aftertax income do not include the effects of interest charges on taxes.

[c]In each year, the rate of return on assets is the same for both companies as the rate of return on common shareholders' equity for No-Debt Company: 10 percent, 7 percent, and 4 percent, respectively.

$40,000 at a 10 percent annual rate. No-Debt Company raises all its capital from common shareholders. Both companies pay income taxes at the rate of 30 percent.

Consider first a good earnings year. Both companies earn $10,000 before interest charges (but after taxes, except for tax effects of interest charges).[5] This represents a rate of return on assets for both companies of 10 percent (= $10,000/ $100,000). Leveraged Company's net income is $7,200 [= $10,000 − (1 − .30 tax rate) × (.10 interest rate × $40,000 borrowed)], representing a rate of return on common shareholders' equity of 12.0 percent (= $7,200/$60,000). Net income of No-Debt Company is $10,000, representing a rate of return on shareholders' equity of 10 percent. Leverage increased the rate of return to shareholders of Leveraged Company, because the capital contributed by the long-term debtors earned 10 percent but required an aftertax interest payment of only 7 percent [= (1 − .30 tax rate) × (.10 interest rate)]. This additional 3 percent return on each dollar of assets increased the return to the common shareholders.

Although leverage increased the return to common stock equity during the good earnings year, the increase would be larger if a greater proportion of the assets was financed with long-term borrowing and the firm was made riskier. For example, assume that the assets of $100,000 were financed with $50,000 of long-term borrowing and $50,000 of shareholders' equity. Net income of Leveraged Company in this case would be $6,500 [= $10,000 − (1 − .30 tax rate) × (.10 × $50,000 bor-

————————————————————————

[5]Income before taxes and before interest charges is $14,286; $10,000 = (1 − .30) × $14,286.

rowed)]. The rate of return on common stock equity would be 13 percent (= $6,500/$50,000). This compares with a rate of return on common stock equity of 12 percent when long-term debt was only 40 percent of the total capital provided.

Financial leverage increases the rate of return on common stock equity when the rate of return on assets is higher than the aftertax cost of debt. The greater the proportion of debt in the capital structure, however, the greater the risk borne by the common shareholders. Of course, debt cannot be increased without limit; as more debt is added to the capital structure, the risk of default or insolvency becomes greater. Lenders, including investors in a firm's bonds, require a higher and higher return (interest rate) to compensate for this additional risk. A point will be reached when the aftertax cost of debt will exceed the rate of return that can be earned on assets. At this point, leverage can no longer increase the potential rate of return to common stock equity. For most large manufacturing firms, liabilities represent between 30 percent and 60 percent of total capital.

Exhibit 6.7 also demonstrates the effect of leverage in a neutral earnings year and in a bad earnings year. In the neutral earnings year, the rate of return to common shareholders is neither increased nor decreased by leverage, because the return on assets is 7 percent and the aftertax cost of long-term debt is also 7 percent. In the bad earnings year, the return on assets of 4 percent is less than the aftertax cost of debt of 7 percent. The return on common stock equity therefore drops — to only 2 percent — below the rate of return on assets. Clearly, financial leverage can work in two ways. It can enhance owners' rate of return in good years, but owners run the risk that bad earnings years will be even worse than they would be without the borrowing.

## Disaggregating the Rate of Return on Common Shareholders' Equity

The rate of return on common shareholders' equity can be disaggregated into several components (in a manner similar to the disaggregation of the rate of return on assets) as follows:

$$\begin{matrix} \text{Rate of Return} \\ \text{on Common} \\ \text{Shareholders'} \\ \text{Equity} \end{matrix} = \begin{matrix} \text{Profit Margin Ratio} \\ \text{(after interest} \\ \text{expense and} \\ \text{preferred dividends)} \end{matrix} \times \begin{matrix} \text{Total} \\ \text{Assets} \\ \text{Turnover} \\ \text{Ratio} \end{matrix} \times \begin{matrix} \text{Leverage} \\ \text{Ratio.} \end{matrix}$$

The profit margin percentage indicates the portion of the revenue dollar left over for the common shareholders after all operating costs have been covered and all claims of creditors and preferred shareholders have been subtracted. The total assets turnover, as discussed earlier, indicates the revenues generated from each dollar of assets. The *leverage ratio* indicates the extent to which capital (= total assets) has been provided by common shareholders. The larger the leverage ratio, the smaller the portion of capital provided by common shareholders and the larger the proportion provided by creditors and preferred shareholders. Thus, the larger the leverage ratio, the greater the extent of financial leverage.

The disaggregation of the rate of return on common shareholders' equity ratio for Horrigan Corporation for Year 4 is as follows:

$$\frac{\$60}{\frac{1}{2}(\$360 + \$410)} = \frac{\$\ 60}{\$475} \times \frac{\$475}{\frac{1}{2}(\$520 + \$650)} \times \frac{\frac{1}{2}(\$520 + \$650)}{\frac{1}{2}(\$360 + \$410)}$$

15.6 percent  = 12.6 percent ×      .81     ×     1.5.

Exhibit 6.8 shows the disaggregation of the rate of return on common share-holders' equity for Horrigan Corporation for Year 2, Year 3, and Year 4. Most of the increase in the rate of return on common shareholders' equity can be attributed to an increasing profit margin over the 3-year period plus an increase in total assets turnover in Year 4. The leverage ratio remained reasonably stable over this period.

## Earnings per Share of Common Stock

A third measure of profitability is *earnings per share* of common stock. This ratio is computed by dividing net income attributable to common stock by the average number of common shares outstanding during the period.

Earnings per share for Horrigan Corporation for Year 4 is calculated as follows:

$$\frac{\text{Net Income} - \text{Preferred Stock Dividend}}{\text{Weighted Average Number of Common Shares Outstanding during the Period}^6} = \frac{\$60 - \$0}{16 \text{ shares}} = \$3.75 \text{ per share.}$$

Earnings per share were $1.28 (= $16/12.5) for Year 2 and $2.19 (= $34/15.5) for Year 3.

If a firm has securities outstanding that can be converted into or exchanged for common stock, it may be required to present two earnings-per-share amounts: *primary earnings per share* and *fully diluted earnings per share*. For example, some firms issue convertible bonds or convertible preferred stock that can be exchanged directly for shares of common stock. Also, many firms have employee stock option plans under which shares of the company's common stock may be acquired by employees under special arrangements. If the convertible securities were converted

---

**Exhibit 6.8** —————————————————————

**HORRIGAN CORPORATION**
**Disaggregation of Rate of Return**
**on Common Shareholders' Equity**

|  | Rate of Return on Common Shareholders' Equity = | Profit Margin × | Total Assets Turnover × | Leverage Ratio |
|---|---|---|---|---|
| Year 2........ | 7.0% | = 7.6% × | .65 × | 1.4 |
| Year 3........ | 10.3 | = 11.0 × | .67 × | 1.4 |
| Year 4........ | 15.6 | = 12.6 × | .81 × | 1.5 |

---

[6]Exhibit 6.1 indicates that the par value of a common share is $10 and that the common stock account has a balance of $160 million throughout Year 4. The shares outstanding were therefore 16 million.

or the stock options were exercised and additional shares of common stock were issued, the amount conventionally shown as earnings per share would probably decrease, or become diluted. When a firm has outstanding securities that, if exchanged for shares of common stock, would decrease earnings per share by 3 percent or more, a dual presentation of primary and fully diluted earnings per share is required.[7]

**Primary Earnings per Share**   In calculating earnings per share, adjustments may be made to the conventionally calculated amount for securities that are nearly the same as common stock. The principal value of these *common stock equivalents* arises from their capability of being exchanged for, or converted into, common stock rather than from their own periodic cash yields over time. Stock options and warrants are always common stock equivalents. Convertible bonds and convertible preferred stock may or may not be common stock equivalents. If the return from these convertible securities at the date of their issue is substantially below the return available from other debt or preferred stock investments, it is presumed that the securities derive their value primarily from their conversion privileges and are therefore common stock equivalents. Adjustments are then made in calculating primary earnings per share for the dilutive effects of these securities.

**Fully Diluted Earnings per Share**   As the name implies, fully diluted earnings per share indicates the maximum possible dilution that would occur if all options, warrants, and convertible securities outstanding at the end of the accounting period were exchanged for common stock. Therefore, this amount represents the maximum limit of possible dilution that could take place on the date of the balance sheet. All securities convertible into or exchangeable for common stock, whether or not classified as common stock equivalents, enter into the calculation of fully diluted earnings per share.

Firms that do not have convertible or other potentially dilutive securities outstanding compute earnings per share in the conventional manner. Firms with outstanding securities that have the potential for materially diluting earnings per share as conventionally computed must present dual earnings-per-share amounts.

**Interpreting Earnings per Share**   Earnings per share has been criticized as a measure of profitability because it does not consider the amount of assets or capital required to generate that level of earnings. Two firms with the same earnings and earnings per share will not be equally profitable if one of the firms requires twice the amount of assets or capital to generate those earnings as does the other firm.

Earnings-per-share amounts are also difficult to interpret when comparing firms. For example, assume that two firms have identical earnings, common shareholders' equity, and rates of return on common shareholders' equity. One firm may have a lower earnings per share simply because it has a larger number of shares

---

[7]Accounting Principles Board, *Opinion No. 15,* "Earnings per Share," 1969.

outstanding (perhaps due to the use of a lower par value for its shares or to different earnings retention policies; see Problem 21 at the end of this chapter).

**Price-Earnings Ratio**  Earnings-per-share amounts are often compared with the market price of the stock. This is usually expressed as a *price-earnings ratio* (= market price per share/earnings per share). For example, the common stock of Horrigan Corporation sells for $40 per share at the end of Year 4. The price-earnings ratio, often called the P/E ratio, is 10.67 to 1 (= $40/$3.75). The relation is sometimes expressed by saying that "the stock is selling at 10.7 times earnings."

The price-earnings ratio is often presented in tables of stock prices and in financial periodicals. These published P/E ratios must be interpreted cautiously, however. In cases in which a firm has discontinued operations or extraordinary gains and losses, the reader must ascertain whether the published ratio is based on income from continuing operations alone or on final net income. Also, the published P/E ratios for firms operating at a net loss for the most recent year are sometimes reported as positive numbers. This occurs because the publisher (e.g., Value Line) converts the net loss for the year to a longer-run expected profit amount to calculate the P/E ratio.

## Summary of Profitability Analysis

Three broad measures for assessing a firm's profitability have been discussed in this chapter. Because the rate of return on assets and rate of return on common shareholders' equity relate earnings to some measure of the capital required to generate those earnings, most of our attention has been focused on these two profitability measures.

Exhibit 6.9 summarizes the analysis discussed. On the most general level, the concern is with overall measures of profitability and the effectiveness of financial

**Exhibit 6.9** _____

**Profitability Ratios**

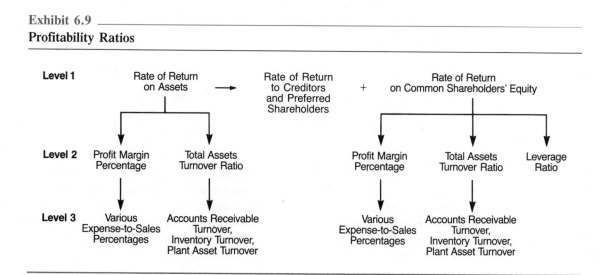

leverage. On the next level, the overall measures of profitability are disaggregated into profit margin, asset turnover, and leverage components. On the third level, the profit margin and asset turnover ratios are further disaggregated to gain additional insights into reasons for changes in profitability. The depth of analysis required in any particular case depends on the differences or changes in profitability observed.

## Analysis of Risk _____

The second parameter in investment decision making is risk. There are various factors that affect the risk of business firms:

1. Economy-wide factors, such as increased inflation or interest rates, unemployment, or recessions.

2. Industry-wide factors, such as increased competition, lack of availability of raw materials, changes in technology, or increased government antitrust actions.

3. Firm-specific factors, such as labor strikes, loss of facilities due to fire or other casualty, or poor health of key managerial personnel.

The ultimate risk is that a firm will be forced into bankruptcy and creditors and investors will lose the capital they provided to the firm.

When assessing risk, the focus is generally on the relative *liquidity* of a firm. Cash and near-cash assets provide a firm with the resources needed to adapt to the various dimensions of risk as potential losses arise; that is, liquid resources provide a firm with financial flexibility. Cash is also the connecting link that permits the operating, investing, and financing activities of a firm to continue running smoothly and effectively.

When assessing liquidity, time is of critical importance. Consider the three questions that follow:

1. Does a firm have sufficient cash to repay a loan due tomorrow?

2. Will the firm have sufficient cash to repay a note due in 6 months?

3. Will the firm have sufficient cash to repay bonds due in 5 years?

In answering the first question, the analysis would probably focus on the amount of cash on hand and in the bank relative to obligations coming due tomorrow. In answering the second question, consideration would be given to the amount of cash expected to be generated from operations during the next 6 months, as well as to any new borrowing, relative to obligations coming due during that period. In answering the third question, the focus would shift to the longer-run cash-generating ability of a firm relative to the amount of long-term debt that would become due.

# Measures of Short-Term Liquidity Risk

This section discusses four measures for assessing *short-term liquidity risk:* (1) the current ratio, (2) the quick ratio, (3) the operating cash flow to current liabilities ratio, and (4) the working capital turnover ratio.

# Current Ratio

The *current ratio* is calculated by dividing current assets by current liabilities. It is commonly expressed as a ratio such as "2 to 1" or "2:1," meaning that current assets are twice as large as current liabilities. The current ratio of Horrigan Corporation on December 31, Year 1, Year 2, Year 3, and Year 4, is

| | Current Ratio $=$ | Current Assets / Current Liabilities |
|---|---|---|
| December 31, Year 1 ............................. | $\dfrac{\$\ 50}{\$\ 40} =$ | 1.25 to 1.0 |
| December 31, Year 2 ............................. | $\dfrac{\$\ 80}{\$\ 50} =$ | 1.60 to 1.0 |
| December 31, Year 3 ............................. | $\dfrac{\$100}{\$\ 60} =$ | 1.67 to 1.0 |
| December 31, Year 4 ............................. | $\dfrac{\$171}{\$\ 90} =$ | 1.90 to 1.0 |

The current ratio is presumed to indicate the ability of the firm to meet its current obligations, and it is therefore of particular significance to short-term creditors. Although an excess of current assets over current liabilities is generally considered desirable from the creditor's viewpoint, changes in the trend of the ratio may be difficult to interpret. For example, when the current ratio is larger than 1 to 1, an increase of equal amount in both current assets and current liabilities results in a decline in the ratio, whereas equal decreases result in an increased current ratio.

In a recession period, business is contracting, current liabilities are paid, and even though current assets may be at a low point, the ratio may go to high levels. In a boom period, just the reverse effect may occur. In other words, a very high current ratio may accompany unsatisfactory business conditions, whereas a falling ratio may accompany profitable operations.

Furthermore, the current ratio is susceptible to "window dressing"; that is, management can take deliberate steps to produce a financial statement that presents a better current ratio at the balance sheet date than the average or normal current ratio. For example, toward the close of a fiscal year normal purchases on account may be delayed. Or loans to officers, classified as noncurrent assets, may be collected and the proceeds used to reduce current liabilities. These actions may be taken so that the current ratio will appear as favorable as possible in the annual financial statements at the balance sheet date.

Although the current ratio is probably the most common liquidity ratio presented in statement analysis, there are limitations in its use. Its trends are difficult to interpret and, if overemphasized, it can easily lead to undesirable business practices as well as misinterpretation of financial condition.

## Quick Ratio

A variation of the current ratio, usually known as the *quick ratio* or *acid test ratio,* is computed by including in the numerator of the fraction only those current assets that could be converted quickly into cash. The numerator customarily includes cash, marketable securities, and receivables, but it would be better to make a study of the facts in each case before deciding whether to include receivables and to exclude inventories. In some businesses, the inventory of merchandise might be converted into cash more quickly than the receivables of other businesses.

Assuming that the accounts receivable of Horrigan Corporation are included but that the inventory is excluded, the quick ratio on December 31, Year 1, Year 2, Year 3, and Year 4, is as follows:

| | Quick Ratio $=$ | Cash, Marketable Securities, Accounts Receivable |
|---|---|---|
| | | Current Liabilities |
| December 31, Year 1 ........................ | $\dfrac{\$36}{\$40} =$ | .90 to 1.0 |
| December 31, Year 2 ........................ | $\dfrac{\$50}{\$50} =$ | 1.0 to 1.0 |
| December 31, Year 3 ........................ | $\dfrac{\$54}{\$60} =$ | .90 to 1.0 |
| December 31, Year 4 ........................ | $\dfrac{\$88}{\$90} =$ | .98 to 1.0 |

Whereas the current ratio increased steadily over the period, the quick ratio remained relatively constant. The increase in the current ratio resulted primarily from a build-up of inventories.

## Operating Cash Flow to Current Liabilities

Both the current ratio and quick ratio can be criticized because they are calculated using amounts at a specific point in time. If financial statement amounts at that particular time are unusually large or small, the resulting ratios will not reflect more normal conditions.

To overcome these deficiencies, the *operating cash flow to current liabilities ratio* can be calculated. The numerator of this ratio is cash flow from operations for the year. The denominator is average current liabilities for the year. The operating cash flow to current liabilities ratios for Horrigan Corporation for Year 2, Year 3, and Year 4 are as follows:

| | Operating Cash Flow to Current Liabilities | = | Cash Flow from Operations / Average Current Liabilities |
|---|---|---|---|
| Year 2...................... | $\dfrac{\$12}{\frac{1}{2}(\$40 + \$50)}$ | = | 26.7 percent |
| Year 3...................... | $\dfrac{\$32}{\frac{1}{2}(\$50 + \$60)}$ | = | 58.2 percent |
| Year 4...................... | $\dfrac{\$41}{\frac{1}{2}(\$60 + \$90)}$ | = | 54.7 percent |

A ratio of 40 percent or more[8] is common for a healthy firm. Thus the liquidity of Horrigan Corporation improved dramatically between Year 2 and Year 3. The decrease between Year 3 and Year 4 is primarily due to a build-up in current liabilities (which, in turn, is probably related to the build-up in inventories noted previously).

## Working Capital Turnover Ratio

The *operating cycle* of a firm is a sequence of activities in which

1. Inventory is purchased on account from suppliers.
2. Inventory is sold on account to customers.
3. Customers pay amounts due.
4. Suppliers are paid amounts due.

This cycle occurs continually for most business firms. The longer the cycle, the longer the time that funds are tied up in receivables and inventories. The interest cost on funds required to carry receivables and inventory reduces net income and hurts profitability. Funds tied up in receivables and inventory also have negative effects on the short-run liquidity of a firm. The more quickly inventory and receivables are turned into cash, the more liquid a firm is.

The *working capital turnover ratio* is a measure of the length of the operating cycle. It is calculated by dividing sales by the average working capital for the year. Working capital is equal to current assets minus current liabilities. The working capital turnover ratio for Horrigan Corporation is as follows:

_____

[8]Cornelius Casey and Norman Bartczak, "Using Operating Cash Flow Data to Predict Financial Distress: Some Extensions," *Journal of Accounting Research* (Spring 1985): 384–401.

| | Working Capital = | Sales |
|---|---|---|
| | Turnover Ratio | Average Working Capital |
| Year 2........................... | $\dfrac{\$210}{\frac{1}{2}(\$10 + \$30)} =$ | 10.5 times |
| Year 3........................... | $\dfrac{\$310}{\frac{1}{2}(\$30 + \$40)} =$ | 8.9 times |
| Year 4........................... | $\dfrac{\$475}{\frac{1}{2}(\$40 + \$81)} =$ | 7.9 times |

The turnover rate has decreased over the 3-year period, primarily because inventories net of current liabilities increased faster than sales.

The working capital turnover ratio is often converted to the number of days required for one revolution of the operating cycle by dividing the turnover ratio into 365 days. Thus working capital turned over on average every 34.8 days (= 365/ 10.5) during Year 2. The corresponding amounts for Year 3 and Year 4 were 41.0 days and 46.2 days, respectively.

The working capital turnover ratio varies significantly across firms depending on the nature of their businesses. For grocery stores it is approximately 12 times per year, whereas for a construction company the turnover is sometimes less than once per year. When using the working capital turnover ratio to evaluate short-term liquidity, the analyst must be aware of the type of business in which the firm is involved.

## Summary of Short-Term Liquidity Analysis

The current and quick ratios give snapshot measures of liquidity at particular times. These ratios for Horrigan Corporation are at reasonably adequate levels at the end of each year, although they indicate a build-up of inventories in Year 4.

The cash flow from operations to current liabilities and the working capital turnover ratios provide measures of short-term liquidity for a period of time. Both ratios indicate a significant improvement in liquidity between Year 2 and Year 3, primarily due to increased cash flow from operations. Both ratios decreased during Year 4 because of the build-up of inventory. However, the levels of the ratios during Year 4 do not yet indicate serious short-term liquidity problems for Horrigan Corporation. Given the growth rate in sales during the past 2 years (approximately 50 percent per year), a build-up of inventories may be justified.

## Measures of Long-Term Liquidity Risk

Measures of *long-term liquidity risk* are used in evaluating a firm's ability to meet interest and principal payments on long-term debt and similar obligations as they become due. If the payments cannot be made on time, a firm becomes insolvent and may have to be reorganized or liquidated.

Perhaps the best indicator for assessing long-term liquidity risk is a firm's ability to generate profits over a period of years. If a firm is profitable, it will either generate sufficient cash from operations or be able to obtain needed capital from creditors and owners. The measures of profitability discussed previously are therefore applicable for this purpose as well. Three other measures of long-term liquidity risk are debt ratios, the cash flow from operations to total liabilities ratio, and the number of times that interest charges are covered.

## Debt Ratios

There are several variations of the debt ratio, but the one most commonly encountered in financial analysis is the *long-term debt ratio*. It reports the portion of the firm's long-term capital that is furnished by debt holders. To calculate this ratio, divide total long-term debt by the sum of total long-term debt and total shareholders' equity.

Another form of the debt ratio is the *debt-equity ratio*. To calculate the debt-equity ratio, divide total liabilities (current and noncurrent) by total equities (= liabilities plus shareholders' equity = total assets).

Exhibit 6.10 shows the two forms of the debt ratio for Horrigan Corporation on December 31, Year 1, Year 2, Year 3, and Year 4. In general, the higher these ratios, the higher the likelihood that the firm may be unable to meet fixed interest and principal payments in the future. The decision for most firms is how much financial leverage, with its attendant risk, they can afford to assume. Funds obtained from issuing bonds or borrowing from a bank have a relatively low interest cost but require fixed, periodic payments that increase the likelihood of bankruptcy.

In assessing the debt ratios, analysts customarily vary the standard in direct relation to the stability of the firm's earnings and cash flows from operations. The more stable the earnings and cash flows, the higher the debt ratio that is considered acceptable or safe. The debt ratios of public utilities are customarily high, frequently on the order of 60 to 70 percent. The stability of public utility earnings and cash flows makes these ratios acceptable to many investors who would be dissatis-

**Exhibit 6.10** ————————————————————————————————

**HORRIGAN CORPORATION**
**Debt Ratios**

| $\text{Long-Term Debt Ratio} = \dfrac{\text{Total Long-Term Debt}}{\text{Total Long-Term Debt plus Shareholders' Equity}}$ | | $\text{Debt-Equity Ratio} = \dfrac{\text{Total Liabilities}}{\text{Total Liabilities plus Shareholders' Equity}}$ | |
|---|---|---|---|
| Dec. 31, Year 1 ... | $\dfrac{\$ 50}{\$210} = 24$ percent | Dec. 31, Year 1 .... | $\dfrac{\$ 90}{\$250} = 36$ percent |
| Dec. 31, Year 2 ... | $\dfrac{\$ 50}{\$350} = 14$ percent | Dec. 31, Year 2 .... | $\dfrac{\$100}{\$400} = 25$ percent |
| Dec. 31, Year 3 ... | $\dfrac{\$100}{\$460} = 22$ percent | Dec. 31, Year 3 .... | $\dfrac{\$160}{\$520} = 31$ percent |
| Dec. 31, Year 4 ... | $\dfrac{\$150}{\$560} = 27$ percent | Dec. 31, Year 4 .... | $\dfrac{\$240}{\$650} = 37$ percent |

fied with such high leverage for firms with less stable earnings and cash flows. The debt ratios of Horrigan Corporation are about average for an industrial firm.

Because several variations of the debt ratio appear in corporate annual reports, care in comparing debt ratios among firms is necessary.

## Cash Flow from Operations to Total Liabilities Ratio

The debt ratios give no recognition to the varying liquidity of assets for covering various levels of debt. The *cash flow from operations to total liabilities ratio* overcomes this deficiency. This cash flow ratio is similar to the one used in assessing short-term liquidity risk, but here *all* liabilities (both current and noncurrent) are included in the denominator. The cash flow from operations to debt ratio for Horrigan Corporation is as follows:

| | Cash Flow from Operations to Debt Ratio | = | Cash Flow from Operations / Average Total Liabilities |
|---|---|---|---|
| Year 2................ | $\dfrac{\$12}{\frac{1}{2}(\$90 + \$100)}$ | = | 12.6 percent |
| Year 3................ | $\dfrac{\$32}{\frac{1}{2}(\$100 + \$160)}$ | = | 24.6 percent |
| Year 4................ | $\dfrac{\$41}{\frac{1}{2}(\$160 + \$240)}$ | = | 20.5 percent |

A ratio of 20 percent or more is normal for a financially healthy company. Thus the long-term liquidity risk decreased significantly between Year 2 and Year 3 but increased again in Year 4.

## Interest Coverage: Times Interest Charges Earned

Another measure of long-term liquidity risk is the number of times that interest charges are earned, or covered. This ratio is calculated by dividing net income before interest and income tax expenses by interest expense. For Horrigan Corporation, the *times interest charges earned ratios* for Year 2, Year 3, and Year 4 are as follows:

| | Times Interest Charges Earned | = | Net Income before Interest and Income Taxes / Interest Expense |
|---|---|---|---|
| Year 2.......... | $\dfrac{\$16 + \$5 + \$\ 7}{\$5}$ | = | 5.6 times |
| Year 3.......... | $\dfrac{\$34 + \$10 + \$14}{\$10}$ | = | 5.8 times |
| Year 4.......... | $\dfrac{\$60 + \$16 + \$26}{\$16}$ | = | 6.4 times |

Thus, whereas the bonded indebtedness increased sharply during the 3-year period, the growth in net income before interest and income taxes was sufficient to provide increasing coverage of the fixed interest charges.

The purpose of this ratio is to indicate the relative protection of bondholders and to assess the probability that the firm will be forced into bankruptcy by a failure to meet required interest payments. If periodic repayments of principal on long-term liabilities are also required, the repayments might also be included in the denominator of the ratio. The ratio would then be described as the number of times that *fixed charges* were earned, or covered.

The times interest or fixed charges earned ratios can be criticized as measures for assessing long-term liquidity risk because these ratios use earnings rather than cash flows in the numerator. Interest and other fixed payment obligations are paid with cash, not with earnings. When the value of the ratio is relatively low (for example, two to three times), some measure of cash flows, such as cash flow from operations, may be preferable in the numerator.

## Summary of Long-Term Liquidity Analysis

Long-term liquidity analysis focuses on the amount of debt (particularly long-term debt) in the capital structure and the adequacy of earnings and cash flows for debt service — making interest and principal payments as they become due. Although both short- and long-term debt of Horrigan Corporation have increased over the 3-year period, increases in sales, earnings, and cash flows from operations all appear to be increasing sufficiently to cover the current levels of debt.

# Limitations of Ratio Analysis _____

For convenient reference, Exhibit 6.11 summarizes the calculation of the ratios discussed in this chapter.

The analytical computations discussed in this chapter have a number of limitations that should be kept in mind when preparing or using them. Several of the more important limitations are the following:

1.  The ratios are based on financial statement data and are therefore subject to the same criticisms as the financial statements (for example, use of acquisition cost rather than current replacement cost or net realizable value; the latitude permitted firms in selecting from among various generally accepted accounting principles).

2.  Changes in many ratios are strongly associated with each other. For example, the changes in the current ratio and quick ratio between two different times are often in the same direction and approximately proportional. It is therefore not necessary to compute all the ratios to assess a particular dimension of profitability or risk.

3.  When comparing the size of a ratio between periods for the same firm, one must recognize conditions that have changed between the periods being com-

**Exhibit 6.11** ————————————————————————————————————————————————————

## Summary of Financial Statement Ratios

| Ratio | Numerator | Denominator |
|---|---|---|
| **Profitability Ratios** | | |
| Rate of Return on Assets .... | Net Income + Interest Expense (net of tax effects)[a] | Average Total Assets during the Period |
| Profit Margin Ratio (before interest effects)..... | Net Income + Interest Expense (net of tax effects)[a] | Revenues |
| Various Expense Ratios ...... | Various Expenses | Revenues |
| Total Assets Turnover Ratio .................... | Revenues | Average Total Assets during the Period |
| Accounts Receivable Turnover Ratio ........... | Net Sales on Account | Average Accounts Receivable during the Period |
| Inventory Turnover Ratio ..... | Cost of Goods Sold | Average Inventory during the Period |
| Plant Asset Turnover Ratio .................... | Revenues | Average Plant Assets during the Period |
| Rate of Return on Common Shareholders' Equity ....... | Net Income − Preferred Stock Dividends | Average Common Shareholders' Equity during the Period |
| Profit Margin Ratio (after interest expense and preferred dividends) ............... | Net Income − Preferred Stock Dividends | Revenues |
| Leverage Ratio.............. | Average Total Assets during the Period | Average Common Shareholders' Equity during the Period |
| Earnings per Share of Stock[b].................... | Net Income − Preferred Stock Dividends | Weighted-Average Number of Common Shares Outstanding during the Period |

*continued*

pared (for example, different product lines or geographic markets served, changes in economic conditions, changes in prices).

4.  When comparing ratios of a particular firm with those of similar firms, one must recognize differences between the firms (for example, use of different methods of accounting, differences in the method of operations, type of financing, and so on).

Results of financial statement analyses cannot be used by themselves as direct indications of good or poor management. Such analyses merely indicate areas that might be investigated further. For example, a decrease in the turnover of raw materials inventory, ordinarily considered to be an undesirable trend, may reflect the accumulation of scarce materials that will keep the plant operating at full capacity during shortages when competitors have been forced to restrict operations or to close down. Ratios derived from financial statements must be combined with an investigation of other facts before valid conclusions can be drawn.

**Exhibit 6.11** *(continued)* _____

| Ratio | Numerator | Denominator |
|---|---|---|
| **Short-Term Liquidity Ratios** | | |
| Current Ratio .............. | Current Assets | Current Liabilities |
| Quick or Acid Test Ratio ..... | Highly Liquid Assets (ordinarily cash, marketable securities, and receivables)[c] | Current Liabilities |
| Cash Flow from Operations to Current Liabilities Ratio .................... | Cash Flow from Operations | Average Current Liabilities during the Period |
| Working Capital Turnover Ratio .................... | Revenues | Average Working Capital during the Period |
| **Long-Term Liquidity Ratios** | | |
| Long-Term Debt Ratio ....... | Total Long-Term Debt | Total Long-Term Debt Plus Shareholders' Equity |
| Debt-Equity Ratio ........... | Total Liabilities | Total Equities (total liabilities plus shareholders' equity) |
| Cash Flow from Operations to Total Liabilities Ratio .................... | Cash Flow from Operations | Average Total Liabilities during the Period |
| Times Interest Charges Earned .................. | Net Income before Interest and Income Taxes | Interest Expense |

[a]If a consolidated subsidiary is not owned entirely by the parent corporation, the minority interest share of earnings must also be added back to net income. See the description in Chapter 13.

[b]This calculation can be more complicated when there are convertible securities, options, or warrants outstanding.

[c]Receivables conceivably could be excluded for some firms and inventories included for others. Such refinements are seldom employed in practice.

# Summary _____

This chapter began with the question, "Should you invest your inheritance in a certificate of deposit or in the shares of common stock of Horrigan Corporation?" Analysis of Horrigan Corporation's financial statements indicates that it has been a growing, profitable company with few indications of either short-term or long-term liquidity problems. At least three additional inputs are necessary before making the investment decision. First, consideration must be given to sources of information other than the financial statements to ascertain whether information relevant for projecting rates of return or for assessing risk needs to be considered. Second, you must make a decision about your attitude toward, or willingness to assume, risk. Third, you must decide if you think the stock market price of the shares makes them an attractive purchase.[9] It is at this stage in the investment decision that the analysis becomes particularly subjective.

# Problem 1 for Self-Study ——————————————

Exhibit 6.12 presents an income statement for Year 2, and Exhibit 6.13 presents a comparative balance sheet for Cox Corporation as of December 31, Year 1 and Year 2. Using information from these financial statements, compute the following ratios. The income tax rate is 30 percent. Cash flow from operations totals $3,300.

**a.** Rate of return on assets.

**b.** Profit margin ratio (before interest and related tax effects).

**c.** Cost of goods sold to sales percentage.

**d.** Selling expense to sales percentage.

**e.** Total assets turnover.

**f.** Accounts receivable turnover.

**g.** Inventory turnover.

**h.** Plant asset turnover.

**Exhibit 6.12** ————————————————————————————————

## COX CORPORATION
### Income and Retained Earnings Statement for Year 2

| | | |
|---|---:|---:|
| Sales Revenue . . . . . . . . . . . . . . . . . . . . . . . . . . . . . . . . . . . . . . . . . . . . . . . | | $30,000 |
| Less Expenses: | | |
|   Cost of Goods Sold . . . . . . . . . . . . . . . . . . . . . . . . . . . . . . . . . . . . . . . | $18,000 | |
|   Selling . . . . . . . . . . . . . . . . . . . . . . . . . . . . . . . . . . . . . . . . . . . . . . . . . . | 4,500 | |
|   Administrative . . . . . . . . . . . . . . . . . . . . . . . . . . . . . . . . . . . . . . . . . . . . | 2,500 | |
|   Interest . . . . . . . . . . . . . . . . . . . . . . . . . . . . . . . . . . . . . . . . . . . . . . . . . . | 700 | |
|   Income Taxes . . . . . . . . . . . . . . . . . . . . . . . . . . . . . . . . . . . . . . . . . . . . | 1,300 | |
|     Total Expenses . . . . . . . . . . . . . . . . . . . . . . . . . . . . . . . . . . . . . . . | | 27,000 |
| Net Income . . . . . . . . . . . . . . . . . . . . . . . . . . . . . . . . . . . . . . . . . . . . . . . . . | | $ 3,000 |
| Less Dividends: | | |
|   Preferred . . . . . . . . . . . . . . . . . . . . . . . . . . . . . . . . . . . . . . . . . . . . . . . . | $ 100 | |
|   Common . . . . . . . . . . . . . . . . . . . . . . . . . . . . . . . . . . . . . . . . . . . . . . . . | 700 | 800 |
| Increase in Retained Earnings for Year 2 . . . . . . . . . . . . . . . . . . . . . . | | $ 2,200 |
| Retained Earnings, December 31, Year 1 . . . . . . . . . . . . . . . . . . . . . . | | 4,500 |
| Retained Earnings, December 31, Year 2 . . . . . . . . . . . . . . . . . . . . . . | | $ 6,700 |

——————

[9]Other important factors cannot be discussed here but are in finance texts. Perhaps the most important question of all is how a particular investment fits in with the investor's entire portfolio. Modern research suggests that the suitability of a potential investment depends more on the attributes of the other components of an investment portfolio and the risk attitude of the investor than it does on the attributes of the potential investment itself.

**Exhibit 6.13** ——————————————————————————————
COX CORPORATION
Comparative Balance Sheet
December 31, Year 1 and Year 2

| | December 31 | |
|---|---|---|
| | Year 1 | Year 2 |
| **Assets** | | |
| **Current Assets:** | | |
| Cash . . . . . . . . . . . . . . . . . . . . . . . . . . . . . . . . . . . . . . . . . . . . . . . . . . . | $    600 | $    750 |
| Accounts Receivable . . . . . . . . . . . . . . . . . . . . . . . . . . . . . . . . . . . . . . | 3,600 | 4,300 |
| Merchandise Inventories . . . . . . . . . . . . . . . . . . . . . . . . . . . . . . . . . . . | 5,600 | 7,900 |
| Prepayments . . . . . . . . . . . . . . . . . . . . . . . . . . . . . . . . . . . . . . . . . . . . . | 300 | 380 |
| Total Current Assets . . . . . . . . . . . . . . . . . . . . . . . . . . . . . . . . . . . . | $10,100 | $13,330 |
| **Property, Plant, and Equipment:** | | |
| Land . . . . . . . . . . . . . . . . . . . . . . . . . . . . . . . . . . . . . . . . . . . . . . . . . . . | $    500 | $    600 |
| Buildings and Equipment (net) . . . . . . . . . . . . . . . . . . . . . . . . . . . . . | 9,400 | 10,070 |
| Total Property, Plant, and Equipment . . . . . . . . . . . . . . . . . . . . . . | $ 9,900 | $10,670 |
| Total Assets . . . . . . . . . . . . . . . . . . . . . . . . . . . . . . . . . . . . . . . . . . . | $20,000 | $24,000 |
| **Liabilities and Shareholders' Equity** | | |
| **Current Liabilities:** | | |
| Notes Payable . . . . . . . . . . . . . . . . . . . . . . . . . . . . . . . . . . . . . . . . . . | $ 2,000 | $ 4,000 |
| Accounts Payable . . . . . . . . . . . . . . . . . . . . . . . . . . . . . . . . . . . . . . . | 3,500 | 3,300 |
| Other Current Liabilities . . . . . . . . . . . . . . . . . . . . . . . . . . . . . . . . . . | 1,500 | 1,900 |
| Total Current Liabilities . . . . . . . . . . . . . . . . . . . . . . . . . . . . . . . . . | $ 7,000 | $ 9,200 |
| **Noncurrent Liabilities:** | | |
| Bonds Payable . . . . . . . . . . . . . . . . . . . . . . . . . . . . . . . . . . . . . . . . . | 4,000 | 2,800 |
| Total Liabilities . . . . . . . . . . . . . . . . . . . . . . . . . . . . . . . . . . . . . . . | $11,000 | $12,000 |
| **Shareholders' Equity:** | | |
| Preferred Stock . . . . . . . . . . . . . . . . . . . . . . . . . . . . . . . . . . . . . . . . | $ 1,000 | $ 1,000 |
| Common Stock . . . . . . . . . . . . . . . . . . . . . . . . . . . . . . . . . . . . . . . . . | 2,000 | 2,500 |
| Additional Paid-in Capital . . . . . . . . . . . . . . . . . . . . . . . . . . . . . . . . . | 1,500 | 1,800 |
| Retained Earnings . . . . . . . . . . . . . . . . . . . . . . . . . . . . . . . . . . . . . . . | 4,500 | 6,700 |
| Total Shareholders' Equity . . . . . . . . . . . . . . . . . . . . . . . . . . . . . . | $ 9,000 | $12,000 |
| Total Liabilities and Shareholders' Equity . . . . . . . . . . . . . . . . . . . . | $20,000 | $24,000 |

**i.** Rate of return on common shareholders' equity.

**j.** Profit margin (after interest).

**k.** Leverage ratio.

**l.** Current ratio (both dates).

**m.** Quick ratio (both dates).

**n.** Cash flow from operations to current liabilities.

**o.** Working capital turnover.

**p.** Long-term debt ratio (both dates).

**q.** Debt-equity ratio (both dates).

**r.** Cash flow from operations to total liabilities.

**s.** Time interest charges earned.


## Suggested Solution

**a.** Rate of return on assets $= \dfrac{\$3{,}000 + (1 - .30)(\$700)}{.5(\$20{,}000 + \$24{,}000)} = 15.9$ percent.

**b.** Profit margin ratio $= \dfrac{\$3{,}000 + (1 - .30)(\$700)}{\$30{,}000} = 11.6$ percent.

**c.** Cost of goods sold to sales percentage $= \dfrac{\$18{,}000}{\$30{,}000} = 60.0$ percent.

**d.** Selling expense to sales percentage $= \dfrac{\$4{,}500}{\$30{,}000} = 15.0$ percent.

**e.** Total assets turnover $= \dfrac{\$30{,}000}{.5(\$20{,}000 + \$24{,}000)} = 1.4$ times per year.

**f.** Accounts receivable turnover $= \dfrac{\$30{,}000}{.5(\$3{,}600 + \$4{,}300)} = 7.6$ times per year.

**g.** Inventory turnover $= \dfrac{\$18{,}000}{.5(\$5{,}600 + \$7{,}900)} = 2.7$ times per year.

**h.** Plant asset turnover $= \dfrac{\$30{,}000}{.5(\$9{,}900 + \$10{,}670)} = 2.9$ times per year.

**i.** Rate of return on common shareholders' equity $= \dfrac{\$3{,}000 - \$100}{.5(\$8{,}000 + \$11{,}000)} =$ 30.5 percent.

**j.** Profit margin (after interest) $= \dfrac{\$3{,}000 - \$100}{\$30{,}000} = 9.7$ percent.

**k.** Leverage ratio $= \dfrac{.5(\$20{,}000 + \$24{,}000)}{.5(\$8{,}000 + \$11{,}000)} = 2.3$.

**l.**   Current ratio

December 31, Year 1: $\dfrac{\$10,100}{\$7,000} = 1.4:1.$

December 31, Year 2: $\dfrac{\$13,330}{\$9,200} = 1.4:1.$

**m.**   Quick ratio

December 31, Year 1: $\dfrac{\$4,200}{\$7,000} = .6:1.$

December 31, Year 2: $\dfrac{\$5,050}{\$9,200} = .5:1.$

**n.**   Cash flow from operations to current liabilities $= \dfrac{\$3,300}{.5(\$7,000 + \$9,200)} =$ 40.7 percent.

**o.**   Working capital turnover $= \dfrac{\$30,000}{.5(\$3,100 + \$4,130)} = 8.3$ times per year.

**p.**   Long-term debt ratio

December 31, Year 1: $\dfrac{\$4,000}{\$13,000} = 30.8$ percent.

December 31, Year 2: $\dfrac{\$2,800}{\$14,800} = 18.9$ percent.

**q.**   Debt-equity ratio

December 31, Year 1: $\dfrac{\$11,000}{\$20,000} = 55.0$ percent.

December 31, Year 2: $\dfrac{\$12,000}{\$24,000} = 50.0$ percent.

**r.**   Cash flow from operations to total liabilities $= \dfrac{\$3,300}{.5(\$11,000 + \$12,000)} =$ 28.7 percent.

**s.**   Times interest charges earned $= \dfrac{\$3,000 + \$1,300 + \$700}{\$700} = 7.1$ times.

## Problem 2 for Self-Study ——————————————

Exhibit 6.14 presents a ratio analysis for Abbott Corporation for Year 1 to Year 3.

**a.**   What is the likely explanation for the decreasing rate of return on assets?

**b.**   What is the likely explanation for the increasing rate of return on common shareholders' equity?

**c.**   What is the likely explanation for the behavior of the current and quick ratios?

**d.**   What is the likely explanation for the decreases in the two cash flow from operations to liabilities ratios?

Exhibit 6.14 _____

## ABBOTT CORPORATION
Ratio Analysis

|  | Year 1 | Year 2 | Year 3 |
|---|---|---|---|
| Rate of Return on Assets ............................ | 10.0% | 9.6% | 9.2% |
| Profit Margin (before interest and related tax effects) ..... | 6.0% | 6.1% | 6.1% |
| Total Assets Turnover ................................. | 1.7 | 1.6 | 1.5 |
| Cost of Goods Sold/Revenues ........................ | 62.5% | 62.3% | 62.6% |
| Selling Expenses/Revenues ......................... | 10.3% | 10.2% | 10.4% |
| Interest Expense/Revenues ........................... | 1.5% | 2.0% | 2.5% |
| Accounts Receivable Turnover ....................... | 4.3 | 4.3 | 4.2 |
| Inventory Turnover .................................. | 3.2 | 3.4 | 3.6 |
| Plant Asset Turnover ................................. | .8 | .7 | .6 |
| Rate of Return on Common Shareholders' Equity ........ | 14.0% | 14.2% | 14.5% |
| Profit Margin (after interest) .......................... | 5.1% | 4.9% | 4.6% |
| Leverage Ratio ...................................... | 1.6 | 1.8 | 2.1 |
| Current Ratio ....................................... | 1.4 | 1.3 | 1.2 |
| Quick Ratio ........................................ | 1.0 | .9 | 1.0 |
| Cash Flow from Operations to Current Liabilities ......... | 38.2% | 37.3% | 36.4% |
| Working Capital Turnover ............................. | 4.8 | 5.0 | 5.2 |
| Long-Term Debt Ratio ............................... | 37.5% | 33.8% | 43.3% |
| Debt-Equity Ratio .................................... | 37.5% | 44.4% | 52.4% |
| Cash Flow from Operations to Total Liabilities ........... | 16.3% | 13.4% | 11.1% |
| Times Interest Charges Earned ...................... | 6.7 | 5.1 | 4.1 |

## Suggested Solution

a. Because the profit margin (before interest expense and related tax effects) is stable over the 3 years, the decreasing rate of return on assets is attributable to a decreasing total assets turnover, which in turn is caused primarily by a decreasing plant asset turnover (the accounts receivable turnover is stable while the inventory turnover increases). Explanations for a decreasing plant asset turnover include (1) acceleration of capital expenditures in anticipation of higher sales in the future and (2) decreasing use of plant capacity so that depreciation expense must be covered by fewer units sold.

b. Because the rate of return on assets is decreasing, the increasing rate of return on common shareholders' equity must be the result of increased financial leverage. The increased financial leverage is evident from the leverage ratio, the percentage of interest expense to sales, and the difference between the profit margin measures before and after interest expense.

c. Because the primary difference between the current and quick ratios relates to inventories, the decreasing current ratio coupled with a stable quick ratio must be caused by more efficient inventory management. This explanation is supported by the increasing inventory turnover.

d. Given the stability of the profit margin (before interest expense and related tax effects) and the accounts receivable turnover and given the increased inventory turnover, we must look to the impact of interest expense on operating cash flows for the explanation. The increasing debt load has decreased the profit margin (after interest) and drained greater and greater amounts of cash for interest payments. These drains on operating cash flows, coupled with increasing amounts of debt (particularly long-term debt), have driven the cash flow ratios down.

# Questions, Exercises, Problems, and Cases _____

## Questions

1. Review the meaning of the following concepts or terms discussed in this chapter.

   a. Return and risk.
   b. Time-series analysis.
   c. Cross-section analysis.
   d. Profitability.
   e. Rate of return on assets.
   f. Profit margin ratio.
   g. Total assets turnover ratio.
   h. Accounts receivable turnover ratio.
   i. Inventory turnover ratio.
   j. Plant asset turnover ratio.
   k. Rate of return on common shareholders' equity.
   l. Financial leverage.
   m. Leverage ratio.

   n. Earnings per share.
   o. Primary and fully diluted earnings per share.
   p. Short-term liquidity risk.
   q. Current ratio.
   r. Quick ratio or acid test.
   s. Operating flow to current liabilities ratio.
   t. Working capital turnover ratio.
   u. Long-term liquidity risk.
   v. Long-term debt ratio.
   w. Debt-equity ratio.
   x. Cash flow from operations to total liabilities ratio.
   y. Times interest charges earned.

2. Describe several factors that might limit the comparability of a firm's financial statement ratios over several periods.

3. Describe several factors that might limit the comparability of one firm's financial statement ratios with those of another firm in the same industry.

4. "I can understand why interest expense is added back to net income in the numerator of the rate of return on assets, but I don't see why an adjustment is made for income taxes." Provide an explanation.

5. One company president stated, "The operations of our company are such that we must turn inventory over once every 4 weeks." Another company president in a similar industry stated, "The operations of our company are such that we can live comfortably with a turnover of four times each year." Explain what these two company presidents probably had in mind.

6. It has been suggested that for any given firm at a particular time there is an optimal inventory turnover ratio. Explain.

7. Under what circumstances will the rate of return on common shareholders' equity be greater than the rate of return on assets? Under what circumstances will it be less?

8. A company president recently stated, "The operations of our company are such that we can effectively use only a small amount of financial leverage." Explain.

9. Define financial leverage. As long as a firm's rate of return on assets exceeds its aftertax cost of borrowing, why doesn't the firm increase borrowing to as close to 100 percent of financing as possible?

10. Illustrate with amounts how a decrease in working capital can accompany an increase in the current ratio.

## Exercises

11. *Calculation and disaggregation of rate of return on assets.* The following data are taken from the most recent annual reports of Alabama Company and Carolina Company.

|  | Alabama Co. | Carolina Co. |
|---|---|---|
| Revenues.................................... | $2,000,000 | $2,400,000 |
| Expenses other than Interest and Income Taxes ... | 1,700,000 | 2,150,000 |
| Interest Expense .............................. | 100,000 | 50,000 |
| Income Tax Expense at 30 Percent ............. | 60,000 | 60,000 |
| Net Income .................................... | 140,000 | 140,000 |
| Average Total Assets during the Year............ | 1,500,000 | 1,000,000 |

a. Calculate the rate of return on assets for each company.
b. Disaggregate the rate of return in part **a** into profit margin and total assets turnover components.
c. Comment on the relative profitability of the two companies.

12. *Profitability analysis for two types of retailers.* The following information is taken from the annual reports of two companies, one of which is a retailer of quality men's clothes and the other of which is a discount household goods store. Neither company had any interest-bearing debt during the year. Identify which of these companies is likely to be the clothing retailer and which is likely to be the discount store. Explain.

|  | Company A | Company B |
|---|---|---|
| Sales........................................ | $3,000,000 | $3,000,000 |
| Net Income ................................... | 60,000 | 300,000 |
| Average Total Assets ......................... | 600,000 | 3,000,000 |

**13.** *Analysis of accounts receivable for two companies.* The following information relates to the activities of Tennessee Corporation and Kentucky Corporation for the current year.

| | Tennessee Corp. | Kentucky Corp. |
|---|---|---|
| Sales on Account........................ | $4,050,000 | $2,560,000 |
| Accounts Receivable, January 1 .......... | 960,000 | 500,000 |
| Accounts Receivable, December 31 ....... | 840,000 | 780,000 |

   **a.** Compute the accounts receivable turnover of each company.
   **b.** Compute the average number of days that accounts receivable are outstanding for each company.
   **c.** Which company is managing its accounts receivable more efficiently?

**14.** *Analysis of inventories over 4 years.* The following information relates to the activities of Carlson Corporation.

| | Year 1 | Year 2 | Year 3 | Year 4 |
|---|---|---|---|---|
| Sales.............................. | $1,000 | $2,500 | $5,000 | $8,000 |
| Cost of Goods Sold.................... | 600 | 1,550 | 3,150 | 5,120 |
| Average Inventory ..................... | 200 | 550 | 1,170 | 2,050 |

   **a.** Compute the inventory turnover for each year.
   **b.** Compute the average number of days that inventories are held for each year.
   **c.** How well has Carlson Corporation been managing its inventories?

**15.** *Analysis of plant assets over 4 years.* The following information relates to Steele Company.

| | Year 1 | Year 2 | Year 3 | Year 4 |
|---|---|---|---|---|
| Sales.............................. | $500 | $800 | $1,500 | $3,000 |
| Average Plant Assets ................... | 400 | 670 | 1,290 | 2,630 |
| Expenditures on Plant Assets ........... | 250 | 500 | 1,200 | 2,700 |

   **a.** Compute the plant asset turnover for each year.
   **b.** How well has Steele Company been managing its investment in plant assets?

16. *Calculation and disaggregation of rate of return on common shareholders' equity*. The following data are taken from the financial statements of Maine Corporation.

| | Year 1 | Year 2 | Year 3 | Year 4 |
|---|---|---|---|---|
| Revenues............................ | $2,000 | $2,250 | $2,500 | $2,750 |
| Net Income ......................... | 160 | 180 | 200 | 220 |
| Average Total Assets ................. | 1,000 | 1,160 | 1,333 | 1,517 |
| Average Common Shareholders' Equity ... | 500 | 592 | 694 | 809 |

a. Calculate the rate of return on common shareholders' equity.
b. Disaggregate the rate of return on common shareholders' equity into profit margin, total assets turnover, and leverage components.
c. How has the profitability of Maine Corporation changed over the 4 years?

17. *Profitability analysis for three companies*. The following data show five items from the financial statements of three companies for a recent year.

| | Company A | Company B | Company C |
|---|---|---|---|
| **For Year** | | | |
| Revenues......................... | $28,947,200 | $13,639,900 | $9,716,900 |
| Income before Interest and Related Taxes[a] ......................... | 4,295,800 | 824,600 | 156,400 |
| Net Income to Common Shareholders[b] . | 2,915,800 | 522,600 | 148,600 |
| **Average during Year** | | | |
| Total Assets ....................... | 77,107,200 | 10,885,000 | 1,532,400 |
| Common Shareholders' Equity ........ | 29,769,200 | 5,118,800 | 743,830 |

[a]Net Income + Interest Expense $\times$ (1 − Tax Rate).
[b]Net Income − Preferred Stock Dividends.

a. Compute the profit margin ratio (after interest) for each company. Which company seems to be the most successful according to this ratio?
b. On average, how many dollars of sales does each of the companies earn for each dollar's worth of assets held during the year?
c. Compute the rate of return on assets for each company. Which company seems to be the most successful according to this ratio?
d. Compute the rate of return on common shareholders' equity for each company. Which company seems to be the most successful according to this ratio?
e. The three companies are American Telephone & Telegraph, Safeway Stores, and Sears, Roebuck and Company. (Dollar amounts shown are actually in thousands.) Which of the companies corresponds to A, B, and C? What clues did you use in reaching your conclusion?

18. *Relation of profitability to financial leverage*.
    a. Compute the ratio of return on common shareholders' equity in each of the following independent cases.

| Case | Total Assets | Interest-Bearing Debt | Common Share-holders' Equity | Rate of Return on Assets | Aftertax Cost of Interest-Bearing Debt |
|------|------|------|------|------|------|
| A .............. | $200 | $100 | $100 | 6% | 6% |
| B .............. | 200 | 100 | 100 | 8 | 6 |
| C .............. | 200 | 120 | 80 | 8 | 6 |
| D .............. | 200 | 100 | 100 | 4 | 6 |
| E .............. | 200 | 50 | 100 | 6 | 6 |
| F .............. | 200 | 50 | 100 | 5 | 6 |

   b. In which cases is leverage working to the advantage of the common shareholders?

19. *Analysis of financial leverage*. The Borrowing Company has total assets of $100,000 during the year. It has borrowed $20,000 at a 10 percent annual rate and pays income taxes at a rate of 30 percent of pretax income. Shareholders' equity is $80,000.
    a. What must net income be for the rate of return on shareholders' equity to equal the rate of return on assets?
    b. What is the rate of return on common shareholders' equity for the net income determined in part **a**?
    c. What must income before interest and income taxes be to achieve this net income?
    d. Repeat parts **a, b,** and **c,** assuming borrowing of $80,000 and common shareholders' equity of $20,000.
    e. Compare the results from the two different debt-equity relations. What generalizations can be made?

20. *Ratio analysis of profitability and risk*. Refer to the following data for the Adelsman Company.

| | Year 1 | Year 2 | Year 3 |
|------|------|------|------|
| Rate of Return on Common Shareholders' Equity .... | 8% | 10% | 11% |
| Earnings per Share ............................... | $3.00 | $4.00 | $4.40 |
| Net Income/Total Interest Expense[a] ............... | 10 | 5 | 4 |
| Debt-Equity Ratio (liabilities/all equities) ............. | 20% | 50% | 60% |

[a]Note that this computation does not represent "times interest earned" as defined in the chapter.

The income tax rate was 30 percent in each year, and 100,000 common shares were outstanding throughout the period.
    a. Did the company's profitability increase over the 3-year period? How can you tell? (*Hint:* Compute the rate of return on assets.)

**b.** Did risk increase? How can you tell?

**c.** Are shareholders better off in Year 3 than in Year 1?

**21.** *Interpreting changes in earnings per share.* Company A and Company B both start Year 1 with $1 million of shareholders' equity and 100,000 shares of common stock outstanding. During Year 1, both companies earn net income of $100,000, a rate of return of 10 percent on common shareholders' equity. Company A declares and pays $100,000 of dividends to common shareholders at the end of Year 1, whereas Company B retains all its earnings and declares no dividends. During Year 2, both companies earn net income equal to 10 percent of shareholders' equity at the beginning of Year 2.

    **a.** Compute earnings per share for Company A and for Company B for Year 1 and for Year 2.

    **b.** Compute the rate of growth in earnings per share for Company A and Company B, comparing earnings per share in Year 2 with earnings per share in Year 1.

    **c.** Using the rate of growth in earnings per share as the criterion, which company's management appears to be doing a better job for its shareholders? Comment on this result.

**22.** *Working backwards from profitability ratios to financial statement data.* The revenues of Lev Company were $1,000 for the year. A financial analyst computed the following ratios for Lev Company, using the year-end balances for balance sheet amounts. The Lev Company has no preferred shares outstanding.

| | |
|---|---|
| Debt-Equity Ratio (all liabilities/all equities) ......................... | 75 percent |
| Income Tax Expense as a Percentage of Pretax Income............. | 30 percent |
| Net Income as a Percentage of Revenue .......................... | 14 percent |
| Rate of Return on Common Shareholders' Equity ................... | 10 percent |
| Rate of Return on Assets ....................................... | 6 percent |

From this information, compute each of the following items:

    **a.** Interest expense.

    **b.** Income tax expense.

    **c.** Total expenses.

    **d.** Net income.

    **e.** Total assets.

    **f.** Total liabilities.

**23.** *Effect of financing strategy on earnings per share (CMA adapted).* The Virgil Company is planning to invest $10 million in an expansion program that is expected to increase income before interest and taxes by $2.5 million. Currently, Virgil Company has total equities of $40 million, 25 percent of which is debt and 75 percent of which is shareholders' equity, represented by 1 million shares. The expansion can be financed by issuing 200,000 new shares at $50 each or by issuing long-term debt at an annual interest rate of 10 percent. The following is an excerpt from the most recent income statement.

| Earnings before Interest and Taxes............................. | $10,500,000 |
| Less: Interest Charges ......................................... | 500,000 |
| Earnings before Income Taxes .................................. | $10,000,000 |
| Income Taxes (at 30 percent) .................................. | 3,000,000 |
| Net Income ...................................... | $ 7,000,000 |

Assume that Virgil Company maintains its current earnings on its present assets, achieves the planned earnings from the new program, and that the tax rate remains at 30 percent.

**a.** What will be earnings per share if the expansion is financed with debt?

**b.** What will be earnings per share if the expansion is financed by issuing new shares?

**c.** At what level of earnings before interest and taxes will earnings per share be the same, regardless of which of the two financing programs is used?

**d.** At what level of earnings before interest and taxes will the rate of return on shareholders' equity be the same, regardless of which of the two financing plans is used?

**24.** *Relation between book and market rates of return.* Net income attributable to common shareholders' equity of Florida Corporation during the current year was $250,000. Earnings per share were $.50 during the period. The average common shareholders' equity during the year was $2,500,000. The market price at year-end was $6.00.

**a.** Calculate the rate of return on common shareholders' equity for the year.

**b.** Calculate the rate of return currently being earned on the market price of the stock (the ratio of earnings per common share to market price per common share).

**c.** Why is there a difference between the rates of return calculated in parts **a** and **b**?

**25.** *Calculation and interpretation of short-term liquidity ratios.* The following data are taken from the financial statements of Maloney Corporation.

| For the Year | | Year 2 | Year 3 | Year 4 |
|---|---|---|---|---|
| Revenues................................. | | $245 | $270 | $281 |
| Cash Flow from Operations.............. | | 79 | 105 | 137 |

| On December 31 | Year 1 | Year 2 | Year 3 | Year 4 |
|---|---|---|---|---|
| Quick Assets......................... | $200 | $225 | $330 | $350 |
| Current Assets ....................... | 320 | 375 | 420 | 455 |
| Current Liabilities .................... | 200 | 250 | 300 | 350 |

**a.** Compute the current and quick ratios as of December 31 of each of the Years 1 through 4.

**b.** Compute the cash flow from operations to current liabilities ratio and the working capital turnover ratio for each of the Years 2 through 4.

**c.** How has the short-term liquidity risk of Maloney Corporation changed over the 3-year period?

26. *Calculating changes in current ratio and working capital.* Merchandise inventory costing $30,000 is purchased on account. Indicate the effect (increase, decrease, no effect) of this transaction on (1) working capital and (2) the current ratio, assuming that current assets and current liabilities immediately before the transaction were as follows:

**a.** Current assets, $120,000; current liabilities, $120,000.
**b.** Current assets, $120,000; current liabilities, $150,000.
**c.** Current assets, $120,000; current liabilities, $80,000.

27. *Relation of profitability to short-term liquidity.* Following is a schedule of the current assets and current liabilities of the Lewis Company.

| | December 31 | |
| --- | --- | --- |
| | Year 2 | Year 1 |
| **Current Assets:** | | |
| Cash ................................................ | $  355,890 | $  212,790 |
| Accounts Receivable ............................... | 389,210 | 646,010 |
| Inventories ........................................ | 799,100 | 1,118,200 |
| Prepayments ....................................... | 21,600 | 30,000 |
| Total Current Assets ........................... | $1,565,800 | $2,007,000 |
| **Current Liabilities:** | | |
| Accounts Payable ................................. | $  152,760 | $  217,240 |
| Accrued Payroll, Taxes, etc. ..................... | 126,340 | 318,760 |
| Notes Payable .................................... | 69,500 | 330,000 |
| Total Current Liabilities ....................... | $  348,600 | $  866,000 |

During Year 2, the Lewis Company operated at a loss of $100,000. Depreciation expense during Year 2 was $30,000.

**a.** Calculate the current ratio for each date.
**b.** Calculate the amount of cash provided by operations for Year 2.
**c.** Explain how the improved current ratio is possible under the Year 2 operating conditions.

28. *Calculation and interpretation of long-term liquidity ratios.* The following data are taken from the financial statements of Michigan Corporation.

| For the Year | Year 2 | Year 3 | Year 4 |
| --- | --- | --- | --- |
| Net Income before Interest and Income Taxes .................................. | $  200 | $  325 | $  360 |
| Cash Flow from Operations ....................... | 115 | 155 | 184 |
| Interest Expense ................................ | 40 | 50 | 60 |

| On December 31 | Year 1 | Year 2 | Year 3 | Year 4 |
|---|---|---|---|---|
| Current Liabilities ...................... | $ 200 | $ 250 | $ 304 | $ 362 |
| Total Liabilities ....................... | 500 | 650 | 822 | 1,018 |
| Total Assets ......................... | 1,000 | 1,250 | 1,522 | 1,818 |

    **a.** Compute the long-term debt ratio and the debt-equity ratio at the end of each of the Years 1 through 4.

    **b.** Compute the cash flow from operations to total liabilities ratio and the times interest charges earned ratio for each of the Years 2 through 4.

    **c.** How has the long-term liquidity risk of Michigan Corporation changed over this 3-year period?

**29.** *Effect of various transactions on financial statement ratios.* Indicate the immediate effects (increase, decrease, no effect) of each of the following independent transactions on (1) the rate of return on common shareholders' equity, (2) the current ratio, and (3) the debt-equity ratio. State any necessary assumptions.

    **a.** Merchandise inventory costing $205,000 is purchased on account.

    **b.** Merchandise inventory costing $120,000 is sold on account for $150,000.

    **c.** Collections from customers on accounts receivable total $100,000.

    **d.** Payments to suppliers on accounts payable total $160,000.

    **e.** A machine costing $40,000, on which $30,000 of depreciation had been taken, is sold for $10,000.

    **f.** Dividends of $80,000 are declared. The dividends will be paid during the next accounting period.

    **g.** Common stock is issued for $75,000.

    **h.** A machine costing $60,000 is acquired. Cash of $10,000 is given, and a note for $50,000 payable 5 years from now is signed for the balance of the purchase price.

**30.** *Effect of various transactions on financial statement ratios.* Indicate the effects (increase, decrease, no effect) of the following independent transactions on (1) earnings per share, (2) working capital, and (3) the quick ratio, where accounts receivable are *included* but merchandise inventory is *excluded* from quick assets. State any necessary assumptions.

    **a.** Merchandise inventory costing $240,000 is sold on account for $300,000.

    **b.** Dividends of $160,000 are declared. The dividends will be paid during the next accounting period.

    **c.** Merchandise inventory costing $410,000 is purchased on account.

    **d.** A machine costing $80,000, on which $60,000 depreciation had been taken, is sold for $20,000.

    **e.** Merchandise inventory purchased for $7,000 cash is returned to the supplier because it is defective. A cash reimbursement is received.

    **f.** Ten thousand shares of $10 par value common stock are issued on the last day of the accounting period for $15 per share. The proceeds are used to acquire the assets of another firm composed of the following: accounts receivable, $30,000; merchandise inventory, $60,000; plant and equipment, $100,000. The acquiring firm also agrees to assume current liabilities of $40,000 of the acquired company.

## Problems and Cases

**31.** *Calculation of profitability and risk ratios.* The following data are taken from the financial statements of the Press Company:

|  | January 1 | December 31 |
|---|---|---|
| Current Assets .................................. | $180,000 | $210,000 |
| Noncurrent Assets .............................. | 255,000 | 275,000 |
| Current Liabilities ............................... | 85,000 | 78,000 |
| Long-Term Liabilities ........................... | 30,000 | 75,000 |
| Common Stock (10,000 shares) .................. | 300,000 | 300,000 |
| Retained Earnings .............................. | 20,000 | 32,000 |

|  | Operations for Year |
|---|---|
| Net Income ..................................... | 84,000 |
| Interest Expense ............................... | 3,000 |
| Income Taxes (30 percent rate) .................. | 36,000 |
| Cash Provided by Operations .................... | 30,970 |
| Dividends Declared ............................. | 72,000 |

Calculate the following ratios:
**a.** Rate of return on assets.
**b.** Rate of return on common shareholders' equity.
**c.** Earnings per share of common stock.
**d.** Current ratio (both months).
**e.** Cash flow from operations to current liabilities.
**f.** Debt-equity ratio (both months).
**g.** Cash flow from operations to total liabilities.
**h.** Times interest charges earned.

**32.** *Calculation of profitability and risk ratios.* The comparative balance sheets, income statement, and statement of cash flows of Solinger Electric Corporation for the current year are shown in Exhibits 6.15, 6.16, and 6.17.
**a.** Calculate the ratios listed in Exhibit 6.11 for Solinger Electric Corporation for the current year. You may omit expense ratios. Balance sheet ratios should be computed at both the beginning and end of the year. The income tax rate is 30 percent.
**b.** Was Solinger Electric Corporation successfully leveraged during the current year?
**c.** Assume that the bonds were issued on November 1. At what annual interest rate were the bonds apparently issued?
**d.** If Solinger Electric Corporation earns the same rate of return on assets next year as it realized this year, and if it issues no more debt, will the firm be successfully leveraged next year?

Exhibit 6.15 ———————————————————————————————————

**SOLINGER ELECTRIC CORPORATION**
Comparative Balance Sheets
(Problem 32)

|  | January 1 | December 31 |
|---|---|---|
| # Assets | | |
| **Current Assets:** | | |
| Cash . . . . . . . . . . . . . . . . . . . . . . . . . . . . . . . . . . . . . . . . . | $ 30,000 | $  3,000 |
| Accounts Receivable . . . . . . . . . . . . . . . . . . . . . . . . . . . . | 20,000 | 55,000 |
| Merchandise Inventory . . . . . . . . . . . . . . . . . . . . . . . . . | 40,000 | 50,000 |
| Total Current Assets . . . . . . . . . . . . . . . . . . . . . . . . | $ 90,000 | $108,000 |
| **Noncurrent Assets:** | | |
| Buildings and Equipment (cost) . . . . . . . . . . . . . . . . . . . | $100,000 | $225,000 |
| Accumulated Depreciation . . . . . . . . . . . . . . . . . . . . . . . | (30,000) | (40,000) |
| Total Noncurrent Assets . . . . . . . . . . . . . . . . . . . . . . | $ 70,000 | $185,000 |
| Total Assets . . . . . . . . . . . . . . . . . . . . . . . . . . . . . . . | $160,000 | $293,000 |
| # Liabilities and Shareholders' Equity | | |
| **Current Liabilities:** | | |
| Accounts Payable—Merchandise Suppliers . . . . . . . . . | $ 30,000 | $ 50,000 |
| Accounts Payable—Other Suppliers . . . . . . . . . . . . . . . | 10,000 | 12,000 |
| Salaries Payable . . . . . . . . . . . . . . . . . . . . . . . . . . . . . . | 5,000 | 6,000 |
| Total Current Liabilities . . . . . . . . . . . . . . . . . . . . . . | $ 45,000 | $ 68,000 |
| **Noncurrent Liabilities:** | | |
| Bonds Payable . . . . . . . . . . . . . . . . . . . . . . . . . . . . . . . | 0 | 100,000 |
| Total Liabilities . . . . . . . . . . . . . . . . . . . . . . . . . . . . | $ 45,000 | $168,000 |
| **Shareholders' Equity:** | | |
| Common Stock ($10 par value) . . . . . . . . . . . . . . . . . . | $100,000 | $100,000 |
| Retained Earnings . . . . . . . . . . . . . . . . . . . . . . . . . . . . | 15,000 | 25,000 |
| Total Shareholders' Equity . . . . . . . . . . . . . . . . . . . . | $115,000 | $125,000 |
| Total Liabilities plus Shareholders' Equity . . . . . . . . . | $160,000 | $293,000 |

Exhibit 6.16 ———————————————————————————————————

**SOLINGER ELECTRIC CORPORATION**
Income Statement for the Current Year
(Problem 32)

| | |
|---|---|
| Sales Revenue . . . . . . . . . . . . . . . . . . . . . . . . . . . . . . . . . . . . . . . . . . . . . | $125,000 |
| Less Expenses: | |
| Cost of Goods Sold . . . . . . . . . . . . . . . . . . . . . . . . . . . . . . . . . . . . . . . . | $ 60,000 |
| Salaries . . . . . . . . . . . . . . . . . . . . . . . . . . . . . . . . . . . . . . . . . . . . . . . . . . | 24,428 |
| Depreciation . . . . . . . . . . . . . . . . . . . . . . . . . . . . . . . . . . . . . . . . . . . . . | 10,000 |
| Interest . . . . . . . . . . . . . . . . . . . . . . . . . . . . . . . . . . . . . . . . . . . . . . . . . . | 2,000 |
| Income Taxes . . . . . . . . . . . . . . . . . . . . . . . . . . . . . . . . . . . . . . . . . . . . | 8,572 |
| Total Expenses . . . . . . . . . . . . . . . . . . . . . . . . . . . . . . . . . . . . . . . . . | $105,000 |
| Net Income . . . . . . . . . . . . . . . . . . . . . . . . . . . . . . . . . . . . . . . . . . . . . . | $ 20,000 |

Exhibit 6.17 _____

**SOLINGER ELECTRIC CORPORATION**
Statement of Cash Flows for the Current Year
(Problem 32)

| | | |
|---|---:|---:|
| *Operations:* | | |
| Net Income .......................................... | $20,000 | |
| Additions: | | |
|   Depreciation Expense ............................. | 10,000 | |
|   Increase in Accounts Payable: | | |
|     Merchandise Suppliers ........................... | 20,000 | |
|     Other Suppliers ................................ | 2,000 | |
|   Increase in Salaries Payable........................ | 1,000 | |
| Subtractions: | | |
|   Increase in Accounts Receivable .................... | (35,000) | |
|   Increase in Merchandise Inventory .................. | (10,000) | |
| Cash Flow from Operations............................ | | $ 8,000 |
| *Investing:* | | |
|   Acquisition of Buildings and Equipment ............... | | (125,000) |
| *Financing:* | | |
|   Issuance of Bonds................................. | $100,000 | |
|   Dividends......................................... | (10,000) | |
| Cash Flow from Financing ............................ | | 90,000 |
| Net Change in Cash ................................. | | $ (27,000) |

33. *Calculation of profitability and risk ratios.* Comparative balance sheets, income statement, and statement of cash flows of Nykerk Electronics Corporation for the current year are presented in Exhibits 6.18, 6.19, and 6.20, respectively.

Exhibit 6.18 _____

**NYKERK ELECTRONICS CORPORATION**
Comparative Balance Sheets
(all dollar amounts in thousands)
(Problem 33)

| | December 31 | January 1 |
|---|---:|---:|
| ## Assets | | |
| **Current Assets:** | | |
| Cash ........................................... | $ 1,600 | $ 1,400 |
| Accounts Receivable (net) ........................ | 2,600 | 2,500 |
| Inventories ...................................... | 7,300 | 6,900 |
|   Total Current Assets .......................... | $11,500 | $10,800 |
| **Noncurrent Assets:** | | |
| Plant and Equipment............................. | $ 5,200 | $ 4,500 |
|   Less Accumulated Depreciation .................. | 1,300 | 1,000 |
| Net Plant and Equipment.......................... | $ 3,900 | $ 3,500 |
| Land ........................................... | 1,200 | 1,200 |
|   Total Noncurrent Assets ........................ | $ 5,100 | $ 4,700 |
|   Total Assets .................................. | $16,600 | $15,500 |

*continued*

**Exhibit 6.18** *(continued)* ————————————————————————

| | December 31 | January 1 |
|---|---|---|
| **Liabilities and Shareholders' Equity** | | |
| **Current Liabilities:** | | |
| Accounts Payable .............................. | $ 1,600 | $ 1,700 |
| Accrued Payables ............................... | 800 | 900 |
| Income Taxes Payable .......................... | 300 | 200 |
| Notes Payable ................................. | 1,900 | 1,200 |
|    Total Current Liabilities ......................... | $ 4,600 | $ 4,000 |
| **Long-Term Liabilities:** | | |
| Bonds Payable (8 percent) ...................... | $ 2,000 | $ 2,100 |
| Mortgage Payable .............................. | 200 | 200 |
|    Total Long-Term Liabilities ...................... | $ 2,200 | $ 2,300 |
|    Total Liabilities ................................ | $ 6,800 | $ 6,300 |
| **Shareholders' Equity:** | | |
| Preferred Stock (6 percent, $100 par) .............. | $ 2,000 | $ 2,000 |
| Common Stock ($1 par) .......................... | 500 | 500 |
| Additional Paid-in Capital ........................ | 2,500 | 2,500 |
|    Total Contributed Capital ....................... | $ 5,000 | $ 5,000 |
| Retained Earnings ............................... | 4,800 | 4,200 |
|    Total Shareholders' Equity ...................... | $ 9,800 | $ 9,200 |
|    Total Liabilities and Shareholders' Equity .......... | $16,600 | $15,500 |

**a.** Calculate the ratios listed in Exhibit 6.11 for Nykerk Electronics Corporation for the current year. You may omit expense ratios. Balance sheet ratios should be computed at both the beginning and end of the year. The income tax rate is 30 percent.

**b.** Was Nykerk Electronics Corporation successfully leveraged during the year?

**34.** *Analysis of profitability and risk for two companies.* Exhibits 6.21 and 6.22 present the income statements and balance sheets of Illinois Corporation and Ohio Corporation.

Cash flow provided by operations was $600,000 for Illinois Corporation and $550,000 for Ohio Corporation.

Assume that the balances in asset and equity accounts at year-end approximate the average balances during the period. The income tax rate is 30 percent. On the basis of this information, which company is

**a.** More profitable?

**b.** Less risky in terms of short-term liquidity?

**c.** Less risky in terms of long-term liquidity?

Use financial ratios, as appropriate, in doing your analysis.

Exhibit 6.19 ————————————————————————————————————

**NYKERK ELECTRONICS CORPORATION**
**Statement of Income and Retained Earnings for the Current Year**
**(all dollar amounts in thousands)**
**(Problem 33)**

| | | |
|---|---:|---:|
| **Revenues:** | | |
| Sales.................................................... | | $26,500 |
| Less Sales Allowances, Returns, and Discounts ............ | | 600 |
| Net Sales................................................ | | $25,900 |
| Interest and Other Revenues .............................. | | 200 |
| Total Revenues ......................................... | | $26,100 |
| | | |
| **Expenses:** | | |
| Cost of Goods Sold....................................... | | $20,500 |
| Selling and Administrative Expenses: | | |
| Selling Expenses ....................................... | $2,120 | |
| Administrative Expenses ............................... | 1,300 | |
| Depreciation .......................................... | 300 | |
| Total Selling and Administrative Expenses................... | | 3,720 |
| Interest Expense ......................................... | | 180 |
| Income Tax Expense ...................................... | | 500 |
| Total Expenses....................................... | | $24,900 |
| Net Income ............................................. | | $ 1,200 |
| | | |
| **Dividends:** | | |
| Dividends on Preferred Shares............................ | $ 120 | |
| Dividends on Common Shares ........................... | 480 | |
| Total Dividends...................................... | | 600 |
| Addition to Retained Earnings for Year..................... | | $   600 |
| Retained Earnings, January 1............................. | | 4,200 |
| Retained Earnings, December 31 .......................... | | $ 4,800 |

Exhibit 6.20 ————————————————————————————————————

**NYKERK ELECTRONICS CORPORATION**
**Statement of Cash Flows for the Current Year**
**(all dollar amounts in thousands)**
**(Problem 33)**

| | | |
|---|---:|---:|
| *Operations:* | | |
| Net Income ............................................. | | $1,200 |
| Additions: | | |
| Depreciation Expense ................................... | | 300 |
| Increase in Income Taxes Payable ...................... | | 100 |
| Subtractions: | | |
| Increase in Accounts Receivable ........................ | | (100) |
| Increase in Inventories ................................. | | (400) |
| Decrease in Accounts Payable .......................... | | (100) |
| Decrease in Accrued Payables.......................... | | (100) |
| Cash Flow from Operations................................. | | $ 900 |
| *Investing:* | | |
| Purchase of Plant and Equipment ........................ | | (700) |

*continued*

**Exhibit 6.20** *(continued)* —————————————————————

*Financing:*

| | |
|---|---|
| Issuance of Bank Note . . . . . . . . . . . . . . . . . . . . . . . . . . . . . . . . . . . | $  700 |
| Preferred Stock Dividend . . . . . . . . . . . . . . . . . . . . . . . . . . . . . . . | (120) |
| Common Stock Dividend . . . . . . . . . . . . . . . . . . . . . . . . . . . . . . . | (480) |
| Redemption of Bonds Payable . . . . . . . . . . . . . . . . . . . . . . . . | (100) |
| Cash Flow from Financing . . . . . . . . . . . . . . . . . . . . . . . . . . . . . . . | 0 |
| Net Change in Cash . . . . . . . . . . . . . . . . . . . . . . . . . . . . . . . . . . . . | $ 200 |

**Exhibit 6.21** —————————————————————————————————

## Income Statements for the Current Year
## (Problem 34)

| | Illinois Corp. | Ohio Corp. |
|---|---|---|
| Sales. . . . . . . . . . . . . . . . . . . . . . . . . . . . . . . . . . . . . . . . . | $4,300,000 | $3,000,000 |
| Less Expenses: | | |
|   Cost of Goods Sold. . . . . . . . . . . . . . . . . . . . . . . . . . . . | $2,800,000 | $1,400,000 |
|   Selling and Administrative Expenses. . . . . . . . . . . . . | 482,860 | 697,140 |
|   Interest Expense . . . . . . . . . . . . . . . . . . . . . . . . . . . . | 100,000 | 200,000 |
|   Income Tax Expense . . . . . . . . . . . . . . . . . . . . . . . . . | 275,140 | 210,860 |
|   Total Expenses. . . . . . . . . . . . . . . . . . . . . . . . . . . . . . | $3,658,000 | $2,508,000 |
|     Net Income . . . . . . . . . . . . . . . . . . . . . . . . . . . | $  642,000 | $  492,000 |

**Exhibit 6.22** —————————————————————————————————

## Balance Sheets, December 31
## (Problem 34)

| | Illinois Corp. | Ohio Corp. |
|---|---|---|
| **Assets** | | |
| Cash . . . . . . . . . . . . . . . . . . . . . . . . . . . . . . . . . . . . . . . . . | $  100,000 | $   50,000 |
| Accounts Receivable (net) . . . . . . . . . . . . . . . . . . . . . . . . | 700,000 | 400,000 |
| Merchandise Inventory . . . . . . . . . . . . . . . . . . . . . . . . . . | 1,200,000 | 750,000 |
| Plant and Equipment (net) . . . . . . . . . . . . . . . . . . . . . . . . | 4,000,000 | 4,800,000 |
|   Total Assets . . . . . . . . . . . . . . . . . . . . . . . . . . . . . . . | $6,000,000 | $6,000,000 |
| | | |
| **Liabilities and Shareholders' Equity** | | |
| Accounts Payable . . . . . . . . . . . . . . . . . . . . . . . . . . . . . . | $  725,000 | $  289,000 |
| Income Taxes Payable . . . . . . . . . . . . . . . . . . . . . . . . . . . | 275,000 | 211,000 |
| Long-Term Bonds Payable (10 percent) . . . . . . . . . . . . | 1,000,000 | 2,000,000 |
| Common Stock . . . . . . . . . . . . . . . . . . . . . . . . . . . . . . . . | 2,000,000 | 2,000,000 |
| Retained Earnings . . . . . . . . . . . . . . . . . . . . . . . . . . . . . . | 2,000,000 | 1,500,000 |
|   Total Liabilities and Shareholders' Equity . . . . . . . . . | $6,000,000 | $6,000,000 |

**Exhibit 6.23** ————————————————————————————————————————————————————
**Data for Ratio Detective Exercise**
**(Problem 35)**

| | Company Numbers | | | | | | |
|---|---|---|---|---|---|---|---|
| | (1) | (2) | (3) | (4) | (5) | (6) | (7) |
| **Balance Sheet at End of Year** | | | | | | | |
| Current Receivables .......... | 0.31% | 29.11% | 6.81% | 25.25% | 3.45% | 38.78% | 17.64% |
| Inventories.................. | 7.80 | 0.00 | 3.14 | 0.00 | 6.45 | 14.94 | 20.57 |
| Net Plant and Equipment* ...... | 8.50 | 9.63 | 11.13 | 19.88 | 49.87 | 15.59 | 37.60 |
| All Other Assets.............. | 2.16 | 7.02 | 25.59 | 32.93 | 24.05 | 15.54 | 30.07 |
| Total Assets ................. | 18.77% | 45.76% | 46.67% | 78.06% | 83.82% | 84.85% | 105.88% |
| *Cost of Plant and Equipment (gross) .......... | 14.64% | 14.80% | 19.57% | 29.03% | 79.03% | 24.80% | 59.73% |
| Current Liabilities ............. | 6.08% | 9.82% | 6.41% | 17.49% | 14.83% | 35.28% | 27.68% |
| Long-Term Liabilities .......... | 2.12 | 7.96 | 0.00 | 0.00 | 0.00 | 8.33 | 1.33 |
| Owners' Equity ............... | 10.57 | 27.98 | 40.26 | 60.57 | 68.99 | 41.24 | 76.87 |
| Total Equities .............. | 18.77% | 45.76% | 46.67% | 78.06% | 83.82% | 84.85% | 105.88% |
| **Income Statement for Year** | | | | | | | |
| Revenues..................... | 100.00% | 100.00% | 100.00% | 100.00% | 100.00% | 100.00% | 100.00% |
| Cost of Goods Sold (excluding depreciation) or Operating Expenses[a] ...... | 78.97 | 53.77 | 48.21 | 59.07 | 68.62 | 60.88 | 33.29 |
| Depreciation .................. | 1.04 | 1.39 | 1.72 | 2.07 | 4.07 | 1.09 | 3.02 |
| Interest Expense ............. | 0.16 | 0.52 | 0.00 | 0.08 | 0.02 | 1.35 | 0.73 |
| Advertising Expense .......... | 3.72 | 0.00 | 11.43 | 0.06 | 4.39 | 2.93 | 2.28 |
| Research and Development Expense .................. | 0.00 | 1.00 | 0.00 | 0.00 | 0.15 | 0.00 | 9.06 |
| Income Taxes ................. | 1.28 | 0.53 | 9.59 | 6.52 | 7.87 | 3.78 | 8.55 |
| All Other Items (net) .......... | 13.34 | 18.88 | 18.58 | 24.52 | 6.40 | 24.39 | 27.66 |
| Total Expenses.............. | 98.51% | 76.09% | 89.53% | 92.32% | 91.52% | 94.42% | 84.59% |
| Net Income .................. | 1.50% | 23.92% | 10.47% | 7.68% | 8.49% | 5.59% | 15.41% |

*continued*

35. *Detective analysis — identify company*. In this problem, you become a financial analyst/detective. The condensed financial statements in Exhibit 6.23 are constructed on a percentage basis. In all cases, total sales revenues are shown as 100.00%. All other numbers were divided by sales revenue for the year. The 13 companies (all corporations except for the accounting firm) shown here represent the following industries:

   (1)  Advertising and public opinion survey firm.
   (2)  Beer brewery.
   (3)  Department store chain (that carries its own receivables).
   (4)  Distiller of hard liquor.
   (5)  Drug manufacturer.
   (6)  Finance company (lends money to consumers).
   (7)  Grocery store chain.
   (8)  Insurance company.
   (9)  Manufacturer of tobacco products, mainly cigarettes.

**Exhibit 6.23** *(continued)* ———————————————————

| | Company Numbers | | | | | |
|---|---|---|---|---|---|---|
| | (8) | (9) | (10) | (11) | (12) | (13) |
| **Balance Sheet at End of Year** | | | | | | |
| Current Receivables .................... | 12.94% | 9.16% | 25.18% | 27.07% | 13.10% | 653.94% |
| Inventories............................. | 15.47 | 56.89 | 79.53 | 0.00 | 1.62 | 0.00 |
| Net Plant and Equipment* ............... | 70.29 | 28.36 | 19.22 | 2.64 | 251.62 | 2.88 |
| All Other Assets........................ | 18.37 | 26.42 | 24.72 | 223.91 | 23.68 | 200.37 |
| Total Assets .......................... | 117.07% | 120.83% | 148.65% | 253.62% | 290.02% | 857.19% |
| *Cost of Plant and Equipment (gross) ..................... | 167.16% | 42.40% | 35.08% | 4.45% | 320.90% | 3.81% |
| Current Liabilities ...................... | 19.37% | 33.01% | 20.42% | 161.37% | 28.01% | 377.56% |
| Long-Term Liabilities ........................ | 20.62 | 34.07 | 36.09 | 10.62 | 115.50 | 280.79 |
| Owners' Equity ........................ | 77.08 | 53.75 | 92.14 | 81.63 | 146.51 | 198.84 |
| Total Equities ....................... | 117.07% | 120.83% | 148.65% | 253.62% | 290.02% | 857.19% |
| **Income Statement for Year** | | | | | | |
| Revenues................................ | 100.00% | 100.00% | 100.00% | 100.00% | 100.00% | 100.00% |
| Cost of Goods Sold (excluding depreciation) or Operating Expenses[a] ................ | 81.92 | 57.35 | 42.92 | 82.61 | 45.23 | 47.69 |
| Depreciation ........................... | 5.81 | 1.90 | 1.97 | 0.05 | 14.55 | 0.00 |
| Interest Expense ....................... | 1.23 | 2.69 | 3.11 | 1.07 | 7.15 | 24.33 |
| Advertising Expense .................... | 0.00 | 6.93 | 13.04 | 0.00 | 0.00 | 0.00 |
| Research and Development Expense............................. | 0.76 | 0.00 | 0.00 | 0.00 | 0.71 | 0.00 |
| Income Taxes........................... | 2.15 | 7.47 | 10.63 | 3.92 | 8.73 | 12.89 |
| All Other Items (net) .................... | 3.81 | 14.82 | 17.99 | 2.97 | 11.51 | −5.57 |
| Total Expenses....................... | 95.68% | 91.16% | 89.66% | 90.62% | 87.88% | 79.34% |
| Net Income ........................... | 4.32% | 8.84% | 10.34% | 9.38% | 12.11% | 20.65% |

[a]Represents operating expenses for the following companies: Advertising/public opinion survey firm, insurance company, finance company, and the public accounting partnership.

 **(10)** Public accounting (CPA) partnership.
 **(11)** Soft drink bottler.
 **(12)** Steel manufacturer.
 **(13)** Utility company.
 Use whatever clues you can to match the companies in Exhibit 6.23 with the industries listed above. You may find it useful to refer to average industry ratios compiled by Dun & Bradstreet, Prentice-Hall, Robert Morris Associates, and the Federal Trade Commission. Copies of these documents can be found in most libraries.

**36.** *Interpretation of ratio analysis.* Exhibit 6.24 presents a ratio analysis for Sarwark Company.
   **a.** What is the likely explanation for the stable rate of return on assets coupled with the decreasing rate of return on common shareholders' equity?
   **b.** What is the likely reason for the increasing plant asset turnover?

**37.** *Interpretation of ratio analysis.* Exhibit 6.25 presents a ratio analysis for Widdicombe Corporation for Year 1 through Year 3.
   **a.** What is the likely explanation for the increasing rate of return on assets coupled with the decreasing rate of return on shareholders' equity?
   **b.** How effectively has the firm been managing its inventories?
   **c.** What is the likely explanation for the increasing total assets turnover?

**38.** *Case analysis of bankruptcy.* On October 2, 1975, W. T. Grant Company filed for bankruptcy protection under Chapter XI of the Bankruptcy Act. At that time, it reported assets of $1.02 billion and liabilities of $1.03 billion. The company had operated at a profit for most years prior to 1974, but it reported an operating loss of $177 million for its fiscal year January 31, 1974, to January 31, 1975.
   The accompanying Exhibits 6.26 through 6.29 contain:

   **1.** Balance sheets, income statements, and statements of cash flows for W. T. Grant Company for the 1971 through 1975 fiscal periods.

   **2.** Additional financial information about W. T. Grant Company, the retail industry, and the economy for the same period.

**Exhibit 6.24** _____

**SARWARK COMPANY**
**Ratio Analysis**
**(Problem 36)**

|  | Year 1 | Year 2 | Year 3 |
|---|---|---|---|
| Rate of Return on Assets ....................... | 10.1% | 10.2% | 9.9% |
| Profit Margin (before interest and related tax effects)................................... | 11.9% | 10.0% | 9.6% |
| Total Assets Turnover ........................... | 0.85 | 1.02 | 1.03 |
| Cost of Goods Sold/Revenues .................. | 72.4% | 73.9% | 73.8% |
| Selling and Administrative Expenses/Revenues .... | 10.5% | 10.4% | 10.5% |
| Interest Expense/Revenues...................... | 2.1% | 3.5% | 4.0% |
| Income Tax Expense/Revenues ................. | 4.2% | 4.1% | 3.8% |
| Accounts Receivable Turnover .................. | 4.6 | 4.7 | 4.6 |
| Inventory Turnover.............................. | 3.7 | 3.6 | 3.7 |
| Plant Asset Turnover............................ | 1.2 | 1.5 | 1.7 |
| Rate of Return on Common Shareholders' Equity .. | 15.5% | 15.2% | 14.7% |
| Current Ratio .................................. | 1.6:1 | 1.4:1 | 1.2:1 |
| Quick Ratio ................................... | .9:1 | .7:1 | .5:1 |
| Total Liabilities/Total Liabilities and Shareholders' Equity ......................... | 42.0% | 48.0% | 60.0% |
| Long-Term Liabilities/Total Liabilities and Shareholders' Equity ......................... | 25.0% | 26.0% | 25.0% |
| Revenues as Percentage of Year 1 Revenues ..... | 100% | 115% | 130% |
| Assets as Percentage of Year 1 Assets ........... | 100% | 113% | 125% |
| Capital Expenditures as Percentage of Year 1 Capital Expenditures ......................... | 100% | 112% | 120% |

Prepare an analysis that explains the major causes of Grant's collapse. You may find it useful to refer to financial and nonfinancial data presented in other sources, such as *The Wall Street Journal*, in addition to that presented here. Assume an income tax rate of 48 percent.

**Exhibit 6.25** ─────────────────────────────────────────
**WIDDICOMBE CORPORATION**
**Ratio Analysis**
**(Problem 37)**

|  | Year 1 | Year 2 | Year 3 |
|---|---|---|---|
| Rate of Return on Assets ......................... | 10% | 11% | 12% |
| Profit Margin (before interest and related taxes)...... | 18% | 16% | 14% |
| Total Assets Turnover............................ | .56 | .69 | .86 |
| Cost of Goods Sold/Revenues .................... | 62% | 63% | 65% |
| Selling and Administrative Expenses/Revenues ...... | 8% | 10% | 10% |
| Interest Expense/Revenues........................ | 16% | 12% | 8% |
| Income Tax Expense/Revenues ................... | 4% | 5% | 7% |
| Accounts Receivable Turnover .................... | 2.6 | 2.5 | 2.4 |
| Inventory Turnover............................... | 3.2 | 2.8 | 2.5 |
| Fixed Asset Turnover ............................ | .3 | .5 | .7 |
| Rate of Return on Common Shareholders' Equity .... | 18% | 16% | 14% |
| Profit Margin (after interest)...................... | 10% | 10% | 10% |
| Asset Turnover .................................. | .56 | .69 | .86 |
| Leverage Ratio .................................. | 3.2 | 2.3 | 1.6 |
| Revenues as Percentage of Year 1 Revenues ....... | 100% | 102% | 99% |
| Assets as Percentage of Year 1 Assets ............ | 100% | 104% | 105% |
| Net Income as Percentage of Year 1 Net Income .... | 100% | 102% | 99% |
| Capital Expenditures as Percentage of Year 1 Capital Expenditures .......................... | 100% | 90% | 85% |

Exhibit 6.26 _____

# W. T. GRANT COMPANY
## Comparative Balance Sheets
## (Problem 38)

| | January 31 | | | | |
| --- | --- | --- | --- | --- | --- |
| | **1971** | **1972** | **1973** | **1974** | **1975** |
| **Assets** | | | | | |
| Cash and Marketable Securities.... | $ 34,009 | $ 49,851 | $ 30,943 | $ 45,951 | $ 79,642 |
| Accounts Receivable.............. | 419,731 | 477,324 | 542,751 | 598,799 | 431,201 |
| Inventories...................... | 260,492 | 298,676 | 399,533 | 450,637 | 407,357 |
| Other Current Assets ............ | 5,246 | 5,378 | 6,649 | 7,299 | 6,581 |
| Total Current Assets ........... | $719,478 | $831,229 | $ 979,876 | $1,102,686 | $ 924,781 |
| Investments..................... | 23,936 | 32,367 | 35,581 | 45,451 | 49,764 |
| Property, Plant, and Equipment (net) ......................... | 61,832 | 77,173 | 91,420 | 100,984 | 101,932 |
| Other Assets.................... | 2,382 | 3,901 | 3,821 | 3,862 | 5,790 |
| Total Assets .................. | $807,628 | $944,670 | $1,110,698 | $1,252,983 | $1,082,267 |
| **Equities** | | | | | |
| Short-Term Debt.................. | $246,420 | $237,741 | $ 390,034 | $ 453,097 | $ 600,695 |
| Accounts Payable ................ | 118,091 | 124,990 | 112,896 | 103,910 | 147,211 |
| Current Deferred Taxes ........... | 94,489 | 112,846 | 130,137 | 133,057 | 2,000 |
| Total Current Liabilities .......... | $459,000 | $475,577 | $ 633,067 | $ 690,064 | $ 749,906 |
| Long-Term Debt .................. | 32,301 | 128,432 | 126,672 | 220,336 | 216,341 |
| Noncurrent Deferred Taxes ........ | 8,518 | 9,664 | 11,926 | 14,649 | — |
| Other Long-Term Liabilities ........ | 5,773 | 5,252 | 4,694 | 4,195 | 2,183 |
| Total Liabilities ................. | $505,592 | $618,925 | $ 776,359 | $ 929,244 | $ 968,430 |
| Preferred Stock .................. | $ 9,600 | $ 9,053 | $ 8,600 | $ 7,465 | $ 7,465 |
| Common Stock................... | 18,180 | 18,529 | 18,588 | 18,599 | 18,599 |
| Additional Paid-in Capital ......... | 78,116 | 85,195 | 86,146 | 85,910 | 83,914 |
| Retained Earnings ............... | 230,435 | 244,508 | 261,154 | 248,461 | 37,674 |
| Total ......................... | $336,331 | $357,285 | $ 374,488 | $ 360,435 | $ 147,652 |
| Less Cost of Treasury Stock ....... | (34,295) | (31,540) | (40,149) | (36,696) | (33,815) |
| Total Shareholders' Equity ....... | $302,036 | $325,745 | $ 334,339 | $ 323,739 | $ 113,837 |
| Total Equities .................. | $807,628 | $944,670 | $1,110,698 | $1,252,983 | $1,082,267 |

Exhibit 6.27 _____

## W. T. GRANT COMPANY
## Statement of Income and Retained Earnings
## (Problem 38)

| | Years Ended January 31 | | | | |
|---|---|---|---|---|---|
| | **1971** | **1972** | **1973** | **1974** | **1975** |
| Sales....................... | $1,254,131 | $1,374,811 | $1,644,747 | $1,849,802 | $1,761,952 |
| Concessions ................. | 4,986 | 3,439 | 3,753 | 3,971 | 4,238 |
| Equity in Earnings ............ | 2,777 | 2,383 | 5,116 | 4,651 | 3,086 |
| Other Income ................ | 2,874 | 3,102 | 1,188 | 3,063 | 3,376 |
| Total Revenues ............ | $1,264,768 | $1,383,735 | $1,654,804 | $1,861,487 | $1,772,652 |
| Cost of Goods Sold........... | $ 843,192 | $ 931,237 | $1,125,261 | $1,282,945 | $1,303,267 |
| Selling, General, and Administration .............. | 329,768 | 373,816 | 444,377 | 518,280 | 540,953 |
| Interest...................... | 18,874 | 16,452 | 21,127 | 51,047 | 199,238 |
| Taxes: Current ............... | 21,140 | 13,487 | 9,588 | (6,021) | (19,439) |
| Deferred .............. | 11,660 | 13,013 | 16,162 | 6,807 | (98,027) |
| Other Expenses .............. | 557 | 518 | 502 | — | 24,000 |
| Total Expenses............. | $1,225,191 | $1,348,523 | $1,617,017 | $1,853,058 | $1,949,992 |
| Net Income .................. | $ 39,577 | $ 35,212 | $ 37,787 | $ 8,429 | $ (177,340) |
| Dividends.................... | (20,821) | (21,139) | (21,141) | (21,122) | (4,457) |
| Other........................ | — | — | — | — | (28,990) |
| Change in Retained Earnings ... | $ 18,756 | $ 14,073 | $ 16,646 | $ (12,693) | $ (210,787) |
| Retained Earnings— Beg. of Period ............. | 211,679 | 230,435 | 244,508 | 261,154 | 248,461 |
| Retained Earnings— End of Period .............. | $ 230,435 | $ 244,508 | $ 261,154 | $ 248,461 | $ 37,674 |

## Exhibit 6.28 ————————————————————————————————————

**W. T. GRANT COMPANY**
Statement of Cash Flows
(Problem 38)

| | Years Ended January 31 | | | | |
|---|---|---|---|---|---|
| | **1971** | **1972** | **1973** | **1974** | **1975** |
| **Sources of Cash:** | | | | | |
| New Financing: | | | | | |
| Short-Term Bank Borrowing .......... | $ 64,288 | — | $152,293 | $ 63,063 | $147,898 |
| Issue of Long-Term Debt ............. | — | $100,000 | — | 100,000 | — |
| Sale of Common Stock: | | | | | |
| To Employees..................... | 5,218 | 7,715 | 3,492 | 2,584 | 886 |
| On Open Market .................. | — | 2,229 | 174 | 260 | — |
| Other Sources (net).................... | — | — | 2,307 | — | — |
| Total Sources of Cash .......... | $ 69,506 | $109,944 | $158,266 | $165,907 | $148,784 |
| **Uses of Cash:** | | | | | |
| Net Income ....................... | $ 39,577 | $ 35,212 | $ 37,787 | $ 8,429 | $(177,340) |
| Additions: | | | | | |
| Depreciation and Other ........... | 9,619 | 10,577 | 12,004 | 13,579 | 14,587 |
| Decrease in Accounts Receivable ... | — | — | — | — | 121,351 |
| Decrease in Inventories ........... | — | — | — | — | 43,280 |
| Increase in Accounts Payable....... | 13,947 | 6,900 | — | — | 42,028 |
| Increase in Deferred Taxes ......... | 14,046 | 18,357 | 17,291 | 2,920 | — |
| Subtractions: | | | | | |
| Equity in Earnings and Other ....... | (2,470) | (1,758) | (1,699) | (1,344) | (16,993) |
| Increase in Accounts Receivable .... | (51,464) | (57,593) | (65,427) | (56,047) | — |
| Increase in Inventories ............. | (38,365) | (38,184) | (100,857) | (51,104) | — |
| Increase in Prepayments ........... | (209) | (428) | (1,271) | (651) | (11,032) |
| Decrease in Accounts Payable...... | — | — | (12,093) | (8,987) | — |
| Decrease in Deferred Taxes ........ | — | — | — | — | (101,078) |
| Cash Used by Operations .............. | $ 15,319 | $ 26,917 | $114,265 | $ 93,205 | $ 85,197 |
| Reduction in Financing: | | | | | |
| Repayment of Short-Term Borrowing (net) ............................. | — | $ 8,680 | — | — | — |
| Retirement of Long-Term Debt ........ | $ 1,538 | 5,143 | $ 1,760 | $ 6,336 | $ 3,995 |
| Reacquisition of Preferred Stock ...... | 948 | 308 | 252 | 618 | — |
| Reacquisition of Common Stock....... | 13,224 | — | 11,466 | 133 | — |
| Dividends......................... | 20,821 | 21,138 | 21,141 | 21,122 | 4,457 |
| Total for Reductions in Financing.. | $ 36,531 | $ 35,269 | $ 34,619 | $ 28,209 | $ 8,452 |
| Investments in Noncurrent Assets: | | | | | |
| Property, Plant, and Equipment ....... | $ 16,141 | $ 25,918 | $ 26,250 | $ 23,143 | $ 15,535 |
| Investments in Securities ............. | 436 | 5,951 | 2,040 | 5,700 | 5,182 |
| Total for Investments............. | $ 16,577 | $ 31,869 | $ 28,290 | $ 28,843 | $ 20,717 |
| Other Uses (net) ...................... | $ 47 | $ 47 | — | $ 642 | $ 727 |
| Total Uses of Cash .............. | $ 68,474 | $ 94,102 | $177,174 | $150,899 | $115,093 |
| **Increase (decrease) in Cash**.......... | $ 1,032 | $ 15,842 | $ (18,908) | $ 15,008 | $ 33,691 |

**Exhibit 6.29** ⸺⸺⸺⸺⸺⸺⸺⸺⸺⸺⸺⸺⸺⸺⸺⸺⸺⸺⸺⸺⸺⸺⸺⸺

## Additional Information
## (Problem 38)

| | Fiscal Years Ending January 31 | | | | |
|---|---|---|---|---|---|
| | 1971 | 1972 | 1973 | 1974 | 1975 |
| **W. T. Grant Company** | | | | | |
| Range of Stock Price, Dollar per Share[a] ....... | $41\frac{7}{8}$–$70\frac{5}{8}$ | $34\frac{3}{4}$–$48\frac{3}{4}$ | $9\frac{7}{8}$–$44\frac{3}{8}$ | $9\frac{5}{8}$–41 | $1\frac{1}{2}$–12 |
| Earnings per Share in Dollars................ | $2.64 | $2.25 | $2.49 | $0.76 | $(12.74) |
| Dividends per Share in Dollars............... | $1.50 | $1.50 | $1.50 | $1.50 | $ 0.30 |
| Number of Stores .......................... | 1,116 | 1,168 | 1,208 | 1,189 | 1,152 |
| Total Store Area, Thousands of Square Feet ... | 38,157 | 44,718 | 50,619 | 53,719 | 54,770 |

| | 1970 | 1971 | 1972 | 1973 | 1974 |
|---|---|---|---|---|---|
| **Retail Industry[b]** | | | | | |
| Total Chain Store Industry Sales in Millions of Dollars................................ | $6,969 | $6,972 | $7,498 | $8,212 | $8,714 |

| | 1970 | 1971 | 1972 | 1973 | 1974 |
|---|---|---|---|---|---|
| **Aggregate Economy[c]** | | | | | |
| Gross National Product in Billions of Dollars.... | $1,075.3 | $1,107.5 | $1,171.1 | $1,233.4 | $1,210 |
| Bank Short-Term Lending Rate .............. | 8.48% | 6.32% | 5.82% | 8.30% | 11.28% |

[a]Source: *Standard and Poor's Stock Reports.*

[b]Source: *Standard Industry Surveys.*

[c]Source: *Survey of Current Business.*

# Part Three
# Measuring and Reporting Assets and Equities Using Generally Accepted Accounting Principles _____

# Chapter 7    The Liquid Assets: Cash, Marketable Securities, and Receivables _____

## Overview of Part Three _____

By now, most of the basic concepts of financial accounting, its purpose, theoretical framework, some of its procedures, and tools for analyzing financial statements have been introduced. From this point onward, generally accepted accounting principles (GAAP) are discussed in approximate balance sheet order: liquid assets in Chapter 7, inventories in Chapter 8, noncurrent assets in Chapter 9, and liabilities and owners' equity in Chapters 10, 11, and 12. Chapter 13, somewhat out of balance sheet order, focuses on accounting for long-term investments in securities of other companies. Before we examine GAAP for liquid assets, the nature and development of accounting principles are explored.

### Nature and Development of Generally Accepted Accounting Principles

*Generally accepted accounting principles,* or *GAAP,* are the accounting methods and procedures used in preparing financial statements. This section considers the nature of these principles and the process through which they develop.

**Nature of Accounting Principles**    To understand the nature of principles in accounting, contrast them with principles in physics and mathematics. Physicists and other natural scientists evaluate a principle (or theory) by asking how well the predictions of the principle correspond with physically observed phenomena. Mathematicians evaluate a principle (or theorem) by comparing its internal consistency with the structure of definitions and underlying axioms. In accounting, principles stand or fall on their general acceptability to preparers and users of accounting reports. Unlike those in the physical sciences, principles in accounting do not exist naturally, merely awaiting discovery. Unlike mathematics, accounting has no structure of definitions and concepts that can be used unambiguously to develop accounting principles. For example, one generally accepted accounting principle requires land to be stated at its acquisition cost as long as it is held by a firm. Changes in the market value of the land are not reflected in the financial statements until the land is sold. This accounting principle cannot be proven to be correct. It has simply been judged to be the generally acceptable method of accounting for land. Accounting principles might more aptly be called "accounting conventions."

**Development of Accounting Principles**   Accounting principles result from an essentially political process. Various persons or groups have power, or authority, in the decision process that yields generally accepted accounting principles. The next few paragraphs describe the most important participants in this process.

**Congress**   By enacting the Securities Act of 1933, Congress accepted the ultimate legal authority to prescribe the methods of accounting used in preparing financial statements for shareholders of publicly owned corporations. Congress has delegated its authority to the *Securities and Exchange Commission (SEC),* an agency of the federal government. Whereas the SEC has *legal* authority to prescribe accounting principles, since 1938 it has delegated most of the responsibility for developing accounting principles to the accounting profession.[1] Typically, the SEC serves as an advisor or consultant on proposed accounting principles. In a few instances, the SEC has effectively exerted its legal authority by disagreeing with positions taken within the accounting profession.

In recent years, the pronouncements of the SEC have been primarily concerned with format and disclosure in the financial statements rather than with valuation and measurement. The SEC requires that specific financial statement information be included in the annual report to shareholders, and the annual report, along with certain supplementary information, must then be included in the annual report submitted to the SEC (known as the *10-K report*).[2]

**Accounting Profession**   The accounting profession comprises practicing public accountants, financial executives, controllers, academics, and others. Most accounting principles have been developed by officially appointed committees or boards within the accounting profession.

Between 1938 and 1959, the Committee on Accounting Procedure of the American Institute of Certified Public Accountants issued *Bulletins* on various topics. Between 1959 and 1973, the Accounting Principles Board (APB) of the American Institute of Certified Public Accountants issued *Opinions*. These *Bulletins* and *Opinions*, unless superceded, still constitute generally accepted accounting principles. The APB consisted of individuals from the accounting profession, with many representatives from public accounting firms.

Since 1973, the *Financial Accounting Standards Board (FASB)* has been the major agency outside the federal government responsible for developing accounting

---

[1]Securities and Exchange Commission, *Accounting Series Release No. 4,* 1938. The SEC reaffirmed its delegation of responsibility by recognizing the Financial Accounting Standards Board in *Accounting Series Release No. 150,* 1973. Reissued in Section 101 of *Codification of Financial Reporting Policies.*

[2]Securities and Exchange Commission, *Accounting Series Releases No. 279, 280, and 281,* 1980. Reissued in Section 101 and 102 of *Codification of Financial Reporting Policies.*

principles. The FASB includes substantial representation from several groups of statement preparers and users in addition to members from the public accounting profession. The members of the FASB serve on a full-time basis, having severed all relations with their previous employers. This independence of board members reduces chances for undue influence by previous employers and adds credibility to the standard-setting process. The FASB issues *Statements of Financial Accounting Standards,* which represent generally accepted accounting principles. In contrast to the SEC's emphasis on disclosure, pronouncements of the FASB tend to deal more with valuation and measurement issues.

The process by which the FASB sets accounting principles has two noteworthy attributes. First, the FASB follows a due process procedure in its deliberations; second, it attempts to relate specific *Standards* to general-purpose financial statement objectives.

The FASB generally follows these procedures:

1. The FASB identifies a reporting issue and places it on the agenda.

2. The technical staff of the FASB, in consultation with a group of knowledgeable persons in the accounting and business community (formed in a "task force"), prepares a *Discussion Memorandum (DM)* on the reporting issue. The *DM* is intended to be an impartial discussion of the major questions to be considered by the board.

3. The *DM* is "exposed" to the public for a period of at least 60 days.

4. The FASB holds a public hearing on the contents of the *DM*. Individuals and organizations have an opportunity to comment on the questions raised and to indicate support for particular positions.

5. The FASB, after considering the oral and written comments received, prepares an *Exposure Draft* of a proposed financial accounting standard. The *Exposure Draft* takes a definitive position on the major issues under consideration.

6. The *Exposure Draft* is exposed to the public for a period of at least 30 days.

7. Frequently, a second public hearing is held. The comments this time are directed at the content of the proposed standard.

8. After additional consideration of the comments received, the FASB either (a) adopts the proposed standard as an official *Statement of Financial Accounting Standard,* (b) revises the proposed standard before making it official, in some cases allowing additional opportunities for public comment (in effect, returning to step 6), (c) delays issuance of an official standard but keeps the issue on its active agenda, or (d) decides not to issue an official standard and takes the issue off its agenda.

The FASB's due process procedure recognizes that the standard-setting process is political and that all constituents must be given an opportunity to speak. It also recognizes that accounting standards are judged according to their acceptability to several groups. By involving the various preparer and user groups in the deliberation process, the FASB hopes that these groups will be able to make more informed recommendations and be more tolerant of viewpoints that differ from their own.

A second attribute of the FASB's standard-setting process is its effort to relate specific accounting standards to more general-purpose financial statement objectives. Chapter 1 discussed these objectives. This approach results from criticisms directed at the FASB's predecessors that they attempted to solve problems without a conceptual framework. Unless accounting pronouncements derive from some underlying set of objectives or purposes of financial statements, the pronouncements can become internally inconsistent. Time will tell whether the FASB can be more successful in relating its pronouncements to a conceptual framework for financial reporting than were its predecessors.

**Other Participants**   Income tax legislation and administration also have had a substantial impact on adequate accounting and reporting. Although the income tax requirements do not establish principles and practices for general external reporting, they influence the choice of acceptable procedures. Individual users of financial statements can offer their own opinions on proposed standards to the FASB and thereby influence the standard-setting process.

**Future Development of Accounting Principles**   Unless Congress or the SEC unexpectedly decides to exert its legal authority, there is little reason to anticipate that the future development of accounting principles will differ from the past. The process will continue to be political, with opposing interests attempting to exert influence on the decision process. Positions taken or opinions rendered by participants in this process must be carefully developed and marketed if the positions are to become generally acceptable to others.

The rest of this chapter presents the generally accepted accounting principles for liquid assets.

# Liquidity and Moneylike Assets ——————————————

Chapters 5 and 6 point out that *liquidity* is essential for business operations. An *insolvent* company, one that cannot pay its bills and meet its commitments as they mature, will not survive no matter how large its owners' equity. Most bankrupt companies show positive owners' equity on their balance sheets at the time of bankruptcy. Bankruptcy is usually caused by an inability to meet debts as they become due. One of the largest bankruptcies occurred in 1970 when the Penn Central Transportation Company was placed into bankruptcy by its parent holding company, the Penn Central Company. At that time, Penn Central Transportation Company had almost $2 billion of shareholders' equity, including some $500 million of retained earnings. Nevertheless, the company became insolvent because it could not meet ''only'' a few hundred million dollars in obligations due at that time.

The availability of moneylike assets determines a firm's liquidity. Cash, marketable securities, accounts receivable, and notes receivable are the principal liquid assets of a business. These assets generally appear at their current cash, or cash equivalent, values on the balance sheet.

# Cash

*Cash* is the most liquid asset. It is also the most vulnerable because of its susceptibility to theft or embezzlement. This section considers cash inclusions and valuation as well as cash management and control.

## Cash Inclusions and Valuation

To be counted as cash on the balance sheet, an item should be freely available for use as a medium of exchange. Coins, currency, travelers' checks, and undeposited checks qualify. Most cash is cash in the bank in the form of *demand deposits,* savings accounts, and *certificates of deposit*. Although banks can restrict the immediate withdrawal of funds from savings accounts and certificates of deposit, these items are usually sufficiently available for use to be included in cash. Cash includes *foreign currency* unless a firm's ability to use the currency is severely restricted. For example, foreign currency held by a division located in a country that forbids the outflow of funds would not be included in the Cash account but in some other account. Also, funds set aside or restricted for a particular purpose would not be included. For example, firms are often required to establish sinking funds to retire outstanding debt. The cash in a sinking fund appears as Investments, rather than as Cash, on the balance sheet.

The Cash account frequently excludes compensating balances. A *compensating balance* generally takes the form of a minimum checking account balance that must be maintained in connection with a borrowing arrangement with a bank. For example, a firm might borrow $5 million from a bank and agree to maintain a 10 percent (= $500,000) compensating balance in a noninterest-bearing checking account. This arrangement results in a reduction of the amount effectively borrowed and an increase in the interest rate effectively paid by the borrower. Unless compensating balances are adequately disclosed, incorrect assessments of a firm's liquidity can occur.

The SEC requires that legally restricted deposits held as compensating balances against short-term borrowing arrangements be separated from Cash but included among current assets. Compensating balances held against long-term borrowing arrangements should be included under noncurrent assets, preferably Investments. When compensating balance arrangements exist but the firm may legally use the cash, the nature of the arrangements and the amounts involved should be disclosed in a note to the financial statements.[3]

Once an item meets the criteria to be included in cash, there are few valuation problems. Cash is normally stated at its face amount. Foreign currency must be translated to its U.S. dollar–equivalent amount using the exchange rate on the balance sheet date.

---

[3]Securities and Exchange Commission, *Accounting Series Release No. 148,* "Amendments to Regulations S-X and Related Interpretations and Guidelines Regarding the Disclosure of Compensating Balances and Short-Term Borrowing Arrangements," 1973. Reissued in Section 203 of *Codification of Financial Reporting Policies.*

## Cash Management

The management of cash involves two distinct goals. First, a firm establishes a system of internal controls to ensure that cash is safeguarded from theft or embezzlement. Typical internal control procedures include separating duties of individuals handling cash receipts and disbursements, depositing cash receipts immediately, disbursing cash only by authorized checks, and preparing bank account reconciliations regularly.

Second, management wants to regulate cash amounts to balance the conflicting goals of having enough cash to conduct business effectively while not losing the earnings that invested cash can generate. Cash on hand or in checking accounts generally does not earn interest. During inflationary periods, idle cash loses purchasing power and decreases in real value. Thus a firm does not want to maintain excessive cash balances. On the other hand, a firm does not want to run short of cash and be unable to meet its obligations or be unable to take advantage of cash discounts.

A weekly or monthly budget of cash receipts and disbursements aids cash management. Such a budget indicates both the amounts and times when excess cash will be available for investment or when additional borrowing will become necessary.

## Marketable Securities _____

A business may find itself with more cash than it needs for current and near-term business purposes. Rather than allow cash to remain unproductive, the business may invest some of its currently excess cash in income-yielding securities, such as U.S. government bonds or stocks or bonds of other companies. Such liquid assets appear under the caption *Marketable Securities* in the Current Assets section of the balance sheet.

A business may also acquire securities intending to hold them for a longer period. Accounting treats such securities as long-term *investments*. This section considers the classification and valuation of securities held either temporarily as current assets or as long-term investments.

### Classification of Securities

Securities appear as "marketable securities" among current assets as long as they can be readily converted into cash *and* management intends to do so when it needs cash. Securities that do not meet both of these criteria appear under Investments on the balance sheet.

**Example 1**   Morrissey Manufacturing Corporation invested $150,000 of temporarily excess funds in U.S. Treasury notes. The notes mature in 3 months. This investment appears among marketable securities because the notes can be sold at any time, and even if not sold, the cash will be collected within 3 months.

**Example 2**  Suppose that Morrissey Manufacturing Corporation acquired 20-year bonds of Greer Electronics Company instead of the U.S. Treasury notes. Its intent in acquiring the bonds is the same as before, the investment of temporarily excess cash. These bonds similarly appear as marketable securities.

**Example 3**  West Corporation acquired shares of Xerox Corporation on the open market for $10 million. West Corporation plans to hold these shares as a long-term investment. Even though the shares of Xerox Corporation are readily marketable, they are not classified as marketable securities, because West Corporation does not intend to turn the securities into cash within a reasonably short period. These securities appear as long-term Investments on the balance sheet.

In published financial statements, all securities properly classified as the current asset Marketable Securities appear together on a single line on the balance sheet. As will be discussed later, however, the accounting for *marketable debt securities* and *marketable equity securities* may differ.

## Valuation of Marketable Securities as Temporary Investments

Marketable securities are initially recorded at acquisition cost, which includes the purchase price plus any commissions, taxes, and other costs incurred. For example, if marketable securities are acquired for $10,000 plus $300 for commissions and taxes, the entry is as follows:

| | | |
|---|---|---|
| Marketable Securities . . . . . . . . . . . . . . . . . . . . . . . . . . . . . . . . . . . . . . . . . . . . . | 10,300 | |
| Cash . . . . . . . . . . . . . . . . . . . . . . . . . . . . . . . . . . . . . . . . . . . . . . . . . . . . | | 10,300 |

Dividends on marketable securities become revenue when declared. Interest revenue is recognized when earned. Assuming that $250 of dividends was declared and $300 of interest was earned on marketable securities and these amounts have not yet been received in cash, the entry is as follows:

| | | |
|---|---|---|
| Dividends and Interest Receivable . . . . . . . . . . . . . . . . . . . . . . . . . . . . | 550 | |
| Dividend Revenue . . . . . . . . . . . . . . . . . . . . . . . . . . . . . . . . . . . . . . . . | | 250 |
| Interest Revenue . . . . . . . . . . . . . . . . . . . . . . . . . . . . . . . . . . . . . . . . | | 300 |

There is nothing unusual about the valuation of marketable securities at date of acquisition or the recording of dividends and interest. Valuing marketable securities after acquisition, however, departs from strict historical cost accounting.

**Marketable Equity Securities**  Financial Accounting Standards Board *Statement of Financial Accounting Standards No. 12* (1975) requires the *portfolio* of marketable equity securities (that is, common stock, preferred stock, stock options, and warrants) classified as current assets to be stated at the lower of acquisition cost or market value at the end of each period.[4]

Under the *lower-of-cost-or-market method,* accounting recognizes decreases in the market value of a portfolio of marketable equity securities as holding losses each period as the decreases occur, even though a market transaction or exchange has not taken place. Accounting recognizes subsequent increases in the market value of the portfolio, up to the original acquisition cost, as holding gains.

The FASB decided that showing marketable securities at acquisition cost when their objectively observable market value declines *below* cost distorts the income and financial position of the firm. When market values rise *above* acquisition cost, the amounts are just as objectively observable, but the FASB does not permit increasing income and asset amounts above cost and recognizing income for unrealized holding gains. The FASB thinks that doing so departs too much from historical cost accounting. The FASB chose to apply lower of cost or market to the entire portfolio, rather than security by security, because "many enterprises regard their portfolios of marketable equity securities . . . as collective assets . . ." and the security-by-security approach would "be unduly conservative and at variance with the manner in which enterprises generally view their investment in marketable equity securities."[5]

The credit to reduce the carrying amount of the current asset Marketable Equity Securities is made to a contra account usually called Allowance for Excess of Cost of Marketable Securities over Market Value. Using a separate contra account enables the simultaneous identification of both the acquisition cost and the amount of decline in the market value of the portfolio. This is necessary to enable subsequent write-ups to original acquisition cost, but no further. The portfolio cannot be stated at an amount greater than the original acquisition cost; that is, the allowance account can never have a debit balance. The following sections illustrate the procedures for applying the lower-of-cost-or-market method.

**Example 4**   Wolfson Company acquired various marketable equity securities during Year 1 as shown in Exhibit 7.1.[6] The entry to record the acquisition of securities during Year 1 is as follows:

| | | |
|---|---|---|
| Marketable Securities ....................................... | 100,000 | |
|   Cash ..................................................... | | 100,000 |

---

[4]"Market value," as defined by Financial Accounting Standards Board, *Statement No. 12,* "Accounting for Certain Marketable Securities," is the quoted market price for both buyers and sellers excluding brokerage commissions, taxes, and similar costs.

[5]Financial Accounting Standards Board, *Statement No. 12,* par. 31.

[6]In reality, a firm holding these securities for 4 years would probably classify them as investments, not as current assets. For purposes of illustration, we have shown the accounting for a portfolio of marketable securities over several years.

Exhibit 7.1 ————————————————————————————————————
## WOLFSON COMPANY
## Data for Illustration of Accounting for Marketable Equity Securities

| Security | Date Acquired | Acquisition Cost | Market Value Dec. 31, Year 1 | Dec. 31, Year 2 | Dec. 31, Year 3 | Dec. 31, Year 4 |
|---|---|---|---|---|---|---|
| Company A ......... | 4/1/Year 1 | $ 50,000 | $53,000 | $54,000 | $52,000 | $43,000 |
| Company B ......... | 6/1/Year 1 | 30,000 | 27,000 | 22,000 | —ᵃ | — |
| Company C ......... | 8/1/Year 1 | 20,000 | 16,000 | 23,000 | 24,000 | —ᵇ |
| Total ............ | | $100,000 | $96,000 | $99,000 | $76,000 | $43,000 |

ᵃHoldings of Company B sold during Year 3 for $32,000.
ᵇHoldings of Company C sold during Year 4 for $17,000.

**Unrealized Holding Loss**  At the end of Year 1, the portfolio of marketable equity securities had an aggregate acquisition cost of $100,000 (= $50,000 + $30,000 + $20,000) and an aggregate market value of $96,000 (= $53,000 + $27,000 + $16,000). A write-down of $4,000 recognizes the *unrealized holding loss on marketable securities.*

---

| | | |
|---|---|---|
| Unrealized Holding Loss on Valuation of Marketable Securities .... | 4,000 | |
| Allowance for Excess of Cost of Marketable Securities over Market Value........................................ | | 4,000 |

Entry to adjust credit balance in allowance account from its current zero balance to $4,000.

---

The loss account appears in the income statement for Year 1 among the expenses.[7] The allowance account appears as a contra account to marketable securities on the balance sheet at the end of Year 1. Exhibits 7.2 and 7.7 illustrate the required disclosures.

Because the lower-of-cost-or-market method applies to the entire portfolio rather than to individual securities, the amount of the decline in market value below cost is not recorded separately for each security. As in this example, gains on some securities may offset losses on others.

**Recovery of Unrealized Holding Loss**  Assume that there are no acquisitions or dispositions of marketable equity securities during Year 2 and that the market value of the portfolio at the end of Year 2 increases to $99,000. The valuation of the portfolio of securities is increased (but never to an amount greater than original acquisition cost). The entry is as follows:

---

[7]For income tax purposes, losses (or gains) are reported only when realized, generally by sale.

| | | |
|---|---|---|
| Allowance for Excess of Cost of Marketable Securities over Market Value . . . . . . . . . . . . . . . . . . . . . . . . . . . . . . . . . . . . . . . . . . . . . | 3;000 | |
|     Recovery of Unrealized Holding Loss on Valuation of Marketable Securities . . . . . . . . . . . . . . . . . . . . . . . . . . . . . . . . . . | | 3,000 |
| To increase valuation of marketable securities by reducing allowance account. | | |

The debit entry decreases the credit balance in the allowance account to $1,000. The Recovery of Unrealized Holding Loss on Valuation of Marketable Securities account appears in the income statement for Year 2 as a revenue, or gain. See Exhibit 7.2 for illustrative disclosures.

**Realized Gain or Loss through Sale**  Upon selling an individual marketable equity security, the realized gain or loss is the difference between the selling price and the original acquisition cost of the individual security, regardless of the related balance in the allowance account. For example, if the securities of Company B are sold during Year 3 for $32,000, the entry to record the sale during Year 3 is as follows:

| | | |
|---|---|---|
| Cash . . . . . . . . . . . . . . . . . . . . . . . . . . . . . . . . . . . . . . . . . . . . . . . . . . . . . | 32,000 | |
|     Marketable Securities . . . . . . . . . . . . . . . . . . . . . . . . . . . . . . . . . . . . | | 30,000 |
|     Realized Holding Gain on Sale of Marketable Securities . . . . . . | | 2,000 |
| To recognize realized holding gain of $2,000 (= $32,000 proceeds of sale − $30,000 original cost). | | |

The realized holding gain appears in the income statement for Year 3; see Exhibit 7.2.[8] The aggregate acquisition cost of the portfolio at the end of Year 3 decreases to $70,000 (= $50,000 + $20,000). The aggregate market value of the portfolio at the end of Year 3 is $76,000 (= $52,000 + $24,000). Because aggregate market value exceeds aggregate cost, the allowance account should have a zero balance so that the portfolio appears at cost on the balance sheet. Because the allowance account has a $1,000 credit balance carried over from Year 2, the following entry at the end of Year 3 reduces the allowance account to zero.

| | | |
|---|---|---|
| Allowance for Excess of Cost of Marketable Securities over Market Value . . . . . . . . . . . . . . . . . . . . . . . . . . . . . . . . . . . . . . . . . . . . . | 1,000 | |
|     Recovery of Unrealized Holding Loss on Valuation of Marketable Securities . . . . . . . . . . . . . . . . . . . . . . . . . . . . . . . . . . | | 1,000 |
| To increase valuation of marketable securities by reducing the allowance. | | |

---

[8]The gain would also be taxable.

Exhibit 7.2 _____

## WOLFSON COMPANY
### Items in Income Statement and Balance Sheet
### Illustrating Transactions in Marketable Equity Securities
### as Temporary Investments — Current Assets

| | Year 1 | Year 2 | Year 3 | Year 4 |
|---|---|---|---|---|
| **Excerpts from Income Statement for Year** | | | | |
| Other Items (assumed) before Taxes ....................... | $300,000 | $300,000 | $300,000 | $300,000 |
| Realized Gain (Loss) on Sale of Marketable Equity Securities..................... | — | — | 2,000 | (3,000) |
| Unrealized Holding Loss on Valuation of Marketable Equity Securities ............. | (4,000) | — | — | (7,000) |
| Recovery of Unrealized Holding Loss on Valuation of Marketable Equity Securities .... | — | 3,000 | 1,000 | — |
| Income before Taxes ........... | $296,000 | $303,000 | $303,000 | $290,000 |
| | | | | |
| **Balance Sheet Items at Year-End** | | | | |
| Marketable Securities at Cost ..... | $100,000 | $100,000 | $ 70,000 | $ 50,000 |
| Less Allowance for Excess of Cost of Marketable Equity Securities over Market Value.... | (4,000) | (1,000) | — | (7,000) |
| Marketable Equity Securities at Lower of Cost or Market[a] .... | $ 96,000 | $ 99,000 | $ 70,000 | $ 43,000 |

[a]Notes to the financial statements must disclose separately the unrealized gains on all securities with gains and the unrealized losses on securities with losses. Exhibit 7.7 illustrates these disclosures. Consider, for example, the first column shown here and the underlying data reported in the preceding exhibit. Unrealized gains on securities with gains (Company A) total $3,000, whereas unrealized losses on securities with losses (Company B and Company C) total $7,000 [= ($30,000 − $27,000) + ($20,000 − $16,000)]. Both the amounts of the unrealized gains of $3,000 and the unrealized losses of $7,000 appear in notes, whereas the net unrealized loss of $4,000 (= $7,000 − $3,000) appears in the Allowance account for the year. For the third year shown here, the notes disclose that the aggregate market value of the securities exceeds their cost by $6,000.

The securities appear at $70,000 on the December 31, Year 3, balance sheet in Exhibit 7.2. Income for Year 3 increases by $1,000 plus the realized gain of $2,000.

**Realized Loss and Unrealized Loss**  The data for Year 4 illustrate the simultaneous realization of a loss on the sale of one security and further unrealized holding losses on securities still held. Holdings of Company C that had cost $20,000 are sold for $17,000. The journal entry is as follows:

| | | |
|---|---|---|
| Cash ...................................................... | 17,000 | |
| Realized Holding Loss on Sale of Marketable Securities .......... | 3,000 | |
|    Marketable Securities ...................................... | | 20,000 |
| Sale of holding of Company C for $3,000 less than original cost. | | |

**Exhibit 7.3** ————————————————————

## WOLFSON COMPANY
**Items in Income Statement and Balance Sheet**
**Illustrating Transactions in Long-Term**
**Investments in Marketable Equity Securities**

| | Year 1 | Year 2 | Year 3 | Year 4 |
|---|---|---|---|---|
| **Excerpts from Income Statement for Year** | | | | |
| Other Items (Assumed) before Taxes .................... | $300,000 | $300,000 | $300,000 | $300,000 |
| Realized Gain (Loss) on Sale of Investments in Marketable Equity Securities ............ | — | — | 2,000 | (3,000) |
| Income before Taxes ........... | $300,000 | $300,000 | $302,000 | $297,000 |
| | | | | |
| **Excerpts from Balance Sheet Items at Year-End Asset Section** | | | | |
| Investments in Marketable Equity Securities at Cost ............ | $100,000 | $100,000 | $ 70,000 | $ 50,000 |
| Less Allowance for Excess of Cost of Investments in Marketable Equity Securities over Market Value ............ | (4,000) | (1,000) | — | (7,000) |
| Marketable Equity Securities at Lower of Cost or Market .... | $ 96,000 | $ 99,000 | $ 70,000[a] | $ 43,000 |
| | | | | |
| **Owners' Equity Section** | | | | |
| Contributed Capital (Assumed) ... | $200,000 | $200,000 | $200,000 | $200,000 |
| Retained Earnings (Assumed) ... | 400,000 | 450,000 | 500,000 | 600,000 |
| Net Unrealized Loss on Investments in Marketable Equity Securities ............ | ( 4,000) | ( 1,000) | — | ( 7,000) |
| Total Owners' Equity ............ | $596,000 | $649,000 | $700,000 | $793,000 |

[a]The captions on the balance sheet or the notes must disclose that the market value on December 31, Year 3, is $76,000. See Exhibit 7.1.

Securities held at the end of Year 4 have an aggregate cost of $50,000 and an aggregate market value of $43,000. Thus the ending balance in the allowance account must be $7,000. Because it had a zero balance at the start of the year, the journal entry is as follows:

| | | |
|---|---|---|
| Unrealized Holding Loss on Valuation of Marketable Securities .... | 7,000 | |
|    Allowance for Excess of Cost of Marketable Securities over Market Value.......................................... | | 7,000 |
| Adjustment of balance in allowance account from zero to $7,000. | | |

Income for Year 4 is decreased for the realized loss of $3,000 and for the unrealized holding loss of $7,000. See Exhibit 7.2.

**Recapitulation** Under lower-of-cost-or-market accounting for equity securities held as current assets, the balance sheet shows the cost of the portfolio in one account and the allowance to reduce that cost to market value if less than cost in another account. The income statement for the period will show any of the following that occur: income from dividends declared during the period; gains or losses realized during the period; unrealized holding losses during the period on securities held at the end of the period; and recoveries of previously recognized unrealized holding losses.

**Marketable Debt Securities** FASB *Statement No. 12* addressed only marketable equity securities. The accounting for marketable debt securities follows *Accounting Research Bulletin No. 43* (Chapter 3A), which prescribes acquisition cost as the valuation method except ''where market value is less than cost by a substantial amount . . . , the amount to be included as a current asset should not exceed the market value.''

As a practical matter, many firms use lower of cost or market for marketable debt securities as well.

## Valuation of Marketable Securities as Long-Term Investments

Businesses may acquire equity securities of another firm as a long-term investment. The motive for acquisition may be either passive or active. With a passive investment, the owning firm hopes to accumulate wealth by receiving dividends and realizing capital gains on selling the equity securities. The owning firm does not, however, actively control or significantly influence the activities of the other firm. (In this sense, an individual's purchase of shares of stock is usually passive.) In contrast, a firm can acquire shares of another company with hope of controlling or significantly influencing the other company's activities.

When the owner of securities can play an active role in the management of the investee company, the owner can influence the company's dividend policy. Under lower-of-cost-or-market accounting, one potentially major component of reported income is the dividends declared by the investee company. Because those who set GAAP are wary of accounting principles that allow management to manipulate income through manipulating the dividends of an investee company, the accounting for active investments in equity securities differs from that presented here for passive investments.

Chapter 13 discusses the criteria used for judging whether investments are active or passive and the accounting for active investments. The general rule is that an investment of less than 20 percent of the outstanding shares is presumed to be passive, but when the ownership is 20 percent or more, the investment is presumed to be active.

Passive investments are accounted for with a lower-of-cost-or-market method similar to that previously explained for temporary holdings, but with one important difference. The decrease in the market value of a portfolio of equity securities classified as Investments is *not* recognized as a loss in calculating net income during the period when the decrease occurs, as is done for marketable securities classified as current assets. Instead, the debit is to an account called Net Unrealized Loss on

Investments in Marketable Equity Securities, which is an owners' equity contra account. The account appears in the owners' equity section, usually below Retained Earnings. The account always has a debit (or zero) balance and reduces the other amounts (credit balances) of owners' equity. The difference in accounting treatments results from the FASB's view that "the present concepts of income require authoritative clarification with respect to the recognition of unrealized gains and losses on long-term assets. Such clarification is beyond the scope of this Statement."[9]

Exhibit 7.3 illustrates the accounting for long-term investments in marketable securities. It uses the same data as in the illustration of accounting for temporary investments. The amounts shown in Exhibits 7.2 and 7.3 differ primarily because of the treatment of unrealized holding losses and recoveries of unrealized holding losses. In Exhibit 7.3, these items do not affect net income as they arise but appear separately in owners' equity, reducing it. Exhibit 12.1 in Chapter 12 illustrates the balance sheet presentation of the owners' equity contra account.

## Transfer of Securities between Current and Noncurrent Portfolios

The same holding of equity securities may be classified either as a current asset or as a noncurrent asset, depending on the owner's intentions. The owner can transfer a security from the current asset portfolio to the noncurrent asset portfolio or vice versa. If the market price of the security is *less* than its cost on the date of transfer, generally accepted accounting principles require a "dual transaction assumption." FASB *Statement No. 12* (paragraph 10) requires a transfer between portfolios of a security whose cost exceeds market value to be treated as though the security were sold for cash equal to market value at the time of transfer and immediately repurchased at the same price. Thus the transfer between portfolios of a security with market value less than cost establishes a realized loss and a new cost basis. Assume, for example, that equity securities had been purchased for $50,000 and held as a current asset while the market price declined to $40,000. The investment has been accounted for using the lower-of-cost-or-market basis. If the firm decides to reclassify the investment as a long-term investment, the following entry is made:

| | | |
|---|---|---|
| Realized Loss on Reclassification of Marketable Security as a Noncurrent Asset .................................... | 10,000 | |
| Investments (Noncurrent Asset) ............................... | 40,000 | |
|     Marketable Securities (Current Asset) ...................... | | 50,000 |

The loss appears on the income statement for the year;[10] the cost basis of the noncurrent asset is $40,000; subsequent increases in market value, even to $50,000, are not recognized in the accounts.

---

[9]Financial Accounting Standards Board, *Statement No. 12,* par. 30.
[10]The loss would not be deductible in computing taxable income until the securities were actually sold.

If the market value of the securities exceeds their cost at the time of transfer, *no* gain is recognized. The securities are transferred at cost.

## Order of Procedures for Lower-of-Cost-or-Market Method

Students often find the treatment of the various events relating to investments in marketable securities confusing — the recording of realized gains or losses (through sale or through reclassification from current to noncurrent or vice versa), the recording of unrealized losses, the recovery of unrealized losses, and the valuation of the allowance account. To minimize the chance for error, analyze and record transactions in the following order:

1. Record any *realized* gains or losses, from whatever source (sale, reclassification from current to noncurrent portfolio, or vice versa).

2. Compare the market value of the portfolio at the end of the period with its acquisition cost to ascertain the required credit balance in the allowance account (= cost less market value if cost exceeds market value, and zero otherwise).

3. Prepare a journal entry to adjust the allowance account from its zero or credit balance at the start of the period to its required credit or zero balance at the end of the period.
   a. If the adjustment requires a credit to the allowance account, debit the Unrealized Loss account, which appears in the income statement if the securities are current assets but in the owners' equity section of the balance sheet if the securities are long-term investments.
   b. If the adjustment requires a debit to the allowance account, for current assets credit the Recovery of Unrealized Loss account, which appears on the income statement, and for long-term investments credit the Unrealized Loss account, which appears on the balance sheet.

Individual securities are valued at cost, not at the lower of cost or market with separate valuation allowances; only the portfolio is valued at lower of cost or market.

The Marketable Securities and Investment accounts are controlling accounts that show the sum of all the recorded acquisition costs of all the individual securities in the portfolios. When a security is removed from a portfolio, its acquisition cost must be taken out of the Marketable Securities or Investment account.

## Evaluation of Lower of Cost or Market

For many years, some accounting theorists have argued that marketable securities should be shown at market value, whether greater or less than cost. Their very marketability makes valuing them on a current basis reasonably objective. The market value of the securities is the most relevant value for assessing a firm's liquidity. The FASB has taken the position, however, that it will not permit the write-up of marketable securities to an amount greater than acquisition cost.

Keep in mind that the total gain (or loss) on the holding of a security is the difference between the cash received on disposal less the original cash cost; over sufficiently long time spans, income equals cash in less cash out. The write-downs and write-ups, if any, merely allocate that income to the various accounting periods between the dates of purchase and sale as market conditions change.

# Accounts Receivable ————————————————————

The third liquid asset this chapter considers is accounts receivable. Trade accounts receivable typically arise when goods or services are sold on account. The entry is as follows:

| | | |
|---|---|---|
| Accounts Receivable......................................... | 250 | |
|     Sales Revenue ............................................. | | 250 |

Receivables sometimes arise from transactions other than sales. For example, advances may be made to officers or employees, deposits may be made to guarantee performance or cover potential damages, or claims may be made against insurance companies, governmental bodies, common carriers, or others. These receivables are classified as either current assets or investments, depending on the expected collection date. This section focuses on trade accounts receivable, considering both their valuation and their management.

## Accounts Receivable Valuation

Individual accounts receivable are initially recorded at the amount owed by each customer. The recording is made either in a subsidiary ledger (manual accounting system) or in a separate data file of a computer memory. The sum of the amounts in individual customers' accounts appears in the master, or control, account for Accounts Receivable. The Accounts Receivable account records the total of the amounts in individual customers' accounts.

The amount in the master account for Accounts Receivable is reduced for estimated uncollectible accounts, sales discounts, and sales returns and allowances. The reporting objective is to state accounts receivable at the amount expected to be collected in cash. The difference between the amounts owed by customers and the amounts expected to be collected in cash must be charged against income. The charge against income for expected uncollectible amounts, sales discounts, and sales returns and allowances is preferably made in the period when the sales occur. In this way, revenue and net income for a period will reflect the amounts expected to be collected for services rendered during the period.

## Uncollectible Accounts

Whenever credit is extended to customers, some accounts will almost certainly never be collected. Most businesses should prefer to have some customers who do not pay their bills: for most firms, the optimal amount of uncollectibles is not zero.

If a firm is to have no uncollectible accounts, it must screen credit customers carefully, which is costly. Furthermore, the firm would deny credit to many customers who would pay their bills even though they could not pass a credit check designed to weed out all potential uncollectibles. Some of the customers who are denied credit will take their business elsewhere and sales will be lost. As long as the amount *collected* from credit sales to a given class of customers exceeds the cost of goods sold and the other costs of serving that class of customers, the firm will be better off selling to that class than losing the sales. The rational firm should prefer granting credit to a class of customers who have a high probability of paying their bills rather than losing their business, even though there may be some uncollectible accounts within the class.

For example, assume that gross margin — selling price less cost of goods sold — on credit sales to a new class of customers, such as college freshmen, is 40 percent of credit sales. A firm could then afford uncollectible accounts of up to 40 percent of the credit sales to the new customers and still show increased net income, as long as all other costs of serving customers remain constant.

This does not suggest, of course, that a firm should grant credit indiscriminately or ignore collection efforts for uncollected accounts receivable. A cost/benefit analysis of credit policy should dictate a strategy that results in some amount of uncollectible accounts, an amount that is reasonably predictable before any sales are made.

Firms use two methods of accounting for uncollectible accounts: (1) the direct write-off method and (2) the allowance method.

## Direct Write-off Method

The direct write-off method recognizes losses from uncollectible accounts in the period in which a specific customer's account is determined to be uncollectible. For example, if it is decided that the account receivable of John Mahoney for $200 has become uncollectible, the following entry would be made:

---

| | | |
|---|---|---|
| Bad Debt Expense .......................................... | 200 | |
|     Accounts Receivable....................................... | | 200 |
| To record loss from an uncollectible customer's account. | | |

---

The direct write-off method has three important shortcomings. First, the loss from uncollectible accounts is usually not recognized in the period in which the sale occurs and revenue is recognized. Too much income is recognized in the period of sale and too little in the period of write-off. Second, the amount of losses from uncollectible accounts recognized in any period is susceptible to intentional misrepresentation, because it is difficult to ascertain just when a particular account becomes uncollectible. Third, the amount of accounts receivable on the balance sheet does not reflect the amount of cash expected to be collected. The direct write-off method is not appropriate for financial reporting when such losses are significant in amount, occur frequently, and are reasonably predictable, as in retail stores. The direct write-off method is required for income tax reporting.

## Allowance Method

When amounts of uncollectibles can be estimated with reasonable precision, GAAP require an alternative procedure, *the allowance method* for uncollectibles. (Chapter 11 discusses the accounting issues raised when a firm uses the allowance method for financial reporting, as it must, and the direct write-off method for tax returns, as it must.) The allowance method involves the following:

1. Estimating the amount of uncollectible accounts that will occur over time in connection with the sales of each period.

2. Making an adjusting entry reducing income of the period for the estimated uncollectible amount.

3. Making a corresponding adjustment to the amount of accounts receivable so that the balance sheet figure reports the amount expected to be collected.

The adjusting entry involves a debit to reduce income and a credit to Allowance for Uncollectible Accounts, which is an account contra to the total of Accounts Receivable. The credit must be made to a contra account rather than to Accounts Receivable because no specific individual account is being written off at the time of entry. Because the Allowance for Uncollectible Accounts is a contra account to Accounts Receivable, its balance at the end of the period appears on the balance sheet as a deduction from Accounts Receivable.

Views differ as to the type of account — expense or revenue contra — debited when providing for estimated uncollectibles. Many firms debit Bad Debt Expense and include its amount among total expenses on the income statement. Their rationale is that a certain amount of bad debts is a necessary cost of generating revenues. On the other hand, using a revenue contra account permits net sales to be shown at the amount of cash expected to be collected. When the provision is debited to an expense account and included among total expenses on the income statement, net sales will overstate the amount of cash expected to be received. Advocates of using a revenue contra account point out that uncollectible accounts cannot theoretically be an expense. An expense is a gone asset. Accounts that were not expected to be collected at the time of recording were never assets to begin with. Although the arguments for using a revenue contra account may be persuasive, Bad Debt Expense is the account debited in this book because that account is more widely used in practice.

To illustrate the allowance method, assume that 2 percent of the credit sales made during the present period are estimated never to be collected. If sales on account are $90,000, the entry to reduce the amount of Accounts Receivable to the amount expected to be collected would be as follows:

| | | |
|---|---|---|
| Bad Debt Expense ......................................... | 1,800 | |
| Allowance for Uncollectible Accounts ....................... | | 1,800 |

To record estimate of uncollectible accounts arising from current period's sales (.02 × $90,000).

When a particular customer's account is judged uncollectible, it is written off against the Allowance for Uncollectible Accounts. If, for example, it is decided that a balance of $200 due from John Mahoney will not be collected, the entry to charge off the account is as follows:

| | | |
|---|---|---|
| Allowance for Uncollectible Accounts ......................... | 200 | |
| Accounts Receivable ...................................... | | 200 |

To write off John Mahoney's account.

The entry to write off specific accounts may be made during the period, as information about specific customers' accounts is obtained, or at the end of the period when adjusting entries are recorded.

Under the allowance method, the income for the period of sale is reduced by the amount of uncollectibles that is estimated to arise from that period's sales. Some time later, when the attempts at collection are finally abandoned, the specific account is written off. Net assets are not affected by writing off the specific account. The reduction in net assets took place earlier, when the Allowance for Uncollectible Accounts was credited in the entry recognizing the estimated amount of eventual uncollectibles.

## Estimating Uncollectibles

Accountants use two basic methods for calculating the amount of the adjustment for uncollectible accounts: the *percentage-of-sales method* and the *aging-of-accounts-receivable method*. The first requires fewer computations than the second, but the second method provides a useful check on the first.

**Percentage-of-Sales Method**   The easiest method in most cases is to multiply the total sales on account during the period by an appropriate percentage, because it seems reasonable to assume that uncollectible account amounts will vary directly with the volume of credit business. (The examples on pages 279 to 280 used the percentage-of-sales method.) The percentage to be used is estimated by studying the experience of the business or by inquiring into the experience of similar enterprises. The rates found in use will generally be within the range of $\frac{1}{4}$ percent to 2 percent of credit sales.

To illustrate, assume that sales on account total $1,500,000, and experience indicates that the appropriate percentage of uncollectible accounts is 2 percent. The entry is as follows:

| | | |
|---|---|---|
| Bad Debt Expense ........................................... | 30,000 | |
|   Allowance for Uncollectible Accounts ....................... | | 30,000 |

To provide for estimate of uncollectibles computed as a percentage of sales.

If cash sales occur in a relatively constant proportion to credit sales, the estimated uncollectibles percentage, proportionately reduced, can be applied to the total sales for the period. The total amount of all sales may be more readily available than that for sales on account.

**Aging-of-Accounts-Receivable Method**   A more costly, but more accurate, method of calculating the amount of the adjustment, called *aging the accounts,* involves classifying each customer's account as to the length of time for which the account has been uncollected. Common intervals used for classifying individual accounts receivable are as follows:

1. Not yet due.
2. Past due 30 days or less.
3. Past due 31 to 60 days.
4. Past due 61 to 180 days.
5. Past due more than 180 days.

The accountant presumes that the balance in the Allowance for Uncollectible Accounts should be large enough to cover substantially all accounts receivable past due for more than 6 months and smaller portions of the more recent accounts. The actual portions are estimated from experience.

As an example of the adjustment to be made, assume that the present balance in the Accounts Receivable account is $850,000 and the balance in the Allowance for Uncollectible Accounts before the adjusting entry for the period is $36,000. An aging of the Accounts Receivable balance ($850,000) shown in Exhibit 7.4 results in an estimate that $68,000 of the accounts will probably become uncollectible. The adjustment requires the Allowance for Uncollectible Accounts balance to be

**Exhibit 7.4** _____

**Illustration of Aging Accounts Receivable**

| Classification of Accounts | Amount | Estimated Uncollectible Percentage | Estimated Uncollectible Amounts |
|---|---|---|---|
| Not yet due .......................... | $680,000 | 0.5 percent | $ 3,400 |
| 1–30 days past due ................. | 60,000 | 6.0 | 3,600 |
| 31–60 days past due ............... | 30,000 | 25.0 | 7,500 |
| 61–180 days past due .............. | 50,000 | 50.0 | 25,000 |
| More than 180 days past due .......... | 30,000 | 95.0 | 28,500 |
| | $850,000 | | $68,000 |

$68,000, an increase of $32,000. The adjusting entry at the end of the period is as follows:

---

| | | |
|---|---|---|
| Bad Debt Expense .......................................... | 32,000 | |
|   Allowance for Uncollectible Accounts ........................ | | 32,000 |

To increase Allowance account to $68,000 computed by an aging analysis; $68,000 − $36,000 = $32,000.

---

Even when the percentage-of-sales method is used, aging the accounts should be done periodically to check on the accuracy of the percentage being used. If the aging analysis shows that the balance in the Allowance for Uncollectible Accounts is apparently too large or too small, the percentage of sales to be charged to the Bad Debt Expense account can be lowered or raised.

When the percentage-of-sales method is used, the periodic provision for uncollectible accounts (for example, $30,000) is merely added (credited) to the amounts provided in previous periods in the account Allowance for Uncollectible Accounts. When the aging method is used, the balance in the account Allowance for Uncollectible Accounts is adjusted (for example, by $32,000) to reflect the desired ending balance. If the percentage used under the percentage-of-sales method reasonably reflects collection experience, the *balance* in the allowance account should be approximately the same at the end of each period under both of these methods of estimating uncollectible accounts.

Exhibit 7.5 illustrates the operation of the allowance method for uncollectibles over two periods. In the first period the percentage method is used. In the second period the aging method is used. Normally, a firm would use the same method in all periods.

## Sales Discounts

Often the seller of merchandise offers a reduction from its invoice price for prompt payment. Such reductions are called *sales discounts* or *cash discounts*.[11] There is nothing incongruous in the proposition that goods may have two prices: a cash price or a higher price if goods are sold on credit. The seller offers a cash discount not only as an interest allowance on funds paid before the bill is due — the implied interest rate is unreasonably large — but also as an incentive for prompt payment so that additional bookkeeping and collection costs can be avoided.

The goods are sold for a certain price if prompt payment is made, and a penalty is added in the form of a higher price if the payment is delayed. The bills rendered by some public utilities illustrate this approach. The amount of sales discount made available to customers, then, should be considered as an adjustment in measuring net sales revenue.

The need to prepare income statements for relatively short periods leads to alternative possibilities for recording sales discounts and computing the amount of

---

[11]See the glossary at the back of the book for the definition of a discount and a summary of the various contexts where this word is used in accounting.

## Exhibit 7.5

### Review of the Allowance Method of Accounting for Uncollectible Accounts

**Transactions in the First Period:**

(1) Sales are $1,000,000.

(2) Cash of $937,000 is collected from customers in payment of their accounts.

(3) At the end of the first period, it is estimated that uncollectibles will be 2 percent of sales; .02 × $1,000,000 = $20,000.

(4) Specific accounts totaling $7,000 are written off as uncollectible.

(5) The revenue and expense accounts are closed.

**Transactions in the Second Period:**

(6) Sales are $1,200,000.

(7) Specific accounts totaling $22,000 are written off during the period as information on their uncollectibility becomes known. The debit balance of $9,000 will remain in the Allowance account until the adjusting entry is made at the end of the period; see (9).

(8) Cash of $1,100,000 is collected from customers in payment of their accounts.

(9) An aging of the accounts receivable shows that the amount in the Allowance account should be $16,000. The amount of the adjustment is $25,000. It is computed as the difference between the desired $16,000 credit balance and the current $9,000 debit balance in the Allowance account.

(10) The revenue and expense accounts are closed.

| Cash | | Accounts Receivable | | Allowance for Uncollectible Accounts | | |
|---|---|---|---|---|---|---|
| | | (1) 1,000,000 | | | | 20,000  (3) |
| (2)  937,000 | | | 937,000 (2) | | | |
| | | | 7,000  (4) | (4) | 7,000 | |
| Bal. ? | | Bal.  56,000 | | | | 13,000  Bal. |
| | | (6) 1,200,000 | | | | |
| | | | 22,000 (7) | (7) | 22,000 | |
| (8) 1,100,000 | | | 1,100,000 (8) | | | |
| | | | | | | 25,000  (9) |
| Bal. ? | | Bal.  134,000 | | | | 16,000  Bal. |

| Bad Debt Expense | | Sales Revenue | |
|---|---|---|---|
| (3)  20,000 | | | 1,000,000 (1) |
| Closed (5) | (5) Closed | | |
| (9)  25,000 | | | 1,200,000 (6) |
| Closed (10) | (10) Closed | | |

sales discounts reported for a period. The issue is whether the amount of cash discount should be deducted from sales revenue in the period when the sales revenue is recognized or in the period of cash collection. In computing the amount of sales discounts recognized for a period, the major alternatives are the following:

1. To recognize discounts when taken by the customer, without regard to the period of sale (called the *gross price method*).

2. To estimate the total amount of discounts that will be taken on the sales made during the period (called the *allowance method*).

3. To record sales amounts reduced by all discounts made available to customers and to recognize additional revenue when a discount lapses (called the *net price method*).

Intermediate accounting texts discuss these methods.

## Sales Returns

When a customer returns merchandise, the sale has been canceled, and an entry to reverse the sale would be appropriate. In analyzing sales activities, however, management may be interested in the amount of goods returned. If so, a sales contra account is used to accumulate the amount of *sales returns* for a particular period.

A cash refund, such as might be made in a retail store when a customer returns merchandise that had been purchased for cash, would be entered as follows:

| | | |
|---|---|---|
| Sales Returns............................................... | 23 | |
|     Cash..................................................... | | 23 |

This treatment assumes that the return occurred before entries were made to recognize the reduction in inventory and the related cost of goods sold. If the return occurs after cost of goods sold has been recognized, the following entry must also be made:

| | | |
|---|---|---|
| Merchandise Inventory ....................................... | 16 | |
|     Cost of Goods Sold....................................... | | 16 |
| To reduce cost of goods sold by the cost (or net realizable value, if lower) of returned goods. | | |

Return of goods by a customer who buys on account usually involves the preparation of a credit memorandum, which is the reverse of a sales invoice. The credit memorandum lists the goods that have been returned and indicates the amount that is to be allowed the customer. The entry to record the issuance of the credit is normally a debit to the Sales Returns and a credit to the Accounts Receivable accounts.

Misleading sales and income amounts can result if goods are returned in a period after the one of sale. If there is no adjustment in the period of sale for estimated returns, the sales and income amounts for the period of sale are overstated, because they reflect transactions that are later canceled. Further, income statement amounts of sales and income are correspondingly understated in the period when the goods are returned. An allowance method for estimated returns similar to that for estimated uncollectible accounts could be used. However, because the amounts of sales returns for most businesses are usually relatively small, an allowance method is not often used.

## Sales Allowances

A *sales allowance* is a reduction in price granted to a customer, usually after the goods have been delivered and found to be unsatisfactory or damaged. Again, as for sales returns, the effect is a reduction in the sales revenue, but it may be desirable to accumulate the amount of such adjustments as a separate item. An account, Sales Allowances, may be used for this purpose, or a combined account title Sales Returns and Allowances may be used. The record-keeping problems are similar to those caused by sales returns.

## Presentation of Sales Adjustments in the Income Statement

In discussing the complications that accompany accounts receivable, several adjustments to sales have been introduced. All of these adjustments — for uncollectible accounts, for discounts, for returns, and for allowances — are illustrated in the Alexis Company's income statement, Exhibit 7.6, which appears later in this chapter.

## Turning Receivables into Cash

A firm may find itself temporarily short of cash and unable to borrow from its usual sources. In such instances, accounts receivable can be used to obtain funds. A firm may *assign* its accounts receivable to a bank or finance company to obtain a loan. The borrowing company physically maintains control of the accounts receivable, collects amounts remitted by customers, and then forwards the proceeds to the lending institution. Alternatively, the firm may *pledge* its accounts receivable to the lending agency. If the borrowing firm is unable to make loan repayments when due, the lending agency has the power to sell the accounts receivable to obtain payment. Finally, the accounts receivable may be *factored* to a bank or finance company to obtain cash. In this case, the accounts receivable are sold to the lending institution, which physically controls the receivables and collects payments from customers. If accounts receivable have been assigned or pledged, a footnote to the financial statements should indicate this fact: the collection of such accounts receivable will not increase the liquid resources available to the firm to pay general trade creditors. Accounts receivable that have been factored will not appear on the balance sheet, because they have been sold.

# Notes Receivable ————————————————————

The last liquid asset this chapter considers is notes receivable. Many business transactions involve written promises to pay sums of money at a future date. These written promises are called *promissory notes*. The holder of a promissory note has a liquid asset, notes receivable. A promissory note is a written contract in which one person, known as the *maker,* promises to pay to another person, known as the *payee,* a definite sum of money. The money may be payable either on demand or at a definite future date. A note may or may not provide for the payment of interest in addition to the principal amount.

Promissory notes are used most commonly in connection with obtaining loans at banks or other institutions, in the purchase of various kinds of property, and as a temporary settlement of an open or charge account balance when payment cannot be made within the usual credit period. A note may be *secured* by a mortgage on real estate (land and buildings) or personal property (machinery and merchandise) or by the deposit of specific collateral (stock certificates, bonds, and so forth). If the secured note is not collected at maturity, the lender can take possession of the real estate, personal property, or other collateral, sell it, and apply the proceeds to the repayment of the note. Any proceeds in excess of the amount due under the note are then paid to the borrower. Alternatively, the note may be *unsecured,* in which case it has about the same legal position as an account receivable.

## Calculation of Interest Revenue

Interest is the price paid for the use of borrowed funds. From the lender's point of view, it is revenue. The interest price is usually expressed as a percentage rate of the principal, with the rate being stated on an annual basis. Thus, a 2-month, 12 percent note would have interest equal to 2 percent of the principal; a 4-month, 15 percent note would have interest equal to 5 percent of principal, and so on. Because interest is a payment for the use of borrowed funds for a period of time, it accrues with the passage of time. Although interest accrues every day (indeed, every time the clock ticks), firms usually record interest only at the time of payment or at the end of an accounting period.

Most short-term notes receivable from customers are based on *simple interest* calculations.[12] The general formula for the calculation of simple interest is

Interest = Base (Principal or Face) × Interest Rate × Elapsed Time.

For example, the interest at the rate of 12 percent a year on $20,000 is $200 for 1 month, $400 for 2 months, $1,200 for 6 months, and so on. The calculation for shorter periods is complicated by the odd number of days in a year and the variations in the number of days in a month. Simple interest at the rate of 12 percent a year on $20,000 for 90 days would be $20,000 × .12 × 90/365, or $592, if an exact computation were made. For many purposes, especially the calculation of accrued interest, a satisfactory approximation of the correct interest can be obtained by assuming that the year has 360 days and that each month is one-twelfth of a year. Thus 30 days is the equivalent of 1 month, and 60 days is the equivalent of 2 months or one-sixth of a year. Under this method, the interest at 12 percent on $20,000 for 90 days would be the same as the interest for 3 months or one-quarter of a year, or $600. Keep in mind that nearly all quotations of simple interest rates state the rate per year, unless some other period is specifically mentioned. In the formula for simple interest, Principal × Rate × Elapsed Time, "time" should be expressed in terms of years or portions of a year, because the rate is the rate per year.

For the sake of uniformity and simplicity, the following rules are used for the calculation of interest throughout the text and problems:

---

[12]Most long-term notes involve compound interest, discussed in Appendix A.

1.  When the maturity terms are given in months, consider 1 month to be one-twelfth of a year; 3 months to be one-fourth of a year; 6 months to be one-half of a year, and so on, regardless of the actual number of days in the period. This is equivalent to regarding any 1-month period as being 30 days in a 360-day year.

2.  When the maturity terms are given in days, use the 360-day year. Consider 30 days to be one-twelfth of a year, 60 days to be one-sixth of a year, 17 days to be 17/360 of a year, and so on. Calculate maturity dates and elapsed time by using the actual number of days.

## Accounting for Interest-Bearing Notes Receivable

The notes to be discussed in this section, so-called interest-bearing notes, are those that indicate a face, or principal, amount together with explicit interest at a stated fair market rate for the time period stated in the note.[13] For example, the basic elements of such a note might read: "Two months after date (June 30), the Suren Company promises to pay to the order of the Mullen Company $3,000 with interest from date at the rate of 12 percent per annum." At the maturity date, August 31, the maturity value would be the face amount of $3,000 plus interest of $60 calculated in accordance with the preceding discussion ($60 = $3,000 $\times$ .12 $\times$ 2/12), or a total of $3,060.

The transactions related to a note receivable discussed in this section are the following: receipt of note, interest recognition at an interim date, transfer prior to maturity, and collection at maturity date.

**Receipt of Notes and Collection at Maturity**  Promissory notes usually are received from customers in connection with sales or with the settlement of an open account receivable. The customer is usually the maker, but the customer may transfer a note that has been received from another. It is common practice to allow the customer full credit for the face value and accrued interest, if any, although a different value might be agreed on in some instances.

If on June 30 the Mullen Company received a 60-day, 12-percent note for $3,000, dated June 30, from the Suren Company to apply on its account, the entry would be as follows:

| | | |
|---|---|---|
| June 30 Notes Receivable..................................... | 3,000 | |
| Accounts Receivable — Suren Company .............. | | 3,000 |

---

[13]Both non-interest-bearing notes, where the face amount is the same as the maturity value, and notes where the stated rate differs from the fair market rate, involve compound interest calculations; Chapters 10 and 11 discuss them.

Exhibit 7.6 _____

## ALEXIS COMPANY
## Income Statement Illustration of Sales and Sales Adjustments
## Partial Income Statement for the Year Ended June 30, Year 2

| | | | |
|---|---:|---:|---:|
| **Revenues:** | | | |
| Sales—Gross ..................................... | | $515,200 | |
| Less Sales Adjustments: | | | |
| Discounts Taken[a] ............................ | $23,600 | | |
| Allowances ................................... | 11,000 | | |
| Estimated Uncollectibles[b] ...................... | 10,300 | | |
| Returns........................................ | 8,600 | | |
| Total Sales Adjustments ...................... | | 53,500 | |
| Net Sales........................................ | | | $461,700 |

[a]The gross price method is used. If the net price method were used, discounts taken would not be shown and there would be an addition to revenue for the amount of sales discounts that lapsed.

[b]Most companies would call this account Bad Debt Expense and list it among the expenses.

Assuming that the accounting period of the Mullen Company is the calendar year, the entry upon collection at maturity would be as follows:

| | | |
|---|---:|---:|
| Aug. 31 Cash ................................................ | 3,060 | |
| Notes Receivable .................................... | | 3,000 |
| Interest Revenue .................................... | | 60 |

Assuming instead that the accounting period of the Mullen Company is 1 month, the interest adjustment at the interim date, July 31, would be as follows:

| | | |
|---|---:|---:|
| July 31 Interest Receivable .................................... | 30 | |
| Interest Revenue .................................... | | 30 |
| ($3,000 × .12 × 30/360 = $30.) | | |

The entry upon collection at maturity would then be as follows:

| | | |
|---|---:|---:|
| Aug. 31 Cash ................................................ | 3,060 | |
| Notes Receivable .................................... | | 3,000 |
| Interest Receivable .................................... | | 30 |
| Interest Revenue .................................... | | 30 |

Exhibit 7.7 _____

## ALEXIS COMPANY
## Detailed Illustration of Current Assets
## Balance Sheet (Excerpts) June 30, Year 1 and Year 2

|  | June 30, Year 2 | June 30, Year 1 |
|---|---|---|
| **Current Assets:** | | |
| Cash in Change and Petty Cash Funds..................... | $ 1,000 | $ 800 |
| Cash in Bank ............................................ | 13,000 | 11,000 |
| Cash Held as Compensating Balances...................... | 1,500 | 1,500 |
| Certificates of Deposit................................. | 8,000 | 7,500 |
| Marketable Securities, Acquisition Cost ................ | $30,000 | $25,000 |
| Less Allowance for Excess of Cost of Marketable Securities over Market Value (on June 30, Year 1, market value of $31,000 exceeds cost) ................ | (3,000) | — |
| Marketable Securities at Lower of Cost or Market (see Note A)............................................ | 27,000 | 25,000 |
| Notes Receivable (see Note B) .......................... | 12,000 | 10,000 |
| Interest and Dividends Receivable....................... | 500 | 400 |
| Accounts Receivable, Gross ............................. | $58,100 | $57,200 |
| Less Allowance for Uncollectible Accounts .............. | (3,600) | (3,500) |
| Accounts Receivable, Net .............................. | 54,500 | 53,700 |
| Merchandise Inventory[a] ............................... | 72,000 | 67,000 |
| Prepayments........................................... | 4,800 | 4,300 |
| Total Current Assets ................................ | $194,300 | $181,200 |

**Note A.** Gross unrealized holding gains and gross unrealized holding losses on Marketable Securities are as follows:

|  | June 30, Year 2 | June 30, Year 1 |
|---|---|---|
| Gross Unrealized Holding Gains ......................... | $7,000 | $7,000 |
| Gross Unrealized Holding Losses ........................ | (10,000) | (1,000) |
| Net Unrealized Holding Gain (Loss) ..................... | ($3,000) | $6,000 |

**Note B.** The amount shown for Notes Receivable does not include notes with a face amount of $2,000 that have been discounted with recourse at The First National Bank. The company is contingently liable for these notes, should the makers not honor them at maturity. The estimated amount of our liability is zero.

_____

[a]Additional required disclosures for this item omitted here. See Chapter 8.

_____

At the maturity date, the note may be collected (as illustrated previously), renewed, partially collected with renewal of the balance, or dishonored by the maker. These other possibilities involve more advanced accounting procedures and are not discussed in this book.

**Transfer of Notes Receivable**   To obtain cash, a note may be transferred to another party *without recourse*. This procedure is equivalent to a sale of the note, because the transferor has no further liability even if the maker fails to pay at maturity.

If Mullen Company transferred without recourse the 2-month, 12 percent, $3,000 note to Lane Trust Company for $3,030, 1 month after the date of the note, the entry would be as follows:

| July 31 Cash............................................... | 3,030 | |
| Notes Receivable .................................... | | 3,000 |
| Interest Revenue .................................... | | 30 |
| To record transfer of note without recourse. | | |

Most businesses that "purchase" notes are, however, unwilling to acquire them without recourse. Such firms do not want to be responsible for investigating the creditworthiness of the maker or for any collection efforts required for dishonored notes. Consequently, most notes that are transferred are done so *with recourse*.

A transfer with recourse places a potential or "contingent" obligation on the transferor if the maker fails to pay at maturity. Such a transfer is not a completed transaction because of the possibility that the transferor will have to pay the note in case the maker defaults at maturity.

Chapter 10 discusses *contingent obligations*, such as those for notes transferred with recourse or for the potential loss arising from an unsettled damage suit. Contingent obligations do not appear in the accounts, but are disclosed in notes to the balance sheet.

If Mullen Company transferred with recourse the 60-day, 12 percent, $3,000 note to Lane Trust Company 1 month after the date of the note, the entry would be the same as if the note was transferred without recourse. If Mullen Company prepared financial statements before Lane Trust Company collected from the maker, however, the notes to Mullen's balance sheet would contain a statement such as the following:

> *Contingencies.* The firm is contingently liable for a note transferred and accrued interest thereon to the Lane Trust Company. The face value of the transferred note is $3,000.

## Illustration of Balance Sheet Presentation _____

The balance sheet accounts discussed in this chapter include Cash, Certificates of Deposit, Marketable Securities, Notes Receivable, Accounts Receivable, and the Allowance for Uncollectible Accounts. Exhibit 7.6 (page 288) shows how transactions affecting these accounts appear in the income statement. Exhibit 7.7 (page 289) illustrates the presentation of these items in the balance sheet, which includes all of the current assets for the Alexis Company as of June 30, Year 1 and Year 2.

## Summary _____

This chapter has examined the accounting for cash and other liquid (or cashlike) assets. Among the questions addressed were the following:

1. What items are included in each of the liquid asset accounts?

2. At what amount are they stated?

3. Are there any restrictions on the use of particular liquid assets?

# Appendix 7.1:
# Effect of Transactions Involving Liquid Assets
# on the Statement of Cash Flows _____

## Marketable Securities

The statement of cash flows treats transactions in marketable securities held as noncurrent assets as investing activities. Transactions involving marketable securities held as current assets affect the working capital section of the statement of cash flows.

## Accounts Receivable

Transactions changing accounts receivable are operating activities. A change in accounts receivable is added to or subtracted from net income to derive cash flow from operations in preparing the statement of cash flows.

# Problem 1 for Self-Study _____

Refer to the data in Exhibits 7.1 and 7.2 showing transactions in marketable securities for the Wolfson Company over 4 years. Assume that in addition to those transactions, Wolfson Company purchased 1,000 shares of Company D on October 1, Year 1, for $40 per share, $40,000 in total. Shares of Company D had a market value of $45 per share at the end of Year 1, $35 per share at the end of Year 2, $30 per share at the end of Year 3, and $50 per share at the end of Year 4.

a.  What are the amounts of each of the following at the end of each of the 4 years: Marketable Securities at Cost, Allowance for Excess of Cost of Marketable Securities over Market Value, and Marketable Securities at Lower of Cost or Market? What is the Unrealized Loss (or Recovery of Unrealized Loss) for each of the 4 years?

b.  If early in Year 2 Wolfson Company sells 900 shares of Company D at $30 each, $27,000 in total, what is the realized gain or loss for Year 2 and the Unrealized Holding Loss or Recovery of Unrealized Holding Loss for Year 2?

c.  Ignore the information in part b. During Year 2, Wolfson Company transferred all 1,000 shares of Company D to its noncurrent asset portfolio of Investments at a time when these shares had an aggregate market value of $38,000. What is income before taxes for Year 2?

d.  Ignore information in parts b and c. Now assume that the securities of all four companies have been classified as the noncurrent asset Investments from the time of acquisition. During Year 3, Wolfson Company sold 400 shares of Company D for $38 per share and transferred the remaining 600 shares to a current asset account, Marketable Securities, at a time when the share price was $35 each. What is income before taxes for Year 3?

e.  Ignore information in parts **b, c,** and **d.** Now assume that Wolfson Company left its holdings of Company D intact until the last day of Year 2, when it sold some shares for $35 per share. If the correct balance on the balance sheet at the end of Year 2 for marketable securities valued at lower of cost or market is $109,500, how many shares were sold on December 31, Year 2?

## Suggested Solution

**a.**  See Exhibit 7.8.

**b.**  Realized Loss = $900 \times (\$40 - \$30) = \$9,000$. December 31 valuation of remaining portfolio is as follows:

| | |
|---|---:|
| At Cost: $100,000 + (100 × $40) .................................... | $104,000 |
| At Market: $99,000 + (100 × $35) .................................... | $102,500 |
| Required Allowance ................................................. | $   1,500 |
| Allowance at Start of Year ......................................... | 0 |
| Unrealized Holding Loss for Year ................................... | $   1,500 |

**c.**

| | |
|---|---:|
| Other Items before Taxes ........................................... | $300,000 |
| Realized Loss on Transfer of Securities between Portfolios (= $40,000 − $38,000) ........................................ | (2,000) |
| Unrealized Holding Loss of Securities A, B, and C.................... | (1,000) |
| Income before Taxes ................................................ | $297,000 |

**d.**

| | |
|---|---:|
| Other Items before Taxes ........................................... | $300,000 |
| Realized Loss on Sales 400 × ($40 − $38) ........................................... | (800) |
| Realized Loss on Transfer 600 × ($40 − $35) ........................................... | (3,000) |
| Income before Taxes ................................................ | $296,200 |

**Exhibit 7.8** ————————————————————————————————————————

**Problem 1 for Self-Study**
**(Suggested Solution to Part a)**

| Marketable Securities | Year 1 | Year 2 | Year 3 | Year 4 |
|---|---|---|---|---|
| At Cost........................... | $140,000 | $140,000 | $110,000 | $90,000 |
| Allowance ....................... | — | (6,000) | (4,000) | — |
| At Lower of Cost or Market ......... | $140,000 | $134,000 | $106,000 | $90,000 |
| Unrealized Loss for Year ........... | — | $  (6,000) | — | — |
| Recovery of Unrealized Loss for Year ....................... | — | — | $   2,000 | $   4,000 |

**e.** Let $x$ represent number of shares of Company D remaining, so that:

| Marketable Securities (December 31, Year 2): | |
|---|---|
| At Cost ............................................. | $100,000 + $40x |
| Allowance ........................................... | (1,000 + 5x) |
| At Lower of Cost or Market ........................... | $ 99,000 + $35x |

If the correct balance is $109,500, then $35x$ is $10,500 and $x$ is 300 shares; 700 (= 1,000 − 300) shares were sold.

# Problem 2 for Self-Study _____

Refer to the data in Exhibit 7.5 showing sales and collection activities for two periods. At the end of the third period, the *unadjusted* trial balance included the following accounts and amounts: Accounts Receivable, $75,000 debit; Allowance for Uncollectible Accounts, $8,000 debit; Bad Debt Expense, zero (adjusting entries have not yet been made); Sales Revenue, $1,300,000. No further specific accounts receivable need to be written off for the period.

**a.** Reconstruct the transactions of the third period, assuming that all sales were made on account.

**b.** What were the total cash collections for the third period from customers who paid their accounts?

**c.** Reconstruct the transactions of the third period, assuming that only $1 million of the $1.3 million total sales were made on account.

**d.** What were the total cash collections for the third period, including collections both from customers who paid cash and from customers who paid their accounts?

**e.** Does one need to know the actual split of sales between cash sales and sales on account to know the total amount of cash collected from customers — that is, the sum of cash sales and collections on account? Why or why not?

**f.** Assume that 2 percent of all sales for the third period is estimated to be uncollectible. What is the adjusting entry to be made at the end of the third period for estimated uncollectibles? What net balance of Accounts Receivable will appear on the balance sheet at the end of the third period?

**g.** Independent of the answer to the preceding part, assume that an aging of accounts receivable indicates that the amount in Allowance for Uncollectibles appropriate for the status of outstanding accounts at the end of the third period is $20,000. What is the adjusting entry to be made at the end of the third period for estimated uncollectibles? What amount of sales less bad debt expense will be reported for the third period?

## Suggested Solution

a. Sales were $1,300,000, debited to Accounts Receivable. Specific accounts receivable of $24,000 (= $16,000 credit at start of period plus $8,000 debit by the end of period) were written off with debits to the Allowance for Uncollectibles account and credits to Accounts Receivable. Thus the balance in accounts receivable before cash collections was $1,410,000 (= $134,000 + $1,300,000 − $24,000). Because the ending balance is actually $75,000, the cash collections from customers who bought on account are $1,335,000 (= $1,410,000 − $75,000).

b. Cash collections of $1,335,000, as derived in part **a**.

c. Sales were $1,300,000, debited $300,000 to Cash and $1,000,000 to Accounts Receivable. Specific accounts receivable of $24,000 were written off with debits to the Allowance for Uncollectibles account and credits to Accounts Receivable. The amount is derived as in part **a**. The write-off of specific accounts left a balance of $1,110,000 (= $134,000 + $1,000,000 − $24,000), but the actual ending balance was $75,000, so $1,035,000 (= $1,110,000 − $75,000) of accounts must have been collected in cash.

d. Total collections of $1,335,000 = $300,000 cash sales plus $1,035,000 from collections on account.

e. No. Once cash from a sale on account has been collected, the overall effect of the sale on the financial statements is identical with a cash sale. Thus cash sales and collected credit sales have the same effects on the financial statements.

---

f. Bad Debt Expense ........................................   26,000
    Allowance for Uncollectible Accounts ....................        26,000
Amount is equal to .02 × $1,300,000. Ending balance in the allowance account is $18,000 (= $26,000 credit less $8,000 debit).

---

The net Accounts Receivable balance at the end of the third period is $57,000 (= $75,000 − $18,000).

---

g. Bad Debt Expense ........................................   28,000
    Allowance for Uncollectible Accounts ....................        28,000
A $28,000 credit is required to establish a $20,000 credit balance in an account with a tentative $8,000 debit balance.

---

Sales less bad debt expense are $1,272,000 (= $1,300,000 gross sales less $28,000 adjustment for uncollectibles). The net Accounts Receivable balance at the end of the third period is $55,000 (= $75,000 − $20,000).

# Questions, Exercises, Problems, and Cases ————————

## Questions

1. Review the meaning of the following concepts or terms discussed in this chapter.

   a. Generally accepted accounting principles (GAAP).

   b. Securities and Exchange Commission (SEC).

   c. Financial Accounting Standards Board (FASB).

   d. Liquidity.

   e. Insolvent.

   f. Cash.

   g. Demand deposits.

   h. Certificate of deposit.

   i. Foreign currency.

   j. Compensating balance.

   k. Marketable securities.

   l. Investments (noncurrent).

   m. Marketable debt securities.

   n. Marketable equity securities.

   o. Lower-of-cost-or-market method.

   p. Unrealized holding loss on marketable securities.

   q. Recovery of unrealized holding loss on marketable securities.

   r. Realized gain or loss on marketable securities.

   s. Direct write-off method.

   t. Allowance method for uncollectibles.

   u. Aging of accounts receivable.

   v. Sales discounts, returns, and allowances.

   w. Factoring.

   x. Simple interest.

   y. Recourse.

   z. Contingent obligation.

2. What purpose is served by having a broad set of financial reporting objectives, such as those issued by the FASB?

3. Generally accepted accounting principles are the methods of accounting used by publicly held firms in preparing their financial statements. A principle in physics, such as the law of gravity, serves as a basis for developing theories and explaining the relations among physical objects. In what ways are generally accepted accounting principles similar to and different from principles of physics?

4. The text states that the standard-setting process is essentially political in nature. Yet the FASB strives to relate its pronouncements to a broad set of financial reporting objectives. Do you see any inconsistency between these two approaches to standard setting?

5. Describe the differences among a *Discussion Memorandum,* an *Exposure Draft* of a proposed financial accounting standard, and a *Financial Accounting Standard.*

6. What evidence of cash control have you observed in a cafeteria? A department store? A theater? A gasoline station?

7. The Tastee Delight ice cream stores prominently advertise on signs in the stores that the customer's purchase is free if the clerk does not present a receipt. Oakland's Original hot dog stand says that the customer's purchase is free if the cash register receipt contains a red star. What control purposes do such policies serve?

8. Current assets are defined as those assets that are expected to be turned into cash or sold or consumed within the next operating cycle. Cash is not always classified as a current asset, however. Explain.

9. Does application of the lower-of-cost-or-market valuation method to the portfolio of marketable equity securities or to each marketable equity security individually result in the most conservative asset values and net income amounts?

10. Which of the two methods for treating uncollectible accounts (direct write-off or allowance) implies recognizing revenue reductions earlier rather than later? Why?

11. **a.** An old wisdom in tennis holds that if your first serves are always good, you are not hitting them hard enough. An analogous statement in business might be that if you have no uncollectible accounts, you probably are not selling enough on credit. Comment on the validity of this statement.
    **b.** When are more uncollectible accounts better than fewer uncollectible accounts?
    **c.** When is a higher percentage of uncollectible accounts better than a lower one?

12. The customary method of accounting for sales results in adequate reporting for returns when the goods are returned in the same period in which they are sold. If the goods are returned in a period subsequent to that of the sale, distortion of the reported income results. Explain how sales returns may produce each of the described effects.

13. Under what circumstances will the Allowance for Uncollectible Accounts have a debit balance during the accounting period? The balance sheet figure for the Allowance for Uncollectible Accounts at the end of the period should never show a debit balance. Why?

14. What is the effect on the financial statements of discounting, or transferring, a note with recourse versus one without recourse?

## Exercises

15. *Inclusions in Cash account.* Indicate if each of the following items should be included in Cash on the balance sheet. If not, indicate how the item should be reported.
    **a.** Cash that has been collected from customers and is awaiting deposit in the firm's checking account.
    **b.** Cash left in cash registers each day to serve as a change fund.
    **c.** Cash set aside in a special savings account to accumulate funds to replace equipment as it wears out. The firm is not legally obligated to use the funds for this purpose.
    **d.** Cash set aside in a special savings account to accumulate funds to retire debt as it becomes due. The firm is legally obligated to use the funds for this purpose.
    **e.** A postdated check received from a customer. The check is dated 60 days after the date of the balance sheet.

    **f.**   A money order received from a customer.

    **g.**   Postage stamps.

    **h.**   Cash held for small miscellaneous expenditures, such as freight charges and executive lunches.

    **i.**   Cash in a checking account that must be maintained at a certain minimum level in accordance with a written loan agreement for a 6-month loan.

**16.** *Inclusions in Cash account.* You are asked to compute the amount that should be shown as Cash on the balance sheet as of December 31 for Zeff Transportation Company from the following information.

    **a.**   Coins, currency, and checks received from customers on December 31 but not yet deposited amounted to $6,500.

    **b.**   The cash fund held for making small miscellaneous cash expenditures normally has a balance of $100, but expenditures of $22 were made on December 31.

    **c.**   The firm's postage meter was "filled" on December 31 and contains $500 in postage.

    **d.**   The books indicate that the balance in the firm's checking account on December 31 was $45,800. When the bank statement was received on the next January 10, it was learned that one customer's check for $800, deposited on December 28, was returned for insufficient funds. In addition, during December the bank collected $2,200 for a note receivable from one of Zeff's customers and added the amount to Zeff's bank account. The note had a face value of $2,000 and interest of $200.

    **e.**   A certificate of deposit for a face value of $10,000 was acquired on July 1 of this year and matures on June 30 of next year. Simple interest of 12 percent per year accumulates on the note and is payable at maturity with the principal.

    **f.**   British sterling currency of £10,000 is held. The exchange rate on December 31 is $1.60 per pound sterling.

**17.** *Effect of compensating balances on effective interest rate.* Davidoff Corporation borrowed $1 million from the local bank on July 1. The bank charged Davidoff Corporation interest at its prime lending rate of 13.5 percent. The principal and interest on the loan are repayable on the following June 30. Davidoff Corporation must maintain a $100,000 compensating balance in an interest-free checking account at the bank during the term of the loan.

    **a.**   What is the effective annual interest rate that Davidoff Corporation is paying on this loan?

    **b.**   What message to Davidoff Corporation is implicit in the bank's requirement that a compensating balance be maintained?

**18.** *Classifying marketable securities.* Indicate the classification of each of the following securities in the balance sheet of Bower Corporation on December 31.

    **a.**   U.S. Treasury bills, acquired on October 15. The bills mature next April 15.

    **b.**   Shares of Brazil Coffee Corporation, a major supplier of raw materials for Bower Corporation's products.

**c.** Shares of Overland Transportation Company. The shares were originally acquired as a temporary investment of excess cash. Overland Transportation Company has been so profitable that Bower Corporation plans to increase its ownership percentage, eventually obtaining 51 percent of the outstanding shares.

**d.** American Telephone and Telegraph Company bonds that mature in 3 years. The bonds were acquired with a cash advance from a customer on a contract for the manufacture of machinery, and they will be sold as needed to pay costs of manufacturing. The manufacturing process will take 3 years.

**19.** *Journal entries for holdings of marketable equity securities.* The following list gives all events for Germont Company's actions with respect to its current asset portfolio of marketable equity securities during the period August, Year 1, through January, Year 2.

8/21 Germont Company purchases 1,000 shares of Grenvil Company for $15 per share. In addition, it pays $150 in brokerage commissions to its stockbroker.

9/1 The stockbroker calls Germont Company to report that Grenvil Company shares closed on the preceding day at $18 per share.

9/30 Grenvil Company declares a dividend of $.25 per share.

10/25 Germont Company receives a dividend check for $250.

12/31 The stockbroker calls Germont Company to report that Grenvil Company shares closed the year at $11 per share. The books are closed for the year.

1/31 Germont Company sells 600 shares for $13 per share, the closing price for the day. Brokerage commissions, deducted from the proceeds, are $100.

1/31 Germont Company prepares an up-to-date balance sheet as part of an application for a loan.

Prepare dated journal entries as required by these events. Ignore income taxes.

**20.** *Journal entries for portfolio of marketable equity securities.* The aggregate cost and aggregate market value of the portfolio of marketable equity securities, current assets, of Elson Corporation at various dates follow.

| Date | Aggregate Cost | Aggregate Market Value |
|---|---|---|
| December 31, Year 1 | $150,000 | $130,000 |
| December 31, Year 2 | 160,000 | 144,000 |
| December 31, Year 3 | 170,000 | 185,000 |
| December 31, Year 4 | 180,000 | 168,000 |

Give the journal entry required at the end of each year, assuming that the accounting period is the calendar year.

21. *Journal entries for the allowance method.* The trial balance of the Walker Company at the end of its first year of operations included $20,000 of outstanding customers' accounts. An analysis revealed that 80 percent of the total credit sales of the year had been collected and that no accounts had been charged off as uncollectible.

   The auditor estimated that 2 percent of the total credit sales would be uncollectible. On the next January 31, the account of H. J. Williams, who had owed a balance of $300 for 6 months, was judged uncollectible and was written off.

   On July 1, the amount owed by H. J. Williams, previously written off, was collected in full.

   Present dated journal entries to record the following:
   a.  Adjustment for estimated uncollectible accounts on December 31.
   b.  Write-off of the H. J. Williams account on January 31.
   c.  Collection of the H. J. Williams account on July 1. Assume that it is believed there is evidence that the account should never have been written off as uncollectible and that total uncollectibles are likely not to be different from the original estimates.

22. *Journal entries for the allowance method.* The trial balance of the Biddle Company at the end of its first year of operations included $25,000 of outstanding customers' accounts. An analysis revealed that 90 percent of the total credit sales of the year had been collected and that no accounts had been charged off as uncollectible.

   The auditor estimated that 1 percent of the total credit sales would be uncollectible. On the next January 31, the account of Robert Jesse, who had owed a balance of $500 for 6 months, was judged uncollectible and was written off. ·

   On August 1, the amount owed by Robert Jesse, previously written off, was collected in full.

   Present dated journal entries to record the following:
   a.  Adjustment for estimated uncollectible accounts for December 31.
   b.  Write-off of the Robert Jesse account on January 31.
   c.  Collection of the Robert Jesse account on August 1. Assume that it is believed there is evidence that the account should never have been written off as uncollectible and that total uncollectibles are likely not to be different from the original estimates.

23. *Reconstructing events when allowance method is used.* The balance sheets of Wilton Corporation on December 31, Year 1 and Year 2, showed gross accounts receivable of $8,300,000 and $9,700,000, respectively. The balances in the Allowance for Uncollectible Accounts account at the beginning and end of Year 2, after closing entries, were credits of $750,000 and $930,000, respectively. The income statement for Year 2 shows that the expense for estimated uncollectible accounts was $300,000, which was 1 percent of sales. All sales are made on account. There were no recoveries during Year 2 of accounts written off in previous years.

Give all the journal entries made during Year 2 that have an effect on Accounts Receivable and Allowance for Uncollectible Accounts.

**24.** *Aging accounts receivable.* Love Company's accounts receivable show the following balances by age:

| Age of Accounts | Balance Receivable |
|---|---|
| 0–30 Days........................................................ | $300,000 |
| 31–60 Days ..................................................... | 75,000 |
| 61–120 Days ................................................... | 30,000 |
| More than 120 Days ........................................ | 15,000 |

The credit balance in the Allowance for Uncollectible Accounts is now $6,000.

Love Company's independent auditors suggest that the following percentages should be used to compute the estimates of amounts that will eventually prove uncollectible: 0–30 days, .5 of 1 percent; 31–60 days, 1 percent; 61–120 days, 10 percent; and more than 120 days, 60 percent.

Prepare a journal entry that will carry out the auditor's suggestion.

**25.** *Aging accounts receivable.* Rozay Company's accounts receivable show the following balances:

| Age of Accounts | Balance Receivable |
|---|---|
| 0–30 Days......................................... | $500,000 |
| 31–60 Days ....................................... | 175,000 |
| 61–120 Days ..................................... | 80,000 |
| More than 120 Days ........................... | 40,000 |

An adjusting entry based on the percentage-of-sales method has already been made for the period. The credit balance in the Allowance for Uncollectible Accounts is now $30,000. The Bad Debt Expense account has a balance of $35,000.

Analysis of recent collection experience suggests that the following percentages should be used to compute the estimates of amounts that will eventually prove uncollectible: 0–30 days, .5 of 1 percent; 31–60 days, 1 percent, 61–120 days, 10 percent; and more than 120 days, 40 percent.

Prepare the indicated adjusting entry.

**26.** *Simple interest computations.* Calculate simple interest on a base of $6,000 for the following intervals and rates, using a 360-day year.
  **a.**  60 days at 12 percent.
  **b.**  90 days at 9 percent.
  **c.**  60 days at 16 percent.
  **d.**  15 days at 16 percent.
  **e.**  5 months, 15 days at 12 percent.

**27.** *Journal entries for notes.* On May 10, the Dukes Company receives a note from one of its customers, Salk Builders, Inc., to apply on its account. The 6-month,

12 percent note for $6,000, issued on May 10, is valued at its face amount, $6,000.

On July 25, the Dukes Company endorses the note and transfers it with recourse to the Beaver Company to settle an account payable. The note is valued at its face amount plus accrued interest.

On November 12, the Dukes Company is notified that the note was paid at maturity.

**a.** Present dated entries on the books of the Dukes Company, assuming that it closes its books quarterly on March 31, June 30, and so on.

**b.** Present dated entries on the books of the Beaver Company, assuming that it closes its books quarterly on March 31, June 30, and so on.

## Problems and Cases

**28.** *Journal entries and financial statement presentation of marketable equity securities.* The following information summarizes data about the marketable equity securities held as current assets of Albion Corporation.

| | | | | | Market Value | |
|---|---|---|---|---|---|---|
| Security | Date Acquired | Acquisition Cost | Date Sold | Selling Price | Dec. 31, Year 1 | Dec. 31, Year 2 |
| A ........... | 1/5/Year 1 | $40,000 | 11/5/Year 2 | $50,000 | $45,000 | — |
| B ........... | 6/12/Year 1 | 85,000 | — | — | 75,000 | $82,000 |
| C ........... | 2/22/Year 2 | 48,000 | — | — | — | 46,000 |
| D ........... | 3/25/Year 2 | 25,000 | 11/5/Year 2 | 18,000 | — | — |
| E ........... | 4/25/Year 2 | 36,000 | — | — | — | 40,000 |

**a.** Give all journal entries relating to these marketable equity securities during Year 1 and Year 2, assuming that the accounting period is the calendar year.

**b.** Indicate the manner in which marketable securities would be presented in the balance sheet and related notes on December 31, Year 1.

**c.** Indicate the manner in which marketable securities would be presented in the balance sheet and related notes on December 31, Year 2.

**29.** *Journal entries and financial statement presentation of marketable equity securities.* The following information summarizes data about the marketable equity securities held as current assets of Booth Corporation.

| | | | | | Market Value | |
|---|---|---|---|---|---|---|
| Security | Date Acquired | Acquisition Cost | Date Sold | Selling Price | Dec. 31, Year 1 | Dec. 31, Year 2 |
| A ........... | 1/5/Year 1 | $30,000 | 11/5/Year 2 | $50,000 | $45,000 | — |
| B ........... | 6/12/Year 1 | 95,000 | — | — | 70,000 | $82,000 |
| C ........... | 2/22/Year 2 | 50,000 | — | — | — | 46,000 |
| D ........... | 3/25/Year 2 | 30,000 | 11/5/Year 2 | 18,000 | — | — |
| E ........... | 4/25/Year 2 | 40,000 | — | — | — | 50,000 |

a.   Give all journal entries relating to these marketable equity securities during Year 1 and Year 2, assuming that the accounting period is the calendar year.

b.   Indicate the manner in which marketable securities would be presented in the balance sheet and related notes on December 31, Year 1.

c.   Indicate the manner in which marketable securities would be presented in the balance sheet and related notes on December 31, Year 2.

**30.** *Financial statement presentation of marketable equity securities.* Exhibit 7.9 gives data on Sprouse Company's holdings of marketable securities for Year 1 and Year 2. There were no sales of securities during Year 1. During Year 2, Sprouse Company purchased new shares in Security F. During Year 2, the following sales of securities took place:

| | Net Proceeds of Sale | Cost | Realized Gain (Loss) |
|---|---|---|---|
| Security A ......................... | $125,000 | $100,000 | $ 25,000 |
| Security B ......................... | 65,000 | 100,000 | (35,000) |
| | $190,000 | $200,000 | $(10,000) |

The valuation allowances required at December 31, Year 2, are as follows:

| | Charged against Income | Charged against Equity |
|---|---|---|
| In Current Assets: | | |
|   Cost $900,000 less Market $850,000 ................... | $50,000 | |
| In Noncurrent Assets: | | |
|   Cost $650,000 less Market $540,000 ................... | | $110,000 |

Ignore income taxes.

a.   Prepare in parallel columns for year-end Year 2 and Year 1 the data that appear in the December 31, Year 2, balance sheet.

b.   Prepare a suitable footnote to accompany the balance sheet for December 31, Year 2.

**31.** *Marketable securities: journal entries and working backwards (adapted from a problem by S. Zeff).* During Year 2, Fitz Company sold marketable equity securities that had been classified as current assets for $46,000 cash. The securities had a market value of $41,000 on December 31, Year 1.

In the company's December 31, Year 2, balance sheet, marketable equity securities were shown as follows:

| | |
|---|---|
| **Current Assets:** | |
| Marketable Equity Securities—At Cost .............................. | $176,000 |
| Less Allowance for Excess of Cost of Marketable Equity Securities over Market Value...................................... | (23,000) |
| Net Balance (lower of cost or market) .............................. | $153,000 |

**Exhibit 7.9** _____

**SPROUSE COMPANY**
**Data on Marketable Securities**
**(Problem 30)**

|  | Year 2 | | Year 1 | |
| --- | --- | --- | --- | --- |
|  | Cost | Market | Cost | Market |
| In Current Assets: | | | | |
| Security A ................. | $100,000 | $100,000 | $200,000 | $250,000 |
| B ................. | 200,000 | 150,000 | 300,000 | 250,000 |
| C ................. | 200,000 | 175,000 | 200,000 | 150,000 |
| D ................. | 150,000 | 100,000 | 150,000 | 200,000 |
| E ................. | 50,000 | 100,000 | 50,000 | 75,000 |
| F ................. | 200,000 | 225,000 | — | — |
| Total of Portfolio.............. | $900,000 | $850,000 | $900,000 | $925,000 |
| In Noncurrent Assets: | | | | |
| Security G ................. | $300,000 | $200,000 | $300,000 | $200,000 |
| H ................. | 100,000 | 190,000 | 100,000 | 250,000 |
| I ................. | 250,000 | 150,000 | 250,000 | 250,000 |
| Total of Portfolio.............. | $650,000 | $540,000 | $650,000 | $700,000 |

The company's income statements included the following:

|  | Year 1 | Year 2 |
| --- | --- | --- |
| Realized Holding Loss on Sale of Marketable Securities....................................................... | $(9,000) | $(13,000) |
| Unrealized Holding Loss on Valuation of Marketable Securities ................................ |  | (11,000) |
| Recovery of Unrealized Holding Loss on Valuation of Marketable Securities............................... | 4,000 |  |

During Year 2, the company purchased marketable equity securities, classified as current assets, at a cost of $28,000. Fitz Company's reported net incomes for Year 1 and Year 2 were $80,000 and $110,000, respectively.

Assume that the company has been keeping its accounting records correctly.

**a.** What entry was made during Year 2 for the sale of the marketable equity securities?

**b.** What was the balance of the current asset Marketable Equity Securities — At Cost in the December 31, Year 1, balance sheet?

**c.** What was the balance in the Allowance account in the December 31, Year 1, balance sheet?

**d.** Suppose that all of the company's marketable equity securities had been classified as *noncurrent* assets from the very beginning. All of the other facts remain the same. What would the company's net incomes have been for Year 1 and Year 2? Ignore income tax effects.

**32.** *Effects of applying lower of cost or market to entire portfolios rather than to individual securities*. Information relating to the marketable equity securities of TSS Company follows.

| | | | | | Market Value | |
|---|---|---|---|---|---|---|
| Security | Date Acquired | Acquisition Cost | Date Sold | Selling Price | Dec. 31, Year 1 | Dec. 31, Year 2 |
| H ......... | 4/26/Year 1 | $18,000 | 2/9/Year 2 | $15,000 | $16,000 | — |
| I .......... | 5/25/Year 1 | 25,000 | 8/10/Year 2 | 26,000 | 24,000 | — |
| J.......... | 11/24/Year 1 | 12,000 | — | — | 14,000 | $15,000 |
| K ......... | 2/26/Year 2 | 34,000 | — | — | — | 33,500 |
| L ......... | 12/17/Year 2 | 8,000 | — | — | — | 7,800 |

a. Compute both the realized and the unrealized gain or loss for Year 1, applying lower of cost or market to the entire portfolio.

b. Compute both the realized and the unrealized gain or loss for Year 2, applying lower of cost or market to the entire portfolio.

c. Repeat steps **a** and **b**, but assume that lower of cost or market is applied individually to each security rather than to the portfolio of securities. This treatment does not conform to generally accepted accounting principles.

d. Does application of lower of cost or market at the level of the portfolio or at the level of individual securities result in the more conservative asset values and measures of earnings?

**33.** *Allowance method: working backwards*. The sales, all on account, of the Needles Company in Year 1, its first year of operations, were $600,000. Collections totaled $500,000. On December 31, Year 1, it was estimated that 1.5 percent of all sales would probably be uncollectible. On that date, specific accounts in the amount of $3,000 were written off.

The company's *unadjusted* trial balance (after all nonadjusting entries were made) on December 31, Year 2, included the following accounts and balances:

| | | |
|---|---|---|
| Accounts Receivable (Dr.) ................................ | $60,000 | |
| Allowance for Uncollectible Accounts (Dr.)................... | 4,000 | |
| Bad Debt Expense ....................................... | — | |
| Sales (Cr.) .............................................. | | $700,000 |

In Year 2, Needles Company switched to the aging method for estimating uncollectibles. It estimated that the Year 2 ending balance of accounts receivable contained $12,000 of probable uncollectibles. You may assume, although it is not necessary to do so (why?), that all sales in Year 2 were made on account. Present journal entries for the following:

a. Transactions and adjustments of Year 1 related to sales and customers' accounts.

**b.** Transactions of Year 2 resulting in the previously listed trial balance amounts.

**c.** Adjustment for estimated uncollectibles for Year 2.

**34.** *Reconstructing events when allowance method is used.* The amounts in certain accounts on January 1, and before adjusting entries on December 31, are as follows:

|  | January 1 | December 31 |
|---|---|---|
| Accounts Receivable............................. | $400,000 Dr. | $ 500,000 Dr. |
| Allowance for Uncollectible Accounts ............ | 30,000 Cr. | 20,000 Dr. |
| Bad Debt Expense ............................. | 0 | 0 |
| Sales......................................... | 0 | 2,000,000 Cr. |

During the year, 90 percent of sales were on account and 3 percent of credit sales were judged to be uncollectible. During the year, one account for $1,500 was collected, although it had been written off as uncollectible during the preceding year. When the written-off account was reinstated, the credit was to the Allowance account.

**a.** Give the journal entries made during the year that explain the changes in the four previously listed accounts.

**b.** Give any adjusting entries required on December 31.

**35.** *Estimating percentage of uncollectibles.* The data in the following schedule pertain to the first 8 years of the Glidden Company's credit sales and experiences with uncollectible accounts.

| Year | Credit Sales | Related Uncollectible Accounts | Year | Credit Sales | Related Uncollectible Accounts |
|---|---|---|---|---|---|
| 1 ......... | $200,000 | $5,100 | 5 ......... | $500,000 | $6,000 |
| 2 ......... | 300,000 | 6,450 | 6 ......... | 550,000 | 5,400 |
| 3 ......... | 400,000 | 7,450 | 7 ......... | 560,000 | 5,750 |
| 4 ......... | 450,000 | 8,000 | 8 ......... | 580,000 | 5,950 |

Glidden Company has not previously used an Allowance for Uncollectible Accounts but has merely charged accounts written off directly to Bad Debt Expense.

What percentage of credit sales for a year would you recommend Glidden Company to charge to the bad debt expense account if the allowance method was adopted at the end of year 8?

**36.** *Decision to extend credit to a new class of customers.* The Feldman Company has a gross margin on credit sales of 30 percent; that is, cost of goods sold on account is 70 percent of sales on account. Uncollectible accounts amount to 2 percent of credit sales. If credit is extended to a new class of customers, credit sales will increase by $10,000, 8 percent of the new credit sales will be uncollectible, and all other costs, including interest to finance extra inventories, will increase by $1,000.

   **a.**  Would Feldman Company be better or worse off if it extended credit to the new class of customer, and by how much?

   **b.**  How would your answer to part **a** differ if $3,000 of the $10,000 increase in credit sales had been made anyway as sales for cash? (Assume that the uncollectible amount on new credit sales is $800.)

**37.**  *Decision to extend credit: working backwards to uncollectible rate.* The Hanrahan Company has credit sales of $100,000 and a gross margin on those sales of 25 percent, with 3 percent of the credit sales uncollectible. If credit is extended to a new class of customers, sales will increase by $40,000, other expenses will increase by $2,500, and uncollectibles will be 5 percent of *all* credit sales. Verify that Hanrahan Company will be $3,500 better off if it extends credit to the new customers. What percentage of the new credit sales are uncollectible?

**38.**  *Journal entries for notes.* On November 1, Year 1, the Atlas Company receives a note from one of its customers to apply on its open account receivable. The 9-month, 18 percent note for $8,000, issued November 1, Year 1, is valued at its face amount.

   On January 31, Year 2, the Atlas Company endorses the note and transfers it with recourse to First National Bank in return for a cash payment of $8,100. The company's checking account at this bank is increased for the proceeds, $8,100.

   On August 1, Year 2, the Atlas Company is notified by the bank that the note was collected from the customer at maturity.

   Atlas Company closes its books annually on December 31.

   Present dated journal entries on the books of Atlas Company relating to this note.

**39.**  *Reconstructing events from journal entries.* Give the likely transaction or event that would result in making each of the independent journal entries that follow.

| | | |
|---|---:|---:|
| **a.** Notes Receivable ..................................... | 300 | |
| Accounts Receivable .............................. | | 300 |
| **b.** Marketable Securities ................................ | 10,000 | |
| Cash .......................................... | | 10,000 |
| **c.** Bad Debt Expense..................................... | 2,300 | |
| Allowance for Uncollectible Accounts................. | | 2,300 |
| **d.** Unrealized Loss on Valuation of Marketable Equity | | |
| Securities ........................................ | 4,000 | |
| Allowance for Excess of Cost of Marketable Equity | | |
| Securities over Market Value ...................... | | 4,000 |
| **e.** Cash ............................................... | 295 | |
| Notes Receivable ................................. | | 285 |
| Interest Revenue ................................. | | 10 |
| **f.** Cash ............................................... | 1,200 | |
| Loss on Sale of Marketable Securities ................... | 200 | |
| Marketable Securities ............................ | | 1,400 |

| | | |
|---|---:|---:|
| **g.** Allowance for Uncollectible Accounts . . . . . . . . . . . . . . . . . . . | 450 | |
|     Accounts Receivable . . . . . . . . . . . . . . . . . . . . . . . . . . . . | | 450 |
| **h.** Allowance for Excess of Cost of Marketable Equity | | |
|     Securities over Market Value . . . . . . . . . . . . . . . . . . . . . . . | 1,000 | |
|     Recovery of Unrealized Loss on Valuation of | | |
|       Marketable Equity Securities . . . . . . . . . . . . . . . . . . . . . | | 1,000 |
| **i.** Bad Debt Expense . . . . . . . . . . . . . . . . . . . . . . . . . . . . . . . . | 495 | |
|     Accounts Receivable . . . . . . . . . . . . . . . . . . . . . . . . . . . . | | 495 |
| **j.** Accounts Receivable . . . . . . . . . . . . . . . . . . . . . . . . . . . . . . | 285 | |
|     Allowance for Uncollectible Accounts . . . . . . . . . . . . . . . . | | 285 |

**40.** *Cash flow statement effects.* Refer to the Simplified Statement of Cash Flows in Exhibit 5.15 on page 188. Eleven of the lines in the statement are numbered. Ignore the unnumbered lines in responding to the questions that follow.

Assume that the accounting cycle is complete for the period and that all of the financial statements have been prepared. It is then discovered that a transaction has been overlooked. That transaction is recorded in the accounts, and all of the financial statements are corrected. Define *funds* as cash.

For each of the following transactions or events, indicate which of the numbered lines of the funds statement is affected and by how much. Ignore income tax effects.

**a.** Estimated uncollectibles equal to 1 percent of the year's sales of $1 million are recognized. An entry is made increasing the Allowance for Uncollectible Accounts.

**b.** The specific account receivable of Eli Worman in the amount of $2,000 is written off by a firm using the allowance method.

**c.** The specific account receivable of Eli Worman in the amount of $3,000 is written off by a firm using the direct write-off method.

**d.** A firm owns short-term marketable securities. Dividends of $30,000 are declared on the shares owned. The payment will be received next period.

**41.** *Preparing statement of cash flows (adapted from a problem by S. Baiman).* Exhibit 7.10 shows comparative balance sheets and an income statement of Trimolet Company for Year 2.

Prepare the Year 2 statement of cash flows.

**42.** *Analysis of financial statement disclosures of marketable equity securities held as investments.* A recent annual report of Warner Communications, Inc. (WCI), contained the following information about its investments in marketable equity securities (noncurrent assets). Dollar amounts appear in thousands.

| | Year 2 | Year 1 |
|---|---:|---:|
| **Noncurrent Asset Section of Balance Sheet** | | |
| Marketable Equity Securities Carried at Lower of Cost | | |
|   or Market . . . . . . . . . . . . . . . . . . . . . . . . . . . . . . . . . . . . . | $44,143 | $96,571 |
| **Owners' Equity Section of Balance Sheet** | | |
| Net Unrealized Loss on Marketable Equity Securities . . . . . . . | (3,887) | (18,736) |

Exhibit 7.10 ——————————————————————————————————

**TRIMOLET COMPANY**
**Comparative Balance Sheets and Income Statement**
**(Problem 41)**

| | December 31 | |
|---|---|---|
| **Balance Sheets** | **Year 1** | **Year 2** |
| Cash ........................................... | $ 50,000 | $130,000 |
| Accounts Receivable............................. | 100,000 | 110,000 |
| Less Allowance for Uncollectibles ...................... | (20,000) | (25,000) |
| Inventory ........................................ | 100,000 | 90,000 |
| Prepaid Rent...................................... | 220,000 | 250,000 |
| Total Assets ................................. | $450,000 | $555,000 |
| Accounts Payable ................................ | $ 20,000 | $ 40,000 |
| Capital Stock..................................... | 200,000 | 135,000 |
| Retained Earnings................................ | 230,000 | 380,000 |
| Total Equities ................................ | $450,000 | $555,000 |

| **Year 2 Income Statement** | |
|---|---|
| Gross Sales ...................................... | $500,000 |
| Less Sales Discounts .............................. | 5,000 |
| Net Sales..................................... | $495,000 |
| Cost of Goods Sold................................ | $200,000 |
| Bad Debt Expense ................................ | 15,000 |
| Rent Expense..................................... | 30,000 |
| Income Tax Expense .............................. | 100,000 |
| Total Expenses.................................... | $345,000 |
| Net Income ...................................... | $150,000 |

*Note:* During Year 2, $6,000 in specific accounts receivables were defaulted upon and written off as uncollectible.

**a.** What was the cost of marketable securities on hand at the end of Year 1?

**b.** Is the amount shown for these securities on hand at the end of Year 2 their cost or their market value? How do you know?

**c.** Assume that no new securities were acquired during Year 2. What was the cost of securities sold during Year 2?

**d.** Assume that on December 31, Year 2, WCI decided to sell its entire portfolio of securities early in Year 3 and, in anticipation of that event, reclassified the entire portfolio as a current asset. Give the journal entries that WCI would make, and indicate the effect of these entries on both the income statement for Year 2 and total owners' equity at the end of Year 2.

**43.** *Analysis of financial statement disclosures for marketable equity securities.* Exhibit 7.11 reproduces the marketable equity securities note of Sunshine Mining Company for a recent year, with dates changed for convenience. Assume that no holdings of current marketable securities were held at the end of Year 1, that no current marketable securities were sold during Year 2, and that no noncurrent marketable securities were purchased or transferred to the current

Exhibit 7.11 _____

**SUNSHINE MINING COMPANY**
**Data on Marketable Equity Securities**
**(all dollar amounts in thousands)**
**(Problem 43)**

| Marketable Equity Securities | Cost | Market Value | Balance Sheet Carrying Value |
|---|---|---|---|
| At December 31, Year 2: | | | |
| Current Marketable Securities.......... | $ 7,067 | $ 4,601 | $ 4,601 |
| Noncurrent Marketable Securities ...... | $ 6,158 | $ 8,807 | $ 6,158 |
| At December 31, Year 1: | | | |
| Noncurrent Marketable Securities ...... | $21,685 | $11,418 | $11,418 |

portfolio during Year 2. The income statement for Year 2 shows a realized loss on sale of noncurrent marketable securities of $3,068,000.

a. What amount for net unrealized gain or loss on noncurrent marketable securities appears on the balance sheet for the end of Year 1?

b. What amount for net unrealized gain or loss on noncurrent marketable securities appears on the balance sheet for the end of Year 2?

c. What were the proceeds of sale of noncurrent marketable securities sold during Year 2?

d. What amount for unrealized loss on holdings of marketable securities appears on the income statement for Year 2?

44. *Analysis of opportunity to manage income with selective sales from portfolio of marketable equity securities.* Insurance companies report holdings of marketable equity securities at market value on the balance sheet, but report only *realized* gains and losses in the income statement. Unrealized gains (losses) are credited (debited) directly to a balance sheet Owners' Equity account. The treatment of both gains and losses on all an insurance company's equity holdings is like that required by FASB *Statement No. 12* for losses on long-term investments in equity securities by noninsurance companies.

Assume that an insurance company has been in business long enough to hold a portfolio of equity securities, some of which have unrealized holding gains (market price increases since acquisition), whereas others have unrealized losses (market price decreases since acquisition). Its income can be manipulated as follows: If more income is wanted, sell securities with unrealized gains; if less income is wanted, sell securities with unrealized losses. Over long time spans, income can be smoothed, even if it cannot be managed arbitrarily. Limits to income management are imposed by the overall portfolio performance.

Sears, Roebuck and Co. owns 100 percent of Allstate Insurance Company. Sears's reported income includes only the realized gains and losses on Allstate's investments.

Exhibit 7.12 presents data for a recent decade for various items reported by Sears and Allstate. Column (1) shows Sears's income as reported, and column

Exhibit 7.12 ————————————————————————————————————————————

## SEARS, ROEBUCK AND CO. AND ALLSTATE INSURANCE COMPANY
Data on Income, Realized Holding Gains, and Unrealized Holding Gains
(all dollar amounts in millions)
(Problem 44)

| | In Reported Income (Loss) Items | | Allstate's Aftertax Realized Investment Gains (Losses) for Year (3) | Allstate's Unrealized Gains (Losses) for Year (4) | Size of Manageable Income Pool at Year-End (Pretax) | | |
|---|---|---|---|---|---|---|---|
| | Reported Total[a] | | | | Unrealized Gains on Securities with Gains (5) | Unrealized (Losses) on Securities with Losses (6) | Net Unrealized Pretax Gains (Losses) (7) |
| Year | Dollars (1) | Percent Change (2) | | | | | |
| 1 | $679.9 | | $26.1 | $(258.7) | NR | NR | $ (63.2) |
| | | −24.8 | | | | | |
| 2 | 511.4 | | 10.8 | (422.1) | NR | NR | (498.8) |
| | | 2.2 | | | | | |
| 3 | 522.6 | | 11.8 | 271.8 | $104.3 | $(304.6) | (200.3) |
| | | 32.9 | | | | | |
| 4 | 694.5 | | 8.0 | 129.6 | 140.2 | (211.0) | (70.8) |
| | | 20.7 | | | | | |
| 5 | 838.0 | | 1.7 | 26.2 | 128.4 | (172.2) | (43.8) |
| | | 10.0 | | | | | |
| 6 | 921.5 | | 16.0 | 36.5 | 156.2 | (162.0) | (5.8) |
| | | −12.1 | | | | | |
| 7 | 810.1 | | 24.9 | 79.5 | 234.6 | (121.1) | 113.5 |
| | | −25.2 | | | | | |
| 8 | 606.0 | | 52.5 | 76.5 | 391.0 | (118.4) | 272.6 |
| | | 7.3 | | | | | |
| 9 | 650.1 | | 58.0 | (103.8) | 227.8 | (159.7) | 68.1 |
| | | 32.5 | | | | | |
| 10 | 861.2 | | 31.5 | 123.0 | 374.7 | (133.8) | 240.9 |

[a]As originally reported, not as restated in subsequent reports for accounting changes.

NR: Not reported or disclosed.

Column (1): Taken from Sears's income statements; includes amounts in column (3) but not amounts in column (4).

Columns (3), (4), (5), and (6): Taken from Allstate's financial statements and notes thereto in the Sears's annual reports.

Column (7) = column (5) + column (6), if not separately reported.

(3) shows Allstate's realized gains and losses, after taxes, on its investments in equity securities.

Columns (5) through (7) show the magnitude of Sears/Allstate's opportunity for managing earnings. Examine Year 4, for example. At the end of Year 4, Allstate had $140.0 million of unrealized gains in its portfolio. Presumably, Allstate's, and hence Sears's, income could have been larger by up to $140.2 million (about 20 percent) before taxes. Similarly, at the end of Year 4 Allstate had $211.0 million of unrealized losses in its portfolio. Presumably, Allstate's income could have been smaller by $211.0 million (about 30 percent) before taxes.[14] Of course, these opportunities for income management implicit in the data in columns (5) through (7) are not independent of each other. If, for example, Allstate had realized all of the gains available at the end of Year 4, there would have been substantially smaller (perhaps zero) unrealized gains at the end of Year 5.

———————————

[14]These percentages are calculated before allowing for the effect of any income tax assessed against the gains and losses once they are realized. The effective income tax rate on such gains and losses is difficult to estimate before realization, and it is possible, by timing the realization of gains and losses judiciously, that the effective rate could be far below the statutory rate.

**a.** Compute the year-to-year changes in Sears's income *before* realized gains.

**b.** Compare these changes with the year-to-year changes in Sears's reported net income; analyze Sears's use of unrealized gains and losses in the All-state portfolio of marketable equity securities to smooth income over time.

45. *Management of marketable securities portfolios to affect income and financial statement ratios.* The chief financial officer (CFO) of Easton Company is nervous about the state of the company's financial affairs, as reflected in its tentative post-closing trial balance at the end of the current year, which appears in Exhibit 7.13. The CFO worries that the current ratio is too low.

Several years ago, the company borrowed $6 million in the form of a long-term bond issue, maturing 15 years from now and carrying an interest rate of 7.5 percent per year. Interest rates have increased substantially since then, and comparable borrowings would now cost the firm more than 10 percent per year. The CFO worries about terms of the bond agreement that require the firm to maintain a ratio of current assets to current liabilities of at least 1.20 to 1.00. If the current ratio falls below that amount, the bond issue becomes due imme-

**Exhibit 7.13** ————————————————————————

**EASTON COMPANY**
**Tentative Post-Closing Trial Balance at Current Year-End**
**(all dollar amounts in thousands)**
**(Problem 45)**

|  | Dr. | Cr. |
|---|---|---|
| Allowance for Excess of Cost of Marketable Securities over Market Value (current asset contra) .............. |  | $ 2,500 |
| Current Liabilities ..................................... |  | 5,500 |
| Investments in Marketable Equity Securities (noncurrent assets) ................................ | $ 3,000 |  |
| Marketable Equity Securities (current assets), at Cost .... | 3,500 |  |
| Noncurrent Liabilities.................................. |  | 6,000 |
| Other Current Assets ................................ | 5,000 |  |
| Other Noncurrent Assets, Net......................... | 12,000 |  |
| Owners' Equity Accounts ............................. |  | 9,500 |
| Totals ......................................... | $23,500 | $23,500 |

## Holdings of Equity Securities

|  | Cost | Year-End Market Value |
|---|---|---|
| **Current Assets:** |  |  |
| Company A ......................................... | $ 2,000 | $ 600 |
| Company B ......................................... | 1,500 | 400 |
| Total ......................................... | $ 3,500 | $ 1,000 |
|  |  |  |
| **Noncurrent Assets:** |  |  |
| Company C ......................................... | $ 1,000 | $ 5,000 |
| Company D ......................................... | 2,000 | 1,600 |
| Total ......................................... | $ 3,000 | $ 6,600 |

diately, rather than maturing at its original maturity date, which is still 15 years in the future. The CFO knows it will be costly to borrow new funds to replace the old ones and ponders the company's recent success in holding down its amounts of receivables and inventories, both sound management practices that reduce current assets but also reduce the current ratio.

Over the past several years Easton Company has acquired various holdings of marketable equity securities, some as current assets and some as noncurrent assets. Data on these holdings appear in Exhibit 7.13. The holdings of any one company were acquired in a single transaction. The CFO wonders what, if anything, can be done with the holdings of marketable equity securities to keep the call provision of the bond issue from being triggered.

The chief executive officer (CEO) of Easton Company has discussed these problems with the CFO and has raised another issue. The CEO's compensation package contains a bonus clause. As things now stand, the CEO will not receive a bonus because income for the year is $1.5 million short of the minimum for a bonus to be earned. Neither the CFO nor the CEO wants the firm to incur any extra income tax payments, as will become payable at a rate of 40 percent on any gains realized on sale of securities. Both the CEO and the CFO seek your advice.

**a.** Is the bond issue in danger of being declared due for current payment? Why or why not?

**b.** What actions, if any, can management of Easton Company undertake to protect the outstanding bond issue from coming due at the end of the current year without having to pay additional income taxes? Provide journal entries that record the actions you suggest. What is the effect on income? On owners' equity?

**c.** What actions, if any, can management undertake to boost reported income sufficiently so that the CEO will receive a bonus? Provide journal entries that record the actions you suggest. How will these actions affect the current ratio?

# Chapter 8  Inventories: The Source of Operating Profits ─────────

In the last 15 years, many major U.S. corporations have changed their accounting for inventories and cost of goods sold. As a result, these corporations reported net income that was hundreds of millions of dollars smaller than would have been reported without the change. Paradoxically, perhaps, these firms made themselves better off by changing. This chapter explains how a firm can be better off reporting smaller, rather than larger, net income. Income tax effects bring about this result. This chapter also introduces the choices that a firm must make in accounting for inventories and shows the impact of these decisions on reported expenses and net income for the period. The choices made in accounting for inventories can make two companies that are otherwise alike appear to be different.

## Inventory Terminology ──────────────────────

The term *inventory* means a stock of goods or other items owned by a firm and held for sale or for processing before being sold as part of a firm's ordinary business operations. Tools, for example, are inventory in the hands of a tool manufacturer or hardware store but not in the hands of a carpenter. Marketable securities are inventory in the hands of a securities dealer but not in the hands of a manufacturer.

Goods held for sale by a retail or wholesale business are called *merchandise inventory;* goods held for sale by a manufacturing concern are called *finished goods inventory*. The inventories of manufacturing firms also include *raw materials* (materials being stored that will become part of goods to be produced) and *work in process* (partially completed products in the factory). The balance sheet may also include inventories of supplies to be consumed in administrative, selling, and manufacturing operations.

To "inventory" a stock of goods means to prepare a list of the items on hand at some specified date, to assign a unit cost to each item, and to calculate the total cost of the goods.

# Significance of Accounting for Inventories _____

Financial accounting attempts to measure periodic income. Accounting for inventories affects income measurement by assigning costs to various accounting periods as expenses. The total cost of goods available for sale during a period must be allocated between the current period's use (cost of goods sold, an expense) and the amounts carried forward to future periods (end-of-period inventory, an asset now but later an expense).

## Inventory Equation

The *inventory equation* helps one understand accounting for inventory. In the following equation, all quantities are measured in physical units.

$$\underbrace{\text{Beginning Inventory + Additions}}_{\text{Goods Available for Use or Sale}} - \text{Withdrawals} = \text{Ending Inventory.}$$

If we begin a period with 2,000 pounds of sugar (beginning inventory) and if we purchase (add) 4,500 pounds during the period, there are 6,500 (= 2,000 + 4,500) pounds available for use. If we use (withdraw) 5,300 pounds during the period, there should be 1,200 pounds of sugar left at the end of the period (ending inventory).

The inventory equation can also be rewritten as follows:

$$\underbrace{\text{Beginning Inventory + Additions}}_{\text{Goods Available for Use or Sale}} - \text{Ending Inventory} = \text{Withdrawals.}$$

If we begin the period with 2,000 pounds of sugar, if we purchase 4,500 pounds of sugar, and if we observe 1,200 pounds of sugar on hand at the end of the period, we know that 5,300 (= 2,000 + 4,500 − 1,200) pounds of sugar were used or otherwise withdrawn from inventory during the period. The sum of Beginning Inventory plus Additions is usually called "Goods available for use or sale." In this example, there are 6,500 pounds of sugar available for use.

If accounting were concerned merely with tracing physical quantities, no conceptual problems in accounting would arise for inventories. But, of course, accounting reports on dollar amounts, not on physical quantities. When prices remain constant, inventory accounting problems are minor, because all items carry the same per-unit cost. Any variation in the values of inventories results only from changes in quantities. The major problems in inventory accounting arise because the unit acquisition costs of inventory items fluctuate over time.

To illustrate, suppose that an appliance store has a beginning inventory of one television set, TV set 1, which cost $250. Suppose further that two TV sets are purchased during the period, TV set 2 for $290 and TV set 3 for $300, and that one TV set is sold for $550. The three TV sets are exactly alike in all physical respects; only their costs differ. Assume that there is no way to know which TV set was sold.

The inventory equation can be written as follows, with all quantities measured in dollars of cost:

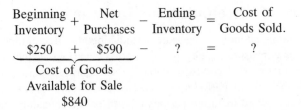

$$\underbrace{\begin{matrix}\text{Beginning} \\ \text{Inventory}\end{matrix} + \begin{matrix}\text{Net} \\ \text{Purchases}\end{matrix}}_{\substack{\text{Cost of Goods} \\ \text{Available for Sale} \\ \$840}} - \begin{matrix}\text{Ending} \\ \text{Inventory}\end{matrix} = \begin{matrix}\text{Cost of} \\ \text{Goods Sold.}\end{matrix}$$

If financial statements are prepared with amounts measured in dollar terms, some assumption must be made about which TV set was sold. There are at least four assumptions that can be made in applying the inventory equation to compute the Cost of Goods Sold expense for the income statement and the ending inventory for the balance sheet. Exhibit 8.1 shows these assumptions. As the inventory equation and the TV set example both show, the higher the Cost of Goods Sold, the lower the Ending Inventory. Which particular pair of numbers appears — one in the income statement and one in the balance sheet — reflects the cost flow assumption, a major accounting issue discussed later in the chapter.

## Problems of Inventory Accounting

The remainder of this chapter discusses four problems of inventory accounting:

1. The costs to be included in acquisition cost.
2. The valuation basis to be used for items in inventory.
3. The frequency of carrying out inventory computations — periodically or perpetually.
4. The cost flow assumption to be used to trace the movement of costs into and out of inventory, which may not parallel the physical movement of goods.

Because income tax laws affect some of a firm's choices in accounting for inventories, income taxes are discussed at appropriate places.

The following discussion can be divided into four distinct sections: computation of acquisition cost, subsequent valuation, timing of inventory computations, and cost flow assumptions. These four distinct problems should be kept in mind as the discussion proceeds.

**Exhibit 8.1** ————————————————————————————————————————————
**Assumptions for Inventory Illustrations**

| Assumed Item Sold | Cost of Goods Available for Sale (beginning inventory plus purchases)[a] | = Cost of Goods Sold (for income statement) | + Ending Inventory (for balance sheet) |
|---|---|---|---|
| TV Set 1 ..................... | $840 | $250 | $590 |
| TV Set 2 ..................... | 840 | 290 | 550 |
| TV Set 3 ..................... | 840 | 300 | 540 |
| Average TV Set ............... | 840 | 280[b] | 560[b] |

[a]Cost of goods available for sale = Cost of (TV set 1 + TV set 2 + TV set 3) = ($250 + $290 + $300) = $840.

[b]Average cost of a TV set = $840/3 = $280.

# Problem 1:
# Costs Included in Inventory at Acquisition _____

## Components of Inventory Cost

The amount on a balance sheet for inventory includes all costs incurred to acquire goods and prepare them for sale. For a merchandising firm, such costs should include purchasing, transportation, receiving, unpacking, inspecting, and shelving costs, as well as any bookkeeping and office costs for recording purchases.[1] The example on page 37 (in Chapter 2), showing the computation of the cost of some equipment, applies to inventory as well.

For a manufacturing firm, inventory costs include direct materials, direct labor, and manufacturing overhead. In a manufacturing firm, *all* production costs are debited to Work-in-Process Inventory; the process of recording these manufacturing costs is straightforward. The later allocation of costs in Work-in-Process Inventory to individual items transferred to the Finished Goods Inventory is not conceptually difficult, but it requires special techniques of cost accounting beyond the scope of this book. (See the glossary definition of *flow of costs*.) The procedure followed is called *full absorption costing* and is required for both external financial and income tax reporting.[2]

## The Purchase Transaction

The purchase transaction includes receiving goods, inspecting them, and recording the purchase. Legally, *purchases* should be recorded in the formal accounting records when title to the goods passes. The timing of title passage is often a technical question whose answer depends on many circumstances of the transaction. For convenience, the accountant usually recognizes purchases only after the invoice and

---

[1]Because the amounts involved are often relatively small, and because it is difficult to assign a definite dollar amount for many of these costs to specific purchases, practice has tended to restrict the actual additions to a few significant items that can easily be identified with particular goods, such as transportation costs. The costs of operating a purchasing department, the salaries and expenses of buyers, the costs of the receiving and warehousing departments, and the costs of handling and shelving must, for tax purposes, be included in inventory cost. For financial reporting purposes, many firms include these costs in inventory as well, although practice is not uniform.

[2]An alternative procedure, known as *variable costing* (or sometimes *direct costing*), may be superior for internal management purposes.

In the variable costing procedure, product costs are classified into variable manufacturing costs (those that tend to vary with output) and fixed manufacturing costs (those that tend to be relatively unaffected in the short run by the number of units produced). Nonvariable (fixed) manufacturing costs are treated in the same way as selling and administrative costs; that is, they are treated as expenses assigned to the period of incurrence rather than as costs assignable to the product produced. Nonvariable manufacturing costs are charged in their entirety against revenues in calculating net income for the period.

When full absorption costing is used, unit costs of products manufactured tend to vary inversely with the total number of units produced because a given amount of fixed costs is allocated to all the units produced. The larger the number of units produced, the smaller the per-unit cost.

Generally accepted accounting principles prohibit the issuing of financial statements based on variable costing. Because variable costing is not a generally accepted accounting principle, managerial accounting courses discuss the criticism of full absorption costing and suggested benefits of variable costing for internal management uses.

the goods are received and inspected. Adjustments may be made at the end of the accounting period to reflect the legal formalities for goods in transit that belong to the purchaser or for goods on hand that still belong to the seller.

## Merchandise Purchases Adjustments

The invoice price of goods purchased seldom measures the total acquisition cost. Additional costs are incurred in transporting and handling the goods; deductions may be required for cash discounts, goods returned, and other adjustments of the invoice price. All of these adjustments could be debited or credited to the Merchandise Inventory account. Frequently, however, a number of contra and adjunct accounts are used for these adjustments so that a more complete analysis of the cost of purchases is available. Purchase Discounts, Freight-in, Purchase Returns, and Purchase Allowances accounts are used to provide the needed detail. The accounting for purchase adjustments closely parallels the accounting for sales adjustments discussed in Chapter 7.

The largest adjustment to the invoice price of merchandise is likely to be that for *purchase discounts*. Sellers often offer a discount from the invoice price for prompt payment. For example, the terms of sale "2/10, net/30" mean that a 2 percent discount from invoice price is offered if payment is made within 10 days, and otherwise the full invoice price is due within 30 days.[3] Purchase discounts become a reduction in the purchase price. Two methods for recording purchases and the later treatment at time of payment (depending on whether the discount is actually taken) are the *gross price method* and the *net price method*. Problem 28 at the end of the chapter describes and illustrates these methods of record keeping.

## Problem 2: Bases of Inventory Valuation ——————————

The basis for valuing inventory — the rule for assigning a cost to a physical unit — affects both periodic net income and the amount at which inventories appear on the balance sheet. At least five valuation bases are used for one purpose or another: acquisition cost, current cost measured by replacement cost, current cost measured by net realizable value, lower of (acquisition) cost or market, and standard cost. Some of the following discussion reviews fundamentals considered in Chapter 2. Generally accepted accounting principles require the use of the lower-of-cost-or-market basis for most purposes.

### Acquisition Cost Basis

The *acquisition cost basis* values units in inventory at their historical cost until sold. In accounting, the terms *acquisition cost* and *historical cost* mean the same thing.

---

[3]Problem 28 at the end of Appendix A demonstrates that the interest rate implied in these terms of sales is about 45 percent per year; that is, a purchaser who does not take such a discount is borrowing money at an interest rate of about 45 percent per year. Most purchasers find it advantageous to take such discounts and to borrow elsewhere at lower rates.

Using acquisition costs implies using the *realization convention:* Gains (or losses) caused by increases (or decreases) in the market value of assets do not appear in income until the particular assets are sold. When the acquisition cost basis is used, only sales transactions affect income. Any changes in the value of inventory items occurring between the time of acquisition and the time of sale are not recognized. The figure shown on the balance sheet for inventory becomes out of date to the extent that prices have changed since the items were acquired. The longer the period of time since acquisition, the more likely it is that the current value of the inventory will differ from its acquisition cost.

## Current Cost Basis

A current cost basis values units in inventory at a current market price. Two current cost bases discussed here are (1) current entry value, often called replacement cost, and (2) current exit value, often called net realizable value. When inventories are stated at current cost, gains and losses from changes in prices are recognized during the holding period that elapses between acquisition (or production) and the time of sale.

Whereas acquisition cost for inventory shows objective, verifiable information that may be out of date, current cost shows up-to-date information, which can be more useful, but the amount shown may be more difficult to measure and to audit.

**Replacement Cost (Entry Value)**  The *replacement cost* of an item at a given time is the amount a firm would have to pay to acquire the item at that time. In computing replacement cost, one assumes a fair market (or arm's-length) transaction between a willing buyer and a willing seller. One also assumes that the inventory is bought in the customary fashion in the customary quantities. Replacement cost does not imply the forced purchase of inventory by a frantic buyer from a hoarding seller (which probably implies a premium price) or purchases of abnormally large quantities (which often can be bought at a lower-than-normal price) or purchases of abnormally small quantities (which usually cost more per unit to acquire).

**Net Realizable Value (Exit Value)**  The amount that a firm could realize as a willing seller (not a distressed seller) in an arm's-length transaction with a willing buyer in the ordinary course of business is *net realizable value*. The measurement of net realizable value can present problems for items of inventory not yet ready for sale (for example, partially complete inventory in a manufacturing firm). Additional manufacturing costs will have to be incurred before the item can be sold. Also, a sales commission and other selling costs, such as packaging and freight costs, will probably be incurred. In these cases, net realizable value is the estimated final selling price of the inventory less the estimated costs necessary to make the item ready for sale and to sell it. As examples, consider agricultural products and precious metals on hand at the close of an accounting period. These are often stated at net realizable value. It may be easier to estimate a market price less selling costs than to measure the historical cost of a bushel of apples harvested from an orchard.

## Lower-of-Cost-or-Market Basis

The *lower-of-cost-or-market valuation basis* is the lesser of the two amounts — acquisition cost or market value — the latter generally measured as replacement cost.[4]

A decline of $5,000 in the market value of inventory is recognized with the following entry:

---

| | | |
|---|---|---|
| Loss from Decline in Value of Inventory . . . . . . . . . . . . . . . . . . . . . . | 5,000 | |
|   Inventory . . . . . . . . . . . . . . . . . . . . . . . . . . . . . . . . . . . . . . . . . . . | | 5,000 |

---

The entry directly credits the Inventory account, not a contra account as is done for marketable securities (explained in Chapter 7), because subsequent recoveries in market value are not recorded as gains. Under some approaches to inventory accounting, the previous entry is not recorded explicitly; instead, the loss appears as a higher cost of goods sold. Consider, for example, the calculation in Exhibit 8.2 of cost of goods sold when beginning inventory is $19,000, purchases are $100,000, and ending inventory has a cost of $25,000 but has a market value of $20,000.

Note that cost of goods sold is $5,000 larger under the lower-of-cost-or-market basis than under the acquisition cost basis. The loss of $5,000 is not reported separately, but income will be $5,000 smaller than when the acquisition cost basis is used. If the amount of the write-down to market is so large that the reader of the statements will be misled without separate disclosure of the decline in market value, the write-down can be shown as an adjustment to cost of goods sold or as a loss, separately reported as part of operating activities.

The lower-of-cost-or-market basis for inventory valuation is called a conservative policy because (1) losses from decreases in market value are recognized before

**Exhibit 8.2** _____

### Calculating Cost of Goods Sold Illustrating
### Different Bases of Inventory Valuation

| | Cost Basis | Lower-of-Cost-or Market Basis |
|---|---|---|
| Beginning Inventory . . . . . . . . . . . . . . . . . . . . . . . . . . . . . . . . . | $ 19,000 | $ 19,000 |
| Purchases . . . . . . . . . . . . . . . . . . . . . . . . . . . . . . . . . . . . . . . . | 100,000 | 100,000 |
| Goods Available for Sale . . . . . . . . . . . . . . . . . . . . . . . . . . . | $119,000 | $119,000 |
| Less Ending Inventory . . . . . . . . . . . . . . . . . . . . . . . . . . . . . | (25,000) | (20,000) |
| Cost of Goods Sold . . . . . . . . . . . . . . . . . . . . . . . . . . . . . . . . | $ 94,000 | $ 99,000 |

---

[4] Actually, the definition of "market value" in the computation of lower of cost or market is more complex than mere replacement cost. Market value is replacement cost but no more than net realizable value nor less than the quantity net realizable value reduced by a normal profit margin on sales of items of this type. See the glossary definition of *lower of cost or market*.

goods are sold, but gains from increases in market value are not recorded before a sale takes place; and (2) inventory figures on the balance sheet are never greater, but may be less, than acquisition cost. In other words, *holding losses* are reported currently, whereas *holding gains* are not reported until the goods are sold.

Over sufficiently long time spans, however, income equals cash in less cash out. For any one unit, there is only one total gain or loss figure — the difference between its selling price and its acquisition cost. The valuation rule merely determines how this gain or loss is spread over the accounting periods between acquisition and final disposition. When the lower-of-cost-or-market basis is used, the net income of the present period may be conservatively lower than if the acquisition cost basis was used, but if so, the net income of a later period, when the unit is sold, will be higher.

## Standard Costs

*Standard cost* is a predetermined estimate of what items of manufactured inventory *should* cost. Studies of past and estimated future cost data provide the basis for standard costs. Manufacturing firms frequently use standard cost systems for internal performance measurement and control. Managerial and cost accounting texts discuss these uses. Standard cost is also used occasionally as the valuation basis for preparing financial statements. Units in inventory may be valued at standard cost, especially in the preparation of monthly or quarterly statements.[5]

## Generally Accepted Accounting Basis for Inventory Valuation

Accounting uses a historical cost basis for most assets. Because the market value of some inventory items can be significantly less than acquisition cost, either because of price changes for this kind of inventory in general or because of physical deterioration of the particular items in an inventory, generally accepted accounting principles require lower of cost or market for inventory.[6] This is the same as saying that market values must be used in some cases. Computing market value requires both replacement cost and net realizable value amounts. Thus generally accepted accounting principles for inventory valuation and measurement of cost of goods sold require a combination of three valuation bases: acquisition cost, replacement cost, and net realizable value. In a period of rising prices, replacement cost and net realizable value are likely to be higher than acquisition cost, so valuation at cost and the lower of cost or market usually give the same valuation.

---

[5]If so, any excess of actual cost over standard cost (called an *unfavorable variance*) is usually debited to cost of goods sold or to other expenses of the period. If actual cost is less than standard cost, the favorable variance is usually credited to cost of goods sold.

[6]Committee on Accounting Procedure, *Accounting Research Bulletin No. 43,* "Inventory Pricing," Chapter 4, Statements 5 and 6, AICPA, 1953.

# Problem 3: Timing of Computations ————————

Two principal approaches to calculating the physical quantity and dollar amount of an inventory are the *periodic* inventory system and the *perpetual* inventory system. The periodic inventory system is less expensive to use than the perpetual system because it involves fewer accounting computations, but the perpetual inventory system provides useful information not provided by the periodic system.

## Periodic Inventory System

In a *periodic inventory system,* the ending inventory figure results from making a physical count of units on hand at the end of an accounting period and multiplying the quantity on hand by the cost per unit. Then the inventory equation is used to calculate the withdrawals that represent the cost-of-goods-sold expense. The following form of the inventory equation computes the cost of goods sold under a periodic system:

$$\underbrace{\begin{array}{l}\text{Beginning} \\ \text{Inventory} \\ \text{(known)}\end{array} + \begin{array}{l}\text{Purchases} \\ \text{(known)}\end{array}}_{\begin{array}{c}\text{Goods Available} \\ \text{for Use or Sale}\end{array}} - \begin{array}{l}\text{Ending} \\ \text{Inventory} \\ \text{(counted} \\ \text{and costed)}\end{array} = \begin{array}{l}\text{Cost of} \\ \text{Goods Sold} \\ \text{(solved for).}\end{array}$$

When a periodic system is used, no entry is made for withdrawals (cost of goods sold) until the inventory on hand at the end of the accounting period is counted and costed.

To illustrate the periodic system, assume that sales during the year amounted to $165,000. The entries made to record sales during the year would have the combined effect of the following entry:

| | | |
|---|---|---|
| Cash and Accounts Receivable ............................. | 165,000 | |
| Sales..................................................... | | 165,000 |
| Sales recorded for the entire year have this effect. | | |

At the end of the year, a physical count is taken, inventory costs are assigned, and the cost of the withdrawals is computed from the inventory equation. Exhibit 8.2 derives cost of goods sold for the lower-of-cost-or-market basis embedded in a periodic inventory system. We assume that all purchases have been debited to the Merchandise Inventory account. The cost-of-goods-sold expense is recognized in a single entry:

| | | |
|---|---|---|
| Cost of Goods Sold........................................ | 99,000 | |
| Merchandise Inventory .................................... | | 99,000 |
| Cost of goods sold recognized under a periodic inventory system. | | |

A periodic inventory system generates no separate information to aid in controlling the amount of inventory *shrinkage* (the general name for losses such as breakage, theft, evaporation, and waste). All goods not in the physical ending inventory count are assumed to have been either sold or used. Any losses from shrinkage appear in the cost of goods sold amount. Furthermore, physically counting the inventory at the end of the accounting period can seriously interfere with normal business operations for several days. Some firms using the periodic inventory system even close down and engage a large staff in physically counting the items on hand. Preparing income statements more frequently than once a year is expensive when the inventory figures result only from physically counting inventories.[7]

## Perpetual Inventory System

In a *perpetual (continuous)* inventory system, cost of goods sold is calculated and recorded whenever an item is taken from inventory. A perpetual inventory system requires a constant tracing of costs as items move into and out of inventory. Such entries as the following may be made from day to day:

| | | |
|---|---|---|
| Accounts Receivable......................................... | 800 | |
|   Sales...................................................... | | 800 |
| Cost of Goods Sold.......................................... | 475 | |
|   Finished Goods Inventory ..................................... | | 475 |
| To record the cost of goods withdrawn from inventory and sold for $800. | | |

After postings for a period have been completed, the balance in the Merchandise Inventory account is the cost of the goods that *should* be on hand. Statements can be prepared without carrying out a physical count of inventory. In a perpetual inventory system, the following form of the inventory equation computes goods expected to remain in the ending inventory after each acquisition or withdrawal:

$$\underbrace{\underset{\text{(known)}}{\text{Beginning Inventory}} + \underset{\text{(known)}}{\text{Purchases}}}_{\text{Goods Available for Use or Sale}} - \underset{\text{(recorded)}}{\text{Withdrawals}} = \underset{\text{(solved for)}}{\text{Ending Inventory}}.$$

Using a perpetual inventory system does not eliminate the need to take a physical inventory in which the items of inventory on hand are counted and costed. A physical count and assignment of costs to remaining items enables measurement of any loss from shrinkage. The loss is the difference between the amounts in the Inventory account and the cost of the goods actually on hand. To illustrate, assume that a book balance for inventory shows $10,000, while the physical count reveals the inventory on hand costs $9,200. The entry to record the shrinkage is as follows:

_____

[7]The gross margin method and retail inventory methods provide for approximating ending inventory costs when counts cannot easily be taken. Intermediate accounting texts discuss these methods, but Problems 30 and 31 at the end of this chapter introduce them.

| | | |
|---|---|---|
| Loss from Inventory Shrinkage ............................... | 800 | |
| Merchandise Inventory ....................................... | | 800 |

To write down inventory from book amount of $10,000 to actual amount of $9,200.

The credit reduces the book amount of inventory from its recorded amount, $10,000, to the correct amount, $9,200. The debit is to a Loss account or, if immaterial, to Cost of Goods Sold. In either case, it reduces net income for the current period.

Some businesses using a perpetual approach make a complete physical check at the end of the accounting period, in the same way as when a periodic inventory is used. But others use a more effective procedure. Rather than taking the inventory of all items at one time, the count may be staggered throughout the period. For example, a college bookstore may check actual physical amounts of textbooks with the inventory account amounts at the end of the school year, whereas the comparison for beach wear might be done in November. All items should be counted at least once during every year, but not all items need to be counted at the same time. The count of a particular item should be scheduled for a time when the stock on hand is near its low point for the year.

## Choosing between Periodic and Perpetual Inventory Systems

A perpetual inventory system helps maintain up-to-date information on quantities actually on hand. It is justified when being "out of stock" may lead to costly consequences, such as customer dissatisfaction or the need to shut down production lines. In such cases, a perpetual inventory system might keep track of the physical quantities of inventory but not the dollar amounts. Controlling losses is easier under a perpetual system, because inventory records always indicate the goods that should remain. A periodic inventory system usually costs less than a perpetual inventory system, but it provides no data on shrinkages.

As with other choices that have to be made in business, costs should be compared with benefits. A periodic inventory system is likely to be cost-effective when being out of stock will not be extremely costly, when there is a large volume of items with a small value per unit, or when items are hard to steal or pilfer. Perpetual inventory systems are cost-effective when there is a small volume of high-value items or when running out of stock is costly.

As the cost of record keeping with computers declines, the cost of perpetual inventories declines. Their use, therefore, increases over time.

## Problem 4: Cost Flow Assumptions _____

### Specific Identification and the Need for a Cost Flow Assumption

Individual units sold can sometimes be physically matched with a specific purchase. If so, no special problems arise in ascertaining the acquisition cost of the units withdrawn from inventory and the cost of the units still on hand. For example, cost can be marked on the unit or on its container, or the unit can be traced back to its purchase invoice or cost record. The inventory and cost of goods sold of an automobile dealer or of a dealer in diamonds or fur coats might be computed using specific identification of costs.

In most cases, however, new items are mixed with old units on shelves, in bins, or in other ways, and physical identification is not feasible. Accounting traces cost flows, not flows of goods. Moreover, to assume that cost flows differ from physical flows of goods may be desirable (for reasons to be discussed in this section).

## Flow of Historical Costs

The inventory costing problem arises because of two unknowns in the inventory equation:

$$\underbrace{\begin{array}{c} \text{Beginning} \\ \text{Inventory} \\ \text{(known)} \end{array} + \begin{array}{c} \text{Net} \\ \text{Purchases} \\ \text{(known)} \end{array}}_{\substack{\text{Goods Available} \\ \text{for Use or Sale}}} = \begin{array}{c} \text{Cost of} \\ \text{Goods Sold} \\ \text{(unknown)} \end{array} + \begin{array}{c} \text{Ending} \\ \text{Inventory} \\ \text{(unknown).} \end{array}$$

We know the costs of the beginning inventory and net purchases but not the amounts for cost of goods sold and ending inventory. The question is whether to compute amounts for the units in ending inventory using the most recent costs, the oldest costs, the average cost, or some other choice. Of course, the question could have been put in terms of computing amounts for the cost of goods sold, for once we place an amount on one unknown quantity, the inventory equation automatically determines the amount of the other. The sum of the two unknowns, Cost of Goods Sold and Ending Inventory, must equal the cost of goods available for sale (= beginning inventory plus net purchases). The higher the cost assigned to one unknown, the lower must be the cost assigned to the other.

When prices are changing, no historical cost-based accounting method for costing ending inventory and cost of goods sold allows the accountant to show recent costs on both the income statement and the balance sheet. Consider, for example, a period of rising prices. If recent, higher acquisition prices are used in measuring cost of goods sold for the income statement, older, lower acquisition prices must be used in costing the ending inventory for the balance sheet. As long as cost of goods sold and ending inventory are based on acquisition costs, financial statements can present current amounts in the income statement or the balance sheet, but not in both. Of course, combinations of current and out-of-date information can appear in both statements.

If more than one purchase is made of the same item at different prices and specific identification is not feasible, some assumption must be made about the flow of costs. The accountant computes the acquisition cost applicable to the units remaining in the inventory using one of three *cost flow assumptions:*

1. First-in, first-out (FIFO)
2. Last-in, first-out (LIFO)
3. Weighted average

The following demonstrations of each of these methods use the TV set example introduced earlier and repeated at the top of Exhibit 8.3. The example of the three TV sets illustrates most of the important points about the cost flow assumption required in accounting for inventories and cost of goods sold. The first problem for self-study at the end of this chapter illustrates the techniques more realistically but contains no new concepts.

## First-In, First-Out

The *first-in, first-out* cost flow assumption, abbreviated *FIFO,* assigns the cost of the earliest units acquired to the withdrawals and the cost of the most recent acquisitions to the ending inventory. This cost flow assumes that the oldest materials and goods are used first. This cost flow assumption conforms to good business practice in managing physical flows, especially in the case of items that deteriorate or become obsolete. Column (1) of Exhibit 8.3 illustrates FIFO. TV set 1 is assumed to be sold, whereas TV sets 2 and 3 are assumed to remain in inventory. The designation FIFO refers to the cost flow of units sold. A parallel description for ending inventory is last-in, still-here, or LISH.

## Last-In, First-Out

The *last-in, first-out* cost flow assumption, abbreviated *LIFO,* assigns the cost of the latest units acquired to the withdrawals and the cost of the oldest units to the ending inventory. Some theorists argue that LIFO matches current costs to current revenues and, therefore, that LIFO better measures income. Column (3) of Exhibit 8.3 illustrates LIFO. The $300 cost of TV set 3 is assumed to leave, whereas the costs of TV sets 1 and 2 are assumed to remain in inventory. The designation of LIFO refers to the cost flow for units sold. A parallel description for ending inventory is first-in, still-here, or FISH.

Firms have increasingly used LIFO since it first became acceptable for income tax reporting in 1939. In a period of consistently rising prices, LIFO results in a higher cost of goods sold, a lower reported periodic income, and lower current income taxes than either FIFO or weighted-average cost flow assumptions.

LIFO usually does not reflect physical flows but is used because it produces a cost-of-goods-sold figure based on more up-to-date prices. In a period of rising prices, LIFO's higher (than FIFO's) cost-of-goods-sold figure reduces reported income and income taxes. Income tax factors are discussed in a later section.

## Weighted Average

Under the *weighted-average* cost flow assumption, the average of the costs of all goods available for sale (or use) during the accounting period, including the cost applicable to the beginning inventory, must be calculated.[8] The weighted-average

---

[8]This description is technically correct only when a periodic inventory system is used. The first problem for self-study at the end of this chapter explores the procedures for applying the weighted-average method in a perpetual inventory system.

**Exhibit 8.3** _____

## Comparison of Cost Flow Assumptions, Historical Cost Basis

**Assumed Data**

| | |
|---|---:|
| Beginning Inventory: TV Set 1 Cost . . . . . . . . . . . . . . . . . . . . . . . . . . . . . . . . . . . . . . . . | $250 |
| Purchases:          TV Set 2 Cost . . . . . . . . . . . . . . . . . . . . . . . . . . . . . . . . . . . . . . . . | 290 |
|                     TV Set 3 Cost . . . . . . . . . . . . . . . . . . . . . . . . . . . . . . . . . . . . . . . . | 300 |
| Cost of Goods Available for Sale . . . . . . . . . . . . . . . . . . . . . . . . . . . . . . . . . . . . . . . . | $840 |
| Sales: One TV set . . . . . . . . . . . . . . . . . . . . . . . . . . . . . . . . . . . . . . . . . . . . . . . . . . | $550 |

| | Cost Flow Assumption | | |
|---|---|---|---|
| **Financial Statements** | **FIFO**<br>**(1)** | **Weighted Average**<br>**(2)** | **LIFO**<br>**(3)** |
| Sales. . . . . . . . . . . . . . . . . . . . . . . . . . . . . . . . . . . . . . . | $550 | $550 | $550 |
| Cost of Goods Sold . . . . . . . . . . . . . . . . . . . . . . . . | 250[a] | 280[b] | 300[c] |
| Gross Margin on Sales . . . . . . . . . . . . . . . . . . . . . . | $300 | $270 | $250 |
| Ending Inventory . . . . . . . . . . . . . . . . . . . . . . . . . . | $590[d] | $560[e] | $540[f] |

[a]TV set 1 costs $250.

[b]Average TV set costs $280 (= $840/3).

[c]TV set 3 costs $300.

[d]TV sets 2 and 3 cost $290 + $300 = $590.

[e]Two average TV sets cost 2 × $280 = $560.

[f]TV sets 1 and 2 cost $250 + $290 = $540.

cost is applied to the units on hand at the end of the month. Column (2) in Exhibit 8.3 illustrates the weighted-average cost flow assumption. The weighted-average cost of TV sets available for sale during the period is $280 [$= \frac{1}{3} \times$ ($250 + $290 + $300)]. Cost of Goods Sold is thus $280, and ending inventory is $560 (= 2 × $280).

## Comparison of Cost Flow Assumptions

FIFO results in balance sheet figures that are closest to current cost, because the latest purchases dominate the ending inventory amounts. Remember LISH — last-in, still-here. The cost-of-goods-sold expense tends to be out of date, however, because FIFO assumes that the earlier prices of the beginning inventory and the earliest purchases are charged to expense. When prices rise, FIFO usually leads to the highest reported net income of the three methods, and when prices fall it leads to the smallest.

Because LIFO ending inventory can contain costs of items acquired many years previously, LIFO produces balance sheet figures usually much lower than current costs. LIFO's cost-of-goods-sold figure closely approximates current costs. Exhibit 8.4 summarizes the differences between FIFO and LIFO. Of the cost flow assumptions, LIFO usually implies the smallest net income when prices are rising (highest

Exhibit 8.4 _____

### Age of Information about Inventory Items

| Cost Flow Assumption | Income Statement | Balance Sheet | Inventory-on-Hand Assumption |
|---|---|---|---|
| FIFO . . . . . . . . . . . . . . . . . . . | Old Prices | Current Prices . . . . . . . . . . . . . . | LISH |
| LIFO . . . . . . . . . . . . . . . . . . . | Current Prices | Very[a] Old Prices . . . . . . . . . . . . | FISH |

[a]The oldest prices on the FIFO income statement are just over 1 year old in nearly all cases, and the *average* price on the FIFO income statement (for a year) is slightly more than $\frac{1}{2}$ year old. The larger the rate of inventory turnover, the closer the average age on the income statement is to $\frac{1}{2}$ year. LIFO balance sheet items are generally much older than FIFO income statement items, with some costs from the 1940s in many cases.

cost of goods sold) and the largest when prices are falling (lowest cost of goods sold). Also, LIFO results in the least fluctuation in reported income in businesses where selling prices tend to change as current prices of inventory items change.

The weighted-average cost flow assumption falls between the other two in its effect on both the balance sheet and the income statement. It is, however, much more like FIFO than like LIFO in its effects on the balance sheet. When inventory turns over rapidly, the weighted-average inventory costs reflect current prices almost as much as FIFO.

## A Closer Look at LIFO's Effects on Financial Statements

As was previously discussed, LIFO usually presents a cost-of-goods-sold figure that reflects current costs. It also generally has the practical advantage of deferring income taxes. If a firm uses a LIFO flow assumption in its income tax return, it must also use LIFO in its financial reports to shareholders.

In the last 15 years, many firms, including Du Pont, General Motors, Eastman Kodak, and Sears, have switched from FIFO to LIFO. Given the rapid rate of price increases over the past decade, the switch from FIFO to LIFO has resulted in substantially lower cash payments for income taxes. For example, when Du Pont and General Motors switched from FIFO to LIFO, they each lowered current income taxes by about $150 million. At the same time, these firms reported lower net income to shareholders than would have been reported if FIFO had still been used.[9]

**LIFO Layers**   In any year when purchases exceed sales, the quantity of units in inventory increases. The amount added to inventory for that year is called a *LIFO inventory layer*. For example, assume that a firm acquires 10 TV sets each year and sells 8 TV sets each year for 4 years. Its inventory at the end of the fourth year would be 8 units. The cost of the 8 units under LIFO is the costs of sets numbered 1 and 2 (from the first year), 11 and 12 (from the second year), 21 and 22 (from the third year), and 31 and 32 (from the fourth year). Common terminology would say that this firm has four LIFO layers, each labeled with its year of acquisition. The

_____

[9]Thus the apparent paradox in the introduction to this chapter is explained.

**Exhibit 8.5** _____

**Data for Illustration of LIFO Dips**
**(Inventory at January 1, Year 5)**

| LIFO Layers | | Cost | |
|---|---|---|---|
| Year Purchased | Number of Units | Per Unit | Total Cost |
| 1 ..................................... | 100 | $ 50 | $ 5,000 |
| 2 ..................................... | 110 | 60 | 6,600 |
| 3 ..................................... | 120 | 80 | 9,600 |
| 4 ..................................... | 130 | 100 | 13,000 |
| | 460 | | $34,200 |

physical units on hand would almost certainly be the most recently acquired units in Year 4, but they would appear on the balance sheet at costs incurred for purchases during each of the 4 years.

**Dipping into LIFO Layers**   A firm using LIFO must be mindful of dipping into old LIFO layers. LIFO reduces current taxes in periods of rising prices and rising inventory quantities. If inventory quantities decline, however, the opposite effect occurs in the year of the decline: Older, lower costs per unit of prior years' LIFO layers leave the balance sheet and are charged to expense.

   If a firm must for some reason reduce end-of-period physical inventory quantities below what they were at the beginning of the period, cost of goods sold will be based on the current period's purchases plus a portion of the older and lower costs in the beginning inventory. Such a firm will have lower cost of goods sold as well as larger reported income and income taxes in that period than if the firm had been able to maintain its ending inventory at beginning-of-period levels.

**Example of Dip into LIFO Layers**   Assume that LIFO inventory at the beginning of Year 5 consists of 460 units with a total cost of $34,200; see Exhibit 8.5. Assume that the cost at the end of Year 5 is $120 per unit. If, for some reason, Year 5 ending inventory drops to 100 units, all 360 units purchased in Year 2 through Year 4 will also enter cost of goods sold. These 360 units cost $29,200 (= $6,600 + $9,600 + $13,000), but the current cost of comparable units is $43,200 (= 360 units × $120 per unit). Cost of goods sold will be $14,000 (= $43,200 − $29,200) smaller than if quantities had not declined because of the dip into old LIFO layers of inventory. Income subject to income taxes will be $14,000 larger than if inventory had been purchased so that quantities had not declined from 460 to 100 units.

**Annual Report of Disclosure of Dip into LIFO Layers**   Many firms actually using LIFO have inventory layers built up since the 1940s, and the costs of the early units are often as little as 10 percent of the current cost. For these firms, a dip into old layers will substantially increase income. A footnote from an earlier annual report of USX Corporation (formerly U.S. Steel) illustrates this phenomenon:

Because of the continuing high demand throughout the year, inventories of many steel-making materials and steel products were unavoidably reduced and could not be replaced during the year. Under the LIFO system of accounting, used for many years by U.S. Steel, the net effect of all the inventory changes [reductions] was to increase income for the year by about $16 million [about 5 percent].

In recent years, USX has shortened its explanation; for example, in a year when it reported a loss of $36 million, it said:

Cost of sales has been reduced and income from all operations increased by $621 million . . . from the liquidations of LIFO inventories.

**LIFO's Effects on Purchasing Behavior**  Consider the quandary faced by a purchasing manager of a LIFO firm nearing the end of a year when the quantity sold has exceeded the quantity purchased so far during the year. If the year ends with sales greater than purchases, the firm will dip into old LIFO layers and will have to pay increased taxes. Assume that the purchasing manager thinks current prices for the goods are abnormally high and prefers to delay making purchases until prices drop, presumably in the next year. However, waiting implies dips into old LIFO layers during this period and higher taxes. Buying now may entail higher inventory and carrying costs.

LIFO can induce firms to manage LIFO layers and cost of goods sold in a way that would be unwise in the absence of tax effects. LIFO also gives management the opportunity to manipulate income: Under LIFO, end-of-year purchases, which can be manipulated, affect net income for the year.

**LIFO Balance Sheet**  LIFO usually leads to a balance sheet amount for inventory so much less than current costs that it may mislead readers of financial statements. For example, in recent years USX has reported that the cost of its ending inventory based on LIFO is about one-half of what it would have been had FIFO been used. USX's inventory on the balance sheet, reported assuming LIFO cost flow, comprises about 10 percent of total assets. Using FIFO cost flow, inventory would be about 25 percent of total assets.

Consider the current ratio (= current assets/current liabilities). Some financial statement analysts use the current ratio to assess the short-term liquidity of a company. If LIFO is used in periods of rising prices while inventory quantities are increasing, the amount of inventory included in the numerator will be much smaller than it would be if the inventory was valued at current prices. Hence, the unwary reader may underestimate the liquidity of a company that uses a LIFO cost flow assumption.

Similarly, the calculation of inventory turnover (= cost of goods sold/average inventory during the period) can be drastically affected by the use of LIFO. Again referring to the USX example, the inventory turnover ratio from the financial statements constructed assuming LIFO cost flow is about twice as large as would result from FIFO cost flow. One of the self-study problems at the end of this chapter explores this phenomenon.

## The Impact of FIFO versus LIFO on Financial Statements: An Illustration

No accounting method for inventories based on historical cost can simultaneously report current data in both the income statement and the balance sheet. If a firm reports current prices in the income statement under LIFO, its balance sheet amount for ending inventory contains some *very* old costs. The SEC is concerned that readers of financial statements not be misled by out-of-date information. It requires firms using LIFO to disclose in notes to the financial statements the amounts by which LIFO inventories would have increased if they had been recorded at FIFO or current cost.[10] From this disclosure and the inventory equation, we can compute what a LIFO firm's income would have been if it had instead been using FIFO. In this way, the financial statements of firms using LIFO can be made more comparable with the financial statements of firms using FIFO.

A note to the financial statements of General Electric Company states, in part:

If the FIFO method of inventory accounting had been used to value all inventories, they would have been $2,240 [million] higher than reported at [year end and] $1,950 [million] higher at [the beginning of the year].

General Electric's beginning inventories under LIFO amounted to $3,161 million, its ending inventory amounted to $3,343 million, and its cost of goods sold totaled $17,751 million. Exhibit 8.6 demonstrates the calculation of cost of goods sold on a FIFO basis. Recall from the inventory equation:

$$\frac{\text{Beginning}}{\text{Inventory}} + \text{Purchases} - \frac{\text{Ending}}{\text{Inventory}} = \frac{\text{Cost of}}{\text{Goods Sold}}.$$

FIFO's higher beginning inventory increases the reported cost of goods available for sale and the cost of goods sold by $1,950 million, relative to LIFO. FIFO's higher ending inventory decreases cost of goods sold by $2,240 million, relative to LIFO. Hence, the cost of goods sold is $2,240 million minus $1,950 million, or $290 million less under FIFO than it would be under LIFO. General Electric's pretax income would be $290 million more under FIFO than under the LIFO flow assumption actually used.

The choice of cost flow assumption can significantly affect financial statements and their interpretation. During periods of substantial price change, no other choice among generally accepted financial accounting principles affects financial statements for most companies as much as the cost flow assumption for inventory.

# Identifying Operating Margin and Holding Gains ———

In general, the reported net income under FIFO exceeds that under LIFO during periods of rising prices. This higher reported net income results from including a

---

[10]The excess of current cost over LIFO cost of inventories is referred to by some managers as the *LIFO reserve*. For reasons discussed in the glossary at the back of the book, the term *reserve* is objectionable, although it continues to be used. A term such as *inventory valuation allowance* is as descriptive as *LIFO reserve* and is less likely to mislead.

## Exhibit 8.6

**Derivation of FIFO Income Data for LIFO Company
Inventory Data from Financial Statements and
Footnotes of General Electric Company
(all dollar amounts in millions)**

(Amounts shown in **boldface** appear in
GE's financial statements.
Other amounts are computed
as indicated.)

| | LIFO Cost Flow Assumption (actually used) | + | Excess of FIFO over LIFO Amount | = | FIFO Cost Flow Assumption (hypothetical) |
|---|---|---|---|---|---|
| Beginning Inventory............. | **$ 3,161** | | **$ 1,950** | | $ 5,111 |
| Purchases .................... | 17,933[a] | | 0 | | 17,933 |
| Cost of Goods Available for Sale . | $21,094 | | **$ 1,950** | | $23,044 |
| Less Ending Inventory .......... | **3,343** | | **2,240** | | 5,583 |
| Cost of Goods Sold............. | **$17,751** | | $ (290) | | $17,461 |
| Sales........................ | **$24,959** | | 0 | | **$24,959** |
| Less Cost of Goods Sold........ | **17,751** | | $ (290) | | 17,461 |
| Gross Margin on Sales.......... | **$ 7,208** | | $ 290 | | $ 7,498 |

[a]Computation of Purchases not presented in financial statements:

Purchases = Cost of Goods Sold + Ending Inventory − Beginning Inventory,
$17,933 =    **$17,751**    +    **$3,343**    −    **$3,161.**

larger realized holding gain in reported net income under FIFO than under LIFO. This section illustrates the significance of holding gains in the calculation of net income under FIFO and LIFO.

The conventionally reported gross margin (sales minus cost of goods sold) comprises:

1. An operating margin.

2. A *realized* holding gain (or loss).

(*Unrealized* holding gains and losses do not appear in income, but they can sometimes be computed from information in notes to the financial statements.)

The difference between the selling price of an item and its replacement cost at the time of sale is called an *operating margin*. This operating margin gives some indication of the relative advantage that a particular firm has in the market for its goods, such as a reputation for quality or service. The difference between the current replacement cost of an item and its acquisition cost is called a *holding gain* (or *loss*). It reflects the change in cost of an item during the period the inventory item is held. Holding gains indicate increasing prices and the skill (or luck) of the purchasing department in timing acquisitions.

To demonstrate the calculation of the operating margin and holding gain, consider the TV set example discussed in this chapter. The acquisition cost of the three items available for sale during the period is $840. Assume that one TV set is sold for $550. The replacement cost of the TV set at the time it was sold is $320. The current replacement cost at the end of the period for each item in ending inventory is $350.

Exhibit 8.7 ———————————————————————————————

**Reporting of Operating Margins and Holding Gains
for TV Sets Using the Periodic Inventory Method**

| | Cost Flow Assumption | | | |
|---|---|---|---|---|
| | FIFO | | LIFO | |
| Sales Revenue . . . . . . . . . . . . . . . . . . . . . . . . . . . . . . . . . . . . . | $550 | | $550 | |
| Less Replacement Cost of Goods Sold . . . . . . . . . . . . . . . . . | 320 | | 320 | |
| Operating Margin on Sales . . . . . . . . . . . . . . . . . . . . . . . . . . . | | $230 | | $230 |
| *Realized Holding Gain on TV Sets:* | | | | |
| Replacement Cost (at time of sale) of Goods Sold . . . . . . . . | $320 | | $320 | |
| Less Acquisition Cost of Goods Sold (FIFO—TV set 1; LIFO—TV set 3) . . . . . . . . . . . . . . . . . . | 250 | | 300 | |
| Realized Holding Gain on TV Sets (inventory profit) . . . . . . . | | 70 | | 20 |
| Conventionally Reported Gross Margin[a] . . . . . . . . . . . . . . . . . | | $300 | | $250 |
| *Unrealized Holding Gain:* | | | | |
| Replacement Cost of Ending Inventory (2 × $350) . . . . . . . . | $700 | | $700 | |
| Less Acquisition Cost of Ending Inventory (FIFO—TV sets 2 and 3; LIFO—TV sets 1 and 2) . . . . . | 590 | | 540 | |
| Unrealized Holding Gain on TV Sets . . . . . . . . . . . . . . . . . . . | | 110 | | 160 |
| Economic Profit on Sales and Holding Inventory of TV Sets (not reported in financial statements) . . . . . . . . . . | | $410 | | $410 |

[a]Note that Exhibit 8.3 stops here.

The top portion of Exhibit 8.7 illustrates the separation of the conventionally reported gross margin into the operating margin and the realized holding gain.

The operating margin is the difference between the $550 selling price and the
$320 replacement cost at the time of sale. The operating margin of $230 is the same
under both the FIFO and LIFO cost flow assumptions. The *realized holding gain* is
the difference between cost of goods sold based on replacement cost and cost of
goods sold based on acquisition cost. The realized holding gain under FIFO is larger
than under LIFO, because the earlier purchases at lower costs are charged to cost of
goods sold under FIFO. The larger realized holding gain explains why net income
under FIFO is typically larger than under LIFO during periods of rising prices. In
conventional financial statements, the realized holding gain does *not* appear separately, as in Exhibit 8.7. Sometimes the realized holding gain on inventory is called
*inventory profit*.

The calculation of an unrealized holding gain on units in ending inventory also
appears in Exhibit 8.7. The *unrealized holding gain* is the difference between the
current replacement cost of the ending inventory and its acquisition cost.[11] This
unrealized gain on ending inventory does not appear in the income statement as
presently prepared. The unrealized holding gain under LIFO exceeds that under
FIFO, because earlier purchases with lower costs remain in ending inventory under

———————————————————————————

[11]The unrealized holding gain for a given year on items on hand both at the beginning and at the end of
the year is the difference between year-end current cost and beginning-of-year current cost. The examples in this chapter do not illustrate this complication; all items on hand at the end of the year are
purchased during the year. See the glossary definition of *inventory profit* for an illustration of the
computation of holding gains for the year where the beginning inventory includes unrealized holding
gains from preceding periods.

LIFO. The sum of the operating margin plus all holding gains (both realized and unrealized), called "Economic Profit" in Exhibit 8.7, is the same under FIFO and LIFO. Most of the holding gain under FIFO (that is, the realized portion) is recognized in computing net income each period, whereas most of the holding gain under LIFO (that is, the unrealized portion) is not currently recognized in the income statement. Instead, under LIFO, the unrealized holding gain remains unreported as long as the older acquisition costs are shown on the balance sheet as ending inventory.

The total increase in wealth for a period includes both realized and unrealized holding gains. That total increase, $410 in the example, is independent of the cost flow assumption, but does not appear in financial statements under currently accepted accounting principles.

## Summary ——————————————————————————————————————

Inventory measurements affect both the cost-of-goods-sold expense on the income statement for the period and the amount shown for the asset "inventory" on the balance sheet at the end of the period. The sum of the two must equal the beginning inventory plus the cost of purchases, at least in accounting based on acquisition costs and market transactions. The allocation between expense and asset depends primarily on the valuation basis and the cost flow assumption used.

Additional inventory problems include dealing with the inclusions (absorption and variable costing, with absorption costing required for financial reporting) and timing inventory computations (periodic and perpetual approaches).

Common business terminology often inhibits clear thinking about the four problems because the term "inventory method" is so often used. For example, the terms "absorption costing method," "acquisition cost method," "perpetual method," and "LIFO method" are often encountered, but these are not alternatives to one another. An inventory method results from a combination of choices, one from each of the following:

1. Inclusion: absorption or variable costing.
2. Basis: historical cost, lower of cost or market, current cost, or standard cost, among others.
3. Frequency of computations: periodic or perpetual.
4. Cost flow assumption: FIFO, LIFO, or weighted average.

Be prepared for the ambiguous use of the term "inventory method," realizing that one of several distinctions may be at issue.

## Appendix 8.1:
## Effects of Transactions Involving Inventory
## on the Statement of Cash Flows ——————————————————

All transactions involving inventory affect the operations section of the statement of cash flows. None of the transactions involving inventory discussed in this chapter requires special adjustments in deriving cash flow from operations.

Consider, for example, the adjusting entry to recognize cost of goods sold in a periodic inventory system:

| | | |
|---|---|---|
| Cost of Goods Sold........................................ | 12,000 | |
|    Inventory ............................................... | | 12,000 |

Although this entry recognizes an expense that does not use cash, it does reduce the net balance in the Inventory account. Reductions in Inventory, like other reductions in current assets, appear in the operating section of the statement of cash flows as an addition to net income in deriving cash flow from operations. Refer to Exhibit 5.15 on page 188. The expense reduces income and cash from operations; the reduction in Inventory increases cash from operations. The total leaves cash from operations unchanged, which is correct because cash did not change.

Or, consider the entry recognizing the acquisition of inventory on account:

| | | |
|---|---|---|
| Inventory ............................................... | 140,000 | |
|    Accounts Payable ........................................ | | 140,000 |

The current asset for Inventory increases, absorbing cash from operations, but the current liability for Accounts Payable also increases, providing cash from operations. The net effect is that cash provided by operations does not change. Later, when the payable is paid, the entry is as follows:

| | | |
|---|---|---|
| Accounts Payable ......................................... | 140,000 | |
|    Cash.................................................... | | 140,000 |

The current liability Accounts Payable declines, absorbing cash from operations.

# Appendix 8.2:
# Current Cost Basis Removes
# the Need for a Cost Flow Assumption _____

The preceding sections have illustrated the difficulty in constructing useful financial statements in historical cost accounting for inventory in times of changing prices. If a FIFO cost flow assumption is used, the income statement reports out-of-date cost of goods sold. If a LIFO cost flow assumption is used, the balance sheet reports out-of-date ending inventory. (See Exhibit 8.4.)

A current cost basis for inventory allows up-to-date information to be shown on both statements, eliminating the need for a cost flow assumption. But using a current cost basis requires the accountant to make estimates of current costs. Some accountants find the resulting loss of objectivity and verifiability outweighs the

Exhibit 8.8 ————————————————————————————————————
Using Replacement Cost Data to Analyze Components of Income

## Assumed Data

| | | |
|---|---|---:|
| Beginning Inventory: TV Set 1 Cost ............................... | | $250 |
| Purchases: | TV Set 2 Cost ............................... | 290 |
| | TV Set 3 Cost ............................... | 300 |
| Historical Cost of Goods Available for Sale .......................... | | $840 |
| Sales: One TV Set for ........................................ | | $550 |
| Replacement Cost of TV Sets on: | | |
| Date of Sale ............................................... | | $320 |
| At End of Period ........................................... | | $350 |

## Income Statement

| | |
|---|---:|
| Sales................................................... | $550 |
| Replacement Cost of Goods Sold ................................ | 320 |
| Operating Margin ........................................... | $230 |
| Holding Gains for Year[a] (see calculation below)..................... | 180 |
| Economic Profit ........................................... | $410 |

**Calculation of Holding Gains for Year**

| | |
|---|---:|
| Replacement Cost at Time of Sale[a] ............................. | $ 320 |
| Replacement Cost of Ending Inventory (2 × $350) .................. | 700 |
| Total Replacement Cost......................................... | $1,020 |
| Historical Cost of Goods Available for Sale .......................... | 840 |
| Total Holding Gains for Year..................................... | $ 180 |
| Ending Inventory (two TV sets, $350 current cost each) .............. | $ 700 |

[a]To give some recognition to the realization convention, the total holding gain might be divided into realized and unrealized portions. To do so requires knowing the acquisition cost of the TV set sold, and that requires a cost flow assumption. As Exhibit 8.7 indicates, if a LIFO assumption is made, then the realized holding gain is $20 and the realized income of $250 could be shown intermediate between the operating margin of $230 and the economic income of $410.

potential benefits from using current cost data. Other accountants think that the benefits of current data outweigh the costs of having less auditable numbers.

Exhibit 8.8 illustrates the TV set example when both cost of goods sold and ending inventory are valued at replacement cost.

The first income figure of $230, labeled *Operating Margin*, gives the selling price less replacement cost of goods sold at the time of sale. This number may have significance for companies operating in unregulated environments. The significance can perhaps be understood by considering the following assertion. If the retailer of the TV sets pays out more than $230 in other expenses, taxes, and dividends, there will be insufficient funds retained in the firm for it to replace inventory and to continue carrying out the same physical operations next period as it did this period. On the date of sale, a new TV set costs $320; the historical cost of the TV set sold, whether $250 or $300 or some amount in between, does not help the retailer to understand the costs required to maintain its productive assets intact, given the *current* economic conditions.

The second income item shown in Exhibit 8.8 is called *Holding Gains*. During the period, holding gains of $180 occurred on the TV sets held in inventory. At the time of sale, the replacement cost of TV sets increased to $320. Thus the holding gain on three TV sets, on the date of sale of one of them, was $120 [= 3 × $320 − ($250 + $290 + $300)]. By the end of the accounting period there was another $60 [= 2 × ($350 − $320)] of holding gain on the two TV sets still held in inventory as the replacement cost increased to $350 from $320.

The $410 income figure shown after the inclusion of holding gains may also be significant. It represents the firm's increase in wealth without regard to the realization convention. Some economists define income as the change in wealth during the period. They judge realization through arm's-length transactions to be unimportant. Economic income, including all holding gains, is $410 in the example.

In recent years, generally accepted accounting principles have allowed (but have not required) firms to disclose the current cost of goods sold computed at the time of sale and the current cost of ending inventory. Such information makes measuring operating margin and holding gains possible.

# Problem 1 for Self-Study ———————————————————

Exhibit 8.9 presents data on beginning amounts of, additions to, and withdrawals from the inventory of item X during June. Beginning inventory is assumed to be 100 units costing $10 each in all cases.[12]

**Exhibit 8.9** ——————————————————————————
**Data for Illustration of Inventory Calculations**

| Item X | Units | Unit Cost | Total Cost |
|---|---|---|---|
| Beginning Inventory, June 1 .......................... | 100 | $10.00 | $1,000 |
| Purchases, June 7.................................... | 400 | 11.00 | 4,400 |
| Purchases, June 12 ................................. | 100 | 12.50 | 1,250 |
| Total Goods Available for Sale at Cost............... | 600 | | $6,650 |
| Withdrawals, June 5 ................................. | 25 | | ? |
| Withdrawals, June 10 ............................... | 10 | | ? |
| Withdrawals, June 15 ............................... | 200 | | ? |
| Withdrawals, June 25 ............................... | 260 | | ? |
| Total Withdrawals during June ...................... | 495 | | ? |
| Ending Inventory, June 30........................... | 105 | | ? |
| Replacement Cost per Unit, June 30 ................. | | $13.60 | |

———————————————————

[12]To simplify the problem, beginning inventory is shown as having the same opening valuation of $1,000 under all cost flow assumptions. If costs had varied in the past, the opening unit costs would differ across cost flow assumption.

**a.** Compute cost of goods sold and ending inventory using a FIFO cost flow assumption. Note that periodic and perpetual approaches give the same results.

**b.** Compute cost of goods sold and ending inventory using a LIFO cost flow assumption with a periodic inventory.

**c.** Compute cost of goods sold and ending inventory using a LIFO cost flow assumption with a perpetual inventory.

**d.** Compute cost of goods sold and ending inventory using a weighted-average cost flow assumption in a periodic inventory.

**e.** Compute cost of goods sold and ending inventory using a weighted-average cost flow assumption in a perpetual inventory.

## Suggested Solution

**a.** See Exhibit 8.10.  **d.** See Exhibit 8.13.

**b.** See Exhibit 8.11.  **e.** See Exhibit 8.14.

**c.** See Exhibit 8.12.

**Exhibit 8.10** _____

### Ending Inventory and Cost-of-Goods-Sold Computation
### Using a Periodic Inventory and a FIFO Cost Flow Assumption

**Item X**

**Ending Inventory Computation**

| | |
|---|---:|
| 100 units @ $12.50 (from June 12 purchase)............................... | $1,250 |
| 5 units @ $11.00 (from June 7 purchase) .................................. | 55 |
| Ending Inventory, June 30............................................... | $1,305 |

**Cost-of-Goods-Sold Computation**

| | |
|---|---:|
| Cost of Goods Available for Sale......................................... | $6,650 |
| Less Ending Inventory .................................................. | 1,305 |
| Cost of Goods Sold..................................................... | $5,345 |

**Exhibit 8.11** _____

### Ending Inventory and Cost-of-Goods-Sold Computation
### Using a Periodic Inventory and a LIFO Cost Flow Assumption

**Item X**

**Ending Inventory Computation**

| | |
|---|---:|
| 100 units @ $10.00 (from beginning inventory) ............................ | $1,000 |
| 5 units @ $11.00 (from first purchase, June 7) ............................ | 55 |
| Ending Inventory at Cost ............................................... | $1,055 |

**Cost-of-Goods-Sold Computation**

| | |
|---|---:|
| Cost of Goods Available for Sale......................................... | $6,650 |
| Less Ending Inventory .................................................. | 1,055 |
| Cost of Goods Sold..................................................... | $5,595 |

Exhibit 8.12 ————————————————————————————————————————————————

**Ending Inventory and Cost-of-Goods-Sold Computation
Using a Perpetual Inventory and a LIFO Cost Flow Assumption**

# Item X, Cost-of-Goods-Sold Computation

| | Received | | | Issued | | | Balance | | |
|---|---|---|---|---|---|---|---|---|---|
| **Date** | **Units** | **Cost** | **Amount** | **Units** | **Cost** | **Amount** | **Units** | **Cost** | **Amount** |
| 6/1 . . . . . . . . . . . . . . . . . . . . . | | | | | | | 100 | $10.00 | $1,000 |
| 6/5 . . . . . . . . . . . . . . . . . . . . . | | | | 25 | $10.00 | $ 250 | 75 | 10.00 | 750 |
| 6/7 . . . . . . . . . . . . . . . . . . . . . | 400 | $11.00 | $4,400 | | | | 75 | 10.00 | 750 |
| | | | | | | | 400 | 11.00 | 4,400 |
| 6/10 . . . . . . . . . . . . . . . . . . . . | | | | 10 | 11.00 | 110 | 75 | 10.00 | 750 |
| | | | | | | | 390 | 11.00 | 4,290 |
| 6/12 . . . . . . . . . . . . . . . . . . . . | 100 | 12.50 | 1,250 | | | | 75 | 10.00 | 750 |
| | | | | | | | 390 | 11.00 | 4,290 |
| | | | | | | | 100 | 12.50 | 1,250 |
| 6/15 . . . . . . . . . . . . . . . . . . . . | | | | 100 | 12.50 | 1,250 | 75 | 10.00 | 750 |
| | | | | 100 | 11.00 | 1,100 | 290 | 11.00 | 3,190 |
| 6/25 . . . . . . . . . . . . . . . . . . . . | | | | 260 | 11.00 | 2,860 | 75 | 10.00 | 750 |
| | | | | | | | 30 | 11.00 | 330 |
| Cost of Goods Sold . . . . . . . | | | | | | $5,570 | | | |

**Ending Inventory Computation**

| | |
|---|---|
| 75 units @ $10.00 . . . . . . . . . . . . . . . . . . . . . . . . . . . . . . . . . . . . . . . . . . . . . . . . . . . . . . . . . . . . . . . . . . . . . . | $ 750 |
| 30 units @ $11.00 . . . . . . . . . . . . . . . . . . . . . . . . . . . . . . . . . . . . . . . . . . . . . . . . . . . . . . . . . . . . . . . . . . . . . . | 330 |
| Ending Inventory . . . . . . . . . . . . . . . . . . . . . . . . . . . . . . . . . . . . . . . . . . . . . . . . . . . . . . . . . . . . . . . . . . . | $1,080 |

**Alternative Cost-of-Goods-Sold Computation**

| | |
|---|---|
| Cost of Goods Available for Sale . . . . . . . . . . . . . . . . . . . . . . . . . . . . . . . . . . . . . . . . . . . . . . . . . . . . . . . . . . | $6,650 |
| Less Ending Inventory . . . . . . . . . . . . . . . . . . . . . . . . . . . . . . . . . . . . . . . . . . . . . . . . . . . . . . . . . . . . . . . . | 1,080 |
| Cost of Goods Sold . . . . . . . . . . . . . . . . . . . . . . . . . . . . . . . . . . . . . . . . . . . . . . . . . . . . . . . . . . . . . . . . . . | $5,570 |

Exhibit 8.13 ————————————————————————————————————————

**Ending Inventory and Cost-of-Goods-Sold Computation Using Periodic
Inventory and a Weighted-Average Cost Flow Assumption**

**Ending Inventory Computation**

| | | | |
|---|---|---|---|
| 6/1 | 100 units @ $10.00 . . . . . . . . . . . . . . . . . . . . . . . . . . . . . . . . . . . . . . . | $1,000 |
| 6/7 | 400 units @ $11.00 . . . . . . . . . . . . . . . . . . . . . . . . . . . . . . . . . . . . . . . | 4,400 |
| 6/12 | 100 units @ $12.50 . . . . . . . . . . . . . . . . . . . . . . . . . . . . . . . . . . . . . . . | 1,250 |
| | 600 units @ $11.08 (= $6,650/600) . . . . . . . . . . . . . . . . . . . . . . . . . . . | $6,650 |
| Ending Inventory (105 units @ $11.08) . . . . . . . . . . . . . . . . . . . . . . . . . . . . . . . . . . . . . . | $1,163 |

**Cost-of-Goods-Sold Computation**

| | |
|---|---|
| Cost of Goods Available for Sale . . . . . . . . . . . . . . . . . . . . . . . . . . . . . . . . . . . . . . . | $6,650 |
| Less Ending Inventory . . . . . . . . . . . . . . . . . . . . . . . . . . . . . . . . . . . . . . . . . . . . | 1,163 |
| Cost of Goods Sold . . . . . . . . . . . . . . . . . . . . . . . . . . . . . . . . . . . . . . . . . . . . . | $5,487[a] |

[a]Because of rounding error, this number is *not* 495 (= 600 − 105) units × $11.08 = $5,485. In general, the weighted-average unit price should be applied either to ending inventory or to cost of goods sold. After being applied to one, the other is found from the inventory equation.

**Exhibit 8.14** ————————————————————————————————————————————

Ending Inventory and Cost-of-Goods-Sold Computation
Using a Perpetual Inventory and a Weighted-Average Cost Flow Assumption

## Item X, Cost-of-Goods-Sold and Ending Inventory Computation

| Date | Received | | | Issued | | | Balance | | |
|---|---|---|---|---|---|---|---|---|---|
| | **Units** | **Cost** | **Amount** | **Units** | **Cost** | **Amount** | **Units** | **Total Cost** | **Unit Cost[a]** |
| 6/1...................... | | | | | | | 100 | $1,000 | $10.00 |
| 6/5...................... | | | | 25 | $10.00 | $ 250 | 75 | 750 | 10.00 |
| 6/7...................... | 400 | $11.00 | $4,400 | | | | 475 | 5,150 | 10.84 |
| 6/10..................... | | | | 10 | 10.84 | 108 | 465 | 5,042 | 10.84 |
| 6/12..................... | 100 | 12.50 | 1,250 | | | | 565 | 6,292 | 11.14 |
| 6/15..................... | | | | 200 | 11.14 | 2,228 | 365 | 4,064 | 11.13[b] |
| 6/25..................... | | | | 260 | 11.13 | 2,894 | 105 | 1,170 | 11.14[b] |
| Cost of Goods Sold....... | | | | | | $5,480 | | | |

**Alternative Cost-of-Goods-Sold Computation**

| | |
|---|---|
| Cost of Goods Available for Sale................................................. | $6,650 |
| Less Ending Inventory ........................................................... | 1,170 |
| Cost of Goods Sold............................................................... | $5,480 |

[a]Unit cost = Total cost/Units.

[b]Note how the rounding effects change the unit cost even though no new units were acquired. The unit costs for 6/15 and 6/25 are conceptually equivalent.

## Problem 2 for Self-Study ————————————————————————————————————

Refer to the data for Item X in Exhibits 8.10 and 8.11, which show cost of goods sold and ending inventory in a periodic inventory and which use FIFO and LIFO cost flow assumptions, respectively. Assume that the 495 units withdrawn from inventory were sold for $15 each, $7,425 in total. Construct a schedule that both separates operating margin from holding gains and separates realized holding gains from unrealized holding gains. Show the results for FIFO and LIFO in parallel columns. The total of operating margin and realized holding gain should be equal to the gross margin reported in historical cost income statements. The total of operating margin and all holding gains should be the same for LIFO as for FIFO.

### Suggested Solution

See Exhibit 8.15.

## Problem 3 for Self-Study ————————————————————————————————————

American Steel Company uses a LIFO cost flow assumption for inventories. Its year-end financial statements show the following amounts:

## Exhibit 8.15

### Reporting of Operating Margins and Holding Gains for Item X

| | Cost Flow Assumption | | | |
| --- | --- | --- | --- | --- |
| | FIFO | | LIFO | |
| **Periodic Inventory Method** | | | | |
| Sales Revenue from Item X (495 × $15.00) ....... | $7,425 | | $7,425 | |
| Less Replacement Cost of Goods Sold [(25 × $10.00) + (10 × $11.00) + (460 × $12.50)] .......................... | 6,110 | | 6,110 | |
| Operating Margin on Sales of Item X ........... | | $1,315 | | $1,315 |
| *Realized Holding Gain on Item X:* | | | | |
| Replacement Cost of Goods Sold ............... | $6,110 | | $6,110 | |
| Less Acquisition Cost of Goods Sold (FIFO—Exhibit 8.10; LIFO—Exhibit 8.11) ...... | 5,345 | | 5,595 | |
| Realized Holding Gain on Item X.............. | | 765 | | 515 |
| Conventionally Reported Gross Margin........... | | $2,080 | | $1,830 |
| *Unrealized Holding Gain on Item X:* | | | | |
| Replacement Cost of Ending Inventory (105 × $13.60; see Exhibit 8.9) ............... | $1,428 | | $1,428 | |
| Less Acquisition Cost of Ending Inventory (FIFO—Exhibit 8.10; LIFO—Exhibit 8.11) ...... | 1,305 | | 1,055 | |
| Unrealized Holding Gain on Item X............. | | 123 | | 373 |
| Economic Profit on Sales and Holding Inventory of Item X ......................... | | $2,203 | | $2,203 |

## Problem 3 for Self-Study *(continued)*

| | |
| --- | --- |
| Balance Sheet Inventories: | |
| Beginning of Year ................................................ | $1,500,000 |
| End of Year....................................................... | $1,700,000 |
| Income Statement Amounts: | |
| Cost of Goods Sold............................................... | $8,000,000 |
| Income before Taxes ............................................. | 800,000 |
| Net Income (40 percent tax rate)................................... | 480,000 |
| Supplementary Information in Notes on Inventory Provide Data on the Excess of FIFO Cost over Reported LIFO Cost of Inventory: | |
| Beginning of Year ................................................ | $1,650,000 |
| End of Year....................................................... | $1,850,000 |

a. Compute the inventory turnover ratio from the published financial statements based on LIFO cost flow.

b. Compute the income before taxes assuming FIFO cost flow.

c. Compute the net income assuming FIFO cost flow and an income tax rate of 40 percent.

d. Compute the inventory turnover ratio from the financial statements as they would appear using FIFO cost flow.

## Suggested Solution

**a.** $\text{Inventory Turnover} = \dfrac{\text{Cost of Goods Sold}}{\text{Average Inventory During Year}}$

$$= \dfrac{\$8,000,000}{.5(\$1,500,000 + \$1,700,000)}$$

$$= 5 \text{ times per year.}$$

**b.** Pretax income would be larger by the amount that cost of goods sold would be smaller. Cost of goods sold would be smaller by $200,000 = $1,850,000 − $1,650,000. See Exhibit 8.6.

**c.** Net income would be larger by the amount found in part **b** multiplied by (1 − income tax rate) = $200,000 × .60 = $120,000.

**d.** $\dfrac{\text{Inventory}}{\text{Turnover}} = \dfrac{\text{Cost of Goods Sold}}{\text{Average Inventory during Year}}$

$$= \dfrac{\$8,000,000 - \$200,000}{.5[(\$1,500,000 + \$1,650,000) + (\$1,700,000 + \$1,850,000)]}$$

$$= \dfrac{\$7,800,000}{\$3,350,000}$$

$$= 2.33 \text{ times per year.}$$

# Questions, Exercises, Problems, and Cases ——————

## Questions

**1.** Review the meaning of the following concepts or terms discussed in this chapter.

| | |
|---|---|
| **a.** Inventory (as both a noun and a verb). | **m.** Periodic inventory system. |
| **b.** Inventory equation. | **n.** Shrinkages. |
| **c.** Full absorption costing. | **o.** Perpetual inventory system. |
| **d.** Variable (direct) costing. | **p.** Cost flow assumption. |
| **e.** Purchases. | **q.** First-in, first-out (FIFO). |
| **f.** Purchase discounts. | **r.** Last-in, first-out (LIFO). |
| **g.** Acquisition cost basis. | **s.** Weighted average. |
| **h.** Realization convention. | **t.** LIFO inventory layer contrasted to LIFO reserve. |
| **i.** Replacement cost. | |
| **j.** Net realizable value. | **u.** Realized holding gain. |
| **k.** Lower-of-cost-or-market basis. | **v.** Inventory profit. |
| **l.** Standard cost. | **w.** Unrealized holding gain. |

**2.** Under what circumstances would the perpetual and periodic inventory systems both yield the same inventory amount if the weighted-average flow assumption were used?

3. Assume no changes in physical quantities during the period. During a period of rising prices, will the FIFO or LIFO cost flow assumption result in the higher ending inventory amount? The lower amount?

   Which cost flow assumption will result in the higher ending inventory amount during a period of declining prices? The lower inventory amount?

4. **a.** During a period of rising prices, will a FIFO or LIFO cost flow assumption result in the higher cost of goods sold? The lower cost of goods sold? Assume no changes in physical quantities during the period.

   **b.** Which cost flow assumption, LIFO or FIFO, will result in the higher cost of goods sold during a period of declining prices? The lower cost of goods sold?

5. ''Cost flow assumptions for inventory are required only because specific identification of items sold is costly. Specific identification is theoretically superior to any cost flow assumption and eliminates the possibility of income manipulation available with some cost flow assumptions.''

   Comment.

6. Assume that a steel manufacturer and a retailing firm have identical sales and income and that the costs of their purchased inputs of goods and services increase at the same rate. The steel company has inventory turnover of about four times per year, whereas the retailer has inventory turnover of about ten times per year.

   Which of the two firms is likely to benefit more by switching from FIFO to LIFO? Explain.

7. ''LIFO provides a more meaningful income statement than FIFO, even though it provides a less meaningful balance sheet.'' Does it ever? Does it always?

8. Assume that the cost basis for inventory is changed from historical cost to current cost, that current costs exceed historical costs at the end of the year of change, and that all year-end inventory is sold during the following year. Ignore income tax effects.

   What will be the impact of the change on net income for the year of change? On income for the following year? On total income over the 2 years?

9. Would you expect to find a periodic or perpetual inventory system used in each of the following situations?
   **a.** The greeting card department of a retail store.
   **b.** The fur coat department of a retail store.
   **c.** Supplies storeroom for an automated production line.
   **d.** Automobile dealership.
   **e.** Wholesale dealer in bulk salad oil.
   **f.** Grocery store.
   **g.** College bookstore.
   **h.** Diamond ring department of a jewelry store.
   **i.** Ballpoint pen department of a jewelry store.

10. A noted accountant once claimed that firms using a LIFO cost flow assumption will find that historical cost of goods sold is *greater* than replacement cost of

goods sold computed as of the time of sale. Under what circumstances is this assertion likely to be true? (*Hint:* Compare the effects of periodic and perpetual approaches on LIFO cost of goods sold.) Do you agree that the assertion is likely to be true?

## Exercises

11. *Journal entries for periodic and perpetual inventories.* Goods that cost $1,500 are sold for $2,000 cash. Present the normal journal entries at the time of the sale:
    a.   When a periodic inventory is used.
    b.   When a perpetual inventory is used.

12. *Effect of inventory errors (adapted from a problem by S. Zeff).* Pollack Company reported net income of $106,000 in Year 1 and $88,000 in Year 2. Early in Year 3, Pollack Company discovered that it had *overstated* its Year 1 ending inventory by $6,000 and had *understated* its Year 2 inventory by $10,000.

    What should have been the company's reported net incomes for Year 1 and Year 2? Ignore income taxes.

13. *Computations involving different cost flow assumptions.* Hanna Company's raw material inventory at September 1 and the purchases during September were as follows:

| | | |
|---|---:|---:|
| 9/1   Inventory.................................... | 1,000 pounds | $ 4,500 |
| 9/5   Purchased .................................. | 3,000 pounds | 13,500 |
| 9/14 Purchased .................................. | 3,500 pounds | 17,500 |
| 9/27 Purchased .................................. | 3,000 pounds | 16,500 |
| 9/29 Purchased .................................. | 1,000 pounds | 8,000 |

The inventory at September 30 was 1,800 pounds.

Assume a periodic inventory system. Compute the cost of the inventory on September 30 under each of the following cost flow assumptions:
    a.   FIFO.
    b.   Weighted average.
    c.   LIFO.

14. *Compute acquisition cost of inventory and record sales transaction using perpetual inventory.* Ducru Company ordered from an overseas supplier 10,000 shirts that had a list price of $12 each, requesting the normal trade discount. The invoice arrived showing a discount of 40 percent from list price. Ducru Company paid its customs broker $750 for taxes and paid a trucking company $250 to deliver the goods. Later, it sold 1,000 shirts for $12 each on account. Ducru Company uses a perpetual inventory.

    Prepare journal entries to record the sales transaction.

15. *Over sufficiently long time spans, income is cash in less cash out; cost flow assumptions.* Gazin Company was in business for 4 years. Exhibit 8.16 shows its purchases and sales during that 4-year period. Ignore income taxes.

**Exhibit 8.16** _____

**GAZIN COMPANY**
**Purchases and Sales**
**(Exercise 15)**

|  | Purchases | | Sales | |
|---|---|---|---|---|
|  | Units | Unit Cost | Units | Unit Price |
| Year 1.......................... | 12,000 | $10 | 9,000 | $15 |
| Year 2.......................... | 11,000 | 11 | 10,000 | 17 |
| Year 3.......................... | 10,000 | 12 | 11,000 | 19 |
| Year 4.......................... | 9,000 | 13 | 12,000 | 21 |
| Totals ...................... | 42,000 | | 42,000 | |

**a.** Compute income for each of the 4 years assuming FIFO cost flow.
**b.** Compute income for each of the 4 years assuming LIFO cost flow.
**c.** Compare total income over the 4-year period. Does the cost flow assumption matter?

**16.** *Over sufficiently long time spans, income is cash in less cash out; cost basis for inventory.* The Sales Company began business on January 1, Year 1. Information concerning merchandise inventories, purchases, and sales for the first 3 years of operations follows:

|  | Year 1 | Year 2 | Year 3 |
|---|---|---|---|
| Sales..................................... | $300,000 | $330,000 | $450,000 |
| Purchases ............................. | 280,000 | 260,000 | 350,000 |
| Inventories, Dec. 31: |  |  |  |
| At cost ................................ | 80,000 | 95,000 | 95,000 |
| At market............................. | 75,000 | 80,000 | 100,000 |

**a.** Compute the gross margin on sales (sales minus cost of goods sold) for each year, using the lower-of-cost-or-market basis in valuing inventories.
**b.** Compute the gross margin on sales (sales minus cost of goods sold) for each year, using the acquisition cost basis in valuing inventories.
**c.** Indicate your conclusion about whether the lower-of-cost-or-market basis of valuing inventories is conservative.

**17.** *When goods available for sale exceed sales, income can be manipulated, even when specific identification is used.* Langoa Company has 300 identical TV sets available for sale during December, when it expects to sell 200 sets for $500 each. These TV sets were acquired as follows: 100 in June for $200 each, 100 in August for $300 each, and 100 in November for $250 each. Assume that sales for December are 200 units at $500 each.
**a.** Compute gross margin for December assuming FIFO.
**b.** Compute gross margin for December assuming specific identification of sales and sets sold to minimize reported income for tax purposes.

    **c.**  Compute gross margin for December assuming specific identification of sales and sets sold to maximize reported income for the purpose of increasing the store manager's profit-sharing bonus for the year.

**18.** *Computations involving cost flow assumptions and periodic or perpetual approaches.* The following information concerning Arpesfeld Company's inventory of raw materials is available:

| | |
|---|---|
| Nov. 2 Inventory............................................ | 4,000 pounds @ $5 |
| 9 Issued ............................................. | 3,000 pounds |
| 16 Purchased ......................................... | 7,000 pounds @ $6 |
| 23 Issued ............................................. | 3,000 pounds |
| 30 Issued ............................................. | 3,000 pounds |

Compute the cost of goods sold and the cost of ending inventory on November 30 for each of the following combinations of inventory systems and cost flow assumptions.

**a.**  Periodic FIFO.

**b.**  Periodic weighted average.

**c.**  Periodic LIFO.

**d.**  Perpetual FIFO.

**e.**  Perpetual weighted average.

**f.**  Perpetual LIFO.

**19.** *Computing cost of goods sold under various treatments of cost flows with periodic and perpetual systems.* The Central Supply Company has in its inventory on May 1 three units of item K, all purchased on the same date at a price of $60 per unit. Information relative to item K is as follows:

| Date | Explanation | Units | Unit Cost | Tag Number |
|---|---|---|---|---|
| May 1 ................. | Inventory | 3 | $60 | K–515,516,517 |
| 3 ................. | Purchase | 2 | 65 | K–518,519 |
| 12 ................. | Sale | 3 | | K–515,518,519 |
| 19 ................. | Purchase | 2 | 76 | K–520,521 |
| 25 ................. | Sale | 1 | | K–516 |

Compute the cost of units sold in accordance with the following:

**a.**  Specific identification of units sold.

**b.**  FIFO cost flow assumption and periodic inventory system.

**c.**  FIFO cost flow assumption and perpetual inventory system.

**d.**  LIFO cost flow assumption and periodic inventory system.

**e.**  LIFO cost flow assumption and perpetual inventory system.

**f.**  Weighted-average cost flow assumption and perpetual inventory system.

**g.**  Weighted-average cost flow assumption and periodic inventory system.

**20.** *LIFO provides opportunity for income manipulation.* Lagrange Company began the year with 20,000 units of product on hand that cost $10 each. During the year, it produced another 30,000 units at a cost of $18 each. Sales for the year were expected to total 50,000 units. During November, the company had to make a decision about production for the remainder of the year. No additional units needed to be produced this year beyond the 30,000 units already produced. Up to 60,000 additional units could be produced; the cost would be $22 per unit regardless of the quantity produced. The company uses a periodic LIFO inventory. Assume that sales are 50,000 units for the year at an average price of $25 per unit.

a. What production level for the remainder of the year gives the largest cost of goods sold for the year? What is that cost of goods sold?

b. What production level for the remainder of the year gives the smallest cost of goods sold for the year? What is that cost of goods sold?

c. Compare the gross margins implied by the two production plans devised in the preceding parts.

21. *Calculations combining cost basis and cost flow assumptions.* The Sanlex Company started the year with no inventories on hand. It manufactured two batches of inventory, 100 units each, which were identical except that the variable costs of producing the first batch were $120 and the variable costs of producing the second batch were $200 because of rising prices. By the end of the year, Sanlex Company had sold 75 units from the first batch for $300 and none of the second batch. The ending inventory had a market value of $305. Total fixed manufacturing costs for the year were $160. Under the absorption costing procedure, $100 of fixed manufacturing costs allocated to units produced remained in inventory at the close of the year. Selling and administrative expenses for the year were $40.

Prepare for the Sanlex Company a statement of pretax income for the year under each of the following sets of assumptions.

a. FIFO, acquisition cost basis.

b. LIFO, acquisition cost basis.

c. FIFO, lower-of-cost-or-market basis.

22. *Analysis of annual report; usage of LIFO.* The notes to the financial statements in a recent report of Sears, Roebuck and Company contained the following statement.

> If the physical quantity of goods in inventory at [year-end and the beginning of the year] . . . were to be replaced, the estimated expenditures of funds required would exceed the amounts reported by approximately $670 million and $440 million, respectively.

Sears uses LIFO.

a. How much higher or lower would Sears's pretax reported income have been if its inventories had been valued at current costs rather than with a LIFO cost flow assumption?

b. Sears reported $606 million net income for the year. Assume tax expense equal to 46 percent of pretax income. By what percentage would Sears's net income have increased if a FIFO flow assumption had been used?

23. *Effects on statement of cash flows.* Indicate the effect on Cash Flow from Operations of the following independent transactions. Include the effects of income taxes, assuming a rate of 40 percent of pretax income. Assume also that the accounting methods used on the tax return are the same as on the financial statements and that taxes have been paid in cash.

   **a.** A firm using the lower-of-cost-or-market basis for inventories writes ending inventory down by $100,000.

   **b.** A firm has been using FIFO. It switches to LIFO at the end of the current year and finds that the cost of goods sold is $200,000 larger than it would have been under FIFO.

24. *Reconstructing financial statement data from information on effects of liquidations of LIFO layers.* The inventory footnote to the annual report of the Alcher Company reads in part as follows:

   > Because of continuing high demand throughout the year, inventories were unavoidably reduced and could not be replaced. Under the LIFO system of accounting, used for many years by Alcher Company, the net effect of all the inventory changes was to increase pretax income by $600,000 over what it would have been had inventories been maintained at their physical levels at the start of the year.

   The price of Alcher Company's merchandise purchases was $18 per unit during the year, after having risen erratically over past years. Alcher Company uses a periodic inventory method. Its inventory positions at the beginning and end of the year are summarized as follows:

   | Date | Physical Count of Inventory | LIFO Cost of Inventory |
   |------|-----------------------------|------------------------|
   | January 1..................................... | 300,000 units | $    ? |
   | December 31 ............................... | 200,000 units | $2,600,000 |

   **a.** What was the average cost per unit of the 100,000 units removed from the January 1 LIFO inventory?

   **b.** What was the January 1 LIFO cost of inventory?

25. *Separating operating margin from holding gains.* On January 1, the merchandise inventory of Revsine Appliance Store consisted of 1,000 units acquired for $450 each. During the year, 2,500 additional units were acquired at an average price of $600 each, while 2,300 units were sold for $900 each. The replacement cost of these units at the time they were sold averaged $600 during the year. The replacement cost of units on December 31 was $750 per unit.

   **a.** Calculate cost of goods sold under both FIFO and LIFO cost flow assumptions.

   **b.** Prepare partial income statements showing gross margin on sales as revenues less cost of goods sold under both FIFO and LIFO cost flow assumptions.

  **c.** Prepare partial income statements, separating the gross margin on sales into operating margins and realized holding gains, under both FIFO and LIFO.

  **d.** Append to the bottom of the statements prepared in part **c** a statement showing the amount of unrealized holding gains and the total of realized income plus unrealized holding gains.

  **e.** If you did the previous steps correctly, the totals in part **d** are the same for both FIFO and LIFO. Is this equality a coincidence? Why or why not?

## Problems and Cases

**26.** *Effect of inventory errors.* On December 30, Year 1, merchandise amounting to $1,000 was received by the Warren Company and was counted in its December 31 listing of all inventory items on hand. The invoice was not received until January 4, Year 2, at which time the acquisition was recorded as a Year 2 acquisition. The acquisition should have been recorded for Year 1. Assume that the error was never discovered by the firm. Warren Company uses a periodic inventory system. Indicate the effect (overstatement, understatement, none) on each of the following amounts. Ignore income taxes.
  **a.** Inventory, 12/31/Year 1.
  **b.** Inventory, 12/31/Year 2.
  **c.** Cost of goods sold, Year 1.
  **d.** Cost of goods sold, Year 2.
  **e.** Net income, Year 1.
  **f.** Net income, Year 2.
  **g.** Accounts payable, 12/31/Year 1.
  **h.** Accounts payable, 12/31/Year 2.
  **i.** Retained earnings, 12/31/Year 2.

**27.** *Analysis of adjunct and contra accounts used for purchases and sales.* The accounts listed below might appear in the records of a retail store. Their use is never required, but accounts such as these often provide details about purchase activity useful to management. From the name of the account and your understanding of the accounting for purchases and sales, indicate:
  **a.** Whether the account is a permanent account (to appear as such on the balance sheet) or a temporary account (to be closed at the end of the accounting period).
  **b.** The normal balance, debit or credit, in the account. If the account is a temporary one, give the normal balance prior to closing.
  **c.** If the account is a temporary one, the kind of account it is closed to — balance sheet asset, balance sheet liability, balance sheet owners' equity through a revenue account, or balance sheet owners' equity through an expense (or revenue contra) account.
  **(1)** Merchandise Purchases.
  **(2)** Merchandise Purchase Allowances.
  **(3)** Merchandise Purchase Returns.
  **(4)** Purchase Returns.
  **(5)** Sales Tax on Purchases.

**(6)** Freight-in on Purchases.

**(7)** Sales Allowances.

**(8)** Allowance for Sales Discounts.

**(9)** Federal Excise Taxes Payable on Sales.

(The next three items should not be attempted until Problem 28 has been read.)

**(10)** Purchase Discounts.

**(11)** Purchase Discounts Taken.

**(12)** Purchase Discounts Lost.

28. *Gross and net price methods for treating purchase discounts.* The chapter mentioned two alternatives for treating discounts on merchandise purchases that are often used in practice: (1) the gross price method, which recognizes the amount of discounts taken on payments made during the period, without regard to the period of purchase, and (2) the net price method, which deducts all discounts made available from the gross purchase invoice prices at the time of purchase. This problem explains the two methods.

**Alternative 1: Gross Price Method**  The gross price method of accounting for purchases records invoices at the gross price and accumulates the amount of discounts taken on payments made. Suppose that goods with a gross invoice price of $1,000 are purchased 2/10, net/30. (That is, a 2 percent discount from invoice price is offered if payment is made within 10 days, and the full invoice price is due in any case within 30 days.) The entries to record the purchase and the payment (1) under the assumption that the payment is made in time to take the discount and (2) under the assumption that the payment is made too late to take advantage of the discount are as follows:

| Gross Price Method | (1) Discount Taken | | (2) Discount Not Taken | |
|---|---|---|---|---|
| Purchases (or Inventory) .................... | 1,000 | | 1,000 | |
| Accounts Payable ...................... | | 1,000 | | 1,000 |
| To record purchase. | | | | |
| Accounts Payable ......................... | 1,000 | | 1,000 | |
| Cash .................................... | | 980 | | 1,000 |
| Purchase Discounts (or Inventory).......... | | 20 | | — |
| To record payment. | | | | |

The balance in the Purchase Discounts account is deducted from the balance in the Purchases account in calculating net purchases for a period. Such a deduction approximates the results achieved by treating purchase discounts as a reduction in purchase price at the time of purchase. An approximation results because the total adjustment includes discounts taken on payments made this period, without regard to the period of purchase.

An accurate adjustment requires eliminating the discounts taken related to purchases of previous periods while including the amount of discounts available at the end of the accounting period that are expected to be taken during the following period. This refinement in the treatment of purchase discounts seldom appears in practice.

**Alternative 2: Net Price Method**   In recording purchases, the purchase discount is deducted from the gross purchase price immediately upon receipt of the invoice, and the net invoice price is used in the entries. The example used previously of a $1,000 invoice price for goods subject to a 2 percent cash discount would be recorded as follows under the net price method:

| Net Price Method | (1) Discount Taken | | (2) Discount Not Taken | |
|---|---|---|---|---|
| Purchases (or Inventory) ........................... | 980 | | 980 | |
| Accounts Payable .............................. | | 980 | | 980 |
| To record purchase. | | | | |
| Accounts Payable ................................ | 980 | | 980 | |
| Purchase Discounts Lost .......................... | — | | 20 | |
| Cash........................................ | | 980 | | 1,000 |
| To record payment. | | | | |

The balance in the Purchase Discounts Lost account could be added to the cost of the merchandise purchased and, therefore, viewed as an additional component of goods available for sale. Most accountants believe, however, that discounts lost should be shown as general operating expenses rather than as additions to the cost of purchases, because lost discounts may indicate an inefficient office force or inadequate financing. In this text, we treat purchase discounts lost as expenses unless an explicit contrary statement is made.

a.   Attempt to decide which of these two alternatives is preferable and why. You might find working part **b**, below, helpful in making your decision.

b.   Prepare a journal form with two pairs of columns, one headed Net Price Method and the other headed Gross Price Method. Using this journal form, show summary entries for the following events in the history of Evans and Foster, furniture manufacturers.

   (1)   During the first year of operations, materials with a gross invoice price of $60,000 are purchased. All invoices are subject to a 2 percent cash discount if paid within 10 days.

   (2)   Payments to creditors during the year amount to $53,000, settling $54,000 of accounts payable at gross prices.

   (3)   Of the $6,000, gross, in unpaid accounts at the end of the year, the discount time has expired on one invoice amounting to $400. It is expected that all other discounts will be taken. This expectation is reflected in the year-end adjustment.

   (4)   During the first few days of the next period, all invoices are paid in accordance with expectations.

**29.** *Gross and net price methods for recording purchase discounts.* (This problem should not be attempted until Problem 28 has been read.) The following are selected transactions of the Skousen Appliance Store:

**(1)** A shipment of refrigerators with a gross invoice price of $15,000 is received from the Standard Electric Company. Terms are 2/30, n/60.

**(2)** Part of the shipment of **(1)** is returned. The gross invoice price of the returned goods is $1,200, and a credit memorandum for this amount is received from the Standard Electric Company.

**(3)** The invoice of the Standard Electric Company is paid in time to take the discount.

**a.** Give entries on the books of the Skousen Appliance Store, assuming that the net price method is used.

**b.** Give entries on the books of the Skousen Appliance Store, assuming that the gross price method is used.

**30.** *Fundamentals of the gross margin method for approximating inventory amounts.* The merchandise inventory of Parks Store was destroyed by fire on July 4. The accounting records were saved and provided the following information:

| | |
|---|---|
| Cost of Merchandise Inventory on Hand, January 1 .................... | $ 45,000 |
| Purchases of Merchandise, January 1 to July 4........................ | 125,000 |
| Sales, January 1 to July 4........................................... | 180,000 |

The average retail markup over cost of goods sold during the year before the fire was 50 percent of the acquisition cost; that is, selling price was equal to 150 percent of cost.

**a.** Estimate the cost of the goods on hand at the time of the fire.

**b.** Give the journal entry to record the loss, assuming that it was uninsured.

**c.** Give the journal entry to record the loss, assuming that all goods were fully insured for their acquisition cost.

**31.** *Fundamentals of the retail inventory method for approximating inventory amounts.* Refer to the data in the preceding problem. Assume that the store owner does not know the average retail markup over cost for the destroyed goods. The accounting records show that the total sales revenue during the 4 years preceding the fire amounted to $1,000,000 and the total cost of goods sold over the same period was $650,000.

**a.** Assume that the ratio of sales prices to cost of goods sold for the last 4 years reflects this year's operations as well. Estimate the cost of the goods destroyed in the fire.

**b.** Assume the same facts as before, except that the $1,000,000 represents the original selling price of the goods sold during the last 4 years. Certain goods were marked down before sale so that the actual sales revenue was only $975,000. Assuming that the same percentage of goods was marked down by the same price percentage during the first 6 months of this year as in the previous 4 years, estimate the cost of the goods destroyed by the fire.

32. *Detailed comparison of various choices for inventory accounting.* The Harrison Corporation was organized and began retailing operations on January 1, Year 1. Purchases of merchandise inventory during Year 1 and Year 2 were as follows:

| | Quantity Purchased | Unit Price | Acquisition Cost |
|---|---|---|---|
| 1/10/Year 1 .......................... | 1,000 | $10 | $10,000 |
| 6/30/Year 1 .......................... | 400 | 15 | 6,000 |
| 10/20/Year 1 ......................... | 200 | 16 | 3,200 |
| Total Year 1 ...................... | 1,600 | | $19,200 |

| | Quantity Purchased | Unit Price | Acquisition Cost |
|---|---|---|---|
| 2/18/Year 2 .......................... | 300 | $18 | $ 5,400 |
| 7/15/Year 2 .......................... | 100 | 20 | 2,000 |
| 12/15/Year 2 ......................... | 500 | 22 | 11,000 |
| Total Year 2 ...................... | 900 | | $18,400 |

The number of units sold during Year 1 and Year 2 was 900 units and 1,100 units, respectively. Harrison Corporation uses a periodic inventory system.

a. Calculate the cost of goods sold during Year 1 under the FIFO cost flow assumption.

b. Calculate the cost of goods sold during Year 1 under the LIFO cost flow assumption.

c. Calculate the cost of goods sold during Year 1 under the weighted-average cost flow assumption.

d. Calculate the cost of goods sold during Year 2 under the FIFO cost flow assumption.

e. Calculate the cost of goods sold during Year 2 under the LIFO cost flow assumption.

f. Calculate the cost of goods sold during Year 2 under the weighted-average cost flow assumption.

g. For the 2 years taken as a whole, will FIFO or LIFO result in reporting the larger net income? What is the difference in net income for the 2-year period under FIFO as compared to LIFO? Assume an income tax rate of 40 percent for both years.

h. Which method, LIFO or FIFO, should Harrison Corporation probably prefer and why?

33. *Continuation of preceding problem introducing current cost concepts.* (This problem should not be attempted until Problem 32 has been done.) Assume the same data for the Harrison Corporation as given in the previous problem. In addition, assume the following:

| | |
|---|---:|
| **Selling Price per Unit:** | |
| Year 1...................................................................... | $25 |
| Year 2...................................................................... | 30 |
| **Average Current Replacement Cost:** | |
| Year 1...................................................................... | $15 |
| Year 2...................................................................... | 20 |
| **Current Replacement Cost:** | |
| December 31, Year 1 ....................................................... | $17 |
| December 31, Year 2 ....................................................... | 22 |

   **a.** Prepare an analysis for Year 1 that identifies operating margins, realized holding gains and losses, and unrealized holding gains and losses for the FIFO, LIFO, and weighted-average cost flow assumptions.

   **b.** Repeat part **a** for Year 2.

   **c.** Demonstrate that over the 2-year period, income plus holding gains before taxes of Harrison Corporation are independent of the cost flow assumption.

**34.** *Decision making and cost basis for inventories.* Imagine that you take frequent business trips. You have discovered a major airline's Bonus Travel tickets, which enable the holder to fly round trip anywhere that the airline flies. These tickets are bought and sold by special ticket brokers, and their price fluctuates almost daily in the market place. The schedule shown here presents data on tickets purchased and used.

| Ticket Number | When Bought | Price Paid | When Used |
|---|---|---|---|
| 1 .............................. | May | $400 | May |
| 2 .............................. | May | 400 | ? |
| 3 .............................. | May | 425 | June |
| 4 .............................. | June | 450 | July |
| 5 .............................. | June | 475 | August |
| 6 .............................. | June | 500 | September |
| 7 .............................. | July | 440 | ? |
| 8 .............................. | August | 550 | ? |

In October, you decide to take a good friend with you on a weekend vacation to New York and to use two of the tickets you have for the trip. At the time you take the October vacation, you have three tickets in your desk drawer: numbers 2, 7, and 8. During the week of the trip you have the option to purchase new tickets for $600 each, and your broker offers to buy tickets from you or anyone else for $480 each.

   Your friend wants to reimburse you for the "cost" of the travel but has not made clear what is meant by *cost*. Your friend does not intend to audit the cost you quote. What is the "cost" of your friend's travel under each of the following sets of facts?

   **a.** For the trip you use ticket numbers 2 and 8, putting the friend's name on ticket 2 and yours on ticket 8.

   **b.** For the trip you use ticket numbers 2 and 8, putting the friend's name on ticket 8 and yours on ticket 2.

**c.** Just before you depart, your broker, in tribute to your being such a good customer, offers you one ticket for the bargain price of $480 and offers to sell you other tickets for $600. You purchase the ticket, but not until after the vacation weekend. For the trip you use ticket numbers 2 and 8, putting the friend's name on ticket 2 and yours on ticket 8.

**d.** Same facts as **c**, except that you do purchase the bargain-priced ticket and use it during the vacation, putting your friend's name on it.

**e.** Indicate how your answers to parts **a** through **d** change (if they do) when you assume that your traveling companion is a business associate, not your friend, and the trip is a business trip, not a vacation.

**f.** Should the cost you impose on your friend or your business associate depend on which particular ticket happens to be used in travel?

35. *Exploring the relation between replacement cost of goods sold and historical LIFO cost of goods sold.* The points to grasp in this problem are as follows:

**(1)** LIFO cost of goods sold is generally larger in a periodic inventory than in a perpetual inventory.

**(2)** LIFO cost of goods sold for most companies is insignificantly different from replacement cost of goods sold (using replacement costs as of the time of sale).

**(3)** Historical LIFO cost of goods sold in a periodic inventory is likely to be larger, although not significantly, than the replacement cost of goods sold (using replacement cost at the time of sale).

The data in Exhibit 8.17 are hypothetical. They are constructed from ratios of Safeway Stores, a firm selling grocery products. Sales revenue for the year is $2,820,000. All expenses (including income taxes) other than cost of goods sold are $144,000 for the year. Exhibit 8.17 shows cost of goods available for sale. The costs of the grocery items for this company increase during the year at a steady rate of about 1 percent per month. The company starts the year with an inventory equal to $1\frac{1}{2}$ months' sales. These items were acquired at the end of December of Year 1 for $300,000. At the end of each month during Year 2, the firm is assumed to acquire inventory in physical quantities equal to the next month's sales requirements. We assume that all sales occur at mid-month during each month and that all purchases occur at the end of a month, with the goods to be sold during the next month. (These artificial assumptions capture the reality of a firm acquiring inventory on average $\frac{1}{2}$ month before it is sold and having an inventory turnover rate of about eight times per year.) Identical physical quantities are purchased and sold each month.

Exhibit 8.17 shows the actual cost of the items purchased at the end of each month and the replacement cost of those items if they had been acquired at mid-month.

At the end of the year, ending physical inventory is equal in amount to $1\frac{1}{2}$ months' sales, which is the same as the physical quantity on hand at the start of the year.

**a.** Compute LIFO historical cost of goods sold and net income for Year 2 using a periodic inventory system.

**b.** Compute LIFO historical cost of goods sold and net income for Year 2 using a perpetual inventory system.

**Exhibit 8.17** ————————————————————————————————————————
**Data for Problem 35**

| | Replacement Cost of Goods Measured at | |
| --- | --- | --- |
| | Sales Dates (mid-month) | Purchases Dates (end of month) |
| December Year 1.............................. | — | $ 300,000 |
| January Year 2................................ | $ 201,000 | 202,000 |
| February Year 2............................... | 203,000 | 204,000 |
| March Year 2 ................................ | 205,000 | 206,000 |
| April Year 2.................................. | 207,000 | 208,000 |
| May Year 2 .................................. | 209,000 | 210,000 |
| June Year 2 .................................. | 211,000 | 212,000 |
| July Year 2 .................................. | 213,000 | 214,000 |
| August Year 2................................. | 215,000 | 216,000 |
| September Year 2 ............................. | 217,000 | 218,000 |
| October Year 2................................ | 219,000 | 220,000 |
| November Year 2.............................. | 221,000 | 222,000 |
| December Year 2.............................. | 223,000 | 224,000 |
| Replacement Cost of Goods Sold at Times of Sale . | $2,544,000 | |
| Cost of Goods Available for Sale.................. | | $2,856,000 |

c.   Compute net income for Year 2 using replacement cost of goods sold at the time of sale.

d.   What is the percentage difference between the largest and smallest cost-of-goods-sold figures computed in the preceding three parts?

e.   What is the percentage error in using LIFO costs of goods sold to approximate replacement cost of goods sold? (Compute percentage errors for both LIFO periodic and LIFO perpetual calculations.)

f.   Would you expect that most companies using LIFO for tax purposes do so with a periodic inventory system or with a perpetual inventory system? Why?

36. *Comparing LIFO and FIFO with declines in inventory quantities.* The LIFO Company and the FIFO Company both manufacture paper and cardboard products. Prices of timber, paper pulp, and finished paper products have generally increased by about 5 percent per year through the *start of this year*. Inventory data for the beginning and end of the year are as follows:

| | Inventory Amounts | |
| --- | --- | --- |
| | January 1 | December 31 |
| LIFO Company Inventory (last-in, first-out; historical cost)................................ | $19,695,000 | $15,870,000 |
| FIFO Company Inventory (first-in, first-out; lower of cost or market) ................................ | 46,284,000 | 38,250,000 |

Income statements for the two companies for the year ending December 31 are as follows:

|  | LIFO Company | FIFO Company |
| --- | --- | --- |
| Sales..................................... | $57,000,000 | $129,000,000 |
| Expenses: |  |  |
| Cost of Goods Sold....................... | $44,580,000 | $108,000,000 |
| Depreciation ............................ | 5,400,000 | 12,000,000 |
| General Expenses ........................ | 2,220,000 | 5,400,000 |
| Income Taxes (40 percent of pretax income) . | 1,920,000 | 1,440,000 |
| Total Expenses......................... | $54,120,000 | $126,840,000 |
| Net Income ............................. | $ 2,880,000 | $ 2,160,000 |

a. Assuming that the prices for timber, paper pulp, and finished paper had remained unchanged during the year, how would the two companies' respective inventory choices have affected the interpretation of their financial statements for the year?

b. How would the answer to part **a** differ if prices at the end of the year had been lower than at the beginning of the year?

c. How would the answer to part **a** differ if prices at the end of the year had been higher than at the beginning of the year?

**37.** *LIFO layers influence purchasing behavior and provide opportunity for income manipulation.* The Wilson Company sells chemical compounds made from expensium. The company has used a LIFO inventory flow assumption for many years. The inventory of expensium on December 31, 1987, consisted of 4,000 pounds from 1978 through 1987 at prices ranging from $30 to $52 per pound. Exhibit 8.18 shows the layers of 1987 ending inventory.

Expensium costs $62 per pound during 1988, but the purchasing agent expects its price to fall back to $52 per pound in 1989. Sales for 1988 require 7,000 pounds of expensium. Wilson Company wants to carry a stock of 4,000 pounds of inventory. The purchasing agent suggests that the inventory of expensium should be allowed to decrease from 4,000 to 600 pounds by the end of 1988 and be replenished to the desired level of 4,000 pounds early in 1989.

The controller argues that such a policy would be foolish. If inventories are allowed to decrease to 600 pounds, the cost of goods sold will be extraordinarily low (because the older LIFO layers will be consumed) and income taxes will be extraordinarily high. He suggests that 1988 purchases should be planned to maintain an end-of-year inventory of 4,000 pounds.

Assume that sales for 1988 do require 7,000 pounds of expensium, that the prices for 1988 are as forecast, and that the income tax rate for Wilson Company is 40 percent.

a. Calculate the cost of goods sold and end-of-year LIFO inventory for 1988, assuming that the controller's advice is followed and inventory at the end of 1988 is 4,000 pounds.

Exhibit 8.18 _____
WILSON COMPANY
Layers of 1987 Year-End Inventory
(Problem 37)

| Year Acquired | Purchase Price per Pound | 1987 Year-End Inventory | |
| --- | --- | --- | --- |
| | | Pounds | Cost |
| 1978 .............................. | $30 | 2,000 | $ 60,000 |
| 1983 .............................. | 46 | 200 | 9,200 |
| 1984 .............................. | 48 | 400 | 19,200 |
| 1987 .............................. | 52 | 1,400 | 72,800 |
| | | 4,000 | $161,200 |

**b.** Calculate the cost of goods sold and end-of-year LIFO inventory for 1988, assuming that the purchasing agent's advice is followed and inventory at the end of 1988 is 600 pounds.

**c.** Assuming that the controller's, not the purchasing agent's, advice is followed, calculate the tax savings for 1988 and the extra cash costs for inventory.

**d.** What should Wilson Company do?

**e.** Management of Wilson Company wants to know what discretion it has to vary income for 1988 by planning its purchases of expensium. If the controller's policy is followed, aftertax income for 1988 will be $50,000. What is the range, after taxes, of income that can be achieved by the purposeful management of expensium purchases?

**38.** *Reconstructing underlying events from ending inventory amounts (adapted from CPA examination).* The Burch Corporation began a merchandising business on January 1, Year 1. It acquired merchandise costing $100,000 in Year 1, $125,000 in Year 2, and $135,000 in Year 3. Exhibit 8.19 presents information about Burch Corporation's inventory as it would appear on the balance sheet under different inventory methods.

In answering each of the following questions, indicate how the answer is deduced. You may assume that in any one year, prices moved only up or down but not both.

**a.** Did prices go up or down in Year 1?

**b.** Did prices go up or down in Year 3?

**c.** Which inventory method would show the highest income for Year 1?

**d.** Which inventory method would show the highest income for Year 2?

**e.** Which inventory method would show the highest income for Year 3?

**f.** Which inventory method would show the lowest income for all 3 years combined?

**g.** For Year 3, how much higher or lower would income be on the FIFO cost basis than it would be on the lower-of-cost-or-market basis?

Exhibit 8.19 _____

**BURCH CORPORATION**
**Inventory Valuations for Balance Sheet under Various Assumptions**
**(Problem 38)**

| December 31 | LIFO Cost | FIFO Cost | Lower of FIFO Cost or Market |
|---|---|---|---|
| Year 1............................ | $40,200 | $40,000 | $37,000 |
| Year 2............................ | 36,400 | 36,000 | 34,000 |
| Year 3............................ | 41,800 | 44,000 | 44,000 |

39. *Detailed comparison of various choices for inventory accounting.* The Freeman Corporation was organized and began retailing operations on January 1, Year 1. Purchases of merchandise inventory during Year 1 and Year 2 were as follows:

| | Quantity Purchased | Unit Price | Acquisition Cost |
|---|---|---|---|
| 1/10/Year 1 ............................ | 600 | $10 | $ 6,000 |
| 6/30/Year 1 ............................ | 200 | 12 | 2,400 |
| 10/20/Year 1 ............................ | 400 | 15 | 6,000 |
| Total Year 1 ........................ | 1,200 | | $14,400 |

| | Quantity Purchased | Unit Price | Acquisition Cost |
|---|---|---|---|
| 2/18/Year 2 ............................ | 500 | $18 | $ 9,000 |
| 7/15/Year 2 ............................ | 500 | 20 | 10,000 |
| 12/15/Year 2 ............................ | 800 | 24 | 19,200 |
| Total Year 2 ........................ | 1,800 | | $38,200 |

The number of units sold during Year 1 and Year 2 was 1,000 units and 1,500 units, respectively. Freeman Corporation uses a periodic inventory system.

a.  Calculate the cost of goods sold during Year 1 under the FIFO cost flow assumption.

b.  Calculate the cost of goods sold during Year 1 under the LIFO cost flow assumption.

c.  Calculate the cost of goods sold during Year 1 under the weighted-average cost flow assumption.

d.  Calculate the cost of goods sold during Year 2 under the FIFO cost flow assumption.

e.  Calculate the cost of goods sold during Year 2 under the LIFO cost flow assumption.

f.  Calculate the cost of goods sold during Year 2 under the weighted-average cost flow assumption.

g.  For the 2 years taken as a whole, will FIFO or LIFO result in reporting the larger net income? What is the difference in net income for the 2-year period under FIFO as compared to LIFO? Assume an income tax rate of 40 percent for both years.

h.  Which method, LIFO or FIFO, should Freeman Corporation probably prefer and why?

40. *Continuation of preceding problem introducing current cost concepts.* (This problem should not be attempted until Problem 39 has been done.) Assume the same data for the Freeman Corporation as given in the previous problem. In addition, assume the following:

| | |
|---|---:|
| **Selling Price per Unit:** | |
| Year 1.................................................................. | $25 |
| Year 2.................................................................. | 30 |
| **Average Current Replacement Cost:** | |
| Year 1.................................................................. | $14 |
| Year 2.................................................................. | 22 |
| **Current Replacement Cost:** | |
| December 31, Year 1 ................................................. | $16 |
| December 31, Year 2 ................................................. | 25 |

a.  Prepare an analysis for Year 1 that identifies operating margins, realized holding gains and losses, and unrealized holding gains and losses for the FIFO, LIFO, and weighted-average cost flow assumptions.

b.  Repeat part **a** for Year 2.

c.  Demonstrate that over the 2-year period, income plus holding gains before taxes of Freeman Corporation are independent of the cost flow assumption.

41. *Analysis of financial statement ratios affected by cost flow assumptions.* A recent annual report of General Motors Corporation contained the following in the section "Financial Review: Management's Discussion and Analysis." (Dates have been changed for convenience.)

> General Motors' liquidity can be measured by its current ratio (ratio of current assets to current liabilities). For the years ended December 31, Year 2 and Year 1, the current ratio, based on LIFO inventories, was 1.13 and 1.09, respectively. The LIFO method, while improving Corporate cash flow, adversely affects the current ratio. . . . If inventories were valued at FIFO, the current ratio would be 1.21 and 1.18, at the ends of Year 2 and Year 1, respectively.

Assume an income tax rate of 46 percent and assume that current assets were $14,043 million and $13,714 million at the end of Year 2 and Year 1, respectively.

a.  Compute the difference between FIFO and LIFO inventories at the ends of Year 2 and Year 1.

   **b.** How did the use of LIFO affect cash flow for Year 2?

   **c.** By how much has the use of LIFO improved cash flow since the time it was adopted?

**42.** *Analysis of disclosures from published financial reports on effects of changing from average cost to LIFO.* The following is adapted from various disclosures in the annual reports of E. I. duPont de Nemours & Company in the year it switched from average cost to LIFO for most of its inventories as well as in the 2 following years. Assume an income tax rate of 48 percent.

**Year 1**  During the year, Du Pont changed its cost flow assumption for most of its inventories from average cost to LIFO to achieve a better matching of current costs with revenues. Net income was reduced by $249.6 million, 27 percent, for the year.

**Year 2**  During the year, inventory quantities were reduced from the abnormally high levels at the start of the year. This resulted in liquidation of LIFO inventory quantities carried at costs lower than those prevailing during the year. The effect was to increase net income by approximately $36.4 million.

**Year 3**  If inventory had been valued at current cost, rather than at historical cost using a LIFO cost flow assumption, the amounts on the balance sheet would have exceeded the amounts reported by $490 million at end of the year and by $410 million at the beginning of the year.

   **a.** By how much did LIFO cost of goods sold in Year 1 differ from the amount computed with an average-cost cost flow assumption?

   **b.** Why does a liquidation of LIFO layers, such as in Year 2, increase net income?

   **c.** By how much did cost of goods sold for Year 2 differ from the amount that would have been reported had the layers not been liquidated? Give the amount and indicate whether this represents an increase or decrease in cost of goods sold.

   **d.** Why might the company not have changed back to average cost for Year 2?

   **e.** Assume that an average-cost cost flow assumption gives ending inventory amounts that are approximately the same as current costs. What were the savings in taxes for Year 3 that resulted from Du Pont's using LIFO rather than average cost?

   **f.** Why might Du Pont choose a cost flow assumption for inventory that reduces reported income?

**43.** *Effects of cost flow assumptions on reported income.* Exhibit 8.20 shows data for the General Electric Company's inventories for a period of years (1) under the LIFO assumption as actually used and (2) under FIFO as inventories would have been if it had been used.

   **a.** Compute the pretax income for years 2 through 6, assuming that a FIFO cost flow assumption had been used.

Exhibit 8.20 _____

**GENERAL ELECTRIC COMPANY**
**(all dollar amounts in millions)**
**(Problem 43)**

| End of Year | LIFO Ending Inventory | FIFO Ending Inventory |
|---|---|---|
| 1 ........................................... | $1,611.7 | $1,884.5 |
| 2 ........................................... | 1,759.0 | 2,063.1 |
| 3 ........................................... | 1,986.2 | 2,415.9 |
| 4 ........................................... | 2,257.0 | 3,040.7 |
| 5 ........................................... | 2,202.9 | 3,166.6 |
| 6 ........................................... | 2,354.4 | 3,515.2 |

| For the Year | Pretax Operating Income Using LIFO |
|---|---|
| 2 ........................................... | $  897.2 |
| 3 ........................................... | 1,011.6 |
| 4 ........................................... | 1,000.7 |
| 5 ........................................... | 1,174.0 |
| 6 ........................................... | 1,627.5 |

| End of Year | Current Assets | Current Liabilities |
|---|---|---|
| 2 ........................................... | $3,979.3 | $2,869.7 |
| 3 ........................................... | 4,485.4 | 3,492.4 |
| 4 ........................................... | 5,222.6 | 3,879.5 |
| 5 ........................................... | 5,750.4 | 4,163.0 |
| 6 ........................................... | 6,685.0 | 4,604.9 |

**b.** Calculate the percentage change in pretax income for each of the years 3 through 6 under both LIFO and FIFO (that is, the increase in pretax income in Year 3 relative to Year 2, the increase in pretax income in Year 4 relative to Year 3, and so on).

**c.** Calculate the percentage change in pretax income between Year 2 and Year 6 (that is, the 5-year period taken as a whole) under both LIFO and FIFO.

**d.** Did the quantity of items in inventory increase or decrease during each of the years 3 through 6? How can you tell?

**e.** Did the acquisition cost of items in inventory increase or decrease during each of the years 3 through 6? How can you tell?

**f.** Assume for this part that the inventory value under LIFO of $1,611.7 at the end of Year 1 is the initial LIFO layer. This layer may be viewed as the bottom layer on a cake. Construct a figure showing the addition or subtraction of LIFO layers for each of the years 2 through 6.

**g.** The current assets and current liabilities of the General Electric Company at the end of years 2 through 6 using a LIFO cost flow assumption are shown in Exhibit 8.20. Compute General Electric's current ratio for each year using the data given.

**h.** Recompute General Electric's current ratio for each year using a FIFO cost flow assumption for inventories. Although it is unrealistic to do so, assume for this part that there are no changes in income taxes payable or in current liabilities. (To make the figures realistic after taxes, ending LIFO inventory should be increased by about one-half the difference between FIFO and LIFO ending inventory amounts. Why? Do not make this adjustment in working the problem, however.)

# Chapter 9    Plant, Equipment, and Intangible Assets: The Source of Operating Capacity ─────

Assets are future benefits, short-lived or long-lived. A business acquires a short-lived asset such as insurance coverage in one period and uses up its benefits within a year. To reap the benefits of a long-lived asset the owner uses it for several years. In this case, the accountant allocates the cost of the asset over the several accounting periods of benefit. This general process is called *amortization*. Amortization of plant assets, which include the fixtures, machinery, equipment, and physical structures of a business, is called *depreciation*.

In addition to its plant assets, companies such as Exxon and Santa Fe Industries own natural resources, called *wasting assets*. Oil wells, coal mines, uranium deposits, and other natural resources are eventually used up. Amortization of the cost of these wasting assets is called *depletion*.

Businesses may also acquire intangible assets, and although there are many examples, several well-known ones are everyday words, such as Coca-Cola, Kleenex, and Xerox, all famous trademarks. A firm may purchase a McDonald's or Kentucky Fried Chicken franchise. Other intangible assets are goodwill, copyrights, and patents. Although such intangibles may have indefinite economic lives, the accountant generally amortizes their costs to the periods of benefit. There is no specific term for the amortization of intangibles; the general term *amortization* is used to describe the process of writing off the cost of all intangibles.

Most of this chapter treats depreciation, because plant assets are the most common long-lived assets and depreciation problems are typical of almost all other amortization problems.[1]

─────────────

[1] The terms *plant assets* and *fixed assets* are often used interchangeably. They refer to long-lived assets used in the operations of trading, service, and manufacturing enterprises and include land, buildings, machinery, and equipment. The ordinary usage of the terms *plant assets* and *fixed assets* often does not adequately encompass the class of long-lived assets that includes all land, buildings, machinery, and equipment. *Plant assets* is sometimes used too narrowly to mean only items in a factory or plant. *Fixed assets* is sometimes used too narrowly to mean only items such as land and buildings that are immovable.

The problems of plant asset valuation and depreciation measurement conveniently divide into the consideration of four separate kinds of events:

1. Recording the acquisition of the asset.
2. Recording its use over time.
3. Recording adjustments for changes in capacity or efficiency and for repairs or improvements.
4. Recording its retirement or other disposal.

## Acquisition of Plant Assets _____

The cost of a *plant asset* includes all charges necessary to prepare it for rendering services, and it is often recorded in a series of transactions. Thus the cost of a piece of equipment will be the sum of the entries to recognize the invoice price (less any discounts), transportation costs, installation charges, and any other costs incurred before the equipment is ready for use. See the example on page 37.

Computing the acquisition cost of an asset acquired in a trade-in transaction presents special problems. A trade-in transaction involves both the retirement of an old asset and the acquisition of a new one. Although its problems might be discussed with acquisitions, this chapter discusses trade-in transactions in the section on retirements. Computing the acquisition cost of a self-constructed asset presents other problems, discussed next.

### Self-Constructed Asset

When a firm constructs its own buildings or equipment, many entries to record the labor, material, and overhead costs will normally be required before the total cost is recorded. FASB *Statement No. 34* requires the firm to also include *interest paid during the construction period* as part of the cost of the asset being constructed.[2] The amount of interest included is based on the entity's actual borrowings and interest payments. It is intended to be the interest cost incurred during periods of asset acquisition that in principle could have been avoided if the assets had not been acquired.

If there is a specific new borrowing in connection with the asset being constructed, the interest rate on that borrowing is used. If the expenditures on plant exceed such specific new borrowings, the interest rate to be applied to such excess is the weighted average of rates applicable to other borrowings of the enterprise. There may not be specific new borrowings; then the average interest rate on old borrowings is used to compute the total amount to be capitalized. The total amount of interest included cannot exceed total interest costs for the period. The capitalization of interest into plant during construction reduces otherwise reportable interest

_____

[2]Financial Accounting Standards Board, *Statement of Financial Accounting Standards No. 34,* "Capitalization of Interest Cost," 1979.

expense and increases income during periods of construction. In later periods, the plant will have higher depreciation charges, reducing income.

**Example**  Assume the following long-term debt structure:

| | |
|---|---:|
| Construction Loan at 15 Percent on Building under Construction . . . . . . . . . . . | $1,000,000 |
| Other Borrowings at 12 Percent Average Rate . . . . . . . . . . . . . . . . . . . . . . . . . | 3,600,000 |
| Total Long-Term Debt . . . . . . . . . . . . . . . . . . . . . . . . . . . . . . . . . . . . . . . . . . . | $4,600,000 |

The account Building under Construction has an average balance during the year of $3,000,000. The amount of interest to be capitalized is based on all of the new construction-related borrowings ($1,000,000) and enough of the older borrowings ($2,000,000) to bring the total to $3,000,000. The interest capitalized is computed as follows:

| | |
|---|---:|
| $1,000,000 × .15 . . . . . . . . . . . . . . . . . . . . . . . . . . . . . . . . . . . . . . . . . . . . . . . | $150,000 |
| $2,000,000 × .12 . . . . . . . . . . . . . . . . . . . . . . . . . . . . . . . . . . . . . . . . . . . . . . . | 240,000 |
| $3,000,000 | $390,000 |

The entries to record interest and to capitalize the required amounts might be as follows:

| | | |
|---|---:|---:|
| Interest Expense . . . . . . . . . . . . . . . . . . . . . . . . . . . . . . . . . . . . . . . . . . | 582,000 | |
|    Interest Payable . . . . . . . . . . . . . . . . . . . . . . . . . . . . . . . . . . . . . . . . | | 582,000 |
| To record all interest as expense: $582,000 = (.15 × $1,000,000) + (.12 × $3,600,000) = $150,000 + $432,000. | | |

| | | |
|---|---:|---:|
| Building under Construction . . . . . . . . . . . . . . . . . . . . . . . . . . . . . . . . . . | 390,000 | |
|    Interest Expense . . . . . . . . . . . . . . . . . . . . . . . . . . . . . . . . . . . . . . . . | | 390,000 |
| The amount capitalized reduces interest expense and increases the recorded cost of the building. | | |

The preceding two entries might be combined into one as follows:

| | | |
|---|---:|---:|
| Interest Expense . . . . . . . . . . . . . . . . . . . . . . . . . . . . . . . . . . . . . . . . . . | 192,000 | |
| Building under Construction . . . . . . . . . . . . . . . . . . . . . . . . . . . . . . . . . . | 390,000 | |
|    Interest Payable . . . . . . . . . . . . . . . . . . . . . . . . . . . . . . . . . . . . . . . . | | 582,000 |
| The amount for Interest Expense is a plug. | | |

Both total interest for the year, $582,000, and the amount capitalized, $390,000, must be disclosed in notes. The income statement will report interest expense — $192,000 in the example. The amount shown in future years for depreciation of the plant will be larger than otherwise because of interest capitalization in earlier years. Over the life of the asset, from construction through retirement, total income is unaffected by capitalizing interest, because the increased income in the construction period is later exactly offset with larger depreciation charges. Over sufficiently long time spans, total expense must equal total cash expenditure.

# Depreciation — Fundamental Concepts _____

## Purpose of Depreciation

Most plant assets can be kept intact and in usable operating condition for more than a year, but, except for land, they eventually must be retired from service. *Depreciation* systematically allocates the cost of these assets to the periods of their use.

**Allocation of Cost**   The cost of a depreciating asset is the price paid for a series of future services. The asset account is like a prepayment, similar to prepaid rent or insurance — a payment in advance for services to be received. As the asset is used in each accounting period, a portion of the investment in the asset is treated as the cost of the service received and is recognized as an expense of the period or as part of the cost of goods produced during the period.

Depreciation is a process of cost allocation, not one of valuation. This chapter discusses the problems of *allocating* assets' costs to the periods of benefit. A depreciation problem will exist whenever (1) funds are invested in services to be rendered by a plant asset and (2) at some date in the future, the asset must be retired from service with a residual value less than its original cost.

No uniquely correct amount for the periodic charge for depreciation can be computed. The cost of the plant asset is a *joint cost* of the several benefited periods; that is, each of the periods of the asset's use benefits from its services. There is usually no single correct way to allocate a joint cost. The depreciation process assigns periodic charges that reflect systematic calculations.

**Return of Capital**   A business attempts to earn both a return *of* capital and a return *on* capital. Before there can be a return *on* capital (as measured by accounting profits), all costs must be recovered. The purpose of amortization is to charge against revenues the cost of noncurrent assets. To understand the role of amortization in this process, reconsider the installment method and the cost-recovery-first method of recognizing revenue, introduced in Chapter 4. In the cost-recovery-first method, there is no accounting income until all costs are recovered. The accounting under cost recovery first charges to expense an amount equal to cash collections so that there is no accounting income until all anticipated costs have been debited to expense. In contrast, under the installment method, costs are allocated over the time of cash collections so that each dollar collected represents identical proportions of cost recovery and profits.

In accounting for noncurrent assets, one might, in principle, debit expense and credit plant assets so that there is no profit until the costs of plant assets have been written off. The early periods of a noncurrent asset's life could have no income, but the later periods would show no expense for plant and, consequently, larger net income. Instead, accounting estimates the life of the noncurrent asset and writes off its cost over its life, in principle allowing each period to show both cost recovery and income. The amortization process provides for the gradual return of the investment in a noncurrent asset. In historical cost accounting, the process is designed to provide a return of the cost of the asset, no more and no less.[3] But the return of costs is designed to occur over the asset's life, not all in the early periods of its life.

## Depreciation Is Not a Decline in Value

In ordinary conversation depreciation frequently means a decline in *value*. Over the entire service life of a plant asset, there is a decline in the asset's value from acquisition until it is retired from service. The charge made to the operations of each accounting period does not result from declines in value during that period but rather from the process of ensuring a return of capital invested. If, in a given period, an asset increases in value, there will still be depreciation during that period. There have been two partially offsetting processes: (1) a holding gain on the asset, which usually is not recognized in historical cost-based accounting and (2) depreciation of the asset's historical cost to achieve a return of investment.

## The Causes of Depreciation

The causes of depreciation are the causes of decline in an asset's service potential and of its ultimate retirement. Unless the asset must eventually be retired from its planned use, there is no depreciation. When the services provided by land do not diminish over time, land is not depreciated; all costs are recovered when the land is sold. Many factors lead to the retirement of assets from service, but the causes of decline in service potential can be classified as either *physical* or *functional*.

The physical factors include such things as ordinary wear and tear from use, chemical action such as rust or electrolysis, and the effects of wind and rain.

The most important functional (nonphysical) cause is *obsolescence*. Inventions, for example, may result in new processes that reduce the unit cost of production to the point where continued operation of old equipment is not economical, even though it may be relatively unimpaired physically. Firms replace computers that work as well as when they were acquired because new, smaller computers occupy less space and compute faster. Retail stores often replace display cases and storefronts long before they are worn out to make the appearance of the store more attractive. Changed economic conditions may also become functional causes of

---

[3]As inflation has become a major economic problem, accountants increasingly recognize that basing depreciation charges on acquisition costs will not, in most cases, charge amounts to expense that are sufficient to maintain the productive capacity of the business. Basing depreciation on acquisition costs will enable a business to recover its initial cash investment but will not necessarily provide enough to replace the physical productive capacity purchased with the cash.

depreciation, such as when an old airport becomes inadequate and must be abandoned, and a new, larger one is built to meet the requirements of heavier traffic, or when an increase in the cost of gasoline causes a reduction in demand for automobile products, which results in a reduced scale of operations in automobile manufacturing.

Identifying the specific causes of depreciation is not essential for measuring it. Almost any physical asset will eventually have to be retired from service, and in some cases the retirement will become necessary at a time when physical deterioration is negligible. Understanding the specific causes can, nevertheless, help in estimating an asset's useful life.

# Depreciation Accounting Problems ———————————

The three principal accounting problems in allocating the cost of an asset over time are as follows:

1. Measuring the depreciable basis of the asset.
2. Estimating its useful service life.
3. Deciding on the pattern of expiration of asset cost over the useful service life.

## Depreciable Basis of Plant Assets — Cost less Salvage Value

Depreciation charges in historical cost accounting are based on the acquisition cost of the asset less the estimated residual value — the amount to be received when the asset is retired from service. The amounts invested in an asset that will be recovered when the asset is retired do not need to be recovered through depreciation charges. Recall that land is not depreciated because its cost will be recovered at the time of sale. Similarly, the amount estimated to be recovered from a depreciating plant asset at its retirement does not need to be depreciated; that portion of the initial investment is recovered at retirement.

**Estimating Salvage Value**  Depreciation charges are based on the difference between acquisition cost and the asset's estimated salvage value or net residual value. The terms *salvage value* and *net residual value* refer to estimated proceeds on disposition of an asset less all removal and selling costs. Salvage value must be an estimate at any time before the asset is retired. Hence, before retirement, the terms *salvage value* and *estimated salvage value* are synonymous.

For buildings, common practice assumes a zero salvage value. This treatment rests on the assumption that the cost to be incurred in tearing down the building will approximate the sales value of the scrap materials recovered. For other assets, however, the salvage value may be substantial and should be taken into account in making the periodic depreciation charge. For example, a car rental firm will replace its automobiles at a time when other owners can use the cars for several years more. The rental firm will be able to recover a substantial part of acquisition cost (and return of part of the capital invested) from the sale of used cars. Past experience usually forms the best basis for estimating salvage value. (Salvage value can be negative. Consider, for example, the cost of dismantling a nuclear electricity-generating plant.)

Estimates of salvage value are necessarily subjective. Disputes over estimated salvage value have led to many disagreements between Internal Revenue Service agents and taxpayers. Partly to reduce such controversy, the Internal Revenue Code has been amended to provide that salvage value may be ignored entirely in calculating depreciation for tax reporting. When calculating depreciation in problems in this text, take the entire salvage value into account unless explicit contrary instructions are given.

**Unit of Account**  Whenever feasible, depreciation should be computed for individual items such as a single building, machine, or automobile. Where similar items are in use and each one has a relatively small cost, individual calculations may be impracticable and the depreciation charge is usually calculated for the group as a whole. Furniture and fixtures, tools, and telephone poles are examples of assets that are usually depreciated in groups. Group depreciation techniques are treated in more advanced financial accounting courses. The basic principles of depreciating individual items discussed here apply, however, to group depreciation situations.

## Estimating Service Life

The depreciation calculation requires an estimate of the economic *service life* of the asset. In making the estimate, both the physical and the functional causes of depreciation must be considered. Experience with similar assets, corrected for differences in the planned intensity of use or alterations in maintenance policy, is usually the best guide for this estimate.

Despite abundant data from experience, estimating service lives for financial reporting is the most difficult task in the entire depreciation calculation. Allowing for obsolescence is particularly difficult because most obsolescence results from forces outside the firm. Estimates will probably prove to be incorrect. For this reason, estimates of assets' useful service life are reconsidered every few years.

Income tax laws allow shorter lives to be used in computing depreciation for tax reporting, but when these lives are shorter than the economic lives of the assets, they should not be used for financial reporting.

In 1981 and 1986, Congress enacted legislation for the *Accelerated Cost Recovery System (ACRS)*. Under ACRS, almost all assets are grouped into one of seven classes as follows:

| Class | Examples |
|---|---|
| 3-year | Some racehorses; almost no others. |
| 5-year | Cars, trucks, some manufacturing equipment, research and development property. |
| 7-year | Office equipment, railroad cars, locomotives. |
| 10-year | Vessels, barges, land improvements. |
| 20-year | Municipal sewers. |
| 27.5-year | Residential rental property. |
| 31.5-year | Nonresidential buildings. |

## Pattern of Expiration of Costs

Once the cost is measured and both salvage value and service life are estimated, the total of depreciation charges for the whole life of the asset has been determined. If salvage value is assumed to be zero, the entire cost will be depreciated. The problem remains of selecting the pattern for allocating those charges to the specific years of the life. Depreciation based on the passage of time follows one of five basic patterns. They are labeled E, A, S, D, and N in Figures 9.1 and 9.2.

The next section discusses the patterns in more detail. A represents accelerated depreciation; S, straight-line depreciation; D, decelerated depreciation. (Understanding the terms *accelerated* and *decelerated* is easier if you compare the depreci-

**Figure 9.1** ————————————————————————————————————
**Patterns of Writing Off Costs: Book Value over Economic Life of Asset**

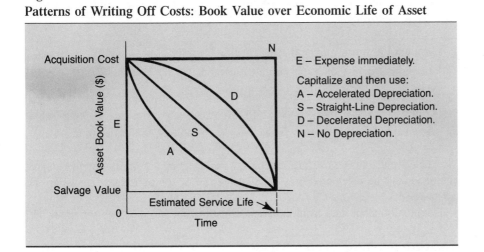

**Figure 9.2** ————————————————————————————————————
**Patterns of Annual Depreciation Charge over Economic Life of Asset**

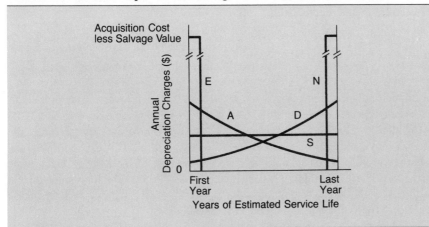

ation charges in the early years to straight-line depreciation. See Figure 9.2.) Pattern D is not used in financial reporting, but it is useful for certain managerial accounting problems (see Problem 39 at the end of this chapter). Pattern E represents immediate expensing of the item; all costs are charged to the period when the cost is incurred. The section on tangibles discusses this pattern. Pattern N represents the situation, such as for land, where there are no periodic amortization charges. The asset is shown on the books at acquisition cost until sold or otherwise retired.

# Depreciation Methods _____

All depreciation methods systematically allocate the cost of the asset minus its estimated salvage value to the periods in which it is used. The methods discussed here are as follows:

1. Straight-line (time) method (pattern S).
2. Production or use (straight-line use) method.
3. Declining-balance methods (pattern A).
4. Sum-of-the-years'-digits method (pattern A).
5. Accelerated Cost Recovery System for tax reporting (pattern A).

When a depreciable asset is acquired or retired during an accounting period, depreciation should be calculated only for that portion of the period during which the asset is used.

## The Straight-Line (Time) Method

The allocation method most commonly used for financial reporting is the *straight-line (time) method*. Under the straight-line method, the cost of the asset, less any estimated salvage value, is divided by the number of years of its expected life to arrive at the annual depreciation.

$$\text{Annual Depreciation} = \frac{\text{Cost less Estimated Salvage Value}}{\text{Estimated Life in Years}}.$$

For example, if a machine costs $12,000, has an estimated salvage value of $1,000, and has an expected useful life of 5 years, the annual depreciation will be $2,200 [= ($12,000 − $1,000)/5]. Occasionally, instead of a positive salvage value, the cost of removal exceeds the gross proceeds on disposition. This excess of removal costs over gross proceeds should be added to the cost of the asset in making the calculation. Thus, if a building is constructed for $3,700,000 and it is estimated that it will cost $500,000 to remove it at the end of 25 years, the annual depreciation would be $168,000 [= ($3,700,000 + $500,000)/25].

## Production or Use (Straight-Line Use) Method

Many assets are not used uniformly over time. Manufacturing plants often have seasonal variations in operation so that certain machines may be used 24 hours a day at one time and 8 hours or less a day at another time of year. Trucks are not likely to receive the same amount of use in each year of their lives. The straight-line (time) method of depreciation may result in depreciation patterns unrelated to usage patterns.

When the rate of usage varies over periods and when the total usage of an asset over its life can be estimated, a straight-line depreciation method based on actual production or usage during the period may be used. For example, depreciation of a truck for a period could be based on the ratio of miles driven during the period to total miles expected to be driven over the truck's life. The depreciation cost per unit (mile) of use is as follows:

$$\text{Depreciation Cost per Unit} = \frac{\text{Cost less Estimated Salvage Value}}{\text{Estimated Number of Units}}.$$

Assume that a truck costs $54,000, has an estimated salvage value of $4,000, and is expected to be driven 200,000 miles before it is retired from service. The depreciation per mile is $.25 [= ($54,000 − $4,000)/200,000]. If the truck is operated 2,000 miles in a given month, the depreciation charge for the month is 2,000 × $.25 = $500.

## Accelerated Depreciation

The earning power of some plant assets declines as the assets grow older. Cutting tools lose some of their precision; printing presses must be shut down more frequently for repairs; rent receipts from an old office building are lower than those from a new one. Some assets provide more and better services in the early years of their lives while requiring increasing amounts of maintenance as they grow older. Where this is the case, methods that recognize larger depreciation charges in early years and progressively smaller depreciation charges later may be justified. Such methods are referred to as *accelerated depreciation* methods because the depreciation charges in the early years of the asset's life are larger than in later years. Accelerated depreciation leads to a pattern such as A in Figures 9.1 and 9.2.

Even when depreciation charges for a year are computed from an accelerated method, amounts are allocated within a year on a straight-line basis. Thus depreciation charges for a month are $\frac{1}{12}$ the annual amount.

## Declining-Balance Methods

The *declining-balance method* is one accelerated depreciation method. In this method, the depreciation charge is calculated by multiplying the net book value of the asset (cost less accumulated depreciation) at the start of each period by a fixed rate. The estimated salvage value is not subtracted from the cost in making the depreciation calculation, but the asset cannot be written down below its estimated

Exhibit 9.1 ————————————————————————————————————————
## 200 Percent Declining-Balance Depreciation
## Asset with 5-Year Life

| Year | Acquisition Cost (1) | Accumulated Depreciation as of Jan. 1 (2) | Net Book Value as of Jan. 1 = (1) − (2) (3) | Depreciation Rate (4) | Depreciation Charge for the Year = (3) × (4) (5) |
|---|---|---|---|---|---|
| 1 ..... | $5,000 | $   0 | $5,000 | .40 | $2,000 |
| 2 ..... | 5,000 | 2,000 | 3,000 | .40 | 1,200 |
| 3 ..... | 5,000 | 3,200 | 1,800 | .40 | 720 |
| 4 ..... | 5,000 | 3,920 | 1,080 | a | 540 |
| 5 ..... | 5,000 | 4,460 | 540 | a | 540 |

aThe firm switches to straight-line write-off of the remaining balance over the remaining life, or $540 (= $1,080/2), during the last 2 years.

salvage value. Because the net book value declines from period to period, the result is a declining periodic charge for depreciation throughout the life of the asset.[4] A method sometimes used is the *200-percent* (or *double*) *declining-balance* method. An asset with an estimated 10-year life would be depreciated at a rate of 20 percent (= $\frac{1}{10} \times 2$) per year of the book value at the start of the year. Under declining-balance methods, the firm switches to straight-line depreciation of the remaining book value at the time when straight line provides higher depreciation charges. If a machine costing $5,000 is purchased on January 1, Year 1, and it is estimated to have a 5-year life, a 40 percent (= $\frac{1}{5} \times 2$) rate would be used for 3 years and then the firm would switch to straight-line depreciation. The depreciation charges, assuming zero salvage value, would be calculated as shown in Exhibit 9.1.

## Sum-of-the-Years'-Digits Method

Another accelerated depreciation method is the *sum-of-the-years'-digits method*. Under this method, the depreciation charge is calculated by applying a fraction, which diminishes from year to year, to the cost less estimated salvage value of the asset. The numerator of the fraction is the number of years of remaining life at the beginning of the year for which the depreciation calculation is being made. The

—————————————————

[4]Under the declining-balance method, as strictly applied, the fixed depreciation rate used is one that will charge the cost less salvage value of the asset over its service life. The formula for computing the rate is

$$\text{Depreciation Rate} = 1 - \sqrt[n]{\frac{s}{c}} = 1 - \left(\frac{s}{c}\right)^{1/n}.$$

In this formula $n$ = estimated periods of service life, $s$ = estimated salvage value, and $c$ = cost.

Estimates of salvage value have a profound effect on the rate. Unless a positive salvage value is assumed, the rate is 100 percent — that is, all depreciation is charged in the first period. For an asset costing $10,000 with an estimated life of 5 years, the depreciation rate is 40 percent per period if salvage value is $778, but it is 60 percent if salvage value is $102.

The effect of small changes in salvage value on the rate and the seeming mathematical complexity of the formula have resulted in widespread use of approximations or rules of thumb instead of the formula.

**Exhibit 9.2** ————————————————————————
**Sum-of-the-Years'-Digits Depreciation**
**Asset with 5-Year Life, $5,000 Cost, and $200 Estimated Salvage Value**

| Year | Acquisition Cost less Salvage Value (1) | Remaining Life in Years (2) | Fraction = (2)/15 (3) | Depreciation Charge for the Year = (3) × (1) (4) |
|---|---|---|---|---|
| 1 ..................... | $4,800 | 5 | 5/15 | $1,600 |
| 2 ..................... | 4,800 | 4 | 4/15 | 1,280 |
| 3 ..................... | 4,800 | 3 | 3/15 | 960 |
| 4 ..................... | 4,800 | 2 | 2/15 | 640 |
| 5 ..................... | 4,800 | 1 | 1/15 | 320 |
| | | | | $4,800 |

denominator is the sum of all such numbers, one for each year of estimated service life; if the service life is $n$ years, the denominator for the sum-of-the-years'-digits method is $1 + 2 + \cdots + n$.[5]

Consider an asset costing $5,000 purchased January 1, Year 1, which has an estimated service life of 5 years and an estimated salvage value of $200. The sum of the years' digits is 15 ($= 1 + 2 + 3 + 4 + 5$).[6] The depreciation charges appear in Exhibit 9.2.

## Accelerated Cost Recovery System for Income Tax Reporting

For income tax reporting, firms generally use the Accelerated Cost Recovery System (ACRS), which specifies depreciation charges accelerated in three distinct ways. First, the depreciable lives themselves are generally shorter than economic lives. (Straight-line depreciation for a shorter period will produce depreciation charges accelerated when compared to straight-line over a longer period.) Second, for assets other than buildings, ACRS provides for depreciation over the specified life based on the 150-percent and 200-percent declining-balance depreciation method, which is more rapid than straight-line. ACRS assumes, however, that each asset is acquired at mid-year of the year of acquisition, so the first-year percentage represents only a half-year of depreciation. Third, ACRS allows the entire depreciable basis to be written off over the depreciation period; salvage value is ignored.

Assets in the 3-year, 5-year, 7-year, and 10-year classes are depreciated using the 200-percent declining-balance method. Assets in the 15-year and 20-year classes are depreciated using the 150-percent declining-balance method. Assets in the 27.5-year and 31.5-year classes must be depreciated on a straight-line basis. Exhibit 9.3 shows the percentage of an asset's cost to be depreciated under ACRS for tax reporting for 200-percent declining-balance classes of property.

---

[5]A formula useful for summing the numbers 1 through $n$ is $1 + 2 + \cdots + n = n(n + 1)/2$.

[6]That is, according to the formula given in the previous footnote, $1 + 2 + 3 + 4 + 5 = 5 \times 6/2 = 15$.

**Exhibit 9.3** _____

**Accelerated Cost Recovery System**

**Percentage of Depreciable Cost Allowed by Year of Asset's Life**

| Recovery Year | Property Class | | | |
|---|---|---|---|---|
| | 3-Year | 5-Year | 7-Year | 10-Year |
| 1[a] ................................... | 33.3% | 20.0% | 14.3% | 10.0% |
| 2 ..................................... | 44.4 | 32.0 | 24.5 | 18.0 |
| 3 ..................................... | 14.8 | 19.2 | 17.5 | 14.4 |
| 4 ..................................... | 7.5 | 11.5 | 12.5 | 11.5 |
| 5 ..................................... | | 11.5 | 8.9 | 9.2 |
| 6 ..................................... | | 5.8 | 8.9 | 7.4 |
| 7 ..................................... | | | 8.9 | 6.6 |
| 8 ..................................... | | | 4.5 | 6.6 |
| 9 ..................................... | | | | 6.6 |
| 10 ..................................... | | | | 6.6 |
| 11 ..................................... | | | | 3.1 |
| Total ................................. | 100.0% | 100.0% | 100.0% | 100.0% |

[a]Assets are generally assumed to be acquired at mid-point of first year, independent of actual acquisition dates. In the first year, ACRS allows only one-half year of depreciation. So, for example, the first-year charge for an asset in the 5-year class is computed as 20-percent = $\frac{1}{2}$(for first half-year) × 2(for 200%-declining-balance) × $\frac{1}{5}$(for five-year life).

An automobile with a 7-year economic life (for financial reporting) is in the 5-year property class for ACRS. If it costs $12,000 and has $2,200 estimated salvage value, the ACRS deductions for the tax return would be $2,400 (= .20 × $12,000) in the first year; $3,840 (= .32 × $12,000) in the second year; $2,304 (= .192 × $12,000) in the third year; $1,380 (= .115 × $12,000) in the fourth and fifth years; and $696 (= .058 × $12,000) in the sixth year; which contains the last half-year of the asset's life. Note that ACRS ignores salvage value, so if the asset is retired for $2,200, there will be a taxable gain on retirement of $2,200. Only rarely would depreciation based on ACRS be appropriate for financial reporting.[7]

## Compound Interest Methods

Compound interest methods are seldom used in financial accounting, but they are theoretically sound for many management decisions. For plant assets producing equal annual net inflows of cash, compound interest depreciation leads to a pattern like D in Figures 9.1 and 9.2. This text does not illustrate compound interest methods, but see Problem 39 at the end of this chapter.

## Factors in Choosing the Depreciation Method

Depreciation affects both income reported in the financial statements and taxable income on tax returns. A firm does not need to choose the same depreciation method for both financial and tax reporting purposes. If it chooses different methods

_____

[7]For financial reporting under the straight-line method, this automobile would have depreciation charges of $1,400 [= ($12,000 − $2,200)/7] per year for 7 years and would have a book value of $2,200 at the end of the seventh year.

for the two purposes, the difference between depreciation in the financial statements and on the tax return leads to a problem in accounting for income taxes, discussed in Chapter 11.

**Tax Reporting**   It seems clear that in selecting depreciation methods for tax reporting, the goal of the firm should be to maximize the present value of the reductions in tax payments from claiming depreciation. Earlier deductions are worth more than later ones, because a dollar saved today is worth more than a dollar saved tomorrow. Congress has presented business firms with several permissible alternatives under ACRS to follow in determining the amount of depreciation to be deducted each year. A firm will generally choose the alternative that meets the general goal of allowing it to pay the least amount of tax, as late as possible, within the law. This goal is sometimes called the *least and latest rule*.

**Financial Reporting**   Financial reporting for long-lived assets seeks an income statement that realistically measures the expiration of the assets' benefits and provides a reasonable pattern of cost recovery. No one knows, however, just what portion of the service potential of a long-lived asset expires in any one period. The cost of the plant asset is a joint cost of the several periods of use, and no uniquely correct way of allocating joint costs exists. All that can be said is that financial statements should report depreciation charges based on reasonable estimates of asset expirations.

Since 1987, the income tax laws interact with financial reporting by levying additional income tax on a corporation as a function of the amount by which pretax financial statement income exceeds taxable income on the tax return. The functional relation is complicated, but we can safely say that many firms have a tax incentive to minimize the excess of financial pretax income over taxable income. Thus, many firms that use some form of accelerated depreciation for tax reporting have an incentive to use accelerated depreciation for financial reporting as well.

Chapter 15 discusses more fully the firm's selection from alternative accounting principles, including the choice of depreciation methods.

## Accounting for Periodic Depreciation

The debit made in the entry to record periodic depreciation is usually either to an expense account or to a product cost account. In a manufacturing concern, the depreciation of factory buildings and equipment is a product cost, a part of the cost of work-in-process and finished goods. Depreciation on sales equipment is a selling expense. Depreciation on office equipment is a general or administrative expense. The matching credit for periodic depreciation could, in principle, be made directly to the asset account affected, such as buildings or equipment. Although such an entry is sometimes made, usually the credit is to a contra-asset account. This leaves the acquisition cost of the asset undisturbed and permits easy computation of the total amount written off through depreciation. The effect, however, is precisely the same as a direct credit to the asset account. Accumulated Depreciation is the title of the contra-asset account credited.

The entry to record periodic depreciation of office facilities, a period expense, is as follows:

| | | |
|---|---|---|
| Depreciation Expense . . . . . . . . . . . . . . . . . . . . . . . . . . . . . . . . . . . . . . . . | 1,500 | |
|    Accumulated Depreciation . . . . . . . . . . . . . . . . . . . . . . . . . . . . . . . . | | 1,500 |

The entry to record periodic depreciation of manufacturing facilities, a product cost, is as follows:

| | | |
|---|---|---|
| Work-in-Process Inventory . . . . . . . . . . . . . . . . . . . . . . . . . . . . . . . . . . . . | 1,500 | |
|    Accumulated Depreciation . . . . . . . . . . . . . . . . . . . . . . . . . . . . . . . . | | 1,500 |

The Depreciation Expense account is closed at the end of the accounting period as a part of the regular closing-entry procedure. The Work-in-Process Inventory account is an asset. Product costs, such as depreciation on manufacturing facilities, accumulate in the Work-in-Process account until the goods being produced are completed and transferred to Finished Goods Inventory. The Accumulated Depreciation account remains open at the end of the period and appears on the balance sheet as a deduction from the asset account to which it refers. The balance in the Accumulated Depreciation account usually represents the total charges in accounting periods prior to the balance sheet date for the depreciation on assets currently in use. The difference between the balance of the asset account and the balance of its accumulated depreciation account is called the *book value* of the asset.

## Changes in Periodic Depreciation

The original depreciation schedule for a particular asset may require changing. Estimates of useful life (and of salvage value as well) may be judged incorrect in light of new information, which may become apparent at any time during the asset's life. The accuracy of the estimates improves as retirement approaches. If the misestimate has a material impact, corrective action must be taken. The generally accepted procedure is to make no adjustment for the past misestimate, but to spread the remaining undepreciated balance less the new estimate of salvage value over the new estimate of remaining service life of the asset.

To illustrate the accounting for *changes in periodic depreciation,* assume the following facts. An office machine was purchased on January 1, Year 1, for $9,200. It was estimated that the machine would be operated for 15 years with a salvage value of $200. The depreciation charge recorded for each of the years from Year 1 through Year 5 under the straight-line method would have been $600 [= ($9,200 − $200)/15]. On December 31, Year 6, before the books are closed for the year, it is decided that a total useful life of 10 years is more likely, but the salvage estimate of $200 is still reasonable.

The accepted procedure for recognizing this substantial decrease in service life is to revise the future depreciation so that the correct total will be accumulated in the Accumulated Depreciation account at the end of the revised service life. No adjustments of amounts previously recorded may be made. In our example, the total

**Figure 9.3**

**Revised Depreciation Schedule**

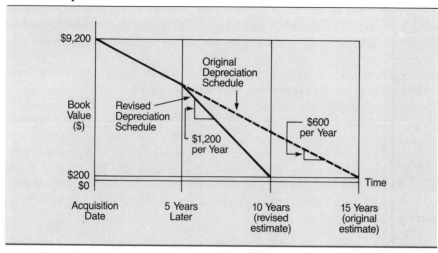

**Asset's service life estimate is decreased from 15 to 10 years at the start of Year 6. The straight-line method is used. Asset costs $9,200 and has estimated salvage value of $200.**

amount of acquisition cost yet to be depreciated before the Year 6 adjustments is $6,000 [= ($9,200 − $200) − (5 × $600)]. The new estimate of the remaining life is 5 years (the year just ended plus the next 4), so the new annual depreciation charge is $1,200 (= $6,000/5). The only change in the accounting procedure is to substitute the new amount of $1,200 for the former annual depreciation of $600. The depreciation entry on December 31, Year 6, and each year thereafter would be as follows:

| | | |
|---|---|---|
| Depreciation Expense . . . . . . . . . . . . . . . . . . . . . . . . . . . . . . . . . . . . . . . | 1,200 | |
|    Accumulated Depreciation . . . . . . . . . . . . . . . . . . . . . . . . . . . . . . . . . | | 1,200 |
| To record depreciation for Year 6 based on revised estimates. | | |

Figure 9.3 illustrates the revised depreciation path.

# Repairs and Improvements _____

Depreciation is not the only cost of using a plant asset. Repair and maintenance costs during the life of the asset will be incurred. The repair policy adopted by the business will often affect the depreciation rate. If, for example, machinery, trucks, and other plant assets are checked and repaired frequently, such assets will have a longer useful life and, therefore, a lower depreciation rate than otherwise. The more commonly used estimates of service life and depreciation rates assume that normal repairs will be made during the life of an asset.

Repairs must be distinguished from improvements (sometimes called *betterments*). *Repairs* do not extend estimated service life materially or otherwise increase productive capacity. They restore future benefits to originally estimated levels. *Improvements* involve making an asset substantially better, improving its productive capacity. Repairs maintain or restore service potential; improvements and betterments extend service beyond that originally anticipated.

Deciding whether a particular expenditure is a repair, treated as a period expense, or an improvement, treated as an asset, can be difficult. The line between maintaining service and improving or extending it is not distinct. Some expenditures may both restore and extend service potential. Consider, for example, an aircraft engine repair during which improved alloy materials are installed where inferior alloy parts had been used before. There is frequent disagreement between the Internal Revenue Service and taxpayers, as well as among accountants, over this question in specific situations.

**Unit of Account Sometimes Distinguishes Repair from Improvement**  Some assets are actually composites of assets. Consider, for example, a truck, which might simplistically be thought of as a chassis, an engine, and a set of tires.

Although some major parts of a composite asset may have shorter lives than the asset as a whole, accounting for them with separate asset accounts is frequently not feasible. Thus the cost of a replacement set of tires is usually charged to repairs expense, although the tires could be treated as a separate asset. In some cases, composite assets are disaggregated for the purposes of depreciation. Exhibit 9.4 illustrates the effects on the timing and amounts of depreciation and repair expense of treating a truck either as a single asset or as a group of assets. At the time the truck is acquired, replacing the tires every second year and the engine after 3 years was anticipated. The repair to the windows in Year 5 was not. The truck has a 6-year life and zero estimated salvage value. When the truck is depreciated as a single asset, replacement of tires or the engine is a repair. When separate accounts are used, replacing the tires is an improvement, the acquisition of a new asset.

## Retirement of Assets _____

When an asset is retired from service, the cost of the asset and the related amount of accumulated depreciation must be removed from the books. As part of this entry, the amount received from the sale or trade-in and any difference between that amount and book value must be recorded. The difference between the proceeds received on retirement and book value is a gain (if positive) or a loss (if negative). Before making the entry to write off the asset and its accumulated depreciation, an entry is made to bring the depreciation up to date; that is, the depreciation that has occurred between the start of the current accounting period and the date of disposition is recorded.

To illustrate the retirement of an asset, assume sales equipment that cost $5,000, that was expected to last 4 years, and that had an estimated salvage value of

**Exhibit 9.4** ————————————————————————

**Unit of Account Influences Depreciation and Maintenance Charges**
Truck: Cost $48,000; 6-Year Life
Engine: Cost $9,000; 3-Year Life
Tires: Cost $1,200; 2-Year Life
Windows: Repair Cost $800 in Year 5
(straight-line depreciation)

| | Depreciation of | | | | |
|---|---|---|---|---|---|
| | **Truck** | **Engine** | **Tires** | **Maintenance** | **Total Expense** |
| **Separate Asset Accounts** | | | | | |
| Year 1......... | $ 6,300[a] | $ 3,000[b] | $  600[c] | — | $ 9,900 |
| Year 2......... | 6,300 | 3,000 | 600 | — | 9,900 |
| Year 3......... | 6,300 | 3,000 | 600[c] | — | 9,900 |
| Year 4......... | 6,300 | 3,000[b] | 600 | — | 9,900 |
| Year 5......... | 6,300 | 3,000 | 600[c] | $   800[d] | 10,700 |
| Year 6......... | 6,300 | 3,000 | 600 | — | 9,900 |
| | $37,800 | $18,000 | $3,600 | $   800 | $60,200 |
| **Single Asset Account** | | | | | |
| Year 1......... | $ 8,000[e] | — | — | — | $ 8,000 |
| Year 2......... | 8,000 | — | — | $ 1,200[f] | 9,200 |
| Year 3......... | 8,000 | — | — | 9,000[g] | 17,000 |
| Year 4......... | 8,000 | — | — | 1,200[f] | 9,200 |
| Year 5......... | 8,000 | — | — | 800[d] | 8,800 |
| Year 6......... | 8,000 | — | — | — | 8,000 |
| | $48,000 | | | $12,200 | $60,200 |

[a]Truck: ($48,000 − $9,000 − $1,200)/6.

[b]Engine: $9,000/3.

[c]Tires: $1,200/2.

[d]Window repair.

[e]$48,000/6.

[f]Tires.

[g]Engine.

$200 is depreciated on a straight-line basis at $1,200 [= ($5,000 − $200)/4] per year. Depreciation has been recorded for 2 years, and the equipment is sold at mid-year in the third year. The depreciation from the start of the accounting period to the date of sale of $600 [= ½ × ($5,000 − $200)/4] is recorded.

———————————————————————————————————————

| | | |
|---|---|---|
| Depreciation Expense........................................ | 600 | |
| Accumulated Depreciation ................................... | | 600 |
| To record depreciation charges up to the date of sale. | | |

———————————————————————————————————————

The book value of the asset is now its cost less 2½ years of straight-line depreciation of $1,200 per year or $2,000 (= $5,000 − $3,000). The entry to record the retirement of the assets depends on the amount of the selling price.

1. Suppose that the equipment was sold for cash at its book value of $2,000. The entry to record the sale would be as follows:

| | | |
|---|---|---|
| Cash . . . . . . . . . . . . . . . . . . . . . . . . . . . . . . . . . . . . . . . . . . . . . . . . | 2,000 | |
| Accumulated Depreciation . . . . . . . . . . . . . . . . . . . . . . . . . . . . . . | 3,000 | |
|     Equipment . . . . . . . . . . . . . . . . . . . . . . . . . . . . . . . . . . . . . . . . . | | 5,000 |

2. Suppose that the equipment was sold for $2,300 cash, more than its book value. The entry to record the sale would be as follows:

| | | |
|---|---|---|
| Cash . . . . . . . . . . . . . . . . . . . . . . . . . . . . . . . . . . . . . . . . . . . . . . . . | 2,300 | |
| Accumulated Depreciation . . . . . . . . . . . . . . . . . . . . . . . . . . . . . . | 3,000 | |
|     Equipment . . . . . . . . . . . . . . . . . . . . . . . . . . . . . . . . . . . . . . . . . | | 5,000 |
|     Gain on Retirement of Equipment . . . . . . . . . . . . . . . . . . . . . . . | | 300 |

3. Suppose that the equipment was sold for $1,500 cash, less than its book value. The entry to record the sale would be as follows:

| | | |
|---|---|---|
| Cash . . . . . . . . . . . . . . . . . . . . . . . . . . . . . . . . . . . . . . . . . . . . . . . . | 1,500 | |
| Accumulated Depreciation . . . . . . . . . . . . . . . . . . . . . . . . . . . . . . | 3,000 | |
| Loss on Retirement of Equipment . . . . . . . . . . . . . . . . . . . . . . . . | 500 | |
|     Equipment . . . . . . . . . . . . . . . . . . . . . . . . . . . . . . . . . . . . . . . . . | | 5,000 |

## Trade-in Transactions

Instead of being sold when it is retired from service, the asset may be traded in on a new unit, a common practice for automobiles. The *trade-in transaction* can best be viewed as a sale of the old asset followed by a purchase of the new asset. The accounting for trade-in transactions determines simultaneously the gain or loss on disposal of the old asset and the acquisition cost recorded for the new asset. The procedures depend on the data available about the market value of the asset traded in and the cash equivalent cost of the new asset.

**Using Market Value of Old Asset**  If the fair market value of the old asset traded in can be found, that amount plus the cash given up generally determines the valuation of the new asset. Assume that used equipment originally costing $5,000 with $3,000 of accumulated depreciation has a fair market value of $1,300 and is traded in on a new piece of equipment, along with an additional $5,500 of cash. The entries could be as follows:

| | | |
|---|---|---|
| Accumulated Depreciation ..................................... | 3,000 | |
| Trade-in Allowance ........................................... | 1,300 | |
| Loss on Disposition of Equipment ............................. | 700 | |
|     Equipment ............................................... | | 5,000 |

To record disposition of old equipment; plug for loss.

| | | |
|---|---|---|
| Equipment ................................................... | 6,800 | |
|     Trade-in Allowance ........................................ | | 1,300 |
|     Cash ..................................................... | | 5,500 |

To record acquisition of new equipment; plug for cost of new equipment. The Trade-in Allowance account is a temporary account, used to make clearer the sequence of computations. It splits the transaction into two components — the sale of the old asset and purchase of the new.

The Trade-in Allowance account is not required. This transaction could be recorded in a single entry as follows:

| | | |
|---|---|---|
| Equipment ................................................... | 6,800 | |
| Accumulated Depreciation ..................................... | 3,000 | |
| Loss on Disposition of Equipment ............................. | 700 | |
|     Equipment ............................................... | | 5,000 |
|     Cash ..................................................... | | 5,500 |

Single entry for trade-in.

Note that the list price of the new equipment does not affect the entries shown above. Valuation of the used asset in established secondhand markets almost always offers more reliable information than quoted list prices.

**Using Market Value of New Asset**  If a reliable valuation of the used asset is not available, the lowest available cash price for the new asset (which is sometimes the list price) will determine the valuation of the new asset, as well as the gain or loss on disposition of the old asset. If the list price of the new equipment in the preceding example was $7,000 and there was no other reliable information available, the entries would be as follows:

| | | |
|---|---|---|
| Equipment ................................................... | 7,000 | |
|     Cash ..................................................... | | 5,500 |
|     Trade-in Allowance ........................................ | | 1,500 |

To record acquisition at list price; plug for trade-in allowance.

| | | |
|---|---|---|
| Accumulated Depreciation ..................................... | 3,000 | |
| Trade-in Allowance ........................................... | 1,500 | |
| Loss on Disposition of Equipment ............................. | 500 | |
|     Equipment ............................................... | | 5,000 |

To record disposition of old equipment. Loss is determined by list price of new equipment.

The single entry to record the trade-in, using the list price of the new equipment, would be as follows:

| | | |
|---|---|---|
| Equipment . . . . . . . . . . . . . . . . . . . . . . . . . . . . . . . . . . . . . . . . . . . . . . . . . . . . | 7,000 | |
| Accumulated Depreciation . . . . . . . . . . . . . . . . . . . . . . . . . . . . . . . . . . . . . | 3,000 | |
| Loss on Disposition of Equipment . . . . . . . . . . . . . . . . . . . . . . . . . . . . . | 500 | |
|     Equipment . . . . . . . . . . . . . . . . . . . . . . . . . . . . . . . . . . . . . . . . . . . . . . . . . . | | 5,000 |
|     Cash . . . . . . . . . . . . . . . . . . . . . . . . . . . . . . . . . . . . . . . . . . . . . . . . . . . . . . . . | | 5,500 |
| Plug for Loss, which is determined by list price of new equipment. | | |

**Income Tax Rules**  The income tax regulations do not permit the recognition of a gain or loss on the trade-in of an old asset in acquiring a new, similar asset. Instead, the cost of the new asset is assumed to be the book value of the used asset plus the cash paid. There can be no gain or loss. The tax rules are designed to reduce opportunity for manipulation of taxable income in trade-in transactions where, typically, the list price of new assets and offsetting trade-in allowances are subject to arbitrary offsetting adjustments. In the illustration used in this section, the entries for tax purposes would be as follows:

| | | |
|---|---|---|
| Accumulated Depreciation . . . . . . . . . . . . . . . . . . . . . . . . . . . . . . . . . . . . . | 3,000 | |
| Trade-in Allowance . . . . . . . . . . . . . . . . . . . . . . . . . . . . . . . . . . . . . . . . . . | 2,000 | |
|     Equipment . . . . . . . . . . . . . . . . . . . . . . . . . . . . . . . . . . . . . . . . . . . . . . . . . . | | 5,000 |
| To record disposition of old equipment at book value; no gain or loss can be recognized. | | |
| Equipment . . . . . . . . . . . . . . . . . . . . . . . . . . . . . . . . . . . . . . . . . . . . . . . . . . . . | 7,500 | |
|     Cash . . . . . . . . . . . . . . . . . . . . . . . . . . . . . . . . . . . . . . . . . . . . . . . . . . . . . . . . | | 5,500 |
|     Trade-in Allowance . . . . . . . . . . . . . . . . . . . . . . . . . . . . . . . . . . . . . . . . . . | | 2,000 |
| To record acquisition of new equipment. Cost of new equipment is a plug. | | |

The single entry to record the trade-in would be as follows:

| | | |
|---|---|---|
| Equipment . . . . . . . . . . . . . . . . . . . . . . . . . . . . . . . . . . . . . . . . . . . . . . . . . . . . | 7,500 | |
| Accumulated Depreciation . . . . . . . . . . . . . . . . . . . . . . . . . . . . . . . . . . . . . | 3,000 | |
|     Equipment . . . . . . . . . . . . . . . . . . . . . . . . . . . . . . . . . . . . . . . . . . . . . . . . . . | | 5,000 |
|     Cash . . . . . . . . . . . . . . . . . . . . . . . . . . . . . . . . . . . . . . . . . . . . . . . . . . . . . . . . | | 5,500 |
| Single entry to record trade-in for tax purposes. No gain or loss can be recognized; book value of new equipment is a plug. | | |

**Summary of Accounting for Trade-ins**  For financial reporting, trade-in transactions are recorded using the market value of the asset traded in or the market value of the new asset acquired, depending on which market value is more objectively measurable. An exception occurs when such recording results in a gain and the trade-in transaction involves similar assets. In this case, no gain is recognized and the new asset is recorded at the book value of the old asset plus the cash paid in the trade-in transaction.[8] The rule is designed to reduce opportunity for manipulating reported income with trade-in transactions.


# Wasting Assets and Depletion _____

The costs of finding natural resources and preparing to extract them from the earth should be capitalized and amortized. Whether all costs of exploration or only the costs of the successful explorations should be capitalized into the asset accounts remains an open accounting question. Generally accepted accounting principles allow two treatments. Under *full costing,* the costs of all explorations (both successful and unsuccessful) are capitalized so long as the expected benefits from the successful explorations will more than cover the cost of all explorations. Under *successful efforts costing,* only the costs of the successful efforts are capitalized; the costs of unsuccessful exploration efforts become expenses of the period when the fact becomes apparent that the efforts will not result in productive sites.[9]

Amortization of *wasting assets,* or natural resources, is called *depletion.* The depletion method most often used is the *units-of-production method.* For example, if $4.5 million in costs are incurred to discover an oil well that contains an estimated 1.5 million barrels of oil, then the costs of $4.5 million would be amortized (depleted) at the rate of $3 (= $4,500,000/1,500,000) for each barrel of oil removed from the well. The major accounting problem of extractive industries stems from uncertainty about the eventual total of units that will result from exploratory efforts.


## Percentage Depletion Allowances

In some special circumstances, the tax laws permit computation of depletion in measuring taxable income as a percentage of the revenues secured from the sale of the minerals each year. The total of depletion charges over the life of the asset is not limited to costs incurred if this method, known as *percentage depletion,* is used. In financial accounting, depletion allocates the cost of natural resources to the periods when the resources are used. The *percentage depletion allowance* is a device instituted by Congress to make the search for natural resources more attractive than it otherwise would be. The effect of percentage depletion is to allow some firms to deduct, on income tax returns over the life of the asset, amounts larger than the total of costs incurred. Financial statement expense over the life of the asset must be equal to the acquisition cost of the asset in a historical cost system; therefore, percentage depletion is not permitted by generally accepted accounting principles.

---

[8]In the highly unlikely situation in which cash is received by the party making the trade-in, some gain is recognized; Accounting Principles Board, *Opinion No. 29,* "Accounting for Nonmonetary Transactions," 1973. (See *trade-in transaction* in the glossary at the back of the book.)

[9]Financial Accounting Standards Board, *Statement of Financial Accounting Standards No. 25,* "Suspension of Certain Accounting Requirements for Oil and Gas Producing Companies," 1979.

# Intangible Assets and Amortization _____

Assets can provide future benefits without having physical form. Such assets are called *intangibles*. Examples are research costs, advertising costs, patents, trade secrets, know-how, trademarks, and copyrights. The first problem with intangibles is to decide

1. whether expenditures made to acquire or develop intangibles have future benefits and can be quantified with a sufficient degree of precision that they should be *capitalized* (set up as assets) and amortized over time; or

2. whether they have no future benefits and thus are expenses of the period in which the costs are incurred.

If the latter is chosen, the immediate expensing of the asset's cost appears as pattern E in Figures 9.1 and 9.2.

The second problem to solve is how to amortize the costs if they have been capitalized. Deciding the period of amortization (the estimated service life) is difficult. Amortization of capitalized intangibles is usually recorded using the straight-line method, but other methods can be used if they seem appropriate. This section discusses some common intangibles and the issues involved in deciding whether to expense or to capitalize their costs. In generally accepted accounting principles, no intangible assets acquired after 1970 can be amortized over a period longer than 40 years.[10]

## Research and Development

One common intangible is the benefit provided by expenditures on *research and development (R&D)*. Such costs are incurred for various reasons. Perhaps the firm seeks to develop a technological or marketing advance in order to have an edge on competition. Or it might wish to explore possible applications of existing technology to design a new product or improve an old one. Other research may be undertaken in response to a government contract, in preparing for bids on potential contracts, or in pursuit of "discoveries," with no specific product in mind. Whatever the reason, practically all research costs will yield their benefits, if any, in future periods. Herein lies the accounting issue: Should research and development costs be charged to expense immediately as they are incurred, or should they be capitalized and amortized over future periods?

Generally accepted accounting principles require immediate expensing of research and development costs.[11] This requirement is based on arguments that the future benefits from most R&D efforts are too uncertain to warrant capitalization and that writing them off as soon as possible is more conservative. Nevertheless, some accountants believe that there must be future benefits in many cases or R&D efforts would not be pursued. They think that R&D costs should be matched with the benefits produced by the R&D expenditures through the capitalization procedure, with amortization over the benefited periods. This procedure is not allowed.

---

[10]Accounting Principles Board, *Opinion No. 17*, "Intangible Assets," 1970.

[11]Financial Accounting Standards Board, *Statement of Financial Accounting Standards No. 2*, "Accounting for Research and Development Costs," 1974.

## Advertising

Advertising expenditures are designed to increase sales, currently and in the future, but there is a lag between the incurrence of these costs and their impact. The impact of advertising probably extends into subsequent periods.

Although generally accepted accounting principles allow capitalizing and then amortizing advertising costs, common practice immediately expenses all advertising costs, regardless of the timing of their impact (see pattern E in Figures 9.1 and 9.2). Those supporting this practice argue that (1) it is more conservative to do so; (2) it is almost impossible to quantify the future effects and timing of benefits derived from these costs; and (3) when these costs remain stable from year to year, income is not affected by the capitalization policy after the first few years. Nevertheless, some accountants support the capitalization treatment because doing so will better report assets and match costs with resulting benefits.

Many companies that market branded products to consumers own major economic assets that do not appear on their balance sheets. Consider, for example, the Procter & Gamble Corporation (P&G), which owns such well-known brand names as Tide and Crest. In recent years, P&G's net income has been about $900 million and its total accounting assets have been on the order of $9 billion. Thus its accounting rate of return has been approximately 10 percent. In recent years P&G has spent about $3 billion per year on advertising. If P&G had capitalized its advertising costs and amortized them over 3 years, its assets would be about $4.5 billion larger and its accounting rate of return would be on the order of 7 percent. Rates of return computed from accounting data for firms with substantial economic benefits in the form of intangibles, not recognized as accounting assets, may be misleadingly large.

## Patents

A patent is a right obtained from the federal government to exclude others from the benefits of an invention. The legal life of patent protection may be as long as 17 years, although the economic life of the patent may be considerably less. The accounting for patent costs depends on whether the patent was purchased from another party or developed internally. If purchased, the cost is capitalized. If developed internally, the total cost of product development and patent application is expensed, as required for all R&D costs.[12] Purchased patent costs are usually amortized over the shorter of (1) the remaining legal life or (2) its estimated economic life. If for some reason the patent becomes worthless, the remaining capitalized cost is recognized immediately as an expense of that period.

## Goodwill

*Goodwill* is an intangible asset that will be mentioned here only briefly. More details follow in Chapter 13. Goodwill arises from the purchase of one company or operating unit by another company and is measured as the difference between the

---

[12]*SFAS No. 2* does not give reasoning to justify this distinction in accounting treatments of purchased versus developed patents.

amount paid for the acquired company as a whole and the sum of the current values of its individual assets less its liabilities. Thus goodwill will appear in the financial statements of the company making the acquisition. Under present practice, goodwill (and other intangibles) acquired after October 1970 must be amortized over a time period not longer than 40 years.[13]

## Summary

Three major classes of long-lived operating assets are plant assets, wasting assets (nonrenewable natural resources), and intangibles. The major accounting problems for each class are the same: (1) calculating the cost of the asset to be capitalized as an asset, (2) estimating the total period of benefit or the amount of expected benefits, and (3) assigning the cost to the benefited periods or units produced in a systematic and reasonable fashion so that investment in the asset is recovered through charges to income.

The chapter emphasized depreciable plant assets and their depreciation. The amount to be charged off is equal to acquisition cost reduced by any salvage value. The period (or number of units) of benefit is estimated from experience or, for tax reporting, is taken from guidelines set by the Internal Revenue Service. The pattern of depreciation charges over the asset's life is usually based on some systematic method; the most common method for financial reporting is straight-line depreciation.

If the asset is retired before the end of the estimated service life for an amount different from its book value, a gain or loss will be recognized. If the asset is traded in on another asset, a gain or loss may or may not be recognized, depending on the terms of the transaction.

Intangibles such as trademarks, copyrights, patents, and computer programs are among the most valuable resources owned by some firms. The accounting treatment of purchased intangibles is the same as for tangible assets. For most intangibles developed within a firm, accounting requires the immediate expensing of the development costs. The firms most likely to be affected are service, rather than manufacturing, companies.

## Appendix 9.1:
## Plant Assets and the
## Statement of Cash Flows

In the statement of cash flows, the periodic depreciation charge is an addback in the Operations section. It represents an expense that does not use cash but that instead uses a noncurrent asset.

---

[13]APB, *Opinion No. 17.*

## The Retirement Entries in the Statement of Cash Flows

The cash received from the disposition of a plant asset is treated as a nonoperating source of funds. It appears on the cash flow statement in the Investing section as a source, Proceeds from Disposition of Noncurrent Assets.

The loss on retirement of equipment reduces net income but does not use cash. Thus, in deriving cash from operations using the indirect method, the amount of the loss is an addback to net income. Its presentation is similar to that for depreciation expense.

If there is a gain on retirement of equipment, the total proceeds from disposition of the asset are shown as an Investing source of funds, and this requires treating the gain on retirement as a subtraction in computing cash from operations when the indirect method is used. The subtraction would be classified under the general heading of Revenues Not Producing Cash from Operations, because all cash produced is shown under the heading of Proceeds from Disposition of Noncurrent Assets.

# Problem 1 for Self-Study _____

Purdy Company acquired two used trucks from Foster Company. Although the trucks were not identical, they both cost $15,000. Purdy Company knew when it negotiated the purchase price that the first truck required extensive engine repair, expected to cost about $4,000. The repair was made the week after acquisition and actually cost $4,200. Purdy Company thought the second truck was in normal operating condition when it negotiated the purchase price but discovered upon taking possession of the truck that certain bearings needed replacing. The cost of this repair, made the week after acquisition, was $4,200.

**a.** What costs should be recorded in the accounts for the two trucks?

**b.** If the amounts recorded in part **a** are different, distinguish between the two "repairs."

## Suggested Solution

**a.** First truck recorded at $19,200. Second truck recorded at $15,000, with $4,200 debited to expense or loss.

**b.** At the time the first truck was acquired, Purdy Company knew it would have to make the "repair." The purchase price was presumably reduced because of the known cost to be incurred. At the time of acquisition, the cost was anticipated to be required in order to produce the expected service potential of the asset. The fact that the cost was $4,200, rather than "about $4,000," does not seem to violate the Purdy Company's expectations at the time it acquired the truck. If the repair had cost significantly more than $4,000 — say, $7,000 — then the excess would be loss or expense.

The second truck was assumed to be operable when the purchase price was agreed upon. The cost of the repair was incurred to bring about the level of service potential already thought to have been acquired. There are no more future benefits after the repair than had been anticipated at the time of acquisition. Therefore, the $4,200 is expense or loss.

## Problem 2 for Self-Study _____

Jensen Company purchased land with a building standing on it as the site for a new plant it planned to construct. The company received bids from several independent contractors for demolition of the old building and construction of the new one. It rejected all bids and undertook demolition and construction using company labor, facilities, and equipment.

All transactions relating to these properties were debited or credited to a single account, Real Estate. Various items in the Real Estate account are described below. The Real Estate account is to be closed. All amounts in it should be taken out and reclassified into one of the following accounts:

**(1)** Land account.

**(2)** Buildings account.

**(3)** Revenue, gain, or expense contra account.

**(4)** Expense, loss, or revenue contra account.

**(5)** Some other account.

You may reclassify amounts of the following transactions into two or more of these accounts. If you use (5), some other account, indicate the nature of the account.

**a.** Cost of land, including old building.

**b.** Legal fees paid to bring about purchase of land and to transfer its title.

**c.** Invoice cost of materials and supplies used in construction.

**d.** Direct labor and materials cost incurred in demolition of old building.

**e.** Direct costs of excavating raw land to prepare it for the foundation of the new building.

**f.** Discounts earned for prompt payment of item **c**.

**g.** Interest for year on notes issued to finance construction.

**h.** Amounts equivalent to interest on Jensen Company's own funds used in construction that would have been invested in marketable securities if an independent contractor had been used. The amount was debited to Real Estate and credited to Interest Revenue so that the cost of the real estate would be comparable to its cost if it had been built by an independent contractor.

**i.** Depreciation for period of construction on trucks that were used both in construction and in regular company operations.

**j.** Proceeds of sale of materials salvaged from old buildings. These were debited to Cash and credited to Real Estate.

**k.** Cost of building permits.

**l.** Salaries of certain corporate engineering executives. These can be allocated between Salary Expense and Real Estate. The portion debited to Real Estate represents an estimate of the portion of the time spent during the year on planning and construction activities for the new building.

**m.** Payments for property taxes on plant site owed by its former owner but assumed by Jensen Company.

**n.** Payments for property taxes on plant site during construction period.

**o.** Insurance premiums to cover workers engaged in demolition and construction activities. The insurance policy contains various deductible clauses, requiring the company to pay the first $5,000 of damages from any accident.

**p.** Cost of injury claims for $2,000 paid by the company because the amount was less than the deductible amount in the policy.

**q.** Costs of new machinery to be installed in building.

**r.** Installation costs for the machinery in part **q**.

**s.** Profit on construction of new building (computed as the difference between lowest independent contractor's bid and the actual construction cost). This was debited to Real Estate and credited to Construction Revenue.

## Suggested Solution

**(1)** a, b, d, j, l, m, o, p

**(2)** c, e, f, g, i, k, l, n, o, p

**(3)** —

**(4)** h, i, p, s

**(5)** i, q, r

## Comments and Explanations

**f.** The reduction in cost of materials and supplies will reduce the cost of the buildings. The actual accounting entries depend on the method used to record the potential discount. These issues are not discussed in this book, but see Problem 28 at the end of Chapter 8.

**h.** Although one capitalizes explicit interest, one may not capitalize opportunity-cost interest or interest imputed on one's own funds used. The adjusting entry credits Real Estate and debits Interest Revenue or its contra account. In any case, the debit reduces income, removing the revenue that had been recognized by the company.

**i.** Computation of the amounts to be allocated requires an estimate. Once the amounts are estimated, they are debited to Building or to Depreciation Expense and Work-in-Process Inventory, as appropriate, for the regular company operations.

**j.** Credit to Land account, reducing its cost.

**l.** Allocate to Land and Building, based on an estimate of how time was spent. Given the description, most of these costs are probably for the building. If all of the salaries had been debited to Real Estate, some must be reclassified as Salary Expense.

**m.** Part of the cost of the land.

**n.** Capitalized as part of the Building account for the same reasons that interest during construction is capitalized. Some accountants would treat this item as expense. In any case, this item can be an expense for tax reporting.

**p.** Most accountants would treat this as an expense or loss for the period. Others would treat it as part of the cost of the building for the same reason that the explicit insurance cost is capitalized. If, however, the company was irrational in acquiring insurance policies with deductible clauses, this item would be expense or loss. Accounting usually assumes that most managements make rational decisions most of the time. In any case, this item can be treated as an expense or loss for tax reporting.

**q.** Debit to Machine and Equipment account, an asset account separate from Building.

**r.** Treat the same as the preceding item; installation costs are part of the cost of the asset. See Chapter 2, page 37.

**s.** The effect of recognizing revenue is reversed. The Real Estate account is credited and Construction Revenue or its contra account is debited.

## Problem 3 for Self-Study _____

Central States Electric Company constructs a nuclear power generating plant at a cost of $200 million. The plant is expected to last 50 years before being retired from service. The company estimates that at the time the plant is retired from service, $20 million in "decommissioning costs" (costs to dismantle the plant and dispose of the radioactive materials) will be incurred. Straight-line depreciation is computed and charged once per year, at year-end.

During the eleventh year of operation, new regulations governing nuclear waste disposal are enacted. The estimated decommissioning costs increase from $20 million to $24 million.

During the thirty-first year of operation, the life of the plant is revised. It will last 60 years in total, not 50 years.

At the end of the thirty-fifth year, the plant is sold to another utility company for $80 million.

**a.** What is the depreciation charge for the first year?

**b.** What is the depreciation charge for the eleventh year?

**c.** What is the depreciation charge for the thirty-first year?

**d.** Record the journal entry for the sale of the plant at the end of the thirty-fifth year.

### Suggested Solution

(All dollar amounts in millions.)

**a.** $4.4 per year = ($200 + $20)/50 years.

**b.** $4.5 per year = ($200 + $20 + $4 − $4.4 per year × 10 years)/40 years remaining life,
= ($224 − $44)/40,
= $180/40.

**c.** $3.0 per year = ($180 − $4.5 × 20 years)/30 years remaining life,
= ($180 − $90)/30,
= $90/30.

**d.** Accumulated depreciation at time of sale
= ($4.4 × 10) + ($4.5 × 20) + ($3.0 × 5) = $149.0.

---

**December 31 of Year 35**

| | | |
|---|---|---|
| Cash . . . . . . . . . . . . . . . . . . . . . . . . . . . . . . . . . . . . . . . . . . . . . . . . . . . . . | 80.0 | |
| Accumulated Depreciation on Power Plant . . . . . . . . . . . . . . . . . . . . . | 149.0 | |
| Power Plant. . . . . . . . . . . . . . . . . . . . . . . . . . . . . . . . . . . . . . . . . . . . . . . | | 200.0 |
| Gain on Disposal of Plant . . . . . . . . . . . . . . . . . . . . . . . . . . . . . . . . . . | | 29.0 |

---

# Questions, Exercises, Problems, and Cases _____

## Questions

**1.** Review the meaning of the following concepts or terms discussed in this chapter.

**a.** Amortization.
**b.** Plant asset.
**c.** Interest during construction.
**d.** Depreciation.
**e.** Joint cost.
**f.** Value.
**g.** Salvage or residual value.
**h.** Service or depreciable life.
**i.** Accelerated Cost Recovery System (ACRS)
**j.** Straight-line (time and use) methods.
**k.** Declining-balance methods.
**l.** Sum-of-the-years'-digits method.

**m.** Treatment of changes in periodic depreciation (estimates of useful lives and residual values) of long-lived assets.
**n.** Repairs and maintenance.
**o.** Improvements.
**p.** Trade-in transaction.
**q.** Wasting assets.
**r.** Depletion.
**s.** Percentage depletion allowance.
**t.** Intangibles.
**u.** Capitalize.
**v.** Research and development (R&D).
**w.** Goodwill.

**2. a.** "Accounting for depreciating assets would be greatly simplified if accounting periods were only long enough or the life of the assets short enough." What is the point of the quotation?

**b.** "The major purpose of depreciation accounting is to provide funds for the replacement of assets as they wear out." Do you agree? Explain.

**3.** "Showing both acquisition cost and accumulated depreciation amounts separately provides a rough indication of the relative age of the firm's long-lived assets."

**a.** Assume that the Dickens Company acquired an asset with a depreciable cost of $100,000 several years ago. Accumulated depreciation as of December 31, recorded on a straight-line basis, is $60,000. The depreciation charge for the year is $10,000. What is the asset's depreciable life? How old is the asset?

b. Assume straight-line depreciation. Devise a formula that, given the depreciation charge for the year and the asset's accumulated depreciation, can be used to determine the age of the asset.

4. a. What is the effect of capitalizing interest on reported net income summed over all the periods of the life of a given self-constructed asset, from building through use until eventual retirement? Contrast with a policy of expensing interest as incurred.

b. Consider a company engaging in increasing dollar amounts of self-construction activity each period during periods when interest rates do not decline. What is the effect on reported income each year of capitalizing interest in contrast to expensing interest as incurred?

## Exercises

5. *Classification of expenditure as asset or expense.* For each of the following expenditures or acquisitions, indicate the type of account debited. Classify the account as asset other than product cost, product cost (Work-in-Process Inventory), or expense. If the account debited is an asset account, specify whether it is current or noncurrent.

a. $150 for repairs of office machines.
b. $1,500 for emergency repairs to an office machine.
c. $250 for maintenance of delivery trucks.
d. $5,000 for a machine acquired in return for a 3-year note.
e. $4,200 for research and development staff salaries.
f. $3,100 for newspaper ads.
g. $6,400 for wages of factory workers engaged in production.
h. $3,500 for wages of factory workers engaged in installing equipment.
i. $2,500 for salaries of the office work force.
j. $1,000 for legal fees incurred in acquiring an ore deposit.
k. $1,200 for a 1-year insurance policy beginning next month.
l. $1,800 for U.S. Treasury notes, to be sold to pay the next installment due on income taxes.
m. $4,000 for royalty payment on a patent used in manufacturing.
n. $10,000 for purchase of a trademark.
o. $100 filing fee for copyright registration application.

6. *Journal entries for trade-in transactions and depreciation.* On April 30, Year 6, the Tico Wholesale Company acquired a new machine with a fair market value of $14,000. The seller agreed to accept in payment the company's old machine, $7,000 in cash, and a 12 percent, 1-year note for $4,000.

The old machine was purchased on January 1, Year 1, for $10,000. It was estimated that the old machine would be useful for 8 years, after which it would have a salvage value of $400. It is estimated that the new machine will have a service life of 10 years and a salvage value of $800.

Assuming that the Tico Company uses the straight-line method of depreciation and closes its books annually on December 31, give the entries that were made in Year 6.

**7.** *Computations and journal entries for retirement of plant.* On July 1, 1965, a building and land were purchased for $96,000 by The Hub, a retail clothing store. Of this amount, $40,000 was allocated to the land and the remainder to the building. The building is depreciated on a straight-line basis.

On July 1, 1987 (no additions or retirements having been recorded in the meanwhile), the net book value of the building was $25,200. On March 31, 1988, the building and site were sold for $60,000. The fair market value of the land was $50,000 on this date.

The firm closes its books annually at June 30. Give the entries required on March 31, 1988. (*Hint:* First compute what the annual depreciation charges must be, based on the facts given.)

**8.** *Journal entries for plant acquisition, depreciation, and retirement.* Journalize the following transactions:
  **a.** A piece of office equipment is purchased for $850 cash.
  **b.** Depreciation of $170 for 1 year is recorded.
  **c.** The equipment is sold for $400. At the time of the sale, Accumulated Depreciation shows a balance of $340. Depreciation of $170 for the year of the sale has not yet been recorded.

**9.** *Journal entries for revising estimate of life.* Give the journal entries for the following selected transactions of the Eagle Manufacturing Company. The company uses the straight-line method of calculating depreciation and closes its books annually on December 31.
  **a.** A machine is purchased on November 1, 1979, for $30,000. It is estimated that it will be used for 10 years and that it will have a salvage value of $600 at the end of that time. Give the journal entry for the depreciation at December 31, 1979.
  **b.** Record the depreciation for the year ending December 31, 1980.
  **c.** In August 1985, it is decided that the machine will probably be used for a total of 12 years and that its salvage value will be $400. Record the depreciation for the year ending December 31, 1985.
  **d.** The machine is sold for $1,000 on March 31, 1990. Record the entries of that date, assuming that depreciation is recorded as indicated in part **c**.

**10.** *Straight-line depreciation, working backwards.* On March 1, one of the buildings owned by the Metropolitan Storage Company was destroyed by fire. The cost of the building was $100,000. The balance in the Accumulated Depreciation account at January 1 was $38,125. A service life of 40 years with a zero salvage value had been estimated for the building. The company uses the straight-line method. The building was not insured.
  **a.** Give the journal entries made at March 1.
  **b.** If there have been no alterations in the service life estimate, how many years previously was the building acquired?

**11.** *Journal entries to correct accounting errors.* Give correcting entries for the following situations. In each case, the firm uses the straight-line method of depreciation and closes its books annually on December 31. Recognize all gains and losses currently.

**a.** A cash register was purchased for $300 on January 1, 1983. It was depreciated at a rate of 10 percent of original cost per year. On June 30, 1988, it was sold for $200 and a new cash register was acquired for $500. The bookkeeper made the following entry to record the transaction:

| | | |
|---|---|---|
| Store Equipment .................................... | 300 | |
| Cash .......................................... | | 300 |

**b.** A used truck was acquired for $4,000. Its cost, when new, was $6,000, and the bookkeeper made the following entry to record the purchase:

| | | |
|---|---|---|
| Truck........................................... | 6,000 | |
| Accumulated Depreciation .......................... | | 2,000 |
| Cash .......................................... | | 4,000 |

**c.** A testing mechanism was purchased on April 1, 1986, for $600. It was depreciated at a 10 percent annual rate. On June 30, 1988, it was stolen. The loss was not insured, and the bookkeeper made the following entry:

| | | |
|---|---|---|
| Theft Loss ......................................... | 600 | |
| Testing Mechanism ................................ | | 600 |

**12.** *Journal entries for acquisition of asset with a note and subsequent recognition of depreciation and interest.* The Grogan Manufacturing Company started business on January 1, 1986. At that time it acquired machine A for $20,000, payment being made by check.

Because of an expansion in the volume of business, machine B, costing $25,000, was acquired on September 30, 1987. A check for $15,000 was issued, with the balance to be paid in annual installments of $2,000 plus interest at the rate of 12 percent on the unpaid balance. The first installment is due on September 30, 1988.

On June 30, 1988, machine A was sold for $13,000 and a larger model, machine C, was acquired for $30,000.

All installments are paid on time.

All machines have an estimated life of 10 years with an estimated salvage value equal to 10 percent of acquisition cost. The company closes its books on December 31. The straight-line method is used.

Prepare dated journal entries to record all transactions through December 31, 1988, including year-end adjustments but excluding closing entries.

13. *Cost of self-constructed assets.* The Dickhaut Manufacturing Company purchased a plot of land for $90,000 as a plant site. There was a small office building on the plot, conservatively appraised at $20,000, which the company will continue to use with some modification and renovation. The company had plans drawn for a factory and received bids for its construction. It rejected all bids and decided to construct the plant itself. The following are additional items that management believes should be included in plant asset accounts:

|  |  |
|---|---:|
| (1) Materials and Supplies | $200,000 |
| (2) Excavation | 12,000 |
| (3) Labor on Construction | 140,000 |
| (4) Cost of Remodeling Old Building into Office Building | 13,000 |
| (5) Interest on Money Borrowed by Dickhaut[a] | 6,000 |
| (6) Interest on Dickhaut's Own Money Used | 9,000 |
| (7) Cash Discounts on Materials Purchased | 7,000 |
| (8) Supervision by Management | 10,000 |
| (9) Workman's Compensation Insurance Premiums | 8,000 |
| (10) Payment of Claims for Injuries Not Covered by Insurance | 3,000 |
| (11) Clerical and Other Expenses of Construction | 8,000 |
| (12) Paving of Streets and Sidewalks | 5,000 |
| (13) Architect's Plans and Specifications | 4,000 |
| (14) Legal Costs of Conveying Land | 2,000 |
| (15) Legal Costs of Injury Claim | 1,000 |
| (16) Income Credited to Retained Earnings Account, Being the Difference between the Foregoing Cost and the Lowest Contractor's Bid | 11,000 |

[a]This interest is the entire amount of interest paid during the construction period.

Show in detail the items to be included in the following accounts: Land, Factory Building, Office Building, and Site Improvements. Explain why you excluded any items that you did not include in the four accounts.

14. *Calculations for various depreciation methods.* Calculate the depreciation charge for the first and second years of the asset's life in each of the following cases.

| Asset | Cost | Estimated Salvage Value | Life (years) | Depreciation Method |
|---|---|---|---|---|
| a. Blast Furnace | $800,000 | $25,000 | 20 | 150% Declining-Balance |
| b. Hotel | 500,000 | 50,000 | 45 | Straight-Line |
| c. Typewriter | 800 | 80 | 8 | Sum-of-the-Years'-Digits |
| d. Tractor | 18,000 | 1,500 | 10 | Double-Declining-Balance (use twice the straight-line rate) |
| e. Delivery Truck | 22,000 | 5,200 | 6 | Sum-of-the-Years'-Digits |
| f. Delivery Truck | 22,000 | 5,200 | 5 | Accelerated Cost Recovery System |

15. *Calculations for various depreciation methods.* On January 1, 1988, the Central Production Company acquired a new turret lathe for $36,000. It was estimated to have a useful life of 4 years and no salvage value. The company closes its books annually on December 31. Indicate the amount of the depreciation charge for each year of the asset's life under
    a. the straight-line method.
    b. the declining-balance method at twice the straight-line rate.
    c. the sum-of-the-years'-digits method.
    d. ACRS depreciation, assuming that the lathe belongs to the 5-year property class. (*Hint:* There will be depreciation charges in each of 6 calendar years.)
    e. Assume now that the lathe was acquired on April 1, 1988. Indicate the amount of the depreciation charge for each of the years from 1988 to 1993, using the sum-of-the-years'-digits method. (*Hint:* Depreciation charges for a year, however they are computed, are allocated on a straight-line basis to periods *within* a year.)

16. *Amount of interest capitalized during construction.* Chan Company builds some of its own chemical processing plants. At the start of the year the Construction-in-Process account had a balance of $1 million. Construction activity occurred uniformly throughout the year. At the end of the year the balance was $5 million. The borrowings of the company during the year were as follows:

| | |
|---|---:|
| New Construction Loans at 20 Percent per Year . . . . . . . . . . . . . . . . . . . | $ 2,000,000 |
| Old Bond Issues Maturing at Various Times, Averaging 10 Percent Rate . . . . . . . . . . . . . . . . . . . . . . . . . . . . . . . . . . . . . . . . . . . . . | 8,000,000 |
| Total Interest-Bearing Debt . . . . . . . . . . . . . . . . . . . . . . . . . . . . . . . . . . . . | $10,000,000 |

    a. Compute the amount of interest to be capitalized into the Construction-in-Process account for the year.
    b. Present journal entries for interest for the year.

17. *Calculations for various depreciation methods.* A machine is acquired for $8,900. It is expected to last 8 years and to be operated for 25,000 hours during that time. It is estimated that its salvage value will be $1,700 at the end of that time. Calculate the depreciation charge for each of the first 3 years using
    a. the straight-line (time) method.
    b. the sum-of-the-years'-digits method.
    c. the declining-balance method using a 25 percent rate.
    d. the units-of-production method. Operating times are as follows: first year, 3,500 hours; second year, 2,000 hours; third year, 5,000 hours.

18. *Revision of estimated service life changes depreciation schedule.* The Slowpoke Shipping Company buys a new car for $10,000 on January 1, 1987. It is estimated that it will last 6 years and have a salvage value of $1,000. Early in 1989, it is discovered that the car will last only an additional 2 years, or 4 years in total. The company closes its books on December 31. Present a table show-

ing the depreciation charges for each year from 1987 to 1990, using each of the methods listed below.

**a.** The straight-line method.

**b.** The sum-of-the-years'-digits method.

19. *Retirement of plant assets.* The Lindahl Manufacturing Company acquires a new machine for $7,200 on July 1, 1984. It is estimated that it will have a useful life of 6 years and a salvage value of $900. The company closes its books annually on June 30.

    **a.** Compute the depreciation charges for each year of the asset's life assuming the straight-line method.

    **b.** If the machine was sold for $700 on October 30, 1989, give the journal entries that would be made on that date.

20. *Trade-in transactions.* The Twombly Company purchased a new panel truck in May 1986. The truck cost $18,600. It was estimated that the truck would be driven for 100,000 miles before being traded in and that its salvage value at that time would be $2,600.

    Odometer readings were as follows:

| | |
|---|---|
| December 31, 1986 | 12,000 |
| December 31, 1987 | 50,000 |
| December 31, 1988 | 82,000 |
| June 16, 1989 | 98,000 |

On June 16, 1989, the truck was traded in for a new one with a list price of $22,000. The old truck had a fair market of $2,600, but the dealer allowed $3,000 on it toward the list price of the new one. The balance of the purchase price was paid by check.

    **a.** Compute the depreciation charges for each year through 1988, using a "production or use" method.

    **b.** Record the entries for June 16, 1989, assuming that the list price of the new truck is unreliable whereas the fair market value of the old one is reliable.

    **c.** Record the entries for June 16, 1989, assuming that there were no reliable estimates for the fair market value of the old truck.

21. *Working backwards to derive proceeds of disposition of plant.* Balance sheets of Rasmussen Company at the beginning and end of the year contained the following data:

| | End of Year | Beginning of Year |
|---|---|---|
| Property, Plant, and Equipment (at cost) | $350,000 | $300,000 |
| Accumulated Depreciation | 165,000 | 170,000 |
| Net Book Value | $185,000 | $130,000 |

During the year, machinery and equipment was sold at a gain of $2,000. New machinery and equipment was purchased at a cost of $80,000. Depreciation charges on machinery and equipment for the year amounted to $20,000.

Calculate the proceeds received from the sale of the machinery and equipment.

**22.** *Cash flow statement; loss on disposal of plant.* Refer to the data in Problem 18 at the end of Chapter 5 on page 195 for the Harris Company. Assume that the proceeds of sale of the equipment amount to $400 rather than $2,000. As a result, net income declines from $39,000 to $37,400, and dividends are reduced from $30,000 to $28,400. All other items remain unchanged. Prepare a statement of cash flows for Year 5.

**23.** *Cash flow statement; gain on disposal of plant.* Refer to the data in Problem 18 at the end of Chapter 5 on page 195 for the Harris Company. Assume that the proceeds of sale of the equipment amount to $3,000 rather than $2,000. As a result, net income increases from $39,000 to $40,000, and dividends are increased from $30,000 to $31,000. All other items remain unchanged. Prepare a statement of cash flows for Year 5.

**24.** *Whether a single asset account or separate asset accounts are used affects classification of expenditures as repairs or improvements.* Lafleur Company purchased a delivery truck for $20,000 at the start of Year 1. The truck is expected to last for 4 years, but the engine is expected to be replaced at the end of Year 2 at a cost of $6,000. Lafleur Company must choose between depreciating the truck as a single unit or as two separate assets — the engine and the rest of the truck. The company uses straight-line depreciation for financial reporting.

**a.** Compute total expense for each of the 4 years of the truck's life, depreciating the entire cost of $20,000 in a single asset account.

**b.** Compute total expense for each year of the truck's life, depreciating the engine and the rest of the truck in separate asset accounts.

## Problems and Cases

**25.** *Allocation of cost in "basket" purchases.* In each of the following situations, compute the amounts of gain or loss to be shown on the income statement for the year, as well as the amount of asset to be shown on the balance sheet as of the end of the year. Show the journal entry or entries required, and provide reasons for your decisions.

**a.** A company wishes to acquire a 5-acre site for a new warehouse. The land it wants is part of a 10-acre site that the owner insists must be purchased as a whole for $18,000. The company purchases the land, spends $2,000 in legal fees for rights to divide the site into two 5-acre plots, and immediately offers half of the land for resale. The two best offers are as follows:

**(1)** $12,000 for the east half.

**(2)** $13,000 for the west half.

The company sells the east half for $12,000.

   **b.** The same data as in part **a**, except the two best offers are as follows:
    **(1)** $5,000 for the east half.
    **(2)** $12,000 for the west half.
    The company sells the west half for $12,000.

**26.** *Composite depreciation versus individual-item depreciation.* The Alexander Company acquired three used machine tools for a total price of $49,000. Costs to transport the machine tools from the seller to Alexander Company's factory were $1,000. The machine tools were renovated, installed, and put to use in manufacturing the firm's products. The costs of renovation and installation were as follows:

| | Machine Tool A | Machine Tool B | Machine Tool C |
|---|---|---|---|
| Renovation Costs........................ | $1,700 | $800 | $950 |
| Installation Costs ........................ | 300 | 550 | 250 |

The machine tools have the following estimated lives: tool A, 4 years; tool B, 10 years; tool C, 6 years.

   **a.** Assume that each machine tool is capitalized in a separate asset account and that the remaining life of each machine tool is used as the basis for allocating the joint costs of acquisition. Compute the depreciable cost of each of the three machine tools.

   **b.** Present journal entries to record depreciation charges for years 1, 5, and 8, given the assumption in part **a**. Use the straight-line method.

   **c.** Assume that the three machine tools are treated as one composite asset in the accounts. If management decides to depreciate the entire cost of the composite asset on a straight-line basis over 10 years, what is the depreciation charge for each year?

   **d.** Which treatment, **a** or **c**, should management of the Alexander Company probably prefer for tax purposes and why?

**27.** *Effect on statement of cash flows.* Refer to the Simplified Statement of Cash Flows in Exhibit 5.15 on page 188. Eleven lines in the statement are numbered. Ignore the unnumbered lines in responding to the questions that follow.

    Assume that the accounting cycle is complete for the period and that all of the financial statements have been prepared. It is then discovered that a transaction has been overlooked. That transaction is recorded in the accounts, and all of the financial statements are corrected. For each of the following transactions, indicate which of the numbered lines of the statement is affected and by how much. Ignore income tax effects.

   **a.** A machine that cost $10,000 and that has $7,000 of accumulated depreciation is sold for $4,000 cash.

   **b.** A machine that cost $10,000 and that has $7,000 of accumulated depreciation is sold for $2,000 cash.

   **c.** A machine that cost $10,000 and that has $7,000 of accumulated depreciation is traded in on a new machine. The new machine has a cash price of

$12,000. A trade-in allowance for the old machine of $4,000 is given, so $8,000 cash is paid.

**d.** A fire destroys a warehouse. The loss is uninsured. The warehouse cost $80,000 and at the time of the fire had accumulated depreciation of $30,000.

**e.** Refer to the facts of part **d**. Inventory costing $70,000 was also destroyed. The loss was uninsured. Record the effects of only these new facts.

**28.** *Effects of recording errors on financial statements*. O'Keefe Company manufactures small machine tools. Its inventory turnover (= cost of goods sold ÷ average inventory during year) is about 3. The company uses a FIFO cost flow assumption. During the current year, inventory increased. The firm depreciates its plant assets over 7 years, using the straight-line method. Below are described several transactions and the incorrect way these events were recorded. Indicate the effect of the mistake (overstatement, understatement, no effect) on each of the following items:

**(1)** Plant Assets (net of depreciation), end of current year.
**(2)** Selling, General, and Administrative Expenses for the current year.
**(3)** Cost of Goods Sold for the current year.
**(4)** Total Assets, end of next year.
**(5)** Net Income for next year.
**(6)** Owners' Equity, end of next year.

For example, if the effect of recording is that net income is too low, the right response is *understatement*.

**a.** During the current year, expenditures for testing a new factory machine were debited to Work-in-Process Inventory.

**b.** During the current year, the company completed self-construction of a warehouse for finished goods, but it failed to charge any general supervisory overhead costs of construction to the plant account. All costs were expensed.

**c.** The local electric utility installed new time-of-day metering devices to enable peak-load pricing of electricity. The O'Keefe Company paid the utility a $5,000 deposit, which will be returned in 3 years if the meters have not been negligently damaged by the company. O'Keefe Company debited this payment to Work-in-Process Inventory.

**d.** Maintenance cost of office machines was debited to Accumulated Depreciation on Plant Assets.

**e.** Maintenance of factory machines was debited to Accumulated Depreciation on Plant Assets.

**f.** In the current year, O'Keefe acquired new land to be used for a warehouse. It incorrectly debited the cost of independent appraisals of the property to general expenses rather than to a plant account.

**g.** O'Keefe Company carried out a significant rearrangement of its factory plant layout during the current year and properly accounted for all costs that were recorded. A bill from Stephens Moving Company will not arrive until the next year. When it is paid, the amount will be debited to a general expense account.

**29.** *Preparing statement of cash flows (adapted from a problem by S. Baiman).* Exhibit 9.5 shows comparative balance sheets, an income statement for Year 2, and supplementary notes of Ormes Company.

Prepare the Year 2 statement of cash flows, with funds defined as cash.

Exhibit 9.5 ————————————————————————————
**ORMES COMPANY**
**Comparative Balance Sheets and Income Statement**
**(Problem 29)**

|  | December 31 | |
| --- | --- | --- |
|  | Year 1 | Year 2 |
| **Balance Sheets** | | |
| Cash ................................................ | $ 30,000 | $130,000 |
| Accounts Receivable.................................. | 100,000 | 120,000 |
| Less Allowance for Uncollectibles ..................... | (20,000) | (25,000) |
| Inventory .......................................... | 100,000 | 80,000 |
| Plant and Equipment.................................. | 700,000 | 750,000 |
| Accumulated Depreciation ........................... | (380,000) | (500,000) |
| Total Assets ..................................... | $530,000 | $555,000 |
| Accounts Payable .................................. | $ 20,000 | $ 30,000 |
| Capital Stock....................................... | 200,000 | 145,000 |
| Retained Earnings .................................. | 310,000 | 380,000 |
| Total Equities .................................... | $530,000 | $555,000 |

**Year 2 Income Statement**

| | |
| --- | --- |
| Net Sales........................................... | $495,000 |
| Gain on Sale of Equipment .......................... | 110,000 |
| | $605,000 |
| Cost of Goods Sold.................................. | $200,000 |
| Bad Debt Expense .................................. | 15,000 |
| Depreciation Expense................................ | 140,000 |
| Income Tax Expense ................................ | 100,000 |
| Total Expenses..................................... | $455,000 |
| Net Income ....................................... | $150,000 |

Notes: (1) During Year 2, Ormes acquired property, plant, and equipment at a cost of $200,000.

(2) During Year 2 Ormes did not collect on any accounts receivable that had previously been written off.

(3) All depreciation charges are expensed.

(4) Dividends declared have been paid in cash.

**30.** *Trade-ins (adapted from a problem by S. Zeff).* Werner Company traded in a machine for an essentially identical machine. The journal entry, which correctly reflects the application of proper accounting practice, was as follows:

| | | |
|---|---|---|
| Machine ............................................... | 33,400 | |
| Accumulated Depreciation ............................... | 12,700 | |
| Loss on Disposition ...................................... | 3,700 | |
| Machine ............................................ | | 29,800 |
| Cash .............................................. | | 20,000 |

**a.** What is the fair market value of the old machine?

**b.** Show the entry for the trade-in as it would be made in accordance with income tax regulations.

**c.** Suppose that all the facts of the trade-in were the same except that the amount of cash given was $15,000 instead of $20,000, changing the $3,700 loss to a $1,300 gain. Give the journal entry that should be made.

**31.** *Capitalizing versus expensing advertising costs: effects on financial statements and rate of return.* The Consumer Products Company has $300,000 of total assets. The company has been earning $45,000 per year and generating $45,000 per year of cash flow from operations. Each year the Consumer Products Company distributes its earnings by paying $45,000 cash to owners. Management believes that a new advertising campaign now will lead to increased sales over the next 4 years. The anticipated net cash flows of the project are as follows:

| Beginning of Year | Net Cash Inflow (outflow) |
|---|---|
| 1 ................................................. | ($24,000) |
| 2, 3, and 4............................................ | 10,000 each year |

Assume that the advertising campaign is undertaken, that cash flows are as planned, and that the Consumer Products Company makes payments to owners of $45,000 at the end of the first year and $47,000 at the end of each of the next 3 years. Assume that there are no interest expenses in any year. Ignore any income tax effects.

**a.** Compute net income and the rate of return on assets of the Consumer Products Company for each of the 4 years, assuming that advertising expenditures are expensed as they occur. Use the year-end balance of total assets in the denominator of the rate-of-return calculation.

**b.** Compute net income and the rate of return on assets of the Consumer Products Company for each year of the project, assuming that advertising costs are capitalized and then amortized on a straight-line basis over the last 3 years. Use the year-end balance of total assets in the denominator of the rate of return on assets.

**c.** How well has the management of the Consumer Products Company carried out its responsibility to its owners? On what basis do you make this judgment? Which method of accounting seems to reflect performance more adequately?

32. *Accounting for intangibles.* In Year 1, Epstein Company acquired the assets of Falk Company, which included various intangibles. Discuss the accounting for the acquisition in Year 1, and in later years, for each of the following items.

   a. Registration of the trademark Thyrom® for thyristors expires in 3 years. Epstein Company believes that the trademark has a fair market value of $100,000. It expects to continue making and selling Thyrom thyristors indefinitely.

   b. The design patent covering the ornamentation of the containers for displaying Thyrom thyristors expires in 5 years. The Epstein Company thinks that the design patent has a fair market value of $30,000 and expects to continue making the containers indefinitely.

   c. An unpatented trade secret on a special material used in manufacturing thyristors is viewed as having a fair market value of $200,000.

   d. Refer to the trade secret in part **c**. Suppose that in Year 2 a competitor discovers the trade secret, but does not disclose the secret to other competitors. How should the accounting policies be changed?

   e. During Year 1, the Epstein Company produced a sales promotion film, *Using Thyristors for Fun and Profit,* at a cost of $45,000. The film is licensed to purchasers of thyristors for use in training their employees and customers. The film is copyrighted.

33. *Expensing versus capitalizing advertising costs for firm advertising every year.* Equilibrium Company plans to spend $60,000 at the beginning of each of the next several years advertising the company's brand names and trademarks. As a result of the advertising expenditure for a given year, aftertax income (not counting advertising expense) is expected to increase by $24,000 a year for 3 years, including the year of the expenditure itself. Equilibrium Company has other aftertax income of $20,000 per year. The controller of Equilibrium Company wonders what will be the effect on the financial statements of following one of two accounting policies with respect to advertising expenditures:

   (1) Expensing the advertising costs in the year of expenditure.

   (2) Capitalizing the advertising costs and amortizing them over 3 years, including the year of the expenditure itself.

   Assume that the company does spend $60,000 at the beginning of each of 4 years and that the planned increase in income occurs. Ignore income tax effects.

   a. Prepare a 4-year condensed summary of net income, assuming that policy (1) is followed and advertising costs are expensed as incurred.

   b. Prepare a 4-year condensed summary of net income, assuming that policy (2) is followed and advertising costs are capitalized and amortized over 3 years. Also compute the amount of Deferred Advertising Costs (asset) to be shown on the balance sheet at the end of each of the 4 years.

   c. In what sense is policy (1) a conservative policy?

   d. What will be the effect on net income and on the balance sheet if Equilibrium Company continues to spend $60,000 each year and the effects on aftertax income continue as in the first 4 years?

34. *Improvements versus repairs or maintenance.* The balance sheet of Woolf's Department Store shows a building with an original cost of $800,000 and

accumulated depreciation of $660,000. The building is being depreciated on a straight-line basis over 40 years. The remaining depreciable life of the building is 7 years. On January 2 of the current year, an expenditure of $28,000 was made on the street-level display windows of the store. Indicate the accounting for the current year if the expenditure of $28,000 was made under each of the following circumstances. Each of these cases is to be considered independently, except where noted. Ignore income tax effects.

**a.** Management decided that improved display windows would make the store's merchandise seem more attractive. The windows are a worthwhile investment.

**b.** A violent hailstorm on New Year's Day destroyed the display windows previously installed. There was no insurance coverage for this sort of destruction. The new windows installed are physically identical to the old windows. The old windows had a book value of $28,000 at the time of the storm.

**c.** Vandals destroyed the display windows on New Year's Day. There was no insurance coverage for this sort of destruction. The new windows installed are physically identical to the old windows. The old windows had a book value of $28,000 at the time of the destruction.

**d.** The old display windows were constructed of nonshatterproof glass. Management had previously considered replacing its old nonshatterproof windows with new ones but had decided that there was zero benefit to the firm in doing so. New shatterproof windows are installed because a new law was passed requiring that all stores must have shatterproof windows on the street level. The alternative to installing the new windows was to shut down the store. In responding to this part, assume zero benefits result from the new windows. Part **e** considers the more realistic case of some benefits.

**e.** Management had previously considered replacing its old nonshatterproof windows with new ones but decided that the new windows were worth only $7,000 (that is, would produce future benefits of only $7,000) and so were not a worthwhile investment. However, a new law (see part **d**) now requires the store to do so (or else shut down), and the new windows were installed.

35. *Capitalizing versus expensing; if capitalized, what amortization period?* In each of the following situations, compute the amounts of revenue, gain, expense, and loss to be shown on the income statement for the year and the amount of asset to be shown on the balance sheet as of the end of the year. Show the journal entry or entries required, and provide reasons for your decisions. Straight-line amortization is used. The reporting period is the calendar year. The situations are independent of each other, except where noted.

**a.** Because of a new fire code, a department store must install an additional fire escape on its building. Management had previously considered installing the additional fire escape. It had rejected the idea because it had already installed a modern sprinkler system, which was even more cost-effective. The new code gives management no alternative except to close the store. The fire escape is acquired for $28,000 cash on January 1. The building is expected to be demolished 7 years from the date the fire escape is installed.

 **b.** Many years ago, a firm acquired shares of stock in the General Electric Company for $100,000. On December 31, the firm acquired a building with an appraised value of $1 million. The company paid for the building by giving up its shares in the General Electric Company at a time when equivalent shares traded on the New York Stock Exchange for $1,050,000.

 **c.** Same data as part **b**, except that the shares of stock represent ownership in Small Timers, Inc., whose shares are traded on a regional stock exchange. The last transaction in shares of Small Timers, Inc., occurred on December 27. Using the prices of the most recent trades, the shares of stock of Small Timers, Inc. given in exchange for the building have a market value of $1,050,000.

 **d.** A company decides that it can save $3,500 a year for 10 years by switching from small panel trucks to larger delivery vans. To do so requires remodeling costs of $18,000 for various garages. The first fleet of delivery vans will last for 5 years, and the garages will last for 20 years. The garages are remodeled on January 1.

 **e.** A company drills for oil. It sinks ten holes during the year at a cost of $1 million each. Nine of the holes are dry, but the tenth is a gusher. By the end of the year, the oil known to be recoverable from the gusher has a net realizable value of $40 million, and Amoco has offered to buy the well for $40 million. No oil was extracted during the year.

 **f.** A company manufactures aircraft. During the current year, all sales were to the government under defense contracts. The company spent $400,000 on institutional advertising to keep its name before the business community. It expects to resume sales of small jet planes to corporate buyers in 2 years.

 **g.** A company runs a large laboratory that has, over the years, found marketable ideas and products worth tens of millions of dollars. On average, the successful products have a life of 10 years. Expenditures for the laboratory this year were $1,500,000.

 **h.** A textile manufacturer gives $250,000 to the Textile Engineering Department of a local university for basic research in fibers. The results of the research, if any, will belong to the general public.

 **i.** On January 1, an automobile company incurs costs of $6 million for specialized machine tools necessary to produce a new model automobile. Such tools last for 6 years, on average, but the new model automobile is expected to be produced for only 3 years.

 **j.** On January 1, an airline purchased a fleet of airbuses for $100 million cash. The airbuses have an expected useful life of 10 years and no salvage value. At the same time the airline purchased for cash $20 million of spare parts for use with those airbuses. The spare parts have no use, now or in the future, other than replacing broken or worn-out airbus parts. During the first year of operation, no spare parts were used.

 **k.** Refer to the data in the preceding part. In the second year of operation, $1 million of spare parts were used.

**36.** *Effect on net income of changes in estimates for depreciable assets.* A major airline has $3 billion of assets, including airplanes costing $2.5 billion with net book value of $1.6 billion. It earns income equal to approximately 6 percent of total assets. Airplanes have been depreciated for financial reporting purposes on a straight-line basis over 10-year lives to a salvage value equal to 10 percent of original cost. The airlines has announced a change in depreciation policy; it will use 14-year lives and salvage values equal to 12 percent of original cost. The airplanes are all 4 years old. Assume an income tax rate of 34 percent.

What will be the approximate impact on net income of the change in depreciation policy? Compute both dollar and percentage effects.

37. *Analysis of financial statements and supplemental disclosures; effect of depreciation method on financial statement ratios.* Exhibit 9.6 reproduces information from a recent annual report of the General Electric Company (GE). GE discloses that it uses the sum-of-the-years'-digits method of depreciation for financial reporting. Assume that GE depreciates all of its assets using a 16-year life with zero estimated salvage value and that the assets are $4\frac{1}{2}$ years old.

**Exhibit 9.6** _____

**GENERAL ELECTRIC COMPANY**
**Condensed Balance Sheet at Year-End**
**(all dollar amounts in millions)**
**(Problem 37)**

| | | | |
|---|---|---|---|
| Current Assets ...................... | $10,356 | Current Liabilities: ..... | $ 8,153 |
| Plant and Equipment at | | Noncurrent Liabilities and | |
| Cost ........................... | 13,843 | Owners' Equity ...... | 13,462 |
| Accumulated Depreciation ............. | (6,535) | | $21,615 |
| Other Assets ....................... | 3,951 | | |
| | $21,615 | | |

**Other Data for Year**

| | |
|---|---|
| Depreciation Charge for Year ............................................. | $  964 |
| Additions to Plant and Equipment during the Year......................... | 1,608 |
| Plant and Equipment, Beginning of Year ................................... | 12,705 |
| Accumulated Depreciation, Beginning of Year.............................. | 5,861 |
| Income before Interest Charges (net of income tax effects) ................. | 2,040 |

a.  Demonstrate that the data in the balance sheet are approximately consistent with GE's using sum-of-the-years'-digits depreciation and assumptions that assets have 16-year lives and are $4\frac{1}{2}$ years old.

b.  Compute the depreciation charge for the year and the amount of accumulated depreciation that would appear on the balance sheet if GE used straight-line depreciation.

c.  Reconstruct GE's balance sheet for year-end as it would appear if GE used straight-line depreciation. Assume no change in income tax expense.

d.  Compute GE's rate of return on assets [= income before interest charges (net of tax effects) divided by end-of-year assets]. First use the financial statements as reported, and then use the financial statements as they would appear if GE used straight-line depreciation.

e.  What was the cost and the accumulated depreciation on plant and equipment retired during the year?

**38.** *Analysis of financial statement disclosure of effects of depreciation policy.* A recent annual report of Caterpillar Tractor Company contained the following statement of depreciation policy:

> Depreciation is computed principally using accelerated methods for both income tax and financial reporting purposes. These methods result in a larger allocation of the cost of buildings, machinery, and equipment to operations in the early years of the lives of assets than does the straight-line method.

Then Caterpillar disclosed the amounts for "Buildings, Machinery, and Equipment — Net" as they would appear if the straight-line method had always been used. Exhibit 9.7 shows these amounts and other data from the financial statements for three recent years.

Exhibit 9.7 _____
**CATERPILLAR TRACTOR COMPANY**
**Excerpts from Annual Report**
**(all dollar amounts in millions)**
**(Problem 38)**

| | Year 3 | Year 2 | Year 1 |
|---|---|---|---|
| **Buildings, Machinery, and Equipment — Net:** | | | |
| As Reported ..................................... | $3,339 | $3,300 | $2,928 |
| If Straight-Line Depreciation Were Used............. | 4,020 | 3,894 | 3,431 |
| **Depreciation Expense Reported** .................. | 505 | 448 | 370 |

a. What amounts would be reported for depreciation expense for Years 2 and 3 if the straight-line method had always been used?

b. Now assume a 40 percent tax rate. Assume also that straight-line depreciation had always been used for both income tax and financial reporting purposes, and that Buildings, Machinery, and Equipment — Net on the balance sheet amounted to $4,020 at the end of Year 3. What other items on the balance sheet for the end of Year 3 would probably change and by how much?

**39.** *Straight-line depreciation is probably too conservative; it usually writes off an asset's cost faster than future benefits disappear.* (This problem requires material from Appendix A.) Assets are acquired for their future benefits — the future cash flows they produce, either cash inflows or savings of cash outflows. As the near-term cash flows are received, the future benefits decline, but the future cash flows come closer to being received, *increasing* the value of the future benefits. The present value of future cash flows may, in total, increase or decrease during any one year. This problem explores changes in the present value of future cash flows with the passage of time and illustrates the phenomenon that for many business projects the present value of future benefits (that is, future cash flows) declines at a rate much slower than implied by straight-line depreciation.

Pasteur Company plans to acquire an asset that will have a 10-year life and that promises to generate cash flows of $10,000 per year at the end of each of the 10 years of its life. Given the risk of the project that uses the asset, Pasteur Company judges that a 12 percent rate is appropriate for discounting its future cash flows. Using a 12-percent discount rate, the present value of $1 received at the end of each of the next 10 years is $5.65022 (see Table 4 at the back of the book; 10-period row, 12 percent column). Because the project is expected to generate $10,000 per year, the present value of the cash flows is $56,502 (= $10,000 × 5.65022). Assume that Pasteur Company purchases the asset for exactly $56,502 at the beginning of Year 1. Exhibit 9.8 shows for each year the present value of the cash flows remaining at the beginning of each year of the asset's life. The numbers in column (3) are derived by multiplying $10,000 by the number appearing in Table 4, 12 percent column, for the number of periods remaining in the asset's life. Column (4) shows the percentage of the asset's present value of the cash flows remaining, and column (5) shows the percentage loss in present value of cash flows during the preceding year.

Column (6) shows the percentage write-off in cost each year using straight-line depreciation — 10 percent per year. Note that the decline in pres-

**Exhibit 9.8** _____

**Pattern of Expiration of Future Benefits Measured as the
Net Present Value of Future Cash Flows
(Problem 39)**

Asset Costs $56,502 and Has 10-Year Life.
Asset Yields $10,000 per Year of Cash Inflow.
Discount Rate = 12 Percent per Year

| Beginning of Year (1) | Years Remaining (2) | Present Value of Remaining Cash Flows (3) | Percentage of Present Value of Cash Flows Remaining (4) | Percentage of Loss in Value during Preceding Year (5) | Straight-Line Depreciation for Preceding Year (6) |
|---|---|---|---|---|---|
| 1 ........ | 10 | $56,502 | 100% | | |
| 2 ........ | 9 | 53,282 | 94 | 6% | 10% |
| 3 ........ | 8 | 49,676 | 88 | 6 | 10 |
| 4 ........ | 7 | 45,638 | 81 | 7 | 10 |
| 5 ........ | 6 | 41,114 | 73 | 8 | 10 |
| 6 ........ | 5 | 36,048 | 64 | 9 | 10 |
| 7 ........ | 4 | 30,373 | 54 | 10 | 10 |
| 8 ........ | 3 | 24,018 | 43 | 11 | 10 |
| 9 ........ | 2 | 16,901 | 30 | 13 | 10 |
| 10 ........ | 1 | 8,929 | 16 | 14 | 10 |
| 11 ........ | 0 | 0 | 0 | 16 | 10 |
| Total .... | | | | 100% | 100% |

Column (3) derived from Table 4 (at back of book), 12 percent column, row corresponding to number in column (2) here, multiplied by $10,000.

Column (4) = number in column (3)/$56,502.

Column (5) = column (4) preceding year − column (4) this year.

ent value of cash flows is less than straight-line in the first 5 years but greater in the last 4 years.

**a.** Construct an exhibit similar to Exhibit 9.8 for an asset with a 5-year life promising $10,000 of cash flows at the end of each year. Use a discount rate of 15 percent per year. The asset costs $33,522. Compare the resulting decline in present value with straight-line depreciation.

**b.** Now consider another asset with a 5-year life with risk appropriate for a 15 percent discount rate. This asset also has net present value of cash flows of $33,522, but the expected cash flows are $11,733 at the end of the first year, $10,767 at the end of the second year, $9,722 at the end of the third year, $8,716 at the end of the fourth year, and $7,710 at the end of the fifth year. Construct an exhibit similar to Exhibit 9.8 for this asset. You should find that the present value of future cash flows disappears at the rate of 20 percent of $33,522 per year, the initial present value.

**c.** Using the results of your work, comment on the nature of conservatism of straight-line depreciation.

**40.** *Analysis of financial statements to compute the change in property and plant assets required to sustain sales growth (developed from a suggestion by K. Schipper).* Exhibit 9.9 shows data from several recent years for the General Electric Company (GE). Assume that analysis of GE's markets indicates that GE can sustain sales growth of 10 percent per year for the next several years. The corporate treasurer must plan ways to raise the new funds that will be required to finance the expansion of assets needed to support such increased sales. Assume that GE's financial policy calls for financing new property and plant with long-term financing, owners' equity (including earnings and retentions), and long-term borrowings. Financing for current assets, such as receivables and inventory, can be generated with current liabilities, such as increases in payables and short-term bank borrowings.

Past relations appear in Exhibit 9.9; note the computation of the fixed asset turnover ratio and the total asset turnover ratio. These ratios show the average amount of sales per dollar of investment in plant and equipment and the average amount of sales per dollar of investment in total assets. The total asset turnover ratio averages 1.42, indicating that $1.42 of sales requires about $1.00 of total assets. Putting it another way, about $.70 (= $1/1.42) of assets is required for each dollar of sales. The average fixed asset turnover ratio of 4.94 indicates that about $1 of net property and plant is required for $4.94 of sales, or that $1 of sales requires about $.20 (= $1/4.94) of property and plant. From these data, management has tentatively concluded that to increase sales by $1 will require about $.70 of new assets, of which about $.20 will be invested in new property and plant, with the remaining $.50 being invested in current assets such as receivables and inventories. Thus to increase sales by 10 percent, or $2.7 billion, will require about $1.9 (= .70 × $2.7) billion of new funds, with about $540 million (= .20 × $2.7 billion) required from long-term sources.

Can you sharpen and improve this analysis? Consider the *incremental* sales achieved by past incremental investments in both property/plant and total assets. Consider that turnover ratios deal with average relations, whereas the questions at issue require analysis of incremental relations—how much additional investment is required for additional sales.

Exhibit 9.9 ————————————————————————————————————————————

**GENERAL ELECTRIC COMPANY**
Data on Sales, Plant/Equipment, and Total Assets
(all dollar amounts in millions)

| Year (1) | Sales (2) | Dollar Change from Preceding Year (3) | Balance Sheet Total Net of Accumulated Depreciation, December 31 (4) | Dollar Change from Preceding Year (5) | New Acquisitions for Year (6) | Balance Sheet Total, December 31 (7) | Dollar Change from Preceding Year (8) | Turnover Ratios Fixed Assets (9) | Turnover Ratios Total Assets (10) |
|---|---|---|---|---|---|---|---|---|---|
| 12 | $27,240 | $2,281 | $6,844 | $1,064 | $2,025 | $20,942 | $2,431 | 4.32 | 1.38 |
| 11 | 24,959 | 2,498 | 5,780 | 1,167 | 1,948 | 18,511 | 1,867 | 4.80 | 1.42 |
| 10 | 22,461 | 2,807 | 4,613 | 590 | 1,262 | 16,644 | 1,608 | 5.20 | 1.42 |
| 9 | 19,654 | 2,135 | 4,023 | 439 | 1,055 | 15,036 | 1,339 | 5.17 | 1.37 |
| 8 | 17,519 | 1,822 | 3,584 | 228 | 823 | 13,697 | 1,647 | 5.05 | 1.36 |
| 7 | 15,697 | 1,592 | 3,356 | 175 | 740 | 12,050 | 1,309 | 4.80 | 1.38 |
| 6 | 14,105 | 187 | 3,181 | 565 | 588 | 10,741 | 1,372 | 4.87 | 1.40 |
| 5 | 13,918 | 1,973 | 2,616 | 255 | 813 | 9,369 | 1,045 | 5.59 | 1.57 |
| 4 | 11,945 | 1,471 | 2,361 | 224 | 735 | 8,324 | 922 | 5.31 | 1.52 |
| 3 | 10,474 | 917 | 2,137 | 111 | 501 | 7,402 | 514 | 5.03 | 1.47 |
| 2 | 9,557 | 723 | 2,026 | 277 | 711 | 6,888 | 689 | 5.06 | 1.46 |
| 1 | 8,834 | | 1,749 | | 685 | 6,199 | | | |
| Weighted average | | | | | | | | 4.94 | 1.42 |

Columns (2), (4), (6), (7): taken from annual reports.

Columns (3), (5), (8): amount for a given year computed by subtracting amount for preceding year from amount for given year, using data in preceding column.

$$\text{Column (9)} = \frac{\text{Column (2)}}{.5 \times [\text{Column (4)} + \text{Column (4), Preceding Year}]}.$$

$$\text{Column (10)} = \frac{\text{Column (2)}}{.5 \times [\text{Column (7)} + \text{Column (7), Preceding Year}]}.$$

# Chapter 10 Liabilities: Introduction _____

This chapter and the next two examine the accounting concepts and procedures for the right-hand side of the balance sheet, which shows the sources of a firm's financing. The funds used to acquire assets come from two sources: owners and nonowners. Chapter 12 discusses owners' equity. This chapter and Chapter 11 discuss obligations incurred by a business as a result of raising funds from nonowners. Banks and creditors providing debt on a long-term basis understand their role as providers of funds. Suppliers and employees, who do not require immediate cash payment for goods provided or services rendered, usually do not think of themselves as contributing to a firm's funds, but they do. Likewise, customers who advance cash to a firm before delivery of a good or service provide funds to the firm. The obligations of a business to these nonowning contributors of funds are *liabilities*.

A thorough understanding of liabilities requires knowledge of compound interest and present value computations. In these computations, payments made at different times are made comparable by taking into account the interest that cash can earn over time. Appendix A at the back of the book introduces the computations.

## Basic Concepts of Liabilities _____

In accounting, an obligation is generally recognized as a *liability* of an entity if it has three essential characteristics:[1]

**1.** The obligation involves a probable future sacrifice of resources — a future transfer of cash, goods, or services or the forgoing of a future cash receipt — at a specified or determinable date. The cash equivalent value of resources to be sacrificed must be measurable with reasonable precision.

_____

[1]Financial Accounting Standards Board, *Statement of Financial Accounting Concepts No. 6,* "Elements of Financial Statements" 1985, par. 36.

**2.** The entity has little or no discretion to avoid the transfer.

**3.** The transaction or event giving rise to the entity's obligation has already occurred.

**Example 1**  Miller Corporation's employees have earned wages and salaries that will not be paid until the next payday, 2 weeks after the end of the current accounting period. Suppliers are owed substantial amounts for goods sold to Miller Corporation, but these debts are not due for 10 to 30 days after the end of the period. Miller Corporation owes the federal and state governments for taxes, but the payments are not due until the 15th of next month. Each of these items meets the three criteria to be a liability. Thus the items are shown as liabilities under titles such as Wages Payable, Salaries Payable, Accounts Payable, and Taxes Payable.

**Example 2**  When Miller Corporation sells television sets, it gives a warranty to repair or replace any faulty parts or faulty sets within 1 year after sale. This obligation meets the three criteria of a liability. Because some television sets will surely need repair, the future sacrifice of resources is probable. The obligation to make repairs is Miller Corporation's. The transaction giving rise to the obligation, the sale of the television set, has already occurred.

The amount is not known with certainty, but Miller Corporation has had sufficient experience with its own television sets to be able to estimate with reasonable precision what the expected costs of repairs or replacements will be. The repairs or replacements will occur within a time span, 1 year, known with reasonable precision. Miller Corporation will thus show Estimated Liability for Warranty Payments on its balance sheet.

**Example 3**  Miller Corporation has signed a binding contract to supply certain goods to a customer within the next 6 months. In this case, there is an obligation, definite time, and definite amount (of goods, if not cash), but there has been no past or current transaction. Chapter 2 pointed out that accounting does not recognize assets or liabilities for *executory contracts* — the mere exchange of promises where there is no mutual performance. Without some mutual performance, there is no current or past benefit. Thus no liability is shown in this case.

**Example 4**  Facts are the same as in Example 3, except that the customer has made a $10,000 cash deposit upon signing the order. Here there has been more than an exchange of promises. The customer has paid cash and Miller Corporation has accepted it. It will show a liability called Advances from Customers in the amount of $10,000. The remainder of the order is still executory and is not recognized in accounting. Such arrangements are called ''partially executory contracts.''

**Example 5**  Miller Corporation has signed a 3-year, noncancelable lease with the IBM Corporation to make payments of $30,000 per month for the use of a computer system with a 3-year life. Definite amounts are due at definite times, and a transaction has occurred—a computer system has been received. Miller Corporation will show a liability called Present Value of Future Payments under Capital Leases on its balance sheet.

**Example 6**  Miller Corporation is defendant in a class action lawsuit alleging damages of $10 million. The lawsuit was filed by customers who claim to have been injured by misleading advertising about Miller Corporation's television sets. Lawyers retained by the corporation think that there is an adequate defense to the charges. Because there is no obligation to make a payment at a reasonably definite time, there is no liability. The notes to the financial statements will disclose the existence of the lawsuit, but no liability will appear on the balance sheet.

**Example 7**  Miller Corporation has signed a contract promising to employ its president for the next 5 years and to pay the president a salary of $250,000 per year. The salary is to be increased in future years at the same rate as the Consumer Price Index, published by the U.S. government, increases. Miller Corporation has an obligation to make payments (although the president may quit at any time without penalty). The payments are of reasonably certain amounts and are to be made at definite times. At the time the contract is signed, no mutual performance has occurred; the contract is purely executory. Because a transaction is deemed not to have taken place, no liability appears on the balance sheet. A liability will, of course, arise as the president performs services over time.

**Example 8**  Miller Corporation has signed a contract with Interstate Oil Pipeline Company to ship at least 10,000 barrels of crude oil per month for the next 3 years. Miller Corporation must pay for the shipping services, whether or not it actually ships oil. An arrangement such as this, called a *throughput contract,* is not recorded as a liability, because the event giving rise to the obligation is viewed as being actual shipment, which has not yet occurred. Such an obligation is merely disclosed in notes. Similarly, obligations for *take-or-pay contracts,* where the purchaser must pay for certain quantities of goods, whether or not the purchaser actually takes delivery of the goods, is not a formal liability. Take-or-pay contracts must be disclosed.[2] Both throughput and take-or-pay contracts are viewed as executory.

## Valuation

In historical cost accounting, liabilities appear on the balance sheet as the present value of payments to be made in the future. The interest rate used in computing the present value amount throughout the life of a liability is the interest rate appropriate for the specific borrower at the time the liability was initially incurred; that is, the *historical* interest rate is used.

---

[2]Financial Accounting Standards Board, *Statement of Financial Accounting Standards No. 47,* ''Disclosure of Long-Term Obligations,'' 1981.

As Chapter 2 mentions, most current liabilities appear at the amount payable because the difference between the amount ultimately payable and its present value is immaterial.

## Classification

Liabilities are generally classified on the balance sheet as current or noncurrent. The criterion used for dividing current from noncurrent liabilities is the length of time that will elapse before payment must be made. The dividing line between the two is the length of the operating cycle, usually 1 year.

## Contingencies — Potential Obligations _____

One of the criteria used by accountants to recognize a liability is that there is a probable future sacrifice of resources. The world of business and law is full of uncertainties. At any given time a firm may find itself potentially liable for events that have occurred in the past. Contingencies of this nature are not recognized as accounting liabilities. They are potential future obligations rather than current obligations. The potential obligations arise from events that occurred in the past but whose outcome is not now known. Whether an item becomes a liability, and how large a liability it will become, depends on a future event, such as the outcome of a lawsuit.

Suppose that a company is sued for damages in a formal court proceeding for an accident involving a customer who was visiting the company. The suit is not scheduled for trial until after the end of this accounting period. If the company's lawyers and auditors agree that the outcome is likely to be favorable for the company or that, if unfavorable, the amount of the damage settlement will not be large, no liability will be recognized on the balance sheet. The notes to the financial statements, however, must disclose significant contingencies.

The FASB has said that an estimated loss from a contingency should be recognized in the accounts only if both of the following conditions are met:[3]

**(a)** Information available prior to the issuance of the financial statements indicates that it is probable that an asset had been impaired or that a liability had been incurred. . . .

**(b)** The amount of the loss can be reasonably estimated.

An example suggested by the FASB *Statement* is that of a toy manufacturer who has sold products for which a safety hazard has been discovered. The toy manufacturer thinks it is likely that liabilities have been incurred. Test **(b)** would be met if experi-

_____

[3]Financial Accounting Standards Board, *Statement of Financial Accounting Standards No. 5*, "Accounting for Contingencies," 1975. When information indicates it is probable that an asset has been impaired or a liability has been incurred, and an estimate of the amount has been made but the estimate is a range, the lower end of the range is to be used. For example, if the estimated loss is a range from $1 million to $1.5 million, the amount $1 million would be used.

ence or other information enabled the manufacturer to make a reasonable estimate of the loss. The journal entry would be as follows:

| | | |
|---|---|---|
| Loss from Damage Claim ................................... | 50,000 | |
|     Estimated Liability for Damages ........................... | | 50,000 |
| To recognize estimated liability for expected damage arising from safety hazard of toys sold. | | |

The debit in this entry is to a loss account (presented among other expenses on the income statement), and the credit is to an *estimated liability,* which should be treated on the balance sheet as a current liability, similar to the Estimated Warranty Liability account. In practice, an account with the title Estimated Liability for Damages would seldom, if ever, appear in published financial statements, because it would be perceived as an admission of guilt. Such an admission is likely to adversely affect the outcome of the lawsuit. The liability account would be combined with others for financial statement presentation.

The term *contingency,* or sometimes *contingent liability,* is used only when the item is not recognized in the accounts but rather in the footnotes. (A note receivable sold with recourse, described in Chapter 7, is another example of a contingency.) A recent annual report of General Motors illustrates the disclosure of contingencies as follows.

> **Note 17. Contingent Liabilities**  There are serious potential liabilities under government regulations pertaining primarily to environmental, fuel economy and safety matters, but the ultimate liability under these regulations is not expected to have a material adverse effect on the Corporation's consolidated financial position. There are also various claims and pending actions against the Corporation and its subsidiaries with respect to commercial matters, including warranties and product liability, civil rights, antitrust, patent matters, taxes and other matters arising out of the conduct of the business. Certain of these actions purport to be class actions, seeking damages in very large amounts. The amounts of liability on these claims and actions at . . . [year-end] were not determinable but, in the opinion of the management, the ultimate liability resulting should not have a material adverse effect on the Corporation's consolidated financial position.

## Current Liabilities

Current liabilities are those due within the current operating cycle, normally 1 year. They include accounts payable to creditors, payroll accruals, short-term notes payable, taxes payable, and a few others. Current liabilities are continually discharged and replaced with new ones in the course of business operations.

These obligations will not be paid for several weeks or months after the current balance sheet date. Their present value is therefore less than the amount that will be paid. Nevertheless, these items are shown at the full amount to be paid, because the difference is usually so small that separate accounting for the difference and subsequent interest expense is judged not to be worth the trouble.

## Accounts Payable to Creditors

Companies seldom pay for goods and services when received. Payment is usually deferred until a bill is received from the supplier. Even then the bill may not be paid immediately, but instead it may be accumulated with other bills until a specified time of the month when all bills are paid. Because explicit interest is not paid on these accounts, management tries to obtain as much capital as possible from its creditors by delaying payment as long as possible. However, failure to keep promises to creditors according to schedule can lead to poor credit ratings and to restrictions on future credit.

## Wages, Salaries, and Other Payroll Items

When employees earn wages, they owe part of their earnings to governments for income and other taxes. They may also owe other amounts for union dues and insurance plans. These amounts, although wage expense of the employer, are not paid directly to employees but are paid on their behalf to the governments, unions, and insurance companies.

In addition, the employer must pay various payroll taxes and may have agreed to pay for other fringe benefits because wages were earned. Employers owe federal Social Security taxes (called *FICA taxes,* for Federal Insurance Contributions Act) for each employee, as well as both federal and state unemployment compensation taxes (called *FUTA taxes,* for Federal Unemployment Tax Act). The rates for FICA and FUTA taxes vary over time; the amounts used in this book are approximately correct.[4]

Employers often provide paid vacations to employees who have worked for more than 6 months or a year. The employer must accrue the costs of the earned but unused vacations (including the payroll taxes and fringe benefits on them) at the time the employees earn them, not at the later time when employees take vacations and are paid. In this way, the accountant will charge each quarter of the year with a portion of the cost of vacations, rather than allocating all to the summer, when most employees take the majority of their vacation days.

**Example 9**   Assume that employees earn $100,000, that the employees' withholding rates for federal income taxes average 20 percent, that the employees' withholding rates for state income taxes average 4 percent, and that employees owe 10 percent of their wages for Social Security taxes. In addition, employees in aggregate owe $500 for union dues to be withheld by the employer and $3,000 for health insurance plans.

---

[4]Readers interested in exact tax rates should consult a current tax manual, such as those published by Commerce Clearing House, Prentice-Hall, and others.

The employer must pay FICA taxes of 10 percent of gross wages and FUTA taxes of 3.5 percent on the first $40,000 of gross wages. Part (2.7 percent) of the FUTA tax is payable to the state government and part (0.8 percent) is payable to the federal government. The employer owes $4,500 for payments to provide life and health insurance coverage. Employees have earned vacation pay estimated to be $4,000; estimated employer payroll taxes and fringe benefits are 18 percent of the gross amount.

The journal entries that follow record these wages. If some of the wages were earned by production workers, some of the debits would be to Work-in-Process Inventory rather than to Wage and Salaries Expense. Although three journal entries are used (one for payments to employees, one for employer payroll taxes, and one for the accrual for estimated vacation pay), in practice these might be prepared as 11 separate entries or even as a single entry.

| | | |
|---|---|---|
| Wages and Salaries Expense ............................... | 100,000 | |
| U.S. Withholding Taxes Payable ........................... | | 20,000 |
| State Withholding Taxes Payable........................... | | 4,000 |
| FICA Taxes Payable ...................................... | | 10,000 |
| Withheld Dues Payable to Union ........................... | | 500 |
| Insurance Premiums Payable .............................. | | 3,000 |
| Wages and Salaries Payable .............................. | | 62,500 |
| Record wage expense; plug for $62,500 actually payable to employees. | | |
| | | |
| Wages and Salaries Expense ............................... | 15,900 | |
| FICA Taxes Payable ...................................... | | 10,000 |
| FUTA Taxes Payable to U.S. Government..................... | | 320 |
| FUTA Taxes Payable to State Government ................... | | 1,080 |
| Insurance Premiums Payable .............................. | | 4,500 |
| Employer's expense for amounts not payable directly to employees. The debit is a plug. | | |
| | | |
| Wages and Salaries Expense ............................... | 4,720 | |
| Estimated Vacation Wages and Fringes Payable .............. | | 4,720 |
| Estimate of vacation pay and fringes thereon earned during the current period; .18 × $4,000 = $720. | | |

On payday, the employer pays $62,500 to employees, discharging the direct liability to them. The employer writes checks at various times to the federal government, the state government, the union, and the insurance companies. Such checks may be sent as often as twice a week (for withheld income and FICA taxes, if the amounts are sufficiently large) or as seldom as once or twice per year (for life insurance). The insurance might be paid in advance, with the debit being made to Prepaid Insurance; if so, the credits when wages are recorded will be to the Prepaid Insurance account. The amounts paid to employees taking vacation are debited to the liability account Estimated Vacation Wages and Fringes Payable, not to an expense account.

# Short-Term Notes and Interest Payable

Businesses obtain interim financing for less than a year from banks or other creditors in return for a short-term note called a *note payable*. Chapter 7 discusses such notes from the point of view of the lender, or note holder. The treatment of these notes by the borrower is the mirror image of the treatment by the lender. Where the lender records an asset, the borrower records a liability. When the lender records interest receivable and revenue, the borrower records interest payable and expense.

# Income Taxes Payable

Businesses organized as corporations must pay federal income taxes based on their taxable income from business activities. In contrast, businesses organized as partnerships or sole proprietorships do not pay income taxes. Instead, the income of the business entity is taxed to the individual partners or sole proprietor. Each partner or sole proprietor adds his or her share of business income to income from all other (nonbusiness) sources in preparing an individual income tax return.

The rules for computing the income tax on corporations change. The rates and schedules of payments mentioned here should not be taken as an indication of the exact procedure in force at any particular time, but rather as an indication of the type of accounting procedures that are involved.

Corporations must estimate the amount of taxes that will be due for the year and make quarterly payments equal to one-fourth of the estimated tax. This is frequently described as "pay-as-you-go" taxation. For a corporation on a calendar-year basis, and using 1988 as an example, 25 percent of the estimated tax for 1988 must be paid by April 15, 1988, 50 percent by June 15, 1988, 75 percent by September 15, 1988, and the entire estimated tax for 1988 must be paid by December 15, 1988.

The estimated income, and hence the estimated tax, may change as the year passes. The corporation must report such changed estimates quarterly. The amount of the quarterly payment is revised to reflect the new estimated tax and takes into account the cumulative payments made during previous quarters of the year. The final income tax return for the year is due by March 15, 1989. Any difference between the actual tax liability for 1988 and the cumulative tax payments during 1988 must be paid by March 15, 1989. The law provides for penalties if the amount estimated is substantially less than the actual tax liability.

If income statements are prepared more often than quarterly, or if the end of the reporting period does not coincide with the tax payment period, it becomes necessary to estimate the income tax for the reporting period so that a more accurate measurement can be made of the net income for the period. Monthly (or other short-period) estimates of the tax are likely to be undependable because of various special provisions in the tax law. During the early quarters of the year, it is not clear which of the special provisions the corporation will ultimately be able to use. One can only prepare the best possible estimate of tax in the light of earnings of the year to date and the prospects for the remainder of the year.

Exhibit 10.1 _____

**Estimating Quarterly Income Tax Payments
and Final Payments of Actual Taxes**

| Date | Estimates of Taxable Income for Year 1 | Amounts Payable for Income Taxes of Year 1 |
|---|---|---|
| **Year 1** | | |
| April 15............... | $1,000,000 | $100,000[a] |
| June 15 ............... | 1,000,000 | 100,000[b] |
| September 15 .......... | 1,000,000 | 100,000[c] |
| December 15 .......... | 1,000,000 | 100,000[d] |
| **Year 2** | | |
| March 15 .............. | 1,100,000[e] | 40,000[f] |

[a] $.25 \times [.40 \times (\$1,000,000)]$.
[b] $.50 \times [.40 \times (\$1,000,000)] - \$100,000$.
[c] $.75 \times [.40 \times (\$1,000,000)] - \$200,000$.
[d] $1.00 \times [.40 \times (\$1,000,000)] - \$300,000$.
[e] Actual income for Year 1 was $1,100,000.
[f] $.40 \times (\$1,100,000) - \$400,000$.

**Illustration of Income Tax Computations**   Exhibit 10.1 illustrates the procedures over several quarterly payments. The income tax rate is assumed to be 40 percent. The related journal entries are of two types and could be combined as follows:

| | | |
|---|---|---|
| Income Tax Expense ......................................... | 100,000 | |
| Income Taxes Payable ..................................... | | 100,000 |
| To accrue quarterly payment. | | |
| Income Taxes Payable ...................................... | 100,000 | |
| Cash ..................................................... | | 100,000 |
| To make payment. | | |

## Deferred Performance Liabilities

Another current liability arises when a firm receives cash from customers for goods or services to be delivered in the future. This liability, unlike the preceding ones, is discharged by delivering goods or services rather than by paying cash. This liability represents unearned, and therefore unrecognized, revenue; that is, cash is received before the goods or services are furnished to the customer.

An example of this type of liability is the advance sale of theater tickets, say, for $20,000. Upon the sale, the following entry is made:

| | | |
|---|---|---|
| Cash ...................................................... | 20,000 | |
| Advances from Customers................................... | | 20,000 |
| Tickets are sold for cash, but there is no revenue until service is rendered. | | |

These deferred performance obligations qualify as liabilities. The account credited is called Advances from Customers or Liability for Advance Sales. After the theater performance, or after the tickets have expired, revenue is recognized and the liability is removed.

---

| | | |
|---|---|---|
| Advances from Customers..................................... | 20,000 | |
|    Performance Revenue ...................................... | | 20,000 |
| Service has been rendered and revenue is recognized. | | |

---

Deferred performance liabilities also arise in connection with the sale of magazine subscriptions, transportation tickets, and service contracts.

A related type of deferred performance liability arises when a firm provides a warranty for free service or repairs for some period after the sale. At the time of sale, the firm can only estimate the likely amount of warranty liability. If sales during the accounting period are $28,000, and the firm estimates that an amount equal to 4 percent of the sales revenue will eventually be used to satisfy warranty claims, the entry is as follows:

---

| | | |
|---|---|---|
| Accounts Receivable........................................ | 28,000 | |
| Warranty Expense ........................................... | 1,120 | |
|    Sales..................................................... | | 28,000 |
|    Estimated Warranty Liability ................................ | | 1,120 |
| To record sales and estimated payment to be made for warranties on items sold. | | |

---

Note that this entry recognizes the warranty expense in the period when revenue is recognized, even though the repairs may be made in a later period. Thus warranty expense is matched with associated revenues. Because the expense is recognized, the liability is created. In this case, neither the amount nor the due date of the liability is definite, but they are reasonably certain. FASB *Statement No. 5,* discussed earlier, requires the accrual of the expense and related warranty liability when the amounts can be "reasonably estimated."

As expenditures of, say, $175 are made next period for repairs under the warranty, the entry is as follows:

---

| | | |
|---|---|---|
| Estimated Warranty Liability ................................... | 175 | |
|    Cash (or other assets consumed for repairs) .................. | | 175 |
| Repairs made. No expense is recognized now; all expense was recognized in the period of sale. | | |

---

With experience, the firm will adjust the percentage of sales it charges to Warranty Expense. Its goal is to achieve a credit balance in the Estimated Warranty Liability account at each balance sheet date that reasonably estimates the actual cost of repairs to be made under warranties outstanding at that time. The accounting for warranties is an allowance method, similar in many ways to the allowance method for uncollectibles discussed in Chapter 7.

The allowance method of accounting for warranties (and bad debts) may not be used for tax reporting. For tax purposes, expense is recognized in the period when cash or other assets are used to discharge the obligation.

# Long-Term Liabilities

The principal long-term liabilities are mortgages, notes, bonds, and leases. The significant differences between long-term and short-term liabilities are that (1) interest on long-term liabilities is ordinarily paid at regular intervals during the life of a long-term obligation, whereas interest on short-term debt is usually paid in a lump sum at maturity; and (2a) the principal of long-term obligations is often paid back in installments, or (2b) special funds are accumulated by the borrower for retiring long-term liabilities.

Accounting for all long-term liabilities generally follows the same procedures. Those procedures are outlined next and illustrated throughout the rest of this chapter and Chapter 11.

## Procedures for Recording Long-Term Liabilities

Long-term liabilities are initially recorded at the present value of all promised payments using the market interest rate at the time the liability is incurred. This market interest rate is also used to compute the amount of interest expense throughout the life of the liability. A portion (perhaps all) of each cash payment represents interest expense. Any excess of cash payment over interest expense is used to reduce the liability itself (often called the *principal*). If a given payment is not sufficient to discharge the entire interest expense that has accrued since the last payment date, the liability principal increases by the excess of interest expense over cash payment.

Retirement of long-term liabilities can occur in several ways, but the process is the same. The net amount shown on the books for the obligation is debited, the asset given up in return (usually cash) is credited, and any difference is recognized as a gain or loss on retirement of the debt.

## Mortgages and Interest-Bearing Notes

In a *mortgage* contract, the lender takes legal title to certain property of the borrower, with the provision that the title reverts to the borrower when the loan is repaid in full. (In a few states, the lender merely acquires a lien on the borrower's property rather than legal title to it.) The mortgaged property is *collateral* for the loan.[5] The customary terminology designates the lender as the *mortgagee* and the borrower as the *mortgagor*.[6]

As long as the mortgagor meets the obligations under the mortgage agreement, the mortgagee does not have the ordinary rights of an owner to possess and use the property. If the mortgagor defaults on either the principal or interest payments, the mortgagee can usually arrange to have the property sold for his or her benefit through a process called *foreclosure*. The mortgagee has first rights to the proceeds from the foreclosure sale for satisfying any unpaid claim. If there is an excess, it is paid to the mortgagor. If the proceeds are insufficient to pay the remaining loan, the lender becomes an unsecured creditor of the borrower for the unpaid balance.

A note is similar to a mortgage except that no property is typically pledged as collateral.

## Accounting for Mortgages and Interest-Bearing Notes

Some of the more common problems in accounting for mortgages appear in the following illustration.

On October 1, Year 1, the Western Company borrows $125,000 for 5 years from the Home Savings and Finance Company to obtain funds for additional working capital. As collateral, Western Company pledges to Home Savings and Finance Company several parcels of land that it owns and that are on its books at a cost of $50,000. Interest is charged on the unpaid balance of the loan principal at an interest rate of 12 percent per year compounded semiannually. Payments are due on April 1 and October 1 of each year. Western agrees to make 10 payments over the 5 years of the mortgage so that when the last payment is made on October 1, Year 6, the loan and all interest will have been paid. The first nine payments are to be $17,000 each. The tenth payment is to be just large enough to discharge the balance of the loan. The Western Company closes its books annually on December 31. (The derivation of the semiannual payment of $17,000 appears in Example 11 in Appendix A at the end of the book.)

The entries from the time the mortgage is issued through December 31, Year 2, assuming annual closings on December 31, are as follows:

| | | | |
|---|---|---|---|
| 10/1/Year 1 | Cash ........................................ | 125,000 | |
| | Mortgage Payable ........................... | | 125,000 |
| | Loan obtained from Home Savings and Finance Company for 5 years at 12 percent compounded semi-annually. | | |

---

[5]Accountants are generally careful to use the word *collateral*, rather than *security*, in this context. Whether the loan is ''secured'' is a matter of legal judgment; moreover, accountants do not wish to imply that the value of the collateral will be sufficient to be able to satisfy the debt, as ''secured'' might imply.

[6]When you borrow money to finance a home purchase, you give the bank a mortgage, not vice versa.

As Example 11 in Appendix A shows, $125,000 is approximately equal to the present value of 10 semiannual cash payments of $17,000, each discounted at 12 percent compounded semiannually.

| | | | |
|---|---|---|---|
| 12/31/Year 1 | Interest Expense............................... | 3,750 | |
| | Interest Payable ........................... | | 3,750 |
| | Adjusting entry: Interest expense on mortgage from 10/1/Year 1 to 12/31/Year 1. | | |

Interest expense on the loan for the first 6 months is $7,500 (= .12 × $125,000 × 6/12). To simplify the calculations, accounting typically assumes that the interest accrues evenly over the 6-month period. Thus interest expense for the 3-month period (October, November, and December) is one-half of the $7,500, or $3,750.

| | | | |
|---|---|---|---|
| 4/1/Year 2 | Interest Expense ............................... | 3,750 | |
| | Interest Payable................................. | 3,750 | |
| | Mortgage Payable ............................. | 9,500 | |
| | Cash......................................... | | 17,000 |
| | Cash payment made requires an entry. Interest expense on mortgage from 1/1/Year 2 to 4/1/Year 2, payment of 6 months' interest, and reduction of loan by the difference, $17,000 − $7,500 = $9,500. | | |

After the cash payment on April 1, Year 2, the unpaid principal of the loan is $115,500 (= $125,000 − $9,500). Interest expense during the second 6-month period is based on this unpaid principal amount.

| | | | |
|---|---|---|---|
| 10/1/Year 2 | Interest Expense ............................... | 6,930 | |
| | Mortgage Payable............................. | 10,070 | |
| | Cash ........................................ | | 17,000 |
| | Cash payment made requires an entry. Interest expense for the period 4/1/Year 2 to 10/1/Year 2 is $6,930 [= .12 × ($125,000 − $9,500) × 6/12]. The loan is reduced by the difference, $17,000 − $6,930 = $10,070. | | |
| 12/31/Year 2 | Interest Expense............................... | 3,163 | |
| | Interest Payable ........................... | | 3,163 |
| | Adjusting entry: Interest expense from 10/1/Year 2 to 12/31/Year 2 = [.12 × ($125,000 − $9,500 − $10,070) × 3/12]. | | |

## Amortization Schedule

Exhibit 10.2 presents an amortization schedule for this mortgage. For each period it shows the balance at the beginning of the period, the interest for the period, the payment for the period, the reduction in principal for the period, and the balance at

## Exhibit 10.2 _____

### Amortization Schedule for $125,000 Mortgage (or note), Repaid in 10 Semiannual Installments of $17,000, Interest Rate of 12 Percent, Compounded Semiannually

**Semiannual Journal Entry**

Dr. Interest Expense ................  Amount in Column (3)
Dr. Mortgage (or Note) Payable .......  Amount in Column (5)
    Cr. Cash .....................           Amount in Column (4)

| 6-Month Period (1) | Loan Balance Start of Period (2) | Interest Expense for Period (3) | Payment (4) | Portion of Payment Reducing Principal (5) | Loan Balance End of Period (6) |
|---|---|---|---|---|---|
| 0 .................. | | | | | $125,000 |
| 1 .................. | $125,000 | $7,500 | $17,000 | $ 9,500 | 115,500 |
| 2 .................. | 115,500 | 6,930 | 17,000 | 10,070 | 105,430 |
| 3 .................. | 105,430 | 6,326 | 17,000 | 10,674 | 94,756 |
| 4 .................. | 94,756 | 5,685 | 17,000 | 11,315 | 83,441 |
| 5 .................. | 83,441 | 5,006 | 17,000 | 11,994 | 71,448 |
| 6 .................. | 71,448 | 4,287 | 17,000 | 12,713 | 58,734 |
| 7 .................. | 58,734 | 3,524 | 17,000 | 13,476 | 45,259 |
| 8 .................. | 45,259 | 2,715 | 17,000 | 14,285 | 30,974 |
| 9 .................. | 30,974 | 1,858 | 17,000 | 15,142 | 15,832 |
| 10 ................. | 15,832 | 950 | 16,782 | 15,832 | 0 |

Note: In preparing this table, calculations were rounded to the nearest cent. Then, for presentation, results were rounded to the nearest dollar.

Column (2) = column (6) from previous period.

Column (3) = .06 × column (2).

Column (4) is given, except row 10, where it is the amount such that column (4) = column (2) + column (3).

Column (5) = column (4) − column (3).

Column (6) = column (2) − column (5).

the end of the period. (The last payment, $16,782 in this case, often differs slightly from the others because of the cumulative effect of rounding errors.) All long-term liabilities have analogous amortization schedules, which aid in understanding the timing of payments to discharge the liability. Amortization schedules for various long-term liabilities appear throughout this chapter and the next.

## Bonds _____

When funds can be borrowed from one lender, the firm usually issues mortgages or notes. When larger amounts are needed, the firm may have to borrow from the general investing public with a bond issue. Bonds are used primarily by corporations and governmental units. The distinctive features of a bond issue are as follows:

1. A *bond indenture,* or agreement, is drawn up that shows in detail the terms of the loan and the rights and duties of the borrower and other parties to the contract. To provide some protection to bondholders, bond indentures typically limit the borrower's right to declare dividends and to make other distributions to owners.

2. *Bond certificates* are used. Engraved certificates are prepared, each one representing a portion of the total loan. The usual minimum denomination in business practice is $1,000, although smaller denominations are occasionally used. Government bonds have been issued in denominations as small as $50.

3. If property is pledged as collateral for the loan (as in a mortgage bond), a *trustee* is named to hold title to the property serving as collateral. The trustee acts as the representative of the bondholders and is usually a bank or trust company.

4. An agent is appointed, usually a bank or trust company, to act as *registrar* and *disbursing agent.* The borrower deposits interest and principal payments with the disbursing agent, who distributes the funds to the bondholders.

5. Most bonds are *coupon bonds.* Coupons attached to the bond certificate represent promises to make interest payments throughout the life of the bond. When a coupon comes due, the bondholder cuts it off and deposits it with a bank. The bank sends the coupon through the bank clearing system to the disbursing agent, who deposits the payment in the bondholder's account at the bank.

6. The entire bond issue is usually issued by the borrower to an investment banking firm or to a group of investment bankers known as a *syndicate,* which takes over responsibility for selling the bonds to the investing public. Members of the syndicate usually bear the risks and rewards of interest rate fluctuations during the period while the bonds are being sold to the public.

## Types of Bonds

*Mortgage bonds* carry a mortgage on real estate as collateral for the repayment of the loan. *Collateral trust bonds* are usually collateralized by stocks and bonds of other corporations. The most common type of corporate bond, except in the railroad and public utility industries, is the *debenture bond.* This type carries no special collateral; instead, it is issued on the general credit of the business. To give added protection to the bondholders, provisions are usually included in the bond indenture that limit the dividends that can be declared or the amount of subsequent long-term debt that can be incurred. *Convertible bonds* are debentures that the holder can exchange, possibly after some specific period of time has elapsed, for a specific number of shares of common stock.

Almost all bonds provide for the payment of interest at regular intervals, usually semiannually. The amount of interest is typically expressed as a percentage of the principal. For example, a 12-percent, 10-year, semiannual coupon bond with face amount of $1,000 promises to pay $60 every 6 months. Here, we assume, the first payment occurs 6 months after the issue date. A total of 20 payments are made. At the time of the final $60 coupon payment, the $1,000 principal is also due. The coupon rate is 12 percent in this case. The principal amount of a bond is its face, or par, value. The terms *face value* and *par value* are synonymous in this context. In general, the par amount multiplied by the coupon rate equals the amount of cash paid per year, whether in quarterly, semiannual, or annual installments. By far the majority of corporate bonds provide for semiannual coupon payments. A bond can be issued and subsequently traded in the marketplace for amounts below par, at par, or above par.

## Proceeds of a Bond Issue

The amount received by the borrower will usually differ from the par value of the bonds issued. The difference arises because the coupon rate printed on the bond certificates differs from the interest rate the market requires given the risk of the borrower, the general level of interest rates in the economy, and other factors. Whatever the market rate, at time of issue or at any time thereafter, the annual cash payments for a bond remain the product of the face value multiplied by the coupon rate. If the coupon rate is less than the rate the market requires the firm to pay, the bonds will sell for less than par; the difference between par and the selling price is called the *discount* on the bond. The issuer will pay the full amount at maturity. The difference between the face amount and the proceeds of the initial issue is part of the interest the market requires the borrower to pay. Even though the payment occurs at maturity, the accounting procedures are designed to record that interest systematically over the life of the bond. If the coupon rate is larger than the rate the market requires, the bonds will sell above par; the difference between the selling price and par is called the *premium* on the bond.

The presence of a discount or premium by itself indicates nothing about the credit standing of the borrower. A firm with a credit standing that would enable it to borrow funds at 11 percent might issue 10 percent bonds that would sell at a discount, whereas another firm with a lower credit standing that would require it to pay 11.5 percent on loans might issue 12 percent bonds that would sell at a premium.

**Issued at Par** The Macaulay Corporation issues $100,000 face value of 12 percent semiannual coupon debenture bonds. The bonds are dated July 1, Year 1. The principal amount is repayable 5 years later, on July 1, Year 6. Interest payments (coupons) are due on July 1 and January 1 of each year. The coupon payments promised at each interest payment date total $6,000. Figure 10.1 presents a time

**Figure 10.1** ————————————————————————————————————————

**Time Line for 5-Year Semiannual Coupon Bonds with 12-Percent Annual Coupons ($100,000 Par Value, Issued at Par)**

| +$100,000 | | | | | | | | | | −$100,000 |
|---|---|---|---|---|---|---|---|---|---|---|
| | −$6,000 | −$6,000 | −$6,000 | −$6,000 | −$6,000 | −$6,000 | −$6,000 | −$6,000 | −$6,000 | −$6,000 |
| 7/1/Y1 | 1/1/Y2 | 7/1/Y2 | 1/1/Y3 | 7/1/Y3 | 1/1/Y4 | 7/1/Y4 | 1/1/Y5 | 7/1/Y5 | 1/1/Y6 | 7/1/Y6 |

line for the two sets of cash flows associated with this bond. Assuming that the issue was taken by Penman & Company, investment bankers, on July 1, Year 1, at a rate to yield exactly 12 percent compounded semiannually, the calculation of the proceeds to Macaulay would be as follows (Appendix A at the back of the book explains the present value calculations):

| | |
|---|---:|
| (a) Present Value of $100,000 to Be Paid at the End of 5 Years . . . . . . . . . . . . . | $ 55,839 |
| (Appendix Table 2 at the back of the book shows the present value of $1 to be paid in 10 periods at 6 percent per period to be $.55839; $100,000 × .55839 = $55,839.) | |
| (b) Present Value of $6,000 to Be Paid Each 6 Months for 5 Years . . . . . . . . . | 44,161 |
| (Appendix Table 4 shows the present value of an ordinary annuity of $1 per period for 10 periods discounted at 6 percent to be $7.36009; $6,000 × 7.36009 = $44,161.) | |
| Total Proceeds. . . . . . . . . . . . . . . . . . . . . . . . . . . . . . . . . . . . . . . . . . . . . . . . . . . . . | $100,000 |

The issue price would be stated as 100.0 (that is, 100 percent of par), which implies that the market interest rate is 12 percent compounded semiannually, the same as the coupon rate.

**Issued at Less than Par**  Assume that these same bonds were issued at a price to yield 14 percent compounded semiannually. The promised cash flows after July 1, Year 1, associated with these bonds (payment of periodic interest plus repayment of principal) are identical to those in the time line shown in Figure 10.1. These future cash flows would be discounted to their present value using a 14 percent discount rate compounded semiannually. The calculation of the issue proceeds (that is, initial market price) would be as follows (why "12-percent" bonds can be issued to yield 14 percent is discussed on page 433):

| | |
|---|---:|
| (a) Present Value of $100,000 to Be Paid at the End of 5 Years . . . . . . . . . . . . . | $50,835 |
| (Present value of $1 to be paid in 10 periods at 7 percent per period is $.50835; $100,000 × .50835 = $50,835.) | |
| (b) Present Value of $6,000 to Be Paid Each 6 Months for 5 Years . . . . . . . . . . . | 42,141 |
| (Present value of an ordinary annuity of $1 per period for 10 periods, discounted at 7 percent per period = $7.02358; $6,000 × 7.02358 = $42,141.) | |
| Total Proceeds. . . . . . . . . . . . . . . . . . . . . . . . . . . . . . . . . . . . . . . . . . . . . . . . . . . . . | $92,976 |

If the issue price were stated on a conventional pricing basis in the market at 92.98 (92.98 percent of par), the issuing price would be $92,980. This amount implies a market yield of slightly less than 14 percent compounded semiannually.

**Issued at More than Par**  Assume that the bonds were issued at a price to yield 10 percent compounded semiannually. The cash flows after July 1, Year 1, would again be identical to those shown in Figure 10.1. They would be discounted at 10 percent compounded semiannually to calculate their present value. The calculation of the proceeds would be as follows:

| | |
|---|---|
| (a) Present Value of $100,000 to Be Paid at the End of 5 Years . . . . . . . . . . . . . | $ 61,391 |
| (Present value of $1 to be paid in 10 periods at 5 percent per period is $.61391; $100,000 × .61391 = $61,391.) | |
| (b) Present Value of $6,000 to Be Paid Each 6 Months for 5 Years . . . . . . . . . | 46,330 |
| (Present value of an ordinary annuity at $1 per period for 10 periods, discounted at 5 percent per period = $7.72173; $6,000 × 7.72173 = $46,330.) | |
| Total Proceeds. . . . . . . . . . . . . . . . . . . . . . . . . . . . . . . . . . . . . . . . . . . . . . . . . . . . . . | $107,721 |

If the issue price were stated on a conventional pricing basis in the market at 107.72 (107.72 percent of par), the issuing price would be $107,720.[7] The price would imply a market yield of slightly more than 10 percent compounded semiannually.

## Bond Tables

These tedious calculations do not need to be made every time a bond issue is analyzed. *Bond tables* show the results of calculations like those just described. Tables 5 and 6 at the back of the book are examples of such tables. Table 5 shows the price for 10-percent semiannual coupon bonds as a percent of par for various market interest rates (yields) and years to maturity. Table 6 shows market rates and implied prices for 12-percent semiannual coupon bonds. (Some modern calculators make the calculations represented by these tables in a few seconds.)

The percentages of par shown in these tables represent the present value of the bond indicated. Because the factors are expressed as a percent of par, they have to be multiplied by 10 to find the price of a $1,000 bond. If you have never used bond tables before now, turn to Table 6 after Appendix A at the back of the book and find in the 5-year row the three different prices for the three different market yields used in the preceding examples. Notice further that a bond will sell at par if and only if it has a market yield equal to its coupon rate.

These tables are useful whether a bond is being issued by a corporation or resold later by an investor. The approach to computing the market price will be the same in either case, although their years to maturity will be fewer than the original term of the bond. The following generalizations can be made regarding bond prices:

_____

[7]In many contexts, bond prices are quoted in dollars plus thirty-seconds of a dollar. A bond selling for about 107.721 percent of par would be quoted at 107$\frac{23}{32}$, which would be written as 107.23. In order to read published bond prices, you must know whether the information after the "decimal" point refers to fractions expressed in one-hundredths or in thirty-seconds. (If you are reading published bond prices and see any number larger than 31 after the decimal point, you can be sure that one-hundredths are being used. If you see many prices, but none of the numbers shown after the point is larger than 31, you can be reasonably sure that thirty-seconds are being used.)

1. When the market interest rate equals the coupon rate, the market price will equal par.

2. When the market interest rate is greater than the coupon rate, the market price will be less than par.

3. When the market interest rate is less than the coupon rate, the market price will be greater than par.

## Accounting for Bonds Issued at Par

The following illustration covers the more common problems associated with bonds issued at par.

We use the data presented in the previous sections for the Macaulay Corporation, where the bonds were issued at par, and we assume that the books are closed semiannually on June 30 and December 31. The entry at the time of issue would be as follows:

| | | | |
|---|---|---|---|
| 7/1/Year 1 | Cash........................................... | 100,000 | |
| | Debenture Bonds Payable...................... | | 100,000 |
| | $100,000 of 12 percent, 5-year bonds issued at par. | | |

The entries for interest would be made at the end of the accounting period and on the interest payment dates. Entries through January 1, Year 2, would be as follows:

| | | | |
|---|---|---|---|
| 12/31/Year 1 | Interest Expense ............................. | 6,000 | |
| | Interest Payable ........................... | | 6,000 |
| 1/1/Year 2 | Interest Payable ........................... | 6,000 | |
| | Cash ..................................... | | 6,000 |
| | To record payment of 6 months' interest. | | |

**Bond Issued between Interest Payment Dates** The actual date that a bond is issued seldom coincides with one of the payment dates. Assuming that these same bonds were actually brought to market on September 1 rather than July 1, and that they were issued at par, the purchasers of the bonds would be expected to pay Macaulay Corporation for 2 months' interest in advance. After all, on the first coupon Macaulay Corporation promises a full $6,000 for 6 months' interest, but it would have had the use of the borrowed funds for only 4 months. The purchasers of the bonds would pay $100,000 plus 2 months' interest of $2,000 $(= .12 \times $100,000 \times \frac{2}{12})$ and would get the $2,000 back when the first coupons were redeemed. The journal entry made by Macaulay Corporation, the issuer, would be as follows:

| 9/1/Year 1 | Cash............................................. | 102,000 | |
| | Bonds Payable................................ | | 100,000 |
| | Interest Payable.............................. | | 2,000 |

To record issue of bonds at par between interest payment dates. The purchasers pay an amount equal to
interest for the first 2 months but will get it back when
the first coupons are redeemed.

## Accounting for Bonds Issued at Less than Par

The following illustrates the more common problems associated with bonds issued
for less than par.

Assume the data presented for the Macaulay Corporation, where 12-percent,
$100,000–par value, 5-year bonds were issued to yield 14 percent compounded
semiannually. The issue price was shown previously to be $92,976. The journal
entry at the time of issue would be as follows:

| 7/1/Year 1 | Cash............................................. | 92,976 | |
| | Debenture Bonds Payable....................... | | 92,976 |

The issuance of these bonds for $92,976, instead of the $100,000 par value, indicates that 12 percent is not a sufficiently high rate of interest for the bonds to induce
purchasers to pay par value in the open market. If purchasers of these bonds paid the
$100,000 par value, they would earn only 12 percent compounded semiannually,
the coupon rate. Purchasers desiring a rate of return of 14 percent will postpone
their purchases until the market price drops to $92,976. At this price, purchasers of
the bonds will earn the 14 percent return they require. The return will be composed
of ten $6,000 coupon payments over the next 5 years plus $7,024 (= $100,000 −
$92,976) as part of the payment at maturity.

For Macaulay Corporation, the total interest expense over the life of the bonds
is equal to $67,024 (periodic interest payments totaling $60,000 plus $7,024 paid at
maturity). The total interest expense of $67,024 is allocated to the periods of the
loan using the effective interest method.

**Interest Expense under the Effective Interest Method**  Under the *effective interest method,* interest expense each period is equal to the market interest rate at the
time the bonds were initially issued (14 percent compounded semiannually in this
example) multiplied by the book value of the liability at the beginning of the interest
period. For example, interest expense for the period from July 1, Year 1, to December 31, Year 1, the first 6-month period, is $6,508 (= .07 × $92,976). The bond
indenture provides that only $6,000 (= .06 × $100,000) needs to be paid on January 1, Year 2. This amount is equal to the coupon rate times the par value of the
bonds. The difference between the interest expense of $6,508 and the interest cur-
rently payable of $6,000 is added to the book value of the bond and will be paid as

part of the principal amount at maturity. The journal entry made on December 31, Year 1, to recognize interest for the last 6 months of Year 1 is as follows:

| | | | |
|---|---|---|---|
| 12/31/Year 1 | Interest Expense............................. | 6,508 | |
| | Interest Payable ........................... | | 6,000 |
| | Debenture Bonds Payable ................... | | 508 |
| | To recognize interest expense for 6 months. | | |

The Interest Payable account will appear as a current liability on the balance sheet at the end of Year 1. Debenture Bonds Payable of $93,484 (= $92,976 + $508) will appear on the balance sheet as a noncurrent liability.

On January 1, Year 2, the first periodic cash payment is made.

| | | | |
|---|---|---|---|
| 1/1/Year 2 | Interest Payable................................ | 6,000 | |
| | Cash........................................ | | 6,000 |
| | To record payment of interest for 6 months. | | |

Interest expense for the second 6 months (from January 1, Year 2, through June 30, Year 2) is $6,544 (= .07 × $93,484). It is larger than the $6,508 for the first 6 months because the recorded book value of the liability at the beginning of the second 6 months is larger. The journal entry on June 30, Year 2, to record interest expense is as follows:

| | | | |
|---|---|---|---|
| 6/30/Year 2 | Interest Expense............................. | 6,544 | |
| | Interest Payable ........................... | | 6,000 |
| | Debenture Bonds Payable ................... | | 544 |
| | To recognize interest expense for 6 months. | | |

An amortization schedule for these bonds over their 5-year life appears in Exhibit 10.3. Column (3) shows the periodic interest expense, and column (6) shows the book value that appears on the balance sheet at the end of each period.

The effective interest method of recognizing interest expense on a bond has the following financial statement effects:

1. Interest expense on the income statement will be a constant percentage of the recorded liability at the beginning of each interest period. This percentage will be equal to the market interest rate for these bonds when they were initially issued. When bonds are issued for less than par value, the dollar amount of interest expense will increase each period as the recorded book value amount increases.

2. On the balance sheet at the end of each period, the bonds will be stated at the present value of the remaining cash outflows discounted at the market interest

## Exhibit 10.3 _____

### Effective Interest Amortization Schedule for $100,000 of 12-Percent, 5-Year Bonds Issued for 92.976 Percent of Par to Yield 14 Percent, Interest Payable Semiannually

**Semiannual Journal Entry**

Dr. Interest Expense . . . . . . . . . . . . . . . . .  Amount in Column (3)
   Cr. Cash . . . . . . . . . . . . . . . . . . . . . . .  Amount in Column (4)
   Cr. Debenture Bonds Payable . . . .  Amount in Column (5)

| Period (6-month intervals) (1) | Liability at Start of Period (2) | Effective Interest: 7 Percent per Period (3) | Coupon Rate: 6 Percent of Par (4) | Increase in Recorded Book Value of Liability (5) | Liability at End of Period (6) |
|---|---|---|---|---|---|
| 0 . . . . . . . . . . . . . |  |  |  |  | $92,976 |
| 1 . . . . . . . . . . . . . | $92,976 | $ 6,508 | $ 6,000 | $ 508 | 93,484 |
| 2 . . . . . . . . . . . . . | 93,484 | 6,544 | 6,000 | 544 | 94,028 |
| 3 . . . . . . . . . . . . . | 94,028 | 6,582 | 6,000 | 582 | 94,610 |
| 4 . . . . . . . . . . . . . | 94,610 | 6,623 | 6,000 | 623 | 95,233 |
| 5 . . . . . . . . . . . . . | 95,233 | 6,666 | 6,000 | 666 | 95,899 |
| 6 . . . . . . . . . . . . . | 95,899 | 6,713 | 6,000 | 713 | 96,612 |
| 7 . . . . . . . . . . . . . | 96,612 | 6,763 | 6,000 | 763 | 97,375 |
| 8 . . . . . . . . . . . . . | 97,375 | 6,816 | 6,000 | 816 | 98,191 |
| 9 . . . . . . . . . . . . . | 98,191 | 6,873 | 6,000 | 873 | 99,064 |
| 10 . . . . . . . . . . . . . | 99,064 | 6,936 | 6,000 | 936 | 100,000 |
| Total . . . . . . . . . . . |  | $67,024 | $60,000 | $7,024 |  |

Note: In preparing this table, calculations were rounded to the nearest cent. Then, for presentation, results were rounded to the nearest dollar.

Column (2) = column (6) from previous period.

Column (3) = .07 × column (2).

Column (4) is given.

Column (5) = column (3) − column (4).

Column (6) = column (2) + column (5).

rate when the bonds were initially issued. For example, on July 1, Year 2, just after a coupon payment has been made, the present value of the remaining cash payments will be as follows:

| | | |
|---|---|---|
| (a) Present Value of $100,000 to Be Paid at the End of 4 Years . . . . . . . . . . | | $58,201 |
| (Appendix Table 2 shows the present value of $1 to be paid at the end of 8 periods discounted at 7 percent to be $.58201; $100,000 × .58201 = $58,201.) | | |
| (b) Present Value of 8 Remaining Semiannual Interest Payments Discounted at 14 Percent, Compounded Semiannually . . . . . . . . . . . . . . . . . . . . . . . . . | | 35,827 |
| (Appendix Table 4 shows the present value of an ordinary annuity of $1 per period for 8 periods discounted at 7 percent to be $5.97130; $6,000 × 5.97130 = $35,827.) | | |
| Total Present Value . . . . . . . . . . . . . . . . . . . . . . . . . . . . . . . . . . . . . | | $94,028 |

The amount $94,028 appears in column (6) of Exhibit 10.3 for the liability at the end of the second 6-month period.

**Discount on Bonds Payable Account**  The preceding description of the recording of bonds issued below par value shows the book value of the bonds directly in the Bonds Payable account. Some accountants prefer to show Bonds Payable at par value with a liability contra account, titled Discount on Bonds Payable, carrying the amount by which par value must be reduced to book value. If the Discount on Bonds Payable account was used, the balance sheet on June 30, Year 2, after two semiannual interest periods, would show:

| | |
|---|---:|
| Bonds Payable — Par Value . . . . . . . . . . . . . . . . . . . . . . . . . . . . . . . . . . . . . . . . . . . . . | $100,000 |
| Less Discount on Bonds Payable . . . . . . . . . . . . . . . . . . . . . . . . . . . . . . . . . . . . . . . | (5,972) |
| Bonds Payable — Net Book Value . . . . . . . . . . . . . . . . . . . . . . . . . . . . . . . . . . . . . . . | $ 94,028 |

## Accounting for Bonds Issued for More than Par

The following discussion illustrates the more common problems associated with bonds issued for more than par.

Assume the data presented for the Macaulay Corporation, in which 12-percent, $100,000–par value, 5-year bonds were issued to yield approximately 10 percent compounded semiannually. The issue price, derived previously, was $107,721. The journal entry at the time of issue would be as follows:

| | | | |
|---|---|---:|---:|
| 7/1/Year 1 | Cash . . . . . . . . . . . . . . . . . . . . . . . . . . . . . . . . . . . . . . . . . . . . . | 107,721 | |
| | Debenture Bonds Payable . . . . . . . . . . . . . . . . . . . . . . | | 107,721 |

The firm borrows $107,721. The issuance of these bonds for $107,721, instead of the $100,000 par value, indicates that 12 percent is a higher rate of interest for the bonds than the purchasers demand. If purchasers of these bonds paid the $100,000 par value, they would earn 12 percent compounded semiannually, the coupon rate. Purchasers requiring a rate of return of only 10 percent will bid up the market price to $107,721. At this price, purchasers of the bonds will earn only the 10 percent demanded return. The return comprises ten $6,000 coupon payments over the next 5 years reduced by $7,721 (= $107,721 − $100,000) lent but not repaid at maturity.

For Macaulay Corporation, the total interest expense over the life of the bonds is equal to $52,279 (periodic interest payments totaling $60,000 less $7,721 of principal not repaid at maturity).

**Interest Expense under the Effective Interest Method**  Under the effective interest method, interest expense each period is equal to the market interest rate at the time the bonds were initially issued (10 percent compounded semiannually in this example) multiplied by the recorded book value of the liability at the beginning of the interest period. For example, interest expense for the period from July 1, Year 1, to December 31, Year 1, the first 6-month period, is \$5,386 (= .05 × \$107,721). The bond indenture provides that \$6,000 (= .06 × \$100,000) is to be paid on January 1, Year 2. This amount equals the coupon rate times the face value of the bonds. The difference between the payment of \$6,000 and the interest expense of \$5,386 reduces the amount of the liability. The journal entry made on December 31, Year 1, to recognize interest for the last 6 months of Year 1 is as follows:

| | | | |
|---|---|---|---|
| 12/31/Year 1 | Interest Expense ............................. | 5,386 | |
| | Debenture Bonds Payable ..................... | 614 | |
| | Interest Payable ........................... | | 6,000 |
| | To recognize interest expense for 6 months. | | |

The Interest Payable account appears as a current liability on the balance sheet at the end of Year 1. Debenture Bonds Payable of \$107,107 (= \$107,721 − \$614) appears as a noncurrent liability.

On January 1, Year 2, the first periodic cash payment is made.

| | | | |
|---|---|---|---|
| 1/1/Year 2 | Interest Payable................................ | 6,000 | |
| | Cash........................................ | | 6,000 |
| | To record payment of interest for 6 months. | | |

Interest expense for the second 6 months (from January 1, Year 2, through June 30, Year 2) is \$5,355 (= .05 × \$107,107) and it is smaller than the \$5,386 for the first 6 months because the unpaid balance of the liability at the beginning of the second 6 months is smaller. The journal entry on June 30, Year 2, to record interest expense is as follows:

| | | | |
|---|---|---|---|
| 6/30/Year 2 | Interest Expense ............................. | 5,355 | |
| | Debenture Bonds Payable ..................... | 645 | |
| | Interest Payable ........................... | | 6,000 |
| | To recognize interest expense for 6 months. | | |

An amortization schedule for these bonds over their 5-year life appears in Exhibit 10.4. Column (3) shows the periodic interest expense, and column (6) shows the book value that appears on the balance sheet at the end of the period.

The effective interest method of recognizing interest expense on a bond has the following financial statement effects:

1. Interest expense on the income statement will be a constant percentage of the recorded liability at the beginning of each interest period. This percentage will be equal to the market interest rate when the bonds were initially issued. When bonds are issued for more than par value, the dollar amount of interest expense will decrease each period as the unpaid liability decreases to the amount to be paid at maturity.

Exhibit 10.4 ———————————————————————————

## Effective Interest Amortization Schedule for $100,000 of 12-Percent, 5-Year Bonds Issued for 107.721 Percent of Par to Yield 10 Percent, Interest Payable Semiannually

**Semiannual Journal Entry**
Dr. Interest Expense . . . . . . . . . . . . . . . .     Amount in Column (3)
Dr. Debenture Bonds Payable . . . . . . . .     Amount in Column (5)
    Cr. Cash . . . . . . . . . . . . . . . . . . . . . .                                   Amount in Column (4)

| Period (6-month Intervals) (1) | Liability at Start of Period (2) | Effective Interest: 5 Percent per Period (3) | Coupon Rate: 6 Percent of Par (4) | Decrease in Recorded Book Value of Liability (5) | Liability at End of Period (6) |
|---|---|---|---|---|---|
| 0 . . . . . . . . . . . . . . . . |  |  |  |  | $107,721 |
| 1 . . . . . . . . . . . . . . . . | $107,721 | $ 5,386 | $ 6,000 | $ 614 | 107,107 |
| 2 . . . . . . . . . . . . . . . . | 107,107 | 5,355 | 6,000 | 645 | 106,462 |
| 3 . . . . . . . . . . . . . . . . | 106,462 | 5,323 | 6,000 | 677 | 105,785 |
| 4 . . . . . . . . . . . . . . . . | 105,785 | 5,289 | 6,000 | 711 | 105,074 |
| 5 . . . . . . . . . . . . . . . . | 105,074 | 5,254 | 6,000 | 746 | 104,328 |
| 6 . . . . . . . . . . . . . . . . | 104,328 | 5,216 | 6,000 | 784 | 103,544 |
| 7 . . . . . . . . . . . . . . . . | 103,544 | 5,177 | 6,000 | 823 | 102,721 |
| 8 . . . . . . . . . . . . . . . . | 102,721 | 5,136 | 6,000 | 864 | 101,857 |
| 9 . . . . . . . . . . . . . . . . | 101,857 | 5,093 | 6,000 | 907 | 100,950 |
| 10 . . . . . . . . . . . . . . . . | 100,950 | 5,050 | 6,000 | 950 | 100,000 |
| Total . . . . . . . . . . . . |  | $52,279 | $60,000 | $7,721 |  |

Column (2) = column (6) from previous period.

Column (3) = .05 × column (2).

Column (4) is given.

Column (5) = column (4) − column (3).

Column (6) = column (2) − column (5).

2.  On the balance sheet at the end of each period, the bonds will be stated at the present value of the remaining cash flow discounted at the market interest rate when the bonds were initially issued. For example, on July 1, Year 2, just after the coupon payment is made, the present value of the remaining cash payments will be as follows:

(a) Present Value of $100,000 to Be Paid at the End of 4 Years. . . . . . . . .     $ 67,684
    (Appendix Table 2 shows the present value of $1 to be paid at the end of 8 periods discounted at 5 percent to be $.67684; $100,000 × .67684 = $67,684.)

(b) Present Value of 8 Remaining Semiannual Interest Payments Discounted at 10 Percent, Compounded Semiannually . . . . . . . . . . . . . . . .     38,779
    (Appendix Table 4 shows the present value of an ordinary annuity of $1 per period for 8 periods discounted at 5 percent to be $6.46321; $6,000 × 6.46321 = $38,779.)

Total Present Value . . . . . . . . . . . . . . . . . . . . . . . . . . . . . . . . . . . . . . . . . . . .     $106,463

The amount $106,462, different because of rounding effects, appears in column (6) of Exhibit 10.4 for the liability at the end of the second 6-month period.

**Premium on Bonds Payable Account**  The preceding description of the recording of bonds issued above par value shows the book value of the bonds directly in the Bonds Payable account. Some accountants prefer to show Bonds Payable at par value with a liability adjunct account,[8] titled Premium on Bonds Payable, carrying the amount added to par value to show book value. If the Premium on Bonds Payable account was used, the balance sheet on June 30, Year 2, after two semiannual interest periods, would show:

| | |
|---|---:|
| Bonds Payable — Par Value | $100,000 |
| Plus Premium on Bonds Payable | 6,462 |
| Bonds Payable — Net Book Value | $106,462 |

## Bond Retirement

Many bonds remain outstanding until the stated maturity date. Refer to Exhibit 10.3, the Macaulay example, where the 12-percent coupon bonds were issued to yield 14 percent. The company pays the final coupon, $6,000, and the face amount, $100,000, on the stated maturity date. The entries are as follows:

| | | | |
|---|---|---:|---:|
| 7/1/Year 6 | Interest Expense | 6,936 | |
| | Cash | | 6,000 |
| | Debenture Bonds Payable | | 936 |
| | See Row 10 of Exhibit 10.3. | | |
| | Debenture Bonds Payable | 100,000 | |
| | Cash | | 100,000 |
| | Retirement at maturity of bonds. | | |

**Retirement before Maturity**  A firm sometimes purchases its own bonds on the open market before maturity. Because market interest rates constantly change, the purchase price will seldom equal the recorded book value of the bonds. Assume that Macaulay Corporation originally issued its 12-percent coupon bonds to yield 14 percent compounded semiannually. Assume that 3 years later, on July 1, Year 4, interest rates in the marketplace have increased so that the market currently requires a 15 percent interest rate to be paid by Macaulay Corporation. Refer to Table 6 at the back of the book, 2-year row, 15 percent column, which shows that 12-percent bonds with 2 years until maturity will sell in the marketplace for 94.9760 percent of par if the current interest rate is 15 percent compounded semiannually.

---

[8]An *adjunct account* accumulates additions to another account; contrast with a contra account, which accumulates subtractions from another account.

The marketplace is not constrained by the principles of historical cost accounting. Even though Macaulay Corporation shows the Debenture Bonds Payable on the balance sheet at $96,612 (see row 6 of Exhibit 10.3), the marketplace puts a price of only $94,976 on the entire bond issue. From the point of view of the marketplace, these bonds are the same as 2-year bonds issued on July 1, Year 4, at an effective yield of 15 percent, so they carry a discount of $5,024 (= $100,000 − $94,976).

If on July 1, Year 4, Macaulay Corporation purchased $10,000 of par value of its own bonds, it would have to pay only $9,498 (= .94976 × $10,000) for those bonds, which have book value of $9,661. The journal entries made at the time of purchase would be as follows:

| | | | |
|---|---|---:|---:|
| 7/1/Year 4 | Interest Expense .................................. | 6,713 | |
| | Interest Payable................................. | | 6,000 |
| | Debenture Bonds Payable....................... | | 713 |
| | See row 6 of Exhibit 10.3. | | |
| | Interest Payable................................. | 6,000 | |
| | Cash.......................................... | | 6,000 |
| | To record payment of coupons, as usual. | | |
| | Debenture Bonds Payable........................ | 9,661 | |
| | Cash.......................................... | | 9,498 |
| | Gain on Retirement of Bonds.................... | | 163 |
| | To record purchase of bonds for less than the current amount shown in the accounting records. | | |

If the bonds are shown at face value, offset with a separate Discount on Bonds Payable account, the entry to record retirement would be as follows:

| | | |
|---|---:|---:|
| Debenture Bonds Payable .................................... | 10,000 | |
| Discount on Bonds Payable ............................... | | 339 |
| Cash ...................................................... | | 9,498 |
| Gain on Retirement of Bonds .............................. | | 163 |
| The discount account is retired along with the bonds themselves; book value of bonds retired is $9,661 (= $10,000 − $339). | | |

The adjustment to give equal debits and credits in the retirement entry is a gain that arises because the firm is able to retire a liability recorded at one amount, $9,661, for a smaller cash payment, $9,498. This gain actually occurred as interest rates increased between Year 1 and Year 4. In historical cost accounting, the gain is reported only when realized — in the period of bond retirement. This phenomenon is analogous to a firm's purchasing marketable securities, holding those securities as prices increase, selling the securities in a subsequent year, and reporting all the gain in the year of sale. It is caused by the historical cost accounting convention of recording amounts at historical cost and not recording increases in wealth until those increases are realized in arm's-length transactions with outsiders.

During the 1970s, interest rates jumped upward from their levels in the 1960s. Many companies had issued bonds in the 1960s at prices near par, with coupon rates of only 3 or 4 percent per year. When interest rates in the 1970s jumped to 12 or 15 percent per year, these bonds traded in the market for substantial discounts from face value. Many companies repurchased their own bonds, recording substantial gains in the process. (In one year Pan American World Airlines was able to report profits after 7 consecutive years of losses. Pan Am had gains on bond retirement that year in excess of the entire amount of reported net income.)

Because there is no alternative in historical cost accounting to showing a gain (or loss) on bond retirement (the debits must equal the credits) and because the FASB is reluctant to let companies manage their own reported income by timing the repurchase of bonds, it generally requires that gains and losses on bond retirements be reported in the income statement as extraordinary items.[9] Such items are included in net income, but with a separate caption. (See the discussion in Chapter 4.) Because bond retirements are financing transactions, the gains (or losses) do not produce (or use) cash from operations. Adjustments must therefore be made to net income for gains (subtractions) and for losses (additions) in deriving cash provided by operations if the indirect method is used.

**Serial Bonds**  The bond indenture may require the issuing firm to make a special provision for retiring the bond issue. There are two major types of retirement provisions. One provides that certain portions of the principal amount will come due on a succession of maturity dates; the bonds of such issues are known as *serial bonds*. (The bonds considered so far in this chapter are not serial bonds.)

**Sinking Fund Bonds**  The other major type of retirement provision in bond indentures requires the firm to accumulate a fund of cash or other assets that will be used to pay the bonds when the maturity date arrives or to reacquire and retire portions of the bond issue.[10] Funds of this type are commonly known as *sinking funds*, although *bond retirement funds* would be a more descriptive term. The trustee of the bond issue usually holds the sinking fund. It appears on the balance sheet as a noncurrent asset in the Investments section.

**Refunded Bonds**  Some bond indentures make no provision for installment repayment or for accumulating sinking funds for the payment of the bonds when they come due. These bonds are usually well protected with property held by trustees as collateral or by the high credit standing of the issuer. In such cases, the entire bond liability may be paid at maturity out of cash in the bank at that time. Quite commonly, however, this procedure is not followed. Instead the bond issue is *refunded* — a new set of bonds is issued to obtain the funds to retire the old ones when they come due.

_____

[9]Financial Accounting Standards Board, *Statement of Financial Accounting Standards No. 4*, "Reporting Gains and Losses from Extinguishment of Debt," 1975. An exception is mentioned in the next footnote.

[10]Gain or loss on bond retirement is part of ordinary income when it results from bond retirement in accord with sinking fund provisions (FASB *Statement of Financial Accounting Standards No. 4*). The gain or loss, like the gain or loss on voluntary bond retirement, does not produce or use cash from operations. Similarly, it requires an adjustment to net income in deriving cash from operations in the statement of cash flows if the indirect method is used.

**Callable Bonds**  A common provision gives the issuing company the right to retire portions of the bond issue before maturity if it so desires, but does not require it to do so. To facilitate such reacquisition and retirement of the bonds, the bond indenture can provide that the bonds be *callable;* that is, the issuing company has the right to reacquire its bonds at prices specified in the bond indenture. When the bonds are called, the trustee will not immediately pay a subsequent coupon presented for redemption. Rather, the trustee will notify the holder to present all remaining coupons and the bond principal for payments equal to the call price plus accrued interest.

The *call price* is usually set a few percentage points above the par value and declines as the maturity date approaches. Because the call provision may be exercised by the issuing company at a time when the market interest rate is less than the coupon rate, callable bonds usually are priced in the marketplace for something less than bonds that are otherwise similar but noncallable.

Assume, for example, that a firm issued 12 percent semiannual coupon bonds at a discount, implying a borrowing rate higher than 12 percent. Later, market interest rates and the firm's credit standing allow it to borrow at 10 percent. If $100,000 of par value bonds with a current book value of $98,000 are called at 105, the entry, in addition to the one to record the accrued interest expense, would be as follows:

| | | |
|---|---:|---:|
| Debenture Bonds Payable . . . . . . . . . . . . . . . . . . . . . . . . . . . . . . . . . . . . | 98,000 | |
| Loss on Retirement of Bonds . . . . . . . . . . . . . . . . . . . . . . . . . . . . . . . . | 7,000 | |
| Cash . . . . . . . . . . . . . . . . . . . . . . . . . . . . . . . . . . . . . . . . . . . . . . . . . . | | 105,000 |
| Bonds called and retired. The loss is an extraordinary item unless the retirement results from a sinking fund provision. | | |

The loss recognized on bond retirement, like the analogous gain, is generally classified as an extraordinary item in the income statement.

The market rate of interest a firm must pay to borrow depends on two factors: the general level of interest rates and its own creditworthiness. If the market rate of interest has risen since bonds were issued (or the firm's credit rating has declined), the bonds will sell in the market at less than issue price. A firm that wanted to retire such bonds would not *call* them, because the call price is typically greater than the face value. Instead the firm would probably purchase its bonds on the open market and realize a gain on the bonds' retirement.

# Unifying Principles of Accounting for Long-Term Liabilities _____

Long-term liabilities are obligations to pay fixed amounts at definite future times more than 1 year in the future. The obligations appear on the balance sheet at the present value of the future payments. The present value computations use the historical rate of interest—the market interest rate on the date the obligation was incurred.

The methods of accounting for all long-term liabilities and related expenses are conceptually and procedurally identical. The liability is initially recorded at the cash equivalent value received, which equals the present value of the future contractual payments using the interest rate appropriate for the borrower on the date the loan begins. At any subsequent interest accrual or interest payment date, Interest Expense is computed by multiplying the book value of the liability by the historical interest rate. The amount of interest expense increases liabilities. The amount of any cash payment made reduces the liabilities. The difference between interest expense and the cash payment increases or decreases the book value of the liability for the next accounting period.

Amortization schedules, such as those in Exhibits 10.2, 10.3, 10.4, 10.5, and in Chapter 11, illustrate this unchanging procedure for a variety of long-term liabilities.

## Summary _____

A liability is an obligation by an entity involving a probable future sacrifice of resources. The amount of the obligation and the timing of its payment can be estimated with reasonable certainty. The transaction causing the obligation to arise has already occurred.

Accounting for long-term liabilities is accomplished by recording these obligations at their present value at the date the obligation is incurred (which equals the cash equivalent value received at the time of the borrowing) and then showing the change in that present value as the maturity date of the obligation approaches. In historical cost accounting, the interest rate used throughout the life of the liability is the firm's borrowing rate at the time the liability was originally incurred. Retirement of long-term liabilities can be brought about in a variety of ways, but in each case the process is the same. The net book value of the obligation is offset against the net assets given in return, usually cash, with gain or loss on retirement recognized as appropriate.

## Appendix 10.1: Long-Term Liabilities and the Statement of Cash Flows _____

### Interest on Bonds Issued for Less than Par and the Statement of Cash Flows

Recognizing interest expense on bonds issued for less than par may require special treatment in computing cash flow from operations in the statement of cash flows. Refer to Exhibit 10.3. Interest expense reported for the first 6 months is $6,508 — $6,000 in coupon payments and $508 in increased principal amount. Notice that only $6,000 of cash was used for the expense. There was an increase in Interest Payable of $6,000 followed by discharge of that current liability with cash payment. The remainder of the interest expense, $508, is an increase in the noncurrent liability Debenture Bonds Payable. Consequently, there must be an addition to net income in computing cash flow from operations in the statement of cash flows when the indirect method is used. The amount of the addback is the amount of the expense that did not use cash, or $508.

## Bonds Issued at a Premium

Interest expense on bonds originally issued above par is less than the periodic amounts of cash disbursed. Because the amount of cash disbursed exceeds interest expense, there must be a subtraction in the statement of cash flows in deriving cash flow from operations when the indirect method is used. The amount subtracted is the excess of cash disbursed over interest expense.

# Problem 1 for Self-Study

Avner Company issues a 3-year, $100,000 note bearing interest at the rate of 15 percent per year — that is, Avner Company promises to pay $15,000 at the end of 1 year, $15,000 at the end of 2 years, and $115,000 at the end of 3 years. The market interest rate on the date the note is issued is 10 percent.

**a.** Compute the proceeds Avner Company receives for its note.

**b.** Prepare an amortization schedule similar to Exhibit 10.2 for the life of the note.

**c.** Prepare journal entries that would be made on three dates: the date of issue, 6 months after the date of issue (assuming the books were closed then), and 1 year after the date of issue, assuming an interest payment is made then.

## Suggested Solution

**a.**

| | |
|---|---:|
| Present Value of 1 Payment of $100,000 Discounted at 10 Percent for 3 Periods (see Table 2, 3-period row, 10 percent column: $100,000 × .75131) ............................................. | $ 75,131 |
| Present Value of 3 Payments of $15,000, Discounted at 10 Percent (see Table 4, 3-period row, 10 percent column: $15,000 × 2.48685) ......... | 37,303 |
| Net Proceeds from Issue of Note .................................... | $112,434 |

**b.**  See Exhibit 10.5.

**c.**

| | | |
|---|---:|---:|
| Cash ................................................. | 112,434 | |
| Note Payable ....................................... | | 112,434 |
| Proceeds of issue of note. | | |
| | | |
| Interest Expense ....................................... | 5,622 | |
| Interest Payable ..................................... | | 5,622 |
| See Exhibit 10.5; accrual of 6 months' interest = $11,243/2. | | |
| | | |
| Interest Expense ....................................... | 5,621 | |
| Interest Payable ....................................... | 5,622 | |
| Notes Payable ........................................ | 3,757 | |
| Cash .............................................. | | 15,000 |

Interest expense for the remainder of the first year and cash payment made. Excess of cash payment over interest expense reduces note principal.

Exhibit 10.5 _____

**Amortization Schedule for Note with Face Value of $100,000 Issued for $112,434, Bearing Interest at the Rate of 15 Percent of Face Value per Year, Issued to Yield 10 Percent (Problem 1 for Self-Study)**

| Yearly Periods (1) | Loan Balance Start of Period (2) | Interest Expense for Period (3) | Payment (4) | Portion of Payment Reducing Book Value of Liability (5) | Loan Balance End of Period (6) |
|---|---|---|---|---|---|
| 0 .............. | | | | | $112,434 |
| 1 .............. | $112,434 | $11,243 | $ 15,000 | $ 3,757 | 108,677 |
| 2 .............. | 108,677 | 10,868 | 15,000 | 4,132 | 104,545 |
| 3 .............. | 104,545 | 10,455 | 115,000 | 104,545 | 0 |

Column (2) = column (6) from previous period.

Column (3) = .10 × column (2).

Column (4) is given.

Column (5) = column (4) − column (3).

Column (6) = column (2) − column (5).

# Problem 2 for Self-Study _____

This problem illustrates the unifying principles of accounting for long-term liabilities described on page 443. Assume that the books are closed once per year, so that adjusting entries are made once per year. The market rate of interest for the borrowing firm on the day the loan is taken is 10 percent, compounded annually. Each of the following steps will be performed for each of the obligations:

**(1)** Compute the initial issue proceeds received by the firm issuing the obligation (that is, borrowing the cash) on the date of issue.

**(2)** Give the journal entry for issue of the liability and receipt of cash.

**(3)** Show the journal entry or entries for interest accrual and cash payment, if any, at the end of the first year, and recompute the book value of all liabilities related to the borrowing at the end of the first year.

**(4)** Show the journal entry or entries for interest accrual and cash payment at the end of the second year, and recompute the book value of all liabilities related to the borrowing at the end of the second year.

Perform these steps for each of the following borrowings:

**a.** The firm issues a single-payment note on the first day of the first year, promising to pay $1,000 on the last day of the second year.

**b.** The firm issues a 10-percent *annual* coupon bond, promising to pay $100 on the last day of the first year and $1,100 (= $1,000 + $100) on the last day of the second year.

**c.** The firm issues an 8-percent *annual* coupon bond, promising to pay $80 on the last day of the first year and $1,080 (= $1,000 + $80) on the last day of the second year.

**d.** The firm issues a 12-percent *annual* coupond bond, promising to pay $120 on the last day of the first year and $1,120 (= $1,000 + $120) on the last day of the second year.

**e.** The firm issues a level-payment note (like a mortgage or installment note), promising to pay $576.19 on the last day of the first year and another $576.19 on the last day of the second year.

## Suggested Solution

**Comments** Exhibit 10.6 shows the accounting for five types of long-term monetary liabilities stated at the present value of future cash flows. The accounting for each of these monetary liabilities follows a common procedure.

**1.** Compute the initial amount of cash received by the borrower as well as the historical interest rate. Sometimes both of these will be known; sometimes the cash received will be known and the interest rate must be inferred by calculation. Sometimes, as Exhibit 10.6 illustrates in all five cases, the interest rate is known and the initial cash received must be computed.

    **a.** To compute the initial amount of cash received, given the contractual payments and the market interest rate, multiply each of the contractual payments by the present value factor (as from Table 2 at the back of the book) for a single payment of $1 to be received in the future. Exhibit 10.6 shows the present value factors at 10 percent interest for payments to be received in 1 year (.90909) and in 2 years (.82645).

    **b.** Computing the market interest rate, given the initial cash proceeds and the series of contractual payments, requires finding the *internal rate of return* of the series of cash flows. Appendix A illustrates this process.

       Exhibit 10.6 shows that only the 10-percent coupon bond and the level-payment note have initial cash proceeds equal to $1,000. The difference in amounts arises because each of the items has a different present value, in spite of the fact that each, loosely speaking, would be called a "$1,000 liability."

**2.** Record a journal entry debiting cash and crediting the monetary liability with the amount of cash received. This presentation showing the common theme uses the generic account title Monetary Liability, although in practice more descriptive titles would be used, as would contra accounts (for the 8-percent bond and single-payment note) or adjunct accounts (for the 12-percent bond).

**3.** At a contractual payment date or at the end of an accounting period, whichever comes first, compute interest expense as the book value of the liability at the beginning of the period multiplied by the historical interest rate. Debit the computed amount to interest expense and credit the liability account.

       If a cash payment is made, credit cash and debit the liability. The book value of the liability is now equal to the beginning balance plus interest expense recorded less cash payments made, if any.

       Exhibit 10.6 does not illustrate this fact directly, but if you were to return to step 1 at this point and compute the present value of the remaining contractual payments using the historical interest rate (10 percent in the examples), that present value would equal the book value computed after step 3.

4.  At each payment date, or at each period-end closing date, repeat step 3. Eventually, when the final payment is made (as illustrated at the bottom of Exhibit 10.6), the entire amount of the liability plus interest will have been discharged. The remaining liability is zero.

# Problem 3 for Self-Study ————————————————————

Generally accepted accounting principles require long-term monetary liabilities to be stated at the present value of the future cash flows discounted at the market rate of interest appropriate to the monetary items at the time they were initially recorded. APB *Opinion No. 21* specifically excludes from present value valuation those obligations that arise from warranties. Warranties, being nonmonetary liabilities, are stated at the estimated cost of providing warranty goods and services in the future.

Assume that the estimated future costs of a 3-year warranty plan on products sold during Year 1 are as follows:

| Year | Expected Cost |
|---|---|
| 2 ........................................................... | $ 500,000 |
| 3 ........................................................... | 600,000 |
| 4 ........................................................... | 900,000 |
| Total ................................................... | $2,000,000 |

Actual costs coincided with expectations as to both timing and amount.

a.  Prepare the journal entries for each of the years 1 through 4 for this warranty plan following current generally accepted accounting principles.

b.  Now assume that generally accepted accounting principles allow these liabilities to be shown at their present value. Prepare the journal entries for each of the years 1 through 4 for this warranty plan assuming that the warranty liability is stated at the present value of the future costs discounted at 10 percent. To simplify the calculations, assume that all warranty costs are incurred on December 31 of each year.

c.  What theoretical arguments can be offered for the valuation basis in part **b**?

## Suggested Solution

a. ————————————————————————————

| | | | |
|---|---|---|---|
| Year 1 | Warranty Expense .............................. | 2,000,000 | |
| | Estimated Warranty Liability................... | | 2,000,000 |
| Year 2 | Estimated Warranty Liability...................... | 500,000 | |
| | Cash and Other Accounts .................... | | 500,000 |
| Year 3 | Estimated Warranty Liability...................... | 600,000 | |
| | Cash and Other Accounts .................... | | 600,000 |
| Year 4 | Estimated Warranty Liability...................... | 900,000 | |
| | Cash and Other Accounts .................... | | 900,000 |

**Exhibit 10.6** _____

## Accounting for Long-Term Monetary Liabilities
## Based on the Present Value of Future Cash Flows

| | a. Single-Payment Note of $1,000 Maturing in 2 Years | | | b. Two-Year Annual Coupon Bond—10 Percent ($100) Coupons | | |
|---|---|---|---|---|---|---|
| | Amount | Dr. | Cr. | Amount | Dr. | Cr. |
| **(1)** Compute Present Value of Future Contractual Payments Using Historical Interest Rate on Day Monetary Liability Is First Recorded. Rate is 10.0 Percent | | | | | | |
| (a) 1 Year Hence .................................... | $      0 | | | $  100.00 | | |
| (b) 2 Year Hence .................................... | $1,000.00 | | | $1,100.00 | | |
| Multiply Payment by Present Value Factors (Table 2) | | | | | | |
| .90909 × (a) .......................................... | $      0 | | | $   90.91 | | |
| .82645 × (b) .......................................... | 826.45 | | | 909.09 | | |
| (c) Total Present Value ............................... | $  826.45 | | | $1,000.00 | | |
| **(2)** Record Initial Liability and Cash or Other Assets Received from Step 1. | | | | | | |
| Dr. Cash or Other Assets ......................... | | 826.45 | | | 1,000.00 | |
| Cr. Monetary Liability ......................... | | | 826.45 | | | 1,000.00 |
| **(3)** First Recording (payment date or end of period): End of First Year | | | | | | |
| (a) Compute Interest Expense as Monetary Liability × Historical Interest Rate | | | | | | |
| Amount on Line 1(c) × .10 ......................... | $   82.64 | | | $  100.00 | | |
| (b) Record Interest Expense | | | | | | |
| Dr. Interest Expense ............................. | | 82.64 | | | 100.00 | |
| Cr. Monetary Liability ......................... | | | 82.64 | | | 100.00 |
| (c) Record Cash Payment (if any) | | | | | | |
| Dr. Monetary Liability ............................. | | — | | | 100.00 | |
| Cr. Cash .................................... | | | — | | | 100.00 |
| (d) Compute Book Value of Monetary Liability | | | | | | |
| Beginning Balance.............................. | $  826.45 | | | $1,000.00 | | |
| Add Interest Expense ............................. | 82.64 | | | 100.00 | | |
| Subtotal ......................................... | $  909.09 | | | $1,100.00 | | |
| Subtract Cash Payment (if any) .................... | — | | | (100.00) | | |
| = Ending Balance ............................... | $  909.09 | | | $1,000.00 | | |
| **(4)** Second Recording: End of Second Year | | | | | | |
| (a) Compute Interest Expense as Monetary Liability × Historical Interest Rate Amount on Line 3(d) × .10 ................................... | $   90.91 | | | $  100.00 | | |
| (b) Record Interest Expense | | | | | | |
| Dr. Interest Expense ............................. | | 90.91 | | | 100.00 | |
| Cr. Monetary Liability ......................... | | | 90.91 | | | 100.00 |
| (c) Record Cash Payment (if any) | | | | | | |
| Dr. Monetary Liability ............................. | | 1,000.00 | | | 1,100.00 | |
| Cr. Cash .................................... | | | 1,000.00 | | | 1,100.00 |
| (d) Compute Book Value of Monetary Liability | | | | | | |
| Beginning Balance.............................. | $  909.09 | | | $1,000.00 | | |
| Add Interest Expense ............................. | 90.91 | | | 100.00 | | |
| Subtotal ......................................... | $1,000.00 | | | $1,100.00 | | |
| Subtract Cash Payment (if any) .................... | (1,000.00) | | | (1,100.00) | | |
| = Ending Balance ............................... | $      0 | | | $      0 | | |

| c. Two-Year Annual Coupon Bond—8 Percent ($80) Coupons | | | d. Two-Year Annual Coupon Bond—12 Percent ($120) Coupons | | | e. Level-Payment Note—Annual Payments of $576.19 | | |
|---|---|---|---|---|---|---|---|---|
| Amount | Dr. | Cr. | Amount | Dr. | Cr. | Amount | Dr. | Cr. |
| $ 80.00 | | | $ 120.00 | | | $ 576.19 | | |
| $1,080.00 | | | $1,120.00 | | | $ 576.19 | | |
| $ 72.73 | | | $ 109.09 | | | $ 523.81 | | |
| 892.57 | | | 925.62 | | | 476.19 | | |
| $ 965.30 | | | $1,034.71 | | | $1,000.00 | | |
| | 965.30 | | | 1,034.71 | | | 1,000.00 | |
| | | 965.30 | | | 1,034.71 | | | 1,000.00 |
| $ 96.53 | | | $ 103.47 | | | $ 100.00 | | |
| | 96.53 | | | 103.47 | | | 100.00 | |
| | | 96.53 | | | 103.47 | | | 100.00 |
| | 80.00 | | | 120.00 | | | 576.19 | |
| | | 80.00 | | | 120.00 | | | 576.19 |
| $ 965.30 | | | $1,034.71 | | | $1,000.00 | | |
| 96.53 | | | 103.47 | | | 100.00 | | |
| $1,061.83 | | | $1,138.18 | | | $1,100.00 | | |
| (80.00) | | | (120.00) | | | (576.19) | | |
| $ 981.83 | | | $1,018.18 | | | $ 523.81 | | |
| $ 98.18 | | | $ 101.82 | | | $ 52.38 | | |
| | 98.18 | | | 101.82 | | | 52.38 | |
| | | 98.18 | | | 101.82 | | | 52.38 |
| | 1,080.00 | | | 1,120.00 | | | 576.19 | |
| | | 1,080.00 | | | 1,120.00 | | | 576.19 |
| $ 981.83 | | | $1,018.18 | | | $ 523.81 | | |
| 98.18 | | | 101.82 | | | 52.38 | | |
| $1,080.01 | | | $1,120.00 | | | $ 576.19 | | |
| (1,080.00) | | | (1,120.00) | | | (576.19) | | |
| $ 0[a] | | | $ 0 | | | $ 0 | | |

[a]Rounding error of $.01.

**b.** The present value of the future cost amounts on December 31, Year 1, discounted at 10 percent, is $1,626,594, computed as follows:

| | | |
|---|---|---:|
| Year 2: | $500,000 × .90909 | $ 454,545 |
| Year 3: | $600,000 × .82645 | 495,870 |
| Year 4: | $900,000 × .75131 | 676,179 |
| Total | | $1,626,594 |

| | | | |
|---|---|---:|---:|
| Year 1 | Warranty Expense | 1,626,594 | |
| | Estimated Warranty Liability | | 1,626,594 |
| Year 2 | Interest Expense | 162,659 | |
| | Estimated Warranty Liability | | 162,659 |
| | .10 × $1,626,594 = $162,659. | | |
| Year 2 | Estimated Warranty Liability | 500,000 | |
| | Cash and Other Accounts | | 500,000 |
| Year 3 | Interest Expense | 128,925 | |
| | Estimated Warranty Liability | | 128,925 |
| | .10 × ($1,626,594 + $162,659 − $500,000) = $128,925. | | |
| Year 3 | Estimated Warranty Liability | 600,000 | |
| | Cash and Other Accounts | | 600,000 |
| Year 4 | Interest Expense | 81,818 | |
| | Estimated Warranty Liability | | 81,818 |
| | .10 × ($1,626,594 + $162,659 − $500,000 + $128,925 − $600,000) = .10 × $818,178 = $81,818. | | |
| Year 4 | Estimated Warranty Liability | 899,996 | |
| | Interest Expense | 4 | |
| | Cash | | 900,000 |

There is a rounding error of $4 in the Estimated Warranty Liability account at the end of Year 4. Interest expense for Year 4 is, therefore, increased by $4.

**c.** The goods and services provided under the warranty plan must first be acquired for cash. Thus, even though customers will receive goods and services, the firm must expend cash at some point. To be consistent with monetary liabilities, these amounts would be discounted to their present value.

# Questions, Exercises, Problems, and Cases ——————

## Questions

**1.** Review the meaning of the following concepts or terms discussed in this chapter.
   **a.** Liability.
   **b.** Executory contract.
   **c.** Contingent liability and estimated liability.

| | |
|---|---|
| **d.** FICA taxes. | **l.** Yield or effective rate of bond. |
| **e.** FUTA taxes. | **m.** Bond tables. |
| **f.** Mortgage, mortgagee, mortgagor. | **n.** Amortization of bonds using the effective interest method. |
| **g.** Collateral. | |
| **h.** Bond indenture. | **o.** Serial bonds. |
| **i.** Coupon bond. | **p.** Sinking fund. |
| **j.** Debenture bond. | **q.** Bond refunding. |
| **k.** Convertible bond. | **r.** Call price. |

2. For each of the following items, indicate whether the item meets all of the criteria of a liability. If so, how is it valued?
   **a.** Interest accrued but not paid on a note.
   **b.** Advances from customers for goods and services to be delivered later.
   **c.** Confirmed orders from customers for goods and services to be delivered later.
   **d.** Mortgages payable.
   **e.** Bonds payable.
   **f.** Product warranties.
   **g.** Fifteen-year cancelable lease on an office building.
   **h.** Damages the company must pay if a pending lawsuit is lost.
   **i.** Cost of restoring strip-mining sites after mining operations are completed.
   **j.** Contractual promises to purchase natural gas for each of the next 10 years.

3. Describe the similarities and differences between the allowance method for uncollectibles (see Chapter 7) and the allowance method for estimated warranty costs.

4. Generally accepted accounting principles specifically require the accrual of earned but unpaid wages and fringe benefits thereon, as well as the accrual of earned but unused vacation pay under most circumstances. Generally accepted accounting principles do not mention fringe benefits (such as FICA, FUTA, insurance, and pensions) attached to vacation pay. Explain why the text might say that accrual of these items is required even though there is no specific pronouncement that mentions such a requirement.

5. A noted accountant once remarked that the optimal number of faulty TV sets for the General Electric Company to sell is "not zero," even if GE promises to repair all faulty GE sets that break down, for whatever reason, within 2 years of purchase. Why could the optimal number be "not zero"?

6. A private school has a reporting year ending June 30. It hires teachers for the 10-month period September of one year through June of the following year. It contracts to pay teachers in 12 monthly installments over the period September of one year through August of the next year. For the current academic year, the total contractual salaries to be paid to teachers is $360,000. How should this amount be accounted for in the financial statements issued June 30, at the end of the academic year?

7. While shopping in a store on July 5, 1986, a customer slipped on the floor and sustained back injuries. On January 15, 1987, the customer sued the store for $1 million. The case came to trial on April 30, 1987. The jury's verdict was rendered on June 15, 1987, with the store being found guilty of gross negligence. A damage award of $400,000 was granted to the customer. The store, on June 25, 1987, appealed the decision to a higher court on the grounds that certain evidence had not been admitted by the lower court. The higher court ruled on November 1, 1987, that the evidence should have been admitted. The lower court reheard the case beginning on March 21, 1988. Another jury, on April 20, 1988, again found the store guilty of gross negligence and awarded $500,000. On May 15, 1988, the store paid the $500,000 judgment. When should a loss from these events be recognized by the store? Explain your reasoning.

8. What factors determine the amount of money a firm actually receives when it offers a bond issue to the market?

9. A call premium is the difference between the call price of a bond and its par value. What is the purpose of such a premium?

10. Why does a company that gives trading stamps to its customers usually not have a problem of estimating a liability for the cost of goods to be given to customers who redeem their stamps?

11. If a company borrows $1,000,000 by issuing, at par, 20-year, 10 percent bonds with semiannual coupons, the total interest expense over the life of the issue is $2,000,000 (= 20 × .10 × $1,000,000). If a company undertakes a 20-year mortgage or note with an implicit borrowing rate of 10 percent, the annual payments are $1,000,000/8.51356 = $117,460. (See Table 4 at the end of the book, 20-period row, 10 percent column.) The total mortgage payments are $2,349,200 (= 20 × $117,460), and the total interest expense over the life of the note or mortgage is $1,349,200 (= $2,349,200 − $1,000,000).

    Why are the amounts of interest expense different for these two means of borrowing for the same length of time at identical interest rates?

12. Are high-quality, long-term bonds always sound investments? A friend has $20,000 to invest to pay for a child's education expenses. The funds will be needed in 4 years. The friend believes that the 10-percent semiannual coupon bonds of the U.S. government maturing in the year 2010 are as safe and sound an investment as any available. What advice can you give?

13. Critics of historical cost accounting for long-term debt argue that the procedures give management unreasonable opportunity to "manage" income with the timing of bond retirements. What phenomenon do these critics have in mind?

14. What purposes do restrictions placed on borrowing firms by bond indentures serve?

## Exercises

15. *Journal entries for payroll.* During the current period, office employees earned wages of $200,000. Fifteen percent of this amount must be withheld from

payments for federal income taxes, 4 percent must be withheld for state income taxes, and 8 percent must be deducted for Social Security taxes. The employer must pay 8 percent of gross wages for Social Security taxes, 2 percent for state FUTA taxes, and 1 percent for federal FUTA taxes. The employer has promised to contribute 4 percent of gross wages to a profit-sharing fund, whose proceeds are used to pay workers when they retire. Employees earned vacation pay estimated to be $9,000; estimated fringes are 20 percent of that amount.

   **a.**   Prepare journal entries for these wage-related items.

   **b.**   What is total wage and salary expense?

**16.** *Journal entries for payroll.* Prepare journal entries for the following wages, fringes, and accruals of Bages Company. Factory employees earned $90,000 and office employees earned $60,000. The employer must withhold from employees' paychecks and pay to taxing authorities 15 percent of employees' wages to the federal government, 3 percent to the state government, and 8 percent to the federal government for withheld Social Security taxes. The employer owes an additional 8 percent for Social Security taxes and 3 percent for FUTA taxes — 2 percent to the state government and 1 percent to the federal government. The employer pays all costs of insurance plans; it owes $5,000 for health and life insurance premiums. Employees who have been working for a year or more are awarded paid vacations. During the current period, employees earning 90 percent of the gross wages are expected to earn paid vacations, which is estimated to be 4 percent of their gross wages. Payroll taxes and fringe benefits are estimated to be 20 percent of vacation pay.

**17.** *Computations and journal entries for income taxes payable.* The Siegal Company files its income tax returns on a calendar-year basis and issues financial statements quarterly as of March 31, June 30, and so on. All income taxes are estimated and paid at the rate of 40 percent of taxable income. The following data are applicable to the company's income tax for Year 1.

---

**Year 1**

| | |
|---|---|
| Mar. 31........ | It is estimated that total taxable income for Year 1 will be about $15 million. The first quarter's financial statements are prepared. |
| April 15........ | The first payment on estimated taxes is made. |
| June 15 ....... | It is now estimated that total taxable income for the year will be about $17 million. The second payment on estimated taxes is made. |
| June 30 ....... | The second quarter's financial statements are prepared. |
| Sept. 15....... | It is now estimated that total taxable income for the year will be about $16 million. The third payment on estimated taxes is made. |
| Sept. 30....... | The third quarter's financial statements are prepared. |
| Dec. 15 ....... | It is now estimated that total taxable income for the year will be about $17.5 million. The fourth payment on estimated taxes is made. |
| Dec. 31 ....... | Income for the year is $17,750,000. Financial statements for the year are prepared. |
| **Year 2** | |
| Mar. 15........ | The balance of taxes for Year 1 is paid. |

---

    **a.** Prepare schedules showing

        **(1)** For tax returns: estimated taxes for year, cumulative payments due, and payment made for each payment date.

        **(2)** For financial statements: tax expenses for the quarterly reports and annual report.

    **b.** Record the transactions related to Year 1 income taxes in journal entry form.

    **c.** Present the T-accounts for Cash, Prepaid Income Taxes (if necessary), Income Taxes Payable, and Income Tax Expense.

**18.** *Journal entries for estimated warranty liabilities and subsequent expenditures.* A new product introduced by Junn Company carries a 2-year warranty against defects. The estimated warranty costs as a percentage of dollar sales are 3 percent in the year of sale and 5 percent in the next year. Sales (all on account) and actual warranty expenditures (all paid in cash) for the first 2 years of the product's life were as follows:

|  | Sales | Actual Warranty Expenditures |
|---|---|---|
| Year 1 | $400,000 | $10,000 |
| Year 2 | 500,000 | 35,000 |

    **a.** Prepare journal entries for the events of Year 1 and Year 2. Closing entries are not required.

    **b.** What is the balance in the Estimated Warranty Liability account at the end of Year 2?

**19.** *Using bond tables.* The Gonedes Company issues 12-percent semiannual coupon bonds maturing in 10 years. The face amount of the bonds is $1 million. The net cash proceeds to Gonedes Company from the bond issue amounts to $944,907.

    What interest rate will be used in applying the effective interest method over the life of this bond issue?

**20.** *Using bond tables.* Refer to Table 6 for 12-percent semiannual coupon bonds issued to yield 13 percent per year compounded semiannually. All of the questions that follow refer to $1 million face value of such bonds.

    **a.** What are the initial issue proceeds for bonds issued to mature in 30 years?

    **b.** What is the book value of those bonds after 5 years?

    **c.** What is the book value of the bonds when they have 20 years until maturity?

    **d.** What are the initial issue proceeds of bonds issued to mature in 20 years? (Compare your answer to part **a.**)

    **e.** Write an expression for interest expense for the last 6 months before maturity.

    **f.** If the market rate of interest on the bonds is 14 percent, what is the market value of the bonds when they have 20 years to maturity?

    **g.** When the bonds have 10 years until maturity, they trade in the market for 112.46 percent of par. What is the effective market rate at that time?

**21.** *Using bond tables; computing interest expense.* Refer to Table 5 in the back of the book for 10-percent semiannual coupon bonds. On January 1, Year 1, Souverain Company issued $1 million face value, 10-percent semiannual coupon bonds maturing in 20 years (on December 31, Year 20) at a price to yield 14 percent per year, compounded semiannually. Use the effective interest method of computing interest expense.

    **a.** What were the proceeds of the original issue?
    **b.** What was the interest expense for the first half of Year 1?
    **c.** What was the interest expense for the second half of Year 1?
    **d.** What was the book value of the bonds on January 1, Year 6 (when the bonds have 15 years until maturity)?
    **e.** What was the interest expense for the first half of Year 6?

**22.** *Using present value tables for bond computations.* Refer to Tables 2 and 4, which appear after Appendix A. Assume that $100,000 par value, 8-percent semiannual coupon bonds maturing in 10 years are issued to yield 10 percent per year, compounded semiannually.

    **a.** Compute the initial issue proceeds.
    **b.** Compute interest expense for the first year the bonds are outstanding.

**23.** *Using present value tables for bond computations.* Refer to Tables 2 and 4, which appear after Appendix A. Assume that $100,000 par value, 8-percent semiannual coupon bonds maturing in 10 years are issued to yield 10 percent per year, compounded semiannually.

    **a.** Compute the book value of the bonds 2 years after issue.
    **b.** Compute the market value of the bonds 2 years after issue if the bonds then have a market yield of 6 percent, compounded semiannually.

**24.** *Cash flow statement effects; gain or loss on bond retirement.* Refer to the data in Exercise 21 for Souverain Company.

    **a.** By what amount did cash used for debt service differ from interest expense, and how does this amount affect the statement of cash flow's derivation of cash provided by continuing operations for Year 1?
    **b.** On January 1, Year 11 (when bonds have 10 years to maturity), $100,000 face value of bonds are purchased in the open market and retired. The market rate of interest at the time of purchase is 12 percent compounded semiannually. What gain or loss will Souverain Company report?

**25.** *Journal entry for short-term note payable.* On December 1, the O'Brien Company obtained a 90-day loan for $15,000 from the Twin City State Bank at an annual interest rate of 12 percent. On the maturity date the note was renewed for another 30 days, with a check being issued to the bank for the accrued interest. The O'Brien Company closes its books annually at December 31.

    **a.** Present entries on the books of the O'Brien Company to record the issue of the note, the year-end adjustment, the renewal of the note, and the payment of cash at maturity of the renewed note.

**b.** Present entries at maturity date of the O'Brien Company's original note for the following variations in the settlement of the note.
   **(1)** The original note is paid at maturity.
   **(2)** The note is renewed for 30 days; the new note bears interest at 15 percent per annum. Interest on the old note was not paid at maturity.

26. *Partial amortization schedule for note.* The Holmes Sales Company sells a building lot to N. Wolfe on September 1 for $27,000. The down payment is $3,000, and minimum payments of $265 a month are to be made on the contract. Interest at the rate of 12 percent per annum on the unpaid balance is deducted from each payment, and the balance is applied to reduce the principal. Payments are made as follows: October 1, $265; November 1, $265; December 1, $600; January 2, $265.

   Prepare a partial amortization schedule showing payments, interest and principal, and remaining liability at each of these dates. Round amounts to the nearest dollar.

27. *Partial amortization schedule for mortgage.* Lynne Michals secures a mortgage loan of $112,000 from the Oakley National Bank. The terms of the mortgage require monthly payments of $1,660. The interest rate to be applied to the unpaid balance is 9 percent per year.

   Prepare a partial amortization schedule showing payments, interest and principal, and remaining liability for the first 4 months of the loan. Round amounts to the nearest dollar.

28. *Journal entries for effective interest method of computing bond interest.* On October 1, Year 1, Howell Stores, Inc., issues 20-year, first mortgage bonds with a face value of $1,000,000. The proceeds of the issue are $1,060,000. The bonds bear interest at the rate of 10 percent per year, payable semiannually at April 1 and October 1. The bonds are issued to yield 9.3 percent per year, compounded semiannually. Howell Stores, Inc., closes its books annually at December 31. Round amounts to the nearest dollar.

   Present dated journal entries related to the bonds from October 1, Year 1, through October 1, Year 2, inclusive.

29. *Amortization schedule for bonds.* Hanouille Company issues 10-percent semi-annual coupon bonds maturing 5 years from the date of issue. Interest of 5 percent of the face value of $100,000 is payable January 1 and July 1. The bonds are issued to yield 12 percent, compounded semiannually.
   **a.** What are the initial issue proceeds received by Hanouille Company?
   **b.** Construct an amortization schedule for this bond issue, similar to Exhibit 10.3.
   **c.** Assume that at the end of the third year of the bond's life, $10,000 face value of bonds are called and retired for 103 percent of par. Give the journal entry to record the retirement.

30. *Accounting for bond issue and subsequent interest, including journal entries.* The Central Power Company issued $2 million bonds in two series, A and B. Each series had face amount of $1 million and was issued at prices to yield 11 percent. Issue A contained semiannual 10-percent coupons. Issue B contained

12-percent semiannual coupons. Issues A and B both mature 30 years from issue date.

Answer the following questions for issue A. Round amounts to the nearest dollar.

**a.** What is the issuing price of the bonds?

**b.** Make the journal entry for the date of bond issue.

**c.** Show the journal entries made on the first semiannual interest payment date.

**d.** Repeat part **c** for the second and third payment dates.

**31.** *Accounting for bond issue and subsequent interest, including journal entries.* Refer to the data in Exercise 30. Work the problem for issue B.

## Problems and Cases

**32.** *Allowance method for warranties; reconstructing transactions.* Colantoni Company sells appliances, all for cash. All acquisitions of appliances during a year are debited to the Merchandise Inventory account. The company provides warranties on all its products, guaranteeing to make repairs within 1 year of the date of sale as required for any of its appliances that break down. The company has many years of experience with its products and warranties.

The schedule shown in Exhibit 10.7 contains trial balances for the Colantoni Company at the ends of Year 1 and Year 2. The trial balances for the end of Year 1 are the Adjusted Preclosing Trial Balance (after all adjusting entries

**Exhibit 10.7** _____
## COLANTONI COMPANY
### (Problem 32)

| Trial Balances—End of Year 1 | Adjusted Preclosing | | Post-Closing | |
|---|---|---|---|---|
| | Dr. | Cr. | Dr. | Cr. |
| Estimated Liability for Warranty Repairs.................. | | $   6,000 | | $   6,000 |
| Merchandise Inventory ......... | $  100,000 | | $100,000 | |
| Sales........................ | | 800,000 | | |
| Warranty Expense ............. | 18,000 | | | |
| All Other Accounts............. | 882,000 | 194,000 | 110,000 | 204,000 |
| Totals .................... | $1,000,000 | $1,000,000 | $210,000 | $210,000 |

| Trial Balance—End of Year 2 | Unadjusted Trial Balance | |
|---|---|---|
| | Dr. | Cr. |
| Estimated Liability for Warranty Repairs................. | $   15,000 | |
| Merchandise Inventory ............................. | 820,000 | |
| Sales.............................................. | | $1,000,000 |
| Warranty Expense .................................. | — | — |
| All Other Accounts.................................. | 265,000 | 100,000 |
| Totals ......................................... | $1,100,000 | $1,100,000 |

have been properly made) and the final Post-Closing Trial Balance. The trial balance shown for the end of Year 2 is taken before any adjusting entries of any kind, although entries have been made to the Estimated Liability for Warranty Repairs account during Year 2 as repairs have been made. Colantoni Company closes its books once each year.

At the end of Year 2, the management of Colantoni Company analyzes the appliances sold within the preceding 12 months. All appliances in the hands of customers that are still covered by warranty are classified as follows: those sold on or before June 30 (more than 6 months old), those sold after June 30 but on or before November 30 (more than 1 month but less than 6 months old), and those sold on or after December 1. One-half of 1 percent of the appliances sold more than 6 months ago are estimated to require repair, 5 percent of the appliances sold 1 to 6 months before the end of the year are estimated to require repair, and 8 percent of the appliances sold within the last month are assumed to require repair. From this analysis, management estimates that $5,000 of repairs would still have to be made in Year 3 on the appliances sold in Year 2. Ending inventory on December 31, Year 2, is $120,000.

   **a.** What were the total acquisitions of merchandise inventory during Year 2?

   **b.** What was the cost of goods sold for Year 2?

   **c.** What was the dollar amount of repairs made during Year 2?

   **d.** What was the Warranty Expense for Year 2?

   **e.** Give journal entries for repairs made during Year 2, for the warranty expense for Year 2, and for cost of goods sold for Year 2.

**33.** *Nonmonetary liabilities; reconstructing transactions.* The Myrtle Lunch sells coupon books that patrons may use later to purchase meals. Each coupon book sells for $17 and has a face value of $20; that is, each book can be used to purchase meals with menu prices of $20. On July 1, redeemable unused coupons with face value of $1,500 were outstanding. During July, 250 coupon books were sold; during August, 100; and during September, 100. Cash receipts exclusive of coupons were $1,200 in July, $1,300 in August, and $1,250 in September. Coupons with a face value of $2,700 were redeemed by patrons during the 3 months.

   **a.** If the Myrtle Lunch had a net income of $500 for the quarter ending September 30, how large were expenses?

   **b.** What effect, if any, do the July, August, and September coupon sales and redemptions have on the right-hand side of the September 30 balance sheet?

**34.** *Nonmonetary liabilities; journal entries.* The Lambert Company sells service contracts to repair copiers at $300 per year. When a contract is signed, the $300 fee is collected and the Service Contract Fees Received in Advance account is credited. Revenues on contracts are recognized on a quarterly basis during the year in which the coverage is in effect. On January 1, 1,000 service contracts were outstanding. Of these, 500 expired at the end of the first quarter, 300 at the end of the second quarter, 150 at the end of the third quarter, and 50 at the end of the fourth quarter. Sales and service during the year came to these amounts (assume that all sales occurred at the beginning of the quarter):

| | Sales of Contracts | Service Expenses |
|---|---|---|
| First Quarter ................... | $120,000 (400 contracts) | $50,000 |
| Second Quarter ............... | 240,000 (800 contracts) | 60,000 |
| Third Quarter ................. | 90,000 (300 contracts) | 45,000 |
| Fourth Quarter ................ | 60,000 (200 contracts) | 55,000 |

**a.** Prepare journal entries for the first three quarters of the year for the Lambert Company. Assume that quarterly reports are prepared on March 31, June 30, and September 30.

**b.** What is the balance in the Service Contract Fees Received in Advance account on December 31?

35. *Journal entries for purchase with existing mortgage; subsequent interest entries.* On June 1, the Loebbecke Company purchases a warehouse from F. S. Brandon for $600,000, of which $100,000 is assigned to the land and $500,000 to the building. There is a mortgage on the property payable to the Dixie National Bank that, together with the accrued interest, will be assumed by the purchaser. It bears interest at the rate of 12 percent per year. The balance due on the mortgage is $240,000. The mortgage principal will be paid on April 1 and October 1 of each year in installments of $20,000 each. The principal payments of $20,000 are in addition to the interest of 6 percent per 6-month period on the outstanding balance. A 10-year second mortgage for $150,000 is issued to F. S. Brandon; it bears interest at the rate of 15 percent per year, payable on June 1 and December 1. A check is drawn to complete the purchase.

Loebbecke Company closes its books once a year on December 31. Prepare journal entries for June 1, October 1, and December 1.

36. *Accounting for investment in bonds.* On April 1, Year 1, the Oliver Company acquired $1,000,000 par value of bonds of the Bret Company for $1,398,000. Costs of acquisition amounted to an additional $2,000. The bonds bear interest at 15 percent per year payable on March 31 and September 30, and they mature on March 31, Year 10.

**a.** Present the journal entry on the books of the Oliver Company for April 1, Year 1.

**b.** Present the journal entry (or entries) for the sale of the bonds on August 1, Year 4, at 103.5 percent plus accrued interest, when the bonds have a book value of $1,267,000, after interest accrual on that date.

37. *Operations of a syndicate and risk of interest rate fluctuations.* During October 1979, IBM arranged with a syndicate of investment bankers to borrow $1 billion. IBM and the syndicate reached agreement on IBM's borrowing rate and the amounts the syndicate would pay to IBM on a Friday. Over the weekend, the Federal Reserve System took actions that drastically increased interest rates. The members of the syndicate were responsible for any difference between the amount they had obligated themselves to pay to IBM and the amount for which they could sell the bonds during the following week.

**a.** Did the syndicate gain or lose by the change in interest rates over the weekend?

**b.** What sorts of actions might members of the syndicate take to insulate themselves from involuntary speculation in interest rates over the weekend?

**38.** *Preparing statement of cash flows (adapted from a problem by S. Baiman).* Exhibit 10.8 shows comparative balance sheets, an income statement for Year 2, and supplementary notes of Branaire Company.

Exhibit 10.8 ———————————————————————————

**BRANAIRE COMPANY**
**Comparative Balance Sheets and Income Statement**
**(Problem 38)**

| | December 31 | |
| --- | --- | --- |
| | Year 1 | Year 2 |
| **Balance Sheets** | | |
| Cash......................................................... | $ 30,000 | $130,000 |
| Accounts Receivable.................................... | 100,000 | 120,000 |
| Less Allowance for Uncollectibles .................... | (20,000) | (25,000) |
| Inventory ................................................ | 140,000 | 150,000 |
| Plant and Equipment.................................... | 800,000 | 855,000 |
| Accumulated Depreciation ............................ | (380,000) | (500,000) |
| Total Assets ...................................... | $670,000 | $730,000 |
| Accounts Payable ...................................... | $ 20,000 | $ 25,000 |
| Bonds Payable ......................................... | 100,000 | 110,000 |
| Premium on Bonds Payable ........................... | 40,000 | 44,000 |
| Capital Stock............................................. | 200,000 | 206,000 |
| Retained Earnings ...................................... | 310,000 | 345,000 |
| Total Equities ..................................... | $670,000 | $730,000 |
| | | |
| **Year 2 Income Statement** | | |
| Net Sales................................................. | | $495,000 |
| Gain on Sale of Equipment ............................ | | 110,000 |
| | | $605,000 |
| Cost of Goods Sold...................................... | | $200,000 |
| Bad Debt Expense ...................................... | | 15,000 |
| Depreciation Expense................................... | | 140,000 |
| Income Tax Expense ................................... | | 100,000 |
| Total Expenses....................................... | | $455,000 |
| Income before Extraordinary Items .................... | | $150,000 |
| Extraordinary Loss on Bond Retirement................. | | 4,000 |
| Net Income ........................................... | | $146,000 |

Notes:

(1) During Year 2, Branaire sold property, plant, and equipment that had originally cost $100,000.

(2) All depreciation charges are expensed.

(3) Dividends declared have been paid in cash.

(4) New bonds due in 15 years were issued for $10,000 more than face value.

(5) Bonds with face value of $20,000 and unamortized premium of $6,000 were retired at a loss (which has no income tax effects).

Prepare the Year 2 statement of cash flows.

**39.** *Cash flow statement effects.* Refer to the Simplified Statement of Cash Flows in Exhibit 5.15 on page 188. Eleven of the lines in the statement are numbered. Ignore the unnumbered lines in responding to the questions that follow.

Assume that the accounting cycle is complete for the period and that all of the financial statements have been prepared. It is then discovered that a transaction has been overlooked. That transaction is recorded in the accounts, and all of the financial statements are corrected. For each of the following transactions, indicate which of the numbered lines of the statement of cash flows is affected and by how much. Ignore income tax effects.

a.  Bonds are issued for $100,000 cash.

b.  Bonds with a fair market value of $100,000 are issued for a building.

c.  Bonds with a book value of $100,000 are retired for $90,000 cash.

d.  Bonds with a book value of $100,000 are called for $105,000 cash and retired.

e.  Interest expense and expenditures for the first half of a year on bonds are recorded. The bonds have a face value of $100,000 and a book value at the beginning of the year of $90,000. The coupon rate is 10 percent, paid semiannually in arrears, and the bonds were originally issued to yield 12 percent, compounded semiannually.

f.  Interest expense and expenditures for the first half of a year on bonds are recorded. The bonds have a face value of $100,000 and a book value at the beginning of the year of $105,000. The coupon rate is 12 percent, paid semiannually in arrears, and the bonds were originally issued to yield 10 percent, compounded semiannually.

**40.** *Managing income and the debt-equity ratio through bond retirement.* Meyney Company issued $40 million of 5-percent semiannual coupon bonds many years ago at par. The bonds now have 20 years until scheduled maturity. Because market interest rates have risen to 12 percent, the market value of the bonds has dropped to 63 percent of par. Meyney Company has $5 million of current liabilities and $35 million of owners' equity in addition to the $40 million of long-term debt in its financial structure. The debt-equity ratio is 56% [= ($40 + $5)/($5 + $40 + $35)]. (Owners' equity includes an estimate of the current year's income.) The president of Meyney Company is concerned about boosting reported income for the year, which is about $8 million in the absence of any other actions. Also, the debt-equity ratio appears to be larger than that of other firms in the industry. The president wonders what would be the impact on net income and the debt-equity ratio of issuing at par new 12-percent semiannual coupon bonds to mature in 20 years and using the proceeds to retire the outstanding bond issue. Assume that such action is taken and that any gain on bond retirement is taxable at the rate of 40 percent.

a.  Prepare the journal entries for the issue of new bonds in amount required to raise funds to retire the old bonds, retirement of the old bonds, and income tax effects.

b.  What is the effect on income for the year? Give both dollar and percentage amounts.

c.  What is the debt-equity ratio after the transaction?

**41.** *Comparison of straight-line and effective interest methods of amortizing bond discount.* IBM established the IBM Credit Corporation (IBMCC) on May 1, 1981. On July 1, 1981, IBMCC issued $150 million of zero coupon notes due July 1, 1988. Zero coupon notes promise to pay a single amount (in this case, $150 million) at maturity (in this case, 7 years after issue date). The issue was marketed at a price to yield 14 percent, compounded semiannually. The notes are redeemable at the option of IBMCC at any time, in whole or in part, at 100 percent of the principal amount.

Interest expense on IBMCC's financial statements is computed using the effective interest method, and on IBMCC's tax return amortizing original-issue bond discount in equal semiannual amounts. Assume an income tax rate of 46 percent.

The financial statements of IBMCC present the following data about long-term debt for December 31, 1981:

|  | (all dollar amounts in thousands) |
|---|---|
| 14⅜% Notes Due July, 1986 ............................... | $100,000 |
| Zero Coupon Notes Due July, 1988 ....................... | 150,000 |
|  | $250,000 |
| Less Unamortized Discount, Related Principally to the Zero Coupon Notes..................................... | 87,762 |
|  | $162,238 |

**a.** What were the proceeds to IBMCC from issue of the zero coupon notes?
**b.** What interest expense was reported on the income statement for these notes for the 6-month period ending December 31, 1981?
**c.** What was the interest deduction on the tax return for 1981 for these notes?
**d.** What was the amount of "Unamortized Discount . . ." that relates only to the zero coupon notes on the balance sheet at year-end 1981?
**e.** A news story in 1982 reported the following:

> . . . [T]he Treasury wants to plug a tax loophole that has enabled companies to borrow billions of dollars cheaply. . . . At issue is a tax break granted to companies issuing . . . "zero-coupon" bonds . . . and other deeply discounted debt instruments, which pay very low interest rates.

Describe the advantages to issuers and purchasers of zero coupon bonds. Give your interpretation of the tax loophole alleged by the Treasury. Be specific in your response by indicating the dollar amount of "loophole" used by IBMCC in 1981. What tax policy with respect to zero coupon bonds would you recommend?

**42.** *Financial institutions holding bonds of issuers in financial difficulties may find the book value and the market value of the bonds to be quite different; should this change be recognized in accounting; troubled debt restructuring.* On January 1, 1982, First National Bank (FNB) acquired $10 million of face value bonds issued on that date by Occidental Oceanic Power Systems (OOPS). The bonds carried 12-percent semiannual coupons and were to mature 20 years from the issue date. The bonds were issued by OOPS, and purchased by FNB, at par.

By 1987, OOPS was in severe financial difficulty and threatened to default on the bonds. After much negotiation with FNB (and other creditors), it agreed to repay the bond issue, but only on less burdensome terms. OOPS agreed to pay 5 percent per year, semiannually, for 25 years and to repay the principal on January 1, 2012, or 25 years after the negotiation. FNB will receive $250,000 every 6 months starting July 1, 1987, and $10 million on January 1, 2012. By January 1, 1987, OOPS was being charged 20 percent per year, compounded semiannually, for its new long-term borrowings.

**a.** What is the value of the bonds that FNB holds? In other words, what is the present value of the newly promised cash payments when discounted at OOPS's current borrowing rate?

**b.** Consider two accounting treatments for this negotiation (called a "troubled debt restructuring" by the FASB in *SFAS No. 15*).

**(1)** Write down the bonds to the value computed in the preceding part, and base future interest revenue computations on that new book value and the new historical interest rate of 20 percent per year, compounded semiannually. (What loss would FNB recognize?)

**(2)** Make no entry to record the negotiation and record interest revenue as the amount of cash, $250,000, received semiannually.

Over the new life of the bond issue, how will total income vary as a function of the method chosen?

**c.** Which of these two methods would you recommend and why? (In *SFAS No. 15*, the FASB chose the second method for troubled debt restructurings such as the one in this problem. In some troubled debt restructurings, those where the future undiscounted cash flows are less than the book value of the debt on the creditor's books, the creditor must recognize a loss equal to the excess of book value over the sum of the undiscounted future promised cash flows.)

# Chapter 11  Liabilities: Interest Imputation, Leases, Off-Balance-Sheet Financing, Deferred Income Taxes, and Pensions _____

The preceding chapter discussed the concept of an accounting liability and described the accounting for current liabilities, long-term notes, and long-term bonds. This chapter examines more advanced issues in liability recognition, valuation, and accounting. The chapter treats the accounting for long-term notes payable where the historical interest rate must be imputed, the accounting for leases and pensions, problems in accounting for income taxes, and off-balance-sheet financing.

## Contracts and Long-Term Notes: Interest Imputation _____

Real estate is often purchased on a *land contract*. Equipment is frequently acquired on the installment plan, and the liability is called an *equipment contract*. Such contracts usually require periodic payments. Sometimes the contract provides for an explicit interest rate. Many contracts, however, do not state an explicit interest rate. Instead, carrying charges are added to the purchase price, and the total is divided over a certain number of months without any specific charge being indicated for interest. The principal or "face" in this case includes *implicit interest*.

Generally accepted accounting principles require that all long-term liabilities, including those carrying no explicit interest, be stated at the present value of the future cash payments. The interest rate used in discounting is the rate appropriate for the particular borrower at the time the obligation is incurred, given the amount and terms of the borrowing arrangement. It is called the *imputed interest rate*. The difference between the present value and the face value of the liability represents interest to be recognized over the period of the loan. The next two sections discuss two acceptable ways to compute the present value of the liability and the amount of imputed interest.

# Base Interest Rate on Market Value of Asset

The first approach uses the market value of the assets acquired as a basis for computing the present value of the liability. For example, assume that a piece of equipment can be bought for $10,500 cash. The equipment is purchased in return for a single-payment note with face amount of $16,000 payable in 3 years. The implied interest rate is about 15 percent per year (that is, $1.15^3 \times \$10,500$ is approximately equal to $16,000). The journal entry using this approach would be as follows:

| | | |
|---|---|---|
| Equipment ................................................ | 10,500 | |
| Note Payable ......................................... | | 10,500 |
| To record purchase of equipment using the known cash price. The amount for the note is inferred from the known cash price of the equipment. | | |

At the end of each accounting period that intervenes between the acquisition of the equipment and repayment of the note, journal entries are made for depreciation of the equipment. These are not shown. Journal entries must also be made to recognize interest expense. Assume that the note was issued at the beginning of a year. The entries for the 3 years would be as follows:

| | | |
|---|---|---|
| (1) Interest Expense ........................................ | 1,575 | |
| Note Payable ....................................... | | 1,575 |
| Entry made 1 year after issuance of note. Interest is .15 × $10,500. The amount is not paid in cash but is added to the principal amount of the liability. | | |
| (2) Interest Expense ........................................ | 1,811 | |
| Note Payable ....................................... | | 1,811 |
| Entry made 1 year after entry (1), 2 years after issuance of note. Interest is .15 × ($10,500 + $1,575). | | |
| (3) Interest Expense ........................................ | 2,114 | |
| Note Payable ....................................... | | 2,114 |
| Entry made 1 year after entry (2) at maturity of note to increase liability to its maturity amount, $16,000. Interest = $16,000 − ($10,500 + $1,575 + $1,811), which is approximately equal to .15 × ($10,500 + $1,575 + $1,811); the difference is the accumulated rounding error caused by using 15 percent as the implicit interest rate rather than the exact rate, which is 15.074 percent. | | |
| (4) Note Payable ........................................... | 16,000 | |
| Cash ................................................. | | 16,000 |
| To repay note at maturity. | | |

Of the $16,000 paid at maturity, $5,500 represents interest accumulated on the note since its issue.

## Use of Market Interest Rate to Establish Market Value of Asset and Present Value of Note

If the firm purchased used equipment with the same 3-year note, it might be unable to establish a reliable estimate of the current market value of the asset acquired. To find the present value of the note, the firm would then use throughout the 3-year life of the note the interest rate it would have to pay for a similar loan in the open market at the time that it acquired the equipment. This is the second acceptable method for quantifying the amount of the liability and computing the imputed interest. Suppose that the firm's borrowing rate for single-payment notes such as the one in the previous example is 12 percent compounded annually, rather than 15 percent. The present value at 12 percent per year of the $16,000 note due in 3 years is $11,388 (= $16,000 × .71178; see Appendix Table 2 at the back of the book, 3-period row, 12 percent column). The entry to record the purchase of used equipment and payment with the note would be as follows:

| | | |
|---|---|---|
| Equipment .................................................. | 11,388 | |
| Note Payable ........................................... | | 11,388 |

To record purchase of equipment. Cost of equipment is inferred from known interest rate.

Entries would be made at the end of each period to recognize interest expense (using the 12 percent borrowing rate) and to increase the principal amount of the liability. After the third period, the principal amount of the liability would be $16,000. See Exercise 19 at the end of the chapter.

## Total Expense Is Independent of Interest Rate

In the first case, the equipment is recorded at $10,500 and there is $5,500 of imputed interest. In the second case, the equipment is recorded at $11,388 and there is $4,612 of imputed interest. The total expense over the combined lives of the note and the equipment — interest plus depreciation — is the same, $16,000, no matter which interest rate is used. Over sufficiently long time periods, total expense equals the total cash expenditure; accrual accounting affects only the timing of the expense recognition.

## Long-Term Notes Held as Receivables

A note that is the long-term liability of the borrower is a long-term asset of the lender. Generally accepted accounting principles require the lender to show the asset in the Long-Term Note Receivable account at its present value. The rate at which the lender discounts the note should in theory be the same as that used by the borrower, but in practice the two rates sometimes differ. The lender's accounting mirrors the borrower's: The lender has interest revenue where the borrower has interest expense.

# Leases ————————————————————————————

Many firms acquire rights to use assets through long-term noncancelable leases. A company might, for example, agree to lease an office suite for 5 years or an entire building for 40 years, promising to pay a fixed periodic fee for the duration of the lease. Promising to make an irrevocable series of lease payments commits the firm just as surely as a bond indenture or mortgage, and the accounting is similar in many cases. This section examines two methods of accounting for long-term leases: the operating lease method and the capital lease method.

   To illustrate these two methods, suppose that Myers Company wants to acquire a computer that has a 3-year life and costs $45,000. Assume that Myers Company must pay 15 percent per year to borrow money for 3 years. The computer manufacturer is willing to sell the equipment for $45,000 or to lease it for 3 years. Myers Company is responsible for property taxes, maintenance, and repairs of the computer whether leased or purchased.

   Assume that the lease is signed on January 1, Year 1, and that payments on the lease are due on December 31, Year 1, Year 2, and Year 3. In practice, lease payments are usually made in advance, but the computations in the example are simpler if we assume payments at the end of the year. Compound interest computations show that each lease payment must be $19,709. (The present value of $1 paid at the end of this year and each of the next 2 years is $2.28323 when the interest rate is 15 percent per year. See Table 4 at the end of the book, 15-percent column, 3-period row. Because the lease payments must have present value of $45,000, each payment must be $45,000/2.28323 = $19,709.)

## Operating Lease Method

In an *operating lease,* the owner, or lessor, transfers only the rights to use the property to the lessee for specified periods of time. At the end of the lease period, the property is returned to the lessor. For example, car rental companies lease cars by the day or week on an operating basis. If the Myers Company lease is cancelable and Myers Company can stop making payments and return the computer at any time, the lease is considered an operating lease. No entry would be made on January 1, Year 1, when the lease is signed, and the following entry would be made on December 31, Year 1, Year 2, and Year 3:

| | | |
|---|---|---|
| Rent Expense . . . . . . . . . . . . . . . . . . . . . . . . . . . . . . . . . . . . . . . . . . . . . . . . . . | 19,709 | |
|   Cash . . . . . . . . . . . . . . . . . . . . . . . . . . . . . . . . . . . . . . . . . . . . . . . . . . . . | | 19,709 |
| To recognize annual expense of leasing computer. | | |

## Capital Lease Method

If this lease is noncancelable, the arrangement is a form of borrowing to purchase the computer. It would be accounted for as a *capital lease*.[1] This treatment recognizes the signing of the lease as the simultaneous acquisition of a long-term asset, called a *leasehold,* and the incurring of a long-term liability for lease payments. At the time the lease is signed, both the leasehold and the liability are recorded on the books at the present value of the liability, $45,000 in the example.

The entry made at the time Myers Company signed its 3-year noncancelable lease would be as follows:

| | | |
|---|---|---|
| Asset — Computer Leasehold .................................. | 45,000 | |
| Liability — Present Value of Lease Obligation ................. | | 45,000 |
| To recognize acquisition of asset and the related liability. | | |

At the end of the year, two separate entries must be made. The leasehold is a long-term asset, and like most long-term assets, it must be amortized over its useful life. The first entry made at the end of each year recognizes the amortization of the leasehold asset. Assuming that Myers Company uses straight-line amortization of its leasehold, the entries made at the end of Year 1, Year 2, and Year 3 would be as follows:

| | | |
|---|---|---|
| Amortization Expense (on Computer Leasehold) ................ | 15,000 | |
| Asset — Computer Leasehold ............................... | | 15,000 |

(An alternative treatment credits a contra-asset account, Accumulated Amortization of Computer Leasehold.) The second entry made at the end of each year recognizes the lease payment, which is part payment of interest on the liability and part reduction in the liability itself. The entries made at the end of each of the 3 years, based on the amortization schedule in Exhibit 11.1, would be as follows:

| | | |
|---|---|---|
| December 31, Year 1: | | |
| Interest Expense ......................................... | 6,750 | |
| Liability — Present Value of Lease Obligation ................... | 12,959 | |
| Cash ................................................... | | 19,709 |
| To recognize lease payment, interest on liability for year (.15 × $45,000 = $6,750), and the plug for reduction in the liability. The present value of the liability after this entry is $32,041 = $45,000 − $12,959. | | |

---

[1]Financial Accounting Standards Board, *Statement of Financial Accounting Standards No. 13,* "Accounting for Leases," 1976, reissued and reinterpreted 1980.

December 31, Year 2:

| | | |
|---|---|---|
| Interest Expense . . . . . . . . . . . . . . . . . . . . . . . . . . . . . . . . . . . . . . . . . . . . . | 4,806 | |
| Liability—Present Value of Lease Obligation . . . . . . . . . . . . . . . . . . . | 14,903 | |
| Cash . . . . . . . . . . . . . . . . . . . . . . . . . . . . . . . . . . . . . . . . . . . . . . . . . . . . | | 19,709 |

To recognize lease payment, interest on liability for year (.15 × $32,041 = $4,806), and the plug for reduction in the liability. The present value of the liability after this entry is $17,138 = $32,041 − $14,903.

Dec. 31, Year 3:

| | | |
|---|---|---|
| Interest Expense . . . . . . . . . . . . . . . . . . . . . . . . . . . . . . . . . . . . . . . . . . . . . | 2,571 | |
| Liability—Present Value of Lease Obligation . . . . . . . . . . . . . . . . . . . | 17,138 | |
| Cash . . . . . . . . . . . . . . . . . . . . . . . . . . . . . . . . . . . . . . . . . . . . . . . . . . . . | | 19,709 |

To recognize lease payment, interest on liability for year (.15 × $17,138 = $2,571), and the plug for reduction in the liability. The present value of the liability after this entry is zero (= $17,138 − $17,138).

Exhibit 11.1 shows the amortization schedule for this lease. Note that its form is exactly the same as in the mortgage amortization schedule shown in Exhibit 10.2.

## Accounting Method Determines Timing, but Not Amount, of Total Expense

Notice that, in the capital lease method, the total expense over the 3 years is $59,127, comprising $45,000 (= $15,000 + $15,000 + $15,000) for amortization expense and $14,127 (= $6,750 + $4,806 + $2,571) for interest expense. This is exactly the same as the total expense recognized under the operating lease method

## Exhibit 11.1 _____

**Amortization Schedule for $45,000 Lease Liability, Repaid in Three Annual Installments of $19,709 Each, Interest Rate 15 Percent, Compounded Annually**

**Annual Journal Entry**

| | |
|---|---|
| Dr. Interest Expense . . . . . . . . . . . . . . . . . | Amount in Column (3) |
| Dr. Liability—Present Value of Lease Obligations. . . . . . . . . . . . . . . . . . . . . . . | Amount in Column (5) |
| Cr. Cash . . . . . . . . . . . . . . . . . . . . . . | Amount in Column (4) |

| Year (1) | Lease Liability, Start of Year (2) | Interest Expense for Year (3) | Payment (4) | Portion of Payment Reducing Lease Liability (5) | Lease Liability, End of Year (6) |
|---|---|---|---|---|---|
| 0 . . . . . . . . . . . . . . . . | | | | | $45,000 |
| 1 . . . . . . . . . . . . . . . . | $45,000 | $6,750 | $19,709 | $12,959 | 32,041 |
| 2 . . . . . . . . . . . . . . . . | 32,041 | 4,806 | 19,709 | 14,903 | 17,138 |
| 3 . . . . . . . . . . . . . . . . | 17,138 | 2,571 | 19,709 | 17,138 | 0 |

Column (2) = column (6), previous period.  Column (5) = column (4) − column (3).

Column (3) = .15 × column (2).  Column (6) = column (2) − column (5).

Column (4) is given.

Exhibit 11.2 ——————————————————————————————

**Comparison of Expense Recognized under
Operating and Capital Lease Methods**

| | Expense Recognized Each Year Under | |
|---|---|---|
| Year | Operating Lease Method | Capital Lease Method |
| 1 ......................... | $19,709 | $21,750 (= $15,000  + $ 6,750) |
| 2 ......................... | 19,709 | 19,806 (=   15,000  +   4,806) |
| 3 ......................... | 19,709 | 17,571 (=   15,000  +   2,571) |
| Total ...................... | $59,127[a] | $59,127 (= $45,000[b] + $14,127[c]) |

[a]Rent expense.

[b]Amortization expense.

[c]Interest expense.

described previously ($19,709 × 3 = $59,127). The capital lease method recognizes expense sooner than does the operating lease method, as summarized in Exhibit 11.2. But, over sufficiently long time periods, expense is equal to the cash expenditure. One difference between the operating lease method and the capital method is the *timing* of the expense recognition. The other difference is that the capital lease method recognizes both the asset (leasehold) and the liability on the balance sheet.

## Choosing the Accounting Method

When a journal entry debits an asset account and credits a liability account, the debt-equity ratio increases, making the company appear more risky. Thus, given a choice, most managements prefer not to show an asset and a related liability on the balance sheet. These managements prefer an operating lease to either an installment purchase or a capital lease, where both the asset and liability appear on the balance sheet. Many managements would also prefer to recognize expenses later rather than sooner for financial reporting. These preferences have led managements to structure asset acquisitions so that the financing takes the form of an operating lease.

**Conditions Requiring Capital Lease Accounting**  The FASB has provided detailed rules of accounting for long-term noncancelable leases. A lease must be accounted for as a capital lease if it meets any one of four conditions.[2]

A lease is a capital lease if it extends for at least 75 percent of the asset's life, or if it transfers ownership to the lessee at the end of the lease term, or if it seems likely that ownership will be transferred to the lessee because of a "bargain purchase" option. A bargain purchase option gives the lessee the right to purchase the asset for a price less than the expected fair market value of the asset when the option is exercised. These three conditions are relatively easy to avoid in lease contracts if a firm prefers to treat a lease as an operating rather than a capital lease.

—————————————

[2]FASB, *Statement of Financial Accounting Standards No. 13*, par. 7.

The most difficult of the four conditions to avoid compares the contractual lease payments discounted at an ''appropriate'' market interest rate with 90 percent of the fair market value of the asset at the time the lease is signed. (The interest rate must be appropriate given the creditworthiness of the lessee.) If the present value of the contractual lease payments equals or exceeds 90 percent of the fair market value of the asset at the time the lease is signed, the lease is a capital lease. Many lessors do not wish to lease assets where they have more than 10 percent of the asset's value at risk. The major risks and rewards of ownership have therefore been transferred from the lessor (landlord) to the lessee. In economic substance, the lessee has acquired an asset, and has agreed to pay for it under a long-term contract, to be recognized as a liability.

## Effects on Lessor

The lessor (landlord) generally uses the same criteria for classifying a lease as a capital lease or an operating lease as does the lessee (tenant). At the time that a capital lease is signed, the lessor recognizes revenue in an amount equal to the present value of all future lease payments and recognizes expense (analogous to cost of goods sold) in an amount equal to the book value of the leased asset. The difference between the revenue and expense is the lessor's gain on the sale of the asset. The lease receivable is recorded like any other long-term receivable at the present value of the future cash flows. Interest revenue is then recognized over the collection period of the payments. Lessors tend to prefer capital lease accounting for financial reporting, because it enables the recognition of a gain on the sale of the asset on the date the lease is signed. Under the operating lease method, all lease revenue is recognized gradually over time as lease payments are received.

# Off-Balance-Sheet Financing[3] _____

Firms generally obtain debt financing either directly from banks and other financial institutions or by issuing bonds to investors. These arrangements result in a debit to cash and a credit to a liability account, as well as an increase in the debt-equity ratio. Under some other financing arrangements, the resulting obligations do not have to be recorded on the balance sheet as liabilities.

## Keeping Debt off the Balance Sheet

To be an accounting liability, an obligation must be incurred for a past or current benefit received — the event or transaction giving rise to the obligation must already have happened. If the obligation arises from an executory contract, in which both

---

[3]This section was developed from materials by Richard Dieter, David L. Landsittel, John E. Stewart, and Arthur R. Wyatt, all of Arthur Andersen & Co. See Landsittel and Stewart, ''Off-Balance Sheet Financing; Commitments and Contingencies,'' in *Handbook of Modern Accounting,* 3rd ed., edited by S. Davidson and R. L. Weil (New York: McGraw-Hill, 1983), chap. 26.

parties have exchanged only promises but there has been no event in which economic risk is transferred, accounting typically does not recognize a liability. The FASB's criterion for recognizing a long-term liability focuses on the transfer of risks and rewards of ownership, not just on the undertaking of commitments to make fixed payments.

**Example (Land Option)**  Miller Corporation wants to acquire land costing $25 million, on which it will build a shopping center. It could borrow the $25 million from its bank, paying interest at 12 percent, and buy the land outright from the seller. If it does so, both an asset and a liability will appear on the balance sheet. Instead, it borrows $5 million and purchases from the seller for $5 million an option to buy the land from the seller at any time within the next 6 years for a price of $20 million. The option costs Miller Corporation $5 million immediately and provides for continuing option payments of $2.4 million per year, which is just equal to Miller Corporation's borrowing rate multiplied by the remaining purchase price of the land: $2.4 million = .12 × $20 million. Although Miller Corporation does not need to continue payments and can let the option lapse at any time, it also has an obligation to begin developing on the site immediately. Because it has invested a substantial sum in the option, will invest more, and will begin immediately to develop the land, Miller Corporation is almost certain to exercise its option before it expires. The seller of the land can take the option contract to the bank and borrow $20 million, paying interest at Miller Corporation's borrowing rate, 12 percent per year. The continuing option payments from Miller Corporation will be sufficient to enable the seller to make its payments to the bank. Generally accepted accounting principles view Miller Corporation as having acquired an option for $5 million, rather than having acquired land costing $25 million in return for $5 million cash and a liability of $20 million. As a result, Miller Corporation keeps $20 million of debt off the balance sheet until it borrows more funds to exercise the option.

The techniques for *off-balance-sheet financing* generally exploit the requirement that to be a liability in accounting, there must have been mutual performance; that is, benefits must have been received in the past that obligate the firm to make payments in the future. When the mutual performance will occur in the future (as in executory contracts), accounting typically does not recognize a liability. In this example, the buyer is viewed as not yet having performed beyond purchasing an option, even though the terms of the option make its eventual exercise by Miller Corporation a virtual certainty. Similarly, the seller is viewed as having sold only an option, not the land itself.

## Why Remove Debt from the Balance Sheet?

When debt is left off the balance sheet, ratios that have proved useful to analysts for many years (such as the debt-equity ratio) will appear more favorable to the borrower. One motive may be to prevent an adverse debt-equity ratio from developing later. The entity may foresee reaching the danger point in its debt-equity relations based on historical standards. Future credit ratings might be lowered, and future borrowing costs might increase.

## Accounting's Response

The accounting profession has begun to recognize that certain off-balance-sheet financing arrangements have the economic substance of notes or bonds and should be recognized as accounting liabilities. For leases (discussed earlier in this chapter), the accounting profession attempted for more than 10 years to develop a set of criteria that clearly specify which lease obligations must be recognized as liabilities.[4] The FASB has dealt with the transactions on a case-by-case basis, without having promulgated principles to deal with all such transactions. Some accountants think that there will never be a satisfactory solution until accounting requires the recording of a liability whenever there is an obligation to pay a reasonably definite amount at a reasonably definite time, independent of the executory nature of the contract.

# Income Tax Accounting and Deferred Income Taxes _____

As discussed throughout this book, a firm often selects different methods of accounting for financial and tax reporting. In most cases, the total amount of revenue or expense recognized over the life of an asset or other item will be the same for these two purposes. However, the *timing* of recognition may differ. For example, the total depreciation recognized for both financial and tax reporting over an asset's life is its acquisition cost. In the early years, tax depreciation for an asset will exceed depreciation recognized for financial reporting, so that taxable income will be less than financial statement income before taxes. In later years, depreciation for tax reporting will be less than that for financial reporting, so that taxable income will exceed income before taxes.[5]

The use of different accounting methods for financial and tax reporting creates a problem in measuring income tax expense each period.

1. Should income tax expense be equal to the income taxes actually payable each period based on taxable income, or

2. Should income tax expense be equal to the income taxes that would have been payable if the methods of accounting used for financial reporting had also been used for tax reporting?

---

[4]See the discussion earlier in this chapter. If lease payments are sufficiently large in present value relative to the value of the asset leased, the FASB judges that the risks and rewards of ownership have been transferred from the lessor to the lessee; the lessee will record both an asset and a liability. If the contractual lease payments have sufficiently small relative present value, even though they are material in amount, the FASB views the contract as executory. The lessor has an obligation to provide future services and the lessee will pay for those services as used.

[5]The term *financial statement income,* although descriptive, is somewhat cumbersome. Throughout this section, the term *book income* is used to refer to net income before taxes reported in the financial statements and *taxable income* is used to refer to the amount reported on the income tax return. Similarly, the terms *book purposes* and *tax purposes* differentiate the financial statements from the income tax return.

## Illustration

Assume that Burns, Inc., pays combined federal and local income taxes at the rate of 40 percent of taxable income. Burns purchases a plant asset for $120,000 that has a 6-year estimated service life and an estimated salvage value of zero. After paying for the costs of running and maintaining the asset, the firm enjoys a $30,000-per-year excess of revenue over expenses (except depreciation and taxes). In addition to the $30,000 from the plant asset, other pretax income for each year is $70,000. Burns uses straight-line depreciation for financial reporting and ACRS for taxes.

As Chapter 9 indicated, ACRS classifies most plants assets (except buildings) into five cost recovery periods: 3, 5, 7, 10, and 15 years. The ACRS cost recovery period is not determined by the estimated service life of the plant asset but instead by the defined plant asset categories. Assume for the purpose of this illustration that the asset being considered is 5-year recovery property. The cost recovery (depreciation) tax deductions for assets in this category are approximately 20 percent in the first year, 32 percent in the second, 19 percent in the third, 12 percent in the fourth, 11 percent in the fifth, and 6 percent in the sixth.[6]

Thus, in the first year the new plant asset is used, depreciation for financial reporting will be $20,000 (= $120,000/6) and on the tax return will be $24,000 (= $120,000 × .20). In the second year depreciation for financial reporting will be $20,000 (= $120,000/6), but on the tax return it will be $38,400 (= $120,000 × .32).

Exhibit 11.3 summarizes the computation of taxes for tax purposes and for financial reporting.

The first column in Exhibit 11.3 shows the amounts from the tax return for the first, second, and sixth years. Note that nothing changes over time other than the depreciation deduction and taxes payable. As depreciation increases from Year 1 to Year 2, taxes payable decrease. As depreciation decreases from Year 2 to Year 6, taxes payable increase. The middle column shows book income resulting from an income statement (not allowed by GAAP) where income tax expense is equal to income taxes payable. Note that pretax book income is the same — $80,000 — in all years, but that aftertax net income increases from $49,600 in Year 1 to $55,360 in Year 2 and then declines to $42,880 by Year 6. The pattern results from fluctuations in income taxes payable over the 6 years: $30,400; $24,640; $30,880; $34,240; $34,720; and $37,120. [All six of these numbers appear in column (8) of Exhibit 11.4, discussed later.]

Those who set generally accepted accounting principles are uncomfortable with the notion that reported income (as in the middle column) would fluctuate merely because different accounting methods were used for tax and for book purposes. Consequently, in this case, generally accepted accounting principles require the income tax expense for financial reporting to be based on pretax *book* income, not on taxes actually payable. The third column of Exhibit 11.3 shows the required accounting. Note that aftertax net income in each year equals that of the first year, just as pretax income in each year equals that of the first year.

---

[6]See Exhibit 9.3 on page 376 for more exact percentages, which are rounded here for arithmetic convenience. For tax reporting, only one-half year of depreciation (20 percent) is taken in the year of acquisition, even though the asset was acquired early in the year. Another half-year of depreciation (6 percent) is claimed on the tax return in the sixth year.

## Exhibit 11.3

**BURNS, INC.**
**Deferred Income Tax Computations**

| | Tax Return | Book Income Using Taxes Payable (not acceptable) | Financial Reporting (required) |
|---|---|---|---|
| **First Year** | | | |
| Other Pretax Income . . . . . . . . . . . . . . . . . . . . . . . | $70,000 | $70,000 | $70,000 |
| Excess of Revenues over Expenses except Depreciation from Plant Asset . . . . . . . . . . . . . . | 30,000 | 30,000 | 30,000 |
| Depreciation . . . . . . . . . . . . . . . . . . . . . . . . . . . . . | (24,000) | (20,000) | (20,000) |
| Income before Taxes . . . . . . . . . . . . . . . . . . . . . | $76,000 | $80,000 | $80,000 |
| Income Taxes Currently Payable (at 40 percent) . . . . . . . . . . . . . . . . . . . . . . . . . | $30,400 | | |
| Income Tax Expense (at 40 percent): | | | |
| On Taxable Income . . . . . . . . . . . . . . . . . . . . . . | | (30,400) | |
| On Pretax Book Income . . . . . . . . . . . . . . . . . | | | (32,000) |
| Net Income . . . . . . . . . . . . . . . . . . . . . . . . . . . . | | $49,600 | $48,000 |
| **Second Year** | | | |
| Other Pretax Income . . . . . . . . . . . . . . . . . . . . . . . | $70,000 | $70,000 | $70,000 |
| Excess of Revenues over Expenses except Depreciation from Plant Asset . . . . . . . . . . . . . . | 30,000 | 30,000 | 30,000 |
| Depreciation . . . . . . . . . . . . . . . . . . . . . . . . . . . . . | (38,400) | (20,000) | (20,000) |
| Income before Taxes . . . . . . . . . . . . . . . . . . . . . | $61,600 | $80,000 | $80,000 |
| Income Taxes Currently Payable (at 40 percent) . . . . . . . . . . . . . . . . . . . . . . . . . | $24,640 | | |
| Income Tax Expense (at 40 percent): | | | |
| On Taxable Income . . . . . . . . . . . . . . . . . . . . . . | | (24,640) | |
| On Pretax Book Income . . . . . . . . . . . . . . . . . | | | (32,000) |
| Net Income . . . . . . . . . . . . . . . . . . . . . . . . . . . . | | $55,360 | $48,000 |
| **Sixth Year** | | | |
| Other Pretax Income . . . . . . . . . . . . . . . . . . . . . . . | $70,000 | $70,000 | $70,000 |
| Excess of Revenues over Expenses except Depreciation from Plant Asset . . . . . . . . . . . . . . | 30,000 | 30,000 | 30,000 |
| Depreciation . . . . . . . . . . . . . . . . . . . . . . . . . . . . . | (7,200) | (20,000) | (20,000) |
| Income before Taxes . . . . . . . . . . . . . . . . . . . . . | $92,800 | $80,000 | $80,000 |
| Income Taxes Currently Payable (at 40 percent) . . . . . . . . . . . . . . . . . . . . . . . . . | $37,120 | | |
| Income Tax Expense (at 40 percent): | | | |
| On Taxable Income . . . . . . . . . . . . . . . . . . . . . . | | (37,120) | |
| On Pretax Book Income . . . . . . . . . . . . . . . . . | | | (32,000) |
| Net Income . . . . . . . . . . . . . . . . . . . . . . . . . . . . | | $42,880 | $48,000 |

## Rationale for Deferred Tax Accounting

Relative to straight-line depreciation, ACRS "borrows" income tax deductions in the early years from later years. The fluctuation in taxable income is predictable during the first year, because it results from a difference in the depreciation methods used in financial statements and the tax return. The tax reduction in the first 3 years, relative to the last 3 years, is a difference that will reverse with the mere passage of time. Generally accepted accounting principles require the reported net income to be the same in each year because pretax income on the financial statements is the same each year.[7] The required accounting matches income tax expense and pretax book income rather than income tax expense and taxable income. The rationale is that income taxes will become payable in future years when the difference between book and taxable income reverses. This future cash outflow is an expense of the current period to be matched against pretax book income much the same as future warranty costs are an expense of the period when the warranteed product is sold.

## Temporary Differences versus Permanent Differences

In general, the problem of accounting for income taxes arises from differences in timing between financial reporting of revenues and expenses and tax reporting of these items. A *timing difference* is any item of revenue or expense that appears on the financial statements in one period but on the tax return in a different period. The total amounts appearing over time on the financial statements and the tax return are identical. Only the timing differs. The following list shows some of the ways in which the timing differences can arise.

1. Depreciation for tax purposes is different from that shown in the financial records in a given period because ACRS is used for taxes and a different method is used for books. Total depreciation over the asset's entire life is generally the same for book and for tax purposes.

2. Income from credit sales is sometimes recognized for financial reporting in the year of sale, but it is recognized for tax purposes in the year that cash is collected from customers. Total income from the credit sale is the same for book and for tax purposes, but the timing of income recognition differs.

3. Some income from long-term construction projects is recognized for financial reporting on the percentage-of-completion basis but on tax returns under the completed contract basis. Total income is again the same for book and for tax purposes, but its timing differs.

4. Expenses for uncollectible accounts are reported in the period of sale for financial reporting (using the allowance method), but they are reported on the tax return in the period when the uncollectible amount is written off (using the direct write-off method). In this case, financial statement income is *less* than taxable income in the year the timing difference originates.

5. Expenses for estimated warranty costs appear on the financial statements in the year of sale, but tax deductions are allowed only later, when expenditures for

---

[7]Accounting Principles Board, *Opinion No. 11*, 1967. But see also the income tax release of the FASB, expected to be issued in late 1987.

repairs are made. In this case, financial statement income is again *less* than taxable income in the year the timing difference originates.

Timing differences are the major type of *temporary differences*. In addition to timing differences, temporary differences include items that arise in situations where the cost basis of assets (or book value of liabilities) for tax reporting differs from their cost (or book value) for financial reporting. For example, a temporary difference that is not a timing difference may arise when a firm acquires a machine in purchasing all the assets of another company or division. In such a purchase, the acquiring firm's book value of the newly acquired machine is its fair market value on the date of acquisition. However, its depreciable cost for tax purposes is usually the amount remaining undepreciated on the tax books of the firm selling its assets to the new owner. Such temporary differences raise issues beyond the scope of this text.

Some differences between reported income and taxable income will never reverse, because the tax laws single them out for special treatment. These include items of revenue that are never taxed or expenses that are never deductible in computing income taxes payable. An example is interest revenue on tax-exempt municipal bonds held as assets. Such tax-exempt interest is part of reported income but is never part of taxable income. Differences between reported income and taxable income that never reverse are called *permanent differences*. Although permanent differences appear in financial statement income, they do not affect income tax expense.

Permanent differences do cause a difference, however, between the *effective income tax rate* (income tax expense divided by pretax income on the financial statements) and the *statutory income tax rate* (generally 34 percent for corporations). Consider, for example, a firm with book income before taxes of $1 million, which includes $100,000 of interest from holdings of tax-exempt municipal bonds. The taxable income is $900,000 (= $1,000,000 − $100,000) and the federal income tax expense is equal to $306,000 (= .34 × $900,000). The effective income tax rate (= income tax expense/pretax book income) is 30.6 percent (= $306,000/ $1,000,000), even though the statutory federal income tax rate is 34 percent. The SEC requires firms to disclose what caused the effective tax rate to differ from the statutory tax rate. The last schedule in Exhibit 11.5, which appears later in this chapter, illustrates the required disclosure.

## Accounting Procedures for Income Taxes Where Timing or Other Temporary Differences Exist

Where there are timing differences for depreciation because the straight-line method is used for financial reporting but ACRS is used for taxes, generally accepted accounting principles require income tax *expense* on the financial statements to be computed as though straight-line depreciation over the estimated service life had been used on the tax return.[8] Under such an assumption, income tax expense in the

---

[8]The preceding description and following examples assume that the statutory income tax rate is not expected to change over the period before the timing difference reverses. If tax rates are expected to change, the computations are more complex. Intermediate accounting texts discuss the required accounting procedures.

## Exhibit 11.4

**BURNS, INC.**
**Summary of Deferred Income Tax Liability Account**

**Annual Journal Entry**

| | |
|---|---|
| Dr. Income Tax Expense ............................... | Amount in Column (5) |
| or Dr. Deferred Income Tax Liability ..................... | Amount in Column (9) |
| Cr. Deferred Income Tax Liability ..................... | Amount in Column (10) |
| Cr. Income Taxes Payable ............................... | Amount in Column (8) |

| | Income before Depreciation and Tax Expenses (2) | Financial Statements | | | Tax Returns | | | Deferred Income Tax Liability Account | | |
|---|---|---|---|---|---|---|---|---|---|---|
| Year (1) | | Depreciation Expense (3) | Pretax Income (4) | Tax Expense (5) | Depreciation Deduction (6) | Taxable Income (7) | Taxes Payable (8) | Debit (9) | Credit (10) | Credit Balance at Year-End (11) |
| 1 .......... | $100,000 | $ 20,000 | $ 80,000 | $ 32,000 | $ 24,000 | $ 76,000 | $ 30,400 | | $1,600 | $ 1,600 |
| 2 .......... | 100,000 | 20,000 | 80,000 | 32,000 | 38,400 | 61,600 | 24,640 | | 7,360 | 8,960 |
| 3 .......... | 100,000 | 20,000 | 80,000 | 32,000 | 22,800 | 77,200 | 30,880 | | 1,120 | 10,080 |
| 4 .......... | 100,000 | 20,000 | 80,000 | 32,000 | 14,400 | 85,600 | 34,240 | $2,240 | | 7,840 |
| 5 .......... | 100,000 | 20,000 | 80,000 | 32,000 | 13,200 | 86,800 | 34,720 | 2,720 | | 5,120 |
| 6 .......... | 100,000 | 20,000 | 80,000 | 32,000 | 7,200 | 92,800 | 37,120 | 5,120 | | 0 |
| | | $120,000 | $480,000 | $192,000 | $120,000 | $480,000 | $192,000 | | | |

Column (4) = column (2) − column (3).

Column (5) = .40 × $80,000.

Column (6) = ACRS: 20 percent, 32 percent, 19 percent, 12 percent, 11 percent, and 6 percent of $120,000.

Column (7) = column (2) − column (6).

Column (8) = column (7) × .40.

Column (9) and (10) = column (5) − column (8); if positive, appears in column (10); if negative, appears in column (9).

Column (11) = Sum of entries in column (10) reduced by column (9).

Burns, Inc., example would be $32,000 each year. Because only $30,400 is payable in the first year and $24,640 in the second year, the following entries would be made:

---

| | | |
|---|---|---|
| Income Tax Expense ........................................ | 32,000 | |
| Income Tax Payable ..................................... | | 30,400 |
| Deferred Income Tax Liability ............................... | | 1,600 |
| First-year income tax entry; expense exceeds cash payment; liability is created. | | |
| | | |
| Income Tax Expense ........................................ | 32,000 | |
| Income Taxes Payable ..................................... | | 24,640 |
| Deferred Income Tax Liability ............................... | | 7,360 |
| Second-year income tax entry; expense exceeds cash payment; liability is increased. | | |

---

For this one asset, the $1,600 tax not paid in the first year and the $7,360 not paid in the second year are not forgiven by the government. Instead, these payments are merely delayed. If Burns had only this one asset, the additional taxes would be paid in later years. The bottom panel of Exhibit 11.3 shows the computation of Income Taxes Payable in the sixth year to be $37,120. Because the financial statements will have Income Tax Expense computed under the assumption that straight-line depreciation is used on the tax return, the reported Income Tax Expense will remain $32,000. Because the actual tax payment must be $37,120, however, the journal entry to recognize the income tax expense for the sixth year is as follows:

---

| | | |
|---|---|---|
| Income Tax Expense ........................................ | 32,000 | |
| Deferred Income Tax Liability ............................... | 5,120 | |
| Income Tax Payable ........................................ | | 37,120 |
| Sixth-year income tax entry; expense is less than cash payment; liability is reduced. | | |

---

The amounts of expense not paid in cash in the early years are credited to the Deferred Income Tax Liability account. Later, when cash payments exceed reported expense, the liability account is debited and its balance is reduced. Exhibit 11.4 shows a summary of the entries in Burns' Deferred Income Tax Liability account for the 6 years during which it uses the plant asset. Observe that the total tax expense in column (5) shown on the financial statements over the asset's life is the same as the total taxes payable on the tax returns in column (8). Using the accelerated method on the tax returns defers payment and thus leads to a lower present value of taxes paid.

## Summary of Income Tax Accounting for Temporary and Timing Differences

Income tax *expense* always refers to the financial statements; income taxes *payable* refers to the amount on the tax return.

Exhibit 11.5 ———————————————————————————————————————

### GENERAL PRODUCTS COMPANY
### Illustrative Disclosure in Notes about Income Taxes
### Excerpts from Financial Statements[a]
### (all dollar amounts in millions)

| Amounts from Income Statement[b] | Year 3 | Year 2 | Year 1 |
|---|---|---|---|
| Income before Income Tax Expense ................... | $3,012 | $2,955 | $2,770 |
| Income Tax Expense ..................................... | 902 | 962 | 869 |
| Net Income ............................................... | $2,110 | $1,993 | $1,901 |

| Details of Income Tax Expense | Year 3 | Year 2 | Year 1 |
|---|---|---|---|
| U.S. Federal Income Taxes: | | | |
| Estimated Amount Payable ......................... | $ 674 | $ 739 | $ 690 |
| Effect of Temporary Differences ...................... | 14 | (21) | (13) |
| U.S. Income Tax Expense ........................... | $ 688 | $ 718 | $ 677 |
| Foreign Income Taxes ................................. | 177 | 221 | 166 |
| State and Local Income Tax Expense ................. | 37 | 23 | 26 |
| Total Income Tax Expense ........................... | $ 902 | $ 962 | $ 869 |

| Effect of Temporary Differences on U.S. Federal Income Taxes: Increase or (Decrease) in Income Tax Expense | Year 3 | Year 2 | Year 1 |
|---|---|---|---|
| Tax over Book Depreciation ........................... | $ 58 | $ 33 | $ 26 |
| Margin on Installment Sales[c] .......................... | 6 | (9) | (5) |
| Bad Debt Expense Exceeding Write-off of Uncollectible Accounts[d] ............................. | (18) | (17) | (10) |
| Warranty Expense Exceeding Current Warranty Costs[e] .... | (32) | (28) | (24) |
| Total Temporary Differences[f] .......................... | $ 14 | $ (21) | $ (13) |

*continued*

Income taxes payable computed on the tax return result from accounting principles selected by the firm to minimize the present value of the cash burden for income taxes. Income tax expense shown in the financial statements results from a measure of taxable income computed using the financial statement's accounting principles for temporary differences, rather than the tax return's accounting principles. The excess of income tax expense over income taxes payable, if any, is credited to the Deferred Income Taxes balance sheet account. The excess of income taxes payable over income tax expense, if any, is debited to the Deferred Income Taxes balance sheet account. If the Deferred Income Taxes account has a credit balance, it appears on the balance sheet as a liability. If the Deferred Income Taxes account has a debit balance, it appears on the balance sheet among the assets.

## Disclosure of Deferred
## Income Taxes in Financial Statements

Notes to financial statements contain a wealth of information about income taxes. Among the items of information included is the amount of deferred tax expense for

**Exhibit 11.5** (continued) _____

| Reconciliation from Statutory to Effective Income Tax Rates | Year 3 | Year 2 | Year 1 |
|---|---|---|---|
| U.S. Federal Statutory Rate . . . . . . . . . . . . . . . . . . . . . . . . . . | 34.0% | 34.0% | 34.0% |
| Reduction in Taxes Resulting from: | | | |
|     Earnings of DISCs[g] Taxed at Lower Rates . . . . . . . . . . . . | (2.1) | (0.7) | (1.2) |
|     Income from Tax-Exempt Investments . . . . . . . . . . . . . . . . | (0.7) | (0.2) | (0.6) |
|     Exclusion of 80% of Intercorporate Dividends Received . . | (0.8) | (0.1) | (0.5) |
|     Foreign Income Taxed at Rate Lower than 34% . . . . . . . . | (0.5) | (0.4) | (0.3) |
| Effective Income Tax Rate[h] . . . . . . . . . . . . . . . . . . . . . . . . . . | 29.9% | 32.6% | 31.4% |

*Authors' Notes: Notes such as these do not usually appear in published financial statements.*

[a]Adapted from disclosures of General Electric and Sears, Roebuck.

[b]The information in this first schedule does not appear in the note specifically describing income taxes of the typical published financial statement.

[c]For book purposes General Products Company recognizes revenues on installment sales at the time of sale, while for tax purposes it uses the installment method.

[d]General Products Company uses the allowance method for book purposes and, as required, the direct write-off method for tax purposes.

[e]For book purposes, General Products Company recognizes estimated warranty expense (and the related liability) at the time of sale, but, as required, it takes a tax deduction for warranty costs only when repairs and replacements under warranty are actually made.

[f]All these temporary differences are timing differences. The word *timing* might be used in the caption, rather than the word *temporary*.

[g]See glossary definition of *DISC*.

[h]Income Tax Expense/Income before Income Tax Expense; see first schedule in this exhibit.

the year caused by each of the several important timing differences. Exhibit 11.5 for General Products Company illustrates this disclosure. (Exhibit 11.5 is adapted from the actual notes of General Electric and Sears, Roebuck.)

Typically, the financial statements do not disclose the amount of deductions claimed on the tax return. The information in the notes about deferred taxes can be used to deduce many of them. For example, the financial statements of Burns, Inc., for the first year in our example show depreciation expense of $20,000. The notes would disclose both that the deferred tax expense caused by depreciation timing differences was $1,600 and that the income tax rate was 40 percent of pretax income. From these data, we can deduce that depreciation claimed on the tax return exceeded depreciation expense on the financial statements by $4,000 (= $1,600/.40). Thus depreciation claimed on the tax return must have been $24,000 (= $20,000 + $4,000).

Similarly, for General Products Company in Year 1 (see Exhibit 11.5), depreciation on the tax return exceeded book depreciation expense by $76.5 million (= $26 million/.34).

# Criticisms of the Accounting for Deferred Income Taxes

The accounting for *deferred income taxes* has been subject to criticism for many years.

**Benefits Ignored** Deferred tax accounting for timing differences conceals the benefit conveyed by tax rules that delay tax payments. Note that the income statements of Burns, Inc., would look the same as the third column in Exhibit 11.3 if straight-line depreciation was used on the tax return. (In fact, Income Tax Expense on Burns's financial statement is computed *assuming* that straight-line depreciation is used on the tax return.) Taxes paid later are less burdensome than taxes paid sooner, but deferred tax accounting conceals this benefit.

**Payments Deferred Indefinitely** A going concern using accelerated cost recovery on the tax return may be able to defer payment of deferred taxes indefinitely. Taxes are levied on overall operations, not on individual assets. Although timing differences for earlier acquisitions do reverse, new acquisitions create new timing differences that offset the reversals if asset acquisitions at least remain level in dollar amounts over time. If increasing amounts are spent each year on new assets, the new timing differences will exceed the reversing timing differences, and the credit balance in the deferred tax account will grow. If the firm continues to acquire depreciable assets each year (in dollar amounts no less than it acquired in the preceding year), then in every year Income Taxes Payable will be *less than or equal to* Income Tax Expense computed as generally accepted accounting principles require. In no year will there be a net debit entry to the Deferred Income Tax account on the balance sheet.

Tax payments will exceed tax expense (as in Years 4, 5, and 6 of the Burns example) only when the firm stops acquiring new assets while it continues to earn taxable income. Few firms shrink in size (as is required for the income taxes payable to exceed income tax expense) and at the same time remain profitable. Most shrinking firms owe no taxes because they fail to earn taxable income.

The deferred tax is probably not going to be paid, and if it is, the time when payment will finally be made is uncertain.[9]

---

[9]Whether timing differences actually reverse remains a controversial question among accounting writers. A majority agree with generally accepted accounting principles on the matter of computing and recognizing deferred income taxes. They argue that the reasons offered against recognizing deferred income tax liabilities also support a conclusion that Accounts Payable are not liabilities either. After all, accounts payable are never paid off in the aggregate for a going concern; in fact, the amount of Accounts Payable usually grows over time.

The critical difference between accounts payable and income taxes, however, is that income taxes are levied on the income of a firm as a whole. Losses or deductions from one project can offset gains or income from another. The government does not tax a firm asset by asset. If a firm shrinks and becomes bankrupt, having no taxable income, the government does not ask for income tax payments; creditors (those who are due to be paid for the Accounts Payable) will be entitled to payment (or partial payment) from the remaining assets as the firm winds down its business. Accounts Payable do have significance as liabilities even though they may increase year after year. There has been empirical work on this issue of whether there are any, many, or few firms that find taxes payable exceeding tax expense because of reversals of depreciation timing differences.

**Not an Obligation**   The amount on the balance sheet for deferred income taxes is not an obligation (to the federal government or to anyone else). The government levies taxes on taxable income as shown on the tax return and only as it is earned. It does not automatically levy a tax because depreciation deductions decline. The government does not suggest to Burns, Inc., in Years 1, 2, and 3 that the firm will also be profitable in Years 4 and 5 or that it has in Years 1, 2, and 3 a liability for taxes due in Years 4 and 5.

**Undiscounted Amount**   Finally, note that obligations for deferred income taxes are shown as undiscounted amounts, not at the present value of those amounts. All other long-term obligations reported on the balance sheet are shown at the present value of the future cash payments. The present value is computed using the historical interest rate appropriate for the firm, as borrower, on the date the obligation is first recorded. The FASB indicated that it decided not to consider discounting of deferred taxes at the time it issued the Exposure Draft for the new *Statement of Financial Accounting Standards on Income Taxes* for several reasons, including the complexity of the process and its wish to consider discounting in a broad context as it applies to several accounting issues.[10]

# Pensions _____

Under a *pension plan,* an employer promises to make payments to employees after they retire. Private pension plan systems have grown so rapidly in number and size over the last several decades that the major asset of many individuals is the present value of their pension benefits and a significant obligation of many firms results from their pension promises. The basic operations of a pension plan are simple, but the concepts can be lost in a variety of details. In a pension plan,

1.   The employer sets up a pension plan, specifying the eligibility of employees, the types of promises to employees, the method of funding, and the pension plan administrator.[11]

2.   The employer computes a pension expense each period according to some formula. The employer debits Pension Expense for that amount and credits Pension Liability. This process is called "expensing pension obligations."

3.   The employer transfers cash to the plan each period according to some formula. The employer debits Pension Liability and credits Cash. This process is called

---

The interested reader can refer to the data presented in the *Journal of Accountancy,* April 1977, pages 53–59. These data show that for 3,100 companies over 19 years (nearly 60,000 company years), there are about 700 cases (slightly more than 1 percent) of a firm's remaining profitable while its depreciable assets shrink in size for the year. See also *Journal of Accountancy,* October 1984, pages 138–142.

[10]See FASB, *Proposed Statement of Financial Accounting Standards, Accounting for Income Taxes,* September 1986, paragraph 153.

[11]Pension law distinguishes the *plan administrator* (who has the fiduciary responsibility for the plan) from the *funding agent* (who receives cash payments and invests them). This discussion does not distinguish between the functions of these two agents in the pension process.

"funding pension liabilities." The amounts funded in this step are usually, but not necessarily, the same as the amounts expensed each period in step 2.

The preceding steps comprise the employer's accounting for pensions. The employer is sometimes called the plan sponsor. The following steps are carried out by the pension plan.

1. The plan receives cash each period from the plan sponsor. In the accounting records of the pension plan, Cash is debited and Liability for Payments to Employees is credited.

2. Funds received are invested to generate income. The income is not part of the employer's (sponsor's) income for the period but is reported in separate financial statements of the pension plan. The fund debits its Investment asset account and credits Investment Revenue.

3. The plan makes payments to those entitled to receive them. The plan debits Liability for Payments to Employees and credits Cash.

FASB *Statement No. 87* (1985) governs the *employer's* accounting and reporting for the pension plan. FASB *Statement No. 35* (1980) governs the *administrator's* accounting and reporting for the pension plan.

## Introduction to Pension Plans

There are almost as many different kinds of pension plans as there are employers who have them. The basic variables of a pension plan are the following:

1. Its requirement for contributions by employers and employees.

2. Vesting provisions.

3. Funding provisions.

4. The kinds of promises made by the employer.

5. Treatment of past service obligation if any.

Each of these variables is explained and discussed.

**Contributions**  Under a *noncontributory plan,* the employee makes no explicit contribution of funds to the pension plan; only the employer contributes. Under a *contributory plan,* both the employee and the employer contribute, but they do not necessarily contribute equal amounts. An employee retains a claim to the explicit contributions under virtually all plans. The employee's rights to the employer's contributions are determined by the vesting provisions. The rest of this section considers noncontributory plans or, if the plan is contributory, only the employer's contributions.

**Vesting Provisions**  An employee's rights under a pension plan may be fully vested or partially vested. When the rights are *fully vested,* the pension benefits purchased with the employer's contributions cannot be taken away from the employee. (These benefits are partially insured by an agency of the federal government.) If the rights are not vested, the employee will lose rights to the employer's contributions if he or she leaves the company. Under *partially vested* (or "graded vesting") plans, rights vest gradually. For example, an employee in the second year of work may have no vested rights, but by the time he or she has been employed for 7 years, all rights will be vested. The nature of vesting provisions will influence the present value of the expected pension liabilities generated during an accounting period. If employees leave their jobs, their rights (and therefore the employer's liabilities) are less if the benefits are only partially vested than if the benefits are fully vested.

Federal pension law (primarily, the Pension Reform Act of 1974, called the *Employee Retirement Income and Security Act* or *ERISA*) requires that an employee's benefits from contributions by the employer must become vested according to one of several formulas. These generally provide for full vesting by the time the employee has worked for the employer for 7 years.

**Funding Provisions**  A pension plan may be fully funded or partially funded. Under a *fully funded plan*, the employer pays cash to an outside trustee, such as an insurance company, equal to the present value of all expected pension liabilities. *Partially funded plans* have cash available in an amount less than the present value of all pension obligations. ERISA mandates certain minimum funding requirements for corporate pension plans.

## Employer Promises

Employers make essentially two different kinds of pension promises to employees:

1.  Some employers make promises about the amounts to be contributed to the pension plan without specifying the benefits to be received by retired employees. Such plans are *defined-contribution* (or *profit-sharing*) *plans*. Employer inputs, or contributions to the plan, are defined. The amounts eventually received by employees depend on the investment performance of the pension fund.

2.  Most employers make promises about the amount each employee will receive during retirement based on wages earned and number of years of employment. The plan does not specify the amounts the employer will contribute to the plan. Such plans are called *defined-benefit plans*. Payments to employees are defined. The employer must make contributions to the plan so that those amounts plus their earnings are large enough to make the promised payments.

**Defined-Contribution Plans**  In a defined-contribution plan, the employer promises to contribute an amount determined by formula to each employee's pension account. Zenith Electronics Corporation, for example, promises to contribute between 6 and 12 percent of income before the contribution (the exact amount depending on some other factors) to the pension plan each year. An employee's share in the company's pension fund depends on his or her annual compensation. Another employer might agree to contribute an amount equal to 5 percent of an employee's salary to a pension fund. Subject to reasonable investment risks, the funds are managed to produce as large a series of payments as possible during the employee's retirement. No specific promises are made to employees about the amount of the eventual pension. Inputs are defined; total outputs depend on investment performance.

The accounting for defined-contribution plans is straightforward. If the employer contributes $75,000 to a trustee to be managed for employees' retirement benefits, the journal entry is as follows:

| | | |
|---|---|---|
| Pension Expense . . . . . . . . . . . . . . . . . . . . . . . . . . . . . . . . . . . . . . . . . . . . . . . . . . . | 75,000 | |
|   Cash . . . . . . . . . . . . . . . . . . . . . . . . . . . . . . . . . . . . . . . . . . . . . . . . . . . . . | | 75,000 |

Other than periodically overseeing the activities of the plan administrator to ensure that investment policies are being carried out prudently, the employer's obligation under the pension plan is largely completed once the cash is paid to the plan administrator. Neither the assets of the pension plan nor the amounts expected to be paid to retired employees appear in the employer's financial statements. The income from pension fund investments each period is not included in the net income of the employer but in separate financial statements of the plan.

**Defined-Benefit Plans**  Under a defined-benefit plan, the employer promises the employee a series of retirement payments based on a formula. The typical formula takes into account the employee's length of service and some measure of average earnings. For example, the employer might promise to pay during retirement an annual pension equal to a stated percentage of the average annual salary earned during the 5 highest-paid working years for all employees. The percentage might increase by 2 percentage points for each year of service, so that an employee with 40 years of service would get a pension equal to 80 percent of his or her average salary during the 5 highest-paid working years. The defined-benefit formula is

$$\begin{matrix} \text{Pension Benefit} \\ \text{per Year during} \\ \text{Retirement} \end{matrix} = .02n \times \begin{matrix} \text{Average Salary for} \\ \text{the 5 Highest-Paid} \\ \text{Years of} \\ \text{Employment,} \end{matrix}$$

where $n$ is the number of years of the employee's employment. Payments are defined by formula; the exact amount to be paid later to employees is not known currently and therefore must be estimated. This amount depends on factors such as mortality, inflation, and future wages.

The employer must set aside funds to fulfill its pension obligations to employees and report expenses for these amounts. The amount depends on (among other factors) the rate of return to be earned on pension fund investments. Because defined-benefit pension plans are based on numerous estimates, accounting for such plans must be able to cope with new information as it becomes apparent.

**Comparison of Types of Promises**  Most corporate pension plans are defined-benefit plans. Federal pension law, known as ERISA, has made defined-contribution plans more attractive than they had been previously. The number of defined-contribution plans is increasing, but such plans remain a minority. Some employees prefer a defined-benefit plan because it reduces the employee's risk in planning for retirement. Employers tend to prefer defined-contribution plans because of the reduced uncertainty of pension expenses and contributions and because defined-benefit plans are more highly regulated by governments than are defined-contribution plans. The plan used in any given firm is likely to be the result of labor–management negotiations.

## Generally Accepted Accounting Principles by Employers for Defined-Benefit Plans

**Current Service Benefits: Service Costs**   Generally accepted accounting principles[12] require the employer with a defined-benefit plan to show as a cost of the period the present value of the pension liabilities generated by employees' service during the period. The expense for pensions earned during a given period is called the *service cost* of that period. ERISA generally requires the liabilities generated for service costs during the period to be funded in the current period. For example, if actuarial calculations show the expected present value of pension obligations arising from labor services for the year to be $500,000, the entry to recognize the expense is as follows:[13]

| | | |
|---|---|---|
| Pension Expense (Service Costs) .......................... | 500,000 | |
|    Pension Liability ......................................... | | 500,000 |
| To recognize pension expense for current service and related liability. | | |

When the pension plan is funded, the entry, assuming that $500,000 is paid to the plan administrator, is as follows:

| | | |
|---|---|---|
| Pension Liability ......................................... | 500,000 | |
|    Cash .................................................... | | 500,000 |
| To fund pension liability. | | |

Because federal law generally requires companies to fund pension expense for service costs in the same year that it is recognized, most companies show no Pension

_____

[12]Financial Accounting Standards Board, *Statement of Financial Accounting Standards No. 87,* 1985.

[13]If the wages of the workers involved were debited to product cost accounts (such as Work-in-Process Inventory), the pension costs would be product costs, not period expenses. In the rest of this chapter we assume that all pension costs are debited to Pension Expense to simplify the illustrations.

Liability account for current service on their balance sheets. In such cases, the effect of the two entries shown previously is often recorded in a single entry, as follows:

| | | |
|---|---|---|
| Pension Expense (Service Costs) . . . . . . . . . . . . . . . . . . . . . . . . . . . . . | 500,000 | |
| Cash . . . . . . . . . . . . . . . . . . . . . . . . . . . . . . . . . . . . . . . . . . . . . . . . . . . . . | | 500,000 |
| To recognize pension expense for current service and its immediate funding. | | |

## Prior Service Benefits

When a pension plan is adopted, current employees will usually receive retroactive credit for years of work performed before the plan's adoption. Moreover, from time to time the pension plan may be made more generous; that is, the benefits promised to employees during retirement may be "sweetened." At the time the plan is made more generous, employees will usually be given credit for those prior years when the defined-benefit formula is applied.

Consider, for example, the defined-benefit formula introduced earlier: Pension $= .02n \times$ Average Salary for 5 Highest-Paid Years. Assume that after an employee has been working for 10 years, the plan is sweetened so that the first factor in the formula is changed to .025 from .02. A question arises as to which $n$ should be used in applying the new formula. Should $n$ be the number of years between the time of sweetening and retirement, or should it be the total number of years the employee will have worked by retirement, which will be 10 larger than the first number? Most plan adoptions and sweetenings use the total work life, not just the time between adoption (or sweetening) and retirement. As a result, the creation or sweetening of a pension plan usually creates employer obligations to pay pension benefits for prior years' work, which are called *prior service obligations*.

The present value of the unfunded prior service obligation is recognized as a liability in the accounting records.[14]

## Generally Accepted Accounting Principles by the Plan for Defined-Benefit Pensions

The pension plan receives the cash paid by the employer/sponsor and invests it until it is paid to retired employees. The plan keeps its own accounting records and makes disclosures according to rules in FASB *Statement No. 35*. The plan reports its assets, usually investments of various sorts, at fair market value. The fluctuations in market value each year are part of the earnings or losses of the pension plan.

**Illustrative Pension Disclosure**   Generally accepted accounting principles require the employer to make certain minimum disclosures for pension plans. Exhibit 11.6 on pages 490 to 491 illustrates the required disclosure for the General Products Company.

---

[14]The matching debit will be to an intangible asset account or to an owners' equity contra account, depending on circumstances too complex for discussion here. See an intermediate accounting text.

# Appendix 11.1:
# Effects on Statement of Cash Flows _____

## Interest Imputation

The process described in the chapter for imputing interest on a long-term, single-payment note results in the recognition of interest expense even though no cash is disbursed (at least until the last period, when the note is discharged). In deriving cash flow from operations when the indirect method is used, an addback must be made to net income for the amount of expense that is credited to the long-term liability account rather than to the Cash account.

## Deferred Income Taxes

Refer to the example for Burns, Inc., in Exhibit 11.4. In the first year, income tax expense exceeds income taxes payable by $1,600. That $1,600 of tax expense did not use cash, so an addback to net income is required in the statement of cash flows in deriving cash flow from operations when the indirect method is used. The $1,600 of expense increases the noncurrent liability for deferred income taxes.

In the sixth year, more cash ($37,120) is used than the amount of the expense ($32,000) reported in the income statement. Consequently, there must be a subtraction of $5,120 (= $37,120 − $32,000) in the statement of cash flows to derive cash flow from operations when the indirect method is used.

The statement of cash flows for Ellwood Corporation in Exhibit 14.3 on page 608 illustrates the addback to net income for deferred taxes in arriving at cash flow from operations. See also Exhibit 15.5 for Kaplan Corporation on page 639.

## Pensions

When pension expense is recorded, income decreases and a liability for pensions increases. When pension liabilities are funded, cash and liabilities are both reduced. Thus, when pension funding is the same amount each period as pension expense, no pension-related adjustments to net income are required in deriving cash flow from operations. If pension expense exceeds pension funding, an addback of the excess is required in deriving cash flow from operations when the indirect method is used. (When pension expense differs from pension funding, other issues arise that are beyond the scope of this discussion.)

# Problem 1 for Self-Study _____

The Chang Company purchased a truck from Guttman's Auto Agency. The truck had a list price of $25,000, but discounts of 10 to 15 percent from list prices are common in purchases of this sort. Chang Company paid for the truck by giving a noninterest-bearing note due 2 years from the date of purchase. The note had a maturity value of $28,730. The rate of interest that Chang Company paid to borrow on secured 2-year loans ranged from 10 to 15 percent during the period when the purchase occurred.

## Exhibit 11.6 ————————————————————————————

GENERAL PRODUCTS COMPANY
Illustrative Disclosure in Notes about Pensions
Excerpts from Financial Statements[a]
(all dollar amounts in millions)

## Total Pension Expense for All Pension Plans[b].

| For the Year | Year 5 | Year 4 | Year 3 |
|---|---|---|---|
| Single-Employer Defined Benefit Plans................. | $143 | $107 | $ 92 |
| Multi-Employer Plans[c]................................ | 102 | 79 | 68 |
| Defined Contribution Plans[d]........................... | 51 | 47 | 41 |
| Total Pension Expense............................... | $296 | $233 | $201 |

## Expense for Defined-Benefit Pension Plans

| For the Year[e] | | Year 5 | | Year 4 |
|---|---|---|---|---|
| Expense for Service during the Year[f] ..... | | $   349 | | $   335 |
| Interest Cost on Projected Benefit Obligation[g].......................... | | 1,074 | | 1,020 |
| Actual Return on Plan Assets[h] .......... | $2,739 | | $2,465 | |
| Amount Deferred to Future Periods[i] ...... | (1,672) | | (1,430) | |
| Amount Reducing Current Year Expense[j] . | $ 1,067 | (1,067) | $1,035 | (1,035) |
| Amortization of Excess of Market Value of Plan Assets over Projected Benefit Obligation on Adoption of SFAS No. 87, Reducing Pension Expense[k]........................... | | (213) | | (213) |
| Net Pension Expense for Year ........... | | $   143 | | $   107 |

*Authors' Notes: Notes such as these do not usually appear in published financial statements.*

[a]Adapted from disclosures of Anheuser-Busch, General Electric, and Inland Steel.

[b]The company has several types of plans; this schedule summarizes the expenses from all of them.

[c]Some unions have pension plans covering employees who work for many different companies. The company contributes to the union plan for the unionized employees covered by those plans.

[d]The company has defined contribution plans for some of its top-level managers who are willing to accept the risks of uncertain investment performance between now and the time they retire.

[e]Ordinarily, three years of data would be shown in this schedule and the next. Only two years are shown here.

[f]This is the service cost for benefits earned by employees during the current year. Computations take into account employees' expected future salary increases.

[g]Each year, the company computes the present value of benefits already earned by employees assuming that employees will be granted salary increases between now and the time they retire. This amount represents the accumulation of interest during the current year on the present value amount, or projected benefit obligation, at the beginning of the year.

[h]The company funds its pension obligations by turning cash over to an independent trustee. The trustee invests the cash and receives the investment earnings. This line shows the amount of earnings on the investments during the year.

[i]Not all of the earnings referred to on the preceding line can be used to reduce pension expense in the year earned. Some, the amount shown on this line, is deferred to the future. The effect is to smooth variable investment experience over time.

**Exhibit 11.6** *(continued)* _____

# Reconciliation of Projected Benefit Obligation with Net Pension Obligation for Defined-Benefit Pension Plans

| December 31 | Year 5 | Year 4 |
|---|---|---|
| Accumulated Benefit Obligation[l] | | |
| Vested Benefits[m] | $11,960 | $11,590 |
| Nonvested Benefits[n] | 298 | 285 |
| Total Accumulated Benefit Obligation | $12,258 | $11,875 |
| Effect of Projected Compensation Increases[o] | 2,588 | 2,507 |
| Projected Benefit Obligation[o] | $14,846 | $14,382 |
| Less: Current Market Value of Plan Assets | (17,547) | (16,915) |
| Unrecognized *SFAS No. 87* Transition Gain (being amortized over 15 years)[p] | 2,130 | 2,343 |
| Other Unrecognized Net Experience Gains[q] | 2,538 | 2,460 |
| Unrecorded Pension Obligation Based on Projected Benefit Obligation | $ 1,977 | $ 2,270 |

[Other schedules, not shown, give the market value of assets for several preceding years and the causes of the changes in those amounts for each year.]

_____

[j]This line shows the amount of investment earnings reducing pension expense for the current year.

[k]*SFAS No. 87* provided for a method of computing pension obligations different from preceding pension GAAP. As a result of this and the favorable stock market experience in the years preceding the adoption of the new standard, many companies found that when they adopted the pension computations, the market value of pension plan assets exceeded the present value of the pension obligations, even when the effect of expected future salary increases for employees is taken into account. This excess, called the ''transition gain,'' can be applied to fund future pension costs and is amortized gradually into income. The company is amortizing the amount over 15 years on a straight-line basis. By the end of Year 5, the amortization period had 10 more years to run. The amounts for the current year appear on this line.

[l]At any time, one can compute the net present value of benefits earned by employees, assuming that current salaries will not change. This is called the ''accumulated'' benefit obligation, because future salary increases, although expected, have not yet occurred.

[m]Most pension plans require employees to work for the company for several years before they can be paid the retirement benefits they have earned during their working years. Once the employee has worked sufficiently long to be entitled to receive a benefit, that benefit is called ''vested.'' Until then, the benefits are called ''nonvested.'' Vested benefits appear on this line.

[n]These are the nonvested benefits; see the preceding note.

[o]When the effect of expected future salary increases is taken into account for a defined benefit plan, the present value of benefits already earned is larger than when the computations are based only on current and past salaries. The amounts on this line show the effect of expected future salary increases on the present value of benefits already earned by current employees.

[p]See note k above. This represents the amount of the excess (called *transition gain*) that remains to be taken into income over the remaining 10 years.

[q]See note i above. In addition to investment earnings being recognized in income gradually, mortality experience and employee termination rates deviate from projections. The amount on this line, which could be negative, is the net of these experience effects caused by actual investment income, mortality, and termination rates being different from initial projections.

**a.** Record the acquisition of the truck on Chang Company's books assuming that the fair market value of the truck is computed using a 10-percent discount from list price.

**b.** What imputed interest rate will be used for computing interest expense throughout the loan if the acquisition is recorded as in part **a**?

**c.** Record the acquisition of the truck on Chang Company's books, assuming that the estimated interest rate Chang Company must pay to borrow is deemed reliable and is 12 percent per year.

**d.** Record the acquisition of the truck on Chang Company's books, assuming that the interest rate Chang Company must pay to borrow is 1 percent per month.

**e.** Prepare journal entries to record the loan and to record interest over 2 years, assuming that the truck is recorded at $23,744 and the interest rate implicit in the loan is 10 percent per year.

**f.** Throughout, this book has stressed that over sufficiently long time periods, total expense is equal to cash outflow. In what sense is the total expense for this transaction the same, independent of the interest rate (and, therefore, the interest expense)?

### Suggested Solution

**a.**

| | | |
|---|---|---|
| Truck.................................................... | 22,500 | |
|     Note Payable ...................................... | | 22,500 |

.90 × $25,000 = $22,500.

**b.** $28,730/$22,500 = 1.27689$. The truck has fair market value of $22,500 $(= .90 \times \$25,000)$; $(1 + r)^2 = 1.27689$, which implies that $r = \sqrt{1.27689} - 1 = .13$, or 13 percent per year. In other words, $22,500 grows to $28,730 in 2 years when the interest rate is 13 percent per period.

**c.**

| | | |
|---|---|---|
| Truck.................................................... | 22,903 | |
|     Note Payable ...................................... | | 22,903 |

$(1.12)^{-2} = .79719$; $.79719 \times \$28,730 = \$22,903$.

**d.** $(1.01)^{-24} = .78757$. (See Table 2 at end of book, 24-period row, 1-percent column.) $.78757 \times \$28,730 = \$22,627$.

| | | |
|---|---|---|
| Truck.................................................... | 22,627 | |
|     Note Payable ...................................... | | 22,627 |

| | | |
|---|---:|---:|
| **e.** Truck.............................................. | 23,744 | |
|     Note Payable ....................................... | | 23,744 |
|     Year 1: | | |
|     Interest Expense (= .10 × $23,744) ...................... | 2,374 | |
|       Note Payable ....................................... | | 2,374 |
|     Year 2: | | |
|     Interest Expense [= .10 × ($23,744 + $2,374)] .............. | 2,612 | |
|       Note Payable ....................................... | | 2,612 |
|     Balance in Note Payable Account at End of Year 2 ......... | | $28,730 |

**f.** Total expense equals interest expense on the note and depreciation on the truck. Interest expense is $28,730 less the amount at which the truck is recorded. Depreciation expense is equal to the amount at which the truck is recorded less estimated salvage value. Thus, over the life of the truck, or 2 years, whichever is longer, the total expense equals $28,730 less salvage value of the truck.

# Problem 2 for Self-Study _____

Landlord Company, as lessor, entered into a long-term lease agreement with Tenant Company, as lessee. The present value of the lease payments exceeded the lessor's cost of manufacturing the asset. Both companies accounted for the lease as an operating lease, whereas they should have accounted for it as a capital lease. What effect — understated, overstated, or none — would this error have on each of the following items in the financial statements of each of the companies for the first year of the lease?

**a.** Current assets.

**b.** Liabilities.

**c.** Revenue.

**d.** Expense.

**e.** Net income.

**f.** Retained earnings.

## Suggested Solution

| | | Tenant Company | Landlord Company |
|---|---|---|---|
| **a.** | Current Assets.................................. | None | Understated[a] |
| **b.** | Liabilities..................................... | Understated | None |
| **c.** | Revenue....................................... | None | Understated[b] |
| **d.** | Expense ...................................... | Understated | Understated[b] |
| **e.** | Net Income.................................... | Overstated | Understated[b] |
| **f.** | Retained Earnings ............................ | Overstated | Understated[b] |

[a]Lease receivables are part current and part noncurrent. Asset is all noncurrent.

[b]In a capital lease, the lessor treats the signing of the lease as an installment sale. The lessor has sales revenue, cost of goods sold, and a new asset, the long-term receivable.

## Problem 3 for Self-Study

The accounting records of Wilson Company disclose the following data on book and taxable income for Year 1 through Year 4.

| | Year 1 | Year 2 | Year 3 | Year 4 |
|---|---|---|---|---|
| (1) Pretax Book Income............. | $90,000 | $90,000 | $90,000 | $90,000 |
| (2) Temporary Differences (Reducing) or Increasing Book Income to Taxable Income............... | ($20,000) | ($10,000) | $15,000 | $ 5,000 |
| (3) Permanent Differences Increasing (or Decreasing) Taxable Income...................... | ($ 8,000) | $ 6,000 | ($ 4,000) | $ 2,000 |

The income tax rate is 40 percent of taxable income.

**a.** Compute taxable income on which income taxes are payable.

**b.** Compute the book amount on which income tax expense is based for each year.

**c.** Give the journal entries to record income tax expense, income taxes payable, and deferred income taxes for each year.

**d.** Compute aftertax net income for each year.

**e.** What is the balance in the Deferred Income Taxes account on the balance sheet at the end of Year 4?

### Suggested Solution

**a.** Taxable income on the tax return each year is line (1) plus or minus line (2) plus or minus line (3): Year 1, $62,000; Year 2, $86,000; Year 3, $101,000; and Year 4 — $97,000.

**Exhibit 11.7** _____

### WILSON COMPANY
### (Suggested Solution to Problem 3 for Self-Study)

| | Year 1 | | Year 2 | | Year 3 | | Year 4 | |
|---|---|---|---|---|---|---|---|---|
| **Journal Entries** | | | | | | | | |
| Income Tax Expense[a]...... | 32,800 | | 38,400 | | 34,400 | | 36,800 | |
| Deferred Income Taxes .... | — | | — | | 6,000 | | 2,000 | |
| Income Taxes Payable[b] | | 24,800 | | 34,400 | | 40,400 | | 38,800 |
| Deferred Income Taxes | | 8,000 | | 4,000 | | — | | — |
| **Income Statement** | | | | | | | | |
| Pretax Book Income ....... | $90,000 | | $90,000 | | $90,000 | | $90,000 | |
| Income Tax Expense ...... | (32,800) | | (38,400) | | (34,400) | | (36,800) | |
| Net Income ............... | $57,200 | | $51,600 | | $55,600 | | $53,200 | |

[a].40 of amounts in answer to part **b**.

[b].40 of amounts in answer to part **a**.

**b.** Income tax expense for each year is based on line (1) plus or minus line (3): Year 1, $82,000; Year 2, $96,000; Year 3, $86,000; and Year 4, $92,000.

**c.** See Exhibit 11.7.

**d.** See Exhibit 11.7.

**e.** $4,000 credit = $8,000 credit + $4,000 credit − $6,000 debit − $2,000 debit.

# Problem 4 for Self-Study _____

The Dominiak Company reports the following information about its financial statements and tax return for a year:

| | |
|---|---:|
| Depreciation Expense from Financial Statements . . . . . . . . . . . . . . . . . . . . . . . . . | $270,000 |
| Financial Statement Pretax Income . . . . . . . . . . . . . . . . . . . . . . . . . . . . . . . . . . . . | 160,000 |
| Income Tax Expense from Financial Statements . . . . . . . . . . . . . . . . . . . . . . . . . | 36,000 |
| Income Taxes Payable from Tax Returns . . . . . . . . . . . . . . . . . . . . . . . . . . . . . . . | 24,000 |

Taxable income is taxed at a combined federal and state income tax rate of 40 percent. Permanent differences result from interest on municipal bonds that is shown as revenue in the financial statements but is exempt from income taxes. Timing differences result from the use of accelerated depreciation for tax returns and straight-line depreciation for financial reporting.

Reconstruct the financial statements and the tax return for the year, identifying the components of timing differences and permanent differences.

## Suggested Solution

See Exhibit 11.8 on page 496.

# Problem 5 for Self-Study _____

Refer to the income tax data for General Products Company in Exhibit 11.5. Assume a marginal tax rate of 34 percent.

**a.** By how much did the bad debt expense for uncollectible accounts in Year 3 differ from the deduction on the tax return for accounts written off?

**b.** Was the book expense larger or smaller than the tax deduction? How can you tell?

## Suggested Solution

**a.** $52.9 million = $18 million/.34.

**b.** Larger. The negative number ($18 million) in the schedule showing the effect of timing differences indicates that taxes payable exceed tax expense because of

Exhibit 11.8 _____

**DOMINIAK COMPANY**
**Illustration of Timing Differences and Permanent Differences**
**(Suggested Solution to Problem 4 for Self-Study)**

| | Financial Statements | Type of Difference | Income Tax Return |
|---|---|---|---|
| Operating Income except Depreciation .... | $360,000 (6) | — | $360,000 (4) |
| Depreciation ......................... | (270,000) (g) | Timing | (300,000) (3) |
| Municipal Bond Interest ................ | 70,000 (5) | Permanent | — |
| Taxable Income ...................... | — | | $ 60,000 (2) |
| Pretax Income ...................... | $160,000 (g) | | |
| Income Taxes Payable at 40 Percent ..... | | | $ 24,000 (g) |
| Income Tax Expense at 40 Percent of $90,000 = $160,000 − $70,000, Which Is Book Income Excluding Permanent Differences ............... | (36,000) (g) | | |
| Net Income ......................... | $124,000 (1) | | |

Order and derivation of computations:

(g) Given.

(1) $124,000 = $160,000 − $36,000.

(2) $60,000 = $24,000/.40.

(3) Timing difference for depreciation is ($36,000 − $24,000)/.40 = $30,000. Because income taxes payable are less than income tax expense, we know that depreciation deducted on tax return exceeds depreciation expense on financial statements. Thus the depreciation deduction on the tax return is $300,000 = $270,000 + $30,000.

(4) $360,000 = $300,000 + $60,000.

(5) Taxable income on financial statements is $90,000 = $36,000/.40. Total financial statement income before taxes, including permanent differences, is $160,000. Hence permanent differences are $160,000 − $90,000 = $70,000.

(6) $160,000 + $270,000 − $70,000 = $360,000. See also (4), for check.

uncollectible accounts. Therefore, taxable income is larger than book income for this item, taken by itself, because the book expense for bad debts exceeds the tax deduction for accounts written off.

## Problem 6 for Self-Study _____

Edwards Company adopts a defined-benefit pension plan at the beginning of Year 1. The service costs for Year 1 and Year 2 are $40,000 and $45,000, respectively. These amounts are expensed and funded in full on December 31 of each year. Assume that the pension fund actually earns 9 percent during Year 2.

**a.** Give journal entries for service cost made by Edwards Company for Year 1 and Year 2.

**b.** What is the dollar value of the investments in the pension fund at the end of Year 2 before the Year 2 contribution is recorded?

c.  Assuming that the pension fund is expected to earn only 8 percent in each year, what is the dollar amount of actual earnings in excess of the projected earnings for Year 2?

## Suggested Solution

a.

|  | Year 1 | | Year 2 | |
|---|---|---|---|---|
| Pension Expense (Service Costs)............ | 40,000 | | 45,000 | |
| Pension Liability ...................... | | 40,000 | | 45,000 |
| To recognize expense. | | | | |
| Pension Liability ........................ | 40,000 | | 45,000 | |
| Cash ............................... | | 40,000 | | 45,000 |
| To fund liability with payments to pension plan. | | | | |

b.  $43,600 = 1.09 \times \$40,000$.

c.  $436 = \$43,600 \times (1.09 - 1.08)$.

## Questions, Exercises, Problems, and Cases ——————————

### Questions

1. Review the meaning of the following concepts or terms discussed in this chapter.
   a.  Implicit interest.
   b.  Imputed interest rate.
   c.  Operating lease.
   d.  Capital lease.
   e.  Off-balance-sheet financing.
   f.  Timing difference.
   g.  Temporary difference.
   h.  Permanent difference.
   i.  Effective income tax rate.
   j.  Statutory income tax rate.
   k.  Deferred income tax expense and liability.
   l.  Pension plan.
   m.  Defined-contribution plan.
   n.  Defined-benefit plan.
   o.  Service cost.

2. In what sense is the historical cost accounting for noncurrent liabilities subsequent to the date of issuance based on historical costs?

3. Brealey Company negotiated a 5-year loan for $1 million with its bank. The terms of the loan specify that the interest rate can be changed as the bank chooses but that the company can repay the loan at any time. Interest is to be paid quarterly. How should Brealey Company classify this note on its balance sheet?

4. Demonstrate that the amortization schedule in Exhibit 11.1 conforms to the "unifying principles of accounting for long-term liabilities" described on pages 442 and 443 of Chapter 10.

5. Why is the question, "Who enjoys the potential rewards and bears the risks of an asset?" important for lease accounting?

6. In what ways is the economic substance of a capital lease entered into by a lessee similar to, and different from, that of an installment purchase?

7. Distinguish between the lessee's accounting for a capital lease and for an installment purchase.

8. In what sense is the total expense from a lease independent of the lessee's method of accounting for it?

9. "Deferred income taxes might be viewed as an interest-free loan from the government." Do you agree? Why or why not?

10. Most large firms report income tax expense that is a lower percentage of book, pretax income than the statutory income tax rate. What might cause this difference?

11. Why do many managements find off-balance-sheet financing attractive?

12. How should the deferred income tax liability be treated by an analyst who wishes to study the debt-equity ratio of a business?

13. Under what circumstances will the Deferred Income Taxes account reduce to a zero balance?

14. You have been called to testify before a Congressional committee on income taxation. One committee member states: "My staff has added up the amounts shown for Deferred Income Taxes on the balance sheets of the 500 largest U.S. corporations. If we collected these amounts immediately, we could reduce the national deficit by billions of dollars. After all, I have to pay my taxes as they become due each year. Why shouldn't corporations have to do the same?" How would you respond?

15. What are the economic and accounting differences between a defined-benefit pension plan and a defined-contribution plan?

16. Why does the amendment ("sweetening") of a defined-benefit plan ordinarily increase the prior service obligation, whereas a change with the same cost in a defined-contribution plan does not?

17. The Hicks Company is adopting a defined-benefit pension plan. Who — the employee or the Hicks Company — is more likely to bear the risks and rewards of fluctuating market returns on funds invested to pay the pension?

## Exercises

18. *Nature of liabilities.*
    a. For each of the following items, indicate if the item meets all of the criteria of the accountant's usual definition of a liability.
    b. If the item is recognized as a liability, how is the amount of the liability computed?
    (1) A 15-year cancelable lease on an office building.
    (2) A 20-year noncancelable lease on a factory building.
    (3) Deferred income taxes.
    (4) The anticipated future cost of restoring strip-mining sites after mining operations are completed.

**(5)** An obligation to pay pensions under a defined-benefit formula for labor services incurred during current year.

**19.** *Journal entries for land contract with imputed interest.* Refer to the example on page 466 of this chapter where equipment is acquired in exchange for a single-payment note for $16,000 due in 3 years. The issuer of the note pays 12 percent interest for borrowings of this sort. The present value of the note on the date of issue is $11,388. Assume that the note is issued on January 1, Year 1, and that the firm closes its books annually.

Provide adjusting entries for the end of Years 1, 2, and 3 and for the payment of the note at maturity.

**20.** *Effects of leases on statement of cash flows.* Refer to the Simplified Statement of Cash Flows in Exhibit 5.15 on page 188. Eleven of the lines in the statement are numbered. Ignore the unnumbered lines in responding to the following questions.

Assume that the accounting cycle is complete for the period and that all of the financial statements have been prepared. It is then discovered that a transaction has been overlooked. That transaction is recorded in the accounts, and all of the financial statements are corrected. For each of the following transactions, indicate which of the numbered lines of the statement of cash flows is affected and by how much. Ignore income tax effects except where taxes are explicitly mentioned.

For the following questions, assume that an asset with an economic life of 10 years costing $100,000 is leased for $19,925 per year, paid at the end of each year.

**a.** The lessor, using the operating lease method, records depreciation for the year.

**b.** The lessor, using the operating lease method, records receipt of a cash payment for the year. Revenue has not previously been recognized.

**c.** The lessee, using the operating lease method, records payment of cash for the year. Expense has not previously been recognized.

**d.** The lessor, using the capital lease method, records receipt of cash at the end of the first year and uses an interest rate of 15 percent per year. Interest is $15,000, and $4,925 is recorded for receipt of principal. No entries have previously been made recognizing revenue.

**e.** The lessee, using the capital lease method, records payment of cash for the first year and uses an interest rate of 15 percent per year. Interest is $15,000, and payment of principal amounts to $4,925.

**21.** *Effects of income taxes on statement of cash flows.* Refer to the instructions in the preceding exercise. For each of the following transactions, indicate which of the numbered lines of the statement of cash flows is affected and by how much. Assume an income tax rate of 40 percent of taxable income.

**a.** Pretax financial statement income is $200,000. Depreciation claimed on the tax return exceeds depreciation expense on the financial statements by $50,000. An entry is made to record income tax expense and *accrual* of amounts payable, because no previous entry for taxes has been made.

**b.** Pretax financial statement income is $300,000. Warranty deductions allowed on the tax return are less than warranty expense on the financial statements by $40,000. An entry is made to record income tax expense and payment of amounts payable, because no previous entry for taxes has been made.

**c.** Pretax financial statement income is $300,000. Deductions for bad debts allowed on the tax return are less than bad debt expense on the financial statements by $40,000. An entry is made to record income tax expense and payment of amounts payable, because no previous entry for taxes has been made.

**d.** Nontaxable municipal bond interest of $10,000 is received. No previous entry has been made for this interest. All effects of this transaction, including income tax effects (if any), are recorded.

**22.** *Working backwards from income tax disclosure to deduce elements of income tax return.* Refer to the income tax data for General Products Company in Exhibit 11.5. Assume a combined marginal tax rate of 40 percent.

**a.** By how much did the book bad debt expense for uncollectible accounts in Year 2 differ from the deduction on the tax return for accounts written off?

**b.** Was the book expense larger or smaller than the tax deduction? How can you tell?

**23.** *Amortization schedule for note where explicit interest differs from market rate of interest.* Garstka Company acquires a computer from Berney's Computer Store. The cash price (fair market value) of the computer is $50,568. Garstka Company gives a 3-year, interest-bearing note with maturity value of $60,000. The note requires annual interest payments of 9 percent of face value, or $5,400 per year. The interest rate implicit in the note is 16 percent per year.

**a.** Prepare an amortization schedule for the note.

**b.** Prepare journal entries for Garstka Company over the life of the note.

**24.** *Operating lease accounting (adapted from CPA examination).* The Jackson Company manufactured a piece of equipment at a cost of $7 million, which it held for resale from January 1 to June 30 at a price of $8 million. On July 1, Jackson leased the equipment to the Crystal Company. The lease, which is appropriately recorded as an operating lease for accounting purposes, is for a 3-year period. Equal monthly payments under the lease are $115,000 and are due on the first of the month. The first payment was made on July 1. The equipment is being depreciated on a straight-line basis over an 8-year period starting at inception of lease with no residual value expected.

**a.** As a result of these facts, what expense should Crystal record for the current year ended December 31? Show supporting computations in good form.

**b.** Considering the previous facts, what income or loss before income taxes should Jackson record for the year ended December 31? Show supporting computations in good form.

**25.** *Computations and journal entries for income taxes with both timing and permanent differences.* Joyce Company reported the following amounts for book and tax purposes for its first 3 years of operations:

| | . | Year 1 | Year 2 | Year 3 |
|---|---|---|---|---|
| Pretax Book Income ...................... | | $300,000 | $280,000 | $440,000 |
| Taxable Income .......................... | | 240,000 | 320,000 | 340,000 |

The differences between book and taxable income were attributable to the use of different depreciation methods. The income tax rate was 40 percent during all years.

**a.** Give the journal entry to record income tax expense for each year.

**b.** Assume, for this part, that $10,000 of interest on state and municipal bonds was included in the pretax book income amounts shown above for each year but properly excluded from taxable income. Give the journal entry to record income tax expense for each year.

26. *Income tax timing differences from differing methods of revenue recognition.* Refer to the data in Exhibit 4.3 on page 142 showing income over a 5-year period under various methods of revenue and income recognition. Use the following methods of accounting for financial statements and for tax returns. Assume an income tax rate of 40 percent. Compute income tax expense, income taxes payable, and deferred income taxes for each period. Put this information into journal entry form.

**a.** Use the percentage-of-completion method on the financial statements and the completed contract method on the tax return.

**b.** Use the cost-recovery-first method on the financial statements and the installment method on the tax return.

27. *Deriving permanent and timing differences from financial statement disclosures.* Gigondas Company reports the following information for a year:

| | |
|---|---|
| Financial Statement Pretax Income ................................. | $106,000 |
| Income Tax Expense .............................................. | 52,000 |
| Income Taxes Payable for This Year ............................... | 16,000 |
| Income Tax Rate on Taxable Income ............................... | 40 Percent |

The company has both permanent and temporary differences between book and taxable income.

**a.** What is the amount of temporary differences for the year? Give the amount, and indicate whether the effect is to make reported income larger or smaller than taxable income.

**b.** What is the amount of permanent differences for the year? Give the amount, and indicate whether the effect is to make reported income larger or smaller than taxable income.

28. *Journal entries for pension plan.* On January 1, Year 1, Kayco Company institutes a defined-benefit pension plan without credit given to employees for prior years' work. That is, prior service benefits are not awarded to current employees. The present value of the benefits earned by employees during both Year 1

and Year 2 is $700,000 at the end of each of those years. Kayco Company designates the Retirement Insurance Company as the trustee of the pension plan and deposits all funding payments with the insurance company at the end of each year. Kayco Company plans to fund each year an amount equal to the pension expense recognized for the year.

Show the journal entries that Kayco Company would make on December 31, Year 1 and Year 2, for its pension plan and related expenses.

29. *Working backwards from income tax disclosure to deduce elements of income tax return.* Refer to the income tax data for General Products Company in Exhibit 11.5. Assume a combined marginal tax rate of 36 percent.

    **a.** By how much did the book depreciation expense in Year 2 differ from the depreciation deduction on the tax return?

    **b.** Was the book expense larger or smaller than the tax deduction? How can you tell?

## Problems and Cases

30. *Comparing expense for operating lease with capital lease.* Maher Company has calculated that the annual payment in arrears to amortize a $1 million loan over 25 years at 15 percent interest is $154,700.

    **a.** What is rent expense for the first year of an operating lease when the rent payment is $154,700?

    **b.** What is lease expense for the first year of a 25-year capital lease for use of an asset costing $1 million requiring annual payments in arrears of $154,700? Use straight-line amortization of leasehold.

    **c.** How much larger in percentage terms is the lessee's expense in the first year under the capital lease than under the operating lease?

31. *Criteria for classifying leases as operating or capital.* Assume that Rich's Department Stores is about to sign four separate leases for stores in four separate shopping centers. Each of the stores would cost $20 million if purchased outright, and each has an economic life of 20 years. Assume that the company currently must pay interest at the rate of 10 percent per year on long-term borrowing when sound collateral backs the loan. The lease payments are to be made at the end of each year in all four cases.

Based on the information given here, decide whether each of the four leases requires accounting as operating leases or as capital leases. Give your reasoning.

| | Lease Term | Annual Lease Payment |
|---|---|---|
| **a.** Cumberland Mall.................................... | 16 Years | $2,500,000 |
| **b.** Normandale Center ................................ | 16 Years | 2,600,000 |
| **c.** Eastbrook Haven ................................... | 12 Years | 2,600,000 |
| **d.** Peachtree Parkview ............................... | 12 Years | 2,700,000 |

32. *Comparison of borrow/buy with operating and capital leases.* The Carom Company plans to acquire, as of January 1, Year 1, a computerized cash regis-

ter system that costs $100,000 and has a 5-year life and no salvage value. The company is considering two plans for acquiring the system.

**(1)** Outright purchase. To finance the purchase, $100,000 of par-value, 10-percent semiannual coupon bonds will be issued January 1, Year 1, at par.

**(2)** Lease. The lease requires five annual payments to be made on December 31, Year 1, Year 2, Year 3, Year 4, and Year 5. The lease payments are such that they have a present value of $100,000 on January 1, Year 1, when discounted at 10 percent per year.

Straight-line amortization methods will be used for all depreciation and amortization computations for assets.

**a.** Verify that the amount of the required lease payment is $26,380 by constructing an amortization schedule for the five payments. Note that there will be a $2 rounding error in the fifth year. Nevertheless, you may treat each payment as being $26,380 in the rest of the problem.

**b.** What balance sheet accounts will be affected if plan (1) is selected? If plan (2) is selected, the lease is cancelable, and the operating lease treatment is used? If plan (2) is selected, the lease is noncancelable, and the capital lease treatment is used?

**c.** What will be the total depreciation and interest expenses for the 5 years under plan (1)?

**d.** What will be the total expenses for the 5 years under plan (2) if the lease were able to be accounted for as an operating lease? As a capital lease?

**e.** Why are the answers in part **d** the same? Why are the answers in part **c** different from those in part **d**?

**f.** What will be the total expenses for Year 1 under plan (1)? Under plan (2) accounted for as an operating lease? Under plan (2) accounted for as a capital lease?

**g.** Repeat part **f** for the fifth year, Year 5.

**33.** *Analysis of risks and rewards of lease contracts.* Pan American World Air Lines (Pan Am) leased three Boeing 707 aircraft in 1963 from Sally Leasing Company (Sally). The aircraft had a purchase price of $6.64 million each. The leases covered 13-year terms, were noncancelable, contained no purchase options, and required monthly payments of $71,115. The rental cost per month of $71,115 was several hundred dollars less than Pan Am would have had to pay for conventional financing at the then-prevalent interest rate.

**a.** What, if anything, did Pan Am give up in return for its savings of several hundred dollars per month for 13 years? What, if anything, did Sally Leasing Company get for giving up several hundred dollars per month for 13 years?

**b.** Who bore the risks and rewards of ownership in these leases?

**c.** Verify that the interest rate implicit in the lease contract is about three-fourths of 1 percent per month.

**d.** Assume that FASB *Statement No. 13* had been in effect when these leases were signed. To ascertain how the leases would be accounted for, what further information would you need?

**34.** *Behavior of deferred income tax account when new assets are acquired every year.* Equilibrium Company has adopted a program of purchasing a new machine each year. It uses ACRS on its income tax return and straight-line depreciation on its financial statements. Each machine costs $12,000 installed, has an economic life of 6 years for financial reporting, and is in the 5-year property class for ACRS. ACRS deductions are 20, 32, 19, 12, 11, and 6 percent of cost in each of the first 6 years, respectively.

   **a.**  Calculate the total depreciation deduction on the tax return for each of the first 7 years in accordance with ACRS.

   **b.**  Calculate depreciation for each year using the straight-line method of depreciation.

   **c.**  Calculate the annual difference in depreciation charges using the results from parts **a** and **b**.

   **d.**  Calculate the annual increase in the Deferred Income Taxes account for the balance sheet by multiplying the tax rate, 40 percent, by the amount found in the preceding part.

   **e.**  Calculate year-end balances for the Deferred Income Taxes account on the balance sheet.

   **f.**  If Equilibrium Company continues to follow its policy of buying a new machine every year for $12,000, what will happen to the balance in the Deferred Income Taxes account on the balance sheet?

**35.** *Accounting for deferred income taxes using net present values of payments expected to be made.* The FASB may eventually require the use of discounting in the accounting for deferred income taxes. Assume that it were to require firms to record income tax expense and liability for the *present value* of payments to be made when timing differences reverse. In all respects, the methods were to conform to the principles of historical cost accounting for liabilities.

    Describe the estimates firms would have to make, the journal entries that would be required on first recording the deferred tax liability, and the subsequent entries in subsequent periods as the reversal approaches and occurs.

**36.** *Possible accounting treatments for prior service obligations.* When a company adopts a defined-benefit pension plan giving credit to current employees for prior service, an obligation, perhaps one involving large amounts, arises.

    Assume that the amount is immediately credited to liability when it comes into existence. What accounts might be debited? Give justifications for debiting an asset account or an expense account.

**37.** *Interpreting financial statement disclosure about timing differences.* Refer to Exhibit 11.5, a note to the financial statements of General Products Company.

   **a.**  What is the combined average federal, state, and local income tax rate that General Products Company appeared to pay in Year 3?

    In the remainder of this problem, assume that the marginal income tax rate is 40 percent of pretax income; that is, if General Products Company earned another $1, it would have additional income tax expense of $.40.

   **b.**  By how much did depreciation claimed on the tax return exceed depreciation expense reported in the financial statements for the Year 3?

   **c.**  Warranty costs are not deductible on the tax return until actual repairs or replacements are made. Estimated warranty expenses are shown in the financial statements whenever they can be computed with a reasonable degree of precision. Did warranty expense on the financial statements exceed deductions for warranty costs on the tax return or vice versa in Year 3? How can you tell? By how much?

**38.** *Deferred taxes arising from using different methods of amortizing bond discount on financial statements and tax return; statement of cash flows effects (adapted from a case by J. Patell and R. Weil).* Refer to Problem 41 in Chapter 10 concerning the zero coupon notes of IBM Credit Corporation (IBMCC). Exhibit 11.9 reproduces the funds statement of cash flows and income tax footnote from IBMCC's annual report.

    **a.** Assume an income tax rate of 46 percent. What was the deferred tax for 1981 arising ''from the timing differences between financial and tax report-

**Exhibit 11.9** _____

**IBM CREDIT CORPORATION**
**Statement of Cash Flows for the Period**
**May 1, 1981, to December 31, 1981**
**(all dollar amounts in thousands)**
**(Problem 38)**

| | | |
|---|---:|---:|
| **Funds (cash and cash equivalents) at May 1**. . . . . . . . . . | | $ — |
| *Operations:* | | |
|   Net Earnings . . . . . . . . . . . . . . . . . . . . . . . . . . . . . . . . . . . . . | $ 9,867 | |
|   Increase in Amounts Due to IBM Corporation . . . . . . . . . . | 97,162 | |
|   Change in Deferred Charges and Other Assets, Taxes, and Other Accruals . . . . . . . . . . . . . . . . . . . . . . . . . . . . | 7,392 | |
|   Cash Flow from Operations . . . . . . . . . . . . . . . . . . . . . . . . | | $114,421 |
| *Investing:* | | |
|   Purchase of Installment Payment Agreement Receivables, Net of Collections . . . . . . . . . . . . . . . . . . | | (689,553) |
| *Financings:* | | |
|   Commercial Paper . . . . . . . . . . . . . . . . . . . . . . . . . . . . . . . . | $318,426 | |
|   Long-Term Debt . . . . . . . . . . . . . . . . . . . . . . . . . . . . . . . . . | 162,238 | |
|   Capital Contributions . . . . . . . . . . . . . . . . . . . . . . . . . . . . . | 95,000 | |
|   Cash Flow from Financings . . . . . . . . . . . . . . . . . . . . . . . . | | 575,664 |
| **Funds (cash and cash equivalents) at December 31** . . . . | | $ 532 |

*Income Tax Footnote Concerning 8-Month Period, May 1–December 31, 1981*

    Taxes: The components of the provision for income taxes, in thousands of dollars, are as follows:

**U.S. Federal:**

| | |
|---|---:|
| Current . . . . . . . . . . . . . . . . . . . . . . . . . . . . . . . . . . . . . . . . . . . . . . . . . . . . . . . . | $2,548 |
| Deferred . . . . . . . . . . . . . . . . . . . . . . . . . . . . . . . . . . . . . . . . . . . . . . . . . . . . . . . | 1,033 |
| | 3,581 |
| **State and Local:** | |
| Current . . . . . . . . . . . . . . . . . . . . . . . . . . . . . . . . . . . . . . . . . . . . . . . . . . . . . . . . | $1,269 |
| Deferred . . . . . . . . . . . . . . . . . . . . . . . . . . . . . . . . . . . . . . . . . . . . . . . . . . . . . . . | 225 |
| | $1,494 |
|   Total Provision . . . . . . . . . . . . . . . . . . . . . . . . . . . . . . . . . . . . . . . . . . . . . . | $5,075 |

Deferred taxes arise primarily from timing differences between financial and tax reporting of the amortization of original issue discount on the zero coupon notes.

ing of the amortization of the original issue discount on zero coupon notes''? Did this amount increase or decrease the credit balance for deferred taxes on the balance sheet?

**b.** Refer to the statement of cash flows for IBMCC. What lines of this statement were affected by the issue of the zero coupon notes, by the interest expense on them, and by the related income taxes, including the effects of timing differences? By how much were these lines affected?

39. *Analysis of data on operating leases; hypothetical capitalization of contractual lease payments.* FASB *Statement of Financial Accounting Standards (SFAS) No. 13* does not require the capitalization onto the balance sheet of assets and liabilities relating to contractual lease payments when the lease qualifies as an operating lease. Although a lessee (tenant) commits itself for a substantial amount of minimum lease payments, because the length of the lease term is sufficiently short and the present value of the lease payments sufficiently small, the resulting leases are viewed as executory contracts. In other words, the lessor will provide services in the future and the lessee will pay for those services as used. In this regard, contractual payments under operating leases are treated in the same way as employment contracts, which also commit the firm to fixed payments in the future in return for future services.

Some retailing companies own their stores or acquire their premises under capital leases. Other retailing companies acquire the use of store facilities under operating leases, contracting to make future payments. An analyst comparing the potential long-term solvency of retailing companies (particularly those who own versus those who rent) may wish to make adjustments to published financial statements to account for the fixed payments the renting firm has promised to make.

Exhibit 11.10 reproduces information from recent annual reports of J. C. Penney Company, Inc., and the Sears, Roebuck Merchandising Group. The data include the disclosures mandated by *SFAS No. 13* for operating leases. J. C. Penney goes beyond the minimal requirement to report the present value of the future contractual payments on operating leases. Assume that Sears's fixed payments after Year 5 are $50 million per year for 12 years and that all payments for operating leases occur at year-end.

**a.** Compute both the debt-equity ratio (total liabilities/total equities) and the long-term debt ratio [= long-term debt/(long-term debt + owners' equity)] for both J. C. Penney and Sears from the published financial statements.

**b.** Estimate the present value of Sears's minimum rent payments under operating leases. Assume a 12 percent annual discount rate.

**c.** Recompute the ratios in part **a**, assuming that the present values of the minimum contractual payments under operating leases are capitalized. What would be the implied journal entry for this capitalization?

40. *Deducing pretax effects of accounting transaction from aftertax data.* A footnote disclosure on inventories from a recent annual report of Deere & Company appeared as follows:

Substantially all inventories owned by Deere & Company and its
United States subsidiaries are valued at cost on the "last-in, first-out"
(LIFO) method.

During the fourth quarter, the company's inventories declined due
to the lower level of production. As a result, lower costs which pre-
vailed in prior years were matched against current year revenues, the
effect of which was to increase net income by $20.8 million or
31 cents per share.

During the fourth quarter, in conjunction with an examination
completed by the Internal Revenue Service of certain prior years'
United States Federal income tax returns, the company increased the
valuation of its slow-moving service parts inventories. As a result net
income was increased by $13.2 million or 20 cents per share.

If all the company's inventories had been valued on a current cost
basis, which approximates FIFO, inventories at year-end were estimated to be $1,885 million compared with approximately $1,941 million at the beginning of the year.

The balance sheet reported inventories of $760.9 million at the end of the year
and $872.0 million at the beginning of the year. Assume an income tax rate of
46 percent.

**a.** The second paragraph refers to inventory declines caused by lower production levels. By how much did the costs of the older inventories "matched

**Exhibit 11.10** ⎯⎯⎯⎯⎯⎯⎯⎯⎯⎯⎯⎯⎯⎯⎯⎯⎯⎯⎯⎯⎯⎯⎯⎯⎯⎯⎯⎯⎯⎯⎯⎯⎯
**J. C. PENNEY COMPANY, INC.,**
**and SEARS, ROEBUCK AND CO. (MERCHANDISING GROUP)**
**Financial Statement Excerpts**
**(all dollar amounts in millions)**
**(Problem 39)**

| | J. C. Penney | Sears |
|---|---|---|
| **Balance Sheet Data at End of Year 0** | | |
| Current Liabilities . . . . . . . . . . . . . . . . . . . . . . . . . . . . . . . . . . . . . . . . . . | $2,070 | $2,181 |
| Long-Term Debt . . . . . . . . . . . . . . . . . . . . . . . . . . . . . . . . . . . . . . . . . . . | 1,384 | 188 |
| Owners' Equity . . . . . . . . . . . . . . . . . . . . . . . . . . . . . . . . . . . . . . . . . . . | 3,228 | 4,318 |
| Total . . . . . . . . . . . . . . . . . . . . . . . . . . . . . . . . . . . . . . . . . . . . | $6,682 | $6,687 |
| | | |
| **Minimum Payments Due under Operating Leases** | | |
| Year 1 . . . . . . . . . . . . . . . . . . . . . . . . . . . . . . . . . . . . . . . . . . . . . . . . . . | $ 195 | $ 212 |
| Year 2 . . . . . . . . . . . . . . . . . . . . . . . . . . . . . . . . . . . . . . . . . . . . . . . . . . | 186 | 181 |
| Year 3 . . . . . . . . . . . . . . . . . . . . . . . . . . . . . . . . . . . . . . . . . . . . . . . . . . | 172 | 138 |
| Year 4 . . . . . . . . . . . . . . . . . . . . . . . . . . . . . . . . . . . . . . . . . . . . . . . . . . | 167 | 110 |
| Year 5 . . . . . . . . . . . . . . . . . . . . . . . . . . . . . . . . . . . . . . . . . . . . . . . . . . | 157 | 89 |
| Thereafter . . . . . . . . . . . . . . . . . . . . . . . . . . . . . . . . . . . . . . . . . . . . . . | 1,855 | 604 |
| Total . . . . . . . . . . . . . . . . . . . . . . . . . . . . . . . . . . . . . . . . . . . . . . . . . | $2,732 | $1,334 |
| Amounts Representing Interest . . . . . . . . . . . . . . . . . . . . . . . . . . . . . . | (1,832) | ? |
| Net Present Value . . . . . . . . . . . . . . . . . . . . . . . . . . . . . . . . . . . . . . . | $ 900 | $ ? |

against current year revenues'' differ from current costs? Give the amount and whether it was larger or smaller.

**b.** How much did the dip into old LIFO layers, referred to in the second paragraph, cost Deere in extra income tax payments?

**c.** The extract refers to resolution of a dispute with the IRS. What was the most likely cause of the dispute?

**d.** As a result of the settlement with the IRS, Deere changed the balance sheet amount of its inventories. What was the amount of the change? Indicate whether it was an increase or a decrease.

**e.** How much has Deere reduced its income taxes payable since it adopted LIFO?

**41.** *Analysis of attempts to achieve off-balance-sheet financing [adapted from ''Off-Balance-Sheet Financing,'' Case 4.1 in* Accounting and Auditing Case Studies *(The Trueblood Professors' Seminar), The Touche Ross Foundation and The American Accounting Association, 1983, pp. 21–22].* Container Company has developed a process for manufacturing plastic bottles at a cost lower than any competitor's. Gigantic Drugs, Inc., has offered to purchase so many of the bottles that Container will have to build a new plant just to fill Gigantic's orders. The new plant will be built next to Gigantic's plant, with a conveyor belt to carry the bottles into Gigantic's plant. Container Company will operate the plant. The problem is that Container does not have, and is unable to raise, sufficient funds to finance construction of the new plant. Gigantic is willing to provide its financial backing to raise the necessary funds but has insufficient cash to finance the project. Moreover, it is unwilling to borrow the funds if doing so increases the recorded debt on its balance sheet because of potential default on some of its own debt covenants and some other new plans it has to raise funds by borrowing. The financial executives of Container and Gigantic have devised two plans to finance the plant while attempting to satisfy Gigantic's requirements. Under both plans, Container will create a subsidiary, Borrower Company, to borrow all the funds required from a bank to build the plant.

**Plan 1** Borrower will lease the plant to Gigantic for 40 years, with lease payments matched in size and timing to Borrower's debt service payments to the bank. Gigantic is sufficiently solvent and profitable that its promised lease payments and the plant itself will induce a bank to provide 100 percent financing at Gigantic's borrowing rate. Borrower would contract with Container so that Container will manage the new plant.

**Plan 2** Gigantic will sign a 40-year contract to purchase bottles from the new plant. It will buy all the bottles produced by the plant when it operates at normal capacity. Contractual payments will cover all variable manufacturing costs, debt service on the bank loan, and the payments to Container to manage the new plant. If Gigantic does not wish to purchase the entire output of the plant and if Borrower is unable to sell the bottles to other bottle users, Gigantic will agree to make a cash payment to Borrower for the difference so that Borrower can meet all its cash obligations. Any cash that Borrower can generate from selling bottles to other bottle users for amounts larger than variable manufacturing costs will reduce the payments Gigantic makes to Borrower.

Discuss these two plans from two perspectives.

a.  Consider the auditor who must decide whether each arrangement requires recognition on the balance sheet or whether footnote disclosure is enough.

b.  Consider an investment banker who is planning to bid on the new bond issue Gigantic will use to raise funds for a different purpose. The banker must take into account, among other things, Gigantic's entire financial structure.

42. *Analysis of take-or-pay contract including capitalization of future payments and possible losses.* Natural gas pipelines sign take-or-pay contracts with producers of natural gas. Under these contracts the pipelines agree to purchase the natural gas in fixed (or computable) quantities at fixed (or computable) prices or to pay for the gas even if they do not take delivery. By the mid-1980s, there was a large quantity of natural gas contracted for relative to the amounts that could be sold by the pipelines. A *Business Week* article on the subject said:

> Most of the unfavorable contracts were hastily signed after the cold winters of 1977 and 1978, when the gas shortage assumed crisis proportions. The pipeline industry faced the prospect of . . . lawsuits over its inability to supply contracted-for fuel. . . . Aggressively bidding for new supplies, the pipelines bought their way out of the problem — and into an even greater mess. They now find themselves stuck with massive numbers of "take-or-pay" agreements. . . . The fear of another icy, gasless winter, some say, drove pipeline executives to close one bad deal after another. Tenneco . . . had 4 billion cu. ft. per day of gas available for delivery and sales of just over 2 billion cu. ft. per day. . . . [The] costs [of natural gas had] soared to $3.48 per thousand cu. ft. . . . and price escalators in many contracts threaten to keep costs rising, especially after [price] controls expire. . . .

The financial statements of Tenneco showed total assets of $17.4 billion, current liabilities of $6.9 billion, long-term debt of $5.0 billion, and owners' equity of $5.5 billion. Notes to the statements indicate that some of Tenneco's take-or-pay contracts extend 25 years into the future.

a.  Compute the long-term debt ratio [= long-term debt/(long-term debt + owners' equity)] from the financial statement data.

b.  Compute the present value of the obligation to take 4 billion cubic feet of gas per day for 10 years. Assume a price of $3.50 per thousand cubic feet, a year of 300 days, and a discount rate of 15 percent per year. Payments occur at year-end.

c.  Assume that these contractual payments are capitalized on the balance sheet and that an asset is recorded in the same amount. Compute the long-term debt ratio.

**d.** Now assume that Tenneco will be able to sell only 60 percent of the contracted-for gas. The other 40 percent will be paid for, but because it is not taken, there is no offsetting asset for this amount, only a loss. Assume that the loss is tax deductible and assume an income tax rate of 46 percent. Recompute owners' equity and the long-term debt ratio for the financial statements excerpted previously.

**43.** *Attempts to achieve off-balance-sheet financing (adapted from materials by R. Dieter, D. Landsittel, J. Stewart, and A. Wyatt).* Brion Company wishes to raise $50 million cash but, for various reasons, does not wish to do so in a way that results in a newly recorded liability. It is sufficiently solvent and profitable that its bank is willing to lend up to $50 million at the prime interest rate. Brion Company's financial executives have devised six different plans, described in the following sections.

**Transfer of Receivables with Recourse** Brion Company will transfer to Credit Company its long-term accounts receivable, which call for payments over the next 2 years. Credit Company will pay an amount equal to the present value of the receivables less an allowance for uncollectibles as well as a discount because it is paying now but will collect cash later. Brion Company must repurchase from Credit Company at face value any receivables that become uncollectible in excess of the allowance. In addition, Brion Company may repurchase any of the receivables not yet due at face value less a discount specified by formula and based on the prime rate at the time of the initial transfer. (This option permits Brion Company to benefit if an unexpected drop in interest rates occurs after the transfer.) The accounting issue is whether the transfer is a sale (where Brion Company debits Cash, credits Accounts Receivable, and debits expense or loss on transfer) or whether the transfer is merely a loan collateralized by the receivables (where Brion Company debits Cash and Credits Notes Payable at the time of transfer).

**Product Financing Arrangement** Brion Company will transfer inventory to Credit Company, who will store the inventory in a public warehouse. Credit Company may use the inventory as collateral for its own borrowings, whose proceeds will be used to pay Brion Company. Brion Company will pay storage costs and will repurchase all the inventory within the next 4 years at contractually fixed prices plus interest accrued for the time elapsed between the transfer and later repurchase. The accounting issue is whether the inventory is sold to Credit Company, with later repurchases treated as new acquisitions for Brion's inventory, or whether the transaction is merely a loan, with the inventory remaining on Brion's balance sheet.

**Throughput Contract** Brion Company requires a branch line of a railroad to be built from the main rail line to carry raw material directly to its own plant. It could, of course, borrow the funds and build the branch line itself. Instead, it will sign an agreement with the railroad to ship specified amounts of material each month for 10 years. Even if it does not ship the specified amounts of material, it will pay the agreed shipping costs. The railroad will take the contract to its bank and, using it as collateral, borrow the funds to build the branch line. The accounting issue is whether Brion Company would debit asset for future rail services and credit liability for payments to the railroad. The alternative is to make no accounting entry except when Brion makes payments to the railroad.

**Construction Partnership**   Brion Company and Mission Company will jointly build a plant to manufacture chemicals both need in their own production processes. Each will contribute $5 million to the project, called Chemical. Chemical will borrow another $40 million from a bank, with Brion, only, guaranteeing the debt. Brion and Mission are each to contribute equally to future operating expenses and debt service payments of Chemical, but, in return for its guaranteeing the debt, Brion will have an option to purchase Mission's interest for $20 million 4 years hence. The accounting issue is whether or not Brion Company would recognize a liability for the funds borrowed by Chemical; because of the debt guarantee, debt service payments will ultimately be Brion Company's responsibility. Alternatively, the debt guarantee is a commitment merely to be disclosed in notes to Brion Company's financial statements.

**Research and Development Partnership**  Brion Company will contribute a laboratory and preliminary finding about a potentially profitable gene-splicing discovery to a partnership, called Venture. Venture will raise funds by selling the remaining interest in the partnership to outside investors for $2 million and borrowing $48 million from a bank with Brion Company guaranteeing the debt. Although Venture will operate under the management of Brion Company, it will be free to sell the results of its further discoveries and development efforts to anyone, including Brion Company. Brion Company is not obligated to purchase any of Venture's output. The accounting issue is whether the liability would be recognized by Brion Company. (Would it make any difference if Brion Company has either the *option* to purchase or an *obligation* to purchase the results of Venture's work?)

**Hotel Financing**  Brion Company owns and operates a profitable hotel. It could use the hotel as collateral for a conventional mortgage loan. Instead, it considers selling the hotel to a partnership for $50 million cash. The partnership will sell ownership interests to outside investors for $5 million and borrow $45 million from a bank on a conventional mortgage loan, using the hotel as collateral. Brion Company guarantees the debt. The accounting issue is whether Brion Company would record the liability for the guaranteed debt of the partnership.

Consider each of these proposed arrangements from the viewpoint of the auditor (who must decide whether the transaction will result in a liability to be recorded or whether footnote disclosure will suffice) and from the viewpoint of an investment banker (who must assess the financing structure of Brion Company in order to make a competitive bid on a proposed new underwriting of Brion Company common shares).

# Exhibit 11.11

## ALCOA, GENERAL ELECTRIC, and USX
Pension and Other Data
(all dollar amounts in millions)
(Problem 44)

| | Alcoa | | General Electric | | USX | |
|---|---|---|---|---|---|---|
| | SFAS No. 35 (decelerated) | Inside Company (accelerated) | SFAS No. 35 (decelerated) | Inside Company (accelerated) | SFAS No. 35 (decelerated) | Inside Company (accelerated) |
| **End of Year** | | | | | | |
| Present Value of Pension Plan Benefits as Based on Actuarial Cost Method | $ (1) | $ (2) | $ (4) | $ (5) | $ (7) | $ (8) |
| Current Market Value of Assets in Pension Fund | 773 | (3) | 4,968 | (6) | 5,100 | (9) |
| Unfunded Obligation of Pension Plan | $ 305 | $492 | $ 840 | $1,036 | $ 0 | $1,000 |
| Owner's Equity | $2,529 | | $7,362 | | $4,895 | |
| **For Year** | | | | | | |
| Net Income (loss) | $ 505 | | $1,409 | | $ (293) | |

**44.** *Analyzing pension disclosure; changes in cost methods.* The employer's costs of a single employee's pension is the amount required to fund the pension promises over the employee's retirement years measured on the date the pension payments start. Assume that amount can be estimated at any time with reasonable precision. Once the accountant estimates that amount, the problem remains of allocating the costs to the individual years when the employee works. Various methods of allocating that cost, called "actuarial cost methods," can be used. Choosing an actuarial cost method is much like choosing a depreciation method; the method can be straight-line, accelerated, or decelerated. In 1980, to achieve more uniformity in pension reporting, the FASB (in *SFAS No. 35*) required all pension plans to use a specific decelerated method. Many companies had been using accelerated or straight-line methods, which recognize the pension expenses faster than the decelerated method. Alcoa, General Electric, and USX, among others, disclosed for several years the fact that for financial reporting and internal purposes, they used a method different (and more conservative) than the FASB-required method. Exhibit 11.11 reproduces data from the annual reports of these companies based on the FASB-required method and the more conservative method used inside the companies.

**a.** Fill in the missing numbers (1) through (9) in Exhibit 11.11. Keep in mind that changing the method for allocating costs to specific periods has no effect on the current market value of the assets in the pension fund.

**b.** By how much does the change in cost methods change expense for the year for these companies? Does the change in cost methods appear to be material for the companies?

# Chapter 12  Owners' Equity ————————————————

The economic resources of a firm come from two major sources — nonowners and owners. When nonowners provide funds to a firm, the sources of these funds appear on the balance sheet as liabilities, discussed in Chapters 10 and 11. When owners provide funds, the sources of these funds appear on the balance sheet as *owners' equity*.

The accounting equation states that

$$\text{Assets} = \text{Liabilities} + \text{Owners' Equity},$$

or

$$\text{Assets} - \text{Liabilities} = \text{Owners' Equity}.$$

Many readers of financial statements think of owners' equity as being calculated as assets minus liabilities. However, double-entry record keeping provides a continuous, independent calculation of owners' equity. This chapter discusses owners' equity for corporations. The corporate organization is used for at least three reasons.

1. The corporate form provides the owner (shareholder) with limited liability; that is, should the corporation become insolvent, creditors' claims are limited to the assets of the corporate entity. The corporation's creditors cannot claim the assets of the individual owners. On the other hand, creditors of partnerships and sole proprietorships have a claim on both the owners' personal and business assets to settle such firms' debts.

2. The corporate form allows raising funds by issuing shares. The general public can acquire the shares in varying amounts. Individual investments can range from a few dollars to billions of dollars.

3. The corporate form makes transfer of ownership interests relatively easy, because individual shares can be sold by current owners to others without interfering with the ongoing operations of the business. Ongoing changes in ownership do not affect the continuity of the management and of operations.

This chapter discusses the accounting for capital contributed by owners; the accounting for income earned by the firm, which may be retained or distributed to owners; and other changes in owners' equity accounts.

# Capital Contributions ————————————————

The *corporation* is a legal entity separate from its owners. Individuals or other entities make capital contributions under a contract between themselves and the corporation.[1] Because those who contribute funds receive certificates for shares of stock, they are known as "stockholders" or "shareholders." The rights and obligations of a shareholder are governed by the following:

1. The corporation laws of the state in which incorporation takes place.

2. The articles of incorporation or *charter*. This is a contract between the firm and the state in which the business is incorporated. The state grants to the firm the privileges of operating as a corporation for certain stated purposes and of obtaining its capital through the issue of shares of stock.

3. The *bylaws* of the corporation. The board of directors adopts bylaws, which are the rules and regulations governing the internal affairs of the corporation.

4. The stock contract. Each type of *capital stock* has its own provisions as to such matters as voting, sharing in earnings, distribution of earnings, and sharing in assets in case of dissolution.

Some "closely held" corporations have a small number of shareholders and operate much like partnerships. The few people involved agree to the amount of capital to be contributed, elect each other to be members of the board of directors and officials of the firm, and agree on policies regarding dividends and salaries. They may restrict the transfer of shares to outsiders, and may even become liable for debts of the corporation by endorsing its notes and bonds.

## Issue of Shares of Stock

The accounting for the initial issue of shares of stock for cash is as follows:

| | | |
|---|---|---|
| Cash . . . . . . . . . . . . . . . . . . . . . . . . . . . . . . . . . . . . . . . . . . . . . . . . | 1,250,000 | |
| Capital Stock . . . . . . . . . . . . . . . . . . . . . . . . . . . . . . . . . . . . . . . . . . | | 1,250,000 |
| Issue of shares of capital stock. | | |

In addition to exchanges for cash, stock is sometimes issued in exchange for property, for personal services rendered, or in settlement of a liability. The entry in these cases is the same as the one illustrated here, but the debit will be made to the accounts for property or services received or the liability settled. The amount for the entry should be the fair market value of the product, property, or services received, or, if this amount is not reasonably estimable, the fair market value of the stock issued.[2]

---

[1]In accounting for owners' equity, the term *contribution* almost never means a gift; capital given to the corporation as a gift is specifically called *donated capital*.

[2]Accounting Principles Board, *Opinion No. 29*, "Accounting for Nonmonetary Transactions," 1973.

## Classes of Shares

Corporate charters often authorize the issue of more than one class of shares, each representing ownership in the business. Most shares issued are either *common* or *preferred*. Occasionally there may be several classes of common or preferred shares, each with different rights and privileges. All corporations have at least one class of shares. They are usually called common shares, but they may be designated by another name, such as class A shares. Preferred shares may be issued, but do not need to be.

*Common shares* have the claim to the corporation's earnings after commitments to creditors and preferred shareholders have been satisfied. Frequently, common shares are the only voting shares of the company. In the event of corporate dissolution, all of the proceeds of asset disposition, after settling the claims of creditors and required distributions to preferred shareholders, are distributed to the common shareholders.

*Preferred shares* have special privileges. Although these privileges vary considerably from issue to issue, a preferred share usually entitles its holder to dividends at a certain rate, which must be paid before dividends can be paid to common shareholders. Sometimes, though, these dividends may be postponed or omitted. If the provisions of the stock contract designate the preferred dividends as *cumulative*, all current and previously postponed dividends must be paid before any dividends on common shares can be paid.

Many preferred shares issued by corporations in recent years have been callable. *Callable preferred shares* can be reacquired by the corporation at a specified price, which may vary according to a preset time schedule. Callability is commonly thought to benefit the corporation. If financing becomes available at a lower cost than the rate fixed for the preferred shares, a corporation may wish to reduce the relatively fixed commitment of preferred dividends (as compared to common) by exercising its option to call the preferred shares. This option is valuable to the corporation but makes the shares less attractive to potential owners. Other things being equal, noncallable shares will be issued for a higher price than callable shares. Thus the degree to which the corporation benefits by making shares callable is not clear-cut.

Preferred shares with a conversion feature have also become increasingly popular. *Convertible preferred shares* may be converted by their owner into a specified number of common shares at a specified time. The conversion privilege may appear advantageous to both the individual shareholder and the corporation. The preferred shareholder enjoys the security of a relatively assured dividend as long as the shares are held. The shareholder also has the opportunity to realize capital appreciation by converting the shares into common stock if the market price of the common shares rises sufficiently. Because of this feature, the change in the market price of convertible preferred shares will often parallel changes in the market price of the common shares.

The firm may also benefit from the conversion option. By including it in the issue, the company is usually able to specify a lower dividend rate on the preferred than otherwise would have been required to issue the shares for a given price.

Some preferred stock issues carry mandatory redemption features; that is, the issuing firm is required to repurchase the shares from their holders, paying for them a specified dollar amount at a specified future time. Other preferred stock issues are redeemable for specific dollar amounts at the option of the holder under certain conditions. Because such redeemable preferred share issues have some of the characteristics of debt, they must be disclosed separately in the shareholders' equity section of the balance sheet.[3]

Separate accounts are used for each class of shares. On the balance sheet, each class of shares appears separately, often with a short description of the major features of the shares, and preferred shares customarily appear before common shares.

## Par Value and No-Par Shares

Shares of capital stock often have either a *par* or a *stated value*. The articles of incorporation specify the amount, which is printed on the face of the stock certificates. The par value of common stock has some legal significance but little economic substance. For legal reasons, accountants separate par value from other contributed capital amounts.[4] The par value rarely denotes the market value of the shares, except perhaps at the date of original issue. Readers of financial statements can usually assume merely that the shareholders in the corporation have invested an amount at least equal to the par value of all common shares. Par value of preferred stock is more meaningful. The dividend rate specified in the preferred stock contract (for example, 9 percent) is almost always based on par value. Any preference as to assets in liquidation that preferred shareholders may have is usually related to the par value of the preferred shares, although some preferred stock contracts may specify a liquidation value different from par value.

Although preferred shares usually have a par value, common shares without a par value are widely used. When no-par-value shares are issued, the amount actually contributed can be credited directly to the capital stock account.

The *book value* of a share of common stock — the total common shareholders' equity divided by the number of shares outstanding — is almost always greater than the par value of the shares. The excess results from retained earnings and from capital contributions in excess of par or stated value.

## Contributions in Excess of Par Value

Shares are usually issued for amounts greater than par. Typically, individuals who purchase newly issued shares from a corporation some years after the corporation

---

[3]Securities and Exchange Commission, *Accounting Series Release No. 268*, "Presentation in Financial Statements of 'Redeemable Preferred Stock,'" 1979. Reissued in Section 101 of *Codification of Financial Reporting Policies*. See also FASB, *Statement of Financial Accounting Standards (SFAS) No. 47*, 1981.

[4]The original legal concept was that par value represented an investment to be maintained by the corporation for the protection of creditors. The investment level was called "legal" or "statutory" or "stated" capital, and many states have prohibited corporations from declaring dividends out of such capital. The concept is now obsolete, because creditors have found more effective ways to protect themselves, such as through specific limitations in debt contracts on corporate financing behavior.

began operations pay a higher price per share to compensate current shareholders for the additional assets provided by the retention of earnings, as well as for increases in the market values of assets over their book values. The corporation credits its capital stock account with only the par value of the shares issued. The excess of issue proceeds over par (or stated) value is credited to an account called *Additional Paid-in Capital*. The title Capital Contributed in Excess of Par (Stated) Value is more descriptive but too cumbersome to be widely used. Sometimes the title used is Premium on Capital Stock.

If par-value shares are used, the credit to the Additional Paid-in Capital account is always the difference between the amount received and the par value of the shares issued to the shareholders. Thus the entry to record the issue of 100 shares with a par value of $10 per share for $10,000 would be as follows:

| | | |
|---|---:|---:|
| Cash . . . . . . . . . . . . . . . . . . . . . . . . . . . . . . . . . . . . . . . . . . . . . . . . . . . . . . . . . . | 10,000 | |
|     Capital Stock—Par Value . . . . . . . . . . . . . . . . . . . . . . . . . . . . . . . . . . | | 1,000 |
|     Additional Paid-in Capital . . . . . . . . . . . . . . . . . . . . . . . . . . . . . . . . . . | | 9,000 |
| Issue of shares for amount greater than par value. | | |

## Treasury Shares

Shares of stock reacquired by the issuing corporation are called *treasury stock* or *treasury shares*. The firm may reacquire its own shares for later distribution under stock option plans or for stock dividends. (Stock option plans and stock dividends are discussed later in this chapter.) The firm may also consider treasury shares a worthwhile use for idle funds. Treasury shares are not entitled to dividends or to voting rights, because they are not considered to be outstanding shares for these purposes. Treasury shares held may be reissued, or resold, on the market.

**Accounting for Treasury Shares**   The fundamental principle of accounting for treasury shares is that a corporation does not report profit or loss on transactions involving its own shares. Even though the firm may sell (technically, reissue) the shares for more than their acquisition cost, the "gain" is not reported in income. Similarly, the firm may subsequently reissue shares for less than their acquisition cost, but even so, the "loss" is not part of net income. The adjustments for reissue of treasury shares are made directly to the contributed capital accounts, bypassing the income statement and, generally, the Retained Earnings account.

When common shares are reacquired, a Treasury Shares–Common account is debited with the total amount paid to reacquire the shares.

| | | |
|---|---:|---:|
| Treasury Shares—Common . . . . . . . . . . . . . . . . . . . . . . . . . . . . . . . . . . | 11,000 | |
|     Cash . . . . . . . . . . . . . . . . . . . . . . . . . . . . . . . . . . . . . . . . . . . . . . . . . . . . . . . | | 11,000 |
| $11,000 paid to reacquire 1,000 common shares. | | |

If the treasury shares are later reissued by the corporation, Cash is debited with the amount received and the Treasury Shares account is credited with the cost of the shares. The reissue price will usually differ from the amount paid to acquire the treasury shares. If the reissue price is greater than the acquisition price, the Additional Paid-in Capital account is credited to make the entry balance. Assuming that the 1,000 shares reacquired in the entry illustrated previously were reissued for $14,000, the entry would be as follows:

| | | |
|---|---:|---:|
| Cash . . . . . . . . . . . . . . . . . . . . . . . . . . . . . . . . . . . . . . . . . . . . . . . . . . . . . . . . . | 14,000 | |
| Treasury Shares — Common . . . . . . . . . . . . . . . . . . . . . . . . . . . . . . . . | | 11,000 |
| Additional Paid-in Capital . . . . . . . . . . . . . . . . . . . . . . . . . . . . . . . . . . . | | 3,000 |
| Reissue of 1,000 shares of treasury stock at a price greater than acquisition cost. | | |

If the reissue price is less than the amount paid, the debit to balance the entry is usually made to Additional Paid-in Capital, as long as there is a sufficient credit balance in that account. If there is not, the additional balancing debit is made directly to Retained Earnings. This debit to Retained Earnings is viewed to be similar to a dividend, not an expense or loss reported in the income statement.

**Disclosure of Treasury Shares** The Treasury Shares account appears contra to total shareholders' equity. Chapter 7 introduced the direct debits to shareholders' equity required for declines in market value of the portfolio of investments in marketable equity securities. The debits for such price declines are generally shown as a negative number either before or after Retained Earnings. An annual report of Warner Communications, Inc., illustrates the disclosures of these two deductions from shareholders' equity; see Exhibit 12.1.

**Exhibit 12.1** _____

**WARNER COMMUNICATIONS, INC.**
**Presentation of Shareholders' Equity in Balance Sheet**
**(all dollar amounts in thousands)**

| **Shareholders' Equity** | |
|---|---:|
| Convertible Preferred Shares Issued, Par Value $1 per Share, 20,000,000 Shares Authorized . . . . . . . . . . . . . . . . . . . . . . . . . . . . . . . . . . . . . . . . . . | — |
| Common Shares Issued, Par Value $1 per Share, 40,000,000 Shares Authorized . . . . . . . . . . . . . . . . . . . . . . . . . . . . . . . . . . . . . . . . . . | $ 28,407 |
| Paid-in Capital . . . . . . . . . . . . . . . . . . . . . . . . . . . . . . . . . . . . . . . . . . . . . . . . | 136,373 |
| Retained Earnings . . . . . . . . . . . . . . . . . . . . . . . . . . . . . . . . . . . . . . . . . . . . . | 487,568 |
| Net Unrealized Loss on Investments in Equity Securities . . . . . . . . . . . . . . . . . . . | (3,887) |
| | $648,461 |
| Less Common Shares in Treasury, at Cost . . . . . . . . . . . . . . . . . . . . . . . . . . . | (33,540) |
| Total Shareholders' Equity . . . . . . . . . . . . . . . . . . . . . . . . . . . . . . . . . . . . . . . . | $614,921 |

## Should a Firm Raise New Funds by Issuing Shares or Bonds?

A major consideration in the issue of common or preferred shares is that dividends are not deductible in calculating taxable income. However, bond interest is deductible. Thus the aftertax accounting cost of borrowing is usually less than the aftertax accounting cost of issuing shares, even though the interest rate on the bonds is higher than the dividend rate. Exhibit 12.2 illustrates this phenomenon. The accounting figures, however, do not reflect the economic costs of risk. When bonds are issued, both preferred and common shares become more risky, because bond-holders have a claim on future cash flows senior to the claim of shareholders. When preferred shares are issued, common shares become more risky. When shares become more risky, all else being equal, the rate of return on those shares required by the market increases. (For a given dollar amount of return from an investment in a share, this means that the price of the share must fall.) Even though a project financed with a bond issue may result in a larger earnings-per-share increase than one financed by a common stock issue, one cannot conclude that raising new funds by borrowing is better than raising new funds with share issues. As Chapter 6

**Exhibit 12.2** _____

### Accounting Benefit of Raising New Funds by Borrowing Rather than by Issuing Common Shares (financial leverage)

**Assumptions (before new funds are raised)**
Income Tax Rate (combined Federal and State): 37.5 Percent
Net Income: $216,000
Shares Outstanding: 90,000
Market Price per Share: $20.00
Earnings per Share: $2.40 (= $216,000/90,000 shares)

**Assumptions about New Project**
Requires New Funds of $1,000,000
Generates Income before Financing Charges and Taxes of $192,000 per Year

**Assumptions about New Financing Options**
Issue $1,000,000 of Bonds at Par with Annual Coupon Rate of 10 Percent
_or_ Issue 50,000 New Common Shares at $20 Each

## Pro Forma Income Statements after New Financing

|  | Issue Bonds | Issue Shares |
|---|---|---|
| Income from New Project before Interest and Taxes.... | $192,000 | $192,000 |
| Less Interest Expense (= .10 × $1,000,000)........... | (100,000) | — |
| Less Additional Income Taxes at 37.5 Percent......... | (34,500) | (72,000) |
| Additional Income ................................... | $ 57,500 | $120,000 |
| Previously Earned Income ........................... | 216,000 | 216,000 |
| Net Income ........................................ | $273,500 | $336,000 |
| Shares Outstanding................................. | 90,000 | 140,000 |
| Earnings per Share ................................. | $3.04 | $2.40 |
| Rate of Return on Market Value of Share of $20....... | 15.2% | 12.0% |

pointed out, leverage (the raising of funds by borrowing) is a two-edged sword. Corporate finance texts discuss whether there is an optimal way to raise new funds.

If the new project undertaken by the firm illustrated in Exhibit 12.2 has the same risk characteristics as the other, older projects of the firm, it is likely that the market value after either form of financing will remain at about $20 per share. If so, the return required by the market of the bond-financed firm will increase from 12.0 percent to 15.2 percent. Although projected earnings per share increase, so does risk.

# Retained Earnings ————————————————————————————

After a new business has become established and profitable, it usually generates additional owners' equity from undistributed earnings. These undistributed earnings represent the accumulated periodic net income remaining after dividends have been declared. Retaining earnings increases shareholders' equity and provides capital for expansion or for replacing assets at higher costs.

## Net Income and Cash Position

One misconception about net income is that it represents a fund of cash available for distribution or expansion. Earnings from operations usually involve cash at some stage: Goods are sold to customers, the cash is collected, more goods are acquired, bills are paid, more sales are made, and so on. However, *assets generated by earnings do not remain in the form of cash.*[5] Only under the most unlikely conditions, where net plant and equipment, inventories, receivables, and liabilities remain at constant amounts, would earnings correspond to the increase in cash. The statement of cash flows shows how the cash provided by operations (and other sources) is used during a period.

A well-managed firm keeps its cash at a reasonable minimum. If cash starts to accumulate, the firm may pay some obligations, increase its inventory, buy more equipment, or declare dividends. Thus there is no way of knowing how retaining earnings affects the individual asset and liability accounts. The only certain statement is that an increase in retained earnings results in increased *net assets* (that is, an increase in the excess of all assets over all liabilities).

## Cash Dividends

The shareholders of a corporation do not directly control distributions of corporate assets generated by net income. State laws and corporation bylaws almost always

---

[5]For many businesses, increased net income is frequently associated with decreased cash, whereas contraction of net income may be accompanied by an increase in cash. In the first stages of a business decline, cash may start to build up from the liquidation of inventories and receivables that have not been replaced, as well as from postponing replacement or expansion of plant. When conditions improve, inventories and receivables are expanded, new plant is acquired, and a cash shortage may develop.

delegate the authority to declare dividends to the board of directors. When a dividend is declared, the entry is as follows:

| | | |
|---|---|---|
| Retained Earnings . . . . . . . . . . . . . . . . . . . . . . . . . . . . . . . . . . . . . . . . . . | 150,000 | |
|    Dividends Payable . . . . . . . . . . . . . . . . . . . . . . . . . . . . . . . . . . . . . . . . . | | 150,000 |
| To record declaration of dividends. (Sometimes an account called Dividends or Dividends Declared is debited. The Dividends account is a temporary account and is closed with a debit to Retained Earnings at the end of the period.) | | |

Once the board of directors declares a dividend, the dividend becomes a legal liability of the corporation. Dividends Payable is shown as a current liability on the balance sheet if the dividends have not been paid at the end of the accounting period. When the dividends are paid, the entry is as follows:

| | | |
|---|---|---|
| Dividends Payable . . . . . . . . . . . . . . . . . . . . . . . . . . . . . . . . . . . . . . . . . | 150,000 | |
|    Cash . . . . . . . . . . . . . . . . . . . . . . . . . . . . . . . . . . . . . . . . . . . . . . . . . . | | 150,000 |

A distribution of a corporation's assets other than cash to its shareholders is called a *dividend in kind* or a *property dividend*. Such dividends are accounted for just like cash dividends, except that when the dividend is paid, the asset given up, rather than cash, is credited. The amount debited to Retained Earnings is the fair market value of the assets distributed. Any gain or loss is part of income for the period.

## Stock Dividends

The retention of earnings may lead to a substantial increase in shareholders' equity, which represents a relatively permanent commitment by shareholders to the business. The commitment is relatively permanent because the net assets generated have been invested in operating assets such as inventories and plant. To indicate such a permanent commitment of reinvested earnings, the board of directors may declare a *stock dividend*. The accounting involves a debit to Retained Earnings and a credit to the contributed capital accounts. When a stock dividend is declared, shareholders receive additional shares of stock in proportion to their existing holdings. If a 5 percent stock dividend is issued, each shareholder receives one additional share for every 20 shares held before the dividend.

Generally accepted accounting principles require that the valuation of the newly issued shares be based on the market value of the shares issued. For example, the directors of a corporation may decide to declare a stock dividend of 10,000 additional shares of common stock with a par value of $10 per share at a time when the market price of a share is $40. The entry would be as follows:

| | | |
|---|---|---|
| Retained Earnings . . . . . . . . . . . . . . . . . . . . . . . . . . . . . . . . . . . . . . . . . . . | 400,000 | |
| Common Stock — Par . . . . . . . . . . . . . . . . . . . . . . . . . . . . . . . . . . . . . | | 100,000 |
| Additional Paid-in Capital . . . . . . . . . . . . . . . . . . . . . . . . . . . . . . . . | | 300,000 |

Declaration of a stock dividend — recorded using market price of shares to quantify the amounts: $40 × 10,000 shares = $400,000.

The stock dividend relabels a portion of the retained earnings that had been legally available for dividend declarations as a more permanent form of owners' equity. A stock dividend formalizes the fact that some of the funds represented by past earnings have been used for plant expansion, to replace assets at increased prices, or to retire bonds. Such funds are therefore unavailable for cash dividends.

Stock dividends have little economic substance for shareholders: The same ownership is spread over more pieces of paper. If the distributed shares are of the same type as those held before, each shareholder's proportionate interest in the capital of the corporation and proportionate voting power have not changed. Although the book value per common share (total common shareholders' equity divided by number of common shares outstanding) decreases, a proportionately larger number of shares will be held, so the total book value of each shareholder's interest will remain unchanged. The market value per share should decline, but, all else being equal, the total market value of an individual's shares will not change. To describe such a distribution of shares as a ''dividend'' — meaning a distribution of earnings — is potentially misleading. It is, nevertheless, generally accepted terminology.

# Dividend Policy _____

The directors, in considering whether to declare cash dividends, must conclude both (1) that declaring a dividend is legal and (2) that it is financially expedient.

## Statutory Limits on Dividends

State corporation laws limit directors' freedom to declare dividends. These limitations are designed to protect creditors whose interests might be jeopardized because neither shareholders nor directors are liable for debts of the corporation.

Generally, the laws provide that dividends ''may not be paid out of capital'' but must be ''paid out of earnings.'' The wording and interpretation of this rule varies among states. ''Capital'' is usually defined as being equal to the total amount paid in by shareholders. Some states allow dividends to be declared out of the earnings of the current period even though Retained Earnings are negative because of accumulated losses from previous periods.

For most companies, statutory limits have little influence on the accounting for shareholders' equity and dividends. A balance sheet does not spell out all the legal details of amounts available for dividends, but it ought to disclose information necessary for the user to apply the legal rules of the state in which the business is incorporated. For example, state statutes can provide that "treasury shares may be acquired only with retained earnings." In other words, dividends cannot exceed the amount of Retained Earnings reduced by the cost of currently held treasury shares. If treasury shares are acquired under these circumstances, the amount of this limit on dividends should appear in a footnote to the balance sheet.[6]

The statutory requirements for declaring dividends can be met by building up a balance in retained earnings. Such a balance does not mean that a fund of cash is available for the dividends. Managing cash is a specialized problem of corporate finance; cash for dividends must be anticipated just as well as cash for the purchase of equipment, the retirement of debts, and so on. Borrowing from the bank to pay the regular dividend is not unsound if the corporation's financial condition justifies the resulting increase in liabilities.

## Contractual Limits on Dividends

Contracts with bondholders, other lenders, and preferred shareholders often limit dividend payments and thereby compel the retention of earnings. A bond contract may require the retirement of the debt to be made "out of earnings." Such a provision involves curtailing dividends so that the necessary debt service payments, plus any dividends, do not exceed the amount of net income for the period. Such a provision forces the shareholders to increase their investment in the business by limiting the amount of dividends that might otherwise be made available to them. Financial statement notes must disclose significant limitations on dividend declarations.

The notes to a recent financial statement of Sears, Roebuck and Co. contain the following disclosure:

> **Dividend payments** are restricted by several statutory and contractual factors, including:
>
> Certain indentures relating to the long-term debt of Sears, Roebuck and Co., which represent the most restrictive contractual limitation on the payment of dividends, provide that the company cannot take specified actions, including the declaration of cash dividends, which would cause its consolidated unencumbered assets, as defined [in the indentures, not in the annual report], to fall below 150 percent of its consolidated liabilities, as defined. At . . . [year-end], $1.8 billion in retained income [of a total of $9.7 billion of retained earnings] could be paid in dividends to shareholders under the most restrictive indentures. [Dividends for the year were approximately $640 million.]

## Dividends and Corporate Financial Policy

Dividends are generally less than the legal maximum. The directors may allow retained earnings to increase as a matter of corporate financial policy for several of the following reasons:

---

[6]Accounting Principles Board, *Opinion No. 6,* "Status of Accounting Research Bulletins," 1965.

1. Earnings are not reflected in a corresponding increase of available cash.

2. Restricting dividends in prosperous years may permit continued dividend payments in poor years.

3. Funds may be needed for expansion of working capital or plant and equipment.

4. Reducing the amount of borrowings, rather than paying dividends, may seem prudent.

The statement of cash flows helps the reader understand how cash provided by operations and other sources has been used.

**Stabilization of Dividends**  Many corporate shareholders want to receive a predictable cash return. To accommodate such shareholders and to create a general impression of stability, directors commonly attempt to declare a regular dividend. They try to maintain the regular dividend through good years and bad. When earnings and financial policy permit, they may declare extra dividends.

**Financial Policy**  Some shareholders prefer a policy that restricts dividends in order to finance expansion. When dividends are declared, such shareholders use the funds received to acquire an equivalent amount of the new shares issued to finance the expansion. These shareholders would be saved transaction costs if earnings were retained. If the corporation pays dividends, the shareholders must pay income taxes on the receipts before they can be reinvested. If the funds were reinvested directly by the corporation, there would be a deferral of, and possibly a permanent avoidance of, personal income taxes.

Other shareholders may want a steady flow of cash but do not wish to sell a portion of their shares to raise cash. Such shareholders would resent being forced to reinvest in the corporation when expansion is financed through the curtailing of dividends. They may change their investment to corporations that declare regular dividends.

How to finance expansion is a problem of managerial finance, not accounting. Research in finance suggests that, within wide limits, what policy a firm chooses makes little difference as long as it tends to follow the same policy over time. Shareholders who want earnings reinvested can invest in shares of firms that finance expansion with earnings, whereas others who want a steady cash flow can invest in shares of firms that regularly pay dividends.

# Other Changes in Owners' Equity Accounts ───────────
## Stock Splits

*Stock splits* (or, more technically, *splitups*) are like stock dividends. Additional shares of stock are issued to shareholders in proportion to their existing holdings. No additional assets are brought into the firm. In a stock split, the par value of all the stock in the issued class is reduced. A corporation may, for example, have 1,000 shares of $10-par-value stock outstanding, and, by a stock split, exchange those shares for 2,000 shares of $5-par-value stock (a two-for-one split), or 4,000 shares of $2.50-par-value stock (a four-for-one split), or any number of shares of no-par stock. If the shares outstanding have no par value, the shareholders keep the existing certificates and receive the new ones.

A stock split generally does not require a journal entry. The amount of retained earnings is not reduced. The amount shown in the capital stock account represents a larger number of shares. Of course, the additional number of shares held by each shareholder must be recorded in the subsidiary capital stock records. Sometimes stock splits are accounted for as stock dividends with a transfer from Retained Earnings to the Contributed Capital account. If so, the amounts are based on the market value of the shares on the date of the split. There is no easy way to distinguish stock splits from stock dividends. Usually small percentage distributions are treated as stock dividends and larger ones as stock splits.

A stock split (or a stock dividend) usually reduces the market value per share, all other factors remaining constant, in inverse proportion to the split (or dividend). Thus a two-for-one split could be expected to result in a 50 percent reduction in the market price per share. Therefore, stock splits have usually been used to keep the market prices per share from rising to a price level unacceptable to management. For example, the board of directors might think that a market price of $30 to $40 is an effective trading range for its stock. (This is a purely subjective estimate, and it is almost never supported by convincing evidence.) If the share prices have risen to $60 in the market, the board of directors may declare a two-for-one split. The only certain result of stock splits and dividends is increased record-keeping costs. Stock splits and stock dividends are used primarily by corporations whose stocks are currently (or soon to be) traded in a public market.

## Stock Options

Often, as part of employee compensation plans, employees are granted options to purchase shares in their company. *Stock options* present two kinds of accounting problems: (1) recording the granting of the option and (2) recording its exercise or lapse.

**Granting the Option**  The generally accepted accounting treatment[7] for options usually results in no entry being made at the time the options are granted. The *exercise price* of an option is the price the option holder will have to pay to acquire a share of stock. If the exercise price is equal to the market price of the stock on the date the option is granted, the granting of the option is not viewed as resulting in compensation to the employee or expense to the employer, and no entry is made. If the exercise price is less than the market price of the stock on the date of the grant, compensation expense may have to be recognized under some circumstances, which may have adverse income tax consequences.

**Exercise or Lapse**  When the option is exercised, the conventional entry simply treats the transaction as an issue of shares at the option price.

---

[7]Accounting Principles Board, *Opinion No. 25*, ''Accounting for Stock Issued to Employees,'' 1972.

| Cash . . . . . . . . . . . . . . . . . . . . . . . . . . . . . . . . . . . . . . . . . . . . . . . . . . . . . . . . . | 35,000 | |
|---|---|---|
| Common Shares—Par . . . . . . . . . . . . . . . . . . . . . . . . . . . . . . . . . . . | | 5,000 |
| Additional Paid-in Capital . . . . . . . . . . . . . . . . . . . . . . . . . . . . . . . . . | | 30,000 |

To record issue of 1,000 shares of $5-par-value stock upon exercise
of options and receipt of $35,000 cash.

If the option lapses or expires without being exercised, no entry is required.

**Disclosure of Options**   Generally accepted accounting principles require the terms
of options granted, outstanding, and exercised during a period to be disclosed in text
or notes accompanying the financial statements. Exhibit 12.3 illustrates the typical
disclosure on stock options for the General Products Company.

## Stock Rights and Warrants

Opportunities to buy shares of stock may be granted through *stock rights* and *stock
warrants*.

**Stock Rights**   Stock rights are similar to stock options, but differ in some respects.
Stock options are granted to employees, are nontransferable, and are a form of
compensation. In contrast, stock rights are granted to current shareholders and can
usually be traded in public markets. They are generally exercisable for only a
limited time but occasionally are good indefinitely. Stock rights are ordinarily associated with attempts to raise new capital for a firm from current shareholders.
Journal entries are not necessary when stock rights are granted to current shareholders. When the rights are exercised, the entry is like the one to record the issue of
new shares at the price paid.

**Stock Warrants**   Stock warrants are issued to the general investing public for cash.
They are exercisable for a limited period in most cases. Assume that a corporation

**Exhibit 12.3** ——————————————————————————————————
**GENERAL PRODUCTS COMPANY**
Disclosure of Employee Stock Options

| Stock Options | Shares Subject to Option | Average per Share | |
|---|---|---|---|
| | | Option Price | Market Price |
| Balance at December 31, Year 1 . . . . . . | 2,388,931 | $45 | $72 |
| Options Granted . . . . . . . . . . . . . . . . . . . . | 475,286 | 77 | 77 |
| Options Exercised . . . . . . . . . . . . . . . . . . | (297,244) | 42 | 76 |
| Options Terminated . . . . . . . . . . . . . . . . . | (90,062) | 45 | — |
| Balance at December 31, Year 2 . . . . . . | 2,476,911 | 50 | 83 |
| Options Granted . . . . . . . . . . . . . . . . . . . . | 554,965 | 75 | 75 |
| Options Exercised . . . . . . . . . . . . . . . . . . | (273,569) | 42 | 74 |
| Options Terminated . . . . . . . . . . . . . . . . . | (58,307) | 52 | — |
| Balance at December 31, Year 3 . . . . . . | 2,700,000 | 54 | 77 |

issues warrants for $15,000 cash. The holders are allowed to purchase 10,000 shares for $20 each. The entry would be as follows:

| | | |
|---|---|---|
| Cash . . . . . . . . . . . . . . . . . . . . . . . . . . . . . . . . . . . . . . . . . . . . . . . . . . | 15,000 | |
|    Common Stock Warrants . . . . . . . . . . . . . . . . . . . . . . . . . . . . . . . . . | | 15,000 |

To record issue of warrants to the public. The Common Stock Warrants account would normally be included with Additional Paid-in Capital for balance sheet presentation.

When the rights contained in these warrants are exercised and 10,000 shares of $5-par-value common stock are issued in exchange for the warrants plus $200,000, the entry would be as follows:

| | | |
|---|---|---|
| Cash . . . . . . . . . . . . . . . . . . . . . . . . . . . . . . . . . . . . . . . . . . . . . . . . . . | 200,000 | |
| Common Stock Warrants . . . . . . . . . . . . . . . . . . . . . . . . . . . . . . . . . | 15,000 | |
|    Common Stock — Par Value . . . . . . . . . . . . . . . . . . . . . . . . . . . . . . | | 50,000 |
|    Additional Paid-in Capital . . . . . . . . . . . . . . . . . . . . . . . . . . . . . . . | | 165,000 |

To record the issue of 10,000 shares for $200,000 cash and the redemption of warrants. (The amount originally received for the warrants is transferred to Additional Paid-in Capital.)

If the warrants expire without having been exercised, the entry would be as follows:

| | | |
|---|---|---|
| Common Stock Warrants . . . . . . . . . . . . . . . . . . . . . . . . . . . . . . . . . | 15,000 | |
|    Additional Paid-in Capital . . . . . . . . . . . . . . . . . . . . . . . . . . . . . . . | | 15,000 |

To record expiration of common stock warrants and the transfer to permanent contributed capital.

## Convertible Bonds

Typically, *convertible bonds* are semiannual coupon bonds like the ones discussed in Chapter 10 — with one added feature. The holder of the bond can *convert* the bond into shares of stock. The bond indenture specifies the number of shares to be received when the bond is converted into stock, the dates when conversion can occur, and other details. Convertible bonds are usually callable.

Investors often find convertible bonds attractive. The bond's owner is promised a regular interest payment. In addition, should the company's business be so successful that its share price rises on the stock market, the holder of the bond can convert the investment from debt into equity; the creditor has become an owner and can share in the good fortune of the company.[8] Of course, an investor does not get

_____

[8]In recent years, the brokers' commission fees for trading convertible bonds have often been less than those for comparable dollar amounts of trades in the underlying common shares.

something for nothing. Because of the potential participation in the earnings of the company once the bonds are converted into common shares, an investor in the bonds must accept a lower interest rate than would be received if the bonds were not convertible into stock. From the company's point of view, convertible bonds allow borrowing at lower rates of interest than is required on ordinary debt, but the company must promise to give up an equity interest if the bonds are converted. The purchaser of the convertible bond is paying something for the option to acquire common stock later. Thus a portion of the proceeds from the issue of convertible bonds actually represents a form of capital contribution, even though it is not so recorded.

**Issue of Convertible Bonds**  Suppose, for example, that the Johnson Company's credit rating would allow it to issue $100,000 of ordinary 10-year, 14-percent semiannual coupon bonds at par. The firm prefers to issue convertible bonds with a lower coupon rate. Assume that Johnson Company issues at par $100,000 of 10-year, 10-percent semiannual coupon bonds, but each $1,000 bond is convertible into 50 shares of Johnson Company $5-par-value common stock. (The entire issue is convertible into 5,000 shares.) The following entry is required:

| | | |
|---|---|---|
| Cash . . . . . . . . . . . . . . . . . . . . . . . . . . . . . . . . . . . . . . . . . . . . . . . . . . . . . . . | 100,000 | |
|    Convertible Bonds Payable . . . . . . . . . . . . . . . . . . . . . . . . . . . . . . . . . . | | 100,000 |
| Issue of convertible bonds at par. | | |

This entry effectively treats convertible bonds just like ordinary, nonconvertible bonds, and it records the value of the conversion feature at zero. (Generally accepted accounting principles do recognize the potential issue of common stock implied by the conversion feature in the calculations of earnings-per-share figures.)

**Recognizing the Value of the Conversion Feature Is Not Permitted**  Appendix Table 5 (for 10-percent coupon bonds) indicates that 10-percent, 10-year semiannual (nonconvertible) coupon bonds sell for about 79 percent of par when the market rate of interest is 14 percent. Thus, if the 10 percent convertible bonds can be issued at par, the conversion feature must be worth about 21 ($= 100 - 79$) percent of par. Then 21 percent of the proceeds from the bond issue actually would be a capital contribution by the bond buyers for the right to acquire common stock later. The entry to record the substance of the issue of these 10-percent convertible bonds at par would be as follows:

| | | |
|---|---|---|
| Cash . . . . . . . . . . . . . . . . . . . . . . . . . . . . . . . . . . . . . . . . . . . . . . . . . . . . . . | 100,000 | |
|    Convertible Bonds Payable . . . . . . . . . . . . . . . . . . . . . . . . . . . . . . . . . . | | 79,000 |
|    Additional Paid-in Capital . . . . . . . . . . . . . . . . . . . . . . . . . . . . . . . . . . . | | 21,000 |
| Issue of 10-percent semiannual coupon convertible bonds at a time when ordinary 10-percent bonds could be issued for 79 percent of par. | | |

Notice that the calculation of the amounts for this entry requires knowing the proceeds of an issue of nonconvertible bonds that are otherwise similar to the convertible bonds. Because auditors often believe that they are unable to ascertain this information in a reasonably objective manner, generally acceptable accounting principles do not allow the previous journal entry.[9] The entry would be simply a debit to Cash and a credit to Convertible Bonds Payable for $100,000.

**Conversion of Bonds**   Assume that the common stock of the Johnson Company increases in the market to $30 a share so that one $1,000 bond, which is convertible into 50 shares, can be converted into shares with a market value of $1,500. If the entire convertible issue was converted into common shares at this time, 5,000 shares of $5-par-value stock would be issued on conversion.

The usual entry to record the conversion of bonds into shares ignores current market prices in the interest of simplicity and merely shows the swap of shares for bonds at their book value.

| | | |
|---|---|---|
| Convertible Bonds Payable . . . . . . . . . . . . . . . . . . . . . . . . . . . . . . . . . . . . | 100,000 | |
|    Common Shares—$5 Par. . . . . . . . . . . . . . . . . . . . . . . . . . . . . . . . . . | | 25,000 |
|    Additional Paid-in Capital . . . . . . . . . . . . . . . . . . . . . . . . . . . . . . . . . | | 75,000 |
| To record conversion of 100 convertible bonds with book value of $100,000 into 5,000 shares of $5-par-value stock. | | |

An allowable alternative treatment recognizes that market prices provide information useful in quantifying the market value of the shares issued. Under the alternative treatment, when the market price of a share is $30 and the fair market value of the 5,000 shares issued on conversion is $150,000, the journal entry made would be as follows:

| | | |
|---|---|---|
| Convertible Bonds Payable . . . . . . . . . . . . . . . . . . . . . . . . . . . . . . . . . . . . | 100,000 | |
| Loss on Conversion of Bonds . . . . . . . . . . . . . . . . . . . . . . . . . . . . . . . . | 50,000 | |
|    Common Shares—$5 Par. . . . . . . . . . . . . . . . . . . . . . . . . . . . . . . . . . | | 25,000 |
|    Additional Paid-in Capital . . . . . . . . . . . . . . . . . . . . . . . . . . . . . . . . . | | 125,000 |
| To record conversion of 100 convertible bonds into 5,000 shares of $5-par-value stock at a time when the market price is $30 per share. | | |

The alternative entry results in the same total owners' equity: smaller retained earnings (because the Loss on Conversion of Bonds will reduce current net income and thus Retained Earnings) but larger contributed capital. It is equivalent to the following two entries:

_____

[9]Accounting Principles Board, *Opinion No. 14*, ''Accounting for Convertible Debt and Debt Issued with Stock Purchase Warrants,'' 1969. The APB stated that, in reaching its conclusions, less weight was given to the practical difficulties than to some other considerations, which were spelled out in the *Opinion*. The dissent to this *Opinion*, expressed by several members of the Board, indicated preference for the treatment recognizing the implied capital contribution.

| | | |
|---|---|---|
| Cash ............................................... | 150,000 | |
| Common Shares—$5 Par................................. | | 25,000 |
| Additional Paid-in Capital .................................. | | 125,000 |
| To record issue of 5,000 shares of $5-par-value stock at $30 per share. | | |
| | | |
| Convertible Bonds Payable ................................. | 100,000 | |
| Loss on Retirement of Bonds .............................. | 50,000 | |
| Cash ..................................................... | | 150,000 |
| Retirement by purchase for $150,000 of 100 convertible bonds carried on the books at $100,000. | | |

## Potential Dilution of Earnings per Share

Chapter 6 explained that earnings per share of common stock is conventionally calculated by dividing net income attributable to the common shareholders by the weighted-average number of shares of common stock outstanding during the period. When a firm has outstanding securities that, if exchanged for common stock, would decrease earnings per share as conventionally calculated, the earnings-per-share calculations become somewhat more complicated. Stock options, stock rights, warrants, and convertible bonds all have the potential of reducing earnings per share and must be taken into account in calculating earnings per share. These complications are discussed in intermediate accounting books, but are introduced in Problem 41 at the end of this chapter.

# Reported Income and Retained Earnings Adjustments _____

## The Income Statement Reconsidered

What is the purpose of the income statement? It is *not* primarily to show net income for the period. The reader of the financial statements can generally ascertain net income by subtracting the beginning balance of Retained Earnings from its ending balance and adding dividends. The purpose of the income statement is to show the *causes* of income.[10] Then a company's performance can be compared with other companies or with itself over time, and more informed projections can be made about the future.

To help the reader understand the causes of income, generally accepted accounting principles require the separate reporting of various income components:

1. Income from continuing operations.

2. Income from operations to be discontinued.

_____

[10]Parallel statements can be made about the statement of cash flows. The purpose of the statement of cash flows is *not* primarily to report the change in cash for the period. That can be deduced by subtracting the balance in the Cash account at the start of the period from that at the end of the period. The purpose is to report the *causes* of the changes in the Cash account.

3. Gain or loss from disposal of discontinued operations.

4. Income from extraordinary items.

5. Adjustments to income resulting from changes in accounting principles.

Items 2 and 3 appear on the income statement under the combined heading of "Discontinued Operations." The FASB has defined criteria for the classification of items into these five categories.

Analysis of financial statements often focuses on income from continuing operations in making projections and buy/sell recommendations or in computing price/earnings ratios. As a result, some managements have attempted to report "good" news in the continuing operations section of the income statement and "bad" news elsewhere. For example, before Accounting Principles Board *Opinion No. 30,* issued in 1973, prescribed rules for classifying an item as extraordinary, most extraordinary items found in published income statements were losses ("bad news"). Managements found ways to justify including nearly all gains ("good news") in income before extraordinary items.

The FASB continues to refine the exceptional cases for items to be excluded from income from continuing operations in order to make the income statement more useful to readers and less susceptible to management whim.

## Direct Adjustments to Retained Earnings

Most items that cause the total of retained earnings to change during a period result from transactions reported in the income statement for that period. The major exception to this general rule is dividend declarations. Dividend declarations are distributions that reduce the balance in the Retained Earnings account but do not affect reported income. Two other exceptions to the general rule that changes in retained earnings arise from current operations and other current transactions are the *correction of errors* and *prior-period adjustments*.

**Correction of Errors**  Errors result from such actions as miscounting inventories, arithmetic mistakes, and misapplications of accounting principles. Such errors, if they are material, are corrected with direct debits or credits to the Retained Earnings account. Assume, for example, that merchandise inventory is discovered to be $10,000 less than was reported at the end of the previous period and that cost of goods sold was computed last period using a periodic inventory method, as follows:

$$\frac{\text{Cost of}}{\text{Goods Sold}} = \frac{\text{Beginning}}{\text{Inventory}} + \text{Purchases} - \frac{\text{Ending}}{\text{Inventory}}.$$

The following entry (ignoring income tax effects) would be made this period:

| | | |
|---|---|---|
| Retained Earnings . . . . . . . . . . . . . . . . . . . . . . . . . . . . . . . . . . . . . . . . . . . . . . . | 10,000 | |
|    Merchandise Inventory . . . . . . . . . . . . . . . . . . . . . . . . . . . . . . . . . . . . . . . . | | 10,000 |
| Correction of inventory error. Last period's cost of goods sold was too small; income was overstated. | | |

**Prior-Period Adjustments**   Assume that the Internal Revenue Service disallowed certain deductions on the firm's tax return of 4 years ago, increasing income tax expense for that year and reducing income for that year. Two treatments of this and similar events are worth considering. Some accountants believe that the income statement for the current period will be more useful if the resulting decrease in Retained Earnings is shown only in the statement reconciling the changes in retained earnings and not in the current income statement. They argue that the time-series trend in reported income will be more meaningful if net income for the prior period is adjusted and the current period's income is unaffected. Other accountants believe that users of financial statements may overlook disclosures of this sort that do not appear in the current income statement, which they think is the most closely studied of the financial statements. These accountants believe that all revenues, gains, expenses, and losses relating to the earnings activity of a firm should be reported in current and future income statements. If a loss is treated as a direct adjustment of retained earnings at the beginning of the period, it will not have appeared in the income statement originally issued for any period.

The FASB requires the latter treatment: Nearly "all items of profit and loss recognized during a period, including accruals of estimated losses from loss contingencies, shall be included in the determination of net income for that period."[11] The rarely occurring exceptions relate to income tax loss carryforwards of purchased subsidiaries.

**New Information about Accounting Estimates Does Not Result in Direct Adjustments of Retained Earnings**   New information often becomes available that helps refine estimates required to apply accounting principles, such as the amount of uncollectible accounts or the service lives of depreciable assets. Earlier chapters have pointed out that this information is incorporated by current and future adjustments to reported revenues and expenses, not by direct adjustments to retained earnings. Refer, for example, to Figure 9.3, which illustrates the use of information about a long-term asset's service life. Although in principle the accounting rules may require an adjustment of previously reported expenses with direct adjustments of the Retained Earnings account, the FASB generally takes the position that items affecting retained earnings should appear in the income statement for some current or future period. Otherwise, management might be tempted to be optimistic in current reporting, with later direct reductions in the Retained Earnings account.

# Disclosure of Changes in Owners' Equity ———————————

The changes in all owners' equity accounts must be explained in the annual reports to shareholders.[12] As previous chapters have pointed out, the reconciliation of retained earnings may appear in the balance sheet, in a statement of income and retained earnings, or in a separate statement.

---

[11]Financial Accounting Standards Board, *Statement of Financial Accounting Standards No. 16*, "Prior Period Adjustments," 1977, par. 10.

[12]Accounting Principles Board, *Opinion No. 12*, "Omnibus Opinion — 1967," 1967.

Exhibit 12.4 _____

MICHIGAN COMPANY
Consolidated Statement of Shareholders' Equity
(all dollar amounts in millions)

| Line Number[a] | | Capital Stock | | Capital in Excess of Par Value of Shares | Retained Earnings | Treasury Shares | Total Share-holders' Equity |
|---|---|---|---|---|---|---|---|
| | | Shares | Amount | | | | |
| | Balance, January 1, Year 1 ...... | 101.5 | $253.7 | $379.5 | $5,328.1 | $(56.5) | $5,904.8 |
| (1) | Net Income ..................... | | | | 906.5 | | 906.5 |
| (2) | Cash Dividends.................. | | | | (317.1) | | (317.1) |
| (3) | Common Stock Issued under Certain Employee Stock Plans........... | 0.2 | 0.5 | 9.9 | | | 10.4 |
| (4) | Conversion of Debentures ........ | | | 0.6 | | 10.2 | 10.8 |
| (5) | Capital Stock Retired ............. | (2.5) | (6.2) | (9.5) | (140.9) | | (156.6) |
| | Balance, December 31, Year 1 .... | 99.2 | 248.0 | $380.5 | $5,776.6 | $(46.3) | $6,358.8 |
| (1) | Net Income ..................... | | | | 360.9 | | 360.9 |
| (2) | Cash Dividends.................. | | | | (298.1) | | (298.1) |
| (3) | Common Stock Issued under Certain Employee Stock Plans........... | 0.1 | 0.2 | 1.8 | | | 2.0 |
| (4) | Conversion of Debentures ........ | | | 1.4 | | 30.6 | 32.0 |
| (5) | Capital Stock Retired ............. | (5.7) | (14.2) | (21.8) | (194.0) | | (230.0) |
| | Balance, December 31, Year 2 .... | 93.6 | $234.0 | $361.9 | $5,645.4 | $(15.7) | $6,225.6 |

[a]This caption and the line numbers do not appear on the original statement. The line numbers correspond to the journal entries in Exhibit 12.5.

A recent annual report contained the Consolidated Statement of Shareholders' Equity reproduced as Exhibit 12.4 for the Michigan Company. The 2-year comparative statement shows separate columns for capital stock at par, capital contributed in excess of par value, retained earnings, treasury shares, and total shareholders' equity. The statement shows opening balances, net income, cash dividends, stock issued under employee option plans, capital stock retired, and capital stock issued on conversion of convertible bonds.

## Journal Entries for Changes in Owners' Equity

To review the accounting for owners' equity, Exhibit 12.5 reconstructs the journal entries made for Year 1 and Year 2 that resulted in the changes in owners' equity disclosed in Exhibit 12.4. The amounts in the entries in Exhibit 12.5 represent millions of dollars, and the journal entries are numbered in the same way as the lines in Exhibit 12.4 to which they apply.

## Summary _____

Accounting for owners' equity in a corporation is based on the premise that there should be a separate account for each source of capital contributed by owners. The sources of capital from shareholders include the following:

**Exhibit 12.5** ⎯⎯⎯⎯⎯⎯⎯⎯⎯⎯⎯⎯⎯⎯⎯⎯⎯⎯⎯⎯⎯⎯⎯⎯⎯⎯⎯⎯⎯
**MICHIGAN COMPANY**
**Journal Entries Illustrating Transactions Involving**
**Owners' Equity, Years 1 and 2**
**(all dollar amounts in millions)**

| Entry and Explanation | Year 1 | | Year 2 | |
|---|---|---|---|---|
| (1) Income Summary ................................... | 906.5 | | 360.9 | |
| Retained Earnings ............................... | | 906.5 | | 360.9 |
| Net income for the year, recorded assuming that an Income Summary account is used. This entry in effect closes all temporary revenue and expense accounts, with the credit balance being reported as income for the year. | | | | |
| (2) Retained Earnings ................................... | 317.1 | | 298.1 | |
| Cash (or Dividends Payable) ...................... | | 317.1 | | 298.1 |
| Cash dividends declared. | | | | |
| (3) Cash .......................................... | 10.4 | | 2.0 | |
| Capital Stock ..................................... | | 0.5 | | 0.2 |
| Capital Account in Excess of Par Value of Stock ...... | | 9.9 | | 1.8 |
| Common stock issued under certain employee stock plans. | | | | |
| (4) Convertible Debentures (Bonds) ...................... | 10.8 | | 32.0 | |
| Treasury Stock.................................... | | 10.2 | | 30.6 |
| Capital Account in Excess of Par Value of Stock ...... | | 0.6 | | 1.4 |
| Common stock issued on conversion of convertible debentures (bonds). The shares "issued" on conversion were shares reissued from a block of treasury shares that had cost $10.2 (for Year 1) and $30.6 (for Year 2). | | | | |
| (5) Capital Stock ....................................... | 6.2 | | 14.2 | |
| Capital Account in Excess of Par Value of Stock ........ | 9.5 | | 21.8 | |
| Earnings Retained for Use in the Business ............. | 140.9 | | 194.0 | |
| Cash ......................................... | | 156.6 | | 230.0 |
| Retirement of capital stock acquired for cash. When shares are acquired for the treasury, the debit is usually to a Treasury Stock account, shown as a contra to all of shareholders' equity. In this case, the shares are "retired," so the specific amounts for Capital Account in Excess of Par Value and Earnings Retained for Use in the Business corresponding to these shares are identified. The debits are to these accounts and to the Capital Stock account, rather than to a single contra account. | | | | |

1. Receipts from issues of stock at par or stated value.

2. Receipts in excess of par or stated value of stock issues.

3. Earnings retentions.

Most changes in retained earnings are reported in the income statement. Dividend declarations are the major exception.

# Problem 1 for Self-Study ⎯⎯⎯⎯⎯⎯⎯⎯⎯⎯⎯⎯⎯⎯⎯⎯⎯⎯⎯⎯⎯

Exhibit 12.6 shows the owners' equity accounts for Lorla Corporation at the end of Year 1 and Year 2. During Year 2, Lorla Corporation issued new shares of stock for $40 a share and reacquired 60 shares for the treasury at $42 per share. Still later in

Exhibit 12.6 _____

**LORLA CORPORATION**
Owners' Equity Accounts
(Problem 1 for Self-Study)

| | December 31 | |
| --- | ---: | ---: |
| | Year 1 | Year 2 |
| Common Stock ($5 par value) ............................. | $ 5,000 | $ 5,500 |
| Additional Paid-in Capital ................................... | 30,000 | 33,620 |
| Net Unrealized Loss on Investments in Marketable Equity Securities ......................................... | (900) | (800) |
| Retained Earnings ......................................... | 60,000 | 67,300 |
| | $94,100 | $105,620 |
| Less Cost of Treasury Shares ............................. | — | (840) |
| Total Owners' Equity ..................................... | $94,100 | $104,780 |

the year, it sold some of the treasury shares. Revenues for Year 2 were $90,000, and net income was $10,000.

Reconstruct all of the transactions involving owners' equity accounts for Year 2, and show the journal entries for those transactions.

## Suggested Solution

| | | |
| --- | ---: | ---: |
| Cash ........................................................ | 4,000 | |
|     Common Stock ($5 par value) ........................... | | 500 |
|     Additional Paid-in Capital ................................. | | 3,500 |

Because the Common Stock account went up by $500 and the par value is $5 per share, 100 shares (= $500/$5 per share) must have been issued. The issue price was $40 per share; hence the cash raised was $4,000 (= $40 × 100 shares).

| | | |
| --- | ---: | ---: |
| Treasury Shares ........................................... | 2,520 | |
|     Cash ................................................... | | 2,520 |

Acquisition of 60 shares for the treasury at $42 per share; 60 × $42 = $2,520.

| | | |
| --- | ---: | ---: |
| Cash ........................................................ | 1,800 | |
|     Treasury Shares ........................................ | | 1,680 |
|     Additional Paid-in Capital ................................. | | 120 |

Because the year-end balance in the treasury shares account is $840, 20 shares (= $840/$42 per share) must remain in the treasury. Thus 40 (= 60 − 20) shares were resold. Because the year-end Additional Paid-in Capital account is $120 larger [= $33,620 − ($30,000 + $3,500)] than is explained by the issue of new shares, a "gain" of $120 must have been realized on the resale of the shares from the treasury. Because 40 shares were resold, the total "gain" was $120, and the "gain" per share must have been $3 (= $120/40 shares). Thus the total resale price per share must have been $45 (= $42 + $3). Cash raised must have been $1,800 = $45 per share × 40 shares.

| | | |
| --- | ---: | ---: |
| Allowance for Excess of Cost over Market Value of Investments in Marketable Equity Securities .................. | 100 | |
|     Recovery of Unrealized Loss on Investment in Marketable Equity Securities ............................. | | 100 |

Market value of the portfolio of investments in marketable equity securities has increased by $100 during the year.

| | | |
|---|---|---|
| Revenue Accounts........................................... | 90,000 | |
| Expense Accounts......................................... | | 80,000 |
| Retained Earnings......................................... | | 10,000 |

Closing entries for revenue and expense accounts, given that revenues were $90,000 and net income was $10,000 for the year.

| | | |
|---|---|---|
| Retained Earnings.......................................... | 2,700 | |
| Dividends Payable........................................ | | 2,700 |

The Retained Earnings account increased by only $7,300 for the year. Dividends must have been $10,000 − $7,300 = $2,700.

# Problem 2 for Self-Study ————————————————————

Patell Company owns 100,000 shares of the General Electric Company, which it has held as an investment. The shares had cost $2 million, $20 each, and now have a fair market value of $50 each. Patell Company declares a dividend in kind, distributing the shares of the General Electric Company to its shareholders.

**a.** Prepare the journal entry to record the declaration. Under generally accepted accounting principles, dividends in kind are recorded at the market value, not the cost, of the assets distributed.

**b.** Prepare a journal entry that would record the dividend using the cost of the shares. This treatment is not generally acceptable.

**c.** Compare the effects on net income, retained earnings, and total owners' equity of the two treatments.

## Suggested Solution

**a.**

| | | |
|---|---|---|
| Retained Earnings....................................... | 5,000,000 | |
| Investments.......................................... | | 2,000,000 |
| Gain on Disposition of Investments .................... | | 3,000,000 |

The gain appears on the income statement and is closed to Retained Earnings.

**b.**

| | | |
|---|---|---|
| Retained Earnings....................................... | 2,000,000 | |
| Investments.......................................... | | 2,000,000 |

**c.** Net income is larger when the dividend is recorded at fair market value. In both cases, Retained Earnings and total owners' equity decline by $2 million. The difference is that in the former treatment, income is increased by $3 million, the holding gain on the shares, which offsets the larger debit to retained earnings for the larger amount of dividend recognized.

# Questions, Exercises, Problems, and Cases _____

## Questions

**1.** Review the meaning of the following concepts or terms discussed in this chapter.

**a.** Corporation.
**b.** Corporate charter.
**c.** Corporate bylaws.
**d.** Capital stock, common shares, preferred shares.
**e.** Cumulative preferred shares.
**f.** Callable preferred shares.
**g.** Convertible preferred shares.
**h.** Par or stated value.
**i.** Additional paid-in capital.

**j.** Treasury shares.
**k.** Earnings are not cash.
**l.** Stock dividend.
**m.** Stock split.
**n.** Stock option.
**o.** Stock right.
**p.** Stock warrant.
**q.** Convertible bond.
**r.** Correction of error.
**s.** Prior-period adjustment.

**2.** Under what circumstances would you expect par value stock to be issued at a price in excess of par? What is the entry to record such an issue?

**3.** A construction corporation is attempting to borrow money on a note secured by some of its property. A bank agrees to accept the note, provided that the president of the corporation will personally endorse it. What is the point of this requirement?

**4.** "Par value of preferred stock is frequently a significant figure, but par value of common stock possesses little significance." Why may par value of preferred stock be significant?

**5.** Why is the amount in the Retained Earnings account for a profitable, growing company that has been in business for several decades unlikely to be of much value for predicting future dividend declarations?

**6.** What is treasury stock? How is it reported on the balance sheet?

**7.** A certain corporation retained almost all of its earnings, only rarely paying a cash dividend. When some of the shareholders objected, the reply of the president was "Why do you want cash dividends? You would just have to go to the trouble of reinvesting them. Where can you possibly find a better investment than our own company?" Comment.

**8.** Compare the position of a shareholder who receives a cash dividend with that of one who receives a stock dividend.

**9.** At the annual shareholders' meeting, the president of the Santa Cris Corporation made the following statement: "The net income for the year, after taxes, was $1,096,000. The directors have decided that the corporation can afford to distribute only $500,000 as a cash dividend." Are the two sentences of this statement compatible?

**10.** The text says, "Convertible bonds are usually callable." The call feature is included so that the issuer can force conversion of the bonds. Explain.

**11.** Are accumulated, but unpaid, dividends to preferred shareholders, which must be paid before dividends can be declared on common shares, liabilities? Explain.

**12.** What are prior-period adjustments? Why do some accountants think that GAAP should only rarely allow them?

**13.** Interest on bonds is deductible for tax purposes. Dividends on preferred stock issues are not. Assume that a company can raise $100 million either by issuing bonds promising 12 percent annual interest or by issuing preferred shares, convertible into common stock shares promising 12 percent annual dividends. The firm expects to continue to have income (in excess of all interest payments) taxable at the combined rate of 40 percent per year.

   **a.** Which of the two financing methods will show a larger income available for common shares?

   **b.** Why does this book suggest that, in spite of the answer to part **a**, one financing method is not necessarily preferred to the other?

## Exercises

**14.** *Effects of transactions involving owners' equity.* Indicate whether each of the following statements is true or false and justify your response. Ignore the effects of income taxes.

   **a.** Cash dividends reduce the book value per share of capital stock.

   **b.** A stock dividend does not affect the Retained Earnings account.

   **c.** Investing 50 percent of net income in government bonds has no effect on the amount legally available for dividends.

   **d.** Stock dividends reduce the book value per share of capital stock.

   **e.** The declaration of a cash dividend does not reduce the amount of the shareholders' equity.

   **f.** The distribution of a stock dividend tends to reduce the market value per share of capital stock.

   **g.** A stock split generally does not affect the Retained Earnings account.

   **h.** A stock dividend declaration is usually accompanied by a reduction in par or stated value per share.

**15.** *Effects of transactions on Retained Earnings and owners' equity.* Indicate the effect of each of the following transactions on (1) the balance in the Retained Earnings account and (2) the total shareholders' equity.

   **a.** Bonds are issued at a discount.

   **b.** A check is written to the Internal Revenue Service for additional income taxes levied on past years' income (no previous entry).

   **c.** A stock split is voted by the directors. The par value per share is reduced from $20 to $5, and each shareholder is given four new shares in exchange for each old share.

   **d.** The manager is voted a bonus of $35,000 by the directors.

   **e.** Notes payable in the face amount of $50,000 are paid by check.

   **f.** A dividend in preferred stock is issued to common shareholders (no previous entry).

   **g.** Securities held as a long-term investment are sold at book value.

   **h.** A building site is received by the company as a donation from the local chamber of commerce.

   **i.** A building is sold for less than its book value.

**16.** *Journal entries for transactions involving owners' equity.* Present the journal entries for each of the following transactions. These transactions do not relate to the same set of records.

**a.** The shares of no-par stock of a corporation are selling on the market at $100 a share. To bring the market value down to a "more popular" figure, the board of directors votes to issue four shares to shareholders in exchange for each share already held by them. The shares are issued.

**b.** The treasurer of the corporation reports that cash on hand exceeds normal requirements by $300,000. Pending a decision by the board of directors on the final disposition of the funds, investments in marketable securities in the amount of $299,600 are made.

**c.** The net income for the year is $150,000. The directors vote to issue 1,000 shares of 10 percent, $100-par-value preferred stock as a stock dividend on the 2,500 shares of no-par common stock outstanding. The preferred's market price is $102 a share. The common's market price is $50 a share.

**d.** After the books are closed and the financial statements are issued, it is discovered that an arithmetic error was made in calculating depreciation on office equipment for the preceding period. The depreciation expense was $8,000 too large.

**17.** *Analyzing changes in owners' equity accounts.* The comparative balance sheet of the Forty-Misty Company shows the following data:

|  | Dec. 31, Year 1 | Dec. 31, Year 2 |
|---|---|---|
| Common Stock...................................... | $1,200,000 | $1,320,000 |
| Retained Earnings .................................. | 460,000 | 400,000 |
| Total Shareholders' Equity .......................... | $1,660,000 | $1,720,000 |

During Year 2, common shareholders received $60,000 in cash dividends and $120,000 in stock dividends. A refund on Year 0 taxes of $30,000 was received on March 1, Year 2, and was credited directly to Retained Earnings. A loss on retirement of plant assets of $5,600 occurred during the year and was debited directly to Retained Earnings.

**a.** What net income was reported for Year 2, after the accounting was done as described?

**b.** What net income should actually have been reported for Year 2? Show your calculations.

**18.** *Analyzing changes in owners' equity accounts.* The comparative balance sheet of the Royal Corporation shows the following information:

|  | Dec. 31, Year 1 | Dec. 31, Year 2 |
|---|---|---|
| Preferred Stock (6 percent) .......................... | $ 750,000 | $ 600,000 |
| Common Stock...................................... | 1,400,000 | 1,550,000 |
| Retained Earnings .................................. | 324,000 | 372,000 |
| Total Shareholders' Equity .......................... | $2,474,000 | $2,522,000 |

During Year 2, stock dividends of $150,000 were issued to common shareholders; in addition, common shareholders received $70,000 in cash dividends. The preferred shareholders received $36,000 in cash dividends. On July 1, Year 2, preferred stock with a par value of $150,000 was called at 104; that is, $156,000 was paid to retire the shares. The call premium was debited to the Common Stock account.

What net income was reported to shareholders for Year 2?

19. *Journal entries for transactions involving owners' equity.* Give journal entries for the following transactions.

   a.   Outstanding shares of stock are acquired by the issuing corporation for its treasury at a cost of $100,000.

   b.   Dividends of $220,000 are declared on preferred stock.

   c.   A dividend is paid to common shareholders consisting of shares of preferred stock in the same corporation with a par value of $200,000.

   d.   A dividend is paid to common shareholders consisting of shares of no-par common stock in the same corporation. The amount assigned to these shares of stock is $600,000.

   e.   The building is mortgaged for $100,000, and this amount is distributed to the common shareholders as a cash dividend.

20. *Journal entries for transactions involving owners' equity and other accounts.* Give journal entries, if required, for the following transactions, which are unrelated unless otherwise specified:

   a.   The regular quarterly dividend is declared on the 10-percent, $100-par-value preferred stock. There are 10,000 shares authorized and 8,000 shares issued, of which 1,600 shares have been reacquired and are held in the treasury.

   b.   The dividend on the preferred stock (see part a) is paid.

   c.   A stock dividend of $250,000 of no-par common stock is issued to common shareholders.

   d.   A building replacement fund of $125,000 is created. The fund is to be used to purchase a new building when the present one becomes inadequate.

   e.   Bonds with $500,000 par value are retired at par out of the sinking fund created for that purpose.

   f.   The shares of no-par stock of the corporation are selling on the market at $300 a share. To bring the market value down to a more popular price and thereby broaden the distribution of its stockholdings, the board of directors votes to issue four extra shares to shareholders for each share already held by them. The shares are issued.

21. *Journal entries for transactions involving owners' equity.* Journalize the following transactions:

   a.   A cash dividend of $2 a share is declared on the outstanding preferred stock. There are 5,000 shares authorized, 3,000 shares issued, and 100 shares reacquired and held in the treasury.

   b.   A cash dividend of $1 a share is declared on the no-par common stock, of which there are 10,000 shares authorized, 7,000 shares issued, and 1,000 shares reacquired and held in the treasury.

c. The dividend on the preferred stock is paid.

d. The dividend on the common stock is paid.

22. *Restrictions on dividend declarations.* Daley Company has total retained earnings of $100 million and has acquired treasury shares at a cost of $25 million. Its loan agreements limit dividend declarations that would reduce retained earnings below $60 million. The corporation laws of the state of Daley Company's incorporation do not allow dividend declarations if the amount of retained earnings is less than the cost of treasury shares held.

What is the maximum amount of dividends that Daley Company can declare?

23. *Stock splits and stock splits accounted for as stock dividends.* The Horngren Company has 5 million common shares outstanding, with par value of $5 per share and retained earnings of $600 million. The common shares have a market price of $80 each. The board of directors wishes to increase the number of shares in circulation to 10 million either by declaring a two-for-one stock split or by declaring a 100 percent stock dividend to be accounted for as a stock split.

a. Give journal entries for each of these treatments.

b. Explain the relative advantages and disadvantages of each.

24. *Transactions to incorporate and run a business.* The following events relate to shareholders' equity transactions of the Richardson Copper Company during the first year of its existence. Present journal entries for each of the transactions.

a. January 2. Articles of incorporation are filed with the State Corporation Commission. The authorized capital stock consists of 5,000 shares of $100-par-value preferred stock that offers an 8 percent annual dividend, and 50,000 shares of no-par common stock. The original incorporators are issued 100 shares of common stock at $20 per share; cash is collected for the shares. A stated value of $20 per share is assigned to the common stock.

b. January 6. 1,600 shares of common stock are issued for cash at $20 per share.

c. January 8. 3,000 shares of preferred stock are issued at par.

d. January 9. Certificates for the shares of preferred stock are issued.

e. January 12. The tangible assets and goodwill of Richardson Copper Works, a partnership, are acquired in exchange for 600 shares of preferred stock and 10,000 shares of common stock. The tangible assets acquired are valued as follows: inventories, $40,000; land, $45,000; buildings, $80,000; and equipment, $95,000.

f. July 3. The semiannual dividend on the preferred stock outstanding is declared, payable July 25, to shareholders of record on July 12.

g. July 5. Operations for the first 6 months have been profitable, and it is decided to expand. The company issues 20,000 shares of common stock for cash at $33 per share.

h. July 25. The preferred stock dividend declared July 3 is paid.

i. October 2. The directors declare a dividend of $1 per share on the common stock, payable October 25, to shareholders of record on October 12.

j. October 25. The dividend on common stock declared on October 2 is paid.

**25.** *Transactions to incorporate and run a business.* The following data are selected from the records of capital stock and retained earnings of the Wheellock Company. Present journal entries for these transactions.

a. July 5, Year 1. Articles of incorporation are filed with the secretary of state. The authorized capital stock consists of 1,000 shares of 6-percent preferred stock with a par value of $100 per share and 10,000 shares of no-par common stock.

b. July 8, Year 1. The company issues 3,000 shares of common stock for cash at $60 per share.

c. July 9, Year 1. The company issues 6,000 shares of common stock for the assets of the partnership of Wheellock and Wheellock. Their assets are valued as follows: accounts receivable, $30,000; inventories, $60,000; land, $80,000; buildings, $90,000; and equipment, $100,000.

d. July 13, Year 1. 750 shares of preferred stock are issued at par for cash.

e. December 31, Year 1. The balance in the Income Summary account, after closing all expense and revenue accounts, is $300,000 credit. The account is to be closed to the Retained Earnings account.

f. January 4, Year 2. The regular semiannual dividend on the preferred stock and a dividend of $2 per share on the common stock are declared. The dividends are payable on February 1.

g. February 1, Year 2. The dividends declared on January 4 are paid.

h. July 2, Year 2. The regular semiannual dividend on the preferred stock is declared. The dividend is payable on August 1.

i. August 1, Year 2. The dividend declared on July 2 is paid.

**26.** *Accounting for convertible bonds.* On January 2, Year 1, the Oklahoma Corporation issues $1 million of 20-year, $1,000-par-value, 10-percent semiannual coupon bonds at par. Each $1,000 bond is convertible into 40 shares of $1-par-value common stock. The Oklahoma Corporation's credit rating is such that it would have to issue 15 percent semiannual coupon bonds if the bonds were not convertible and if they were to be issued at par. On January 2, Year 5, the bond issue is converted into common stock. The common stock has a market price of $45 a share on January 2, Year 5.

Present the journal entries made under generally accepted accounting principles on January 2, Year 1 and Year 5, to record the issue and conversion of the issue.

# Problems and Cases

**27.** *Granting stock options to executives involves an element of compensation.* Assume that accounting were to require recognition of compensation expense on the date that stock options were granted to an employee. A precise measure of the amount of the compensation expense would not be possible, but various approximations could be made. How might the accountant put a dollar amount on the compensation expense granted through stock options? You may assume that the exercise price is the market price on the date the option is granted.

**28.** *Market reaction to stock dividends.* Chapter 7 of *Accounting Research Bulletin No. 43,* issued in 1953, presented the rules of accounting for stock dividends

Exhibit 12.7 _____

**CHELEX COMPANY**
**Shareholders' Equity as of December 31**
**(Problem 29)**

| | |
|---|---:|
| Capital Stock ($10 par value) . . . . . . . . . . . . . . . . . . . . . . . . . . . . . . . . . . . | $ 50,000 |
| Additional Paid-in Capital . . . . . . . . . . . . . . . . . . . . . . . . . . . . . . . . . . . . . . . | 78,000 |
| Retained Earnings . . . . . . . . . . . . . . . . . . . . . . . . . . . . . . . . . . . . . . . . . . . . | 10,000 |
| Less 300 Shares Held in Treasury . . . . . . . . . . . . . . . . . . . . . . . . . . . . . . . | (6,000) |
|    Total Shareholders' Equity . . . . . . . . . . . . . . . . . . . . . . . . . . . . . . . . . . . | $132,000 |

and stock splits. Paragraph 10 provides reasons for the rules; it says that the rules are justified by ". . . those instances, which are by far the most numerous, where the issuances [of stock dividends] are so small in comparison with the shares previously outstanding that they do not have any apparent effect upon the share market price and, consequently, the market value of the shares previously held remains substantially unchanged."
  Comment.

**29.** *Reconstructing transactions involving owners' equity.* The Chelex Company began business on January 1. Its balance sheet on December 31 contained the shareholders' equity section shown in Exhibit 12.7.
  During the year, Chelex Company engaged in the following capital stock transactions, which comprise all capital transactions of the year:
**(1)** Issued shares for $25 each.
**(2)** Acquired a block of 500 shares for the treasury in a single transaction.
**(3)** Reissued some of the treasury shares.
Assuming that these were all of the capital stock transactions during the year, answer the following questions:
**a.** How many shares were issued for $25?
**b.** What was the price at which the treasury shares were acquired?
**c.** How many shares were reissued from the block of treasury shares?
**d.** What was the price at which the treasury shares were issued?
**e.** What journal entries must have been made during the year?

**30.** *Reconstructing transactions involving owners' equity.* The Worman Company began business on January 1. Its balance sheet on December 31 contained the shareholders' equity section shown in Exhibit 12.8.
  During the year, Worman Company engaged in the following capital stock transactions:
**(1)** Issued shares for $30 each.
**(2)** Acquired a block of 1,000 shares for the treasury in a single transaction.
**(3)** Reissued some of the treasury shares.
Assuming that these were the only capital stock transactions during the year, answer the following questions:
**a.** How many shares were issued for $30 each?
**b.** What was the price at which the treasury shares were acquired?

**Exhibit 12.8** _____

**WORMAN COMPANY**
**Shareholders' Equity as of December 31**
**(Problem 30)**

| | |
|---|---:|
| Capital Stock ($5 par value) ........................................ | $ 50,000 |
| Additional Paid-in Capital ......................................... | 254,800 |
| Retained Earnings ................................................. | 25,000 |
| Less 600 Shares Held in Treasury ................................ | (16,800) |
| Total Shareholders' Equity ....................................... | $313,000 |

**c.** How many shares were reissued from the block of treasury shares?

**d.** What was the price at which the treasury shares were reissued?

**e.** What journal entries must have been made during the year?

**31.** *Effects on statement of cash flows.* Refer to the Simplified Statement of Cash Flows in Exhibit 5.15 on page 188. Eleven of the lines in the statement are numbered. Ignore the unnumbered lines in responding to the following questions.

Assume that the accounting cycle is complete for the period and that all of the financial statements have been prepared. It is then discovered that a transaction has been overlooked. The transaction is recorded in the accounts, and all of the financial statements are corrected. For each of the following transactions, indicate which of the numbered lines of the statement of cash flows is affected and by how much. Ignore income tax effects.

**a.** Common shares are issued for $200,000.

**b.** Common shares originally issued for $50,000 are repurchased for $75,000 and retired.

**c.** Convertible bonds with a book value of $100,000 and a market value of $240,000 are converted into common shares with a par value of $10,000 and a market value of $240,000.

**d.** Treasury shares acquired for $20,000 are reissued for $15,000.

**e.** A stock dividend is declared. The par value of the shares issued is $1,000, and their market value is $300,000.

**f.** A cash dividend of $70,000 is declared and paid.

**g.** A previously declared cash dividend of $70,000 is paid.

**h.** Stock rights are exercised. The shares have a par value of $1,000 and market value of $35,000 on the date of exercise. The exercise price is $20,000, and $20,000 cash is received.

**32.** *Dilutive effects of stock options.* Refer to the schedule in Exhibit 12.3 on page 527, which shows employee stock option data for the General Products Company (GP). At December 31, Year 3, there were 2.7 million options outstanding to purchase shares at an average of $54 per share. Total shareholders' equity at December 31, Year 3, was about $2.5 billion.

**a.** If GP were to issue 2.7 million shares in a public offering at the market price per share on December 31, Year 3, what would be the proceeds of the issue?

**b.** If GP were to issue 2.7 million shares to employees who exercised all outstanding stock options, what would be the proceeds of the issue?

**c.** Are GP's shareholders better off under **a** or under **b**?

**d.** The text accompanying the stock option data in the GP annual report reads, in part, as follows:

> Option price under these plans is the full market value of General Products common stock on date of grant. Therefore, participants in the plans do not benefit unless the stock's market price rises, thus benefiting all share owners. . . .

GP seems to be saying that shareholders are not harmed by these options, whereas your answers to parts **a** and **b** show that shareholders are worse off when options are exercised than when shares are issued to the public. Attempt to reconcile GP's statement with your own analysis in parts **a** and **b**.

33. *Dividends in kind.* In the mid-1970s, American Express Company held shares of Donaldson, Lufkin & Jenrette, Inc. (DLJ) as an investment. These shares had cost about $27 million but had a market value of about $6 million. The shares were carried on the books as a long-term investment at cost. (These events occurred before the FASB issued *SFAS No. 12* requiring such items to be carried at lower of cost or market.) During a year when its income was about $200 million, American Express distributed the shares of DLJ as a dividend in kind to its own shareholders. The annual report of American Express said that in management's opinion the difference between the cost and the market value of the DLJ investment "did not represent a permanent impairment in value. . . . Accordingly, the entire carrying value of the DLJ investment . . . was charged to retained earnings." Ignore income tax effects.

**a.** What journal entry did American Express apparently make?

**b.** What journal entries would have been made had the dividend in kind been recorded at market value of the assets distributed?

**c.** What are the differences in these two treatments on net income and retained earnings?

34. *Reporting nonrecurring gains in the income statement.* After American Airlines lost a DC-10 in a Chicago crash, it collected about $37 million in insurance payments. The original cost of the DC-10 was $18 million, and at the time of the crash its net book value was $11 million. Ignore income tax effects.

**a.** Give the journal entry American Airlines made on loss of the plane.

**b.** How do you think this transaction, which represented a significant fraction of American Airline's income for the period, should be reported in the financial statements?

35. *Dividend policy and dividend reinvestment plans.* Many companies have automatic dividend reinvestment plans. Shareholders notify the company that they wish to reinvest all cash dividends in common shares. The company arranges to have common shares purchased at current market value for the accounts of the shareholders.

General Products Company, which has 231.5 million shares of common stock outstanding, has such an automatic dividend reinvestment plan. At the end of last year it declared and paid a dividend of $2 per share. Holders of 10 percent of the shares have elected the automatic dividend reinvestment option. The market price of a share on the date of reinvestment is $60. General Products Company instructs a stock broker to purchase the required shares on the New York Stock Exchange.

a.  Give the journal entries, if any, that General Products Company makes for the dividend declaration and for the automatic reinvestment of dividends.

b.  A shareholder complained that if the company would refrain from paying dividends, only to have them reinvested, it would save paperwork and the shareholders would save income taxes. Comment.

36. *Dilution of earnings per share.* In May of Year 1, the A-Tat Company issued 100,000 shares of no-par, convertible preferred stock for $50 a share. The shares promised a dividend of $6. All shares were issued for cash. These shares were convertible into common stock (par value $1 per share) at a rate of 5 shares of common stock for each share of preferred. The preferred shares are *not* regarded as equivalent to common shares in the calculation of earnings per share.

The company's earnings increased sharply during the next 4 years, and during January of Year 5, all shares of preferred were converted into common shares. One million common shares were outstanding before conversion of the shares. If the conversion had not taken place, the net income to common for Year 5 would have been $3,000,000. Other data are as follows:

|  | May, Year 1 | Jan., Year 5 |
|---|---|---|
| **Market Prices:** | | |
| A-Tat Common Stock ........................... | $10 | $ 20 |
| A-Tat $6 Preferred Stock ....................... | 50 | 100 |
| Book Value per A-Tat Common Share (before conversion of preferred) ..................... | 14 | 18 |

a.  Prepare journal entries to record the issuance and conversion of the preferred stock.

b.  Compute earnings per common share before conversion of the shares. What was the effect of the conversion on book values and on earnings per common share?

c.  Did the conversion of the preferred shares into common stock lead to a dilution of the common shareholders' equity? Explain your reasoning.

37. *Accounting for detachable warrants.* After several years of rapid expansion, the Alcher Company approached the State National Bank for a $1 million, 5-year loan. The bank was willing to lend the money at an interest rate of 12 percent per year. Alcher Company then approached an individual investor who was willing to provide the same funds for only 8 percent per year, provided that the Alcher Company gave the investor an option to purchase 20,000 shares of Alcher Company $5-par-value common stock for $20 per share at any time within 5 years of the initial date of the loan.

Alcher weighed both opportunities and decided to borrow from the investor. At the time of the loan, the common shares had a market price of $15 per share. Five years after the initial date of the loan, the investor exercised the option and purchased 20,000 shares for $20 each. At that time, the market price of the common shares was $45 each.

**a.** Did the use of the detachable warrants (the technical name for the option granted to the investor) reduce the Alcher Company's cost of borrowing?

**b.** How should the loan and annual interest payments of $80,000 be recorded in the books of the Alcher Company to reflect the economic reality of the transaction?

**c.** How might the exercise of the warrants (and the purchase of the 20,000 shares) be recorded?

**d.** Did exercise of the option dilute the owners' equity of the other shareholders on the date the option was exercised?

**e.** What disclosures during the life of the loan do you think appropriate? Why?

**38.** *Comprehensive review of accounting for owners' equity.* The shareholders' equity section of the balance sheet of the Reis Corporation at December 31 is as follows:

**Shareholders' Equity**

| | |
|---|---:|
| Common Stock—$10 Par Value, 500,000 Shares Authorized and 100,000 Shares Outstanding............................... | $1,000,000 |
| Additional Paid-in Capital......................................... | 500,000 |
| Retained Earnings .................................................. | 3,000,000 |
| Total Shareholders' Equity....................................... | $4,500,000 |

**a.** Calculate the total book value and the book value per common share as of December 31.

**b.** For each of the following transactions or events, give the appropriate journal entry and determine the total book value and the book value per common share of the Reis Corporation after the transaction. The transactions and events are independent of each other, except where noted.

**(1)** A 10-percent stock dividend is declared when the market price of Reis Corporation's common stock is $60 per share.

**(2)** A two-for-one stock split is declared, and the par value of the common stock is reduced from $10 to $5 per share. The new shares are issued immediately.

**(3)** Ten thousand shares of Reis Corporation's common stock are purchased on the open market for $50 per share and held as treasury stock.

**(4)** Ten thousand shares of Reis Corporation's common stock are purchased on the open market for $30 per share and held as treasury stock.

**(5)** The shares acquired in (3) are sold for $70 per share.

**(6)** The shares acquired in (3) are sold for $40 per share.

**(7)** The shares acquired in (3) are sold for $30 per share.

**(8)** Options to acquire 10,000 shares of Reis Corporation stock are exercised by officers for $15 per share.

**(9)** Same as (8), except that the exercise price is $50 per share.

**(10)** Convertible bonds with a book value of $300,000 and a market value of $340,000 are exchanged for 10,000 shares of common stock having a market value of $34 per share. No gain or loss is recognized on the conversion of bonds.

**(11)** Same as (10), except that gain or loss is recognized on the conversion of bonds into stock. Ignore income tax effects.

**c.** Using the results from part **b**, summarize the transactions and events that result in a reduction in:

**(1)** Total book value.

**(2)** Book value per share.

**39.** *Evaluation of various financing alternatives (adapted from a case by C. Mitchell).* In early January, B. R. Baine, President of Franco Incorporated, a diversified public company, faced the problem of determining the means of financing a major project recently approved by the board of directors. This project requires an investment of $1,000,000 and is expected to produce an operating income before financing costs and income taxes of $200,000 a year, with the principal returned at the end of the fifth year. Franco Incorporated is subject to an income tax rate of 40 percent.

The corporate treasurer has advised B. R. that the following alternative sources of financing are available:

**(1)** Issue new common shares at $20 per share.

**(2)** Arrange a 5-year bank loan with 14 percent interest payable annually in arrears.

**(3)** Issue 5-year convertible bonds at par with 10 percent interest payable annually. Each $1,000 bond would be convertible into 45 common shares.

**(4)** Issue cumulative, redeemable, convertible $1.75 preferred shares. The preferred shares are redeemable in 5 years at their issue price and convertible into common shares on the basis of one common share for each preferred share. The preferred shares would be issued at $25 per share. Other income is expected to be $420,000 per year with earnings per share of $2.10.

Analyze the forms of financing and their impact on earnings per share.

**40.** *Reconstructing events affecting owners' equity.* Exhibit 12.9 reproduces the statement of changes in owners' equity accounts for Granof Company for Year 2.

**a.** Identify the most likely events or transaction for each of the events numbered (1) to (6) in the exhibit.

**b.** Prepare journal entries for each of these events or transactions.

**41.** *Case introducing earnings-per-share calculations for a complex capital structure.* The Layton Ball Corporation has a relatively complicated capital structure. In addition to common shares, it has issued stock options, warrants, and convertible bonds. Exhibit 12.10 summarizes some pertinent information about

Exhibit 12.9 _____

## GRANOF COMPANY
### Statement of Changes in Owners' Equity Accounts for Year 2
### (Problem 40)

| | Common Shares | | | | | |
| | Market Value per Share[a] | Number of Shares | Par Value | Additional Paid-in Capital | Retained Earnings | Total Owners' Equity |
|---|---|---|---|---|---|---|
| Balances, Dec. 31, Year 1.................. | $100 | 2,000,000 | $12,000,000 | $48,000,000 | $40,000,000 | $100,000,000 |
| **Events Causing Changes** | | | | | | |
| (1) ....................... | 105 | 4,000,000 | — | — | — | — |
| (2) ....................... | 40 | 600,000 | 1,200,000 | 22,800,000 | (24,000,000) | — |
| (3) ....................... | 45 | 100,000 | 200,000 | 4,300,000 | — | 4,500,000 |
| (4) ....................... | 48 | 50,000 | 100,000 | 1,400,000 | — | 1,500,000 |
| (5) ....................... | 50 | — | — | — | 45,000,000 | 45,000,000 |
| (6) ....................... | 53 | — | — | — | (6,750,000) | (6,750,000) |
| Balances, Dec. 31, Year 2.................. | | 6,750,000 | $13,500,000 | $76,500,000 | $54,250,000 | $144,250,000 |

[a]Before event.

these items. Net income for the year is $9,500, and the income tax rate used in computing income tax expense is 40 percent of pretax income.

a.   First, ignore all items of capital except for the common shares. Calculate earnings per common share.

b.   In past years, employees have been issued options to purchase shares of stock. Exhibit 12.10 indicates that the price of the common stock through-

Exhibit 12.10 _____

## LAYTON BALL CORPORATION
### Information on Capital Structure for Earnings-per-Share Calculation
### (Problem 41)

Assume the following data about the capital structure and earnings for the Layton Ball Corporation for the year:

| | |
|---|---|
| Number of Common Shares Outstanding throughout the Year ..... | 2,500 shares |
| Market Price per Common Share throughout the Year ............ | $25 |
| Options Outstanding during the Year: | |
| Number of Shares Issuable on Exercise of Options ............ | 1,000 shares |
| Exercise Price per Share .................................... | $15 |
| Warrants Outstanding during the Year: | |
| Number of Shares Issuable on Exercise of Warrants ........... | 2,000 shares |
| Exercise Price per Share .................................... | $30 |
| Convertible Bonds Outstanding: | |
| Number (issued 15 years ago) ............................... | 100 bonds |
| Proceeds per Bond at Time of Issue (= par value) ............. | $1,000 |
| Shares of Common Issuable on Conversion (per bond) ......... | 10 shares |
| Coupon Rate (per year) ..................................... | $4\frac{1}{6}$ percent |

out the year was $25 but that the stock options could be exercised at any time for $15 each. The holder of an option is allowed to surrender it along with $15 cash and receive one share in return. Thus the number of shares would be increased, which would decrease the earnings-per-share figure. The company would, however, have more cash. Assume that the holders of options tender them, along with $15 each, to purchase shares. Assume that the company uses the cash to purchase shares for the treasury at a price of $25 each. Compute a new earnings-per-share figure. (Treasury shares are *not* counted in the denominator of the earnings-per-share calculation.)

c.  Exhibit 12.10 indicates that there were also warrants outstanding in the hands of the public. Anyone who owns such a warrant is allowed to turn in that warrant, along with $30 cash, to purchase one share of stock. If the warrants were exercised, there would be more shares outstanding, which would reduce earnings per share. However, the company would have more cash, which it could use to purchase shares for the treasury, reducing the number of shares outstanding. Assume that all holders of warrants exercise them. Assume that the company uses the cash to purchase outstanding shares for the treasury. Compute a new earnings-per-share figure. (Ignore the information about options and the calculations in part **b** at this point.) Note that a rational warrant holder would *not* exercise his or her warrants for $30 when a share could be purchased for $25.

d.  There were also convertible bonds outstanding. A holder of a convertible bond is entitled to trade in that bond for 10 shares. If a bond was converted, the number of shares would increase, which would tend to reduce earnings per share. On the other hand, the company would not have to pay interest and thus would have no interest expense on the bond, because it would no longer be outstanding. This would tend to increase income and earnings per share. Assume that all holders of convertible bonds convert their bonds into shares. Compute a new net income figure (do not forget income tax effects on income of the interest saved) and a new earnings-per-share figure. (Ignore the information about options and warrants and the calculations in parts **b** and **c** at this point.)

e.  Now consider all the previous calculations. Which sets of assumptions from parts **b**, **c**, and **d** would lead to the lowest possible earnings per share when they are all made simultaneously? Compute a new earnings per share under the most restrictive set of assumptions about reductions in earnings per share.

f.  Accountants publish several earnings-per-share figures for companies with complicated capital structures and complicated events during the year. *The Wall Street Journal,* however, publishes only one figure in its daily columns (where it reports the price-earnings ratio — the price of a share of stock divided by its earnings per share). Which of the figures computed previously for earnings per share do you think should be reported by *The Wall Street Journal* as *the* earnings-per-share figure? Why?

# Chapter 13  Long-Term Investments in Corporate Securities _____

For a variety of reasons, corporations often acquire the *marketable securities* (bonds and capital stock) of other corporations. For example, a corporation may temporarily hold excess cash that is not needed for operations. Rather than permit the cash to remain idle in its bank account, the corporation may acquire the bonds or capital stock of another corporation. Relatively short-term holdings of corporate securities are usually classified as Marketable Securities and are shown in the Current Assets section of the balance sheet. Chapter 7 discusses the accounting for such marketable securities.

A corporation may also acquire another corporation's capital stock for some more long-term purpose.[1] For example, a firm may acquire shares of common stock of a major raw materials supplier to help assure continued availability of raw materials. Or a firm may wish to diversify its operations by acquiring a controlling interest in an established firm in some new area of business. Long-term investments in corporate securities are typically classified on the asset side of the balance sheet in a separate section called ''Investments.'' Both Chapter 7 and this chapter discuss the accounting for long-term investments in capital stock.

## Types of Long-Term Investments _____

The accounting for long-term investments depends on the purpose of the investment and on the percentage of voting stock that one corporation owns of another. Refer to Figure 13.1. Three types of long-term investments can be identified.

1.  *Minority, passive investments* — Shares of capital stock of another corporation are viewed as a good long-term investment and are acquired for the dividends

---

[1]Industrial firms seldom acquire bonds of other corporations as long-term investments. Consequently, this chapter focuses on long-term investments in capital stock.

## Figure 13.1 ⎯⎯⎯⎯⎯⎯⎯⎯⎯⎯⎯⎯⎯⎯⎯⎯⎯⎯⎯⎯⎯⎯⎯⎯⎯

### Types of Intercorporate Investments in Capital Stock

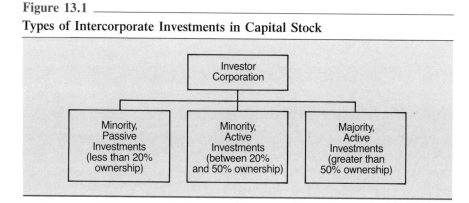

and capital gains (increases in the market price of the shares) anticipated from owning the shares. The percentage owned of the other corporation's shares is not so large that the acquiring company can control or exert significant influence over the other company. Generally accepted accounting principles view investments of less than 20 percent of the voting stock of another company as minority, passive investments in most cases.[2]

2. *Minority, active investments* — Shares of another corporation are acquired so that the acquiring corporation can exert significant influence over the other company's activities. This significant influence is usually at a broad policy-making level through representation on the other corporation's board of directors. Because the shares of capital stock of most publicly held corporations are widely dispersed among numerous individuals, many of whom do not vote their shares, significant influence can be exerted over another corporation with ownership of less than a majority of the voting stock. Generally accepted accounting principles view investments of between 20 and 50 percent of the voting stock of another company as minority, active investments "unless evidence indicates that significant influence cannot be exercised."[3]

3. *Majority, active investments* — Shares of another corporation are acquired so that the acquiring corporation can be sure to control the other company. This control is typically at both the broad policy-making level and at the day-to-day operational level. Ownership of more than 50 percent of the voting stock of another company implies an ability to control, unless there is evidence to the contrary.[4]

---

[2]Accounting Principles Board (APB), *Opinion No. 18,* "The Equity Method of Accounting for Investments in Common Stock," 1971.

[3]APB, *Opinion No. 18;* Financial Accounting Standards Board, *Interpretation No. 35,* "Criteria for Applying the Equity Method of Accounting for Investments in Common Stock," 1981.

[4]A corporation may be unable to exercise its control over another corporation, despite the ownership of a majority of the voting stock, if the other corporation is in bankruptcy proceedings and under the control of a court or if it is in a foreign country where the government imposes severe restrictions on withdrawal of assets from the country.

The sections that follow discuss the accounting for these three types of investments. Throughout the chapter, the acquiring corporation is designated P, for *purchaser* or for *parent,* depending on the context, and the acquired corporation is designated S, for *seller* or for *subsidiary.*

## Minority, Passive Investments _____

If a firm does not own a sufficient percentage of the voting stock of another corporation to control or significantly influence it (assumed to be 20 percent or more under generally accepted accounting principles), the management of the investment involves two activities: awaiting the receipt of dividends and deciding when the investment should be sold for a capital gain or loss. Minority, passive investments must be accounted for by using the *lower-of-cost-or-market method.* Chapter 7 describes and illustrates the lower-of-cost-or-market method for both marketable securities classified as Current Assets (that is, those planned to be sold within a short period when cash is needed) and minority, passive investments classified as Investments (that is, those held for some long-term purpose). The following summarizes the lower-of-cost-or-market method for minority, passive investments:

1. Investments are initially recorded at acquisition cost.

2. Dividends received or receivable each period are recognized as dividend revenue.

3. At the end of each period, the market value of the portfolio of noncurrent marketable equity securities is compared to the acquisition cost of the portfolio. The amount shown on the balance sheet for these investments is the lower of acquisition cost or current market value.

   Assume that a portfolio of marketable equity securities held as long-term investments had an acquisition cost of $100,000. The portfolio has a market value of $95,000 at the end of a firm's first year of operations. The following entry would be made at year-end:

| | | |
|---|---|---|
| Unrealized Holding Loss on Valuation of Marketable Equity Investments.......................................... | 5,000 | |
| Allowance for Excess of Cost of Investments over Market Value....................................... | | 5,000 |

The account debited, Unrealized Holding Loss on Valuation of Marketable Equity Investments, is included as a negative amount in the shareholders' equity section of the balance sheet, typically between Additional Paid-in Capital and Retained Earnings. See Exhibit 12.1 on page 519. The unrealized loss is not included in the calculation of net income for the period. The suggested rationale is that these investments are acquired for their long-term capital gains (plus dividends). Short-term changes in market value, therefore, should not affect periodic earnings. The account credited, Allowance for Excess of Cost of

Investments over Market Value, is a contra account to the Investments in Securities account. Using it permits the net investments to be shown at the lower of cost or market while retaining the amount of acquisition cost in the Investment in Securities account.

Subsequent increases in the market value of the portfolio up to, but not exceeding, the original cost of the investments in the portfolio are debited to the asset contra and credited to the balance sheet shareholders' equity account for unrealized losses.

**4.** When a particular minority, passive investment is sold, the difference between the selling price and the acquisition cost of the investment is recognized as a gain or loss. Thus all changes in market value between the time an investment is acquired and when it is sold are reflected in net income in the period of sale. The net amount shown for investments on the asset side of the balance sheet reflects the *potential* future holding loss on the portfolio of such investments.

You may find it helpful to review the illustration of the lower-of-cost-or-market method for minority, passive investments in Chapter 7.

# Minority, Active Investments _____

When less than a majority of the voting stock of another corporation is owned, judgment is required in ascertaining when significant influence can be exercised. For the sake of uniformity, generally accepted accounting principles presume that one company can significantly influence another company when 20 percent or more of the voting stock of the other company is owned. Significant influence may be present when less than 20 percent is owned, but in these cases management must demonstrate to the independent accountants that it exists.

Minority, active investments, generally those where ownership is between 20 and 50 percent, must be accounted for using the *equity method*. Under the equity method, the firm owning shares in another firm recognizes as revenue (expense) each period its share of the net income (loss) of the other firm. Dividends received from S are not recognized as income but as a return of investment. In the discussion that follows, we designate the firm owning shares as P and the firm whose shares are owned as S.

## Equity Method: Rationale

The rationale for using the equity method when significant influence is present can be best understood by considering the financial statement effects of using the lower-of-cost-or-market method in these circumstances. Under the lower-of-cost-or-market method, P recognizes income or loss on the income statement only when it receives a dividend or sells all or part of the investment. Suppose, as often happens, that S follows a policy of financing its own growing operations through retention of earnings and consistently declares dividends significantly less than its net income. The market price of S's shares will probably increase to reflect the retention of assets generated by earnings. Under the lower-of-cost-or-market method, P will continue to show the investment at acquisition cost and P's only reported income from the investment will be the modest dividends received. P, because of its ownership percentage, can influence the dividend policy of S and thereby the amount of income recognized under the lower-of-cost-or-market method. Under these conditions, the lower-of-cost-or-market method may not reasonably reflect the earnings of S generated under P's influence. The equity method is designed to provide a better measure of a firm's earnings and of its investment when, because of its ownership interest, significant influence can be exerted over the operations and dividend policy of another firm.

## Equity Method: Procedures

Under the equity method, the initial purchase of an investment is recorded at acquisition cost, the same as under the lower-of-cost-or-market method. Each period Company P treats as revenue its proportionate share of the periodic earnings, not the dividends, of Company S. Dividends declared by S are then treated by P as a reduction in its Investment in S account.

Suppose that P acquires 30 percent of the outstanding shares of S for $600,000. The entry to record the acquisition would be as follows:

---

(1) Investment in Stock of S . . . . . . . . . . . . . . . . . . . . . . . . . . . . . . . . .   600,000
    Cash . . . . . . . . . . . . . . . . . . . . . . . . . . . . . . . . . . . . . . . . . . . . . . .       600,000
    Investment made in 30 percent of Company S.

---

Between the time of the acquisition and the end of P's next accounting period, S reports income of $80,000. P, using the equity method, would record the following:

---

(2) Investment in Stock of S . . . . . . . . . . . . . . . . . . . . . . . . . . . . . . . . .   24,000
    Revenue from Investments . . . . . . . . . . . . . . . . . . . . . . . . . . . . . . .       24,000
    To record 30 percent of income earned by investee, accounted
    for using the equity method. Revenue account title often used in
    practice is Equity in Earnings of Unconsolidated Affiliates.

---

If S pays a dividend of $30,000 to holders of common stock, P would be entitled to receive $9,000 and would record the following:

---

(3) Cash . . . . . . . . . . . . . . . . . . . . . . . . . . . . . . . . . . . . . . . . . . . . . . . .   9,000
    Investment in Stock of S . . . . . . . . . . . . . . . . . . . . . . . . . . . . . . . .       9,000
    To record dividends received from investee, accounted for using
    the equity method, and the resulting reduction in the investment
    account.

---

Notice that the credit is to the Investment in S account. P records income earned by S as an *increase* in investment. The dividend becomes a return of investment and *decreases* the Investment account.[5]

Suppose that S subsequently reports earnings of $100,000 and also pays dividends of $40,000. P's entries would be as follows:

---

| | | |
|---|---|---|
| (4) Investment in Stock of S...................................... | 30,000 | |
|    Revenue from Investments.............................. | | 30,000 |
| (5) Cash ....................................................... | 12,000 | |
|    Investment in Stock of S................................ | | 12,000 |

To record revenue and dividends from investee, accounted for using equity method.

---

P's Investment in S account now has a balance of $633,000 as follows:

**Investment in Stock of S**

| | | | | |
|---|---|---|---|---|
| (1) | 600,000 | 9,000 | (3) |
| (2) | 24,000 | 12,000 | (5) |
| (4) | 30,000 | | |
| | | | |
| Bal. | 633,000 | | |

If P now sells one-fourth of its shares for $165,000, P's entry to record the sale would be as follows:

---

| | | |
|---|---|---|
| Cash....................................................... | 165,000 | |
|    Investment in Stock of S .................................... | | 158,250 |
|    Gain on Sale of Investment in S ........................... | | 6,750 |
| ($\frac{1}{4}$ × $633,000 = $158,250.) | | |

---

The equity method as described here is simple enough to use. To make financial reports that use the equity method more realistic, generally accepted accounting principles require some modification of the entries under certain circumstances, described next.

---

[5]Students often have difficulty understanding journal entry (3), particularly the credit by the investor when a dividend is paid by the investee company. The transactions and entries are analogous to an individual's ordinary savings account at a local bank. Assume that you put $600,000 in a savings account, that later interest of 4 percent (or $24,000) is added by the bank to the account, and that still later you withdraw $9,000 from the savings account. Journal entries (1) through (3) in the text could be recorded for these three events, with slight changes in the account titles: Investment in S changes to Savings Account, and Revenue from Investments changes to Interest Revenue.

The cash withdrawal reduces the amount invested in the savings account. Similarly, the declaration of a cash dividend by an investee company accounted for with the equity method reduces the investor's investment in the company. The investor, Company P, owns a sufficiently large percentage of the voting shares that it can "require" Company S to declare a dividend, just as you can require the savings bank to remit cash to you almost whenever you choose.

Even though S does not declare all of its earnings in dividends, P reports its proportionate share of S's earnings as income. But this income is not currently taxable to P. Consequently, there will sometimes be an entry in the deferred tax account. Calculating the amount of the deferred tax charge presents issues too complex for this introductory text.

An additional complication in using the equity method arises when the acquisition cost of P's shares exceeds P's proportionate share of the book value of the net assets (= assets − liabilities) or shareholders' equity of S at the date of acquisition. For example, assume that P acquires 25 percent of the stock of S for $400,000 when the total shareholders' equity of S is $1 million. The excess of P's cost over book value acquired is $150,000 (= $400,000 − .25 × $1,000,000). Under the equity method, the excess is generally *goodwill*. Goodwill must be amortized over a period not greater than 40 years.[6] Accounting for goodwill, including its amortization, is discussed in Appendix 13.1.

On the balance sheet, an investment accounted for with the equity method appears in the Investments section. The amount shown will be equal to the acquisition cost of the shares plus P's share of S's undistributed earnings since the date the shares were acquired, unless the acquisition involved some amount of goodwill. On the income statement, P shows its share of S's income as a revenue each period. (The financial statements of the investee, S, are not affected by the accounting method used by the investor, P.)

## Majority, Active Investments ——————————————————————

When one firm, P, owns more than 50 percent of the voting stock of another company, S, P can control the activities of S. This control can be both at a broad policy-making level and at a day-to-day operational level. The majority investor in this case is called the *parent* and the majority-owned company is called the *subsidiary*. Generally accepted accounting principles require that the financial statement of majority-owned companies be combined, or *consolidated*, with those of the parent.[7]

### Reasons for Legally Separate Corporations

There are many reasons why a business firm prefers to operate as a group of legally separate corporations rather than as a single legal entity. From the standpoint of the parent company, the more important reasons for maintaining legally separate subsidiary companies include the following:

1.  To reduce financial risk. Separate corporations may be used for mining raw materials, transporting them to a manufacturing plant, producing the product,

---

[6]Accounting Principles Board, *Opinion No. 17*, "Intangible Assets," 1970.

[7]Until recently, firms had some choice in this matter, being able either to use the equity method or to consolidate majority-owned investments in companies whose operations differed in form from those of the parent. *Statement of Financial Accounting Standards No. 94*, 1987, of the FASB restricts the accounting choices for majority-owned subsidiaries.

and selling the finished product to the public. If any one part of the total process proves to be unprofitable or inefficient, losses from insolvency will fall only on the owners and creditors of the one subsidiary corporation.

2. To meet more effectively the requirements of state corporation laws and tax legislation. If an organization does business in a number of states, it is often faced with overlapping and inconsistent taxation, regulations, and requirements. Organizing separate corporations to conduct the operations in the various states may be more economical.

3. To expand or diversify with a minimum of capital investment. A firm may absorb another company by acquiring a controlling interest in its voting stock. The result may be accomplished with a substantially smaller capital investment, as well as with less difficulty, inconvenience, and risk, than if a new plant had been constructed or the firm had geared up for a new line of business.

## Purpose of Consolidated Statements

For a variety of reasons, then, a single economic entity may exist in the form of a parent and several legally separate subsidiaries. (The General Electric Company, for example, consists of about 150 legally separate companies.) A consolidation of the financial statements of the parent and each of its subsidiaries presents the results of operations, financial position, and changes in cash flows of an affiliated group of companies under the control of a parent, essentially as if the group of companies were a single entity. The parent and each subsidiary are legally separate entities, but they operate as one centrally controlled *economic entity*. Consolidated financial statements generally provide more useful information to the shareholders of the parent corporation than would separate financial statements of the parent as investor and each subsidiary as an operating company.

Consolidated financial statements also generally provide more useful information than does use of the equity method. The parent, because of its voting interest, can effectively control the use of all of the subsidiary's assets. Consolidation of the individual assets, liabilities, revenues, and expenses of both the parent and the subsidiary provides a more realistic picture of the operations and financial position of the single economic entity.

In a legal sense, consolidated statements merely supplement, and do not replace, the separate statements of the individual corporations, although it is common practice to present only the consolidated statements in published annual reports.

## Consolidation Policy

Consolidated financial statements are generally prepared when the two following criteria are met:

1. The parent owns more than 50 percent of the voting stock of the subsidiary.

2. There are no important restrictions on the ability of the parent to exercise control of the subsidiary.

Ownership of more than 50 percent of the subsidiary's voting stock implies an ability to exert control over the activities of the subsidiary. For example, the parent can control the subsidiary's corporate policies and dividend declarations. There may be situations, however, where control of the subsidiary's activities cannot be carried out effectively, despite the ownership of a majority of the voting stock. For example, the subsidiary may be located in a foreign country that has severely restricted the withdrawal of funds from that country. Or the subsidiary may be in bankruptcy and under the control of a court-appointed group of trustees. In these cases, the financial statements of the subsidiary probably will not be consolidated with those of the parent. When the parent owns more than 50 percent of the shares but cannot exercise control, so that consolidated statements are not prepared, the lower-of-cost-or-market method must be used.

**Example 1** General Motors, General Electric, and Westinghouse, among others, have wholly owned finance subsidiaries. These subsidiaries make a portion of their loans to customers who wish to purchase the products of the parent company. The financial statements of these subsidiaries are consolidated with those of the parent company. The assets of these subsidiaries are largely receivables. Some argue that statement readers may be misled as to the relative liquidity of these firms when consolidated statements are prepared and the assets of the parent — largely noncurrent manufacturing plant and equipment — are combined with the more liquid assets of the finance subsidiary. The counter argument is that these entities operate as a single integrated unit so that consolidated financial statements depict more accurately the nature of their operating relationships.

**Example 2** A major mining corporation owns a mining subsidiary in South America. The government of the country enforces stringent control over cash payments outside the country. The company is not able to control the use of all the assets, despite the ownership of a majority of the voting shares. Therefore, it does not prepare consolidated statements with the subsidiary.

## Disclosure of Consolidation Policy

The summary of significant accounting principles in financial statements includes a statement about the *consolidation policy* of the parent. If a significant majority-owned subsidiary is not consolidated, the notes will disclose that fact. A recent annual report of American Home Products Corporation contained the following:

*Notes to Consolidated Financial Statements*

1. *Summary of Significant Accounting Policies: . . . Principles of Consolidation:* The accompanying consolidated financial statements include the accounts of the Company and its subsidiaries with the exception of those subsidiaries described in Note 3 which are accounted for on a cash basis. . . .

3. *Provision for Impairment of Investment in Certain Foreign Locations:* [During the preceding year], the Corporation recorded a charge of

$50,000,000 recognizing the impairment of its investment in its subsidiaries in South America, except for its investment in Brazil. The provision was made after determining that the continued imposition of constraints such as dividend restrictions, exchange controls, price controls and import restrictions in these countries so severely impede management's control of the economic performance of the businesses that continued inclusion of these subsidiaries in the consolidated financial statements is inappropriate. The Company is continuing to operate these businesses, which for the most part are self-sufficient; however, the investments have been deconsolidated and earnings are recorded on a cash [similar to lower-of-cost-or-market] basis. Net sales from these operations aggregated $97,790,000, $95,084,000, and $100,045,000 [in the last three years]. . . . Net income included in the consolidated statements of income was approximately $2,200,000 . . . and $2,000,000 [for the last two years].

## Understanding Consolidated Statements

This section discusses three concepts essential for understanding consolidated financial statements:

1. The need for intercompany eliminations.
2. The meaning of consolidated net income.
3. The nature of the external minority interest.

**Need for Intercompany Eliminations**  State corporation laws typically require each legally separate corporation to maintain its own set of books. Thus, during the accounting period, the accounting records of each corporation will record transactions of that entity with all other entities (both affiliated and nonaffiliated). At the end of the period, each corporation will prepare its own set of financial statements. The consolidation of these financial statements basically involves summing the amounts for various financial statement items across the separate company statements. The amounts resulting from the summation must be adjusted, however, to eliminate double counting resulting from *intercompany transactions*. Consolidated financial statements are intended to reflect the results that would be achieved if the affiliated group of companies were a single company. Consolidated financial statements reflect only the transactions between the consolidated entity and others outside the group.

The eliminations to remove intercompany transactions typically appear on a *consolidation work sheet* and not on the books of any of the legal entities being consolidated. The consolidated financial statements are then prepared directly from the work sheet. There are generally no separate books for the consolidated entity.

To illustrate the need for, and the nature of, *elimination entries,* refer to the data for Company P and Company S in Exhibit 13.1. Column (1) shows the balance sheet and income statement data for Company P taken from its separate company books. Column (2) shows similar data for Company S. Column (3) sums the amounts from columns (1) and (2). The amounts in column (3) include the effects of

## Exhibit 13.1

### Illustrative Data for Preparation of Consolidated Financial Statements

| | Single-Company Statements | | |
|---|---|---|---|
| | Company P (1) | Company S (2) | Combined (3) = (1) + (2) |
| **Condensed Balance Sheets on December 31** | | | |
| **Assets:** | | | |
| Accounts Receivable......................................... | $ 200,000 | $ 25,000 | $ 225,000 |
| Investment in Stock of Company S (at equity) ................. | 705,000 | — | 705,000 |
| Other Assets.............................................. | 2,150,000 | 975,000 | 3,125,000 |
| Total Assets ......................................... | $3,055,000 | $1,000,000 | $4,055,000 |
| | | | |
| **Equities:** | | | |
| Accounts Payable ........................................ | $ 75,000 | $ 15,000 | $ 90,000 |
| Other Liabilities.......................................... | 70,000 | 280,000 | 350,000 |
| Common Stock........................................... | 2,500,000 | 500,000 | 3,000,000 |
| Retained Earnings ........................................ | 410,000 | 205,000 | 615,000 |
| Total Equities ....................................... | $3,055,000 | $1,000,000 | $4,055,000 |
| | | | |
| **Condensed Income Statement for Current Year** | | | |
| **Revenues:** | | | |
| Sales..................................................... | $ 900,000 | $ 250,000 | $1,150,000 |
| Equity in Earnings of Company S ............................ | 48,000 | — | 48,000 |
| Total Revenues ...................................... | $ 948,000 | $ 250,000 | $1,198,000 |
| | | | |
| **Expenses:** | | | |
| Cost of Goods Sold (excluding depreciation) ................... | $ 440,000 | $ 80,000 | $ 520,000 |
| Depreciation Expense...................................... | 120,000 | 50,000 | 170,000 |
| Administrative Expenses ................................... | 80,000 | 40,000 | 120,000 |
| Income Tax Expense ...................................... | 104,000 | 32,000 | 136,000 |
| Total Expenses....................................... | $ 744,000 | $ 202,000 | $ 946,000 |
| Net Income .............................................. | $ 204,000 | $ 48,000 | $ 252,000 |
| Dividend Declarations ..................................... | 50,000 | 13,000 | 63,000 |
| Increase in Retained Earnings for the Year.................... | $ 154,000 | $ 35,000 | $ 189,000 |

several intercompany items and, therefore, do not represent the correct amounts for *consolidated* assets, equities, revenues, or expenses.

**Eliminating Double Counting of Intercompany Payables** For example, separate company records indicate that $12,000 of Company S's accounts receivable represent amounts payable by Company P. The current assets underlying this transaction are effectively counted twice in column (3): once as part of Accounts Receivable on Company S's books and a second time as Cash (Other Assets) on Company P's books. Also, the liability shown on Company P's books is included in the combined amount for Accounts Payable in column (3), even though the amount is not payable to an entity external to the consolidated group. To eliminate double counting on the asset side and to report Accounts Payable at the amount payable to external entities, an elimination entry must be made to reduce the amounts for Accounts Receivable and Accounts Payable in column (3) by $12,000.

**Eliminating Double-Counting of Investment**  To consider a more complex example, Company P's balance sheet shows an asset, Investment in Stock of Company S. The subsidiary's balance sheet shows its individual assets. When the two balance sheets are added together in column (3), the sum shows both Company P's investment in Company S's assets and the assets themselves. Company P's account, Investment in Stock of Company S, must therefore be eliminated from the sum of the balance sheets. Because the consolidated balance sheet must maintain the accounting equation, corresponding eliminations must be made on the right-hand, or equities, side in this case.

To understand the eliminations from the right-hand side of the balance sheet, recall that the right-hand side shows the sources of the firm's financing. Company S is financed by creditors (liabilities) and by owners (shareholders' equity). In this case, Company P owns 100 percent of Company S's voting shares. Thus the assets on the consolidated balance sheet of the single economic entity are financed by the creditors of both companies and by Company P's shareholders. In other words, the equities of the consolidated entity are the liabilities of both companies but the shareholders' equity of Company P alone. If the shareholders' equity accounts of Company S were added to those of Company P, the financing from Company P's shareholders would be counted twice (once on the parent's books and once on the subsidiary's books). Hence, when Company P's investment account is eliminated from the sum of the two companies' assets, the accounting equation is maintained by eliminating the shareholders' equity accounts of Company S.

**Eliminating Double-Counting of Income**  Similarly, certain intercompany items must be eliminated from the sum of income statement accounts so that the operating performance of the consolidated entity can be meaningfully presented. Company P's accounts show Equity in Earnings of Company S of $48,000. Company S's records show individual revenues and expenses that net to $48,000. If the revenues and expenses of the two companies were merely summed, as is done in column (3) of Exhibit 13.1, the earnings of Company S would be double-counted. The account Equity in Earnings of Company S must, therefore, be eliminated in preparing consolidated statements (illustrated later in the chapter).

**Eliminating Intercompany Sales**  Another example of an intercompany item involves intercompany sales of inventory. Separate company records indicate that Company S sold merchandise to Company P for $40,000 during the year. None of this inventory remains in Company P's inventory on December 31. The merchandise inventory items sold are included in Sales Revenue on both Company S's books (sale to Company P) and on Company P's books (sale to external entity). Thus sales are overstated from the standpoint of the consolidated entity. Likewise, Cost of Goods Sold of both companies includes the separate company cost of the goods sold. To eliminate double counting, the intercompany sale from Company S to Company P must be eliminated (illustrated later).

To complete this example, suppose that the subsidiary sells to the parent but that the parent has not yet sold the goods to the public. The subsidiary will have recorded profits on the sale, but from the standpoint of the overall economic entity, no profits for shareholders have actually been realized, because the items are still in the inventory of the overall economic entity. Consequently, profits from the subsidiary's sales to the parent that have not been realized by subsequent sales to outsiders are eliminated from consolidated net income and balance sheet amounts. The consolidated income statement attempts to show sales, expenses, and net income figures that report the results of operations of the group of companies as though they were a single company.

A later section illustrates the adjustment to convert column (3) of Exhibit 13.1 to a consolidated basis.

**Consolidated Income**  The amount of consolidated net income for a period exactly equals the amount that the parent would show on its separate company books from applying the equity method; that is, consolidated net income is

$$\begin{array}{ccc} \text{Parent Company's} & \text{Parent Company's} & \text{Profit (or + Loss)} \\ \text{Net Income from} & + \text{ Share of Subsidiary's} & - \text{ on Intercompany} \\ \text{Its Own Activities} & \text{Net Income} & \text{Transactions.} \end{array}$$

A consolidated income statement differs from an income statement where the equity method has been used in the *components* presented. Under the equity method for an unconsolidated subsidiary, the parent's share of the subsidiary's net income minus gain (or plus loss) on intercompany transactions appears on a single line, Equity in Earnings of Unconsolidated Subsidiary. In a consolidated income statement, the individual revenues and expenses of the subsidiary (less intercompany adjustments) are combined with those of the parent, and the account, Equity in Earnings of Unconsolidated Subsidiary, shown on the parent's books, is eliminated.[8]

**External Minority Interest in Consolidated Subsidiary**  In many cases, the parent does not own 100 percent of the voting stock of a consolidated subsidiary. The owners of the remaining shares of voting stock are called *external minority shareholders* or the *minority interest*.[9] These shareholders have a proportionate interest in the net assets (= total assets − total liabilities) of the subsidiary as shown on the subsidiary's separate corporate records. They also have a proportionate interest in the earnings of the subsidiary.

**Should the Minority Interest in Net Assets Appear in the Consolidated Balance Sheet?**  An issue in the generally accepted accounting principles for consolidated statements is whether the statements should show only the parent's share of the

---

[8]The equity method is sometimes referred to as a *one-line consolidation* because the individual revenues and expenses of the subsidiary are netted in the one account, Equity in Earnings of Unconsolidated Subsidiary.

[9]Do not confuse this minority interest in a consolidated subsidiary with a firm's own minority investments, discussed earlier. The minority *interest* belongs to others outside the parent and its economic entity. The parent's minority *investments* are merely those for which the parent owns less than 50 percent of the shares.

assets and liabilities of the subsidiary or whether they should show all of the subsidiary's assets and liabilities along with the minority interests in them. The generally accepted accounting principle is to show all of the assets and liabilities of the subsidiary, because the parent, with its controlling voting interest, can effectively direct the use of all the assets and liabilities, not merely an amount equal to the parent's percentage of ownership. The consolidated balance sheet and income statement in these instances, however, must disclose the interest of the minority shareholders in the subsidiary that has been consolidated.

The amount of the minority interest shown on the balance sheet is generally the result of multiplying the common stockholders' equity of the subsidiary by the minority's percentage of ownership. For example, if the common shareholders' equity (or assets minus liabilities) of a consolidated subsidiary totals $500,000 and the minority owns 20 percent of the common stock, the minority interest shown on the consolidated balance sheet is $100,000 (= .20 × $500,000).

The minority interest typically appears among the equities on the consolidated balance sheet between the liabilities and shareholders' equity. See, for example, Exhibit 15.6 on page 640. Note that "Minority Interest" is shown among the liabilities but is not clearly labeled as one. This presentation is typical of many published financial statements. The right-hand side of the balance sheet contains only liabilities and owners' equity items, so the minority interest should appear as one or the other. Because the minority interest has no maturity date, it does not meet the criteria to be a liability discussed in Chapter 10. It is therefore classified as part of owners' equity by some companies.

The amount of the minority interest in the subsidiary's income, shown on the consolidated income statement, is generally the result of multiplying the subsidiary's net income by the minority's percentage of ownership. The consolidated income is allocated to show the portions applicable to the parent company and the portion of the subsidiary's income applicable to the minority interest. Refer to Exhibit 15.4 for Kaplan Corporation on page 638. Notice the deduction of $40 million for the Minority Interest in Earnings of Heimann Corporation before the consolidated net income figure for Year 2. The consolidated net income includes only that portion of net income of subsidiary companies allocable to the shareholders of Kaplan Corporation. Typically, the minority interest in the subsidiary's income appears as a deduction in calculating consolidated net income.

## Limitations of Consolidated Statements

The consolidated statements do not replace those of individual corporations; rather, they supplement those statements and aid in their interpretation. Creditors must rely on the resources of one corporation and may be misled if forced to rely entirely on a consolidated statement that combines the data of a company in good financial condition with those of one verging on insolvency. Dividends can legally be declared only from the retained earnings of one corporation. Where the parent company does not own all of the shares of the subsidiary, the outside or minority stockholders can judge the dividend constraints, both legal and financial, only by inspecting the subsidiary's statements.

# Preparing Consolidated Financial Statements ——————

This section illustrates the preparation of consolidated financial statements for Company P and Company S. Knowing how to construct consolidated financial statements is not essential for learning how to interpret and to analyze them, but it helps.

## Data for the Illustration

The single-company financial statements of Company P and Company S appear in Exhibit 13.1 on page 562. The following additional information is to be considered in preparing the consolidated financial statements.

**1.** Company P acquired 100 percent of the outstanding shares of Company S for $650,000 cash on January 1, Year 1. At the time of acquisition, the book value of the shareholders' equity of Company S was $650,000, comprising the following account balances:

| Company S, January 1, Year 1 | |
| --- | --- |
| Common Stock................................................... | $500,000 |
| Retained Earnings ............................................... | 150,000 |
| Total Shareholders' Equity....................................... | $650,000 |

Company P made the following journal entry on its books at the time of acquisition:

| | | |
| --- | --- | --- |
| Investment in Stock of Company S ........................ | 650,000 | |
| Cash.......................................................... | | 650,000 |

**2.** Company P records its investment in the shares of Company S using the equity method. The increase in Retained Earnings of Company S since January 1, Year 1, the date of acquisition, has been $55,000 (= $205,000 − $150,000). This increase has been reflected in the Investment in Company S account on Company P's books: $705,000 = $650,000 + $55,000.

**3.** At December 31, Year 4, $12,000 of Company S's accounts receivable represented amounts payable by Company P.

**4.** During Year 4, Company S sold merchandise to Company P for $40,000. None of that merchandise remains in Company P's inventory as of December 31, Year 4.

## Work Sheet Preparation

Preparing consolidated statements for Company P and Company S requires the following steps, characteristic of the consolidation procedure:

**A.** Elimination of the parent company's investment account.

**B.** Elimination of intercompany receivables and payables.

**C.** Elimination of intercompany sales and purchases.

This illustration starts with the information in single-company, preclosing trial balances. These data appear in the first two pairs of columns of the work sheet in Exhibit 13.2, which contain the same information as the first two columns of Exhibit 13.1. Note that the amounts shown for Retained Earnings are the balances as of January 1, Year 4. Revenue, expense, and dividend declaration accounts for Year 4 have not yet been closed to Retained Earnings. The fourth pair of columns in Exhibit 13.2 shows the amounts on a consolidated basis for Company P and Company S. The amounts in the last pair of columns horizontally sum the amounts in the other columns — Company P items, Company S items, plus adjustments and eliminations. These adjustments and eliminations, discussed in the sections that follow, are recorded only on a work sheet to prepare consolidated statements, not in the accounting records of either company.

**A. Elimination of Parent Company's Investment Account**   Company P acquired the shares of Company S for a price equal to their book value ($650,000). Since acquisition, Company P has used the equity method and has recorded the increase in Retained Earnings of Company S ($55,000) in its investment account. To avoid double counting the net assets of Company S (the assets themselves on Company S's balance sheet and Company P's investment in them on Company P's balance sheet), the investment account must be eliminated. The elimination is as follows:

| | | |
|---|---:|---:|
| (1) Common Stock (Company S)............................. | 500,000 | |
| Retained Earnings, January 1, Year 4 (Company S) .......... | 170,000 | |
| Equity in Earnings of Company S (Company P) .............. | 48,000 | |
| Dividends Declared (Company S)......................... | | 13,000 |
| Investment in Stock of Company S (Company P)........... | | 705,000 |

Aside from the minority interest, if any, the owners' equity of the consolidated entity is provided by the shareholders of the parent. There is no minority interest in this example. Thus the owners' equity of the subsidiary comes entirely from the parent's financing. If the owners' equity of the parent and of the subsidiary were merely added together, equities would be counted twice. When Company P's investment account is eliminated to avoid double counting of net assets, the subsidiary's owners' equity accounts — corresponding to the parent's investment — are eliminated to avoid double counting of the equities. The total amount eliminated is equal to the balance in the investment account ($705,000). This amount is also equal to the total shareholders' equity of Company S on December 31, Year 4 ($500,000 + $205,000; see Exhibit 13.1). Because the elimination is being made to a preclosing trial balance, the revenue, expense, and dividend declaration accounts of Company S have not yet been closed to Company S's Retained Earnings. Thus, in addition to eliminating the common stock of Company S ($500,000), the bal-

# Exhibit 13.2

## COMPANY P and COMPANY S
### Work Sheet to Derive Consolidated Financial Statements Based on Data from Preclosing Trial Balances for Year 4

| Trial Balance Accounts | Company P Debit | Company P Credit | Company S Debit | Company S Credit | Adjustments and Eliminations Debit | Adjustments and Eliminations Credit | P and S Consolidated Debit | P and S Consolidated Credit |
|---|---|---|---|---|---|---|---|---|
| Accounts Receivable | $ 200,000 | | $ 25,000 | | | (2) $ 12,000 | $ 213,000 | |
| Investment in Stock of Company S | 705,000 | | — | | | (1) 705,000 | — | |
| Other Assets | 2,150,000 | | 975,000 | | | | 3,125,000 | |
| Accounts Payable | | $ 75,000 | | $ 15,000 | (2) $ 12,000 | | | $ 78,000 |
| Other Liabilities | | 70,000 | | 280,000 | | | | 350,000 |
| Common Stock | | 2,500,000 | | 500,000 | (1) 500,000 | | | 2,500,000 |
| Retained Earnings, January 1, Year 4: | | | | | | | | |
| Company P | | 256,000 | | | | | | 256,000 |
| Company S | | | | 170,000 | (1) 170,000 | | | |
| Sales | | 900,000 | | 250,000 | (3) 40,000 | | | 1,110,000 |
| Equity in Earnings of Company S | | 48,000 | | — | (1) 48,000 | | | |
| Cost of Goods Sold | 440,000 | | 80,000 | | | (3) 40,000 | 480,000 | |
| Depreciation Expense | 120,000 | | 50,000 | | | | 170,000 | |
| Administrative Expenses | 80,000 | | 40,000 | | | | 120,000 | |
| Income Taxes | 104,000 | | 32,000 | | | | 136,000 | |
| Dividends Declared | 50,000 | | 13,000 | | | (1) 13,000 | 50,000 | |
| Totals | $3,849,000 | $3,849,000 | $1,215,000 | $1,215,000 | $770,000 | $770,000 | $4,294,000 | $4,294,000 |

ances in Retained Earnings of Company S on January 1, Year 4 ($170,000), the Equity in Earnings of Company S for Year 4 ($48,000), and the Dividends Declared by Company S during Year 4 ($13,000) are eliminated. The balance in the account Equity in Earnings of Company S equals Company S's net income for the year. This account is eliminated and replaced with the individual revenues less expenses of Company S (whose difference is also Company S's net income) in the consolidated income statement.

**B.  Elimination of Intercompany Receivables and Payables**  A parent may sell goods on account to, or buy goods on account from, a subsidiary and treat the resulting obligation as an account receivable or an account payable. The subsidiary will treat the obligation as an account payable or an account receivable. A parent often makes loans to subsidiaries that appear among the parent's asset as Notes Receivable, Investment in Bonds, or Advances to Subsidiary. The subsidiary would show Notes Payable, Bonds Payable, or Advances from Parent in its liabilities. A single company would not show Accounts Receivable and Accounts Payable for departments within the company. These transactions are eliminated from the consolidated balance sheet so that the resulting statement appears as that of a single company.

In the illustration, Company S's accounts receivable include $12,000 due to it from Company P. The entry to record the elimination of the intercompany receivables and payables in Exhibit 13.2 is as follows:

```
(2) Accounts Payable ......................................   12,000
       Accounts Receivable ..................................          12,000
    To eliminate intercompany payables and receivables.
```

**C.  Elimination of Intercompany Sales and Purchases**  Sales between consolidated companies should not be reported in a consolidated income statement, any more than transfers from Work-in-Process Inventory to Finished Goods Inventory should be reported as sales within a single company. During Year 4, Company P acquired $40,000 of merchandise inventory from Company S. Eliminating intercompany sales requires a debit to Sales (of the selling corporation) and a credit to Inventories or Cost of Goods Sold of the purchasing corporation, depending on whether it has yet computed Cost of Goods Sold. In this illustration, Company P has already computed its cost of goods sold from the inventory equation:

$$\text{Cost of Goods Sold} = \text{Beginning Inventory} + \text{Purchases} - \text{Ending Inventory}$$
$$= \text{Goods Available for Sale} - \text{Ending Inventory}.$$

Therefore, the offsetting credit to eliminate intercompany sales must be to the Cost of Goods Sold account.

```
(3) Sales ................................................   40,000
       Cost of Goods Sold ..................................          40,000
    To eliminate intercompany sales and purchases.
```

## Exhibit 13.3 _____

**Balance Sheet and Income Statement Assuming that
Company S Is Not Consolidated and Company S Is Consolidated**

|  | Company P Unconsolidated (Equity Method) (1) | Company P and Company S Consolidated (2) |
|---|---|---|
| **Balance Sheet** | | |
| **Assets:** | | |
| Accounts Receivable......................... | $ 200,000 | $ 213,000 |
| Investment in Stock of S Company ............ | 705,000 | — |
| Other Assets................................ | 2,150,000 | 3,125,000 |
| Total Assets ........................... | $3,055,000 | $3,338,000 |
| | | |
| **Equities:** | | |
| Accounts Payable ......................... | $  75,000 | $  78,000 |
| Other Liabilities............................. | 70,000 | 350,000 |
| Common Stock............................. | 2,500,000 | 2,500,000 |
| Retained Earnings ......................... | 410,000 | 410,000 |
| Total Equities ........................... | $3,055,000 | $3,338,000 |

Company S sold goods to Company P, and Company P sold the goods outside the consolidated pair of companies. In the absence of the elimination of intercompany sales, these sales would be counted twice. The profits on the sales would be computed properly, but the amount of gross sales and purchases (Cost of Goods Sold) would be inflated. To see that profits are computed properly, even without the elimination, assume that the goods cost Company S $30,000 and that Company P sold them for $45,000. In the single-company income statements, Company S profits are $10,000 (= $40,000 − $30,000) as a result of the sale to Company P. Company P profits are $5,000 (= $45,000 − $40,000) as a result of its sales to others. Total profits of the consolidated group from these transactions are $15,000, or Company P's revenue of $45,000 less Company S's cost of $30,000. The elimination of intercompany sales does not change the consolidated sales to outsiders, the consolidated cost of goods sold to outsiders, or consolidated profit.

If either company holds bonds or long-term notes of the other, there would be a similar elimination of the "borrower's" interest expense and of the "lender's" interest revenue.

## Statement Preparation

Once the consolidation work sheet has been completed, the consolidated statements can be prepared. Column (2) of Exhibit 13.3 presents a consolidated balance sheet on December 31, Year 4, and a consolidated income statement for Year 4 for Company P and Company S. To make comparisons easier, column (1) of Exhibit 13.3 repeats the balance sheet and income statement for Company P alone,

**Exhibit 13.3** *(continued)* _____

|  | Company P Unconsolidated (Equity Method) (1) | Company P and Company S Consolidated (2) |
|---|---|---|
| **Income Statement** | | |
| **Revenues:** | | |
| Sales..................................... | $ 900,000 | $1,110,000 |
| Equity in Earnings of Company S .............. | 48,000 | — |
| Total Revenues ........................... | $ 948,000 | $1,110,000 |
| | | |
| **Expenses:** | | |
| Cost of Goods Sold......................... | $ 440,000 | $ 480,000 |
| Depreciation Expense....................... | 120,000 | 170,000 |
| Administrative Expenses ..................... | 80,000 | 120,000 |
| Income Taxes .............................. | 104,000 | 136,000 |
| Total Expenses............................ | $ 744,000 | $ 906,000 |
| Net Income ............................... | $ 204,000 | $ 204,000 |

assuming that Company S is *not* consolidated and the Investment in Stock of Company S is accounted for using the equity method. Note the following aspects of using the equity method for an unconsolidated subsidiary versus consolidating that subsidiary:

1.  When a subsidiary is not consolidated, the parent's balance sheet will show the investment in the subsidiary's net assets in a single investment account. When the subsidiary is consolidated, the investment account is replaced with the individual assets and liabilities of the subsidiary.

2.  Consolidated retained earnings are the same amount as would result when the parent uses the equity method for an unconsolidated subsidiary.

3.  When a subsidiary is not consolidated, the parent's interest in the earnings of the subsidiary appears on the single line, Equity in Earnings of Company S, on the parent's income statement. When the subsidiary is consolidated, the individual revenues and expenses of the subsidiary replace the Equity in Earnings of S account.

4.  Consolidated net income is the same amount as that which results when the parent uses the equity method for an unconsolidated subsidiary.

# Summary _____

Businesses acquire stock in other businesses for a variety of reasons and in a variety of ways. The acquisition of stock of another company as a long-term investment is generally recorded as follows:

| | | |
|---|---|---|
| Investment in S ............................................. | X | |
|    Cash or Other Consideration Given........................... | | X |

The investment account is recorded at the amount of cash given or the market value of other consideration exchanged.

The accounting for the investment subsequent to acquisition depends on the ownership percentage. The lower-of-cost-or-market method is generally used when the parent owns less than 20 percent. The equity method is generally used when the parent owns at least 20 percent, but not more than 50 percent, of the stock of another company. The equity method will also be used when the investor company can exercise significant influence even when the percentage owned is less than 20 percent. Consolidated statements are prepared when the parent owns more than 50 percent of the voting shares of another company, but the lower-of-cost-or-market method may be used if control cannot be exercised. Exhibit 13.4 summarizes the accounting for investments subsequent to the acquisition.

Under the lower-of-cost-or-market method, income is recognized only when dividends become receivable by the investor or when the securities are sold.

Consolidated statements and the equity method both have the same effect on net income. The parent shows as income its proportional share of the acquired firm's periodic income after acquisition. Income statement amounts of revenues and expenses will be larger under the consolidation method, however, because the revenues and expenses of the acquired company are combined with those of the parent. Balance sheet components will be larger under the consolidation method than under the equity method, because the individual assets and liabilities of the acquired company will be substituted for the investment balance on the parent company's books.

# Appendix 13.1:
# Some Complexities in Consolidation _____

The illustrations in Exhibits 13.1 and 13.2 were simplified. This appendix considers two situations encountered in consolidated statements that were not illustrated in this chapter. These are:

1.  Acquisition price of subsidiary exceeds book value acquired.
2.  Less than 100 percent of the subsidiary's stock is acquired, resulting in a minority interest.

Refer to the data in Exhibits 13.1 and 13.2, and to steps A through C for worksheet preparation listed on page 567.

## Acquisition Price Exceeds Book Value Acquired

Suppose that Company P had paid $700,000, rather than $650,000, for its 100 percent investment in Company S. The $50,000 difference in purchase price represents the amount paid for Company S's assets in excess of their book value, for

**Exhibit 13.4** _____

## Effects of Various Methods of Accounting for Long-Term Investments in Corporate Securities

| Method of Accounting | Balance Sheet | Income Statement | Statements of Cash Flows |
|---|---|---|---|
| Lower-of-cost-or-market method (generally used when ownership percentage is less than 20 percent). | Investment account shown at lower of acquisition cost or current market value as a noncurrent asset. Unrealized losses resulting from decline in market value below cost are credited to an asset contra and debited to an unrealized loss account that is shown as a negative component of owners' equity. | Dividends declared by investee shown as revenue of investor. Gains and losses (from original cost) are reported in income only as realized in arm's-length transactions with outsiders. | Dividends received from investee included in cash provided by operations of investor. |
| Equity method (generally used when ownership percentage is at least 20 percent but not more than 50 percent). | Investment account shown at cost plus share of investee's net income less share of investee's dividends since acquisition. | Equity in investee's net income shown as revenue in period that investee earns income. | Equity in investee's undistributed earnings is subtracted from net income to derive cash provided by operations of investor. Cash from operations is thus increased only by the amount of dividend received. |
| Consolidation (generally used when ownership percentage is greater than 50 percent). | Investment account is eliminated and replaced with individual assets and liabilities of subsidiary. Minority interest in subsidiary's net assets shown among equities. | Individual revenues and expenses of subsidiary are combined with those of parent. Minority interest in subsidiary's net income shown as a subtraction. | Individual sources and uses of cash of subsidiary are combined with those of parent. Minority interest in net income is added to net income to obtain cash provided by operations. |

goodwill, or for both. Assume that on the date of acquisition, January 1, Year 1, the book value of Company S's recorded assets and liabilities equaled their market values at that time. The fact that Company P was willing to pay $700,000 for recorded assets having book values and market values equal to $650,000 means that Company S must have had *unrecorded* assets of $50,000 on January 1, Year 1. The $50,000 of unrecorded assets represents goodwill. Generally accepted accounting principles[10] require goodwill to be amortized over a period not exceeding 40 years. Assume that Company P chose a 40-year amortization period. On its separate company books, Company P would have made the following entry during each of the years 1 through 4:

| | | |
|---|---|---|
| Amortization Expense . . . . . . . . . . . . . . . . . . . . . . . . . . . . . . . . . . . . . . | 1,250 | |
| Investment in Stock of Company S . . . . . . . . . . . . . . . . . . . . . . . . . . | | 1,250 |

To recognize amortization of goodwill; $1,250 = ($700,000 − $650,000)/40.

In preparing the consolidation work sheet at the end of Year 4, entry (1) would be the same as that shown in Exhibit 13.2. After entry (1), the Investment in Stock of

_____

[10]Accounting Principles Board, *Opinion No. 17.*

Company S would still have a debit balance of $45,000 [= $50,000 − (4 × $1,250)]. This amount represents the *unamortized* goodwill arising from the acquisition. A work sheet entry should be made to reclassify this amount from the investment account to goodwill. The entry is as follows:

| | | |
|---|---|---|
| Goodwill .................................................. | 45,000 | |
|     Investment in Stock of Company S .......................... | | 45,000 |
| To reclassify goodwill. | | |

The consolidated balance sheet on December 31, Year 4, will show goodwill of $45,000 [= $50,000 − (4 × $1,250)]. Consolidated net income for Year 4 will now be $202,750 (= $204,000 − $1,250) to reflect amortization expense for Year 4. Consolidated retained earnings will be $405,000 [= $410,000 − (4 × $1,250)]. The statement of cash flows will show an addback of $1,250 for amortization expense that did not use cash.

## Recognizing External, Minority Interest

Now assume that Company P had acquired only 90 percent of the capital stock of Company S on January 1, Year 1, at its book value. In this case, other individuals or entities own the remaining 10 percent of the shares. These individuals or entities represent an external minority interest in the earnings and net assets of Company S.

The net assets, or shareholders' equity, of Company S are allocable to Company P and to the minority shareholders as shown in Exhibit 13.5. Assuming that Company P has acquired its 90 percent interest in Company S for book value, it would have paid $585,000 (= .90 × $650,000) on January 1, Year 1. The Investment in Stock of Company S account would have been recorded initially at this amount in Company P's books. Between Year 1 and Year 4, Company P would

**Exhibit 13.5** _____
**Allocation of Shareholders' Equity of Company S
to Company P and Minority Interest Shareholders**

| | Total (1) | To Company P (90 percent) (2) | To Minority Shareholders (10 percent) (3) |
|---|---|---|---|
| January 1, Year 1: Common Stock ...... | $500,000 | $450,000 | $50,000 |
|                        Retained Earnings ... | 150,000 | 135,000 | 15,000 |
| Increase in Retained Earnings, January 1, Year 1–December 31, Year 3............................. | 20,000 | 18,000 | 2,000 |
|    Subtotal .......................... | $670,000 | $603,000 | $67,000 |
| Net Income for Year 4 ................. | 48,000 | 43,200 | 4,800 |
| Dividends Declared for Year 4 .......... | (13,000) | (11,700) | (1,300) |
| December 31, Year 4 ................. | $705,000 | $634,500 | $70,500 |

have increased the investment account for 90 percent of Company S's earnings and decreased the investment account for 90 percent of Company S's dividends. Thus the Investment in Stock of Company S account would show a balance of $634,500 on December 31, Year 4 [see column (2) of Exhibit 13.5]. The work sheet elimination entry for the investment account would be as follows:

| | | |
|---|---|---|
| Common Stock (Company S)..................................... | 450,000 | |
| Retained Earnings, January 1 (Company S) .................... | 153,000 | |
| Equity in Earnings of Company S (Company P)................. | 43,200 | |
|    Dividends Declared (Company S) ............................ | | 11,700 |
|    Investment in Stock of Company S (Company P) .............. | | 634,500 |

The minority interest constitutes the remaining balances in Company S's shareholders' equity accounts. The work sheet entry to recognize the minority interest is as follows:

| | | |
|---|---|---|
| Common Stock (Company S) .................................... | 50,000 | |
| Retained Earnings (Company S) .............................. | 17,000 | |
| Minority Interest in Earnings of Company S .................... | 4,800 | |
|    Dividends Declared (Company S) ............................ | | 1,300 |
|    Minority Interest in Net Assets of Company S ................ | | 70,500 |

The account Minority Interest in Earnings of Company S is "created" on the consolidation work sheet. It does not appear as an account on either of the separate company's books. It represents the external minority interest in the earnings of Company S and is shown as a deduction in calculating consolidated net income. Consolidated net income is, therefore, $199,200 (= $204,000 − $4,800).

The account Minority Interest in Net Assets of Company S is, likewise, created on the consolidation work sheet. It represents the external minority interest in the net assets of Company S, a *consolidated* subsidiary. It is shown on the right-hand side of the consolidated balance sheet, usually between liabilities and shareholders' equity.

The consolidated statement of cash flows starts with the net income of $199,200 to shareholders of Company P. Amounts are added back for the minority interest in S's undistributed earnings for the year of $3,500 (= $4,800 − $1,300) and for depreciation ($170,000), neither of which uses cash. The only use of cash is the $50,000 of dividends paid by the parent.

Parts **f** through **i** of the Problem for Self-Study review the material in this appendix.

# Appendix 13.2:
# Effects in the Statement of Cash Flows _____

## Equity Method

When Company P uses the lower-of-cost-or-market method to account for its investment in Company S, all dividend revenues recognized in computing net income also generally produce cash. Therefore, no adjustment to net income is normally required in calculating cash flow from operations.

However, accounting for investments using the equity method requires an adjustment to net income to compute cash flow from operations. Suppose that Company P prepares its financial statements at the end of a year during which transactions (1) through (5), described in pages 556 and 557, occurred. P's revenue from its investment in S is $54,000. This amount is the sum of the revenue recognized in transactions (2) and (4). P's income (ignoring income tax effects) increased $54,000 because of its investment. However, P's cash increased by only $21,000 [transactions (3) and (5)] as a result of S's dividends. Consequently, there must be a *subtraction* from net income of $33,000 (= $54,000 − $21,000) in computing cash flow from operations to show that cash did not increase by as much as the amount of revenue recognized under the equity method.

In preparing P's statement of cash flows using the indirect method, the following change in a noncurrent asset account would have to be explained:

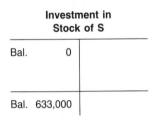

**Investment in
Stock of S**

| | | |
|---|---|---|
| Bal. | 0 | |
| Bal. | 633,000 | |

The entries to explain this debit change of $633,000 would be as follows:

| | | |
|---|---|---|
| Investment in Stock of S ...................................... | 600,000 | |
|     Cash (Investing — Acquisition of Investment) ................ | | 600,000 |
| To recognize use of cash for an investment in a noncurrent asset. | | |
| Investment in Stock of S ...................................... | 33,000 | |
|     Cash (Operations: Subtraction — Undistributed Income under | | |
|       Equity Method) ......................................... | | 33,000 |
| To recognize that cash was not increased by the full amount of revenue recognized under the equity method. | | |

Keep in mind that these two entries are not formally made in the accounting records, but are made only in the work sheet used for preparing the statement of cash flows.

## Minority Interest

The minority interest share of earnings is deducted in calculating consolidated net income. This deduction did not require the use of cash. Consequently, there must be an addback to derive cash flow from operations in the statement of cash flows when the indirect method is used. See Exhibit 15.5, which illustrates this addback.

# Appendix 13.3:
# Accounting for Corporate Acquisitions _____

When one corporation acquires all, or substantially all, of another corporation's common stock in a single transaction, the transaction is called a *corporate acquisition*. Two methods of accounting for corporate acquisitions are permitted under generally accepted accounting principles, depending on the manner in which the acquisition is structured: the purchase method or the pooling-of-interests method.

## Purchase Method

The purchase method uses acquisition cost accounting. The Investment in Subsidiary account on the parent's books is recorded initially at the amount of cash or the market value of other consideration given in the exchange. When the consolidation work sheet is prepared, any difference between the amount in the investment account on the date of acquisition and the book value of the net assets acquired is allocated to individual assets and liabilities to write them up or down to their market values. Any excess of the purchase price over the market values of the individual assets and liabilities is then allocated to goodwill. Thus, under the purchase method, the assets and liabilities of the acquired company are reported in the consolidated balance sheet at the date of acquisition at their market values. The consolidated income statement in subsequent periods will show expenses (depreciation and amortization) based on these market values. The principles of the purchase method have implicitly been used throughout this chapter.

## Pooling-of-Interests Method

The pooling-of-interests method accounts for a corporate acquisition as the uniting of ownership interests of two companies by exchange of equity (common stock) securities. The exchange of equity interests is viewed as a change in *form*, not in *substance;* that is, the shareholders of the predecessor companies become shareholders in the new combined enterprise. Each of the predecessor companies continues carrying out its operations as before. Because there is no change in the substance of either the ownership interest or the nature of the activities of the enterprises involved, no new basis of accountability arises. In other words, the book values of the assets and liabilities of the predecessor companies are carried over to the new combined, or consolidated, enterprise. Unlike the purchase method, assets and liabilities do not reflect market values at the date of acquisition on the consolidated balance sheet.

## Illustration of Purchase and Pooling-of-Interests Methods

To illustrate the purchase and pooling-of-interests methods, assume that Company P and Company S decide to combine operations. Management estimates that the combination will save $50,000 a year in expenses of running the combined businesses. Columns (1) and (2) in Exhibit 13.6 show abbreviated single-company financial statements for Company P and Company S before combination. Company S has 20,000 shares of stock outstanding that sell for $84 per share in the market. The market value of Company S as a going concern is, therefore, $1,680,000. As shown in column (3), S's shareholders have $1,230,000 of equity not recorded on the books. Of this $1,230,000, $400,000 is attributable to undervalued noncurrent assets, and $830,000 is attributable to goodwill. Company P has 100,000 shares outstanding, which have a $5 par value and sell for $42 each in the market. Income taxes are ignored.

**Purchase Method** To carry out the acquisition, P issues (sells) 40,000 additional shares on the market for $42 each, or $1,680,000 in total, and uses the proceeds to purchase all shares of S for $84 each. (Each share of S is, in effect, "sold" for two shares of P.) P has acquired 100 percent of the shares of S and now owns S.

P's acquisition of S will be accounted for using the purchase method. Under these conditions, P will amortize the revalued asset costs over 5 years and the goodwill over 40 years. Consolidated financial reports under the purchase method are shown in Exhibit 13.6 in column (4). The consolidated balance sheet is the sum of columns (1) and (3), except for the shareholders' equity section. Since P issued 40,000 new shares for $42 each, the Common Stock account shows 140,000 shares at $5 par value. The Additional Paid-in Capital account shows P's former Additional Paid-in Capital plus the addition arising from the new stock issue: $200,000 + [40,000 × ($42 − $5)] = $1,680,000. The retained earnings of the consolidated enterprise are equal to P's retained earnings.

The consolidated income statement, when the acquisition is treated as a purchase, starts with the combined incomes before consolidation. To that amount is added the cost savings of $50,000 resulting from the more efficient operations of the combination. Then both the additional depreciation expense arising from the asset revaluations and the goodwill amortization expense are subtracted. The reported consolidated net income, as projected, is $409,250.

**Pooling of Interests** Now, examine the accounting for the acquisition as shown in column (5), assuming that it qualifies for the pooling-of-interests method. Assume that P issued the 40,000 shares of stock directly to the owners of S in return for their shares. The balance sheet items, except for the individual shareholders' equity accounts, are merely the sum of the single-company amounts shown in columns (1) and (2). The shareholders' equity after pooling must then equal total shareholders' equity before pooling.

The common stock of the pooled enterprise must equal the par value of the shares outstanding after pooling. After pooling there are 140,000 shares outstanding with a par value of $700,000. The general rule is that the pooled retained earnings balance is the sum of the retained earnings before pooling. The example illustrates

## Exhibit 13.6

## Consolidated Statements Comparing Purchase and Pooling-of-Interests Methods

| | Historical Cost | | S Shown at Current Values (3) | Companies P and S Consolidated at Date of Acquisition | |
| --- | --- | --- | --- | --- | --- |
| | P (1) | S (2) | | Purchase (4) | Pooling of Interests (5) |
| **Balance Sheets** | | | | | |
| **Assets:** | | | | | |
| Current Assets ............................ | $1,500,000 | $450,000 | $ 450,000 | $1,950,000 | $1,950,000 |
| Long-Term Assets less Accumulated Depreciation .......................... | 1,700,000 | 450,000 | 850,000 | 2,550,000 | 2,150,000 |
| Goodwill ................................. | — | — | 830,000 | 830,000 | — |
| Total Assets ......................... | $3,200,000 | $900,000 | $2,130,000 | $5,330,000 | $4,100,000 |
| | | | | | |
| **Equities:** | | | | | |
| Liabilities ................................ | $1,300,000 | $450,000 | $ 450,000 | $1,750,000 | $1,750,000 |
| Common Stock ($5 par) .................. | 500,000 | 100,000 | 100,000 | 700,000[a] | 700,000[a] |
| Additional Paid-in Capital ................ | 200,000 | 150,000 | 150,000 | 1,680,000[b] | 250,000[e] |
| Retained Earnings ....................... | 1,200,000 | 200,000 | 200,000 | 1,200,000[c] | 1,400,000[d] |
| Unrecorded Equity at Current Valuation ...... | — | — | 1,230,000 | — | — |
| Total Liabilities and Shareholders' Equity ... | $3,200,000 | $900,000 | $2,130,000 | $5,330,000 | $4,100,000 |

### Income Statements (ignoring income taxes)[h]

| | | | | | |
| --- | --- | --- | --- | --- | --- |
| Precombination Income .................... | $ 300,000 | $160,000 | | $ 460,000 | $ 460,000 |
| From Combination: | | | | | |
| Cost Savings (projected) ................... | — | — | | 50,000 | 50,000 |
| Extra Depreciation Expense ................ | — | — | | (80,000)[f] | — |
| Amortization of Goodwill.................... | — | — | | (20,750)[g] | — |
| Net Income ........................... | $ 300,000 | $160,000 | | $ 409,250[h] | $ 510,000[h] |
| Number of Common Shares Outstanding..... | 100,000 | 20,000 | | 140,000 | 140,000 |
| Earnings per Share ....................... | $3.00 | $8.00 | | $2.92 | $3.64 |

### Rate of Return Ratios

| | | | | | |
| --- | --- | --- | --- | --- | --- |
| Return on Assets (Net Income[i]/Total Assets) ............... | 9.4% | 17.8% | | 7.7% | 12.4% |
| Return on Common Shareholders' Equity (Net Income/Owners' Equity) ............. | 15.8 | 35.6 | | 11.4 | 21.7 |

Assumptions: (1) Company S has 20,000 shares outstanding that sell for $84 each in the market.

(2) Company P's shares sell for $42 each in the market. Company P issues 40,000 shares for the purpose of acquiring Company S.

[a]P's 100,000 original shares plus 40,000 new shares at $5 par.
[b]P's $200,000 original additional paid-in capital plus 40,000 × ($42 − $5).
[c]P's retained earnings.
[d]Sum of P's and S's retained earnings.
[e]Plug to equate pooled shareholders' equity to the sum of all the shareholders' equity accounts of the combining companies before combination.
[f]1/5 × ($850,000 − $450,000).
[g]1/40 × $830,000.
[h]As projected.
[i]The numerator would usually be adjusted for the aftertax effects of interest. This example assumes no interest expense for either company.

the general rule. The total paid-in capital (par value plus additional paid-in capital) after pooling will generally equal the sum of the paid-in capital accounts of the firms before pooling. Thus the additional paid-in capital of the pooled firm is, ordinarily, the plug to equate the pooled paid-in capital with the sum of the paid-in capital accounts before pooling.

The income statement resulting from a pooling of interests shows the same revenues and cost savings as those following a purchase. There are, however, no extra depreciation and amortization expenses resulting from increased asset valuations and the recognition of goodwill. Consequently, the pooled enterprise projects net income of $510,000 and shareholders' equity of $2,350,000 (a rate of return on shareholders' equity of 21.7 percent), whereas the identical acquisition accounted for using the purchase method projects smaller income ($409,250) and larger shareholders' equity of $3,580,000 (a rate of return on shareholders' equity of 11.4 percent). Notice that the earnings-per-share figure — one often scrutinized by financial analysts — under the pooling-of-interests method is 25 percent larger than under the purchase method.

This example, if anything, understates the difference between the purchase and pooling methods. Notice that S's market value before the merger is less than four times ($1,680,000/$450,000 = 3.7) its book value. In practice, poolings of interests have occurred when the ratio of market value to book value was as high as ten or more to one. Thus the amortization charges of the purchased subsidiary's assets can be many times larger than the amortization of the pooled subsidiary's assets.

## Managing Earnings

Pooling of interests not only keeps reported expenses from increasing after the merger, it may also allow the management of the pooled companies to manage the reported earnings in an arbitrary way. Suppose, as has happened, that Company P merges with an old, established firm, Company F, which has produced commercial movie films. These films, made in the 1940s and 1950s, were amortized so that by the 1980s the book value of these films is close to zero. But the market value of the films is much larger than zero, because television stations and cable networks find that old movies please their audiences. If Company P purchases Company F, the old films will be shown on the consolidated balance sheet at the films' current market value. If Company P merges with Company F using the pooling-of-interests method, the films will be shown on the consolidated balance sheet at their near-zero book values. Then, when Company P wants to boost reported earnings for the year, it can sell some old movies to a television or cable network and report a large gain. Actually, of course, the owners of Company F enjoyed this gain when their stock was "sold to" (or exchanged with) Company P for current asset values, not the obsolete book values.

Those who defend pooling-of-interests accounting argue that the management of the pooled enterprise has no more opportunity to manage earnings than did the management of Company F before the pooling. Management of Company F can sell old movies any time it chooses and report handsome gains. The problem is caused by the historical cost basis of accounting, which recognizes gains only when there has been a market transaction. Defenders of pooling argue that there is no reason to penalize the management of a merged company relative to the management of an established company with many assets undervalued on its books. Opponents of pooling reply that it was the management of Company F that earned the holding gains, whereas it is the management of Company P that will be able to report them as realized gains under pooling.

In summary, if the acquisition qualifies as a purchase, the reported income of the combined enterprise may be reduced by additional depreciation and amortization expenses. The extra depreciation and amortization expenses result from recognizing increased asset valuations and, perhaps, goodwill. If the acquisition qualifies as a pooling of interests, reported income for the consolidated enterprise will ordinarily be larger than for the same consolidated enterprise accounted for as a purchase.

## Problem for Self-Study ————————————————————

Reynolds Corporation acquired as long-term investments shares of common stock of Company R, Company S, and Company T on January 2. These are the only long-term investments in securities of Reynolds Corporation. Data relating to the acquisitions follow.

| Company | Percentage Acquired | Book Value and Market Value of Total Net Assets on January 2 | Acquisition Cost | Net Income for Year | Dividends Declared for Year | Market Value of Shares Owned on December 31 |
|---|---|---|---|---|---|---|
| R ................ | 10% | $5,000,000 | $ 540,000 | $1,000,000 | $400,000 | $ 520,000 |
| S ................ | 30 | 5,000,000 | 1,700,000 | 1,000,000 | 400,000 | 1,710,000 |
| T ................ | 100 | 5,000,000 | 5,000,000 | 1,000,000 | 400,000 | 5,200,000 |

Any goodwill arising from the acquisitions is amortized over 10 years.

**a.** Give the journal entries made to acquire the shares of Company R and to account for the investment during the year, using the lower-of-cost-or-market method.

**b.** Give the journal entries made to acquire the shares of Company S and to account for the investment during the year, using the equity method.

**c.** Give the journal entries made to acquire the shares of Company T and to account for the investment during the year, using the equity method.

**d.** Give the consolidation work sheet entry to eliminate the Investment in Stock of Company T account at the end of the year, assuming that the equity method is used and that the work sheet is based on preclosing trial balance amounts. Company T had $2,000,000 in its Common Stock account throughout the year and a zero balance in Additional Paid-in Capital.

**e.** Repeat part **d**, but assume that the work sheet is based on post-closing trial balance amounts.

Parts **f** through **i** should not be worked until Appendix 13.1 has been read.

**f.**   Assume that the shares of Company T had been acquired for $5,500,000, instead of $5,000,000. Give the journal entries made during the year to acquire the shares of Company T and to account for the investment, using the equity method. Any excess of cost over book value is considered goodwill and is amortized over 10 years.

**g.**   Refer to part **f**. Give the consolidation work sheet entry to eliminate the Investment in Stock of Company T account, assuming the work sheet is based on preclosing trial balance data.

**h.**   Assume that Reynolds Corporation had paid $4,000,000 for 80 percent of the shares of Company T on January 2. Give the journal entries made during the year to acquire the shares of Company T and to account for the investment, using the equity method.

**i.**   Refer to part **h**. Give the consolidation work sheet entries to eliminate the Investment in Stock of Company T account and to recognize the external minority interest in Company T, assuming the work sheet is based on preclosing trial balance data.

## Suggested Solution

| | | |
|---|---:|---:|
| **a.**  Investment in Stock of Company R . . . . . . . . . . . . . . . . . . . . . . . . | 540,000 | |
| Cash . . . . . . . . . . . . . . . . . . . . . . . . . . . . . . . . . . . . . . . . . . . . . . | | 540,000 |
| To record acquisition of shares of Company R. | | |
| Cash and Dividends Receivable . . . . . . . . . . . . . . . . . . . . . . . . . . | 40,000 | |
| Dividend Revenue . . . . . . . . . . . . . . . . . . . . . . . . . . . . . . . . . | | 40,000 |
| To record dividends received or receivable. | | |
| Unrealized Holding Loss on Valuation of Marketable Equity | | |
| Investments . . . . . . . . . . . . . . . . . . . . . . . . . . . . . . . . . . . . . . . . . | 20,000 | |
| Allowance for Excess of Cost of Investments over | | |
| Market Value . . . . . . . . . . . . . . . . . . . . . . . . . . . . . . . . . . . . . | | 20,000 |
| To write down portfolio (Company R only) of minority, passive investments to market value; $20,000 = $540,000 − $520,000. | | |
| **b.**  Investment in Stock of Company S . . . . . . . . . . . . . . . . . . . . . . . . | 1,700,000 | |
| Cash . . . . . . . . . . . . . . . . . . . . . . . . . . . . . . . . . . . . . . . . . . . . . . | | 1,700,000 |
| To record acquisition of shares of Company S. | | |
| Investment in Stock of Company S . . . . . . . . . . . . . . . . . . . . . . . . | 300,000 | |
| Equity in Earnings of Company S . . . . . . . . . . . . . . . . . . . . . | | 300,000 |
| To accrue share of Company S's earnings; $300,000 = .30 × $1,000,000. | | |
| Cash and Dividends Receivable . . . . . . . . . . . . . . . . . . . . . . . . . . | 120,000 | |
| Investment in Stock of Company S . . . . . . . . . . . . . . . . . . . . | | 120,000 |
| To record dividends received or receivable. | | |
| Amortization Expense . . . . . . . . . . . . . . . . . . . . . . . . . . . . . . . . . . | 20,000 | |
| Investment in Stock of Company S . . . . . . . . . . . . . . . . . . . . | | 20,000 |
| To record amortization of goodwill implicit in purchase price; $20,000 = ($1,700,000 − $1,500,000)/10. | | |

**c.** Investment in Stock of Company T ......................... 5,000,000
  Cash .................................................           5,000,000
  To record acquisition of shares of Company T.

Investment in Stock of Company T ......................... 1,000,000
  Equity in Earnings of Company T .....................         1,000,000
  To accrue earnings of Company T; $1,000,000 = 100% × $1,000,000.

Cash and Dividends Receivable.......................... 400,000
  Investment in Stock of Company T .....................       400,000
  To record dividends received or receivable.

**d.** Common Stock........................................ 2,000,000
Retained Earnings (January 2)........................... 3,000,000
Equity in Earnings of Company T ........................ 1,000,000
  Dividends Declared ..................................       400,000
  Investment in Stock of Company T .....................     5,600,000
  To eliminate investment account on consolidation work sheet.

**e.** Common Stock........................................ 2,000,000
Retained Earnings (December 31)......................... 3,600,000
  Investment in Stock of Company T .....................     5,600,000
  To eliminate investment account on consolidation work sheet.

**f.** Investment in Stock of Company T ......................... 5,500,000
  Cash .................................................      5,500,000
  To record acquisition of shares of Company T.

Investment in Stock of Company T ......................... 1,000,000
  Equity in Earnings of Company T .....................    1,000,000
  To accrue earnings of Company T.

Cash and Dividends Receivable.......................... 400,000
  Investment in Stock of Company T .....................     400,000
  To record dividends received or receivable.

Amortization Expense ................................... 50,000
  Investment in Stock of Company T .....................     50,000
  To record amortization of goodwill implicit in purchase price; $50,000 = ($5,500,000 − $5,000,000)/10.

**g.** Common Stock........................................ 2,000,000
Retained Earnings ...................................... 3,000,000
Equity in Earnings of Company T ........................ 1,000,000
Goodwill .............................................. 450,000
  Dividends Declared ..................................     400,000
  Investment in Stock of Company T .....................   6,050,000
  To eliminate investment account on consolidation work sheet; $6,050,000 = $5,500,000 + $1,000,000 − $400,000 − $50,000.

**h.** Investment in Stock of Company T ......................... 4,000,000
  Cash .................................................     4,000,000
  To record acquisition of shares of Company T.

| | | |
|---|---|---|
| Investment in Stock of Company T ....................... | 800,000 | |
|     Equity in Earnings of Company T ..................... | | 800,000 |

To accrue share of Company T's earnings; $800,000 = .80 × $1,000,000.

| | | |
|---|---|---|
| Cash or Dividends Receivable ......................... | 320,000 | |
|     Investment in Stock of Company T .................... | | 320,000 |

To record dividends received or receivable; $320,000 = .80 × $400,000.

---

**i.**

| | | |
|---|---|---|
| Common Stock......................................... | 1,600,000 | |
| Retained Earnings ..................................... | 2,400,000 | |
| Equity in Earnings of Company T ...................... | 800,000 | |
|     Dividends Declared ................................. | | 320,000 |
|     Investment in Stock of Company T ................... | | 4,480,000 |

To eliminate investment account on consolidation work sheet; $4,480,000 = $4,000,000 + $800,000 − $320,000.

| | | |
|---|---|---|
| Common Stock......................................... | 400,000 | |
| Retained Earnings ..................................... | 600,000 | |
| Minority Interest in Earnings of Company T.............. | 200,000 | |
|     Dividends Declared ................................. | | 80,000 |
|     Minority Interest in Net Assets of Company T........... | | 1,120,000 |

To recognize external minority interest in Company T.

---

# Questions, Exercises, Problems, and Cases _____

## Questions

1. Review the meaning of the following concepts or terms discussed in this chapter.
   a. Marketable securities classified as current assets or as long-term investments.
   b. Minority, passive investments.
   c. Significant influence by an investor over an investee.
   d. Minority, active investments.
   e. Majority, active investments.
   f. Lower-of-cost-or-market method for long-term investments.
   g. Equity method.
   h. Parent.
   i. Subsidiary.
   j. Consolidated financial statements.
   k. Economic entity versus legal entity.
   l. Consolidation policy.
   m. Intercompany transactions.
   n. Adjustments and eliminations in a consolidation work sheet.
   o. Minority interest in a consolidated subsidiary.
   p. Goodwill.

2. Unrealized holding losses from price declines of marketable equity securities classified as current assets are recognized as they arise in calculating net income. Similar unrealized holding losses from long-term investments accounted for using the lower-of-cost-or-market method are not recognized as they arise in calculating net income. What is the rationale for this difference in accounting treatment?

**3.** Compare and contrast each of the following pairs of accounts.
    **a.** Unrealized Holding Loss on Valuation of Marketable Equity Securities, and Unrealized Holding Loss on Valuation of Marketable Equity Investments.
    **b.** Allowance for Excess of Cost of Marketable Securities over Market Value, and Allowance for Excess of Cost of Investments over Market Value.
    **c.** Dividend Revenue, and Equity in Earnings of Unconsolidated Affiliates.
    **d.** Equity in Earnings of Unconsolidated Affiliate, and Minority Interest in Earnings of Consolidated Subsidiary.
    **e.** Minority Interest in Earnings of Consolidated Subsidiary, and Minority Interest in Net Assets of Consolidated Subsidiary.

**4.** "Dividends received or receivable from another company may be either an item of revenue in calculating net income or a return of investment, depending on the method of accounting used." Explain.

**5.** Why is the equity method sometimes called a *one-line consolidation?* Consider both the balance sheet and the income statement in your response.

**6.** Distinguish between minority investments in other companies and the minority interest in a consolidated subsidiary.

**7.** "Net income will be the same independent of whether an investment in a subsidiary is accounted for using the equity method and not consolidated or whether the subsidiary is consolidated. Total assets will be different, however, depending on whether or not the subsidiary is consolidated." Explain.

## Exercises

**8.** *Amount of income recognized under various methods of accounting for investments.* On January 1, Buyer Company acquired common stock of X Company. At the time of acquisition, the book value and fair market value of X Company's net assets were $200,000. During the year, X Company earned $50,000 and declared dividends of $40,000. How much income would Buyer Company report for the year from its investment under the assumption that it did the following:
    **a.** Paid $30,000 for 15 percent of the common stock and uses the lower-of-cost-or-market method to account for its investment in X Company.
    **b.** Paid $40,000 for 15 percent of the common stock and uses the lower-of-cost-or-market method to account for its investment in X Company.
    **c.** Paid $60,000 for 30 percent of the common stock and uses the equity method to account for its investment in X Company.
    **d.** Paid $80,000 for 30 percent of the common stock and uses the equity method to account for its investment in X Company? Give the maximum income that Buyer Company can report from the investment.

**9.** *Balance sheet and income effects of alternative methods of accounting for investments.* On January 1, P acquired common stock of S. At the time of acquisition, the book value and market value of S's net assets were $400,000. During the current year, S earned $80,000 and declared dividends of $50,000. Indicate the amount shown for Investment in S on the balance sheet on December 31 and the amount of income P would report for the year from its invest-ment under the assumption that P did the following:

   **a.** Paid $40,000 for a 10 percent interest in S and uses the lower-of-cost-or-market method. The market value of S on December 31 was $400,000.

   **b.** Same as part **a**, except that the market value of S on December 31 was $390,000.

   **c.** Paid $45,000 for a 10 percent interest in S and uses the lower-of-cost-or-market method. The market value of S on December 31 was $450,000.

   **d.** Paid $160,000 for a 40 percent interest in S and uses the equity method.

   **e.** Paid $180,000 for a 40 percent interest in S and uses the equity method. Goodwill is amortized over 40 years.

**10.** *Journal entries under various methods of accounting for investments.* Johnson Corporation made three long-term intercorporate investments on January 2. Data relating to these investments for the year are as follows:

| Company | Percentage Acquired | Book Value and Market Value of Net Assets on January 2 | Acquisition Cost | Net Income for the Year | Dividends Declared during the Year |
|---|---|---|---|---|---|
| X ....... | 20% | $2,000,000 | $ 400,000 | $200,000 | $ 80,000 |
| Y ....... | 25 | 3,000,000 | 800,000 | 300,000 | 120,000 |
| Z ....... | 30 | 4,000,000 | 1,300,000 | 400,000 | 160,000 |

Give the journal entries to record the acquisition of these investments and to apply the equity method during the year. Goodwill is amortized over 20 years.

**11.** *Journal entries under various methods of accounting for investments.* Maddox Corporation made three long-term intercorporate investments on January 2. Data relating to these investments are as follows:

| Company | Percentage Acquired | Book Value and Market Value of Net Assets on January 2 | Acquisition Cost | Net Income for Year | Dividends Declared during the Year | Market Value of Shares Held on December 31 |
|---|---|---|---|---|---|---|
| A ................. | 10% | $1,800,000 | $ 200,000 | $100,000 | $40,000 | $ 180,000 |
| B ................. | 25 | 1,800,000 | 500,000 | 100,000 | 40,000 | 510,000 |
| C ................. | 60 | 1,800,000 | 1,400,000 | 100,000 | 40,000 | 1,431,000 |

Assume that these were the only three intercorporate investments of Maddox Corporation. Goodwill is amortized over 40 years.

   **a.** Give the journal entries on Maddox Corporation's books to record these acquisitions of common stock and to account for the intercorporate invest-ments under generally accepted accounting principles. The investment in Company C is not consolidated. Be sure to include any required year-end adjusting entries.

   **b.** Assuming that the financial statements of Company C are consolidated with those of Maddox Corporation, that the investment in Company C is accounted for using the equity method, and that the consolidation work sheet is based on preclosing trial balance data, give the work sheet entry to eliminate the Investment in Stock of Company C account on December 31. The Common Stock account of Company C has a balance of $1,000,000, and Additional Paid-in Capital has a zero balance.

c.  Refer to part **b**. Give the consolidation work sheet entry to recognize the minority interest in Company C on December 31.

12. *Consolidation policy and principal consolidation concepts.* The CAR Corporation manufactures computers in the United States. It owns 75 percent of the voting stock of Charles of Canada, 80 percent of the voting stock of Alexandre de France (in France), and 90 percent of the voting stock of R Credit Corporation (a finance company). The CAR Corporation prepares consolidated financial statements consolidating Charles of Canada, uses the equity method for R Credit Corporation, and uses the lower-of-cost-or-market method for its investment in Alexandre de France. Data from the annual reports of these companies are given in the following exhibit:

| | Percentage Owned | Net Income | Dividends | Accounting Method |
|---|---|---|---|---|
| CAR Corporation Consolidated......... | — | $1,000,000 | $ 70,000 | — |
| Charles of Canada ..... | 75% | 100,000 | 40,000 | Consolidated |
| Alexandre de France[a] ... | 80 | 80,000 | 50,000 | Lower of Cost or Market |
| R Credit Corporation .... | 90 | 120,000 | 100,000 | Equity |

[a]Market value of shares exceeds cost.

a.  Which, if any, of the companies is incorrectly accounted for by CAR according to generally accepted accounting principles?

Assuming the accounting for the three subsidiaries shown above to be correct, answer the following questions.

b.  How much of the net income reported by CAR Corporation Consolidated is attributable to the operations of the three subsidiaries?

c.  What is the amount of the minority interest now shown on the income statement, and how does it affect net income of CAR Corporation Consolidated?

d.  If all three subsidiaries had been consolidated, what would have been the net income of CAR Corporation Consolidated?

e.  If all three subsidiaries had been consolidated, what would have been the minority interest shown on the income statement?

13. *Equity method and consolidation elimination entries.* The Hart Company acquired control of the Keller Company on January 2 by purchasing 80 percent of its outstanding stock for $700,000. The entire excess of cost over book value acquired is attributed to goodwill, which is amortized over 40 years. The shareholder's equity accounts of the Keller Company appeared as follows on January 2 and December 31 of the current year:

|  | Jan. 2 | Dec. 31 |
| --- | --- | --- |
| Common Stock....................................... | $600,000 | $600,000 |
| Retained Earnings ................................... | 200,000 | 420,000 |

Keller Company had earnings of $250,000 and declared dividends of $30,000 during the year. The accounts receivable of the Hart Company at December 31 included $4,500 that is due it from the Keller Company. Hart Company accounts for its investment in Keller Company on its single-company books using the equity method.

**a.** Give the journal entries to record the acquisition of the shares of Keller Company and to apply the equity method during the year on the books of Hart Company.

**b.** Give the required elimination entries for a consolidation work sheet at the end of the year, assuming that the work sheet is based on preclosing trial balance data.

**14.** *Equity method and consolidation elimination entries.* The Roe Company purchased 80 percent of the common stock of Danver Company on January 2 at book value for $480,000. The total common stock of Danver Company at this date was $450,000, and the retained earnings balance was $150,000. During the year, net income of the Danver Company was $90,000; dividends declared were $36,000. The Roe Company uses the equity method to account for the investment.

**a.** Give the journal entry made by Roe Company during the year to account for its investment in Danver Company.

**b.** Give the elimination entry for the investment account, assuming that the consolidation work sheet is based on preclosing trial balance data.

**15.** *Equity method and consolidation work sheet entries.* The Little Company is a subsidiary of the Butler Company and is accounted for using the equity method on the single-company books of the Butler Company.

**a.** Present journal entries for the following selected transactions. Record the set of entries on the books of the Little Company separately from the set of entries on the books of the Butler Company.

**(1)** On January 2, the Butler Company acquired on the market, for cash, 80 percent of all the common stock of the Little Company. The outlay was $325,000. The total contributed capital of the stock outstanding was $300,000; the retained earnings balance was $80,000. The excess of cost over book value acquired is all attributed to goodwill and is amortized over 10 years.

**(2)** The Little Company purchased materials for $23,000 from the Butler Company on account at the latter's cost.

**(3)** The Little Company obtained an advance of $9,000 from the Butler Company. The funds were deposited in the bank.

**(4)** The Little Company paid $19,000 on the purchases in (2).

**(5)** The Little Company repaid $7,500 of the loan received from the Butler Company in (3).

(6) The Little Company declared and paid a dividend of $24,000 during the year.

(7) The net income of the Little Company for the year was $40,000.

b. Prepare the adjustment and elimination entries that would be necessary in the preparation of the December 31 consolidated balance sheet, recognizing the effects of only the previously listed transactions. Assume that the work sheet is based on preclosing financial statement data.

16. *Intercompany inventory transactions between consolidated entities.* Company P owns 70 percent of a consolidated subsidiary, Company S. During the year, Company P's sales to Company S amounted to $50,000. The cost of those sales was $35,000. The following data are taken from the two companies' income statements:

|  | Company P | Company S |
| --- | --- | --- |
| Sales........................................ | $120,000 | $250,000 |
| Cost of Goods Sold............................. | 70,000 | 150,000 |

a. Compute consolidated sales and consolidated cost of goods sold for the year, assuming that Company S sold all the goods purchased from Company P.

b. Compare the consolidated sales, cost of goods sold, and gross margin on sales to the sum of the sales, cost of goods sold, and gross margins of the separate companies.

17. *Working backwards to consolidation relationships.* A parent company owns shares in one other company. It has owned them since the other company was formed. The parent company has retained earnings from its own operations independent of intercorporate investments of $100,000. The consolidated balance sheet shows no goodwill and shows retained earnings of $160,000. Consider each of the following questions independently of the others.

a. If the parent owns 80 percent of its consolidated subsidiary, what are the retained earnings of the subsidiary?

b. If the subsidiary has retained earnings of $96,000, what fraction of the subsidiary does the parent own?

c. If the subsidiary had not been consolidated but instead had been accounted for by the equity method, how much revenue in excess of dividends received would the parent have recognized from the investment?

18. *Working backwards from consolidated income statements.* Sealco Enterprises published the consolidated income statement for the year that is shown in Exhibit 13.7. The unconsolidated affiliate retained 20 percent of its earnings of $100,000 during the year, having paid out the rest as dividends. The consolidated subsidiary earned $200,000 during the year and declared no dividends.

a. What percentage of the unconsolidated affiliate does Sealco Enterprises own?

b. What dividends did Sealco Enterprises receive from the unconsolidated affiliate during the year?

Exhibit 13.7 ──────────────────────────────────────────────────

## SEALCO ENTERPRISES
### Consolidated Income Statement
### (Problem 18)

| | | |
|---|---:|---:|
| **Revenues:** | | |
| Sales............................................... | | $1,000,000 |
| Equity in Earnings of Unconsolidated Affiliate............. | | 40,000 |
| Total Revenues ...................................... | | $1,040,000 |
| | | |
| **Expenses:** | | |
| Cost of Goods Sold (excluding depreciation) ............. | | $ 650,000 |
| Administrative Expenses ............................. | | 100,000 |
| Depreciation Expense................................. | | 115,000 |
| Amortization of Goodwill............................. | | 5,000 |
| Income Tax Expenses: | | |
| Currently Payable ................................ | $42,000 | |
| Deferred......................................... | 10,000 | 52,000 |
| Total Expenses........................................ | | $ 922,000 |
| Income of the Consolidated Group ..................... | | $ 118,000 |
| Less Minority Interest in Earnings of Consolidated Subsidiary ......................................... | | 30,000 |
| Net Income to Shareholders ........................... | | $ 88,000 |

**c.** What percentage of the consolidated subsidiary does Sealco Enterprises own?

19. *Working backwards from the statement of cash flows.* Lesala Corporation purchased most of the common stock of its subsidiary in Year 1. The subsidiary earned $1 million in Year 3 but declared no dividends. Exhibit 13.8 is an excerpt from Lesala Corporation's financial statements issued for Year 3.

   **a.** What percentage of the consolidated subsidiary does Lesala Corporation own?

Exhibit 13.8 ──────────────────────────────────────────────────

## LESALA CORPORATION
### Consolidated Statement of Cash Flows for Year 3

| | | |
|---|---:|---:|
| **Operations:** | | |
| Consolidated Net Income............................. | | $3,000,000 |
| Additions: | | |
| Depreciation of Plant............................. | $150,000 | |
| Amortization of Goodwill Arising from Acquisition of Consolidated Subsidiary ..................... | 10,000 | |
| Minority Interest in Earnings of Consolidated Subsidiary ..................................... | 200,000 | |
| Increases in Current Liabilities .................... | 75,000 | |
| Subtractions: | | |
| Increases in Current Assets Other than Cash....... | (90,000) | 345,000 |
| Cash Provided by Operations ....................... | | $3,345,000 |

    **b.** Goodwill arising from the acquisition of the consolidated subsidiary is being amortized, using the straight-line method, to show the minimum charges allowed by generally accepted accounting principles. What was the excess of the subsidiary's market value as a going concern over the market value of the actual assets shown on its books as of the date of acquisition? Assume that the acquisition occurred on January 1, Year 1.

**20.** *Effect of transactions on the statement of cash flows.* Refer to the Simplified Statement of Cash Flows in Exhibit 5.15 on page 188. Eleven of the lines in the statement are numbered. Ignore the unnumbered lines in responding to the questions that follow.

    Assume that the accounting cycle is complete for the period and that all of the financial statements have been prepared. It is then discovered that a transaction has been overlooked. The transaction is recorded in the accounts, and all of the financial statements are corrected. For each of the following transactions or events, indicate which of the numbered lines of the statement of cash flows is affected and by how much. Ignore income tax effects.

    **a.** A 40-percent-owned affiliate accounted for with the equity method earns $25,000 and pays dividends of $10,000.

    **b.** A 40-percent-owned affiliate accounted for with the equity method reports a loss for the year of $12,500.

    **c.** Minority interest in income of a consolidated subsidiary is recognized in the amount of $20,000.

    **d.** Minority interest in the losses of a consolidated subsidiary is recognized in the amount of $8,000.

    **e.** A 100-percent-owned consolidated subsidiary sold merchandise to the parent company for $10,000. The subsidiary's cost of the goods sold was $6,000. The parent sold the merchandise for $12,000. An elimination of the intercompany transactions is made.

    **f.** The *investment* in the noncurrent portfolio of equity securities accounted for with the lower-of-cost-or-market method is written down from $10,000 to $8,000.

    **g.** A dividend of $7,000 is received on shares held as an *investment* and accounted for with the lower-of-cost-or-market method.

    **h.** The market value of the portfolio of equity securities accounted for as *current assets* (Marketable Securities) is $5,000 less than the net amount shown for the same portfolio on the balance sheet at the end of the previous accounting period. The amount in the allowance contra to the Marketable Securities account is changed.

    **i.** The market value of the portfolio of marketable equity securities in part **h** increases $3,000 by the end of the next accounting period. The amount in the allowance contra to the Marketable Securities account is changed.

**21.** *Effect of errors on financial statements.* Using the notation O/S (overstated), U/S (understated), or No (no effect), indicate the effects on assets, liabilities, and net income of each of the independent errors that follow. Ignore income tax effects.

a.  In applying the lower-of-cost-or-market method to the portfolios of marketable equity investments, dividends received were incorrectly credited to the Investment account.

b.  The market value of the portfolio of marketable equity investments at the end of a firm's first year of operations was $5,000 less than its cost. The firm neglected to make the required journal entry in applying the lower-of-cost-or-market method.

c.  In applying the equity method, P correctly accrued its share of S's net income for the year. However, when a dividend was received, Dividend Revenue was credited.

d.  P acquired 30 percent of S on January 1 of the current year for an amount in excess of the market value of S's net assets. P correctly accounted for its share of S's net income and dividends for the year but neglected to amortize any of the excess purchase price.

e.  During the current year, P sold inventory items to S, its wholly owned subsidiary, at a profit. These inventory items were sold by S, and P was paid for them before the end of the year. No elimination entry was made for this intercompany sale on the consolidation work sheet. Indicate the effect of this error on consolidated assets, liabilities, and net income.

f.  Refer to part **e**. Assume that one-fourth of these goods were not sold by S during the year and therefore remain in ending inventory.

g.  Refer to part **e**. Assume that S owes P $10,000 for intercompany purchases at year-end. No elimination entry is made for this intercompany debt. Indicate the effect on consolidated assets, liabilities, and net income.

h.  P owns 90 percent of S. The minority interest in consolidated subsidiaries is treated as part of shareholders' equity. In preparing a consolidated work sheet, no entry was made to accrue the minority interest's share of S's net income or of S's net assets.

## Problems and Cases

22.  *Consolidation work sheet for wholly owned subsidiary purchased at book value.* The trial balances of High Company and Low Company on December 31 of the current year appear in Exhibit 13.9.

High Company acquired all of the common stock of Low Company on January 1 of this year for $80,000. The receivables of High Company and the liabilities of Low Company contain $5,000 of advances from High Company to Low Company. Prepare a consolidation work sheet for High Company and Low Company for the year. The adjustments and eliminations columns should contain entries to

(1) Eliminate the investment account.

(2) Eliminate intercompany receivables and payables.

23.  *Consolidation work sheet entries for less than wholly owned subsidiary purchased for more than book value.* Refer to the data for High Company and Low Company in Problem 22. Give the consolidation work sheet adjustment and elimination entries under each of the following independent situations:

## Exhibit 13.9 ————————————————————————————

## HIGH COMPANY and LOW COMPANY
### Preclosing Trial Balances
### (Problems 22 and 23)

| | High Company | Low Company |
|---|---|---|
| **Debits:** | | |
| Cash . . . . . . . . . . . . . . . . . . . . . . . . . . . . . . . . . . . . . . . . . . | $ 50,000 | $ 5,000 |
| Accounts Receivable . . . . . . . . . . . . . . . . . . . . . . . . . . . . . | 80,000 | 15,000 |
| Investment in Stock of Low Company (at equity) . . . . . . . . . | 90,000 | — |
| Other Assets . . . . . . . . . . . . . . . . . . . . . . . . . . . . . . . . . . . | 360,000 | 100,000 |
| Cost of Goods Sold . . . . . . . . . . . . . . . . . . . . . . . . . . . . . . | 160,000 | 60,000 |
| Selling and Administrative Expenses . . . . . . . . . . . . . . . . . . | 50,000 | 20,000 |
| Income Tax Expense . . . . . . . . . . . . . . . . . . . . . . . . . . . . . | 40,000 | 10,000 |
| Totals . . . . . . . . . . . . . . . . . . . . . . . . . . . . . . . . . . . . | $830,000 | $210,000 |
| | | |
| **Credits:** | | |
| Accounts Payable . . . . . . . . . . . . . . . . . . . . . . . . . . . . . . . | $ 70,000 | $ 30,000 |
| Bonds Payable . . . . . . . . . . . . . . . . . . . . . . . . . . . . . . . . . | 100,000 | — |
| Common Stock . . . . . . . . . . . . . . . . . . . . . . . . . . . . . . . . . . | 150,000 | 50,000 |
| Retained Earnings . . . . . . . . . . . . . . . . . . . . . . . . . . . . . . . | 200,000 | 30,000 |
| Sales Revenue . . . . . . . . . . . . . . . . . . . . . . . . . . . . . . . . . | 300,000 | 100,000 |
| Equity in Earnings of Low Company . . . . . . . . . . . . . . . . . . | 10,000 | — |
| Totals . . . . . . . . . . . . . . . . . . . . . . . . . . . . . . . . . . . . | $830,000 | $210,000 |

a.  High Company paid $100,000, instead of $80,000, for all of the common
    stock of Low Company on January 1. The market values of Low Com-
    pany's recorded assets and liabilities equaled their book values. Goodwill
    is amortized over 10 years. The Investment in Stock of Low Company
    account showed a balance of $108,000 on December 31.

b.  High Company paid $64,000 for 80 percent of the common stock of Low
    Company on January 1. The Investment in Stock of Low Company account
    showed a balance of $72,000 on December 31.

24.  *Consolidation work sheet for less than wholly owned subsidiary purchased for*
    *book value.* The preclosing trial balances of Company L and Company M on
    December 31, Year 2, are shown in Exhibit 13.10. Company L acquired 90
    percent of the common stock of Company M on January 2, Year 1, for
    $270,000. On this date, the shareholders' equity accounts of Company M were
    as follows:

| | |
|---|---|
| Common Stock . . . . . . . . . . . . . . . . . . . . . . . . . . . . . . . . . . . . . . . . . . . . . . . . . . . . | $100,000 |
| Retained Earnings . . . . . . . . . . . . . . . . . . . . . . . . . . . . . . . . . . . . . . . . . . . . . . . . . . | 200,000 |
| Total . . . . . . . . . . . . . . . . . . . . . . . . . . . . . . . . . . . . . . . . . . . . . . . . . . . . . . . . . | $300,000 |

During Year 2, Company L sold merchandise costing $30,000, on account, to
Company M for $40,000. Of the amount, $10,000 remains unpaid at year-end.
Company M sold all of the merchandise during Year 2.

**Exhibit 13.10** _____
**COMPANY L and COMPANY M**
**Preclosing Trial Balances**
**(Problem 24)**

|  | Company L | Company M |
|---|---|---|
| **Debits:** | | |
| Receivables..................................... | $ 60,000 | $130,000 |
| Investment in Stock of Company M................ | 319,500 | — |
| Other Assets.................................... | 761,500 | 285,000 |
| Cost of Goods Sold.............................. | 550,000 | 150,000 |
| Other Expenses ................................. | 120,000 | 10,000 |
| Dividends Declared ............................. | 30,000 | 15,000 |
| Totals ...................................... | $1,841,000 | $590,000 |
| | | |
| **Credits:** | | |
| Accounts Payable .............................. | $ 80,000 | $ 20,000 |
| Other Liabilities................................ | 90,000 | 40,000 |
| Common Stock.................................. | 400,000 | 100,000 |
| Retained Earnings .............................. | 435,000 | 230,000 |
| Sales Revenue.................................. | 800,000 | 200,000 |
| Equity in Earnings of Company M ................ | 36,000 | — |
| Totals ...................................... | $1,841,000 | $590,000 |

a. Prepare a consolidation work sheet for Company L and Company M for Year 2. The adjustments and eliminations columns should contain entries to do the following:

(1) Eliminate the investment account.

(2) Eliminate intercompany sales.

(3) Eliminate intercompany receivables and payables.

(4) Recognize the minority interest.

b. Prepare a consolidated statement of income and retained earnings for Year 2 and a consolidated balance sheet as of December 31, Year 2.

25. *Consolidation work sheet for less than wholly owned subsidiary purchased for more than book value.* The condensed balance sheets of the Ely Company and the Sims Company at December 31 appear in Exhibit 13.11. The receivables of the Ely Company and the liabilities of the Sims Company contain an advance from the Ely Company to the Sims Company of $5,500. The Ely Company acquired 85 percent of the capital stock of the Sims Company on the market at January 2 of this year for $80,000. At that date, the balance in the Retained Earnings account of the Sims Company was $30,000. Amortize goodwill, if any, over 40 years.

Prepare a consolidation work sheet for Ely Company and Sims Company. The adjustment and elimination columns should contain entries to do the following:

(1) Eliminate the Investment in the Sims Company account.

(2) Eliminate intercompany obligations.

(3) Recognize the minority interest.

Exhibit 13.11 ————————————————————————
**ELY COMPANY and SIMS COMPANY**
**Balance Sheet Data**
**(Problem 25)**

| | Ely Company | Sims Company |
|---|---|---|
| **Assets** | | |
| Cash............................................... | $ 60,000 | $  5,000 |
| Receivables....................................... | 120,000 | 15,000 |
| Investment in Sims Company Stock (at equity) .......... | 88,200 | — |
| Other Assets...................................... | 540,000 | 100,000 |
| | $808,200 | $120,000 |
| **Liabilities and Shareholders' Equity** | | |
| Current Liabilities .................................. | $250,000 | $ 30,000 |
| Common Stock..................................... | 400,000 | 50,000 |
| Retained Earnings .................................. | 158,200 | 40,000 |
| | $808,200 | $120,000 |

**26.** *Consolidation work sheet subsequent to year of acquisition.* The condensed balance sheets of Companies R and S on December 31, Year 2, are shown in Exhibit 13.12.

*Additional Information:*

Company R owns 90 percent of the capital stock of Company S. The stock of Company S was acquired on January 1, Year 1, when Company S's retained earnings amounted to $20,000.

Company R holds a note issued by Company S in the amount of $8,200.

Excess of cost over book value acquired is all attributable to goodwill, to be amortized over 40 years.

Prepare a work sheet for a consolidated balance sheet.

Exhibit 13.12 ————————————————————————
**COMPANY R and COMPANY S**
**Balance Sheet Data**
**(Problem 26)**

| | Company R | Company S |
|---|---|---|
| **Assets** | | |
| Cash............................................ | $ 18,000 | $ 13,000 |
| Accounts and Notes Receivable.................... | 90,000 | 25,000 |
| Inventories...................................... | 220,000 | 125,000 |
| Investment in Stock of Company S (at equity) ....... | 312,450 | — |
| Plant Assets ..................................... | 300,000 | 212,000 |
| Total Assets .................................. | $940,450 | $375,000 |

*continued*

Exhibit 13.12 (*continued*) _____

## Liabilities and Shareholders' Equity

| | | |
|---|---:|---:|
| Accounts and Notes Payable ..................... | $ 55,000 | $ 17,000 |
| Dividends Payable............................... | — | 12,500 |
| Other Liabilities................................ | 143,000 | 11,000 |
| Common Stock.................................. | 600,000 | 250,000 |
| Capital Contributed in Excess of Stated Value ....... | — | 50,000 |
| Retained Earnings .............................. | 142,450 | 34,500 |
| Total Liabilities and Shareholders' Equity.......... | $940,450 | $375,000 |

27. *Purchase versus pooling: balance sheet.* Marmee Company and Small Enterprises agree to merge at a time when the balance sheets of the two companies are as shown in the following exhibit:

| | Marmee Company | Small Enterprises |
|---|---:|---:|
| Assets........................................... | $700,000 | $312,000 |
| Liabilities ....................................... | $150,000 | $100,000 |
| Common Stock ($1 par)........................... | 160,000 | 64,000 |
| Additional Paid-in Capital ......................... | 120,000 | 34,000 |
| Retained Earnings ................................ | 270,000 | 114,000 |
| Total Equities ................................ | $700,000 | $312,000 |

Marmee issues 50,000 shares with market value of $800,000 to the owners of Small in return for their 64,000 shares, which represent equity of $212,000 (= $312,000 of assets − $100,000 of liabilities). The excess of Marmee's cost ($800,000) over the book value of Small's assets acquired ($212,000) results from Small's book value of assets being $448,000 less than their current value and from $140,000 of goodwill ($800,000 − $212,000 = $448,000 + $140,000).

Prepare consolidated balance sheets as of the merger date, assuming that the merger is treated as

a. A purchase.

b. A pooling of interests.

28. *Purchasing versus pooling: income statement.* Refer to the data in Problem 27. Partial single-company income statements for Marmee Company and Small Enterprises are shown here for the first year after the merger.

|  | Marmee Company | Small Enterprises |
|---|---|---|
| Sales.......................................... | $2,000,000 | $1,500,000 |
| Other Revenues................................. | 50,000 | 10,000 |
| Total Revenues .............................. | $2,050,000 | $1,510,000 |
| Expenses Except Income Taxes................... | 1,700,000 | 1,300,000 |
| Pretax Income ............................... | $ 350,000 | $ 210,000 |

Make the following assumptions:

**(1)** The income tax rate for the consolidated firm is 40 percent.

**(2)** Where necessary, the extra asset costs that must be recognized in the consolidated statement are amortized over 5 years, and the goodwill is amortized over 40 years.

**(3)** Amortization of asset costs and goodwill arising from the purchase are not deductible from taxable income in calculations for tax returns.

**(4)** Small Enterprises declared no dividends.

Prepare consolidated income statements and consolidated earnings per share for the first year following the merger. Assume that the merger is treated as

**a.** A purchase.

**b.** A pooling of interests.

**29.** *Effects of consolidating companies with different asset and equity structures.* General Manufacturing (G.M.) Company manufactures heavy-duty industrial equipment and consumer durable goods. To enable its customers to make convenient credit arrangements, G.M. Company organized General Manufacturing Credit Corporation several years ago. G.M. Credit Corporation is 100 percent owned by G.M. Company. In its single-company records, G.M. Company accounts for its investment in G.M. Credit Corporation using the equity method. Refer to the comparative balance sheets and income statements for the two companies in Exhibits 13.13 and 13.14.

**a.** Prepare a worksheet to consolidate G.M. Credit Corporation's accounts with those of G.M. for Year 1.

**b.** Now consider G.M. Company's published financial statements, in which it consolidates the Credit Corporation. Notice that when a 100-percent-owned affiliate — accounted for with the equity method on the parent's single-company books — is consolidated, the effect on balance sheet totals and subtotals can be summarized as follows:

**(1)** Total owners' equity on the parent's books remains unchanged.

**(2)** Total liabilities on the parent's books increases by the amount of the affiliate's total liabilities (assuming that there are no intercompany receivables and payables).

**(3)** Total assets on the parent's books increase net by an amount equal to the affiliate's liabilities. (All of the affiliate's assets are put onto the parent's books, but the parent's investment in the affiliate, an amount equal to the affiliate's owners' equity, is removed. The net effect is to increase assets by the amount of the affiliate's total assets − affiliate's owners' equity = affiliate's liabilities.)

Exhibit 13.13 _____

**GENERAL MANUFACTURING COMPANY**
**Single-Company Books**
**(all dollar amounts in millions)**
**(Problems 29, 30, 31)**

| | December 31 | | |
|---|---|---|---|
| **Balance Sheet** | **Year 3** | **Year 2** | **Year 1** |
| Investment in G.M. Credit Corporation ......... | $   260.0 | $   231.9 | $   190.0 |
| Other Assets ................................. | 7,141.8 | 6,655.9 | 6,008.5 |
|   Total Assets ............................ | $ 7,401.8 | $6,887.8 | $6,198.5 |
| Total Liabilities ............................. | $ 4,317.2 | $4,086.0 | $3,644.9 |
| Shareholders' Equity ........................ | 3,084.6 | 2,801.8 | 2,553.6 |
|   Total Equities ........................... | $ 7,401.8 | $6,887.8 | $6,198.5 |

| **Income Statement** | **Year 3** | **Year 2** | **Year 1** |
|---|---|---|---|
| Sales...................................... | $10,387.6 | $9,546.4 | $8,813.6 |
| Equity in Net Earnings of Credit Corporation.... | 41.1 | 30.9 | 19.9 |
|   Total Revenues ......................... | $10,428.7 | $9,577.3 | $8,833.5 |
| Expenses.................................. | (9,898.7) | (9,105.5) | (8,505.0) |
| Net Income ................................ | $   530.0 | $   471.8 | $   328.5 |

Exhibit 13.14 _____

**GENERAL MANUFACTURING CREDIT CORPORATION**
**(all dollar amounts in millions)**
**(Problems 29, 30, 31)**

| | December 31 | | |
|---|---|---|---|
| **Balance Sheet** | **Year 3** | **Year 2** | **Year 1** |
| Total Assets ............................... | $2,789.5 | $2,358.7 | $2,157.0 |
| Total Liabilities ............................ | $2,529.5 | $2,126.8 | $1,967.0 |
| Capital Stock............................... | $  110.0 | $   90.0 | $   55.0 |
| Retained Earnings .......................... | 150.0 | 141.9 | 135.0 |
| Shareholders' Equity ........................ | $  260.0 | $  231.9 | $  190.0 |
| Total Equities .............................. | $2,789.5 | $2,358.7 | $2,157.0 |

| **Statement of Income and Retained Earnings** | **Year 3** | **Year 2** | **Year 1** |
|---|---|---|---|
| Revenues................................... | $  319.8 | $  280.0 | $  247.5 |
|   Less Expenses ........................... | 278.7 | 249.1 | 227.6 |
| Net Income ................................ | $   41.1 | $   30.9 | $   19.9 |
|   Less Dividends ........................... | 33.0 | 24.0 | 15.0 |
| Earnings Retained for Year ................... | $    8.1 | $    6.9 | $    4.9 |
| Retained Earnings at January 1 ............... | 141.9 | 135.0 | 130.1 |
| Retained Earnings at December 31............ | $  150.0 | $  141.9 | $  135.0 |

    **c.** Compute the following ratios for G.M. from its single-company books for Year 1. (Refer to Exhibit 6.11 if you have forgotten how to compute these ratios.)

        **(1)** Rate of return on assets. (Insufficient information is given to allow an addback to the numerator for interest payments net of tax effects; ignore that adjustment to net income that is ordinarily required. Use the year-end balance of total assets for the year's average.)

        **(2)** Debt-equity ratio.

    **d.** For Year 1, compute the two ratios required in part **c**, using G.M.'s consolidated statements derived in part **a**.

    **e.** Compare the results in parts **b** and **c**. What conclusions can you draw from this exercise about comparing financial ratios for companies that own finance subsidiaries with those of companies that do not?

**30.** Repeat Problem 29 for Year 2.

**31.** Repeat Problem 29 for Year 3.

**32.** *Impact of consolidation of finance subsidiaries on debt ratios.* This problem illustrates the impact that consolidation has on financial statements. Sears, Roebuck & Co. and J. C. Penney Company are large retailers who have similar operations. Both companies have organized financing subsidiaries. Each subsidiary borrows funds in credit markets and lends the funds to customers who purchase goods or services from the retailers. Each subsidiary is 100-percent-owned by its parent company. Sears has, for many years, consolidated its financing subsidiary (Sears, Roebuck Acceptance Corp.) in published financial statements. Prior to 1987, Penney used the equity method for its financing subsidiary (J. C. Penney Financial Corporation) and showed the separate financial statements of the financing subsidiary in notes to the published financial statements.

    In this problem we focus on the debt ratio, because the effects are easy to illustrate. Other ratios could be used as well. Throughout this text, the debt-equity ratio has been defined as

$$\text{Debt-Equity Ratio} = \frac{\text{Total Liabilities}}{\text{Total Equities}}.$$

Many financial analysts prefer to use a form of the debt ratio such as

$$\text{Debt Ratio} = \frac{\text{Total } \textit{Long-Term} \text{ Debt}}{\text{Total Shareholders' Equity}}.$$

Such analysts believe that this version of the debt ratio focuses more attention on the risk of companies being analyzed. (The notion is that the percentage of current liabilities to total equities is, to a large degree, determined by the nature of the business and that so long as current assets are as large as current liabilities, the percentage of current liabilities in total equities is not important.)

    The accompanying Exhibit 13.15 shows pertinent data from financial statements for both Sears and Penney issued before 1987. Both versions of the debt ratio mentioned previously are presented. The data for Sears are taken directly from the financial statements. For Penney, the exhibit shows data from

Exhibit 13.15 _____

**Effect of Consolidation Policy**
**(all dollar amounts in millions)**
**(Problem 32)**

| | J. C. Penney Company | | | Sears, Roebuck & Co. |
|---|---|---|---|---|
| | **Financial Statements as Issued (1)** | **Financing Subsidiary Statements as Shown in Notes (2)** | **Hypothetical Financial Statements if Subsidiary Were Consolidated (3)** | **Financial Statements as Issued (4)** |
| Total Assets ................................ | $3,483.8 | $1,458.1 | ? | $12,711.5 |
| Total Liabilities ............................. | 1,567.2 | 1,078.9 | ? | 6,774.6 |
| Long-Term Debt............................. | 355.5 | 517.0 | ? | 1,563.5 |
| Shareholders' Equity ........................ | 1,916.6 | 379.2 | ? | 5,936.9 |
| Debt-Equity Ratio (Total Liabilities/ Total Equities)............................... | 45.0% | 74.0% | 58.0% | 53.3% |
| Long-Term Debt/Shareholders' Equity ............ | 18.5% | 136.3% | 45.5% | 26.3% |

the published balance sheet in column (1), shows data from the statements of the financing subsidiary in column (2), and presents a column for Penney's hypothetical financial statements, assuming consolidation of the financing subsidiary. Column (3) represents the accounting for Penney that is analogous to Sears' accounting.

**a.** Complete column (3) for Penney. (The ratios shown are correct; you can check your work from them.) You may find the summary in part **b** of Problem 29 to be useful.

**b.** As measured by the debt ratios, which company appears to be the more risky? Which company do you think is more risky and why?

**c.** Assume that the managements of Penney and Sears are both considering additional long-term financing to raise funds. Managements of both companies are concerned about how the marketplace will react to new debt financing on the one hand or new common share issues on the other. How are financial analysts who are concerned with risk (as measured in part by debt ratios) likely to react to these two companies? How are managements of the two companies likely to react in making their financing decisions if they anticipate the reaction of financial analysts?

**33.** *Preparation of statement of cash flows (adapted from a problem by S. Baiman).* Exhibit 13.16 presents a comparative balance sheet for Cherry Corporation for Year 6. The following additional information is obtained.

*Additional Information:*

**(1)** For the year ended December 31, Year 6, Cherry reported net income of $496,000.

**(2)** Uncollectible accounts receivable of $4,500 were written off as a result of defaults.

Exhibit 13.16 _____

**CHERRY CORPORATION**
**Comparative Balance Sheets**
**(Problem 33)**

| | December 31 | |
| --- | --- | --- |
| | Year 6 | Year 5 |

# Assets

Current Assets

| | | |
| --- | --- | --- |
| Cash . . . . . . . . . . . . . . . . . . . . . . . . . . . . . . . . . . . . . . | $ 450,000 | $ 287,000 |
| Accounts Receivable (net of allowance for doubtful accounts) . . . . . . . . . . . . . . . . . . . . . . . . . . . | 645,000 | 550,000 |
| Inventories . . . . . . . . . . . . . . . . . . . . . . . . . . . . . . . . . . | 460,000 | 298,000 |
| Total Current Assets . . . . . . . . . . . . . . . . . . . . . . . . | $1,555,000 | $1,135,000 |
| Investments: | | |
| Common Stock of Roy Co. (3 percent) . . . . . . . . . . . . | $ 0 | $ 39,000 |
| Common Stock of Zuber Co. (45 percent) . . . . . . . . . | 246,300 | 0 |
| Plant Assets . . . . . . . . . . . . . . . . . . . . . . . . . . . . . . . . . | 455,000 | 381,000 |
| Less Accumulated Depreciation . . . . . . . . . . . . . . . . . . . | (193,000) | (144,000) |
| Patents (net) . . . . . . . . . . . . . . . . . . . . . . . . . . . . . . . . | 26,000 | 19,000 |
| Total Assets . . . . . . . . . . . . . . . . . . . . . . . . . . . . . . | $2,089,300 | $1,430,000 |

# Liabilities and Shareholders' Equity

Current Liabilities:

| | | |
| --- | --- | --- |
| Dividends Payable . . . . . . . . . . . . . . . . . . . . . . . . . . . . . | $ 181,000 | $ 0 |
| Accounts Payable . . . . . . . . . . . . . . . . . . . . . . . . . . . . | 170,000 | 70,000 |
| Accrued Liabilities . . . . . . . . . . . . . . . . . . . . . . . . . . . . | 24,800 | 41,800 |
| Total Current Liabilities . . . . . . . . . . . . . . . . . . . . . . . | $ 375,800 | $ 111,800 |
| Long-Term Bonds Payable . . . . . . . . . . . . . . . . . . . . . . | 223,000 | 180,000 |
| Less Unamortized Bond Discount . . . . . . . . . . . . . . . . . . | (49,000) | (47,000) |
| Total Liabilities . . . . . . . . . . . . . . . . . . . . . . . . . . . . | $ 549,800 | $ 244,800 |
| Preferred Stock at Par ($2) . . . . . . . . . . . . . . . . . . . . . . | $ 60,000 | $ 53,000 |
| Additional Paid-in Capital — Preferred . . . . . . . . . . . . . . | 6,000 | 2,500 |
| Common Stock at Par ($10) . . . . . . . . . . . . . . . . . . . . . . | 752,000 | 700,000 |
| Additional Paid-in Capital — Common . . . . . . . . . . . . . . | 20,000 | 9,600 |
| Retained Earnings . . . . . . . . . . . . . . . . . . . . . . . . . . . . . | 701,500 | 420,100 |
| Total Shareholders' Equity . . . . . . . . . . . . . . . . . . . . . . | $1,539,500 | $1,185,200 |
| Total Liabilities and Shareholders' Equity . . . . . . . . | $2,089,300 | $1,430,000 |

**(3)** Bad debt expense on Year 6 sales on account is estimated to be $5,000.

**(4)** On January 3, Year 6, Cherry acquired 45 percent of the outstanding common stock of Zuber Co. To consummate this transaction, Cherry paid $72,000 cash and issued 3,500 shares of its preferred stock and 2,400 shares of its common stock. The market price of Cherry's preferred stock on January 3, Year 6, was $3 a share, and the market price of its common stock was $12 a share. The market value of the cash and stock given up by Cherry was equal to its share of Zuber's net book value. The investment in

Zuber is accounted for on Cherry's financial statement using the equity method. For the year ended December 31, Year 6, Zuber Co. reported $320,000 of net income and declared and paid cash dividends of $20,000.

(5) Cherry's investment in the common stock of Roy Co. was made in Year 2 and represented a 3-percent interest. On January 1, Year 6, Cherry sold this investment for $46,000. In addition, Cherry acquired new plant assets at a cost of $81,000. Plant assets with a cost of $22,000 and accumulated depreciation of $17,600 were sold for $3,200. The remaining increase in plant assets resulted from major improvements that were accounted for properly as capital expenditures.

(6) Amortization of patents for Year 6 was $3,000. A new patent was acquired for cash.

(7) On January 2, Year 6 (before the purchase of Zuber), Cherry declared and issued a 4-percent stock dividend on its common stock. The market price of the common stock on that date was $12 a share. On December 31, Year 6, cash dividends of $145,000 on the common stock and $36,000 on the preferred stock were declared.

(8) During Year 6, bonds with a face value of $20,000 and unamortized bond discount of $3,000 were repurchased for $17,000. During Year 6, bond discount of $4,000 was amortized against interest expense. During Year 6, new bonds were issued at a discount.

a. Prepare a T-account work sheet for a statement of cash flows.

b. Prepare a statement of cash flows for Cherry Corporation for Year 6.

# Chapter 14    Statement of Cash Flows: Another Look _____

Chapter 5 introduced the statement of cash flows, discussing its rationale and illustrating a T-account approach for preparing the statement. Subsequent chapters have described briefly the impact of various transactions on the statement of cash flows. This chapter synthesizes these chapter-by-chapter discussions by providing a comprehensive example of a statement of cash flows.

## Review of T-Account Procedure for Preparing Statement of Cash Flows _____

The statement of cash flows is typically prepared after the balance sheet and income statement. The procedure described and illustrated in Chapter 5 is summarized as follows:

**Step 1**   Obtain a balance sheet for the beginning and end of the period for which the statement of cash flows is to be prepared.

**Step 2**   Prepare a T-account work sheet. At the top of the work sheet is a master T-account for cash. The T-account has sections labeled Operations, Investing, and Financing. The beginning and ending balances in cash and cash equivalents are entered in the master T-account. The T-account work sheet is completed by preparing a T-account for each balance sheet account other than cash and cash equivalents and entering the beginning and ending balances.

**Step 3**   Explain the change in the master cash account between the beginning and end of the period by explaining, or accounting for, the changes in the other balance sheet accounts. This step is accomplished by reconstructing the entries originally made in the accounts during the period and entering them in appropriate T-accounts on the work sheet. Once the changes in these other balance sheet accounts have been explained, the change in cash and cash equivalents will have been explained.

**Step 4**   Prepare a statement of cash flows using information in the T-account work sheet.

# Comprehensive Illustration of
# Statement of Cash Flows _____

Data for Ellwood Corporation for Year 2 is used in this comprehensive illustration of the statement of cash flows. Exhibit 14.1 presents a comparative balance sheet as of December 31, Year 1 and Year 2; Exhibit 14.2 presents an income statement for Year 2; and Exhibit 14.3 presents a statement of cash flows. In the sections that follow, each of the line items in Exhibit 14.3 is discussed.

**Line 1: Net Income**   The income statement indicates that net income for the period was $1,000. The work sheet entry presumes that cash is provisionally increased by the amount of net income.

| | | |
|---|---|---|
| (1a) Cash (Operations — Net Income) ......................... | 1,000 | |
| Retained Earnings ..................................... | | 1,000 |

**Line 2: Depreciation Expense Addback**   Internal records indicate that depreciation of $500 was included in cost of goods sold and depreciation of $200 was included in selling and administrative expenses. None of this $700 of depreciation required an operating cash outflow during Year 2. Thus it must be added back to net income in deriving cash flow from operations.

| | | |
|---|---|---|
| (2a) Cash (Operations — Depreciation Expense Addback) ........ | 700 | |
| Accumulated Depreciation ............................. | | 700 |

**Line 3: Amortization of Patent**   The treatment of patent amortization is identical to that of depreciation. Company records indicate that patent amortization of $150 was recorded during Year 2 and was included in cost of goods sold. The work sheet entry is as follows:

| | | |
|---|---|---|
| (3a) Cash (Operations — Amortization Expense Addback)......... | 150 | |
| Accumulated Amortization............................. | | 150 |

**Line 4: Minority Interest in Consolidated Earnings**   The financial statements in Exhibits 14.1, 14.2, and 14.3 are consolidated statements for Ellwood Corporation and its majority-owned subsidiaries. Ellwood does not own all of the stock of some of its consolidated subsidiaries. The minority shareholders in these subsidiaries have a claim on the earnings of their respective subsidiaries. The income statement in Exhibit 14.2 indicates that the minority interest in earnings of $50 has been subtracted in computing consolidated net income. This amount does not use cash

Exhibit 14.1 _____

**ELLWOOD CORPORATION**
Consolidated Balance Sheet

| | December 31 | |
| --- | --- | --- |
| | Year 1 | Year 2 |
| **Assets** | | |
| **Current Assets:** | | |
| Cash . . . . . . . . . . . . . . . . . . . . . . . . . . . . . . . . . . . . . . . . . . . . . . . . . . . . | $ 1,150 | $ 1,050 |
| Certificate of Deposit . . . . . . . . . . . . . . . . . . . . . . . . . . . . . . . . . . . . . | 1,800 | 980 |
| Accounts Receivable (net) . . . . . . . . . . . . . . . . . . . . . . . . . . . . . . . . . | 3,400 | 4,300 |
| Inventories . . . . . . . . . . . . . . . . . . . . . . . . . . . . . . . . . . . . . . . . . . . . . . | 1,500 | 2,350 |
| Prepayments . . . . . . . . . . . . . . . . . . . . . . . . . . . . . . . . . . . . . . . . . . . . . | 800 | 600 |
| Total Current Assets . . . . . . . . . . . . . . . . . . . . . . . . . . . . . . . . . . | $ 8,650 | $ 9,280 |
| **Investments:** | | |
| Investment in Company A (15%) . . . . . . . . . . . . . . . . . . . . . . . . . . . | $ 1,200 | $ 1,200 |
| Investment in Company B (40%) . . . . . . . . . . . . . . . . . . . . . . . . . . . | 2,100 | 2,420 |
| Total Investments . . . . . . . . . . . . . . . . . . . . . . . . . . . . . . . . . . . . . | $ 3,300 | $ 3,620 |
| **Property, Plant, and Equipment:** | | |
| Land . . . . . . . . . . . . . . . . . . . . . . . . . . . . . . . . . . . . . . . . . . . . . . . . . . . | $ 1,000 | $ 1,000 |
| Buildings . . . . . . . . . . . . . . . . . . . . . . . . . . . . . . . . . . . . . . . . . . . . . . | 8,600 | 8,900 |
| Equipment . . . . . . . . . . . . . . . . . . . . . . . . . . . . . . . . . . . . . . . . . . . . . | 10,840 | 11,540 |
| Less Accumulated Depreciation . . . . . . . . . . . . . . . . . . . . . . . . . . . . | (6,240) | (6,490) |
| Total Property, Plant, and Equipment . . . . . . . . . . . . . . . . . . . . . . | $14,200 | $14,950 |
| **Intangible Assets:** | | |
| Patent . . . . . . . . . . . . . . . . . . . . . . . . . . . . . . . . . . . . . . . . . . . . . . . . . . | $ 2,550 | $ 2,550 |
| Less Accumulated Amortization . . . . . . . . . . . . . . . . . . . . . . . . . . . . | (600) | (750) |
| Total Intangible Assets . . . . . . . . . . . . . . . . . . . . . . . . . . . . . . . . | $ 1,950 | $ 1,800 |
| Total Assets . . . . . . . . . . . . . . . . . . . . . . . . . . . . . . . . . . . . . . . . . | $28,100 | $29,650 |

*continued*

and must be added back to net income to compute cash flow from operations. The analytic entry on the work sheet is as follows:

---

| | | |
| --- | --- | --- |
| (4a) Cash (Operations—Minority Interest Addback) . . . . . . . . . . . . . . | 50 | |
| Minority Interest in Consolidated Subsidiary . . . . . . . . . . . . . . | | 50 |

---

The balance sheet in Exhibit 14.1 indicates that the account titled Minority Interest in Consolidated Subsidiary increased during Year 2 by $30 (= $230 − $200). Because the account increased by $50 for the minority interest in earnings, dividends of $20 must have been paid to these shareholders during the year. The work sheet entry for these dividends is discussed in conjunction with the consideration of dividends on Line 23.

**Line 5: Deferred Income Taxes**  Notes to the financial statements of Ellwood Corporation indicate that income tax expense of $300 is composed of $200 of

**Exhibit 14.1** (continued) _____

| | December 31 | |
| --- | :---: | :---: |
| | Year 1 | Year 2 |

# Liabilities and Shareholders' Equity

**Current Liabilities:**

| | | |
| --- | ---: | ---: |
| Bank Notes Payable ......................................... | $ 2,000 | $ 2,750 |
| Accounts Payable .......................................... | 2,250 | 3,000 |
| Warranties Payable ........................................ | 1,200 | 1,000 |
| Advances from Customers................................... | 600 | 900 |
| Total Current Liabilities .................................... | $ 6,050 | $ 7,650 |

**Noncurrent Liabilities:**

| | | |
| --- | ---: | ---: |
| Bonds Payable ............................................ | $ 2,820 | $ 1,370 |
| Capitalized Lease Obligation ............................... | 1,800 | 2,100 |
| Deferred Income Taxes .................................... | 550 | 650 |
| Total Noncurrent Liabilities................................. | $ 5,170 | $ 4,120 |
| Minority Interest in Consolidated Subsidiary ................... | $ 200 | $ 230 |

**Shareholders' Equity:**

| | | |
| --- | ---: | ---: |
| Preferred Stock .......................................... | $ 1,000 | $ 1,200 |
| Common Stock............................................ | 2,000 | 2,100 |
| Additional Paid-in Capital .................................. | 4,000 | 4,200 |
| Retained Earnings ........................................ | 9,930 | 10,530 |
| Total .................................................... | $16,930 | $18,030 |
| Less Cost of Treasury Stock ............................... | (250) | (380) |
| Total Shareholders' Equity ................................. | $16,680 | $17,650 |
| Total Liabilities and Shareholders' Equity .................... | $28,100 | $29,650 |

**Exhibit 14.2** _____

## ELLWOOD CORPORATION
### Consolidated Income Statement for Year 2

**Revenues:**

| | |
| --- | ---: |
| Sales..................................................... | $10,500 |
| Interest and Dividends .................................... | 320 |
| Equity in Earnings of Affiliate ............................. | 480 |
| Gain on Sale of Equipment ................................ | 50 |
| Total Revenues ....................................... | $11,350 |

**Expenses:**

| | |
| --- | ---: |
| Cost of Goods Sold....................................... | $ 6,000 |
| Selling and Administration ................................. | 3,550 |
| Interest .................................................. | 450 |
| Income Taxes ............................................ | 300 |
| Total Expenses........................................ | $10,300 |
| Net Income before Minority Interest........................ | $ 1,050 |
| Less Minority Interest in Earnings ......................... | (50) |
| Net Income .............................................. | $ 1,000 |

Exhibit 14.3 _____

## ELLWOOD CORPORATION
### Consolidated Statement of Cash Flows for Year 2

| | | |
|---|--:|--:|
| *Operations:* | | |
| (1) Net Income . . . . . . . . . . . . . . . . . . . . . . . . . . . . . . . . . . . . . . . . . . . | $ 1,000 | |
| Noncash Revenues, Expenses, Gains, and Losses Included in Income: | | |
| (2) Depreciation of Buildings and Equipment . . . . . . . . . . . . . . . . . . | 700 | |
| (3) Amortization of Patent . . . . . . . . . . . . . . . . . . . . . . . . . . . . . . . . . | 150 | |
| (4) Minority Interest in Consolidated Earnings . . . . . . . . . . . . . . . . . | 50 | |
| (5) Deferred Income Taxes . . . . . . . . . . . . . . . . . . . . . . . . . . . . . . . . | 100 | |
| (6) Amortization of Bond Premium. . . . . . . . . . . . . . . . . . . . . . . . . . . | (50) | |
| (7) Gain on Sale of Equipment. . . . . . . . . . . . . . . . . . . . . . . . . . . . . | (30) | |
| (8) Equity in Undistributed Earnings of Affiliate. . . . . . . . . . . . . . . . . | (320) | |
| (9) Decrease in Prepayments . . . . . . . . . . . . . . . . . . . . . . . . . . . . . . | 200 | |
| (10) Increase in Accounts Payable . . . . . . . . . . . . . . . . . . . . . . . . . . | 750 | |
| (11) Increase in Advances on Contracts . . . . . . . . . . . . . . . . . . . . . . | 300 | |
| (12) Increase in Accounts Receivable (Net) . . . . . . . . . . . . . . . . . . . | (900) | |
| (13) Increase in Inventories. . . . . . . . . . . . . . . . . . . . . . . . . . . . . . . . | (850) | |
| (14) Decrease in Warranties Payable . . . . . . . . . . . . . . . . . . . . . . . . | (200) | |
| Cash Flow from Operations. . . . . . . . . . . . . . . . . . . . . . . . . . . . . . . . . | | $ 900 |
| *Investing:* | | |
| (15) Sale of Equipment. . . . . . . . . . . . . . . . . . . . . . . . . . . . . . . . . . . | $ 180 | |
| (16) Acquisition of Equipment . . . . . . . . . . . . . . . . . . . . . . . . . . . . . . | (1,300) | |
| (17) Acquisition of Building through Capital Lease. . . . . . . . . . . . . . . | (300) | |
| Cash Flow from Investing . . . . . . . . . . . . . . . . . . . . . . . . . . . . . . . . . . | | (1,420) |
| *Financing:* | | |
| (18) Short-Term Bank Borrowing . . . . . . . . . . . . . . . . . . . . . . . . . . . . | $ 750 | |
| (19) Long-Term Bonds Issued. . . . . . . . . . . . . . . . . . . . . . . . . . . . . . | 400 | |
| (20) Capital Lease Obligation Incurred in Acquisition of Building . . . . . . . . . . . . . . . . . . . . . . . . . . . . . . . . . . . . . . . . . | 300 | |
| (21) Preferred Stock Issued. . . . . . . . . . . . . . . . . . . . . . . . . . . . . . . . | 200 | |
| (22) Common Stock Issued on Conversion of Bonds . . . . . . . . . . . . | 300 | |
| (23) Dividends . . . . . . . . . . . . . . . . . . . . . . . . . . . . . . . . . . . . . . . . . | (420) | |
| (24) Retirement of Long-Term Debt at Maturity . . . . . . . . . . . . . . . . . | (1,500) | |
| (25) Conversion of Long-Term Bonds and Common Stock . . . . . . . . | (300) | |
| (26) Acquisition of Common Stock. . . . . . . . . . . . . . . . . . . . . . . . . . . | (130) | |
| Cash Flow from Financing. . . . . . . . . . . . . . . . . . . . . . . . . . . . . . . . . . | | (400) |
| Net Change in Cash . . . . . . . . . . . . . . . . . . . . . . . . . . . . . . . . . . . . . . | | $ (920) |

currently payable taxes and $100 of deferred income taxes. The $100 of deferred income taxes reduced net income but did not require a cash outflow during Year 2. This amount must, therefore, be added back to net income.

| | | |
|---|--:|--:|
| (5a) Cash (Operations — Deferred Tax Addback) . . . . . . . . . . . . . . . | 100, | |
| Deferred Income Taxes . . . . . . . . . . . . . . . . . . . . . . . . . . . . . . | | 100 |

**Line 6: Amortization of Bond Premium**  Included in Bonds Payable on the balance sheet is one series of bonds that were initially issued at a premium (that is, the

coupon rate exceeded the required market rate of interest). The bond premium must be amortized over the life of the bonds as a reduction in interest expense. The entry made in the accounting records for this bond during the period was as follows:

| | | |
|---|---|---|
| (6) Interest Expense ....................................... | 300 | |
|     Bonds Payable ......................................... | 50 | |
|         Cash ............................................... | | 350 |

Cash of $350 was expended even though only $300 of interest expense had been subtracted in computing net income. An additional $50 must be subtracted from net income to derive cash flow from operations.

| | | |
|---|---|---|
| (6a) Bonds Payable ........................................ | 50 | |
|        Cash (Operations — Bond Premium Amortization | | |
|          Subtraction) ......................................... | | 50 |

Note that cash used for interest expense is classified as an operating, not a financing, activity because it is viewed as a cost of carrying out operations.

**Line 7: Gain on Sale of Equipment**  The accounting records indicate that a machine originally costing $600 and on which accumulated depreciation of $450 had been taken was sold for $180 during Year 2. The journal entry made to record this sale was as follows:

| | | |
|---|---|---|
| (7) Cash .................................................. | 180 | |
|     Accumulated Depreciation................................. | 450 | |
|         Equipment........................................... | | 600 |
|         Gain on Sale of Equipment ............................. | | 30 |

The cash proceeds of $180 are shown on Line 15 as an increase in cash from an investing activity. The $30 gain on the sale is included in net income on Line 1. To avoid overstating the amount of cash derived from this sale, the $30 gain must be subtracted from net income in computing cash from operations.

| | | |
|---|---|---|
| (7a) Cash (Investing — Sale of Equipment)..................... | 180 | |
|     Accumulated Depreciation ............................... | 450 | |
|         Equipment .......................................... | | 600 |
|         Cash (Operations — Gain on Sale of Equipment | | |
|          Subtraction) ......................................... | | 30 |

Note that all cash proceeds are classified as investing activities and none as operating activities. Most firms acquire and sell plant assets with the objective of providing a capacity to carry out operations rather than as a means of generating operating income.

If plant assets are sold at a loss instead of a gain, the loss must be added back to net income in deriving cash flow from operations. The typical work sheet entry would be as follows:

| | | |
|---|---|---|
| Cash (Investing — Sale of Equipment) . . . . . . . . . . . . . . . . . . . . . . . . . . | X | |
| Accumulated Depreciation . . . . . . . . . . . . . . . . . . . . . . . . . . . . . . . . . . . | X | |
| Cash (Operations — Loss on Sale of Equipment Addback) . . . . . . . . | X | |
|     Equipment . . . . . . . . . . . . . . . . . . . . . . . . . . . . . . . . . . . . . . . . . . . . . . . | | X |

**Line 8: Equity in Undistributed Earnings of Affiliate**  The balance sheet indicates that Ellwood Corporation owns 40 percent of the common stock of Company B. During Year 2, Company B earned $1,200 and paid $400 of dividends. Ellwood Corporation made the following entries on its books during the year.

| | | |
|---|---|---|
| (8) Investment in Company B. . . . . . . . . . . . . . . . . . . . . . . . . . . . . . . . . . | 480 | |
|     Equity in Earnings of Affiliate . . . . . . . . . . . . . . . . . . . . . . . . . . . | | 480 |
|   Cash . . . . . . . . . . . . . . . . . . . . . . . . . . . . . . . . . . . . . . . . . . . . . . . . . . | 160 | |
|     Investment in Company B. . . . . . . . . . . . . . . . . . . . . . . . . . . . . . | | 160 |
|   .40 × $400 = $160. | | |

Net income of Ellwood Corporation on Line 1 of Exhibit 14.3 includes $480 of equity income. Only $160 of cash was received. Thus a subtraction of $320 (= $480 − $160) must be made from net income in deriving cash from operations.

| | | |
|---|---|---|
| (8a) Investment in Company B. . . . . . . . . . . . . . . . . . . . . . . . . . . . . . . . . | 320 | |
|     Cash (Operations — Equity in Undistributed Earnings | | |
|       Subtraction) . . . . . . . . . . . . . . . . . . . . . . . . . . . . . . . . . . . . . . . | | 320 |

The investment in Company A shown in the balance sheet in Exhibit 14.1 is accounted for using the lower-of-cost-or-market method. During Year 2, dividends of $100 were received and included in Interest and Dividends on the income statement. Because these dividends provided cash, no adjustment is made to net income in computing cash flow from operations.

**Line 9: Decrease in Prepayments**  Because prepayments decreased by $200 during Year 2, less cash was expended during Year 2 for new prepayments than was amortized from prepayments of earlier years. Thus $200 must be added to net income for this credit change in an operating current asset account.

(9a) Cash (Operations—Decrease in Prepayments) .............  200
   Prepayments ........................................    200

**Line 10: Increase in Accounts Payable**  An increase in accounts payable indicates that more costs were incurred on account and cash payments delayed than the amount paid during Year 2 for previous purchases on account. This increase in accounts payable, a credit change in an operating current liability account, implicitly increases cash from operations.

(10a) Cash (Operations—Increase in Accounts Payable).........  750
   Accounts Payable...................................    750

**Line 11: Increase in Advances from Customers**  The $300 increase in customer advances means that $300 more cash was received during Year 2 than was recognized as revenue. The excess must be added to net income in deriving cash flow from operations.

(11a) Cash (Operations—Increase in Advances
   on Contracts).......................................  300
   Advances from Customers ..........................    300

**Line 12: Increase in Accounts Receivable**  The increase in accounts receivable indicates that less cash was collected from customers than the amount shown for sales on account. Thus the increase in accounts receivable, a debit change in an operating current asset account, must be subtracted from net income.

(12a) Accounts Receivable ...................................  900
   Cash (Operations—Increase in Accounts Receivable) ..    900

Note that this entry automatically incorporates the effect of any change in the Allowance for Uncollectible Accounts. Separate work sheet entries could be made for the change in gross accounts receivable and allowance for uncollectible accounts.

**Line 13: Increase in Inventories**  The increase in inventories indicates that more merchandise was purchased than was sold during Year 2. Thus more cash was used than the amount shown for cost of goods sold.[1] A subtraction from net income is required for this debit change in an operating current asset account.

_____

[1]To correctly compute the cash flow effect, the change in accounts payable must also be considered. See Line 10.

| (13a) Inventories ........................................... | 850 | |
| Cash (Operations—Increase in Inventories) .......... | | 850 |

**Line 14: Decrease in Warranties Payable**  Recall that Warranties Payable is increased for the estimated cost of future warranty services on products sold during the period and is decreased by the actual cost of warranty services performed. During Year 2, $200 more in costs was incurred and paid in cash than was included in expenses on the income statement. This decrease in Warranties Payable, a debit change in an operating current liability account, must be subtracted from net income.

| (14a) Warranties Payable .................................... | 200 | |
| Cash (Operations—Decrease in Warranties Payable) .. | | 200 |

Cash flow from operations is $900 for Year 2.

**Line 16: Acquisition of Equipment**  Equipment costing $1,300 was acquired during Year 2. The analytic entry for this investing activity is as follows:

| (16a) Equipment ........................................... | 1,300 | |
| Cash (Investing—Acquisition of Equipment) .......... | | 1,300 |

**Line 17: Acquisition of Building through Capital Lease**  A long-term lease was signed during Year 2 for a building. This lease was classified as a capital lease and recorded in the accounts as follows:

| (17) Building............................................... | 300 | |
| Capitalized Lease Obligations ....................... | | 300 |

Note that this entry does not affect cash. It does affect the investing and financing activities of Ellwood Corporation and can be shown either in the statement of cash flows or in a supplementary schedule. Ellwood Corporation indicates the transaction in its statement of cash flows with the following work sheet entry:

| (17a) Cash (Financing—Capital Lease Obligation Incurred in Acquisition of Building) .................... | 300 | |
| Cash (Investing—Acquisition of Building through Capital Lease) .................................... | | 300 |

Cash flow from investing activities was a cash outflow of $1,420 during Year 2.

**Line 18: Short-Term Borrowing**   Ellwood Corporation borrowed $750 during Year 2 from its bank under a short-term borrowing arrangement. Even though this loan is short-term, it is classified as a financing rather than an operating activity. The analytic entry on the work sheet is as follows:

| | | |
|---|---|---|
| (18a) Cash (Financing—Short-Term Bank Borrowing)............ | 750 | |
| Bank Note Payable ................................ | | 750 |

**Line 19: Long-Term Bonds Issued**   Long-term bonds totaling $400 were issued during Year 2.

| | | |
|---|---|---|
| (19a) Cash (Financing—Long-Term Bonds Issued) .............. | 400 | |
| Bonds Payable ..................................... | | 400 |

**Line 21: Preferred Stock Issued**   Preferred stock totaling $200 was issued during the year.

| | | |
|---|---|---|
| (21a) Cash (Financing—Preferred Stock Issued)................ | 200 | |
| Preferred Stock ..................................... | | 200 |

**Lines 22 and 25: Conversion of Debt to Common Stock**   The conversion of debt to common stock is a transaction that does not directly affect cash but represents a financing transaction. It is disclosed on Lines 22 and 25 in offsetting amounts.

| | | |
|---|---|---|
| (22a) Cash (Financing—Issue of Common Stock in Bond Conversion) ................................ | 300 | |
| Cash (Financing—Conversion of Long-Term Bonds into Common Stock) ............................. | | 300 |

**Line 23: Dividends**   Ellwood Corporation declared and paid $400 of dividends to its shareholders during Year 2. In addition, a consolidated subsidiary paid $20 of dividends to minority shareholders (see discussion of Line 4). The analytic entry is as follows:

| | | |
|---|---|---|
| (23a) Retained Earnings ...................................... | 400 | |
| Minority Interest in Consolidated Subsidiary................ | 20 | |
| Cash (Financing—Dividends) ........................ | | 420 |

**Exhibit 14.4** _____

**ELLWOOD CORPORATION**
T-Account Work Sheet

**Cash**

✔ 2,950

*Operations*

| | | | | | |
|---|---|---|---|---|---|
| Net Income | (1a) | 1,000 | 50 | (6a) | Bond Premium Amortization |
| Depreciation Expense Addback | (2a) | 700 | 30 | (7a) | Gain on Sale of Equipment |
| Amortization Expense Addback | (3a) | 150 | 320 | (8a) | Equity in Undistributed Earnings |
| Minority Interest in Consolidated Subsidiary | (4a) | 50 | 900 | (12a) | Increase in Accounts Receivable |
| Deferred Income Taxes | (5a) | 100 | 850 | (13a) | Increase in Inventories |
| Decrease in Prepayment | (9a) | 200 | 200 | (14a) | Decrease in Warranties Payable |
| Increase in Accounts Payable | (10a) | 750 | | | |
| Increase in Advances from Customers | (11a) | 300 | | | |

*Investing*

| | | | | | |
|---|---|---|---|---|---|
| Sale of Equipment | (7a) | 180 | 1,300 | (16a) | Acquisition of Equipment |
| | | | 300 | (17a) | Acquisition of Building through Capital Lease |

*Financing*

| | | | | | |
|---|---|---|---|---|---|
| Capital Lease Obligation Incurred in Acquisition of Building | (17a) | 300 | 300 | (22a) | Conversion of Long-Term Bonds into Common Stock |
| Short-Term Borrowing | (18a) | 750 | 420 | (23a) | Dividends |
| Long-Term Bonds Issued | (19a) | 400 | 1,500 | (24a) | Retirement of Long-Term Debt |
| Preferred Stock Issued | (21a) | 200 | 130 | (26a) | Acquisition of Common Stock |
| Common Stock Issued on Conversion of Bonds | (22a) | 300 | | | |

✔ 2,030

| **Accounts Receivable** | | **Inventories** | | **Prepayments** | |
|---|---|---|---|---|---|
| ✔ 3,400 | | ✔ 1,500 | | ✔ 800 | |
| (12a) 900 | | (13a) 850 | | | 200 (9a) |
| ✔ 4,300 | | ✔ 2,350 | | ✔ 600 | |

| **Investment in Company A** | | **Investment in Company B** | | **Land** | |
|---|---|---|---|---|---|
| ✔ 1,200 | | ✔ 2,100 | | ✔ 1,000 | |
| | | (8a) 320 | | | |
| ✔ 1,200 | | ✔ 2,420 | | ✔ 1,000 | |

| **Buildings** | | **Equipment** | | **Accumulated Depreciation** | |
|---|---|---|---|---|---|
| ✔ 8,600 | | ✔ 10,840 | | | 6,240 ✔ |
| (17a) 300 | | (16a) 1,300 | 600 (7a) | (7a) 450 | 700 (2a) |
| ✔ 8,900 | | ✔ 11,540 | | | 6,490 ✔ |

*continued*

**Exhibit 14.4** *(continued)* ————————————————————————————————————————

| Patent | | Accumulated Amortization | | Bank Notes Payable | |
|---|---|---|---|---|---|
| ✔ 2,550 | | | 600 ✔ | | 2,000 ✔ |
| | | | 150 (3a) | | 750 (18a) |
| ✔ 2,550 | | | 750 ✔ | | 2,750 ✔ |

| Accounts Payable | | Warranties Payable | | Advances from Customers | |
|---|---|---|---|---|---|
| | 2,250 ✔ | | 1,200 ✔ | | 600 ✔ |
| | 750 (10a) | (14a)  200 | | | 300 (11a) |
| | 3,000 ✔ | | 1,000 ✔ | | 900 ✔ |

| Bonds Payable | | Capitalized Lease Obligation | | Deferred Income Taxes | |
|---|---|---|---|---|---|
| | 2,820 ✔ | | 1,800 ✔ | | 550 ✔ |
| (6a)  50 | 400 (19a) | | 300 (17a) | | 100 (5a) |
| (22a)  300 | | | | | |
| (24a) 1,500 | | | | | |
| | 1,370 ✔ | | 2,100 ✔ | | 650 ✔ |

| Minority Interest in Consolidated Subsidiary | | Preferred Stock | | Common Stock | |
|---|---|---|---|---|---|
| | 200 ✔ | | 1,000 ✔ | | 2,000 ✔ |
| (23a)  20 | 50 (4a) | | 200 (21a) | | 100 (22a) |
| | 230 ✔ | | 1,200 ✔ | | 2,100 ✔ |

| Additional Paid-in Capital | | Retained Earnings | | Treasury Stock | |
|---|---|---|---|---|---|
| | 4,000 ✔ | | 9,930 ✔ | ✔ 250 | |
| | 200 (22a) | (23a)  400 | 1,000 (1a) | (26a) 130 | |
| | 4,200 ✔ | | 10,530 ✔ | ✔ 380 | |

**Line 24: Retirement of Long-Term Debt**   Ellwood Corporation retired $1,500 of long-term debt at maturity and would make the following work sheet entry:

| | | |
|---|---|---|
| (24a) Bonds Payable ........................................ | 1,500 | |
| Cash (Financing — Retirement of Long-Term Debt) ....... | | 1,500 |

If the debt had been retired prior to maturity, it is likely that a gain or loss would have been recognized. The gain or loss would have been eliminated from net income in computing cash flow from operations, and the full amount of cash used to retire the debt would have been classified as a financing activity.

**Line 26: Acquisition of Common Stock**   Common stock costing $130 was acquired during Year 2.

| | | |
|---|---|---|
| (26a) Treasury Stock ........................................ | 130 | |
| Cash (Financing — Acquisition of Common Stock) ........ | | 130 |

Net cash outflow for financing totaled $400 during the year.

Exhibit 14.4 on pages 614 and 615 presents a T-account work sheet for Ellwood Corporation for Year 2.

# Problems and Cases _____

1.  *Effects on Statement of Cash Flows*. Refer to Exhibit 5.15, where a simplified statement of cash flows is presented. For each of the transactions that follow, indicate the number(s) of the line(s) in Exhibit 5.15 that would be affected assuming that funds are defined as cash and cash equivalents. If net income is affected, be sure to indicate if it increases or decreases. Ignore income tax effects.
    a.  Long-term bonds are retired, using funds in a bond sinking fund.
    b.  A cash dividend is received from an unconsolidated subsidiary accounted for using the equity method.
    c.  Accounts are written off as uncollectible when the allowance method is used.
    d.  Marketable securities are purchased for cash.
    e.  Land is sold for an amount greater than its acquisition cost.
    f.  A firm's annual cash contribution to a bond sinking fund is made.
    g.  A fully amortized patent is written off.
    h.  Land is given in settlement of annual legal fees of the corporate attorney.
    i.  Preferred stock is converted into common stock.
    j.  Inventory items are written down to reflect a lower-of-cost-or-market valuation.

    **k.** The Deferred Income Tax (Credit) account is increased for the year.

    **l.** The Premium on Bonds Payable account is amortized for the year.

    **m.** A majority interest in the common stock of a supplier is acquired by issuing long-term convertible bonds.

    **n.** The liability account Rental Fees Received in Advance is reduced when the rental services are provided.

    **o.** A 10-percent stock dividend is declared and issued.

    **p.** Long-term debt maturing within the next year is reclassified as a current liability.

    **q.** Provision is made for estimated uncollectible accounts when the allowance method is used.

    **r.** Income is recognized using the percentage-of-completion method for long-term contracts.

    **s.** Land is donated to a firm by a local government as an inducement to locate manufacturing facilities in the area.

    **t.** Long-term investments in securities are written down to reflect a lower-of-cost-or-market valuation.

    **u.** Research and development costs are paid during the period.

    **v.** Depreciation is recorded on selling and administrative facilities.

    **w.** Depreciation is recorded on manufacturing facilities.

    **x.** Treasury stock is sold for an amount less than its repurchase price.

    **y.** A 6-month loan is obtained from a local bank.

**2.** Work Problem 41 in Chapter 7.

**3.** Work Problem 29 in Chapter 9.

**4.** Work Problem 38 in Chapter 10.

**5.** Work Problem 33 in Chapter 13.

**6.** *Preparation of statement of cash flows (adapted from CPA examination).* The management of Hatfield Corporation, concerned over a decrease in cash, has provided you with the comparative analysis of changes in account balances between December 31, Year 4, and December 31, Year 5, shown in Exhibit 14.5.

    During Year 5, the following transactions occurred:

**(1)** New machinery was purchased for $386,000. In addition, certain obsolete machinery, having a book value of $61,000, was sold for $48,000. No other entries were recorded in Machinery and Equipment or related accounts other than provisions for depreciation.

**(2)** Hatfield paid $2,000 of legal costs in a successful defense of a new patent, which was correctly debited to the Patents account. Amortization of patents amounting to $4,200 was recorded.

**(3)** Preferred stock, par value $100, was purchased at 110 and subsequently canceled. The premium paid was charged to retained earnings.

**(4)** On December 10, Year 5, the board of directors declared a cash dividend of $.20 per share payable to holders of common stock on January 10, Year 6.

Exhibit 14.5 _____

**HATFIELD CORPORATION**
Changes in Account Balances between December 31, Year 4, and
December 31, Year 5

| | December 31 | |
|---|---|---|
| | Year 5 | Year 4 |
| **Debit Balances** | | |
| Cash .............................................. | $ 145,000 | $ 186,000 |
| Accounts Receivable ............................. | 255,000 | 273,000 |
| Inventories ....................................... | 483,000 | 538,000 |
| Securities Held for Plant Expansion Purposes......... | 150,000 | — |
| Machinery and Equipment ......................... | 927,000 | 647,000 |
| Leasehold Improvements .......................... | 87,000 | 87,000 |
| Patents .......................................... | 27,800 | 30,000 |
| Totals........................................ | $2,074,800 | $1,761,000 |
| **Credit Balances** | | |
| Allowance for Uncollectible Accounts................. | $ 16,000 | $ 17,000 |
| Accumulated Depreciation of Machinery and Equipment | 416,000 | 372,000 |
| Allowance for Amortization of Leasehold Improvements | 58,000 | 49,000 |
| Accounts Payable.................................. | 232,800 | 105,000 |
| Cash Dividends Payable ............................ | 40,000 | — |
| Current Portion of 6-Percent Serial Bonds Payable .... | 50,000 | 50,000 |
| 6-Percent Serial Bonds Payable .................... | 250,000 | 300,000 |
| Preferred Stock ................................... | 90,000 | 100,000 |
| Common Stock .................................... | 500,000 | 500,000 |
| Retained Earnings ................................ | 422,000 | 268,000 |
| Totals........................................ | $2,074,800 | $1,761,000 |

(5) A comparative analysis of retained earnings as of December 31, Year 5 and
Year 4, is presented as follows:

| | December 31 | |
|---|---|---|
| | Year 5 | Year 4 |
| Balance, January 1 .............................. | $268,000 | $131,000 |
| Net Income ...................................... | 195,000 | 172,000 |
| | $463,000 | $303,000 |
| Dividends Declared .............................. | (40,000) | (35,000) |
| Premium on Preferred Stock Repurchased .......... | (1,000) | — |
| Balance, December 31 ........................... | $422,000 | $268,000 |

(6) Accounts totaling $3,000 were written off as uncollectible during Year 5.

a. Prepare a T-account work sheet for the preparation of a statement of cash
flows.

**b.** Prepare a formal statement of cash flows for Hatfield Corporation for the year ending December 31, Year 5.

7. *Preparation of statement of cash flows (adapted from CPA examination).* Bencivenga Company has prepared its financial statements for the year ended December 31, Year 6, and for the 3 months ended March 31, Year 7. You have been asked to prepare a statement of cash flows for the 3 months ended March 31, Year 7. The company's balance sheet data at December 31, Year 6, and March 31, Year 7, are shown in Exhibit 14.6, and its income statement data for the 3 months ended March 31, Year 7, are shown in Exhibit 14.7. You have previously satisfied yourself as to the correctness of the amounts presented.

Your discussion with the company's controller and a review of the financial records have revealed the following information:

**(1)** On January 8, Year 7, the company sold marketable securities for cash. These securities had been held for more than 6 months. No marketable securities were purchased during Year 7.

**Exhibit 14.6** ———————————————————————
**BENCIVENGA COMPANY**
**Balance Sheet**

|  | Dec. 31, Year 6 | Mar. 31, Year 7 |
|---|---|---|
| Cash | $ 25,300 | $ 87,400 |
| Marketable Securities | 16,500 | 7,300 |
| Accounts Receivable (net) | 24,320 | 49,320 |
| Inventory | 31,090 | 48,590 |
| Total Current Assets | $ 97,210 | $192,610 |
| Land | 40,000 | 18,700 |
| Building | 250,000 | 250,000 |
| Equipment | — | 81,500 |
| Accumulated Depreciation | (15,000) | (16,250) |
| Investment in 30-Percent-Owned Company | 61,220 | 66,980 |
| Other Assets | 15,100 | 15,100 |
| Total Assets | $448,530 | $608,640 |
| | | |
| Accounts Payable | $ 21,220 | $ 17,330 |
| Dividend Payable | — | 8,000 |
| Income Taxes Payable | — | 34,616 |
| Total Current Liabilities | $ 21,220 | $ 59,946 |
| Other Liabilities | 186,000 | 186,000 |
| Bonds Payable | 50,000 | 115,000 |
| Discount on Bonds Payable | (2,300) | (2,150) |
| Deferred Income Taxes | 510 | 846 |
| Preferred Stock | 30,000 | — |
| Common Stock | 80,000 | 110,000 |
| Dividends Declared | — | (8,000) |
| Retained Earnings | 83,100 | 146,998 |
| Total Equities | $448,530 | $608,640 |

**Exhibit 14.7** _____

**BENCIVENGA COMPANY**
**Income Statement Data for the 3 Months Ended March 31, Year 7**

| | |
|---|---:|
| Sales...................................................... | $242,807 |
| Gain on Sale of Marketable Securities ............................... | 2,400 |
| Equity in Earnings of 30-Percent-Owned Company.................... | 5,880 |
| Gain on Condemnation of Land ..................................... | 10,700 |
|    Total Revenues ............................................. | $261,787 |
| Cost of Sales ...................................................... | $138,407 |
| General and Administration Expenses ............................... | 22,130 |
| Depreciation ...................................................... | 1,250 |
| Interest Expense ................................................... | 1,150 |
| Income Taxes ..................................................... | 34,952 |
|    Total Expenses............................................. | $197,889 |
| Net Income ...................................................... | $ 63,898 |

**(2)** The company's preferred stock is convertible into common stock at a rate of one share of preferred for two shares of common. The preferred stock and common stock have par values of $2 and $1, respectively.

**(3)** On January 17, Year 7, three acres of land were condemned. An award of $32,000 in cash was received on March 22, Year 7. Purchase of additional land as a replacement is not contemplated by the company.

**(4)** On March 25, Year 7, the company purchased equipment for cash.

**(5)** On March 29, Year 7, bonds payable were issued by the company at par for cash.

**(6)** The investment in the 30-percent-owned company included an amount attributable to goodwill of $3,220 at December 31, Year 6. Goodwill is being amortized at an annual rate of $480.

**a.** Prepare a T-account work sheet for the preparation of a statement of cash flows, defining funds as cash and cash equivalents.

**b.** Prepare a formal statement of cash flows for Bencivenga Company for the 3 months ending March 31, Year 7.

**8.** *Preparation of statement of cash flows (adapted from CPA examination).* Exhibit 14.8 presents a comparative statement of financial position for Kenwood Corporation as of December 31, Year 1 and Year 2. Exhibit 14.9 presents an income statement for Year 2. The following additional information has been obtained.

**(1)** On February 2, Year 2, Kenwood issued a 10-percent stock dividend to shareholders of record on January 15, Year 2. The market price per share of the common stock on February 2, Year 2, was $15.

**(2)** On March 1, Year 2, Kenwood issued 3,800 shares of common stock for land. The common stock and land had current market values of approximately $40,000 on March 1, Year 2.

**(3)** On April 15, Year 2, Kenwood repurchased long-term bonds with a face and book value of $50,000. The gain of $22,000 was reported as an extraordinary item on the income statement.

Exhibit 14.8 ————————————————————————————

## KENWOOD CORPORATION
## Statement of Financial Position

| | December 31 | |
| --- | --- | --- |
| | Year 2 | Year 1 |

# Assets

| | | |
| --- | --- | --- |
| Current Assets: | | |
| Cash ........................................... | $ 100,000 | $ 90,000 |
| Accounts Receivable (net of allowance for doubtful accounts of $10,000 and $8,000, respectively).... | 210,000 | 140,000 |
| Inventories ..................................... | 260,000 | 220,000 |
| Total Current Assets .......................... | $ 570,000 | $ 450,000 |
| Land ........................................... | 325,000 | 200,000 |
| Plant and Equipment............................. | 580,000 | 633,000 |
| Less Accumulated Depreciation .................... | (90,000) | (100,000) |
| Patents......................................... | 30,000 | 33,000 |
| Total Assets ................................... | $1,415,000 | $1,216,000 |

# Liabilities and Shareholders' Equity

| | | |
| --- | --- | --- |
| Liabilities: | | |
| Current Liabilities: | | |
| Accounts Payable ............................. | $ 260,000 | $ 200,000 |
| Accrued Liabilities ............................ | 200,000 | 210,000 |
| Total Current Liabilities ...................... | $ 460,000 | $ 410,000 |
| Deferred Income Taxes ........................ | 140,000 | 100,000 |
| Long-Term Bonds (due December 15, Year 13)..... | 130,000 | 180,000 |
| Total Liabilities .............................. | $ 730,000 | $ 690,000 |
| Shareholders' Equity: | | |
| Common Stock, Par Value $5, Authorized 100,000 Shares, Issued and Outstanding 50,000 and 42,000 Shares, Respectively.................... | $ 250,000 | $ 210,000 |
| Additional Paid-In Capital........................ | 233,000 | 170,000 |
| Retained Earnings ............................. | 202,000 | 146,000 |
| Total Shareholders' Equity ................... | $ 685,000 | $ 526,000 |
| Total Liabilities and Shareholders' Equity ........... | $1,415,000 | $1,216,000 |

(4) On June 30, Year 2, Kenwood sold equipment costing $53,000, with a book value of $23,000, for $19,000 cash.

(5) On September 30, Year 2, Kenwood declared and paid a $.04 per share cash dividend to shareholders of record on August 1, Year 2.

(6) On October 10, Year 2, Kenwood purchased land for $85,000 cash.

(7) Deferred income taxes represent timing differences relating to the use of different depreciation methods for income tax and financial statement reporting.

a. Prepare a T-account work sheet for the preparation of a statement of cash flows.

b. Prepare a formal statement of cash flows for Kenwood Corporation for the year ended December 31, Year 2.

Exhibit 14.9 ———————————————————————————

## KENWOOD CORPORATION
### Income Statement for the Year Ended December 31, Year 2

| | |
|---|---:|
| Sales.......................................................... | $1,000,000 |
| Expenses: | |
|   Cost of Goods Sold......................................... | $ 560,000 |
|   Salary and Wages ......................................... | 190,000 |
|   Depreciation ............................................ | 20,000 |
|   Amortization ............................................ | 3,000 |
|   Loss on Sale of Equipment ................................. | 4,000 |
|   Interest ................................................ | 16,000 |
|   Miscellaneous .......................................... | 8,000 |
| Total Expenses........................................... | $ 801,000 |
| Income before Income Taxes and Extraordinary Item ................. | $ 199,000 |
| Income Taxes | |
|   Current ................................................ | $ 50,000 |
|   Deferred ............................................... | 40,000 |
| Provision for Income Taxes ................................... | $ 90,000 |
| Income before Extraordinary Item ............................. | $ 109,000 |
| Extraordinary Item—Gain on Repurchase of Long-Term Bonds | |
|   (net of $10,000 income tax) ............................... | 12,000 |
| Net Income .................................................. | $ 121,000 |
| Earnings per Share: | |
|   Income before Extraordinary Item ........................... | $2.21 |
|   Extraordinary Item ........................................ | .24 |
|   Net Income ............................................. | $2.45 |

9. *Preparation of statement of cash flows (adapted from CPA examination).* The comparative balance sheets for the Plainview Corporation are shown in Exhibit 14.10.

The following additional information relates to Year 5 activities:

(1) The Retained Earnings account was analyzed as follows:

| | | |
|---|---:|---:|
| Retained Earnings, December 31, Year 4 ............ | | $758,200 |
| Add Net Income after Extraordinary Items | | |
|   (loss of $3,000) ................................ | | 236,580 |
| Subtotal ...................................... | | $994,780 |
| Deduct: | | |
|   Cash Dividends .................................. | $130,000 | |
|   Loss on Reissue of Treasury Stock................ | 3,000 | |
|   Stock Dividend ................................... | 100,200 | 233,200 |
| Retained Earnings, December 31, Year 5 ............ | | $761,580 |

(2) On January 2, Year 5, marketable securities costing $110,000 were sold for $127,000. The proceeds from this sale, the funds in the bond sinking fund, and the amount received from the issuance of the 8-percent deben-

**Exhibit 14.10** _____

PLAINVIEW CORPORATION
Comparative Balance Sheets
December 31, Year 5 and Year 4

|  | Year 5 | Year 4 |
|---|---|---|
| **Assets** | | |
| Cash | $ 142,100 | $ 165,300 |
| Marketable Securities (at cost) | 122,800 | 129,200 |
| Accounts Receivable (net) | 312,200 | 371,200 |
| Inventories | 255,200 | 124,100 |
| Prepayments | 23,400 | 22,000 |
| Bond Sinking Fund | — | 63,000 |
| Investment in Subsidiary (at equity) | 134,080 | 152,000 |
| Plant and Equipment (net) | 1,443,700 | 1,534,600 |
| Total Assets | $2,433,280 | $2,561,400 |
| **Equities** | | |
| Accounts Payable | $ 238,100 | $ 213,300 |
| Notes Payable—Current | — | 145,000 |
| Accrued Payables | 16,500 | 18,000 |
| Income Taxes Payable | 97,500 | 31,000 |
| Deferred Income Taxes (noncurrent) | 127,900 | 128,400 |
| 6-Percent Mortgage Bonds Payable (due Year 17) | — | 300,000 |
| Premium on Mortgage Bonds | — | 10,000 |
| 8-Percent Debentures Payable (due Year 25) | 125,000 | — |
| Common Stock, $10 Par Value | 1,033,500 | 950,000 |
| Additional Paid-In Capital | 67,700 | 51,000 |
| Retained Earnings | 761,580 | 758,200 |
| Treasury Stock—at Cost of $3 per Share | (34,500) | (43,500) |
| Total Equities | $2,433,280 | $2,561,400 |

tures were used to retire the 6-percent mortgage bonds. Any gain or loss on the retirement is taxed currently at 40 percent.

(3) The treasury stock was reissued on February 28, Year 5. All "losses" on the reissue of treasury stock are charged to retained earnings.

(4) The stock dividend was declared on October 31, Year 5, when the market price of Plainview Corporation's stock was $12 per share.

(5) On April 30, Year 5, a fire destroyed a warehouse that cost $100,000 and on which depreciation of $65,000 had accumulated. The loss was not insured.

(6) Plant and equipment transactions consisted of the sale of a building at its book value of $4,000 and the purchase of machinery for $28,000.

(7) Accounts receivable written off as uncollectible were $16,300 in Year 4 and $18,500 in Year 5. Expired insurance was $4,100 recorded in Year 4 and $3,900 in Year 5.

**(8)** The subsidiary, which is 80-percent owned, reported a loss of $22,400 for Year 5.

**a.** Prepare a T-account work sheet for Plainview Corporation for Year 5, defining funds as cash and cash equivalents.

**b.** Prepare a formal statement of cash flows for the year ending December 31, Year 5.

# Part Four
# Synthesis

# Chapter 15 Significance and Implications of Alternative Accounting Principles _____

The independent accountant expresses an unqualified opinion on a firm's financial statements by stating that the statements were prepared in accordance with generally accepted accounting principles. Previous chapters have described and illustrated the important accounting principles currently employed in preparing financial statements. This chapter focuses on the following questions:

1. What criteria should a firm use in selecting its accounting principles from among those that are considered "generally acceptable"?

2. What are the effects of using alternative accounting principles on the principal financial statements?

3. What are the effects of using alternative accounting principles on investors' decisions to invest their capital resources?

One who understands the significance and implications of alternative generally accepted accounting principles is a more effective reader and interpreter of published financial statements. Throughout this chapter, the terms *accounting principles, methods,* and *procedures* are used interchangeably.

## Summary of Generally Accepted Accounting Principles _____

This section lists the major currently acceptable accounting principles, most of which have been discussed in previous chapters. These accounting principles may be classified into two broad groups based on the flexibility permitted to firms in selecting alternative methods of accounting for a specific item. In some instances, the firm has wide flexibility in choosing among alternative methods, such as in selecting depreciation methods. In other instances, the specific conditions associated with a transaction or event dictate the method of accounting that must be used. For example, the method of accounting for investments in the common stock of other firms depends partly on the ownership percentage. Thus a particular firm does not have wide flexibility in selecting its accounting methods in all instances.

**Revenue Recognition**   Revenue may be recognized at the time goods are sold or services are rendered, as is typically done under the accrual basis of accounting, at the time cash is collected (installment method or cost-recovery-first method), or as production progresses (percentage-of-completion method for long-term contracts).

**Uncollectible Accounts**   A firm may recognize expense for uncollectible accounts in the period when revenue is recognized (allowance method) or, if the amount of uncollectibles is unpredictable, in the period when specific accounts are found to be uncollectible (direct write-off method). For tax purposes, a firm must use the direct write-off method under all circumstances.

**Inventories**   A firm may cost inventories on one of several bases: acquisition cost, lower of acquisition cost or market, standard cost, and, in the case of some by-products and precious minerals, net realizable value. When the cost of the goods cannot be specifically identified, the firm must make a cost flow assumption. The cost flow assumption may be FIFO, LIFO, or weighted average, although LIFO must generally be used for financial reports if it is used for income tax returns.

**Investments in Securities**   A firm accounts for investments in the common stock securities of other firms using either the lower-of-cost-or-market method or the equity method, or else it prepares consolidated statements. The method used depends primarily on the percentage of outstanding shares that are held.

**Machinery, Equipment, and Other Depreciable Assets**   These plant assets may be depreciated using the straight-line, double-declining-balance, sum-of-the-years'-digits, or units-of-production method. Estimates of service lives for similar assets may differ among firms.

**Leases**   A firm may set up as an asset and subsequently amortize the rights to use property acquired under lease (capital lease method) or give no recognition to the lease except at the time that lease payments are due each period (operating lease method). Likewise, the lessor can set up the rights to receive future lease payments as a receivable at the inception of the lease (capital lease method) or give no recognition to the lease except to the extent that lease payments become due each period (operating lease method). Whether the capital or operating lease method is used depends on such factors as the life of the lease relative to the life of the leased asset and the present value of the lease payments relative to the market value of the leased property. The facts of each lease agreement determine the method to be used. Both the lessor and the lessee will generally use the same method for a given lease.

The preceding list of alternative acceptable accounting principles is not exhaustive. Also, remember that a firm does not always have a choice of methods. The factors that a firm might consider in selecting its accounting principles are discussed next.

# The Firm's Selection of Alternative Accounting Principles _____

The methods of accounting used for income tax and financial reporting purposes generally do not have to be the same. (An exception is the requirement that if LIFO is used for income tax purposes, it must in general also be used for financial reporting.) Because the firm may pursue different objectives for financial and tax reporting, the selection of accounting principles for the two types of reports is discussed separately.[1]

## Financial Reporting Purposes

**Accurate Presentation**  One of the criteria for assessing the usefulness of accounting information is *accuracy in presentation* of the underlying events and transactions. This criterion may be used by the firm as a basis for selecting its methods of accounting. For example, assets have been defined as resources having future service potential and expenses defined as a measurement of the cost of services consumed during the period. In applying the accuracy criterion, the firm would select the inventory cost flow assumption and depreciation method that most accurately measured the pattern of services consumed during the period and the amount of services still available at the end of the period. As a basis for selecting an accounting method, this approach has at least one serious limitation. The accountant can seldom directly observe the services consumed and the service potential remaining. Without this information the accountant cannot ascertain which accounting principles lead to the most accurate presentation of the underlying events. This criterion can serve only as a normative criterion toward which the development and selection of accounting principles should be directed.

**Conservatism**  In choosing among alternative generally acceptable methods, the firm may select the set that provides the most conservative measure of net income. Considering the uncertainties involved in measuring benefits received as revenues and services consumed as expenses, some have suggested that a conservative measure of earnings should be provided, thereby reducing the possibility of unwarranted optimism by users of financial statements. As a criterion for selecting accounting principles, *conservatism* implies that methods should be chosen that minimize cumulative reported earnings. That is, expenses should be recognized as quickly as possible, and the recognition of revenue should be postponed as long as possible. This reporting objective would lead to selecting the double-declining-balance or sum-of-the-years'-digits depreciation method, selecting the LIFO cost flow assumption if periods of rising prices are anticipated, and expensing intangible development costs in the year incurred.

---

[1]The Tax Reform Act of 1986 imposed an alternative minimum tax on corporations. Included in the base for the alternative minimum tax are timing differences between book income and taxable income. At least with respect to the alternative minimum tax, the selection of accounting methods for financial and tax reporting are not independent.

The rationale for conservatism as a reporting objective has been challenged. Over the whole life of the firm, income is equal to cash receipts minus cash expenditures. Thus, to the extent that net income of earlier periods is smaller, earnings of later periods must be larger. The ''later'' periods when income must be larger may, however, be many periods later, sometimes even the last period of the firm's existence. Also, some statement users may be misled by earnings reports based on conservative reporting principles. Consider, for example, investors who sell shares because they believe that the firm is not operating in a sufficiently profitable manner with the resources available, when earnings reported in a manner less biased toward conservatism would not have induced the sale. Or consider the potential investors who do not purchase securities because they are misled by the published conservative statement of earnings.

**Profit Maximization**   A reporting objective having an effect opposite to conservatism may be employed in selecting among alternative generally accepted accounting principles. Somewhat loosely termed *reported profit maximization,*[2] this criterion suggests the selection of accounting methods that maximize cumulative reported earnings. That is, revenue should be recognized as quickly as possible, and the recognition of expense should be postponed as long as possible. For example, the straight-line method of depreciation would be used, and when periods of rising prices were anticipated the FIFO cost flow assumption would be selected. The use of profit maximization as a reporting objective is an extension of the notion that the firm is in business to generate profits, and it should present as favorable a report on performance as possible within currently acceptable accounting methods. Some firm's managers, whose compensation depends in part on reported earnings, prefer larger reported earnings to smaller. Profit maximization is subject to a similar, but mirror-image, criticism as the use of conservatism as a reporting objective. Reporting income earlier under the profit maximization criterion must mean that smaller income will be reported in some later period.

**Income Smoothing**   A final reporting objective that may be used in selecting accounting principles is *income smoothing*. This criterion suggests selecting accounting methods that result in the smoothest earnings trend over time. As discussed later in this chapter, empirical research has shown that changes in stock prices are related to changes in earnings. Advocates of income smoothing suggest that if a company can minimize fluctuations in earnings, the perceived risk of investing in shares of its stock will be reduced and, all else being equal, its stock price will be higher. Note that this reporting criterion suggests that net income, not revenues and expenses individually, is to be smoothed. As a result, the firm must consider the total pattern of its operations before selecting the appropriate accounting methods. For example, the straight-line method of depreciation may provide the smoothest amount of depreciation expense on a machine over its life. If, however, the productivity of the machine declines with age so that revenues decrease in later

---

[2]The concept of profit maximization as a reporting objective is not the same as the profit maximization dictum of microeconomics.

years, net income using the straight-line method may not provide the smoothest net income stream.

**Summary** The principal message of this section is that accurate presentation, although perhaps a desirable reporting objective, is not operational for selecting accounting principles. As a result, firms may select from among the methods included in the set of generally acceptable accounting principles using whatever reporting criterion they choose.

Where does this flexibility permitted in selecting accounting principles leave the user of financial statements? Accounting Principles Board *Opinion No. 22* requires firms to disclose the accounting principles used in preparing financial statements, either in a separate statement or as a note to the principal statements.[3] The effect of alternative accounting principles on investment decisions is discussed later in the chapter.

### Income Tax Reporting Purposes

In selecting accounting procedures for income tax purposes, the corporation's objective should be to select those methods that minimize the present value of the stream of income tax payments. The operational rule, sometimes called the *least and latest rule,* is to pay the least amount of taxes as late as possible within the law. The least and latest rule generally translates into a policy of recognizing expenses as quickly as possible and postponing the recognition of revenue as long as possible. This policy might be altered somewhat if income tax rates are expected to change, or if the firm had losses in earlier years and can carry those losses forward to offset taxable income of the current year.

The desire to recognize expenses as quickly as possible suggests the adoption of the LIFO inventory cost flow assumption, accelerated depreciation, and immediate expensing of research and development, advertising, and similar costs. Using the installment basis of recognizing revenue is generally desirable for income tax purposes where permitted by the Internal Revenue Code and Regulations, because it results in postponing the recognition of revenue and the resulting income tax payments until cash is collected.

## An Illustration of the Effects of Alternative Accounting Principles on a Set of Financial Statements _____

This section illustrates the effects of using different accounting principles on a set of financial statements. The illustration has been constructed so that the accounting principles used create significant differences in the financial statements. Therefore, inferences about the usual magnitude of the effects of alternative methods should not be drawn from this example.

---

[3]Accounting Principles Board, *Opinion No. 22,* "Disclosure of Accounting Policies," 1972.

# The Scenario

On January 1, two corporations are formed to operate merchandising businesses. The two firms are alike in all respects except for their methods of accounting. Conservative Company chooses the accounting principles that will minimize its reported net income. High Flyer Company chooses the accounting principles that will maximize its reported net income. The following events occur during the year.

1. Both corporations issue 2 million shares of $10-par-value stock on January 1, for $20 million cash.

2. Both firms acquire equipment on January 1 for $14 million cash. The equipment is estimated to have a 10-year life and zero salvage value.

3. Both firms make the following purchases of merchandise inventory:

| Date | Units Purchased | Unit Price | Cost of Purchases |
|---|---|---|---|
| January 1............................. | 170,000 | @$60 | $10,200,000 |
| May 1 .................................. | 190,000 | @$63 | 11,970,000 |
| September 1 .......................... | 200,000 | @$66 | 13,200,000 |
| Total ................................ | 560,000 | | $35,370,000 |

4. During the year, both firms sell 420,000 units at an average price of $100 each. All sales are made for cash.

5. During the year, both firms have selling, general, and administrative expenses, excluding depreciation, of $2.7 million.

6. The income tax rate is assumed to be 34 percent.

# Accounting Principles Used

The methods of accounting used by each firm in preparing its financial statements are described in the following sections.

**Inventory Cost Flow Assumption** Conservative Company makes a LIFO cost flow assumption, whereas High Flyer Company makes a FIFO assumption. The method chosen by each firm is used for both its financial reports and income tax returns. Because the beginning inventory is zero, the cost of goods available for sale by each firm is equal to the purchases during the year of $35,370,000. Both firms have 140,000 units in ending inventory. Conservative Company therefore reports a cost of goods sold of $26,970,000 [= $35,370,000 − (140,000 × $60)], whereas High Flyer Company reports a cost of goods sold of $26,130,000 [= $35,370,000 − (140,000 × $66)]. Income tax regulations generally require a firm to use LIFO in its financial reports if it uses LIFO for its tax return. High Flyer Company does not want to use LIFO in its financial reports and therefore forgoes the tax savings opportunities from using it for tax purposes.

**Depreciation**  Conservative Company decides to depreciate its equipment using the double-declining-balance method in its financial statements, whereas High Flyer Company decides to use the straight-line method. Conservative Company therefore reports depreciation expense of $2.8 million (= $2 \times \frac{1}{10} \times$ $14,000,000), whereas High Flyer Company reports depreciation expense of $1.4 million (= $\frac{1}{10} \times$ $14,000,000) to shareholders. Both companies compute depreciation for tax purposes using a 7-year life, the double-declining balance depreciation method, and the initial half-year depreciation convention. Depreciation on the tax return is $2.0 million for the year.

## Comparative Income Statements

Exhibit 15.1 presents comparative income statements for Conservative Company and High Flyer Company for the year ending December 31. For each company, the revenues and expenses (except for depreciation) reported in the financial statements are the same as reported in the income tax return.

**Exhibit 15.1** _____

**Comparative Income Statements Based on Different Accounting Principles for the Year Ending December 31**
**(all dollar amounts in thousands, except for per-share amounts)**

| | Conservative Company | | High Flyer Company | |
| --- | --- | --- | --- | --- |
| | Financial Statement | Tax Return | Financial Statement | Tax Return |
| Sales Revenue . . . . . . . . . . . . . . . . . . . | $42,000.0 | $42,000.0 | $42,000.0 | $42,000.0 |
| Expenses: | | | | |
| Cost of Goods Sold . . . . . . . . . . . . . | $26,970.0 | $26,970.0 | $26,130.0 | $26,130.0 |
| Depreciation on Equipment[b] . . . . . . | 2,800.0 | 2,000.0 | 1,400.0 | 2,000.0 |
| Other Selling, General, and Administrative . . . . . . . . . . . . | 2,700.0 | 2,700.0 | 2,700.0 | 2,700.0 |
| Expenses before Income Taxes . . . . . | $32,470.0 | $31,670.0 | $30,230.0 | $30,830.0 |
| Net Income before Income Taxes . . . . . . . . . . . . . . . . . . | $ 9,530.0 | $10,330.0 | $11,770.0 | $11,170.0 |
| Income Tax Expense[a] . . . . . . . . . . . . . | 3,240.2 | | 4,001.8 | |
| Net Income . . . . . . . . . . . . . . . . . . . . . | $ 6,289.8 | | $ 7,768.2 | |
| Earnings per Share (2,000,000 shares outstanding) . . . | $3.14 | | $3.88 | |
| [a]Computation of Income Taxes: Income before Taxes . . . . . . . . . . . . . | $ 9,530.0 | $10,330.0 | $11,770.0 | $11,170.0 |
| Income Tax Expense (at 34 percent) . . . . . . . . . . . . . . . . | $ 3,240.2 | | $ 4,001.8 | |
| Income Tax Currently Payable . . . . . | | $ 3,512.2 | | $ 3,797.8 |
| [b]Income Taxes Deferred by Timing Differences for Depreciation: Dr. = .34 ($2,000 − $2,800) . . . . | $ (272.0) | | | |
| Cr. = .34 ($2,000 − $1,400) . . . . | | | | $ 204.0 |

Conservative Company reports $800 million (= $2,800,000 − $2,000,000) more depreciation in the financial statements than in the tax return. The $800 million difference is viewed as a timing difference. Income taxes payable currently of $3,512,200 exceed income tax expense of $3,240,200. The $272,000 difference (= $3,512,200 − $3,240,200) is debited to Prepaid Income Taxes on the balance sheet.

High Flyer Company reports $600 million (= $1,400 million − $2,000 million) less depreciation in the financial statements than in the tax return. This $600 million difference is also a timing difference. Because taxes currently payable are less than income tax expense, a deferred tax appears on the equities side of the balance sheet.

Note in this illustration that reported net income and earnings per share of High Flyer Company are significantly larger than for Conservative Company.

## Comparative Balance Sheets

Exhibit 15.2 presents comparative balance sheets for Conservative Company and High Flyer Company as of December 31. Merchandise inventory and equipment (net) as well as total assets of Conservative Company are stated at lower amounts than those of High Flyer Company. The only real difference between the economic positions of each company is the amount of cash. The difference in the amount of cash is attributable to the payment of different amounts of income taxes by the two firms. Note that Conservative Company has more cash because it paid smaller income taxes. One could argue that it is better off than High Flyer Company.

The differences in the amounts at which merchandise inventory and equipment (net) are stated result from the different accounting methods used by the two companies. The amounts shown for Conservative Company are smaller than the corre-

**Exhibit 15.2** _____

**Comparative Balance Sheets Based on Alternative
Accounting Principles, December 31
(all dollar amounts in thousands)**

|  | Conservative Company | High Flyer Company |
|---|---|---|
| **Assets:** | | |
| Cash...................................................... | $ 6,417.8 | $ 6,132.2 |
| Merchandise Inventory ................................ | 8,400.0 | 9,240.0 |
| Equipment (at acquisition cost)....................... | 14,000.0 | 14,000.0 |
| Less Accumulated Depreciation ...................... | (2,800.0) | (1,400.0) |
| Prepaid Income Taxes ................................ | 272.0 | — |
| Total Assets ..................................... | $26,289.8 | $27,972.2 |
| **Equities:** | | |
| Deferred Income Taxes ............................... | — | $ 204.0 |
| Common Stock......................................... | $20,000.0 | 20,000.0 |
| Retained Earnings .................................... | 6,289.8 | 7,768.2 |
| Total Equities ..................................... | $26,289.8 | $27,972.2 |

sponding amounts for High Flyer Company because a larger portion of the costs incurred during the period by Conservative Company has been recognized as an expense. Conservative Company also shows Prepaid Income Taxes of $272,000 arising from timing differences in depreciation for financial and tax reporting.

In the equities portion of the balance sheet, High Flyer Company reports deferred income taxes resulting from differences in the timing of depreciation on equipment in the financial statements and income tax return.

Note the effect of using alternative accounting principles on the rate of return on total assets ratio (= net income/total assets). Conservative Company reports a smaller amount of net income but also a smaller amount of total assets. One may expect the rate of return on total assets of the two firms to approximate each other more closely than either net income or total assets individually. Significant differences in the ratio for the two firms are still observable in this illustration, however. The rate of return on total assets for Conservative Company is 27.2 percent [= $6,289,800/($20,000,000 + $26,289,800)/2], and for High Flyer Company it is 33.2 percent [= $7,972,200/($20,000,000 + $27,972,200)/2].

Exhibit 15.3 presents comparative statements of cash flows for Conservative Company and High Flyer Company. The amount of cash provided by Conservative Company's operations is larger than for High Flyer Company. The difference of $285.6 million (= $417.8 million − $132.2 million) results from the difference in the amount of income taxes paid. These companies paid different amounts of income taxes because they used different cost flow assumptions for inventories on their tax returns, which is shown as follows:

| | |
|---|---:|
| Conservative Company: LIFO Cost of Goods Sold . . . . . . . . . . . . . . . . . . . . . . . . | $26,970 |
| High Flyer Company: FIFO Cost of Goods Sold . . . . . . . . . . . . . . . . . . . . . . . . . | 26,130 |
| Difference in Cost of Goods Sold and Taxable Income . . . . . . . . . . . . . . . . . . . . | $    840 |
| Tax Rate . . . . . . . . . . . . . . . . . . . . . . . . . . . . . . . . . . . . . . . . . . . . . . . . . . . . . | 34% |
| Difference in Cash Flow . . . . . . . . . . . . . . . . . . . . . . . . . . . . . . . . . . . . . . . . . . | $    285.6 |

Note that the use of different depreciation methods *on the financial statements* does not affect cash flows and the statement of cash flows. As long as these firms use the same depreciation method on their tax returns, cash flows will be the same. Thus the statement of cash flows tends to be affected much less by alternative generally accepted accounting principles than are the balance sheet and income statement.

## Moral of the Illustration

To interpret published financial statements, the analyst must be aware of which accounting principles from the set of alternative generally accepted accounting principles are used. When reports of several companies are compared, the amounts shown should be adjusted where possible for the different accounting methods used. The techniques for making some of these adjustments were illustrated in previous chapters (for example, LIFO to FIFO cost flow assumption). The notes to the

Exhibit 15.3 ————————————————————————

**Comparative Statements of Cash Flows**
**for the Year Ending December 31**
**(all dollar amounts in thousands)**

| | Conservative Company | High Flyer Company |
|---|---|---|
| **Operations:** | | |
| Net Income . . . . . . . . . . . . . . . . . . . . . . | $6,289.8 | $7,768.2 |
| Additions: | | |
| Depreciation Expense . . . . . . . . . . . . . . | 2,800.0 | 1,400.0 |
| Deferred Tax Credit . . . . . . . . . . . . . . . . | — | 204.0 |
| Subtractions: | | |
| Deferred Tax Debit . . . . . . . . . . . . . . . . | ( 272.0) | |
| Increase in Merchandise | | |
| Inventory . . . . . . . . . . . . . . . . . . . . . . | (8,400.0) | (9,240.0) |
| Cash Flow from Operations . . . . . . . . . . | $    417.8 | $    132.2 |
| **Investing:** | | |
| Acquisition of Equipment . . . . . . . . . . . . | (14,000.0) | (14,000.0) |
| **Financing:** | | |
| Issue of Common Stock . . . . . . . . . . . . . | 20,000.0 | 20,000.0 |
| Net Change in Cash . . . . . . . . . . . . . . . . | $ 6,417.8 | $ 6,132.2 |

financial statements will disclose the accounting methods used, but not necessarily
the data required to make appropriate adjustments.


## Assessing the Effects of Alternative
## Accounting Principles on Investment Decisions ————————

Previous sections of this chapter emphasized the flexibility that firms have in selecting accounting procedures and the possible effects of using different accounting
procedures on the financial statements. We now focus briefly on a related and
important question: Do investors accept financial statement information as presented, or do they somehow filter out all or most of the differences in the financial
statements of various firms that result from differences in the methods of accounting
employed? If investors accept financial statement information as presented, without
adjustments for the methods of accounting used, then two firms, otherwise identical
except for the accounting procedures employed, might receive a disproportionate
amount of capital funds. The use of alternative accounting principles could lead to
a misallocation of resources in the economy. On the other hand, if investors make
adjustments for the different accounting procedures in analyzing the financial statements of various firms, perhaps the policy maker does not need to be concerned
over the variety of acceptable accounting principles. If investors do make such
adjustments, increased disclosure of the procedures followed may be more important than greater uniformity in accounting principles.

The effect of alternative accounting principles on investment decisions has been the subject of extensive debate among public accountants, academics, personnel in government agencies, and financial statement users.

Those who believe that investors can be misled point to examples where the market prices of particular firms' shares of stock have decreased dramatically after the effects of using specific accounting procedures have been carefully analyzed and reported in the financial press.[4] In these examples it is often difficult, however, to judge whether the price change is attributable to the disclosure of the effects of using particular accounting procedures or to other, more temporary factors affecting the specific firm, its industry, or all firms in the economy. Also, it is difficult to generalize on the effects of using alternative accounting principles on investment decisions from isolated and anecdotal examples.

An expanding number of empirical research studies, on the other hand, have supported the view that investors at the aggregate market level are rarely misled by the accounting methods employed. This research has developed from the theory and empirical evidence that the stock market is efficient, in the sense that market prices adjust quickly and in an unbiased manner to new information.[5] Unlike the examples supporting the view that investors are misled, these empirical studies have been based on data for a large number of firms over long time periods. Also, an effort has been made in these studies to control for the effects of economy-wide and industry effects on market price changes.

Several studies have shown that changes in earnings are associated with changes in market prices and, therefore, indicate that information contained in the financial statements is used by investors in making their resource allocation decisions. Several studies have examined the effects of *changes* in the methods of accounting on market prices, and a third group of studies looked at *differences* in the methods of accounting across firms. The results of these last two groups of studies have been mixed, with several studies supporting the position that investors are misled and several studies supporting the position that they are not misled. The methodology used in many of these studies has been extensively criticized, so the full implications are not clear.[6]

Research regarding the effects of alternative accounting principles on investment decisions has not progressed sufficiently for any consensus to have been reached. The research that has been conducted has been described here briefly to emphasize an important point. It is not obvious, as it might first appear, that the

---

[4]For several examples, see Abraham J. Briloff, *More Debits Than Credits* (New York: Harper & Row, 1976). For an analysis of these examples, see George Foster, "Briloff and the Capital Market," *Journal of Accounting Research* 17 (Spring 1979): 262–274.

[5]See Eugene F. Fama, "Efficient Capital Markets: A Review of Theory and Empirical Work," *Journal of Finance* 25 (May 1970): 383–417.

[6]For a review of these studies, see Ray Ball and George Foster, "Corporate Financial Reporting: A Methodological Review of Empirical Research," *Studies in Current Methodologies in Accounting: A Critical Evaluation,* supplement to *Journal of Accounting Research* 20 (1982): 117–148; and Baruch Lev and James A. Ohlson, "Market-Based Empirical Research: A Review, Interpretation, and Extension," Ibid.: 249–322.

current flexibility permitted firms in selecting accounting principles necessarily misleads investors and results in a misallocation of resources.[7]

## Development of Principles in Accounting _____

Chapter 7 indicated that the development of generally accepted accounting principles is essentially a political process. Various persons or groups have power or authority in the decision process, including Congress and the Securities and Exchange Commission, the courts, professional accounting organizations and their members, business firms, and financial statement users. Although Congress has the ultimate authority to specify acceptable accounting methods, it has delegated that authority in almost all cases to the Securities and Exchange Commission. The Commission has indicated that it will generally accept the pronouncements of the Financial Accounting Standards Board on accounting principles. The role of the private sector versus the public sector in setting accounting principles and regulating professional accounting practice continues, however, to be the subject of extensive debate.

## Summary _____

The structure of accounting principles might be depicted as shown in Figure 15.1. The *universe* of possible accounting principles is encircled by a dashed line because of the difficulty in defining the relative size, or boundaries, of circle A. The process of specifying the principles designated as *generally acceptable* (the subset of principles from circle A represented by circle B) is political in nature. Congress and the

**Figure 15.1** _____

**Structure of Accounting Principles**

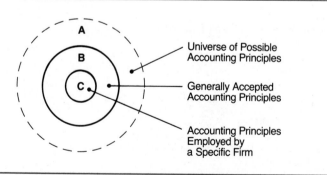

[7]For a description of the theoretical framework and a summary of the empirical work behind this position, see Nicholas J. Gonedes and Nicholas Dopuch, "Capital Market Equilibrium, Information-Production, and Selecting Accounting Techniques: Theoretical Framework and Review of Empirical Work," *Studies on Financial Accounting Objectives: 1974,* supplement to *Journal of Accounting Research* 12 (1974): 48–129; and Thomas R. Dyckman and Dale Morse, *Efficient Capital Markets and Accounting: A Critical Analysis,* 2nd ed. (Englewood Cliffs, N.J.: Prentice-Hall, 1986).

Securities and Exchange Commission have the legal authority to make the selection, but most of the responsibility for doing so has, in effect, been delegated to the Financial Accounting Standards Board. The individual firm's selection of accounting principles (the subset of principles from circle B represented by circle C) may be based on a criterion of accurate presentation. However, because benefits received and services consumed are seldom observable events and are therefore difficult to measure, reaching consensus on which generally accepted accounting principles provide an accurate or fair presentation is difficult. This chapter suggests that a firm might pursue a specific reporting objective, such as conservatism, profit maximization, or income smoothing, in selecting its accounting principles.

Before we can know whether circle B should be widened or narrowed, we must learn whether investors accept financial statement information as presented or whether they make adjustments to recognize the effects of using alternative accounting principles. This question has been, and continues to be, the subject of extensive research.

# Master Review Problem for Self-Study _____

A set of financial statements for Kaplan Corporation follows, including a consolidated income statement (Exhibit 15.4) and a consolidated statement of cash flows (Exhibit 15.5) for Year 2, and a comparative consolidated balance sheet (Exhibit 15.6) on December 31, Year 1 and Year 2. Following the financial statements is a series of notes providing additional information on certain items in the financial statements. Respond to each of the questions on pages 643 and 644, using informa-

**Exhibit 15.4** _____
**KAPLAN CORPORATION**
**Consolidated Income Statement for Year 2**
**(all dollar amounts in thousands)**

| | |
|---|---:|
| **Revenues:** | |
| Sales........................................................ | $12,000 |
| Equity in Earnings of Unconsolidated Affiliates ............................ | 300 |
| Dividend Revenue ........................................... | 20 |
| Gain on Sale of Marketable Securities ..................................... | 30 |
| Total Revenues ............................................. | $12,350 |
| **Expenses:** | |
| Cost of Goods Sold.......................................... | $ 7,200 |
| Selling and Administrative ................................... | 2,689 |
| Loss on Sale of Equipment .................................. | 80 |
| Unrealized Loss from Price Decline of Marketable Equity Securities ........... | 20 |
| Interest (Notes 7 and 8)...................................... | 561 |
| Total Expenses............................................. | $10,550 |
| Net Income before Income Taxes and Minority Interest ..................... | $ 1,800 |
| Income Tax Expense ........................................ | 540 |
| Net Income before Minority Interest.......................... | $ 1,260 |
| Minority Interest in Earnings of Heimann Corporation ...................... | 40 |
| Net Income ................................................ | $ 1,220 |

## Exhibit 15.5 _____

## KAPLAN CORPORATION
Consolidated Statement of Cash Flows for Year 2
(all dollar amounts in thousands)

| | | |
|---|---:|---:|
| *Operations:* | | |
| Net Income | $1,220 | |
| Additions: | | |
| Depreciation | 560 | |
| Deferred Taxes | 120 | |
| Loss on Sale of Equipment | 80 | |
| Minority Interest in Undistributed Earnings of | | |
|    Consolidated Subsidiaries | 34 | |
| Amortization of Discount on Bonds | 28 | |
| Amortization of Goodwill | 10 | |
| Unrealized Loss from Price Declines of Marketable Securities | 20 | |
| Increase in Accounts Payable | 1,355 | |
| Increase in Interest Payable | 100 | |
| Increase in Income Taxes Payable | 125 | |
| Subtractions: | | |
| Gain on Sale of Marketable Securities | (30) | |
| Equity in Earnings of Affiliates in | | |
|    Excess of Dividends Received | (180) | |
| Amortization of Premium on Bonds | (28) | |
| Increase in Accounts Receivable | (550) | |
| Increase in Inventories | (520) | |
| Increase in Prepayments | (170) | |
| Decrease in Salaries Payable | (200) | |
| Cash Flow from Operations | | $1,974 |
| *Investing:* | | |
| Sale of Marketable Securities | $ 210 | |
| Sale of Equipment | 150 | |
| Investment in Johnson Corporation | (50) | |
| Purchase of Marketable Securities | (300) | |
| Acquisition of: Land | (100) | |
|           Building | (300) | |
|           Equipment | (1,400) | |
| Cash Flow from Investing | | (1,790) |
| *Financing:* | | |
| Increase in Notes Payable | $1,000 | |
| Common Stock Issued | 500 | |
| Treasury Stock Sold | 15 | |
| Dividends | (250) | |
| Cash Flow from Financing | | 1,265 |
| Net Change in Cash | | $1,449 |

tion from the financial statements and notes. It is suggested that you study the statements and notes carefully before attempting to respond to the questions.

• Note 1: Summary of Accounting Policies

• *Basis of consolidation.* The financial statements of Kaplan Corporation are consolidated with Heimann Corporation, an 80 percent-owned subsidiary acquired on January 2, Year 1.

**Exhibit 15.6** _____

**KAPLAN CORPORATION**
Consolidated Balance Sheets
December 31, Year 1 and Year 2
(all dollar amounts in thousands)

| | December 31, Year 1 | December 31, Year 2 |
|---|---|---|
| **Assets** | | |
| **Current Assets:** | | |
| Cash . . . . . . . . . . . . . . . . . . . . . . . . . . . . . . . . . . . . . . . . . . . | $ 1,470 | $ 2,919 |
| Marketable Securities (Note 2) . . . . . . . . . . . . . . . . . . . . . . . | 450 | 550 |
| Accounts Receivable (net; Note 3) . . . . . . . . . . . . . . . . . . . | 2,300 | 2,850 |
| Inventories (Note 4) . . . . . . . . . . . . . . . . . . . . . . . . . . . . . . . . | 2,590 | 3,110 |
| Prepayments . . . . . . . . . . . . . . . . . . . . . . . . . . . . . . . . . . . . . | 800 | 970 |
| Total Current Assets . . . . . . . . . . . . . . . . . . . . . . . . . . . . | $ 7,610 | $10,399 |
| | | |
| **Investments** (Note 5): | | |
| Investment in Maher Corporation (10 percent) . . . . . . . . . . . | $ 200 | $ 185 |
| Investment in Johnson Corporation (30 percent) . . . . . . . . . | 310 | 410 |
| Investment in Burton Corporation (40 percent) . . . . . . . . . . . | 800 | 930 |
| Total Investments . . . . . . . . . . . . . . . . . . . . . . . . . . . . . . . | $ 1,310 | $ 1,525 |
| | | |
| **Property, Plant, and Equipment:** | | |
| Land . . . . . . . . . . . . . . . . . . . . . . . . . . . . . . . . . . . . . . . . . . . . | $ 400 | $ 500 |
| Buildings . . . . . . . . . . . . . . . . . . . . . . . . . . . . . . . . . . . . . . . . | 800 | 940 |
| Equipment . . . . . . . . . . . . . . . . . . . . . . . . . . . . . . . . . . . . . . . | 3,300 | 3,800 |
| Total Cost . . . . . . . . . . . . . . . . . . . . . . . . . . . . . . . . . . . . . | $ 4,500 | $ 5,240 |
| Less Accumulated Depreciation . . . . . . . . . . . . . . . . . . . . . . . | (1,200) | (930) |
| Net Property, Plant, and Equipment . . . . . . . . . . . . . . . . . | $ 3,300 | $ 4,310 |
| Goodwill (Note 6) . . . . . . . . . . . . . . . . . . . . . . . . . . . . . . . . . . | 90 | 80 |
| Total Assets . . . . . . . . . . . . . . . . . . . . . . . . . . . . . . . . . . . | $12,310 | $16,314 |

*continued*

- *Marketable securities.* Marketable securities are stated at the lower of ac- quisition cost or market.

- *Accounts receivable.* Uncollectible accounts of customers are accounted for using the allowance method.

- *Inventories.* Inventories are computed using a last-in, first-out (LIFO) cost flow assumption.

- *Investments.* Investments of less than 20 percent of the outstanding com- mon stock of other companies are accounted for using the lower-of-cost- or-market method. Investments of 20 to 50 percent of the outstanding common stock of unconsolidated affiliates and subsidiaries are accounted for using the equity method.

- *Buildings and equipment.* Depreciation for financial reporting purposes is calculated using the straight-line method. For income tax purposes, accel- erated depreciation is used.

**Exhibit 15.6** (*continued*) _____

| | December 31, Year 1 | December 31, Year 2 |
|---|---|---|
| **Liabilities and Shareholders' Equity** | | |
| **Current Liabilities:** | | |
| Note Payable (Note 7) ............................. | $ — | $ 1,000 |
| Accounts Payable .................................. | 1,070 | 2,425 |
| Salaries Payable ................................... | 800 | 600 |
| Interest Payable .................................... | 300 | 400 |
| Income Taxes Payable ............................. | 250 | 375 |
| Total Current Liabilities ........................ | $ 2,420 | $ 4,800 |
| **Long-Term Liabilities:** | | |
| Bonds Payable (Note 8) ............................ | $ 6,209 | $ 6,209 |
| Deferred Income Taxes ............................ | 820 | 940 |
| Total Long-Term Liabilities ....................... | $ 7,029 | $ 7,149 |
| Minority Interest .................................. | $ 180 | $ 214 |
| **Shareholders' Equity:** | | |
| Common Shares ($10 par value) ...................... | $ 500 | $ 600 |
| Additional Paid-in Capital ............................ | 800 | 1,205 |
| Unrealized Loss on Valuation of Investments ........... | (25) | (40) |
| Retained Earnings .................................. | 1,436 | 2,406 |
| Total .............................................. | $ 2,711 | $ 4,171 |
| Less Treasury Shares (at cost) ....................... | (30) | (20) |
| Total Shareholders' Equity ......................... | $ 2,681 | $ 4,151 |
| Total Liabilities and Shareholders' Equity ............. | $12,310 | $16,314 |

- *Goodwill.* Goodwill is amortized over a period of 10 years.

- *Interest on long-term debt.* Interest expense on bonds payable is recognized using the effective interest method.

- *Deferred income taxes.* Deferred income taxes are provided for timing differences between book income and taxable income.

- Note 2: Marketable securities are shown net of an allowance for market price declines below acquisition cost of $50,000 on December 31, Year 1, and $70,000 on December 31, Year 2.

- Note 3: Accounts receivable are shown net of an allowance for uncollectible accounts of $200,000 on December 31, Year 1, and $250,000 on December 31, Year 2. Bad debt expense of $120,000 is included in Selling and Administrative Expenses.

- Note 4: Inventories consist of the following:

| | December 31, Year 1 | December 31, Year 2 |
|---|---|---|
| Raw Materials..................................... | $ 330,000 | $ 380,000 |
| Work in Process............................. | 460,000 | 530,000 |
| Finished Goods ............................ | 1,800,000 | 2,200,000 |
| Total ..................................... | $2,590,000 | $3,110,000 |

The current cost of inventories exceeded the amounts determined on a LIFO basis by $420,000 on December 31, Year 1, and $730,000 on December 31, Year 2.

- Note 5: Burton Corporation had a net income of $400,000 and paid dividends of $75,000 in Year 2.

## BURTON CORPORATION
### (all dollar amounts in thousands)

| | December 31, Year 1 | December 31, Year 2 |
|---|---|---|
| **Balance Sheet** | | |
| Cash and Marketable Securities................ | $ 760 | $ 840 |
| Accounts Receivable (net)..................... | 6,590 | 7,400 |
| Other Assets.................................. | 1,050 | 1,260 |
| Total Assets ............................. | $8,400 | $9,500 |
| | | |
| Notes Payable Due within 1 Year .............. | $3,900 | $4,300 |
| Long-Term Note Payable ...................... | 2,000 | 2,000 |
| Other Liabilities.............................. | 500 | 875 |
| Common Stock................................ | 100 | 100 |
| Additional Paid-in Capital..................... | 1,500 | 1,500 |
| Retained Earnings ........................... | 400 | 725 |
| Total Equities ............................ | $8,400 | $9,500 |

| | Year 2 |
|---|---|
| **Statement of Income and Retained Earnings** | |
| Revenues....................................................... | $920 |
| Expenses....................................................... | 520 |
| Net Income .................................................... | $400 |
| Less Dividends................................................. | (75) |
| Retained Earnings, December 31, Year 1 ............................ | 400 |
| Retained Earnings, December 31, Year 2 ............................ | $725 |

- Note 6: On January 2, Year 1, Kaplan Corporation acquired 80 percent of the outstanding common shares of Heimann Corporation by issuing 20,000 shares of Kaplan Corporation common stock. The Kaplan Corporation shares were selling on January 2, Year 1, for $40 a share. Any difference between the acquisition price and the book value of the net assets acquired was considered goodwill and is being amortized over a period of 10 years from the date of acquisition.

- Note 7: The note payable included under current liabilities is a 1-year note due on January 2, Year 3. The note requires annual interest payments on December 31 of each year.

- Note 8: Bonds payable are as follows:

|  | December 31, Year 1 | December 31, Year 2 |
|---|---|---|
| 4-Percent, $2,000,000 Bonds Due Dec. 31, Year 7, with Interest Payable Semiannually...... | $1,800,920 | $1,829,390 |
| 10-Percent, $3,000,000 Bonds Due Dec. 31, Year 11, with Interest Payable Semiannually .... | 3,407,720 | 3,379,790 |
| 8-Percent, $1,000,000 Bonds Due on Dec. 31, Year 17, with Interest Payable Semiannually .... | 1,000,000 | 1,000,000 |
| Total ...................................... | $6,208,640 | $6,209,180 |

a. Marketable securities costing $180,000 were sold during Year 2. Ascertain the price at which these securities were sold.

b. Refer to part **a**. Compute the cost of marketable securities purchased during Year 2.

c. What was the amount of specific customers' accounts written off as uncollectible during Year 2?

d. Assume that all sales are made on account. Compute the amount of cash collected from customers during the year.

e. Compute the cost of units completed and transferred to the finished goods inventory during Year 2.

f. Direct labor and overhead costs incurred in manufacturing during the year totaled $4,500,000. Determine the cost of raw materials purchased during Year 2.

g. Assume that the amounts disclosed in Note 4 for the current cost of inventories represent the amounts that would be obtained from using a first-in, first-out (FIFO) cost flow assumption. What would cost of goods sold have been if FIFO, rather than LIFO, had been used?

h. Prepare an analysis that explains the causes of the changes in each of the three intercorporate investment accounts.

i. Prepare an analysis that explains the change in each of the four following accounts during Year 2: Land, Building, Equipment, and Accumulated Depreciation.

j. Give the journal entry made on Kaplan Corporation's books on January 2, Year 1, when it acquired Heimann Corporation.

k. Compute the book value of the net assets of Heimann Corporation on January 2, Year 1.

l. Compute the total amount of dividends declared by Heimann Corporation during Year 2.

m. The 4-percent bonds payable were initially priced to yield 6 percent compounded semiannually. The 10-percent bonds were initially priced to yield 8 percent compounded semiannually. Using the appropriate present value tables at the back of the book, demonstrate that $1,800,920 and $3,407,720 (see Note 8) were the correct valuations of these two bond issues on December 31, Year 1.

n. Calculate the amount of interest expense and any change in the valuation of the bond liability for Year 2 on each of the three long-term bond issues (see Note 8).

o. Compute the amount of income taxes actually paid during Year 2.

p. On July 1, Year 2, Kaplan Corporation issued 10,000 shares of its common stock on the open market for $50 a share. Prepare an analysis explaining the change during Year 2 in each of the following accounts: Common Shares, Additional Paid-in Capital, Retained Earnings, Treasury Shares.

## Suggested Solution

| | |
|---|---:|
| a. Cost of Marketable Securities Sold........................................ | $180,000 |
| Gain on Sale (from Income Statement) .............................. | 30,000 |
| Selling Price...................................................... | $210,000 |

| | |
|---|---:|
| b. Marketable Securities at Cost on December 31, Year 1 | |
| ($450,000 + $50,000) ........................................... | $500,000 |
| Plus Purchases ................................................... | ? |
| Less Cost of Marketable Securities Sold............................. | (180,000) |
| Marketable Securities at Cost on December 31, Year 2 | |
| ($550,000 + $70,000) ........................................... | $620,000 |

The cost of marketable securities purchased during Year 2 was $300,000.

| | |
|---|---:|
| c. Allowance for Uncollectible Accounts, December 31, Year 1 ............ | $200,000 |
| Plus Provision for Uncollectible Accounts during Year 2 ................ | 120,000 |
| Less Specific Customers' Accounts Written Off as Uncollectible | |
| during Year 2....................................................... | (?) |
| Allowance for Uncollectible Accounts, December 31, Year 2 ............ | $250,000 |

Specific customers' accounts written off as uncollectible during Year 2 totaled $70,000.

**d.**

| | |
|---|---:|
| Gross Accounts Receivable, December 31, Year 1[a]................... | $ 2,500 |
| Plus Sales during the Year........................................ | 12,000 |
| Less Gross Accounts Receivable, December 31, Year 2[b].............. | (3,100) |
| Accounts Collected or Written Off................................... | $11,400 |
| Less Write-Offs ................................................... | (70) |
| Cash Collected during Year ........................................ | $11,330 |

[a]$2,300 + $200.

[b]$2,850 + $250.

**e.**

| | |
|---|---:|
| Finished Goods Inventory, December 31, Year 1 ................... | $1,800,000 |
| Plus Cost of Units Completed during the Year ..................... | ? |
| Less Cost of Units Sold during the Year........................... | (7,200,000) |
| Finished Goods Inventory, December 31, Year 2 ................... | $2,200,000 |

The cost of units completed was $7,600,000.

**f.**

| | |
|---|---:|
| Work in Process Inventory, December 31, Year 1 ................... | $ 460,000 |
| Plus Cost of Raw Materials Used .................................. | ? |
| Plus Direct Labor and Manufacturing Overhead Costs Incurred ....... | 4,500,000 |
| Less Cost of Units Completed ..................................... | (7,600,000) |
| Work-in-Process Inventory, December 31, Year 2................... | $ 530,000 |

The cost of raw materials used during Year 2 was $3,170,000.

| | |
|---|---:|
| Raw Materials Inventory, December 31, Year 1 .................... | $ 330,000 |
| Plus Cost of Raw Materials Purchased ............................ | ? |
| Less Cost of Raw Materials Used................................. | (3,170,000) |
| Raw Materials Inventory, December 31, Year 2 .................... | $ 380,000 |

The cost of raw materials purchased was $3,220,000.

**g.**

| | LIFO | Difference | FIFO |
|---|---:|---:|---:|
| Inventory, December 31, Year 1 ......... | $ 2,590,000 | $420,000 | $ 3,010,000 |
| Purchases plus Costs Incurred .......... | 7,720,000 | — | 7,720,000 |
| Goods Available ....................... | $10,310,000 | $420,000 | $10,730,000 |
| Less Inventory, December 31, Year 2 .... | 3,110,000 | 730,000 | 3,840,000 |
| Cost of Goods Sold ................... | $ 7,200,000 | $310,000 | $ 6,890,000 |

Cost of goods sold under FIFO would have been $6,890,000.

**h.** **Investment in Maher Corporation (lower-of-cost-or-market method):**

| | |
|---|---:|
| Balance, December 31, Year 1 ..................................... | $200,000 |
| Plus Additional Investments ........................................ | 0 |
| Less Sale of Investments ........................................... | 0 |
| Less Increase in Unrealized Loss on Valuation of Investments ......... | 15,000 |
| Balance, December 31, Year 2 ..................................... | $185,000 |

**Investment in Johnson Corporation (equity method):**

| | |
|---|---:|
| Balance, December 31, Year 1 ..................................... | $310,000 |
| Plus Additional Investments ....................................... | 50,000 |
| Plus Equity in Earnings (total equity in earnings of $300,000 from income statement minus equity in earnings of Burton Corporation of $160,000) ....................................... | 140,000 |
| Less Sale of Investments .......................................... | 0 |
| Less Dividend Received (plug) ..................................... | (90,000) |
| Balance, December 31, Year 2 ..................................... | $410,000 |

**Investment in Burton Corporation (equity method):**

| | |
|---|---:|
| Balance, December 31, Year 1 ..................................... | $800,000 |
| Plus Additional Investments ....................................... | 0 |
| Plus Equity in Earnings (.40 × $400,000) .......................... | 160,000 |
| Less Sale of Investments .......................................... | 0 |
| Less Dividends Received (.40 × $75,000) .......................... | (30,000) |
| Balance, December 31, Year 2 ..................................... | $930,000 |

**i.** **Land:**

| | |
|---|---:|
| Balance, December 31, Year 1 ..................................... | $ 400,000 |
| Plus Acquisitions................................................. | 100,000 |
| Less Disposals ................................................... | 0 |
| Balance, December 31, Year 2 ..................................... | $ 500,000 |

**Building:**

| | |
|---|---:|
| Balance, December 31, Year 1 ..................................... | $ 800,000 |
| Plus Acquisitions................................................. | 300,000 |
| Less Retirements (plug) .......................................... | (160,000) |
| Balance, December 31, Year 2 ..................................... | $ 940,000 |

**Equipment:**

| | |
|---|---:|
| Balance, December 31, Year 1 ..................................... | $3,300,000 |
| Plus Acquisitions................................................. | 1,400,000 |
| Less Disposals (plug)............................................. | (900,000) |
| Balance, December 31, Year 2 ..................................... | $3,800,000 |

**Accumulated Depreciation:**

| | |
|---|---:|
| Balance, December 31, Year 1 ..................................... | $1,200,000 |
| Plus Depreciation for Year 2 ...................................... | 560,000 |
| Less Accumulated Depreciation on Building Retired (plug)............ | (160,000) |
| Less Accumulated Depreciation on Equipment Sold (see below) ...... | (670,000) |
| Balance, December 31, Year 2 ..................................... | $ 930,000 |

| | |
|---|---:|
| Selling Price of Equipment Sold .................................... | $  150,000 |
| Loss on Sale of Equipment ....................................... | 80,000 |
| Book Value of Equipment Sold ................................... | $  230,000 |
| | |
| Cost of Equipment Sold (from above) ............................ | $  900,000 |
| Less Accumulated Depreciation on Equipment Sold................. | (670,000) |
| Book Value of Equipment Sold ................................... | $  230,000 |

**j.**

| | | |
|---|---:|---:|
| Investment in Heimann Corporation ....................... | 800,000 | |
| Common Stock (20,000 × $10) ........................ | | 200,000 |
| Additional Paid-in Capital (20,000 × $30) .............. | | 600,000 |

**k.**

| | |
|---|---:|
| Cost of Investment in Heimann Corporation .......................... | $800,000 |
| Goodwill, $80,000 + (2 × $10,000) ................................... | (100,000) |
| Book Value of Net Assets Acquired ................................ | $700,000 |

Eighty percent acquired; so book value of Heimann on date of acquisition is $700,000/.80 = $875,000.

**l.**

| | |
|---|---:|
| Minority Interest in Heimann Corporation, January 2, Year 2 ............ | $180,000 |
| Plus Minority Interest in Earnings of Heimann Corporation (from income statement) ........................................ | 40,000 |
| Less Minority Interest in Dividends of Heimann Corporation (plug)....... | (6,000) |
| Minority Interest in Heimann Corporation, December 31, Year 2 (from balance sheet) ........................................... | $214,000 |

Total dividends declared were $30,000 (= $6,000/.20).

**m.   4-Percent Bond Issue:**

| | |
|---|---:|
| $40,000 × 9.9540 ..................................................... | $  398,160 |
| $2,000,000 × .70138 ............................................... | 1,402,760 |
| Total...................................................... | $1,800,920 |

**10-Percent Bond Issue:**

| | |
|---|---:|
| $150,000 × 13.59033.................................................. | $2,038,550 |
| $3,000,000 × .45639 ............................................... | 1,369,170 |
| Total...................................................... | $3,407,720 |

| | Liability, Beginning of the Period | Market Interest Rate | Interest Expense | Interest Payable | Addition to or Reduction in Liability | Liability, End of the Period |
|---|---|---|---|---|---|---|
| **n.** | **4-Percent Bond Issue:** | | | | | |
| January 1, Year 2......... | $1,800,920 | .03 | $ 54,028 | $ 40,000 | $14,028 | $1,814,948 |
| July 1, Year 2 ............ | 1,814,948 | .03 | 54,448 | 40,000 | 14,448 | 1,829,396 |
| Total................... | | | $108,476 | $ 80,000 | $28,476 | |
| | | | | | | |
| **10-Percent Bond Issue:** | | | | | | |
| January 1, Year 2......... | 3,407,720 | .04 | $136,309 | $150,000 | $13,691 | $3,394,029 |
| July 1, Year 2 ............ | 3,394,029 | .04 | 135,761 | 150,000 | 14,239 | 3,379,790 |
| Total................... | | | $272,070 | $300,000 | $27,930 | |
| | | | | | | |
| **8-Percent Bond Issue:** | | | | | | |
| January 1, Year 2......... | 1,000,000 | .04 | $ 40,000 | $ 40,000 | $ 0 | $1,000,000 |
| July 1, Year 2 ............ | 1,000,000 | .04 | 40,000 | 40,000 | 0 | 1,000,000 |
| Total................... | | | $ 80,000 | $ 80,000 | $ 0 | |

**o.**

| | |
|---|---|
| Income Taxes Payable, December 31, Year 1......................... | $250,000 |
| Plus Current Income Tax Expense for Year 2 (see below) ............. | 420,000 |
| Less Cash Payment during Year 2..................................... | ? |
| Income Taxes Payable, December 31, Year 2......................... | $375,000 |
| | |
| Total Income Tax Expense ......................................... | $540,000 |
| Less Increase in Deferred Income Taxes ........................... | (120,000) |
| Current Income Tax Expense....................................... | $420,000 |

Cash payments for income taxes totaled $295,000 during Year 2.

| | | Common Shares | | Additional Paid-in Capital | Retained Earnings | Treasury Shares |
|---|---|---|---|---|---|---|
| | | Number of Shares | Amount | | | |
| **p.** | Balance, December 31, Year 1 ............. | 50,000 | $500,000 | $ 800,000 | $1,436,000 | $30,000 |
| | Common Stock Issued on the Open Market. | 10,000 | 100,000 | 400,000 | — | — |
| | Treasury Stock Sold ... | — | — | 5,000 | — | (10,000) |
| | Net Income........... | — | — | — | 1,220,000 | — |
| | Dividends (plug)[a]...... | — | — | — | (250,000) | — |
| | Balance, December 31, Year 2 ............. | 60,000 | $600,000 | $1,205,000 | $2,406,000 | $20,000 |

[a]Or, see statement of cash flows.

# Questions, Exercises, Problems, and Cases ─────────

## Questions

1. Review the meaning of the following concepts or terms discussed in this chapter.
   a. Generally accepted accounting principles.
   b. Accurate presentation.
   c. Conservatism.
   d. Profit maximization.
   e. Income smoothing.
   f. Least and latest rule.
   g. Development of accounting principles is a political process.

2. A critic of accounting stated: "The financial statements are virtually useless because firms have too much latitude in selecting from among generally accepted accounting methods." Another critic of accounting reacted: "I agree that the financial statements are useless, but it is because there is too little latitude in the way certain transactions are accounted for under generally accepted accounting principles." Respond to these statements.

3. "The controversy over alternative generally accepted accounting principles could be solved by requiring all firms to use the same methods of accounting in their financial statements that they use in their tax return." Respond to this proposal.

4. If net income over sufficiently long time periods is equal to cash in minus cash out, why not allow the timing of cash flows to dictate revenue and expense recognition and eliminate alternative generally accepted accounting principles?

5. "The total reported net income over sufficiently long time periods will be the same regardless of whether a firm follows a conservative strategy or a profit-maximizing strategy in selecting its accounting methods." Explain.

6. "The statement of cash flows is affected less by the use of alternative accounting principles than the balance sheet and income statement." Explain.

7. If capital markets react quickly and in an unbiased manner to the release of information, including information contained in the financial statements, what is the benefit of analyzing a set of financial statements?

## Exercises

8. *Identifying generally accepted accounting principles.* Indicate the generally accepted accounting principle or method described in each of the following statements. Explain your reasoning.
   a. This inventory cost flow assumption results in reporting the largest net income during periods of rising prices.
   b. This method of accounting for uncollectible accounts recognizes the implied income reduction in the period of sale.
   c. This method of accounting for long-term investments in the securities of other corporations usually requires an adjustment to net income to calculate cash flow from operations in the statement of cash flows.

    **d.** This method of accounting for long-term leases by the lessee gives rise to a noncurrent liability.

    **e.** This inventory cost flow assumption results in approximately the same balance sheet amount as the FIFO flow assumption.

    **f.** This method of recognizing interest expense on bonds provides a uniform annual rate of interest expense over the life of the bond.

    **g.** During periods of rising prices, this inventory valuation basis produces approximately the same results as the acquisition cost valuation basis.

    **h.** When specific customers' accounts are deemed uncollectible and written off, this method of accounting results in a decrease in the current ratio.

    **i.** This method of depreciation generally provides the largest amounts of depreciation expense during the first several years of an asset's life.

    **j.** This method of accounting for intercorporate investments in securities can result in a decrease in the investor's total shareholders' equity without affecting the Retained Earnings account.

    **k.** This method of recognizing income from long-term contracts generally results in the least amount of fluctuation in earnings over several periods.

    **l.** When specific customers' accounts are deemed uncollectible and are written off, this method of accounting has no effect on working capital.

    **m.** When used in calculating taxable income, this inventory cost flow assumption generally must also be used in calculating net income reported to shareholders.

    **n.** Under this method of accounting for long-term leases of equipment by the lessor, an amount for depreciation expense on the leased equipment will appear on the income statement.

**9.** *Identifying generally accepted accounting principles.* Indicate the accounting principle or procedure apparently being used to record each of the following independent transactions. Indicate your reasoning.

  **a.** Bad Debt Expense ................................... X
      Accounts Receivable ..............................     X
  **b.** Cash ............................................. X
      Dividend Income ..................................     X
  **c.** Unrealized Loss from Price Declines in Marketable
      Securities ...................................... X
      Allowance to Reduce Marketable Securities to Market .     X
  **d.** Cash ............................................. X
      Investment in Affiliated Company ....................     X
      Dividend declared and received from affiliated company.
  **e.** Bad Debt Expense ................................... X
      Allowance for Uncollectible Accounts ................     X

**10.** *Identifying generally accepted accounting principles.* Indicate the accounting principle or procedure apparently being used to record each of the following independent transactions. Give your reasoning.

| | | | |
|---|---|---|---|
| **a.** | Rent Expense (for lease contract)..................... | X | |
| | Cash ............................................... | | X |
| **b.** | Advertising Expense................................. | X | |
| | Deferred Advertising Costs.......................... | | X |
| **c.** | Investment in Affiliated Company ..................... | X | |
| | Equity in Earnings of Affiliated Company ............. | | X |
| **d.** | Allowance for Uncollectible Accounts.................. | X | |
| | Accounts Receivable ............................... | | X |
| **e.** | Loss from Price Decline for Inventories................ | X | |
| | Merchandise Inventories ............................ | | X |
| **f.** | Liability under Long-Term Lease ...................... | X | |
| | Interest Expense ................................... | X | |
| | Cash ............................................... | | X |

11. *Identifying effects of generally accepted accounting principles on reported income.* Indicate the accounting principle that provides the smallest amount of earnings in each of the following cases.
    a. FIFO, LIFO, or weighted-average cost flow assumption for inventories during periods of rising prices.
    b. FIFO, LIFO, or weighted-average cost flow assumption for inventories during periods of declining prices.
    c. Lower-of-cost-or-market or equity method of accounting for long-term investments in the securities of unconsolidated subsidiaries where dividends declared by the subsidiary are less than its earnings.
    d. Sum-of-the-years'-digits or straight-line depreciation method during the first one-third of an asset's life.
    e. Sum-of-the-years'-digits or straight-line depreciation method during the last one-third of an asset's life.
    f. The valuation of inventories at acquisition cost or lower of cost or market.
    g. Lower-of-cost-or-market or equity method of accounting for long-term investments in the securities of unconsolidated subsidiaries where the investee realizes net losses and does not pay dividends.

## Problems and Cases

12. *Impact of capitalizing and amortizing versus expensing when incurred.* South Company and North Company incur $50,000 of advertising costs each year. South Company expenses these costs immediately, whereas North Company capitalizes the costs and amortizes them over 5 years.
    a. Compute the amount of advertising expense and deferred advertising costs each firm would report beginning in the first year that advertising costs are incurred and continuing for 6 years.
    b. For this part, assume that the amount of advertising costs incurred by each firm increases by $10,000 each year. Repeat part **a**.
    c. Comment on the differences noted in parts **a** and **b**.

13. *Impact of alternative accounting principles on two firms.* On January 1, Year 1, two corporations are formed to operate merchandising businesses. The firms

are alike in all respects except for their methods of accounting. Ruzicka Company chooses the accounting principles that will minimize its reported net income. Murphy Company chooses the accounting principles that will maximize its reported net income but, where different procedures are permitted, will use accounting methods that minimize its taxable income. The following events occur during Year 1.

**(1)** Both companies issue 500,000 shares of $1-par-value common shares for $6 per share on January 2, Year 1.

**(2)** Both firms acquire equipment on January 2, Year 1, for $1,650,000 cash. The equipment is estimated to have a 10-year life and zero salvage value.

**(3)** Both firms engage in extensive sales promotion activities during Year 1, incurring costs of $400,000.

**(4)** The two firms make the following purchases of merchandise inventory.

| Date | Units Purchased | Unit Price | Cost of Purchase |
|---|---|---|---|
| January 2 .......... | 50,000 | $6.00 | $  300,000 |
| April 1 ............. | 60,000 | 6.20 | 372,000 |
| August 15 .......... | 40,000 | 6.25 | 250,000 |
| November 30 ....... | 50,000 | 6.50 | 325,000 |
| Total ............. | 200,000 | | $1,247,000 |

**(5)** During the year, both firms sell 140,000 units at an average price of $15 each.

**(6)** Selling, general, and administrative expenses, other than advertising, total $100,000 during the year.

The Ruzicka Company uses the following accounting methods (for both book and tax purposes): LIFO inventory cost flow assumption, accelerated depreciation, and immediate expensing of the costs of sales promotion. The sum-of-the-years'-digits depreciation method is used for financial reporting, and double-declining-balance depreciation is used for tax purposes. Depreciation for tax purposes on this equipment is $235,700 for Year 1.

The Murphy Company uses the following accounting methods: FIFO inventory cost flow assumption for both book and tax purposes, the straight-line depreciation method for book and double-declining-balance depreciation for tax purposes, and capitalization and amortization of the costs of the sales promotion campaign over 4 years for book and immediate expensing for tax purposes.

**a.** Prepare comparative income statements for the two firms for Year 1. Include separate computations of income tax expense. The income tax rate is 30 percent.

**b.** Prepare comparative balance sheets for the two firms as of December 31, Year 1. Both firms have $1 million of outstanding accounts receivable on this date and a single current liability for income taxes payable for the year.

**c.** Prepare comparative statements of cash flows for the two firms for Year 1, defining funds as cash.

**14.** *Impact of two sets of alternative accounting principles on net income and cash flows.* The Langston Corporation is formed on January 2, Year 1, with the issuance at par of 100,000 shares of $10-par-value common stock for cash. During Year 1, the following transactions occur.

**(1)** The assets of the Dee's Department Store are acquired on January 2, Year 1, for $800,000 cash. The market values of the identifiable assets received are as follows: accounts receivable, $200,000; merchandise inventory, $400,000 (200,000 units); store equipment, $150,000; and goodwill, $50,000.

**(2)** Merchandise inventory is purchased during Year 1 as follows:

| Date | Units Purchased | Unit Price | Cost of Purchase |
|------|-----------------|------------|------------------|
| April 1 .............. | 30,000 | $2.10 | $ 63,000 |
| August 1 ........... | 20,000 | 2.20 | 44,000 |
| October 1 .......... | 50,000 | 2.40 | 120,000 |
| Total............. | 100,000 | | $227,000 |

**(3)** During the year, 210,000 units are sold at an average price of $3.20.

**(4)** Extensive training programs are held during the year to acquaint previous employees of Dee's Department Store with the merchandising policies and procedures of Langston Corporation. The costs incurred in the training programs total $50,000.

**(5)** Selling, general, and administrative costs incurred and recognized as an expense during Year 1 are $80,000.

**(6)** The store equipment is estimated to have a 10-year useful life and zero salvage value.

**(7)** The income tax rate is 30 percent. Goodwill arising from a corporate acquisition is not deductible in computing taxable income, and the difference is a permanent difference, not a timing difference.

The management of Langston Corporation is uncertain about the accounting methods that should be used in preparing its financial statements. The choice has been narrowed to two sets of accounting methods, and you have been asked to calculate net income for Year 1 using each set.

Set A consists of the following accounting methods (for book and tax purposes): LIFO inventory cost flow assumption, accelerated depreciation, immediate expensing of the costs of the training program, and amortization of goodwill (for book) over 10 years. Depreciation will be computed using the double-declining-balance method for both book (10-year useful life) and tax (7-year depreciable life) purposes. Depreciation for tax purposes will be $21,430.

Set B consists of the following accounting methods: FIFO inventory cost flow assumption, straight-line depreciation for book and double-declining-balance depreciation for tax purposes, capitalization and amortization of the costs of the training program over 5 years for book and immediate expensing for tax purposes, and amortization of goodwill (for book) over 40 years. Depreciation for tax purposes will be $21,430.

    **a.** Calculate net income for Year 1 under each set of accounting methods.

    **b.** Calculate cash flow from operations under each set of accounting methods. Assume that accounts receivable at year end total $160,000.

15. *Impact of alternative accounting principles on net income, Year 2.* Net income of Miller Corporation for the year ending December 31, Year 2, is $600,000 based on the accounting methods actually used by the firm. You have been asked to calculate the amount of net income that would have been reported under several alternative accounting methods. The income tax rate is 30 percent, and the same accounting methods are used for financial reporting and income tax purposes unless otherwise indicated. Each of the following questions should be considered independently.

    **a.** Miller Corporation acquired a machine costing $300,000 on January 1, Year 2. The machine was depreciated during Year 2 using the straight-line method based on a 5-year useful life and zero salvage value. What would net income have been if the sum-of-the-years'-digits depreciation method had been used?

    **b.** Miller Corporation used the lower-of-cost-or-market method of accounting for its 18-percent investment in the common shares of General Tools Corporation. During Year 2, General Tools Corporation earned $200,000 and paid dividends of $50,000. The market value of General Tools Corporation was the same at the end of Year 2 as it was at the beginning of Year 2. What would net income have been during Year 2 if Miller Corporation continued to account for the investment under the lower-of-cost-or-market method for income tax purposes but used the equity method for financial reporting purposes?

    **c.** Miller Corporation used the FIFO inventory cost flow assumption. Under FIFO, the January 1, Year 2, inventory was $300,000, and the December 31, Year 2, inventory was $320,000. Under LIFO, the January 1, Year 2, inventory would have been $240,000 and the December 31, Year 2, inventory would have been $230,000. What would net income have been if the LIFO inventory cost flow assumption had been used?

16. *Computation of cash provided by operations.* The income statement of Garrett Corporation for Year 5 appears in Exhibit 15.7. An analysis of changes in working capital accounts appears in Exhibit 15.8. Notes to these statements follow.

- Note 1: Garrett Corporation owns 10 percent of the outstanding common shares of Williams Corporation. During Year 5, Williams Corporation earned $2,000,000 and declared dividends of $600,000.

- Note 2: Garrett Corporation owns 30 percent of the outstanding common shares of Knowles Corporation. During Year 5, Knowles Corporation earned $1,000,000 and declared dividends of $400,000.

- Note 3: Depreciation charges of $200,000 and $100,000 are included in Cost of Goods Sold and Selling and Administrative Expenses, respectively.

Exhibit 15.7 _____

GARRETT CORPORATION
Income Statement for Year 5
(Problem 16)

**Revenues:**

| | |
|---|---:|
| Sales.......................................................... | $5,000,000 |
| Interest........................................................ | 100,000 |
| Dividends (Note 1)............................................ | 60,000 |
| Equity in Earnings of Affiliate (Note 2) .................... | 300,000 |
| Recovery of Loss on Valuation of Marketable Equity Securities ........ | 30,000 |
|    Total Revenue .......................................... | $5,490,000 |

**Expenses:**

| | |
|---|---:|
| Cost of Goods Sold (Note 3) ................................. | $3,000,000 |
| Selling and Administrative (Note 3) .......................... | 800,000 |
| Interest....................................................... | 200,000 |
|    Total Expenses........................................ | $4,000,000 |
| Income before Income Taxes .................................. | $1,490,000 |
| Income Tax Expense (Note 4) ................................. | 447,000 |
| Income before Minority Interest ............................. | $1,043,000 |
| Less Minority Interest in Earnings of Consolidated Subsidiary ......... | 160,000 |
| Net Income .................................................. | $  883,000 |

Exhibit 15.8 _____

GARRETT CORPORATION
Analysis of Changes in Working Capital Accounts for Year 5
(Problem 16)

**Increase (Decrease) in Current Assets:**

| | |
|---|---:|
| Cash.......................................................... | $ 70,000 |
| Certificate of Deposit.......................................... | 30,000 |
| Accounts Receivable............................................ | 430,000 |
| Merchandise Inventories......................................... | 370,000 |

**Decrease (Increase) in Current Liabilities:**

| | |
|---|---:|
| Accounts Payable ............................................. | (320,000) |
| Income Taxes Payable ......................................... | (120,000) |
| **Increase in Working Capital** .................................. | $460,000 |

• Note 4: Income Tax Expense is composed of the following:

| | |
|---|---:|
| Current ....................................................... | 247,000 |
| Deferred ...................................................... | 200,000 |
|    Total ...................................................... | 447,000 |

**Exhibit 15.9** ————————————————————————————————————————————

## HICKORY MERCHANDISING COMPANY
Adjusted Trial Balance
(Problem 17)

| | December 31, Year 1 | | December 31, Year 2 | |
|---|---|---|---|---|
| Accounts Payable ................................ | | $ 183,545 | | $ 188,470 |
| Accounts Receivable — Net ........................ | $ 580,335 | | $ 617,530 | |
| Accruals and Withholdings Payable.................. | | 99,800 | | 99,700 |
| Administrative Expenses .......................... | 449,160 | | 447,260 | |
| Bonds Payable (6 percent) ........................ | | 275,000 | | 277,000 |
| Cash........................................... | 114,080 | | 149,485 | |
| Common Stock................................... | | 100,000 | | [        ] |
| Cost of Goods Sold.............................. | 3,207,840 | | 3,220,390 | |
| Depreciation Expense ............................ | 45,710 | | 48,825 | |
| Dividends on Common Shares — Cash and Stock ................ | 50,000 | | [        ] | |
| Dividends on Preferred Shares — Cash .............. | 6,000 | | 6,000 | |
| Dividends Payable................................ | | — | | [        ] |
| Federal and State Income Tax Expense ............ | 74,975 | | 87,675 | |
| Federal and State Income Tax Payable ............. | | 18,750 | | 21,920 |
| Gain on Sale of Plant ............................ | | — | | [        ] |
| Interest Expense on Notes ........................ | 2,900 | | 3,100 | |
| Interest Expense on Bonds ........................ | 19,000 | | 20,000 | |
| Interest and Dividend Revenue..................... | | 16,010 | | 18,070 |
| Inventories...................................... | 616,120 | | 633,690 | |
| Investments in Subsidiaries ....................... | 162,000 | | 162,000 | |
| Notes Payable .................................. | | 51,500 | | 53,400 |
| Notes Receivable................................ | 65,600 | | 68,400 | |
| Plant and Equipment — Net........................ | 391,880 | | [        ] | |
| Preferred Stock ................................. | | 100,000 | | 100,000 |
| Premium on Common Stock ....................... | | 700,000 | | [        ] |
| Prepaid Insurance ............................... | 8,240 | | 7,640 | |
| Retained Earnings ............................... | | [        ] | | [        ] |
| Royalties Revenue................................ | | 37,020 | | 44,285 |
| Sales........................................... | | 4,552,320 | | 4,605,275 |
| Selling Expenses ................................ | 673,530 | | 691,230 | |
| | $6,467,370 | $6,467,370 | $6,739,860 | $6,739,860 |

Compute the amount of cash and cash equivalents provided by operations for Garrett Corporation during Year 5. Your analysis should begin with net income of $883,000.

**17.** *Preparation of three principal financial statements from comprehensive data.* The data in Exhibit 15.9 are taken from the adjusted trial balances of the Hickory Merchandising Company as of December 31, Year 1 and Year 2. The brackets indicate amounts to be found in the solution of the problem.

*Additional Data:*

**(1)** Preferred shares: 6 percent, cumulative, $100 par value; 2,000 shares authorized.

**(2)** Common shares: $1 par value; 150,000 shares authorized.

(3)  On January 10, Year 2, a 10-percent stock dividend was declared on common stock, issuable in common stock. The market price per share was $10, and the dividend was capitalized at $10 per share.

(4)  On March 31 and September 30, Year 2, dividends of 25 cents per share were declared. The dividends were payable on April 20 and October 20, Year 2, respectively. On December 31, Year 2, an extra dividend of $12\frac{1}{2}$ cents per share was declared payable on January 20, Year 3. Note that all dividends, in cash and in shares, have been debited to Dividends accounts, not to Retained Earnings.

(5)  Plant and equipment items having a cost of $39,240 and accumulated depreciation of $32,570 were retired and sold for $15,000. Acquisitions during Year 2 amounted to $71,500.

(6)  The bonds are 30-year bonds and mature on June 30, Year 14. All bonds issued remain outstanding.

a.  Prepare a well-organized comparative statement of income and retained earnings for Year 1 and Year 2.

b.  Prepare a well-organized comparative balance sheet for December 31, Year 1 and Year 2.

c.  Prepare a well-organized statement of cash flows for Year 2.

18. *Preparation of income statement and balance sheet from comprehensive data.* The data in Exhibit 15.10 are taken from the records of the Barr Sales Company.

*Additional Information:*

(1)  During the year the company retired fully depreciated fixtures that had cost $2,000. These were the only dispositions of furniture and fixtures.

(2)  Furniture and fixtures acquired on May 10, Year 2, were financed one-third down; one-third due May 10, Year 3; and one-third due May 10, Year 4.

(3)  On December 9, Year 2, the company sold a parcel of land it had purchased on January 14, Year 2, at a cost of $8,000.

(4)  On June 15, Year 2, the company purchased additional investments at a cost of $3,200. This was the only acquisition during the year. All investments are shown at cost, since market value exceeds cost.

(5)  Merchandise was delivered during the year on customers' deposits in the amount of $1,200. All other deliveries were on account.

(6)  On January 2, Year 2, the board of directors declared a 5-percent stock dividend. The dividend was capitalized at $11 per share.

(7)  On June 20, Year 2, and December 20, Year 2, the board of directors declared the regular semiannual cash dividends of $0.50 per share.

(8)  On June 30, Year 2, the company issued 250 shares of stock for cash.

(9)  Note that all dividends, both in cash and in shares, were debited to Dividends on Common Shares, not to Retained Earnings.

a.  Prepare a well-organized statement of income and retained earnings for Year 2.

b.  Prepare a well-organized comparative balance sheet as of December 31, Year 1 and Year 2.

**Exhibit 15.10** ————————————————————————————————————

**BARR SALES COMPANY**
Trial Balance Data
(Problem 18)

|  | December 31 | |
| --- | --- | --- |
|  | Year 2 Adjusted Trial Balance | Year 1 Post-closing Trial Balance |
| Accounts Payable—Merchandise .............. | $  8,400 | $ 9,160 |
| Accounts Receivable.......................... | 25,100 | 25,900 |
| Accumulated Depreciation ..................... | 4,600 | 5,600 |
| Allowance for Uncollectible Accounts ........... | 400 | 430 |
| Bad Debt Expense ........................... | 800 |  |
| Cash....................................... | 27,802 | 21,810 |
| Common Stock ($10 par value) ................ | 55,000 | 50,000 |
| Cost of Goods Sold.......................... | 155,000 |  |
| Deposits by Customers ....................... | 420 |  |
| Depreciation ................................. | 1,000 |  |
| Dividends on Common Shares (both in cash and in shares) ................ | 8,125 |  |
| Dividends Payable ........................... | 2,750 | 2,500 |
| Federal Income Tax Expense .................. | 3,600 |  |
| Federal Income Tax Payable................... | 3,600 | 2,400 |
| Furniture and Fixtures........................ | 21,000 | 20,000 |
| Gain on Sale of Land ........................ | 1,500 |  |
| Installment Contracts Payable.................. | 2,000 |  |
| Interest Expense on Mortgage ................. | 482 |  |
| Interest Revenue on Investments............... | 500 |  |
| Interest Payable on Mortgage.................. | 50 |  |
| Interest Receivable .......................... | 50 | 30 |
| Investments................................. | 14,000 | 15,000 |
| Loss on Sale of Investments................... | 300 |  |
| Merchandise Inventory ....................... | 33,450 | 31,150 |
| Mortgage Payable (5 percent).................. | 10,122 | 10,140 |
| Other Expenses ............................. | 26,293 |  |
| Premium on Common Shares................... | 4,500 | 4,000 |
| Prepaid Rent................................ | 300 |  |
| Rent Expense ............................... | 3,600 |  |
| Retained Earnings ........................... | 28,860 | 28,860 |
| Sales....................................... | 210,000 |  |
| Sales Commissions........................... | 12,400 |  |
| Sales Commissions Payable ................... | 600 | 800 |

19. *Chrysler discussion case of costly switch from LIFO to FIFO.* In the 1960s, Chrysler switched its inventory cost flow assumption from FIFO to LIFO. It was the only one of the Big Three auto makers to do so at that time. By 1970, Chrysler's inventories had grown and prices of its acquisition for inventory had increased so much that it had saved over $50 million in income taxes by using LIFO. Then, in the 1970s, Chrysler switched from LIFO back to FIFO. To comply with government tax regulations on inventory accounting, Chrysler paid to the government all of the taxes that it had saved from using LIFO over

the entire time it had used LIFO. Chrysler paid the federal government more than $50 million for the privilege of switching from LIFO back to FIFO.

Investigation of why Chrysler would send the government $50 million for the privilege of switching back to FIFO suggests that Chrysler was in danger of violating a covenant in some of its bond indentures with respect to the debt-equity ratio. If the debt-equity ratio rose above a critical value, certain bonds would become due immediately that otherwise would not mature for a decade or more.

Under what conditions would a company not want its old bonds suddenly to come due for immediate payment? Explain. Under what conditions would switching from LIFO to FIFO and incurring an immediate $50 million liability improve Chrysler's position? Explain. What is the purpose of bond indentures such as the one to which Chrysler had agreed? Were the bondholders made better off by Chrysler's actions? Discuss.

20. *Impact of alternative accounting principles on debt ratio.* Two conventional calculations of the debt-equity ratio were introduced in Chapter 6. In this problem we focus on the following definition:

$$\text{Debt Ratio} = \frac{\text{Total Long-Term External Financing}}{\text{Owners' Equity}}.$$

Many analysts use this ratio to assess the risk in the financial structure of a corporation. The higher the debt-equity ratio, other things being equal, the greater the risk. Many analysts construct ratios from the conventional, historical cost financial statements without adjustment. This problem illustrates how the assessment of the relative risk of companies can change as more sophisticated analysis of the financial statements is undertaken. In this problem, various adjustments to the conventional financial statements are made, and new versions of the debt-equity ratio are compared.

The problem may be worked all at once at the end of the course as a review, or it may be worked part by part as the various topics in the course are covered. Each part contains guidance as to when in the course the reader should be ready to work that part.

Data for four companies appear in Exhibit 15.11. The methods are illustrated with the data for General Products Company. The reader is to prepare answers for the three other companies. All data are taken from the financial statements of the various companies for the same year. All dollar amounts are in millions. Income tax effects are ignored, except where noted.

a.  (After Chapter 6.) Compute the debt ratio for each of the companies. Include deferred income taxes with long-term financing in the numerator. For General Products Company the debt ratio is as follows:

$$\frac{\$1,000 + \$0}{\$8,200} = 12.2 \text{ percent.}$$

Which companies appear to be significantly different from the others in terms of financial structure and risk? Discuss.

Exhibit 15.11 ——————————————————————————————————
## Data for Four Companies
### (all dollar amounts in millions)
### (Problem 20)

| | General Products Company | Eastman Kodak | General Motors | Zenith |
|---|---|---|---|---|
| 1. Long-Term Debt .............................. | $1,000 | $ 152.4 | $ 1,668.7 | $ 50.0 |
| 2. Deferred Tax Credits (balance sheet) ............. | —ᵃ | 144.0 | 472.5 | 18.3 |
| 3. Owners' Equity .................................. | 8,200 | 4,026.3 | 14,385.2 | 292.4 |
| 4. Excess of Current (FIFO) Cost over LIFO Cost of Ending Inventory ................... | 2,240 | 330.3 | 299.5 | 9.2 |

ᵃGeneral Products Company reports only deferred tax debits (assets).

**b.** (After Chapter 8.) Chapter 8 pointed out that LIFO companies show old, out-of-date inventory amounts on their balance sheets. The LIFO cost flow assumption has the effect of understating total assets and owners' equity. (Owner's equity is understated because the unrealized holding gains on the inventory are not included in the balance sheet.) The financial statements can be made more realistic by adjusting them with the following entry, which ignores income tax effects:

| | | |
|---|---|---|
| Inventory........................................... | 2,240 | |
|     Owners' Equity ...................................... | | 2,240 |

$2,240 million is the amount shown in General Products Company's notes as the excess of current cost, or FIFO cost, over the balance sheet amount of ending inventory.

The debt-equity ratio for General Products Company after making this inventory adjustment is as follows:

$$\frac{\$1,000 + \$0}{\$8,200 + \$2,240} = \frac{\$1,000}{\$10,440} = 9.6 \text{ percent.}$$

Compute the debt ratio for each of the companies and the percentage change in the ratio from part **a** for each of the firms. On which companies did this adjustment have the most impact?

**c.** (After Chapter 11.) Chapter 11 suggests that certain items shown as liabilities should not be. Note that in most cases Deferred Income Taxes are not even likely to be paid and should perhaps be reclassified as owners' equity. This reclassification can be reflected in the financial statements by making the following entry:

| | | |
|---|---|---|
| Deferred Income Taxes (balance sheet) ............... | a | |
|     Owners' Equity ...................................... | | a |

Amount is that shown in line 2 of Exhibit 15.11. The amount for General Products Company is zero because Deferred Income Taxes has a debit, or asset, balance.

Case-by-case analysis might be required in practice to find out if some of the companies' timing differences are likely to reverse in the foreseeable future. An analysis of these companies' reported items does not reveal any such significant potential reversals.

If all adjustments in parts **a**, **b**, and **c** are made, General Products Company's debt-equity ratio is as follows:

$$\frac{\$1,000}{\$8,200 + 0 + \$2,240} = \frac{\$1,000}{\$10,440} = 9.6 \text{ percent.}$$

Make the adjustments suggested previously and recompute the debt ratio for each of the other three companies. Compute the ratios on a cumulative and noncumulative basis; that is, compute the debt ratio after making each individual adjustment to the ratios computed in part **a**, and then after taking all the adjustments together, compute the percentage change in the ratio for each company. On which of the companies did each of these adjustments have the most impact?

d. What can you infer from this exercise about the debt ratio computed from published financial statements?

21. *Comprehensive review problem.* The principal objective of this book has been to help you develop a sufficient understanding of the accounting process that generates financial statements for external users so that the resulting statements can then be interpreted, analyzed, and evaluated. This problem has been designed partly as a review of the material covered in the book and partly as a means of assessing your progress toward this objective. A partial set of financial statements of Calmes Corporation for Year 2, including consolidated comparative balance sheets at December 31, Year 1 and Year 2, and a consolidated statement of income and retained earnings for Year 2, is presented in Exhibits 15.12 and 15.13. A series of discussion questions and short problems relating to the financial statements of Calmes Corporation are then presented. It is suggested that you study the financial statements before responding to these questions and problems. The following additional information may be helpful.

(1) Machinery and equipment costing $500,000 and with a book value of $100,000 were sold for cash during Year 2.

(2) The only transaction affecting common or preferred stocks during Year 2 was the sale of treasury stock.

(3) The bonds payable have a maturity value of $2 million.

## Part I — Financial Statement Interpretation

For each of the accounts or items in the following list and appearing on the consolidated balance sheets and income statement of the Calmes Corporation, describe the nature of the account or item (that is, the transaction or conditions that resulted in its recognition) and the valuation method used in determining its amount. Respond in descriptive terms rather than using specific numbers from the financial statements of the Calmes Corporation. The first one is provided as an example.

Exhibit 15.12 _____

## CALMES CORPORATION
### Consolidated Statement of Income and Retained Earnings for Year 2 (Problem 21)

**Revenues:**

| | | |
|---|---:|---:|
| Sales................................................. | | $6,000,000 |
| Gain on Sale of Machinery and Equipment.............. | | 100,000 |
| Income from Completed Contracts...................... | | 960,000 |
| Equity in Earnings of Affiliates: | | |
| Calmes Finance Corporation......................... | $900,000 | |
| Richardson Company ............................... | 50,000 | |
| Anthony Corporation .............................. | 50,000 | 1,000,000 |
| Total Revenues ................................... | | $8,060,000 |

**Expenses:**

| | | |
|---|---:|---:|
| Cost of Goods Sold.................................. | | $2,500,000 |
| Employee Payroll.................................... | | 1,500,000 |
| Depreciation of Plant and Equipment and Amortization of Leased Property Rights ............................. | | 500,000 |
| Amortization of Intangibles........................... | | 100,000 |
| Bad Debt Expense ................................... | | 60,000 |
| Interest ............................................ | | 300,000 |
| General Corporate ................................... | | 100,000 |
| Income Taxes—Current ............................. | | 700,000 |
| Income Taxes—Deferred ............................ | | 100,000 |
| Total Expenses..................................... | | $5,860,000 |
| Net Income before Minority Interest.................... | | $2,200,000 |
| Minority Interest in Earnings .......................... | | 200,000 |
| Net Income ......................................... | | $2,000,000 |
| Less: Dividends on Preferred Shares .................. | | 60,000 |
| Dividends on Common Shares .................. | | 840,000 |
| Increase in Retained Earnings ........................ | | $1,100,000 |
| Retained Earnings, January 1, Year 2 ................. | | 1,400,000 |
| Retained Earnings, December 31, Year 2 .............. | | $2,500,000 |
| Primary Earnings per Common Share (based on 1,000,000 average shares outstanding) .............. | | $1.94 |
| Fully Diluted Earnings per Share (assuming conversion of preferred stock) ................................. | | $1.25 |

**a.** Accumulated Costs under Contracts in Process in Excess of Progress Billings — The Calmes Corporation is providing services of some type to specific customers under contract. All costs incurred under the contracts are accumulated in this current asset account. When customers are billed periodically for a portion of the contract price, this account is credited. The account, therefore, reflects the excess of costs incurred to date on uncompleted contracts over the amounts billed to customers. Since the account does not include any income or profit from the contracts (that is, accumulated costs), the firm is apparently using the completed contract method rather than the percentage-of-completion method of recognizing revenues.

**b.** Investment in Calmes Finance Corporation.
**c.** Property Rights Acquired under Lease.
**d.** Goodwill.
**e.** Rent Received in Advance.
**f.** Deferred Income Taxes (balance sheet).
**g.** Minority Interest in Subsidiary (balance sheet).
**h.** Treasury Shares.
**i.** Bad Debt Expense (income statement).

## Part II — Financial Statement Analysis

**a.** Compute the amount of specific customers' accounts written off as uncollectible during Year 2, assuming that there were no recoveries during Year 2 of accounts written off in years prior to Year 2.

**b.** The Calmes Corporation used the LIFO cost flow assumption in computing its cost of goods sold and beginning and ending merchandise inventory amounts. If the FIFO cost flow assumption had been used, the beginning inventory would have been $900,000 and the ending inventory would have been $850,000. Compute the actual gross profit (net sales less cost of goods sold) of the Calmes Corporation for Year 2 under LIFO and the corresponding amount of gross profit if FIFO had been used (ignore income tax effects). Calmes Corporation used the periodic inventory method.

**c.** Refer to part **b**. What can be said about the quantity of merchandise inventory at the beginning and end of Year 2 and the direction of price changes during Year 2? Explain.

**d.** The Calmes Corporation accounts for its three intercorporate investments in unconsolidated affiliates under the equity method. The shares in each of these companies were acquired at book value at the time of acquisition. What were the total dividends declared by these three companies during Year 2? How can you tell?

**e.** The Calmes Corporation accounts for its three intercorporate investments in unconsolidated affiliates using the equity method. The shares in each of these companies were acquired at book value at the time of acquisition. Give the journal entry (entries) that was (were) made during Year 2 in applying the equity method.

**f.** The building was acquired on January 1, Year 1. It was estimated to have a 40-year useful life and zero salvage value at that time. Calculate the amount of depreciation expense on this building for Year 2, assuming that the double-declining-balance method is used.

**g.** Machinery and equipment costing $500,000 and with a book value of $100,000 were sold for cash during Year 2. Give the journal entry to record the disposition.

**h.** The bonds payable carry 6 percent annual coupons. Interest is paid on December 31 of each year. Give the journal entry made on December 31,

**Exhibit 15.13** ——————————————————————————
## CALMES CORPORATION
**Consolidated Balance Sheets**
**December 31**
**(Problem 21)**

|  | Year 2 | Year 1 |
|---|---|---|
| # Assets | | |
| **Current Assets:** | | |
| Cash . . . . . . . . . . . . . . . . . . . . . . . . . . . . . . . . . . . . . . . . . . . . . | $    50,000 | $  100,000 |
| Certificate of Deposit . . . . . . . . . . . . . . . . . . . . . . . . . . . . . . | 150,000 | — |
| Accounts Receivable (net of estimated uncollectibles of $80,000 in Year 2 and $50,000 in Year 1) . . . . . . | 300,000 | 250,000 |
| Merchandise Inventory . . . . . . . . . . . . . . . . . . . . . . . . . . . . | 700,000 | 600,000 |
| Accumulated Costs under Contracts in Process in Excess of Progress Billings . . . . . . . . . . . . . . . . . . . . . | 200,000 | 150,000 |
| Prepayments . . . . . . . . . . . . . . . . . . . . . . . . . . . . . . . . . . . . . . | 100,000 | 100,000 |
| Total Current Assets . . . . . . . . . . . . . . . . . . . . . . . . . . . | $ 1,500,000 | $1,200,000 |
| **Investments (at equity):** | | |
| Calmes Finance Corporation (40-percent owned) . . . . | $ 2,000,000 | $1,100,000 |
| Richardson Company (50-percent owned) . . . . . . . . . . | 500,000 | 450,000 |
| Anthony Company (25-percent owned) . . . . . . . . . . . . . | 100,000 | 50,000 |
| Total Investments . . . . . . . . . . . . . . . . . . . . . . . . . . . . . | $ 2,600,000 | $1,600,000 |
| **Property, Plant, and Equipment:** | | |
| Land . . . . . . . . . . . . . . . . . . . . . . . . . . . . . . . . . . . . . . . . . . . . | $    250,000 | $  200,000 |
| Building . . . . . . . . . . . . . . . . . . . . . . . . . . . . . . . . . . . . . . . | 2,000,000 | 2,000,000 |
| Machinery and Equipment . . . . . . . . . . . . . . . . . . . . . . . . | 4,000,000 | 3,650,000 |
| Property Rights Acquired under Lease . . . . . . . . . . . . . . | 750,000 | 750,000 |
| Total . . . . . . . . . . . . . . . . . . . . . . . . . . . . . . . . . . . . . . . . | $ 7,000,000 | $6,600,000 |
| Less Accumulated Depreciation and Amortization . . . . | (2,000,000) | (1,900,000) |
| Total Property, Plant, and Equipment . . . . . . . . . . . . | $ 5,000,000 | $4,700,000 |
| **Intangibles (at net book value):** | | |
| Patent . . . . . . . . . . . . . . . . . . . . . . . . . . . . . . . . . . . . . . . . . | $    200,000 | $  250,000 |
| Goodwill . . . . . . . . . . . . . . . . . . . . . . . . . . . . . . . . . . . . . . . | 700,000 | 750,000 |
| Total Intangibles . . . . . . . . . . . . . . . . . . . . . . . . . . . . . | $    900,000 | $1,000,000 |
| Total Assets . . . . . . . . . . . . . . . . . . . . . . . . . . . . . . . . . | $10,000,000 | $8,500,000 |

*continued*

Year 2, to recognize interest expense for Year 2, assuming that Calmes Corporation uses the effective interest method.

**i.** Refer to part **h**. What was the effective or market interest rate on these bonds on the date they were issued? Explain.

**j.** The only timing difference between net income and taxable income during Year 2 was in the amount of depreciation expense. If the income tax rate was 30 percent, calculate the difference between the depreciation deduction reported on the tax return and the depreciation expense reported on the income statement.

**Exhibit 15.13** *(continued)* ————————————

| | Year 2 | Year 1 |
|---|---|---|
| **Liabilities and Shareholders' Equity** | | |
| **Current Liabilities:** | | |
| Accounts Payable ............................. | $ 250,000 | $ 200,000 |
| Accrued Liabilities ............................. | 350,000 | 330,000 |
| Salaries Payable ................................ | 150,000 | 120,000 |
| Income Taxes Payable .......................... | 200,000 | 150,000 |
| Rent Received in Advance ....................... | 50,000 | — |
| Other Current Liabilities ......................... | 200,000 | 100,000 |
| Total Current Liabilities ......................... | $ 1,200,000 | $ 900,000 |
| | | |
| **Long-Term Debt:** | | |
| Bonds Payable .................................. | $ 1,824,000 | $1,800,000 |
| Equipment Mortgage Indebtedness ................. | 176,000 | 650,000 |
| Capitalized Lease Obligations ..................... | 500,000 | 550,000 |
| Total Long-Term Debt ........................... | $ 2,500,000 | $3,000,000 |
| | | |
| Deferred Income Taxes .......................... | $ 800,000 | $ 700,000 |
| | | |
| Minority Interest in Subsidiary ..................... | $ 500,000 | $ 300,000 |
| | | |
| **Shareholders' Equity:** | | |
| Convertible Preferred Stock....................... | $ 1,000,000 | $1,000,000 |
| Common Stock.................................. | 1,000,000 | 1,000,000 |
| Additional Paid-in Capital ........................ | 1,000,000 | 900,000 |
| Retained Earnings ............................... | 2,500,000 | 1,400,000 |
| Total ....................................... | $ 5,500,000 | $4,300,000 |
| Less Cost of Treasury Shares ................... | (500,000) | (700,000) |
| Total Shareholders' Equity ..................... | $ 5,000,000 | $3,600,000 |
| Total Liabilities and Shareholders' Equity .......... | $10,000,000 | $8,500,000 |

**k.** Give the journal entry that explains the change in the treasury shares account assuming that there were no other transactions affecting common or preferred shares during Year 2.

**l.** If the original amount of the patent acquired was $500,000, and the patent is being amortized on a straight-line basis, how long ago was the patent acquired?

**m.** The stock of the Anthony Company was acquired on December 31, Year 1. If the same amount of stock was held during the year, but the amount represented only *15-percent* ownership of the Anthony Company, how would the financial statements have differed? Disregard income tax effects and assume the shares' market price exceeds their cost.

**n.** During Year 2, Calmes paid $85,000 to the lessor of property represented on the balance sheet by "Property Rights Acquired under Lease." Property rights acquired under lease have a 10-year life and are being amortized on a straight-line basis. What was the total expense reported by Calmes Corporation during Year 2 from using the leased property?

**o.** How would the financial statements have differed if the Calmes Corporation accounted for inventories on the lower-of-cost-or-market basis and the market value of these inventories had been $680,000 instead of $700,000 at the end of Year 2? Disregard income tax effects.

**p.** If the Minority Interest in Subsidiary represents a 20-percent interest in Calmes Corporation's only consolidated subsidiary, what was the *total* amount of dividends declared by this subsidiary during Year 2? How can you tell?

**q.** Refer to the earnings-per-share amounts in the income statement of Calmes Corporation. How many shares of common stock would be issued if all of the outstanding shares of preferred stock were converted into common stock?

**r.** Insert the missing items of information numbered (3) through (26) in the statement of cash flows of the Calmes Corporation in Exhibit 15.14. Cash flows include cash and cash equivalents. Be sure to include both descriptions of the missing items and their amounts. Provide supporting calculations for each of the missing items in the statement.

**s.** On January 2, Year 3, the Calmes Corporation asked its bank to grant a 6-month loan for $300,000. If approved, the loan would be granted on January 10, Year 3. As the bank's senior credit analyst, you have been asked to assess the liquidity of the Calmes Corporation and present a memorandum summarizing your conclusions. Include any ratios and any other information from the financial statements that you believe are relevant. Also include a summary of information not disclosed in the financial statements that you think the loan officer should consider before making a final decision.

## Part III — Financial Statement Evaluation

**a.** The treasurer of the Calmes Corporation recently remarked, "The value or worth of our company on December 31, Year 2, is $5,000,000, as measured by total shareholders' equity." Describe briefly at least three reasons why the difference between recorded total assets and recorded total liabilities on the balance sheet does not represent the firm's value or worth.

**b.** The accounting profession has been criticized for permitting several generally accepted accounting principles for the same or similar transactions. What are the major arguments for (1) narrowing the range of acceptable methods and (2) continuing the present system of permitting business firms some degree of flexibility in selecting their accounting methods?

**22.** *Comprehensive review problem.* Partial financial statements of Tuck Corporation for Year 2 are presented in Exhibit 15.15 (consolidated statement of income and retained earnings) and Exhibit 15.16 (consolidated balance sheet).

**Exhibit 15.14** _____

## CALMES CORPORATION
## Consolidated Statement of Cash Flows for Year 2
## (Problem 21)
_____

*Operations:*

  (3)_____ ..... $ _____

Add Expenses and Deductions Not Using Cash:

  (4)_____ .....     _____
  (5)_____ .....     _____
  (6)_____ .....     _____
  (7)_____ .....     _____
  (8)_____ .....     _____

Add Credit Changes in Operating Current Asset
  and Current Liability Accounts:

  (9)_____ .....     _____
  (10)_____ .....     _____
  (11)_____ .....     _____
  (12)_____ .....     _____
  (13)_____ .....     _____
  (14)_____ .....     _____

Subtract Revenues and Additions Not Providing
  Cash:

  (15)_____ .....     _____
  (16)_____ .....     _____

Subtract Debit Changes in Operating Current
  Asset and Current Liability Accounts:

  (17)_____ .....     _____
  (18)_____ .....     _____
  (19)_____ .....     _____

Cash Flow from Operations........................        $1,924,000

*Investing:*

  (20)_____ .....     _____
  (21)_____ .....     _____
  (22)_____ .....     _____

Cash Flow from Investing .........................         (700,000)

*Financing:*

  (23)_____ .....     _____
  (24)_____ .....     _____
  (25)_____ .....     _____
  (26)_____ .....     _____

Cash Flow from Financing.........................       (1,124,000)

Net Change in Cash ..............................        $  100,000

**Exhibit 15.15** _____

## TUCK CORPORATION
### Consolidated Statement of Income and Retained Earnings for Year 2
### (Problem 22)

| | | |
|---|---:|---:|
| **Revenues and Gains:** | | |
| Sales.......................................... | $4,000,000 | |
| Gain on Sale of Equipment ........................ | 3,000 | |
| Recovery of Unrealized Loss on Valuation of Marketable Equity Securities ..................... | 4,000 | |
| Rental Revenue ................................. | 240,000 | |
| Dividend Revenue ............................... | 8,000 | |
| Equity in Earnings of Unconsolidated Affiliates ........ | 102,000 | |
| Total Revenues and Gains ...................... | | $4,357,000 |
| | | |
| **Expenses, Losses, and Deductions:** | | |
| Cost of Goods Sold (including depreciation and amortization) .................................... | $2,580,000 | |
| Selling and Administrative Expenses (including depreciation and amortization) ................... | 1,096,205 | |
| Warranty Expense ............................... | 46,800 | |
| Interest Expense ................................ | 165,995 | |
| Loss on Sale of Marketable Equity Securities ......... | 8,000 | |
| Income Tax Expense ............................. | 150,000 | |
| Minority Interest in Earnings of Consolidated Subsidiary | 10,000 | |
| Total Expenses, Losses, and Deductions........... | | 4,057,000 |
| Consolidated Net Income........................... | | $ 300,000 |
| Less Dividends Declared .......................... | | (120,000) |
| Increase in Retained Earnings for Year 2 ............ | | $ 180,000 |
| Retained Earnings, December 31, Year 1 ............ | | 220,000 |
| Retained Earnings, December 31, Year 2 ........... | | $ 400,000 |

Also shown are a statement of accounting policies and a set of notes to the financial statements. After studying these financial statements and notes, respond to each of the following questions.

a. Prepare an analysis that explains the change in Marketable Equity Securities — Net account during Year 2.

b. Calculate the proceeds from sales of marketable equity securities classified as current assets during Year 2.

c. Calculate the amount of the provision for estimated uncollectible accounts made during Year 2.

d. Calculate the amount of cost of goods sold assuming a FIFO cost flow assumption had been used.

e. Give the journal entry(s) to account for the change in the Investment in Thayer Corporation — Net account during Year 2.

f. Calculate the amount of income or loss from the Investment in Thayer Corporation during Year 2.

g. Give the journal entry(s) to account for the change in the Investment in Davis Corporation account during Year 2.

h. Prepare an analysis identifying the factors and the amounts that explain the change in the Minority Interest in Subsidiary account on the balance sheet.

i.  Calculate the balance in the Investment in Harvard Corporation account on Tuck Corporation's books on December 31, Year 2, assuming that the equity method had been used.

j.  Calculate the amount of cash received during Year 2 for rental fees.

k.  Calculate the actual cost of goods and services required to service customers' warranties during Year 2.

l.  Refer to Note 7. Calculate the amount of interest expense on the $1 million, 6-percent bonds for Year 2.

m.  Give the journal entry(s) that accounts for the change in the Mortgage Payable account during Year 2.

n.  The income tax rate is 30 percent. Calculate the difference between the amount of depreciation recognized for financial reporting purposes and the amount recognized for tax reporting.

o.  Give the journal entry made on July 1, Year 2, upon conversion of the preferred stock.

p.  Give the journal entry(s) to account for the change in the Treasury Stock account during Year 2.

q.  Prepare a T-account work sheet for the preparation of a statement of cash flows, defining funds as cash.

## Statement of Accounting Policies

- *Basis of consolidation.* The financial statements of Tuck Corporation are consolidated with Harvard Corporation, a 90-percent-owned subsidiary acquired on January 2, Year 0.

- *Marketable equity securities.* Marketable equity securities are stated at lower of acquisition cost or market.

- *Accounts receivable.* Uncollectible accounts of customers are accounted for using the allowance method.

- *Inventories.* Inventories are measured using a last-in, first-out (LIFO) cost flow assumption.

- *Investments.* Investments of less than 20 percent of the outstanding common stock of other companies are accounted for using the lower-of-cost-or-market method. Investments of 20 to 50 percent of the outstanding common stock of affiliates are accounted for using the equity method.

- *Building, equipment, and leaseholds.* Depreciation for financial reporting purposes is calculated using the straight-line method. For income tax purposes, ACRS depreciation is used.

- *Goodwill.* Goodwill arising from investments in Harvard Corporation is amortized over a period of 20 years.

- *Interest expense on long-term debt.* Interest expense on long-term debt is recognized using the effective interest method.

- *Deferred income taxes.* Deferred income taxes are provided for timing differences between book and taxable income. All timing differences relate to depreciation.

Exhibit 15.16 ————————————————————————————————

**TUCK CORPORATION**
**Consolidated Comparative Balance Sheet**
**(Problem 22)**

|  | December 31, Year 1 | December 31, Year 2 |
|---|---|---|
| **Assets** | | |
| **Current Assets:** | | |
| Cash . . . . . . . . . . . . . . . . . . . . . . . . . . . . . . . . . . . . . . . | $ 240,000 | $ 280,000 |
| Marketable Equity Securities—Net (Note 1) . . . . . | 125,000 | 141,000 |
| Accounts Receivable—Net (Note 2) . . . . . . . . . . . | 1,431,200 | 1,509,600 |
| Inventories (Note 3) . . . . . . . . . . . . . . . . . . . . . . . . . | 1,257,261 | 1,525,315 |
| Prepayments . . . . . . . . . . . . . . . . . . . . . . . . . . . . . . . | 28,000 | 32,000 |
| Total Current Assets . . . . . . . . . . . . . . . . . . . . . | $3,081,461 | $3,487,915 |
| **Investments (Note 4):** | | |
| Investment in Thayer Corporation—Net (15-percent owned) . . . . . . . . . . . . . . . . . . . . . . . . | $ 92,000 | $ 87,000 |
| Investment in Hitchcock Corporation (30-percent owned) . . . . . . . . . . . . . . . . . . . . . . . . | 120,000 | 135,000 |
| Investment in Davis Corporation (40-percent owned) . . . . . . . . . . . . . . . . . . . . . . . . | 215,000 | 298,000 |
| Total Investments . . . . . . . . . . . . . . . . . . . . . . . . | $ 427,000 | $ 520,000 |
| **Property, Plant, and Equipment (Note 5):** | | |
| Land . . . . . . . . . . . . . . . . . . . . . . . . . . . . . . . . . . . . . . | $ 82,000 | $ 82,000 |
| Building . . . . . . . . . . . . . . . . . . . . . . . . . . . . . . . . . . . | 843,000 | 843,000 |
| Equipment . . . . . . . . . . . . . . . . . . . . . . . . . . . . . . . . . | 497,818 | 1,848,418 |
| Leasehold . . . . . . . . . . . . . . . . . . . . . . . . . . . . . . . . . | 98,182 | 98,182 |
| Total Plant Assets at Cost . . . . . . . . . . . . . . . . . . | $1,521,000 | $2,871,600 |
| Less Accumulated Depreciation and Amortization | (376,000) | (413,000) |
| Total Plant Assets—Net . . . . . . . . . . . . . . . . . . | $1,145,000 | $2,458,600 |
| **Intangibles:** | | |
| Goodwill—Net . . . . . . . . . . . . . . . . . . . . . . . . . . . . . | $ 36,000 | $ 34,000 |
| Total Assets . . . . . . . . . . . . . . . . . . . . . . . . . . . . | $4,689,461 | $6,500,515 |

*continued*

## Notes to the Financial Statements

- Note 1: Marketable equity securities are shown net of an allowance for price declines below acquisition cost of $25,000 on December 31, Year 1, and $21,000 on December 31, Year 2. Marketable equity securities costing $35,000 were sold during Year 2. No dividends were received from marketable equity securities during Year 2.

- Note 2: Accounts receivable are shown net of an allowance for uncollectible accounts of $128,800 on December 31, Year 1, and $210,400 on December 31, Year 2. A total of $63,000 of accounts were written off as uncollectible during Year 2.

**Exhibit 15.16** *(continued)* _____

| | Year 1 | Year 2 |
|---|---|---|
| **Liabilities and Shareholders' Equity** | | |
| **Current Liabilities:** | | |
| Note Payable (Note 6) ............................ | $ 100,000 | $ 200,000 |
| Accounts Payable ................................ | 666,100 | 723,700 |
| Rental Fees Received in Advance.................. | 46,000 | 58,000 |
| Estimated Warranty Liability ...................... | 75,200 | 78,600 |
| Interest Payable on Notes ......................... | 1,500 | 2,000 |
| Dividends Payable................................. | 25,000 | 30,000 |
| Income Taxes Payable—Current................... | 140,000 | 160,000 |
| Total Current Liabilities .......................... | $1,053,800 | $1,252,300 |
| **Noncurrent Liabilities:** | | |
| Bonds Payable (Note 7)........................... | $1,104,650 | $1,931,143 |
| Mortgage Payable (Note 8) ....................... | 299,947 | 280,943 |
| Capitalized Lease Obligation (Note 9).............. | 62,064 | 56,229 |
| Deferred Income Taxes .......................... | 130,000 | 145,000 |
| Total Noncurrent Liabilities....................... | $1,596,661 | $2,413,315 |
| Total Liabilities ................................. | $2,650,461 | $3,665,615 |
| **Shareholders' Equity:** | | |
| Minority Interest in Subsidiary ..................... | $ 32,000 | $ 36,500 |
| Convertible Preferred Stock, $100 par Value (Note 10) | 700,000 | 200,000 |
| Common Stock, $10 par Value (Note 11) ............ | 1,000,000 | 1,650,000 |
| Additional Paid-in Capital—Common .............. | 130,000 | 583,600 |
| Unrealized Loss from Price Declines of Marketable Equity Investments ............................ | (16,000) | (21,000) |
| Retained Earnings ............................... | 220,000 | 400,000 |
| Total ......................................... | $2,066,000 | $2,849,100 |
| Less Cost of Treasury Stock (Note 12).............. | (27,000) | (14,200) |
| Total Shareholders' Equity ....................... | $2,039,000 | $2,834,900 |
| Total Liabilities and Shareholders' Equity .......... | $4,689,461 | $6,500,515 |

- Note 3: The valuation of inventories on a FIFO basis exceeded the amounts on a LIFO basis by $430,000 on December 31, Year 1, and by $410,000 on December 31, Year 2.

- Note 4: Net income of Davis Corporation for Year 2 was $217,500. Dividends declared and paid during Year 2 totaled $60,000.

- Note 5: Equipment with a cost of $23,000 and a book value of $4,000 was sold during Year 2. This was the only disposition of property, plant, or equipment during the year.

- Note 6: A 90-day, 9-percent note with a face amount of $100,000 was paid with interest at maturity on January 30, Year 2. On December 1, Year 2,

Tuck Corporation borrowed $200,000 from its local bank, promising to repay the principal plus interest at 12 percent in 6 months.

- Note 7: Bonds Payable on the balance sheet is composed of the following:

|  | December 31, Year 1 | December 31, Year 2 |
|---|---|---|
| $1,000,000, 6-Percent, 20-Year Semiannual Coupon Bonds, Due Dec. 31, Year 16, Priced at $1,125,510 to Yield 5 Percent, Compounded Semiannually, at the Time of Issue ................................ | $1,104,650 | $1,099,823 |
| $1,000,000, 8-Percent, 20-Year Semiannual Coupon Bonds, Due Dec. 31, Year 21, Priced at $828,409 to Yield 10 Percent, Compounded Semiannually, at the Time of Issue ................................ | — | 831,320 |
| Total..................................... | $1,104,650 | $1,931,143 |

- Note 8: Mortgage Payable represents a mortgage on buildings requiring equal installment payments of $40,000 on December 31 of each year. The loan underlying the mortgage bears interest of 7 percent, compounded annually. The final installment payment is due on December 31, Year 12.

- Note 9: The Capitalized Lease Obligation represents a 20-year, noncancelable lease on certain equipment. The lease requires annual payments in advance of $10,000 on January 2 of each year. The last lease payment will be made on January 2, Year 8. The lease is capitalized at the lessee's borrowing rate (at the inception of the lease) of 8 percent.

- Note 10: Each share of preferred stock is convertible into 5 shares of common stock. On July 1, Year 2, holders of 5,000 shares of preferred stock exercised their options. The conversion was recorded using book values.

- Note 11: On October 1, Year 2, 40,000 shares of common stock were issued on the open market for $15 per share.

- Note 12: Treasury Stock is composed of the following:

| | |
|---|---|
| Dec. 31, Year 1: 2,250 Shares at $12 per Share ................... | $27,000 |
| Dec. 31, Year 2: 450 Shares at $12 per Share.................... | $ 5,400 |
| 550 Shares at $16 per Share.................... | 8,800 |
| | $14,200 |

During Year 2, 1,800 shares of treasury stock were sold and 550 shares were acquired.

23. *Selecting accounting methods.* Champion Clothiers, Inc., owns and operates 80 retailing establishments throughout New England, specializing in quality men's and women's clothing. The company was established many years ago by James

Champion and has been run by a member of the Champion family ever since. Currently, Ronald Champion, grandson of the founder, is president and chief executive officer. The company's shares are held by members of the Champion family.

The setting for this case is March of 1988. The following conversation takes place between Ronald Champion and the company's accountant, Tom Morrissey.

*Champion* (President): "Tom, you said on the telephone that the financial statements for 1987 were now complete. How much did we earn last year?"

*Morrissey* (Accountant): "Net income was $800,000, with earnings per share at $1.60. With the $1.20 per share earned in 1985 and $1.38 earned in 1986, we have maintained our 15 percent growth rate in profits."

*Champion:* "That sounds great! Tom, at our board meeting next week I am going to announce that the Champion family has decided to take the company public. We will be issuing shares equal to a 40 percent stake in the company early in 1989. It is important that our earnings for 1988 continue to reflect the growth rate we have been experiencing. By my calculations, we need an earnings per share for 1988 in the neighborhood of $1.84. Does this seem likely?"

*Morrissey:* "I'm afraid not. Our current projections indicate an earnings per share around $1.65 for this year. Major unexpected style changes earlier this year have left us with obsolete inventory that will have to be written off. In addition, increased competition in several of our major markets is putting a squeeze on margins. Even the acquisition of Green Trucking Company in June of this year will not help earnings that much."

*Champion:* "I know you accountants have all kinds of games you can play to doctor up the numbers. There must be something we can do to increase earnings to the desired level. What about our use of LIFO for inventories?"

*Morrissey:* "We have been using LIFO in the past because it reduces income and saves taxes during a period of rising prices. The more recent, higher acquisition costs of inventory items are used in computing cost of goods sold in the income statement. The older, lower acquisition prices are used in the valuation of inventory on the balance sheet. We could switch to FIFO for 1988. That would add about $.21 to earnings per share. However, we would probably have to use FIFO for tax purposes as well, increasing our taxes for the year by about $50,000."

*Champion:* "I don't like paying more taxes, but FIFO certainly more closely approximates the physical flow of our goods. If we decide to stay on LIFO, is there anything we can do in applying the LIFO method that would prop up earnings?"

*Morrissey:* "We now classify our inventory very broadly into two LIFO groups, or pools: one for men's clothing and one for women's clothing. We do this to minimize the possibility of dipping into an old LIFO layer. As you will recall, if we sell more than we purchase during a given period, we dip into an old LIFO layer. These LIFO layers are valued using acquisition costs of the year the layer was added. Some of these layers reflect costs of the mid-50s. When we dip into one of these layers, we have to use these old, lower costs in figuring cost of goods sold and net income. By defining our LIFO pools broadly to include our dollar investment in men's clothing and our dollar investment in women's clothing, we minimize the probability of liquidating an old LIFO layer. We could define our LIFO pools more narrowly to increase the possibility of dipping. We could then let the inventory of particular items run down at the end of the year, dip into the LIFO layer to increase earnings, and then rebuild the inventory early in the next year. I suspect we could add about $.02 a share to 1988 earnings if we went with narrower pools.''

*Champion:* ''We own all of our store buildings and display counters. Is there anything we can do with depreciation expense?''

*Morrissey:* ''We now depreciate these items using the shortest lives allowed and the fastest write-off permitted by tax law. However, unlike LIFO, we do not have to calculate depreciation for financial reporting in the same way as we do for tax reporting. We could depreciate these items over the expected economic life of each asset, which would be longer than the tax life. That should add about $.04 to earnings per share for 1988. We could also use the straight-line depreciation method for financial reporting. While our depreciable assets probably decrease in value faster than the straight-line method would indicate, we would be using the depreciation method that most of our competitors use for financial reporting. The use of straight-line depreciation would add another $.08.''

*Champion:* ''Now you're talking. What else can we do?''

*Morrissey:* ''There are some possibilities with respect to the acquisition of Green Trucking later this year. We currently plan to account for this acquisition using the purchase method. Under the purchase method, we will record the assets (and liabilities) of Green Trucking on our books at their market value on the date of acquisition. Since we expect to pay a price higher than the market value of Green's identifiable assets, there will also be some goodwill recorded.''

*Champion:* ''How does the acquisition affect earnings for 1988?''

*Morrissey:* ''On the plus side, we will include the earnings of Green Trucking from the date of acquisition in June until the end of the year. However, cost of goods sold and depreciation expense must be based on the higher current market values recorded on our books for Green's assets rather than the lower recorded amounts on Green's books. In addition, we will have to amortize the goodwill. I expect to pick up $.08 per share in earnings for 1988 from the Green acquisition, but this is already reflected in my $1.65 estimate for the year.''

*Champion:* ''Can we account for the acquisition any differently?''

*Morrissey:* ''If we can qualify, we may be able to use the pooling-of-interests method. Under the pooling method, we would record Green's assets (and liabilities) on our books at the amounts at which they are stated on Green's books; that is, the older, lower book values would be carried over. This means that cost of goods sold and depreciation expense will be lower this year and in the future than if we used the purchase method. In addition, no goodwill would be recognized and therefore no goodwill amortization would have to be recorded. Also, we would reflect in our earnings for 1988 the earnings of Green Trucking for all of 1988, not just that portion after June. Using the pooling method, earnings per share should increase $.10 more than the purchase method.''

*Champion:* "That sounds great, but what do we have to do to qualify?"

*Morrissey:* "To justify carrying over the old book values of Green Trucking, we have to show that we are merely combining the predecessor companies *and their shareholders*. The shareholders of Green Trucking must receive common stock of Champion Clothiers in exchange for their shares in Green Trucking. The shareholders in each of the predecessor companies then become shareholders in the new combined company (which will carry the Champion name). The Green shareholders would own 10 percent of Champion after the acquisition. Accountants view such a transaction as a change in form rather than in substance and permit the carryover of the old book values of Green.''

*Champion:* "My family may not be too happy about this arrangement, but let's move on.''

*Morrissey:* "Well, there is one thing we can do very easily with our pension plan to improve earnings. When we adopted the pension plan 2 years ago, we gave all employees credit for their service prior to adoption. This created an immediate obligation for past service. We are amortizing this obligation as a charge against earnings over a 10-year period. Generally accepted accounting principles permit us to use 15 years instead of 10 years as the amortization period; that switch would increase earnings per share by $.05 for 1988.''

*Champion:* "All of the things you have suggested deal with the selection or application of accounting methods. Can we do anything with the timing of expenditures to help 1988's earnings?''

*Morrissey:* "Well, painting and other maintenance of our stores scheduled for the last quarter of this year could be postponed until the first quarter of next year. That would add $.02 to earnings per share. In addition, we anticipate running a major advertising campaign just after Christmas. While the advertising expenditure will be made in 1988 and will reduce earnings per share by $.03, all of the benefits of the campaign will be realized in greater sales early in 1989.

*Champion:* "I hadn't realized how much flexibility we had for managing our earnings. Before we decide which choices to make, can you think of any other avenues open to us?''

*Morrissey:* "We could always sell off assets on which we have potential gain. For example, we hold some marketable securities that we purchased last year. Selling those securities would net us an additional $.02 in earnings per share. In addition, we own two parcels of land that we hope to use some day for new stores. These parcels could be sold at a gain of $.04 per share.''

*Champion:* "It strikes me that these alternatives could increase earnings per share for 1988 to the $2.00-plus range. This level is a lot more appealing than the $1.65 per share anticipated for the year. Will we have to do anything to earnings per share for prior years if we adopt any of these alternatives?''

*Morrissey:* "I have set out in Exhibit 15.17 the impact of each of the choices on earnings per share for 1988, as well as any restatement required for prior years. This summary should be helpful as we decide our strategy.''

How much do you think Champion Clothiers should report as earnings per share for 1988?

**Exhibit 15.17** ————————————————————————————

**CHAMPION CLOTHIERS, INC.**
**Alternative Strategies for Managing Earnings per Share**
**(Problem 23)**

| | Impact on Earnings per Share | | | |
|---|---|---|---|---|
| **Alternative** | **1985** | **1986** | **1987** | **1988** |
| Actual or Anticipated ......................... | $1.20 | $1.38 | $1.60 | $1.65 |
| Adoption of FIFO ........................... | +.15 | +.17 | +.20 | +.21 |
| Use of Narrower LIFO Pools................. | +.02 | +.03 | +.02 | +.02 |
| Use of Longer Depreciable Lives ............. | — | — | — | +.04 |
| Adoption of Straight-Line Depreciation ........ | +.05 | +.06 | +.07 | +.08 |
| Adoption of Pooling of Interests .............. | +.02 | +.04 | +.06 | +.10 |
| Amortization of Pension Obligation over 15 Years ............................ | — | — | — | +.05 |
| Deferral of Maintenance ..................... | — | — | — | +.02 |
| Deferral of Advertising ...................... | — | — | — | +.03 |
| Sale of Marketable Securities ................ | — | — | — | +.02 |
| Sale of Land ............................... | — | — | — | +.04 |

# Compound Interest
# Concepts and Applications _____

Money is a scarce resource, which its owner can use to command other resources. Like owners of other scarce resources, owners of money can permit borrowers to rent the use of their money for a period of time. Payment for the use of money differs little from other rental payments, such as those made to a landlord for the use of property or to a car rental agency for the use of a car. Payment for the use of money is called *interest*. Accounting is concerned with interest because it must record transactions in which the use of money is bought and sold.

Accountants and managers are concerned with interest calculations for another, equally important, reason. Expenditures for an asset most often occur before the receipts for services produced by that asset. Money received later is less valuable than money received sooner. The difference in timing affects whether acquiring an asset is profitable. Amounts of money received at different times have different values. Managers use interest calculations to make valid comparisons among amounts of money to be paid or received at different times.

Contracts involving a series of money payments over time, such as bonds, mortgages, notes, and leases, are evaluated by finding the *present value* of the stream of payments. The present value of a stream of payments is a single amount of money at the present time that is the economic equivalent of the entire stream.

# Compound Interest Concepts _____

Interest "cost" is typically stated as a percentage of the amount borrowed per unit of time. Examples are 12 percent per year and 1 percent per month, which are not the same. Another example occurs in the context of discounts on purchases. The terms of sale "2/10, net/30" are equivalent to 2 percent for 20 days. If the discount is not taken, payment can be delayed and the money can be used for up to an extra 20 (= 30 − 10) days.

The amount borrowed or loaned is called the *principal. Compound interest* means that the amount of interest earned during a period is added to the principal and the principal for the next interest period is larger.

For example, if you deposit $1,000 in a savings account that pays compound interest at the rate of 6 percent per year, you will earn $60 by the end of 1 year. If you do not withdraw the $60, then $1,060 will be earning interest during the second year. During the second year your principal of $1,060 will earn $63.60 interest; $60 on the initial deposit of $1,000 and $3.60 on the $60 earned the first year. By the end of the second year, you will have $1,123.60.

When only the original principal earns interest during the entire life of the loan, the interest due at the time the loan is repaid is called *simple interest*. In simple interest calculations, interest on previously earned interest is ignored.[1] The use of simple interest calculations in accounting arises in the following way. If you borrow $10,000 at a rate of 12 percent per year but compute interest for any month as $100 ($= \$10,000 \times .12 \times \frac{1}{12}$), you are using a simple interest calculation. Nearly all economic calculations, however, involve compound interest.

The force, or effect, of compound interest is more substantial than many people realize. For example, compounded annually at 8 percent, money doubles itself in 9 years. Put another way, if you invest $100 at 8 percent compounded annually, you will have $200 in 9 years.

Problems involving compound interest generally fall into two groups with respect to time. First there are the problems for which we want to know the future value of money invested or loaned today. Second there are the problems for which we want to know the present value, or today's value, of money to be received or paid at later dates. In addition, the accountant must sometimes compute the interest rate implicit in certain payment streams.

## Future Value

When $1 is invested today at 12 percent compounded annually, it will grow to $1.12000 at the end of 1 year, $1.25440 at the end of 2 years, $1.40493 at the end of 3 years, and so on, according to the formula

$$F_n = P(1 + r)^n,$$

where

$F_n =$ accumulation or future value

$P =$ one-time investment today

$r =$ interest rate per period

$n =$ number of periods from today.

The amount $F_n$ is the *future value* of the present payment, $P$, compounded at $r$ percent per period for $n$ periods. Table 1 on page 702 shows the future values of $P = \$1$ for various numbers of periods and for various interest rates. Extracts from that table appear here in Table A.1.

_____

[1]If interest earned may be withdrawn, compound interest techniques are relevant. The withdrawn interest can be invested elsewhere to earn additional interest.

## Table A.1

(Excerpt from Table 1)
Future Value of $1 at 8 Percent and 12 Percent per Period
$F_n = (1 + r)^n$

| Number of Periods = $n$ | Rate = $r$ | |
| --- | --- | --- |
| | 8 Percent | 12 Percent |
| 1 | 1.08000 | 1.12000 |
| 2 | 1.16640 | 1.25440 |
| 3 | 1.25971 | 1.40493 |
| 10 | 2.15892 | 3.10585 |
| 20 | 4.66096 | 9.64629 |

## Example Problems in Computing Future Value

**Example 1**  How much will $1,000 deposited today at 8 percent compounded annually be worth 10 years from now?

One dollar deposited today at 8 percent will grow to $2.15892; therefore $1,000 will grow to $1,000 (1.08)^{10} = $1,000 \times 2.15892 = $2,158.92$.

**Example 2**  Macaulay Corporation deposits $10,000 in an expansion fund today. The fund will earn 12 percent per year. How much will the $10,000 grow to in 20 years if the entire fund and all interest earned on it are left on deposit in the fund?

One dollar deposited today at 12 percent will grow to $9.64629 in 20 years. Therefore, $10,000 will grow to $96,463 (= $10,000 \times 9.64629) in 20 years.

## Present Value

The preceding section developed the computation of the future value $F_n$ of a sum of money $P$ deposited or invested today. $P$ is known; $F_n$ is calculated. This section deals with the problems of calculating how much principal, $P$, has to be invested today in order to have a specified amount, $F_n$, at the end of $n$ periods. The future amount, $F_n$, the interest rate, $r$, and the number of periods, $n$, are known; $P$ is to be found. In order to have $1 one year from today when interest is earned at 8 percent, $P$ of .92593 must be invested today. That is, $F_1 = P(1.08)^1$ or $1 = $.92593 \times 1.08$. Because $F_n = P(1 + r)^n$, dividing both sides of the equation by $(1 + r)^n$ yields

$$\frac{F_n}{(1 + r)^n} = P,$$

or

$$P = \frac{F_n}{(1 + r)^n} = F_n(1 + r)^{-n}.$$

## Present Value Terminology

The number $(1 + r)^{-n}$ is the present value of $1 to be received after $n$ periods when interest is earned at $r$ percent per period. The term *discount* is used in this context as follows. The discounted present value of $1 to be received $n$ periods in the future is $(1 + r)^{-n}$ when the discount rate is $r$ percent per period for $n$ periods. The number $r$ is the *discount rate* and the number $(1 + r)^{-n}$ is the *discount factor* for $n$ periods. A discount factor $(1 + r)^{-n}$ is merely the reciprocal, or inverse, of a number, $(1 + r)^n$, in Table A.1. Portions of Table 2 (on page 703), which shows discount factors, or equivalently, present values of $1 for various interest (or discount) rates for various numbers of periods, appear in Table A.2.

## Example Problems in Determining Present Values

**Example 3**  What is the present value of $1 due 10 years from now if the interest (equivalently, the discount) rate $r$ is 8 percent per year?

From Table A.2, 8 percent column, 10-period row, the present value of $1 to be received 10 periods hence at 8 percent is $.46319.

**Example 4**  (This example appears in Chapter 11.) You issue a non-interest-bearing note that promises to pay $16,000 three years from today in exchange for used equipment. How much is that promise worth today if the discount rate appropriate for such notes is 12 percent per period?

One dollar paid 3 years hence discounted at 12 percent has a present value of $.71178. Thus, the promise is worth $16,000 × .71178 = $11,388.

# Changing the Compounding Period: Nominal and Effective Rates ————————————————

"Twelve percent, compounded annually" is the price for a loan; this means that interest is added to or *converted* into principal once a year at the rate of 12 percent. Often, however, the price for a loan states that compounding is to take place more than once a year. A savings bank may advertise that it pays 6 percent, compounded

**Table A.2** ————————————————————————————————————

(Excerpt from Table 2)
Present Value of $1 at 8 Percent and 12 Percent per Period
$P = F_n(1 + r)^{-n}$

| Number of Periods = $n$ | Rate = $r$ | |
|---|---|---|
| | 8 Percent | 12 Percent |
| 1 ..................................................... | .92593 | .89286 |
| 2 ..................................................... | .85734 | .79719 |
| 3 ..................................................... | .79383 | .71178 |
| 10 ..................................................... | .46319 | .32197 |
| 20 ..................................................... | .21455 | .10367 |

quarterly. This means that at the end of each quarter the bank credits savings accounts with interest calculated at the rate 1.5 percent (= 6 percent/4). The interest payment can be withdrawn or left on deposit to earn more interest.

If $10,000 is invested today at 12 percent compounded annually, its future value 1 year later is $11,200. If the rate of interest is stated as 12 percent compounded semiannually, 6 percent interest is added to the principal every 6 months. At the end of the first 6 months, $10,000 will have grown to $10,600, so that the accumulation will be $10,600 × 1.06 = $11,236 by the end of the year. Notice that 12 percent compounded semiannually is equivalent to 12.36 percent compounded annually.

Suppose that the price is quoted as 12 percent, compounded quarterly. An additional 3 percent of the principal will be added to, or converted into, principal every 3 months. By the end of the year, $10,000 will grow to $10,000 × $(1.03)^4$ = $10,000 × 1.12551 = $11,255. Twelve percent compounded quarterly is equivalent to 12.55 percent compounded annually. If 12 percent is compounded monthly, $1 will grow to $1 × $(1.01)^{12}$ = $1.12683 and $10,000 will grow to $11,268. Thus, 12 percent compounded monthly is equivalent to 12.68 percent compounded annually.

For a given *nominal* rate, such as the 12 percent in the examples above, the more often interest is compounded or converted into principal, the higher the *effective* rate of interest paid. If a nominal rate, $r$, is compounded $m$ times per year, the effective rate is equal to $(1 + r/m)^m - 1$.

In practice, to solve problems that require computation of interest quoted at a nominal rate $r$ percent per period compounded $m$ times per period for $n$ periods, simply use the tables for rate $r/m$ and $m \times n$ periods.[2] For example, 12 percent compounded quarterly for 5 years is equivalent to the rate found in the interest tables for $r = 12/4 = 3$ percent for $m \times n = 4 \times 5 = 20$ periods.

## Example Problems in Changing the Compounding Period

**Example 5**  What is the future value 5 years hence of $600 invested at 16 percent compounded semiannually?

Sixteen percent compounded two times per year for 5 years is equivalent to 8 percent per period compounded for 10 periods. Table A.1 shows the value of $F_{10} = (1.08)^{10}$ to be 2.15892. Six hundred dollars, then, would grow to $600 × 2.15892 = $1,295.35.

---

[2]Some savings banks advertise that they compound interest daily or even continuously. The mathematics of calculus provides a mechanism for finding the effective rate when interest is compounded continuously. If interest is compounded continuously at nominal rate $r$ per year, the effective annual rate is $e^r - 1$, where $e$ is the base of the natural logarithms. Tables of values of $e^r$ are widely available. See, for example, *Handbook of Modern Accounting*, 3rd ed., edited by Sidney Davidson and Roman L. Weil (McGraw-Hill, 1983), chap. 9, Exhibit 1. Six percent per year compounded continuously is equivalent to 6.1837 percent compounded annually. Twelve percent per year compounded continuously is equivalent to 12.75 percent compounded annually. Do not confuse the compounding period with the payment period. Some banks, for example, compound interest daily but pay interest quarterly. You can be sure that such banks do not employ clerks or even computers to calculate interest every day. They merely use tables to derive an equivalent effective rate to apply at the end of each quarter.

**Example 6**  How much money must be invested today at 16 percent compounded semiannually in order to have $10,000 ten years from today?

Sixteen percent compounded two times a year for 10 years is equivalent to 8 percent per period compounded for 20 periods. The present value, Table A.2, of $1 received 20 periods hence at 8 percent per period is $.21455. That is, $.21455 invested today for 20 periods at an interest rate of 8 percent per period will grow to $1. To have $10,000 in 20 periods (10 years), $2,146 (= $10,000 × $.21455) must be invested today.

**Example 7**  A local department store offers its customers credit and advertises its interest rate at 18 percent per year, compounded monthly at the rate of $1\frac{1}{2}$ percent per month. What is the effective annual interest rate?

One and one-half percent per month for 12 months is equivalent to $(1.015)^{12} - 1 = 19.562$ percent per year. See Table 1, 12-period row, $1\frac{1}{2}$-percent column where the factor is 1.19562.

**Example 8**  If prices increased at the rate of 6 percent during each of two consecutive 6-month periods, how much did prices increase during the entire year?

If a price index is 100.00 at the start of the year, it will be $100.00 \times (1.06)^2 = 112.36$ at the end of the year. The price change for the entire year is $(112.36/100.00) - 1 = 12.36$ percent.

# Annuities _____

An *annuity* is a series of equal payments made at the beginning or end of equal periods of time. Examples of annuities include monthly rental payments, semiannual corporate bond coupon (or interest) payments, and annual payments to a lessor under a lease contract. Armed with an understanding of the tables for future and present values, you can solve any annuity problem. Annuities arise so often, however, and their solution is so tedious without special tables that annuity problems warrant special study and the use of special tables.

## Terminology for Annuities

The terminology used for annuities can be confusing because not all writers use the same terms. Definitions of the terms used in this text follow.

An annuity whose payments occur at the end of each period is called an *ordinary annuity* or an *annuity in arrears*. Semiannual corporate bond coupon payments are usually paid in arrears or, equivalently, the first payment does not occur until after the bond has been outstanding for 6 months.

An annuity whose payments occur at the beginning of each period is called an *annuity due* or an *annuity in advance*. Rent is usually paid in advance, so a series of rental payments is an annuity due.

A *deferred annuity* is one whose first payment is at some time later than the end of the first period.

Annuities can be paid forever. Such annuities are called *perpetuities*. Bonds that promise payments forever are called *consols*. The British and Canadian governments have issued consols from time to time. A perpetuity can be in arrears or in advance. The only difference between the two is the timing of the first payment.

Annuities can be confusing. Their study is made easier with a time line such as the one shown below.

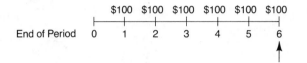

A time line marks the end of each period, numbers the period, shows the payments to be received or paid, and shows the time at which the annuity is valued. The time line above represents an ordinary annuity (in arrears) for six periods of $100 to be valued at the end of period 6. The end of period 0 is "now." The first payment is to be received one period from now.

## Ordinary Annuities (Annuities in Arrears)

The future values of ordinary annuities appear in Table 3 on page 704, portions of which Table A.3 reproduces.

Consider an ordinary annuity for three periods at 12 percent. The time line for the future value of such an annuity is as follows:

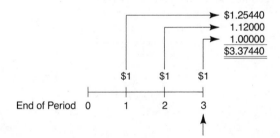

The $1 received at the end of the first period earns interest for two periods, so it is worth $1.25440 at the end of period 3. (See Table A.1.) The $1 received at the end of the second period grows to $1.12000 by the end of period 3, and the $1 received at the end of period 3 is, of course, worth $1.00000 at the end of period 3. The entire annuity is worth $3.37440 at the end of period 3. This is the amount shown in Table A.3 for the future value of an ordinary annuity for three periods at 12 percent. Factors for the future value of an annuity for a particular number of periods are merely the sum of the factors for the future value of $1 for each of the periods. The future value of an ordinary annuity is calculated as follows:

$$\begin{matrix} \text{Future Value of} \\ \text{Ordinary Annuity} \end{matrix} = \begin{matrix} \text{Periodic} \\ \text{Payment} \end{matrix} \times \begin{matrix} \text{Factor for} \\ \text{the Future} \\ \text{Value of an} \\ \text{Ordinary Annuity.} \end{matrix}$$

Table A.3 _____

**(Excerpt from Table 3)**
**Future Value of an Ordinary Annuity of**
**$1 per Period at 8 Percent and 12 Percent**

$$F_A = \frac{[(1 + r)^n - 1]}{r}$$

| Number of Periods = $n$ | Rate = $r$ | |
| --- | --- | --- |
| | 8 Percent | 12 Percent |
| 1 | 1.00000 | 1.00000 |
| 2 | 2.08000 | 2.12000 |
| 3 | 3.24640 | 3.37440 |
| 5 | 5.86660 | 6.35285 |
| 10 | 14.48656 | 17.54874 |
| 20 | 45.76196 | 72.05244 |

Thus,

$$\$3.37440 \quad = \quad \$1 \quad \times \quad 3.37440.$$

Table 4 on page 705 shows the present value of ordinary annuities. Table A.4 reproduces excerpts from Table 4.

The time line for the present value of an ordinary annuity of $1 per period for three periods, discounted at 12 percent, is as follows:

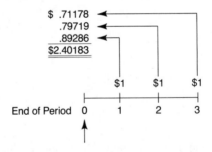

The $1 to be received at the end of period 1 has a present value of $.89286, the $1 to be received at the end of period 2 has a present value of $.79719, and the $1 to be received at the end of period 3 has a present value of $.71178. Each of these numbers comes from Table A.2. The present value of the annuity is the sum of these individual present values, $2.40183, shown in Table A.4.

The present value of an ordinary annuity for $n$ periods is the sum of the present value of $1 received 1 period from now plus the present value of $1 received 2 periods from now, and so on until we add on the present value of $1 received $n$ periods from now. The present value of an ordinary annuity is calculated as follows:

$$\begin{array}{ccc} \text{Present Value} & & \text{Factor for} \\ \text{of an} & = \text{Periodic} \times & \text{the Present} \\ \text{Ordinary Annuity} & \text{Payment} & \text{Value of an} \\ & & \text{Ordinary Annuity.} \end{array}$$

Table A.4 _____

(Excerpt from Table 4)
Present Value of an Ordinary Annuity of
$1 per Period at 8 Percent and 12 Percent

$$P_A = \frac{[1 - (1 + r)^{-n}]}{r}$$

| Number of | Rate = r | |
| Periods = n | 8 Percent | 12 Percent |
|---|---|---|
| 1 | .92593 | .89286 |
| 2 | 1.78326 | 1.69005 |
| 3 | 2.57710 | 2.40183 |
| 5 | 3.99271 | 3.60478 |
| 10 | 6.71008 | 5.65022 |
| 20 | 9.81815 | 7.46944 |

Thus,

$$\$2.40183 \quad = \quad \$1 \quad \times \quad 2.40183.$$

## Example Problems Involving Ordinary Annuities

**Example 9**   An individual plans to invest $1,000 at the end of each of the next 10 years in a savings account. The savings account accumulates interest of 8 percent compounded annually. What will be the balance in the savings account at the end of 10 years?

The time line for this problem is as follows:

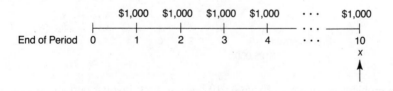

The symbol $x$ denotes the amount to be calculated. Table A.3 indicates that the factor for the future value of an annuity at 8 percent for ten periods is 14.48656. Thus,

$$\begin{array}{ccc} \text{Future Value} & & \text{Factor for} \\ \text{of an} & = \begin{array}{c}\text{Periodic} \\ \text{Payment}\end{array} \times & \text{the Future} \\ \text{Ordinary Annuity} & & \begin{array}{c}\text{Value of an} \\ \text{Ordinary Annuity}\end{array} \end{array}$$

$$x \quad = \$1,000 \times \quad 14.48656$$

$$x \quad = \$14,487.$$

**Example 10**   An individual wishes to receive $60 every 6 months, starting 6 months hence, for the next 5 years. How much must be invested today if the interest rate is 8 percent compounded semiannually?

The time line is as follows:

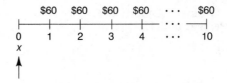

The factor from Table 4 for the present value of an annuity at 4 percent (= 8 percent per year/2 semiannual periods per year) for 10 (= 2 periods per year × 5 years) periods is 8.11090. Thus,

$$
\begin{array}{ccc}
\begin{array}{c}\text{Present Value}\\ \text{of an}\\ \text{Ordinary Annuity}\end{array}
& = \begin{array}{c}\text{Periodic}\\ \text{Payment}\end{array} \times
& \begin{array}{c}\text{Factor for}\\ \text{the Present}\\ \text{Value of an}\\ \text{Ordinary Annuity}\end{array}
\end{array}
$$

$$x \quad = \quad \$60 \ \times \quad 8.11090$$

$$x \quad = \$486.65.$$

If $486.65 is invested today, the principal plus interest compounded on the principal will provide sufficient funds that $60 can be withdrawn every 6 months for the next 5 years.

**Example 11**  (Western Company mortgage example from Chapter 10.) A company borrows $125,000 from a savings-and-loan association. The interest rate on the loan is 12 percent compounded semiannually. The company agrees to repay the loan in equal semiannual installments over the next 5 years. The first payment is to be made 6 months from now. What is the amount of the required semiannual payment?
The time line is as follows:

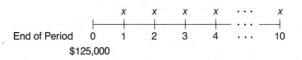

This problem is similar to Example 10 because both involve periodic payments in the future that are discounted to today. In Example 10, the periodic payments were given and the present value was computed. In Example 11, the present value is given and the periodic payment is computed. Table 4 indicates that the present value of annuity at 6 percent (= 12 percent per year/2 semiannual periods per year) for 10 periods (= 2 periods per year × 5 years) is 7.36009. Thus,

$$
\begin{array}{ccc}
\begin{array}{c}\text{Present Value}\\ \text{of an}\\ \text{Ordinary Annuity}\end{array}
& = \begin{array}{c}\text{Periodic}\\ \text{Payment}\end{array} \times
& \begin{array}{c}\text{Factor for}\\ \text{the Present}\\ \text{Value of an}\\ \text{Ordinary Annuity}\end{array}
\end{array}
$$

$$\$125,000 \quad = \quad x \ \times \quad 7.36009$$

$$x \quad = \frac{\$125,000}{7.36009}$$

$$x \quad = \$16,983.$$

Because the periodic payment is being calculated, the present value amount of $125,000 must be divided by the present value factor. (You may examine Exhibit 10.2 to study the amortization table for this loan. The amount of each semiannual payment shown there is $17,000 rather than $16,983, but the last payment is less than $17,000 to compensate for the extra $17 paid in the preceding periods.)

**Example 12**  (Myers Company lease example from Chapter 11.) A company signs a lease acquiring the right to use property for 3 years. Lease payments of $19,709 are to be made annually at the end of this and the next 2 years. The discount, or interest, rate is 15 percent per year. What is the present value of the lease payments?

The time line is as follows:

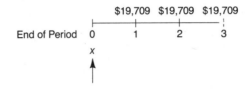

The factor from Table 4 for the present value of an annuity at 15 percent for three periods is 2.28323. Thus,

$$\begin{array}{ccc} \text{Present Value} \\ \text{of an} \\ \text{Ordinary Annuity} \end{array} = \begin{array}{c} \text{Periodic} \\ \text{Payment} \end{array} \times \begin{array}{c} \text{Factor for} \\ \text{the Present} \\ \text{Value of an} \\ \text{Ordinary Annuity} \end{array}$$

$$x \quad = \$19{,}709 \times \quad 2.28323$$

$$x \quad = \$45{,}000.$$

In the Myers Company example in Chapter 11, the cost of the equipment is given at $45,000 and the periodic rental payment is computed with an annuity factor. Thus,

$$\begin{array}{ccc} \text{Present Value} \\ \text{of an} \\ \text{Ordinary Annuity} \end{array} = \begin{array}{c} \text{Periodic} \\ \text{Payment} \end{array} \times \begin{array}{c} \text{Factor for} \\ \text{the Present} \\ \text{Value of} \\ \text{an Annuity} \end{array}$$

$$\$45{,}000 \quad = \quad x \quad \times \ 2.28323$$

$$x \quad = \frac{\$45{,}000}{2.28323}$$

$$x \quad = \$19{,}709.$$

**Example 13**  (Pension funding example.) A company is obligated to make annual payments to a pension fund at the end of each of the next 30 years. The present value of those payments is to be $100,000. What must the annual payment be if the fund is projected to earn interest at the rate of 8 percent per year?

The time line is as follows:

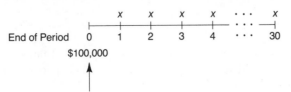

Table 4 indicates that the factor for the present value of $1 paid at the end of the next 30 periods at 8 percent per period is 11.25778. Thus,

$$\begin{array}{c} \text{Present Value} \\ \text{of an} \\ \text{Ordinary Annuity} \end{array} = \begin{array}{c} \text{Periodic} \\ \text{Payment} \end{array} \times \begin{array}{c} \text{Factor for} \\ \text{the Present} \\ \text{Value of an} \\ \text{Ordinary Annuity} \end{array}$$

$$\$100,000 = x \times 11.25778$$

$$x = \frac{\$100,000}{11.25778}$$

$$x = \$8,883.$$

**Example 14**  Mr. Mason is 62 years old. He wishes to invest equal amounts on his sixty-third, sixty-fourth, and sixty-fifth birthdays so that starting on his sixty-sixth birthday he can withdraw $5,000 on each birthday for 10 years. His investments will earn 8 percent per year. How much should be invested on the sixty-third through sixty-fifth birthdays?

The time line for this problem is as follows:

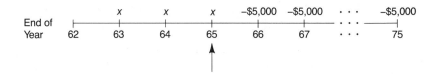

On his sixty-fifth birthday, Mr. Mason needs to have accumulated a fund equal to the present value of an annuity of $5,000 per period for 10 periods, discounted at 8 percent per period. The factor from Table A.4 for 8 percent and 10 periods is 6.71008. Thus,

$$\begin{array}{c} \text{Present Value} \\ \text{of an} \\ \text{Ordinary Annuity} \end{array} = \begin{array}{c} \text{Periodic} \\ \text{Payment} \end{array} \times \begin{array}{c} \text{Factor for} \\ \text{the Present} \\ \text{Value of an} \\ \text{Ordinary Annuity} \end{array}$$

$$x = \$\,5,000 \times 6.71008$$

$$x = \$33,550.$$

The time line now appears as follows:

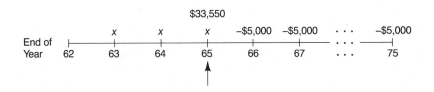

The question now becomes, how much must be invested on Mr. Mason's sixty-third, sixty-fourth, and sixty-fifth birthdays to accumulate to a fund of $33,550 on his sixty-fifth birthday? The factor for the future value of an annuity for three periods at 8 percent is 3.24640. Thus,

$$\begin{array}{ccc}
\begin{matrix}\text{Future Value}\\\text{of an}\\\text{Ordinary Annuity}\end{matrix} & = & \begin{matrix}\text{Periodic}\\\text{Payment}\end{matrix} \times & \begin{matrix}\text{Factor for}\\\text{the Future}\\\text{Value of an}\\\text{Ordinary Annuity}\end{matrix}
\end{array}$$

$$\$33{,}550 \;=\; x \;\times\; 3.24640$$

$$x = \frac{\$33{,}550}{3.24640}$$

$$x = \$10{,}335.$$

In the solution above, all calculations are expressed in terms of equivalent amounts on Mr. Mason's sixty-fifth birthday. That is, the present value of an annuity of $5,000 per period for 10 periods at 8 percent is equal to the future value of an annuity of $10,335 per period for 3 periods at 8 percent and both of these amounts are equal to $33,550. The problem could have been worked by selecting any common time period between Mr. Mason's sixty-second and seventy-fifth birthdays.

One possibility would be to express all calculations in terms of equivalent amounts on Mr. Mason's sixty-second birthday. To solve the problem in this way, first find the present value on Mr. Mason's sixty-fifth birthday of an annuity of $5,000 per period for 10 periods ($33,550 = $5,000 × 6.71008). Discount $33,550 back three periods using Table 2 for the present value of $1 ($26,633 = $33,550 × .79383). The result is the present value of the payments to be made to Mr. Mason *measured as of his sixty-second birthday*. Then find the amounts that must be invested by Mr. Mason on his sixty-third, sixty-fourth, and sixty-fifth birthdays that have a *present value* on his sixty-second birthday equal to $26,633. The calculation is as follows:

$$\begin{array}{ccc}
\begin{matrix}\text{Present Value}\\\text{of an}\\\text{Ordinary Annuity}\end{matrix} & = & \begin{matrix}\text{Periodic}\\\text{Payment}\end{matrix} \times & \begin{matrix}\text{Factor for}\\\text{the Present}\\\text{Value of an}\\\text{Ordinary Annuity}\end{matrix}
\end{array}$$

$$\$26{,}633 \;=\; x \;\times\; 2.57710$$

$$x = \$10{,}335.$$

The amount $10,335 is the same as that found above.

# Perpetuities _____

A periodic payment to be received forever is called a *perpetuity*. Future values of perpetuities are undefined. If $1 is to be received at the end of every period and the discount rate is $r$ percent, the present value of the perpetuity is $\$1/r$. This expression can be derived with algebra or by observing what happens in the expression for the present value of an ordinary annuity of $A$ per payment as $n$, the number of payments, approaches infinity:

$$P_A = \frac{A[1 - (1 + r)^{-n}]}{r}$$

As $n$ approaches infinity, $(1 + r)^{-n}$ approaches 0, so that $P_A$ approaches $A(1/r)$. If the first payment of the perpetuity occurs now, the present value is $A[1 + 1/r]$.

## Examples of Perpetuities

**Example 15**  The Canadian government offers to pay $30 every 6 months forever in the form of a perpetual bond. What is that bond worth if the discount rate is 10 percent compounded semiannually?

Ten percent compounded semiannually is equivalent to 5 percent per 6-month period. If the first payment occurs 6 months from now, the present value is $30/.05 = $600. If the first payment occurs today, the present value is $30 + $600 = $630.

**Example 16**  Every 2 years, Sandra Young gives $20,000 to the university to provide a scholarship for an entering student in a 2-year business administration course. If the university credits 6 percent per year to its investment accounts, how much must Young give to the university to provide such a scholarship every 2 years forever, starting 2 years hence?

A perpetuity in arrears assumes one payment at the end of each period. Here, the period is 2 years. Six percent compounded once a year over 2 years is equivalent to a rate of $(1.06)^2 - 1 = .12360$ or 12.36 percent compounded once per 2-year period. Consequently, the present value of the perpetuity paid in arrears every 2 years is $161,812 (= $20,000/.12360). A gift of $161,812 will be sufficient to provide a $20,000 scholarship forever. If the first scholarship is to be awarded now, the gift must be $181,812 (= $161,812 + $20,000).

## Implicit Interest Rates: Finding Internal Rates of Return _____

In the preceding examples, given the interest rate and stated cash payments, a future value or a present value was computed. Or the required payments were computed given their known future value or their known present value. In some calculations, the present or future value and the periodic payments are known; the implicit interest rate is to be found. For example, Chapter 11 illustrates a case in which the cash price of some equipment is known to be $10,500 and the asset was acquired using a note. The note is non-interest-bearing, has a face value of $16,000, and matures in 3 years. In order to compute interest expense over the 3-year period, the implicit interest rate must be found. The time line for this problem is as follows:

```
            +$10,500     0          0       -$16,000
            ├──────────┼──────────┼──────────┤
End of Year      0          1          2          3
```

The implicit interest rate is $r$, such that

$$\text{(A.1)} \qquad\qquad 0 = \$10{,}500 - \frac{\$16{,}000}{(1 + r)^3}$$

$$\text{(A.2)} \qquad\qquad \$10{,}500 = \frac{\$16{,}000}{(1 + r)^3}$$

That is, the present value of $\$16{,}000$ discounted three periods at $r$ percent per period is $\$10{,}500$. The present value of all current and future cash flows nets to 0 when future flows are discounted at $r$ per period. In general, the only way to find such an $r$ is through trial and error. In cases where $r$ appears only in one term, as here, $r$ can be found analytically. Here, $r = (\$16{,}000/\$10{,}500)^{1/3} - 1 = .1507 = 15.1$ percent.

The general procedure is called *finding the internal rate of return* of a series of cash flows. The internal rate of return of a series of cash flows is the discount rate that equates the net present value of that series of cash flows to 0. The steps in finding the internal rate of return are as follows:

1. Make an educated guess, called the "trial rate," at the internal rate of return. If you have no idea what to guess, try 0.

2. Calculate the present value of all the cash flows (including the one at the end of Year 0).

3. If the present value of the cash flows is 0, stop. The current trial rate is the internal rate of return.

4. If the amount found in step 2 is less than 0, try a larger interest rate as the trial rate and go back to step 2.

5. If the amount found in step 2 is greater than 0, try a smaller interest rate as the new trial rate and go back to step 2.

The iterations below illustrate the process for the example in Equation A.1.

| Iteration Number | Trial Rate = $r$ | Net Present Value: Right-Hand Side of Equation A.1 |
|---|---|---|
| 1 | 0.0% | −$5,500 |
| 2 | 10.0 | − 1,521 |
| 3 | 15.0 | − 20 |
| 4 | 15.5 | 116 |
| 5 | 15.2 | 34 |
| 6 | 15.1 | 7 |

With a trial rate of 15.1 percent, the right-hand side is close enough to 0 that 15.1 percent can be used as the implicit interest rate. Continued iterations would find trial rates even closer to the true rate, which is about 15.0739 percent.

Finding the internal rate of return for a series of cash flows can be tedious and should not be attempted unless one has at least a desk calculator. An exponential feature, which allows the computation of $(1 + r)$ raised to various powers, helps.[3]

## Example Problem Involving Implicit Interest Rates

**Example 17**    The Alexis Company acquires a machine with a cash price of $10,500. It pays for the machine by giving a note promising to make payments equal to 7 percent of the face value, $840, at the end of each of the next 3 years and a single payment of $12,000 in 3 years. What is the implicit interest rate in the loan?

The time line for this problem is as follows:

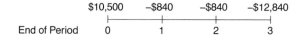

|  | $10,500 | −$840 | −$840 | −$12,840 |
|---|---|---|---|---|
| End of Period | 0 | 1 | 2 | 3 |

The implicit interest rate is $r$, such that[4]

$$\text{(A.3)} \qquad \$10,500 = \frac{\$840}{(1 + r)} + \frac{\$840}{(1 + r)^2} + \frac{\$12,840}{(1 + r)^3}.$$

The internal rate of return is found to the nearest tenth of 1 percent to be 12.2 percent:

| Iteration Number | Trial Rate | Right-Hand Side of Equation A.3 |
|---|---|---|
| 1 ............................................... | 7.0% | $12,000 |
| 2 ............................................... | 15.0 | 9,808 |
| 3 ............................................... | 11.0 | 10,827 |
| 4 ............................................... | 13.0 | 10,300 |
| 5 ............................................... | 12.0 | 10,559 |
| 6 ............................................... | 12.5 | 10,428 |
| 7 ............................................... | 12.3 | 10,480 |
| 8 ............................................... | 12.2 | 10,506 |
| 9 ............................................... | 12.1 | 10,532 |

[3]There are ways to guess the trial rate that will approximate the true rate in fewer iterations than the method described here. If you want to find internal rates of return efficiently with successive trial rates, refer to a mathematical reference book to learn about the "Newton search" method, sometimes called the "method of false position."

[4]Compare this formulation to that in Equation A.1. Note that the left-hand side is 0 in one case but not in the other. The left-hand side can be either nonzero or 0, depending on what seems convenient for the particular context.

# Summary ————————————————————————————

Accountants typically use one of four kinds of compound interest calculations: the present or future value of a single payment or of a series of payments. In working annuity problems, a time line helps in deciding which particular kind of annuity is involved.

# Questions, Exercises, Problems, and Cases ——————————

## Questions

1. Review the following concepts or terms discussed in this appendix.

   a. Present value.

   b. Principal.

   c. Compound interest.

   d. Simple interest.

   e. Future value.

   f. Discounted value.

   g. Discount rate.

   h. Discount factor.

   i. Ordinary annuity (annuity in arrears).

   j. Deferred annuity.

   k. Perpetuity.

   l. Implicit interest rate (internal rate of return).

2. What is interest?

3. Distinguish between simple and compound interest.

4. Distinguish between the discounted present value of a stream of future payments and their net present value. If there is no distinction, then so state.

5. Distinguish between an annuity due and an ordinary annuity.

6. Describe the implicit interest rate for a series of cash flows and a procedure for finding it.

7. Does the present value of a given amount to be paid in 10 years increase or decrease if the interest rate increases? Suppose that the amount were due in 5 years? 20 years? Does the present value of an annuity to be paid for 10 years increase or decrease if the discount rate decreases? Suppose that the annuity were for 5 years? 20 years?

8. Rather than pay you $100 a month for the next 20 years, the person who injured you in an automobile accident is willing to pay a single amount now to settle your claim for injuries. Would you rather an interest rate of 6 percent or 12 percent be used in computing the present value of the lump-sum settlement? Comment or explain.

## Exercises

9. *Effective interest rates.* State the rate per period and the number of periods in

   a. 12 percent per annum, for 5 years, compounded annually.

   b. 12 percent per annum, for 5 years, compounded semiannually.

   c. 12 percent per annum, for 5 years, compounded quarterly.

   d. 12 percent per annum, for 5 years, compounded monthly.

*Exercises 10 through 26 involve calculations of present and future value for single payments and for annuities. To make the exercises more realistic, specific guidance is not given with each individual exercise.*

**10.** Compute the future value of
  **a.**  $100 invested for 5 years at 4 percent compounded annually.
  **b.**  $500 invested for 15 periods at 2 percent compounded once per period.
  **c.**  $200 invested for 8 years at 3 percent compounded semiannually.
  **d.**  $2,500 invested for 14 years at 8 percent compounded quarterly.
  **e.**  $600 invested for 3 years at 12 percent compounded monthly.

**11.** Compute the present value of
  **a.**  $100 due in 30 years at 4 percent compounded annually.
  **b.**  $250 due in 8 years at 8 percent compounded quarterly.
  **c.**  $1,000 due in 2 years at 12 percent compounded monthly.

**12.** Compute the amount (future value) of an ordinary annuity (an annuity in arrears) of
  **a.**  13 rental payments of $100 at $1\frac{1}{2}$ percent per period.
  **b.**  8 rental payments of $850 at 6 percent per period.
  **c.**  28 rental payments of $400 at 4 percent per period.

**13.** Mr. Adams has $500 to invest. He wishes to know how much it will amount to if he invests it at
  **a.**  6 percent per year for 21 years.
  **b.**  8 percent per year for 33 years.

**14.** Ms. Black wishes to have $15,000 at the end of 8 years. How much must she invest today to accomplish this purpose if the interest rate is
  **a.**  6 percent per year?
  **b.**  8 percent per year?

**15.** Mr. Case plans to set aside $4,000 each year, the first payment to be made on January 1, 1985, and the last on January 1, 1990. How much will he have accumulated by January 1, 1990 if the interest rate is
  **a.**  6 percent per year?
  **b.**  8 percent per year?

**16.** Ms. David wants to have $450,000 on her sixty-fifth birthday. She asks you to tell her how much she must deposit on each birthday from her fifty-eighth to sixty-fifth, inclusive, in order to receive this amount. Assume an interest rate of
  **a.**  8 percent per year.
  **b.**  12 percent per year.

**17.** If Mr. Edwards invests $900 on June 1 of each year from 1985 to 1995 inclusive, how much will he have accumulated on June 1, 1996 (note that 1 year elapses after last payment) if the interest rate is
  **a.**  5 percent per year?
  **b.**  10 percent per year?

**18.** Ms. Frank has $145,000 with which she purchases an annuity on February 1, 1985. The annuity consists of six annual payments, the first to be made on

February 1, 1986. How much will she receive in each payment? Assume an interest rate of

**a.**   8 percent per year.

**b.**   12 percent per year.

19. In the preceding Exercises 10 through 18, you have been asked to compute a number. First you must decide what factor from the tables is appropriate and then you use that factor in the appropriate calculation. Notice that the last step could be omitted. You could write an arithmetic expression showing the factor you want to use without actually copying down the number and doing the arithmetic. For example, define the following notation: T($i$, $p$, $r$) means Table $i$ (1, 2, 3, or 4), row $p$ (periods 1 to 20, 22, 24, . . . , 40, 45, 50, 100), and column $r$ (interest rates from $\frac{1}{2}$ percent up to 20 percent). Thus, T(3, 16, 12) would be the factor in Table 3 for 16 periods and an interest rate of 12 percent per period, which is 42.75328. Using this notation, you can write an expression for any compound interest problem. A clerk can evaluate the expression.

You can check that you understand this notation by observing that the following are true statements:

T(1, 20, 8)   =   4.66096
T(2, 12, 5)   =   0.55684
T(3, 16, 12) = 42.75328
T(4, 10, 20) =   4.19247.

In the following questions, write an expression for the correct answer using the notation introduced here, but do not attempt to evaluate the expression.

**a.**   Work the **a** parts of Exercises 10 through 14.

**b.**   Work the **b** parts of Exercises 15 through 18.

**c.**   How might the use of this notation make it easier for your instructor to write examination questions on compound interest?

20. Mr. Grady agrees to lease a certain property for 10 years, at the following annual rentals, payable in advance:

Years 1 and 2—$1,000 per year.
Years 3 to 6—$2,000 per year.
Years 7 to 10—$2,500 per year.

What single immediate sum will pay all of these rents if they are discounted at

**a.**   6 percent per year?

**b.**   8 percent per year?

**c.**   10 percent per year?

21. In order to establish a fund that will provide a scholarship of $3,000 a year indefinitely, with the first award to occur now, how much must be deposited if the fund earns

**a.**   6 percent per period?

**b.**   8 percent per period?

**22.** Consider the scholarship fund in the preceding question. Suppose that the first scholarship is not to be awarded until 1 year from now. How much should be deposited if the fund earns

    **a.** 6 percent per period?

    **b.** 8 percent per period?

    Suppose that the first scholarship is not to be awarded until 5 years from now. How much should be deposited if the fund earns

    **c.** 6 percent per year?

    **d.** 8 percent per year?

**23.** The state helps a rural county maintain a bridge and has agreed to pay $6,000 now and every 2 years thereafter forever toward the expenses. The state wishes to discharge its obligation by paying a single sum to the county now in lieu of the payment due and all future payments. How much should the state pay the county if the discount rate is

    **a.** 8 percent per year?

    **b.** 12 percent per year?

**24.** Find the interest rate implicit in a loan of $100,000 that is discharged with the two annual installments of $55,307 each, paid at the ends of Years 1 and 2.

**25.** A single-payment note has a face value of $140,493, to be paid in 3 years. The note is exchanged for equipment having a fair market value of $100,000, three years before the maturity date on the note.

    What interest rate will be imputed in accounting for the single-payment note?

**26.** A single-payment note has a face value of $67,280, due on maturity of the note. The note is exchanged for land with a fair market value of $50,000, two years before the maturity date on the note.

    **a.** What interest rate will be imputed in accounting for this single-payment note?

    **b.** Construct an amortization schedule for the note using the interest rate imputed. Show book value of the note at the start of each year, interest for each year, amount reducing or increasing book value each year, and book value at the end of the year.

**27.** *Finding implicit interest rates; constructing amortization schedules.* Berman Company purchased a plot of land for possible future development. The land had fair market value of $86,000. Berman Company gave a 3-year interest-bearing note. The note had face value of $100,000 and provided for interest at a stated rate of 8 percent — payments of $8,000 were due at the end of each of 3 years, the last payment coinciding with the maturity of the note's face value of $100,000.

    **a.** What is the interest rate implicit in the note accurate to the nearest tenth of one percent?

    **b.** Construct an amortization schedule for the note for each year, showing the book value of the note at the start of the year, interest for the year, payment for the year, amount reducing or increasing the book value of the note for each payment, and the book value of the note at the end of each year. Use the interest rate found in part **a**. See Exhibit 10.2 for an example of an amortization schedule.

28. The terms of sale "2/10, net/30" mean that a discount of 2 percent from gross invoice price can be taken if the invoice is paid within 10 days and that otherwise the full amount is due within 30 days.
    a.  Write an expression for the implied annual rate of interest being offered, if the entire discount is viewed as being interest for funds received sooner rather than later. (Note that 98 percent of the gross invoice price is being borrowed for 20 days.)
    b.  The tables at the back of the book do not permit the exact evaluation of the expression derived in part **a**. The rate of interest implied is 44.59 percent per year. Use the tables to convince yourself that this astounding (to some) answer must be close to correct.

## Problems and Cases

29. *Present value of a perpetuity.* An oil-drilling company figures that $30,000 must be spent for an initial supply of drill bits and that $10,000 must be spent every month to replace the worn-out bits. What is the present value of the cost of the bits if the company plans to be in business indefinitely and discounts payments at 1 percent per month?

*The following problems involve using future value and present value techniques to solve a variety of realistic problems. No hints as to the specific calculation are given with the problems.*

30. If you promise to leave $35,000 on deposit at the Dime Savings Bank for 4 years, the bank will give you a new car today and your $35,000 back at the end of 4 years. How much are you paying today for the car, in effect, if the bank pays other customers 8 percent interest compounded quarterly (2 percent paid four times per year)?

31. When Mr. Shafer died, his estate after taxes amounted to $300,000. His will provided that Mrs. Shafer would receive $24,000 per year starting immediately from the principal of the estate and that the balance of the principal would pass to the Shafers' children upon Mrs. Shafer's death. The state law governing this estate provided for a *dower* option. If Mrs. Shafer elects the dower option, she renounces the will and can have one-third of the estate in cash now. The remainder will then pass immediately to their children. Mrs. Shafer wants to maximize the present value of her bequest. Should she take the annuity or elect the dower option if she will receive five payments and discounts payments at
    a.  8 percent per year?
    b.  12 percent per year?

32. Mrs. Heileman occasionally drinks beer. She consumes one case in 20 weeks. She can buy beer in disposable bottles for $25.20 per case or for $24.00 a case of returnable bottles if a $3.00 refundable deposit is paid at the time of purchase. If her discount rate is $\frac{1}{4}$ percent per week, how much in present value

dollars does she save by buying the returnables and thereby losing the use of the $3.00 deposit for 20 weeks?

33. When the General Electric Company first introduced the Lucalox ceramic, screw-in light bulb, the bulb cost three-and-one-half times as much as an ordinary bulb but lasted five times as long. An ordinary bulb cost $.50 and lasted about 8 months. If a firm has a discount rate of 12 percent compounded three times a year, how much would it save in present value dollars by using one Lucalox bulb?

34. The Roberts Dairy Company switched from delivery trucks with regular gasoline engines to ones with diesel engines. The diesel trucks cost $2,000 more than the ordinary gasoline trucks, but $600 per year less to operate. Assume that the operating costs are saved at the end of each month. If Roberts Dairy uses a discount rate of 1 percent per month, approximately how many months, at a minimum, must the diesel trucks remain in service for the switch to save money?

35. On January 1, Year 1, Outergarments, Inc., opened a new textile plant for the production of synthetic fabrics. The plant is on leased land; 20 years remain on the nonrenewable lease.

    The cost of the plant was $2 million. Net cash flow to be derived from the project is estimated to be $300,000 per year. The company does not normally invest in such projects unless the anticipated yield is at least 12 percent.

    On December 31, Year 1, the company finds cash flows from the plant to be $280,000 for the year. On the same day, farm experts predict cotton production to be unusually low for the next 2 years. Outergarments estimates the resulting increase in demand for synthetic fabrics to boost cash flows to $350,000 for each of the next 2 years. Subsequent years' estimates remain unchanged. Ignore tax considerations.

    a. Calculate the present value of the future expected cash flows from the plant when it was opened.
    b. What is the present value of the plant on January 1, Year 2, immediately after the reestimation of future incomes?
    c. On January 2, Year 2, the day following the cotton production news release, Overalls Company announces plans to build a synthetic fabrics plant to be opened in 3 years. Outergarments, Inc., keeps its Year 2 to Year 4 estimates, but reduces the estimated annual cash flows for subsequent years to $200,000. What is the value of Outergarments' present plant on January 1, Year 2, after the new projections?
    d. On January 2, Year 2, an investor contacts Outergarments about purchasing a 20 percent share of the plant. If the investor expects to earn at least a 12 percent annual return on the investment, what is the maximum amount that the investor can pay? Assume that the investor and Outergarments, Inc., both know all relevant information and use the same estimates of annual cash flows.

36. *Finding implicit interest rates (truth-in-lending laws reduce the type of deception suggested by this problem).* The Friendly Loan Company advertises that it is willing to lend money for 5 years at the low rate of 8 percent per year. A

potential borrower discovers that a 5-year, $10,000 loan requires that the 8 percent interest be paid in advance, with interest deducted from the loan proceeds. The borrower will collect $6,000 [= $10,000 − (5 × .08 × $10,000)] cash and must repay the "$10,000" loan in five annual installments of $2,000, one each at the end of the next 5 years.

Compute the effective interest rate implied by these loan terms.

**37.** *Deriving net present value of cash flows for decision to dispose of asset.* The Wisher Washer Company purchased a made-to-order machine tool for grinding washing machine parts. The machine cost $100,000 and was installed yesterday. Today, a machine tool is offered that will do exactly the same work but costs only $50,000. Assume that the discount rate is 12 percent, that both machines will last for 5 years, that both machines will be depreciated on a straight-line basis for tax purposes with no salvage value, that the income tax rate is and will continue to be 40 percent, and that Wisher Washer Company earns sufficient income that any loss from disposing of or depreciating the "old" machine can be used to offset other taxable income. Ignore the investment credit.

How much, at a minimum, must the "old" machine fetch on resale at this time to make purchasing the new machine worthwhile?

**38.** *Computation of present value of cash flows; untaxed acquisition, no change in tax basis of assets.* The balance sheet of Lynch Company shows assets of $100,000, net, and owners' equity of $100,000. The assets are all depreciable assets with remaining lives of 20 years. The income statement for the year shows revenues of $700,000, depreciation of $50,000 (= $1,000,000/20 years), no other expenses, income taxes of $260,000 (40 percent of pretax income of $650,000), and net income of $390,000.

Bages Company is considering purchasing all of the stock of Lynch Company. It is willing to pay an amount equal to the present value of the cash flows from operations for the next 20 years discounted at a rate of 10 percent per year.

The transaction will not be taxable; that is, after the purchase, the tax basis of the assets of Lynch Company will remain unchanged, so that depreciation charges will remain at $50,000 per year and income taxes will remain at $260,000 per year. Revenues will be $700,000 per year for the next 20 years.
**a.** Compute the annual cash flows produced by Lynch Company.
**b.** Compute the maximum amount Bages Company should be willing to pay.

**39.** *Computation of present value of cash flows; taxable acquisition, changing tax basis of assets.* Refer to the data in the preceding problem. Assume now that the acquisition is taxable, so that the tax basis of the assets acquired changes after the purchase. If the purchase price is $V, then depreciation charges will be $V/20 per year for 20 years. Income taxes will be 40 percent of pretax income.

What is the maximum Bages Company should be willing to pay for Lynch Company?

**40.** *(Adapted from a problem by S. Zeff.)* Lexie Colleton is the chief financial officer of Rigazzi, and one of her duties is to give advice on investment projects. Today's date is December 31, Year 0. Colleton requires that, to be acceptable, new investments provide a positive net present value when cash flows are discounted at 12 percent per year.

A proposed investment is the purchase of an automatic gonculator, which involves an initial cash disbursement on December 31, Year 0. The useful life of the machine is through Year 9. The machine could be sold for cash of $30,000 on December 31, Year 9. Commercial production is expected to begin on December 31, Year 1.

The machine will be depreciated on a straight-line basis. Ignore income taxes.

During Year 1, the break-in year, the company will perform test runs in order to put the machine in proper working order. It is expected that the total cash outlay for this purpose will be $20,000, incurred at the end of Year 1.

It is expected that the cash disbursements for regular maintenance will be $60,000 at the end of each of Years 2 through 5, inclusive, and $100,000 at the end of each of the Years 6 through 8, inclusive.

Cash receipts from the sale of the product that the machine turns out are expected to be $130,000 at the end of each year from Year 2 through Year 9, inclusive.

a. What is the maximum price that Rigazzi can pay for the automatic gonculator on December 31, Year 0, and still earn a positive net present value of cash flows?

b. Independent of your answer to part **a**, assume the purchase price is $250,000, that Rigazzi will pay for the machine in four equal annual installments starting December 31, Year 1, and an implicit interest rate of 10 percent per year on the installment note. What is the amount of each payment?

# Compound Interest, Annuity, and Bond Tables

# Table 1
Future Value of $1

$$F_n = P(1 + r)^n$$

$r$ = interest rate; $n$ = number of periods until valuation; $P$ = $1

| Periods = n | ½% | 1% | 1½% | 2% | 3% | 4% | 5% | 6% | 7% | 8% | 10% | 12% | 15% | 20% | 25% |
|---|---|---|---|---|---|---|---|---|---|---|---|---|---|---|---|
| 1 | 1.00500 | 1.01000 | 1.01500 | 1.02000 | 1.03000 | 1.04000 | 1.05000 | 1.06000 | 1.07000 | 1.08000 | 1.10000 | 1.12000 | 1.15000 | 1.20000 | 1.25000 |
| 2 | 1.01003 | 1.02010 | 1.03023 | 1.04040 | 1.06090 | 1.08160 | 1.10250 | 1.12360 | 1.14490 | 1.16640 | 1.21000 | 1.25440 | 1.32250 | 1.44000 | 1.56250 |
| 3 | 1.01508 | 1.03030 | 1.04568 | 1.06121 | 1.09273 | 1.12486 | 1.15763 | 1.19102 | 1.22504 | 1.25971 | 1.33100 | 1.40493 | 1.52088 | 1.72800 | 1.95313 |
| 4 | 1.02015 | 1.04060 | 1.06136 | 1.08243 | 1.12551 | 1.16986 | 1.21551 | 1.26248 | 1.31080 | 1.36049 | 1.46410 | 1.57352 | 1.74901 | 2.07360 | 2.44141 |
| 5 | 1.02525 | 1.05101 | 1.07728 | 1.10408 | 1.15927 | 1.21665 | 1.27628 | 1.33823 | 1.40255 | 1.46933 | 1.61051 | 1.76234 | 2.01136 | 2.48832 | 3.05176 |
| 6 | 1.03038 | 1.06152 | 1.09344 | 1.12616 | 1.19405 | 1.26532 | 1.34010 | 1.41852 | 1.50073 | 1.58687 | 1.77156 | 1.97382 | 2.31306 | 2.98598 | 3.81470 |
| 7 | 1.03553 | 1.07214 | 1.10984 | 1.14869 | 1.22987 | 1.31593 | 1.40710 | 1.50363 | 1.60578 | 1.71382 | 1.94872 | 2.21068 | 2.66002 | 3.58318 | 4.76837 |
| 8 | 1.04071 | 1.08286 | 1.12649 | 1.17166 | 1.26677 | 1.36857 | 1.47746 | 1.59385 | 1.71819 | 1.85093 | 2.14359 | 2.47596 | 3.05902 | 4.29982 | 5.96046 |
| 9 | 1.04591 | 1.09369 | 1.14339 | 1.19509 | 1.30477 | 1.42331 | 1.55133 | 1.68948 | 1.83846 | 1.99900 | 2.35795 | 2.77308 | 3.51788 | 5.15978 | 7.45058 |
| 10 | 1.05114 | 1.10462 | 1.16054 | 1.21899 | 1.34392 | 1.48024 | 1.62889 | 1.79085 | 1.96715 | 2.15892 | 2.59374 | 3.10585 | 4.04556 | 6.19174 | 9.31323 |
| 11 | 1.05640 | 1.11567 | 1.17795 | 1.24337 | 1.38423 | 1.53945 | 1.71034 | 1.89830 | 2.10485 | 2.33164 | 2.85312 | 3.47855 | 4.65239 | 7.43008 | 11.64153 |
| 12 | 1.06168 | 1.12683 | 1.19562 | 1.26824 | 1.42576 | 1.60103 | 1.79586 | 2.01220 | 2.25219 | 2.51817 | 3.13843 | 3.89598 | 5.35025 | 8.91610 | 14.55192 |
| 13 | 1.06699 | 1.13809 | 1.21355 | 1.29361 | 1.46853 | 1.66507 | 1.88565 | 2.13293 | 2.40985 | 2.71962 | 3.45227 | 4.36349 | 6.15279 | 10.69932 | 18.18989 |
| 14 | 1.07232 | 1.14947 | 1.23176 | 1.31948 | 1.51259 | 1.73168 | 1.97993 | 2.26090 | 2.57853 | 2.93719 | 3.79750 | 4.88711 | 7.07571 | 12.83918 | 22.73737 |
| 15 | 1.07768 | 1.16097 | 1.25023 | 1.34587 | 1.55797 | 1.80094 | 2.07893 | 2.39656 | 2.75903 | 3.17217 | 4.17725 | 5.47357 | 8.13706 | 15.40702 | 28.42171 |
| 16 | 1.08307 | 1.17258 | 1.26899 | 1.37279 | 1.60471 | 1.87298 | 2.18287 | 2.54035 | 2.95216 | 3.42594 | 4.59497 | 6.13039 | 9.35762 | 18.48843 | 35.52714 |
| 17 | 1.08849 | 1.18430 | 1.28802 | 1.40024 | 1.65285 | 1.94790 | 2.29202 | 2.69277 | 3.15882 | 3.70002 | 5.05447 | 6.86604 | 10.76126 | 22.18611 | 44.40892 |
| 18 | 1.09393 | 1.19615 | 1.30734 | 1.42825 | 1.70243 | 2.02582 | 2.40662 | 2.85434 | 3.37993 | 3.99602 | 5.55992 | 7.68997 | 12.37545 | 26.62333 | 55.51115 |
| 19 | 1.09940 | 1.20811 | 1.32695 | 1.45681 | 1.75351 | 2.10685 | 2.52695 | 3.02560 | 3.61653 | 4.31570 | 6.11591 | 8.61276 | 14.23177 | 31.94800 | 69.38894 |
| 20 | 1.10490 | 1.22019 | 1.34686 | 1.48595 | 1.80611 | 2.19112 | 2.65330 | 3.20714 | 3.86968 | 4.66096 | 6.72750 | 9.64629 | 16.36654 | 38.33760 | 86.73617 |
| 22 | 1.11597 | 1.24472 | 1.38756 | 1.54598 | 1.91610 | 2.36992 | 2.92526 | 3.60354 | 4.43040 | 5.43654 | 8.14027 | 12.10031 | 21.64475 | 55.20614 | 135.5253 |
| 24 | 1.12716 | 1.26973 | 1.42950 | 1.60844 | 2.03279 | 2.56330 | 3.22510 | 4.04893 | 5.07237 | 6.34118 | 9.84973 | 15.17863 | 28.62518 | 79.49685 | 211.7582 |
| 26 | 1.13846 | 1.29526 | 1.47271 | 1.67342 | 2.15659 | 2.77247 | 3.55567 | 4.54938 | 5.80735 | 7.39635 | 11.91818 | 19.04007 | 37.85680 | 114.4755 | 330.8722 |
| 28 | 1.14987 | 1.32129 | 1.51722 | 1.74102 | 2.28793 | 2.99870 | 3.92013 | 5.11169 | 6.64884 | 8.62711 | 14.42099 | 23.88387 | 50.06561 | 164.8447 | 516.9879 |
| 30 | 1.16140 | 1.34785 | 1.56308 | 1.81136 | 2.42726 | 3.24340 | 4.32194 | 5.74349 | 7.61226 | 10.06266 | 17.44940 | 29.95992 | 66.21177 | 237.3763 | 807.7936 |
| 32 | 1.17304 | 1.37494 | 1.61032 | 1.88454 | 2.57508 | 3.50806 | 4.76494 | 6.45339 | 8.71527 | 11.73708 | 21.11378 | 37.58173 | 87.56507 | 341.8219 | 1262.177 |
| 34 | 1.18480 | 1.40258 | 1.65900 | 1.96068 | 2.73191 | 3.79432 | 5.25335 | 7.25103 | 9.97811 | 13.69013 | 25.54767 | 47.14252 | 115.80480 | 492.2235 | 1972.152 |
| 36 | 1.19668 | 1.43077 | 1.70914 | 2.03989 | 2.89828 | 4.10393 | 5.79182 | 8.14725 | 11.42394 | 15.96817 | 30.91268 | 59.13557 | 153.15185 | 708.8019 | 3081.488 |
| 38 | 1.20868 | 1.45953 | 1.76080 | 2.12230 | 3.07478 | 4.43881 | 6.38548 | 9.15425 | 13.07927 | 18.62528 | 37.40434 | 74.17966 | 202.54332 | 1020.675 | 4814.825 |
| 40 | 1.22079 | 1.48886 | 1.81402 | 2.20804 | 3.26204 | 4.80102 | 7.03999 | 10.28572 | 14.97446 | 21.72452 | 45.25926 | 93.05097 | 267.86355 | 1469.772 | 7523.164 |
| 45 | 1.25162 | 1.56481 | 1.95421 | 2.43785 | 3.78160 | 5.84118 | 8.98501 | 13.76461 | 21.00245 | 31.92045 | 72.89048 | 163.9876 | 538.76927 | 3657.262 | 22958.87 |
| 50 | 1.28323 | 1.64463 | 2.10524 | 2.69159 | 4.38391 | 7.10668 | 11.46740 | 18.42015 | 29.45703 | 46.90161 | 117.3909 | 289.0022 | 1083.65744 | 9100.438 | 70064.92 |
| 100 | 1.64667 | 2.70481 | 4.43205 | 7.24465 | 19.21863 | 50.50495 | 131.5013 | 339.3021 | 867.7163 | 2199.761 | 13780.61 | 83522.27 | $117 \times 10^4$ | $828 \times 10^5$ | $491 \times 10^7$ |

# Table 2
## Present Value of $1

$$P = F_n(1 + r)^{-n}$$

$r$ = discount rate; $n$ = number of periods until payment; $P = \$1$

| Periods = $n$ | ½% | 1% | 1½% | 2% | 3% | 4% | 5% | 6% | 7% | 8% | 10% | 12% | 15% | 20% | 25% |
|---|---|---|---|---|---|---|---|---|---|---|---|---|---|---|---|
| 1 | .99502 | .99010 | .98522 | .98039 | .97087 | .96154 | .95238 | .94340 | .93458 | .92593 | .90909 | .89286 | .86957 | .83333 | .80000 |
| 2 | .99007 | .98030 | .97066 | .96117 | .94260 | .92456 | .90703 | .89000 | .87344 | .85734 | .82645 | .79719 | .75614 | .69444 | .64000 |
| 3 | .98515 | .97059 | .95632 | .94232 | .91514 | .88900 | .86384 | .83962 | .81630 | .79383 | .75131 | .71178 | .65752 | .57870 | .51200 |
| 4 | .98025 | .96098 | .94218 | .92385 | .88849 | .85480 | .82270 | .79209 | .76290 | .73503 | .68301 | .63552 | .57175 | .48225 | .40960 |
| 5 | .97537 | .95147 | .92826 | .90573 | .86261 | .82193 | .78353 | .74726 | .71299 | .68058 | .62092 | .56743 | .49718 | .40188 | .32768 |
| 6 | .97052 | .94205 | .91454 | .88797 | .83748 | .79031 | .74622 | .70496 | .66634 | .63017 | .56447 | .50663 | .43233 | .33490 | .26214 |
| 7 | .96569 | .93272 | .90103 | .87056 | .81309 | .75992 | .71068 | .66506 | .62275 | .58349 | .51316 | .45235 | .37594 | .27908 | .20972 |
| 8 | .96089 | .92348 | .88771 | .85349 | .78941 | .73069 | .67684 | .62741 | .58201 | .54027 | .46651 | .40388 | .32690 | .23257 | .16777 |
| 9 | .95610 | .91434 | .87459 | .83676 | .76642 | .70259 | .64461 | .59190 | .54393 | .50025 | .42410 | .36061 | .28426 | .19381 | .13422 |
| 10 | .95135 | .90529 | .86167 | .82035 | .74409 | .67556 | .61391 | .55839 | .50835 | .46319 | .38554 | .32197 | .24718 | .16151 | .10737 |
| 11 | .94661 | .89632 | .84893 | .80426 | .72242 | .64958 | .58468 | .52679 | .47509 | .42888 | .35049 | .28748 | .21494 | .13459 | .08590 |
| 12 | .94191 | .88745 | .83639 | .78849 | .70138 | .62460 | .55684 | .49697 | .44401 | .39711 | .31863 | .25668 | .18691 | .11216 | .06872 |
| 13 | .93722 | .87866 | .82403 | .77303 | .68095 | .60057 | .53032 | .46884 | .41496 | .36770 | .28966 | .22917 | .16253 | .09346 | .05498 |
| 14 | .93256 | .86996 | .81185 | .75788 | .66112 | .57748 | .50507 | .44230 | .38782 | .34046 | .26333 | .20462 | .14133 | .07789 | .04398 |
| 15 | .92792 | .86135 | .79985 | .74301 | .64186 | .55526 | .48102 | .41727 | .36245 | .31524 | .23939 | .18270 | .12289 | .06491 | .03518 |
| 16 | .92330 | .85282 | .78803 | .72845 | .62317 | .53391 | .45811 | .39365 | .33873 | .29189 | .21763 | .16312 | .10686 | .05409 | .02815 |
| 17 | .91871 | .84438 | .77639 | .71416 | .60502 | .51337 | .43630 | .37136 | .31657 | .27027 | .19784 | .14564 | .09293 | .04507 | .02252 |
| 18 | .91414 | .83602 | .76491 | .70016 | .58739 | .49363 | .41552 | .35034 | .29586 | .25025 | .17986 | .13004 | .08081 | .03756 | .01801 |
| 19 | .90959 | .82774 | .75361 | .68643 | .57029 | .47464 | .39573 | .33051 | .27651 | .23171 | .16351 | .11611 | .07027 | .03130 | .01441 |
| 20 | .90506 | .81954 | .74247 | .67297 | .55368 | .45639 | .37689 | .31180 | .25842 | .21455 | .14864 | .10367 | .06110 | .02608 | .01153 |
| 22 | .89608 | .80340 | .72069 | .64684 | .52189 | .42196 | .34185 | .27751 | .22571 | .18394 | .12285 | .08264 | .04620 | .01811 | .00738 |
| 24 | .88719 | .78757 | .69954 | .62172 | .49193 | .39012 | .31007 | .24698 | .19715 | .15770 | .10153 | .06588 | .03493 | .01258 | .00472 |
| 26 | .87838 | .77205 | .67902 | .59758 | .46369 | .36069 | .28124 | .21981 | .17220 | .13520 | .08391 | .05252 | .02642 | .00874 | .00302 |
| 28 | .86966 | .75684 | .65910 | .57437 | .43708 | .33348 | .25509 | .19563 | .15040 | .11591 | .06934 | .04187 | .01997 | .00607 | .00193 |
| 30 | .86103 | .74192 | .63976 | .55207 | .41199 | .30832 | .23138 | .17411 | .13137 | .09938 | .05731 | .03338 | .01510 | .00421 | .00124 |
| 32 | .85248 | .72730 | .62099 | .53063 | .38834 | .28506 | .20987 | .15496 | .11474 | .08520 | .04736 | .02661 | .01142 | .00293 | .00079 |
| 34 | .84402 | .71297 | .60277 | .51003 | .36604 | .26355 | .19035 | .13791 | .10022 | .07305 | .03914 | .02121 | .00864 | .00203 | .00051 |
| 36 | .83564 | .69892 | .58509 | .49022 | .34503 | .24367 | .17266 | .12274 | .08754 | .06262 | .03235 | .01691 | .00653 | .00141 | .00032 |
| 38 | .82735 | .68515 | .56792 | .47119 | .32523 | .22529 | .15661 | .10924 | .07646 | .05369 | .02673 | .01348 | .00494 | .00098 | .00021 |
| 40 | .81914 | .67165 | .55126 | .45289 | .30656 | .20829 | .14205 | .09722 | .06678 | .04603 | .02209 | .01075 | .00373 | .00068 | .00013 |
| 45 | .79896 | .63905 | .51171 | .41020 | .26444 | .17120 | .11130 | .07265 | .04761 | .03133 | .01372 | .00610 | .00186 | .00027 | .00004 |
| 50 | .77929 | .60804 | .47500 | .37153 | .22811 | .14071 | .08720 | .05429 | .03395 | .02132 | .00852 | .00346 | .00092 | .00011 | .00001 |
| 100 | .60729 | .36971 | .22563 | .13803 | .05203 | .01980 | .00760 | .00295 | .00115 | .00045 | .00007 | .00001 | .00000 | .00000 | .00000 |

703

**Table 3**
Future Value of Annuity of $1 in Arrears

$$F = \frac{(1+r)^n - 1}{r}$$

$r$ = interest rate; $n$ = number of payments

| No. of Payments = n | ½% | 1% | 1½% | 2% | 3% | 4% | 5% | 6% | 7% | 8% | 10% | 12% | 15% | 20% | 25% |
|---|---|---|---|---|---|---|---|---|---|---|---|---|---|---|---|
| 1 | 1.00000 | 1.00000 | 1.00000 | 1.00000 | 1.00000 | 1.00000 | 1.00000 | 1.00000 | 1.00000 | 1.00000 | 1.00000 | 1.00000 | 1.00000 | 1.00000 | 1.00000 |
| 2 | 2.00500 | 2.01000 | 2.01500 | 2.02000 | 2.03000 | 2.04000 | 2.05000 | 2.06000 | 2.07000 | 2.08000 | 2.10000 | 2.12000 | 2.15000 | 2.20000 | 2.25000 |
| 3 | 3.01503 | 3.03010 | 3.04523 | 3.06040 | 3.09090 | 3.12160 | 3.15250 | 3.18360 | 3.21490 | 3.24640 | 3.31000 | 3.37440 | 3.47250 | 3.64000 | 3.81250 |
| 4 | 4.03010 | 4.06040 | 4.09090 | 4.12161 | 4.18363 | 4.24646 | 4.31013 | 4.37462 | 4.43994 | 4.50611 | 4.64100 | 4.77933 | 4.99338 | 5.36800 | 5.76563 |
| 5 | 5.05025 | 5.10101 | 5.15227 | 5.20404 | 5.30914 | 5.41632 | 5.52563 | 5.63709 | 5.75074 | 5.86660 | 6.10510 | 6.35285 | 6.74238 | 7.44160 | 8.20703 |
| 6 | 6.07550 | 6.15202 | 6.22955 | 6.30812 | 6.46841 | 6.63298 | 6.80191 | 6.97532 | 7.15329 | 7.33593 | 7.71561 | 8.11519 | 8.75374 | 9.92992 | 11.25879 |
| 7 | 7.10588 | 7.21354 | 7.32299 | 7.43428 | 7.66246 | 7.89829 | 8.14201 | 8.39384 | 8.65402 | 8.92280 | 9.48717 | 10.08901 | 11.06680 | 12.91590 | 15.07349 |
| 8 | 8.14141 | 8.28567 | 8.43284 | 8.58297 | 8.89234 | 9.21423 | 9.54911 | 9.89747 | 10.25980 | 10.63663 | 11.43589 | 12.29969 | 13.72682 | 16.49908 | 19.84186 |
| 9 | 9.18212 | 9.36853 | 9.55933 | 9.75463 | 10.15911 | 10.58280 | 11.02656 | 11.49132 | 11.97799 | 12.48756 | 13.57948 | 14.77566 | 16.78584 | 20.79890 | 25.80232 |
| 10 | 10.22803 | 10.46221 | 10.70272 | 10.94972 | 11.46388 | 12.00611 | 12.57789 | 13.18079 | 13.81645 | 14.48656 | 15.93742 | 17.54874 | 20.30372 | 25.95868 | 33.25290 |
| 11 | 11.27917 | 11.56683 | 11.86326 | 12.16872 | 12.80780 | 13.48635 | 14.20679 | 14.97164 | 15.78360 | 16.64549 | 18.53117 | 20.65458 | 24.34928 | 32.15042 | 42.56613 |
| 12 | 12.33556 | 12.68250 | 13.04121 | 13.41209 | 14.19203 | 15.02581 | 15.91713 | 16.86994 | 17.88845 | 18.97713 | 21.38428 | 24.13313 | 29.00167 | 39.58050 | 54.20766 |
| 13 | 13.39724 | 13.80933 | 14.23683 | 14.68033 | 15.61779 | 16.62684 | 17.71298 | 18.88214 | 20.14064 | 21.49530 | 24.52271 | 28.02911 | 34.35192 | 48.49660 | 68.75958 |
| 14 | 14.46423 | 14.94742 | 15.45038 | 15.97394 | 17.08632 | 18.29191 | 19.59863 | 21.01507 | 22.55049 | 24.21492 | 27.97498 | 32.39260 | 40.50471 | 59.19592 | 86.94947 |
| 15 | 15.53655 | 16.09690 | 16.68214 | 17.29342 | 18.59891 | 20.02359 | 21.57856 | 23.27597 | 25.12902 | 27.15211 | 31.72248 | 37.27971 | 47.58041 | 72.03511 | 109.6868 |
| 16 | 16.61423 | 17.25786 | 17.93237 | 18.63929 | 20.15688 | 21.82453 | 23.65749 | 25.67253 | 27.88805 | 30.32428 | 35.94973 | 42.75328 | 55.71747 | 87.44213 | 138.1085 |
| 17 | 17.69730 | 18.43044 | 19.20136 | 20.01207 | 21.76159 | 23.69751 | 25.84037 | 28.21288 | 30.84022 | 33.75023 | 40.54470 | 48.88367 | 65.07509 | 105.9306 | 173.6357 |
| 18 | 18.78579 | 19.61475 | 20.48938 | 21.41231 | 23.41444 | 25.64541 | 28.13238 | 30.90565 | 33.99903 | 37.45024 | 45.59917 | 55.74971 | 75.83636 | 128.1167 | 218.0446 |
| 19 | 19.87972 | 20.81090 | 21.79672 | 22.84056 | 25.11687 | 27.67123 | 30.53900 | 33.75999 | 37.37896 | 41.44626 | 51.15909 | 63.43968 | 88.21181 | 154.7400 | 273.5558 |
| 20 | 20.97912 | 22.01900 | 23.12367 | 24.29737 | 26.87037 | 29.77808 | 33.06595 | 36.78559 | 40.99549 | 45.76196 | 57.27500 | 72.05244 | 102.44358 | 186.6880 | 342.9447 |
| 22 | 23.19443 | 24.47159 | 25.83758 | 27.29898 | 30.53678 | 34.24797 | 38.50521 | 43.39229 | 49.00574 | 55.45676 | 71.40275 | 92.50258 | 137.63164 | 271.0307 | 538.1011 |
| 24 | 25.43196 | 26.97346 | 28.63352 | 30.42186 | 34.42647 | 39.08260 | 44.50200 | 50.81558 | 58.17667 | 66.76476 | 88.49733 | 118.1552 | 184.16784 | 392.4842 | 843.0329 |
| 26 | 27.69191 | 29.52563 | 31.51397 | 33.67091 | 38.55304 | 44.31174 | 51.11345 | 59.15638 | 68.67647 | 79.95442 | 109.1818 | 150.3339 | 245.71197 | 567.3773 | 1319.489 |
| 28 | 29.97452 | 32.12910 | 34.48148 | 37.05121 | 42.93092 | 49.96758 | 58.40258 | 68.52811 | 80.69769 | 95.33883 | 134.2099 | 190.6989 | 327.10408 | 819.2233 | 2063.952 |
| 30 | 32.28002 | 34.78489 | 37.53868 | 40.56808 | 47.57542 | 56.08494 | 66.43885 | 79.05819 | 94.46079 | 113.2832 | 164.4940 | 241.3327 | 434.74515 | 1181.881 | 3227.174 |
| 32 | 34.60862 | 37.49407 | 40.68829 | 44.22703 | 52.50276 | 62.70147 | 75.29883 | 90.88978 | 110.2181 | 134.2135 | 201.1378 | 304.8477 | 577.10046 | 1704.109 | 5044.710 |
| 34 | 36.96058 | 40.25770 | 43.93309 | 48.03380 | 57.73018 | 69.85791 | 85.06696 | 104.1838 | 128.2588 | 158.6267 | 245.4767 | 384.5210 | 765.36535 | 2456.118 | 7884.609 |
| 36 | 39.33610 | 43.07688 | 47.27597 | 51.99437 | 63.27594 | 77.59831 | 95.83632 | 119.1209 | 148.9135 | 187.1022 | 299.1268 | 484.4631 | 1014.34568 | 3539.009 | 12321.95 |
| 38 | 41.73545 | 45.95272 | 50.71989 | 56.11494 | 69.15945 | 85.97034 | 107.7095 | 135.9042 | 172.5610 | 220.3159 | 364.0434 | 609.8305 | 1343.62216 | 5098.373 | 19255.30 |
| 40 | 44.15885 | 48.88637 | 54.26789 | 60.40198 | 75.40126 | 95.02552 | 120.7998 | 154.7620 | 199.6351 | 259.0565 | 442.5926 | 767.0914 | 1779.09031 | 7343.858 | 30088.66 |
| 45 | 50.32416 | 56.48107 | 63.61420 | 71.89271 | 92.71986 | 121.0294 | 159.7002 | 212.7435 | 285.7493 | 386.5056 | 718.9048 | 1358.230 | 3585.12846 | 18281.31 | 91831.50 |
| 50 | 56.64516 | 64.46318 | 73.68283 | 84.57940 | 112.7969 | 152.6671 | 209.3480 | 290.3359 | 406.5289 | 573.7702 | 1163.909 | 2400.018 | 7217.71628 | 45497.19 | 280255.7 |
| 100 | 129.33370 | 170.4814 | 228.8030 | 312.2323 | 607.2877 | 1237.624 | 2610.025 | 5638.368 | 12381.66 | 27484.52 | 137796.1 | 696010.5 | $783 \times 10^4$ | $414 \times 10^6$ | $196 \times 10^8$ |

*Note:* To convert from this table to values of an annuity in advance, determine the annuity in arrears above for one more period and subtract 1.00000.

# Table 4
Present Value of an Annuity of $1 in Arrears

$$P_A = \frac{1 - (1 + r)^{-n}}{r}$$

$r$ = discount rate; $n$ = number of payments

| No. of Payments = n | ½% | 1% | 1½% | 2% | 3% | 4% | 5% | 6% | 7% | 8% | 10% | 12% | 15% | 20% | 25% |
|---|---|---|---|---|---|---|---|---|---|---|---|---|---|---|---|
| 1 | .99502 | .99010 | .98522 | .98039 | .97087 | .96154 | .95238 | .94340 | .93458 | .92593 | .90909 | .89286 | .86957 | .83333 | .80000 |
| 2 | 1.98510 | 1.97040 | 1.95588 | 1.94156 | 1.91347 | 1.88609 | 1.85941 | 1.83339 | 1.80802 | 1.78326 | 1.73554 | 1.69005 | 1.62571 | 1.52778 | 1.44000 |
| 3 | 2.97025 | 2.94099 | 2.91220 | 2.88388 | 2.82861 | 2.77509 | 2.72325 | 2.67301 | 2.62432 | 2.57710 | 2.48685 | 2.40183 | 2.28323 | 2.10648 | 1.95200 |
| 4 | 3.95050 | 3.90197 | 3.85438 | 3.80773 | 3.71710 | 3.62990 | 3.54595 | 3.46511 | 3.38721 | 3.31213 | 3.16987 | 3.03735 | 2.85498 | 2.58873 | 2.36160 |
| 5 | 4.92587 | 4.85343 | 4.78264 | 4.71346 | 4.57971 | 4.45182 | 4.32948 | 4.21236 | 4.10020 | 3.99271 | 3.79079 | 3.60478 | 3.35216 | 2.99061 | 2.68928 |
| 6 | 5.89638 | 5.79548 | 5.69719 | 5.60143 | 5.41719 | 5.24212 | 5.07569 | 4.91732 | 4.76654 | 4.62288 | 4.35526 | 4.11141 | 3.78448 | 3.32551 | 2.95142 |
| 7 | 6.86207 | 6.72819 | 6.59821 | 6.47199 | 6.23028 | 6.00205 | 5.78637 | 5.58238 | 5.38929 | 5.20637 | 4.86842 | 4.56376 | 4.16042 | 3.60459 | 3.16114 |
| 8 | 7.82296 | 7.65168 | 7.48593 | 7.32548 | 7.01969 | 6.73274 | 6.46321 | 6.20979 | 5.97130 | 5.74664 | 5.33493 | 4.96764 | 4.48732 | 3.83716 | 3.32891 |
| 9 | 8.77906 | 8.56602 | 8.36052 | 8.16224 | 7.78611 | 7.43533 | 7.10782 | 6.80169 | 6.51523 | 6.24689 | 5.75902 | 5.32825 | 4.77158 | 4.03097 | 3.46313 |
| 10 | 9.73041 | 9.47130 | 9.22218 | 8.98259 | 8.53020 | 8.11090 | 7.72173 | 7.36009 | 7.02358 | 6.71008 | 6.14457 | 5.65022 | 5.01877 | 4.19247 | 3.57050 |
| 11 | 10.67703 | 10.36763 | 10.07112 | 9.78685 | 9.25262 | 8.76048 | 8.30641 | 7.88687 | 7.49867 | 7.13896 | 6.49506 | 5.93770 | 5.23371 | 4.32706 | 3.65640 |
| 12 | 11.61893 | 11.25508 | 10.90751 | 10.57534 | 9.95400 | 9.38507 | 8.86325 | 8.38384 | 7.94269 | 7.53608 | 6.81369 | 6.19437 | 5.42062 | 4.43922 | 3.72512 |
| 13 | 12.55615 | 12.13374 | 11.73153 | 11.34837 | 10.63496 | 9.98565 | 9.39357 | 8.85268 | 8.35765 | 7.90378 | 7.10336 | 6.42355 | 5.58315 | 4.53268 | 3.78010 |
| 14 | 13.48871 | 13.00370 | 12.54338 | 12.10625 | 11.29607 | 10.56312 | 9.89864 | 9.29498 | 8.74547 | 8.24424 | 7.36669 | 6.62817 | 5.72448 | 4.61057 | 3.82408 |
| 15 | 14.41662 | 13.86505 | 13.34323 | 12.84926 | 11.93794 | 11.11839 | 10.37966 | 9.71225 | 9.10791 | 8.55948 | 7.60608 | 6.81086 | 5.84737 | 4.67547 | 3.85926 |
| 16 | 15.33993 | 14.71787 | 14.13126 | 13.57771 | 12.56110 | 11.65230 | 10.83777 | 10.10590 | 9.44665 | 8.85137 | 7.82371 | 6.97399 | 5.95423 | 4.72956 | 3.88741 |
| 17 | 16.25863 | 15.56225 | 14.90765 | 14.29187 | 13.16612 | 12.16567 | 11.27407 | 10.47726 | 9.76322 | 9.12164 | 8.02155 | 7.11963 | 6.04716 | 4.77463 | 3.90993 |
| 18 | 17.17277 | 16.39827 | 15.67256 | 14.99203 | 13.75351 | 12.65930 | 11.68959 | 10.82760 | 10.05909 | 9.37189 | 8.20141 | 7.24967 | 6.12797 | 4.81219 | 3.92794 |
| 19 | 18.08236 | 17.22601 | 16.42617 | 15.67846 | 14.32380 | 13.13394 | 12.08532 | 11.15812 | 10.33560 | 9.60360 | 8.36492 | 7.36578 | 6.19823 | 4.84350 | 3.94235 |
| 20 | 18.98742 | 18.04555 | 17.16864 | 16.35143 | 14.87747 | 13.59033 | 12.46221 | 11.46992 | 10.59401 | 9.81815 | 8.51356 | 7.46944 | 6.25933 | 4.86958 | 3.95388 |
| 22 | 20.78406 | 19.66038 | 18.62082 | 17.65805 | 15.93692 | 14.45112 | 13.16300 | 12.04158 | 11.06124 | 10.20074 | 8.77154 | 7.64465 | 6.35866 | 4.90943 | 3.97049 |
| 24 | 22.56287 | 21.24339 | 20.03041 | 18.91393 | 16.93554 | 15.24696 | 13.79864 | 12.55036 | 11.46933 | 10.52876 | 8.98474 | 7.78432 | 6.43377 | 4.93710 | 3.98111 |
| 26 | 24.32402 | 22.79520 | 21.39863 | 20.12104 | 17.87684 | 15.98277 | 14.37519 | 13.00317 | 11.82578 | 10.80998 | 9.16095 | 7.89566 | 6.49056 | 4.95632 | 3.98791 |
| 28 | 26.06769 | 24.31644 | 22.72672 | 21.28127 | 18.76411 | 16.66306 | 14.89813 | 13.40616 | 12.13711 | 11.05108 | 9.30657 | 7.98442 | 6.53351 | 4.96967 | 3.99226 |
| 30 | 27.79405 | 25.80771 | 24.01584 | 22.39646 | 19.60044 | 17.29203 | 15.37245 | 13.76483 | 12.40904 | 11.25778 | 9.42691 | 8.05518 | 6.56598 | 4.97894 | 3.99505 |
| 32 | 29.50328 | 27.26959 | 25.26714 | 23.46833 | 20.38877 | 17.87355 | 15.80268 | 14.08404 | 12.64656 | 11.43500 | 9.52638 | 8.11159 | 6.59053 | 4.98537 | 3.99683 |
| 34 | 31.19555 | 28.70267 | 26.48173 | 24.49859 | 21.13184 | 18.41120 | 16.19290 | 14.36814 | 12.85401 | 11.58693 | 9.60857 | 8.15656 | 6.60910 | 4.98984 | 3.99797 |
| 36 | 32.87102 | 30.10751 | 27.66068 | 25.48884 | 21.83225 | 18.90828 | 16.54685 | 14.62099 | 13.03521 | 11.71719 | 9.67651 | 8.19241 | 6.62314 | 4.99295 | 3.99870 |
| 38 | 34.52985 | 31.48466 | 28.80505 | 26.44064 | 22.49246 | 19.36786 | 16.86789 | 14.84602 | 13.19347 | 11.82887 | 9.73265 | 8.22099 | 6.63375 | 4.99510 | 3.99917 |
| 40 | 36.17223 | 32.83469 | 29.91585 | 27.35548 | 23.11477 | 19.79277 | 17.15909 | 15.04630 | 13.33171 | 11.92461 | 9.77905 | 8.24378 | 6.64178 | 4.99660 | 3.99947 |
| 45 | 40.20720 | 36.09451 | 32.55234 | 29.49016 | 24.51871 | 20.72004 | 17.77407 | 15.45583 | 13.60552 | 12.10840 | 9.86281 | 8.28252 | 6.65429 | 4.99863 | 3.99983 |
| 50 | 44.14279 | 39.19612 | 34.99969 | 31.42361 | 25.72976 | 21.48218 | 18.25593 | 15.76186 | 13.80075 | 12.23348 | 9.91481 | 8.30450 | 6.66051 | 4.99945 | 3.99994 |
| 100 | 78.54264 | 63.02888 | 51.62470 | 43.09835 | 31.59891 | 24.50500 | 19.84791 | 16.61755 | 14.26925 | 12.49432 | 9.99927 | 8.33323 | 6.66666 | 5.00000 | 4.00000 |

*Note:* To convert from this table to values of an annuity in advance, determine the annuity in arrears above for one less period and add 1.00000.

## Table 5
Bond Values in Percent of Par:
10 Percent Semiannual Coupons
Bond value $= 10/r + (100 - 10/r)(1 + r/2)^{-2n}$
$r$ = yield to maturity; $n$ = years to maturity

| Years to Maturity | Market Yield Percent per Year Compounded Semiannually | | | | | | | | | | |
|---|---|---|---|---|---|---|---|---|---|---|---|
| | 8.0 | 9.0 | 9.5 | 10.0 | 10.5 | 11.0 | 12.0 | 13.0 | 14.0 | 15.0 | 20.0 |
| 0.5 | 100.9615 | 100.4785 | 100.2387 | 100.0 | 99.7625 | 99.5261 | 99.0566 | 98.5915 | 98.1308 | 97.6744 | 95.4545 |
| 1.0 | 101.8861 | 100.9363 | 100.4665 | 100.0 | 99.5368 | 99.0768 | 98.1666 | 97.2691 | 96.3840 | 95.5111 | 91.3223 |
| 1.5 | 102.7751 | 101.3745 | 100.6840 | 100.0 | 99.3224 | 98.6510 | 97.3270 | 96.0273 | 94.7514 | 93.4987 | 87.5657 |
| 2.0 | 103.6299 | 101.7938 | 100.8917 | 100.0 | 99.1186 | 98.2474 | 96.5349 | 94.8613 | 93.2256 | 91.6267 | 84.1507 |
| 2.5 | 104.4518 | 102.1950 | 101.0899 | 100.0 | 98.9251 | 97.8649 | 95.7876 | 93.7665 | 91.7996 | 89.8853 | 81.0461 |
| 5.0 | 108.1109 | 103.9564 | 101.9541 | 100.0 | 98.0928 | 96.2312 | 92.6399 | 89.2168 | 85.9528 | 82.8398 | 69.2772 |
| 9.0 | 112.6593 | 106.0800 | 102.9803 | 100.0 | 97.1339 | 94.3770 | 89.1724 | 84.3513 | 79.8818 | 75.7350 | 58.9929 |
| 9.5 | 113.1339 | 106.2966 | 103.0838 | 100.0 | 97.0393 | 94.1962 | 88.8419 | 83.8979 | 79.3288 | 75.1023 | 58.1754 |
| 10.0 | 113.5903 | 106.5040 | 103.1827 | 100.0 | 96.9494 | 94.0248 | 88.5301 | 83.4722 | 78.8120 | 74.5138 | 57.4322 |
| 15.0 | 117.2920 | 108.1444 | 103.9551 | 100.0 | 96.2640 | 92.7331 | 86.2352 | 80.4120 | 75.1819 | 70.4740 | 52.8654 |
| 19.0 | 119.3679 | 109.0250 | 104.3608 | 100.0 | 95.9194 | 92.0976 | 85.1540 | 79.0312 | 73.6131 | 68.8015 | 51.3367 |
| 19.5 | 119.5845 | 109.1148 | 104.4017 | 100.0 | 95.8854 | 92.0357 | 85.0509 | 78.9025 | 73.4701 | 68.6525 | 51.2152 |
| 20.0 | 119.7928 | 109.2008 | 104.4408 | 100.0 | 95.8531 | 91.9769 | 84.9537 | 78.7817 | 73.3366 | 68.5140 | 51.1047 |
| 25.0 | 121.4822 | 109.8810 | 104.7461 | 100.0 | 95.6068 | 91.5342 | 84.2381 | 77.9132 | 72.3985 | 67.5630 | 50.4259 |
| 30.0 | 122.6235 | 110.3190 | 104.9381 | 100.0 | 95.4591 | 91.2751 | 83.8386 | 77.4506 | 71.9216 | 67.1015 | 50.1642 |
| 40.0 | 123.9154 | 110.7827 | 105.1347 | 100.0 | 95.3175 | 91.0345 | 83.4909 | 77.0728 | 71.5560 | 66.7690 | 50.0244 |
| 50.0 | 124.5050 | 110.9749 | 105.2124 | 100.0 | 95.2666 | 90.9521 | 83.3825 | 76.9656 | 71.4615 | 66.6908 | 50.0036 |

**Table 6**
Bond Values in Percent of Par:
12 Percent Semiannual Coupons

Bond value $= 12/r + (100 - 12/r)(1 + r/2)^{-2n}$

$r =$ yield to maturity; $n =$ years to maturity

| Years to Maturity | Market Yield Percent per Year Compounded Semiannually | | | | | | | | | | |
|---|---|---|---|---|---|---|---|---|---|---|---|
| | 8.0 | 9.0 | 10.0 | 11.0 | 11.5 | 12.0 | 12.5 | 13.0 | 14.0 | 15.0 | 20.0 |
| 0.5 | 101.9231 | 101.4354 | 100.9524 | 100.4739 | 100.2364 | 100.0 | 99.7647 | 99.5305 | 99.0654 | 98.6047 | 96.3636 |
| 1.0 | 103.7722 | 102.8090 | 101.8594 | 100.9232 | 100.4600 | 100.0 | 99.5433 | 99.0897 | 98.1920 | 97.3067 | 93.0579 |
| 1.5 | 105.5502 | 104.1234 | 102.7232 | 101.3490 | 100.6714 | 100.0 | 99.3348 | 98.6758 | 97.3757 | 96.0992 | 90.0526 |
| 2.0 | 107.2598 | 105.3813 | 103.5459 | 101.7526 | 100.8713 | 100.0 | 99.1387 | 98.2871 | 96.6128 | 94.9760 | 87.3205 |
| 2.5 | 108.9036 | 106.5850 | 104.3295 | 102.1351 | 101.0603 | 100.0 | 98.9540 | 97.9222 | 95.8998 | 93.9312 | 84.8369 |
| 5.0 | 116.2218 | 111.8691 | 107.7217 | 103.7688 | 101.8620 | 100.0 | 98.1816 | 96.4056 | 92.9764 | 89.7039 | 75.4217 |
| 9.0 | 125.3186 | 118.2400 | 111.6896 | 105.6230 | 102.7585 | 100.0 | 97.3432 | 94.7838 | 89.9409 | 85.4410 | 67.1944 |
| 9.5 | 126.2679 | 118.8899 | 112.0853 | 105.8038 | 102.8449 | 100.0 | 97.2642 | 94.6326 | 89.6644 | 85.0614 | 66.5403 |
| 10.0 | 127.1807 | 119.5119 | 112.4622 | 105.9752 | 102.9266 | 100.0 | 97.1898 | 94.4907 | 89.4060 | 84.7083 | 65.9457 |
| 15.0 | 134.5841 | 124.4333 | 115.3724 | 107.2669 | 103.5353 | 100.0 | 96.6489 | 93.4707 | 87.5910 | 82.2844 | 62.2923 |
| 19.0 | 138.7357 | 127.0750 | 116.8679 | 107.9024 | 103.8283 | 100.0 | 96.3995 | 93.0104 | 86.8065 | 81.2809 | 61.0694 |
| 19.5 | 139.1690 | 127.3445 | 117.0170 | 107.9643 | 103.8565 | 100.0 | 96.3760 | 92.9675 | 86.7351 | 81.1915 | 60.9722 |
| 20.0 | 139.5855 | 127.6024 | 117.1591 | 108.0231 | 103.8832 | 100.0 | 96.3539 | 92.9272 | 86.6683 | 81.1084 | 60.8838 |
| 25.0 | 142.9644 | 129.6430 | 118.2559 | 108.4658 | 104.0822 | 100.0 | 96.1930 | 92.6377 | 86.1993 | 80.5378 | 60.3407 |
| 30.0 | 145.2470 | 130.9570 | 118.9293 | 108.7249 | 104.1960 | 100.0 | 96.1053 | 92.4835 | 85.9608 | 80.2609 | 60.1314 |
| 40.0 | 147.8308 | 132.3480 | 119.5965 | 108.9655 | 104.2982 | 100.0 | 96.0313 | 92.3576 | 85.7780 | 80.0614 | 60.0195 |
| 50.0 | 149.0100 | 132.9248 | 119.8479 | 109.0479 | 104.3316 | 100.0 | 96.0093 | 92.3219 | 85.7307 | 80.0145 | 60.0029 |

# Glossary*

A

**AAA.** *American Accounting Association.*

**Abacus.** A scholarly journal containing articles on theoretical aspects of accounting. Published twice a year by the Sydney University Press, Sydney, Australia.

**abatement.** A complete or partial cancellation of a levy imposed by a government unit.

**abnormal spoilage.** Actual spoilage exceeding that expected when operations are normally efficient. Usual practice treats this cost as an *expense* of the period rather than as a *product cost*. Contrast with *normal spoilage*.

**aboriginal cost.** In public utility accounting, the *acquisition cost* of an *asset* incurred by the first *entity* devoting that asset to public use. Most public utility regulation is based on aboriginal cost. If it were not, then public utilities could exchange assets among themselves at ever-increasing prices in order to raise the rate base and, then, prices based thereon.

**absorbed overhead.** *Overhead* costs allocated to individual products at some *overhead rate*. Also called *applied overhead*.

**absorption costing.** See *full absorption costing*.

**Accelerated Cost Recovery System.** A form of *accelerated depreciation* enacted by the Congress in 1981 and amended in 1986. The system provides percentages of the asset's cost to be depreciated each year for tax purposes. *Salvage value* is ignored. These amounts are generally not used for *financial accounting*.

**accelerated depreciation.** Any method of calculating *depreciation* charges where the charges become progressively smaller each period. Examples are *double-declining-balance* and *sum-of-the-years' digits* methods.

**acceptance.** A written promise to pay that is equivalent to a *promissory note*.

**account.** Any device for accumulating additions and subtractions relating to a single *asset*, *liability*, or *owners' equity* item, including *revenues* and *expenses*.

**account analysis method.** A method of separating *fixed* from *variable costs* involving the classification of the various *production cost accounts*. For example, *direct labor* and *direct material* are classified as variable and *depreciation* on the factory building as fixed.

**account form.** The form of *balance sheet* where *assets* are shown on the left and *equities* are shown on the right. Contrast with *report form*. See also *T-account*.

**account payable.** A *liability* representing an amount owed to a *creditor*, usually arising from purchase of *merchandise* or materials and supplies; not necessarily due or past due. Normally, a *current liability*.

**account receivable.** A claim against a *debtor* usually arising from sales or services rendered; not necessarily due or past due. Normally, a *current asset*.

**accountability center.** *Responsibility center*.

**accountancy.** The British word for *accounting*. In the United States, it means the theory and practice of accounting.

**Accountants' Index.** A publication of the *AICPA* that indexes, in detail, the accounting literature of the period.

**accountant's opinion.** *Auditor's report*.

**accountant's report.** *Auditor's report.* 709

*Many words and phrases in the Glossary are defined in terms of other words and phrases. Terms in a given definition that are themselves (or variants thereof) explained elsewhere under their own listings are *italicized*.

**accounting.** An *information system* conveying information about a specific *entity*. The information is in financial terms and is restricted to information that can be made reasonably precise. The *AICPA* defines accounting as a service activity whose "function is to provide quantitative information, primarily financial in nature, about economic entities that is intended to be useful in making economic decisions."

**accounting changes.** As defined by *APB Opinion No. 20*, a change in (a) an *accounting principle* (such as a switch from *FIFO* to *LIFO* or from *sum-of-the-years'-digits* to *straight-line depreciation*), (b) an accounting estimate (such as estimated useful lives or salvage value of depreciable assets and estimates of *warranty* costs or *uncollectible accounts*), and (c) the reporting *entity*. Changes of type (a) should be disclosed. The cumulative effect of the change on *retained earnings* at the start of the period during which the change was made should be included in reported earnings for the period of change. Changes of type (b) should be treated as affecting only the period of change and, if necessary, future periods. The reasons for changes of type (c) should be disclosed and, in statements reporting on operations of the period of the change, the effect of the change on all other periods reported on for comparative purposes should also be shown. In some cases (such as a change from *LIFO* to other inventory *flow assumptions* or in the method of accounting for long-term construction contracts), changes of type (a) are treated like changes of type (c). That is, for these changes all statements shown for prior periods must be restated to show the effect of adopting the change for those periods as well. See *all-inclusive concept* and *accounting errors*.

**accounting conventions.** Methods or procedures used in accounting. This term tends to be used when the method or procedure has not been given official authoritative sanction by a pronouncement of a group such as the *APB, EITF, FASB*, or *SEC*. Contrast with *accounting principles*.

**accounting cycle.** The sequence of accounting procedures starting with *journal entries* for various transactions and events and ending with the *financial statements* or, perhaps, the *post-closing trial balance*.

**accounting entity.** See *entity*.

**accounting equation.** *Assets = Equities. Assets = Liabilities + Owners' Equity*.

**accounting errors.** Arithmetic errors and misapplications of *accounting principles* in previously published financial statements that are corrected in the current period with direct *debits* or *credits* to *retained earnings*. In this regard, they are treated like *prior-period adjustments*, but, technically, they are not classified by *APB Opinion No. 9* as prior-period adjustments. See *accounting changes* and contrast with changes in accounting estimates as described there.

**accounting event.** Any occurrence that is recorded in the accounting records.

**accounting methods.** *Accounting principles*. Procedures for carrying out accounting principles.

**accounting period.** The time period for which *financial statements* that measure *flows*, such as the *income statement* and the *statement of cash flows*, are prepared. Should be clearly identified on the financial statements. See *interim statements*.

**accounting policies.** *Accounting principles* adopted by a specific *entity*.

**accounting principles.** The methods or procedures used in accounting for events reported in the *financial statements*. This term tends to be used when the method or procedure has been given official authoritative sanction by a pronouncement of a group such as the *APB, EITF, FASB*, or *SEC*. Contrast with *accounting conventions* and *conceptual framework*.

**Accounting Principles Board.** See *APB*.

**accounting procedures.** See *accounting principles*, but usually this term refers to the methods for implementing accounting principles.

**accounting rate of return.** Income for a period divided by average investment during the period. Based on income, rather than discounted cash flows and, hence, is a poor decision making aid or tool. See *ratio*.

*Accounting Research Bulletin. ARB*. The name of the official pronouncements of the former *Committee on Accounting Procedure* of the *AICPA*. Fifty-one bulletins were issued between 1939 and 1959. *ARB No. 43* summarizes the first forty-two bulletins.

*Accounting Research Study. ARS*. One of a series of studies published by the Director of Accounting Research of the *AICPA* "designed to provide professional accountants and others interested in the development of accounting with a discussion and documentation of accounting problems." Fifteen such studies were published between 1961 and 1974.

*The Accounting Review*. Scholarly publication of the *American Accounting Association*.

*Accounting Series Release. ASR*. See *SEC*.

**accounting standards.** *Accounting principles*.

**Accounting Standards Executive Committee.** **AcSEC.** The senior technical committee of the *AICPA* authorized to speak for the AICPA in the areas of *financial accounting* and reporting as well as *cost accounting*.

**accounting system.** The procedures for collecting and summarizing financial data in a firm.

**Accounting Terminology Bulletin. ATB.** One of four releases of the Committee on Terminology of the *AICPA* issued in the period 1953–1957.

**Accounting Trends and Techniques.** An annual publication of the *AICPA* that surveys the reporting practices of 600 large corporations. It presents tabulations of specific practices, terminology, and disclosures along with illustrations taken from individual annual reports.

**accounts receivable turnover.** Net *sales on account* divided by average *accounts receivable*. See *ratio*.

**accretion.** See *amortization*. When a *book value* grows over time, such as a *bond* originally issued at a *discount*, the correct technical term is "accretion," not "amortization." Also, increase in economic worth through physical change, usually said of a natural resource such as an orchard, caused by natural growth. Contrast with *appreciation*.

**accrual.** Recognition of an *expense (or revenue)* and the related *liability (or asset)* that is caused by an *accounting event*, frequently by the passage of time, and that is not signaled by an explicit cash transaction. For example, the recognition of interest expense or revenue (or wages, salaries, or rent) at the end of a period even though no explicit cash transaction is made at that time. Cash flow follows accounting recognition; contrast with *deferral*.

**accrual basis of accounting.** The method of recognizing *revenues* as *goods* are sold (or delivered) and as *services* are rendered, independent of the time when cash is received. *Expenses* are recognized in the period when the related revenue is recognized independent of the time when cash is paid out. *SFAC No. 1* says "accrual accounting attempts to record the financial effects on an enterprise of transactions and other events and circumstances that have cash consequences for the enterprise in the periods in which those transactions, events, and circumstances occur rather than only in the periods in which cash is received or paid by the enterprise." Contrast with the *cash basis of accounting*. See *accrual* and *deferral*. The basis would more correctly be called "accrual/deferral" accounting.

**accrued.** Said of a *revenue (expense)* that has been earned (recognized) even though the related *receivable (payable)* is not yet due. This adjective should not be used as part of an account title. Thus, we prefer to use Interest Receivable (Payable) as the account title, rather than Accrued Interest Receivable (Payable). See *matching convention*. See *accrual*.

**accrued depreciation.** An incorrect term for *accumulated depreciation*. Acquiring an asset with cash, capitalizing it, and then amortizing its cost over periods of use is a process of *deferral* and allocation, not of *accrual*.

**accrued payable.** A *payable* usually resulting from the passage of time. For example, *salaries* and *interest* accrue as time passes. See *accrued*.

**accrued receivable.** A *receivable* usually resulting from the passage of time. See *accrued*.

**accumulated benefit obligation.** See *projected benefit obligation* for definition and contrast.

**accumulated depreciation.** A preferred title for the *contra-asset* account that shows the sum of *depreciation* charges on an asset since it was acquired. Other titles used are *allowance* for *depreciation* (acceptable term) and *reserve* for *depreciation* (unacceptable term).

**accurate presentation.** The qualitative accounting objective suggesting that information reported in financial statements should correspond as precisely as possible with the economic effects underlying transactions and events. See *fair presentation* and *full disclosure*.

**acid test ratio.** *Quick ratio.*

**acquisition cost.** Of an *asset*, the net *invoice* price plus all *expenditures* to place and ready the asset for its intended use. The other expenditures might include legal fees, transportation charges, and installation costs.

**ACRS.** *Accelerated Cost Recovery System.*

**AcSEC.** *Accounting Standards Executive Committee* of the *AICPA*.

**activity accounting.** *Responsibility accounting.*

**activity-based depreciation.** *Production method of depreciation.*

**activity basis.** *Costs* are *variable* or *fixed* (*incremental* or *unavoidable*) with respect to some activity, such as production of units (or the undertaking of some new project). This activity is referred to as the "activity basis."

**actual cost (basis).** *Acquisition* or *historical cost*. Also contrast with *standard cost*.

**actual costing (system).** Method of allocating costs to products using actual *direct materials*, actual *direct labor*, and actual *factory overhead*. Contrast with *normal costing* and *standard cost system*.

**actuarial.** Usually said of computations or analyses that involve both *compound interest* and probabilities, such as the computation of the *present value* of a life-contingent *annuity*. Sometimes the term is used if only one of the two is involved.

**actuarial accrued liability.** A 1981 report of the Joint Committee on Pension Terminology (of various actuarial societies) stated that this term is the preferred one for *prior service cost*.

**additional paid-in capital.** An alternative acceptable title for the *capital contributed in excess of par (or stated) value account*.

**additional processing cost.** *Costs* incurred in processing *joint products* after the *splitoff point*.

**adequate disclosure.** *Fair presentation* of *financial statements* requires *disclosure* of *material* items. This *auditing standard* does not, however, require publicizing all information detrimental to a company. For example, the company may be threatened with a lawsuit and disclosure might seem to require a *debit* to a *loss* account and a *credit* to an *estimated liability*. But the mere making of this entry might adversely affect the actual outcome of the suit. Such entries need not be made although impending suits should be disclosed.

**adjunct account.** An *account* that accumulates additions to another account. For example, Premium on Bonds Payable is adjunct to the liability Bonds Payable; the effective liability is the sum of the two account balances at a given date. Contrast with *contra account*.

**adjusted acquisition (historical) cost.** Sometimes said of the *book value* of a *plant asset*. Also, cost adjusted to a *constant dollar* amount to reflect *general price level changes*.

**adjusted bank balance of cash.** The *balance* shown on the statement from the bank plus or minus amounts, such as for unrecorded deposits or outstanding checks, to reconcile the bank's balance with the correct cash balance. See *adjusted book balance of cash*.

**adjusted basis.** The *basis* used to compute gain or loss on disposition of an *asset* for tax purposes. Also, see *book value*.

**adjusted book balance of cash.** The *balance* shown in the firm's account for cash in bank plus or minus amounts, such as for *notes* collected by the bank or bank service charges, to reconcile the account balance with the correct cash balance. See *adjusted bank balance of cash*.

**adjusted trial balance.** *Trial balance* taken after *adjusting entries* but before *closing entries*. Contrast with *pre* and *post-closing trial balances*. See *unadjusted trial balance* and *post-closing trial balance*. See also *work sheet*.

**adjusting entry.** An entry made at the end of an *accounting period* to record a *transaction* or other *accounting event*, which for some reason has not been recorded or has been improperly recorded during the accounting period. An entry to update the accounts. See *work sheet*.

**adjustment.** A change in an *account* produced by an *adjusting entry*. Sometimes the term is used to refer to the process of restating *financial statement* amounts to *constant dollars*.

**administrative expense.** An *expense* related to the enterprise as a whole as contrasted to expenses related to more specific functions such as manufacturing or selling.

**admission of partner.** Legally, when a new partner joins a *partnership*, the old partnership is dissolved and a new one comes into being. In practice, however, the old accounting records may be kept in use and the accounting entries reflect the manner in which the new partner joined the firm. If the new partner merely purchases the interest of another partner, the only accounting is to change the name for one capital account. If the new partner contributes *assets* and *liabilities* to the partnership, then the new assets must be recognized with debits and the liabilities and other source of capital, with credits. See *bonus method*.

**ADR.** See *asset depreciation range*.

**advances from (by) customers.** A preferred title for the *liability* account representing *receipts* of *cash* in advance of delivering the *goods* or rendering the *service* (that will cause *revenue* to be recognized). Sometimes called "deferred revenue" or "deferred income."

**advances to affiliates.** *Loans* by a parent company to a *subsidiary*. Frequently combined with "investment in subsidiary" as "investments and advances to subsidiary" and shown as a *noncurrent asset* on the parent's *balance sheet*. These advances are eliminated in *consolidated financial statements*.

**advances to suppliers.** A preferred term for the *asset account* representing *disbursements* of cash in advance of receiving *assets* or *services*.

**adverse opinion.** An *auditor's report* stating that the financial statements are not fair or are not in accord with *GAAP*.

**affiliated company.** Said of a company controlling or controlled by another company.

**after closing.** *Post-closing*; said of a *trial balance* at the end of the period.

**after cost.** Said of *expenditures* to be made subsequent to *revenue* recognition. For example, *expenditures* for *repairs* under warranty are after costs. Proper recognition of after costs involves a debit to expense at the time of the sale and a credit to an *estimated liability*. When the liability is discharged, the debit is to the estimated liability and the credit is to the assets consumed.

**agency fund.** An account for *assets* received by governmental units in the capacity of trustee or agent.

**agency theory.** A branch of economics relating the behavior of principals (such as owner non managers or bosses) and their *agents* (such as nonowner managers or subordinates). The principal assigns responsibility and authority to the agent but the agent has his or her own risks and preferences different from those of the principal. The principal is unable to observe all activities of the agent. Thus the principal must be careful about the kinds of observations of or reports sought from the agent, perhaps through an independent *auditor,* and the sorts of incentive contracts that the principal makes with the agent.

**agent.** One authorized to transact business, including executing contracts, for another.

**aging accounts receivable.** The process of classifying *accounts receivable* by the time elapsed since the claim came into existence for the purpose of estimating the amount of uncollectible accounts receivable as of a given date. See *sales contra, estimated uncollectibles* and *allowance for uncollectibles.*

**aging schedule.** A listing of *accounts receivable*, classified by age, used in *aging accounts receivable.*

**AICPA.** American Institute of Certified Public Accountants. The national organization that represents *CPAs*. See *AcSEC*. It oversees the writing and grading of the Uniform CPA Examination. Each state, however, sets its own requirements for becoming a CPA in that state. See *certified public accountant.*

**all-capital earnings rate**. *Rate of return on assets.*

**all-inclusive (income) concept.** Under this concept, no distinction is drawn between *operating* and *nonoperating revenues* and *expenses*; thus the only entries to retained earnings are for *net income* and *dividends*. Under this concept all *income*, *gains*, and *losses* are reported in the *income statement*; thus, events usually reported as *prior-period adjustments* and as *corrections of errors* are included in net income. This concept in its pure form is not the basis of *GAAP*, but *APB Opinions Nos. 9 and 30* move far in this direction. They do permit retained earnings entries for prior-period adjustments and correction of errors.

**allocate.** To spread a *cost* from one *account* to several accounts, to several products, or activities, or to several periods.

**allocation base.** *Joint costs* are assigned to *cost objectives* in some systematic fashion. The allocation base specifies the fashion. For example, the cost of a truck might be assigned to periods based on miles driven during the period; the allocation base is miles. Or, the cost of a factory supervisor might be assigned to product based on *direct labor* hours; the allocation base is direct labor hours.

**allocation of income taxes.** See *deferred income tax.*

**allowance.** A balance sheet *contra account* generally used for *receivables* and depreciable assets. See *sales* (or *purchase*) *allowance* for another use of this term.

**allowance for funds used during construction.** One principle of public utility regulation and rate setting is that customers should pay the full costs of producing the services (e.g., electricity) that they use nothing more and nothing less. Thus an electric utility is even more careful than other businesses to capitalize into an *asset account* the full costs, but no more, of producing a new electric power generating plant. One of the costs of building a new plant is the *interest* cost on money tied up during construction. If *funds* are explicitly borrowed by an ordinary business, the journal entry for interest of $1,000 is typically:

| | | |
|---|---|---|
| Interest Expense ................. | 1,000 | |
|    Interest Payable ............... | | 1,000 |
| Interest expense for the period. | | |

If the firm is constructing a new plant, then another entry would be made capitalizing interest into the plant-under-construction account:

| | | |
|---|---|---|
| Construction Work in Progress ........ | 750 | |
|    Interest Expense ................. | | 750 |
| Capitalize relevant portion of interest relating to construction work in progress into the asset account. | | |

The cost of the *plant asset* is increased; when the plant is used, *depreciation* is charged; the interest will become an expense through the depreciation process in the later periods of use, not currently as the interest is paid. Thus the full cost of the electricity generated during a given period is reported as expense in that period. But suppose, as is common, that the electric utility does not explicitly borrow the funds, but uses some of its own funds, including funds raised from equity issues as well as from debt. Even though there is no explicit interest expense, there is the *opportunity cost* of the funds. Put another way, the cost of the plant under construction is not less in an economic sense just because the firm used its own cash, rather than borrowing. The public utility using its own funds, on which $750 of interest would be payable if the funds had been explicitly borrowed, will make the following entry:

| | |
|---|---|
| Construction Work in Progress . . . . . . . . | 750 |
| Allowance for Funds Used during Construction . . . . . . . . . . . . . | 750 |
| Recognition of interest, an opportunity cost, on own funds used. | |

The allowance account is a form of *revenue*, to appear on the income statement, and will be closed to Retained Earnings, increasing it. On the *funds statement*, it is an income or revenue item not producing funds and so must be subtracted from net income in deriving *funds provided by operations*. *SFAS No. 34* specifically prohibits non utility companies from capitalizing the opportunity cost (interest) on own funds used into plant under construction.

**allowance for uncollectibles** (accounts receivable). A *contra* to Accounts Receivable that shows the estimated amount of *accounts receivable* that will not be collected. When such an allowance is used, the actual *write-off* of specific accounts receivable (*debit* allowance, *credit* specific account) does not affect *revenue* or *expense* at the time of the write off. The revenue reduction is recognized when *bad debt expense* is *debited* and the allowance is credited; the amount of the credit to the allowance may be based on a percentage of sales on account for a period of time or computed from *aging accounts receivable*. This contra account enables an estimate to be shown of the amount of receivables that will be collected without identifying specific uncollectible accounts. See *allowance method*.

**allowance method.** A method of attempting to *match* all *expenses* of a transaction with its associated *revenues*. Usually involves a debit to expense and a credit to an *estimated liability*, such as for estimated warranty expenditures, or a debit to a revenue (*contra*) account and a credit to an asset (*contra*) account, such as in some firms' accounting for uncollectible accounts. See *allowance for uncollectibles* for further explanation. When the allowance method is used for *sales discounts*, sales are recorded at *gross invoice* prices (not reduced by the amounts of discounts made available). An estimate of the amount of discounts to be taken is debited to a *revenue contra account* and *credited* to an allowance account, shown contra to *accounts receivable*.

**American Accounting Association. AAA.** An organization primarily for academic accountants, but open to all interested in accounting. It publishes *The Accounting Review*.

**American Institute of Certified Public Accountants.** See *AICPA*.

**American Stock Exchange. AMEX. ASE.** A public market where various corporate *securities* are traded.

**AMEX.** *American Stock Exchange.*

**amortization.** Strictly speaking, the process of liquidating or extinguishing ("bringing to death") a *debt* with a series of payments to the *creditor* (or to a *sinking fund*). From that usage has evolved a related use involving the accounting for the payments themselves: "amortization schedule" for a mortgage which is a table showing the allocation between *interest* and *principle*. The term has come to mean writing off ("liquidating") the cost of an asset. In this context it means the general process of *allocating acquisition cost* of an asset to either the periods of benefit as *expenses* or to *inventory* accounts as *product costs*. Called *depreciation* for *plant assets, depletion* for *wasting assets* (natural resources), and "amortization" for *intangibles*. *SFAC No. 6* refers to amortization as "the accounting process of reducing an amount by periodic payments or write-downs." The expressions "unamortized debt discount or premium" and "to amortize debt discount or premium" relate to *accruals*, not to *deferrals*. The expressions "amortization of long-term assets" and "to amortize long-term assets" refer to deferrals, not accruals. Contrast with *accretion*.

**analysis of variances.** See *variance analysis*.

**annual report.** A report for shareholders and other interested parties prepared once a year, includes a *balance sheet*, an *income statement*, a *statement of cash flows*, a reconciliation of changes in *owners' equity* accounts, a *summary of significant accounting principles*, other explanatory *notes*, the *auditor's report*, and, comments from management about the year's events. See *10-K* and *financial statements*.

**annuitant.** One who receives an *annuity*.

**annuity.** A series of payments, usually made at equally spaced time intervals.

**annuity certain.** An *annuity* payable for a definite number of periods. Contrast with *contingent annuity*.

**annuity due.** An *annuity* whose first payment is made at the start of period 1 (or at the end of period 0). Contrast with *annuity in arrears*.

**annuity in advance.** An *annuity due*.

**annuity in arrears.** An *ordinary annuity* whose first payment occurs at the end of the first period.

**annuity method of depreciation.** See *compound interest depreciation*.

**antidilutive.** Said of a *potentially dilutive security* that will increase *earnings per share* if it is *exercised* or *converted* into common stock. In computing *primary* and *fully diluted earnings per share*, antidilutive securities may not be assumed to be exercised or converted and hence do not increase reported earnings per share in a given period.

**APB.** Accounting Principles Board of the *AICPA*. It set *accounting principles* from 1959 through 1973, issuing 31 *APB Opinions* and 4 APB *Statements*. It was superseded by the *FASB*.

**APB Opinion.** The name given to pronouncements of the *APB* that make up much of *generally accepted accounting principles*; there are 31 *APB Opinions*, issued from 1962 through 1973.

**APB Statement.** The *APB* issued four *Statements* between 1962 and 1970. The *Statements* were approved by at least two thirds of the Board, but they are recommendations, not requirements. For example, *Statement No. 3* (1969) suggested the publication of *constant dollar financial statements* but did not require them.

**APBs.** An abbreviation used for *APB Opinions*.

**applied cost.** A *cost* that has been *allocated* to a department, product, or activity; need not be based on actual costs incurred.

**applied overhead.** *Overhead costs* charged to departments, products or activities. Also called *absorbed overhead*.

**appraisal.** The process of obtaining a valuation for an *asset* or *liability* that involves expert opinion rather than evaluation of explicit market transactions.

**appraisal method of depreciation.** The periodic *depreciation* charge is the difference between the beginning and end-of-period appraised value of the *asset* if that difference is positive. If negative, there is no charge. Not based on *historical cost* nor, hence, generally accepted.

**appreciation.** An increase in economic worth caused by rising market prices for an *asset*. Contrast with *accretion*.

**appropriated retained earnings.** See *retained earnings, appropriated*.

**appropriation.** In governmental accounting, an *expenditure* authorized for a specified amount, purpose, and time.

**appropriation account.** In governmental accounting, an account set up to record specific authorizations to spend; it is credited with appropriation amounts. *Expenditures* during the period and *encumbrances* outstanding at the end of the period are closed (debited) to this account at the end of the period.

**approximate net realizable value method.** A method of assigning joint costs to *joint products* based on revenues minus *additional processing costs* of the end products.

**ARB.** *Accounting Research Bulletin*.

**arbitrage.** Strictly speaking, the simultaneous purchase in one market and sale in another of a *security* or commodity in hope of making a *profit* on price differences in the different markets. Often this term is loosely used when the item sold is somewhat different from the item purchased; for example, the sale of shares of *common stock* and the simultaneous purchase of a *convertible bond* that is convertible into identical common shares.

**arm's length.** Said of a transaction negotiated by unrelated parties, each acting in his or her own self-interest; the basis for a *fair market value* determination.

**arrears.** Said of *cumulative preferred stock dividends* that have not been declared up to the current date. See *annuity in arrears* for another context.

**ARS.** *Accounting Research Study*.

**articles of incorporation.** Document filed with state authorities by persons forming a corporation. When the document is returned with a certificate of incorporation, it becomes the corporation's *charter*.

**articulate.** Said of the relationship between any operating statement (for example, *income statement* or *statement of cash flows*) and *comparative balance sheets*, where the operating statement explains (or reconciles) the change in some major balance sheet category (for example, *retained earnings* or *working capital*).

**ASE.** *American Stock Exchange*.

**ASR.** *Accounting Series Release*.

**assess.** To value property for the purpose of property taxation; the assessment is computed by the taxing authority. To levy a charge on the owner of property for improvements thereto, such as for sewers or sidewalks.

**assessed valuation.** A dollar amount for real estate or other property used by a government as a basis for levying taxes. The amount may or may not bear some relation to *market value*.

**asset.** *SFAC No. 6* defines assets as "probable future economic benefits obtained or controlled by a particular entity as a result of past transactions . . . An asset has three essential characteristics: (a) it embodies a probable future benefit that involves a capacity, singly or in combination with other assets, to contribute directly or indirectly to future net cash inflows, (b) a particular entity can obtain the benefit and control others' access to it, and (c) the transaction or other event giving rise to the entity's right to or control of the benefit has already occurred." A footnote points out that "probable" means that which can be reasonably expected or believed but is neither certain nor proved. May be *tangible* or *intangible, short-term* (current) or *longterm* (noncurrent).

**asset depreciation range. ADR.** The range of *depreciable lives* allowed by the *Internal Revenue Service* for a specific depreciable *asset*.

**asset turnover.** Net sales divided by average assets. See *ratio*.

**assignment of accounts receivable.** Transfer of the legal ownership of an *account receivable* through its sale. Contrast with *pledging* accounts receivable where the receivables serve as *collateral* for a *loan*.

*ATB.* *Accounting Terminology Bulletin.*

**at par.** Said of a *bond* or *preferred stock* issued or selling at its *face amount*.

**attachment.** The laying claim to the *assets* of a borrower or debtor by a lender or creditor when the borrower has failed to pay debts on time.

**attest.** Rendering of an *opinion* by an auditor that the *financial statements* are fair. This procedure is called the "attest function" of the CPA. See *fair presentation*.

**attribute measured.** When making physical measurements, such as of a person, one needs to decide the units with which to measure, such as inches or centimeters or pounds or grams. One chooses the attribute height or weight independently of the measuring unit English or metric. In conventional accounting the attribute measured is *historical cost* and the measuring unit is *nominal dollars*. Some theorists argue that accounting is more useful when the attribute measured is *current cost*. Others argue that accounting is more useful when the measuring unit is *constant dollars*. Some, including us, think both changes from conventional accounting should be made. The attribute historical cost can be measured in nominal dollars or in constant dollars. The attribute current cost can also be measured in nominal dollars or constant dollars. Choosing between two attributes and two measuring units implies four different accounting systems. Each of these four has its uses.

**audit.** Systematic inspection of accounting records involving analyses, tests, and *confirmations*. See *internal audit*.

**audit committee.** A committee of the board of directors of a *corporation* usually consisting of outside directors who nominate the independent auditors and discuss the auditors' work with them. If the auditors believe certain matters should be brought to the attention of shareholders, the auditors first bring these matters to the attention of the audit committee.

*Audit Guides.* See *Industry Audit Guides*.

**audit program.** The procedures followed by the *auditor* in carrying out the *audit*.

**audit trail.** A reference accompanying an *entry*, or *posting*, to an underlying source record or document. A good audit trail is essential for efficiently checking the accuracy of accounting entries. See *cross-reference*.

**Auditing Research Monograph.** Publication series of the *AICPA*.

**auditing standards.** A set of ten standards promulgated by the *AICPA*, including three general standards, three standards of field work, and four standards of reporting. According to the AICPA, these standards "deal with the measures of the quality of the performance and the objectives to be attained," rather than with specific auditing procedures.

*Auditing Standards Advisory Council.* An *AICPA* committee.

**Auditing Standards Board.** Operating committee of the *AICPA* promulgating auditing rules.

**auditor.** One who checks the accuracy, fairness, and general acceptability of accounting records and statements and then *attests* to them.

**auditor's opinion.** *Auditor's report.*

**auditor's report.** The auditor's statement of the work done and an opinion of the *financial statements*. Opinions are usually unqualified ("clean"), but may be *qualified*, or the auditor may disclaim an opinion in the report. Often called the "accountant's report." See *adverse opinion*.

**AudSEC.** The former Auditing Standards Executive Committee of the *AICPA*, now functioning as the *Auditing Standards Board*.

**authorized capital stock.** The number of *shares* of stock that can be issued by a corporation; specified by the *articles of incorporation*.

**average.** The arithmetic mean of a set of numbers; obtained by summing the items and dividing by the number of items.

**average collection period of receivables.** See *ratio*.

**average-cost flow assumption.** An *inventory flow assumption* where the cost of units is the *weighted average* cost of the *beginning inventory* and purchases. See *inventory equation*.

**average tax rate.** The rate found by dividing *income tax expense* by *net income* before taxes. Contrast with *marginal tax rate, statutory tax rate*.

**avoidable cost.** A *cost* that will cease if an activity is discontinued. An *incremental* or *variable cost*. See *programmed cost*.

# B

**backlog.** Orders for which insufficient *inventory* is on hand for current delivery and which will be filled in a later period.

**backlog depreciation.** In *current cost accounting*, a problem arising for the *accumulated depreciation* on *plant assets*. Consider an *asset* costing $10,000 with a 10-year life depreciated with the *straight-line method*. Assume that a similar asset has a current cost of $10,000 at the end of the first year but $12,000 at the end of the second year. Assume that the depreciation charge is based on the average current cost during the year, $10,000 for the first year and $11,000 for the second. The depreciation charge for the first year is $1,000 and for the second is $1,100 (= .10 × $11,000), so the *accumulated depreciation account* is $2,100 after 2 years. Note that at the end of the second year, 20 percent of the asset's future benefits have been used, so the accounting records based on current costs must show a *net book value* of $9,600 (= .80 × $12,000), which would result if accumulated depreciation of $2,400 were subtracted from a current cost of $12,000. But the sum of the depreciation charges has been only $2,100. The *journal entry* to increase the accumulated depreciation account requires a *credit* to that account of $300. The question arises, what account is to debited? That is the problem of backlog depreciation. Some theorists would *debit* an *income* account and others would *debit* a *balance sheet owners' equity* account without reducing current-period earnings. The answer to the question of what to do with the debit is closely tied to the problem of how *holding gains* are recorded. When the asset account is debited for $2,000 to increase the recorded amount from $10,000 to $12,000, a holding gain of $2,000 must be recorded with a credit. Many theorists believe that whatever account is credited for the holding gains is the same account that should be debited for backlog depreciation. Sometimes called "catch-up depreciation."

**bad debt.** An *uncollectible account receivable*; see *bad debt expense* and *sales contra, estimated uncollectibles*.

**bad debt expense.** The name for the *account debited* in both the *allowance method* for *uncollectibles* and the *direct write-off method*.

**bad debt recovery.** Collection, perhaps partial, of a specific account receivable previously written off as uncollectible. If the *allowance method* is used, the *credit* is usually to the *allowance* account. If the *direct write-off method* is used, the credit is to a *revenue account*.

**bailout period.** In a *capital budgeting* context, the total time that must elapse before net accumulated cash inflows from a project including potential *salvage value* of assets at various times equal or exceed the accumulated cash outflows. Contrast with *payback period*, which assumes completion of the project and uses terminal salvage value. Bailout is superior to payback because bailout takes into account, at least to some degree, the *present value* of the cash flows after termination date being considered. The potential salvage value at any time includes some estimate of the flows that can occur after that time.

**balance.** As a noun, the sum of *debit* entries minus the sum of *credit* entries in an *account*. If positive, the difference is called a debit balance; if negative, a credit balance. As a verb, to find the difference described above.

**balance sheet.** Statement of financial position that shows *Total Assets* = Total Liabilities + Owners' Equity.

**balance sheet account.** An account that can appear on a balance sheet. A *permanent account*; contrast with *temporary account*.

**balloon.** Most *mortgage* and *installment loans* require relative equal periodic payments. Sometimes, the loan requires relatively equal periodic payments with a large final payment. The large final payment is called a "balloon" payment. Such loans are called "balloon" loans. Although a *coupon bond* meets this definition, the term is seldom, if ever, applied to bond loans.

**bank balance.** The amount of the balance in a checking account shown on the *bank statement*. Compare with *adjusted bank balance* and see *bank reconciliation schedule*.

**bank prime rate.** See *prime rate*.

**bank reconciliation schedule.** A schedule that shows how the difference between the book balance of the cash in bank account and the bank's statement can be explained. Takes into account the amount of such items as checks issued that have not cleared or deposits that have not been recorded by the bank as well as errors made by the bank or the firm.

**bank statement.** A statement sent by the bank to a checking account customer showing deposits, checks cleared, and service charges for a period, usually one month.

**bankrupt.** Said of a company whose *liabilities* exceed its *assets* where a legal petition has been filed and accepted under the bankruptcy law. A bankrupt firm is usually, but need not be, *insolvent*.

**base stock method.** A method of inventory valuation that assumes that there is a minimum normal or base stock of goods that must be kept on hand at all times for effective continuity of operations. This base quantity is valued at *acquisition cost* of the inventory on hand in the earliest period when inventory was on hand. The method is not allowable for income tax purposes and is no longer used, but is generally considered to be the forerunner of the *LIFO* method.

**basic accounting equation.** *Accounting equation.*

**basis.** *Acquisition cost*, or some substitute therefore, of an *asset* or *liability* used in computing gain or loss on disposition or retirement. *Attribute measured*. This term is used in both *financial* and *tax reporting*, but the basis of a given item need not be the same for both purposes.

**basket purchase.** Purchase of a group of *assets* (and *liabilities*) for a single price; *costs* must be assigned to each of the items so that the individual items can be recorded in the *accounts*.

**bear.** One who believes that security prices will fall. A "bear market" refers to a time when stock prices are generally declining. Contrast with *bull*.

**bearer bond.** See *registered bond* for contrast and definition.

**beginning inventory.** Valuation of *inventory* on hand at the beginning of the *accounting period*.

**behavioral congruence.** *Goal congruence*.

**betterment.** An *improvement*, usually *capitalized*.

**bid.** An offer to purchase, or the amount of the offer.

**big bath.** A *write off* of a substantial amount of costs previously treated as *assets*. Usually caused when a corporation drops a line of business that required a large investment but that proved to be unprofitable. Sometimes used to describe a situation where a corporation takes a large write off in one period in order to free later periods of gradual write offs of those amounts. In this sense it frequently occurs when there is a change in top management.

**Big Eight.** The eight largest U.S. *public accounting (CPA)* partnerships; in alphabetical order: Arthur Andersen & Co.; Coopers & Lybrand; Deloitte Haskins & Sells; Ernst & Whinney; Peat Marwick Main & Co.; Price Waterhouse & Co.; Touche Ross & Co.; and Arthur Young & Company.

**bill.** An *invoice* of charges and *terms of sale* for *goods* and *services*. Also, a piece of currency.

**bill of materials.** A specification of the quantities of *direct materials* expected to be used to produce a given job or quantity of output.

**board of directors.** The governing body of a corporation elected by the shareholders.

**bond.** A certificate to show evidence of debt. The *par value* is the *principal* or face amount of the bond payable at maturity. The *coupon rate* is the amount of interest payable in one year divided by the principal amount. Coupon bonds have attached to them coupons that can be redeemed at stated dates for interest payments. Normally, bonds carry semiannual coupons.

**bond conversion.** The act of exchanging *convertible bonds* for *preferred* or *common stock*.

**bond discount.** From the standpoint of the issuer of a *bond* at the issue date, the excess of the *par value* of a bond over its initial sales price; at later dates the excess of par over the sum of (initial issue price plus the portion of discount already *amortized*). From the standpoint of a bondholder, the difference between par value and selling price when the bond sells below par.

**bond indenture.** The contract between an issuer of *bonds* and the bondholders.

**bond premium.** Exactly parallel to *bond discount* except that the issue price (or current selling price) is higher than *par value*.

**bond ratings.** Ratings of corporate and *municipal bond* issues by Moody's Investors Service and by Standard & Poor's Corporation, based on the issuer's existing *debt* level, its previous record of payment, the *coupon rate* on the bonds, and the safety of the *assets* or *revenues* that are committed to paying off *principal* and *interest*. Moody's top rating is Aaa; Standard & Poor's is AAA.

**bond redemption.** Retirement of *bonds*.

**bond refunding.** To incur *debt*, usually through the issue of new *bonds*, intending to use the proceeds to retire an *outstanding* bond issue.

**bond sinking fund.** See *sinking fund*.

**bond table.** A table showing the current price of a *bond* as a function of the *coupon rate*, years to *maturity*, and effective *yield to maturity* (or *effective rate*).

**bonus.** Premium over normal *wage* or *salary*, paid usually for meritorious performance.

**bonus method.** When a new partner is admitted to a *partnership* and the new partner is to be credited with *capital* in excess proportion to the amount of *tangible* assets he or she contributes, two methods may be used to recognize this excess, say $10,000. First, $10,000 may be transferred from the old partners to the new one. This is the bonus method. Second, goodwill in the amount of $10,000 may be recognized as an asset with the credit to the new partner's capital account. This is the *goodwill method*. (Notice that the new partner's percentage of total ownership is not the same under the two methods.) If the new partner is to be credited with capital in smaller proportion than the amount of contribution, then there will be bonus or goodwill for the old partners.

**book.** As a verb, to record a transaction. As a noun, usually plural, the *journals* and *ledgers*. As an adjective, see *book value*.

**book cost.** *Book value.*

**book inventory.** An *inventory* amount that results, not from physical count, but from the amount of beginning inventory plus *invoice* amounts of net purchases less invoice amounts of *requisitions* or withdrawals; implies a *perpetual* method.

**book of original entry.** A *journal*.

**book value.** The amount shown in the books or in the *accounts* for an *asset, liability*, or *owners' equity* item. Generally used to refer to the *net* amount of an *asset* or group of assets shown in the account which records the asset and reductions, such as for *amortization*, in its cost. Of a firm, the excess of total assets over total liabilities. *Net assets*.

**book value per share of common stock.** Common *shareholders' equity* divided by the number of shares of *common stock outstanding*. See *ratio*.

**bookkeeping.** The process of analyzing and recording transactions in the accounting records.

**boot.** The additional money paid (or received) along with a used item in a trade-in or exchange transaction for another item. See *trade-in transaction*.

**borrower.** See *loan*.

**branch.** A sales office or other unit of an enterprise physically separated from the home office of the enterprise but not organized as a legally separate *subsidiary*. The term is rarely used to refer to manufacturing units.

**branch accounting.** An accounting procedure that enables the financial position and operations of each *branch* to be reported separately but later combined for published statements.

**breakeven analysis.** See *breakeven chart*.

**breakeven chart.** Two kinds of breakeven charts are shown here. The charts are based on the information for a month shown below. Revenue is $30 per unit.

| Cost Classification | Variable Cost, Per Unit | Fixed Cost, Per Month |
|---|---|---|
| Manufacturing costs: | | |
| Direct material ......... | $ 4 | — |
| Direct labor ............ | 9 | — |
| Overhead.............. | 4 | $3,060 |
| Total manufacturing costs .............. | $17 | $3,060 |
| Selling, general and administrative costs ... | 5 | 1,740 |
| Total costs .......... | $22 | $4,800 |

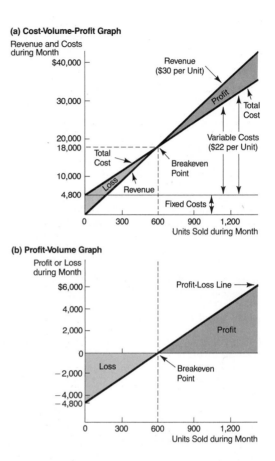

**(a) Cost-Volume-Profit Graph**

**(b) Profit-Volume Graph**

The cost-volume-profit graph presents the relationship of changes in volume to the amount of *profit*, or *income*. On such a graph, total *revenue* and total *costs* for each volume level are indicated and profit or loss at any volume can be read directly from the chart. The profit-volume graph does not show revenues and costs but more readily indicates profit (or loss) at various output levels. Two caveats should be kept in mind about these graphs. Although the curve depicting *variable cost* and total cost is shown as being a straight line for its entire length, it is likely that at low or high levels of output, variable cost would probably differ from $22 per unit. The variable cost figure was probably established by studies of operations at some broad central area of production, called the *relevant range*. For low (or high) levels of activity, the chart may not be applicable. For this reason, the total cost and profit-loss curves are sometimes shown as dotted lines at lower (or higher) volume levels. Second, this chart is simplified because it assumes a single product firm. For a multiproduct firm, the horizontal axis would have to be stated in dollars rather than in physical units of output. Breakeven charts for multiproduct firms necessarily assume that constant proportions of the several products are sold and changes in this mixture as well as in costs or selling prices would invalidate such a chart.

**breakeven point.** The volume of sales required so that total *revenues* and total *costs* are equal. May be expressed in units (*fixed costs/contribution per unit*) or in sales dollars [selling price per unit × (fixed costs/contribution per unit)].

**budget.** A financial plan that is used to estimate the results of future operations. Frequently used to help control future operations. In governmental operations, budgets often become the law.

**budgetary accounts.** In governmental accounting, the accounts that reflect estimated operations and financial condition, as affected by estimated *revenues, appropriations*, and *encumbrances*. In contrast to *proprietary accounts* that record the transactions.

**budgetary control.** Management of governmental (nongovernmental) unit in accordance with an official (approved) *budget* in order to keep total expenditures within authorized (planned) limits.

**budgeted cost.** See *standard cost* for definition and contrast.

**budgeted statements.** *Pro forma statements* prepared before the event or period occurs.

**bull.** One who believes that security prices will rise. A "bull market" refers to a time when stock prices are generally rising. Contrast with *bear*.

**burden.** See *overhead costs*.

**burn rate.** A new business usually begins life with cash-absorbing operating losses, but with a limited amount of cash. The "burn rate" measures how long the new business can survive before operating losses must stop or a new infusion of cash will be necessary. The measurement is ordinarily stated in terms of months.

**business combination**. As defined in *APB Opinion No. 16*, the bringing together into a single accounting *entity* of two or more incorporated or unincorporated businesses. The *merger* will be accounted for either with the *purchase method* or the *pooling-of-interests method*. See *conglomerate*.

**business entity.** *Entity. Accounting entity*.

**bylaws.** The rules adopted by the shareholders of a corporation that specify the general methods for carrying out the functions of the corporation.

**by-product.** A *joint product* whose sales value is so small relative to the sales value of the other joint product(s) that it does not receive normal accounting treatment. The costs assigned to by-products reduce the costs

of the main product(s). By-products are allocated a share of joint costs such that the expected gain or loss upon their sale is zero. Thus, by-products are shown in the *accounts* at *net realizable value*.

## C

**CA.** *Chartered accountant*.

**call**. An option to buy *shares* of a publicly traded corporation at a fixed price during a fixed time span. Contrast with *put*.

**call premium.** See *callable bond*.

**call price.** See *callable bond*.

**callable bond.** A *bond* for which the issuer reserves the right to pay a specific amount, the call price, to retire the obligation before *maturity* date. If the issuer agrees to pay more than the *face amount* of the bond when called the excess of the payment over the face amount is the "call premium."

**Canadian Institute of Chartered Accountants.** The national organization that represents *chartered accountants* in Canada.

**cancelable lease.** See *lease*.

**capacity.** Stated in units of product, the amount that can be produced per unit of time. Stated in units of input, such as *direct labor* hours, the amount of input that can be used in production per unit of time. This measure of output or input is used in allocating *fixed costs* if the amounts producible are normal, rather than maximum, amounts.

**capacity cost.** A *fixed cost* incurred to provide a firm with the capacity to produce or to sell. Consists of *standby costs* and *enabling costs*. Contrast with *programmed costs*.

**capacity variance.** *Production volume variance*.

**capital.** *Owners' equity* in a business. Often used, equally correctly, to mean the total assets of a business. Sometimes used to mean *capital assets*.

**capital asset.** Properly used, a designation for income tax purposes that describes property held by a taxpayer, except *cash*, inventoriable *assets*, goods held primarily for sale, most depreciable property, *real estate, receivables*, certain *intangibles*, and a few other items. Sometimes this term is imprecisely used to describe *plant* and *equipment*, which are clearly not capital assets under the income tax definition. Often the term is used to refer to an *investment* in *securities*.

**capital budget.** Plan of proposed outlays for acquiring long-term *assets* and the means of *financing* the acquisition.

**capital budgeting.** The process of choosing *investment* projects for an enterprise by considering the *present value* of cash flows and deciding how to raise the funds required by the investment.

**capital consumption allowance.** The term used for *depreciation expense* in national income accounting and the reporting of funds in the economy.

**capital contributed in excess of par (or stated) value.** A preferred title for the account that shows the amount received by the issuer for *capital stock* in excess of *par (or stated) value*.

**capital expenditure (outlay).** An *expenditure* to acquire long-term *assets*.

**capital gain.** The excess of proceeds over *cost*, or other *basis*, from the sale of a *capital asset* as defined by the Internal Revenue Code. If the capital asset has been held for a sufficiently long time before sale, then the tax on the gain is computed at a rate lower than is used for other gains and ordinary income.

**capital lease.** A *lease* treated by the *lessee* as both the borrowing of funds and the acquisition of an *asset* to be *amortized*. Both the *liability* and the asset are recognized on the balance sheet. Expenses consist of *interest* on the *debt* and *amortization* of the asset. The *lessor* treats the lease as the sale of the asset in return for a series of future cash receipts. Contrast with *operating lease*.

**capital loss.** A negative capital gain; see *capital gain*.

**capital rationing.** In a *capital budgeting* context, the imposing of constraints on the amounts of total capital expenditures in each period.

**capital stock.** The ownership shares of a corporation. Consists of all classes of *common* and *preferred stock*.

**capital structure.** The composition of a corporation's equities; the relative proportions of *short-term debt*, *long-term debt*, and *owners' equity*.

**capital surplus.** An inferior term for *capital contributed in excess of par (or stated) value*.

**capitalization of a corporation.** A term used by investment analysts to indicate *shareholders' equity* plus *bonds outstanding*.

**capitalization of earnings.** The process of estimating the economic worth of a firm by computing the *net present value* of the predicted *net income* (not *cash flows*) of the firm for the future.

**capitalization rate.** An *interest rate* used to convert a series of payments or receipts or earnings into a single *present value*.

**capitalize.** To record an *expenditure* that may benefit a future period as an *asset* rather than to treat the expenditure as an *expense* of the period of its occurrence. Whether or not expenditures for advertising or for research and development should be capitalized is controversial, but *SFAS No. 2* requires expensing of *R&D* costs. We believe expenditures should be capitalized if they lead to future benefits and thus meet the criterion to be an asset.

**carryback, carryforward, carryover.** The use of losses or tax credits in one period to reduce income taxes payable in other periods. There are two common kinds of carrybacks: for net operating losses and for *capital losses*. They are applied against taxable income. In general, carrybacks are for three years with the earliest year first. Operating losses can be carried forward for fifteen years. Corporate capital loss carryforwards are for five years. The capital loss for individuals can be carried forward indefinitely.

**carrying cost.** Costs (such as property taxes and insurance) of holding, or storing, *inventory* from the time of purchase until the time of sale or use.

**carrying value (amount).** *Book value*.

**CASB.** Cost Accounting Standards Board. A board of five members authorized by the U.S. Congress to "promulgate cost-accounting standards designed to achieve uniformity and consistency in the cost-accounting principles followed by defense contractors and subcontractors under federal contracts." The *principles* promulgated since 1970 by the CASB are likely to have considerable weight in practice where the *FASB* has not established a standard. Although the Congress allowed the CASB to go out of existence in 1980, its standards have the same force as before.

**cash.** Currency and coins, negotiable checks, and balances in bank accounts. For the *statement of cash flows*, "cash" also includes *marketable securities* held as *current assets*.

**cash basis of accounting.** In contrast to the *accrual basis of accounting*, a system of accounting in which *revenues* are recognized when *cash* is received and *expenses* are recognized as *disbursements* are made. No attempt is made to *match revenues* and *expenses* in determining *income*. See *modified cash basis*.

**cash budget.** A schedule of expected cash *receipts* and *disbursements*.

**cash collection basis.** The *installment method* for recognizing *revenue*. Not to be confused with the *cash basis of accounting*.

**cash conversion cycle.** *Cash cycle*.

**cash cycle.** The period of time that elapses during which *cash* is converted into *inventories*, inventories are converted into *accounts receivable*, and receivables are converted back into cash. *Earnings cycle.*

**cash disbursements journal.** A specialized *journal* used to record *expenditures* by *cash* and by *check*. If a *check register* is also used, a cash disbursements journal records only expenditures of currency and coins.

**cash discount.** A reduction in sales or purchase price allowed for prompt payment.

**cash dividend.** See *dividend.*

**cash equivalent value.** A term used to describe the amount for which an *asset* could be sold. *Market value. Fair market price (value).*

**cash flow.** Cash *receipts* minus *disbursements* from a given *asset*, or group of assets, for a given period.

**cash flow statement.** *Statement of cash flows.*

**cash provided by operations.** An important subtotal in the *statement of cash flows*. This amount is the total of revenues producing *cash* less *expenses* requiring cash. Often, the amount is shown as *net income* plus expenses not requiring cash (such as depreciation charges) minus revenues not producing cash (such as revenues recognized under the *equity method* of accounting for a long-term investment). The statement of cash flows maintains the same distinctions between *continuing operations, discontinued operations*, and *income* or *loss* from *extraordinary items* as does the *income statement*.

**cash receipts journal.** A specialized *journal* used to record all *receipts* of *cash*.

**cash (surrender) value of life insurance.** An amount equal, not to the face value of the policy to be paid in event of death, but to the amount that could be realized if the policy were immediately canceled and traded with the insurance company for cash. If a firm owns a life insurance policy, the policy is reported as an asset at an amount equal to this value.

**cash yield.** See *yield.*

**cashier's check.** A bank's own *check* drawn on itself and signed by the cashier or other authorized official. It is a direct obligation of the bank. Compare with *certified check*.

**catch-up depreciation.** *Backlog depreciation.*

**CCA.** *Current cost accounting; current value accounting.*

**central corporate expenses.** General *overhead expenses* incurred in running the corporate headquarters and related supporting activities of a corporation. These expenses are treated as *period expenses*. Contrast with *manufacturing overhead*. A major problem in *line of business reporting* is the treatment of these expenses.

**certificate.** The document that is the physical embodiment of a *bond* or a *share of stock*. A term sometimes used for the *auditor's report*.

**Certified management accountant.** *CMA*.

**certificate of deposit.** Federal law constrains the *rate of interest* that banks can pay. Under current law banks are allowed to pay a rate higher than the one allowed on a *time deposit* if the depositor promises to leave funds on deposit for several months or more. When the bank receives such funds, it issues a certificate of deposit. The depositor can withdraw the funds before maturity if a penalty is paid.

**certified check.** The *check* of a depositor drawn on a bank on the face of which the bank has inserted the words "accepted" or "certified" with the date and signature of a bank official. The check then becomes an obligation of the bank. Compare with *cashier's check*.

**certified financial statement.** A financial statement attested to by an independent *auditor* who is a *CPA*.

**certified internal auditor.** See *CIA*.

**certified public accountant. CPA.** An accountant who has satisfied the statutory and administrative requirements of his or her jurisdiction to be registered or licensed as a public accountant. In addition to passing the Uniform CPA Examination administered by the *AICPA*, the CPA must meet certain educational, experience, and moral requirements that differ from jurisdiction to jurisdiction. The jurisdictions are the 50 states, the District of Columbia, Guam, Puerto Rico, and the Virgin Islands.

**chain discount.** A series of *discount* percentages; for example, if a chain discount of 10 and 5 percent is quoted, the actual, or *invoice*, price is the nominal, or list, price times .90 times .95, or 85.5 percent of invoice price.

**change fund.** Coins and currency issued to cashiers, delivery drivers, and so on.

**changes, accounting.** See *accounting changes.*

**changes in financial position.** See *statement of cash flows.*

**charge.** As a noun, a *debit* to an account; as a verb, to debit.

**charge off.** To treat as a *loss* or *expense* an amount originally recorded as an *asset*; use of this term implies that the charge is not in accord with original expectations.

**chart of accounts.** A list of names and numbers, systematically organized, of *accounts*.

**charter.** Document issued by a state government authorizing the creation of a corporation.

**chartered accountant. CA.** The title used in Australia, Canada, and the United Kingdom for an accountant who has satisfied the requirements of the institute of his or her jurisdiction to be qualified to serve as a *public accountant*. In Canada, each provincial institute or order has the right to administer the examination and set the standards of performance and ethics for Chartered Accountants in its province. For a number of years, however, the provincial organizations have pooled their rights to qualify new members through the Inter-provincial Education Committee and the result is that there are nationally set and graded examinations given in English and French. The pass/fail grade awarded by the Board of Examiners (a subcommittee of the Inter-provincial Education Committee) is rarely deviated from.

**check.** You know what a check is. The Federal Reserve Board defines a check as "a *draft* or order upon a bank or banking house purporting to be drawn upon a deposit of funds for the payment at all events of a certain sum of money to a certain person therein named or to him or his order or to bearer and payable instantly on demand." It must contain the phrase "pay to the order of." The amount shown on the check's face must be clearly readable and it must have the signature of the drawer. Checks need not be dated, although they usually are. The *balance* in the *cash account* is usually reduced when a check is issued, not later when it clears the bank and reduces cash in bank. See *remittance advice*.

**check register.** A *journal* to record *checks* issued.

**CIA.** Certified Internal Auditor. One who has satisfied certain requirements of the *Institute of Internal Auditors* including experience, ethics, education, and passing examinations.

**CICA.** *Canadian Institute of Chartered Accountants*.

**CIF.** Cost, insurance, and freight; a term used in contracts along with the name of a given port to indicate that the quoted price includes insurance, handling, and freight charges up to delivery by the seller at the given port.

**circulating capital.** *Working capital*.

**clean opinion.** See *auditor's report*.

**clean surplus concept.** The notion that the only entries to the *retained earnings* account are to record *net income* and *dividends*. See *comprehensive income*. Contrast with *current operating performance concept*. This concept, with minor exceptions, is now controlling in *GAAP*. (See *APB Opinions* Nos. 9 and 30.)

**clearing account.** An account containing amounts to be transferred to another account(s) before the end of the *accounting period*. Examples are the *income summary* account (whose balance is transferred to *retained earnings*) and the purchases account (whose balance is transferred to *inventory* or to *cost of goods sold*).

**close.** As a verb, to transfer the *balance* of a *temporary* or *contra* or *adjunct* account to the main account to which it relates; for example, to transfer *revenue* and *expense* accounts directly, or through the *income summary* account, to an *owner's equity* account, or to transfer *purchase discounts* to purchases.

**closed account.** An *account* with equal *debits* and *credits*, usually as a result of a *closing entry*. See *ruling an account*.

**closing entries.** The *entries* that accomplish the transfer of balances in *temporary accounts* to the related *balance sheet accounts*. See *work sheet*.

**closing inventory.** *Ending inventory*.

**CMA.** Certificate in Management Accounting. Awarded by the *Institute of Certified Management Accountants* of the *National Association of Accountants* to those who pass a set of examinations and meet certain experience and continuing education requirements.

**CoCoA.** *Continuously contemporary accounting*.

**coding of accounts.** The numbering of *accounts*, as for a *chart of accounts*, which is necessary for computerized accounting.

**coinsurance.** Insurance policies that protect against hazards such as fire or water damage often specify that the owner of the property may not collect the full amount of insurance for a loss unless the insurance policy covers at least some specified "coinsurance" percentage, usually about 80 percent, of the *replacement cost* of the property. Coinsurance clauses induce the owner to carry full, or nearly full, coverage.

**COLA.** Cost-of-living adjustment. See *indexation*.

**collateral.** *Assets* pledged by a *borrower* that will be given up if the *loan* is not paid.

**collectible.** Capable of being converted into *cash*; now, if due; later, otherwise.

**combination.** See *business combination*.

**commercial paper.** *Short-term notes* issued by corporate borrowers.

**commission.** Remuneration, usually expressed as a percentage, to employees based upon an activity rate, such as sales.

**committed costs.** *Capacity costs.*

**Committee on Accounting Procedure. CAP.** Predecessor of the *APB.* The *AICPA's* principles-promulgating body from 1939 through 1959. Its 51 pronouncements are called *Accounting Research Bulletins.*

**common cost.** *Cost* resulting from use of *raw materials*, a facility (for example, plant or machines), or a service (for example, fire insurance) that benefits several products or departments and must be allocated to those products or departments. Common costs result when multiple products are produced together although they could be produced separately; joint costs occur when multiple products are of necessity produced together. Many writers use common costs and *joint costs* synonymously. See *joint costs, indirect costs*, and *overhead.* See *sterilized allocation.*

**common dollar accounting.** *Constant dollar accounting.*

**common monetary measuring unit.** For U.S. corporations, the dollar. See also *stable monetary unit assumption* and *constant dollar accounting.*

**common shares.** *Shares* representing the class of owners who have residual claims on the *assets* and *earnings* of a *corporation* after all *debt* and *preferred shareholders'* claims have been met.

**common stock equivalent.** A *security* whose primary value arises from its ability to be exchanged for *common shares*; includes *stock options, warrants*, and also *convertible bonds* or *convertible preferred stock* whose *effective interest rate* is at the time of issue is less than two-thirds the average Aa corporate bond yield. See *bond ratings.*

**common size statement.** A *percentage statement* usually based on total *assets* or *net sales* or *revenues.*

**company wide control.** See *control system.*

**comparative (financial) statements.** *Financial statements* showing information for the same company for different times, usually two successive years. Nearly all published financial statements are in this form. Contrast with *historical summary.*

**compensating balance.** When a bank lends funds to a customer, it often requires that the customer keep on deposit in his or her checking account an amount equal to some percentage—say, 20 percent—of the loan. The amount required to be left on deposit is the compensating balance. Such amounts effectively increase the *interest rate.* The amounts of such balances must be disclosed in *notes* to the *financial statements.*

**completed contract method.** Recognizing *revenues* and *expenses* for a job or order only when it is finished, except that when a loss on the contract is expected, reve-

nues and expenses are recognized in the period when the loss is first forecast. This term is generally used only for long-term contracts. It is otherwise equivalent to the *sales basis* of *revenue recognition.*

**completed sales basis.** See *sales basis of revenue recognition.*

**compliance audit.** Objectively obtaining and evaluating evidence regarding assertions, actions, and events to ascertain the degree of correspondence between them and established performance criteria.

**composite cost of capital.** See *cost of capital.*

**composite depreciation.** *Group depreciation* of dissimilar items.

**composite life method.** *Group depreciation*, which see, for items of unlike kind. The term may be used when a single item, such as a crane, which consists of separate units with differing service lives, such as the chassis, the motor, the lifting mechanism, and so on, is depreciated as a whole rather than treating each of the components separately.

**compound entry.** A *journal entry* with more than one *debit* or more than one *credit*, or both. See *trade-in transaction* for an example.

**compound interest.** *Interest* calculated on *principal* plus previously undistributed interest.

**compound interest depreciation.** A method designed to hold the *rate of return* on an asset constant. First find the *internal rate of return* on the cash inflows and outflows of the asset. The periodic depreciation charge is the cash flow for the period less the internal rate of return multiplied by the asset's book value at the beginning of the period. When the cash flows from the asset are constant over time, the method is sometimes called the "annuity method" of depreciation.

**compounding period.** The time period for which *interest* is calculated. At the end of the period, the interest may be paid to the lender or added (that is, converted) to principal for the next interest-earning period, which is usually a year or some portion of a year.

**comprehensive budget.** *Master budget.*

**comprehensive income.** Defined in *SFAS No. 3* as "the change in equity (net assets) of an entity during a period from transactions and other events and circumstances from nonowner sources. It includes all changes in equity during a period except those resulting from investments by owners and distributions to owners." In this definition, "equity" means *owners' equity.*

**comptroller.** Same meaning and pronunciation as *controller.*

**conceptual framework.** A coherent system of interrelated objectives and fundamentals, promulgated by the *FASB* primarily through its *SFAC* publications, expected to lead to consistent standards for *financial accounting* and reporting.

**confirmation.** A formal memorandum delivered by the customers or suppliers of a company to its independent *auditor* verifying the amounts shown as receivable or payable. The confirmation document is originally sent by the auditor to the customer. If the auditor asks that the document be returned whether the *balance* is correct or incorrect, then it is called a "positive confirmation." If the auditor asks that the document be returned only if there is an error, it is called a "negative confirmation."

**conglomerate.** *Holding company*. This term is used when the owned companies are in dissimilar lines of business.

**conservatism.** A *reporting objective* that calls for anticipation of all *losses* and *expenses* but defers recognition of *gains* or *profits* until they are *realized* in *arm's-length* transactions. In the absence of certainty, events are to be reported in a way that tends to minimize cumulative income.

**consignee.** See *on consignment*.

**consignment.** See *on consignment*.

**consignor.** See *on consignment*.

**consistency.** Treatment of like *transactions* in the same way in consecutive periods so that financial statements will be more comparable than otherwise. The reporting policy implying that procedures, once adopted, should be followed from period to period by a reporting *entity*. See *accounting changes* for the treatment of inconsistencies.

**consol.** A *bond* that never matures; a *perpetuity* in the form of a bond. Originally issued by Great Britain after the Napoleonic wars to consolidate debt issues of that period. The term arose as an abbreviation for "consolidated annuities."

**consolidated financial statements.** Statements issued by legally separate companies that show financial position and income as they would appear if the companies were one economic *entity*.

**constant dollar.** A hypothetical unit of *general purchasing power*, denoted "C$" by the *FASB*.

**constant dollar accounting.** Accounting where items are measured in *constant dollars*. See *historical cost/constant dollar accounting* and *current cost/constant dollar accounting*.

**constant dollar date.** The time at which the *general purchasing power* of one *constant dollar* is exactly equal to the *general purchasing power* of one *nominal dollar*; that is, the date when C$1 = $1. When the constant dollar date is mid-period, then the nominal amounts of *revenues* and *expenses* spread evenly throughout the period are equal to their constant dollar amounts, but end-of-period *balance sheet* amounts measured in constant mid-period dollars differ from their nominal dollar amounts. When the constant dollar date is at the end of the period, then the constant dollar and nominal dollar amounts on a balance sheet for that date are identical.

**constructive receipt.** An item is included in taxable income when the taxpayer can control funds whether or not cash has been received. For example, *interest* added to *principal* in a savings account is deemed by the *IRS* to be constructively received.

**Consumer Price Index. CPI.** A *price index* computed and issued monthly by the Bureau of Labor Statistics of the U.S. Department of Labor. The index attempts to track the price level of a group of goods and services purchased by the average consumer. The CPI is used in *constant dollar accounting*. Contrast with *GNP Implicit Price Deflator*.

**contingency.** A potential *liability*; if a specified event were to occur, such as losing a lawsuit, a liability would be recognized. The contingency is merely disclosed in notes, rather than shown in the balance sheet. *SFAS No. 5* requires treatment as a contingency until the outcome is "probable" and the amount of payment can be reasonably estimated, perhaps within a range. When the outcome becomes probable (the future event is "likely" to occur) and the amount can be reasonably estimated (using the lower end of a range if only a range can be estimated), then the liability is recognized in the accounts, rather than being disclosed in the notes. A *material* contingency may lead to a qualified, "*subject to*," auditor's opinion. *Gain* contingencies are not recorded in the accounts, but are merely disclosed in notes.

**contingent annuity.** An *annuity* whose number of payments depends upon the outcome of an event whose timing is uncertain at the time the annuity is set up; for example, an annuity payable until death of the *annuitant*. Contrast with *annuity certain*.

**contingent issue (securities).** Securities issuable to specific individuals upon the occurrence of some event, such as the firm's attaining a specified level of earnings.

**contingent liability.** *Contingency*. This term is to be avoided because it refers to something that is not a *liability* on the *balance sheet*.

**continuing appropriation.** A governmental *appropriation* automatically renewed without further legislative action until it is altered or revoked or expended.

**continuing operations.** See *income from continuing operations*.

**continuity of operations.** The assumption in accounting that the business *entity* will continue to operate long enough for current plans to be carried out. The *going-concern assumption*.

**continuous budget.** A *budget* that perpetually adds a period in the future as the period just ended is dropped.

**continuous compounding.** *Compound interest* where the *compounding period* is every instant of time. See *e* for the computation of the equivalent annual or periodic rate.

**continuous inventory method.** The *perpetual inventory* method.

**Continuously Contemporary Accounting. CoCoA.** A name coined by the Australian theorist, Raymond J. Chambers, to indicate a combination of *current value accounting* where amounts are measured in *constant dollars* and based on *exit values*.

**contra account.** An *account*, such as *accumulated depreciation*, that accumulates subtractions from another account, such as machinery. Contrast with *adjunct account*.

**contributed capital.** The sum of the balances in *capital stock* accounts plus *capital contributed in excess of par (or stated) value* accounts. Contrast with *donated capital*.

**contributed surplus.** An inferior term for *capital contributed in excess of par value*.

**contribution approach.** Method of preparing *income statements* that separates *variable costs* from *fixed costs* in order to emphasize the importance of cost behavior patterns for purposes of planning and control.

**contribution margin.** *Revenue* from *sales* less all variable *expenses*. See *gross margin*.

**contribution margin ratio.** *Contribution margin* divided by *net sales*; usually measured from the price and cost of a single unit.

**contribution per unit.** Selling price less *variable costs* per unit.

**contributory.** Said of a *pension plan* where employees, as well as employers, make payments to a pension *fund*. Note that the provisions for *vesting* are applicable only to the employer's payments. Whatever the degree of vesting of the employer's payments, the employee typically gets back all of his or her payments, with interest, in case of death, or other cessation of employment, before retirement.

**control (controlling) account.** A summary *account* with totals equal to those of entries and balances that appear in individual accounts in a *subsidiary ledger*.

Accounts Receivable is a control account backed up with an account for each customer. The balance in a control account should not be changed unless a corresponding change is made in one of the subsidiary accounts.

**control system.** A device for ensuring that actions are carried out according to plan or for safeguarding *assets*. A system for ensuring that actions are carried out according to plan can be designed for a single function within the firm, called "operational control," for autonomous segments within the firm that generally have responsibility for both revenues and costs, called "divisional control," or for activities of the firm as a whole, called "company-wide control." Systems designed for safeguarding *assets* are called "internal control" systems.

**controllable cost.** A *cost* whose amount can be influenced by the way in which operations are carried out, such as advertising costs. These costs can be *fixed* or *variable*. See *programmed costs* and *managed costs*.

**controlled company.** A company, a majority of whose voting shares is held by an individual or corporation. Effective control can sometimes be exercised when less than 50 percent of the shares is owned.

**controller.** The title often used for the chief accountant of an organization. Often spelled *comptroller*.

**conversion.** The act of exchanging a convertible security for another security.

**conversion cost.** *Direct labor* costs plus factory *overhead* costs incurred in producing a product. That is, the cost to convert raw materials to finished products. *Manufacturing cost*.

**conversion period.** *Compounding period*. Also, period during which a *convertible bond* or *convertible preferred stock* can be converted into *common stock*.

**convertible bond.** A *bond* that may be converted into a specified number of shares of *capital stock* during the *conversion period*.

**convertible preferred stock.** *Preferred shares* that may be converted into a specified number of shares of *common stock*.

**co-product.** A product sharing production facilities with another product. For example, if an apparel manufacturer produces shirts and jeans on the same line, these are co-products. Co-products are distinguished from *joint products* and *by-products*, which by their very nature must be produced together, such as the various grades of wood produced in a lumber factory.

**copyright.** Exclusive right granted by the government to an individual author, composer, playwright, and the like for the life of the individual plus 50 years. If the copyright is granted to a firm, then the right extends 75 years after the original publication. The *economic life* of a copyright may be considerably less than the legal life as, for example, the copyright of this book.

**corporation.** A legal entity authorized by a state to operate under the rules of the entity's *charter*.

**correcting entry.** An *adjusting entry* where an improperly recorded *transaction* is properly recorded. Not to be confused with entries that correct *accounting errors*.

**correction of errors.** See *accounting errors*.

**cost.** The sacrifice, measured by the *price* paid or required to be paid, to acquire *goods* or *services*. See *acquisition cost* and *replacement cost*. The term "cost" is often used when referring to the valuation of a good or service acquired. When "cost" is used in this sense, a cost is an *asset*. When the benefits of the acquisition (the goods or services acquired) expire, the cost becomes an *expense* or *loss*. Some writers, however, use cost and expense as synonyms. Contrast with *expense*.

**cost accounting.** Classifying, summarizing, recording, reporting, and allocating current or predicted *costs*. A subset of *managerial accounting*.

**Cost Accounting Standards Board.** See *CASB*.

**cost accumulation.** Bringing together, usually in a single *account*, all *costs* of a specified activity. Contrast with *cost allocation*.

**cost allocation.** Assigning *costs* to individual products or time periods. Contrast with *cost accumulation*.

**cost-based transfer price.** A *transfer price* based on *historical costs*.

**cost behavior.** The functional relation between changes in activity and changes in *cost*. For example, *fixed* versus *variable costs*; *linear* versus *curvilinear cost*.

**cost/benefit criterion.** Some measure of *costs* compared to some measure of *benefits* for a proposed undertaking. If the costs exceed the benefits, then the undertaking is judged not worthwhile. This criterion will not give good decisions unless all costs and benefits flowing from the undertaking are estimated.

**cost center.** A unit of activity for which *expenditures* and *expenses* are accumulated.

**cost effective.** Among alternatives, the one whose benefit, or payoff, per unit of cost is highest. Sometimes said of an action whose expected benefits exceed expected costs whether or not there are other alternatives with larger benefit/cost ratios.

**cost estimation.** The process of measuring the functional relation between changes in activity levels and changes in cost.

**cost flow assumption.** See *flow assumption*.

**cost flows.** Costs passing through various classifications within an entity. See *flow of costs* for a diagram.

**cost method (for investments).** Accounting for an investment in the *capital stock* or *bonds* of another company where the investment is shown at *acquisition cost*, and only *dividends* declared or *interest receivable* is treated as *revenue*.

**cost method (for treasury stock).** The method of showing *treasury stock* in a *contra account* to all other items of *shareholders' equity* in an amount equal to that paid to reacquire the stock.

**cost objective.** Any activity for which a separate measurement of *costs* is desired. Examples include departments, products, and territories.

**cost of capital.** *Opportunity cost* of funds invested in a business. The rate of return required to be earned on an asset before the rational owner will devote that asset to a particular purpose. Sometimes measured as the average rate per year a company must pay for its *equities*. In efficient capital markets, the *discount rate* that equates the expected *present value* of all future cash flows to common shareholders with the market value of common stock at a given time.

The cost of capital is often measured by taking a *weighted average* of the firm's *debt* and various *equity securities*. The measurement so derived is sometimes called the "composite cost of capital," and some analysts confuse this measurement of the cost of capital with the cost of capital itself. For example, if the equities of a firm include substantial amounts for the *deferred income tax liability*, the composite cost of capital will underestimate the true cost of capital, the required rate of return on a firm's assets, because the deferred income tax liability has no explicit cost.

**cost of goods manufactured.** The sum of all costs allocated to products completed during a period; includes materials, labor, and *overhead*.

**cost of goods purchased.** Net purchase price of goods acquired plus costs of storage and delivery to the place where the items can be productively used.

**cost of goods sold.** Inventoriable *costs* that are *expensed* because the units are sold; equals *beginning inventory* plus *cost of goods purchased* or *manufactured* minus *ending inventory*.

**cost of sales.** Generally refers to *cost of goods sold*; occasionally, to *selling expenses*.

**cost or market, whichever is lower.** See *lower of cost or market*.

**cost percentage.** One less *markup percentage*. *Cost* of *goods available for sale* divided by selling prices of goods available for sale (when FIFO is used). With *LIFO, cost* of *purchases* divided by selling price of purchases. See *markup* for further detail on inclusions in calculation of cost percentage.

**cost pool.** *Indirect cost pool*.

**cost principle.** The *principle* that requires reporting *assets* at *historical* or *acquisition cost*, less accumulated *amortization*. This principle is based on the assumption that cost is equal to *fair market value* at the date of acquisition and subsequent changes are not likely to be significant.

**cost-recovery-first method.** A method of *revenue* recognition that *credits inventory* as collections are received until all costs are recovered. Only after costs are completely recovered is *income* recognized. To be used in financial reporting only when the total amount of collections is highly uncertain. Can never be used in income tax reporting. Contrast with the *installment method* where constant proportions of each collection are credited both to cost and to income.

**cost sheet.** Statement that shows all the elements comprising the total cost of an item.

**cost terminology.** The word "cost" appears in many accounting terms. The exhibit on pages 729 through 731 classifies some of these by the distinctions the terms are used to make. Joel Dean was, to our knowledge, the first to attempt such distinctions; we have used some of his ideas here. Some terms have more detailed discussion under their own listings.

**cost-to-cost.** The *percentage-of-completion method* where the estimate of completion is the ratio of costs incurred to date divided by total costs expected to be incurred for the entire project.

**cost-volume-profit analysis.** A study of the sensitivity of *profits* to changes in units sold (or produced), assuming some *semivariable costs* in the cost structure.

**cost-volume-profit graph (chart).** A graph that shows the relation between *fixed costs, contribution per unit, breakeven point*, and *sales*. See *breakeven chart*.

**costing.** The process of calculating the cost of activities, products, or services. The British word for *cost accounting*.

**coupon.** That portion of a *bond* document redeemable at a specified date for *interest* payments. Its physical form is much like a ticket; each coupon is dated and is deposited at a bank, just like a check, for collection or is mailed to the issuer's agent for collection.

**coupon rate.** Of a *bond*, the amount of annual coupons divided by par value. Contrast with *effective rate*.

**covenant.** A promise with legal validity.

**CPA.** See *certified public accountant*. The *AICPA* suggests that no periods be shown in the abbreviation.

**CPI.** *Consumer price index*.

**CPP.** Current purchasing power; usually used as an adjective modifying the word "accounting" to mean the accounting that produces *constant dollar financial statements*.

**Cr.** Abbreviation for *credit*.

**credit.** As a noun, an entry on the right-hand side of an *account*. As a verb, to make an entry on the right-hand side of an account. Records increases in *liabilities, owner's equity, revenues* and *gains*; records decreases in *assets* and *expenses*. See *debit and credit conventions*. Also the ability or right to buy or borrow in return for a promise to pay later.

**credit loss.** The amount of *accounts receivable* that is, or is expected to become, *uncollectible*.

**credit memorandum.** A document used by a seller to inform a buyer that the buyer's *account receivable* is being credited (reduced) because of *errors, returns*, or *allowances*. Also, the document provided by a bank to a depositor to indicate that the depositor's balance is being increased because of some event other than a deposit, such as the collection by the bank of the depositor's *note receivable*.

**creditor.** One who lends.

**cross-reference (index).** A number placed by each *account* in a *journal entry* indicating the *ledger* account to which the entry is posted and placing in the ledger the page number of the journal where the entry was made. Used to link the *debit* and *credit* parts of an entry in the ledger accounts back to the original entry in the journal. See *audit trail*.

**cross-section analysis.** Analysis of *financial statements* of various firms for a single period of time; contrast with time-series analysis where statements of a given firm are analyzed over several periods of time.

**cumulative dividend.** Preferred stock *dividends* that, if not paid, accrue as a commitment that must be paid before dividends to common shareholders can be declared.

**cumulative preferred shares.** *Preferred* shares with *cumulative dividend* rights.

## Cost Terminology: Distinctions among Terms Containing the Word "Cost"

| Terms (Synonyms Given in Parentheses) | | | Distinctions and Comments |
|---|---|---|---|
| | | | 1. The following pairs of terms distinguish the basis measured in accounting. |
| Historical Cost (Acquisition Cost) | vs. | Current Cost | A distinction used in financial accounting. Current cost can be used more specifically to mean replacement cost, net realizable value, or present value of cash flows. "Current cost" is often used narrowly to mean replacement cost. |
| Historical Cost (Actual Cost) | vs. | Standard Cost | The distinction between historical and standard costs arises in product costing for inventory valuation. Some systems record actual costs while others record the standard costs. |
| | | | 2. The following pairs of terms denote various distinctions among historical costs. For each pair of terms, the sum of the two kinds of costs equals total historical cost used in financial reporting. |
| Variable Cost | vs. | Fixed Cost (Constant Cost) | Distinction used in breakeven analysis and in designing cost accounting systems, particularly for product costing. See (4), below, for a further subdivision of fixed costs and (5), below, for an economic distinction closely paralleling this one. |
| Traceable Cost | vs. | Common Cost (Joint Cost) | Distinction arises in allocating manufacturing costs to product. Common costs are allocated to product, but the allocations are more-or-less arbitrary. The distinction also arises in segment reporting and in separating manufacturing from nonmanufacturing costs. |
| Direct Cost | vs. | Indirect Cost | Distinction arises in designing cost accounting systems and in product costing. Direct costs can be traced directly to a cost object (e.g., a product, a responsibility center), whereas indirect costs cannot. |
| Out-of-Pocket Cost (Outlay Cost; Cash Cost) | vs. | Book Cost | Virtually all costs recorded in financial statements require a cash outlay at one time or another. The distinction here separates expenditures to occur in the future from those already made and is used in making decisions. Book costs, such as for depreciation, reduce income without requiring a future outlay of cash. The cash has already been spent. See future vs. past costs in (5), below. |
| Incremental Cost (Marginal Cost; Differential Cost) | vs. | Unavoidable Cost (Inescapable Cost; Sunk Cost) | Distinction used in making decisions. Incremental costs will be incurred (or saved) if a decision is made to go ahead (or to stop) some activity, but not otherwise. Unavoidable costs will be reported in financial statements whether the decision is made to go ahead or not, because cash has already been spent or committed. Not all unavoidable costs are book costs, as, for example, a salary promised but not yet earned, that will be paid even if a no-go decision is made. |
| | | | The economist restricts the term marginal cost to the cost of producing one more unit. Thus the next unit has a marginal cost; the next week's output has an incremental cost. If a firm produces and sells a new product, the related new costs would properly be called incremental, not marginal. If a factory is closed, the costs saved are incremental, not marginal. |
| Escapable Cost | vs. | Inescapable Cost (Unavoidable Cost) | Same distinction as incremental vs. sunk costs, but this pair is used only when the decision maker is considering stopping something — ceasing to produce a product, closing a factory, or the like. See next pair. |
| Avoidable Cost | vs. | Unavoidable Cost | A distinction sometimes used in discussing the merits of variable and absorption costing. Avoidable costs are treated as product cost and unavoidable costs are treated as period expenses under variable costing. |

| Terms (Synonyms Given in Parentheses) | | | Distinctions and Comments |
|---|---|---|---|
| Controllable Cost | vs. | Uncontrollable Cost | The distinction here is used in assigning responsibility and in setting bonus or incentive plans. All costs can be affected by someone in the entity; those who design incentive schemes attempt to hold a person responsible for a cost only if that person can influence the amount of the cost. |

3. In each of the following pairs, used in historical cost accounting, the word "cost" appears in one of the terms where "expense" is meant.

| Terms (Synonyms Given in Parentheses) | | | Distinctions and Comments |
|---|---|---|---|
| Expired Cost | vs. | Unexpired Cost | The distinction is between *expense* and *asset*. |
| Product Cost | vs. | Period Cost | The terms distinguish product cost from period expense. When a given asset is used, is its cost converted into work in process and then finished goods on the balance sheet until the goods are sold or is it an expense shown on this period's income statement? Product costs appear on the income statement as part of cost of goods sold in the period when the goods are sold. Period expenses appear on the income statement with an appropriate caption for the item in the period when the cost is incurred or recognized. |

4. The following subdivisions of fixed (historical) costs are used in analyzing operations. The relation between the components of fixed costs is:

$$\underbrace{\text{Fixed Costs}} = \underbrace{\text{Capacity Costs}} + \text{Programmed Costs}$$

Fixed Costs:
Semifixed Costs + "Pure" Fixed Costs + Fixed Portions of Semivariable Costs

Capacity Costs:
Standby Costs + Enabling Costs

| Terms (Synonyms Given in Parentheses) | | | Distinctions and Comments |
|---|---|---|---|
| Capacity Cost (Committed Cost) | vs. | Programmed Cost (Managed Cost; Discretionary Cost) | Capacity costs give a firm the capability to produce or to sell. Programmed costs, such as for advertising or research and development, may not be essential, but once a decision to incur them it made, they become fixed costs. |
| Standby Cost | vs. | Enabling Cost | Standby costs will be incurred whether capacity, once acquired, is used or not, such as property taxes and depreciation on a factory. Enabling costs, such as for security force, can be avoided if the capacity is unused. |
| Semifixed Cost | vs. | Semivariable Cost | A cost fixed over a wide range but that can change at various levels is a semifixed cost or "step cost." An example is the cost of rail lines from the factory to the main rail line where fixed cost depends on whether there are one or two parallel lines, but are independent of the number of trains run per day. Semivariable costs combine a strictly fixed component cost plus a variable component. Telephone charges usually have a fixed monthly component plus a charge related to usage. |

5. The following pairs of terms distinguish among economic uses or decision-making uses or regulatory uses of cost terms.

| Terms (Synonyms Given in Parentheses) | | | Distinctions and Comments |
|---|---|---|---|
| Fully Absorbed Cost | vs. | Variable Cost (Direct Cost) | Fully absorbed costs refer to costs where fixed costs have been allocated to units or departments as required by generally accepted accounting principles. Variable costs, in contrast, may be more relevant for making decisions, such as in setting prices. |

| Terms (Synonyms Given in Parentheses) | | | Distinctions and Comments |
|---|---|---|---|
| Fully Absorbed Cost | vs. | Full Cost | In full costing, all costs, manufacturing costs as well as central corporate express (including financing expenses), are allocated to product or divisions. In full absorption costing, only manufacturing costs are allocated to product. Only in full costing will revenues, expenses, and income summed over all products or divisions equal corporate revenues, expenses, and income. |
| Opportunity Cost | vs. | Outlay Cost (Out-of-Pocket Cost) | Opportunity cost refers to the economic benefit forgone by using a resource for one purpose instead of for another. The outlay cost of the resource will be recorded in financial records. The distinction arises because a resource is already in the possession of the entity with a recorded historical cost. Its economic value to the firm, opportunity cost, generally differs from the historical cost; it can be either larger or smaller. |
| Future Cost | vs. | Past Cost | Effective decision making analyzes only present and future outlay costs, or out-of-pocket costs. Opportunity costs are relevant for profit maximizing; past costs are used in financial reporting. |
| Short-Run Cost | vs. | Long-Run Cost | Short-run costs vary as output is varied for a given configuration of plant and equipment. Long-run costs can be incurred to change that configuration. This pair of terms is the economic analog of the accounting pair, see (2) above, variable and fixed costs. The analogy is not perfect because some short-run costs are fixed, such as property taxes on the factory, from the point of view of breakeven analysis. |
| Imputed Cost | vs. | Book Cost | In a regulatory setting some costs, for example the cost of owners' equity capital, are calculated and used for various purposes; these are imputed costs. Imputed costs are not recorded in the historical costs accounting records for financial reporting. Book costs are recorded. |
| Average Cost | vs. | Marginal Cost | The economic distinction equivalent to fully absorbed cost of product and direct cost of product. Average cost is total cost divided by number of units. Marginal cost is the cost to produce the next unit (or the last unit). |
| Incremental Cost | vs. | Variable Cost | Whether a cost changes or remains fixed depends on the activity basis being considered. Typically, but not invariably, costs are said to be variable or fixed with respect to an activity basis such as changes in production levels. Typically, but not invariably, costs are said to be incremental or not with respect to an activity basis such as the undertaking of some new venture. For example, consider the decision to undertake the production of food processors, rather than food blenders, which the manufacturer has been making. To produce processors requires the acquisition of a new machine tool. The cost of the new machine tool is incremental with respect to a decision to produce food processors instead of food blenders, but, once acquired, becomes a fixed cost of producing food processors. If costs of direct labor hours are going to be incurred for the production of food processors or food blenders, whichever is produced (in a scenario when not both are to be produced), such costs are variable with respect to production measured in units, but not incremental with respect to the decision to produce processors rather than blenders. This distinction is often blurred in practice, so a careful understanding of the activity basis being considered is necessary for understanding of the concepts being used in a particular application. |

**current asset.** *Cash* and other *assets* that are expected to be turned into cash, sold, or exchanged within the normal operating cycle of the firm, usually one year. Current assets include *cash, marketable securities, receivables, inventory,* and *current prepayments.*

**current cost.** *Cost* stated in terms of current values (of *productive capacity*) rather than in terms of *acquisition cost*. See *net realizable value, current selling price.*

**current cost accounting.** The *FASB's* term for *financial statements* where the *attribute measured* is *current cost.*

**current cost/nominal dollar accounting.** Accounting based on *current cost* valuations measured in *nominal dollars*. Components of *income* include an *operating margin* and *holding gains and losses.*

**current exit value.** *Exit value.*

**current fund.** In governmental accounting, a synonym for general fund.

**current funds.** *Cash* and other assets readily convertible into cash. In governmental accounting, funds spent for operating purposes during the current period. Includes *general, special revenue, debt service,* and *enterprise funds.*

**current (gross) margin.** See *operating margin (based on current costs).*

**current liability.** A debt or other obligation that must be discharged within a short time, usually the *earnings cycle* or one year, normally by expending *current assets.*

**current operating performance concept.** The notion that reported *income* for a period ought to reflect only ordinary, normal, and recurring operations of that period. A consequence is that *extraordinary* and nonrecurring items are entered directly in the Retained Earnings account. Contrast with *clean surplus concept.* This concept is no longer acceptable. (See *APB Opinions Nos. 9* and *30*.)

**current ratio.** Sum of *current assets* divided by sum of *current liabilities.* See *ratio.*

**current realizable value.** *Realizable value.*

**current replacement cost.** Of an *asset,* the amount currently required to acquire an identical asset (in the same condition and with the same service potential) or an asset capable of rendering the same service at a current *fair market price*. If these two amounts differ, the lower is usually used. Contrast with *reproduction cost.*

**current selling price.** The amount for which an *asset* could be sold as of a given time in an *arm's-length* transaction, rather than in a forced sale.

**current service costs.** *Service costs* of a *pension plan.*

**current value accounting.** The form of accounting where all assets are shown at *current replacement cost (entry value)* or *current selling price* or *net realizable value (exit value)* and all *liabilities* are shown at *present value*. Entry and exit values may be quite different from each other so there is no general agreement on the precise meaning of current value accounting.

**current yield.** Of a *bond,* the annual amount of *interest coupons* divided by current market price of the bond. Contrast with *yield to maturity.*

**currently attainable standard cost.** *Normal standard cost.*

**curvilinear (variable) cost.** A continuous, but not necessarily linear (straight-line), functional relation between activity levels and *costs.*

**customers' ledger.** The *ledger* that shows accounts receivable of individual customers. It is the *subsidiary ledger* for the *controlling account,* Accounts Receivable.

**cutoff rate.** *Hurdle rate.*

# D

**days of average inventory on hand.** See *ratio.*

**DCF.** *Discounted cash flow.*

**DDB.** *Double-declining-balance depreciation.*

**debenture bond.** A *bond* not secured with *collateral.*

**debit.** As a noun, an entry on the left-hand side of an *account.* As a verb, to make an entry on the left-hand side of an account. Records increases in *assets* and *expenses*; records decreases in *liabilities, owners' equity,* and *revenues.* See *debit and credit conventions.*

**debit and credit conventions.** The equality of the two sides of the *accounting equation* is maintained by recording equal amounts of *debits* and *credits* for each *transaction.* The conventional use of the *T-account* form and the rules for debit and credit in *balance sheet accounts* are summarized as follows.

### Any Asset Account

| Opening Balance Increase + Dr. Ending Balance | Decrease − Cr. |
|---|---|

### Any Liability Account

| Decrease<br>−<br>Dr. | Opening Balance<br>Increase<br>+<br>Cr.<br>Ending Balance |
|---|---|

### Any Owners' Equity Account

| Decrease<br>−<br>Dr. | Opening Balance<br>Increase<br>+<br>Cr.<br>Ending Balance |
|---|---|

Revenue and expense accounts belong to the owners' equity group. The relationship and the rules for debit and credit in these accounts can be expressed as follows.

### Owners' Equity

| Decrease<br>−<br>Dr.<br>**Expenses** | Increase<br>+<br>Cr.<br>**Revenues** |
|---|---|

| Dr.<br>+<br>* | Cr.<br>− | | Dr.<br>− | Cr.<br>+<br>* |
|---|---|---|---|---|

*Normal balance prior to closing.

**debit memorandum.** A document used by a seller to inform a buyer that the seller is debiting (increasing) the amount of the buyer's *account receivable*. Also, the document provided by a bank to a depositor to indicate that the depositor's *balance* is being decreased because of some event other than payment for a *check*, such as monthly service charges or the printing of checks.

**debt.** An amount owed. The general name for *notes, bonds, mortgages*, and the like that are evidence of amounts owed and have definite payment dates.

**debt-equity ratio.** Total *liabilities* divided by total equities. See *ratio*. Sometimes the denominator is merely total shareholders' equity. Sometimes the numerator is restricted to *long-term debt*.

**debt capital.** *Noncurrent liabilities*. See *debt financing* and contrast with *equity financing*.

**debt financing.** Raising *funds* by issuing *bonds, mortgages*, or *notes*. Contrast with *equity financing*. *Leverage*.

**debt guarantee.** See *guarantee*.

**debt ratio.** *Debt-equity ratio*.

**debt service fund.** In governmental accounting, a *fund* established to account for payment of *interest* and *principal* on all general-obligation *debt* other than that payable from special *assessments*.

**debt service requirement.** The amount of cash required for payments of *interest*, current maturities of *principal* on outstanding *debt*, and payments to *sinking funds* (corporations) or to the *debt service fund* (governmental).

**debtor.** One who borrows.

**decentralized decision making.** A manager of a business unit is given responsibility for that unit's *revenues* and *costs*, being free to make decisions about prices, sources of supply, and the like, as though the unit were a separate business owned by the manager. See *responsibility accounting* and *transfer price*.

**declaration date.** Time when a *dividend* is declared by the *board of directors*.

**declining balance depreciation.** The method of calculating the periodic *depreciation* charge by multiplying the *book value* at the start of the period by a constant percentage. In pure declining balance depreciation the constant percentage is $1 - \sqrt[n]{s/c}$ where $n$ is the *depreciable life*, $s$ is *salvage value*, and $c$ is *acquisition cost*. See *double-declining balance depreciation*.

**deep discount bonds.** Said of *bonds* selling much below (exactly how much is not clear) *par value*.

**defalcation.** Embezzlement.

**default.** Failure to pay *interest* or *principal* on a *debt* when due.

**defeasance.** *Interest rates* have increased over the past several decades. Consequently, the *market value* of *debt* outstanding is substantially less than its *book value* for many firms. In *historical cost accounting* for debt retirements, retiring debt with a *cash* payment less than the book value of the debt results in a gain (generally, an *extraordinary item*). Many firms would like to retire the outstanding debt issues and report the gain. Two factors impede doing so: (1) the gain can be a taxable event generating adverse *income tax* consequences and (2) the transactions costs in retiring all of the debt can be large, in part because not all debt holders can easily be located or persuaded to sell back their bonds to the issuer. The process of "defeasance" is the economic equivalent to retiring a debt issue that saves the issuer from adverse tax consequences and actually having to locate and retire the bonds. The process works as follows. The debt issuing firms turns over to an independent trustee, such as bank, amounts of cash or low risk government bonds sufficient to make all debt service payments on the outstanding debt, including bond retirements, in return for the trustee's commitment to make all debt service payments. The debt issuer effectively retires the outstanding debt. It debits the liability account, credits Cash or Marketable Securities, as appropriate, and credits Extraordinary Gain on Debt Retirement. The trustee is free to retire debt or make debt service payments, whichever it chooses. For income tax purposes, however, the firm's debt is still outstanding. The firm will have taxable interest *deductions* for its still outstanding debt and taxable interest *revenue* on the investments held by the trustee for debt service. In law, the term "defeasance" means "a rendering null and void." This process described here renders the outstanding debt economically null and void, without causing a taxable event.

**defensive interval.** A financial *ratio* equal to the number of days of normal cash *expenditures* covered by *quick assets*. It is defined as

$$\frac{\text{Quick Assets}}{\text{(All Expenses Except Amortization and Others Not Using Funds/365)}}$$

The denominator of the ratio is the cash expenditure per day. This ratio has been found useful in predicting *bankruptcy*.

**deferral.** The accounting process concerned with past *cash receipts* and *payments*; in contrast to *accrual*. Recognizing a liability resulting from a current cash receipt (as for magazines to be delivered) or recognizing an asset from a current cash payment (or for prepaid insurance or a long-term depreciable asset).

**deferral method.** See *flow-through method* (of accounting for the *investment credit*) for definition and contrast.

**deferred annuity.** An *annuity* whose first payment is made sometime after the end of the first period.

**deferred asset.** *Deferred charge*.

**deferred charge.** *Expenditure* not recognized as an *expense* of the period when made but carried forward as an *asset* to be *written off* in future periods, such as for advance rent payments or insurance premiums. See *deferral*.

**deferred cost.** *Deferred charge*.

**deferred credit.** Sometimes used to indicate *advances from customers*.

**deferred debit.** *Deferred charge*.

**deferred expense.** *Deferred charge*.

**deferred gross margin.** *Unrealized gross margin*.

**deferred income.** *Advances from customers*.

**deferred income tax (liability).** An *indeterminate term liability* that arises when the pretax income shown on the tax return is less than what it would have been had the same *accounting principles* and *cost basis* for *assets* and *liabilities* been used in tax returns as used for financial reporting. An anticipated 1987 *SFAS* will require that the firm debit income tax *expense* and credit deferred income tax with the amount of the taxes delayed by using different accounting principles in tax returns from those used in financial reports. See *temporary difference*, *timing difference*, and *permanent difference*. See *installment sales*. If, as a result of temporary differences, cumulative taxable income exceeds cumulative reported income before taxes, the deferred income tax account will have a *debit* balance and will be reported as a *deferred charge*.

**deferred revenue.** Sometimes used to indicate *advances from customers*.

**deferred tax.** See *deferred income tax*.

**deficit.** A *debit balance* in the Retained Earnings account; presented on the balance sheet in a *contra account* to shareholders' equity. Sometimes used to mean negative *net income* for a period.

**defined-benefit plan.** A *pension plan* where the employer promises specific dollar amounts to each eligible employee; the amounts usually depend on a formula which takes into account such things as the employee's earnings, years of employment, and age. The employer's cash contributions and pension expense are adjusted in relation to *actuarial* experience in the eligible employee group and investment performance of the pension *fund*. Sometimes called a "fixed-benefit" pension plan. Contrast with *money purchase plan*.

**defined contribution plan.** A *money purchase (pension) plan* or other arrangement, based on formula or discretion, where the employer makes cash contributions to eligible individual employee *accounts* under the terms of a written plan document. Profit-sharing pension plans are of this type.

**deflation.** A period of declining *general price changes*.

**demand deposit.** *Funds* in a *checking account* at a bank.

**demand loan.** See *term loan* for definition and contrast.

**denominator volume.** Capacity measured in expected number of units to be produced this period; divided into *budgeted fixed costs* to obtain fixed costs applied per unit of product.

**dependent variable.** See *regression analysis*.

**depletion.** Exhaustion or *amortization* of a *wasting asset*, or natural resource. Also see *percentage depletion*.

**depletion allowance.** See *percentage depletion*.

**deposit method (of revenue recognition).** This method of *revenue* recognition does not differ from the *completed sale* or *completed contract method*. In some contexts such as retail land sales, the customer must make substantial payments while still having the right to back out of the deal and receive a refund. When there is uncertainty about whether the deal will be completed but a cash collection is made by the seller, the seller must *credit* deposits, a *liability account*, rather than *revenue*. (In this regard, the accounting differs from the completed contract method where the account credited is off-set against the *work-in-process inventory* account.) When the *sale* becomes complete, a revenue account is credited and the deposit account is *debited*.

**deposit, sinking fund.** Payments made to a *sinking fund*.

**deposits (by customers).** A *liability* arising upon receipt of *cash* (as in a bank, or in a grocery store when the customer pays cash for sodapop bottles to be repaid when the bottles are returned).

**deposits in transit.** Deposits made by a firm but not yet reflected on the *bank statement*.

**depreciable cost.** That part of the *cost* of an asset, usually *acquisition cost* less *salvage value*, that is to be charged off over the life of the asset through the process of *depreciation*.

**depreciable life.** For an *asset*, the time period or units of activity (such as miles driven for a truck) over which *depreciable cost* is to be allocated. For tax returns, depreciable life may be shorter than estimated *service life*.

**depreciation.** *Amortization of plant assets*; the process of allocating the cost of an asset to the periods of benefit — the *depreciable life*. Classified as a *production cost* or a *period expense*, depending upon the asset and whether *absorption* or *variable costing* is used. Depreciation methods described in this glossary include the *annuity method, appraisal method, composite method, compound interest method, production method, replacement method, retirement method, straight line method, sinking fund method,* and *sum-of-the-years'-digits method*.

**depreciation reserve.** An inferior term for *accumulated depreciation*. See *reserve*. Do not confuse with a replacement *fund*.

**Descartes' rule of signs.** In a *capital budgeting* context, the rule says that a series of cash flows will have a nonnegative number of *internal rates of return*. The number is equal to the number of variations in the sign of the cash flow series or is less than that number by an even integer. Consider the following series of cash flows, the first occurring now and the others at subsequent yearly intervals: $-100, -100, +50, +175, -50,$

$+100$. The internal rates of return are the numbers for $r$ that satisfy the equation

$$-100 - \frac{100}{(1 + r)} + \frac{50}{(1 + r)2} + \frac{175}{(1 + r)3} + \frac{50}{(1 + r)4} + \frac{100}{(1 + r)5} = 0.$$

The series of cash flows has three variations in sign: a change from minus to plus, a change from plus to minus, and a change from minus to plus. The rule says that this series must have either one or three internal rates of return; in fact, it has only one, about 12 percent. But also see *reinvestment rate*.

**determination.** See *determine*.

**determine.** The verb "determine" and the noun "determination" are often used (in our opinion, overused) by accountants and those who describe the accounting process. A leading dictionary associates the following meanings with the verb "determine": settle, decide, conclude, ascertain, cause, affect, control, impel, terminate, and decide upon. In addition, accounting writers can mean any one of the following: measure, allocate, report, calculate, compute, observe, choose, and legislate. In accounting, there are two distinct sets of meanings — those encompassed by the synonym "cause or legislate" and those encompassed by the synonym "measure." The first set of uses conveys the active notion of causing something to happen and the second set of uses conveys the more passive notion of observing something that someone else has caused to happen. An accountant who speaks of cost or income "determination" generally means measurement or observation, not causation; management and economic conditions cause costs and income to be what they are. One who speaks of accounting principles "determination" can mean choosing or applying (as in "determining depreciation charges" from an allowable set) or causing to be acceptable (as in the *FASB* "determining" the accounting for *leases*). In the long run, income is cash in less cash out, so management and economic conditions "determine" (cause) income to be what it is. In the short run, reported income is a function of accounting principles chosen and applied, so the accountant "determines" (measures) income. A question such as "Who determines income?" has, therefore, no unambiguous answer. The meaning of "an accountant determining acceptable accounting principles" is also vague. Does the clause mean merely choosing one from the set of generally acceptable principles, or does it mean using professional judgment to decide that some of the generally accepted principles are not correct under the current circumstances? We try never to use "determine" unless we mean "cause." Otherwise we use "measure," "report," "calculate," "compute," or whatever specific verb seems appropriate. We suggest that careful writers will always "determine" to use the most specific verb to convey meaning. "Determine" is seldom the best choice of words to describe a process where those who make decisions often differ from those who apply technique.

**development stage enterprise.** As defined in *SFAS No. 7*, a firm whose planned principal *operations* have not commenced or having commenced, have not generated significant *revenue*. Such enterprises should be so identified, but no special *accounting principles* apply to them.

**differential analysis.** Analysis of *incremental costs*.

**differential cost.** *Incremental cost*. If a total cost curve is smooth (in mathematical terms, differentiable), then the curve graphing the derivative of the total cost curve is often said to show differential costs, the costs increments associated with infinitesimal changes in volume.

**dilution.** A potential reduction in *earnings per share* or *book value* per share by the potential *conversion* of securities or by the potential exercise of *warrants* or *options*.

**dilutive.** Said of a *security* that would reduce *earnings per share* if it were exchanged for *common stock*.

**dipping into LIFO layers.** See *LIFO inventory layer*.

**direct cost.** Cost of *direct material* and *direct labor* incurred in producing a product. See *prime cost*. In some accounting literature, this term is used to mean the same thing as *variable cost*.

**direct costing.** Another, less-preferred, term for *variable costing*.

**direct labor (material) cost.** Cost of labor (material) applied and assigned directly to a product; contrast with *indirect labor (material)*.

**direct labor variance.** *Price* and *quantity variances* for direct labor in *standard costs systems*.

**direct method.** See *statement of cash flows*.

**direct posting.** A method of bookkeeping where *entries* are made directly in *ledger accounts*, without the use of a *journal*.

**direct write-off method.** See *write-off method*.

**disbursement.** Payment by *cash* or by *check*. See *expenditure*.

**DISC.** Domestic International Sales Corporation. A U.S. *corporation*, usually a *subsidiary*, whose *income* is primarily attributable to exports. *Income tax* on 50 percent of a DISC's income is usually deferred for a long period. Generally, this results in a lower overall corporate tax for the *parent* than would otherwise be incurred.

**disclaimer of opinion.** An *auditor's report* stating that an opinion cannot be given on the *financial statements*. Usually results from *material* restrictions on the scope of the audit or from material uncertainties about the accounts which cannot be resolved at the time of the audit.

**disclosure.** The showing of facts in *financial statements, notes* thereto, or the *auditor's report*.

**discontinued operations.** See *income from discontinued operations*.

**discount.** In the context of *compound interest, bonds* and *notes*, the difference between *face* or *future value* and *present value* of a payment. In the context of *sales* and *purchases*, a reduction in price granted for prompt payment. See also *chain discount, quantity discount*, and *trade discount*.

**discount factor.** The reciprocal of one plus the *discount rate*. If the discount rate is 10 percent per period, the discount factor for three periods is $1/(1.10)^3 = (1.10)^{-3} = 0.75131$.

**discount rate.** *Interest rate* used to convert future payments to *present values*.

**discounted bailout period.** In a *capital budgeting* context, the total time that must elapse before discounted value of net accumulated cash flows from a project, including potential *salvage value* at various times of assets, equals or exceeds the *present value* of net accumulated cash outflows. Contrast with *discounted payback period*.

**discounted cash flow. DCF.** Using either the *net present value* or the *internal rate of return* in an analysis to measure the value of future expected cash *expenditures* and *receipts* at a common date. In discounted cash flow analysis, choosing the alternative with the largest *internal rate of return* may give wrong answers when there are *mutually exclusive projects* and the amounts of initial investment are quite different for two of the projects. Consider, to take an unrealistic example to illustrate the point, a project involving an initial investment of $1, with an *IRR* of 60 percent and another project involving an initial investment of $1 million with an IRR of 40 percent. Under most conditions, most firms will prefer the second project to the first, but choosing the project with the larger IRR will lead to undertaking the first, not the second. This shortcoming of choosing between alternatives based on the magnitude of the internal rate or return, rather than based on the magnitude of the *net present value* of the cash flows, is called the "scale effect."

**discounted payback period.** The shortest amount of time which must elapse before the discounted present value of cash inflows from a project, excluding potential *salvage value*, equals the discounted *present value* of the cash outflows.

**discounting a note.** See *note receivable discounted* and *factoring*.

**discounts lapsed (lost).** The sum of *discounts* offered for prompt payment that were not taken (or allowed) because of expiration of the discount period. See *terms of sale*.

**discovery value accounting.** See *reserve recognition accounting*.

**discretionary costs.** *Programmed costs*.

**Discussion Memorandum.** A neutral discussion of all the issues concerning an accounting problem of current concern to the *FASB*. The publication of such a document usually implies that the FASB is considering issuing an *SFAS* or *SFAC* on this particular problem. The discussion memorandum brings together material about the particular problem to facilitate interaction and comment by those interested in the matter. It may lead to an *Exposure Draft*.

**dishonored note.** A *promissory note* whose maker does not repay the loan at *maturity* for a *term loan*, or on demand, for a *demand loan*.

**disintermediation.** Federal law regulates the maximum *interest rate* that both banks and savings and loan associations can pay for *time deposits*. When free-market interest rates exceed the regulated interest ceiling for such time deposits, some depositors withdraw their funds and invest them elsewhere at a higher interest rate. This process is known as "disintermediation."

**distributable income.** The portion of conventional accounting net income that can be distributed to owners (usually in the form of *dividends*) without impairing the physical capacity of the firm to continue operations at current levels. Pretax distributable income is conventional pretax income less the excess of *current cost* of goods sold and *depreciation* charges based on the replacement cost of *productive capacity* over cost of goods sold and depreciation on an *acquisition cost basis*. Contrast with *sustainable income*. See *inventory profit*.

**distribution expense.** *Expense* of selling, advertising, and delivery activities.

**dividend.** A distribution of assets generated from *earnings* to owners of a corporation; it may be paid in cash (cash dividend), with stock (stock dividend), with property, or with other securities (dividend in kind). Dividends, except stock dividends, become a legal liability of the corporation when they are declared. Hence, the owner of stock ordinarily recognizes *revenue* when a dividend, other than a stock dividend, is declared. See also *liquidating dividend* and *stock dividend*.

**dividend yield.** *Dividends* declared for the year divided by market price of the stock as of a given time of the year.

**dividends in arrears.** Dividends on *cumulative preferred stock* that have not been declared in accordance with the preferred stock contract. Such arrearages must usually be cleared before dividends on *common stock* can be declared.

**dividends in kind.** See *dividend*.

**division.** A more or less self-contained business unit which is part of a larger family of business units under common control.

**divisional control.** See *control system*.

**divisional reporting.** *Line-of-business reporting*.

**dollar sign rules.** In presenting accounting statements or schedules, place a dollar sign beside the first figure in each column and beside any figure below a horizontal line drawn under the preceding figure.

**dollar-value LIFO method.** A form of *LIFO* inventory accounting with inventory quantities (*layers*) measured in dollar, rather than physical, terms. Adjustments to account for changing prices are made by use of specific price indexes appropriate for the kinds of items in the inventory.

**Domestic International Sales Corporation.** See *DISC*.

**donated capital.** A *shareholders' equity* account credited when contributions, such as land or buildings, are freely given to the company. Do not confuse with *contributed capital*.

**double entry.** The system of recording transactions that maintains the equality of the accounting equation; each entry results in recording equal amounts of *debits* and *credits*.

**double-declining-balance depreciation. DDB.** *Declining-balance depreciation*, which see, where the constant percentage used to multiply by book value in computing the depreciation charge for the year is $2/n$ and $n$ is the *depreciable life* in periods. *Salvage value* is omitted from the depreciable amount. Thus if the asset cost $100 and has a depreciable life of 5 years, the depreciation in the first year would be $40 = 2/5 \times \$100$, in the second would be $24 = 2/5 \times (\$100 - \$40)$, and in the third year would be $14.40 = 2/5 \times (\$100 - \$40 - \$24)$. By the fourth year, the remaining undepreciated cost could be depreciated under the straight line method at $10.80 = 1/2 \times (\$100 - \$40 - \$24 - \$14.40)$ per year for tax purposes.

**double T-account.** *T-account* with an extra horizontal line showing a change in the account balance to be explained by the subsequent entries into the account, such as:

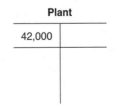

| Plant | |
|---|---|
| 42,000 | |

This account shows an increase in the asset account, plant, of $42,000 to be explained. Such accounts are useful in preparing the *statement of cash flows*; they are not a part of the formal record-keeping process.

**double taxation.** Corporate income is subject to the corporate income tax and the aftertax income, when distributed to owners as dividends, is subject to the personal income tax.

**doubtful accounts.** *Accounts receivable* estimated to be *uncollectible*.

**Dr.** The abbreviation for *debit*.

**draft.** A written order by the first party, called the drawer, instructing a second party, called the drawee (such as a bank) to pay a third party, called the payee. See also *check, cashier's check, certified check, NOW account, sight draft,* and *trade acceptance*.

**drawee.** See *draft*.

**drawer.** See *draft*.

**drawing account.** A *temporary account* used in *sole proprietorships* and *partnerships* to record payments to owners or partners during a period. At the end of the period, the drawing account is closed by crediting it and debiting the owner's or partner's share of income or, perhaps, his or her capital account.

**drawings.** Payments made to a *sole proprietor* or to a *partner* during a period. See *drawing account*.

**dry-hole accounting.** See *reserve recognition accounting* for definition and contrast.

**dual transactions assumption (fiction).** In presenting the *statement of cash flows*, some transactions not involving *cash* accounts are reported as though cash was generated and then used. For example, the issue of *capital stock* in return for the *asset*, land, is reported in the statement of cash flows as though stock were issued for *cash* and cash were used to acquire land. Other examples of transactions that require the dual transaction fiction are the issue of the *mortgage* in return for a noncurrent asset and the issue of stock to bondholders on *conversion* of their *convertible bonds*.

**dual transfer prices.** The *transfer price charged* to the buying *division* differs from that *credited* to the selling division. Such prices make sense when the selling division has excess capacity and, as usual, the *incremental cost* to produce the goods or services being transferred is less than their *fair market value*.

**duality.** The axiom of *double entry* record keeping that every *transaction* is broken down into equal *debit* and *credit* amounts.

# E

**e.** The base of natural logarithms; 2.718281828459045 . . . . If *interest* is compounded continuously during a period at stated rate of $r$ per period, then the effective *interest rate* is equivalent to interest compounded once per period at rate $i$ where $i = e^r - 1$. Tables of $e^r$ are widely available. If 12 percent annual interest is compounded continuously, the effective annual rate is $e^{.12} - 1 = 12.75$ percent.

**earned surplus.** A term once used, but no longer considered proper, for *retained earnings*.

**earnings.** *Income*, or sometimes *profit*.

**earnings cycle.** The period of time that elapses for a given firm, or the series of transactions, during which *cash* is converted into *goods* and *services*, goods and services are sold to customers, and customers pay for their purchases with cash. *Cash cycle*.

**earnings per share (of common stock).** *Net income* to common shareholders (net income minus *preferred dividends*) divided by the average number of *common shares* outstanding; see also *primary earnings per share* and *fully diluted earnings per share*. See *ratio*.

**earnings per share (of preferred stock).** *Net income* divided by the average number of *preferred shares* outstanding during the period. This ratio indicates how well the preferred dividends are covered or protected; it does not indicate a legal share of *earnings*. See *ratio*.

**earnings, retained.** See *retained earnings*.

**earnings statement.** *Income statement*.

**earn-out.** An agreement between two merging firms under which the amount of payment by the acquiring firm to the acquired firm's shareholders depends on the future earnings of the acquired firm or, perhaps of the *consolidated entity*.

**easement.** The acquired right or privilege of one person to use, or have access to, certain property of another. For example, a public utility's right to lay pipes or lines under property of another and to service those facilities.

**economic depreciation.** Decline in *current cost* of an *asset* during a period.

**economic entity.** See *entity*.

**economic life.** The time span over which the benefits of an *asset* are expected to be received. The economic life of a *patent, copyright*, or *franchise* may be less than the legal life. *Service life*.

**economic order quantity.**  In mathematical *inventory* analysis, the optimal amount of stock to order when inventory is reduced to a level called the "reorder point." If $A$ represents the *incremental cost* of placing a single order, $D$ represents the total demand for a period of time in units, and $H$ represents the incremental holding cost during the period per unit of inventory, then the economic order quantity $Q = \sqrt{2AD/H}$. $Q$ is sometimes called the "optimal lot size."

**ED.**  *Exposure Draft.*

**effective interest method.**  A systematic method for computing *interest expense* (or *revenue*) that makes the interest expense for each period divided by the amount of the net *liability (asset)* at the beginning of the period equal to the *yield rate* on the bond at the time of issue (acquisition). Interest for a period is yield rate (at time of issue) multiplied by the net liability (asset) at the start of the period. The *amortization* of discount or premium is the *plug* to give equal *debits* and *credits*. (Interest expense is a debit and the amount of coupon payments is a credit.)

**effective (interest) rate.**  Of a bond, the *internal rate of return* or *yield to maturity* at the time of issue. Contrast with *coupon rate*. If the bond is issued for a price below *par*, the effective rate is higher than the coupon rate; if it is issued for a price greater than par, then the effective rate is lower than the coupon rate. In the context of *compound interest*, when the *compounding period* on a *loan* is different from one year, such as a nominal interest rate of 12 percent compounded monthly, the single payment that could be made at the end of a year that is economically equivalent to the series of interest payments exceeds the quoted nominal rate multiplied by the *principal*. If 12 percent per year is compounded monthly, the effective annual interest rate is 12.683 percent. In general, if the nominal rate is $r$ percent per year and is compounded $m$ times per year, then the effective rate is $(1 + r/m)^m - 1$.

**efficiency variance.**  A term used for the *quantity variance* for labor or *variable overhead* in a *standard cost system*.

**efficient market hypothesis.**  The supposition in finance that securities' prices reflect all available information and react nearly instantaneously and in an unbiased fashion to new information.

**EITF.**  *Emerging Issues Task Force.*

**eliminations.**  *Work sheet* entries to prepare *consolidated statements* that are made to avoid duplicating the amounts of *assets*, *liabilities*, *owners' equity*, *revenues*, and *expenses* of the consolidated *entity* when the accounts of the *parent* and *subsidiaries* are summed.

**Emerging Issues Task Force. EITF.**  A group convened by the *FASB* to deal more rapidly with accounting issues than the FASB's due process procedures can allow. The task force comprises about 20 members from public accounting, industry, and several trade associations. It meets every six weeks. Meetings are chaired by the FASB's director of research. Several FASB board members usually attend and participate. The chief accountant of the SEC has indicated that the SEC will require that published financial statements follow guidelines set by a consensus of the EITF. The EITF requires that nearly all of its members agree on a position before that position is given the label of "consensus." Since 1984, the EITF has become one of the promulgators of *GAAP*.

**employee stock option.**  See *stock option*.

**Employee Stock Ownership Trust (or Plan).**  See *ESOT*.

**employer, employee payroll taxes.**  See *payroll*.

**enabling costs.**  A type of *capacity cost* that will stop being incurred if operations are shut down completely but must be incurred in full if operations are carried out at any level. Costs of a security force or of a quality control inspector for an assembly line might be examples. Contrast with *standby costs*.

**encumbrance.**  In governmental accounting, an anticipated *expenditure*, or *funds* restricted for anticipated expenditure, such as for outstanding purchase orders. *Appropriations* less expenditures less outstanding encumbrances yields unencumbered balance.

**ending inventory.**  The *cost* of *inventory* on hand at the end of the *accounting period*, often called "closing inventory." The dollar amount of inventory to be carried to the subsequent period.

**endorsee.**  See *endorser*.

**endorsement.**  See *draft*. The *payee* signs the draft and transfers it to a fourth party, such as the payee's bank.

**endorser.**  The *payee* of a *note* or *draft* signs it, after writing "Pay to the order of X," transfers the note to person X, and presumably receives some benefit, such as cash, in return. The payee who signs over the note is called the endorser and person X is called the endorsee. The endorsee then has the rights of the payee and may in turn become an endorser by endorsing the note to another endorsee.

**engineering method (of cost estimation).**  Estimates of unit costs of product built up from study of the materials, labor and *overhead* components of the production process.

**enterprise.**  Any business organization, usually defining the accounting *entity*.

**enterprise fund.**  A *fund* established by a governmental unit to account for acquisition, operation, and maintenance of governmental services that are supposed to be self-supporting from user charges, such as for water or airports.

**entity.** A person, *partnership, corporation*, or other organization. The *accounting entity* for which accounting statements are prepared may not be the same as the entity defined by law. For example, a *sole proprietorship* is an accounting entity but the individual's combined business and personal assets are the legal entity in most jurisdictions. Several affiliated corporations may be separate legal entities while *consolidated financial statements* are prepared for the group of companies operating as a single economic entity.

**entity theory.** The view of the corporation that emphasizes the form of the *accounting equation* that says *assets = equities*. Contrast with *proprietorship theory*. The entity theory is less concerned with a distinct line between *liabilities* and *shareholders' equity* than is the proprietorship theory. Rather, all equities are provided to the corporation by outsiders who merely have claims of differing legal standings. The entity theory implies using a *multiple-step* income statement.

**entry value.** The *current cost* of acquiring an asset or service at a *fair market price. Replacement cost.*

**EOQ.** *Economic order quantity.*

**EPS.** *Earnings per share.*

**EPVI.** *Excess present value index.*

**equalization reserve.** An inferior title for the allowance or *estimated liability* account when the *allowance method* is used for such things as maintenance expenses. Periodically, maintenance *expense* is debited and the allowance is credited. As maintenance *expenditures* are actually incurred, the allowance is debited and cash or the other asset expended is credited.

**equities.** *Liabilities* plus *owners' equity*. See *equity*.

**equity.** A claim to *assets*; a source of assets. *SFAS No. 3* defines equity as "the residual interest in the assets of an entity that remains after deducting its liabilities." Usage may be changing so that "equity" will exclude liabilities. We prefer to keep the broader definition, including liabilities, because there is no other single word that serves this useful purpose.

**equity financing.** Raising *funds* by issuance of *capital stock*. Contrast with *debt financing*.

**equity method.** A method of accounting for an *investment* in the stock of another company in which the proportionate share of the earnings of the other company is debited to the investment account and credited to a *revenue* account as earned. When *dividends* are received, *cash* is debited and the investment account is credited. Used in reporting when the investor owns sufficient shares of stock of an unconsolidated company to exercise significant control over the actions of that company. One of the few instances where revenue is recognized without a change in *working capital*.

**equity ratio.** *Shareholders' equity* divided by total *assets*. See *ratio*.

**equivalent production.** *Equivalent units*.

**equivalent units (of work).** The number of units of completed output that would require the same costs as were actually incurred for production of completed and partially completed units during a period. Used primarily in *process costing* calculations to measure in uniform terms the output of a continuous process.

**ERISA.** Employee Retirement Income Security Act of 1974. The federal law that sets most *pension plan* requirements.

**error accounting.** See *accounting errors*.

**escapable cost.** *Avoidable costs*.

**ESOP.** Employee Stock Ownership Plan. See *ESOT*.

**ESOT.** Employee Stock Ownership Trust. A trust *fund* created by a corporate employer that can provide certain tax benefits to the corporation while providing for employee stock ownership. The corporate employer can contribute up to 25 percent of its payroll per year to the trust. The contributions are *deductions* from otherwise taxable income for federal *income tax* purposes. The assets of the trust must be used for the benefit of employees — for example, to fund death or retirement benefits. The assets of the trust are usually the *common stock*, sometimes nonvoting, of the corporate employer. As an example of the potential *tax shelter*, consider the case of a corporation with $1 million of *debt* outstanding, which it wishes to retire, and an annual payroll of $2 million. The corporation sells $1 million of common stock to the ESOT. The ESOT borrows $1 million with the loan guaranteed by, and therefore a *contingency* of, the corporation. The corporation uses the $1 million proceeds of the stock issue to retire its outstanding debt. (The debt of the corporation has been replaced with the debt of the ESOT.) The corporation can contribute $500,000 (= .25 × $2 million payroll) to the ESOT each year and treat the contribution as a deduction for tax purposes. After a little more than two years, the ESOT has received sufficient funds to retire its loan. The corporation has effectively repaid its original $1 million debt with pretax dollars. Assuming an income tax rate of 40 percent, it has saved $400,000 (= .40 × $1 million) of aftertax dollars *if* the $500,000 expense for the contribution to the ESOT for the pension benefits of employees would have been made, in one form or another, anyway. Observe that the corporation could use the proceeds ($1 million in the example) of the stock issued to the ESOT for any of several different purposes: financing expansion, replacing plant assets, or acquiring another company. Basically this same form of pretax dollar financing through pensions is "almost" available with any corporate pension plan, but with one important exception. The trustees of an ordinary pension trust must invest the assets "prudently" and if they do not, they are personally liable to employees. Current judgment about "prudent" investment requires diversification — pension trust assets should be invested in a wide variety of investment opportunities. (Not more than 10 percent of a pension trust's assets can ordinarily be invested in the parent's common stock.) Thus the ordinary pension trust cannot, in practice, invest all, or even most, of its assets in the parent corporation's stock. This constraint does not apply to the investments of an ESOT. All ESOT assets may be invested in the parent company's stock. The ESOT also provides a means for closely held corporations to achieve wider ownership of shares without *going public*. The laws enabling ESOT's provide for independent professional appraisal of shares not traded in public markets and for transactions between the corporation and the ESOT or between the ESOT and the employees to be based on the appraised values of the shares.

**estimated expenses.** See *after cost*.

**estimated liability.** The preferred terminology for estimated costs to be incurred for such uncertain things as repairs under *warranty*. An estimated liability appears on the *balance sheet*. Contrast with *contingency*.

**estimated revenue.** A term used in governmental accounting to designate revenue expected to accrue during a period whether or not it will be collected during the period. A *budgetary account* is usually established at the beginning of the budget period.

**estimated salvage value.** Synonymous with *salvage value* of an *asset* before its retirement.

**estimates, changes in.** See *accounting changes*.

**except for.** Qualification in *auditor's report*, usually caused by a change, approved by the auditor, from one acceptable accounting principle or procedure to another.

**excess present value.** In a *capital budgeting* context, *present value* of (anticipated net cash inflows minus cash outflows including initial cash outflow) for a project.

**excess present value index.** *Present value*, of future *cash* inflows divided by initial cash outlay.

**exchange.** The generic term for a transaction (or more technically, a reciprocal transfer) between one entity and another. In another context, the name for a market, such as the New York Stock Exchange.

**exchange gain or loss.** The phrase used by the *FASB* for *foreign exchange gain or loss*.

**exchange rate.** The *price* of one country's currency in terms of another country's currency. For example, the British pound sterling might be worth $1.60 at a given time. The exchange rate would be stated as "one pound is worth one dollar and sixty cents" or "one dollar is worth £.625 (= £1/$1.60)."

**excise tax.** Tax on the manufacture, sale, or consumption of a commodity.

**ex-dividend.** Said of a stock at the time when the declared *dividend* becomes the property of the person who owned the stock on the *record date*. The payment date follows the ex-dividend date.

**executory contract.** A mere exchange of promises. An agreement providing for payment by a payor to a payee upon the performance of an act or service by the payee, such as a labor contract. Obligations under such contracts generally are not recognized as *liabilities*.

**exemption.** A term used for various amounts subtracted from gross income in computing taxable income. Not all such subtractions are called "exemptions." See *tax deduction*.

**exercise.** When owners of an *option* or *warrant* purchase the security that the option entitles them to purchase, they have exercised the option or warrant.

**exercise price.** See *option*.

**exit value.** The proceeds that would be received if assets were disposed of in an *arm's-length transaction*. *Current selling price. Net realizable value*.

**expected value.** The mean or arithmetic *average* of a statistical distribution or series of numbers.

**expected value of (perfect) information.** Expected *net benefits* from an undertaking with (perfect) information minus expected net benefits of the undertaking without (perfect) information.

**expendable fund.** In governmental accounting, a *fund* whose resources, *principal*, and earnings may be distributed.

**expenditure.** Payment of *cash* for goods or services received. Payment may be made either at the time the goods or services are received or at a later time. Virtually synonymous with *disbursement* except that disbursement is a broader term and includes all payments for goods or services. Contrast with *expense*.

**expense.** As a noun, a decrease in *owners' equity* caused by the using up of *assets* in producing *revenue* or carrying out other activities that are part of the entity's *operations*. A "gone" asset; an expired cost. The amount is the *cost* of the assets used up. Do not confuse with *expenditure* or *disbursement*, which may occur before, when, or after the related expense is recognized.

Use the word "cost" to refer to an item that still has service potential and is an asset. Use the word "expense" after the asset's service potential has been used. As a verb, to designate a past or current expenditure as a current expense.

**expense account.** An *account* to accumulate *expenses*; such accounts are closed at the end of the accounting period. A *temporary owners' equity* account. Also used to describe a listing of expenses by an employee submitted to the employer for reimbursement.

**experience rating.** A term used in insurance, particularly unemployment insurance, to denote changes from ordinary rates to reflect extraordinarily large or small amounts of claims over time by the insured.

**expired cost.** An *expense* or a *loss*.

***Exposure Draft*. ED.** A preliminary statement of the *FASB* (or *APB* between 1962 and 1973) that shows the contents of a pronouncement the Board is considering making effective.

**external reporting.** Reporting to shareholders and the public, as opposed to internal reporting for management's benefit. See *financial accounting* and contrast with *managerial accounting*.

**extraordinary item.** A *material expense* or *revenue* item characterized both by its unusual nature and infrequency of occurrence that is shown along with its income tax effects separately from ordinary income and *income from discontinued operations* on the *income statement*. A *loss* from an earthquake would probably be classified as an extraordinary item. Gain (or loss) on retirement of *bonds* is treated as an extraordinary item under the terms of *SFAS No. 4*.

**F**

**face amount (value).** The nominal amount due at *maturity* from a *bond* or *note* not including contractual interest that may also be due on the same date. The corresponding amount of a stock certificate is best called the *par* or *stated value*, whichever is applicable.

**factoring.** The process of buying *notes* or *accounts receivable* at a *discount* from the holder to whom the debt is owed; from the holder's point of view, the selling of such notes or accounts. When a single note is involved, the process is called "discounting a note."

**factory.** Used synonymously with *manufacturing* as an adjective.

**factory burden.** Manufacturing *overhead*.

**factory cost.** *Manufacturing cost*.

**factory expense.** Manufacturing *overhead*. *Expense* is a poor term in this context because the item is a *product cost*.

**factory overhead.** Usually an item of *manufacturing cost* other than *direct labor* or *direct materials*.

**fair market price (value).** Price (value) negotiated at *arm's-length* between a willing buyer and a willing seller, each acting rationally in his or her own self interest. May be estimated in the absence of a monetary transaction.

**fair presentation (fairness).** When the *auditor's report* says that the *financial statements* "present fairly . . . ," the auditor means that the accounting alternatives used by the entity are all in accordance with *GAAP*. In recent years, however, courts are finding that conformity with *generally accepted accounting principles* may be insufficient grounds for an opinion that the statements are fair. *SAS No. 5* requires that the auditor judge the accounting principles used "appropriate in the circumstances" before attesting to fair presentation.

**FASB.** Financial Accounting Standards Board. An independent board responsible since 1973 for establishing *generally accepted accounting principles*. Its official pronouncements are called *"Statements of Financial Accounting Concepts" ("SFAC")*, *"Statements of Financial Accounting Standards" ("SFAS")*, and *"Interpretations of Financial Accounting Standards."* See also *Discussion Memorandum* and *Technical Bulletin*.

***FASB Interpretation***. An official statement of the *FASB* interpreting the meaning of *Accounting Research Bulletins, APB Opinions*, and *Statements of Financial Accounting Standards*.

***FASB Technical Bulletin.*** See *Technical Bulletin*.

**favorable variance.** An excess of actual *revenues* over expected revenues. An excess of *standard cost* over actual cost.

**federal income tax.** *Income tax* levied by the U.S. government on individuals and corporations.

**Federal Insurance Contributions Act.** See *FICA*.

**Federal Unemployment Tax Act.** See *FUTA*.

**feedback.** The process of informing employees about how their actual performance compares with the expected or desired level of performance in the hope that the information will reinforce desired behavior and reduce unproductive behavior.

**FEI.** *Financial Executives Institute*.

**FICA.** Federal Insurance Contributions Act. The law that sets *"Social Security" taxes* and benefits.

**fiduciary.** Someone responsible for the custody or administration of property belonging to another, such as an executor (of an estate), agent, receiver (in *bankruptcy*), or trustee (of a trust).

**FIFO.** First-in, first-out; the *inventory flow assumption* by which *ending inventory* cost is computed from most recent purchases and *cost of goods sold* is computed from oldest purchases including beginning inventory. See *LISH*. Contrast with *LIFO*.

**finance.** As a verb, to supply with *funds* through the *issue* of stocks, bonds, notes, or mortgages, or through the retention of earnings.

**financial accounting.** The accounting for *assets, equities, revenues*, and *expenses* of a business. Primarily concerned with the historical reporting of the *financial position* and operations of an *entity* to external users on a regular, periodic basis. Contrast with *managerial accounting*.

**Financial Accounting Foundation.** The independent foundation (committee) that raises funds to support the *FASB* and GASB.

**Financial Accounting Standards Advisory Council.** A committee giving advice to the *FASB* on matters of strategy and emerging issues.

**Financial Accounting Standards Board.** *FASB*.

**Financial Executives Institute.** An organization of financial executives, such as chief accountants, *controllers*, and treasurers, of large businesses.

**financial expense.** An *expense* incurred in raising or managing *funds*.

**financial forecast.** See *financial projection* for definition and contrast.

**financial leverage.** See *leverage*.

**financial position (condition).** Statement of the *assets* and *equities* of a firm displayed as a *balance sheet*.

**financial projection.** An estimate of *financial position*, results of *operations*, and changes in cash flows for one or more future periods based on a set of assumptions. If the assumptions are not necessarily the most likely outcomes, then the estimate is called a "projection." If the assumptions represent the most probable outcomes, then the estimate is called a "forecast." "Most probable" means that the assumptions have been evaluated by management and that they are management's judgment of the most likely set of conditions and most likely outcomes.

**financial ratio.** See *ratio*.

**financial reporting objectives.** FASB *Statement of Financial Accounting Concepts No. 1* sets out the broad objectives of financial reporting that are intended to guide the development of specific *accounting standards*.

***Financial Reporting Release.*** Series of releases, issued by the SEC since 1982. Replaces the *Accounting Series Releases*. See *SEC*.

**financial statements.** The *balance sheet, income statement, statement of retained earnings, statement of cash flows*, statement of changes in *owners' equity accounts*, and *notes* thereto.

**financial structure.** *Capital structure.*

**financial year.** The term for *fiscal year* in Australia and Britain.

**financing activities.** Obtaining resources from (a) owners and providing them with a return on and a return of their *investment* and (b) *creditors* and repaying amounts borrowed (or otherwise settling the obligation). See *statement of cash flows*.

**financing lease.** *Capital lease.*

**finished goods (inventory account).** Manufactured product ready for sale; a *current asset (inventory) account*.

**firm.** Informally, any business entity. (Strictly speaking, a firm is a *partnership*.)

**first-in, first-out.** See *FIFO*.

**fiscal year.** A period of 12 consecutive months chosen by a business as the *accounting period* for annual reports. May or may not be a *natural business year* or a calendar year.

**FISH.** An acronym, conceived by George H. Sorter, for *first in, still here*. FISH is the same cost flow assumption as *LIFO*. Many readers of accounting statements find it easier to think about inventory questions in terms of items still on hand. Think of LIFO in connection with *cost of goods sold* but of FISH in connection with *ending inventory*. See *LISH*.

**fixed assets.** *Plant assets.*

**fixed assets turnover.** *Sales* divided by average total *fixed assets*.

**fixed benefit plan.** A *defined-benefit (pension) plan*.

**fixed budget.** A plan that provides for specified amounts of *expenditures* and *receipts* that do not vary with activity levels. Sometimes called a "static budget." Contrast with *flexible budget*.

Flow of Costs (and Sales Revenue)

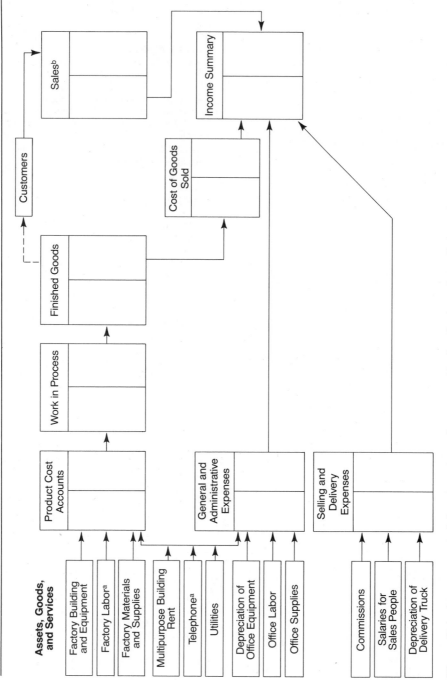

[a]The credit in the entry to record these items is usually to a payable; for all others, the credit is usually to an asset, or to an asset contra account.
[b]When sales to customers are recorded, the Sales account is credited. The debit is usually to Cash or Accounts Receivable.

**fixed charges earned (coverage) ratio.** *Income* before *interest expense* and *income tax expense* divided by interest expense.

**fixed cost (expense).** An *expenditure* or *expense* that does not vary with volume of activity, at least in the short run. See *capacity costs*, which include *enabling costs* and *standby costs*, and *programmed costs* for various subdivisions of fixed costs. See *cost terminology*.

**fixed liability.** *Long-term* liability.

**fixed manufacturing overhead applied.** The portion of *fixed manufacturing overhead cost* allocated to units produced during a period.

**fixed overhead variance.** Difference between *actual fixed manufacturing costs* and fixed manufacturing costs applied to production in a *standard costing system*.

**flexible budget.** *Budget* that projects receipts and expenditures as a function of activity levels. Contrast with *fixed budget*.

**flexible budget allowance.** With respect to manufacturing overhead, the total cost that should have been incurred at the level of activity actually experienced during the period.

**float.** *Checks* whose amounts have been *added* to the depositor's bank account, but not yet subtracted from the *drawer's* bank account.

**flow.** The change in the amount of an item over time. Contrast with *stock*.

**flow assumption.** When a *withdrawal* is made from *inventory*, the cost of the withdrawal must be computed by a flow assumption if *specific identification* of units is not used. The usual flow assumptions are *FIFO*, *LIFO*, and *weighted average*.

**flow of costs.** *Costs* passing through various classifications within an *entity*. See the accompanying diagram for a summary of *product* and *period cost* flows.

**flow-through method.** Accounting for the *investment credit* to show all income statement benefits of the credit in the year of acquisition, rather than spreading them over the life of the asset acquired, called the "deferral method." The *APB* preferred the deferral method in *Opinion No. 2* (1962) but accepted the flow-through method in *Opinion No. 4* (1964). The term is also used in connection with *depreciation* accounting where *straight-line method* is used for financial reporting and an *accelerated* method for tax reporting. Followers of the flow-through method would not recognize a *deferred tax liability*. *APB Opinion No. 11* prohibits the use of the flow-through approach in financial reporting although it has been used by some regulatory commissions.

**FOB.** Free on board some location (for example, FOB shipping point; FOB destination); the *invoice* price includes delivery at seller's expense to that location. Title to goods usually passes from seller to buyer at the FOB location.

**footing.** Adding a column of figures.

**footnotes.** More detailed information than that provided in the *income statement, balance sheet, statement of retained earnings*, and *statement of cash flows*; these are considered an integral part of the statements and are covered by the *auditor's report*. Sometimes called "notes."

**forecast.** See *financial projection* for definition and contrast.

**foreclosure.** The borrower fails to make a required payment on a *mortgage*; the lender takes possession of the property for his or her own use or sale. Assume that the lender sells the property but the proceeds of sale are insufficient to cover the outstanding balance on the loan at the time of foreclosure. Under the terms of most mortgages, the lender becomes an unsecured creditor of the borrower for the still-unrecovered balance of the loan.

**foreign currency.** For *financial statements* prepared in a given currency, any other currency.

**foreign exchange gain or loss.** Gain or loss from holding *net* foreign *monetary items* during a period when the *exchange rate* changes.

**Foreign Sales Corporation.** See *FSC*.

**Form 10-K.** See *10-K*.

**forward exchange contract.** An agreement to exchange at a specified future date currencies of different countries at a specified rate call the "forward rate".

**franchise.** A privilege granted or sold, such as to use a name or to sell products or services.

**free on board.** *FOB*.

**freight-in.** The *cost* of freight or shipping incurred in acquiring *inventory*, preferably treated as a part of the cost of *inventory*. Often shown temporarily in an *adjunct account* that is closed at the end of the period with other purchase accounts to the inventory account by the acquirer.

**freight-out.** The *cost* of freight or shipping incurred in selling *inventory*, treated by the seller as a selling *expense* in the period of sale.

**FSC.** Foreign Sales Corporation. A foreign *corporation* engaging in certain export activities some of whose *income* is exempt from U.S. federal *income tax*. A U.S. corporation need pay no income taxes on *dividends* distributed by an FSC out of *earnings* attributable to certain foreign income.

**full absorption costing.** The method of *costing* that assigns all types of manufacturing costs (*direct material, direct labor,* and *fixed* and *variable overhead*) to units produced; required by *GAAP*. Also called "absorption costing." Contrast with *variable costing.*

**full costing. full costs.** The total cost of producing and selling a unit. Full cost per unit equals *full absorption cost* per unit plus *marketing, administrative, interest,* and other *central corporate expenses,* per unit. The sum of full costs for all units equals total costs of the firm. Often used in *long-term* profitability and pricing decisions.

**full disclosure.** The reporting policy requiring that all significant or *material* information is to be presented in the financial statements. See *fair presentation.*

**fully diluted earnings per share.** Smallest *earnings per share* figure on *common stock* that can be obtained by computing an earnings per share for all possible combinations of assumed *exercise* or *conversion* of *potentially dilutive securities.* Must be reported on the *income statement* if it is less than 97 percent of earnings available to common shareholders divided by the average number of common shares outstanding during the period.

**fully vested.** Said of a *pension plan* when an employee (or his or her estate) has rights to all the benefits purchased with the employer's contributions to the plan even if the employee is not employed by this employer at the time of death or retirement.

**function.** In governmental accounting, said of a group of related activities for accomplishing a service or regulatory program for which the governmental unit is responsible. In mathematics, a rule for associating a number, called the dependent variable, with another number (or numbers), called independent variable(s).

**functional classification.** *Income statement* reporting form in which *expenses* are reported by functions, that is, cost of goods sold, administrative expenses, financing expenses, selling expenses; contrast with *natural classification.*

**fund.** An *asset* or group of assets set aside for a specific purpose. See also *fund accounting.*

**fund accounting.** The accounting for resources, obligations, and *capital* balances, usually of a not-for-profit or governmental *entity,* which have been segregated into *accounts* representing logical groupings based on legal, donor, or administrative restrictions or requirements. The groupings are described as "funds." The accounts of each fund are *self-balancing* and from them a *balance sheet* and an operating statement for each fund can be prepared. See *fund* and *fund balance.*

**fund balance.** In governmental accounting, the excess of assets of a *fund* over its liabilities and reserves; the not-for-profit equivalent of *owners' equity.*

**funded.** Said of a *pension plan* or other obligation when *funds* have been set aside for meeting the obligation when it becomes due. The federal law for pension plans requires that all *normal costs* be funded as recognized. In addition, *prior service cost* of pension plans must be funded over 30 or over 40 years, depending on the circumstances.

**funding.** Replacing *short-term* liabilities with *long-term* debt.

**funds.** Generally *working capital*; current assets less current liabilities. Sometimes used to refer to *cash* or to cash and *marketable securities.*

**funds provided by operations.** See *cash provided by operations.*

**funds statement.** An informal name often used for the *statement of cash flows.*

**funny money.** Said of securities such as *convertible preferred stock, convertible bonds, options,* and *warrants* that have aspects of *common stock* equity but that did not reduce reported *earnings per share* prior to the issuance of *APB Opinions No. 9* in 1967 and *No. 15* in 1969.

**FUTA.** Federal Unemployment Tax Act which provides for taxes to be collected at the federal level, to help subsidize the individual states' administration of their unemployment compensation programs.

**future value.** Value at a specified future date of a sum increased at a specified *interest rate.*

## G

**GAAP.** *Generally accepted accounting principles.* A plural noun.

**GAAS.** *Generally accepted auditing standards.* A plural noun. Not to be confused with *GAS.*

**gain.** Increase in *owners' equity* caused by a transaction not part of a firm's typical, day-to-day operations and not part of owners' *investment* or *withdrawals.* The term "gain" (or "*loss*") is distinguished in two separate ways from related terms. First, gains (and losses) are generally used for nonoperating, incidental, peripheral, or nonroutine transactions: gain on sale of land in contrast to *gross margin* on *sale* of *inventory.* Second, gains and losses are *net* concepts, not gross concepts: gain or loss results from subtracting some measure of *cost* from the measure of inflow. *Revenues* and *expenses,* on the other hand, are gross concepts; their difference is a net concept. Gain is nonroutine and net, *profit* or *margin* is routine and net; revenue is routine and gross. Loss is net but can be either routine ("loss on sale of inventory") or not ("loss on disposal of segment of business").

**gain contingency.** See *contingency.*

**GAS.** *Goods available for sale.* Not to be confused with *GAAS.*

**GASB.** Government Accounting Standards Board. An independent body responsible since 1982 for establishing accounting standards for state and local government units. It is part of the *Financial Accounting Foundation,* parallel to the *FASB,* and currently consists of five members.

**gearing.** British term for *financial leverage.*

**gearing adjustment.** Consider a firm, part of whose assets are *noncurrent liabilities* and who has experience *holding gains* on its *assets* during a period. All of the increase in wealth caused by the holding gains belongs to the owners; none typically belongs to the lenders. Some British accounting authorities believe that published *income statements* should show the part of the holding gain financed with debt in *income* for the period. That part is called the "gearing adjustment."

**general debt.** Debt of a governmental unit legally payable from general revenues and backed by the full faith and credit of the governmental unit.

**general expenses.** *Operating expenses* other than those specifically assigned to cost of goods sold, selling, and administration.

**general fixed asset (group of accounts).** Accounts showing those long-term assets of a governmental unit not accounted for in *enterprise, trust,* or intragovernmental service funds.

**general fund.** Assets and liabilities of a nonprofit entity not specifically earmarked for other purposes; the primary operating fund of a governmental unit.

**general journal.** The formal record where transactions, or summaries of similar transactions, are recorded in *journal entry* form as they occur. Use of the adjective "general" usually implies only two columns for cash amounts or that there are also various *special journals,* such as a *check register* or *sales journal,* in use.

**general ledger.** The name for the formal *ledger* containing all of the financial statement accounts. It has equal debits and credits as evidenced by the *trial balance.* Some of the accounts in the general ledger may be *controlling accounts,* supported by details contained in *subsidiary ledgers.*

**general partner.** Member of *partnership* personally liable for all debts of the partnership; contrast with *limited partner.*

**general price index.** A measure of the aggregate prices of a wide range of goods and services in the economy at one time relative to the prices during a base period. See *consumer price index* and *GNP Implicit Price Deflator.* Contrast with *specific price index.*

**general price level-adjusted statements.** See *constant dollar accounting.*

**general price level changes.** Changes in the aggregate prices of a wide range of goods and services in the economy. These price changes are measured using a *general price index.* Contrast with *specific price changes.*

**general purchasing power.** The command of the dollar over a wide range of goods and services in the economy. The general purchasing power of the dollar is inversely related to changes in a general price index. See *general price index.*

**general purchasing power accounting.** See *constant dollar accounting.*

**generally accepted accounting principles. GAAP.** As previously defined by the *APB* and now by the *FASB,* the conventions, rules, and procedures necessary to define accepted accounting practice at a particular time; includes both broad guidelines and relatively detailed practices and procedures.

**generally accepted auditing standards. GAAS.** The standards, as opposed to particular procedures, promulgated by the *AICPA* (in *Statements on Auditing Standards*) that concern "the auditor's professional quantities" and "the judgment exercised by him in the performance of his examination and in his report." Currently, there are ten such standards: three general ones (concerned with proficiency, independence, and degree of care to be exercised), three standards of field work, and four standards of reporting. The first standard of reporting requires that the *auditor's report* state whether or not the *financial statements* are prepared in accordance with *generally accepted accounting principles.* Thus the typical auditor's report says that the examination was conducted in accordance with generally accepted auditing standards and that the statements are prepared in accordance with generally accepted accounting principles. See *auditor's report.*

**GNP Implicit Price Deflator (Index).** A *price index* issued quarterly by the Office of Business Economics of the U.S. Department of Commerce. This index attempts to trace the price level of all *goods and services* comprising the *gross national product.* Contrast with *consumer price index.*

**goal congruence.** All members of an organization have incentives to perform for a common interest, *shareholder* wealth maximization for a *corporation.*

**going-concern assumption.** For accounting purposes, a business is assumed to remain in operation long enough for all its current plans to be carried out. This assumption is part of the justification for the *acquisition cost* basis, rather than a *liquidation* or *exit value* basis of accounting.

**going public.** Said of a business when its *shares* become widely traded, rather than being closely held by relatively few shareholders. Issuing shares to the general investing public.

**goods.** Items of merchandise, supplies, raw materials, or finished goods. Sometimes the meaning of "goods" is extended to include all *tangible* items, as in the phrase "goods and services."

**goods available for sale.** The sum of *beginning inventory* plus all acquisitions of merchandise or finished goods during an *accounting period*.

**goods in process.** *Work in process.*

**goodwill.** The excess of cost of an acquired firm (or operating unit) over the current *fair market value* of the separately identifiable *net assets* of the acquired unit. Before goodwill is recognized, all identifiable assets, whether or not on the books of the acquired unit, must be given a *fair market value*. For example, a firm has developed a *patent* which is not recognized on its books because of *SFAS No. 2*. If another company acquires the firm, the acquirer will recognize the patent at an amount equal to its estimated fair market value before computing goodwill. Informally, the term is used to indicate the value of good customer relations, high employee morale, a well-respected business name, and so on, that are expected to result in greater than that normal earning power.

**goodwill method.** A method of accounting for the *admission* of a new partner to a *partnership* when the new partner is to be credited with a portion of capital different from the value of the *tangible* assets contributed as a fraction of tangible assets on the partnership. See *bonus method* for a description and contrast.

**Governmental Accounting Standards Advisory Council.** A group that consults with the *GASB* on agenda, technical issues and the assignment of priorities to projects. It consists of more than a dozen members representing various areas of expertise.

**Governmental Accounting Standards Board.** *GASB.*

**GPL.** General price level; usually used as an adjective modifying the word "accounting" to mean *constant dollar accounting*.

**GPLA.** General price level-adjusted accounting; *constant dollar accounting*.

**GPP.** General purchasing power; usually used as an adjective modifying the word "accounting" to mean *constant dollar accounting*.

**graded vesting.** Said of a *pension plan* where not all employee benefits are currently *vested*. By law, the benefits must become vested according to one of several formulas as time passes.

**grandfather clause.** An exemption in new accounting *pronouncements* exempting transactions that occurred before a given date from the new accounting treatment. For example, *APB Opinion No. 17*, adopted in 1970, exempted *goodwill* acquired before 1970 from required *amortization*. The term "grandfather" appears in the title to *SFAS No. 10*.

**gross.** Not adjusted or reduced by deductions or subtractions. Contrast with *net*.

**gross margin.** *Net sales* minus *cost of goods sold*.

**gross margin percent.** $100 \times (1 - \text{cost of goods sold/ net sales}) = 100 \times (\text{gross margin/net sales})$.

**gross national product. GNP.** The market value within a nation for a year of all goods and services produced as measured by final sales of goods and services to individuals, corporations, and governments plus the excess of exports over imports.

**gross price method (of recording purchase or sales discounts).** The *purchase* (or *sale*) is recorded at its *invoice price*, not deducting the amounts of *discounts* available. Discounts taken are recorded in a *contra* account to purchases (or sales). Information on discounts lapsed is not made available, and for this reason, most firms prefer the *net price method* of recording purchase discounts.

**gross profit.** *Gross margin*.

**gross profit method.** A method of estimating *ending inventory* amounts. *Cost of goods sold* is measured as some fraction of sales; the *inventory equation* is then used to value *ending inventory*.

**gross profit ratio.** *Gross margin* divided by *net sales*.

**gross sales.** All *sales* at *invoice* prices, not reduced by *discounts*, *allowances*, *returns*, or other adjustments.

**group depreciation.** A method of calculating *depreciation* charges where similar assets are combined, rather than depreciated separately. No gain or loss is recognized on retirement of items from the group until the last item in the group is sold or retired. See *composite life method*.

**guarantee.** A promise to answer for payment of debt or performance of some obligation if the person liable for the debt or obligation fails to perform. A guarantee is a *contingency* of the *entity* making the promise. Often, the words "guarantee" and "warranty" are used to mean the same thing. In precise usage, however, "guarantee" means promise to fulfill the promise of some person to perform a contractual obligation such as to pay a sum of money, whereas "warranty" is most often used to refer to promises about pieces of machinery or other products. See *warranty*.

# H

**half-year convention.** An assumption used in *tax accounting* under *ACRS*, and sometimes in *financial accounting*, that *depreciable assets* were acquired at mid-year of the year of acquisition. When this convention is used, the *depreciation charge* for the year is computed as one-half the charge that would be used if the assets had been acquired at the beginning of the year.

*Hasselback.* An annual directory of accounting faculty at colleges and universities, which gives information about the faculty's training and fields of specialization. The directory has been compiled for over a decade by James R. Hasselback of Florida State University and is distributed by Prentice-Hall of Englewood Cliffs, New Jersey.

**hidden reserve.** The term refers to an amount by which *owners' equity* has been understated, perhaps deliberately. The understatement arises from an undervaluation of *assets* or overvaluation of *liabilities*. By undervaluing assets on this period's *balance sheet*, *net income* in some future period can be made to look artificially high by disposing of the asset: actual *revenues* less artificially low cost of assets sold yields artificially high net income. There is no *account* that has this title.

**historical cost.** *Acquisition cost; original cost; a sunk cost.*

**historical cost/constant dollar accounting.** Accounting based on *historical cost* valuations measured in *constant dollars*. *Nonmonetary items* are restated to reflect changes in the *general purchasing power* of the dollar since the time the specific *assets* were acquired or *liabilities* were incurred. A *gain* or *loss* is recognized on *monetary items* as they are held over time periods when the general purchasing power of the dollar changes.

**historical summary.** A part of the *annual report* to shareholders that shows important items, such as *net income, revenues, expenses, asset* and *equity* totals, *earnings per share*, and the like, for five or ten periods including the current one. Usually not as much detail is shown in the historical summary as in *comparative statements*, which typically report as much detail for the two preceding years as for the current year. Annual reports may contain both comparative statements and a historical summary.

**holding company.** A company that confines its activities to owning *stock* in, and supervising management of, other companies. A holding company usually owns a controlling interest in, that is more than 50 percent of the voting stock of, the companies whose stock it holds.

Contrast with *mutual fund*. See *conglomerate*. In British usage, the term refers to any company with controlling interest in another company.

**holding gain or loss.** Difference between end-of-period price and beginning-of-period price of an asset held during the period. Realized holding gains and losses are not ordinarily separately reported in financial statements. Unrealized gains are not usually reflected in income at all. Some unrealized losses, such as on inventory or marketable securities, are reflected in income or *owners' equity* as the losses occur; see *lower of cost or market*. See *inventory profit* for further refinement, including *gains* on *assets* sold during the period.

**holding gain or loss net of inflation.** Increase or decrease in the *current cost* of an asset while it is held measured in units of *constant dollars*.

**horizontal analysis.** *Time-series analysis.*

**human resource accounting.** A term used to describe a variety of proposals that seek to report and emphasize the importance of human resources—knowledgeable, trained, and loyal employees—in a company's earning process and total assets.

**hurdle rate.** Required rate of return in a *discounted cash flow* analysis.

**hybrid security.** *Security*, such as a *convertible bond*, containing elements of both *debt* and *owners' equity*.

**hypothecation.** The *pledging* of property, without transfer of title or possession, to secure a loan.

# I

**I.** *Identity matrix.*

**IAA.** *Interamerican Accounting Association.*

**ICMA.** *Institute of Certified Management Accountants.* See *CMA* and *National Association of Accountants.*

**ideal standard costs.** *Standard costs* set equal to those that would be incurred under the best possible conditions.

**identity matrix.** A square *matrix* with ones on the main diagonal and zeros elsewhere; a matrix **I** such that for any other matrix **A**, **IA** = **AI** = **A**. The matrix equivalent to the number one.

**IIA.** *Institute of Internal Auditors.*

**IMA.** *Institute of Management Accounting.* See *CMA* and *National Association of Accountants.*

**implicit interest.** *Interest* not paid or received. See *interest, imputed*. All transactions involving the deferred payment or receipt of cash involved interest, whether explicitly stated or not. The implicit interest on a single-payment *note* is the difference between the amount collected at maturity less the amount lent at the start of the loan. The implicit *interest rate* per year can be computed from

$$\left[\frac{\text{Cash Received at Maturity}}{\text{Cash Lent}}\right]^{(1/t)} - 1.$$

where $t$ is the term of the loan in years; $t$ need not be an integer.

**imprest fund.** *Petty cash fund.*

**improvement.** An *expenditure* to extend the useful life of an *asset* or to improve its performance (rate of output, cost) over that of the original asset. Such expenditures are *capitalized* as part of the asset's cost. Sometimes called "betterment." Contrast with *maintenance* and *repair*.

**imputed cost.** A cost that does not appear in accounting records, such as the *interest* that could be earned on cash spent to acquire inventories rather than, say, government bonds. Or, consider a firm that owns the buildings it occupies. This firm has an imputed cost for rent in an amount equal to what it would have to pay to use similar buildings owned by another. *Opportunity cost.*

**imputed interest.** See *interest, imputed*.

**incentive compatible compensation.** Said of a compensation plan for managers that induces them to act for the interests of owners while acting in their own interests. For example, consider a time of rising prices and increasing inventories when using a *LIFO cost flow assumption* implies having to pay lower *income taxes* than would *FIFO*. A bonus scheme for managers based on accounting *net income* would not be incentive compatible, because the owners will be better off under LIFO, whereas managers will be better off if they report using FIFO. (See *LIFO conformity rule*.) See *goal congruence*.

**income.** *Excess of revenues* and *gains* over *expenses* and *losses* for a period; *net income*. Sometimes used with an appropriate modifier to refer to the various intermediate amounts shown in a *multiple-step income statement*. Sometimes used to refer to revenues, as in "rental income." See *comprehensive income*.

**income accounts.** *Revenue* and *expense accounts*.

**income before taxes.** On the *income statement*, the difference between all *revenues* and *expenses* except *income tax* expense. Contrast with *net income* and *taxable income*.

**income determination.** See *determine*.

**income distribution account.** *Temporary account* sometimes debited when *dividends* are declared; closed to *retained earnings*.

**income from continuing operations.** As defined by APB *Opinion No. 30*, all *revenues* less all *expenses* except for the following: results of operations (including *income tax* effects) that have been or will be discontinued; *gains* or *losses*, including income tax effects, on disposal of segments of the business; gains or losses, including income tax effects, from *extraordinary items*; and the cumulative effect of *accounting changes*.

**income from discontinued operations.** *Income*, net of tax effects, from parts of the business that have been discontinued during the period or are to be discontinued in the near future. Such items are reported on separate line of the *income statement* after *income from continuing operations* but before *extraordinary items*.

**income (revenue) bond.** See *special revenue debt*.

**income smoothing.** A method of timing business *transactions* or choosing *accounting principles* so that variations in reported *income* from year to year are reduced from what they would otherwise be. Although income smoothing is an objective of some managements, it is not an official *accounting principle* or *reporting objective*.

**income statement.** The statement of *revenues, expenses, gains*, and *losses* for the period ending with *net income* for the period. The *earnings-per-share* amount is usually shown on the income statement; the *reconciliation* of beginning and ending balances of *retained earnings* may also be shown in a combined statement of income and retained earnings. See *income from continuing operations, income from discontinued operations, extraordinary items, multiple-step, single-step*.

**income summary.** An *account* used in problem solving that serves as a surrogate for the *income statement*. All *revenues* are closed to the Income Summary as *credits* and all *expenses*, as *debits*. The *balance* in the account, after all other *closing entries* are made, is then closed to the retained earnings or other *owners' equity* account and represents *net income* for the period.

**income tax.** An annual tax levied by the federal and other governments on the income of an entity.

**income tax allocation.** See *deferred tax liability* and *tax allocation: intrastatement*.

**incremental.** An adjective used to describe the change in *cost, expense, investment, cash flow, revenue, profit*, and the like if one or more units are produced or sold or if an activity is undertaken.

**incremental cost.** See *incremental*.

**indenture.** See *bond indenture*.

**independence.** The mental attitude required of the *CPA* in performing the *attest* function. It implies impartiality and that the members of the auditing CPA firm own no stock in the corporation being audited.

**independent accountant.** The *CPA* who performs the *attest* function for a firm.

**independent variable.** See *regression analysis*.

**indeterminate-term liability.** A *liability* lacking the criterion of being due at a definite time. This term is our own coinage to encompass the *minority interest*.

**indexation.** An attempt by lawmakers or parties to a contract to cope with the effects of *inflation*. Amounts fixed in law or contracts are "indexed" when these amounts change as a given measure of price changes. For example, a so-called escalator clause (COLA — cost of living allowance or adjustment) in a labor contract might provide that hourly wages will be increased as the *Consumer Price Index* increases. Many economists have suggested the indexation of numbers fixed in the *income tax* laws. If, for example, the personal *exemption* is $1,000 at the start of the period, prices rise by 10 percent during the period, and the personal exemption is indexed, then the personal exemption would automatically rise to $1,100 (= $1,000 × .10 + $1,000) at the end of the period.

**indirect cost pool.** Any grouping of individual costs that is not identified with a *cost objective*.

**indirect costs.** Costs of production not easily associated with the production of specific goods and services; *overhead costs*. May be *allocated* on some arbitrary basis to specific products or departments.

**indirect labor (material) cost.** An *indirect cost* for labor (material) such as for supervisors (supplies).

**indirect method.** See *statement of cash flows*.

**individual proprietorship.** *Sole proprietorship*.

**Industry Audit Guide.** A series of publications by the *AICPA* providing specific accounting and *auditing principles* for specialized situations. Audit guides have been issued covering government contractors, state and local government units, investment companies, finance companies, brokers and dealers in securities, and many others.

**inescapable cost.** A *cost* that is not *avoidable*. A *cost* that is not *avoidable* because of an action. For example, if two operating rooms in a hospital are closed, but security is still employed, the security costs are "inescapable" with respect to the decision to close the operating rooms.

**inflation.** A time of generally rising prices.

**inflation accounting.** Strictly speaking, *constant dollar accounting*. Some writers use the term, incorrectly, to mean *current cost accounting*.

**information system.** A system, sometimes formal and sometimes informal, for collecting, processing, and communicating data that are useful for the managerial functions of decision making, planning, and control, and for financial reporting under the *attest* requirement.

**insolvent.** Unable to pay debts when due. Said of a company even though *assets* exceed *liabilities*.

**installment.** Partial payment of a debt or collection of a receivable, usually according to a contract.

**installment contracts receivable.** The name used for *accounts receivable* when the *installment method* of recognizing revenue is used. Its *contra account, unrealized gross margin*, is shown on the balance sheet as a subtraction from the amount receivable.

**installment (sales) method.** Recognizing *revenue* and *expense* (or *gross margin*) from a sales transaction in proportion to the fraction of the selling price collected during a period. Allowed by the *IRS* for income tax reporting, but acceptable in *GAAP* (*APB Opinion No. 10*) only when cash collections are uncertain. See *realized* (and *unrealized*) *gross margin*.

**installment sales.** Sales on account where the buyer promises to pay in several separate payments, called *installments*. Sometimes are, but need not be, accounted for on the *installment method*. If installment sales are accounted for with the sales *basis of revenue recognition* for financial reporting but with the installment method for income tax returns, then a *deferred income tax liability* arises.

**Institute of Certified Management Accountants.** See *ICMA*.

**Institute of Internal Auditors. IIA.** The national association of accountants who are engaged in internal auditing and are employed by business firms. Administers a comprehensive professional examination; those who pass qualify to be designated CIA, certified internal auditor.

**Institute of Management Accounting.** See *CMA*.

**insurance.** A contract for reimbursement of specific losses; purchased with insurance premiums. Self-insurance is not insurance but merely the willingness to assume risk of incurring losses while saving the premium.

**intangible asset.** A nonphysical, *noncurrent* right that gives a firm an exclusive or preferred position in the marketplace. Examples are a *copyright, patent, trademark, goodwill, organization costs, capitalized* advertising cost, computer programs, licenses for any of the preceding, government licenses (e.g., broadcasting or the right to sell liquor), *leases*, franchises, mailing lists, exploration permits, import and export permits, construction permits, and marketing quotas.

**Interamerican Accounting Association.** An organization, headquartered in Mexico City, devoted to facilitating interaction between accounting practitioners in Central America, North America, and South America.

**intercompany elimination.** See *eliminations*.

**intercompany profit.** If one *affiliated company* sells to another, and the goods remain in the second company's *inventory* at the end of the period, then the first company's *profit* has not been realized by a sale to an outsider. That profit is called "intercompany profit" and is eliminated from net *income* in *consolidated income statements* or when the *equity method* is used.

**intercompany transaction.** *Transaction* between *parent company* and *subsidiary* or between subsidiaries in a *consolidated entity* whose effects are eliminated in preparing *consolidated financial statements*. See *intercompany profit*.

**intercorporate investment.** A given *corporation* owns *shares* or *debt* issued by another.

**interdepartment monitoring.** One of the advantages of allocating *service department costs* to *production departments* is that those charged with the costs will have an incentive to control the costs incurred in the service department.

**interest.** The charge or cost for using money; expressed as a rate per period, usually one year, called the "interest rate." See *effective interest rate* and *nominal interest rate*.

**interest, imputed.** If a borrower merely promises to pay a single amount, sometime later than the present, then the present value (computed at a *fair market* interest rate, called the "imputed interest rate") of the promise is less than the *face amount* to be paid at *maturity*. The difference between the face amount and the present value of a promise is called imputed interest. See also *imputed cost*.

**interest factor.** One plus the *interest* rate.

**interest method.** See *effective interest method*.

**interest rate.** See *interest*.

**interfund accounts.** In governmental accounting, the accounts that show transactions between funds, especially interfund receivables and payables.

**interim statements.** Statements issued for periods less than the regular, annual *accounting period*. Most corporations are required to issue interim statements on a quarterly basis. The basic issue in preparing interim reports is whether their purpose is to report on the interim period (1) as a self-contained accounting period or (2) as an integral part of the year of which they are a part so that forecasts of annual performance can be made. For example, assume that at the end of the first quarter, a retailer has depleted its *inventory* so that *LIFO cost of goods sold* is artificially low and *net income* is artificially high, relative to their amounts if purchases for inventory had been "normal" and equal to or greater than sales. The retailer expects to purchase inventory sufficiently large so that when cost of goods sold is computed for the year, there will be no *dips into old LIFO layers* and income will not be artificially high. Under the first approach, the quarterly income will be computed from cost of goods sold using data for the dips that have actually occurred by the end of the quarter. Under the second, quarterly income will be computed from cost of goods sold assuming that purchases were equal to "normal" amounts and that there are no dips into old LIFO layers. *APB Opinion No. 28* and the *SEC* require that interim reports be constructed largely to satisfy the second purpose.

**internal audit.** An *audit* conducted by employees to ascertain whether or not *internal control* procedures are working, as opposed to an external audit conducted by a *CPA*.

**internal control.** See *control system*.

**internal rate of return. IRR.** The discount rate that equates the net *present value* of a stream of cash outflows and inflows to zero.

**internal reporting.** Reporting for management's use in planning and control; contrast with *external reporting* for financial statement users.

**Internal Revenue Service. IRS.** Agency of the U.S. Treasury Department responsible for administering the Internal Revenue Code and collecting income, and certain other, taxes.

**International Accounting Standards Committee.** An organization that promotes the establishment of international accounting standards.

**interperiod tax allocation.** See *deferred income tax liability*.

**interpolation.** The estimation of an unknown number intermediate between two (or more) known numbers.

**Interpretations of Statements of Financial Accounting Standards.** See *FASB Interpretations*.

**in the black (red).** Operating at a profit (loss).

**intrastatement tax allocation.** See *tax allocation: intrastatement*.

**inventoriable costs.** _Costs_ incurred that are added to the cost of manufactured products. _Product costs_ (_assets_) as opposed to _period expenses_.

**inventory.** As a noun, the _balance_ in an asset _account_ such as raw materials, supplies, work in process, and finished goods. As a verb, to calculate the _cost_ of goods on hand at a given time or to physically count items on hand.

**inventory equation.** _Beginning inventory_ + net additions − withdrawals = ending inventory. Ordinarily, additions are net purchases and withdrawals are _cost of goods sold_. Notice that ending inventory, to be shown on the balance sheet, and cost of goods sold, to be shown on the income statement, are not independent of each other. The larger is one, the smaller must be the other. In valuing inventories, beginning inventory and net purchases are usually known. In some inventory methods (for example, some applications of the _retail inventory method_), costs of goods sold is measured and the equation is used to find the cost of ending inventory. In most methods, cost of ending inventory is measured and the equation is used to find the cost of goods sold (withdrawals). In _current cost_ (in contrast to _historical cost_) accounting _additions_ (in the equation) include holding gains, whether realized or not. Thus the current cost inventory equation is: Beginning Inventory (at Current Cost) + Purchases (where Current Cost is Historical Cost) + Holding Gains (whether Realized or Not) − Ending Inventory (at Current Cost) = Cost of Goods Sold (Current Cost).

**inventory holding gains.** See _inventory profit_.

**inventory layer.** See _LIFO inventory layer_.

**inventory profit.** This term has several possible meanings. The _historical cost_ data are derived in the conventional manner; the firm uses a _FIFO cost flow assumption_. The _current cost_ data are assumed, but are of the kind that the FASB suggests in _SFAS No. 89_. The term _income from continuing operations_ refers to revenues less expenses based on current, rather than historical, costs. To that subtotal add realized holding gains to arrive at realized (conventional) income. To that, add unrealized holding gains to arrive at _economic income_. The term "inventory profit" often refers (for example in some _SEC_ releases) to the realized holding gain. The amount of inventory profit will usually be material when FIFO is used and prices are rising. Others, including us, prefer to use the term "inventory profit" to refer to the total _holding gain_, but this appears to be a lost cause. In periods of rising prices and increasing inventories, the realized holding gains under a FIFO cost flow assumption will be substantially larger than under LIFO. For example, assume under LIFO that the historical cost of goods sold is $4,800, that historical LIFO cost of beginning inventory is $600, and that historical LIFO cost of ending inventory is $800. Then income from continuing operations, based on current costs, remains $350 (= $5,200 − $4,850), realized holding gains are $50

(= $4,850 − $4,800), realized income is $400 (= $350 + $50), the unrealized holding gain for the year is $250 [= ($1,550 − $800) − ($1,100 − $600)], and economic income is $650 (= $350 + $50 + $250). Because the only real effect of the cost flow assumption is to split the total holding gain into realized and unrealized portions, economic income is the same, independent of the cost flow assumption. The choice of cost flow assumption merely determines the portion reported as realized.

**inventory turnover.** Number of times the average _inventory_ has been sold during a period; _cost of goods sold_ for a period divided by average inventory for the period. See _ratio_.

**invested capital.** _Contributed capital_.

**investee.** A company whose _stock_ is owned by another.

**investing activities.** Lending money and collecting _principal_ (but not _interest_, which is an _operating activity_) on those loans; acquiring and selling _securities_ or productive _assets_ expected to produce _revenue_ over several _periods_.

**investment.** An _expenditure_ to acquire property or other assets in order to produce _revenue_; the _asset_ so acquired; hence a _current_ expenditure made in anticipation of future income. Said of _securities_ of other companies held for the long term and shown in a separate section of the _balance sheet_; in this context, contrast with _marketable securities_.

**investment center.** A _responsibility center_, with control over _revenues, costs_, and _assets_.

**investment credit.** A reduction in income tax liability sometimes granted by the federal government to firms that buy new equipment. This item is a credit, in that it is deducted from the tax bill, not from pretax income. The tax credit has been a given percentage of the purchase price of certain assets purchased. The actual rules and rates have changed over the years. As of 1988, there is no investment credit. See _flow-through_ method and _carryforward_.

**investment tax credit.** _Investment credit_.

**investment turnover ratio.** This term means the same thing as _total assets turnover ratio_, but is sometimes used for a _division_.

**invoice.** A document showing the details of a sale or purchase transaction.

**IRR.** _Internal rate of return_.

**IRS.** _Internal Revenue Service_.

**isoprofit line.** On a graph delimiting feasible production possibilities of two products that require the use of the same, limited resources, a line showing all feasible production possibility combinations with the same *profit* or, perhaps, *contribution margin*.

**issue.** When a corporation exchanges its stock (or bonds) for cash or other assets, the corporation is said to issue, not sell, that stock (or bonds). Also used in the context of withdrawing supplies or materials from inventory for use in operations and drawing of a *check*.

**issued shares.** Those shares of *authorized capital stock* of a *corporation* that have been distributed to the shareholders. See *issue*. Shares of *treasury stock* are legally issued but are not considered to be *outstanding* for the purpose of voting, *dividend declarations,* and *earnings-per-share* calculations.

# J

**JIT.** See *just-in-time inventory*.

**job cost sheet.** A schedule showing actual or budgeted inputs for a special order.

**job development credit.** The name used for the *investment credit* in the 1971 tax law, since repealed, on this subject.

**job (-order) costing.** Accumulation of *costs* for a particular identifiable batch of product, known as a job, as it moves through production.

**joint cost.** Cost of simultaneously producing or otherwise acquiring two or more products, called joint products, that must, by the nature of the process, be produced or acquired together, such as the cost of beef and hides of cattle. Generally, the joint costs of production are allocated to the individual products in proportion to their respective sales value at the *splitoff point*. Other examples include *central corporate expenses, overhead* of a department when several products are manufactured, and *basket purchases*. See *common cost*. See *sterilized allocation*.

**joint cost allocation.** See *joint cost*.

**joint product.** One of two or more outputs with significant value produced by a process that must be produced or acquired simultaneously. See *by-product* and *joint cost*.

**journal.** The place where transactions are recorded as they occur. The book of original entry.

**journal entry.** A recording in a *journal*, of equal *debits* and *credits*, with an explanation of the *transaction*, if necessary.

**Journal of Accountancy.** A monthly publication of the *AICPA*.

**Journal of Accounting and Economics.** Scholarly journal published three times a year by the Graduate School of Management of the University of Rochester.

**Journal of Accounting Research.** Scholarly journal containing articles on theoretical and empirical aspects of accounting. Published three times a year by the Graduate School of Business of the University of Chicago.

**journal voucher.** A *voucher* documenting (and sometimes authorizing) a transaction, leading to an entry in the *journal*.

**journalize.** To make an entry in a *journal*.

**just-in-time inventory (production); JIT.** System of managing *inventory* for manufacturing where each component is purchased or manufactured just before it is used. Contrast with systems where many parts are acquired or manufactured in advance of needs. JIT systems have much smaller, ideally no, carrying costs for inventory, but run higher risks of incurring *stockout costs*.

# K

**kiting.** This term means slightly different things in banking and auditing contexts. In both, however, it refers to the wrongful practice of taking advantage of the *float*, the time that elapses between the deposit of a *check* in one bank and its collection at another. In the banking context, an individual deposits in Bank A a check written on Bank B. He (or she) then writes checks against the deposit created in Bank A. Several days later, he deposits in Bank B a check written on Bank A, to cover the original check written on Bank B. Still later, he deposits in Bank A a check written on Bank B. The process of covering the deposit in Bank A with a check written on Bank B and vice versa is continued until an actual deposit of cash can be arranged. In the auditing context, kiting refers to a form of *window dressing* where the amount of the account Cash in Bank is made to appear larger than it actually is by depositing in Bank A a check written on Bank B without recording the check written on Bank B in the *check register* until after the close of the *accounting period*.

**know-how.** Technical or business information of the type defined under *trade secret*, but that is not maintained as a secret. The rules of accounting for this asset are the same as for other *intangibles*.

# L

**labor variances.** The *price* (or *rate*) and *quantity* (or *usage*) *variances* for *direct labor* inputs in a *standard costing system*.

**land.** An *asset shown at acquisition cost* plus the *cost* of any nondepreciable *improvements*. In accounting, implies use as a plant or office site, rather than as a *natural resource*, such as timberland or farm land.

**lapping (accounts receivable).** The theft, by an employee, of cash sent in by a customer to discharge the latter's *payable*. The theft from the first customer is concealed by using cash received from a second customer. The theft from the second customer is concealed by using the cash received from a third customer, and so on. The process is continued until the thief returns the funds or can make the theft permanent by creating a fictitious *expense* or receivable write-off, or until the fraud is discovered.

**lapse.** To expire; said of, for example, an insurance policy or discounts made available for prompt payment that are not taken.

**last-in, first-out.** See *LIFO*.

**layer.** See *LIFO inventory layer*.

**lead time.** The time that elapses between placing an order and receipt of the *goods or services* ordered.

**lease.** A contract calling for the lessee (user) to pay the lessor (owner) for the use of an asset. A cancelable lease is one the lessee can cancel at any time. A noncancelable lease requires payments from the lessee for the life of the lease and usually has many of the economic characteristics of *debt financing*. Most long-term noncancelable leases meet the usual criteria to be classified as a *liability* but some leases entered into before 1977 need not be shown as a liability. *SFAS No. 13* and the *SEC* require disclosure in notes to the financial statements of the commitments for long-term noncancelable leases. See *capital lease* and *operating lease*.

**leasehold.** The *asset* representing the right of the *lessee* to use leased property. See *lease* and *leasehold improvement*.

**leasehold improvement.** An *improvement* to leased property. Should be *amortized* over *service life* or the life of the lease, whichever is shorter.

**least and latest rule.** Pay the least amount of taxes as late as possible within the law to minimize the *present value* of tax payments for a given set of operations.

**ledger.** A book of accounts. See *general ledger* and *subsidiary ledger*; contrast with *journal*. Book of final entry.

**legal capital.** The amount of *contributed capital* that, according to state law, must remain permanently in the firm as protection for creditors.

**legal entity.** See *entity*.

**lender.** See *loan*.

**lessee.** See *lease*.

**lessor.** See *lease*.

**letter stock.** Privately placed *common shares*; so called because the *SEC* requires the purchaser to sign a letter of intent not to resell the shares.

**leverage.** "Operating leverage" refers to the tendency of *net income* to rise at a faster rate than sales when there are *fixed costs*. A doubling of sales, for example, usually implies a more than doubling of net income. "Financial leverage" (or "capital leverage") refers to the increased rate of return on *owners' equity* (see *ratio*) when an investment earns a return larger than the after-tax *interest rate* paid for *debt* financing. Because the interest charges on debt are usually fixed, any *incremental* income benefits owners and none benefits debtors. When "leverage" is used without a qualifying adjective, it usually refers to financial leverage and means the use of *long-term* debt in securing *funds* for the *entity*.

**leveraged lease.** A special form of lease involving three parties: a *lender*, a *lessor*, and a *lessee*. The lender, such as a bank or insurance company, lends a portion, say 80 percent, of the cash required for acquiring the *asset*. The lessor puts up the remainder, 20 percent, of the cash required. The lessor acquires the asset with the cash, using the asset as security for the loan and leases it to the lessee on a *noncancelable* basis. The lessee makes periodic lease payments to the lessor, who in turn makes payments on the loan to the lender. Typically, the lessor has no obligation for the debt to the lender other than transferring a portion of the receipts from the lessee. If the lessee should default on required lease payments, then the lender can repossess the leased asset. The lessor is usually entitled to deductions for tax purposes for *depreciation* on the asset, for *interest expense* on the loan from the lender, and for any *investment credit*. The lease is leveraged in the sense that the lessor, who enjoys most of the risks and rewards of ownership, usually borrows most of the funds needed to acquire the asset. See *leverage*.

**liability.** An obligation to pay a definite (or reasonably definite) amount at a definite (or reasonably definite) time in return for a past or current benefit. That is, the obligation arises from other than an *executory contract*. A probable future sacrifice of economic benefits arising from present obligations of a particular *entity* to *transfer assets* or to provide services to other entities in the future as a result of past *transactions* or events. *SFAC No. 6* says that "probable" refers to that which can reasonably be expected or believed but is neither certain nor proved. A liability has three essential characteristics: (1) an obligation to transfer assets or services at a specified or determinable date, (2) the entity has little or no discretion to avoid the transfer, and (3) the event causing the obligation has already happened; that is, is not executory.

**lien.** The right of person A to satisfy a claim against person B by holding B's property as security or by seizing B's property.

**life annuity.** A *contingent annuity* in which payments cease at death of a specified person(s), usually the *annuitant(s)*.

**LIFO.** *Last-in, first-out.* An *inventory* flow assumption where the *cost of goods sold* is the cost of the most recently acquired units and the *ending inventory cost* is computed from costs of the oldest units; contrast with *FIFO*. In periods of rising prices and increasing inventories, LIFO leads to higher reported expenses and therefore lower reported income and lower balance sheet inventories than does FIFO. See also *FISH* and *inventory profit*.

**LIFO conformity rule.** The *IRS* requires that companies which use a *LIFO cost flow assumption for income taxes* also use LIFO in computing *income* reported in *financial statements* and forbids disclosure of *pro forma* results from using any other cost flow assumption.

**LIFO, dollar-value method.** See *dollar-value LIFO method*.

**LIFO inventory layer.** The *ending inventory* for a period is likely to be larger than the *beginning inventory*. Under a *LIFO cost flow assumption*, this increase in physical quantities is assigned a cost computed from the prices of the earliest purchases during the year. The LIFO inventory then consists of layers, sometimes called "slices," which typically consist of relatively small amounts of physical quantities from each of the past several years. Each layer carries the prices from near the beginning of the period when it was acquired. The earliest layers will typically (in periods of rising prices) have prices much less than current prices. If inventory quantities should decline in a subsequent period, the latest layers enter cost of goods sold first.

**LIFO reserve.** *Unrealized holding gain* in *ending inventory: current or FIFO historical* cost of ending inventory less LIFO *historical* cost. See *reserve*; a better term for this concept is "excess of current cost over LIFO historical cost."

**limited liability.** Shareholders of corporations are not personally liable for debts of the company.

**limited partner.** Member of a *partnership* not personally liable for debts of the partnership; every partnership must have at least one *general partner* who is fully liable.

**line of business reporting.** See *segment reporting*.

**line of credit.** An agreement with the bank or set of banks for short-term borrowings on demand.

**linear programming.** A mathematical tool for finding profit-maximizing (or cost-minimizing) combinations of products to produce when there are several products that can be produced but there are linear constraints on the resources available in the production processes or on maximum and minimum production requirements.

**line-of-business reporting.** See *segment reporting*.

**liquid.** Said of a business with a substantial amount (the amount is unspecified) of *working capital*, especially *quick assets*.

**liquid assets.** *Cash, current marketable securities*, and, sometimes, *current receivables*.

**liquidating dividend.** *Dividend* declared in the winding up of a business to distribute the assets of the company to the shareholders. Usually treated by recipient as a return of *investment*, not as *revenue*.

**liquidation.** Payment of a debt. Sale of assets in closing down a business or a segment thereof.

**liquidation value per share.** The amount each *share* of stock will receive if the corporation is dissolved. For *preferred stock* with a liquidation preference, a stated amount per share.

**liquidity.** Refers to the availability of *cash*, or near cash resources, for meeting a firm's obligations.

**LISH.** An acronym, conceived by George H. Sorter, for *last in, still here*. LISH is the same cost flow assumption as *FIFO*. Many readers of accounting statements find it easier to think about inventory questions in terms of items still on hand. Think of FIFO in connection with *cost of goods sold* but of LISH in connection with *ending inventory*. See *FISH*.

**list price.** The published or nominally quoted price for goods.

**list price method.** See *trade-in transaction*.

**loan.** An arrangement where the owner of property, called the lender, allows someone else, called the borrower, the use of the property for a period of time that is usually specified in the agreement setting up the loan. The borrower promises to return the property to the lender and, often, to make a payment for use of the property. Generally used when the property is *cash* and the payment for its use is *interest*.

**long-lived (term) asset.** An asset whose benefits are expected to be received over several years. A *noncurrent* asset, usually includes *investments, plant assets*, and *intangibles*.

**long-run. long-term.** A term denoting a time or time periods in the future. How far in the future depends on context. For some securities traders, "long-term" can mean anything beyond the next hour or two. For most managers, it means anything beyond the next year or two. For government policy makers, it can mean anything beyond the next decade or two.

**long-term (construction) contract accounting.** The *percentage of completion method* of *revenue* recognition. Sometimes used to mean the *completed contract method*.

**long-term debt ratio.** *Noncurrent liabilities* divided by total *assets*.

**long-term liability (debt).** *Noncurrent liability*.

**long-term solvency risk.** The risk that a firm will not have sufficient *cash* to pay its *debts* sometime in the *long-run*.

**loophole.** Imprecise term meaning a technicality allowing a taxpayer (or *financial statements*) to circumvent a law's (or *GAAP*'s) intent without violating its letter.

**loss.** Excess of *cost* over net proceeds for a single transaction; negative *income* for a period. A cost expiration that produced no *revenue*. See *gain* for a discussion of related and contrasting terms.

**loss contingency.** See *contingency*.

**lower of cost or market.** A basis for valuation of *inventory* or *marketable equity securities*. The inventory value is set at the lower of *acquisition cost* or *current replacement cost* (market), subject to the following constraints: First, the market value of an item used in the computation cannot exceed its *net realizable value* — an amount equal to selling price less reasonable costs to complete production and to sell the item. Second, the market value of an item used in the computation cannot be less than the net realizable value minus the normal *profit* ordinarily realized on disposition of completed items of this type. The lower-of-cost-or-market valuation is chosen as the lower of acquisition *cost* or replacement cost *(market)* subject to the upper and lower bounds on replacement cost established in the first two steps. Thus,

Market Value = Midvalue of (Replacement Cost, Net Realizable Value, Net Realizable Value less Normal Profit Margin)

Lower of Cost or Market Valuation = Minimum (Acquisition Cost, Market Value).

The accompanying exhibit illustrates the calculation of the lower-of-cost-or-market valuation for four inventory items. Notice that each of the four possible outcomes occurs once in determining lower of cost or market. Item 1 uses acquisition cost; item 2 uses net realizable value; item 3 uses replacement cost; and item 4 uses net realizable value less normal profit.

| | Item | | | |
|---|---|---|---|---|
| | 1 | 2 | 3 | 4 |
| *Calculation of Market Value* | | | | |
| (a) Replacement Cost ....... | $92 | $96 | $92 | $96 |
| (b) Net Realizable Value ..... | 95 | 95 | 95 | 95 |
| (c) Net Realizable Value Less Normal Profit Margin [= (b) − $9] ............ | 86 | 86 | 86 | 86 |
| (d) Market = Midvalue [(a), (b), (c)] | 92 | 95 | 92 | 86 |
| *Calculation of Lower of Cost or Market* | | | | |
| (e) Acquisition Cost ......... | 90 | 97 | 96 | 90 |
| (f) Market [= (d)] .......... | 92 | 95 | 92 | 86 |
| (g) Lower of Cost or Market = Minimum [(e), (f)] ........ | 90 | 95 | 92 | 86 |

Lower of cost or market cannot be used for inventory on tax returns in a combination with a *LIFO cost flow assumption*. In the context of inventory, once the asset is written down, a new "original cost" basis is established and subsequent increases in market value are ignored in the accounts.

In the context of *marketable equity securities* the method is applied separately to short-term and long-term portfolios of securities. Losses in market value on the short-term portfolio (and any subsequent recoveries in value up to original cost) are reported as part of *income from continuing operations* for the period. For the long-term portfolio, the losses (and subsequent recoveries, if any) are *debited* (or *credited*) directly to an *owners' equity contra account*.

Note that hyphens are not used when the term is used as a noun but hyphens are used when the term is used as an adjectival phrase.

**lump-sum acquisition.** *Basket purchase*.

# M

**MD&A.** *Management discussion and analysis* section of *financial statements*.

**maintenance.** *Expenditures* undertaken to preserve an *asset's* service potential for its originally intended life; these expenditures are treated as *period expenses* or *product costs*; contrast with *improvement*. See *repair*.

**make-or-buy decision.** A managerial decision about whether the firm should produce a product internally or purchase it from others. Proper make-or-buy decisions in the short run result when *incremental costs* are the only costs considered in decision making.

**maker (of note) (of check).** One who signs a *note* to borrow. One who signs a *check*; in this context synonymous with drawer; see *draft*.

**management.** Executive authority that operates a business.

**management accounting.** See *managerial accounting*.

*Management Accounting.* Monthly publication of the *NAA*.

**management audit.** An audit conducted to ascertain whether the objectives, policies, and procedures for a firm or one of its operating units are properly carried out. Generally applies only to activities for which qualitative standards can be specified. See *audit* and *internal audit*.

**management by exception.** A principle of management where attention is focused on performance only if it differs significantly from that expected.

**management discussion and analysis.** A discussion of management's views of the company's performance required by the *SEC* since 1974 to be included in the *10-K* and in the *annual report* to shareholders. The information typically contains discussion of such items as liquidity, results of *operations*, *segments*, and the effects of *inflation*.

**managerial (management) accounting.** Reporting designed to enhance the ability of management to do its job of decision making, planning, and control; contrast with *financial accounting*.

**manufacturing cost.** Cost of producing goods, usually in a factory.

**manufacturing expense.** An imprecise, and generally incorrect, alternative title for *manufacturing overhead*.

**manufacturing overhead.** General manufacturing *costs* incurred in providing a capacity to carry on productive activities but that are not directly associated with identifiable units of product. *Fixed* manufacturing overhead costs are treated as a *product cost* under *absorption costing* but as an *expense* of the period under *direct costing*.

**margin.** *Revenue* less specified expenses. See *contribution margin*, *gross margin*, and *current margin*.

**margin of safety.** Excess of actual, or budgeted, sales over *breakeven* sales. Usually expressed in dollars; may be expressed in units of product.

**marginal cost.** The *incremental cost* or *differential cost* of the last unit added to production or the first unit subtracted from production. See *cost terminology*.

**marginal costing.** *Direct costing*.

**marginal revenue.** The increment in *revenue* from sale of one additional unit of product.

**marginal tax rate.** The tax imposed on the next dollar of taxable income generated; contrast with *average tax rate*.

**markdown.** See *markup* for definition and contrast.

**markdown cancellation.** See *markup* for definition and contrast.

**market-based transfer price.** A *transfer price* based on external market, rather than internal company, data.

**market price.** See *fair market price*.

**market rate.** The rate of *interest* a company must pay to borrow *funds* currently. See *effective rate*.

**marketable equity securities.** *Marketable securities* representing *owners' equity* interest in other companies, rather than *loans* to them.

**marketable securities.** *Stocks* and *bonds* of other companies held that can be readily sold on stock exchanges or over-the-counter markets and that the company plans to sell as cash is needed. Classified as *current assets* and as part of "cash" in preparing the *statement of cash flows*. The same securities held for *long-term* purposes would be classified as *noncurrent assets*. *SFAS No. 12* requires the *lower-of-cost-or-market* valuation basis for all marketable equity securities but different accounting treatments (with differing effect on income) depending upon whether the security is a *current* or a *noncurrent* asset.

**markon.** See *markup* for definition and contrast.

**markup.** When a retailer acquires items for *inventory*, the items are given a selling price. The difference between the original selling price and cost is most precisely called "markon," although many business people use the term "markup," and because of confusion of this use of "markup" with its precise definition (see below), "original markup" is sometimes used. If the originally established retail price is increased, the precise term for the amount of price increase is "markup," although "additional markup" is sometimes used. If a selling price is lowered, the terms "markdown" and "markup cancellation" are used. "Markup cancellation" refers to reduction in price following "additional markups" and can, by definition, be no more than the amount of the additional markup; "cancellation of additional markup," although not used, is descriptive. "Markdown" refers to price reductions from the original retail price. A price increase after a markdown is a "markdown cancellation." If original cost is $12 and original selling price is $20, then markon (original markup) is $8; if the price is later increased to $24, the $4 increase is markup (additional markup); if the price is later lowered to $21, the $3 reduction is markup cancellation; if price is lowered further to $17, the $4 reduction comprises $1 markup cancellation and $3 markdown; if price is later increased to $22, the $5 increase comprises $3 of markdown cancellation and $2 of markup (additional markup). Markup cancellations and markdowns are separately counted because the former are deducted (while the latter are not) in computing the selling prices of goods available for sale for the denominator of the *cost percentage* used in the conventional *retail inventory method*.

**markup cancellation.** See *markup* for definition and contrast.

**markup percentage.** *Markup* divided by (acquisition cost plus *markup*).

**master budget.** A *budget* projecting all *financial statements* and their components.

**matching convention.** The concept of recognizing cost expirations *(expenses)* in the same accounting period when the related *revenues* are recognized. Combining or simultaneously recognizing the revenues and expenses that jointly result from the same *transactions* or other events.

**material.** As an adjective, it means relatively important. See *materiality*. Currently, no operational definition exists. As a noun, *raw material*.

**material variances.** *Price* and *quantity variances* for *direct materials* in *standard costing systems*. Sometimes used to mean variances that are significant; see *materiality*.

**materiality.** The concept that accounting should disclose separately only those events that are relatively important (no operable definition yet exists) for the business or for understanding its statements. *SFAC No. 2* suggests that accounting information is material if "the judgment of a reasonable person relying on the information would have been changed or influenced by the omission or misstatement."

**matrix.** A rectangular array of numbers or mathematical symbols.

**matrix inverse.** For a given square *matrix* $\mathbf{A}$, the square matrix inverse is the matrix $\mathbf{A}^{-1}$, such that $\mathbf{AA}^{-1} = \mathbf{A}^{-1}\mathbf{A} = \mathbf{I}$, the *identity matrix*. Not all square matrices have inverses. Those that do not are "singular," those that do are "nonsingular."

**maturity.** The date at which an obligation, such as the *principal* of a *bond* or a *note*, becomes due.

**maturity value.** The amount expected to be collected when a loan reaches *maturity*. Depending upon the context, the amount may be *principal* or principal and *interest*.

**measuring unit.** See *attribute measured* for definition and contrast.

**merchandise.** *Finished goods* bought by a retailer or wholesaler for resale; contrast with finished goods of a manufacturing business.

**merchandise turnover.** *Inventory turnover* for merchandise; see *ratio*.

**merchandising business.** As opposed to a manufacturing or service business, one that purchases (rather than manufactures) *finished goods* for resale.

**merger.** The joining of two or more businesses into a single *economic entity*. See *holding company*.

**minority interest.** A *balance sheet account* on *consolidated statements* showing the *equity* in a less-than-100-percent-owned *subsidiary* company allocable to those who are not part of the controlling (majority) interest. May be classified either as shareholders' equity or as a liability of *indeterminate term* on the consolidated balance sheet. On the *income statement*, the minority's interest in current period's income of the less-than-100-percent-owned subsidiary must be subtracted to arrive at consolidated *net income* for the period.

**minority investment.** A holding of less than 50 percent of the *voting stock* in another corporation. Accounted for with the *equity method* when sufficient shares are owned so that the investor can exercise "significant influence," and with the *lower-of-cost-or-market* otherwise. See *mutual fund*.

**minutes book.** A record of all actions authorized at corporate *board of directors'* or shareholders' meetings.

**mix variance.** Many *standard costing systems* specify combinations of inputs, for example, labor of a certain skill and materials of a certain quality grade. Sometimes combinations of inputs used differ from those contemplated by the standard. The mix variance attempts to report the cost change caused by changing the combination of inputs.

**mixed cost.** A *semifixed* or a *semivariable cost*.

**modified cash basis.** The *cash basis of accounting* with long-term assets accounted for with the *accrual basis of accounting*. Most uses of the term "cash basis of accounting" actually mean "modified cash basis."

**monetary assets and liabilities.** See *monetary items*.

**monetary gain or loss.** The *gain* or *loss* in *general purchasing power* as a result of holding *monetary assets* or liabilities during a period when the *general purchasing power of the dollar* changes. During periods of *inflation*, holders of net monetary assets lose, and holders of net monetary liabilities gain, general purchasing power. During periods of *deflation*, holders of net monetary assets gain, and holders of net monetary liabilities lose, general purchasing power. Explicitly reported in *constant dollar accounting*.

**monetary items.** Amounts fixed in terms of dollars by statute or contract. *Cash, accounts receivable, accounts payable*, and *debt*. The distinction between monetary and nonmonetary items is important for *constant dollar accounting* and for *foreign exchange gain* or *loss* computations. In the foreign exchange context, account amounts denominated in dollars are not monetary items, whereas amounts denominated in any other currency are monetary.

**money.** A word seldom used with precision in accounting, at least in part because economists have not yet agreed on its definition. Economists use the term to refer to both a medium of exchange and a unit of value. See *cash* and *monetary items*.

**money purchase plan.** A *pension plan* where the employer contributes a specified amount of cash each year to each employee's pension fund. Benefits ultimately received by the employee are not specifically defined but depend on the rate of return on the cash invested. Sometimes called a "defined-contribution" pension plan; contrast with *defined-benefit plan*. As of the mid-1980's most corporate pension plans were defined-benefit plans because both the law and *generally accepted accounting principles* for pensions made defined-benefit plans more attractive than money purchase plans. *ERISA* makes money purchase plans relatively more attractive than they had been. We expect the relative number of money purchase plans to increase.

**mortality table.** Data of life expectancies or probabilities of death for persons of specified ages and sex.

**mortgage.** A claim given by the borrower (mortgagor) to the lender (mortgagee) against the borrower's property in return for a loan.

**moving average.** An *average* computed on observations over time. As a new observation becomes available, the oldest one is dropped so that the average is always computed for the same number of observations and only the most recent ones. Sometimes, however, this term is used synonymously with *weighted average*.

**moving average method.** *Weighted-average method.*

**multiple-step.** Said of an *income statement* where various classes of *expenses* and *losses* are subtracted from *revenues* to show intermediate items such as *operating income*, income of the enterprise (operating income plus *interest* income), income to investors (income of the enterprise less *income taxes*), net income to shareholders (income to investors less interest charges), and income retained (income to shareholders less dividends). See *entity theory*.

**municipal bond.** A *bond* issued by a village, town, or city. *Interest* on such bonds is generally exempt from federal *income taxes* and from some state income taxes. Because bonds issued by state and county governments often have these characteristics, such bonds are often called "municipals" as well. Sometimes referred to as "tax exempts."

**mutual fund.** An investment company that issues its own stock to the public and uses the proceeds to invest in securities of other companies. A mutual fund usually owns less than five or ten percent of the stock of any one company and accounts for its investments using current *market values*; contrast with *holding company*.

**mutually exclusive projects.** Competing investment projects, where accepting one project eliminates the possibility of undertaking the remaining projects.

**N**

**NAARS.** *National Automated Accounting Research System.*

**NASDAQ.** National Association of Securities Dealers Automated Quotation System; a computerized system to provide brokers and dealers with price quotations for securities traded *over the counter* as well as for some *NYSE* securities.

**National Association of Accountants. NAA.** A national society generally open to all engaged in activities closely associated with *managerial accounting*. Oversees the administration of the *CMA* Examinations through the Institute of Management Accounting.

**National Automated Accounting Research System. NAARS.** A computer based information retrieval system containing, among other things, the complete text of most public corporate annual reports and *Form 10-K*. The system is available to users through the *AICPA*.

**natural business year.** A 12-month period chosen as the reporting period so that the end of the period coincides with a low point in activity or inventories. See *ratio* for a discussion of analyses of financial statements of companies using a natural business year.

**natural classification.** *Income statement* reporting form in which *expenses* are classified by nature of items as acquired, that is, materials, wages, salaries, insurance, and taxes, as well as depreciation; contrast with *functional classification*.

**natural resources.** Timberland, oil and gas wells, ore deposits, and other products of nature that have economic value. The cost of natural resources is subject to *depletion*. Natural resources are "nonrenewable" (for example, oil, coal, gas, ore deposits) or "renewable" (timberland, sod fields); the former are often called "wasting assets." See also *reserve recognition accounting* and *percentage depletion*.

**negative confirmation.** See *confirmation*.

**negative goodwill.** Refer to *goodwill*. When the purchase price of the company acquired is less than the sum of the *fair market value* of the *net assets* acquired, *APB Opinion No. 16* requires that the valuation of noncurrent assets (except *investments* in *marketable securities*) acquired be reduced until the purchase price equals the adjusted valuation of the fair market value of net assets acquired. If, after the adjusted valuation of noncurrent assets is reduced to zero, the purchase price is still less than the net assets acquired, then the difference is shown as a credit balance in the balance sheet as negative goodwill and is amortized to income over a period not to exceed forty years. For negative goodwill to exist, someone must be willing to sell a company for less than the fair market value of net current assets and marketable securities. Because such a bargain purchase is rare, negative goodwill is rarely found in the financial statements; when it does appear, it generally signals unrecorded obligations, such as for *pensions* or contingent liability in a law suit.

**negotiable.** Legally capable of being transferred by endorsement. Usually said of *checks* and *notes* and sometimes of *stocks* and *bearer bonds*.

**negotiated transfer price.** A *transfer price* set jointly by the buying and selling divisions.

**net.** Reduced by all relevant deductions.

**net assets.** *Owners' equity*; total *assets* minus total *liabilities*.

**net bank position.** From a firm's point of view, *cash* in a specific bank less *loans* payable to that bank.

**net current assets.** *Working capital* = *current assets* − *current liabilities*.

**net current asset value (per share).** *Working capital* divided by the number of common shares outstanding. Many security analysts think that when a common share trades in the market for an amount less than net current asset value, then the shares are undervalued and should be purchased. We find this view naive because it ignores the efficiency of capital markets generally and, specifically, unrecorded obligations such as for some *pension plans*, not currently reported as liabilities in the *balance sheet* under *GAAP*.

**net income.** The excess of all *revenues* and *gains* for a period over all *expenses* and *losses* of the period. See *comprehensive income*.

**net loss.** The excess of all *expenses* and *losses* for a period over all *revenues* and *gains* of the period. Negative *net income*.

**net markup.** In the context of *retail inventory methods*, *markups* less markup cancellations; a figure that usually ignores *markdowns* and markdown cancellations.

**net of tax method.** A nonsanctioned method for dealing with the problem of *income tax allocation*; described in *APB Opinion No. 11*. Deferred tax items are subtracted from specific *asset* amounts rather than being shown as a deferred credit or *liability*.

**net of tax reporting.** Reporting, such as for *income from discontinued operations, extraordinary items*, and *prior-period adjustments*, where the amounts presented in *financial statements* have been adjusted for all income tax effects. For example, if an extraordinary loss amounted to $10,000 and the marginal tax rate were 40 percent, then the extraordinary item would be reported "net of taxes" as a $6,000 loss. Hence, all income taxes may not be reported on one line of the income statement. The taxes will be allocated to *income from continuing operations, income from discontinued operations, extraordinary items*, cumulative effects of *accounting changes*, and *prior-period adjustments*.

**net operating profit.** Income from *continuing operations*.

**net present value.** Discounted or *present value* of all cash inflows and outflows of a project or from an *investment* at a given *discount rate*.

**net price method (of recording purchase or sales discounts).** The *purchase* (or *sale*) is recorded at its *invoice* price less all *discounts* made available under the assumption that nearly all discounts will be taken. Discounts lapsed through failure to pay promptly are debited to an *expense* account. For purchases, management usually prefers to know about the amount of discounts lost because of inefficient operations, not the amounts taken, so that most managers prefer the net price method to the *gross price method*.

**net realizable (sales) value.** A method for *allocating joint costs* in proportion to *realizable values* of the joint products. For example, joint products A and B together cost $100 and A sells for $60 whereas B sells for $90. Then A would be allocated ($60/$150) × $100 = .40 × $100 = $40 of cost while B would be allocated ($90/$150) × $100 = $60 of cost.

**net sales.** Sales (at gross invoice amount) less *returns, allowances*, freight paid for customers, and *discounts* taken.

**net working capital.** *Working capital*; the "net" is redundant in accounting. Financial analysts sometimes mean *current assets* when they speak of working capital, so for them the "net" is not redundant.

**net worth.** A misleading term, to be avoided, that means the same as *owners' equity*.

**New York Stock Exchange. NYSE.** A public market where various corporate *securities* are traded.

**next-in, first-out.** See *NIFO*.

**NIFO.** *Next-in, first-out.* In making decisions, many managers consider *replacement costs* (rather than *historical costs*) and refer to them as NIFO costs.

**no par.** Said of *stock* without a *par value.*

**nominal accounts.** *Temporary accounts,* such as *revenue* and *expense* accounts, as opposed to *balance sheet accounts.* All nominal accounts are *closed* at the end of each *accounting period.*

**nominal amount (value).** An amount stated in dollars, in contrast to an amount stated in *constant dollars.* Contrast with *real amount (value).*

**nominal dollars.** The measuring unit giving no consideration to differences in the *general purchasing power of the dollar* over time. The face amount of currency or coin, a *bond,* an *invoice,* a *receivable* is a nominal dollar amount. When that amount is adjusted for changes in *general purchasing power,* it is converted into a *constant dollar* amount.

**nominal interest rate.** A rate specified on a *debt* instrument, which usually differs from the market or *effective rate.* Also, a rate of *interest* quoted for a year. If the interest is compounded more often than annually, then the *effective interest rate* is higher than the nominal rate.

**noncancelable.** See *lease.*

**nonconsolidated subsidiary.** An *intercorporate investment* where more than 50 percent of the shares of the *subsidiary* are owned but the investment is accounted for with the *cost method* or *lower-of-cost-or-market method.*

**noncontributory.** Said of a *pension plan* where only the employer makes payments to a pension *fund;* contrast with *contributory.*

**noncontrollable cost.** A cost that is not *controllable* by a particular manager.

**noncurrent.** Due more than one year (or more than one *operating cycle*) hence.

**nonexpendable fund.** A governmental fund, whose *principal,* and sometimes earnings, may not be spent.

**non-interest-bearing note.** A *note* that bears no explicit interest. The *present value* of such a note at any time before *maturity* is less than the *face value* so long as *interest rates* are positive. *APB Opinion No. 21* requires that the present value, not face value, of long-term noninterest-bearing notes be reported as the *asset* or *liability* amount in financial statements. For this purpose, the *historical interest rate* is used. See *interest, imputed.*

**nonmanufacturing costs.** All *costs* incurred other than those to produce goods.

**nonmonetary items.** All items that are not monetary; see *monetary items.*

**nonoperating.** In the *income statement* context, said of revenues and expenses arising from transactions incidental to the company's main line(s) of business. In the *statement of cash flows* context, said of all sources or uses of cash other than cash provided by operations. See *operations.*

**nonprofit corporation.** An incorporated *entity,* such as a hospital, with owners who do not share in the earnings. It usually emphasizes providing services rather than maximizing income.

**nonrecurring.** Said of an event that is not expected to happen often for a given firm. Under *APB Opinion No. 30,* the effects of such events should be disclosed separately, but as part of *ordinary* items unless the event is also unusual. See *extraordinary* item.

**normal cost.** Former name for *service cost.*

**normal costing.** Method of charging costs to products using actual *direct materials,* actual *direct labor,* and predetermined *factory overhead rates.*

**normal costing system.** *Costing* based on *actual material* and *labor* costs, but using *predetermined overhead* rates per unit of some *activity basis* (such as *direct labor hours* or machine hours) to apply overhead to production. This rate for overhead to be charged to production is decided at the start of the period. At the end of the period it is multiplied by the actual number of units of the base activity (such as actual direct labor hours worked or actual machine hours used during the period) to apply overhead to production.

**normal spoilage.** Costs incurred because of ordinary amounts of spoilage; such costs should be prorated to units produced as *product costs;* contrast with *abnormal spoilage.*

**normal standard cost. normal standards.** The *cost* expected to be incurred under reasonably efficient operating conditions with adequate provision for an average amount of rework, spoilage, and the like.

**normal volume.** The level of production over a time span, usually 1 year, that will satisfy demand by purchasers and provide for reasonable *inventory* levels.

**note.** An unconditional written promise by the maker (borrower) to pay a certain amount on demand or at a certain future time. See *footnotes* for another context.

**note receivable discounted.** A *note* assigned by the holder to another. The new holder of the note typically pays the old holder an amount less than the *face value* of the note; hence the word ''discounted.'' But this word is used even if the payment by the new holder to the old is at or above face value. If the note is assigned with recourse, it is the *contingent liability* of the assignor until the debt is paid. See *factoring*.

**NOW account.** Negotiable order of withdrawal. A *savings account* on which orders to pay, much like *checks* but technically not checks, can be drawn and given to others who can redeem the order at the savings institution.

**number of days sales in inventory (or receivables).** Days of average inventory on hand (or average collection period for receivables). See *ratio*.

**NYSE.** *New York Stock Exchange*.

# O

**OASD(H)I.** *Old Age, Survivors, Disability, and (Hospital) Insurance.*

**objective.** See *reporting objective* and *objectivity*.

**objective function.** In *linear programming*, the name of the profit or cost criterion to be optimized.

**objectivity.** The reporting policy implying that formal recognition will not be given to an event in financial statements until the magnitude of the events can be measured with reasonable accuracy and is subject to independent verification.

**obsolescence.** A decline in *market value* of an *asset* caused by improved alternatives becoming available that will be more *cost effective*; the decline in market value is unrelated to physical changes in the asset itself. See *partial obsolescence*.

**Occupational Safety and Health Act.** *OSHA.*

**off-balance-sheet financing.** A description often used for an obligation meeting all the tests to be a liability, except that the obligation arises from an *executory contract* and, hence, is not a *liability*. Consider the following example.

Miller Corporation desires to acquire land costing $25 million, on which it will build a shopping center. It could borrow the $25 million from its bank, paying interest at 12 percent, and buy the land outright from the seller. If so, both an asset and a liability will appear on the balance sheet. Instead, it borrows $5 million and purchases for $5 million from the seller an *option* to buy the land from the seller at any time within the next 6 years for a price of $20 million. The option costs Miller Corporation $5 million immediately and provides for continuing "option" payments of $2.4 million per year, which is just equal to Miller Corporation's borrowing rate multiplied by the remaining purchase price of the land: $2.4 million = .12 × $20 million. Although Miller Corporation need not continue payments and can let the option lapse at any time, it also has an obligation to begin developing on the site immediately. Because

Miller Corporation has invested a substantial sum in the option, will invest more, and will begin immediately developing the land, Miller Corporation is almost certain to exercise its option before it expires. The seller of the land can take the option contract to the bank and borrow $20 million, paying interest at Miller Corporation's borrowing rate, 12 percent per year. The continuing option payments from Miller Corporation will be sufficient to enable the seller to make its payments to the bank. *Generally accepted accounting principles* view Miller Corporation as having acquired an option for $5 million, rather than having acquired land costing $25 million in return for $5 million of "debt" off the balance sheet until it borrows more funds to exercise the option.

**Old Age, Survivors, Disability, and (Hospital) Insurance.** The technical name for Social Security under the Federal Insurance Contributions Act (FICA).

**on (open) account.** Said of a *purchase* or *sale* when payment is expected sometime after delivery and no *note* evidencing the *debt* is given or received. The purchaser has generally signed an agreement sometime in the past promising to pay for such purchases according to an agreed time schedule. When a sale (purchase) is made on open account, *Accounts Receivable (Payable)* is *debited (credited)*.

**on consignment.** Said of goods delivered by the owner (the consignor) to another (the consignee) to be sold by the consignee; the owner is entitled to the return of the property or payment of an amount agreed upon in advance. The goods are assets of the consignor. Such arrangements provide the consignor with better protection than an outright *sale on account* to the consignee in case the consignee becomes bankrupt. In event of *bankruptcy*, the consignor can reclaim the goods, without going through lengthy bankruptcy proceedings from which the consignor might recover only a small percentage of the amounts owed to it.

**one-line consolidation.** Said of an *intercorporate investment* accounted for with the *equity method*. The effects of this method on reported *income* and *balance sheet* total *assets* and *equities* are identical to those that would appear if the investee firm were consolidated, even though the income from the investment appears on a single line of the income statement and the net investment appears on a single line in the assets section of the balance sheet.

**open account.** Any *account* with a nonzero *debit* or *credit balance*. See *on (open) account*.

**operating.** An adjective used to refer to *revenue* and *expense* items relating to the company's main line(s) of business. See *operations*.

**operating accounts.** *Revenue, expense,* and *production cost accounts*; contrast with *balance sheet accounts*.

**operating activities.** See *operations*. For purposes of the *statement of cash flows*, all *transactions* and *events* that are neither *financing activities* nor *investing activities*.

**operating budget.** A formal *budget* for the *operating cycle* or for a year.

**operating cycle.** *Earnings cycle*.

**operating expenses.** *Expenses* incurred in the course of *ordinary* activities of an *entity*. Frequently, a classification including only *selling, general*, and *administrative expenses*, thereby excluding *cost of goods sold, interest*, and *income tax* expenses. See *operations*.

**operating lease.** A *lease* accounted for by the *lessee* without showing an *asset* for the lease rights (*leasehold*) or a *liability* for the lease payment obligations. Rental payments of the lessee are merely shown as *expenses* of the period. The asset remains on the lessor's *books* where rental collections appear as *revenues*; contrast with *capital lease*.

**operating leverage.** Usually said of a firm with a large proportion of *fixed costs* in its *total costs*. Consider a book publisher or a railroad; the *incremental costs* of producing another book or transporting another freight car are much less than *average cost*, so the *gross margin* upon sale of the unit is relatively large. Contrast, for example, a grocery store, where the *contribution margin* is usually less than 5 percent of the selling price. For firms with equal profitability, however defined, the one with the larger percentage increase in income from a given percentage increase in unit sales is said to have the larger operating leverage. See *leverage* for contrast of this term with "financial leverage." See *cost terminology* for definition of terms involving the word *cost*.

**operating margin (based on current costs).** *Revenues* from *sales* minus *current cost* of goods sold. A measure of operating efficiency that is independent of the *cost flow assumption* for *inventory*. Sometimes called "current (gross) margin." See *inventory profit* for illustrative computations.

**operating ratio.** See *ratio*.

**operational control.** See *control system*.

**operations.** A word not precisely defined in *accounting*. Generally, operating activities (producing and selling *goods* or *services*) are distinguished from financing activities (raising funds) and *investing activities*. Acquiring goods on account and then paying for them in one month, though generally classified as a financing activity, has the characteristics of a financing activity. Or consider the transaction of selling plant assets for a price in excess of book value. On the *income statement*, the gain is part of income from operations (continuing operations or discontinued operations, depending on the circumstances) but on the *statement of cash flows*, all of the funds received on disposition are reported below the "cash from operations" section, as a nonoperating source of cash, disposition of noncurrent assets. In income tax accounting an "operating loss" results whenever deductions are greater than taxable revenues.

**opinion.** The *auditor's report* containing an attestation or lack thereof. Also, *APB Opinion*.

**opinion paragraph.** Section of *auditor's report*, generally following the *scope paragraph*, giving the auditor's conclusion that the *financial statements* are (rarely, are not) in accordance with *GAAP* and present fairly the *financial position*, changes in financial position, and the results of *operations*.

**opportunity cost.** The *present value* of the *income* (or *costs*) that could be earned (or saved) from using an *asset* in its best alternative use to the one being considered.

**option.** The legal right to buy something during a specified period at a specified price, called the *exercise* price. Employee stock options should not be confused with *put* and *call* options traded in various public markets.

**ordinary annuity.** An *annuity in arrears*.

**ordinary income.** For income tax purposes, reportable *income* not qualifying as *capital gains*.

**organization costs.** The *costs* incurred in planning and establishing an *entity*; example of an *intangible* asset. Often, since the amounts are not *material*, the costs are treated as *expenses* in the period incurred even though the *expenditures* clearly provide future benefits and meet the test to be *assets*.

**original cost.** *Acquisition cost*. In public utility accounting, the acquisition cost of the *entity* first devoting the asset to public use. See *aboriginal cost*.

**original entry.** Entry in a *journal*.

**OSHA.** Occupational Safety and Health Act. The federal law that governs working conditions in commerce and industry.

**outlay.** The amount of an *expenditure*.

**outlier.** Said of an observation (or data point) that appears to differ significantly in some regard from other observations (or data points) of supposedly the same phenomenon. Often used in describing the results of a *regression analysis* when an observation is not "near" the fitted regression equation.

**out-of-pocket.** Said of an *expenditure* usually paid for with cash. An *incremental* cost.

**out-of-stock cost.** The estimated decrease in future *profit* as a result of losing customers because insufficient quantities of *inventory* are currently on hand to meet customers' demands.

**output.** Physical quantity or monetary measurement of *goods* and *services* produced.

**outside director.** A member of a corporate board of directors who is not a company officer and does not participate in the corporation's day-to-day management.

**outstanding.** Unpaid or uncollected. When said of *stock*, the shares issued less *treasury stock*. When said of checks, it means a check issued that did not clear the *drawer's* bank prior to the *bank statement* date.

**over-and-short.** Title for an *expense account* used to account for small differences between book balances of cash and actual cash and vouchers or receipts in *petty cash* or *change funds*.

**overapplied (overabsorbed) overhead.** An excess of costs applied, or *charged*, to product for a period over actual *overhead costs* during the period. A *credit balance* in an overhead account after overhead is assigned to product.

**overdraft.** A check written on a checking account that contains funds less than the amount of the check.

**overhead costs.** Any *cost* not directly associated with the production or sale of identifiable goods and services. Sometimes called "burden" or "indirect costs" and, in Britain, "oncosts." Frequently limited to manufacturing overhead. See *central corporate expenses* and *manufacturing overhead*.

**overhead rate.** Standard, or other predetermined rate at which *overhead costs* are applied to products or to services.

**over-the-counter.** Said of a *security* traded in a negotiated transaction, rather than in an auctioned one on an organized stock exchange, such as the *New York Stock Exchange*.

**owners' equity.** *Proprietorship; assets* minus *liabilities; paid-in capital* plus *retained earnings* of a corporation; partners' capital accounts in a *partnership*; owner's capital account in a *sole proprietorship*.

**P**

**P & L.** Profit and loss statement; *income statement*.

**paid-in capital.** Sum of balances in *capital stock* and *capital contributed in excess of par (or stated) value* accounts. Same as *contributed capital* (minus *donated capital*). Some use the term to mean only *capital contributed in excess of par (or stated value)*.

**paid-in surplus.** See *surplus*.

**paper profit.** A *gain* not yet realized through a *transaction*. An *unrealized holding gain*.

**par.** See *at par* and *face amount*.

**par value.** *Face amount* of a *security*.

**par value method.** The method of accounting for *treasury stock* that *debits* a common stock account with the *par value* of the shares required and allocates the remaining debits between the *additional paid-in capital* and *retained earnings* accounts; contrast with *cost method*.

**parent company.** Company owning more than 50 percent of the voting shares of another company, called the *subsidiary*.

**partial obsolescence.** As technology improves, the economic value of existing *assets* declines. In many cases, however, it will not pay a firm to replace the existing asset with a new one even though the new type, rather than the old, would be acquired if a new acquisition were to be made currently. In these cases, the accountant should theoretically recognize a loss from partial obsolescence from the firm's owning an old, out-of-date asset, but *GAAP* does not permit recognition of partial obsolescence. The old asset will be carried at *cost* less *accumulated depreciation* until it is retired from service so long as the *undiscounted* future *cash flows* from the asset exceed its book value. See *obsolescence*.

**partially funded.** Said of a *pension plan* where not all earned benefits have been funded. See *funded* for funding requirements.

**partially vested.** Said of a *pension plan* where not all employee benefits are *vested*. See *graded vesting*.

**participating dividend.** *Dividend* paid to preferred shareholders in addition to the minimum preferred dividends when the *preferred stock* contract allows such sharing in earnings. Usually applied after dividends on *common stock* have reached a certain level.

**participating preferred stock.** *Preferred stock* with rights to *participating dividends*.

**partner's drawing.** A payment to a partner to be charged against his or her share of income or capital. The name of a *temporary account* to record such payments.

**partnership.** Contractual arrangement between individuals to share resources and operations in a jointly run business. See *general* and *limited partner* and *Uniform Partnership Act*.

**patent.** A right granted for up to 17 years by the federal government to exclude others from manufacturing, using or selling a claimed design, product or plant (e.g., a new breed of rose) or from using a claimed process or method of manufacture. An asset if acquired by purchase. If developed internally, the development costs are *expensed* when incurred under current *GAAP*.

**payable.** Unpaid but not necessarily due or past due.

**pay as you go.** Said of an *income tax* scheme where periodic payments of income taxes are made during the period when the income to be taxed is being earned; in contrast to a scheme where no payments are due until the end of, or after, the period whose income is being taxed. (Called PAYE — pay as you earn — in Britain.) Sometimes used to describe an *unfunded pension plan*, where payments to pension plan beneficiaries are made from general corporate funds, not from cash previously contributed to a pension fund. Not acceptable as a method of accounting for pension plans under *SFAS No. 87* nor as a method of *funding* under *ERISA*.

**payback period.** Amount of time that must elapse before the cash inflows from a project equal the cash outflows.

**payback reciprocal.** One divided by the *payback period*. This number approximates the *internal rate of return* on a project when the project life is more than twice the payback period and the cash inflows are identical in every period after the initial period.

**PAYE.** See *pay as you go*.

**payee.** The person or entity to whom a cash payment is made or who will receive the stated amount of money on a check. See *draft*.

**payout ratio.** *Common stock dividends* declared for a year divided by net *income* to common stock for the year. A term used by financial analysts; contrast with *dividend yield*.

**payroll taxes.** Taxes levied because salaries or wages are paid; for example, *FICA* and unemployment compensation insurance taxes. Typically, the employer pays a portion and withholds part of the employee's wage fund.

**P/E ratio**. *Price-earnings ratio*.

**Pension Benefit Guarantee Corporation. PBGC.** A federal corporation established under *ERISA* to guarantee basic pension benefits in covered pension plans by administering terminated pension plans and placing *liens* on corporate assets for certain unfunded pension liabilities.

**pension fund.** *Fund*, the assets of which are to be paid to retired ex-employees, usually as a *life annuity*. Usually held by an independent trustee and thus is not an *asset* of the employer.

**pension plan.** Details or provisions of employer's contract with employees for paying retirement *annuities* or other benefits. See *funded, vested, service cost, prior service cost, money purchase plan*, and *defined-benefit plan*.

**per books.** An expression used to refer to the *book value* of an item at a specific time.

**percent.** Any number, expressed as a decimal, multiplied by 100.

**percentage depletion (allowance).** Deductible *expense* allowed in some cases by the federal *income tax* regulations; computed as a percentage of gross income from a *natural resource* independent of the unamortized cost of the asset. Because the amount of the total deductions for tax purposes is usually greater than the cost of the asset being *depleted*, many people think the deduction is an unfair tax advantage or *loophole*.

**percentage-of-completion method.** Recognizing *revenues* and *expenses* on a job, order, or contract (a) in proportion to the *costs* incurred for the period divided by total costs expected to be incurred for the job or order ("cost to cost") or (b) in proportion to engineers' or architects' estimates of the incremental degree of completion of the job, order, or contract during the period. Contrast with *completed contract method*.

**percentage statement.** A statement containing, in addition to (or instead of) dollar amounts, ratios of dollar amounts to some base. In a percentage *income statement*, the base is usually either *net sales* or total *revenues* and in a percentage *balance sheet*, the base is usually total *assets*.

**period.** *Accounting period*.

**period cost.** An inferior term for *period expense*.

**period expense (charge).** *Expenditure*, usually based on the passage of time, charged to operations of the accounting period rather than *capitalized* as an asset; contrast with *product cost*.

**periodic inventory.** A method of recording *inventory* that uses data on beginning inventory, additions to inventories, and ending inventory to find the cost of withdrawals from inventory. Contrast with *perpetual inventory*.

**periodic procedures.** The process of making *adjusting entries, closing entries*, and preparing the *financial statements*, usually by use of *trial balances* and *work sheets*.

**permanent account**. An account which appears on the *balance sheet*; contrast with *temporary account*.

**permanent difference.** Difference between reported income and taxable income that will never be reversed and, hence, requires no entry in the *deferred income tax liability* account. An example is the difference between taxable and reportable income from interest earned on state and municipal bonds; contrast with *timing difference* and see *deferred income tax liability*.

**perpetual annuity.**  *Perpetuity.*

**perpetual inventory.**  Records on quantities and amounts of *inventory* that are changed or made current with each physical addition to or withdrawal from the stock of goods; an inventory so recorded. The records will show the physical quantities and, frequently, the dollar valuations that should be on hand at any time. Because *cost of goods sold* is explicitly computed, the *inventory equation* can be used to compute an amount for what *ending inventory* should be. The computed amount of ending inventory can be compared to the actual amount of ending inventory as a *control* device. Contrast with *periodic inventory*.

**perpetuity.**  An *annuity* whose payments continue forever. The *present value* of a perpetuity in *arrears* is *p/r* where *p* is the periodic payment and *r* is the *interest rate* per period. If $100 is promised each year, in arrears, forever, and the interest rate is 8 percent per year, the value of the perpetuity is $1,250 = $100/.08.

**personal account.**  *Drawing account.*

**petty cash fund.**  Currency and coins maintained for expenditures that are made with cash on hand.

**physical units method.**  A method of allocating a *joint cost* to the *joint products* based on a physical measure of the joint products. For example, allocating the cost of a cow to sirloin steak and to hamburger, based on the weight of the meat. This method usually provides nonsensical (see *sterilized allocation*) results unless the physical units of the joint products tend to have the same value.

**physical verification.**  *Verification*, by an *auditor*, performed by actually inspecting items in *inventory, plant assets*, and the like; may be based on statistical sampling procedures; in contrast to mere checking of written records.

**planning and control process.**  General name for the techniques of management comprising the setting of organizational goals and *strategic plans*, *capital budgeting, operations* budgeting, comparison of plans with actual results, performance evaluation and corrective action, and revisions of goals, plans, and budgets.

**plant.**  *Plant assets.*

**plant assets.**  Buildings, machinery, equipment, land, and natural resources. The phrase "property, plant and equipment" is, therefore, a redundancy. In this context, "plant" means buildings.

**plant asset turnover.**  Number of dollars of *sales* generated per dollar of *plant assets*. Equal to sales divided by average *plant assets*.

**pledging.**  The borrower assigns *assets* as security or *collateral* for repayment of a loan.

**pledging of receivables.**  The process of using expected collections on accounts receivable as *collateral* for a loan. The borrower remains responsible for collecting the receivable but promises to use the proceeds for repaying the debt.

**plow back.**  To retain assets generated by earnings for continued investment in the business.

**plug.**  For any *account*, beginning balance + additions − deductions = ending balance; if any three of the four items are known, the fourth can be found by plugging. In making a *journal entry*, often all *debits* are known, as are all but one of the *credits* (or vice versa). Because *double-entry* bookkeeping requires equal debits and credits, the unknown quantity can be computed by subtracting the sum of the known credits from the sum of all the debits (or vice versa). This process is also known as plugging. The unknown found is called the plug. For example, if a *discount* on *bonds payable* is being *amortized* with the *straight-line method*, then *interest expense* is a plug: interest expense = interest payable + discount amortization. See *trade-in transaction* for an example. The term sometimes has a bad connotation for accountants because plugging occurs in a slightly different context: In preparing a *pre-closing trial balance* (or balance sheet), often the sum of the debits does not equal the sum of the credits. Rather than find the error, some accountants are tempted to force equality by changing one of the amounts, with a plugged debit or credit to an account such as Other Expenses. There is really nothing wrong with this procedure if the amount of the error is very small compared to asset totals because it is not cost effective to spend tens or hundreds of dollars in bookkeeper's or accountant's time to find an error of a few dollars. Still, most accounting teachers and auditors gravely frown on the process.

**pooling-of-interests method.**  Accounting for a *business combination* by merely adding together the *book value* of the *assets* and *equities* of the combined firms. Contrast with *purchase method*. Generally leads to a higher reported *net income* for the combined firms than would be reported had the business combination been accounted for as a purchase because the *market values* of the merged assets are generally larger than their book values. *APB Opinion No. 16* states the conditions that, when met, require the pooling-of-interests treatment.

**positive confirmation.**  See *confirmation*.

**post.**  To record entries in an *account* in a *ledger*; usually the entries are transferred from a *journal*.

**post-closing trial balance.** *Trial balance* taken after all *temporary accounts* have been closed.

**post-statement events.** Events with *material* impact that occur between the end of the *accounting period* and the formal publication of the *financial statements*. Such events must be disclosed in notes for the auditor to give a *clean opinion*, even though the events are subsequent to the period being reported on.

**potentially dilutive.** A *security* that may be converted into, or exchanged for, common stock and thereby reduce reported *earnings per share: options, warrants, convertible bonds*, and *convertible preferred stock*.

**PPB.** *Program budgeting*; the second "P" means "plan".

**practical capacity.** Maximum level at which the plant or department can operate efficiently.

**preclosing trial balance.** *Trial balance* taken at the end of the period before *closing entries*. In this sense, an *adjusted trial balance*. Sometimes taken before *adjusting entries* and then is synonymous with *unadjusted trial balance*.

**predetermined (factory) overhead rate.** Rate used in applying *overhead* to products or departments, developed at the start of a period by dividing estimated overhead cost by the estimated number of units of the overhead allocation base (or *denominator volume*) activity. See *normal costing*.

**preemptive right.** The privilege of a *shareholder* to maintain a proportionate share of ownership by purchasing a proportionate share of any new stock issues. Most state corporation laws allow corporations to pay shareholders to waive their preemptive rights or state that preemptive rights exist only if the *corporation charter* explicitly grants them. In practice, then, preemptive rights are the exception, rather than the rule.

**preference as to assets.** The rights of *preferred shareholders* to receive certain payments in case of dissolution before common shareholders receive payments.

**preferred shares.** *Capital stock* with a claim to *income* or *assets* after *bondholders* but before *common shares*. *Dividends* on preferred shares are *income distributions*, not *expenses*. See *cumulative preferred stock*.

**premium.** The excess of issue (or market) price over *par value*. For a different context, see *insurance*.

**premium on capital stock.** Alternative but inferior title for *capital contributed in excess of (par) or stated value*.

**prepaid expense.** An *expenditure* that leads to a *deferred charge* or *prepayment*; strictly speaking, a contradiction in terms because an *expense* is a gone asset and

this title refers to past *expenditures*, such as for rent or insurance premiums, that still have future benefits and thus are *assets*.

**prepaid income.** An inferior alternative title for *advances from customers*. An item should not be called *revenue* or *income* until earned, when goods are delivered or services are rendered.

**prepayments.** *Deferred charges*. *Assets* representing *expenditures* for future benefits. Rent and insurance premiums paid in advance are usually classified as *current* prepayments.

**present value.** Value today (or at some specific date) of an amount or amounts to be paid or received later (or at other, different dates), discounted at some *interest* or *discount rate*.

**price.** The quantity of one *good* or *service*, usually *cash*, asked in return for a unit of another good or service. See *fair market price*.

**price-earnings ratio.** At a given time, the market value of a company's *common stock*, per share, divided by the *earnings per* common *share* for the past year. The denominator is usually based on *income from continuing operations* or, if the analyst thinks the current figure for that amount is not representative — such as when the number is negative — on some estimate of the number. See *ratio*.

**price index.** A series of numbers, one for each period, that purports to represent some *average* of prices for a series of periods, relative to a base period.

**price level.** The number from a *price index* series for a given period or date.

**price level-adjusted statements.** *Financial statements* expressed in terms of dollars of uniform purchasing power. *Nonmonetary* items are restated to reflect changes in general *price levels* since the time specific *assets* were acquired and *liabilities* were incurred. A *gain* or *loss* is recognized on *monetary items* as they are held over time periods when the general *price level changes*. Conventional financial statements show *historical costs* and ignore differences in purchasing power in different periods.

**price variance.** In accounting for *standard costs*, Price Variance = (Actual Cost per Unit − Standard Cost per Unit) × Quantity Purchased.

**primary earnings per share.** Net *income* to *common shareholders* plus *interest* (*net of tax* effects) or *dividends* paid on *common stock equivalents* divided by (weighted average of common share outstanding plus the net increase in the number of common shares that would become *outstanding* if all common stock equivalents were exchanged for common shares with cash proceeds, if any, used to retire common shares).

**prime cost.** Sum of *direct materials* and *direct labor* costs assigned to product.

**prime rate.** The rate for loans charged by commercial banks to their creditworthy customers. Some customers pay even less than the prime rate and others, more. The *Federal Reserve Bulletin* is considered the authoritative source of information about historical prime rates.

**principal.** An amount in which *interest* is charged or earned. The *face amount* of a *loan*. Also, the absent owner (principal) who hires the manager (agent) in a "principal-agent" relationship.

**principle.** See *generally accepted accounting principles*.

**prior-period adjustment.** A *debit* or *credit* made directly to *retained earnings* (that does not affect *income* for the period) to adjust earnings as calculated for prior periods. Such adjustments are now extremely rare. Theory might suggest that corrections of errors in accounting estimates (such as the *depreciable life* or *salvage value* of an asset) should be treated as adjustments to retained earnings. But *GAAP* require that corrections of such estimates flow through current, and perhaps future, *income statements*. See *accounting changes* and *accounting errors*.

**prior service cost.** *Present value* at a given time of a *pension plan's* retroactive *benefits*. "Unrecognized prior service cost" refers to that portion of prior service cost not yet *debited* to *expense*. See *actuarial accrued liability* and *funded*; contrast with *normal cost*.

**pro forma statements.** Hypothetical statements. Financial statements as they would appear if some event, such as a *merger* or increased production and sales, had occurred or were to occur. Pro forma is often spelled as one word.

**proceeds.** The *funds* received from disposition of assets or from the issue of securities.

**process costing.** A method of *cost accounting* based on average costs (total cost divided by the *equivalent units* of work done in a period). Typically used for assembly lines or for products that are produced in a series of steps that are more continuous than discrete.

**product.** *Goods* or *services* produced.

**product cost.** Any *manufacturing cost* that can be inventoried. See *flow of costs* for example and contrast with *period expenses*.

**production cost.** *Manufacturing cost*.

**production cost account.** A *temporary account* for accumulating *manufacturing costs* during a period.

**production department.** A department producing salable *goods* or *services*; contrast with *service department*.

**production method (depreciation).** The depreciable asset (e.g., a truck) is given a *depreciable life* measured, not in elapsed time, but in units of output (e.g., miles) or perhaps in units of time of expected use. Then the *depreciation* charge for a period is a portion of depreciable cost equal to a fraction computed by dividing the actual output produced during the period by the expected total output to be produced over the life of the asset. Sometimes called the "units-of-production (or output) method."

**production method (revenue recognition).** *Percentage-of-completion* method for recognizing *revenue*.

**production volume variance.** Standard fixed *overhead* rate per unit of normal *capacity* (or base activity) times (units of base activity budgeted or planned for a period minus actual units of base activity worked or assigned to product during the period). Often called a "volume variance."

**productive capacity.** In computing *current cost* of *long-term assets*, we are interested in the cost of reproducing the productive capacity (for example, the ability to manufacture one million units a year), not the cost of reproducing the actual physical assets currently used (see *reproduction cost*). Replacement cost of productive capacity will be the same as reproduction cost of assets only in the unusual case when there has been no technological improvement in production processes and the relative prices of goods and services used in production have remained approximately the same as when the currently used ones were acquired.

**profit.** Excess of *revenues* over *expenses* for a *transaction*; sometimes used synonymously with *net income* for the period.

**profit and loss sharing ratio.** The fraction of *net income* or loss allocable to a partner in a *partnership*. Need not be the same fraction as the partner's share of capital.

**profit and loss statement.** *Income statement*.

**profit center.** A unit of activity for which both *revenue* and *expenses* are accumulated; contrast with *cost center*.

**profit margin.** Sales minus all expenses as a single amount. Frequently used to mean ratio of sales minus all *operating* expenses divided by sales.

**profit margin percentage.** *Profit margin* divided by *net sales*.

**profit maximization.** The doctrine that a given set of operations should be accounted for so as to make reported *net income* as large as possible; contrast with *con-*

*servatism*. This concept in accounting is slightly different from the profit-maximizing concept in economics where the doctrine states that operations should be managed to maximize the present value of the firm's wealth, generally by equating *marginal costs* and *marginal revenues*.

**profit sharing plan.** A *defined contribution plan*, where the employer contributes amounts based on *net income*.

**profit variance analysis.** Analysis of the causes of the difference between *budgeted profit* in the *master budget* and the profits earned.

**profit-volume analysis (equation).** See *breakeven analysis*.

**profit-volume graph.** See *breakeven chart*.

**profit-volume ratio.** *Net income* divided by net sales in dollars.

**profitability accounting.** *Responsibility accounting*.

**program budgeting.** Specification and analysis of inputs, outputs, costs, and alternatives that link plans to *budgets*.

**programmed costs.** A *fixed cost* not essential for carrying out operations. Research and development and advertising designed to generate new business are controllable, but once a commitment is made to incur them, they become fixed costs. Sometimes called *managed costs* or *discretionary costs*; contrast with *capacity costs*.

**progressive tax.** Tax for which the rate increases as the taxed base, such as income, increases; contrast with *regressive tax*.

**project financing arrangement.** As defined by *SFAS No. 47*, the financing of an investment project in which the lender looks principally to the *cash flows* and *earnings* of the project as the source of funds for repayment and to the *assets* of the project as *collateral* for the loan. The general *credit* of the project entity is usually not a significant factor, either because the entity is a *corporation* without other assets or because the financing is without direct *recourse* to the entity's owners.

**projected benefit obligation.** The *actuarial present value* at a given date of all pension benefits attributed by a *defined-benefit pension* formula to employee service rendered before that date. The obligation is measured using assumptions as to future compensation levels if the formula incorporates future compensation, as happens, for example, when the eventual pension benefit is based on wages of the last several years of employees' work lives. Contrast to "accumulated benefit obligation," where the obligation is measured using employee compensation levels at the time of the measurement date of the obligation.

**projected financial statement.** *Pro forma* financial statement.

**projection.** See *financial projection* for definition and contrast.

**promissory note.** An unconditional written promise to pay a specified sum of money on demand or at a specified date.

**proof of journal.** The process of checking arithmetic accuracy of *journal entries* by testing for the equality of all *debits* with all *credits* since the last previous proof.

**property dividend.** A *dividend in kind*.

**proprietary accounts.** See *budgetary accounts* for definition and contrast in context of governmental accounting.

**proprietorship.** *Assets* minus *liabilities* of an *entity*; equals *contributed capital* plus *retained earnings*.

**proprietorship theory.** The view of the corporation that emphasizes the form of the *accounting equation* that says *assets − liabilities = owners' equity*; contrast with *entity theory*. The major implication of a choice between these theories deals with the treatment of *subsidiaries*. For example, the view that *minority interest* is an *indeterminate term liability* is based on the proprietorship theory. The proprietorship theory implies using a *single-step income statement*.

**prorate.** To *allocate* in proportion to some base; for example, allocate *service department* costs in proportion to hours of service used by the benefited department. Or, to allocate *manufacturing variances* to product sold and to product added to *ending inventory*.

**prorating variances.** See *prorate*.

**prospectus.** Formal written document describing *securities* to be issued. See *proxy*.

**protest fee.** Fee charged by banks or other financial agencies when items (such as checks) presented for collection cannot be collected.

**provision.** Often the exact amount of an *expense* is uncertain, but must, nevertheless, be recognized currently. The entry for the estimated expense, such as for *income taxes* or expected costs under *warranty*, is:

| | | |
|---|---|---|
| Expense (Estimated) . . . . . . . . . . . . | X | |
| Liability (Estimated) . . . . . . . . . . . | | X |

In American usage, the term "provision" is often used in the expense account title of the above entry. Thus, Provision for Income Taxes is used to mean the estimate of income tax expense. (In British usage, the term "provision" is used in the title for the estimated liability of the above entry, so that Provision for Income Taxes is a balance sheet account.)

**proxy.** Written authorization given by one person to another so that the second person can act for the first, such as to vote shares of stock. Of particular significance to accountants because the *SEC* presumes that financial information is distributed by management along with its proxy solicitations.

**public accountant.** Generally, this term is synonymous with *certified public accountant*. In some jurisdictions, individuals have been licensed as public accountants without being CPAs.

**public accounting.** That portion of accounting primarily involving the *attest* function, culminating in the *auditor's report*.

**PuPU.** An acronym for *p*urchasing *p*ower *u*nit conceived by John C. Burton, former Chief Accountant of the SEC. Those who think *constant dollar accounting* not particularly useful poke fun at it by calling it "PuPU accounting."

**purchase allowance.** A reduction in sales *invoice price* usually granted because the *goods* received by the purchaser were not exactly as ordered. The goods are not returned to the seller, but are purchased at a price lower than originally agreed upon.

**purchase discount.** A reduction in purchase *invoice price* granted for prompt payment. See *sales discount* and *terms of sale*.

**purchase method.** Accounting for a *business combination* by adding the acquired company's assets at the price paid for them to the acquiring company's assets. Contrast with *pooling-of-interests method*. The acquired assets are put on the books at current values, rather than original costs; the subsequent *amortization expenses* are usually larger (and reported income, smaller) than for the same business combination accounted for as a pooling of interests. The purchase method is required unless all the criteria in *APB Opinion No. 16* to be a pooling are met.

**purchase order.** Document authorizing a seller to deliver goods with payment to be made later.

**purchasing power gain or loss.** *Monetary gain or loss*.

**push-down accounting.** Assume that Company A purchases substantially all of the *common shares* of Company B but that Company B must still issue its own *financial statements*. The question arises, shall the *basis* for Company B's *assets* and *equities* be changed on its own books to the same updated amounts at which they are shown on Company A's *consolidated* statements.

When Company B shows the new asset and equity bases reflecting Company A's purchase, Company B is using "push-down accounting," because the new bases are "pushed down" from Company A (where they are required in *GAAP* to Company B (where the new bases would not appear in *historical cost accounting*). Since 1983, the *SEC* has required push-down accounting under some circumstances.

**put.** An option to sell *shares* of a publicly-traded corporation at a fixed price during a fixed time span. Contrast with *call*.

## Q

**qualified report (opinion).** *Auditor's report* containing a statement that the auditor was unable to complete a satisfactory examination of all things considered relevant or that the auditor has doubts about the financial impact of some *material* item reported in the financial statements. See *except for* and *subject to*.

**quantitative performance measure.** A measure of output based on an objectively observable quantity, like units produced or *direct costs* incurred, rather than on an unobservable quantity or one observable only nonobjectively, like quality of service provided.

**quantity discount.** A reduction in purchase price as quantity purchased increases; amount of the discount is constrained by law (Robinson-Patman Act). Not to be confused with *purchase discount*.

**quantity variance.** *Efficiency variance*. In *standard costing systems*, the Standard Price per Unit × (Actual Quantity Used − Standard Quantity That Should Be Used).

**quasi-reorganization.** A *reorganization* where no new company is formed or no court has intervened, as would happen in *bankruptcy*. The primary purpose is to absorb a *deficit* and get a "fresh start."

**quick assets.** *Assets* readily convertible into *cash*; includes cash, *current marketable securities* and *current receivables*.

**quick ratio.** Sum of (*cash, current marketable securities*, and *receivables*) divided by *current liabilities*. Some non-liquid receivables may be excluded from the numerator. Often called the "acid test ratio." See *ratio*.

## R

$R^2$. The proportion of the statistical variance of a *dependent variable* explained by the equation fit to *independent variable(s)* in a *regression analysis*.

**R & D.** See *research and development*.

**Railroad Accounting Principles Board. RAPB.** A board brought into existence by the Staggers Rail Act of 1980 to advise the Interstate Commerce Commission on matters of accounting affecting railroads.

**RAPB.** *Railroad Accounting Principles Board.*

**rate of return on assets.** *Net income* plus aftertax *interest charges* plus *minority interest* in income divided by average total *assets*. Perhaps the single most useful ratio for assessing management's overall operating performance. See *ratio.*

**rate of return on common stock equity.** See *ratio.*

**rate of return on shareholders' (owners') equity.** See *ratio.*

**rate of return (on total capital).** See *ratio* and *rate of return on assets.*

**rate variance.** *Price variance*, usually for *direct labor costs.*

**ratio.** The number resulting when one number is divided by another. Ratios are generally used to assess aspects of profitability, solvency, and liquidity. The commonly used financial ratios are of three kinds: (1) those that summarize some aspect of *operations* for a period, usually a year, (2) those that summarize some aspect of *financial position* at a given moment — the moment for which a balance sheet has been prepared, and (3) those that relate some aspect of operations to some aspect of financial position.

Exhibit 6.11 lists the most common financial ratios and shows separately both the numerator and denominator used to calculate each ratio.

For all ratios that require an average balance during the period, the average is most often derived as one half the sum of the beginning and ending balances. Sophisticated analysts recognize, however, that when companies use a fiscal year different from the calendar year, this averaging of beginning and ending balances may be misleading. Consider, for example, the *rate of return on assets* of Sears, Roebuck & Company, whose fiscal year ends on January 31. Sears chooses a January 31 closing date at least in part because inventories are at a low level and are therefore easy to count — the Christmas merchandise has been sold and the Easter merchandise has not yet all been received. Furthermore, by January 31 most Christmas sales have been collected or returned, so receivable amounts are not unusually large. Thus, at January 31 the amount of total assets is lower than at many other times during the year. Consequently, the denominator of the rate of return on assets, total assets, for Sears is more likely to represent the smallest amount of total assets on hand during the year than the average amount. The return on assets rate for Sears and other companies who choose a fiscal year-end to coincide with low points in the inventory cycle is likely to be larger than if a more accurate estimate of the average amounts of total assets were used.

**raw material.** Goods purchased for use in manufacturing a product.

**reacquired stock.** *Treasury stock.*

**real accounts.** *Balance sheet accounts*; as opposed to *nominal accounts.* See *permanent accounts.*

**real amount (value).** An amount stated in *constant dollars.* For example, if an investment costing $100 is sold for $130 after a period of 10 percent general *inflation*, the *nominal amount* of *gain* is $30 (= $130 − $100) but the real amount of gain is C$20 [= $130 − (1.10 × $100)], where "C$" denotes constant dollars of purchasing power on the date of sale.

**real estate.** *Land* and its *improvements*, such as landscaping and roads, but not buildings.

**realizable value.** *Market value* or, sometimes, *net realizable value.*

**realization convention.** The accounting practice of delaying the recognition of *gains* and *losses* from changes in the market price of *assets* until the assets are sold. However, unrealized losses on *inventory* and *marketable securities* classified as *current assets* are recognized prior to sale when the *lower-of-cost-or-market* valuation basis is used.

**realize.** To convert into *funds.* When applied to a *gain* or *loss*, implies that an *arm's-length transaction* has taken place. Contrast with *recognize*; a loss (as for example on *marketable equity securities*) may be recognized in the financial statements even though it has not yet been realized in a transaction.

**realized gain (or loss) on marketable equity securities.** An income statement account title for the difference between the proceeds of disposition and the *original cost* of *marketable equity securities.*

**realized holding gain.** See *inventory profit* for definition and an example.

**rearrangement costs.** Costs of re-installing assets perhaps in a different location. May be *capitalized* as part of the assets cost, just as is original installation cost.

**recapitalization.** *Reorganization.*

**recapture.** Various provisions of the *income tax* rules require refund by the taxpayer (recapture by the government) of various tax advantages under certain conditions. For example, the tax savings provided by the *investment credit* or by *accelerated depreciation* must be repaid if the item providing the tax savings is retired prematurely.

**receipt.** Acquisition of *cash.*

**receivable.** Any *collectible* whether or not it is currently due.

**receivable turnover.** See *ratio*.

**reciprocal holdings.** Company A owns stock of Company B and Company B owns stock of Company A.

**recognize.** To enter a transaction in the accounts. Not synonymous with *realize*.

**reconciliation.** A calculation that shows how one balance or figure is derived systematically from another, such as a *reconciliation of retained earnings* or a *bank reconciliation schedule*. See *articulate*.

**record date.** *Dividends* are paid on payment date to those who own the stock on the record date.

**recourse.** See *note receivable discounted*.

**recovery of unrealized loss on marketable securities.** An *income statement account title* for the *gain* during the current period on the *current asset* portfolio of *marketable equity securities*. This gain will be *recognized* only to the extent that net losses have been recognized in preceding periods in amounts no smaller than the current gain. (The Allowance for Declines in Marketable Equity Securities account can never have a *debit balance*.)

**redemption.** Retirement by the issuer, usually by a purchase or *call*, of *stocks* or *bonds*.

**redemption premium.** *Call premium*.

**redemption value.** The price to be paid by a corporation to retire *bonds* or *preferred stock* if called before *maturity*.

**refunding bond issue.** Said of a *bond* issue whose proceeds are used to retire bonds already *outstanding*.

**register.** Collection of consecutive entries, or other information, in chronological order, such as a check register or an insurance register, which lists all insurance policies owned. If entries are recorded, it may serve as a *journal*.

**registered bond.** *Principal* of such a *bond* and *interest*, if registered as to interest, is paid to the owner listed on the books of the issuer. As opposed to a bearer bond where the possessor of the bond is entitled to interest and principal.

**registrar.** An *agent*, usually a bank or trust company, appointed by a corporation to keep track of the names of shareholders and distributions of earnings.

**registration statement.** Statement required by the Securities Act of 1933 of most companies wishing to have their securities traded in public markets. The statement discloses financial data and other items of interest to potential investors.

**regression analysis.** A method of *cost estimation* based on statistical techniques for fitting a line (or its equivalent in higher mathematical dimensions) to an observed series of data points, usually by minimizing the sum of squared deviations of the observed data from the fitted line. The cost whose behavior is being explained is called the ''dependent variable;'' the variable(s) being used to estimate cost behavior are called ''independent variable(s).'' If there is more than one independent variable, the analysis is called ''multiple regression analysis.'' See $R^2$, *standard error, t-value*.

**regressive tax.** Tax for which the rate decreases as the taxed base, such as income, increases. Contrast with *progressive tax*.

**Regulation S-X.** The *SEC's* regulation specifying the form and content of financial reports to the SEC.

**rehabilitation.** The improving of a used *asset* via an extensive repair. Ordinary *repairs* and *maintenance* restore or maintain expected *service potential* of an asset and are treated as *expenses*. A rehabilitation improves the asset beyond its current service potential, enhancing the service potential to significantly higher level than before the rehabilitation. Once rehabilitated, the asset may be better, but need not be, than it was when new. *Expenditures* for rehabilitation, like those for *betterments* and *improvements*, are *capitalized*.

**reinvestment rate.** In a *capital budgeting* context, the rate at which cash inflows from a project occurring before the project's completion are invested. Once such a rate is assumed, there will never be multiple *internal rates of return*. See *Descartes' rule of signs*.

**relative performance evaluation.** Setting performance targets and, sometimes, compensation in relation to performance of others, perhaps in different firms or divisions, facing a similar environment.

**relevant cost.** *Incremental cost. Opportunity cost.*

**relevant range.** Activity levels over which costs are linear or for which *flexible budget* estimates and *break-even charts* will remain valid.

**relative sales value method.** *Net realizable (sales) value method.*

**remittance advice.** Information on a *check stub*, or on a document attached to a check by the *drawer*, which tells the *payee* why a payment is being made.

**rent.** A charge for use of land, buildings, or other assets.

**reorganization.** A major change in the *capital structure* of a corporation that leads to changes in the rights, interests, and implied ownership of the various security owners. Usually results from a *merger* or agreement by senior security holders to take action to forestall *bankruptcy*.

**repair.** An *expenditure* to restore an *asset's* service potential after damage or after prolonged use. In the second sense, after prolonged use, the difference between repairs and maintenance is one of degree and not of kind. Treated as an *expense* of the period when incurred. Because repairs and maintenance are treated similarly in this regard, the distinction is not important. A repair helps to maintain capacity intact at levels planned when the *asset* was acquired; contrast with *improvement*.

**replacement cost.** For an asset, the current fair market price to purchase another, similar asset (with the same future benefit or service potential). *Current cost.* See *reproduction cost* and *productive capacity.* See also *distributable income* and *inventory profit.*

**replacement cost method of depreciation.** The original cost *depreciation* charge is augmented by an amount based upon a portion of the difference between the *current replacement cost* of the asset and its *original cost.*

**replacement system of depreciation.** See *retirement method of depreciation* for definition and contrast.

**report.** *Financial statement; auditor's report.*

**report form.** This form of *balance sheet* typically shows *assets* minus *liabilities* as one total. Then, below that appears the components of *owners' equity* summing to the same total. Often, the top section shows *current* assets less current liabilities before *noncurrent assets* less noncurrent liabilities. Contrast with *account form.*

**reporting objectives (policies).** The general purposes for which *financial statements* are prepared. The *FASB* has discussed these in *SFAC No. 1.*

**reproduction cost.** The *cost* necessary to acquire an *asset* similar in all physical respects to another asset for which a *current value* is wanted. See *replacement cost* and *productive capacity* for further contrast.

**required rate of return.** *Cost of capital.*

**requisition.** A formal written order or request, such as for withdrawal of supplies from the storeroom.

**resale value.** *Exit value. Net realizable value.*

**research and development.** Research is activity aimed at discovering new knowledge in hopes that such activity will be useful in creating a new product, process, or service or improving a present product, process, or service. Development is the translation of research findings or other knowledge into a new or improved product, process, or service. *SFAS No. 2* requires that costs of such activities be *expensed* as incurred on the grounds that the future benefits are too uncertain to warrant *capitalization* as an asset. This treatment seems questionable to us because we wonder why firms would continue to undertake R&D if there were no expectation of future benefit; if future benefits exist, then its *costs* should be assets.

**reserve.** When properly used in accounting, the term refers to an account that appropriates *retained earnings* and restricts dividend declarations. Appropriating retained earnings is itself a poor and vanishing practice, so the word should seldom be used in accounting. In addition, used in the past to indicate an asset *contra account* (for example, "reserve for depreciation") or an *estimated liability* for example, "reserve for warranty costs"). In any case, reserve accounts have *credit* balances and are not pools of *funds* as the unwary reader might infer. If a company has set aside a pool of *cash* (or *marketable securities*) to serve some specific purpose such as paying for a new factory, then that cash will be called a *fund.* No other word in accounting is so misunderstood and misused by laymen and "experts" who should know better. A leading unabridged dictionary defines "reserve" as "Cash, or assets readily convertible into cash, held aside, as by a corporation, bank, state or national government, etc. to meet expected or unexpected demands." This definition is absolutely wrong in accounting. Reserves are not funds. For example, a contingency fund of $10,000 is created by depositing cash in a fund and this entry is made:

| | | |
|---|---|---|
| Dr. Contingency Fund . . . . . . . . . . . . . | 10,000 | |
| Cr. Cash . . . . . . . . . . . . . . . . . . . . . . | | 10,000 |

The following entry may accompany this entry, if retained earnings are to be appropriated:

| | | |
|---|---|---|
| Dr. Retained Earnings . . . . . . . . . . . . . | 10,000 | |
| Cr. Reserve for Contingencies . . . . | | 10,000 |

The transaction leading to the first entry is an event of economic significance. The second entry has little economic impact for most firms. The problem with the word "reserve" arises because the second entry can be made without the first — a company can create a reserve, that is appropriate retained earnings, without creating a fund. The problem is at least in part caused by the fact that in common usage, "reserve" means a pool of assets, as in the phrase "oil reserves." The *Internal Revenue Service* does not help in dispelling confusion about the term *reserves.* The federal *income tax* return for corporations uses the title "Reserve for Bad Debts" to mean the "Allowance for Uncollectible Accounts" and speaks of the "Reserve Method" in referring to the *allowance method* for estimating *revenue* or *income* reductions from estimated *uncollectibles.*

**reserve recognition accounting.** In exploration for natural resources, there is the problem of what to do with the expenditures for exploration. Suppose that $10 million is spent to drill 10 holes ($1 million each) and that nine of them are dry whereas one is a gusher containing oil with a *net realizable value* of $40 million. Dry hole, or *successful efforts*, accounting would expense $9 million and *capitalize* $1 million to be *depleted* as the oil was lifted from the ground. *SFAS No. 19*, now suspended, required successful efforts accounting. Full costing would expense nothing, but capitalize the $10 million of drilling costs to be depleted as the oil is lifted from the single productive well. Reserve recognition accounting would capitalize $40 million to be depleted as the oil is lifted, with a $30 million *credit* to *income* or *contributed capital*. The *balance sheet* shows the *net realizable value* of proven oil and gas reserves. The *income statement* has three sorts of items: (1) current income resulting from production or "lifting profit," which is the *revenue* from sales of oil and gas less the expense based on the current valuation amount at which these items had been carried on the balance sheet, (2) profit or loss from exploration efforts where the current value of new discoveries is revenue and all the exploration cost is expense, and (3) gain or loss on changes in current value during the year, which is in other contexts called a *holding gain or loss*.

**residual income.** In an external reporting context, this term refers to *net income* to *common shares* (= net income less *preferred stock dividends*). In *managerial accounting*, this term refers to the excess of income for a *division* or *segment* of a company over the product of the *cost of capital* for the company multiplied by the average amount of capital invested in the division during the period over which the income was earned.

**residual security.** A *potentially dilutive security*. Options, *warrants*, *convertible bonds*, and *convertible preferred stock*.

**residual value.** At any time, the estimated or actual, *net realizable value* (that is, proceeds less removal costs) of an *asset*, usually a depreciable *plant asset*. In the context of depreciation accounting, this term is equivalent to *salvage value* and is preferable to *scrap value*, because the asset need not be scrapped. Sometimes used to mean net *book value*. In the context of a *noncancelable* lease, the estimated value of the leased asset at the end of the lease period. See *lease*.

**responsibility accounting.** Accounting for a business by considering various units as separate entities, or *profit centers*, giving management of each unit responsibility for the unit's *revenues* and *expenses*. Sometimes called "activity accounting." See *transfer price*.

**responsibility center.** Part or *segment* of an organization that is accountable for a specified set of activities. Also called "accountability center." See *cost center*, *investment center*, *profit center*, *revenue center*.

**restricted assets.** Governmental resources restricted by legal or contractual requirements for specific purpose.

**restricted retained earnings.** That part of *retained earnings* not legally available for *dividends*. See *retained earnings, appropriated*. Bond indentures and other loan contracts can curtail the legal ability of the corporation to declare dividends without formally requiring a retained earnings appropriation, but disclosure is required.

**retail inventory method.** Ascertaining cost amounts of *ending inventory* as follows (assuming FIFO): cost of ending inventory = (selling price of *goods available for sale* − sales) × *cost percentage*. Cost of goods sold is then computed from the inventory equation; costs of beginning inventory, purchases and ending inventory are all known. (When *LIFO* is used, the method is similar to the *dollar-value LIFO method*). See *markup*.

**retail terminology.** See *markup*.

**retained earnings.** Net *income* over the life of a corporation less all *dividends* (including capitalization through *stock dividends*); *owners' equity* less *contributed capital*.

**retained earnings, appropriated.** An *account* set up by crediting it and debiting *retained earnings*. Used to indicate that a portion of retained earnings is not available for dividends. The practice of appropriating retained earnings is misleading unless all capital is earmarked with its use, which is not practicable. Use of formal retained earnings appropriations is declining.

**retained earnings statement.** *Generally accepted accounting principles* require that whenever *comparative balance sheets* and an *income statement* are presented, there must also be presented a *reconciliation* of the beginning and ending balances in the *retained earnings account*. This reconciliation can appear in a separate statement, in a combined statement of income and retained earnings, or in the balance sheet.

**retirement method of depreciation.** No entry is recorded for *depreciation expense* until an *asset* is retired from service. Then, an entry is made *debiting* depreciation expense and *crediting* the asset account for the cost of the asset retired. If the retired asset has a *salvage value*, the amount of the debit to depreciation expense is reduced by the amount of salvage value with a corresponding debit to cash, receivables, or salvaged materials. The "replacement system of depreciation" is similar, except that the debit to depreciation expense equals the cost of the new asset less the salvage value, if any, of the old asset. These methods were used by some public utilities. For example, if ten telephone poles are acquired in Year 1 for $60 each and are replaced in Year 10 for $100 each when the salvage value of the old poles is $5 each, then the accounting would be as follows:

**Retirement Method**

| | | |
|---|---|---|
| Plant Assets . . . . . . . . . . . . . . . . . . . . . . . | 600 | |
| Cash . . . . . . . . . . . . . . . . . . . . . . . . . . . | | 600 |
| To acquire assets in Year 1. | | |

| | | |
|---|---|---|
| Depreciation Expense . . . . . . . . . . . . . . . . | 550 | |
| Salvage Receivable . . . . . . . . . . . . . . . . . . | 50 | |
| Plant Assets . . . . . . . . . . . . . . . . . . . . . | | 600 |
| To record retirement and depreciation in Year 10. | | |

| | | |
|---|---|---|
| Plant Assets . . . . . . . . . . . . . . . . . . . . . . . | 1,000 | |
| Cash . . . . . . . . . . . . . . . . . . . . . . . . . . . | | 1,000 |
| To record acquisition of new assets in Year 10. | | |

**Replacement Method**

| | | |
|---|---|---|
| Plant Assets . . . . . . . . . . . . . . . . . . . . . . . | 600 | |
| Cash . . . . . . . . . . . . . . . . . . . . . . . . . . . | | 600 |
| To acquire assets in Year 1. | | |

| | | |
|---|---|---|
| Depreciation Expense . . . . . . . . . . . . . . . . | 950 | |
| Salvage Receivable . . . . . . . . . . . . . . . . . . | 50 | |
| Cash . . . . . . . . . . . . . . . . . . . . . . . . . . . | | 1,000 |
| To record depreciation on old asset in amount quantified by net cost of replacement asset in Year 10. | | |

The retirement method is like *FIFO*, in that the cost of the first assets is recorded as depreciation and the cost of the second assets is put on the balance sheet. The replacement method is like *LIFO* in that the cost of the second assets determines the depreciation expense and the cost of the first assets remains on the balance sheet.

**retirement plan.** *Pension plan.*

**retroactive benefits.** *Pension plan* benefits granted in initiating or amending a *defined-benefit* pension plan that are attributed by the benefit formula to employee services rendered in periods prior to the initiation or amendment. See *prior service costs*.

**return.** A schedule of information required by governmental bodies, such as the tax return required by the *Internal Revenue Service*. Also the physical return of merchandise. See also *return on investment*.

**return of investment. return on capital.** *Income* (before distributions to suppliers of capital) for a period. As a rate, this amount divided by average total assets. *Interest*, net of tax effects, should be added back to *net income* for the numerator. See *ratio*.

**revenue.** The increase in *owners' equity* caused by a service rendered or the sale of goods. The monetary measure of a service rendered. *Sales* of products, merchandise, and services, and earnings from *interest, dividends, rents,* and the like. The amount of revenue is the expected *net present value* of the net assets received. Do not confuse with *receipt* of *funds*, which may occur before, when, or after revenue is recognized. Contrast with *gain* and *income*. See also *holding gain*. Some writers use the term *gross income* synonymously with *revenue*; avoid such usage.

**revenue center.** A *responsibility center* within a firm that has control only over revenues generated; contrast with *cost center*. See *profit center*.

**revenue expenditure.** A phrase sometimes used to mean an *expense*, in contrast to a capital *expenditure* to acquire an *asset* or to discharge a *liability*. Avoid using this phrase; use *period expense* instead.

**revenue received in advance.** An inferior term for *advances from customers*.

**reversal (reversing) entry.** An *entry* in which all *debits* and *credits* are the credits and debits, respectively, of another entry, and in the same amounts. It is usually made on the first day of an *accounting period* to reverse a previous *adjusting entry*, usually an *accrual*. The purpose of such entries is to make the bookkeeper's tasks easier. Suppose that salaries are paid every other Friday, with paychecks compensating employees for the 2 weeks just ended. Total salaries accrue at the rate of $5,000 per 5-day work week. The bookkeeper is accustomed to making the following entry every other Friday:

| | | |
|---|---|---|
| (1) Salary Expense . . . . . . . . . . . . . . . | 10,000 | |
| Cash . . . . . . . . . . . . . . . . . . . . . | | 10,000 |
| To record salary expense and salary payments. | | |

If paychecks are delivered to employees on Friday, November 25, 1988, then the *adjusting entry* made on November 30 (or, perhaps, later) to record accrued salaries for November 28, 29, and 30 would be as follows:

| | | |
|---|---|---|
| (2) Salary Expense . . . . . . . . . . . . . . . . . . | 3,000 | |
| Salaries Payable . . . . . . . . . . . . . . . | | 3,000 |
| To charge November operations with all salaries earned in November. | | |

The Salary Expense account would be closed as part of the November 30 closing entries. On the next pay day, December 9, the salary entry would have to be as follows:

| (3) Salary Expense | 7,000 | |
| Salaries Payable | 3,000 | |
| Cash | | 10,000 |
| To record salary payments split between expense for December (7 days) and liability carried over from November. | | |

To make entry (3), the bookkeeper must look back into the records to see how much of the debit is to Salaries Payable accrued from the previous year so that total debits are properly split between third quarter expense and the liability carried over from the second quarter. Notice that this entry forces the bookkeeper both (a) to refer to balances in old accounts and (b) to make an entry different from the one customarily made, entry (1). The reversing entry, made just after the books have been closed for the second quarter, makes the salary entry for December 9, 1988, the same as that made on all other Friday pay days. The reversing entry merely *reverses* the adjusting entry (2):

| (4) Salaries Payable | 3,000 | |
| Salary Expense | | 3,000 |
| To reverse the adjusting entry. | | |

This entry results in a zero balance in the Salaries Payable account and a credit balance in the Salary Expense account. If entry (4) is made just after the books are closed for November, then the entry on December 9 will be the customary entry (1). Entries (4) and (1) together have exactly the same effect as entry (3).

The procedure for using reversal entries is as follows: The required adjustment to record an accrual (*payable* or *receivable*) is made at the end of an *accounting period*; the closing entry is made as usual; as of the first day of the following period, an entry is made reversing the adjusting entry; when a payment is made (or received), the entry is recorded as though no adjusting entry had been recorded. Whether or not reversal entries are used affects the record-keeping procedures, but not the financial statements.

Also used to describe the entry reversing an incorrect entry before recording the correct entry.

**reverse stock split.** A stock split in which the number of shares *outstanding* is decreased. See *stock split*.

**revolving fund.** A fund whose amounts are continually expended and then replenished; for example, a *petty cash fund*.

**revolving loan.** A *loan* that is expected to be renewed at *maturity*.

**right.** The privilege to subscribe to new *stock* issues or to purchase stock. Usually, rights are contained in securities called warrants and the *warrants* may be sold to others. See also *preemptive right*.

**risk.** A measure of the variability of the *return on investment*. For a given expected amount of return, most people prefer less risk to more risk. Therefore, in rational markets, investments with more risk usually promise, or are expected to yield, a higher rate of return than investments with lower risk. Most people use "risk" and "uncertainty" as synonyms. In technical language, however, these terms have different meanings. "Risk" is used when the probabilities attached to the various outcomes are known, such as the probabilities of heads or tails in the flip of a fair coin. "Uncertainty" refers to an event where the probabilities of the outcomes, such as winning or losing a lawsuit, can only be estimated.

**risk adjusted discount rate.** In a *capital budgeting* context, a decision maker compares projects by comparing their net *present values* for a given *interest* rate, usually the cost of capital. If a given project's outcome is considered to be much more or much less risky than the normal undertakings of the company, then the interest rate used in discounting will be increased (if the project is more risky) or decreased (if less risky) and the rate used is said to be "risk-adjusted."

**risk premium.** Extra compensation paid to an employee or extra *interest* paid to a lender, over amounts usually considered normal, in return for their undertaking to engage in activities more risky than normal.

**ROI.** *Return on investment*, but usually used to refer to a single project and expressed as a ratio: *income* divided by average *cost* of *assets* devoted to the project.

**royalty.** Compensation for the use of property, usually a patent, copyrighted material, or natural resources. The amount is often expressed as a percentage of receipts from using the property or as an amount per unit produced.

**RRA.** See *Reserve recognition accounting*.

**RRR.** Required rate of return.

**rule of 69.** An amount of money invested at $r$ percent per period will double in $69/r + .35$ periods. This approximation is accurate to one tenth of a period for interest rates between 1/4 and 100 percent per period. For example, at 10 percent per period, the rule says that a given sum will double in $69/10 + .35 = 7.25$ periods. At 10 percent per period, a given sum doubles in $7.27+$ periods.

**rule of 72.** An amount of money invested at $r$ percent per period will double in $72/r$ periods. A reasonable approximation but not nearly as accurate as the *rule of 69*. For example, at 10 percent per period, the rule says that a given sum will double in $72/10 = 7.2$ periods.

## An Open Account, Ruled and Balanced
### (Steps indicated in parentheses correspond to steps described in "ruling an account.")

| | Date 1988 | Explanation | Ref. | Debit (1) | Date 1988 | Explanation | Ref. | Credit (2) | |
|---|---|---|---|---|---|---|---|---|---|
| | Jan. 2 | Balance | ✔ | 100.00 | | | | | |
| | Jan. 13 | | VR | 121.37 | Sept. 15 | | J | .42 | |
| | Mar. 20 | | VR | 56.42 | Nov. 12 | | J | 413.15 | |
| | June 5 | | J | 1,138.09 | Dec. 31 | Balance | ✔ | 1,050.59 | (3) |
| | Aug. 18 | | J | 1.21 | | | | | |
| | Nov. 20 | | VR | 38.43 | | | | | |
| | Dec. 7 | | VR | 8.64 | | | | | |
| (4) | 1989 | | | 1,464.16 | 1989 | | | 1,464.16 | (4) |
| (5) | Jan. 1 | Balance | ✔ | 1,050.59 | | | | | |

**rule of 78.** The rule followed by many finance companies for allocating earnings on *loans* among the months of a year on the sum-of-the-months'-digits basis when equal monthly payments from the borrower are to be received. The sum of the digits from 1 through 12 is 78, so 12/78 of the year's earnings are allocated to the first month, 11/78 to the second month, and so on. See *sum-of-the-years'-digits depreciation*.

**ruling (and balancing) an account.** The process of summarizing a series of entries in an *account* by computing a new *balance* and drawing double lines to indicate the information above the double lines has been summarized in the new balance. The process is illustrated above. The steps are as follows. (1) Compute the sum of all *debit* entries including opening debit balance, if any—$1,464.16. (2) Compute the sum of all credit entries including opening credit balance, if any—$413.57. (3) If the amount in (1) is larger than the amount in (2), then write the excess as a credit with a check mark—$1,464.16 − $413.57 = $1,050.59. (4) Add both debit and credit columns, which should both now sum to the same amount, and show that identical total at the foot of both columns. (5) Draw double lines under those numbers and write the excess of debits over credits as the new debit balance with a check mark. (6) If the amount in (2) is larger than the amount in (1), then write the excess as a debit with a check mark. (7) Do steps (4) and (5) except that the excess becomes the new credit balance. (8) If the amount in (1) is equal to the amount in (2), then the balance is zero and only the totals with the double lines beneath them need be shown. This process is illustrated in the accompanying figure.

## S

*SAB.* *Staff Accounting Bulletin* of the *SEC*.

**safe-harbor lease.** A form of *tax-transfer lease*.

**salary.** Compensation earned by managers, administrators, professionals, not based on an hourly rate. Contrast with *wage*.

**sale.** A *revenue* transaction where *goods* or *services* are delivered to a customer in return for cash or a contractual obligation to pay.

**sale and leaseback.** Describes a *financing* transaction where improved property is sold but is taken back for use on a long-term *lease*. Such transactions often have advantageous income tax effects, but usually have no effect on *financial statement income*.

**sales allowance.** A reduction in sales *invoice* price usually given because the *goods* received by the buyer are not exactly what was ordered. The amounts of such adjustments are often accumulated by the seller in a temporary *revenue contra account* having this, or a similar, title. See *sales discount*.

**sales basis of revenue recognition.** *Revenue* is recognized, not as goods are produced nor as orders are received, but only when the sale (delivery) has been consummated and cash or a *receivable* obtained. Most revenue is recognized on this basis. Compare with *percentage-of-completion method* and the *installment method*. Identical with the *completed contract method* but this latter term is ordinarily used only for *long-term* construction projects.

**sales contra, estimated uncollectibles.** A title for the *contra-revenue account* to recognize estimated reductions in income caused by accounts receivable that will not be collected. See *bad debt expense, allowance for uncollectibles*, and *allowance method*.

**sales discount.** Reduction in sales *invoice* price usually offered for prompt payment. See *terms of sale* and *2/10, n/30*.

**sales return.** The physical return of merchandise; the amounts of such returns are often accumulated by the seller in a temporary *revenue contra account*.

**sales value method.** *Relative sales value method*.

**sales volume variance.** *Budgeted Contribution Margin per Unit* × (Planned Sales Volume − Actual Sales Volume).

**salvage value.** Actual or estimated selling price, net of removal or disposal costs, of a used *plant asset* to be sold or otherwise retired. See *residual value*.

**SAS.** *Statement on Auditing Standards* of the *AICPA*.

**scale effect.** See *discounted cash flow*.

**schedule.** Supporting set of calculations that show how figures in a *financial statement* or tax return are derived.

**scientific method.** *Effective interest method* of *amortizing bond discount* or *premium*.

**scrap value.** *Salvage value* assuming item is to be junked. A *net realizable value*. *Residual value*.

**SEC.** Securities and Exchange Commission, an agency authorized by the U.S. Congress to regulate, among other things, the financial reporting practices of most public corporations. The SEC has indicated that it will usually allow the *FASB* to set accounting principles, but it often requires more disclosure than required by the FASB. The SEC's accounting requirements are stated in its *Accounting Series Releases (ASR)*, *Financial Reporting Releases (FRR)*, Accounting and Auditing Enforcement Releases, *Staff Accounting Bulletins*, and *Regulation S-X*. See also *registration statement* and *10-K*.

**secret reserve.** *Hidden reserve*.

**Securities and Exchange Commission.** *SEC*.

**security.** Document that indicates ownership or indebtedness or potential ownership, such as an *option* or *warrant*.

**segment (of a business).** As defined by *APB Opinion No. 30*, ''a component of an *entity* whose activities represent a separate major line of business or class of customer. . . . [It may be] a *subsidiary*, a division, or a department, . . . provided that its *assets*, results of *operations*, and activities can be clearly distinguished, physically and operationally for financial reporting purposes, from the other assets, results of operations, and activities of the entity.'' In *SFAS No. 14* a segment is defined as ''A component of an enterprise engaged in promoting a product or service or a group of related products and services primarily to unaffiliated customers . . . for a profit.''

**segment reporting.** Reporting of *sales, income* and *assets* by *segments of a business*, usually classified by nature of products sold but sometimes by geographical area where goods are produced or sold or by type of customers. Sometimes called ''line of business reporting.'' *Central corporate expenses* are not allocated to the segments.

**self balancing.** A set of records with equal *debits* and *credits* such as the *ledger* (but not individual accounts), the *balance sheet*, and a *fund* in nonprofit accounting.

**self insurance.** See *insurance*.

**selling and administrative expenses.** *Expenses* not specifically identifiable with, nor assigned to, production.

**semifixed costs.** *Costs* that increase with activity as a step function.

**semivariable costs.** *Costs* that increase strictly linearly with activity but that are positive at zero activity level. Royalty fees of 2 percent of sales are variable; royalty fees of $1,000 per year plus 2 percent of sales are semivariable.

**senior securities.** *Bonds* as opposed to *preferred stock; preferred stock* as opposed to *common stock*. The senior security has a claim against *earnings* or *assets* that must be met before the claim of less senior securities.

**sensitivity analysis.** Most decision making requires the use of assumptions. Sensitivity analysis is the study of how the outcome of a decision-making process changes as one or more of the assumptions change.

**serial bonds.** An *issue* of *bonds* that mature in part at one date, another part on another date, and so on; the various maturity dates usually are equally spaced; contrast them with *term bonds*.

**service basis of depreciation.** *Production method*.

**service cost. (current) service cost.** *Pension plan expenses incurred* during an *accounting period* for employment services performed during that period; contrast with *prior service cost* and see *funded*.

**service department.** A department, such as the personnel or computer department, that provides services to other departments rather than direct work on a salable product; contrast with *production department*. Costs of service departments whose services benefit manufacturing operations must be *allocated* as *product costs* under *absorption costing*.

**service life.** Period of expected usefulness of an asset; may not be the same as *depreciable life* for income tax purposes.

**service potential.** The future benefits embodied in an item that cause the item to be classified as an *asset*. Without service potential, there are no future benefits and the item should not be classified as an asset. *SFAS No. 6* suggests that the primary characteristic of service potential is the ability to generate future net cash inflows.

**services.** Useful work done by a person, a machine, or an organization. See *goods and services*.

**setup.** The time or costs required to prepare production equipment for doing a job.

***SFAC.*** *Statement of Financial Accounting Concepts* of the *FASB*.

***SFAS.*** *Statement of Financial Accounting Standards* of the *FASB*.

**shadow price.** One output of a *linear programming* analysis is the potential value of having available more of the scarce resources that constrain the production process; for example, the value of having more time available on a machine tool critical to the production of two products. This value is called a ''shadow price'' or the ''dual value'' of the scarce resource.

**share.** A unit of *stock* representing ownership in a corporation.

**shareholders' equity.** *Proprietorship* or *owners' equity* of a corporation. Because *stock* means inventory in Australian, British, and Canadian usage, the term ''shareholders' equity'' is usually used by Australian, British, and Canadian writers, who do not use the term ''stockholders' equity.''

**short-run. short-term.** The opposite of *long-run* or *long-term*. This pair of terms is equally imprecise.

**short-term.** Current; ordinarily, due within one year.

**short-term liquidity risk.** The risk that an *entity* will not have enough *cash* in the *short run* to pay its *debts*.

**shrinkage.** An excess of *inventory* shown on the *books* over actual physical quantities on hand. Can result from theft or shoplifting as well as from evaporation or general wear and tear.

**sight draft.** A demand for payment drawn by a person to whom money is owed. The *draft* is presented to the borrower's (the debtor's) bank in expectation that the borrower will authorize its bank to disburse the funds. Such drafts are often used when a seller sells goods to a new customer in a different city. The seller is not sure whether the buyer will pay the bill. The seller sends the *bill* of lading, or other evidence of ownership of the goods, along with a sight draft to the buyer's bank. Before the goods can be released to the buyer, the buyer must instruct its bank to honor the sight draft by withdrawing funds from the buyer's account. Once the sight draft is honored, the bill of lading or other document evidencing ownership is handed over to the buyer and the goods become the property of the buyer.

**simple interest.** *Interest* calculated on *principal* where interest earned during periods before maturity of the loan is neither added to the principal nor paid to the lender.

*Interest = principal × interest rate × time*. Seldom used in economic calculations except for periods less than one year; contrast with *compound interest*.

**single-entry accounting.** Accounting that is neither *self-balancing* nor *articulated*; that is, it does not rely on equal *debits* and *credits*. *No journal entries* are made. *Plugging* is required to derive *owners' equity* for the *balance sheet*.

**single proprietorship.** *Sole proprietorship*.

**single-step.** Said of an *income statement* where *ordinary revenue* and *gain* items are shown first and totaled. Then all ordinary *expenses* and *losses* are totaled. Their difference, plus the effect of *income from discontinued operations* and *extraordinary items*, is shown as *net income*; contrast with *multiple-step* and see *proprietorship theory*.

**sinking fund.** *Assets* and their earnings earmarked for the retirement of bonds or other long-term obligations. Earnings of sinking fund investments are taxable income of the company.

**sinking fund method of depreciation.** The periodic charge is an amount so that when the charges are considered to be an *annuity*, the value of the annuity at the end of depreciable life is equal to the *acquisition cost* of the asset. In theory, the charge for a period ought also to include interest on the accumulated depreciation at the start of the period as well. A *fund* of cash is not necessarily, or even usually, accumulated. This method is rarely used.

**skeleton account.** *T-account*.

**slide.** The name of the error made by a bookkeeper in recording the digits of a number correctly with the decimal point misplaced; for example, recording $123.40 as $1,234.00 or as $12.34.

**soak-up method.** The *equity method*.

**Social Security taxes.** Taxes levied by the federal government on both employers and employees to provide *funds* to pay retired persons (or their survivors) who are entitled to receive such payments, either because they paid Social Security taxes themselves or because the Congress has declared them eligible. Unlike a *pension plan*, the Social Security system does not collect funds and invest them for many years. The tax collections in a given year are used primarily to pay benefits for that year. At any given time the system has a multitrillion dollar unfunded obligation to current workers for their eventual retirement benefits. See *Old Age, Survivors, Disability, and (Hospital) Insurance*.

**sole proprietorship.** All *owners' equity* belongs to one person.

**solvent.** Able to meet debts when due.

**SOP.** *Statement of Position* (of *AcSEC* of the *AICPA*).

**sound value.** A phrase used mainly in appraisals of *fixed assets* to mean *fair market value* or *replacement cost* in present condition.

**source of funds.** Any *transaction* that increases *cash* and *marketable securities* held as *current assets*.

**sources and uses statement.** *Statement of cash flows*.

**SOYD.** *Sum-of-the-years'-digits depreciation*.

**special assessment.** A compulsory levy made by a governmental unit on property to pay the costs of a specific improvement, or service, presumed not to benefit the general public but only the owners of the property so assessed. Accounted for in a special assessment fund.

**special journal.** A *journal*, such as a sales journal or cash disbursements journal, to record *transactions* of a similar nature that occur frequently.

**special revenue debt.** Debt of a governmental unit backed only by revenues from specific sources such as tolls from a bridge.

**specific identification method.** Method for valuing *ending inventory* and *cost of goods sold* by identifying actual units sold and in inventory and summing the actual costs of those individual units. Usually used for items with large unit value, such as precious jewelry, automobiles, and fur coats.

**specific price changes.** Changes in the market prices of specific *goods and services*; contrast with *general price level changes*.

**specific price index.** A measure of the price of a specific good or service, or a small group of similar goods or services, at one time relative to the price during a base period; contrast with *general price index*. See *dollar-value LIFO method*.

**spending variance.** In *standard costing systems*, the *price (rate) variance* for *overhead costs*.

**split.** *Stock split*. Sometimes called "splitup."

**splitoff point.** The point where all costs are no longer *joint costs* but can be identified with individual products or perhaps with a smaller number of *joint products*.

**spoilage.** See *abnormal spoilage* and *normal spoilage*.

**spread sheet.** A *work sheet* organized like a *matrix* that provides a two-way classification of accounting data. The rows and columns are both labeled with *account* titles. An entry in a row represents a *debit* whereas an entry in a column represents a *credit*. Thus, the number "100" in the "cash" row and the "accounts receivable" column records an entry debiting cash and crediting accounts receivable for $100. A given row total indicates all debit entries to the account represented by that row and a given column total indicates the sum of all credit entries to the account represented by the column.

**squeeze.** A term sometimes used for *plug*.

**SSARS.** See *Statement on Standards for Accounting and Review Services*.

**stabilized accounting.** *Constant dollar accounting*.

**stable monetary unit assumption.** In spite of *inflation* that appears to be a way of life, the assumption that underlies *historical cost/nominal dollar accounting*—namely that current dollars and dollars of previous years can be meaningfully added together. No specific recognition is given to changing values of the dollar in the usual *financial statements*. See *constant dollar accounting*.

**Staff Accounting Bulletin.** An interpretation issued by the Staff of the Chief Accountant of the *SEC* "suggesting" how the various *Accounting Series Releases* should be applied in practice. The suggestions are effectively part of *GAAP*.

**standard cost.** Anticipated *cost* of producing a unit of output; a predetermined cost to be assigned to products produced. Standard cost implies a norm—what costs should be. Budgeted cost implies a forecast—something likely, but not necessarily a "should," as implied by a norm. Standard costs are used as the benchmark for gauging good and bad performance. Whereas a budget may similarly be used, it need not. A budget may simply be a planning document, subject to changes whenever plans change, whereas standard costs are usually changed annually or when technology significantly changes or costs of labor and materials significantly change.

**standard costing system.** *Product costing* using *standard costs* rather than actual costs. May be based on either *absorption* or *variable costing* principles.

**standard costing.** *Costing* based on *standard costs*.

**standard error (of regression coefficients).** A measure of the uncertainty about the magnitude of the estimated parameters of an equation fit with a *regression analysis*.

**standard manufacturing overhead.** *Overhead costs* expected to be incurred per unit of time and per unit produced.

**standard price (rate).** Unit price established for materials or labor used in *standard cost systems*.

**standard quantity allowed.** The quantity of direct material or direct labor (inputs) that should have been used if the units of output had been produced in accordance with preset *standards*.

**standby costs.** A type of *capacity cost*, such as property taxes, incurred even if operations are shut down completely. Contrast with *enabling costs*.

**stated capital.** Amount of capital contributed by shareholders. Sometimes used to mean *legal capital*.

**stated value.** A term sometimes used for the *face amount of capital stock*, when no *par value* is indicated. Where there is stated value per share, it may be set by the directors (in which case, capital *contributed in excess of stated value* may come into being).

**statement of affairs.** A *balance sheet* showing immediate *liquidation* amounts, rather than *historical costs*, usually prepared when *insolvency* or *bankruptcy* is imminent. The *going-concern assumption* is not used.

**statement of cash flows.** The *FASB* requires that all for-profit companies present a schedule of *cash receipts* and *payments*, classified by *investing, financing*, and *operating activities*. Operating activities may be reported with either the direct method (where only receipts and payments of cash appear) or the indirect method (which starts with *net income* and shows adjustments for *revenues* not currently producing cash and for *expenses* not currently using cash). "Cash" includes cash equivalents such as Treasury bills, commercial paper and *marketable securities* held as *current assets*. Sometimes called the "funds statement." Before 1987, the FASB required the presentation of a similar statement called the *statement of changes in financial position*, which tended to emphasize *working capital*, not cash. See *dual transactions assumption*.

**statement of changes in financial position.** As defined by *APB Opinion No. 19*, a statement that explains the changes in *working capital* (or cash) balances during a period and shows the changes in the working capital (or cash) accounts themselves. This statement has been replaced with the *statement of cash flows*.

*Statement of Financial Accounting Standards. SFAS.* See *FASB*.

*Statement of Financial Accounting Concepts. SFAC.* One of a series of *FASB* publications in its *conceptual framework* for *financial accounting* and reporting. Such statements set forth objectives and fundamentals to be the basis for specific financial accounting and reporting standards.

**statement of financial position.** *Balance sheet.*

*Statement of Position. SOP.* A recommendation on an emerging accounting problem issued by the *AcSEC* of the *AICPA*. The AICPA's Code of Professional Ethics specifically states that *CPAs* need not treat *SOPs* as they do rules from the *FASB*, but a CPA would be wary of departing from the recommendations of a *SOP*.

**statement of retained earnings (income).** A statement that reconciles the beginning-of-period and end-of-period balances in the *retained earnings* account. It shows the effects of *earnings, dividend declarations*, and *prior-period adjustments*.

**statement of significant accounting policies (principles).** *APB Opinion No. 22* requires that every *annual report* summarize the significant *accounting principles* used in compiling the annual report. This summary may be a separate exhibit or the first *note* to the financial statements.

*Statement on Auditing Standards. SAS. No. 1* of this series (1973) codifies all statements on auditing standards previously promulgated by the AICPA. Later numbers deal with specific auditing standards and procedures.

*Statement on Standards for Accounting and Review Services. SSARS.* Pronouncements issued by the *AICPA* on *unaudited financial statements* and unaudited financial information of nonpublic entities.

**static budget.** *Fixed budget.*

**status quo.** Events or costs incurrences that will happen or are expected to happen in the absence of taking some contemplated action.

**statutory tax rate.** The tax rate specified in the *income tax* law for each type of income (for example, *ordinary income, capital gain or loss*).

**step allocation method.** *Step-down method.*

**step cost.** *Semifixed cost.*

**step-down method.** The method for *allocating service department* costs that starts by allocating one service department's costs to *production departments* and to all other service departments. Then a second service department's costs, including costs allocated from the first, are allocated to production departments and to all other service departments except the first one. In this fashion, the costs of all service departments, including previous allocations, are allocated to production departments and to those service departments whose costs have not yet been allocated.

**stepped cost.** *Semifixed cost.*

**sterilized allocation.** Optimal decisions result from considering *incremental costs*, only. *Allocations* of *joint* or *common costs* are never required for optimal decisions. An allocation of these costs that causes the optimal decision choice not to differ from the one that occurs when joint or common costs are unallocated is "sterilized" with respect to that decision. The term was first used in this context by Arthur L. Thomas. Because *absorption costing* requires that all manufacturing costs be allocated to product, and because some allocations can lead to bad decisions, Thomas (and we) advocate that the allocation scheme chosen lead to sterilized allocations that do not alter the otherwise optimal decision. There is, however, no single allocation scheme that is always sterilized with respect to all decisions. Thus, Thomas (and we) advocate that decisions be made on the basis of incremental costs before any allocations.

**stewardship.** The function of management to be accountable for an *entity's* resources, for their efficient use, and for protecting them, as well as is practicable, from adverse impact. Some theorists believe that a primary goal of *accounting* is to aid users of *financial statements* in their assessment of management's performance in stewardship.

**stock.** *Inventory. Capital stock.* A measure of the amount of something on hand at a specific time; in this sense, contrast with *flow*.

**stock appreciation rights.** The employer promises to pay to the employee an amount of *cash* on a certain future date. The amount of cash is the difference between the *market value* of a certain number of *shares* of *stock* in the employer's company on a given future date and some base price set on the date the rights are granted. This form of compensation is sometimes used because both changes in tax laws in recent years have made *stock options* relatively less attractive. *GAAP* computes compensation based on the difference between market value of the shares and the base price set at the time of the grant. *Expense* is recognized as the holder of the rights performs the services required for the rights to be exercised.

**stock dividend.** A so-called *dividend* where additional *shares* of *capital stock* are distributed, without cash payments, to existing shareholders. It results in a *debit* to *retained earnings* in the amount of the market value of the shares issued and a *credit* to *capital stock* accounts. It is ordinarily used to indicate that earnings retained have been permanently reinvested in the business; contrast with a *stock split*, which requires no entry in the capital stock accounts other than a notation that the *par* or *stated value* per share has been changed.

**stock option.** The right to purchase a specified number of shares of *stock* for a specified price at specified times, usually granted to employees; contrast with *warrant*.

**stockout.** A unit of *inventory* is needed in production or to sell to a customer but is unavailable.

**stockout costs.** *Contribution margin* or other measure of *profits* not earned because a seller has run out of *inventory* and is unable to fill a customer's order. May be an extra cost incurred because of delay in filling an order.

**stock right.** See *right*.

**stock split.** Increase in the number of common shares outstanding resulting from the issuance of additional shares to existing shareholders without additional capital contributions by them. Does not increase the total *par* (or *stated*) *value of common stock* outstanding because par (or stated) value per share is reduced in inverse proportion. A three-for-one stock split reduces par (or stated) value per share to one third of its former amount. Stock splits are usually limited to distributions that increase the number of shares outstanding by 20 percent or more; compare with *stock dividend*.

**stock subscriptions.** See *subscription* and *subscribed stock*.

**stock warrant.** See *warrant*.

**stockholders' equity.** See *shareholders' equity*.

**stores.** *Raw materials*, parts, and supplies.

**straight-debt value.** An estimate of what the *market value* of a *convertible bond* would be if the bond did not contain a conversion privilege.

**straight line depreciation.** If the *depreciable life* is *n* periods, then the periodic *depreciation* charge is $1/n$ of the *depreciable cost*. Results in equal periodic charges and is sometimes called "straight time depreciation."

**strategic plan.** A statement of the method for achieving an organization's goals.

**Subchapter S Corporation.** A firm legally organized as a *corporation* but taxed as if it were a *partnership*. The corporations paying their own income taxes are called "C Corporations."

**subject to.** Qualifications in an *auditor's report* usually caused by a *material* uncertainty in the valuation of an item, such as future promised payments from a foreign government or outcome of pending litigation.

**subordinated.** Said of *debt* whose claim on income or assets is junior to, or comes after, claims of other debt.

**subscribed stock.** A *shareholders' equity* account showing the capital that will be contributed as soon as the subscription price is collected. A subscription is a legal contract so that an entry is made *debiting* an *owners' equity contra account* and *crediting* subscribed stock as soon as the stock is subscribed.

**subscription.** Agreement to buy a *security*, or to purchase periodicals, such as magazines.

**subsequent events.** *Post-statement events*.

**subsidiary.** Said of a company more than 50 percent of whose voting stock is owned by another.

**subsidiary (ledger) accounts.** The *accounts* in a *subsidiary ledger*.

**subsidiary ledger.** The *ledger* that contains the detailed accounts whose total is shown in a *controlling account* of the *general ledger*.

**successful efforts accounting.** In petroleum accounting, the *capitalization* of the drilling costs of only those wells that contain gas or oil. See *reserve recognition accounting* for an example.

**sum-of-the-years'-digits depreciation. SYD. SOYD.** An *accelerated depreciation* method for an asset with *depreciable life* of *n* years where the charge in period *i* ($i = 1,...,n$) is the fraction $(n + 1 - i)/[n(n + 1)/2]$ of the *depreciable cost*. If an asset has a depreciable cost of $15,000 and a 5 year depreciable life, for example, the depreciation charges would be $5,000 (= 5/15 × $15,000) in the first year, $4,000 in the second, $3,000 in the third, $2,000 in the fourth, and $1,000 in the fifth. The name derives from the fact that the denominator in the fraction is the sum of the digits from 1 through *n*.

**summary of significant accounting principles.** *APB Opinion No. 22* requires that every *annual report* summarize the significant *accounting principles* used in compiling the annual report. This summary may be a separate exhibit or the first *note* to the financial statements.

**sunk cost.** *Costs* incurred in the past that cannot be affected by, and hence are irrelevant for, current and future decisions, aside from *income tax* effects; contrast with *incremental costs* and *imputed costs*. For example, the *acquisition cost* of machinery is irrelevant to a decision of whether to scrap the machinery. The current *exit value* of the machine is the *opportunity cost* of continuing to own it, and the cost of, say, electricity to run the machine is an incremental cost of its operation. Sunk costs become relevant for decision making when *income taxes* (*gain* or *loss* on disposal of asset) are taken into account, because the cash payment for income taxes depends on the tax basis of the asset. The term should be avoided in careful writing because it is ambiguous. Consider, for example, a machine costing $100,000 with current *salvage* value of $20,000. Some (including us) would say that $100,000 is "sunk;" others would say that only $80,000 is "sunk."

**supplementary statements (schedules).** Statements (schedules) in addition to the four basic *financial statements* (including the *retained earnings* reconciliation as a basic statement).

**surplus.** A word once used but now considered poor terminology; prefaced by "earned" to mean *retained earnings* and prefaced by "capital" to mean *capital contributed in excess of par (or stated) value*.

**surplus reserves.** Of all the words in accounting, *reserve* is the most objectionable and *surplus* is the second most objectionable. This phrase, then, has nothing to recommend it. It means *appropriated retained earnings*.

**suspense account.** A *temporary account* used to record part of a transaction prior to final analysis of that transaction. For example, if a business regularly classifies all sales into a dozen or more different categories but wants to deposit the proceeds of cash sales every day, it may credit a sales suspense account pending detailed classification of all sales into sales, type 1; sales, type 2; and so on.

**sustainable income.** The part of *distributable income* (computed from *current cost* data) that the firm can be expected to earn in the next accounting period if operations are continued at the same levels as during the current period. *Income from discontinued operations*, for example, may be distributable but not sustainable.

**S-X.** See *Regulation S-X*.

**SYD.** *Sum-of-the-years'-digits depreciation. SOYD.*

**T**

**T-account.** Account form shaped like the letter T with the title above the horizontal line. *Debits* are shown to the left of the vertical line, *credits* to the right.

**take-home pay.** The amount of a paycheck; earned wages or *salary* reduced by deductions for *income taxes*, *Social Security taxes*, contributions to fringe benefit plans, union dues, and so on. Take home pay might be as little as half of earned compensation.

**take-or-pay contract.** As defined by *SFAS No. 47*, an agreement between a purchaser and a seller that provides for the purchaser to pay specified amounts periodically in return for products or services. The purchaser must make specified minimum payments even if it does not take delivery of the contracted products or services.

**taking a bath.** To incur a large loss. See *big bath*.

**tangible.** Having physical form. Accounting has never satisfactorily defined the distinction between tangible and intangible assets. Typically, intangibles are defined by giving an exhaustive list and everything not on the list is defined as tangible. See *intangible asset* for such a list.

**target cost.** *Standard cost*.

**tax.** A nonpenal, but compulsory, charge levied by a government on income, consumption, wealth, or other basis, for the benefit of all those governed. The term does not include fines or specific charges for benefits accruing only to those paying the charges, such as licenses, permits, special assessments, admissions fees, and tolls.

**tax allocation: interperiod.** See *deferred income tax liability*.

**tax allocation: intrastatement.** The showing of income tax effects on *extraordinary items, income from discontinued operations*, and *prior-period adjustments* along with these items, separately from income taxes on other income. See *net-of-tax reporting*.

**tax avoidance.** See *tax shelter* and *loophole*.

**tax credit.** A subtraction from taxes otherwise payable, contrast with *tax deduction*.

**tax deduction.** A subtraction from *revenues* and *gains* to arrive at taxable income. Tax deductions are technically different from tax *exemptions*, but the effect of both is to reduce gross income in computing taxable income. Both are different from *tax credits*, which are subtracted from the computed tax itself in determining taxes payable. If the tax rate is the fraction $t$ of pretax income, then a *tax credit* of $1 is worth $1/t$ of *tax deductions*.

**tax evasion.** The fraudulent understatement of taxable revenues or overstatement of deductions and expenses or both; contrast with *tax shelter* and *loophole*.

**tax exempts.** See *municipal bonds*.

**tax shelter.** The legal avoidance of, or reduction in, *income taxes* resulting from a careful reading of the complex income tax regulations and the subsequent rearrangement of financial affairs to take advantage of the regulations. Often the term is used pejoratively, but the courts have long held that an individual or corporation has no obligation to pay taxes any larger than the legal minimum. If the public concludes that a given tax shelter is "unfair," then the laws and regulations can be, and have been, changed. Sometimes used to refer to the investment that permits tax avoidance. See *loophole*.

**tax shield.** The amount of an *expense* that reduces taxable income but does not require *working capital*, such as *depreciation*. Sometimes this term is expanded to include expenses that reduce taxable income and use working capital. A depreciation deduction (or *R&D expense* in the expanded sense) of $10,000 provides a tax shield of $4,600 when the marginal tax rate is 46 percent.

**taxable income.** *Income* computed according to *IRS* regulations and subject to *income taxes*. Contrast with income, net income, income before taxes (in the *income statement*), and *comprehensive income* (a *financial reporting* concept). Use the term "pretax income" to refer to income before taxes on the income statement in financial reports.

**tax-transfer lease.** The Congress has in the past provided business with an incentive to invest in qualifying *plant and equipment* by granting an *investment credit*, which though it occurs as a reduction in *income taxes* otherwise payable, is effectively a reduction in the purchase price of the assets. Similarly, the Congress continues to grant an incentive to acquire such assets by allowing *Accelerated Cost Recovery* (*ACRS*, form of unusually *accelerated depreciation*). Accelerated depreciation for tax purposes allows a reduction of taxes paid in early years of an asset's life, which provides the firm with an increased *net present value* of *cash flows*. Both of these incentives are administered by the *IRS* through the income tax laws, rather than being granted as an outright cash payment by some other government agency. A business with no taxable income in many cases had difficulty reaping the benefits of the investment credit or of accelerated depreciation because the Congress had not provided for tax refunds to those who acquire qualifying assets but who have no taxable income. In principle, a company without taxable income could lease from another firm with taxable income an asset that would otherwise have been purchased by the first company. The second firm acquires the asset, gets the tax reduction benefits from the acquisition, and becomes a lessor, leasing the asset (presumably at a lower price reflecting its own costs lowered by the tax reductions) to the unprofitable company. Such leases were discouraged by the tax laws prior to 1981. That is, although firms could enter into such leases, the tax benefits could not be legally transferred. Under certain restrictive conditions, the tax law allows a profitable firm to earn tax credits and take deductions while leasing to the firm without tax liability in such leases. These leases have sometimes been called "safe-harbor leases."

*Technical Bulletin.* The *FASB* has authorized its staff to issue bulletins to provide guidance on financial accounting and reporting problems. Although the FASB does not formally approve the contents of the bulletins, their contents are presumed to be part of *GAAP*.

**technology.** The sum of a firm's technical *trade secrets* and *know-how*, as distinct from its *patents*.

**temporary account.** *Account* that does not appear on the *balance sheet*. *Revenue* and *expense* accounts, their *adjuncts* and *contras*, production cost accounts, dividend distribution accounts, and purchases-related accounts (which are closed to the various inventories). Sometimes called a "nominal account."

**temporary difference.** Temporary differences include *timing differences* and differences between *taxable income* and pretax income caused by different cost bases for assets. For example, a plant asset might have a cost of $10,000 for financial reporting, but a basis of $7,000 for income tax purposes; this creates a temporary difference which is not a timing difference.

**temporary investments.** Investments in *marketable securities* that the owner intends to sell within a short time, usually one year, and hence classified as *current assets*.

**10-K.** The name of the annual report required by the *SEC* of nearly all publicly held corporations.

**term bonds.** A *bond issue* whose component bonds all mature at the same time; contrast with *serial bonds*.

**term loan.** A loan with a *maturity* date, as opposed to a demand loan which is due whenever the lender requests payment. In practice, bankers and auditors use this phrase only for loans for a year or more.

**terms of sale.** The conditions governing payment for a sale. For example, the terms *2/10, n(et)/30* mean that if payment is made within 10 days of the invoice date, a *discount* of 2 percent from *invoice* price can be taken; the invoice amount must be paid, in any event, within 30 days or it becomes overdue.

**throughput contract.** As defined by *SFAS No. 47*, an agreement between a shipper (processor) and the owner of a transportation facility (such as an oil or natural gas pipeline or a ship) or a manufacturing facility that provides for the shipper (processor) to pay specified amounts periodically in return for the transportation (processing) of a product. The shipper (processor) is obligated to make cash payments even if it does not ship (process) the contracted quantities.

**tickler file.** A collection of *vouchers* or other memoranda arranged chronologically to remind the person in charge of certain duties to make payments (or to do other tasks) as scheduled.

**time-adjusted rate of return.** *Internal rate of return*.

**time cost.** *Period cost*.

**time deposit.** Cash in bank earning interest; contrast with *demand deposit*.

**time-series analysis.** See *cross-section analysis* for definition and contrast.

**times-interest (charges) earned.** Ratio of pretax *income* plus *interest* charges to interest charges. See *ratio*.

**timing difference.** The major type of *temporary difference*. A difference between taxable income and pretax income reported to shareholders that will be reversed in a subsequent period and requires an entry in the *deferred income tax* account. For example, the use of *accelerated depreciation* for tax returns and *straight line depreciation* for financial reporting. Contrast with *permanent difference*.

**total assets turnover.** *Sales* divided by average total *assets*.

**traceable cost.** A *cost* that can be identified with or assigned to a specific product; in contrast to a *joint cost*.

**trade acceptance.** A *draft* drawn by a seller which is presented for signature (acceptance) to the buyer at the time goods are purchased and which then becomes the equivalent of a *note receivable* of the seller and the *note payable* of the buyer.

**trade credit.** One business allows another to buy from it in return for a promise to pay later. As contrasted with consumer credit, where a business extends the privilege of paying later to a retail customer.

**trade discount.** A *discount* from *list price* offered to all customers of a given type; contrast with a *discount* offered for prompt payment and *quantity discount*.

**trade payables (receivables).** *Payables (receivables)* arising in the ordinary course of business transactions. Most accounts payable (receivable) are of this kind.

**trade secret.** Technical or business information such as formulas, recipes, computer programs, and marketing data not generally known by competitors and maintained by the firm as a secret. A famous example is the secret formula for *Coca-Cola* (a registered *trademark* of the company). Compare with *know-how*. Theoretically capable of having an infinite life, this intangible asset is capitalized only if purchased and then amortized over a period not to exceed 40 years. If it is developed internally, then no asset will be shown.

**trade-in.** Acquiring a new *asset* in exchange for a used one and perhaps additional cash. See *boot* and *trade-in transaction*.

**trade-in transaction.** The accounting for a trade-in depends whether or not the asset received is "similar" to the asset traded in and whether the accounting is for *financial statements* or for *income tax* returns. Assume that an old asset cost $5,000, has $3,000 of *accumulated depreciation* (after recording depreciation to the date of the trade-in), and hence has a *book value* of $2,000. The old asset appears to have a market value of $1,500, according to price quotations in used asset markets. The old asset is traded in on a new asset with a list price of $10,000. The old asset and $5,500 cash *(boot)* are given for the new asset. The generic entry for the trade in transaction is:

| | | | |
|---|---|---|---|
| New Asset . . . . . . . . . . . . . . . . . . . . . | A | | |
| Accumulated Depreciation (Old Asset) . . . . . . . . . . . . . . . . . . | 3,000 | | |
| Adjustment on Exchange of Asset . . | B | or | B |
| Old Asset . . . . . . . . . . . . . . . . . . . . . | | | 5,000 |
| Cash . . . . . . . . . . . . . . . . . . . . . . . . | | | 5,500 |

(1) The *list price* method of accounting for trade ins rests on the assumption that the list price of the new asset closely approximates its market value. The new asset is recorded at its list price (A = $10,000 in the example); B is a *plug* (= $2,500 credit in the example). If B requires a *debit* plug, the Adjustment on Exchange of Asset is a *loss*; if a *credit* plug is required (as in the example), the adjustment is a *gain*.

(2) Another theoretically sound method of accounting for trade-ins rests on the assumption that the price quotation from used-asset markets gives a more reliable measure of the market value of the old asset than is the list price a reliable measure of the market value of the new asset. This method uses the *fair market value* of the old asset, $1,500 in the example, to determine B (= $2,000 book value − $1,500 assumed proceeds on disposition = $500 debit or loss). The exchange results in a loss if the book value of the old asset exceeds its market value and in a gain if the market value exceeds the book value. The new asset is recorded on the books by plugging for A (= $7,000 in the example).

(3) For income tax reporting, no gain or loss may be recognized on the trade-in. Thus the new asset is recorded on the books by assuming B is zero and plugging for A (= $7,500 in the example). In practice, firms that wish to recognize the loss currently will sell the old asset directly, rather than trading it in, and acquire the new asset entirely for cash.

(4) *Generally accepted accounting principles (APB Opinion No. 29)* require a variant of these methods. The basic method is (1) or (2), depending on whether the list price of the new asset (1) or the quotation of the old asset's market value (2) is the more reliable indication of market value. If, when applying the basic method, a debit entry, or loss, is required for the Adjustment on Exchange of Asset, then the trade-in is recorded as described in (1) or (2) and the full amount of the loss is recognized currently. If, however, a credit entry, or gain, is required for the Adjustment on Exchange of Asset, then the amount of gain recognized currently depends on whether or not the old asset and the new asset are "similar." If the assets are not similar, then the entire gain is recognized currently. If the assets are similar and cash is not received by the party trading in, then no gain is recognized and the treatment is like that in (3); that is B = 0, plug for A. If the assets are similar and cash is received by the party trading in — a rare case — then a portion of the gain is recognized currently. The portion of the gain recognized currently is the fraction *cash received/fair market value of total consideration received*. (When the list price method, (1), is used, the market value of the old asset is assumed to be the list price of the new asset plus the amount of cash received by the party trading in.)

The results of applying *GAAP* to the example can be summarized as follows:

| More Reliable Information As to Fair Market Value | Old Asset Compared with New Asset | |
|---|---|---|
| | Similar | Not Similar |
| New Asset List Price | A = $7,500 | A = $10,000 |
| | B = 0 | B = 2,500 gain |
| Old Asset Market Price | A = $7,000 | A = $ 7,000 |
| | B = 500 loss | B = 500 loss |

**trademark.** A distinctive word or symbol affixed to a product, its package or dispenser, which uniquely identifies the firm's products and services. See *trademark right*.

**trademark right.** The right to exclude competitors in sales or advertising from using words or symbols that may be confusingly similar to the firm's *trademarks*. Trademark rights last as long as the firm continues to use the trademarks in question. In the United States, trademark rights arise from use and not from government registration. They therefore have a legal life independent of the life of a registration. Registrations last 20 years and are renewable as long as the trademark is being used. Thus, as an asset, purchased trademark rights might, like land, not be subject to amortization if management believes that the life of the trademark is indefinite. In practice, accountants amortize a trademark right over some estimate of its life, not to exceed 40 years. Under *SFAS No. 2*, internally developed trademark rights must be *expensed*.

**trading on the equity.** Said of a firm engaging in *debt financing*; frequently said of a firm doing so to a degree considered abnormal for a firm of its kind. *Leverage*.

**transaction.** A *transfer* (of more than promises — see *executory contract*) between the accounting *entity* and another party, or parties.

**transfer.** *SFAC No. 6* distinguishes "reciprocal" and "nonreciprocal" transfers. In a reciprocal transfer, or "exchange," the entity both receives and sacrifices. In a nonreciprocal transfer the entity sacrifices but does not receive (examples include gifts, distributions to owners) or receives but does not sacrifice (investment by owner in entity). *SFAC No. 6* suggests that the term "internal transfer" is self-contradictory and that the term "internal event" be used instead.

**transfer agent.** Usually a bank or trust company designated by a corporation to make legal transfers of *stock (bonds)* and, perhaps, to pay *dividends (coupons)*.

**transfer price.** A substitute for a *market*, or *arm's length*, *price* used in *profit center*, or *responsibility center*, accounting when one segment of the business "sells" to another segment. Incentives of profit center managers will not coincide with the best interests of the entire business unless transfer prices are properly set.

**transfer pricing problem.** The problem of setting *transfer prices* so that both buyer and seller have *goal congruence* with respect to the parent organization's goals.

**translation gain (or loss).** *Foreign exchange gain (or loss)*.

**transportation-in.** *Freight-in*.

**transposition error.** An error in record keeping resulting from reversing the order of digits in a number, such as recording "32" for "23." If an error of this sort has been made in a number added in a total, then the incorrect total will always differ from the correct total by a number divisible by nine. Thus if *trial balance* sums differ by a number divisible by nine, one might search for a transposition error.

**treasurer.** The name sometimes given to the chief financial officer of a business.

**treasury bond.** A bond issued by a corporation and then reacquired; such bonds are treated as retired when reacquired and an *extraordinary gain or loss* on reacquisition is recognized. Also, a *bond* issued by the U.S. Treasury Department.

**treasury shares.** *Capital stock* issued and then reacquired by the corporation. Such reacquisitions result in a reduction of *shareholders' equity*, and are usually shown on the balance sheet as *contra* to shareholders' equity. Neither *gain* nor *loss* is recognized on transactions involving treasury stock. Any difference between the amounts paid and received for treasury stock transactions is debited (if positive) or credited (if negative) to *additional paid-in capital*. See *cost method* and *par value method*.

**treasury stock.** *Treasury shares.*

**trial balance.** A listing of *account balances*; all accounts with *debit* balances are totaled separately from accounts with *credit* balances. The two totals should be equal. Trial balances are taken as a partial check of the arithmetic accuracy of the entries previously made. See *adjusted, preclosing, postclosing, unadjusted trial balance, plug.*

**troubled debt restructuring.** As defined in *SFAS No. 15*, a concession (changing of the terms of a *debt*) granted by a *creditor* for economic or legal reasons related to the *debtor's* financial difficulty that the creditor would not otherwise consider.

**turnover.** The number of times that *assets*, such as *inventory* or *accounts receivable*, are replaced on average during the period. Accounts receivable turnover, for example, is total sales on account for a period divided by average accounts receivable balance for the period. See *ratio.*

**turnover of plant and equipment.** See *ratio.*

**t-value.** In *regression analysis*, the ratio of an estimated regression coefficient divided by its *standard error.*

**two T-account method.** A method for computing either (1) *foreign exchange gains and losses* or (2) *monetary gains* or *losses* for *constant dollar accounting statements*. The left-hand *T-account* shows actual net balances of *monetary items* and the right-hand T-account shows implied *(common) dollar* amounts.

**2/10, n(et)/30.** See *terms of sale.*

**U**

**unadjusted trial balance.** *Trial balance* before *adjusting* and *closing entries* are made at the end of the period.

**unappropriated retained earnings.** *Retained earnings* not appropriated and therefore against which *dividends* can be charged in the absence of retained earnings restrictions. See *restricted retained earnings.*

**unavoidable cost.** A *cost* that is not an *avoidable cost.*

**uncertainty.** See *risk* for definition and contrast.

**uncollectible account.** An *account receivable* that will not be paid by the *debtor*. If the preferable *allowance method* is used, the entry on judging a specific account to be uncollectible is to *debit* the allowance for uncollectible accounts and to *credit* the specific account receivable. See *bad debt expense* and *sales contra, estimated uncollectibles.*

**unconsolidated subsidiary.** A *subsidiary* not consolidated and, hence, accounted for on the *equity method.*

**uncontrollable cost.** The opposite of *controllable cost.*

**underapplied (underabsorbed) overhead.** An excess of actual *overhead costs* for a period over costs applied, or charged, to products produced during the period. A *debit balance* remaining in an overhead account after overhead is assigned to product.

**underlying document.** The record, memorandum, *voucher*, or other signal that is the authority for making an *entry* into a *journal.*

**underwriter.** One who agrees to purchase an entire *security issue* for a specified price, usually for resale to others.

**undistributed earnings.** *Retained earnings*; typically, this term refers to that amount retained for a given year.

**unearned income (revenue).** *Advances from customers*; strictly speaking, a contradiction in terms.

**unemployment tax.** See *FUTA.*

**unencumbered appropriation.** In governmental accounting, portion of an *appropriation* not yet spent or *encumbered.*

**unexpired cost.** An *asset.*

**unfavorable variance.** In *standard cost* accounting, an excess of expected revenue over actual revenue or an excess of actual cost over standard cost.

**unfunded.** Not *funded*. An obligation or *liability*, usually for *pension costs*, exists but no *funds* have been set aside to discharge the obligation or liability.

**Uniform Partnership Act.** A model law, enacted by many states, to govern the relations between partners where the *partnership* agreement fails to specify the agreed-upon treatment.

**unissued capital stock.** *Stock* authorized but not yet issued.

**units-of-production method.** The *production method of depreciation*.

**unlimited liability.** The legal obligation of *general partners* or the sole proprietor for all debts of the *partnership* or *sole proprietorship*.

**unqualified opinion.** See *auditor's report*.

**unrealized appreciation.** An *unrealized holding gain*; frequently used in the context of *marketable securities*.

**unrealized gross margin (profit).** A *contra* account to *installment accounts receivable* used with the *installment method* of revenue recognition. Shows the amount of profit that will eventually be realized when the receivable is collected. Some accountants show this account as a *liability*.

**unrealized holding gain.** See *inventory profit* for definition and an example.

**unrealized loss on marketable securities.** An *income statement account* title for the amount of *loss* during the current period on the portfolio of *marketable securities* held as *current assets*. *SFAS No. 12* requires that losses caused by declines in price below market be *recognized* in the income statement, even though they have not been *realized*.

**unrecovered cost.** *Book value* of an *asset*.

**usage variance.** *Efficiency variance*.

**use of funds.** Any transaction that reduces funds (however funds is defined).

**useful life.** *Service life*.

# V

**valuation account.** A *contra* account or *adjunct account*. When *marketable securities* are reported at *lower of cost or market*, any declines in market value below cost will be credited to a valuation account. In this way, the acquisition cost and the amount of price declines below cost can both be shown. *SFAC No. 6* says a valuation account is "a separate item that reduces and increases the carrying amount" of an asset (or liability). The accounts are part of the related assets (or liabilities) and are neither assets (nor liabilities) in their own right.

**value.** Monetary worth; the term is usually so subjective that it ought not to be used without a modifying adjective unless most people would agree on the amount; not to be confused with cost. See *fair market value, entry value, exit value*.

**value added.** *Cost* of a product or *work in process*, minus the cost of the material purchased for the product or work in process.

**value variance.** *Price variance*.

**variable annuity.** An *annuity* whose periodic payments depend on some uncertain outcome, such as stock market prices.

**variable budget.** *Flexible budget*.

**variable costing.** This method of allocating costs assigns only *variable manufacturing costs* to product and treats *fixed manufacturing costs* as *period expenses*. Contrast with *full absorption costing*.

**variable costs.** *Costs* that change as activity levels change. Strictly speaking, variable costs are zero when the activity level is zero. See *semivariable costs*. In accounting this term most often means the sum of *direct costs* and variable *overhead*.

**variable overhead variance.** Difference between actual and *standard variable overhead costs*.

**variance.** Difference between actual and *standard costs* or between *budgeted* and actual *expenditures* or, sometimes, *expenses*. The word has completely different meanings in accounting and statistics, where it is a measure of dispersion of a distribution.

**variance analysis (investigation).** The investigation of the causes of *variances* in a *standard costing system*. This term has a different meaning in statistics.

**variation analysis.** Analysis of the causes of changes in items of interest in financial statements such as net *income* or *gross margin*.

**vendor.** A seller. Sometimes spelled, "vender."

**verifiable.** A qualitative *objective* of financial reporting specifying that items in *financial statements* can be checked by tracing back to *underlying documents* — supporting *invoices*, canceled *checks*, and other physical pieces of evidence.

**verification.** The auditor's act of reviewing or checking items in *financial statements* by tracing back to *underlying documents*—supporting *invoices*, canceled *checks*, and other business documents—or sending out *confirmations* to be returned. Compare with *physical verification*.

**vertical analysis.** Analysis of the financial statements of a single firm or across several firms for a particular time, as opposed to *horizontal* or time-series analysis where items are compared over time for a single firm or across firms.

**vested.** Said of an employee's *pension plan* benefits that are not contingent on the employee's continuing to work for the employer.

**visual curve fitting method.** Sometimes, when only rough approximations to the amounts of *fixed* and *variable costs* are required, one need not engage in a formal *regression analysis*, but need merely plot the data and draw in a line by hand that seems to fit the data, using the parameters of that line for the rough approximations.

**volume variance.** *Production volume variance*. Less often, used to mean *sales volume variance*.

**voucher.** A document that signals recognition of a *liability* and authorizes the disbursement of cash. Sometimes used to refer to the written evidence documenting an *accounting entry*, as in the term *journal voucher*.

**voucher system.** A method for controlling *cash* that requires each *check* to be authorized with an approved *voucher*. No *disbursements* of currency or coins are made except from *petty cash funds*.

**W**

**wage.** Compensation of employees based on time worked or output of product for manual labor. But see *take-home pay*.

**warrant.** A certificate entitling the owner to buy a specified number of shares at a specified time(s) for a specified price. Differs from a *stock option* only in that options are granted to employees and warrants are issued to the public. See *right*.

**warranty.** A promise by a seller to correct deficiencies in products sold. When warranties are given, proper accounting practice recognizes an estimate of warranty *expense* and an *estimated liability* at the time of sale. See *guarantee* for contrast in proper usage.

**wash sale.** The sale and purchase of the same or similar *asset* within a short time period. For *income tax* purposes, *losses* on a sale of stock may not be recognized if equivalent stock is purchased within 30 days before or 30 days after the date of sale.

**waste.** Residue of material from manufacturing operations with no sale value. Frequently, it has negative value because additional costs must be incurred for disposal.

**wasting asset.** A *natural resource* having a limited *useful life* and, hence, subject to *amortization*, called *depletion*. Examples are timberland, oil and gas wells, and ore deposits.

**watered stock.** Shares issued for *assets* with *fair market value* less than *par* or *stated value*. The assets are put onto the books at the overstated values. In the law, for shares to be considered watered, the *board of directors* must have acted in bad faith or fraudulently in issuing the shares under these circumstances. The term originated from a former practice of cattlemen who fed cattle (''stock'') large quantities of salt to make them thirsty. The cattle then drank a lot of water before being taken to market. This was done to make the cattle appear heavier and more valuable than otherwise.

**weighted average.** An average computed by counting each occurrence of each value, not merely a single occurrence of each value. For example, if one unit is purchased for $1 and two units are purchased for $2 each, the simple average of the purchase prices is $1.50, but the weighted average price per unit is $5/3 = $1.67. Contrast with *moving average*.

**weighted-average inventory method.** Valuing either *withdrawals* or *ending inventory* at the *weighted-average* purchase price of all units on hand at the time of withdrawal or of computing ending inventory. The *inventory equation* is used to calculate the other quantity. If the *perpetual inventory* method is in use, often called the ''moving average method.''

**where-got, where-gone statement.** A term used by W. M. Cole for a statement much like the *statement of cash flows*.

**window dressing.** The attempt to make financial statements show *operating* results, or *financial position*, more favorable than would be otherwise shown.

**with recourse.** See *note receivable discounted*.

**withdrawals.** *Assets* distributed to an owner. *Partner's drawings*. See *inventory equation* for another context.

**withholding.** Deductions from *salaries* or *wages*, usually for *income taxes*, to be remitted by the employer, in the employee's name, to the taxing authority.

**without recourse.** See *note receivable discounted*.

**work in process (inventory account).** Partially completed product; an asset that is classified as *inventory*.

**work sheet.** A tabular schedule for convenient summary of *adjusting* and *closing entries*. The work sheet usually begins with an *unadjusted trial balance*. Adjusting entries are shown in the next two columns, one for *debts* and one for *credits*. The horizontal sum of each line is then carried to the right into either the *income statement or balance sheet* column, as appropriate. The *plug* to equate the income statement column totals is the income, if a debit plug is required, or loss, if a credit plug is required, for the period. That income will be closed to retained earnings on the balance sheet. The income statement credit columns are the revenues for the period and the debit columns are the expenses (and revenue *contras*) to be shown on the income statement. Work sheet is also used to refer to *schedules* for determining other items appearing on the *financial statements* that require adjustment or compilation.

**working capital.** *Current assets* minus *current liabilities*.

**working papers.** The schedules and analyses prepared by the *auditor* in carrying out investigations prior to issuing an *opinion* on *financial statements*.

**worth.** *Value*. See *net worth*.

**worth-debt ratio.** Reciprocal of the *debt-equity ratio*. See *ratio*.

**write down.** *Write off*, except that not all the assets' cost is charged to expense or *loss*. Generally used for nonrecurring items.

**write off.** *Charge* an *asset* to *expense* or *loss*; that is, *debit* expense (or loss) and *credit* asset.

**write-off method.** A method for treating *uncollectible accounts* that charges *bad debt expense* and credits accounts receivable of specific customers as uncollectible amounts are identified. May not be used when uncollectible amounts are significant and can be estimated. See *bad debt expense, sales contra, estimated uncollectibles* and the *allowance method* for contrast.

**write up.** To increase the recorded *cost* of an *asset* with no corresponding *disbursement* of *funds*; that is, *debit* asset and *credit revenue*, or perhaps, *owners' equity*. Seldom done because currently accepted accounting principles are based on actual transactions. When a portfolio of *marketable equity securities* increases in market value subsequent to a previously recognized decrease, the *book value* of the portfolio is written up — the debit is to the *contra account*.

**Y**

**yield.** *Internal rate of return* of a stream of cash flows. Cash yield is cash flow divided by book value. See also *dividend yield*.

**yield to maturity.** At a given time, the *internal rate of return* of a series of cash flows, usually said of a *bond*. Sometimes called the "effective rate."

**yield variance.** The portion of an *efficiency variance* that is not the *mix variance*.

**Z**

**zero-base(d) budgeting. ZBB.** In preparing an ordinary *budget* for the next period, a manager starts with the budget for the current period and makes adjustments as seem necessary because of changed conditions for the next period. Because most managers like to increase the scope of the activities managed and since most prices increase most of the time, amounts in budgets prepared in the ordinary, incremental way seem to increase period after period. The authority approving the budget assumes operations will be carried out in the same way as in the past and that next period's expenditures will have to be at least as large as the current period's. Thus, this authority tends to study only the increments to the current period's budget. In ZBB, the authority questions the process for carrying out a program and the entire budget for next period. Every dollar in the budget is studied, not just the dollars incremental to the previous period's amounts. The advocates of ZBB claim that in this way: (1) programs or divisions of marginal benefit to the business or governmental unit will more likely be deleted from the program, rather than being continued with costs at least as large as the present ones and (2) alternative, more cost-effective, ways of carrying out programs are more likely to be discovered and implemented. ZBB implies questioning the existence of programs and the fundamental nature of the way they are carried out, not merely the amounts used to fund them. Experts appear to be evenly divided as to whether the middle word should be "base" or "based."

# Index